The Princeton Encyclopedia of Islamic Political Thought

The Princeton Encyclopedia of Islamic Political Thought

Editor

Gerhard Bowering
Yale University

Associate Editors

Patricia Crone
Institute for Advanced Study

Wadad Kadi
University of Chicago

Devin J. Stewart
Emory University

Muhammad Qasim Zaman
Princeton University

Assistant Editor

Mahan Mirza
Zaytuna College

Princeton University Press
Princeton and Oxford

Published by Princeton University Press, 41 William Street,
Princeton, New Jersey 08540
In the United Kingdom: Princeton University Press,
6 Oxford Street, Woodstock, Oxfordshire OX20 1TW

Library of Congress Cataloging-in-Publication Data

The Princeton encyclopedia of Islamic political thought / editor,
Gerhard Böwering ; associate editors, Patricia Crone . . . [et al.] ;
assistant editor, Mahan Mirza.
p. cm.
Includes bibliographical references and index.
ISBN 978-0-691-13484-0 (hardcover : alk. paper) 1. Political
science—Islamic countries—Encyclopedias. 2. Political science—
Islamic Empire—Encyclopedias. 3. Islam and politics—
Encyclopedias. I. Böwering, Gerhard, 1939– II. Crone, Patricia,
1945– III. Mirza, Mahan. IV. Title: Encyclopedia of Islamic
political thought.

JC49.P75 2012
320.55'703—dc23 2012003118

This book has been composed in Times and Myriad Pro.
Printed on acid-free paper.
press.princeton.edu
Printed in the United States of America

10 9 8 7 6 5 4 3 2 1

Contents

Introduction

The Islamic World Today in Historical Perspective

In 2012, the year 1433 of the Muslim calendar, the Islamic population throughout the world was estimated at approximately a billion and a half, representing about one-fifth of humanity. In geographical terms, Islam occupies the center of the world, stretching like a big belt across the globe from east to west. From Morocco to Mindanao, it encompasses countries of both the consumer North and the disadvantaged South. It sits at the crossroads of America, Europe, and Russia on one side and Africa, India, and China on the other. Historically, Islam is also at a crossroads, destined to play a world role in politics and to become the most prominent world religion during the 21st century. Islam is thus not contained in any national culture; it is a universal force.

The cultural reach of Islam may be divided into five geographical blocks: West and East Africa, the Arab world (including North Africa), the Turco-Iranian lands (including Central Asia, northwestern China, the Caucasus, the Balkans, and parts of Russia and the Ukraine), South Asia (including Pakistan, Bangladesh, and many regions in India), and Southeast Asia (the Indonesian archipelago; the Malaysian peninsula; Singapore; and minorities in Thailand, the Philippines, and by extension, Australia). Particularly in the past century, Islam has created the core of a sixth block: small but vigorous communities living on both sides of the Atlantic, in Europe (especially in France, Germany, Great Britain, the Netherlands, and Spain), and the Americas (especially in Canada, the United States, the Caribbean, and Argentina).

Islam has grown consistently throughout history, expanding into new neighboring territories without ever retreating (except on the margins, as in Sicily and Spain, where it was expelled by force, and the Balkans, where it is now regaining its foothold). It began in the seventh century as a small community in Mecca and Medina in the Arabian Peninsula led by its messenger, the Prophet Muhammad (d. 632), who was eventually to unite all the Arab tribes under the banner of Islam. Within the first two centuries of its existence, it came into global prominence through its conquests of the Middle East, North Africa, the Iberian Peninsula, the Iranian lands, Central Asia, and the Indus valley. In the process and aftermath of these conquests, Islam inherited the legacy of the ancient Egyptian and Mesopotamian civilizations, embraced and transformed the heritage of Hellenistic philosophy and science, assimilated the subtleties of Persian statecraft, incorporated the reasoning of Jewish law and the methods of Christian theology, absorbed cultural patterns of Zoroastrian dualism and Manichean speculation, and acquired wisdom from Mahayana Buddhism and Indian philosophy and science. Its great cosmopolitan centers—Baghdad, Cairo, Córdoba, Damascus, and Samarqand—became the furnace in which the energy of these cultural traditions was converted into a new religion and polity. These major cities, as well as provincial capitals of the newly founded Islamic empire, such as Basra, Kufa, Aleppo, Qayrawan, Fez, Rayy (Tehran), Nishapur, and San‘a’, merged the legacy of the Arab tribal tradition with newly incorporated cultural trends. By religious conversion, whether fervent, formal, or forced, Islam integrated Christians of Greek, Syriac, Coptic, and Latin rites and included large numbers of Jews, Zoroastrians, Gnostics, and Manicheans. By ethnic assimilation, it absorbed a great variety of nations, whether through compacts, clientage and marriage, persuasion, and threat or through religious indifference, social climbing, and the self-interest of newly conquered peoples. It embraced Aramaic-, Persian-, and Berber-speaking peoples; accommodated the disruptive incursions of Turks and the devastating invasion of Mongols into its territories; and sent its emissaries, traders, immigrants, and colonists to the lands beyond the Indus valley, the semiarid plains south of the Sahara, and the distant shores of the Southeast Asian islands.

By transforming the world during the ascendancy of the Abbasid Empire (750–1258), Islam created a splendid cosmopolitan civilization built on the Arabic language; the message of its scripture, tradition, and law (Qur’an, hadith, and shari‘a); and the wisdom and science of the cultures newly incorporated during its expansion over three continents. The practice of philosophy, medicine, and the sciences within the Islamic empire was at a level of sophistication unmatched by any other civilization; it secured pride of place in such diverse fields as architecture, philosophy, maritime navigation, and trade and commerce by land and sea and saw the founding of the world's first universities. Recuperating from two centuries of relative political decentralization, it coalesced around the year 1500 into three great empires: the Ottomans in the west with Istanbul as their center, the Safavids in Iran with Isfahan as their hub, and the Mughals in the Indian subcontinent with Agra and Delhi as their axis.

As the Islamic world witnessed the emergence of these three empires, European powers began to expand their influence over the world during the age of global discoveries—westward across the Atlantic into the Americas and eastward by charting a navigational route around Africa into the Indian Ocean—there entering into fierce competition with regional powers along the long-established network of trade routes between China on the one hand and the Mediterranean and East Africa on the other. The European exploration of the East and growing ability to exploit an existing vast trade network, together with the inadvertent but eventually lucrative “discovery” of the New World, were to result in Europe's economic and political hegemony over the Islamic world, with which it had rubbed military and mercantile shoulders since the early Muslim conquests. The early modern Islamic world (and much of the rest of the world) fell behind the West economically and politically with

the advent of the Enlightenment in the 18th century and the Industrial Revolution in the 19th century.

By about 1800, small European nations (e.g., England, France, and Holland) had established rule over large regions of the Islamic world. Their trading companies and imperial outposts in distant Muslim lands were transformed into colonies of European supremacy that were eager to benefit from Western industrialization. It took until the end of World War II for the global geopolitical map to become reorganized into an array of discrete nation-states on the European model. Muslim nations perceived Islam not only as the way of life led by the majority of the population but also as the source of normative principles for social order.

In the 19th century, two diametrically opposed trends would preoccupy the Muslim intelligentsia in their effort to bring about social and religious renewal. Modernism proposed adapting Islam to Western ideals, while revivalism advocated restoring the vigor of the original dynamics of Islam; neither approach would lead to the utopia of a Pan-Islamic caliphate. Islam was now challenged to express itself within the framework of independent nations, with their focus on ethnicity, territoriality, and culture.

At the beginning of the 20th century, the Islamic world witnessed the explosion of Turkish secularism; in its middle period, it sought sovereignty and honor in Arab, Iranian, Pakistani, and Indonesian nationalism; at the end of the 20th century, it became increasingly dominated by militant trends. "Islamism," a fundamentalist reaction to Western ascendancy, called for an Islamic state rigorously based on Islamic law; its public image was dominated by marginal yet high-profile extremists who advocated the use of terrorist attacks and suicide martyr missions to achieve this end. Both Sunni and Shi'i expressions of Islamism—in Algeria, Sudan, Iran, or Afghanistan—were inspired by their belief that if only Muslims were to return to their religious roots, God would grant them success in this world and bliss in the next. The past glory of the Islamic world would be restored, and the West would again study at its feet.

At the beginning of the 21st century, the world has drawn closer together through the power of advanced technology and the speed of global communication, including ubiquitous access to mobile phones and the Internet. Those advances enabled the annihilation of the Twin Towers in New York City on September 11, 2001, and other acts of terror that have occurred since that date. Yet they also may be nurturing a different response of Islam to the modern world, as rumblings of freedom, cries for liberation from corrupt regimes, and calls for democratic forms of government echo from Muslim lands through cyberspace. The nonviolent but persistent 2011 demonstrations in Freedom Square in Egypt may be a sign of a transition from organized martyr-murderer movements to coordinated peaceful agitation for political liberty, respect for human rights, and free exercise of religion for the many polities of Islam.

The Evolution of Islamic Political Thought

The development of Islamic political thought tracks the differing positions Islam has occupied during its political expansion over the course of 14 centuries. Just as Islamic history both preserved its tradition and reshaped its internal culture consistently over this period of expansion, so did Islamic political thought maintain certain principal foundations while undergoing successive stages of evolution. The foundations of Islam neither allow for distinctions between spiritual and temporal, ecclesiastical and civil, or religious and secular categories, nor envisage the same duality of authority accepted in Western political thought as standard, such as God and Caesar, church and state, clergy and laity. Over the centuries, Islamic forms of state and government, power and authority, and rule and loyalty have exhibited great diversity. Although they were all based on the premise of a unity of religion and state, it has nonetheless been impossible for Islam to formulate a norm of political thought that would stand above and apart from its various cultural permutations.

In contrast to the West, the respective realms of religion and state are intimately intertwined in Islam and subject to a process of fluid negotiation; the concepts of authority and duty overshadow those of freedom and the rights of the individual. Islamic political thought not only deals with matters of government, politics, and the state but also addresses questions of acceptable behavior and ethics of both the ruler and the ruled before God. Islamic political thought cannot be measured by Western criteria and standards of political theory. It must be understood from within its own tradition, characterized by a vibrant integration of the secular and sacred in obedience to God and His Prophet. In its very nature, Islam is dynamic, not static, both as a way of life and as a way of monotheistic worship. It is a living reality rather than a frozen system.

Rudimentary but enduring foundations for Islamic political thought were laid beginning with the Prophet's career in Medina. Significant divisions, however, came to the fore under the Umayyad caliphs (658–750), the first Arab dynasty ruling from Damascus. Arabic, the language of Muhammad and his early successors (632–61), was propagated by the conquests of Islam and became established as the language of high Islamic culture and political thought during the caliphate of 'Abd al-Malik (r. 685–705). On the criterion of its scripture (*kitāb*), Islamic political thought enforced the basic principle of obedience to God and His Prophet. That principle was articulated in the nucleus of its creed, the *shahāda*, and extrapolated in oral tradition by the early practice of the community, modeled after the Prophet, which is known as the sunna.

The Umayyad rulers belonging to the Quraysh, Muhammad's tribe, claimed to be the rightful caliphs as heirs to the Prophet but saw their leadership challenged by both the Shi'is, who reserved legitimate leadership for Muhammad's family, and the Kharijis, who advocated that the most meritorious Muslim be the ideal caliph. By the end of the Umayyad caliphate in 750, the stage had been set for Islamic political thought to evolve through five successive periods, the trajectory of which may be summarized as follows.

750–1055. The early medieval formulations of Islamic political thought during the ascendancy of the Abbasid caliphate at Baghdad developed in three directions: those of the clerical class of administrators (*kuttāb*), the schools of legal scholars ('ulama', *fuqahā'*)

and theologians (*mutakallimūn*), and the circles of philosophers (*falāsifa*). Over a period of five centuries, in particular during the caliphates of Harun al-Rashid (r. 781–809) and Ma'mun (r. 813–33), Islamic thinkers integrated the thought patterns of a great variety of peoples, absorbing the intellectual systems brought into its fold by the converted populations of the Iranian empire and the Byzantine provinces. It appropriated the legacy of their learning and the acumen of their political experience with the help of comprehensive translation movements from Greek and Pahlavi into Arabic.

1055–1258. During this stage, Islamic political thought had to address the upheaval caused by Sunni Turkic nomads from Central Asia. Turkic sultans gained effective military control and cut into the economic and administrative strata of an Iran-based society, nominally ruled by the Abbasid caliphs. The Turkic Seljuqs neither intended nor attempted to impose their language, culture, and seminomadic social order on the fabric of the Islamic polity; instead they wholeheartedly adopted Islam as their religion and promoted Persian next to Arabic as a language of higher learning.

1258–1500. After the demise of the attenuated Abbasid caliphate of Baghdad in 1258 during the Mongol invasions, Muslim political thinkers were forced to come to terms with three new political powers in the east: (1) Ilkhanid and then Timurid rule in Iran and Iraq, (2) khanate rule of the Golden Horde from Siberia to the Caucasus and from the Urals to the Danube River, and (3) Delhi-based sultanates in India. Farther to the west, it saw military control pass into the hands of Mamluk Turks and Circassians who, uprooted from their homelands as military slaves, were sold into the households of their patrons and emancipated as converts to Islam to serve as soldiers in the Mamluk armies in Egypt and Syria. Control of the polity was thus usurped by a medley of foreign khanates and slave sultanates, each attempting to claim legitimacy through the manipulation of Islamic symbols of just rule and institutional affiliation with Sufi shaykhs. Faced with this fragmentation, Islamic political thinkers sought to find new paradigms that reflected the effort to overcome the tumultuous breakdown of order. Nonetheless, despite having to endure the devastations of Chingiz Khan (1167–1227) and Tamerlane (1336–1405), the conquered Islamic community managed to integrate the foreign conquerors into its religion and polity.

1500–1800. From about 1500 onward, the division of the Islamic world into sultanates was succeeded by the rise of three separate and flourishing monarchic empires, none of which used Arabic as their official language of discourse and administration. The Turkish-speaking Ottomans, who had conquered Constantinople in 1453 (now named Istanbul as their seat of government), added Syria and Egypt to their empire in 1517 and eventually adopted the title and the legacy of Sunni caliphs. Adopting the Persian idiom, the Safavids established themselves in Iran in 1501 and transformed it into a theocratic Imami Shi'i monarchy. The Mughals, developing a Persian-speaking culture, established their predominantly Sunni rule over India with their victory at Panipat in 1526. In this new threefold constellation, political theory was made to serve the particular vision of rule of each empire rather than that of a universal caliphal culture, and thus Islamic political thought was shaped according to three different modes. Decline set in for all three empires in the 18th century: in the Ottoman lands after Russia gained access to the Black Sea and the Dardanelles in the Treaty of Küçük-Kaynarca (1774) and Napoleon landed in Egypt (1798–1801); in Iran after the murder of Nadir Shah in 1747 and the Qajar accession to power; and in India with a long, agonizing decline after the death of Aurangzeb in 1707 that terminated when the last Mughal emperor was deposed by the British in 1858.

From 1800 onward. The multifarious search for rationales of Islamic political thought from 1800 onward struggled with a situation the world of Islam had never encountered before in its history. It was challenged by a Western culture that had entered its ascendancy. For the first time, Islam neither had the power to conquer nor the capacity to absorb the opposing culture. In response to this anxious and often desperate situation, there gradually emerged revival movements and nationalisms in the Islamic world, whose ideologies covered the spectrum from puritanism, reformism, modernism, secularism, nationalism, and socialism to the extremes of fundamentalism, often termed "Islamism." Its apogees are represented on the one hand by the Iranian Revolution of 1979 and on the other hand by the terrorist attack of September 11, 2001, on the United States.

Rudimentary Foundations of Islamic Political Thought (from Muhammad to 750)

Both Islamic history and Islamic political thought began in the twilight of Late Antiquity with the hijra, the emigration of the Prophet from Mecca to Medina in 622. During his prophetic career in Mecca, Muhammad preached with the expectation of apocalyptic end times, focusing his listeners on their future in the hereafter and reminding them of their individual accountability before God. In Medina, he changed course, dominated by the urge to establish the collective religious unity of a community that would enter history here and now and shape a polity in this world. Once the proclamation of the Qur'an came to an end with the death of the Prophet, eschatological concerns faded; Muslims focused on the victories of the Arab conquest and the resulting exigencies of empire building and the shaping of polity. The caliphs took charge in their succession to the Prophet as leaders of the community. The crisis (*fitna*) of fraternal wars of succession within the ranks of the believers pitted insiders against outsiders, early Arab Muslims against new client converts, orthodox against heterodox, tribes against tribes, regions against regions, and dynasties against dynasties. It gave rise to sects and parties but, ultimately, did not dismantle the body politic even though, from the ninth century onward, it allowed for the separation of political functions between caliphs, military amirs, and viziers administering the state. Neither the bifurcation of the caliphate in the middle of the tenth century into the Muslim East under the Buyid amirs in Baghdad and the Muslim West under the Fatimid caliphs in Cairo (and the Umayyad caliphs in Córdoba) nor the influx of Turks and Mongols in the middle of the 11th and 13th centuries destroyed the cohesive but highly flexible structure of the Islamic polity.

Early medieval Islamic political thought proved masterfully able to build on the rudimentary foundations of the earliest phase of Islam. Although the Qur'an was not designed to be a book of political thought, it included language that Muslim political thinkers adopted in their formulation of essential concepts. In addition, Muhammad's organization of Medinan society through the Constitution of Medina offered a model of applied political thought and a glimpse into the Prophet's pragmatic approach toward the creation of a new polity. The first four caliphs conquered and quickly established themselves as administrators of the core lands of the future empire and encapsulated their political vision in short directives and instructions. In Umayyad times, the caliphs defended Muslim interests, regarding the state as their family's benefice. The people, most of whom were non-Muslim, were regarded as clients under the caliph's patronage, providing the tax revenue needed by the state. As deputy (*khalīfa*) of the Prophet, the ruler oversaw the law and demanded unconditional obedience on the part of his subjects. Differing views about government and society were put down decisively as manifested by the neutralization of the Shi'is and the suppression of the Kharijis. In the dying days of the Umayyad caliphate, the scribe 'Abd al-Hamid (d. 750), founder of the Arabic epistolary style, began a tradition of giving advice to the ruler on personal conduct, administrative and ceremonial matters, and the conduct of war.

Islamic Political Thought in the Early Middle Ages (750–1055)

Upon the accession of the Abbasids as rulers of the empire in 750, the caliph acted as the protector of religion and state (*dīn wa-dawla*) and his government as God's shadow on Earth under whose sheltering protection everyone could find refuge. The clerical class (*kuttāb*) undertook impressive Arabic translations of Persian treatises on Iranian political institutions—a movement spearheaded by its principal proponent, Ibn al-Muqaffa' (ca. 720–56), the champion of the courtly ideal of government (*adab*). *Kitab al-Kharaj* (The book of the land tax), written by the chief judge Abu Yusuf (d. 798) at the behest of caliph Harun al-Rashid, set a precedent for treatises on government and fiscal matters written by 'ulama'. It covered not only the rules of taxation but also legal and ethical principles as applied to social groups. It also defined the caliph as the shepherd of his flock and stressed his obligation to establish divine order. Ma'mun's attempt to establish a high imperial ideal with the primacy of the caliph over the clerical class and the learned elite produced a flourishing high culture infused with the Hellenistic heritage. Neoplatonism, in particular, entered into Islamic political thought through a translation movement of Greek (via Syriac) into Arabic. After the failure of the *miḥna* (trial), the inquisition enforced by an edict of the caliph to impose the theological doctrines of the Mu'tazilis as state creed, the clerical and learned classes found a way to resist caliphal authority in matters of religious doctrine and law.

The seat of the caliphs in the center of the circular capital city of Baghdad, conceived as an ideal city, did not become a throne for a pope-like authority; rather, the caliphate had to acknowledge that the 'ulama', inspired by Shafi'i (d. 820) and Ahmad b. Hanbal (d. 855), held the allegiance of the masses and would exclusively and collectively represent the teaching authority in Sunni Islam on a consensual basis. The situation was very different with the Shi'is, who emphasized the teaching authority of their ideal leader and placed overriding authority in the infallible imam. This view was expounded in the theological works of the Imami Shi'is; it was forcefully articulated by Mufid (948–1022) and Murtada (967–1044), who formulated a response to the Mu'tazili vision incisively presented in the works of the Qadi 'Abd al-Jabbar (935–1025). The Shi'is, a minority weakened by internal dissensions and schisms, were unable to establish their own political theology as normative and endured Sunni ruling institutions by embracing the principle of cautious dissimulation (*taqiyya*). They were sustained by their belief in the hidden presence of the imam and their projection into the future of the Mahdi's apocalyptic return. In the middle of the tenth century, the Qarmati branch of the Isma'ili Shi'is produced its esoteric propaganda of fellowship in the encyclopedic *Epistles* (*Rasa'il*) of the Brethren of Purity (Ikhwan al-Safa'), an anonymous work too arcane to have a practical impact.

The articulate political thought developed by the Muslim philosophers (*falāsifa*) argued for a political society (*madīna*) that evoked the Greek ideal city (*polis*), from where the name of *madīnat al-salām* (city of peace) that the Abbasids adopted for Baghdad, their capital, originated. Farabi (870–950) and Ibn Sina (980–1037), both hailing from Transoxiana, focused on the center of the empire and supported the ideal of the philosopher-king, an ethically perfect individual as head of a virtuous polity. Farabi's ideal of "the virtuous city" (*al-madīna al-fāḍila*) offered a systematic thesis on the state as the perfect society, in which rational integrity and right conduct are the means for achieving supreme felicity (*sa'āda*). Just as the human body has different parts doing different work in a harmonious manner, so too does the body politic require an efficient division of labor. Just as the body has a head to rule it, so too does society have a chief to rule it, guiding society toward becoming an ideal community of the virtuous. Ibn Sina's chapter on governance (*siyāsa*) in his encyclopedic work, *al-Shifa'* (The healing of the soul) stressed the principle of human interdependence and promoted the ideal of the lawgiver who is both philosopher and prophet. Responding to the need for human government in a religious polity and reminding believers of God and the afterlife, the ruler guarantees the observance of the civil (*nāmūs*) and religious law (shari'a).

Anchored in reason (*'aql*) as its ultimate principle and worked out across boundaries of religious affiliations between Muslims and Christians, the political theory of the Islamic philosophers charted an intellectual trajectory that the majority of the Sunni population was unprepared or unwilling to follow. Unlike the philosophical elite, the Sunni masses needed a system of political thought established on the platform of tradition, not abstract reason. Islamic philosophy lacked the institutional basis that an academy would have provided and did not manage to attract the popularly important scholars of law and religion with their deep roots in the literature

of the traditions of the Prophet and his Companions (hadith) and their codices of jurisprudence detailing the stipulations of shari'a and amassing myriad opinions on legal points (fatwa).

Islamic Political Thought in the High Middle Ages (1055–1258)

The political vision of Sunni Islam can be traced in two classical works on public law: the Arabic treatise on *The Principles of Power* (*al-Ahkam al-Sultaniyya*) by Mawardi (974–1058), the honorary chief judge of the Abbasid caliphs, who defined the standard theory of the Sunni caliphate and its institutions from the perspective of the 'ulama', and the *Siyasatnama*, the famous Persian work on statecraft by Nizam al-Mulk (1018–92), chief vizier of the Seljuqs, giving expression to the views of the clerical class (*kuttāb*). Nizam al-Mulk also created the foundations of a network of educational institutions (madrasa) that offered scholars of law and religion lecterns and listeners for the dissemination of their works for many centuries. The *Siyasatnama*, together with the *Qabusnama* written in 1082 by Kay Ka'us, represent the apogee of the literary genre of *naṣīḥat al-mulūk* (advice for rulers)—that is, Mirrors for Princes literature that counseled political leaders on statecraft and diplomacy. Thriving for over a millennium, the genre found its beginnings in the writings of 'Abd al-Hamid and Ibn al-Muqaffa', followed by Jahiz (776–869), Ibn Qutayba (828–89), and Ibn 'Abd Rabbih (860–940); continued with treatises of Sufis and courtiers on ethical conduct in political life; and reached its final flourishing during the Mughal and Ottoman empires.

The impact of medieval Islamic political thought is best exemplified by the classical work of Ghazali (1058–1111), presented with great didactic clarity in his encyclopedic *Revival of the Religious Sciences* (*Ihya' 'Ulum al-Din*), which relied on the legal tradition of the Shafi'i school of law and the orthodox theological tradition of Baqillani (d. 1013) and Juwayni (1028–85). The major achievement of Ghazali's magisterial work, however, was the theological and ethical platform he laid for Islamic political institutions, a platform that enabled the moral and religious renewal of Islamic society. Offering a Sunni theological interpretation of political thought, Fakhr al-Din al-Razi (1149–1209) tried to combine dialectical theology with a modified version of Ibn Sina's philosophy in order to support the doctrine that the existence of the king-emperor—namely, the caliph—is necessary to maintain the order of the world. Following the line of the *Treatise of Ethics* (*Tahdhib al-Akhlaq*) of Miskawayh (936–1030), Nasir al-Din al-Tusi's (1201–74) ethical treatise, *The Nasirean Ethics* (*Akhlaq-i Nasiri*), revived Shi'i political thought during Ilkhanid times through his influence on the Shi'i school of Hilla in the works of Muhaqqiq (1205–77) and Ibn al-Mutahhir (1250–1325). Continued in the work of Dawani (1427–1502), Nasir al-Din al-Tusi's pattern of thought later had a significant impact on political ideas in the Mughal Empire of India.

On the far western periphery of the Islamic world in the Iberian Peninsula, Ghazali's books were burned in public by order of the ruling dynasty, bowing to the agitation of Maliki legal scholars. Significant contributions to Islamic political thought were made in Spain, however, through the works of Ibn Hazm (994–1064), and under Almoravid and Almohad rule, those of Ibn Bajja (d. 1139) and Ibn Tufayl (d. 1185). Political thought in Spain reached its peak with the insightful analysis of state and society by Ibn Rushd (1126–98), supporter of Almohad religious policy and one of the most original minds in all of Islam. According to Ibn Rushd, philosophers were best qualified to interpret scripture, tradition, and law because they possessed the highest form of knowledge. Following Aristotle, he held that right and wrong were determined by nature rather than by divine command and that effective legislation required both theoretical and empirical knowledge.

In the last century of Abbasid rule in Baghdad, Sufism emerged as an organized movement of fraternities or affiliations, building up the infrastructure of Muslim society and shaping the Islamic identity of the polity for centuries to come; in fact, Sufism made a powerful impact on the fabric of Islamic polity that contemporary scholarship has widely overlooked. Sufism had begun in the eighth and ninth centuries in Egypt, Syria, Iraq, and Iran with groups of men of piety leading an ascetic life and seeking mystic experience of union with God. Led by teaching masters called shaykhs (or *pīr*s in Persian), such as Dhu al-Nun (796–860), Bayazid al-Bistami (d. 874), Sahl al-Tustari (816–96), Junayd (d. 910), and Hallaj (857–922), it developed its ideal of poverty (*faqr*) and trust in God (*tawakkul*) and spread its practice of meditative recollection (*dhikr*). Its radical spiritual and social patterns provoked the scholars of law and theology, stirred up urban populations, and challenged public order. After being eclipsed by the Shi'i renaissance of the tenth century, Sufism reframed its path to God as a branch of the Muslim sciences during the Sunni revival under the Seljuq Turks in works such as the *Risala* (*Epistle*) of Qushayri (986–1074). Leading into the caliphate of the Abbasid Nasir (1180–1225), Sufism organized itself into a large number of fraternities (*futuwwa*) and affiliations (*ṭarīqa*), based on a strict order of master and disciples and marked by initiation rites and common prayer ceremonies. Networks of Sufis centers, called "lodges" (*ribāṭ*), paralleled the educational institution of the madrasa and were favored by sultanate governments. The sultans sought sacred legitimization for the secular leadership they had acquired through usurpation by securing the endorsement of Sufi shaykhs, whom they often honored with the title of shaykh al-Islam.

Sufism was influenced by the illuminationist philosophy of Shihab al-Din Yahya al-Suhrawardi (1155–91) and was profoundly undergirded by the monist philosophy of Ibn al-'Arabi (1165–1240), whose pivotal concept of the "perfect man" (*al-insān al-kāmil*) supplied both an ontological and ethical ideal. Yet Sufism engaged the emotions as well as the intellect, tolerating unruly wandering dervishes (*qalandar*) and growing widely popular through its provocative use of Persian love poetry, especially that of Jalal al-Din al-Rumi (1207–73). Drawing upon an image familiar to steppe populations, the Sufis advocated a "tent" of spiritual rule (*wilāya*) over the entire society. The hierarchy of saints (*awliyā'*) would be anchored in a spiritual pole (*quṭb*), who would in turn be supported by his substitutes, the "stakes" (*abdāl*) and "pegs" (*awtād*).

Sufi institutions, often built at the outskirts of urban centers around the tombs of their founders, produced widely used manuals, such as Abu Hafs 'Umar al-Suhrawardi's (1145–1234) *'Awarif al-ma'arif* (Gifts of knowledge) that disseminated the ethical and spiritual ideal of the Sufi way of life and contributed much to the Islamic identity of populations in India, Southeast Asia, and sub-Saharan Africa. Sufism made its principal impact on Islamic political thought and social practice during the turbulent transition from the fragmentation of the Abbasid Empire and the emergence of its three successors. During the sultanate period of Ilkhanids, Timurids, Mamluks, and Delhi sultans, Sufi influence was spread by many orders, among them the Kubrawis in Central Asia, the Shadhilis in Egypt and North Africa, and the Suhrawardis and Chishtis in the Indus and Ganges plains. The three great empires would draw religious and political strength from Sufi resources, the Ottomans from the Mevlevis and Bektashis, the Shi'i Safavids from their Sunni Sufi roots, and the Mughals from the Qadiris and Naqshbandis.

Islamic Political Thought in the Late Middle Ages (1258–1500)

Two writers on Islamic political thought stand out in the Late Middle Ages during the period of fragmentation and before the establishment of the three empires: Ibn Taymiyya (1263–1328) and Ibn Khaldun (1332–1406). Ibn Taymiyya, a Hanbali scholar of law and theology who was active in Damascus and Cairo, engaged in bitter controversies with rationalism, Sufism, Shi'ism, and Christianity. He championed the method of legal reasoning (*ijtihād*) to discern the consensus of the believers and chose the middle ground between reason and tradition as well as between violence and piety. In his main political work, *al-Siyasa al-Shar'iyya* (The book of governance according to the shari'a), Ibn Taymiyya countered the aggressive militarism of the Mamluk sultanate with the regulative idea of government embodied in the rule of Sunni religious law. He proclaimed that religion and state need one another because perfect spiritual and temporal prosperity is achieved only when religion is put into practice by religious law that is enforced by a leader who accepts the duty of commanding good and forbidding evil. Ibn Taymiyya maintained that the principles of the state's power should be applied rigorously through the use of the shari'a enforced by the ruler—an ideal that the Wahhabi movement adopted in the 18th century.

Ibn Khaldun was active in North Africa, Spain, and Egypt during periods of dynastic declines. Although he studied broadly in philosophy, law, and theology, he presented his famous *Muqaddima* (the prolegomena to his world history) as an empirical analysis gleaned from the history of the Berbers and Arabs in North Africa. His study of the history of civilization revealed a cyclical pattern: the rule of nomadic chieftains would gradually evolve into kingship in a civilized society that, in turn, would be overthrown by another nomadic group. To break the cycle, authority of leadership had to emerge from natural dominion, pass through the stage of government by men of intelligence and insight, and stabilize itself in a polity based on the principles of religion laid down by God, as exemplified ideally by the rule of the Prophet and his successors, the caliphs.

Little research has been done on the considerable role women played in the medieval Islamic polity. According to the Qur'an, women are equal to men before God and have similar religious obligations. Though subordinate to men in the public sphere and unequal in many sectors of Islamic law, many women played significant roles in the transmission of hadith, beginning with Muhammad's wives ' A'isha and Umm Salama, in the organization of court life, the education of scholars, and the welfare of Islamic families and children in medieval times. Muslim biographical works quote hundreds of women involved in teaching Islam and transmitting its tradition. Sufi women, such as Rabi'a of Basra (d. 801) and Fatima of Nishapur (d. 849), had an impact on Islamic ethics and Sufi practice; Umm Mu'ayyad al-As'ardi (d. 1218) was an important link in the transmission of collections on hadith; Ibn Taymiyya had a chief disciple in Umm Zaynab (d. 1312); Ibn al-'Arabi (1165–1240) was taught by Fatima of Marchena; and Umm Hani' (d. ca. 1466) taught hadith to groups of students in her house in Cairo. There has been a tendency in secular feminist scholarship to depict premodern women in the Islamic world as utterly backward. Against this backdrop, however, Muslim women now writing on Islam in the contemporary world have begun their own active line of feminist inquiry, which promises to open new vistas on Islamic political thought from a previously neglected sector of Islamic culture.

Since the end of Late Antiquity and through most of the millennium of the Early and Late Middle Ages, the Islamic world had been the leading culture on the globe. It has excelled in philosophy and the natural sciences; in logic and metaphysics; in mathematics, astronomy, and optics; in alchemy and geography; and in medicine and architecture. Its transition from vellum to paper in the eighth century propelled it onto a great curve of literary production in both religious and nonreligious literature. This enormous cultural achievement was accomplished in medieval Islam because the Muslim scholars of medicine and science, the philosophers, and the historians avidly inquired into the roots of world cultures anteceding or surrounding them in India, ancient Iran, and the Hellenistic world. Islamic political thought drew on the classics of Greco-Roman and Irano-Indian antiquity. It also antedated and influenced the appearance of works of political thought in medieval Europe, building a bridge between antiquity and modernity. Islamic political thought developed in a cosmopolitan medieval environment of wide-ranging information about other cultures, with all their riches and restrictions. A significant disruption in this development, however, came about at the turn from the 15th to the 16th century, when the Western world of Europe embarked on a course of profound changes in its vision of the world, religion, society, and politics.

Islamic Political Thought in the Early Modern Period (1500–1800)

The Ottomans, a group of Turkic tribesmen, established a small principality in northwestern Anatolia, crossed into Europe in 1357, and took control of the Balkans, moving their capital from Bursa to Edirne in 1366. Although defeated by Timur at Ankara in 1402, they conquered Constantinople in 1453, making it their new capital of

Istanbul. With the conquest of Egypt and Syria in 1517, the Ottomans established a large Sunni empire over Anatolia, the Balkans, and the regions of the eastern and southern Mediterranean. Constantly engaged in warfare with European powers, they suffered a decisive defeat at Lepanto in 1571 and failed to take Vienna in 1683. Increasingly weakened during the 18th and 19th centuries, they acceded to the rule of Muhammad ʻAli (r. 1805–48) as governor of Egypt in 1805. The Ottoman Empire officially disappeared from the geopolitical map when Atatürk abolished the sultanate in 1922 and founded modern Turkey in 1923.

Ruled by pragmatic sultans, the Ottomans created a strong and loyal military force in the Janissaries, who were recruited as children from the Christian subject populations and raised as Muslims. Organizing themselves around the sultan, the Ottomans integrated the military, the learned, and the bureaucracy into their patrimonial state and gave room to the influences of Sufi orders and folk Islam. Seeing the implementation of justice as their right and duty, the sultans conferred upon judges (qadis) the authority to administer both shariʻa and their innovative and parallel civil law (*qānūn*).

Ottoman rule excelled in practical politics; its range of political theories, however, was modest. The perspective of the ʻulama' can be found in Tursun Beg's (d. ca. 1492) essay and Dede Efendi's (d. 1565) epistle on governance. Abu al-Suʻud (1490–1574), a famous commentator on the Qur'an and appointed as a shaykh al-Islam, worked to strengthen the absolute rule of the sultan as the ultimate religious and civil authority. His fatwas brought the *qānūn* into agreement with the shariʻa and established the principle that the qadis derived their competence from the appointment of the sultan and were obliged to go along with his directives in legal matters. In contrast, Kinalizade (1510–72) followed the philosophical tradition of ethics developed by Nasir al-Din al-Tusi and Dawani, advocating the ideal of the philosopher-king who ruled the virtuous city. His delineation of four status groups—men of the pen, men of the sword, traders, and craftsmen—became the foundation of an ideal social order, known as the "right world order" (*niẓām al-ʻālam*). In practice, however, Ottoman society was organized according to a rougher bipartite order. The ruling class of *ʻaskarī*s (warriors) encompassed the military, the learned, and the bureaucrats; its members were supported by taxes levied on the *riʻāya* (flock), the class of ruled subjects composed of tradesmen, laborers, and minorities.

Mustafa ʻAli (1541–1600) saw religion and the educational madrasa system as the moral and intellectual bases of the state; he emphasized the role of the sultan, *qānūn*, and nationality in forging a unified political community. Aqhisari (1544–1616), a Bosnian qadi, wrote a small book on political reform, titled *Usul al-Hikam fi Nizam al-ʻAlam* (Sources of wisdom on the world order), that advocated justice, counsel, military capability, and piety as the foundations of government. Katib Çelebi (1609–57), the most productive scholar of the Ottoman Empire, analyzed the financial state of the sultanate in his reform tract, *Dustur al-ʻAmal* (Code of action), which was influenced by Ibn Khaldun's work. He formulated his thought in anthropological and medical terms, analogizing the body politic to the human body and its stages of growth and decline. In addition to arguing for a balanced budget, an increase in agricultural production, and a reduction of the armed forces, he also exposed rampant corruption and exploitation of the peasants. Katib Çelebi advocated the rule of a strong and just sultan as a solution to the social problems that he identified.

The Turkic-speaking Safavids of Kurdish origin arose from a Sunni Sufi fraternity that was organized in Azerbaijan by Safi al-Din (d. 1334). There and in the neighboring regions of eastern Anatolia, the movement became militantly Shiʻi under their leader Junayd (1446–60). Led by Shah Ismaʻil (1487–1524), they brought the whole of Iran under their control after overpowering the regional rule of the Timurid Qara Quyunlu and Aq Quyunlu in 1501. In these military endeavors, they relied on the support of Turkic tribesmen, called "Redheads" (Qizilbash) for their distinctive red headgear. Adopting Persian as the language of their monarchy, the Safavid shahs set themselves in opposition to the Sunni Ottomans based at the western flank of their territory. Claiming to be living emanations of the godhead and representatives on Earth of the Mahdi, the Twelfth Imam of Shiʻism, they combined supreme secular and spiritual authority into the office of a single omnipotent ruler. The Safavids imposed Shiʻism as the state religion upon all of Iran. The capital was moved from Tabriz first to Qazvin and then to Isfahan, where Shiʻi Safavid power reached its apex in the reign of Shah ʻAbbas (r. 1587–1629). The Safavid dynasty came to an end with the rise of Nadir Shah (r. 1736–47), a chieftain of Turkic tribesmen, who consolidated his rule over all of Iran, and the subsequent Qajar dynasty (1779–1925), a clan that had served in the Qizilbash army under the Safavids.

In the 16th century, the Safavids imposed Imami Shiʻi beliefs on a largely Sunni population, although the distinction between the two groups was marked by significant ambiguity at the time. Shiʻi political thought came vigorously alive in the work of Karaki (1466–1534), a Lebanese scholar who made the provocative claim to be speaking as the general representative (*al-nā'ib al-ʻāmm*) of the absent imam. Karaki's theory of authority has been accepted and extended from his own time until the present by those scholars known as *uṣūlī*s—that is, those who held that religious authority is derived from the study of jurisprudence (*uṣūl al-fiqh*). In accordance with this view, the scholars of the Safavid realm recognized the leading jurist as *mujtahid al-zamān* (the independent jurist of the age) and treated his authority as absolute.

The *uṣūlī*s were challenged in the 17th century by Muhammad Amin al-Astarabadi (d. 1626–27), whose *al-Fawa'id al-Madaniyya* (Instructive notes from Medina), completed in 1622, inaugurated what came to be known as the *akhbārī* or traditionist school of thought. The *uṣūlī*s favored rational elaboration of the law (*ijtihād*) and the acquiescence of lay Shiʻis to the opinions of qualified jurists (*taqlīd*). The *akhbārī*s saw in revelation the sole source of the law and furthermore claimed that it was most reliably preserved in the *akhbār*, the reports of the imams' words and deeds recorded in the Four Books of Traditions accepted by the Shiʻis. Even the Qur'an, in their view, should properly be understood through the commentary of the imams preserved in these reports. In the later 17th century,

the main spokesman for the *akhbārīs* was Muhsin Fayz Kashani (1598–1680). He popularized the political thought of his period by his *Kingly Mirror*, which integrated Sufi ideas into a treatise that nonetheless maintained the supremacy of revelation and religious law over reason and conscience. The *uṣūlīs*, on the other hand, found their most illustrious proponent in Majlisi (1627–1700), who developed orthodox Imami Shi'ism and brought the state under the direction of the legal scholars, launching attacks against Sufis and philosophers. In the view of Majlisi and similar theorists, the king (shah) was but the instrument of the clerical class and dependent on the leading *mujtahid*. The victory of the *uṣūlīs* over the *akhbārīs* was finally achieved by Muhammad Baqir al-Bihbihani's (1705–91) decisive work, *Risalat al-Akhbar wa-l-Ijtihad* (Epistle on prophetic traditions and legal reasoning).

During three centuries (1200–1500), Muslim rule in India was organized by Afghan and Turkic sultanates ruling mainly from Delhi. The control of the Mughal emperors over the entire subcontinent began with Babur (1483–1530), a descendant of both Chingiz Khan and Tamerlane, who invaded India from the northwest. After Babur's victory at Panipat in 1526, the Sunni Mughal monarchy was extended over almost all of India during the long rule of Akbar the Great (r. 1556–1605). Akbar, a superb though illiterate administrator, abolished the poll tax levied on Hindus; favored a syncretistic religion, called *dīn-i ilāhī* (divine religion); and created a ruling class of appointees (*manṣabdārīs*) consisting of Turks, Afghans, Persians, and Hindus. Dara Shikuh (1615–59), inclined toward the Qadiri Sufi order, inspired the translation of the Upanishads into Persian and championed religious assimilation with Hinduism. His program of religious openness was not to last long when he was executed on the orders of Aurangzeb (r. 1658–1707), his brother and rival. Aurangzeb stood up against the eclectic traditions of his predecessors, breaking the renewed vigor of Hinduism with a reform centered on Islamic values and supported by the Naqshbandi Sufi order. The Mughal Empire lost its glory after Delhi was sacked by Nadir Shah in 1739 and gradually lost all its power under the rule of British colonialism.

The open-minded innovations of the Mughal emperor Akbar broke with traditional patterns of Islamic political thought in an attempt to build a single political community that granted India's Hindu population religious toleration and equal status with their Sunni and Shi'i Muslim neighbors. He also tried to reconcile Muslim sectarian groups with one another. Akbar's views were expounded in the *Regulations of Akbar* (*A'īn-i Akbarī*), which were compiled by his adviser Abu al-Fadl (1551–1602). Claiming infallible monarchical authority and according himself supreme power as the *insān al-kāmil*, Akbar combined the role of king with that of spiritual teacher. Proclaiming himself the highest authority in matters of religious law as well as secular law, he set aside key stipulations of the shari'a and embraced religious tolerance and political equality.

Akbar's and Abu al-Fadl's vision did not survive in India. Ahmad Sirhindi (1564–1624), who stood in the spiritual line of the Naqshbandis, perceived Akbar's ideology as destructive to Islamic law and religion. He came to be called the "renewer" (*mujaddid*) as Islam entered into its second millennium because he wished to restore Islamic values in public and political life, albeit in a form inspired by Sufi piety rather than legalistic rigidity. 'Abd al-Haqq Dihlawi (1551–1642) went a step further and stressed the precedence of religious law over the Sufi path and limited the king's function to upholding the shari'a. Emperor Aurangzeb (1650–1707) repudiated Akbar's tolerance toward Hinduism; he reintroduced a unified legal system of Sunni orthodoxy based on Hanafi law and reimposed the poll tax on non-Muslims. Shah Waliullah (1703–62), a man of encyclopedic learning with roots in the Naqshbandi Sufi affiliation, strove to establish a polity based on the shari'a in India. In his *The Conclusive Argument from God* (*Hujjat Allah al-Baligha*), he applied the Islamic principle of *ijtihād* to the changing circumstances of his time and tried to reconcile the doctrinal differences between the legal scholars and Sufi mystics while rejecting tolerance toward Hindus.

Islamic Political Thought in the Later Modern Period (from 1800 to the Present)

During the 19th century, half of the Islamic world passed under the formal colonial rule of European states—geographically tiny but militarily and economically mighty countries in comparison to the vast Muslim territories they ruled and controlled. The reaction of the Islamic intelligentsia to this overpowering control from without was one of reform and revival from within, spearheaded by social and political reformers, some of whom were journalists rather than scholars steeped in Islamic law and religion. Perhaps the most outstanding figure among them was Jamal al-Din al-Afghani (1839–97). Active in Istanbul, Cairo, Paris, London, India, Russia, and Iran, he devoted his life to the reviving of Muslim intellectual and social life in pamphlets and political articles and agitated for the resurrection of a reformed and purified Islamic identity in the face of European encroachment. He attacked Darwin in his refutation of materialism and asserted that only religion ensures stability of society while materialism causes decay and debasement. Longing to re-create the glory of Islam in a Pan-Islamic state, Afghani argued that Islam's ultimate orientation toward God enabled it to organize the finest possible political community.

Afghani's chief disciple was Muhammad 'Abduh (1849–1905), often seen as the founder of Egyptian modernism. 'Abduh, who had received a traditional education and attended Azhar University, was attracted to mysticism and considered Afghani to be his spiritual guide. He became the editor of the *Egyptian Gazette* and for the last six years of his life served as the grand mufti of Egypt. He wrote several theological treatises, among them a defense of Islam against Christianity, and promulgated his program of reform in *al-Manar* (The lighthouse), a Qur'an commentary that he published in installments and that was later continued as a monthly by his highly educated collaborator Rashid Rida (1865–1935), a man of Syrian descent. 'Abduh's political thought had the overriding goal of returning Islam to its pristine condition, emphasizing the Qur'an and sunna and restoring the role of *ijtihād*. Although the exercise of reason and the adoption of modern natural science

were of paramount importance, reason must defer to the dogmas of religion while prophecy focused on the moral education of the masses. Rida, a prolific writer, refined some of ʻAbduh's points and distinguished between the religious duties (*ʻibādāt*), unchangeable because based on the Qur'an and sunna, and duties toward other Muslims (*muʻāmalāt*), to be reinterpreted by the exercise of reason so as to serve the welfare (*maṣlaḥa*) of the community. Rida believed that the caliphate was indispensible in guaranteeing the coherence of the Muslim community. Faced with the breakup of the Ottoman caliphate in 1923, he proposed a resurrected caliphate preserve the solidarity of all Muslims worldwide.

With roots in the political thought of Ahmad b. Hanbal and Ibn Taymiyya, the modern reform movement of the Salafis began with Afghani, ʻAbduh, and Rida and continued to identify the causes of disintegration of the Muslim community in the infiltration of foreign ideas and practices. The movement taught that Islamic honor and self-respect can be reestablished only if Islam as both a religion and a way of life is redeemed from cultural submission to Western powers. Salafi thinkers called for sweeping reforms in Muslim education, combining the values of traditional pedagogy with the creativity of modern education. They advocated resurrecting the ideal of Islamic law and updating the Arabic language to address the realities of modern life. The Salafis had an impact on Algeria with Ibn Badis (1889–1940), on Morocco with Muhammad ʻAllal al-Fasi (1910–74), and on Tunisia with Muhammad al-Tahir b. ʻAshur (1879–1973).

The puritan movement of the Wahhabis began in the heart of the Arabian Peninsula with Muhammad b. ʻAbd al-Wahhab (1703–92), who insisted on uncompromising monotheism (*tawḥīd*). Islam, he believed, had to be purified from all devotion to anything else (*shirk*): there was no room for saint worship, legal reasoning beyond the Qur'an and sunna, or any innovation (*bidʻa*). He allied himself with ʻAbd al-ʻAziz b. Muhammad b. Suʻud (1765–1803), the leader of the tribal group of Al-Suʻud, becoming shaykh and qadi in the service of the amir and imam. The Saudi-Wahhabi alliance continued with their sons and extended rule over the Hijaz and the key cities of Mecca and Medina. Eradicating anything that might undermine the purity of their beliefs, they destroyed tombs of saints and books of intellectual adversaries, interdicted devotional prayers, and pillaged Shiʻi shrines in Iraq. Muhammad ʻAli, the powerful governor of Egypt under the Ottomans, pushed them back, but the Saudi-Wahhabi state, with Riyad as its capital, was restored under the amirs Turki (d. 1834) and his son Faysal (d. 1865) and the religious authority of ʻAbd al-Rahman (d. 1869), a grandson of Muhammad b. ʻAbd al-Wahhab. After many setbacks and internal rivalries, the Saudi-Wahhabi state was restored in 1902. Over this long history, the Wahhabis expressed the staunchest spirit of politically strategic fundamentalism that inspired many similar movements in other parts of the Islamic world.

Traders brought Islam to West Africa on camelback from the north through the Sahara and to East Africa from the shores of South Arabia, Iran, and India by boat across the Indian Ocean. In West Africa, Sunni Islam of the Maliki legal school became dominant; since the 12th century, Timbuktu developed into a famous seat of commerce and Islamic learning on the Niger River. Dongola on the upper Nile River was taken under Muslim rule in the 14th century after the collapse of Christian Nubia. The vast independent state (often called the "Sokoto caliphate") established at Sokoto by Muhammad Bello at the death of his father ʻUthman b. Fudi (Usman dan Fodio, 1754–1817), who had led a successful four-year jihad against neighboring principalities, became the largest autonomous state in 19th century sub-Saharan Africa.

It was charismatic leadership that transformed sub-Saharan Islamic societies into fundamentalist-inspired states, as can be shown by two examples, one centered on the idea of "the seal of the saints" (*khāṭam al-awliyā'*) and the other on the messianic idea of the Mahdi, the apocalyptic leader of the end times. In West Africa, the Tijani Sufi affiliation was founded in an oasis of Algeria by Ahmad al-Tijani (1737–1815), whose teachings were recorded by a close companion and thereafter elaborated by ʻUmar b. Saʻid al-Futi (1796–1864). Ahmad al-Tijani claimed that the Prophet had appeared to him in a waking vision, appointing him to the spiritual rank of the seal of sainthood (*khātam al-awliyā'*, *quṭb al-aqtāb*), a rank that gave him spiritual domination over the age (*ṣāḥib al-waqt*), exclusive knowledge of the supreme name of God (*ism Allāh al-aʻẓam*), and the power of a vicegerent (*khalīfa*) who alone mediates between God and His creatures. In the middle of the 19th century, ʻUmar b. Saʻid al-Futi, a Fulbe of Senegal, assumed the leadership of the Tijanis and the role of a *mujāhid* (border warrior for the faith), launching a militant anticolonial jihad movement across West Africa from Senegal to Ghana and into Nilotic Sudan. By the middle of the 20th century, the Tijanis were transformed into a revivalist movement among the black Africans as Ibrahim Niasse (1900–1975) extended it among the urban Muslims of Nigeria and Sudan.

In (Nilotic) Sudan, Muhammad Ahmad (1844–85), a Sunni with roots in the Sammani Sufi affiliation, proclaimed himself to be the expected Mahdi in 1881. He learned of his divine election in a colloquy with the Prophet himself. Ahmad advocated a reformist brand of Islam; he aimed to restore the primitive *umma* (community of believers), governed by the Qur'an and sunna, through his activity in supreme succession to the Prophet (*al-khilāfa al-kubrā*) and with the assistance of his chief disciples in the role of successors to the Rightly Guided Caliphs. Retreating (hijra) into the Nuba Mountains together with his followers, named Ansar after the helpers of Muhammad in Medina, he called people to arms in a jihad against Turkish, Egyptian, and British overlords. Ahmad died shortly after conquering Khartoum in 1885. He was succeeded by his son ʻAbdallah b. Muhammad (1885–99) as his deputy (*khalīfa*), who established a Mahdist state that was overthrown by the British in 1898. The revivalist movement of the Ansar, however, continued under the leadership of ʻAbd al-Rahman (1885–1959) and played a decisive role in the Sudan's declaration of independence in 1955. Under the influence of the Muslim Brotherhood, Hasan al-Turabi (b. 1932) worked toward the formation of an Islamic state and the promotion of a fundamentalist regime in Sudan.

Beginning in the ninth century, Islam reached East Africa through traders and seafarers who came from Southern Arabia and Iran and established trading posts on the East African coast. By the 13th century, the Indian Ocean had become a Muslim sea and Muslims controlled the trade from India and Iran to South Arabia and East Africa. Sunni Islam of the Shafi'i legal school laid the religious foundations for the emergence of the Swahili civilization of the Muslim "coastalists" (*sawāḥila*) in East Africa. In 1332, the Muslim world traveler Ibn Battuta (1304–68) was impressed by the Muslim piety he encountered on the island of Kilwa and in the coastal settlements of Mombasa and Mogadishu. Swahili culture remained a coastal phenomenon with only sporadic Islamic inroads into the East African hinterland; in the area of Lake Nyasa, for example, Islam spread among the Yao. In the 16th century, the Portuguese took control of the spice trade away from the Muslims and secured a sea route linking Europe to India. By the end of the 17th century, however, the sultans of Oman reestablished effective rule in East Africa, when they exerted dominance over the island of Zanzibar in 1698 and expelled the Portuguese from the Tanzanian coasts in 1730. In 1832, the sultans of Oman moved their capital to Zanzibar, which had by that time become the center of the Arab slave trade. In the late 19th and early 20th centuries, imperialist European powers (Portugal, France, Germany, Great Britain, and Italy) scrambled among themselves for control of East Africa. Islam, however, began to play a significant political role in the region only in the 20th century as East African states that included large Muslim minorities gained their independence. These states included Tanzania, Mozambique, Kenya, Uganda, and Malawi. Although the Muslims of South Africa, who trace their ancestry to immigrants from South Asia and slaves imported from Southeast Asia, remained a small minority, they attracted worldwide attention in their struggle against the injustice of apartheid.

Islam in India saw its own developments of Islamic political thought in the 19th century. Ahmad Khan (1817–98), known as Sir Sayyid and knighted by the British in 1888, had only a traditional schooling but became the founder of Muslim modernism and the principal force of Islamic revival in India. An advocate of modern education for its Muslims, he published the periodical *Tahdhib al-Akhlaq* (Moral reform) and wrote commentaries on the Bible and the first half of the Qur'an. After the Sepoy Mutiny in 1857, Ahmad Khan worked toward the reconciliation of the British and Muslims in India and founded the Muhammedan Anglo-Oriental College at Aligarh in 1875. Reinterpreting Islam according to his maxim "the work of God—that is, nature and its fixed laws—is identical to the word of God," he emphasized a rational approach to Islam and to social reforms in Muslim culture.

The Sepoy Mutiny in 1857 that led to the formal colonization of India by the British also had an effect on the emergence of two Sunni reform movements among the Urdu-speaking Muslims, the Barelwis, led by Ahmad Riza (1856–1921), and the Deobandis, led by Qasim Nanawtawi (1832–80) and Rashid Ahmad Gangohi (1828–1905). Both movements maintain considerable influence among Muslims in India and Pakistan today. Muhammad Iqbal (1877–1938), an outstanding poet beloved for his commitment to the creation of Pakistan, accused both the West of cheating humanity of its values through the power of its technology and the Muslim society of his day of subsisting in a state of somnolence; in his *Reconstruction of Religious Thought*, he called the whole world to join the dynamism of the "true Islam" of Qur'an and Muhammad, a dynamism that he believed would harness the forces of history for the moral renewal of all humanity.

Islam came to Southeast Asia (Indonesia, Malaysia, Singapore, and Brunei as well as territories in Thailand and Mindanao) discreetly over the sea. From about the 13th century onward, Muslim traders in noticeable numbers sailed to the ports of this island world and its adjacent coasts, forming viable and enduring communities. Sultanates, based in the port cities of Malacca on the Malaysian peninsula (1400–1511) and Demak on Java (1475–1588), constituted little-known early Muslim powers. The 16th and 17th centuries saw the formation of four great Islamic empires with their centers in port cities, formed at (1) Aceh, in northern Sumatra and central Malaysia (1500–1650); (2) Bantam, on western Java and southern Sumatra (1527–1682); (3) Mataram, on central Java, southern Borneo (Kalimantan), and eastern Sumatra (1588–1682); and (4) Macassar, on Celebes and Sumbawa (1605–69). As Sunni Islam of the Shafi'i (Kalimantan) legal tradition spread in Southeast Asia, its law, practice, and essential doctrines took firm roots. In addition, Sufis coming from India to the Malay Peninsula and from the Arabian Peninsula to the archipelago had a significant impact on the formation of the Southeast Asian Muslim polity.

In the 18th and 19th centuries, the Muslims of Southeast Asia were challenged by increasing Dutch colonial supremacy throughout Sumatra, Java, and Borneo, as well as by British colonial administration in Malaysia. At the same time, the fervent practice of the pilgrimage to Mecca kept Southeast Asian Muslims in contact with the world of Islam and facilitated the influence of the Wahhabis and the reformism of 'Abduh and Rashid Rida on Southeast Asian Islam. Journals such as *al-Imam* (The guide) in Singapore and *al-Munir* (The enlightener) in Sumatra imitated *al-Manar*. The development of the *pesantren*, Muslim boarding schools led by groups of religious teachers known as *kyai*, created an infrastructure of traditional Muslim education that propelled the spread of Islam, especially in Java. The most influential puritan movement of the Muhammadiyya, founded in Yogyakarta in 1912, adopted Dutch institutional and Christian missionary approaches and opposed Sufi forms of education. It organized a comprehensive educational system that ranged from primary schools to teacher training colleges and expanded social services to the needy. Wiped out by the Dutch in 1930, it was followed to some degree by the traditionalist Nahdat al-'Ulama', founded in 1926. Indonesia achieved independence in 1945 and adopted the five principles or Pancasila (monotheism, nationalism, humanism, democracy, and social justice) as the philosophical basis for its order of society; Sukarno became the first president (1945–67), followed by Suharto (1967–98). Malaysia gained its independence from the British in 1957; its political system was a mixture of parliamentarianism and authoritarianism. The Malaysian

constitution both guaranteed freedom of religion and made Islam the state religion. Ethnic Malays, who are mainly Muslim, dominated politics, and non-Muslim Malays of Chinese or Indian descent ran the economic and financial sectors. Since 1969, the *dakwah* (*da'wa*) movement has endeavored to invite non-Muslims to embrace Islam and has strived to establish the power of Islam as a total system of *deen* (*dīn*, religion) against Western secularism.

In the 20th century, Europe lost its global leadership during the period of the two world wars, when it experienced the eclipse of fascist nationalism, the downfall of colonial imperialism, and the emergence of the Soviet Union and the United States as the primary shapers of the world order. The Russian revolution and the emergence of the communist systems in the Soviet Union and China left only tangential imprints on Islamic political thought. The forceful entry of the United States into world politics in the aftermath of World War II, however, particularly its projection of military and cultural dominance into Muslim societies, provoked a range of vehement and enduring Islamic reactions. The extremist fringe is characterized by destructive militancy and terrorist movements, such as al-Qaeda, originally a group of American-backed jihadists fighting against the Soviet Union in Afghanistan.

For Islam, the 20th century began with forceful secularist movements and ended with a rising tide of fundamentalist movements seeking to expunge the Western presence from Muslim lands.

In 1924, Atatürk abolished polygamy, shari'a courts, and Qur'an schools in Turkey; he also created national banks, reformed the Turkish alphabet, prohibited the wearing of fez and veil, empowered women to vote and obtain equality in education and employment, and required citizens to use family names rather than simply first names. Turkey became the central example of a cultural and political revolution imposed from the top by an authoritarian regime. The country was divided into urban elites (which acceded to the secularization) and rural masses (which resisted it). Later leaders gradually restored balance to Turkey's society, allowing some expression of Islamic culture and practice to resume. Not all efforts to reappropriate the riches of the Islamic tradition have been violent. The Nur movement, founded by Bediüzzaman Said Nursi (1876–1960), with millions of followers that today form two major branches, was a peaceful revivalist phenomenon manifesting the re-Islamizing trend in Turkey.

On the other side of the spectrum, in the late 20th century, the Islamic world became dominated by fundamentalist movements: the Muslim Brotherhood founded by Hasan al-Banna (1906–49) in Egypt and spearheaded by Sayyid Qutb (1906–66); the Islamic Group, established by Mawdudi (1903–79) in India and Pakistan; and the movement of clerics and mujahidin led by Ayatollah Khomeini (1903–89) that culminated in the Iranian Revolution in 1979. These three movements transformed Islam into a political ideology and were not hesitant to use force to secure their political objectives.

Banna, a school teacher from Isma'iliyya on the Suez Canal, formed the Muslim Brotherhood in order to combat the influence of a corrupt society by bringing the Egyptian youth back to religion. He gave his movement a militant character with a strict chain of command, which consisted of a general guide presiding over the membership, members organized as families and battalions, and a trusted core of its elite defined as a "secret apparatus." His promulgation of the movement's "fundamental law" transformed it publicly into a social and political organization with antiforeign, anti-Zionist, anti-Communist, and antisectarian attitudes. After the Free Officers seized power in 1952 and exiled Farouk, Egypt's last king of Albanian descent, President Nasser cracked down on the Muslim Brotherhood, driving the movement underground. Sayyid Qutb, a journalist who had experienced cultural shock during a visit to America, returned to Egypt in 1951, proclaimed himself to have been reborn a true Muslim, and joined the Muslim Brotherhood. Imprisoned by Nasser for ten years, he wrote the *Signposts on the Way* (*Ma'alim fi al-Tariq*), a manifesto for political revolution through personal discipline and violent jihad, which decried Nasser's Egypt as *jāhiliyya*, a land of ignorance and unbelief. He argued that to resurrect the Muslim polity as a collectivity (*jamā'a*) based on Islamic ethics, a vanguard had to be mobilized by an all-inclusive jihad with the aim of establishing a truly Islamic society.

The Muslim Brotherhood achieved a strong popular appeal through its social programs, which assisted the large lower strata of Muslim society in their neighborhoods. They were unable, however, to offer an agenda that would pull Egypt out of lethargy and overcome corruption. They also contributed to social instability by organizing riots that targeted the minority Coptic populations. Later, small spin-offs of the Muslim Brotherhood had recourse to more extreme forms of violence. In 1977, al-Takfir wa-l-Hijra resorted to kidnapping, and in 1981, Al-Jihad assassinated President Sadat, using the pamphlet of the *Neglected Duty* (*al-Farida al-Gha'iba*) as their manual of action. Not unlike his predecessors, President Mubarak curbed the influence of the Muslim Brotherhood by arresting its leadership. When he was removed from power by peaceful mass demonstrations in 2011, however, the Muslim Brotherhood was taken by surprise and began immediately to reorganize its structure to resonate with the new spirit of freedom. The "Arab Spring," beginning with mass demonstrations in Tunisia and Egypt early in 2011, created enthusiasm but risks devolving into a leaderless revolution. The key challenge facing Muslim advocates for reform would be to identify and empower balanced leadership in the hitherto unfamiliar environment of human rights and democratic freedom.

In India and Pakistan, Mawdudi, an Urdu journalist by profession, became one of the leading interpreters of Islam in the 20th century. Educated as a Hanafi Sunni, he was insulated from Western ideas and the English language but acquired a fluent knowledge of Arabic. Stung by Hindu assertions that Islam had been spread by the sword, he emphasized the spiritual and ethical dimensions of the doctrine of jihad in his *al-Jihad fi al-Islam* (Jihad in Islam), a testimony to his profound conversion to the Muslim faith. For the rest of his life, Mawdudi published his ideas in the monthly *Tarjuman al-Qur'an*, making it the vehicle for his intense anti-Western feelings and his relentless desire to demonstrate the superiority of Islamic culture. For 30 years, Mawdudi worked on his Qur'an commentary, *Tafhim al-Qur'an*, in which he developed his political thought on the Islamic

state. In 1941, he founded the Jama'at-i Islami, a carefully selected group that would disseminate his ideas and implement his plan for an ideal Islamic state that was not confined within national boundaries. Mawdudi was initially opposed to the creation of Pakistan as a separate state, out of fear that the Muslims in India would lose their religious identity. Nevertheless, when the subcontinent was divided in 1947, he opted to move to Pakistan, becoming the decisive force that directed the new nation away from the ideal of a secular state toward that of an Islamic state. Mawdudi met with considerable resistance, enduring a series of imprisonments and, in 1953, even a death sentence that was not carried out. He managed nevertheless to infuse his ideas into the constitution of Pakistan. Toward the end of his life, he supported the move to outlaw the revivalist and messianic movement of the Ahmadis, founded by Mirza Ghulam Ahmad (1835–1908) in India—a move that was accomplished in 1974 by an act of the Pakistan parliament. In 1977, Mawdudi also called for the overthrow of Zulfikar Ali Bhutto, the leader of the People's Party and prime minister of Pakistan, who was executed in 1979.

Khomeini came from a family of strict Shi'i religious leaders in Iran; his father was killed on the orders of Reza Shah (r. 1925–41). Having been educated in Islamic schools and having written extensively on Islamic law and philosophy, Khomeini was recognized as an ayatollah in the 1950s in Qum, where he had moved in 1922 with his teacher 'Abd al-Karim al-Ha'iri. He received the more exalted title of a *marja'* (grand ayatollah) after the death of Ayatollah Borujerdi in 1960. Because he spoke out against Muhammad Reza Shah (r. 1941–79) and against Westernization, he was exiled to Najaf in Iraq in 1964. Asked to leave Iraq in 1978, Khomeini settled in a suburb of Paris and agitated from there for the overthrow of the Shah and the establishment of an Islamic Republic in Iran. After the ouster of the Shah, he returned to his homeland on February 1, 1979, and was acclaimed as the religious leader of the revolution. Khomeini came to power with the help of a network of mosques, the support of the bazaar, and the support of the lower ranks of the military, together with a wide spectrum of leftist, secularist, and conservative traditionalist thinkers.

A new constitution created the Islamic Republic of Iran with Khomeini as its religious leader and legal guardian (*wilāyat al-faqīh*). More generally, a new theocratic political system gave the clerics ultimate control of the state. Although an elected president headed the executive branch, his authority was superseded by that of the legal guardian, who was supported by an advisory council of Shi'i jurists. Under Khomeini's direction, fundamentalist Muslim codes designed to suppress Western influence and restore shari'a were enacted. Women were required to wear the veil, alcohol and Western music were banned, and punishments prescribed by Islamic law were reinstated. Opposition figures were killed, imprisoned, or exiled. The fledging republic managed to survive war with Iraq (1980–88) but was unable to export its Shi'i brand of fundamentalism to other Muslim countries.

Perhaps the thorniest issue for Islamic political thought in the 20th century was the establishment of Israel on native Arab lands in 1948. To make room for Ashkenazi Jewish refugees from Central Europe and Sephardic Jewish immigrants from North Africa and the Middle East after World War II, Palestinian Arabs were driven from their homes without receiving any remuneration and forced to live in refugee camps. Wars in 1967 and 1973 between Israel and its neighbors as well as Israeli bombardments of Beirut in 1982 and cluster bombings of southern Lebanon in July 2006 only deepened Arab resentment. Ongoing construction of new Israeli settlements on the high ground of Palestinian soil west of the Jordan River and dividing walls cutting through Palestinian villages further antagonized the Palestinians, who were promised a two-part quasi-state—the Gaza Strip and West Bank—without territorial, economic, or military sovereignty. While advocates for peace and reconciliation can be found with both liberal Israeli and Palestinian factions, the policies of far-right Israeli leaders have resisted reconciliation and reparation as dangerous weaknesses. American support of Israel created a deep dislike for American policy in the greater Middle East that reverberated throughout the entire Muslim world.

In contemporary times, Pan-Islamism has remained a distant dream, secularism severed the bonds with a long and venerable Islamic heritage while fundamentalist movements forced Islam into a puritanical straitjacket, and militancy brought murder and destruction. Islam has not created a comprehensive system of political thought able to integrate the disparate elements informing its current stage of development. Emerging currents in political Islam are attempting to articulate ideologies and organize movements that aspire to inner purity, ethical strength, personal freedom, and collective dignity. Burdened with political and cultural fragmentation and labeled by the West as violent religion, Islam thirsts for a new paradigm of political thought that will enable it to construct its future as a peaceful order in a pluralistic world.

The Encyclopedia of Islamic Political Thought (EIPT)

In creating the EIPT, our goal was to provide a solid and innovative reference work that would trace the historical roots of Islamic political thought and demonstrate its contemporary importance. The editors first met for a workshop in fall of 2007 at the Institute for Advanced Study in Princeton, where we agreed on a framework for the encyclopedia and drafted a list of entries. The EIPT was conceived as a combination of broad, comprehensive articles on core concepts and shorter entries on specific ideas, movements, leaders, and related topics. We intended to make the EIPT accessible, informative, and comprehensive with respect to the contemporary political and cultural situation of Islam, while also providing in-depth examination of the historical roots of that situation. The core articles on central themes were designated to provide the framework for the reader to integrate and contextualize the information provided by the plethora of articles on more specific subjects. It is our hope that this organizational structure will enable the EIPT to serve as a reference work of the first order for both beginners and specialists and to support undergraduate and graduate courses on Islamic political thought.

The entries appear in alphabetical order for ease of use but fall into five categories: (1) central themes, under the direction of

Gerhard Bowering; (2) modern concepts, institutions, movements, and parties, under Muhammad Qasim Zaman; (3) Islamic law and traditional Islamic societies, under Devin J. Stewart; (4) historical developments, sects and schools, and regions and dynasties, under Patricia Crone; and (5) thinkers, personalities, and statesmen, under Wadad Kadi. In the spring of 2008, Princeton University Press assumed the significant administrative burden of implementing the editorial vision for the encyclopedia by helping the editors to secure contributors and track the encyclopedia's progress toward completion. This undertaking has much evolved during the last four years, and the final product, I believe, constitutes a pioneering venture in this field.

We asked contributors to write for the educated nonspecialist reader, to maintain an objective tone, and to provide recommendations for further reading. We followed the system of transliteration developed by the *International Journal of Middle Eastern Studies* (IJMES), with minor modifications, and have simplified spelling as much as possible.

As chief editor, I would like to thank Mahan Mirza for having become the heart and soul of the project, managing the flow of the contributions and consulting at each and every impasse with myself, the associate editors, and the Press, in countless phone calls and e-mails. Without him, the project would neither have begun nor come to term. My thanks are due equally to Patricia Crone, Wadad Kadi, Devin J. Stewart, and Qasim Zaman for their excellent contributions of core articles and their unstinting dedication to the great variety of articles that crossed their desk at untimely intervals. Without their endurance and patience, the project could not have been steered through many perilous straits. I wish to express particular gratitude to Anne Savarese and her collaborators at the Press (Claire Tilman-McTigue, Diana Goovaerts, Natalie Baan, and others who worked behind the scenes), all of whom went out of their way to overcome the technical hurdles of this project and to bear with all of us as the process lengthened beyond expectation. Finally, I would like to thank the many scholars who contributed to the EIPT, making it an instrument to explain and analyze Islamic political thought for specialists and generally informed readers alike.

GERHARD BOWERING

Alphabetical List of Entries

Alphabetical List of Entries

Topical List of Entries

Central Themes
Historical Developments, Sects and Schools, Regions and Dynasties
Modern Concepts, Institutions, Movements, and Parties
Islamic Law and Traditional Islamic Societies
Thinkers, Personalities, and Statesmen

Central Themes

Edited by Gerhard Bowering

authority
caliph, caliphate
fundamentalism
government
jihad
knowledge
minorities
modernity
Muhammad (570–632)
pluralism and tolerance
Qur'an
revival and reform
shari'a
traditional political thought
'ulama'

Historical Developments, Sects and Schools, Regions and Dynasties

Edited by Patricia Crone

Dynasties

Abbasids (750–1258)
Almohads (1130–1269)
Almoravids (1056–1147)
Ayyubids (1169–1250)
Buyids (945–1062)
Delhi Sultanate (1206–1526)
Fatimids (909–1171)
Ghaznavids (977–1086)
Ghurids (1009–1215)
Ilkhanids (1256–1336)
Mamluks (1250–1517)
Mughals (1526–1857)
Ottomans (1299–1924)
Safavids (1501–1722)
Samanids (819–1005)
Seljuqs (1055–1194)
Timurids (1370–1506)
Umayyads (661–750)

Historical Developments

alliances
bazaar
Brethren of Purity
city (philosophical)
civil war
clients
coinage
Crusades
difference of opinion
excommunication
ghāzī
heresiography
heresy and innovation
hypocrisy
inquisition
Mongols
philosophy
privacy
Qajars (1789–1925)
Rightly Guided Caliphate (632–61)
shāhānshāh
Shahnama
solidarity
theology
Thousand and One Nights
trade and commerce
usurper

Regions

Afghanistan
Algeria
Baghdad
Bangladesh
Beirut
Cairo
Central Asia
China
Delhi
East Africa
Egypt
Ethiopia and Eritrea
Europe
India
Indonesia
Iran
Iraq
Istanbul
Jerusalem
Jordan
Karbala
Lebanon
Malaysia
Mecca and Medina
Morocco
Nigeria
North Africa
North America
Pakistan
Palestine
Saudi Arabia
South Africa
Southeast Asia
Spain and Portugal (Andalus)
Sudan
Syria
Transoxiana
Tunisia
Turkey
West Africa
Yemen

Sects and Schools

'Alawis
Ash'aris
Barelwis
Berbers
Druze
Ibadis
Isma'ilis
Kadızadeli
Karramis
Kharijis
Murji'is
Mu'tazilis
Nizaris
Qadaris
Qarmatians
Shi'ism
Shu'ubis
Sufism
Sunnism
Uighurs
Zahiris
Zaydis

Topical List of Entries

Modern Concepts, Institutions, Movements, and Parties

Edited by Muhammad Qasim Zaman

absolutism
Ahmadis
Aligarh
Amal
anarchism
apartheid
Arab nationalism
Azhar University
Ba'th Party
bazaar
capitalism
censorship
Christian-Muslim relations
citizenship
civil society
colonialism
communism
community
constitutionalism
contracts
coup d'état
culture
democracy
demographics
Deobandis
diplomacy
economic theory
education
elections
environment
equality
ethics
freedom
al-Gama'a al-Islamiyya
globalization
Hamas
Hizbullah
human rights
ideology
imperialism
individualism
international Islamic organizations
international relations
Islamic Jihad
Islamization
Jama'at-i Islami
judicial courts
Khilafat movement (1919–24)
leadership
liberalism
liberation theology
libertarianism
media
minorities, jurisprudence of
modernism
monarchy
Muslim Brotherhood
Muslim League
nationalism
Nation of Islam
nation-state
natural law
nonviolence
Palestinian Liberation Organization (PLO)
Pan-Islamism
Pan-Malaysian Islamic Party (PAS)
parliament
preaching
public opinion
public sphere
al-Qaeda
racism
representation
republicanism
Salafis
secularism
socialism
sovereignty
suicide
Tablighi Jama'at
Taliban
Tanzimat
terrorism
theocracy
treason
veil
violence
West, the
Westernization
women
Young Turks

Islamic Law and Traditional Islamic Societies

Edited by Devin J. Stewart

abdication
abodes of Islam, war, and truce
advice
apocalypse
apostasy
arbitration
'Ashura'
astrology
asylum
ayatollah
blasphemy
brotherhoods
bureaucracy
charity
chivalry
city
collective obligations
commanding right and forbidding wrong
Companions of the Prophet
consensus
Constitution of Medina
consultation
conversion
custom
dissent, opposition, resistance
dissimulation
division of labor
endowment
ethnicity
exegesis
faith
family
fatwa
free will
Friday prayer
friendship
genealogy
God
governance
grievance
guardianship of the jurist
guilds
hadith
hijra
holy places
honor
household
human nature
ijtihād and *taqlīd*
imamate
intercession
jāhiliyya
jizya
judge
jurisprudence
justice
kinship
loyalty
madrasa
Mahdi
martyrdom
masses
mawlid
messianism
military
Mirrors for Princes
mosque
mufti/grand mufti
Nizamiyya

Thinkers, Personalities, and Statesmen

Edited by Wadad Kadi

Contributors

Ahmed Abdel Meguid, *Syracuse University*
Ash'aris; free will; human nature; prophecy

As'ad AbuKhalil, *California State University, Stanislaus*
Lebanon

Camilla Adang, *Tel Aviv University*
Ibn Hazm

Asma Afsaruddin, *Indiana University*
martyrdom

Ahmed Afzaal, *Concordia College*
nonviolence

Irfan Ahmad, *Monash University (Australia)*
Aligarh; Jama'at-i Islami; Mawdudi, Abul al-A'la; Sayyid Ahmad Khan

Sadaf Ahmad, *Lahore University of Management Sciences (Pakistan)*
veil

Farish Ahmad-Noor, *Nanyang Technological University (Singapore) and Erasmus Universias Muhamadiyah Surakarta, Yogjarta (Indonesia)*
Pan-Malaysian Islamic Party (PAS)

Rafiuddin Ahmed, *Elmira College*
Bangladesh

Shahrough Akhavi, *University of South Carolina*
communism; guardianship of the jurist; socialism

Mehmetcan Akpinar, *University of Chicago*
Mawardi

Omar Alí-de Unzaga, *Institute of Ismaili Studies (London)*
Brethren of Purity

Adel Allouche, *Yale University*
Tunisia

Sean W. Anthony, *University of Oregon*
'Ali b. Abi Talib; Hasan b. 'Ali; 'Umar b. al-Khattab; 'Uthman b. 'Affan

Zayde Antrim, *Trinity College (Connecticut)*
Jerusalem; Mecca and Medina

Christopher Anzalone, *McGill University*
propaganda

Saïd Amir Arjomand, *Stony Brook University*
absolutism; monarchy; patrimonial state; al-Sadr, Muhammad Baqir

J. C. Arsenault, *University of Pennsylvania*
community; culture

Mushegh Asatryan, *Yale University*
'Alawis

Fakhreddin Azimi, *University of Connecticut*
Iran

Kathryn Babayan, *University of Michigan*
Isma'il I

Irit Back, *Tel Aviv University*
East Africa; Ethiopia and Eritrea

Roswitha Badry, *University of Freiburg (Germany)*
consultation

Meir M. Bar-Asher, *Hebrew University of Jerusalem*
Druze

Michael Barry, *Princeton University*
Afghanistan

Abbas Barzegar, *Georgia State University*
ayatollah; commanding right and forbidding wrong; source of emulation; al-Zawahiri, Ayman

Shahzad Bashir, *Stanford University*
messianism

Orit Bashkin, *University of Chicago*
'Abd al-Raziq, 'Ali

Mangol Bayat, *Independent scholar*
al-Afghani, Jamal al-Din

Amira K. Bennison, *University of Cambridge*
Algeria; Berbers; Morocco; North Africa

Lindsay J. Benstead, *University of Michigan*
parliament

Herbert Berg, *University of North Carolina, Wilmington*
Muhammad, Elijah; Nation of Islam

Jonathan P. Berkey, *Davidson College*
madrasa

Michal Biran, *Hebrew University of Jerusalem*
Transoxiana

Khalid Yahya Blankinship, *Temple University*
Malik b. Anas; obedience; al-Shaybani, Muhammad b. al-Hasan

Antoine Borrut, *University of Maryland*
'Umar b. 'Abd al-'Aziz

John Bowen, *Washington University in Saint Louis*
West, the

Gerhard Bowering, *Yale University*
Egypt (coauthor); Muhammad; Qur'an; Syria

James Broucek, *Florida State University*
mufti/grand mufti

Jonathan A. C. Brown, *University of Washington*
hadith

Rainer Brunner, *University of Freiburg (Germany)*
Europe; Karbala; Rightly Guided Caliphate

Richard W. Bulliet, *Columbia University*
conversion

Heribert Busse, *University of Kiel (Germany)*
Buyids

Alexander Caeiro, *Erlangen Centre for Islam and Law in Europe*
minorities, jurisprudence of

Yousef Casewit, *Yale University*
Zahiris

Shaojin Chai, *University of Notre Dame*
Uighurs

Ayesha S. Chaudhry, *University of British Columbia*
women

Contributors

Julia Clancy-Smith, *University of Arizona*
'Abd al-Qadir al-Jaza'iri

David Cook, *Rice University*
Mahdi

Michael Cook, *Princeton University*
freedom

Michael Cooperson, *University of California, Los Angeles*
Baghdad; Ma'mun; *Thousand and One Nights*

Robert D. Crews, *Stanford University*
Central Asia; imperialism

Patricia Crone, *Institute for Advanced Study (Princeton, NJ)*
clients; philosophy; Quraysh; sunna; traditional political thought; usurper

Farhad Daftary, *Institute of Ismaili Studies (London)*
Aga Khan; Fatimids; Nizaris; Qarmatians

Hans Daiber, *Frankfurt University (Germany)*
philosopher-king

Stephen F. Dale, *Ohio State University*
Babur, Zahir al-Din

Linda Darling, *University of Arizona*
Ottomans

Lara Deeb, *Scripps College*
Amal; Hizbullah

John Donohue, *Saint Joseph University (Lebanon)*
Beirut; Jordan

Phil Dorroll, *Emory University*
holy places

Racha El Omari, *University of California, Santa Barbara*
theology

Sarah Eltantawi, *Harvard University*
Nigeria

Yanis Eshots, *University of Latvia*
city (philosophical); al-Farabi, Abu Nasr; Ibn Sina, Abu 'Ali

Roxanne L. Euben, *Wellesley College*
fundamentalism

Mohammad Fadel, *University of Toronto*
arbitration; collective obligations; contracts; judicial courts

Khaled Fahmy, *New York University*
Muhammad 'Ali

Schirin H. Fathi, *University of Hamburg (Germany)*
Shari'ati, 'Ali

Maribel Fierro, *Center of Human and Social Sciences of the Consejo Superior de Investigaciones Científicas, Madrid*
Almohads; Almoravids; heresy and innovation; Ibn Tumart; Spain and Portugal (Andalus)

Melissa Finn, *York University (Canada)*
asylum; revolutions

Cornell H. Fleischer, *University of Chicago*
Süleiman the Magnificent (coauthor)

Finbarr Barry Flood, *New York University*
Ghurids

Kathleen Foody, *University of North Carolina, Chapel Hill*
utopia

Bernard K. Freamon, *Seton Hall University*
slavery

Yohanan Friedmann, *Hebrew University of Jerusalem*
Ahmadis; Ahmad Sirhindi; minorities

Patrick D. Gaffney, *University of Notre Dame*
al-Gama'a al-Islamiyya; mosque; preaching; pulpit

Moshe Gammer, *Tel Aviv University*
Shamil

Behrooz Ghamari-Tabrizi, *University of Illinois, Urbana-Champaign*
Westernization

Kambiz GhaneaBassiri, *Reed College*
North America

Dru C. Gladney, *Pomona College*
China

Robert Gleave, *University of Exeter (England)*
Friday prayer; Shi'ism

Andreas Görke, *University of Basel (Switzerland)*
taxation

Frank Griffel, *Yale University*
apostasy; excommunication; natural law

Sebastian Günther, *University of Toronto*
education

Li Guo, *University of Notre Dame*
Mamluks

Joseph Hammond, *Independent scholar*
anarchism; ethnicity

Andras Hamori, *Princeton University*
Ibn al-Muqaffa'

Dyala Hamzah, *Zentrum Moderner Orient (Germany)*
Rida, Muhammad Rashid

M. Şükrü Hanioğlu, *Princeton University*
Abdülhamid II; Atatürk, Mustafa Kemal; Tanizmat; Turkey; Young Turks

Nicholas G. Harris, *University of Pennsylvania*
censorship; punishment; treason

Jan-Peter Hartung, *University of London—School of Oriental and African Studies*
India

Nader Hashemi, *University of Denver*
sovereignty

Sohail H. Hashmi, *Mount Holyoke College*
abodes of Islam, war, and truce; diplomacy; rebellion

Jane Hathaway, *Ohio State University*
household

Bernard Haykel, *New York University*
Ibn 'Abd al-Wahhab, Muhammad; Salafis; Saudi Arabia; al-Shawkani, Muhammad b. 'Ali; Yemen

Paul L. Heck, *Georgetown University*
Abu Yusuf; advice; Bin Laden, Osama; bureaucracy; knowledge; Mulla 'Umar

Robert W. Hefner, *Boston University*
Indonesia; Malaysia

Thomas Hegghammer, *Norwegian Defence Research Establishment (Norway) and New York University Center on Law and Security*
suicide; terrorism
Jocelyn Hendrickson, *Whitman College*
fatwa; hijra
Marcia Hermansen, *Loyola University Chicago*
Shah Waliullah
Edmund Herzig, *University of Manchester (England)*
Safavids
Carole Hillenbrand, *University of Edinburgh*
Crusades
Nathan Hofer, *University of Missouri*
brotherhoods; shaykh, *pīr*
David Hollenberg, *James Madison University*
Isma'ilis
Russell Hopley, *Bowdoin College*
leadership
Steve Howard, *Ohio University*
Taha, Mahmoud Mohamed
Murad Idris, *University of Pennsylvania*
Islamization; masses
Matthew B. Ingalls, *University of Puget Sound*
Tablighi Jama'at; vizier
Brannon Ingram, *University of North Carolina, Chapel Hill*
Zia-ul-Haq
Roy Jackson, *University of Gloucestershire (England)*
authority
Sherman A. Jackson, *University of Michigan*
al-Qarafi, Shihab al-Din
Tariq Jaffer, *Boston University*
Murji'is; al-Razi, Fakhr al-Din
Johannes J. G. Jansen, *Leiden University (Netherlands)*
Faraj, Muhammad 'Abd al-Salam
Maher Jarrar, *American University of Beirut*
Qadaris
Masoud Jafari Jazi, *Teacher Training University, Tehran (Iran)*
Jalal Al-i Ahmad
Shamil Jeppie, *University of Cape Town (South Africa)*
apartheid
David L. Johnston, *University of Pennsylvania*
Christian-Muslim relations; environment
Katrin Jomaa, *Indiana University*
city; quietism and activism
Hadi Jorati, *Yale University*
bazaar; Istanbul
Wadad Kadi, *University of Chicago*
'Abd al-Hamid al-Katib b. Yahya al-'Amiri; Abu Bakr; caliph, caliphate (coauthor); al-Tawhidi, Abu Hayyan
Ahmet T. Karamustafa, *Washington University in Saint Louis*
individualism
Rosemary B. Kellison, *Florida State University*
dissent, opposition, resistance; military; republicanism
John Kelsay, *Florida State University*
jihad
Khaled M. G. Keshk, *DePaul University*
Mu'awiya
Nancy Khalek, *Brown University*
notables
Etan Kohlberg, *Hebrew University of Jerusalem*
Ja'far al-Sadiq
Gudrun Krämer, *Free University of Berlin (Germany)*
al-Banna, Hasan; pluralism and tolerance
Sunil Kumar, *Delhi University (India)*
Delhi; Delhi Sultanate
Mirjam Künkler, *Princeton University*
democracy; theocracy
Timur Kuran, *Duke University*
economic theory; public opinion
Charles Kurzman, *University of North Carolina, Chapel Hill*
liberalism; modernism
Michael Laffan, *Princeton University*
Southeast Asia
Ella Landau-Tasseron, *Hebrew University of Jerusalem*
alliances; Umayyads
Christian Lange, *Utrecht University (Netherlands)*
privacy
Henri Lauziere, *Northwestern University*
secularism
Todd Lawson, *University of Toronto*
apocalypse
Marnia Lazreg, *The City University of New York, Hunter College*
torture
Michael Lecker, *Hebrew University of Jerusalem*
Constitution of Medina
Amalia Levanoni, *University of Haifa (Israel)*
Ibn Jama'a
Milka Levy-Rubin, *Hebrew University of Jerusalem*
Treaty of 'Umar
Keith Lewinstein, *Bridgewater State University*
heresiography; Ibadis; Kharijis
Franklin Lewis, *University of Chicago*
Shahnama
Gideon Libson, *Hebrew University of Jerusalem*
custom
Charles Lindholm, *Boston University*
honor; kinship
Roman Loimeier, *Humboldt University of Berlin (Germany)*
West Africa
Matthew Long, *University of Georgia*
Ibn Khaldun; *jizya*
Joseph E. Lowry, *University of Pennsylvania*
rights; al-Shafi'i, Muhammad b. Idris
Scott C. Lucas, *University of Arizona*
Companions of the Prophet

Loren D. Lybarger, *Ohio University*
Arafat, Yasir; Hamas; Palestine; Palestinian Liberation Organization (PLO)
Gregory Mack, *McGill University*
grievance; jurisprudence
Anas Malik, *Xavier University*
libertarianism
Peter Mandaville, *George Mason University*
international relations
Beatrice Forbes Manz, *Tufts University*
Timurids
Andrew F. March, *Yale University*
constitutionalism; ethics; representation
L. Marlow, *Wellesley College*
Mirrors for Princes
Andrew Marsham, *University of Edinburgh*
oath of allegiance
Nabil Matar, *University of Minnesota*
Ibn Tufayl
Rudi Matthee, *University of Delaware*
'Abbas I
Jane Dammen McAuliffe, *Georgetown University*
exegesis; People of the Book
David Mednicoff, *University of Massachusetts, Amherst*
human rights
Christopher Melchert, *University of Oxford*
Ahmad b. Hanbal
Charles Melville, *University of Cambridge*
Ilkhanids
Matthew Melvin-Koushki, *Yale University*
Khunji, Fazl Allah b. Ruzbihan; Mongols; Qajars; Tamerlane
Yahya M. Michot, *University of Oxford*
Ibn Taymiyya
Gail Minault, *University of Texas at Austin*
Khilafat movement
Mustansir Mir, *Youngstown State University*
Iqbal, Muhammad
Mahan Mirza, *Zaytuna College*
Ahmad, Israr; demographics
Jennifer Mitchell, *Champlain Regional College and Vanier College (Canada)*
citizenship
Yasien Mohamed, *University of the Western Cape (South Africa)*
South Africa
Ebrahim Moosa, *Duke University*
Rahman, Fazlur; revival and reform (coauthor)
Suleiman Ali Mourad, *Smith College*
hypocrisy
Rose E. Muravchick, *University of Pennsylvania*
royal court
John A. Nawas, *Catholic University of Leuven (Belgium)*
inquisition; patronage
Daniel Neep, *University of Exeter (England)*
Arab nationalism; colonialism; coup d'état; nationalism
Nassima Neggaz, *Georgetown University*
Dan Fodio, Usman; Muslim League; Mu'tazilis; Nasser, Gamal Abdel; al-Qaeda; Saladin
Martin Nguyen, *Fairfield University*
piety and asceticism
Erik S. Ohlander, *Indiana University-Purdue University Fort Wayne*
al-Suhrawardi, Abu Hafs 'Umar
Jacob Olidort, *Princeton University*
political ritual
Felicitas Opwis, *Georgetown University*
public interest
Eva Orthmann, *University of Bonn (Germany)*
astrology
Carl F. Petry, *Northwestern University*
Cairo
Matthew Pierce, *Fulbright Scholar Program*
judge
Andrew Polk, *Florida State University*
Mohammed, W. D.
Yasir Qadhi, *Yale University*
Karramis; al-Qaradawi, Yusuf
Junaid Quadri, *McGill University*
endowment
Tahera Qutbuddin, *University of Chicago*
Husayn b. 'Ali
Intisar A. Rabb, *New York University*
governance; police
Bernde Radtke, *Utrecht University (Netherlands)*
Sufism
Shadaab Rahemtulla, *Oxford University*
justice; solidarity; tyranny
Sayeed S. Rahman, *Bryn Mawr College*
mawlid
Ali-Ahmad Rasekh, *Concordia University (Canada)*
'Ashura'
Dietrich Reetz, *Zentrum Moderner Orient (Germany)*
Barelwis; Deobandis
Sajjad H. Rizvi, *University of Exeter (England)*
Dawani, Jalal al-Din; Mir Damad; al-Tusi, Nasir al-Din
Chase W. Robinson, *Royal Holloway, University of London*
civil war
Jared Rubin, *Chapman University*
trade and commerce
Marina Rustow, *Emory University*
intercession; loyalty
Bruce K. Rutherford, *Colgate University*
elections
Kaya Şahin, *Tulane University*
Süleiman the Magnificent (coauthor)
Mashal Saif, *Duke University*
Abbasids

Noah Salomon, *Carleton College*
Sudan
Armando Salvatore, *University of Naples-L'Orientale (Italy)*
civil society; globalization; modernity; public sphere
Sarah Bowen Savant, *Aga Khan University-Institute for the Study of Muslim Civilisations (England)*
genealogy; Shu'ubis
S. Abdallah Schleifer, *American University in Cairo*
media
Warren C. Schultz, *DePaul University*
coinage
Reinhard Schulze, *University of Bern (Switzerland)*
international Islamic organizations; Pan-Islamism
Rachel M. Scott, *Virginia Polytechnic Institute and State University*
equality
Kim Searcy, *Loyola University Chicago*
Mahdi of the Sudan
Mark Sedgwick, *Aarhus University (Denmark)*
'Abduh, Muhammad
Rüdiger Seesemann, *University of Bayreuth (Germany)*
al-Turabi, Hasan
Aram A. Shahin, *James Madison University*
caliph, caliphate (coauthor)
Emad El-Din Shahin, *University of Notre Dame*
Egypt (coauthor); government
Zaid Shakir, *Zaytuna College*
Malcolm X
Maya Shatzmiller, *University of Western Ontario (Canada)*
division of labor
William E. Shepard, *University of Canterbury (New Zealand)*
ideology; *jāhilyya*; Sayyid Qutb
Fiazuddin Shu'ayb, *University of California, Los Angeles*
succession
Thomas Sizgorich, *University of California, Irvine*
violence
Denise Spellberg, *University of Texas at Austin*
'A'isha
Ronald Bruce St John, *Independent scholar*
Qaddafi, Mu'ammar
Amina Steinfels, *Mount Holyoke College*
Aurangzeb
Devin J. Stewart, *Emory University*
abdication; blasphemy; consensus; dissimulation; Fadlallah, Muhammad Husayn; faith; family; God; *ijtihād* and *taqlīd*; Nizamiyya; shari'a; shaykh al-Islam
Frank H. Stewart, *Hebrew University of Jerusalem*
tribalism
W. Craig Streetman, *University of Kentucky*
Ibn Bajja
Mairaj Syed, *Princeton University*
difference of opinion; Sunnism
Ian Talbot, *University of Southampton (England)*
Jinnah, Mohammad 'Ali; Pakistan
Daniella Talmon-Heller, *Ben-Gurion University (Israel)*
Ayyubids
Georges Tamer, *University of Erlangen-Nuremberg (Germany)*
Ibn Rushd
SherAli Tareen, *Franklin and Marshall College*
charity; revival and reform (coauthor)
Amin Tarzi, *Marine Corps University*
Taliban
Sultan Tepe, *University of Illinois at Chicago*
nation-state
Baki Tezcan, *University of California, Davis*
Kadızadeli; racism
Shawkat M. Toorawa, *Cornell University*
friendship; pilgrimage; Pillars of Islam
D. G. Tor, *University of Notre Dame*
ghāzī; Ghaznavids; Samanids; Seljuqs; *shāhānshāh*; sultan
Alexander Treiger, *Dalhousie University*
Ghazali
Charles Tripp, *School of Oriental and African Studies, University of London*
capitalism
Nurit Tsafrir, *Tel Aviv University (Israel)*
Abu Hanifa
Mete Tuncay, *Istanbul Belgi University (Turkey)*
Nazim Hikmet
Paul E. Walker, *University of Chicago*
Hakim bi-Amr Allah
Keith David Watenpaugh, *University of California, Davis*
'Aflaq, Michel; Ba'th Party
Neguin Yavari, *Columbia University*
Khomeini, Ayatollah; Nizam al-Mulk
Isra Yazicioglu, *Saint Joseph's University*
Sa'id Nursi
Hayrettin Yücesoy, *Saint Louis University*
imamate
Mohsen Zakeri, *Frankfurt University (Germany)*
chivalry
Muhammad Qasim Zaman, *Princeton University*
'ulama'
Taymiya R. Zaman, *University of San Francisco*
Akbar the Great; Mughals
Syed Rizwan Zamir, *University of Virginia*
guilds
Malika Zeghal, *University of Chicago*
'Abd al-Rahman, 'Umar; Azhar University; Muslim Brotherhood
Homayra Ziad, *Trinity College (Connecticut)*
liberation theology
Hossein Ziai, *University of California, Los Angeles*
Mulla Sadra
Barbara Zollner, *Birkbeck, University of London*
Islamic Jihad
Aron Zysow, *Princeton University*
Zaydis

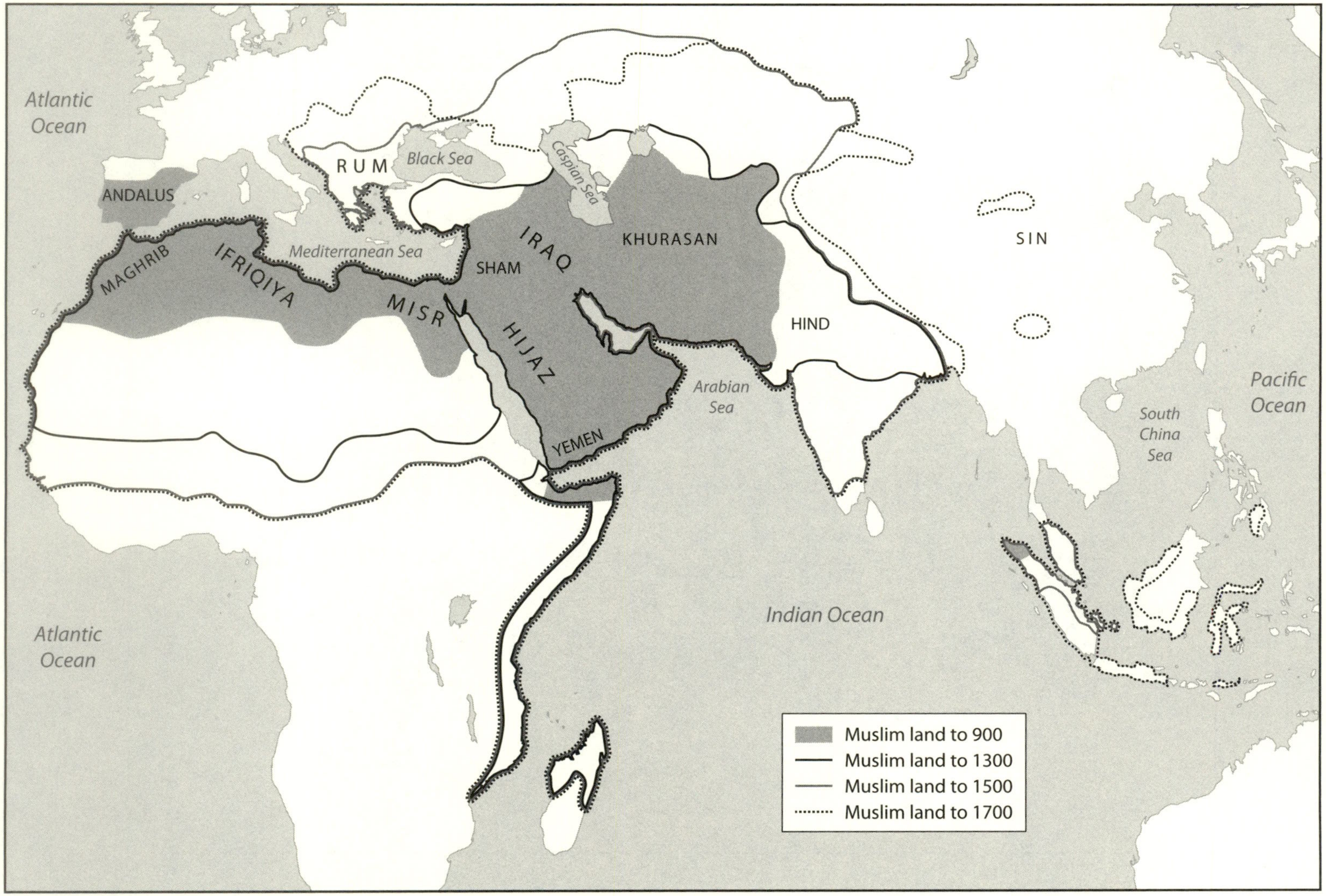

Map 1. The Spread of Islam, 750–1700. Adapted from Malise Ruthven, *Historical Atlas of Islam*, Harvard University Press, 2004, pp. 32–33.

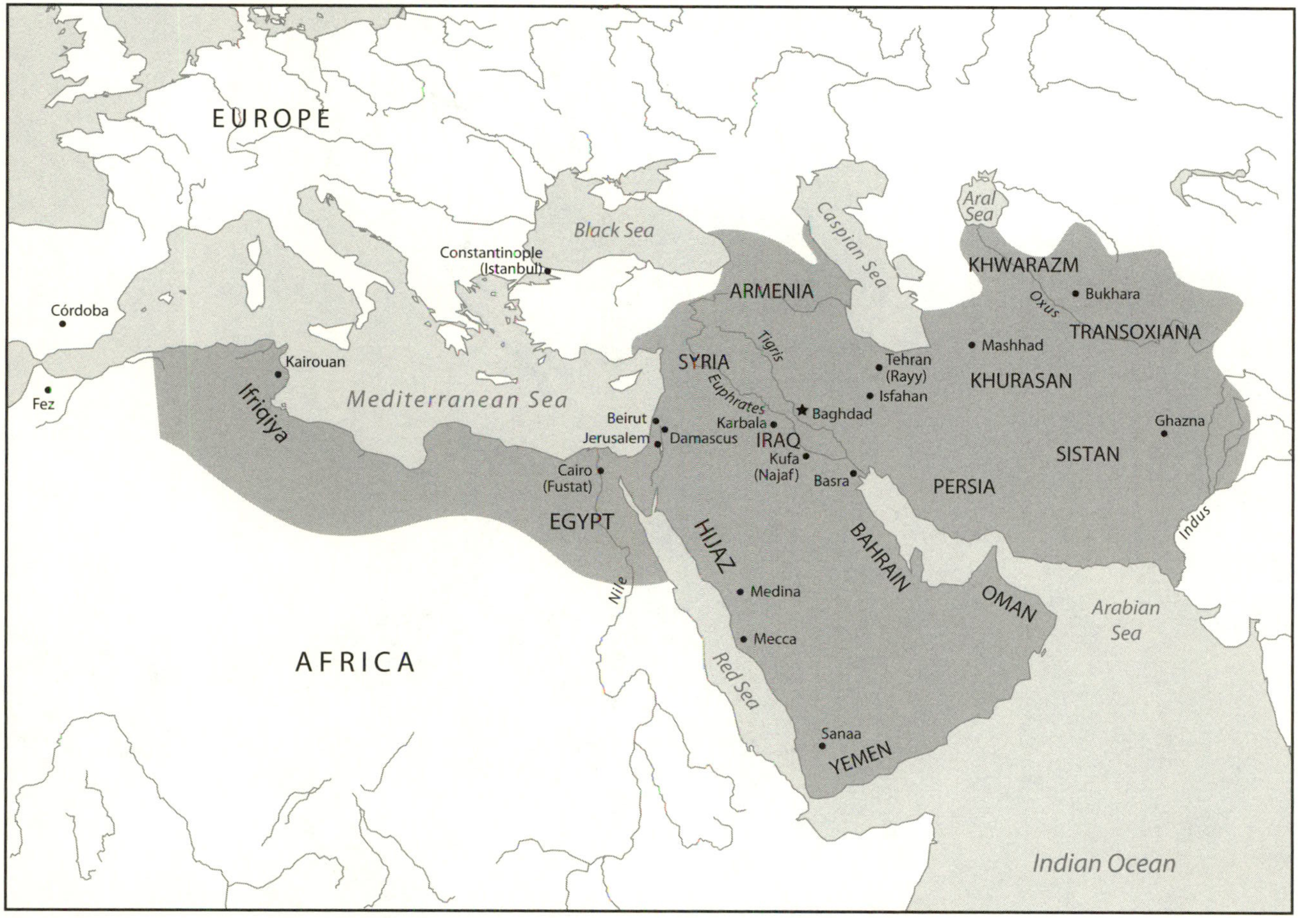

Map 2. The Abbasid Empire. Adapted from Malise Ruthven, *Historical Atlas of Islam*, Harvard University Press, 2004, p. 37.

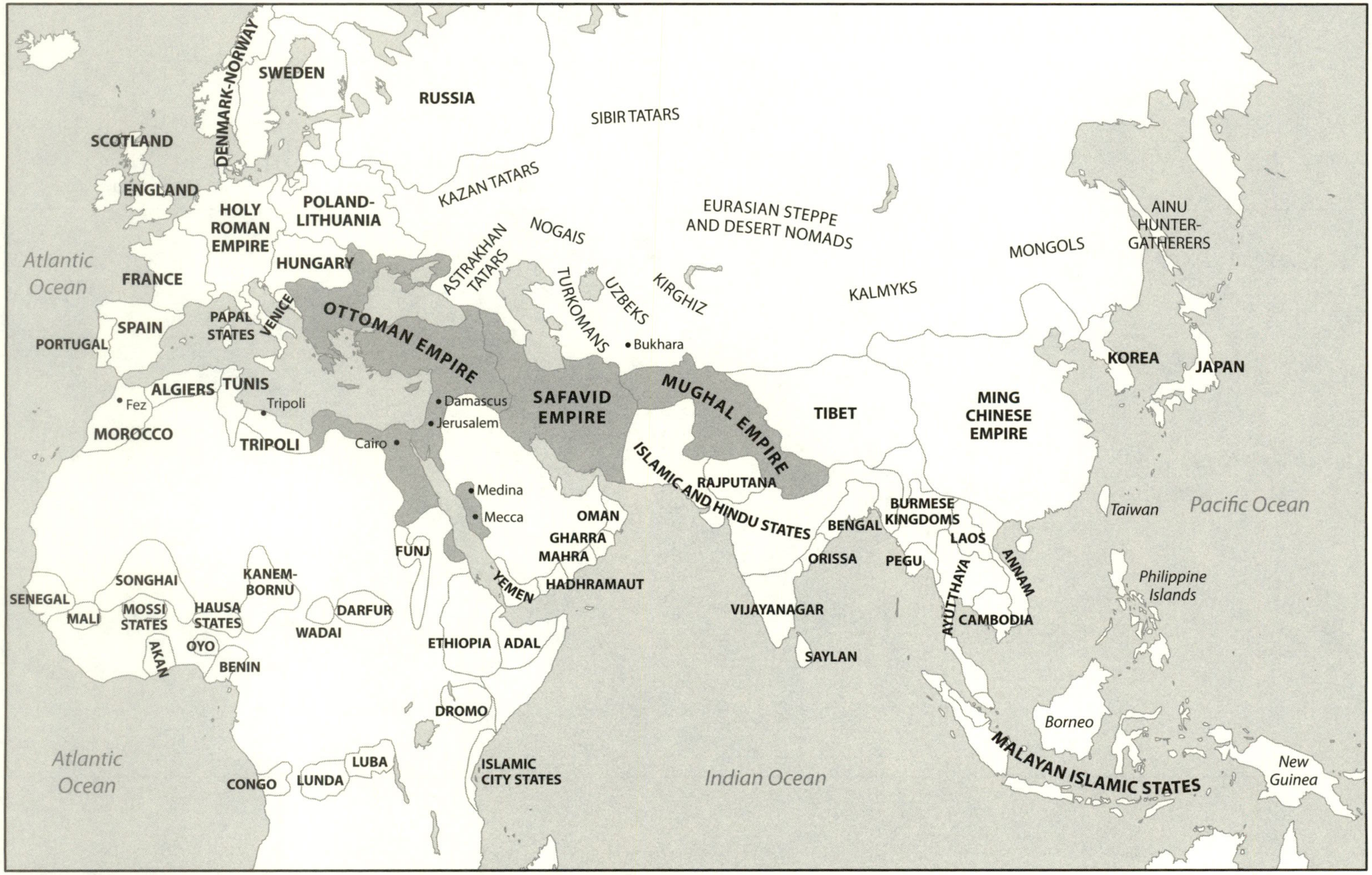

Map 3. Premodern Islamic Empires and States. Adapted from Malise Ruthven, *Historical Atlas of Islam*, Harvard University Press, 2004, p. 54–55.

Map 4. The Muslim World under Colonial Domination (until World War II). Adapted from Malise Ruthven, *Historical Atlas of Islam*, Harvard University Press, 2004, p. 117.

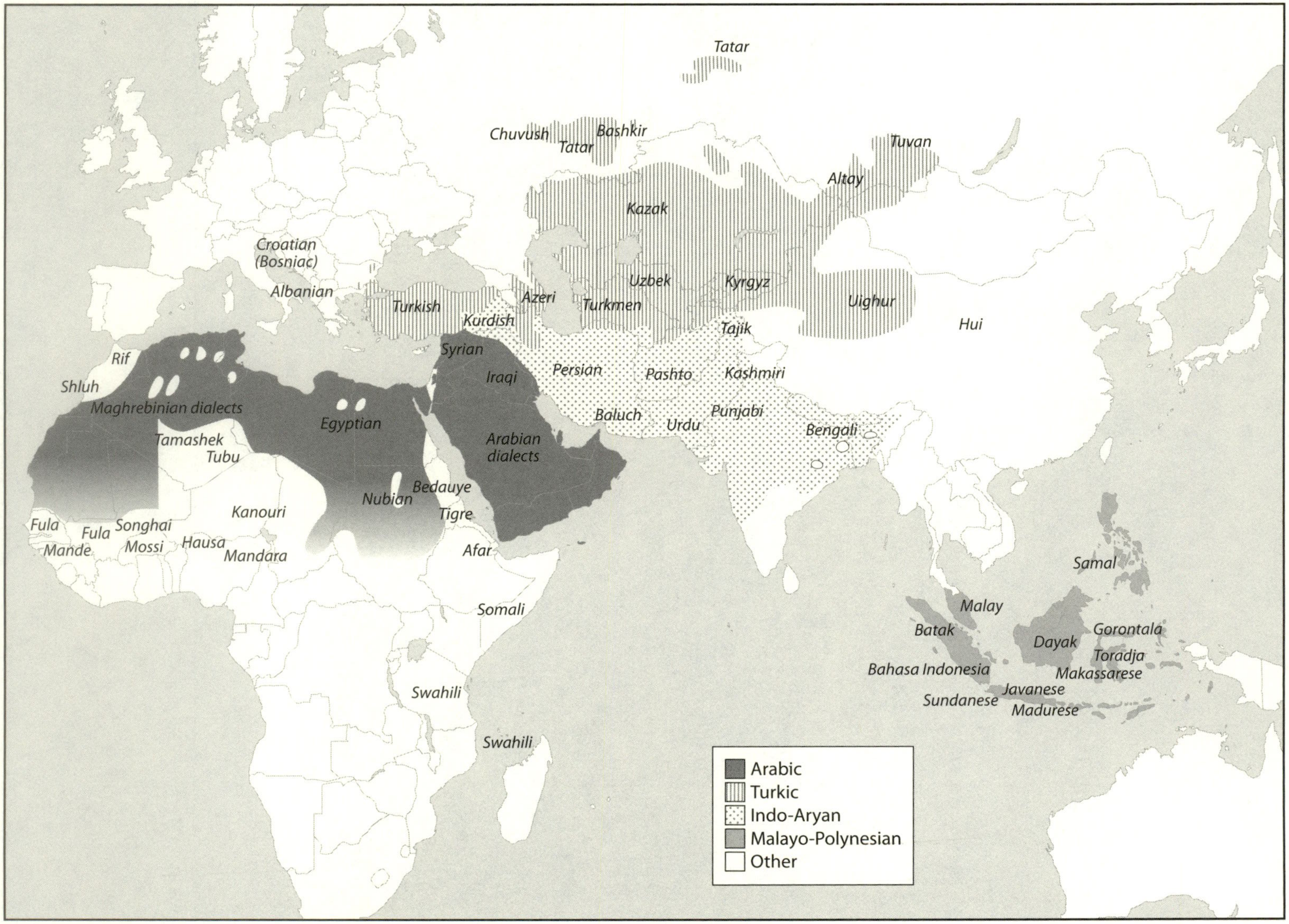

Map 5. Linguistic Regions of Islam. Adapted from Andreas Birken, *Atlas of Islam: 1800–2000*, Brill, 2010, p. 21.

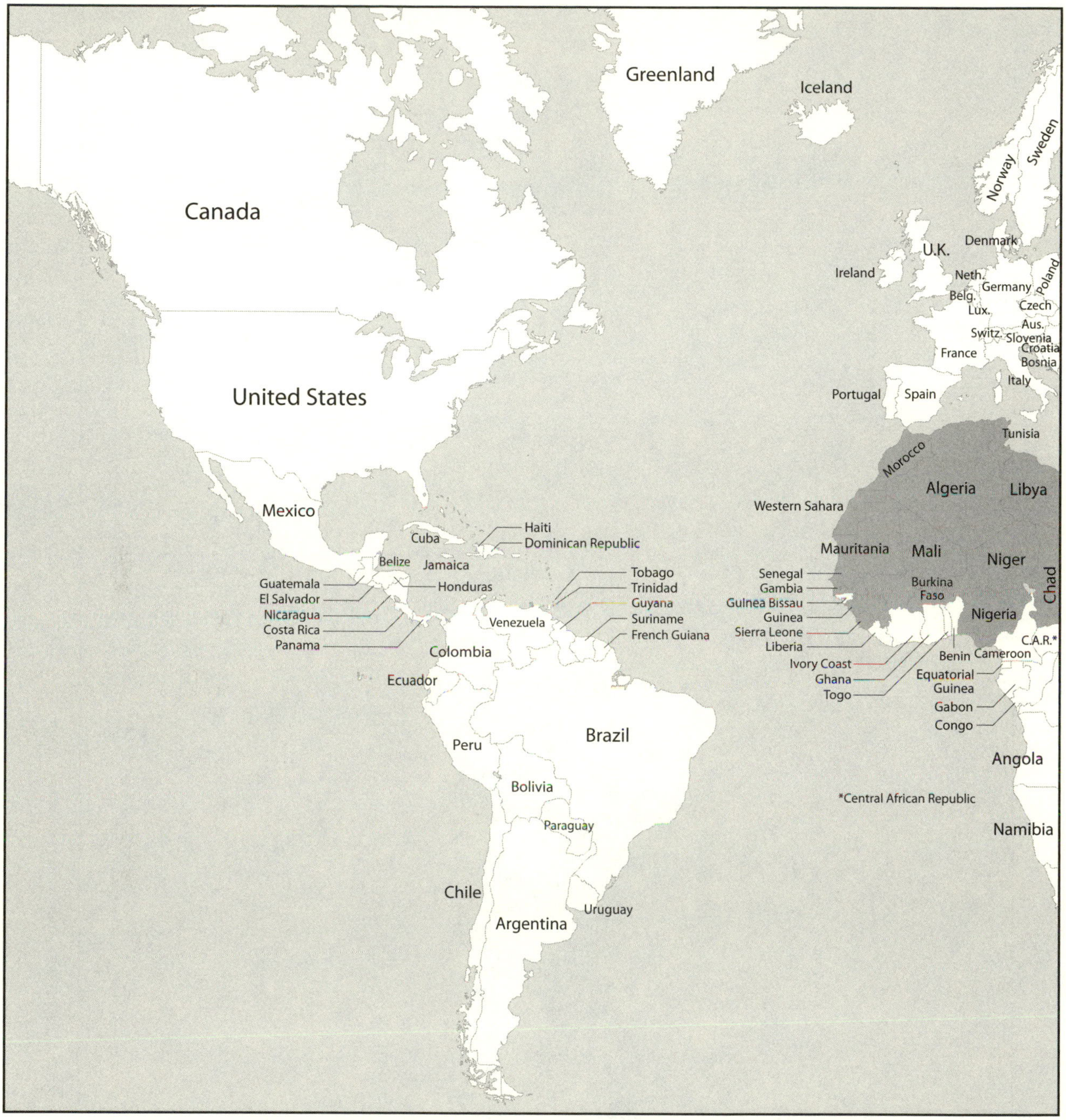

Map 6a–b. Worldwide Muslim Population in 2010 (see table, pp. xlii–xliv). Muslim-majority countries are shaded.

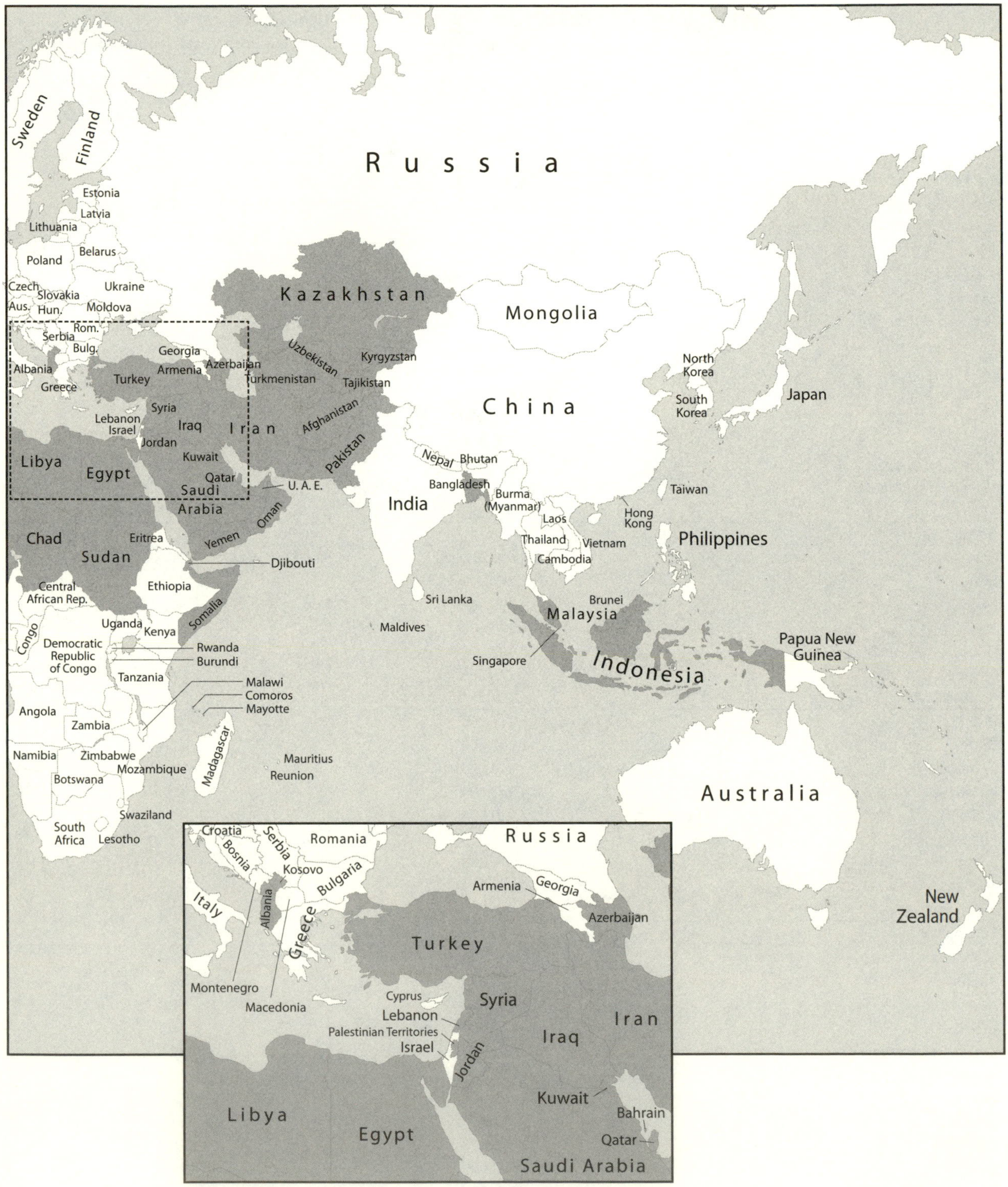
Russia
Sweden
Finland
Estonia
Latvia
Lithuania
Belarus
Poland
Czech
Slovakia
Ukraine
Aus.
Hun.
Moldova
Rom.
Serbia
Bulg.
Albania
Greece
Georgia
Armenia
Azerbaijan
Turkey
Kazakhstan
Uzbekistan
Turkmenistan
Kyrgyzstan
Tajikistan
Mongolia
North Korea
South Korea
Japan
China
Syria
Lebanon
Israel
Iraq
Iran
Afghanistan
Jordan
Kuwait
Pakistan
Nepal
Bhutan
Libya
Egypt
Qatar
Saudi Arabia
U. A. E.
Bangladesh
India
Burma (Myanmar)
Taiwan
Hong Kong
Laos
Thailand
Vietnam
Cambodia
Philippines
Chad
Sudan
Eritrea
Yemen
Oman
Djibouti
Central African Rep.
Ethiopia
Somalia
Sri Lanka
Brunei
Malaysia
Uganda
Kenya
Maldives
Congo
Democratic Republic of Congo
Rwanda
Burundi
Singapore
Indonesia
Papua New Guinea
Tanzania
Malawi
Comoros
Mayotte
Angola
Zambia
Namibia
Zimbabwe
Mozambique
Madagascar
Mauritius
Reunion
Botswana
Australia
Swaziland
South Africa
Lesotho
New Zealand
Croatia
Bosnia
Serbia
Romania
Russia
Kosovo
Bulgaria
Italy
Albania
Greece
Armenia
Georgia
Azerbaijan
Turkey
Montenegro
Macedonia
Cyprus
Syria
Lebanon
Palestinian Territories
Israel
Jordan
Iran
Iraq
Kuwait
Bahrain
Libya
Egypt
Qatar
Saudi Arabia

The Muslim World in 2010: Cultural Blocks and Populations

	Muslim population	Percentage of total population in country
Arabic-Speaking World		
Algeria	34,780,000	98.2
Bahrain	655,000	81.2
Egypt	80,024,000	94.7
Iraq	31,108,000	98.9
Jordan	6,397,000	98.8
Kuwait	2,636,000	86.4
Lebanon	2,542,000	59.7
Libya	6,325,000	96.6
Mauritania	3,338,000	99.2
Morocco	32,381,000	99.9
Oman	2,547,000	87.7
Palestinian territories	4,298,000	97.5
Qatar	1,168,000	77.5
Saudi Arabia	25,493,000	97.1
Sudan	30,855,000	71.4
Syria	20,895,000	92.8
Tunisia	10,349,000	99.8
United Arab Emirates	3,577,000	76.0
Yemen	24,023,000	99.0
South Asia		
Bangladesh	148,607,000	90.4
India	177,286,000	14.6
Maldives	309,000	98.4
Nepal	1,253,000	4.2
Pakistan	178,097,000	96.4
Sri Lanka	1,725,000	8.5
Southeast Asia		
Brunei	211,000	51.9
Burma (Myanmar)	1,900,000	3.8
Cambodia	240,000	1.6
Indonesia	204,847,000	88.1
Malaysia	17,139,000	61.4
Philippines	4,737,000	5.1
Singapore	721,000	14.9
Thailand	3,952,000	5.8
Vietnam	160,000	0.2
Eurasia		
Afghanistan	29,047,000	99.8
Albania	2,601,000	82.1
Azerbaijan	8,795,000	98.4
Belarus	19,000	0.2
Bosnia-Herzegovina	1,564,000	41.6
Bulgaria	1,002,000	13.4
China	23,308,000	1.8
Croatia	56,000	1.3
Cyprus	200,000	22.7
Georgia	442,000	10.5
Greece	527,000	4.7
Hong Kong	91,000	1.3

The Muslim World in 2010: Cultural Blocks and Populations *(continued)*

	Muslim population	Percentage of total population in country
Hungary	25,000	0.3
Iran	74,819,000	99.6
Kazakhstan	8,887,000	56.4
Kosovo	2,104,000	91.7
Kyrgyzstan	4,927,000	88.8
Moldova	15,000	0.4
Mongolia	120,000	4.4
Montenegro	116,000	18.5
Republic of Macedonia	713,000	34.9
Romania	73,000	0.3
Russia	16,379,000	11.7
Serbia	280,000	3.7
Slovenia	49,000	2.4
Taiwan	23,000	0.1
Tajikistan	7,006,000	99.0
Turkey	74,660,000	98.6
Turkmenistan	4,830,000	93.3
Ukraine	393,000	0.9
Uzbekistan	26,833,000	96.5
African Islam		
Angola	195,000	1.0
Benin	2,259,000	24.5
Burkina Faso	9,600,000	58.9
Burundi	184,000	2.2
Cameroon	3,598,000	18.0
Central African Republic	403,000	8.9
Chad	6,404,000	55.7
Comoros	679,000	98.3
Congo	969,000	1.4
Djibouti	853,000	97.0
Equatorial Guinea	28,000	4.1
Eritrea	1,909,000	36.5
Ethiopia	28,721,000	33.8
Gabon	145,000	9.7
Gambia	1,669,000	95.3
Ghana	3,906,000	16.1
Guinea	8,693,000	84.2
Guinea Bissau	705,000	42.8
Ivory Coast	7,960,000	36.9
Kenya	2,868,000	7.0
Liberia	523,000	12.8
Madagascar	220,000	1.1
Malawi	2,011,000	12.8
Mali	12,316,000	92.4
Mauritius	216,000	16.6
Mayotte	197,000	98.8
Mozambique	5,340,000	22.8
Niger	15,627,000	98.3
Nigeria	75,728,000	47.9
Republic of Congo	60,000	1.6

The Muslim World in 2010: Cultural Blocks and Populations *(continued)*

	Muslim population	Percentage of total population in country
Reunion	35,000	4.2
Rwanda	188,000	1.8
Senegal	12,333,000	95.9
Sierra Leone	4,171,000	71.5
Somalia	9,231,000	98.6
South Africa	737,000	1.5
Tanzania	13,450,000	29.9
Togo	827,000	12.2
Uganda	4,060,000	12.0
Western Sahara	528,000	99.6
Zambia	59,000	0.4
Zimbabwe	109,000	0.9
Rest of the World		
Argentina	1,000,000	2.5
Australia	399,000	1.9
Austria	475,000	5.7
Belgium	638,000	6.0
Brazil	204,000	0.1
Canada	940,000	2.8
Colombia	14,000	< 0.1
Cuba	10,000	0.1
Denmark	226,000	4.1
Fiji	54,000	6.3
Finland	42,000	0.8
France	4,704,000	7.5
Germany	4,119,000	5.0
Guyana	55,000	7.2
Honduras	11,000	0.1
Ireland	43,000	0.9
Israel	1,287,000	17.7
Italy	1,583,000	2.6
Japan	185,000	0.1
Luxembourg	11,000	2.3
Mexico	111,000	0.1
Netherlands	914,000	5.5
New Zealand	41,000	0.9
Norway	144,000	3.0
Panama	25,000	0.7
Poland	20,000	0.1
Portugal	65,000	0.6
South Korea	75,000	0.2
Spain	1,021,000	2.3
Suriname	84,000	15.9
Sweden	451,000	4.9
Switzerland	433,000	5.7
Trinidad and Tobago	78,000	5.8
United Kingdom	2,869,000	4.6
United States	2,595,000	0.8
Venezuela	95,000	0.3

Data is from the Pew Forum on Religion & Public Life, *The Future of the Global Muslim Population*, Washington DC: Pew Research Center, January 2011.
Table excludes countries with fewer than 10,000 Muslims.

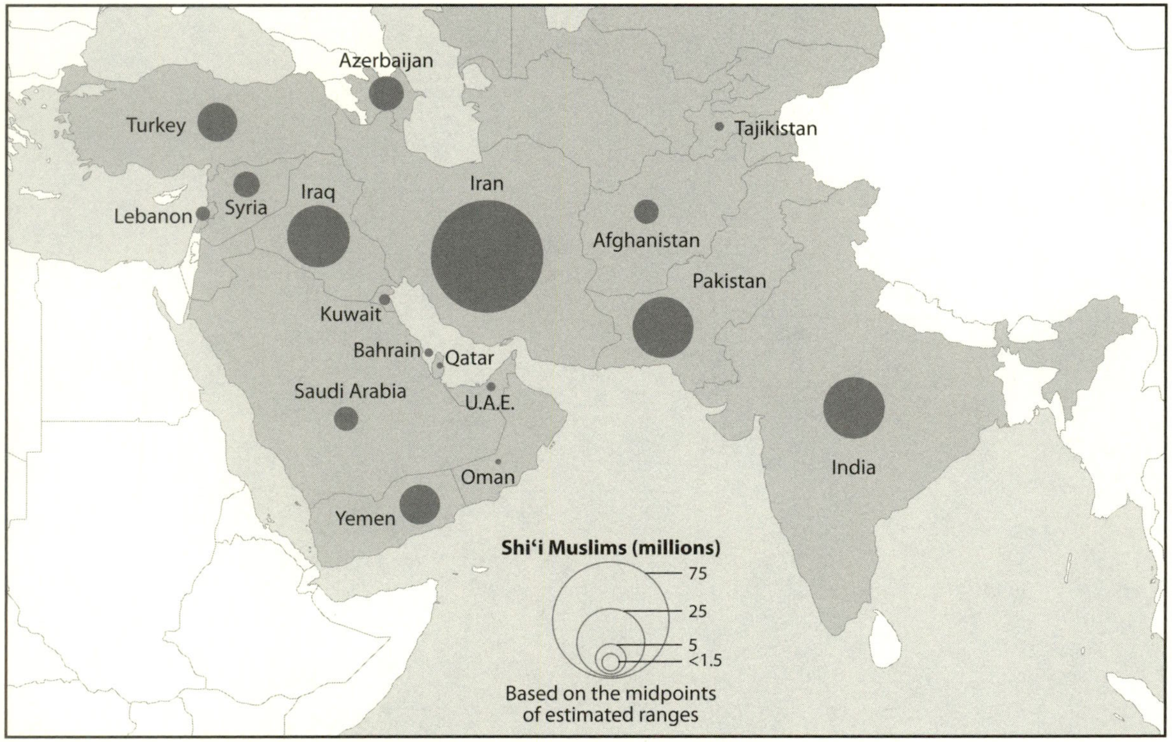

Map 7. Shi'i Population. Adapted from the Pew Forum on Religion & Public Life, *Mapping the Global Muslim Population*, Washington DC: Pew Research Center, October 2009, p. 11.

The Princeton Encyclopedia of Islamic Political Thought

A

‘Abbas I (1571–1629)

Shah ‘Abbas I, the third son of Shah Muhammad Khudabanda (r. 1578–87) and the fifth ruler of the Safavid dynasty (1501–1722), came to power at age 17, at a time when tribal factionalism tore at the fabric of the state and foreign invaders had greatly reduced Iran's territory. Once on the throne, the shah set out to reestablish the authority of his predecessors and to regain the lands they had lost. Unable to fight a war on two fronts, he took on the Uzbeks in the northeast after concluding a peace treaty with the more formidable Ottomans that forced him to give up substantial territory. The resulting stability allowed him to reform Iran's military and financial system. Intent on weakening the fractious Turkoman tribes who had brought the dynasty to power, the shah created a standing army composed of loyal slave soldiers (*ghulāms*), most of whom were Georgians captured during bloody raids in the Caucasus. The revenue required for these measures was raised by converting outlying provinces from state lands ruled as fiefs by tribal leaders to crown lands administered by *ghulāms* directly reporting to the shah.

Shah ‘Abbas's grandest achievement was his selection of Isfahan, a city located in the center of Iran, as the nation's capital. Isfahan was given a new administrative and commercial center consisting of a palace complex, several mosques, and a bazaar, all grouped around a splendid royal square. The shah took various other measures to encourage trade, increasing road security and building many caravansaries throughout the country. To the same end, he deported a large group of Armenians, known for their industriousness, to a newly built suburb of Isfahan, where they were given commercial privileges, including a monopoly on the export of the country's silk.

A master of co-opting rivals and playing off enemies, ‘Abbas conducted an astute, forward-looking foreign policy designed to maximize revenue and to create an anti-Ottoman alliance with Europe's Catholic powers. A desire to forge such an alliance and the need for intermediaries played a role in his decision to allow Christian missionaries to settle and operate in his country. He also welcomed English and Dutch merchants, offering them trading rights, and made use of English naval power to expel the Portuguese from the isle of Hormuz in 1622.

Considering Iran's political fragmentation and its resource-poor economy, Shah ‘Abbas was remarkably successful in his endeavors. In his 40-year reign, he retook the northwestern lands lost by his predecessors, added the Persian Gulf littoral to Safavid control, incorporated parts of Armenia and Georgia with a series of brutal campaigns, seized Qandahar from the Mughals in 1622, and halted the westward expansion of the Ottomans by taking Baghdad a year later. Despite this, some of his policies had long-term negative effects. For fear of a premature challenge to his authority, he brutally dealt with rivals within his family: he killed one of his sons, blinded several of his other sons, and kept their offspring immured in the royal harem. Consequences emerged in the form of inexperienced and mostly weak successors. His conversion of state lands to crown lands generated short-term income but led to long-term exploitation of peasants by landholders interested only in immediate revenue.

Famously down to Earth, Shah ‘Abbas kept an informal style, often mingling with the common people of Isfahan. As gregarious as he was shrewd, and as often cruel as generous, ‘Abbas ultimately was a pragmatic ruler. He is remembered as one of the few kings in Iranian history who was concerned about his people.

See also Iran; Safavids (1501–1722)

Further Reading

Rula Jurdi Abisaab, *Converting Persia: Religion and Power in the Safavid Empire*, 2004; Kathryn Babayan, *Mystics, Monarchs, and Messiahs: Cultural Landscapes of Early Modern Iran*, 2003; David Blow, *Shah Abbas: The Ruthless King Who Became an Iranian Legend*, 2009; Willem Floor, *The Economy of Safavid Persia*, 2000; Rudolph Matthee, *The Politics of Trade in Safavid Iran: Silk for Silver, 1600–1730*, 1999; Andrew Newman, *Safavid Iran: Rebirth of a Persian Empire*, 2006; Sholeh Quinn, *Historical Writing during the Reign of Shah ‘Abbas: Ideology, Imitation and Legitimacy in Safavid Chronicles*, 2000; Roger Savory, *Iranunder the Safavids*, 1980.

RUDI MATTHEE

Abbasids (750–1258)

The Abbasids came to power in 750 by overthrowing their Umayyad predecessors. The Abbasid revolution represented more than a change of dynasty; Abbasid rule substantially transformed the Islamic tradition. Some of the more obvious effects of Abbasid rule were a new concept of the caliphate; a shift in the locus of political power to the eastern city of Baghdad; the establishment of Islam as a predominantly universalist and multiethnic faith (as opposed to an Arab religion); an increase in the rate of conversion; influence and

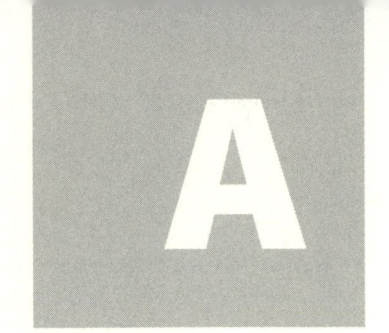

borrowing from Persian culture; and substantial advancements in the fields of science, technology, literature, and philosophy.

The Abbasids derive their name from the Prophet Muhammad’s uncle, ‘Abbas (d. 653), from whom the first Abbasid caliph, Abu al-‘Abbas al-Saffah (r. 750–54), traced his genealogy. By emphasizing this genealogical link, the Abbasids appealed for support from Muhammad’s family and presented themselves as Muhammad’s true successors. Moreover, in their rise to power, the Abbasids painted themselves as champions of Islamic justice who stood in contrast to the morally corrupt Umayyads. Although the Abbasids had begun as morally driven revolutionaries, they soon settled into a dynastic patrimonial monarchy. Shortly after assuming power, the Abbasids also abandoned their sympathy for minority groups such as the Shi‘i factions and began pandering to the numerically stronger proto-Sunnis.

At the time of the Abbasids, the Islamic tradition was still in its nascent stage, and its political drift was unclear. Given the numerical strength of their Persian supporters, the Abbasids adopted both the Iranian tradition of centralized monarchy as well as Iranian practices of government. They developed a secret service and bureaucracy as well as a court culture. The main ideological initiative of the Abbasids was to emphasize their position as God’s deputies and the Prophet’s successors. Over the years, a number of Abbasid rulers echoed statements such as that made by Caliph Mansur (r. 754–75): “I am simply the authority of God on this Earth.”

From among the Abbasids, Caliph Ma’mun (r. 813–33) was the most determined to construct a high imperial ideal that would free the office of deputyship from reliance on the military as well popular religious leaders. To fulfill this aim, he appealed directly to his subjects and emphasized high culture and the intellectual prominence of the caliphate and the ‘ulama’. Ma’mun’s successor, Mu‘tasim (r. 833–42), adopted a similar strategy, but in a more tempered manner. Under Mutawakkil (r. 847–61) the influence of the more literal-minded Sunnis increased and the Mu‘tazilis and neo-Greek philosophers were pushed to the peripheries. Mutawakkil was assassinated by a band of Turkic slave-soldiers, who dominated Baghdadi politics until the Shi‘i Buyids seized Baghdad in 945. Gradually, more and more of the provinces of the caliphate became independent under new dynasties. These new dynasties continued to follow the practices and ideology of patrimonial monarchy as developed under the Abbasids.

Although their empire soon fragmented, the Abbasids remained a local power that symbolically represented the caliphate. Their swift downfall can be attributed to a lack of consistent imperial strategy—they had no defining imperial or state ideology. Although they could have adopted the Shi‘i view of the imamate as their state ideology, the Abbasids abandoned Shi‘ism soon after they ascended to power. In the later Sunni milieu, the unclear role of the deputy was detrimental to their political hold. Moreover, the power of the centralized government was mitigated by the power shared with senior judges in major cities. These judges, although appointed by the deputy, ruled by a law in which they alone, and not the state, possessed authority.

Despite its swift fragmentation, the Abbasid empire had a lasting impact on the religious and political landscape of the current Muslim world. The Iranian tradition of patrimonial monarchy initially adopted by the Abbasids was emulated by all later Islamic dynasties. Moreover, the political precedent set by the Abbasids continued to govern how state officials and citizens understood political authority and the ruler–ruled relationship.

See also Baghdad; Ma’mun (786–833); Umayyads (661–750)

Further Reading

Antony Black, *The History of Islamic Political Thought: From the Prophet to the Present*, 2004; Amira K. Bennison, *The Great Caliphs: The Golden Age of the ‘Abbasid Empire*, 2009; Hugh N. Kennedy, *The Early Abbasid Caliphate: A Political History*, 1981.

MASHAL SAIF

‘Abd al-Hamid al-Katib b. Yahya al-‘Amiri (d. 750)

An early epistolographer credited from medieval times with founding Arabic literary prose, ‘Abd al-Hamid was a third-generation non-Arab Muslim born around 688, probably in al-Anbar in Iraq. He studied most likely in Kufa, where he later worked as a teacher and a peripatetic tutor. He then became a secretary in the Umayyad administration in Damascus, taking up a career that he kept until the end of his life. His work allowed him to be close to at least two influential Umayyad caliphs: Hisham b. ‘Abd al-Malik (r. 724–43) and Marwan b. Muhammad (Marwan II; r. 744–50). This closeness allowed him to write letters on their behalf, to espouse fervently their political cause, and to be their mouthpiece in expressing their ideology. He paid the ultimate price for his loyalty to them when agents of the Abbasid rebels, successfully overthrowing the Umayyads, killed him in 750.

‘Abd al-Hamid’s letters were transmitted and studied by his students and descendants, many of whom served as secretaries in the Abbasid and Tulunid administrations. These and later secretaries and litterateurs praised ‘Abd al-Hamid’s style, crediting him with introducing several innovations into Arabic prose. Combining talent with memorization of fine literature and secretarial training in the chancery, he created a recognizable style that manipulated the possibilities of language and sound and made extensive and creative use of Qur’anic citations and allusions.

‘Abd al-Hamid’s letters filled about 1,000 folios in the late tenth century, but only about 100 pages of them survived. This corpus consists of about 62 complete or fragmentary letters or extracts of letters, 37 of which are major, in addition to several signatory notes and oral sayings. Some of the major letters are descriptive or personal, and one of them is his famous “Letter to the Secretaries,” in which ‘Abd al-Hamid counseled his peers on their education and their behavior toward superiors and colleagues. Most of

those letters, however, are official, dealing by and large with public matters and often written on behalf of identified or unidentified Umayyad caliphs. Some of them address gubernatorial issues, others describe major caliphal activities, and still others hail the victories of the Muslims over the non-Muslims. They analyze potential dissent or actual rebellions, describe the suppression of rebels, or warn rebels or other groups engaged in illegitimate civil activities. Several also examine the issues of obedience, disobedience, and civil discord (*fitna*), and one of them, 'Abd al-Hamid's longest work (about 40 pages), is his famous "Testament to the Crown Prince," in which he counsels the heir apparent of Marwan II on matters moral, religious, political, and military in a manner reminiscent of the Mirrors for Princes political advice genre that was to develop later in Islamic political literature.

'Abd al-Hamid's main contribution to Islamic political thought in his official letters lies in constructing a theoretical framework for Umayyad ideology and in presenting the Umayyads as pious guardians of religion. Theoretically, 'Abd al-Hamid places the Umayyads in a universal historical context: God chose Islam to be his own religion; he sent the Prophet Muhammad at a moment of darkness in human history; and after Muhammad's demise, God created a new institution, the caliphate, which inherited prophethood. The caliphs are thus God's caliphs, whom he mandated to rule and to whom absolute obedience is due, just as it is to God. Therefore, obedience is the means of salvation for all Muslims in this world and the next; any engagement in disobedience or civil strife is fatal.

On the practical level, 'Abd al-Hamid painted a highly religious picture of the Umayyad caliphs. He described them as pious, God-fearing, and utterly helpless without God, and he highlighted several of their activities that had a religious context, such as performing the pilgrimage and fasting during the month of Ramadan. His victory letters hail each triumph as indicative of God's support of the Umayyad caliphs and their being his rightful appointees to the guardianship of the Muslim community. Although almost all of 'Abd al-Hamid's letters use Qur'anic citations and allusions, this use is particularly frequent in his ideologically oriented letters, where the support of God's word acts as the ultimate proof of the rightfulness of the Umayyads' cause.

See also Ibn al-Muqaffa' (ca. 720–56); Mirrors for Princes; Umayyads (661–750)

Further Reading

Ihsan 'Abbas, *'Abd al-Hamid al-Katib wa-ma Tabaqqa min Rasa'ilihi wa-Rasa'il Salim Abi al-Ala'*, 1988; Wadad Kadi, "Early Islamic State Letters: The Question of Authenticity," in *The Byzantine and Early Islamic Near East, I. Problems in the Literary Source Material*, edited by A. Cameron and L. Conrad, 1999; Idem, "The Religious Foundation od Late Umayyad Ideology and Practice," in *Sober Religioso y Poder politico en el Islam,* edited by Manuela Marin, 1994. Hannelore Schonig, *Das Sendschreiben des 'Abdalḥamīd b. Yaḥyā (gest. 132/750) an den Kronprinzen 'Abdallāh b. Marwān II*, 1985.

WADAD KADI

'Abd al-Qadir al-Jaza'iri (1808–83)

Amir 'Abd al-Qadir al-Jaza'iri is best known for his determined resistance to the invading French army in Algeria between 1832 and 1847 and his decisive role in protecting the Christian inhabitants of Damascus during the 1860 uprisings in Lebanon and Syria. He was also an original thinker and writer whose ideas were influenced by the nature of his early instruction; the years spent leading the jihad against, and negotiations with, the French; his time as a political prisoner in France; and his eventual settlement in Damascus.

Born in western Algeria near the city of Mascara to a family of religious notables, he was educated in the port of Azrew by a local scholar (*'ālim*), Tahir b. Ahmad, who instilled in his young pupil an interest in geography, mathematics, and astronomy, in addition to a deep knowledge of the Islamic sciences. Another formative influence was his pilgrimage to the Hijaz in modern Saudi Arabia made with his father beginning in November 1825, which conferred additional socio-spiritual authority upon him. Their sojourn in Egypt during the implementation of Muhammad 'Ali's modernization program exposed the future amir to novel methods of political and military organization, which he later attempted to introduce in his native Algeria. After completing the pilgrimage, father and son spent four months in Damascus, where they studied Naqshbandi teachings and rituals from prominent shaykhs and formed ties of friendship with the local 'ulama'. The two Algerians returned home to the Oran just two years prior to France's occupation of Algeria in 1830.

In 1832, 'Abd al-Qadir was proclaimed the "sultan of the Arabs" for mobilizing tribesmen under his green-and-white flag, which became the symbol of the nationalist movement in the 20th century. After a decade and a half of fighting interspersed with cessations of hostilities against the French military, the amir's movement was exhausted and outnumbered. In 1847, he surrendered to General Louis de La Moricière in exchange for a promise of safe passage either to Alexandria or to Acre, in Palestine. In flagrant violation of the agreement, 'Abd al-Qadir and his large retinue were taken to France and imprisoned until 1852, when the prince-president Louis-Napoleon III released them. The Algerians first settled in Bursa (in Anatolia) and subsequently in Damascus in 1855, where some of his descendants reside to this day. The generous pension accorded by the French state conferred financial security upon the amir, his family, and his followers, allowing the Algerian leader to purchase considerable landholdings in the area. But it also alienated some Damascene notables and 'ulama', who condemned his close ties to the French government in a period of increasing European interventions in the affairs of the Ottoman Empire. Nevertheless, he held classes at the great Umayyad Mosque, lecturing on the Qur'an and the sunna.

During his four years in France, 'Abd al-Qadir entertained wide-ranging contacts with political, military, and even Catholic leaders and thinkers. Soon after his relocation to Damascus, the Paris-based Asiatic Society invited him to become a member. He submitted an essay discussing the thorny issues of Muslim-Christian relations and

the relationship between revelation and human reason, which won him praise. In his treatise *Reminding the Rational Man and Alerting the Neglectful Man*, 'Abd al-Qadir sought to reconcile rational inquiry with religious belief and truth. As David D. Cummings points out, arguments in favor of reconciling modern science with revelation through a reinterpretation of the sources reflected an intellectual movement among some Islamic thinkers and represented a trend that later inspired the Salafis. This might be considered the first phase in the amir's religiospiritual and intellectual trajectory.

The second phase came after the events of the 1860 civil strife in Lebanon and the Hawran, during which 'Abd al-Qadir strove to calm Druze-Christian sectarian conflict, probably because he realized that civil war would provide a pretext for heightened European meddling—a lesson he had surely learned in Algeria. When his efforts failed, he provided shelter to several thousand Christians in his residence in Damascus, sparing them from death at the hands of mobs. His courageous actions earned him kudos not only from the European powers but also from President Abraham Lincoln, and it brought him to the attention of the Masons. In 1862, he performed another pilgrimage, staying in Mecca for an extended period, where he studied Shadhili Sufi teachings. On his way back to Damascus in 1864, he spent time in Alexandria, where he encountered Masonic ideas in one of the city's lodges. One of the biggest controversies among scholars of 'Abd al-Qadir's life and thought revolves around his relationship to the Masons: How receptive or sympathetic was he to Masonic ideas? And did he really become a member, if only for a short period?

From the mid-1860s on, however, his thinking shifted as he became less concerned with "shari'a-minded Sufism," which maintained that the sunna and the law must represent the core of the Sufi way. The amir died and was buried in Damascus in May 1883. But in 1968, the newly independent state of Algeria recalled 'Abd al-Qadir home, repatriating his remains to his native land after an exile of 121 years.

See also Algeria; North Africa

Further Reading

Charles Henry Churchill, *The Life of Abdel Kader: Ex-Sultan of the Arabs of Algeria*, 1868; Julia Clancy-Smith, *Rebel and Saint: Muslim Notables, Populist Protest, Colonial Encounters (Algeria and Tunisia, 1800–1904)*, 1994; David Dean Cummings, *Islamic Reform: Politics and Social Change in Late Ottoman Syria*, 1990; Charles-André Julien, "La conquête et les débuts de la colonisation (1827–1871)," in *Histoire de l'Algérie contemporaine* 1 (1979).

JULIA CLANCY-SMITH

'Abd al-Rahman, 'Umar (b. 1938)

'Umar 'Abd al-Rahman was born in 1938 into a modest family of the rural region of Egypt's northern Nile Delta region. Having lost his sight at a young age, he was placed in the Qur'anic school of his village and followed the customary educational path of rural children at that time. By the age of 11 he had memorized the Qur'an, and after finishing his primary and secondary education, he enrolled in Azhar University in Cairo. In 1965, he graduated from Azhar's Department of Theology and was appointed imam of a provincial mosque by the Ministry of Religious Affairs. Influenced by the ideology of the Muslim Brotherhood, and in particular by the writings of Sayyid Qutb, he became after 1967 openly critical of the regime of Gamal Abdel Nasser; when Nasser died in 1970, 'Abd al-Rahman forbade in one of his sermons praying on Nasser's tomb. This was his first conspicuous opposition to the Egyptian government, and it earned him his first prison sentence.

Even as he was gaining a reputation as a political opponent, 'Abd al-Rahman continued his theological studies at Azhar and obtained a PhD in 1972. Between 1973 and 1977, while teaching in the southern town of Asyut, he came in contact with the Islamist youth of al-Gama'a al-Islamiyya. In the early 1980s, after having taught for some time in Saudi Arabia, he was consulted in matters of Islamic law (*fiqh*) by the leaders of the Gama'a, as well as by the leaders of al-Jihad al-Islami, the group that carried out the assassination of Egyptian president Anwar Sadat in 1981. He was among the defendants in the trial of Sadat's assassins, but in that case he was acquitted. During the 1980s, the Gama'a Islamiyya, though a fragmented group, continued to refer to 'Abd al-Rahman's theological rulings in order to justify its strategy of undertaking violent attacks against practices it deemed un-Islamic and to defend its confrontations with the police and military forces. In 1990, 'Abd al-Rahman left Egypt for the United States and settled in Jersey City, New Jersey, where he continued to preach and criticize the Egyptian regime and American foreign policy. The 1993 attack on the World Trade Center in New York City brought him again to the limelight through his trial over this attack with other codefendants. He was convicted of "seditious conspiracy" and sentenced to life in prison in the United States.

'Abd al-Rahman did not write any books, and his ideas are mainly accessible through his sermons and the transcripts of his testimonies at his trials in Egypt and the United States. Often referring to the body of legal rulings (*fatāwā*) of the influential jurist Ibn Taymiyya, 'Abd al-Rahman holds views of the ideal polity that are similar to those held by Sayyid Qutb and that view parliamentary democracy as a contradiction to the principle of God's sovereignty (*ḥākimiyya*). For him, impious leaders must be eliminated and divine sovereignty implemented through the shari'a in order to realize the ideal polity. The legitimacy of political power is exclusively defined through the concept of obedience (*ṭā'a*) to God and disobedience (*ma'ṣiya*) to whoever fails to obey God, thereby opening up the possibility of political rebellion. He is more precise than Qutb concerning his conception of jihad, which he describes as an armed war against the enemies of Islam and against those societies that, according to him, claim to be Muslim but are in fact societies of *jāhiliyya*, or "ignorance." 'Abd al-Rahman rejects modern interpretations of jihad as being exclusively a defensive war or as

an inner struggle that takes place in the intellectual and spiritual domains. He also explicitly rejects the gradation of categories outlined in classical Islamic legal thought between permissible and impious behavior. For him, there is no category between impiety and Islam. This is why impiety can be immediately recognized and corrected "by the hand," as it is discernible by humans and is not exclusively identifiable by God. ‘Abd al-Rahman's ideas, thus, legitimize the possibility—and even the duty—for any Muslim to intervene in the public sphere to correct behavior that does not conform to Islamic norms.

‘Abd al-Rahman's influence on certain radical Islamist groups in Egypt and beyond has been significant. It seems that, in the eyes of members of a few radical groups in the 1980s and 1990s, he was a legal and theological counsel who played the role of a legitimizing figure: as a shaykh educated at Azhar, he was asked to provide religious justifications for political action. It was extremely rare, however, for scholars educated at Azhar in 20th-century Egypt to express such a radical opposition to the government and to associate themselves with groups advocating violence. Azhar University exemplified the tradition of *naṣīḥa*, the act of speaking the truth—often in subtle ways—to the political sovereign without necessarily acting against him. On the other hand, like many ‘ulama’, ‘Abd al-Rahman envisions the role of the ‘ulama’ as independent from any official religious institution. He conceives of his own function as that of a scholar belonging to an intellectual and religious elite characterized by its access to religious knowledge and piety rather than by its professional or institutional status. The case of ‘Abd al-Rahman also illustrates the division of labor common in Sunni Islam between the carriers of religious knowledge and political activists: scholars might devise and publicly articulate political theologies, but they rarely participate in their implementation.

See also Azhar University; Faraj, Muhammad ‘Abd al-Salam (1954–82); fundamentalism; al-Gama‘a al-Islamiyya; Ibn Taymiyya (1263–1328); Islamic Jihad; *jāhiliyya*; jihad; Muslim Brotherhood; Nasser, Gamal Abdel (1918–70); obedience; rebellion; Sayyid Qutb (1906–66); sovereignty; tyranny; ‘ulama’

Further Reading

Malika Zeghal, *Gardiens de l'islam: Les oulémas d'al Azhar dans l'Egypte contemporaine*, 1996.

MALIKA ZEGHAL

‘Abd al-Raziq, ‘Ali (1887–1966)

A judge, politician, and Islamic political theorist whose views on the caliphate galvanized the Egyptian public sphere during the interwar period, ‘Ali ‘Abd al-Raziq was born in 1867 into a wealthy landowning family in the province of Minya, Egypt. The family was identified with the Liberal Constitutionalists Party (al-Ahrar al-Dusturiyyun), and their house in Cairo hosted prominent intellectuals such as Muhammad ‘Abduh (1849–1905), Rashid Rida (1865–1935), and Ahmad Lufti al-Sayyid (1872–1963). ‘Abd al-Raziq was educated at the Egyptian University in Cairo and at Azhar University, from which he graduated in 1912. Between 1912 and 1915, he studied at Oxford, and upon his return to Egypt, he became a shari‘a court judge in al-Mansura. He was dismissed from Azhar University in 1925 and did not return for two decades until his brother, Mustafa, was appointed grand shaykh of the university. He served as a minister of Awqaf (1948–49) and as a member of the Egyptian parliament, the senate, and the Egyptian Language Academy. He published several works, notably *al-Ijma‘ fi al-Shari‘a al-Islamiyya* (Consensus in Islamic law) in 1947, a volume of his lectures, and an edited collection of his brother's works.

‘Abd al-Raziq's most famous book is his 1925 *al-Islam wa-Usul al-Hukm* (Islam and the principles of governance), which at the time provoked wide discussion in the Egyptian public sphere. The major catalyst for its publication was the abolition of the caliphate by the Turkish state (March 3, 1924) and a series of conferences and public debates regarding the desirability of a new caliph in the modern period (debates in which the Egyptian king Fu'ad was very much involved). Many modern reformers, notably ‘Abd al-Rahman al-Kawakibi (1849–1902) and Rashid Rida, had been fascinated by the concept of the caliph prior to the action of the Turkish state—and *al-Islam wa-Usul al-Hukm* continued these discussions. At that time, controversies were frequent and conformed to a pattern in Egypt: a famous scholar (e.g., Qasim Amin, ‘Abd al-Raziq, Taha Husayn) publishes a text in which he challenges some assumptions; a scandal ensues in which the scholar, though persecuted, cements his position as a precursor of modernity, while Azhar University and the more conservative circles present themselves as the guardians of the shari‘a. This was the case with ‘Abd al-Raziq's work. On May 24, 1925, the noted intellectual and politician Muhammad Husayn Haykal (1888–1956) recommended in his journal *al-Siyasa* that people read *al-Islam wa-Usul al-Hukm*. The next month, Rida published an attack on the book. In August, Azhar University's rector and 24 of its leading ‘ulama’ (backed by King Fu'ad) responded by dismissing ‘Abd al-Raziq from his judgeship, ousting him from Azhar University, and denouncing his book publicly. Husayn and Haykal defended ‘Abd al-Raziq, while some Azharis published books refuting the main arguments of *al-Islam wa Usul al-Hukm*. The question that occupied many intellectuals then and later was whether ‘Abd al-Raziq was advocating a separation between state and church under the veneer of accepting Islamic political theory or attempting to strengthen Islamic political theory from within. Was he, in other words, the Egyptian John Locke or a new Mawardi?

Like many modern Muslim political theorists before him, ‘Abd al-Raziq relies heavily on the Qur'an, as well as on the philosophy of Ibn Khaldun, yet he also draws on scholars such as Aristotle, Plato, Thomas Hobbes, Locke, Thomas Arnold (notably, his work on the caliphate), and other political theorists who wrote on the question of governance.

'Abd al-Raziq opens *al-Islam wa-Usul al-Hukm* by presenting two opinions on the source of the caliph's power: God or (based on Locke's theories) the community (*umma*). Although he does not clarify his own views at this point, the text as a whole seems to support the latter contention.

'Abd al-Raziq's main argument is that the caliphate emerged as a recognized form of political authority during the time of Abu Bakr, not before him. His historical readings of the institution of the caliphate in the post-*Rāshidūn* (Rightly Guided Caliphs) era are rather pessimistic, if not Machiavellian. He argues that nearly every caliph, including Abu Bakr, faced political opposition. While it was possible to assume that the legitimacy of the caliphate should be drawn from the voluntary will of the Muslims (*ikhtiyāriyya*), in reality the caliphate was based on power, and most commonly military power. Rulers in Islam also limited scientific inquiry, and thus despite the flourishing of medieval Islamic sciences and the interest in Greek thought, political science (*al-'ulūm al-siyāsiyya*) was never developed in Islamic thought. This is because of the limitations on political and intellectual freedom under various leaders of the Islamic state, who promulgated the mistaken notion that obedience to political authority should be understood as obedience to God. This misguided view allowed them to establish tyrannies, lead the people astray, and manipulate the meaning of religion in order to rule. What enabled these leaders to control their nations—their command of Muslim armies, the development of cities, and the establishment of various ministries—had very little to do with religion and relied on reason, expertise, and technical knowledge. Nothing, then, prevented Muslims from being like other peoples and developing a theory of politics that would lay the groundwork for a different system of governance.

While 'Abd al-Raziq's opinions should be contextualized within the politics of King Fu'ad and the debates over the question of the caliphate in the Muslim world, the abuse of power under British colonialism in the Middle East also inspired his writings. 'Abd al-Raziq makes mention of the newly appointed Iraqi king, Faysal b. al-Husayn, whose father challenged Ottoman rule with British support, thus guaranteeing that his son, Faysal, would be installed as king. Faysal was made king of Iraq based on the false claims of the British that the Iraqi people had freely elected him. In the same manner that Mu'awiya and his son Yazid had achieved the *bay'a* (oath of allegiance) of their own people—namely, by power—Faysal owed his position to his British backers, yet his rule was represented as reflecting the will of the people. 'Abd al-Raziq was troubled by the new Arab leadership, whose authority had little to do with the will of the people and yet represented itself as democratic. While the need to limit the power of political leaders was a much-discussed theme in modern Islamic political thought (especially in the years preceding the constitutional revolutions in Iran and the Ottoman Empire), 'Abd al-Raziq suggests that the power of the political leader should not be limited (by the 'ulama', consultation, or whatever other power) but rethought altogether.

'Abd al-Raziq argues that neither the Qur'an nor the hadith devotes much space to the issue of the caliphate. To understand this, it was necessary to distinguish between political and religious governance. According to political scientists (*'ulamā' al-siyāsa*), some form of power is needed in order to govern any *umma*, whether it is secular (*lā dīn lahā*) or religious (Jewish, Christian, or Muslim). The nature of this power, however, differs according to whether the mode of governance is constitutional (*dustūriyya*), tyrannical (*istibdādiyya*), republican, or Bolshevik. In fact, part of the discourse of the 'ulama' on leadership (*imāma*) and the caliphate (*khilāfa*) centered on what political science calls governance (*ḥukūma*)—namely, political practices rather than religious ones.

Referencing the *sīra* (life of the Prophet), the chronicles of Tabari, and the hadith literature, 'Abd al-Raziq seeks to establish that the caliphate was an institution that developed historically from less developed forms to more complex ones in tandem with the growth of the Islamic state. The Prophet, in this sense, was a religious leader (*rasūl da'wa dīniyya*) and not a political leader in the fullest sense of the word. Many prophetic messengers (*rasūl*) were not necessarily political leaders; Jesus, one such figure, said famously, "Render unto Caesar the things which are Caesar's, and unto God the things that are God's" (Matthew 22:21). The Prophet did establish an entity that had elements (*maẓāhir*) of governance and traces (*āthār*) of power. Even though jihad was used as a weapon for the expansion of the new faith, its promotion was mostly attained by spiritual and nonviolent means. Evoking the Qur'anic verse "There is no compulsion in religion" (2:256), 'Abd al-Raziq proposes that the Prophet attempted to persuade people to embrace his religion rather than use force and, by extension, establish a state. In fact, the prophetic state (*al-mamlaka al-nabawiyya, al-dawla al-nabawiyya*) did not achieve perfection in terms of its political form but was rather a state in the primitive stages of development (*dawlat al-basāṭa, ḥukūmat al-fiṭra*) led by a man who loved simplicity and was close to the people. Therefore, the prophetic state was one of a kind; today a state without a fixed budget or ministries is inconceivable. The Prophet did not desire to establish a state, much less an empire, and in terms of leadership, he was more akin to Moses and Jesus than any political figure. The Muslims obeyed the Prophet without question because his authority emanated from the divine law. The rule of the Prophet, however, should not be confused with the rule of those who came after him. Islam was a call to reform mankind and a means to achieve happiness and not a political prescription for establishing a state. It was therefore possible that one day the world would experience religious unity, yet it was utterly impossible, and in contradiction to human nature, to have one state for all mankind.

Reflecting on current political theories (such as Pan-Arabism), 'Abd al-Raziq suggests that Islam, as a global and humanistic mission, was neither an Arab religion nor a manifestation of Arab unity, as the Islamic faith did not privilege one nation, language, or historical period over another. True, the Prophet was an Arab and the Qur'an was an Arabic book—yet the Arabs at the time were not unified. They spoke different dialects and lived under different political regimes (some were ruled by the Byzantines; others were independent). Islam did provide the Arabs with certain laws

regarding war, culture, speech, and etiquette, thus offering some form of unity, yet this unity was not intended to form a state because the Prophet's authority was religious in nature, and the Arabs obeyed him based on their faith.

For 'Abd al-Raziq, the transformation to the rule of Abu Bakr typified the shift to an Arab state. It is in the debates between the *muhājirūn* (emigrants) and the *anṣār* (helpers) that 'Abd al-Raziq locates a new political vocabulary relating to governance. Abu Bakr did not intend to be a religious ruler, but his public persona and the people's admiration for him solidified this religious notion. Unlike the Prophet, he was a political leader who had to unite the Arabs as he faced the challenge of the ethnotribal loyalties (*'aṣabiyya*) emblematic of the Arabian political order. However, some of his followers wrongly believed that his authority was like that of Muhammad: Abu Bakr was not seen as replacing Muhammad but rather as a representative of Allah. In this context, the *ridda* (apostasy) wars should be understood as tribal rather than religious wars, relating to the rivalries between Quraysh and Tamim and the desire to keep the leadership of the Arab state within Quraysh. These processes of the consolidation of power, however, should be interpreted as arising out of the particular nature of the new state and not as articles of the Islamic faith. Certainly, there was a heretical group, such as false prophets, within the opposition to Abu Bakr. Yet some of those who rebelled against Abu Bakr could have been Muslims resisting the political hegemony offered by Abu Bakr, not the Islamic religion. The refusal to recognize Abu Bakr's political authority was not in itself a sign of *ridda*, for individuals such as 'Ali b. Abi Talib were not considered *murtaddūn* (apostates) or treated as such. Those who did not want to pay the zakat (alms tax) were not rejecting religion but rather the regime of Abu Bakr.

The ideas put forth by 'Abd al-Raziq were truly revolutionary. On the one hand, he intentionally downplayed or ignored many elements in the Prophet's biography (such as the signing of *'ahd al-umma*, the covenant of the community) in order to support his contention that the Prophet's early community was not a political one. Moreover, by arguing that the prophetic state was a very primordial one at best and that the Prophet was a religious leader whose rule could not, and should not, be emulated by any other leader, 'Abd al-Raziq negated the view, widespread in his time, that the Prophet and the *salaf* (Islam's first generations) should serve as ideals for political figures. Going further, the implications of *al-Islam wa-Usul al-Hukm* were that Muslims should not attempt to emulate the political structure created at the time of the Prophet, as political systems, like all other systems, develop historically and change from time to time.

Unlike Islamists today, or even the Wahhabis during his time, 'Abd al-Raziq was extremely cautious in calling another Muslim *murtadd*, or apostate. His writings marked a clear separation between state and religion, which was reflected not only in his call for democratic regimes in the future but also in his interpretation of the Islamic past. As an Azhari intimately familiar with the Qur'an and the hadith, he was able to amass numerous verses and traditions that accentuated nonviolent methods of proselytization in Islam and illustrated the primitive nature of the early Islamic state. While he recognized the need for the stability brought about by a government, he was critical of the ways in which religiosity was used to support undemocratic regimes. The mentions of democracy, Bolshevism, and tyranny in his writing indicate that he was thinking about current political regimes. His technique was not different from those of many of his contemporaries, who offered their own Qur'anic exegesis to resolve political dilemmas and imbued medieval Islamic concepts with modern meanings. Yet unlike many of his contemporaries, who evoked the idea of *shūrā* (mutual consultation) as a means of curbing the power of the sovereign, 'Abd al-Raziq suggested a new reading of the past that rarely had been offered before—or would be after—to support radical political change.

See also 'Abduh, Muhammad (1849–1905); modernity; Rida, Muhammad Rashid (1865–1935); secularism

Further Reading

Ali Abderraziq, *L'Islam et les fondements du pouvoir*, translated and introduction by Abdou Filali-Ansary, 1994; Souad T. Ali, *A Religion, Not a State: Ali 'Abd al-Raziq's Islamic Justification of Political Secularism*, 2009.

ORIT BASHKIN

abdication

Abdication is a ruler's unilateral decision to give up his position of power. Classical Islamic political theory, including theological and juridical discussions of the imamate, allows the caliph or imam, the supreme ruler of the Muslim community, to abdicate of his own volition. He may do so because he is physically disqualified, such as if his health has deteriorated and he is unable to carry out his duties; because he is morally disqualified, such as if his sinful acts have affected his moral probity; or simply because he no longer wishes to assume the tremendous obligations and grave moral responsibilities that accompany the office. Under the caliphal dynasties of the Umayyads (661–750) and the Abbasids (750–1258), it became standard practice to designate an heir apparent—often two under the Umayyads—who would assume the office in cases of abdication or death.

Abdications occurred quite frequently in the history of the Umayyad and Abbasid caliphates, but they were usually coerced pseudoabdications. For example, the Umayyad caliph Ibrahim b. al-Walid (r. 744) was forced to abdicate when his cousin Marwan II (r. 744–50) had surrounded Damascus and was about to overrun the capital. In 1031, the last Umayyad caliph in Córdoba abdicated under similar circumstances, and his realm was divided into petty principalities. Under the Abbasids, Turkish military commanders and palace factions often dictated caliphal abdications, removing

one member of the ruling family and installing another in order to undermine rival factions. In 866, for example, the caliph Musta'in (r. 862–66) succumbed to pressures from the captains of the Turkish guard to abdicate in favor of his cousin Mu'tazz (r. 866–69); although he was promised that he would be able to retire to Medina with a sufficient income, Mu'tazz did not keep his word, confined Musta'in to Baghdad, then had him assassinated. When other caliphs refused to abdicate, the Turkish commanders deposed them by blinding them in order to disqualify them for the office in the future, imprisoning them indefinitely, or killing them.

The most famous abdication in Islamic history is that of Hasan b. 'Ali, the Prophet's eldest grandson, who in 661 relinquished his claim to the caliphate and recognized Mu'awiya (r. 661–80), governor of Damascus and founder of the Umayyad dynasty, as ruler of the Muslim community. This took place after the assassination of his father, 'Ali b. Abi Talib, by the Khariji rebel Ibn Muljam in Kufa. After 'Ali was assassinated, his followers, the Shi'is, took the oath of allegiance to his son Hasan as caliph. Hasan initially led them from Iraq toward Syria to face Mu'awiya's advancing forces, but ended up accepting a settlement with his opponent. While subsequent Sunni histories claim that Hasan stepped down in recognition of the legitimacy of his opponent's rule, demonstrated by Mu'awiya's ability to garner widespread support and unite the Islamic state and sealed by Hasan's acceptance of a large payment in return, Shi'is maintained that this was a tactical move that did not entail surrender of the 'Alids' claim to the caliphate. Rather, Hasan supposedly intended to avoid further bloodshed after the devastating First Islamic Civil War (656–61), which had erupted following the assassination of 'Uthman b. 'Affan (r. 644–56), the third caliph, and pitted 'Ali against the Prophet's wife 'A'isha and the Umayyad clan and their supporters, and to ensure the safety of his loyal followers, who were faced with overwhelming opposing forces as well as traitors in their midst. In fact, Shi'i sources report that he was wounded in the thigh by a Khariji who had infiltrated his own camp. In later Shi'i thought, Hasan's abdication provided a model for quietist resistance and accommodation with illegitimate political regimes, in contrast to the active resistance embodied by his brother Husayn, who died at the Battle of Karbala in 680 as he sought to lead a revolt against Mu'awiya's son Yazid I (r. 680–83), the first hereditary ruler in Islamic history. Ayatollah Khomeini and other ideologues of the Iranian Revolution of 1979 vocally contrasted the two stances, claiming the superiority of the latter in order to mobilize the populace of Iran against Muhammad Reza Shah (r. 1941–79), the secularizing king of Iran.

The tables would be turned after a fashion when Yazid's son Mu'awiya II (r. 683–84) abdicated for pious reasons in 684. Faced with the need to crush the counter-caliphate of Ibn al-Zubayr (r. 683–92) in the Hijaz, Mu'awiya II chose to abdicate rather than assume the responsibility for conducting what would likely be a bloody military campaign in Mecca, on Islam's holiest ground. Shi'is even claim that he had secretly converted to Shi'ism and did not want to be associated with the massacre of the descendants of the Prophet.

Subsequent Islamic history provides many examples of coerced pseudoabdications. A number of the Ottoman sultans, Safavid shahs, and other rulers were forced to abdicate by military factions aiming to exert greater control over the central government. Such abdications have continued until the present. In 1941, the Western powers forced Reza Shah (r. 1925–41) to abdicate in favor of his son Muhammad Reza Shah (r. 1941–79). Egypt's King Farouk I was forced to abdicate in 1952 after the coup d'etat led by the Free Officers and went into exile in Monaco and Italy. His infant son was proclaimed King Fu'ad II, but the monarchy was officially abolished the next year. The second Hashimi monarch of Jordan, Talal b. 'Abdallah (r. 1951–52), abdicated in favor of his son Hussein in 1952 after he was declared unfit to rule by parliament due to mental illness. Most recently, Egyptian president Husni Mubarak (r. 1981–2011) abdicated under pressure from the Egyptian army after a massive wave of popular protests in the early months of 2011. A striking abdication in recent history is that of 'Abd al-Rahman Siwar al-Dahab, the Sudanese general who overthrew Ja'far al-Numayri's government in 1985. After controlling an interim government as head of the transitional military council, he abdicated in May 1986, handing over power to a democratically elected civilian government headed by Sadiq al-Mahdi, surprising skeptics who doubted that the military would voluntarily relinquish power.

See also caliph, caliphate; military

Further Reading

Juwayni, *A Guide to Conclusive Proofs for the Principles of Belief*, translated by Paul Walker, 2000; Mawardi, *Ordinances of Government*, translated by Wafa H. Wahba, 2001; Al-Shaykh al-Mufid, *Kitab al-Irshad: The Book of Guidance*, translated by I.K.A. Howard, n.d.

DEVIN J. STEWART

'Abduh, Muhammad (1849–1905)

Editor of Egypt's government newspaper during the 'Urabi revolt (1881–82), member of the Paris-based Pan-Islamic revolutionary organization al-'Urwa al-Wuthqa (The Firmest Bond) in 1884, later a member of various Egyptian government commissions, and finally mufti of Egypt (1899–1905), Muhammad 'Abduh is best known as one of the chief founders of the rationalist and modernist movement known to Western scholars as Salafism. His name became synonymous with Islamic reform.

Born in a village in Buhayra province, Egypt, in about 1849, 'Abduh studied at Azhar, where he was a young follower of Afghani (1838–97), a roving Persian intellectual and activist, under whose influence he joined a progressive Masonic lodge where he made connections that would continue throughout his subsequent career. After Afghani's expulsion from Egypt in 1879, 'Abduh remained close to the reform-minded minister Mustafa Riyad Pasha, under

whose patronage he became editor of the government newspaper, *al-Waqa‘i al-Misriyya* (Egyptian events), a post that carried with it the duty of supervising the Egyptian press. Initially reluctant to join the ‘Urabi revolt of 1881 and 1882 against Egypt's hereditary ruler the Khedive Tawfiq, ‘Abduh eventually oriented *al-Waqa‘i* in support of the rebels, evidently hoping that this might advance his constitutionalist agenda. Arrested and imprisoned in the repression that followed the revolt's failure, he was exiled from Egypt and, after a period in Beirut, joined Afghani in Paris in 1884. ‘Abduh edited and wrote much of *al-‘Urwa al-Wuthqa* (The firmest bond), a radical Pan-Islamist and anti-imperialist journal aimed at readers in Egypt and India, then both under British occupation. This journal ceased publication after eight months, partly because the British authorities forbade its distribution in Egypt and India and partly because it ran out of money, but nevertheless was widely influential. The Syrian Islamic activist and journalist Rashid Rida credited his own conversion to Islamic nationalism to his discovery of an old copy of the journal. The significance of the journal lay in its use of Islam and the Qur'an to encourage Pan-Islamic solidarity against Western imperialism. In some ways, it invented modern Islamic radicalism. Given that the journal's radicalism contrasted with ‘Abduh's later moderate stance, some scholars have argued that the primary responsibility for this hard line lay with Afghani rather than ‘Abduh, but others find the evidence for this unconvincing.

After breaking with Afghani in 1885 for reasons that are unclear, ‘Abduh returned to Syria, where he was briefly employed at a pioneering modernist school and wrote one of his most famous works, *Risalat al-Tawhid* (translated into English as *The Theology of Unity*). This short volume, little read in ‘Abduh's lifetime, argues for a rational and scientific understanding of Islam and shows the influence of the French historian François Guizot, whose schema of European history ‘Abduh applied to the Muslim world. Where Guizot credited the Renaissance and Reformation with saving Europe from the Dark Ages and restoring it to the high rationality previously achieved in the Classical world, ‘Abduh looked for an Islamic reformation and renaissance to save Islam from its Dark Age and restore the rationality of the high Abbasid period (750 to 10th century).

Evidently despairing of making much progress in Syria under the repressive regime of the Ottoman Sultan Abdülhamid II, ‘Abduh secured permission to return to Egypt in 1888. He was initially given the minor post of a judge in the provincial town of Banha but gradually proved himself a reliable supporter of the government of Khedive ‘Abbas Hilmi II. He assisted various reform projects and was rewarded in 1895 with a post on the newly created Azhar Administrative Council, where he represented the government's interests. Upon the forced resignation of Hasuna al-Nawawi as grand mufti of Egypt in 1899, ‘Abduh was appointed as his replacement. ‘Abduh's own relationship with the khedive later deteriorated, and as mufti he avoided a fate similar to that of his predecessor thanks only to the intervention of Lord Cromer, the British official who was the effective ruler of Egypt, with whom ‘Abduh had formed an alliance based on common interests and, to some extent, on genuine personal and intellectual sympathy. Even so, ‘Abduh might not have survived much longer as mufti had he not died of cancer in 1905, at the age of 56.

As a member of the Azhar Administrative Council, ‘Abduh delivered at Azhar a series of well-attended public lectures based on Qur'anic texts; these were later collected and edited by Rashid Rida and published under the title *Tafsir al-Manar* (*Al-Manar's* exegesis), a work partly of Rashid Rida's own composition. In the role of mufti, ‘Abduh performed his administrative duties as expected and also delivered a number of modernist fatwas endorsing such religiously problematic institutions as the wearing of the European-style brimmed hat and the use of insurance. These fatwas were published in Rashid Rida's journal *al-Manar* (The lighthouse), which was widely read and extremely influential throughout the Muslim world.

‘Abduh's lectures, fatwas, and occasional newspaper articles during this period are not overtly political. They deal instead with the need for intellectual and social reform. They stress the value of reason, attack adherence to traditional precedent (*taqlīd*), and call for new interpretations of Islam (*ijtihād*). They also stress the value of progressive education (‘Abduh became a keen supporter of the theories of the English liberal philosopher Herbert Spencer) and condemn polygamy as a social and moral abuse. The silence on political issues may, however, be seen as a sort of political statement: that the way forward for the Muslims was, at least for a period, not through conflict with Europe but through cooperation and even emulation. ‘Abduh himself set an example by remaining an active Mason, learning French, taking summer holidays in Switzerland, and dining regularly with Lord Cromer.

After ‘Abduh's death, his writings were collected, edited, and promoted by Rashid Rida, who is thought by some to have used ‘Abduh's name and fame to promote his own rather different agenda. ‘Abduh's association with Rashid Rida, combined with the difference between his political positions before and after his break with Afghani in 1885, produced many different later interpretations of his life. Since his death, ‘Abduh has been widely used to endorse a variety of religious and political positions and is remembered more as a religious than as a political figure.

See also al-Afghani, Jamal al-Din (1838–97); modernism; Pan-Islamism; Rida, Muhammad Rashid (1865–1935); Salafis

Further Reading

Muhammad ‘Abduh, *The Theology of Unity*, translated by Ishaq Masa‘ad and Kenneth Cragg, 1966; Charles Adams, *Islam and Modernism in Egypt: A Study of the Modern Reform Movement Inaugurated by Muhammad ‘Abduh*, 1933; Muhammad al-Haddad, *Muhammad ‘Abduh: Qira'a Jadidah fi Khitab al-Islah al-Dini*, 2003; Albert Hourani, *Arabic Thought in the Liberal Age, 1798–1939*, 1962; Jacques Jomier, *Le commentaire coranique du Manar: tendances modernes de l'exégèse coranique en Égypte*, 1954; Elie Kedourie, *Afghani and ‘Abduh: An Essay on Religious Unbelief and Political Activism in Modern Islam*, 1966; Mark Sedgwick, *Muhammad Abduh*, 2010.

MARK SEDGWICK

Abdülhamid II (1842–1918)

Abdülhamid II, the 34th Ottoman sultan, presided over the promulgation of the first Ottoman Constitution. Son of Sultan Abdülmecid (r. 1839–61), Abdülhamid II ascended the throne on August 31, 1876, amid international crisis and domestic instability. The Eastern Question, dormant since the Paris Treaty of 1856, flared up again in 1875, when rebellions engulfed first Herzegovina and then Bosnia. Subsequent clashes between Muslims and Christians in Bulgaria prompted diplomatic intervention by the Great Powers of Europe and provided the impetus for the deposition of Sultan Abdülaziz (r. 1861–76) by reformist statesmen on May 30, 1876. Abdülaziz's successor, the mentally ill Murad V, disappointed the high hopes of the reformers, who deposed him after a 93-day reign and anointed his younger brother, Abdülhamid, to rule.

The bureaucracy, which sought to reestablish the favorable balance of power that had existed between the imperial court and the Sublime Porte (Ottoman government) in the heyday of the "reforms" (Tanzimat), expected the new sultan to promulgate the empire's first constitution and otherwise keep a low profile. Abdülhamid II, however, had other ideas. Despite the urgent need to present the Europeans with the fait accompli of a constitutional monarchy and thereby deflect pressures for reform, the sultan engaged the bureaucrats in a protracted debate on the nature of the constitution. He insisted on protecting his sovereign rights and compelled the reformers to make crucial concessions, the most important of which was a clause stipulating that the sultan could exile, without trial, individuals who endangered public safety. The announcement of the 119-article constitution was timed to coincide with the opening of the conference of international powers in Istanbul on December 23, 1876. Nevertheless, the Great Powers, unimpressed by the promises of equality for all Ottoman citizens included in the constitution, insisted on sweeping reforms favoring non-Muslims.

In April 1877, soon after the Ottoman government had rejected these demands, Russia declared war. Within less than a year, Russian armies were at the gates of Istanbul, forcing the government to sign one of the most disadvantageous peace treaties in Ottoman history at San Stefano on March 3, 1878. However, the resulting disturbance to the status quo proved too much for the other Great Powers to stomach, and the Congress of Berlin (June–July 1878) reversed some of the treaty's most radical provisions and restored some stability to the region. Abdülhamid II seized the opportunity presented by the war to prorogue the Chamber of Deputies after a mere 162 days in session. Constitutional rule continued in theory, but thereafter the sultan worked relentlessly to strengthen his position and eliminate the threat posed by parliamentary democracy to a polyethnic empire.

Abdülhamid II created a neopatrimonial autocracy combining the legitimizing strictures of Islamic law with the modern ideals of a *Rechtsstaat*—a state ruled by law. As power flowed back to the palace, the Sublime Porte shrank to its former stature as a subservient administrative arm of the state. The sultan vigorously suppressed all forms of opposition and established an effective spy network and a strict mechanism of censorship, which sustained his autocratic rule for more than three decades. The Hamidian regime revived an old Ottoman emphasis on personal loyalty, replacing the reform-era concept of the officialdom's loyalty to the state with that of fealty to the sovereign. The sultan bestowed extra ranks, decorations, and sometimes extravagant personal gifts, such as cash awards and mansions, upon high-ranking bureaucrats who proved exceptionally faithful. However, Abdülhamid II's autocracy did not, as is often maintained, represent a wholesale return to the patrimonialism of the pre-reforms era, for the lower rungs of the bureaucracy answered to their superiors within a strict hierarchy, which was too similar to that found in equivalent European institutions.

Abdülhamid II regarded himself as one of the great reforming sultans of the late Ottoman era; Ottoman propaganda frequently likened him to Peter the Great. He initiated major changes in education, state infrastructure, and the use of technology. The modern system of education established during the reforms era gained further strength. Under his aegis, a host of new colleges sprang up, designed to furnish the bureaucracy with competent officials, ranging from customs officers and veterinarians to governors and experts on agriculture. The provinces were connected to the imperial center through an extensive network of telegraph lines. Extraordinary efforts were invested in developing the Ottoman railway system. Statistics, including socioeconomic ones, came to be widely employed in bureaucratic planning and decision making.

Abdülhamid II also sought to reinvent tradition in an effort to bolster his image and foster a new sense of belonging to a Pan-Ottoman community. He refashioned old Ottoman customs and turned them into pompous, European-style ceremonies. Even Friday sermons acquired ceremonial trappings resembling European imperial rites. The new imperial image was intended to create a sense of belonging among the subjects. Imperial symbols, such as the coat-of-arms, became ubiquitous, appearing on all kinds of objects, ranging from bookbindings to silver artifacts. New maps featured the empire in its glorious entirety, as opposed to the splintered representation of the separate continents in maps of the past.

Abdülhamid II also crafted a new foreign policy. Initially, he adopted a stance of noncommitment and studiously avoided any confrontation with the Great Powers. Acknowledging Ottoman military weakness, he sought to amplify the empire's power by deploying Pan-Islamism as an ideological weapon in his dealings with European colonial powers. He was not only the primary practitioner of Pan-Islamism but also one of its major ideologues, along with Jamal al-Din al-Afghani (d. 1897), whom he invited to Istanbul. Pan-Islamism served as a tool to cement the solidarity of the Muslim subjects of the empire and gave new substance to the official ideology, Ottomanism. It also served as a wild card to stave off pressure for pro-Christian reforms on the part of European powers by threatening them with jihad in their colonies. The Penjdeh

crisis of 1885 between Great Britain and Russia and Lord Robert Salisbury's decision in 1896 to base the defense of British interests in the Near East on Egypt, rather than on efforts to preserve the status quo at the Ottoman Straits, strained Anglo-Ottoman relations and eliminated the 19th-century assurance of British support for the empire in a time of crisis. The loss of the British guarantee compelled Abdülhamid II to switch to a policy of armed neutrality and to promote cordial relations with Germany. The Germans had also altered their strategy toward the Ottoman Empire in favor of their new *Drang nach Osten* (thrust to the East) policy. Although the subsequent Anglo-Russian rapprochement made the sultan lean even more toward Germany, he did not abandon his policy of avoiding alliances with the Great Powers. Likewise, he stuck to his pragmatic aversion to crises with the Great Powers over territories that were already lost to the empire in all but name. Thus he accepted the Bulgarian annexation of Eastern Rumelia (1885) and the British occupation of Egypt (1882). On the other hand, he bitterly contested British expansionism in the Arabian Peninsula and European reform schemes for Macedonia and eastern Anatolia. Similarly, Abdülhamid II rejected the 1901–2 Zionist proposal for settling and organizing Jews in Palestine in exchange for the consolidation of the colossal Ottoman debt.

Soaring debt, exacerbated by the war with Russia and the Great Depression of 1873–96, took a heavy toll on the Ottoman economy. And yet, despite the establishment of the Ottoman Public Debt Organization in 1881, to which a considerable proportion of state revenues were channeled, the economy fared well under Abdülhamid II. He presided over the centralization of the Ottoman economy and the institution of a protectionist trade regime. At his behest, the state made major investments in infrastructure, such as the Baghdad and Hijaz railways, a large irrigation project in the Konya valley, and telegraph lines connecting the Ottoman provinces with the center.

A generation of intellectuals found Abdülhamid II's autocratic regime an oppressive anachronism and fought against it mainly from outside the country. The establishment of a link between these exiles and disaffected members of the military eventually created a revolution. In July 1908, the main Ottoman organization of opposition, the Committee of Union and Progress (CUP), launched the Young Turk Revolution in Macedonia. The CUP forced the sultan to reinstate the Constitution of 1876 and to reconvene the Chamber of Deputies, which had been prorogued for 30 years. Abdülhamid II's second term as a chastened constitutional monarch was considerably shorter than the previous term. On April 27, 1909, the General Assembly, convening after the suppression of the counterrevolution of April 13 and acting on the basis of CUP instructions and a fatwa, deposed Abdülhamid II and placed him under virtual house arrest in Salonica. In 1912, when the city was about to fall to the Greeks, the sultan was transferred back to Istanbul, where he spent his last years at Beylerbeyi Palace until his death.

See also constitutionalism; Europe; Ottomans (1299–1924); revival and reform; Turkey

Further Reading

Selim Deringil, *The Well-Protected Domains: Ideology and the Legitimation of Power in the Ottoman Empire, 1876–1909*, 1998; François Georgeon, *Abdülhamid II: Le Sultan Calife, 1876–1909*, 2003; M. Şükrü Hanioğlu, *The Young Turks in Opposition*, 1995; F.A.K. Yasamee, *Ottoman Diplomacy: Abdülhamid II and the Great Powers, 1878–1888*, 1996.

M. ŞÜKRÜ HANIOĞLU

abodes of Islam, war, and truce

The classical Islamic theory of world order, as outlined in legal treatises on the Islamic state's relations with non-Muslims (*siyar*), divided the world into different realms or abodes (in Arabic, *dār* [sing.], *diyār* [plural]). The number and names of such abodes varied widely in classical sources, but the three that received the most attention among jurists were the abode of Islam (*dār al-islām*), war (*dār al-ḥarb*), and truce (*dār al-ṣulḥ*). Even these three, however, did not receive detailed or consistent elaboration.

Dār al-islām was generally understood as the territory over which Muslims held political sovereignty and in which Islamic law (shari'a) was enforced. *Dār al-islām* was conceived as the abode of the Muslim *umma*, the community of believers, in which Muslim lives, property, honor, and faith were safeguarded. *Dār al-islām* also comprised non-Muslim communities (*dhimmī*s), whose lives, property, and religious autonomy were guaranteed by the Islamic state so long as they did not challenge Muslim sovereignty and paid the poll tax (the *jizya* mentioned in Q. 9:29) or a land tax (the *kharāj*).

Dār al-ḥarb was understood broadly as all territories in which Islamic law did not prevail. According to the majority of jurists, it was the duty of the Muslim ruler to undertake jihad—through peaceful means if possible but through forceful means if necessary—to reduce *dār al-ḥarb* and expand *dār al-islām* whenever the state was militarily and financially able to do so. An area of *dār al-ḥarb* could be incorporated into *dār al-islām* through capitulation (*sulḥan*) or through conquest (*'anwatan*). Conversely, according to jurists of the Hanafi school, three conditions caused a territory to revert from *dār al-islām* to *dār al-ḥarb*: (1) enforcement of non-Islamic laws, (2) contiguity with another territory of *dār al-ḥarb*, and (3) the absence of security for Muslims or *dhimmīs*.

Dār al-ṣulḥ, or the abode of truce, was a third category posited mainly by jurists of the Shafi'i school, although scholars from other schools also employed it or analogous terms. It included areas that could not be objects of jihad because of a truce or other agreement with the Islamic state. Drawing an analogy from the treaty of Hudaybiyya concluded by the Prophet and his Meccan opponents in 628, most jurists held that the maximum term for any truce was ten years, although nothing barred the Muslim ruler

from indefinitely renewing it if he deemed such a truce to be in the Muslims' interest.

These terms are not found in either the Qur'an or the hadith. They appear to have entered Islamic parlance during the late eighth century (second Islamic century), perhaps in an effort by the jurists to revive Islamic unity through renewed military efforts (jihad) in order to expand Islamic rule. The theory of world order in which these abodes played an important part was thus never matched by reality. Yet the terms have continued to be used and debated by Muslims until the present. During the 19th century, Indian 'ulama' divided over the question of whether India under British rule remained *dār al-islām* or had become *dār al-ḥarb*. Similar debates took place from North Africa to Southeast Asia. The terms are still employed today, mainly by fundamentalist writers, although with profound differences from the classical usage. *Dār al-islām* does not exist; instead, it has been replaced by a new *jāhiliyya*, or a corrupted, un-Islamic order, as argued by Mawdudi (d. 1979), the founder of the Jama'at-i Islami in India and Pakistan, and Sayyid Qutb (d. 1966), the chief ideologue of the Egyptian Muslim Brotherhood. For such theorists and activists, reconstituting an authentic *dār al-islām* is now the primary goal of jihad.

See also alliances; asylum; diplomacy; international relations; jihad

Further Reading

Khaled Abou El Fadl, "Islamic Law and Muslim Minorities: The Juristic Discourse on Muslim Minorities from the Second/Eighth to the Eleventh/Seventeenth Centuries," *Journal of Islamic Law and Society* 22, no. 1 (1994); Muhammad Hamidullah, *The Muslim Conduct of State*, 1977; Sohail H. Hashmi, "Political Boundaries and Moral Communities: Islamic Perspectives," in *States, Nations, and Borders: The Ethics of Making Boundaries*, edited by Allen Buchanan and Margaret Moore, 2003; Majid Khadduri, *War and Peace in the Law of Islam*, 1955; Rudolph Peters, *Islam and Colonialism: The Doctrine of Jihad in Modern History*, 1979.

SOHAIL H. HASHMI

absolutism

Traditional monarchy (*salṭana*) in Islam was autocratic. There were no formal checks on the ruler, but he was the protector of religion and enforcer of the divine law (shari'a). In theory, government was not arbitrary but subject to law. This form of government therefore should be characterized as autocracy. The legitimacy of autocracy depended on justice and the observance of divine law. Government without justice was tyranny (*ẓulm*). With political modernization in the latter part of the 19th century, traditional monarchy was described as absolutism (*salṭana muṭlaqa*), in contrast to modern constitutional or conditional (*mashrūṭa*) monarchy, and increasingly decried as despotism (*istibdād*). In the political literature of the late 19th and early 20th centuries, the latter term, *istibdād*, carried the brunt of the pejorative weight traditionally associated with tyranny.

In the 11th century, the historian Abu al-Fadl Muhammad b. Husayn al-Bayhaqi (d. 1077) used the term *istibdād* to describe the arbitrary decisions of the sultan. A few centuries later, Ibn Khaldun (d. 1406) used its derivative verbal forms to describe the consolidation of the power of a single ruler in periods of breakdown and transition within and between various Andalusian and North African dynasties. But the term in its modern sense must be considered a neologism. Aristotle had used the term *despotés* for the authority of the master in the household, or *oikos*, and had further described Persian kingship as "hereditary despotic rule governing in conformity with law." Aristotle's *Politics* was, however, not available to Muslim thinkers in the 19th century. It was through the radical redefinition of absolutism as despotic rule by the great political thinker of the Enlightenment, Montesquieu (d. 1755), that the concept entered modern Muslim political thought, albeit indirectly. The Ottoman regime was depicted fairly favorably by Jean Bodin (d. 1596) in the 16th century, but a Venetian ambassador in 1637 described it as a power "most immoderate, absolute and despotic," and a century later, Montesquieu elaborated on his famous concept of Oriental despotism in sharp contrast to the "moderate" Christian monarchies of Europe. Montesquieu's pejorative reclassification of Aristotle's despotism was achieved by his artful collapse of law into religion in his discussion of the Ottoman (1299–1924) and Safavid (1501–1722) empires. Despotism was an important element of his project of enlightenment in the context of the growing de facto absolutism of the French state and was intended as a warning (through its projection to other civilizations). Although Montesquieu's *Spirit of Laws* was not translated into Arabic, Persian, or Turkish in the 19th century, his influence was transmitted by modern legal education and, more particularly, through Vittorio Alfieri's *De Tirannide* (1800). The term *istibdād* was used in the pejorative sense of absolutism in the last quarter of the 19th century by Khayr al-Din al-Tunisi (d. 1890) and Namık Kemal (d. 1888), and Abdullah Cevdet (d. 1895) used it as the title of his Turkish translation of Alfieri in 1898. Shortly thereafter in 1900, the Syrian 'Abd al-Rahman al-Kawakibi (d. 1902) published his famous *Tabayi' al-Istibdad* (Characteristics of despotism) in Cairo, drawing heavily on that translation (though mistaking Montesquieu for a poet). The constitutionalist writers in the Ottoman Empire, including Egypt and Iran, thus appropriated Montesquieu's characterization of despotism as arbitrary rule without law to describe the autocracy they wished to reform.

In the formal typologies of government in modern public law of the period, absolutism was contrasted to constitutional monarchy and republic, both interestingly rendered as "national sovereignty" (*salṭanat-i millī*) in the Persian tracts. In the polemical literature against despotism, the idea of absolutism constituted a complete break with traditional political thought. In fact, very little attention

was paid to the traditional theory of monarchy that rested on the fear of anarchy and the necessity of order for the effective divine salvation of humankind. Kawakibi mentioned the traditional political philosophy (*siyāsa madaniyya*) a few times in passing and only once cited the hadiths and maxims justifying monarchy, adding that they were conditional upon justice, whereas monarchy loses its legitimacy when it practices tyranny—taken to be the usual form of absolutism.

More recent Pan-Islamic theories of the caliphate, promoted by the Ottoman sultan Abdülhamid II (d. 1918), were also set aside in the constitutionalist literature. In fact, Kawakibi had already put forward a theory of the caliphate as purely a spiritual authority when he moved from Aleppo to Cairo, presumably for the benefit of his uncle's pupil, 'Abbas Hilmi II, the khedive of Egypt. This idea was put forward without regard to the discussion of absolutism and was at odds with it. A quarter of a century later, when Muhammad Rashid Rida (d. 1935) drew on the medieval juristic literature to formulate his modern theory of the caliphate, its dissociation from the concept of absolutism was complete.

In Iran, absolutism was contrasted to the rule of law and became the battle cry of the Constitutional Revolution (1906–11). Kawakibi's *Tabayi' al-Istibdad* was translated into Persian with the same title and published in Tehran in 1907. The period during which autocracy was restored, from June 1908 to July 1909, was called the "Lesser Despotism" (*istibdād-i saghīr*). In *Tanbih al-Umma wa-Tanzih al-Milla*, published in Baghdad in 1909, Mirza Muhammad Husayn Gharavi Na'ini (d. 1936), a constitutionalist Shi'i *mujtahid* (authoritative jurist) of Najaf, drew on Kawakibi's *Tabayi' al-Istibdad* to underscore the illegitimacy of absolutism as a despotic form of government. It was contrasted with constitutional government, for which Na'ini offered a conditional justification within the framework of the traditional Shi'i jurisprudence as the least undesirable form of government during the occultation of the Twelfth Imam. Na'ini's treatise was republished in Tehran in 1955 by Mahmud Taleqani as a plea for the observance of the constitution of 1906 to 1907 and in order to delegitimize the incipient royal dictatorship of Muhammad Reza Shah Pahlavi (d. 1979). Although it was displaced by such terms as *dictatorship*, the notion of absolutism (*istibdād*) did not disappear entirely. Since the Islamic Revolution of 1979 in Iran, a powerful minority of Shi'i clerics have advocated theocratic government—led by clerics—as "healthy absolutism" in their inner circle, arguing publicly that Ayatollah Khomeini (d. 1989) had intended the "Islamic Republic" merely as a transitory form of Islamic government.

See also monarchy

Further Reading

Charles de Secondat Montesquieu, *The Spirit of the Laws*, translated by Anne M. Cohler, Basia Carolyn Miller, and Harold Samuel Stone, 1989; Lucette Valensi, *The Birth of the Despot: Venice and the Sublime Porte*, translated by A. Denner, 1993.

SAÏD AMIR ARJOMAND

Abu Bakr (ca. 573–634)

Abu Bakr b. Abi Quhafa b. 'Amir was the first caliph, or successor, to the Prophet Muhammad to head the Muslim community after Muhammad's death in 632 and until his own death in 634. Like Muhammad, he was a Meccan from the tribe of Quraysh, albeit from the clan of Taym rather than Muhammad's clan of Hashim. Allegedly one of the two earliest male converts to Islam, Abu Bakr had been a merchant in Mecca in pre-Islamic times, and upon his conversion he spent much of his moral and financial capital in support of the cause of Islam. Known as *al-ṣiddīq*, "the trustworthy" or "the upright," Abu Bakr was Muhammad's close friend, chief adviser, and staunch ally, who defended the Prophet's account of his night journey (*isrā'*) from Mecca to Jerusalem. In 622, Muhammad selected him to be his companion in his emigration journey from Mecca to Medina, as is referred to in the Qur'an (9:40), and he later participated in all the expeditions that Muhammad led in the Medinan period.

Political questions surrounded the selection and election of Abu Bakr as caliph since that office was without precedent in Arabia, and his tenure would begin to define it at a critical moment for the Islamic polity, as Muslims moved from God's rule under Muhammad to the appointment of his successors by mere mortals. Abu Bakr's appointment was not without controversy. Immediately following the Prophet's death, a power struggle took place in Medina on the *saqīfa*, or "portico," of the clan of Banu Sa'ida between the Medinan (*anṣār*) and Meccan (*muhājirūn*) Muslims, the former group attempting to share with the Quraysh the leadership of the Muslim community and the latter seeking to keep that leadership exclusively within Quraysh. The *anṣār*'s attempt was thwarted by the decisive intervention of 'Umar b. al-Khattab (d. 644), an influential Companion of the Prophet from his tribe of Quraysh, who proposed that his friend Abu Bakr be the leader of a single, unified community. Later literature legitimates Abu Bakr's claim to rule by the Prophet's demonstrated esteem for him, by his precedence (*sābiqa*) in adopting the new faith and by the Prophet appointing him, during his final illness, to lead the prayer. His exalted position was confirmed when the Prophet married Abu Bakr's daughter 'A'isha (d. 678) when she was nine or ten. This could have been, initially, a political alliance, part of the Prophet's strategy that resulted in each of the first four caliphs being bound to him by marriage. Abu Bakr's prestige, however, was much enhanced when 'A'isha was later acknowledged as the Prophet's favorite wife.

Even after Abu Bakr's acclamation as caliph through an oath of allegiance (*bay'a*) of all Muslims in Medina, including a delayed one by 'Ali b. Abi Talib (d. 661), the Prophet's son-in-law, some continued to believe that 'Ali had a greater claim to rule than Abu Bakr. This tension sowed the seeds for the later division of the Muslim community into Sunni and Shi'i Muslims. Within decades, and more so over the first Islamic centuries, the

rift between the two groups widened. The Shi'is supported the political and religious preeminence of 'Ali and his descendants as imams, and some of them identified Abu Bakr (as well as his two successors) as a usurper who had seized power unjustly despite knowing that the Prophet had appointed 'Ali to lead his community prior to his death. The Sunnis reject as unsubstantiated the claim that the Prophet had designated a successor before he died.

Abu Bakr spent almost his entire reign of over two years (June 8, 632–August 23, 634) as caliph waging wars against the Arab tribes who carried out religiopolitical insurgencies in central and eastern Arabia and in Yemen against the Muslim authority in Medina. Islamic historical literature reads all the opposition movements during Abu Bakr's caliphate in a religious light and put all the activities related to them under the heading of "the apostasy" (*al-ridda*), simultaneously characterizing some of their leaders as "false prophets." Far from being a uniform body of rebellions, some the tribes simply rejected the supremacy of the Medinan authority, refused to pay the prescribed zakat (alms taxes), or declined the invitation to embrace Islam for the first time. The armies that Abu Bakr sent against these "apostates" quelled all their resistance. In the important battle at 'Aqraba' in May 633, Musaylima b. Thumama, the most serious religious and political opponent of the Muslims, was defeated and killed. By the time Abu Bakr had died, Arabia had become unified under Muslim rule, with its center in Medina.

Abu Bakr continued the Prophet's policy of sending expeditions into Syria. The conflicts that ensued with the Byzantines, under the leadership of Usama b. Zayd, signaled the first phase of the Islamic conquests of the vast lands between the Nile and Oxus rivers in 634. It was under Abu Bakr's rule that the incursion into Iraq by the Muslims, under the leadership of Khalid b. al-Walid, started.

Before his death of natural causes in 634, Abu Bakr designated 'Umar b. al-Khattab as his successor, and when he died he was buried next to the Prophet, beneath his own daughter's house in Medina. Overall, and despite its shortness, Abu Bakr's reign was pivotal in that it saved the Muslim community from internal dissolution and reestablished a unified control over fractious Arabian tribes. Sunni Muslims praise him as the first of the four *Rāshidūn*, "Rightly Guided Caliphs" (caliphs who succeeded Muhammad), while many among the Shi'i Muslims malign him as a usurper.

See also 'A'isha (ca. 614–78); caliph, caliphate; Companions of the Prophet; Rightly Guided Caliphate (632–61); succession

Further Reading

Khalil Athamina, "The Pre-Islamic Roots of the Early Muslim Caliphate: The Emergence of Abū Bakr," *Der Islam* 76 (1999); Hugh Kennedy, *The Prophet and the Age of the Caliphate*, 1986; Wilferd Madelung, *The Succession to Muhammad: A Study of the Early Caliphate*, 1997; Miklos Muranyi, "Ein neuer Bericht über die Wahl des ersten Kalifen Abū Bakr," *Arabica* 25 (1978).

WADAD KADI

Abu Hanifa (699–767)

Abu Hanifa was the eponymous founder of the Hanafi school, one of the four orthodox Muslim schools of law, and a leader of the Murji'a, a religiopolitical movement that emerged in seventh-century Iraq in the context of disputes within the Muslim community regarding claims to the caliphate. In response to these disputes and to the schisms they produced (primarily the Shi'is and the Kharijis), the Murji'is proclaimed a neutral position regarding rights to the caliphate—in particular those of the third and fourth caliphs, 'Uthman b. 'Affan and 'Ali b. Abi Talib. They maintained that the judgment on these caliphs should be suspended and left to God. This position, together with a statement implying the renunciation of the extremist Shi'is' exclusive support of 'Ali, is found in *al-Fiqh al-Absat* (The plainest law), an early collection of dogmatic views attributed to Abu Hanifa. On the practical level, however, Abu Hanifa deviated from the Murji'i principle of political neutrality when he contributed money to support Zayd b. 'Ali, the eponym of the Zaydis, who revolted against the Umayyads in 740. Although he excused himself from active participation in Zayd's revolt, Abu Hanifa is said to have justified the uprising by comparing it to the Prophet's fight against the infidels. Moreover, Abu Hanifa advocated for the 'Alid Ibrahim b. 'Abdallah, who rebelled with his brother Muhammad al-Nafs al-Zakiyya against the Abbasids in 762–63.

As Wilferd Madelung has shown, Abu Hanifa differed from the Umayyads regarding the status of newly converted non-Arab populations in the eastern areas of the caliphate. These new converts confessed their belief in Islam, yet they did not necessarily fulfill the requisite religious duties. In line with the Murji'i dogma, which identified faith with the mere confession of belief to the exclusion of performance of religious obligations, Abu Hanifa recognized these converts as Muslims, while the Umayyads denied them this status and continued to impose on them the *jizya*, the tax paid by non-Muslims only. In 734, the new converts' struggle for equality turned into a militant revolt led by extreme Murji'is. Abu Hanifa did not participate in the revolt and served as a mediator between the rebels and the Umayyad caliph Yazid III. This is one example of Abu Hanifa's complex relations with the government: on the one hand he disagreed with its policy, but on the other hand he enjoyed influence in the caliphal court and even cooperated with the caliph. The report that Abu Hanifa was invited by the Abbasid caliph Mansur to help in the construction of Baghdad demonstrates such cooperation.

Abu Hanifa's attitude toward the government was at times critical and reserved (an attitude not uncommon among contemporary religious scholars), but his level of activism in this regard is unclear. In *al-Fiqh al-Absat*, he proclaims the religious duty of *al-amr bi-l-ma'rūf wa-l-nahy 'an al-munkar*—namely, to enjoin a fellow Muslim what is proper and forbid him what is improper. The second part of this duty had an important political implication, for when applied to the authorities, it meant confronting

them by condemning their misconduct. This political implication is related to the question of the religious status of an unjust ruler and the obligation to obey him. Such a ruler was, according to the Murji'i definition, a "sinful believer." This definition did not legitimize dethroning the ruler, but it left an opening for criticizing his wrongdoings. As demonstrated by Michael Cook, the nature of such criticism was the subject of various interpretations, ranging from armed rebellion to the mere avoidance of the authorities. The evidence regarding Abu Hanifa's view on this issue, as presented by Cook, is ambivalent. According to some reports Abu Hanifa espoused the militant option, and at least one person is said to have fought alongside (and have been killed with) the 'Alid Ibrahim upon Abu Hanifa's advice. Other accounts, however, portray him as a quietist who, without denying the religious duty of rebuking the unjust ruler—and the potential revolt this duty implied—discouraged rebellion in practice and refused to take an active part in it. Ultimately, while no evidence exists that Abu Hanifa's support of movements opposing the government ever amounted to actually participating in a revolt, it is clear that he was not of the quietist, obedient type of the following generation of Hanafi-Murji'is.

See also jurisprudence; Murji'is; theology

Further Reading

Abu Hanifa (attributed), *al-Fiqh al-Absat*, edited by M. Z. al-Kawthari, 1368; M. Abu Zahra, *Abu Hanifa: Hayatuhu wa-'Asruhu, ara'uhu wa-Fiqhuhu*, 1947; M. Cook, *Commanding Right and Forbidding Wrong in Islamic Thought*, 2000; *Encyclopaedia of Islam, Three*, s.v. "Abū Ḥanīfa," by H. Yanagihashi, 2007, http://www.brillonline.nl/subscriber/entry?entry=ei3_COM-0151; al-Khatib al-Baghdadi, *Ta'rikh Baghdad*, 1966; W. Madelung, *Religious Trends in Early Islamic Iran*, 1988; J. van Ess, *Theologie und Gesellschaft im 2. und 3. Jahrhundert Hidschra*, 1991.

NURIT TSAFRIR

Abu Yusuf (ca. 731–98)

Abu Yusuf Ya'qub b. Ibrahim al-Ansari, better known as Abu Yusuf, was born in Kufa and died in Baghdad. As both a religious scholar and a dynastic official, he played a pioneering role in the amalgamation of the religious sciences and governing practices of the Abbasid dynasty, which he served in Baghdad first as judge and then as chief judge (*qāḍī al-quḍāt*). He was the first to occupy the post of chief judge, created during the caliphate of Harun al-Rashid for the sake of greater centralization of the judiciary (i.e., appointment and supervision of all Abbasid judgeships).

Abu Yusuf studied with several of the leading scholars of his day and was most devoted to Abu Hanifa (d. 767), whose teachings he and his pupil, Muhammad al-Hasan al-Shaybani (d. 805), developed into a distinct school (*madhhab*) of shari'a. According to Ibn al-Nadim (writing in the latter part of the tenth century), Abu Yusuf was first committed to the preservation of hadith (reports about the first Muslims, the Prophet Muhammad above all, as the source of religious and moral norms) but then, under the tutelage of Abu Hanifa, turned his attention to judicial reasoning (*ra'y*). His teachings are more grounded in prophetic traditions than those of Abu Hanifa, and one of his works, *Kitab al-Athar* (The book of traditions), is a collection of hadith transmitted in Kufa. His work overall, however, shows a strong interest in *fiqh* (i.e., comprehension and articulation of the law and not only transmission of the prophetic heritage). Two surviving works, *al-Radd 'ala Siyar al-Awza'i* (Refutation of the moral teachings of al-Awza'i) and *Ikhtilaf Abi Hanifa wa-Ibn Abi Layla* (The disagreement of Abu Hanifa and Ibn Abi Layla), and two lost works, *Ikhtilaf al-Amsar* and *al-Radd 'ala Malik b. Anas* (as reported by Ibn al-Nadim), as well as extracts from his *Kitab al-Hiyal* (Book of stratagems) preserved in Shaybani's work on the subject of legal artifices, all underscore a developing interest in the nature and purpose of law. His arguments, which sometimes disagree with his master, and his opinions, which sometimes contradict themselves, have been incorporated into the legacy of the Hanafi school of shari'a, as embodied in the legal compendium known as *al-Asl* (The origin), attributed to Shaybani, and *al-Hidaya* (The guidance), compiled by Burhan al-Din Abu l-Hasan 'Ali Marghinani (d. 1197).

The work for which Abu Yusuf is most celebrated is *Kitab al-Kharaj* (The book of the land tax), in which he responds at length to 28 questions posed by the caliph Harun al-Rashid on various aspects of governance. The work is chiefly devoted to fiscal matters but encompasses a wide range of administrative concerns, including the status of non-Muslim subjects, warfare, and the punishment of crime. It does not exhibit the scope and organization of later administrative works, such as the *Kitab al-Kharaj wa-Sina'at al-Kitaba* (The book of the land tax and art of administrative writing) by Qudama b. Ja'far (d. ca. 948), but it does reflect the ongoing Abbasid interest, first seen in *Risala fi al-Sahaba* (Epistle on the caliph's entourage) by Ibn al-Muqaffa' (d. 756), in having a single "book" (i.e., code) of administrative law, especially in matters pertaining to fiscal affairs.

Kitab al-Kharaj seeks to cull administrative and especially fiscal principles from prophetic and communal precedents; from the practices of the first Muslims, notably the Rightly Guided Caliphs; and also from Umayyad policies and the rulings and opinions of legal scholars. The introduction, set in the genre of advice literature, depicts the caliph as a figure who is entrusted by God with the just governance of His servants and who is thus mindful of the counsel of religious scholars. He can therefore expect the obedience of his subjects. The central Qur'anic theme of prosperity (*ṣalāḥ*) over corruption (*fasād*) is given political form in this work by being tied to the judgment (*ra'y*) of the caliph, which is understood to be the mechanism ensuring the achievement of God's will for human society.

This notion is reflected throughout the body of the work, notably in the reiterated confirmation of the authority of the caliph to make and change laws where no clearly revealed precedent exists, especially when doing so serves the interests of Muslims. For example, Abu Yusuf demonstrates that while the status of land in Arabia has been set by prophetic precedent, the caliph is free to adjust taxes as he sees fit for the sake of the public welfare by encouraging cultivation on parcels of land granted to dynastic officials or military commanders: "Do what you judge to be of greater interest for Muslims and more generally beneficial, for both the elite and the masses." Echoing Umayyad sentiment, Abu Yusuf posits that the caliphate, successor to the prophetic office, is indispensable for the political coherency of the abode of Islam, including its non-Muslim elements. The point is that the common good is the purpose of rule, making it worthy of religious obedience.

This early attempt to cast administrative policy as part of Islam's religious purview had far-reaching consequences, giving administrative rulings a firmer grounding in the jurisprudence of Islam (*ḥukm kitābī mardūd ilā uṣūl al-fiqh*, as Qudama b. Ja'far would put it in the seventh section of his aforementioned work). Abbasid policies, such as a system of proportional taxation (*muqāsama*), could henceforth be associated with the practices of 'Umar b. al-Khattab (r. 634–44), the second of the Rightly Guided Caliphs. On a more theoretical level, it could be said that Abu Yusuf sowed the seeds for the later Hanafi view that governance in Islam is advanced by the ruler's assessment of the public interest (*maṣlaḥa*), even if it cannot be tied to a particular shari'a precedent (*dalīl juz'ī*). In general, then, Abu Yusuf paved the way for the idea that policy making in Islam—including the role of shari'a in the process—is a function of principles and not only precedents.

See also Abu Hanifa (699–767); jurisprudence; taxation

Further Reading

Abu Yusuf, *Kitab al-Kharaj*, edited by I. 'Abbas, 1985; A. Ben Shemesh, *Abu Yusuf's Kitab al-Kharaj*, 1969; N. Calder, *Studies in Early Muslim Jurisprudence*, 1993; M. al-Kawthari, *Husn al-Taqadi fi Sirat al-Imam Abi Yusuf al-Qadi*, 1948; Ibn Nadim, *al-Fihrist*, edited by Yusuf 'Ali Tawil, 1996.

PAUL L. HECK

advice

Advice (*naṣīḥa*) usually implies counsel offered to a ruler to guide him in governing the realm. Islam has also produced a robust heritage of spiritual advice—a kind of mentoring on the path to God, as exemplified in *al-Wasaya wa-l-Nasa'ih* (Testimonies and advices) by Abu 'Abdallah al-Harith al-Muhasibi (d. 857) and *Ayyuha al-Walad* (Letter to a disciple) by Ghazali (d. 1111). In general, however, the term refers to political advice for rulers responsible for the affairs and interests of this world. A genre of literature arose around the term with the aim of explaining the art and nature of dynastic rule. A wide range of figures—administrative and court officials, religious scholars, litterateurs, spiritual masters, and philosophers—tried their hand at this genre. The most celebrated examples include *Siyasatnama* (Political administration) by the Seljuq vizier Nizam al-Mulk (d. 1092), *Nasihat al-Muluk* (Advice for rulers) by Ghazali, and *al-Siyasa al-Shar'iyya* (The book of governance according to the shari'a) by Ibn Taymiyya (d. 1328). Despite varied emphases (some works stress pragmatic considerations, whereas others stress piety), the attempt to formulate a model of effective and virtuous governance (i.e., rule pleasing to God) is common to the genre as a whole.

Some religious scholars did try to preserve principles of communal consensus and election when it came to political authority, but Muslim dynasties generally operated according to the divine right of kings (i.e., hereditary rule by a single family); authority implied a system of power based on a hierarchy of personal relations alongside administrative institutions as organs of governance. Yet political authority in this premodern form was still accountable to a set of expectations as elaborated in the genre of advice literature. This literature therefore had a constitutional purpose, applying basic assumptions and norms of governance in Islam to both the person of the ruler and the organization of the polity as a whole. Advice literature, which combined humanistic ethics and divinely revealed wisdom, was not simply a catch-all cultural reservoir but represented a distinct body of knowledge for realizing just and prosperous rule—a kind of premodern political science.

The Qur'an speaks of prophets extending advice to the ruling elite (*mala'*), who invariably dismiss it, jeopardizing not only their standing before God but also their standing among their subjects. (Echoing this, a canonical hadith speaks of religion as *naṣīḥa* in the sense of sincere devotion—to God, his book, his messenger, and both leaders and commoners alike among the Muslims.) In the Qur'anic narrative, this failure to comply with prophetic mentoring results in corruption (*fasād*) and, eventually, political demise, as opposed to the righteous prosperity (*ṣalāḥ*) God intends for human society. In the absence of revealed directives on the constitution of such rule, the Qur'anic narrative thus encouraged Muslims to consider nonrevealed (i.e., secular) sources of advice, notably the works of Perso-Sasanian and Greco-Hellenistic provenance, which greatly contributed to the shaping of Muslim understanding of the characteristics of good governance. Alexander and his philosophical advisor, Aristotle, and Anushirvan and his ministerial counselor, Buzurgmihr, were often held up as exemplars of successful rule because they heeded the advice of the learned. Competence in administering justice was emphasized over personal piety, and an adage had it that rule could last with impiety but not with injustice.

Advice was delivered in the form of letters and treatises; two early pioneers in these forms were 'Abd al-Hamid al-Katib (d. 750) and Ibn al-Muqaffa' (d. 756), high-ranking secretaries in caliphal

employ. Another form was the testimony (*waṣiyya*) of a ruler to his successor. This testimony functioned as a quasi-constitution of the dynastic rule in question, elucidating a theory of governance (usually the necessity of strong rule), the mechanisms of effective statecraft, and the intellectual and moral virtues expected of the ruler so as to be able to undertake the appropriate actions to secure the harmony and prosperity of the realm. Such actions typically included preserving law and order, ensuring justice, and fostering economic activity; managing both commoners and elites, including his own court servitors, administrative personnel, and military commanders; and protecting and promoting orthodox religion (another key component of successful rule), along with justice, which generated political solidarity and good behavior among the subjects.

From the eighth-century treatise of Abu Yusuf (d. 798), chief judge under the Abbasid caliph Harun al-Rashid (r. 786–809), to the 19th-century treatise of Khayr al-Din al-Tunisi (d. 1890), a high-ranking Ottoman official, advice was offered with the aim of promoting prosperity (*salāḥ*)—that is, the worldly interests (*maṣāliḥ*, sing. *maṣlaḥa*) of Muslim society—by methods above and beyond shari'a considerations. The ideal image of the Muslim ruler in advice literature did not look so much to prophetic descent or membership in Quraysh (the influential and respected tribe at the beginnings of Islam) as the essential criterion of governance in Islam (such was the concern of sectarian literature, *kutub al-firaq*). Rather, justice made a ruler worthy of being called the shadow of God on Earth insofar as the office he occupied existed to ensure God's purposes for Muslim society by permitting people to live in harmony and pursue their livelihood in peace. Advice literature, then, formed an important complement to shari'a in decision making relevant to the common good in Muslim society. Indeed, the genre of political advice can be said to have indirectly influenced a greater rationalization of the juristic conceptualization of the public purposes of shari'a (*maqāṣid al-sharī'a*), as can be seen in *Ghiyath al-Umam* (Salvation of the nations) by the celebrated Ash'ari scholar of theology Juwayni (d. 1085).

It is then in the genre of advice literature—even in the case of the aforementioned work of Ibn Taymiyya (which is sometimes seen as driven by pious concerns more than political considerations)—that the idea of rule as a function of the common good is nurtured in Islam. This scenario changed dramatically with the introduction of the nation-state in place of the dynasty as ruler of Muslim society. Advice ceased to be the preserve of the learned elite and became, at least in principle, the work of the electorate (i.e., national citizenry). The purpose of rule here is not virtuous governance per se but rather technical expertise in protecting and promoting political interests—an idea that is not necessarily at odds with the Qur'anic goal of bringing about a just prosperity for believers. The legacy of advice literature, even if no longer produced in its traditional form, is no longer irrelevant to Muslim society, for it establishes an important "secular" aspect to rule in Islam. That is, while the Qur'an called for justice and prosperity, it did not spell out how to achieve such things, which, it would seem, were left to human resources to determine. Thus, advice to rulers, a nonrevealed genre of literature, sought to respond to a goal implied by the revealed message—namely, successful politics (i.e., good governance) as a divine mandate. Rule was never equated with religion but rather cast as its twin, making God's purposes for human society possible in this world. In contrast, the postcolonial moment has seen many Islamist voices advocating for the largely rejected idea in classical Islam that human rule is to be adjudicated and constitutionally defined in terms of shari'a rather than *naṣīḥa*, thereby turning rule into religion—that is, assuming rule in Islam as a product of the revealed message alone, apart from cultural considerations. This is to ignore the long-standing assumption of advice literature, referred to earlier, that rule and religion are not the same even if working in complementary fashion for the overall welfare of Muslim society.

See also Mirrors for Princes

Further Reading

Paul L. Heck, "The Role of Law in 'Abbasid Political Thought: From Ibn al-Muqaffa' (d. 139/756) to Qudāma b. Ja'far (d. 337/948)," in *Occasional Papers of the School of Abbasid Studies, Cambridge, 6–10 July 2002*, edited by J. E. Montgomery, 2004; Louise Marlow and Beatrice Gruendler, eds., *Writers and Rulers: Perspectives on Their Relationship from Abbasid to Safavid Times*, 2004.

PAUL L. HECK

Advice-to-Kings. *See* Mirrors for Princes

al-Afghani, Jamal al-Din (1838–97)

Best known as the founder and prime mover of Pan-Islamism in the second half of the 19th century, Afghani was born in Iran and educated in traditional Shi'i religious schools both in Iran and in the holy centers of Ottoman Iraq. His formal education consisted of Islamic jurisprudence, hadith traditions, and Arabic language, but he was mainly interested in mysticism, philosophy, and theological concepts and schools deemed controversial, if not heretical, by the 'ulama' establishment. He was mostly attracted to the ideas of Sadr al-Din al-Shirazi, known as Mulla Sadra (1572–1640), the brilliant thinker who attempted to reconcile mysticism and philosophy while satisfying religious fundamental principles, and Shaykh Ahmad al-Ahsa'i (1753–1826), the founder of Shaikhism, an important 19th-century speculative Shi'i school of theology that inspired successive generations of prominent Iranian intellectuals. Afghani was also allegedly sympathetic to Babism, the mid-19th-century revolutionary religious movement, but there is no evidence that he ever adhered to its doctrines.

In his late teens, Afghani fled Iran. His political consciousness was then awakened when he visited British-ruled India at the time of the Indian Rebellion of 1857, a revolt that was largely supported by India's Muslim population. Witnessing the event left its mark on the impressionable youth, and the resultant anti-British sentiment defined his future political career as a champion of Muslim struggle against imperialism. In 1870, Afghani arrived in Istanbul by way of Afghanistan and Arabia. At the university, a lecture in which he praised philosophy and discussed prophecy in Islamic philosophical terms led to his expulsion from the Ottoman capital upon the order of the 'ulama'. He then went to Cairo, where over the course of eight years he acquired a solid reputation as the most prominent Islamic intellectual and political leader of his time. In fact, his assumed Afghan Sunni identity dates back to this period, spread by his disciples, who most probably simply believed what he had told them. A Sunni identity proved to be an expedient passport for Afghani, one that facilitated an easy move in Arab and Turkish circles. He rallied around him a small but potentially influential group of Egyptian and Syrian intellectuals, including Muhammad 'Abduh and Rashid Rida, two important turn-of-the-century Muslim Arab religious reformers. In his lectures and private discussions, he severely criticized traditional Islamic teachings, holding the 'ulama' establishment responsible for Muslim intellectual decline. He called for a profound revision of the curriculum of Azhar University so it would include philosophy and science. He likewise directed his relentless assault at the ruling elite, accusing them of corruption, and his political message found eager reception among young Egyptian activists. It was also in Cairo that Afghani joined several British and French Masonic lodges and even attempted to independently establish one. His political intrigues within the Masonic lodges and his anti-British and antigovernment activities, in addition to his teachings declared heretical by the authorities of Azhar University, led to his expulsion from Egypt in 1879. He went back to India, where he stayed until 1882, when he went to Europe.

In Paris, Afghani published, together with fellow political exile Muhammad 'Abduh, an Arabic journal, *al-'Urwa al-Wuthqa* (The firmest bond), which became an important organ for a Pan-Islamic, anti-imperialist movement. It promoted religious institutional reforms to help raise a new generation of Muslims who would be aware of the social and political exigencies of modern times. Seeking solutions to the problems resulting from European encroachment in the Muslim world, Afghani revived the old concept of the Islamic community as a sociopolitical entity. He rose in defense of Islam, which the French freethinking writer Ernest Renan denounced as a backward faith, incompatible with science and responsible for Muslim social and intellectual decline. In London, he met Wilfrid Blunt, a pro-Arab amateur politician with important connections to British government officials to whom Afghani was introduced. He also traveled in the Russian Empire for a period of two years, visiting Moscow and the Muslim regions in the Caucasus and Azerbaijan. Back in Iran in 1886 and 1887 and then again at the end of 1889, he rapidly involved himself with the opposition movement, led by some individual members of the 'ulama' and wealthy merchants who were rising against government corruption and the sale of national economic assets through a growing number of concessions to foreigners. He also began to organize a mass revolt movement until he was once again forced into exile.

From London and Istanbul, where he spent the last six years of his life, Afghani relentlessly called for the formation in Iran of a united political opposition front composed of members of the 'ulama', the merchant class, and the intelligentsia to combat royal tyranny and corruption. He collaborated with other political exiles and religious dissidents at home and abroad to incite the 'ulama' to renounce the time-honored tradition of political quietism and lead the opposition movement against the shah's abuse of power. Two personal letters, one addressed to the leading *mujtahid* (legist) in Samarra and the other to a prominent *mujtahid* in Tehran, display Afghani's ambiguous attitude toward the religious leadership of his time. In both letters, he refers to them in highly exalted terms, acknowledging them as the representatives of the Hidden Imam, divinely appointed to lead the nation and rescue religion from the evildoing of the corrupt shah. He urges them to take action and exercise their power in deposing the "pharaoh" and destroying the "roots of tyranny," restoring "the creed of divine justice," and reviving the Islamic government. The entire nation, put under the control of the "party of the 'ulama'," would then enjoy divine protection. Thus Afghani forcefully promoted the idea that, during the Imam's occultation, the *mujtahids*' authority overpowers that of the temporal ruler. This idea, doctrinally well founded as it may be, was never before exploited by the 'ulama' establishment in either the Safavid or Qajar eras. It was Afghani and his collaborators who first enunciated in explicit terms the religious basis for potential 'ulama' claims to political power. Afghani's letters, while deferential in tone, also sharply criticize the Iranian 'ulama''s political acquiescence bordering on servility; he blames their "silence" for the nation's defenselessness in the hands of foreign powers. Simultaneously flattering and angry and almost threatening, his appeal hardly conceals his manipulative intentions to mobilize the 'ulama' for his own political ends.

The attempt to mobilize the religious leadership for a political rebellion was first successfully tested with the campaign to revoke the concession the shah had granted a British company for the curing and sale of Iran's entire tobacco crop. At the time of the Tobacco Protests (1891–92), Afghani was living abroad, and his own role in the protest was not as prominent as his contemporary and subsequent admirers claimed it to be, but his propaganda and rhetorical skills in staging a mass movement of protest—the first of its kind in modern Iranian history—left a lasting impact. The repeal of the concession marked the peak of Afghani's career as a revolutionary leader. His Pan-Islamic scheme to forge the political unification of all Muslims under the rule of one Muslim monarch, however, proved to be a failure: he was unable to win the ruler's confidence in Afghanistan, Egypt, or Iran. In Istanbul, Sultan Abdülhamid II, initially attracted to the idea of assuming the old Islamic title of caliph, granted his royal patronage until he, too, grew suspicious of the entire movement. Afghani was kept under close surveillance until he died of cancer, surrounded by his faithful followers, who were

to keep up his spirit of revolt. At home and abroad, his so-called Pan-Islamic society included political malcontents, freethinkers and former Babis, social reformers and revolutionaries, as well as opponents of the current minister in power in Iran.

Afghani failed to influence the 'ulama' institutional establishment as he did the activist religious dissidents, who participated in the Tobacco Protests and most subsequent political events. High-ranking *mujtahids*, including Mirza Muhammad Hasan al-Shirazi, in whose name the fatwa banning the consumption of tobacco was issued in protest against the concession, and Mirza Hasan Ashtiyani, who led the revolt in Tehran, did not lay claim to political authority upon Afghani's incitement, despite their role in the movement. Threat of prolonged violence in Tehran realigned Ashtiyani with government forces to restore order. On the other hand, Afghani's reminder of the *mujtahid*s' doctrinal authority was an expedient tactic to appeal to their support for a short-term goal: to arouse public opinion for a mass movement of popular revolt. Mass appeal, he believed, could be successful only in the name of religion, because rational arguments could only be understood by the few educated individuals. He and Malkum Khan, the Armenian convert to Islam who played a major role in the reformist movement, as well as their respective followers, did not seriously consider establishing a theocracy or even an 'ulama'-dominated government. His Pan-Islamism, formed with a group of disparate political and religious dissidents, never became a movement with its own organization, program, and leadership. The so-called Pan-Islamist group increasingly turned their attention to social and political causes, joining the lay reform-minded intelligentsia or more radical revolutionaries. They used the mosques and madrasas as effective forums for the dissemination of new ideas.

Inspired by medieval Islamic philosophy and Shaikhism, Afghani turned against the orthodox teachings of religion. In a notorious lecture delivered in Istanbul in 1870, he defined prophecy as a craft nobler than yet similar to any other. However, he judged philosophy to be loftier and universal. He argued that while prophecy is divinely inspired and varies according to times and conditions, philosophy is based on reason and is needed at all times to enlighten humanity. The Prophet is infallible, the philosopher is not, but the philosopher is the torchbearer leading the way out of ignorance. Elsewhere he attacked institutionalized religion for its anti-intellectualism and its stifling effect on scientific and philosophic inquiry. In his famous *Answer to Renan*, written in Paris, he specifically distinguished Islam from "the manner in which it was propagated in the world" and referred to Islamic science and philosophy as evidence of its past brilliant achievements despite the "heavy yoke" imposed on free investigation by the jurists, the guardians of the holy law. In most of his Persian essays, Afghani relentlessly called for the "renewal" of Muslim societies and culture, urging people to liberate themselves from the "heaviest and most humiliating yokes" imposed upon them by their educators. With the passage of time and his travels to Europe, he also came to denounce the very schools of Islamic philosophy and speculative theology he had earlier admired, although he often relapsed into traditional modes of thinking, attempting to reconcile science, philosophy, and religion in a manner reminiscent of the medieval philosophers. He condemned traditional Islamic thought for ignoring relevant social and political issues. He hailed European science and technology, which he believed to be the source of European world power. Assailing the 'ulama' for discouraging the faithful from learning from the non-Muslims, he wrote in one of his essays, "They have not understood that science is that noble thing that has no connection with any nation, and is not distinguished by anything but itself. . . . Men must be related to science, not science to men." It is this intellectual standing that most defines the legacy of Afghani's activism. He universalized the concept of *'ilm* by divorcing it from the traditional Islamic conception of it as the knowledge of the divine and related religious disciplines, which does not distinguish the sacred from the profane. In fact, he desacralized the concept of *'ilm* as no Muslim philosopher ever had, laying the ground for the secular reforms undertaken by the next generation of lay intellectuals and educators.

Afghani's dedication was not to the "philosophic outlook" in the traditional sense, as Muhsin Mahdi, the late scholar of Islamic philosophy, asserted. Far from being a philosopher, Afghani was a social critic and a polemicist who devoted his most vehement critiques to the 'ulama' establishment he held responsible for the Muslims' cultural and political stagnation. Yet, paradoxically, he appealed to them in deference to their religious authority and social status as the guardians of the holy law when he needed them most for his political activities. That may explain in part his tendencies to argue inconsistently and to contradict himself, leading scholars to depict him either as a true believer, a last representative of the Islamic philosophical tradition, an irreligious opportunist, an Islamic deist, or a genuine nationalist rising in defense of the Muslim struggle against European imperialism.

See also 'Abduh, Muhammad (1849–1905); Pan-Islamism; revival and reform; Rida, Muhammad Rashid (1865–1935)

Further Reading

Sayyid Jamal al-Din Asadabadi al-Afghani, *Maqalat-i Jamaliyya*, 1933; Mangol Bayat, *Mysticism and Dissent: Socioreligious Thought in Qajar Iran*, 1982; Sir Hamilton A. R. Gibb, *Modern Trends in Islam*, 1947; Nikki R. Keddie, *Sayyid Jamāl ad-Dīn "al-Afghānī": A Political Biography*, 1972; Elie Kedourie, *Afghani and 'Abduh: An Essay on Religious Unbelief and Political Activism in Modern Islam*, 1966.

MANGOL BAYAT

Afghanistan

Landlocked between Iran, Pakistan, the former Soviet Central Asian Republics, and, at its narrowest northeastern tip, China, today's Islamic Republic of Afghanistan covers a mostly mountainous and

arid territory slightly larger than France, with a population estimated in 2010 at about 30 million. Afghans today regard themselves as a nation distinct from neighboring Iran and Pakistan, however divided they may be by religion, ethnicity, or other factors.

In religious terms, most Afghans are Sunni Muslims of the Hanafi rite, but Shi'is (both Imami and Isma'ili) constitute a significant minority (some 19 percent as of 2010, according to the *CIA World Factbook*, for example). In ethnic terms, 42 percent of Afghans are Pashtuns, whose tribal values, code of honor, and rivalries between chiefs make up *Pashtūnwalī*, "the Pashtun way," perceived as seamlessly interwoven with *Sunnat*, or "Islamic tradition." The Pashtuns were politically divided by successive 19th-century redefinitions of the Afghan-Indian Frontier, which culminated in the "Durand Line" in 1893 that bisected tribal territories, as drawn by British civil servant Sir Mortimer Durand to ensure British-Indian military control of strategic ridges overlooking the eastern Afghan valleys. Nearly twice as many Pashtuns as in Afghanistan now live to the east of the Durand Line, in modern Pakistan. Within Afghanistan, the Pashtuns have long been divided by the rivalry between two main tribal groups: the Durrani and the Ghilzai.

About 30 percent of Afghans are Tajiks, who are best described as Eastern Iranians. Whereas Pashtuns speak Pashto, Tajiks speak Persian (Dari) and are ethnically related to the Tajiks in the neighboring Republic of Tajikistan and to the large Tajik minority in (predominantly Turkic) Uzbekistan. A third major ethnic group is the Persian-speaking Hazara (mostly Shi'i), who comprise roughly 9 percent of the population and whose descent from the Mongols shows in their distinctly "Asian" features. There are also Turkic-speaking Uzbeks (mostly Hanafis) in Afghanistan, as well as other minorities, such as the Turkmen, Baloch, Qizilbash, Nuristani, and a small number of Sikhs. Tribal political behavior is still extremely important in Afghanistan and northwest Pakistan, coloring religious language and affecting Great Power strategies—such as when both India and post-Soviet Russia between 1994 and 2001, and the United States in late 2001, chose to support an essentially non-Pashtun "Northern Alliance" (mainly ethnic Tajiks, Uzbeks, and Hazaras) against the largely Pashtun Taliban, themselves supplied until September 2001 by Pakistan. Ethnic, sectarian, and territorial splits and resentments—notably the Afghan kingdom's (then Indian- and Soviet-supported) official irredentist refusal to recognize either the Durand Line or Pakistan's retention of the eastern Pashtun zones after British withdrawal from the region in 1947—help explain the region's many conflicts in the recent past and present alike.

The concept of Afghanistan as a nation-state was fostered during the reign of King Amanullah (r. 1919–29). Advised by his mentor Mahmud Tarzi (1866–1935), he committed his government to radical modernizing or "Westernizing" reform along lines broadly similar to those of Atatürk in Turkey and Reza Shah in Iran. However, unlike his counterparts, Amanullah did not enjoy a long tradition of a centralized bureaucratic government buttressed by a powerful army: the king himself was forced into exile in the face of conservative tribal uprisings endorsed by leading clerics in 1929. Nevertheless, the legacy of Amanullah's ideals proved tenaciously successful among the small, urbanized minority. Many of Amanullah's reforms—in education, law, and women's rights and his insistence that all the country's citizens be named "Afghans" (a term reserved before 1923 to the Pashtuns only)—were thus cautiously reintroduced under kings Nadir (r. 1929–33) and Zahir (r. 1933–73) and much enforced under President Daoud (r. 1973–78). The Afghan nationalist idea notably withstood the repeated shocks of a Marxist-Leninist military coup (1978); a Soviet invasion (1979–89); a post-Soviet civil war involving non-Pashtun ethnic factions against Pashtun ones, the latter supported by the Pakistani military high command in the name of endangered Pashtun ethnic supremacy and strict Sunni orthodoxy (1989–96); a Pakistani-supported sectarian and ethnic-based Sunni Pashtun dictatorship (1996–2001); and military intervention from the United States and NATO (since 2001).

Afghans define themselves with reference to their largely successful resistance to British power in the three Anglo-Afghan Wars (1838–42, 1878–80, and 1919), in which they see themselves as having defended their fatherland and Islam alike. Heroes and villains from Islamists to communists are routinely compared to archetypes of the "Three Wars," such as Akbar Khan (the resistance hero of 1838–42), Shah Shuja' (the archtraitor of 1838–42), Malalai (the tribal heroine at the battle of Maiwand in 1880), and King Amanullah (the winner of full independence from Britain in 1919). The victories over the British at Gandamak in 1842 and at Maiwand in 1880, as well as the Independence Treaty of 1919, are commemorated in anniversaries and street names, and every Afghan leader since 1842 has dreaded identification as a treacherous Shah Shuja', relying on foreign troops.

The contemporary Afghan situation can best be understood in the light of this legacy of resistance against foreigners. Military technology, however superior, has never been able to break the recalcitrance of this tribal society, which identifies itself in strongly religious terms and has resisted centralized control when non-Muslim foreigners have threatened its autonomy, either directly or through a local puppet government. In such circumstances, the Afghan response would be to withhold obedience, deny collaboration, and cut communications to the accompaniment of religious denunciation. Targeted assassination of would-be collaborators (usually by members of their own clans to prevent blood feuds) would further reduce the pool of local administrative or military personnel available to the occupying power.

Afghanistan entered the 20th century as one of the two or three most conservative Islamic societies on Earth, a mountain bastion of traditional autonomous tribalism surrounding a handful of lowland towns under royal control. Tensions between tradition, tribalism, Islam, and modernity that continued under various rulers after Amanullah resulted in the development of a somewhat schizophrenic culture with a minuscule autocratic elite in Kabul dedicated to slow Westernizing modernization behind a facade of Islamic conservatism. In 1964, Afghanistan became

a parliamentary monarchy with a constitution, free speech and press, political parties, and elected prime ministers. Nostalgic Afghans regard the Constitutional Period (1964–73) as their last years of peace before the gathering storm. In the course of this storm, the Communist Party, already a major ideological force in the capital and in the army, split into ethnic factions (the Durrani Pashtun *Parcham*, or "Banner," and the Ghilzai Pashtun *Khalq*, or "People," both pro-Soviet, and the non-Pashtun *Shu'la-yi Jawed*, or "Eternal Flame," pro-Chinese), while at the same time diverse Islamist opposition groups formed (e.g., Jamiat-i Islami, mainly Tajik, and Hizb-i Islami, mainly Pashtun, which in turn also further factionalized), all of which made Afghanistan amenable to foreign manipulation.

The Soviet occupation of Afghanistan in the 1980s provoked disparate Afghan factions to rise in generalized anti-Soviet insurgency in the name of both nationalism and Islam, with the direct backing of the United States, China, Pakistan, and Arab allies. But the Afghan mujahidin, or "holy warriors," were never united, again splitting along ethnic or sectarian lines, and after the defeat and withdrawal of the Soviet Army in 1989, their infighting disintegrated into factional war until the Taliban (Students) seized power in Kabul in 1996 with decisive Pakistani military support, claiming to restore stability and strict Sunni Islamic law. The Taliban, a movement of conservative Pashtun madrasa (Muslim school) students who had participated in the war against Soviet occupation, claimed control of over 90 percent of the Afghan territory by the mid-1990s but failed to receive international recognition (except by Pakistan, United Arab Emirates, and Saudi Arabia). In Afghanistan, the Taliban were opposed by what Pakistan called the "Northern Alliance" of mainly non-Pashtun ethnic groups, which, with foreign help, successfully resisted a complete Taliban takeover. Meanwhile, Islamists from outside Afghanistan (mainly the Arab world) who had participated in the jihad against the Soviets found refuge under the Taliban in Afghanistan. Having identified U.S. foreign policy as the root of all problems in the Muslim world, they initiated attacks on U.S. interests from Afghan soil, resulting in the U.S.-led invasion of Afghanistan and global "war on terror" after the attacks on the United States on September 11, 2001. Whether Afghanistan's hitherto remarkable resilience as a nation-state will survive remains to be seen.

See also Central Asia; Mulla 'Umar (b. 1959); Taliban

Further Reading

Thomas Barfield, *Afghanistan, a Cultural and Political History*, 2010; Michael Barry, *Kabul's Long Shadows, Historical Perspectives*, 2011; Idem, *Le royaume de l'insolence*, 2011; Louis Dupree, *Afghanistan*, 1980; Mountstuart Elphinstone, *An Account of the Kingdom of Caubul*, 1815; Vartan Gregorian, *The Emergence of Modern Afghanistan (1838–1946)*, 1969; Leon Poullada, *Reform and Rebellion in Afghanistan, 1919–1929*, 1973; Ahmed Rashid, *Taliban: Islam, Oil and the New Great Game in Central Asia*, 2001.

MICHAEL BARRY

'Aflaq, Michel (1910–89)

A leading Arab intellectual, Michel 'Aflaq was a cofounder and chief ideologue of the Ba'th Party, which, while largely a secular nationalist movement, incorporated Islam as an elemental feature of Arab identity and culture.

Born into a commercial, middle-class, Orthodox Christian family in a suburb of Damascus in the last years of the Ottoman Empire, 'Aflaq came of age in the successor state of Syria during the French colonial rule of the interwar period. He was educated in the city's Orthodox Christian schools until the age of 19, whereupon he earned a scholarship to attend the University of Paris, Sorbonne (1929–34). Exposed to the intellectual and political ferment of Paris in the 1930s, 'Aflaq was increasingly drawn to nationalism, radical leftist politics, and the ideas of the French philosopher Henri Bergson, whose notion of élan vital is reproduced in 'Aflaq's concept of "Arab Spirit." Returning to Damascus upon completing his studies in history and philosophy, he taught at the city's main high school and formed, with fellow teacher Salah al-Din al-Bitar (d. 1980), a political discussion group of like-minded students and young professionals.

The discussion group grew in the early 1940s into a political party, the Hizb al-Ba'th al-'Arabi al-Ishtiraki (Party of Arab Socialist Rebirth), and it held its first congress in 1947, in which 'Aflaq was elected *'amīd* (dean) and served as its chief ideologue until his death. Ba'thism became the state ideology in Syria (1963) and Iraq (1968) and exerted tremendous power over the shape of midcentury nationalism throughout the Arab world, primarily in various Arab unity initiatives. 'Aflaq's influence waned in the 1970s with the rise of military dictatorships in both Syria and Iraq and a regional disaffection with nationalism; nevertheless, elements of his thought persist in the region's political culture, primarily in educational and religious policies.

In 'Aflaq's hands, Ba'thism was less a coherent political system than an eclectic mixture of fascism, Leninism, liberalism, and romantic nationalism. Among its central tenets was the assertion of a secular basis for society, making Arab identity the only prerequisite for membership in an ultramodern, pan-Arab national community. What made an Arab, and by extension the Arab nation, was the "Arab Spirit," and all Arabs—especially members of non-Muslim minorities, like 'Aflaq himself—were equal citizens of that nation.

Crucial to 'Aflaq's thought, and in a departure from the ideas of other non-Muslim Arab nationalists, is that Islam is the foundation of Arab nationalism. However, in his version, Islam was circumscribed as a discrete historical object and a transhistorical constituent element of the "Arab Spirit"; it could not, however, serve as the basis for a political system. This contrasts markedly with contemporary Salafists and mainstream Islamic theologians in its abandonment of the living and historically transcendent nature of Islam. By historicizing Islam as the definitive *cultural* practice of the Arab, 'Aflaq may have asserted a central place for Islam in Arab identity, but that place would be in the service of a largely secular, nationalist, and

socialist agenda; any form of Islamic political theory was, by the same measure, inherently illiberal and antimodern.

A valediction he delivered at the Syrian National University in 1943 titled "In Remembrance of the Arab Prophet," which appears in the 1959 collection of his essays and speeches, *Fi Sabil al-Ba'th* (For the cause of the Ba'th), confirms this role of Islam. 'Aflaq argued that "to the Arabs, the Islamic movement embodied in the life of [Muhammad] is not merely a historical occurrence . . . rather, it is at the very depths . . . and bound fiercely into the life of the Arab." He then concluded, "Islam has renewed the Arab nationality and completed it." Nevertheless, 'Aflaq's writings evidenced only a rudimentary understanding of the religion. In practice, Ba'thists were openly hostile to Islamism and conservative Islam and tended to refuse political accommodation with either, employing Islamic symbols and rhetoric only during moments of political necessity.

A telling example of the way Ba'thists employed Islam is that upon his death in 1989, it was announced that 'Aflaq, who had lived in Iraq since 1975, had converted to Islam and taken the first name Ahmad. Although later confirmed by his children, it is widely believed that the conversion was a ploy by the regime of Saddam Hussein (d. 2006) to help bolster its religious credentials in the face of growing Islamist influence following the Iran-Iraq War (1980–88). It also allowed the Ba'thist state to memorialize the party's founder in a mosque-tomb complex, a building imbued with more religious significance than a traditional monument. After the 2003 U.S.-led occupation of Iraq, 'Aflaq's body was disinterred from the complex, which is situated near Hussein's former presidential palace and was used as barracks by a contingent of U.S. Marines.

See also Arab nationalism; Ba'th Party; Iraq; modernity; nationalism; secularism; socialism; Syria

Further Reading

Michel 'Aflaq, *Fi Sabil al-Ba'th*, 1952; Hanna Batatu, *The Old Social Classes and the Revolutionary Movements in Iraq*, 1978; Eric Davis, *Memories of State*, 2005; John F. Devlin, "The Ba'th Party: Rise and Metamorphosis," *The American Historical Review* 96, no. 5 (1991); Albert Hourani, *Arabic Thought in the Liberal Age*, 1962.

KEITH DAVID WATENPAUGH

Africa. *See* East Africa; North Africa; South Africa; West Africa

Aga Khan

The title of Aga Khan (also Agha Khan), an honorific of Turkic-Mongol-Persian origins meaning "lord and master," was bestowed on the 46th Nizari Isma'ili imam, Hasan 'Ali Shah (1804–81), around 1820 by the contemporary Qajar monarch of Iran, Fath 'Ali Shah (r. 1797–1834). Thereafter, Nizari Isma'ili imams of Shi'i Muslims retained Aga Khan as a hereditary title, with Prince Karim Aga Khan IV, 49th imam, acceding to this position in 1957. He leads this Shi'i community officially designated as the "Shia Imami Ismaili Muslims," who are dispersed through more than 30 countries worldwide. Rooted in the teachings of the early Imami Shi'is, the Nizari imam's office is known as the imamate (or *imāma*) because it represents his hereditary authority as a descendant of the Prophet Muhammad through Muhammad's daughter Fatima and her husband, 'Ali (the first imam).

Hasan 'Ali Shah succeeded to the Isma'ili imamate upon the death of his father, Shah Khalil Allah, in 1817. By then, the Nizari imams had lived, as successors to their ancestors who ruled as the lords of Alamut, in different parts of Iran for more than seven centuries. Around 1820, Fath 'Ali Shah Qajar appointed the youthful Nizari imam to the governorship of Qum, gave him one of his daughters in marriage, and bestowed on him the honorific title of Aga Khan. After a prolonged conflict with the Qajar establishment, the first Aga Khan settled permanently in India in the 1840s. Subsequently, he preoccupied himself with defining the distinctive religious identity of his followers, especially those in South Asia known as the Khojas. The Nizari Isma'ilis frequently practiced *taqiyya*, or precautionary dissimulation, to protect themselves against persecution, disguising themselves variously as Sunnis, Sufis, Twelver Shi'is, or Hindus. As a result, their true religious identity was often obscured and confused.

The first Aga Khan's son and successor, 'Ali Shah Aga Khan II, led the community for a brief four-year period. Upon his death in 1885, his eight-year-old son, Sultan Muhammad Shah (1877–1957), succeeded to the Nizari Isma'ili imamate and became widely known, under his title of Aga Khan, as a Muslim reformer due to his prominent role in Indo-Muslim and international affairs. Guiding the Nizaris for 72 years as their 48th imam, Aga Khan III formulated numerous modernization policies and programs for his community while making further efforts to distinguish the Nizaris from other Muslims. The Nizari identity was specifically articulated in the constitutions that Aga Khan III promulgated for his followers, especially those in India, Pakistan, and East Africa. Reiterating the all-embracing authority of the imam and his office, these constitutions represented the personal law of the community, with articles on marriage, divorce, inheritance, and other matters.

Aga Khan III worked vigorously to reorganize his followers into a modern Muslim community with high standards of health, education, and social welfare, also paying special attention to the emancipation of Isma'ili women and their participation in community affairs. To implement his reforms, Aga Khan III developed a network of national and regional councils for the Nizaris of South Asia and East Africa. According to Nizari teachings, the concepts of *dīn* (religion) and *dunyā* (worldly affairs) are both integral components of the social order, and Aga

Khan III guided the religious and secular affairs of his followers, aiming to sustain a balance between these two domains of life. He often imparted his guidance through his speeches or *farmāns* (written edicts).

Aga Khan III designated his grandson, Karim, as his successor. Accordingly, Prince Karim Aga Khan IV succeeded to the imamate upon the death of his grandfather in 1957. Aga Khan IV continued and substantially extended the modernization policies of his grandfather, also developing a multitude of new programs and institutions of his own for the socioeconomic and educational benefit of his followers. At the same time, Aga Khan IV concerned himself with a variety of social, humanitarian, developmental, and cultural issues of wider interest to Muslims and citizens of Third World countries, especially Asia and Africa. With these objectives in mind, Aga Khan IV created a complex and global institutional network generally known as the Aga Khan Development Network.

Aga Khan IV closely supervised the spiritual and secular affairs of his community from his headquarters near Paris. He regularly visited his followers in different countries and gave them guidance by means of his own *farmāns*. He maintained the elaborate council system of communal organization developed by his grandfather and extended it into new regions in Europe and North America in recognition of the large-scale emigration of Nizaris from East Africa and South Asia to the West since the 1970s.

In 1986, Aga Khan IV issued a new universal constitution for all his followers throughout the world. The preamble of the new constitution, amended in 1998, affirmed all the fundamental Islamic beliefs and then specifically focused on the office of the imamate. It emphasized the imam's *ta'līm*, or authoritative teaching, which guides the Nizaris along the path of spiritual enlightenment as well as improved material life. Indeed, the new Isma'ili constitution stressed the all-important teaching and guiding role of the "imam of the time" by affirming that, by the virtue of his office and in accordance with the beliefs of the Nizari Isma'ilis, the imam enjoys full authority of governance in respect to all religious and communal matters of his followers. The office of the imamate thus provides the Nizari Isma'ilis with appropriate guidance and organizational structures to contextualize and practice their faith under changing circumstances.

See also imamate; Isma'ilis; Nizaris; Shi'ism

Further Reading

Aga Khan III, Sulṭān Muḥammad Shāh. *Selected Speeches and Writings of Sir Sultan Muhammad Shah*, 2 vols., edited by K. K. Aziz, 1997–98; Michel Boivin, *La Rénovation du Shî'isme Ismaélien en Inde et au Pakistan*, 2003; *The Constitution of the Shia Imami Ismaili Muslims*, 1986; Farhad Daftary, *The Ismā'īlīs: Their History and Doctrines*, 2nd ed., 2007; Willi Frischauer, *The Aga Khans*, 1970.

FARHAD DAFTARY

Ahmad, Israr (1932–2010)

Founder of the Islamic revolutionary movement Tanzeem-e-Islami (the Islamic Organization); the research, instructional, and outreach institute Anjuman Khuddam-ul-Qur'an Lahore (Society of the Servants of the Qur'an); and the populist Tehreek-e-Khilafat (Caliphate movement), Israr Ahmad is best known as a scholar of the Qur'an. Born in Hisar (Haryana, India) on April 26, 1932, he was attracted to the Muslim League before moving to Lahore, Pakistan, after partition in 1947. Influenced from a young age by the poet-philosopher Muhammad Iqbal (d. 1938), Ahmad became a sympathizer of the revivalist Mawdudi (d. 1979) and his religiopolitical movement Jama'at-i Islami, as well as an organizer for its student wing, while studying medicine at King Edward Medical College (1950–54). After graduating, Ahmad joined the Jama'at but resigned his membership in 1957 to pursue a popular revolution rather than engage in electoral politics.

Ahmad established himself as an activist-scholar through public lectures and workshops on the Qur'an (*durūs-i Qur'ān*). Soon after receiving a master's degree in Islamic studies from Karachi University in 1965, he published two short Urdu pamphlets (translated into English) that became the cornerstones of his future endeavors. The first, *Obligations Muslims Owe to the Qur'ān*, states that the Qur'an is for the soul what nourishment is for the body. Rather than celebrating the glory of the Qur'an through hollow praise, Ahmad writes that Muslims should recite and study it so as to establish its laws in society and preach its tenets to humanity. The second work, *Islamic Renaissance: The Real Task Ahead*, attributes the failure of revivalist movements such as the Jama'at to the pride of place they give to the legal and political aspects of Islam over its inner dimensions of faith. Ahmad argues that for any Islamic movement to be successful, it must first revitalize the faith of both the masses and intelligentsia by translating and preaching the Qur'an at the popular and philosophical levels.

In devotion to his cause, Ahmad relinquished his medical practice in 1971. He founded the Anjuman in 1972 to fulfill his vision of an intellectual "Islamic Renaissance" and the Tanzeem in 1975 as a revolutionary movement to establish Islamic ethics and law (shari'a) in economics, polity, and society, first in Pakistan and then across the globe. In the early 1980s, during Zia-ul-Haq's regime (1977–88), Ahmad delivered a series of lectures interpreting the life of the Prophet as a revolutionary movement, drawing inspiration from the Indian nationalist leader Mohandas Gandhi and Ayatollah Khomeini's Islamic revolution in Iran. Concerned that his message was not reaching the masses, Ahmad launched the Tehreek-e-Khilafat as a populist front in 1991. Ahmad upheld a nonviolent strategy of civil disobedience and advocated for a political framework identical to that of the United States, complete with its system of checks and balances but with three constitutional provisions: (1) sovereignty would belong to God and not the people, (2) no law could be made contrary to the Qur'an and

sunna, and (3) non-Muslims would be protected minorities rather than equal citizens. Ahmad couched his political thought within a comprehensive theology, cosmogony, and philosophy of history by synthesizing elements of modern thought with the Qur'an and Islamic traditions. He traced his intellectual roots to five influences: (1) traditional Islamic consensus (*ijmāʿ-i ahl al-sunna wa-l-jamāʿa*, Deoband), (2) revivalist thought (*iqāmat-i dīn*, Mawdudi), (3) thematic cohesion in the Qur'an (*naẓm-i Qur'ān*, Amin Ahsan Islahi, d. 1997), (4) perennial wisdom in the Qur'an (*ḥikmat-i Qur'ān*, Iqbal), and (5) his scientific training. In two larger Urdu works, *Jama'at-i Shaykh al-Hind awr Tanzim-i Islami* (The party of Shaykh al-Hind and the Tanzeem) and *Daʿwat-i Rujuʿ ila al-Qur'an ka Manzar wa-pass Manzar* (The historical background of the movement for the return to the Qur'an), Ahmad outlined the development and continuity of Islamic revivalist thought in India from the second Islamic millennium until his time. According to Ahmad, the center of Islamic thought shifted from the Arab world to the Indian subcontinent in the 17th century with the advent of the renewer (*mujaddid*) Ahmad Sirhindi (d. 1624). Ahmad viewed his own contribution as one in a series toward the global revival of Islam, which he believed was destined to emerge from the chosen land of Pakistan at the end of time.

Although the Tanzeem established branches in other parts of the world, including North America, it remained politically insignificant. Having lectured widely in public forums and on television, Ahmad became known primarily as a wise teacher of the Qur'an rather than a jurist-scholar (*faqīh*) or revolutionary leader. In 2002, he transferred leadership of the Tanzeem to his second son but remained president of the Anjuman until his death due to natural causes on April 14, 2010. The Anjuman has carefully recorded and catalogued his various speeches and tracts for dissemination.

See also fundamentalism; Jamaʿat-i Islami; Mawdudi, Abu al-Aʿla (1903–79); nonviolence; Pakistan

Further Reading

Shagufta Ahmad, *Dr. Israr Ahmad's Political Thought and Activities*, 1996; Tanzeem-e-Islami, http://www.tanzeem.org.

MAHAN MIRZA

Ahmad b. Hanbal (780–855)

Abu ʿAbdallah Ahmad b. Muhammad, hadith collector and critic, jurist, and dogmatist, was born in Baghdad in 780 and died there in 855. Premodern sources refer to him as "Abu ʿAbdallah," "Ibn Hanbal," "Ahmad b. Hanbal," or most often simply "Ahmad." He was descended from Arabs who had gone to Khurasan (now northeastern Iran and parts of Afghanistan) and served the Abbasids. At the age of 15, he dedicated himself to the study of the hadith. He first studied in Baghdad, where he had grown up, and then traveled to Kufa, Basra, Mecca, Yemen, and Syria before finally settling down in Baghdad after 820. His first and second wives died after bearing one son each, and a concubine then bore him several more children. They all lived together in a large house, supported mainly by commercial and probably residential properties in Baghdad.

Ibn Hanbal famously suffered in the inquisition (*miḥna*) that the Abbasid caliph Ma'mun (r. 813–33) instituted in 833, requiring religious scholars to testify that the Qur'an was created. The caliph believed he was the arbiter of Islamic orthodoxy. Ibn Hanbal was one of the few to refuse to testify. He was imprisoned and then tried, probably a year later, before Ma'mun's successor, Muʿtasim (r. 833–42). He finally was flogged and released. Hostile sources assert that he confessed, while Hanbali sources say that he lost consciousness (and so could not have been responsible for anything he said). The caliph Mutawakkil (r. 847–61) dismantled the inquisition during the first five years of his reign. Near the end of this period, he summoned Ibn Hanbal to Samarra to teach; however, Ibn Hanbal did not want anything to do with the ruler, refused to eat, and was finally sent home.

Ibn Hanbal's greatest literary monument is the *Musnad* (Solid tradition), a collection of almost 28,000 prophetic hadiths, about 80 percent of which are repeats with variant chains of transmitters (compared to the *Ṣaḥīḥ* [Sound collection] of Bukhari [d. 870] with 7,400 hadiths, about 60 percent of which are repeats). The *Musnad* seems to have been assembled by Ibn Hanbal's son ʿAbdallah (d. 903). Ibn Hanbal generally evaluated hadiths by comparing variant chains of transmitters. If someone's transmissions were too often uncorroborated by parallels from contemporaries, Ibn Hanbal considered that person unreliable. Later hadith critics often quoted his evaluations.

Ibn Hanbal's second greatest literary monument is the *Kitab al-Zuhd* (On renunciation), a collection of sayings concerning the pious life, especially from the early eighth century. The extant version of the book comprises around 2,400 items, but the original was apparently two or three times longer. Perhaps half of it was the contribution of Ibn Hanbal himself, while the remaining half was added by his son ʿAbdallah as he assembled it. Prominent features of the work are a focus on otherworldliness (hence little concern for service in this world), nighttime devotions (which are preferred, as they are less likely to be performed for the sake of being seen), austerity (such as eating little and requiring only the plainest dress and furniture), and the cultivation of sadness and fear (i.e., sadness over past sins and fear of the Judgment to come).

Various followers transmitted Ibn Hanbal's legal opinions, of which several collections (called *masā'il*) are extant. From these early collections, it is evident that he strongly preferred to infer rules from the hadith, from the Prophet if possible, and from Companions if necessary. When confronted with two contradictory hadith reports, he tested their chains of transmitters to see which was more reliable. If they seemed equally good, he might simply state the alternatives without imposing his own opinion. Ibn Hanbal's jurisprudence is distinguished by its ethical character. For example, he regularly tried to protect against exploitation, condemned *ḥiyal*

(legal devices) that respected the letter of the law but contravened its spirit, and required words and actions to have consequences. Many of the opinions ascribed to him in later sources were evidently generated by *takhrīj*, meaning the attribution to Ibn Hanbal of opinions thought to ensue naturally from his principles, even if they were not actually enunciated by him. The Hanbali Sunni school of law takes its name from him.

In theology, he rejected almost all speculation that went beyond what was expressly stated in the Qur'an and hadith. Both friendly and hostile accounts of his stance at the inquisition stress his refusal to debate on rational grounds. He was, if anything, even more hostile to would-be proponents of Sunni *kalām* (dialectical theology) than he was to Murji'is, Qadaris, and other non-Sunni theological groups. He was associated especially with bitter denunciations of those who conceded that, although the Qur'an was not itself created, one's pronunciation of the Qur'an was created. Ibn Hanbal preferred that the question not be discussed.

In politics, Ibn Hanbal was a quietist Sunni. By all accounts, he recognized 'Ali b. Abi Talib as the legitimate fourth caliph, against those who considered that Mu'awiya (r. 661–80) had directly succeeded 'Uthman b. 'Affan (r. 644–56). However, he staunchly rejected Shi'i assertions that some of the Companions had been unrighteous, notably those who acclaimed Abu Bakr (r. 632–34) 'Umar b. al-Khattab (r. 634–44) and opposed 'Ali. He recognized as the imam of his time whoever was the subject of universal agreement. One Hanbali source goes so far as to quote him: "Whoever overcomes them by the sword, so that he becomes caliph and is called the Commander of the Faithful, it is not licit for anyone who believes in God and the Last Day to spend a night not considering him an imam, whether he is pious or reprobate." Accordingly, in 846 he discouraged rebellion against the persecuting caliph Wathiq (r. 842–47).

At the same time, there runs through sources purporting to quote Ibn Hanbal a strong concern on the part of Ibn Hanbal with commanding right and forbidding wrong, meaning rebuke of misbehaving rulers and private correction of misbehavior where the ruler has failed to enforce the law. Ibn Hanbal recognized the duty but recommended caution to avoid provoking any violent reaction from the ruler; he warned not to expect too much of people and not to seek out misbehavior but only to correct such as it presented itself publicly (e.g., to pour out wine in an uncovered container but not to uncover a container one suspects of holding wine). Ibn Hanbal himself went so far as to avoid public prayer in the mosque, which he thought normally to be required, so as to avoid both the caliph's blandishments and the duty of openly rebuking him.

See also hadith; inquisition; Ma'mun (786–833); Sunnism

Further Reading

Michael Cook, *Commanding Right and Forbidding Wrong in Islamic Thought*, 2000; Michael Cooperson, *Classical Arabic Biography: The Heirs of the Prophets in the Age of al-Ma'mun*, 2000; Nimrod Hurvitz, *The Formation of Hanbalism: Piety into Power*, 2002; Christopher Melchert, *Ahmad ibn Hanbal*, 2006; Susan A. Spectorsky, "Ahmad ibn Hanbal's *Fiqh*," *Journal of the American Oriental Society* 102 (1982); Idem, *Chapters on Marriage and Divorce: Responses of ibn Hanbal and ibn Rahwayh*, 1993.

CHRISTOPHER MELCHERT

Ahmadis

The Ahmadi or Ahmadiyya movement in Islam is a modern Muslim messianic movement. It was founded in 1889 in the Indian province of the Punjab by Ghulam Ahmad (1835–1908). Accused of rejecting the Muslim dogma asserting the finality of Muhammad's prophethood, the movement aroused the fierce opposition of the Sunni mainstream. During the period of British rule in India, the controversy was merely a doctrinal dispute between private individuals or voluntary organizations, but when most Ahmadis moved in 1947 to the professedly Islamic state of Pakistan, the issue was transformed into a major constitutional problem. The Sunni Muslim mainstream demanded the formal exclusion of the Ahmadis from the Muslim fold. This objective was attained in 1974: against fierce opposition from the Ahmadis, the Pakistani parliament adopted a constitutional amendment declaring them non-Muslims. In 1984, in the framework of General Zia-ul-Haq's (d. 1988) Islamization trend in Pakistan, the presidential Ordinance no. XX of 1984 transformed the religious observance of the Ahmadis into a criminal offense punishable by three years of imprisonment. The ordinance became an instrument for the harassment and judicial persecution of the Ahmadi community. Following the promulgation of this legal restriction, the headquarters of the Ahmadi movement moved from Rabwa (in Pakistan) to London.

As far as constitutional procedure is concerned, the 1974 amendment is extraordinary. Politicians elected through a secular process arrogated to themselves the authority of an assembly of theologians, discussed a subtle issue of Muslim theology, dealt with matters concerning faith and infidelity, and pronounced judgment on the religious affiliation of a group of citizens. With the adoption of the amendment, Ahmadis, who passionately believed in being Muslims in the fullest sense of the word, were transformed into a non-Muslim minority. Legally, the constitutional amendment should have prevented the Ahmadis only from serving as president and prime minister of Pakistan, who must be Muslims according to the constitution. In practice, it had more serious repercussions. Ahmadis were removed from senior positions in the army, and international Muslim organizations began to adopt anti-Ahmadi resolutions and urged Muslim governments to declare Ahmadis as apostates. In 1975, Pakistan's minister of religious affairs declared that Ahmadis would not be allowed to perform the pilgrimage (hajj) to Mecca, and any Pakistani who wished to perform it would be

obliged to sign a declaration affirming his or her belief in the finality of Muhammad's prophethood.

Before the establishment of Pakistan, Ahmadis developed distinct political thought. Grateful that the British administration allowed them to preach and propagate their version of Islam, the Ahmadis were loyal to the British government. While Ghulam Ahmad would brook no compromise with Christianity and its missionaries in India, he carefully distinguished between Christian missionaries and the British rule to which he gave his staunch support. He repeatedly paid tribute to the British for creating conditions in which the Ahmadis were able not only to extol Islam but also to criticize Christianity. The Ahmadis did not identify with issues that agitated the Muslim world at the beginning of the 20th century. The reverses suffered by the Ottomans during the Balkan wars, which aroused intense feelings of sympathy among mainstream Muslims, left the Ahmadis untouched. Similarly, the Ahmadi movement remained aloof during the anti-British noncooperation movement in the early 1920s. Ahmadi attitudes toward the struggle for Indian independence were ambivalent. Although the Ahmadi leadership expressed sympathy with the aim of the Indian National Congress to improve India's political status, it also maintained that the government must be obeyed and rejected the use of civil disobedience in the political struggle. In the last years before independence and partition, the Ahmadi pronouncements became more outspoken in favor of Indian independence, but even then the movement did not identify with any of the parties that led the nationalist struggle. This allowed the adversaries of the Ahmadis to stigmatize it as a movement that stood by the imperial power and did not share the aspirations of the Indian people at a crucial stage in their history.

The Ahmadis have a distinctive interpretation of jihad. In their view, jihad should be waged in a way appropriate to the threat facing Islam. In the early Muslim period, nascent Islam was in danger of physical extinction, and therefore military jihad was called for. In Ghulam Ahmad's lifetime, Muslims faced the onslaught of Christian missionaries who engaged in slander against Islam and its Prophet. In such a situation, Ahmadis believed Muslims should respond in kind and defend Islam by preaching and refuting the slander rather than by military means. Though this interpretation is specific to the situation of Indian Muslims under British rule, it came to be considered an unchanging principle of the Ahmadi worldview.

In their relationship with the non-Muslim world, the Ahmadis have been engaged in depicting Islam as a liberal, humane, and progressive religion, systematically misrepresented by non-Muslims. This aspect of Ahmadi teaching is well in line with that of modernist Muslim thinkers, though in other matters, such as the seclusion of women, the Ahmadis follow the traditional point of view. One of the most distinctive features of the movement is that the Ahmadis consider the peaceful propagation of their version of Islam among Muslims and non-Muslims alike as essential.

See also apostasy; India; messianism; Pakistan

Further Reading

Bashir al-Din Mahmud Ahmad, *Indian Problem and Its Solution*, ca. 1926; Idem, *Invitation to Aḥmadiyyat*, 1961; Idem, *The Nehru Report and Muslim Rights*, 1930; Ghulam Ahmad, "Government-i angrezi awr jihad" [The British government and jihad], in *Ruhani Khaza'in* [The collected works of Ghulam Ahmad], vol. 17, 1965. English translation: *Review of Religions* 10 (1911); Leonard Binder, *Religion and Politics in Pakistan*, 1961; S. E. Brush, "Ahmadiyyat in Pakistan: Rabwa and the Ahmadis," *Muslim World* 45 (1955); Yohanan Friedmann, *Prophecy Continuous: Aspects of Ahmadi Religious Thought and Its Medieval Background*, 2nd ed., 2003; *Pakistan National Assembly's Verdict on Finality of Prophethood of Hazrat Muhammad (Peace be upon him)*, 1974; Muhammad Zafrullah Khan, *Aḥmadiyyat: The Renaissance of Islam*, 1978.

YOHANAN FRIEDMANN

Ahmad Sirhindi (1564–1624)

An Indian Muslim Sufi, considered by his followers as "the renewer of the second millennium" (of the Islamic era; *mujaddid-i alf-i thānī*), Ahmad Sirhindi was born in Sirhind in East Punjab and received his religious education from several teachers in Sialkot. Because of his scholarship, he was later invited to the court of Emperor Akbar (r. 1556–1605) in Agra. A turning point in his life came in 1599–1600, when he went to Delhi and was initiated into the Naqshbandi order of Sufis by Khwaja Muhammad al-Baqi bi-llah, a prominent Naqshbandi teacher. Subsequently he devoted himself to the propagation of Naqshbandi ideas on Sufism and wrote hundreds of letters in which he explained various points in the doctrine of the Naqshbandis. These letters included ideas that Emperor Jahangir (r. 1605–27) considered arrogant and conducive to heresy. In 1619, Jahangir summoned Sirhindi to his court and imprisoned him. His imprisonment lasted for a year. After his release, Sirhindi continued his Sufi activities until he died in 1624.

Sirhindi's celebrated collection of letters, titled *Maktubat-i Imam-i Rabbani* (Letters of the divine guide), is regarded as a landmark in the development of Islam in the Indian subcontinent. Most letters deal with aspects of Islamic mysticism, but some are relevant to questions of political thought. In a few letters, Sirhindi expresses his views on the desirability of a relationship between devout Muslims and their rulers. At times, he writes that a devout Muslim must refrain from any relationship of this kind and should flee from the rulers' company as he would flee from lions. Nevertheless, he wrote letters to Mughul officials. In some of those letters, he recommended certain individuals for governmental posts or for stipends. In other letters, he urged the officials to strive for the strict implementation of the shari'a by the state. In particular, he demanded the humiliation of the Hindus and the merciless

imposition of the poll tax (*jizya*) on them. He also expressed his joy at the 1606 execution of Arjun, the fifth guru of the Sikhs.

On the basis of these few letters, many modern scholars and thinkers maintain that Sirhindi brought about major changes in the development of Islam in the subcontinent. According to these scholars, Sirhindi reversed the heretical trends of the period of Akbar, restored the pristine purity of Islam, and inspired the orthodox reforms of Emperor Aurangzeb (r. 1658–1707). In mainstream Pakistani historiography, Sirhindi is portrayed as a figure who saved Indian Islam from disintegration. The decisive majority of Sirhindi's letters, however, deal with mystical rather than political issues, and there is no evidence that the Mughal Empire heeded Sirhindi's advice concerning the imposition of Islamic laws on the state. It is reasonably clear that in the 17th century, Sirhindi was not considered a political activist but rather a Sufi who suffered from delusions of grandeur and whose writings were replete with heretical ideas. In addition to his imprisonment by Emperor Jahangir in 1619, Emperor Aurangzeb—who is supposed to have been influenced by Sirhindi's views—proscribed the study of his *Maktubat* in 1679. Sirhindi's primary influence was not as a political thinker but as a mystic: the Mujaddidi branch of the Naqshbandi order that came into being under his influence spread from India into the Ottoman lands in the 18th century and also was influential in Turkey and in Syria.

See also India; Mughals (1526–1857); Sufism

Further Reading

Butrus Abu-Manneh, "The Naqshbandiyya-Mujaddidiyya in the Ottoman Lands in the Early 19th Century," *Die Welt des Islams* 22 (1982); Aziz Ahmad, "Religious and Political Ideas of Shaykh Ahmad Sirhindi," *Rivista degli Studi Orientali* 36 (1961); Burhan Ahmad Faruqi, *The Mujaddid's Conception of Tawhid*, 1940; Yohanan Friedmann, *Shaykh Aḥmad Sirhindī: An Outline of His Thought and a Study of His Image in the Eyes of Posterity*, 2000; J. G. J. ter Haar, *Follower and Heir of the Prophet: Shaykh Ahmad Sirhindi (1564–1624) as Mystic*, 1992; Shaykh Ahmad Sirhindi, *Ithbat al-nubuwwa*. Haydarabad (Sindh), 1963–64; Idem, *Maktubat-i Imam-i Rabbani*, 1889.

YOHANAN FRIEDMANN

'A'isha (ca. 614–78)

'A'isha was the most prominent of the Prophet Muhammad's wives. Daughter of Abu Bakr, Muhammad's close companion and the future first caliph of the Muslim community, she was born in Mecca and was married to the Prophet at the age of nine or ten in a union that some early sources attributed to divine arrangement by the angel Gabriel. Her youth gave her a special status during the Prophet's life, although it did occasionally cause uneasy relations within the Prophet's extended household, such as an accusation of adultery (*al-ifk*), of which she was fully exonerated by a Qur'anic revelation (Q. 24:11–20) containing a sharp rebuke of her accusers.

When the Prophet was ill toward the end of his life in 632, 'A'isha, only 18 and with no children, was acknowledged as his favorite wife, and thus she nursed him in her quarters, where he died and was buried beneath the house. Like all the Prophet's surviving wives, she was forbidden by Qur'anic injunction to remarry (Q. 33:53) and became part of a new female elite known as *ummahāt al-mu'minīn*, or "the Mothers of the Believers." This unique status elevated the Prophet's widows to higher standards of conduct than other women, including the unique command that they speak to men not of their immediate family from behind a *ḥijāb*, or curtain (Q. 33:53).

'A'isha seems to have led a quiet life during the successive caliphates of her father, Abu Bakr, and 'Umar b. al-Khattab. She criticized the policies of the third caliph, 'Uthman b. 'Affan (d. 656), however, claiming that they deviated from her husband's. Muslims heatedly disagreed about 'A'isha's right to publicly criticize the caliph, and 'Uthman rebuked her, reminding her of the Qur'anic verse commanding the wives of the Prophet to "stay in your houses" (Q. 33:33), a reference meant to silence her. This injunction, although never followed literally by the wives of the Prophet, echoed later in the rhetoric of those who condemned 'A'isha.

When 'Uthman was assassinated by Muslim rebels in 656, 'A'isha demanded that his murderers be punished, thus pitting her against the newly elected fourth caliph, 'Ali b. Abi Talib (d. 661). 'Ali had been one of her vocal critics during the incident of the *ifk* (adultery) and had suggested that the Prophet divorce her, but her reasons also included a belief in the importance of establishing *iṣlāḥ*, a final peaceful resolution between 'Ali's party and her own allies (Q. 49:9–10). 'A'isha was supported in her quest by two brothers-in-law and aspirants to the caliphate: her cousin Talha b. 'Ubaydallah and Zubayr b. al-'Awwam (both d. 656).

Speaking in Mecca from behind the curtained sanctuary of the Ka'ba, 'A'isha rallied her male followers to march to war against 'Ali in Basra, Iraq. There, she watched as 'Ali's more numerous forces defeated hers in 656. As Zubayr and Talha perished, 'A'isha did not wield a sword in the conflict but instead urged her troops on to victory from a curtained palanquin. The fiercest fighting took place around her camel, where 70 men are said to have died defending her. When her camel was hamstrung, the conflict, known thereafter as the Battle of the Camel, ended. 'A'isha was treated with respect by 'Ali and was returned by his troops to Medina, where she retired from politics.

'A'isha became a major conduit for her husband's sunna, the precedent that later became a source of Islamic law; about 300 of the "sound," or most authentic, prophetic traditions preserved in the canonical work of Muslim (d. 875) and Bukhari (d. 870) were narrated by her, although the full corpus of her transmission is much larger—more than one thousand traditions.

In medieval Shi'i historiography, 'A'isha is portrayed consistently as the leader of the opposition, a headstrong but powerful woman and ultimately the antithesis of ideal Muslim womanhood. Sunni historians praised her as the Prophet's favorite wife but shifted the blame for her political involvement to her male allies,

emphasizing her lack of leadership. Both Shi'i and Sunni accounts, authored exclusively by men in the premodern period, found in 'A'isha's defeat a precedent to exclude all women from politics.

In the seventh century, 'A'isha's age prompted only praise, which is recorded in the earliest sources. Contemporary non-Muslims, however, often use 'A'isha's marital age in broader critiques of Islam. Many websites, both Muslim and non-Muslim, have focused on 'A'isha's youth as a vexed issue. As a result, her original seventh-century political importance has been overshadowed in contemporary Western debate by what some believe are anachronistic readings of the era in which she lived.

In the 20th and 21st centuries, some Sunni Muslim women found a positive political model in 'A'isha. She left no first-person defense of her political motivations. In only one early account, displaying grief for the dead after her defeat, did she admit "wrongdoing." This suggests that, until her defeat, 'A'isha assumed it was her prerogative to participate in the political life of the first Muslim polity.

See also Abu Bakr (ca. 573–634); 'Ali b. Abi Talib (ca. 599–661); 'Uthman b. 'Affan (ca. 579–656); women

Further Reading

Nabia Abbott, *'A'ishah: The Beloved of Mohammed*, 1942; Kecia Ali, *Sexual Ethics & Islam: Feminist Reflections on Qur'an, Hadith, and Jurisprudence*, 2006; Wilferd Madelung, *The Succession to Muhammad: A Study of the Early Caliphate*, 1997; Fatima Mernissi, *The Veil and the Male Elite: A Feminist Interpretation of Women's Rights in Islam*, translated by Mary Jo Lakeland, 1991; D. A. Spellberg, *Politics, Gender, and the Islamic Past: The Legacy of 'A'isha bint Abi Bakr*, 1994; Barbara Freyer Stowasser, *Women in the Qu'ran, Traditions, and Interpretation*, 1994.

DENISE SPELLBERG

Akbar the Great (1542–1605)

The third and arguably the greatest king of the Mughal Empire, Akbar is responsible for consolidating Mughal power in India. At his accession in 1556, the young king faced threats from supporters of Afghan leader Islam Shah Suri. One of Islam Shah's generals, Samrat Hem Chandra (popularly known as Hemu), challenged Akbar for control of North India, but his forces were defeated by Akbar at Panipat. Within the next five years, Akbar successfully wrested control of India away from the remaining Sur princes.

Akbar's next challenge came from his regent Bairam Khan, whose family had traveled to India from Central Asia with Akbar's grandfather, Zahiruddin Babur. (Babur conquered India in 1526 to establish the Mughal Empire.) Akbar dismissed Bairam Khan from office, sent him on a pilgrimage to Mecca, and replaced him with his own foster brother, Adham Khan. Adham Khan displeased Akbar when he kept all the spoils of a campaign he led into Malwa, and Khan further angered Akbar when he assassinated Akbar's chief minister. Akbar reportedly struck Adham Khan and threw him off a balcony to ensure his death. This event—illustrated in Abu al-Fadl's *Akbarnama* (The book of Akbar), a lavish chronicle commissioned by Akbar—came to be one of the many stories associated with the charisma and power of Akbar.

To secure his power, Akbar marginalized the Uzbek elite at court by cultivating a Persian elite and by forming new alliances with the landed Indian aristocracy. The Uzbek nobles at court had supported the claims of Akbar's half brother, Mirza Hakim, to the throne of Delhi, and Akbar wished to counter their power by forming local alliances. Akbar's campaigns into Rajasthan, his marriage to a Rajput woman, and his appointment of Rajput chiefs to high posts in the government paved the way for a new administrative order. Akbar also constructed four impressive fortresses in the cities of Agra, Lahore, Allahabad, and Ajmer and commissioned the building of a new city, Fatehpur Sikri, which he would use as his capital. In Fatehpur Sikri, Akbar built a tomb for Salim Chishti (d. 1572), the mystic to whose prayers Akbar credited the birth of his son and successor, Prince Salim. Akbar actively recruited the family of Salim Chishti into Mughal service and, by doing so, gained for himself another valuable source of local authority. To challenge the power held by the 'ulama', Akbar seized religious land grants they had gained under Sur rulers and distributed these land grants to learned men of all religious communities. Akbar also abolished the poll tax (*jizya*) and gave himself religious authority over the body of 'ulama' and over all figures who held spiritual legitimacy.

The arrival of the second Islamic millennium in 1592 formed the backdrop for Akbar's personal theology. In Abu al-Fadl's *Akbarnama*, Akbar is portrayed as the embodiment of the divine and as a messianic figure whose coming was foretold by seers and astrologers. As Akbar's historian, Abu al-Fadl created for the king a genealogy beginning with Adam, continuing through the line of Abrahamic prophets, and finally arriving at the immaculate conception that began the line of Akbar's ancestor Timur Gurgan (the legendary Central Asian conqueror known as Tamerlane). A close-knit circle of noblemen at Akbar's court was bound to him by ties of discipleship, similar to the ties between the heads of Sufi orders and their followers. Akbar's religious claims were pluralistic in nature; the emperor embodied the divine at the heart of all religions, and his military prowess, combined with his administrative skills, added to his mystique. When Akbar died in 1605, he left behind a legacy of successful military campaigns, a full treasury, and a centralized, efficient state.

See also messianism; Mughals (1526–1857)

Further Reading

Irfan Habib, ed., *Akbar and His India*, 1992; Ruby Lal, *Domesticity and Power in the Early Mughal World*, 2005; J. F. Richards, *The Cambridge History of India: The Mughal Empire*, 1993; Douglas E. Streusand, *The Formation of the Mughal Empire*, 1989; André Wink, *Akbar*, 2009.

TAYMIYA R. ZAMAN

‘Alawis

‘Alawis are a religious group who live in the southeast of Turkey and Lebanon, as well as in Syria, where they are both the largest religious minority and the ruling political elite. They emerged as a distinct religious movement in the tenth-century Shi‘i milieu of Iraq and were later transplanted to Syria. During the French mandate of Syria after World War I, the French army included large numbers of ‘Alawis, whose military experience enabled them to take power in Syria after France’s withdrawal.

The name of the sect (Arabic, *‘Alawī*) refers to their deification of the first Shi‘i imam ‘Ali b. Abi Talib (d. 661). Originally, however, they were called Nusayris, after their eponymous founder Muhammad b. Nusayr, who lived in the second half of the ninth century. He was succeeded by Husayn al-Khusaybi (d. 957 or 969), who played an important role in the formulation of the Nusayri doctrine. ‘Alawi teachings were preserved in a considerable number of medieval and early modern treatises written by members of the sect, together with accounts of its critics.

Before the second half of the 20th century, ‘Alawis never held political power, so their doctrines pay little attention to the state and politics, mainly focusing on the supernatural realm and man’s relation to it. The core of their belief is the divine nature of ‘Ali, who in different texts is depicted as either God or His manifestation in human form. The creation of the human race is followed by their sin, causing them to fall from the luminous divine realm into the evil material world. However, virtuous believers are able to return to the divine realm along a path (*ṣirāṭ*) that includes numerous degrees of spiritual perfection. Conversely, the sinful are punished by being reborn into other human bodies (*naskh*), or worse, by undergoing transformation (*musūkhiyya*) into animals, plants, and inanimate objects, according to the degree of their sins.

God is imagined as a triad, consisting of the supreme member called Meaning (*ma‘nā*) and His two emanations—His Name (*ism*), also called Veil (*ḥijāb*), and His Gate (*bāb*). The Meaning is utterly transcendent. His first emanation has two functions: to name and conceal Him, hence his two epithets, Name and Veil. The second emanation, the Gate, is called so because he serves as a link between the Meaning and the believers. The divinity’s three aspects are not completely detached from the world of humans but appear to them from time to time in the form of various persons. Most commonly, they appeared to humans in the forms of, respectively, ‘Ali, the Prophet Muhammad, and Salman al-Farisi, Muhammad’s well-known Companion. Besides the triad, there are a number of other spiritual beings, the most important of whom are the five Unique Ones (*aytām*, sing. *yatīm*) who have emanated from the three divine persons.

The three personifications of God are manifested in the material world in seven historical cycles, called Domes (*qibāb*, sing. *qubba*), centered on the persons of biblical and Islamic characters, including prophets and imams. The present cycle is called the *qubba Muḥammadiyya*, referring to the Prophet Muhammad. Some ‘Alawi authors have viewed human history as finite. Thus, according to a 19th-century catechism, at the end of time ‘Ali will appear to free the souls of believers from their graves and return them to the luminous realm. But others believe that the cycles are endless: this world will come to an end, but another will be created thereafter. Despite the numerous common elements between ‘Alawi teachings and mainstream Islam (especially in its Shi‘i form), many of their beliefs have appeared scandalous to both Shi‘i and Sunni Muslims, who have consistently accused them of heresy and immoral practices. Charges of heresy and the lack of political power led ‘Alawis to view secrecy as an essential part of their belief and a condition for belonging to the community. Divulging religious secrets to outsiders became equal to unbelief and led to banishment.

See also ‘Ali b. Abi Talib (ca. 599–661); Shi‘ism; Syria

Further Reading

Meir Bar-Asher and Aryeh Kofsky, *The Nuṣayrī-‘Alawī Religion: An Enquiry into Its Theology and Religion*, 2002; Yaron Friedman, *The Nuṣayrī-‘Alawīs*, 2010; Heinz Halm, *Die Islamische Gnosis*, 1982; Matti Moosa, *Extremist Shiites*, 1988; Tord Olsson, “The Gnosis of Mountaineers and Townspeople: The Religion of the Syrian Alawites, or the Nuṣayrīs,” in *Alevi Identity: Cultural, Religious and Social Perspectives*, edited by Tord Olsson, Elisabeth Özdalga, and Catharina Raudvere, 1998; Edward Salisbury, “The Book of Sulaimân’s First Ripe Fruit, Disclosing the Mysteries of the Nusairian Religion,” *Journal of the American Oriental Society* 8 (1866).

MUSHEGH ASATRYAN

Algeria

Modern political thought in Algeria emerged in the vacuum created by the systemic French conquest of the territories of the Ottoman Beylik (province) of Algiers in the 1840s. This conquest destroyed all but the most resilient local indigenous political institutions, represented by the tribes and Sufi brotherhoods, and immediately implanted French political institutions at the upper levels of the state. It took decades for the traumatized population to regain its political vision. In the early 20th century, however, a new French-educated class of Algerians, patronizingly described by the French as *évolués* (evolved, developed), began to consider both the past and future of their country, thereby laying the foundations of modern Algerian national identity and political thought. This identity was complex: on the one hand, it was traceable to the ancient Berber and Phoenician kingdoms of antiquity, but on the other, it was firmly Arab and politically secular but at the same time culturally Islamic. Whether Algeria existed before *l’Algérie française* was a moot point, and in the face of French colonialism, it was impossible to imagine reconstituting it in anything but a modern guise.

The Algerian political community, however, consisting of groups in both Algeria and France, was divided over what modern Algeria should be. At one end of the spectrum stood the secular socialist trade unionists and at the other end the reformist 'ulama' led by the eminent scholar 'Abd al-Hamid b. Badis (d. 1940). Ibn Badis introduced the Salafism of Muhammad 'Abduh to Algeria and launched an attack on folk Islam, as represented primarily by the Sufi brotherhoods, in favor of an urban middle-class interpretation of the faith consistent with modernity. Although the Algerian War of Independence, spearheaded by the Front de Libération National, traditionally has been seen as both a war of national liberation and a socialist revolution, recent studies indicate the importance of Islam as a popular idiom and motivator of political action, especially in the countryside where jihad rather than revolution galvanized people to participate.

Although the independent state of Algeria prided itself on its nationalist socialist credentials, its citizens proved to be the most open in the region to the Islamist discourse that swept across the Middle East and North Africa from the 1970s onward. One reason for this was the almost complete absence of continuity between the precolonial and postcolonial eras and the consequent alienation of many from the political structures of the new state. Education and an adequate response to the country's social and economic problems might have alleviated this alienation, but in any case, the new political discourse of Islamism received an immediate and significant welcome, especially in cities such as Algiers. What was distinctive about Islamism in Algeria was its strongly nationalist color, despite the apparent contradiction between the communities of Islam and the nation respectively. This can be traced to Ibn Badis himself and his understanding of Salafism as a tool for national revival and identity formation in opposition to external European, and specifically French, attempts to undermine the Algerian political persona. This link between Algerian nationalism and Islam was assisted by the association of the French Empire with Christianity—a link made most clearly by the Cathedral of Notre Dame d'Afrique, established by Cardinal Lavigerie (d. 1892), which sits atop a cliff overlooking the Bay of Algiers.

Although submerged in the halcyon days of the revolution, the Islamic strand had been present from the start of Algeria's engagement with modernity. In the late 20th century, it offered Algerians not a means to evade the nation-state but instead a means to make it accountable and give it authenticity. Islamism is by definition a hegemonic interpretation of Islam, however, and it was rejected not only by the secular-minded army but also by important sectors of the population, most notably the Berber population of Kabylia, who saw it as part of a program of Islamization and Arabization that ignored their contribution to the formation of Algeria and devalued their approach to Islam. The result was the vicious civil war that erupted when the Front Islamique du Salut won the elections in 1992 but were prevented from acceding to power by the army.

See also colonialism; fundamentalism; modernity; nationalism; North Africa; secularism

Further Reading

Amira Bennison, "Opposition and Accommodation to French Colonialism in Early Nineteenth Century Algeria," *Cambridge Review of International Affairs* 11, no. 2 (1998); Alistair Horne, *A Savage War of Peace: Algeria 1954–1962*, 1987; James McDougall, *History and the Culture of Nationalism in Algeria*, 2006; Hugh Roberts, *The Battlefield: Algeria 1988–2002*, 2003; Michael Willis, *The Islamist Challenge in Algeria: A Political History*, 1996.

AMIRA K. BENNISON

'Ali b. Abi Talib (ca. 599–661)

Cousin and son-in-law to the Prophet by marriage to his eldest daughter, Fatima, 'Ali is revered by Shi'is as the first imam and, therefore, the true successor and inheritor (*waṣī*) to the Prophet's legacy (*waṣiyya*) to whom absolute devotion (*walāya*) serves as the precondition of true knowledge of Islam. Sunnis regard him as the last of the so-called Rightly Guided Caliphs (*al-khulafā' al-rāshidūn*). Although universally revered, the biography and station of 'Ali within the Muslim community remain the *locus classicus* of the profoundest sectarian disputes between Sunni and Shi'i believers. 'Ali's bid for the caliphate came in the midst of the Great Schism (*al-fitna al-kubrā*) following the assassination of 'Uthman b. 'Affan in 656. His brief and beleaguered efforts to reunite the *umma* under his leadership ended tragically with his assassination by the blade of one of his renegade followers on January 27, 661.

'Ali's political influence and, for some, his political *right* (*ḥaqq*) to leadership derives from his early and intimate ties with Muhammad, which originate from his early youth. 'Ali ranks among the earliest converts to the new religion (a dispute exists over whether Abu Bakr's conversion preceded 'Ali's or whether 'Ali's status as a minor rendered Abu Bakr's conversion more meritorious). The prominence of place in the political arena publicly accorded to 'Ali by the Prophet, particularly in Medina, is often striking. When instituting the brotherhood pact between prominent Meccan emigrants (*muhājirūn*) and Medinan helpers (*anṣār*), the Prophet chose 'Ali as his brother designate. Muhammad also charged 'Ali, who was renowned as a fierce warrior, with leading numerous raids and key diplomatic missions—for example, the Yemeni tribe Banu Hamdan allegedly converted at his hands—and twice Muhammad delegated him to destroy idols (first those of the Aws and Khazraj, then those of the Ka'ba). Most important for Shi'is, however, was the event transpiring in 632 at Ghadir Khumm, a marsh located between Mecca and Medina. After his return from his final pilgrimage, Muhammad declared to a congregation of Muslims, "Whosoever regards me as his master [*mawlā*], 'Ali is his master." This declaration is vague—the word *mawlā* by no means unambiguously conveys the sense of political or religious leadership.

Shi'is, however, interpreted the event as the Prophet's investiture (*naṣṣ*) of 'Ali with the leadership of the *umma* upon the death of the Prophet, whereas Sunni traditionalists usually regarded the event as evidence of 'Ali's high station in the community, though little more.

After the Prophet's death, Abu Bakr's initiation of the Qurashi caliphate with the help of 'Umar b. al-Khattab and Abu 'Ubayda b. al-Jarrah transpired without 'Ali's consultation, as he reportedly remained in the Prophet's home preparing his corpse for burial. 'Ali was not immediately forthcoming in granting Abu Bakr the oath of allegiance (*bay'a*). The relations between the two worsened when Abu Bakr rejected Fatima's claim to the Prophet's orchard in Fadak. Fatima refused to meet with Abu Bakr ever again and died six months later, at which time 'Ali swore his oath of allegiance. The ownership of Fadak remained a contested issue for centuries; caliphs periodically returned the property to Fatima's descendents or seized it in varying contexts.

Even after the *bay'a*, 'Ali remained disconsolate and at a considerable distance from public life. In marked contrast to his exploits during Muhammad's lifetime, 'Ali participated in neither the wars of apostasy (*ridda*) under Abu Bakr nor the conquests undertaken by 'Umar and 'Uthman. 'Umar, who reportedly disdained 'Ali's "foolishness" (*du'āba*), may have played a direct role in marginalizing his influence from an early date. 'Ali's self-imposed distance and disenfranchisement apparently manifested a silent censure of the first three caliphs. Potentially revealing as well are the reports of his allegedly noncommittal (and consequentially negative) reply to 'Abd al-Rahman b. 'Awf's inquiry during the consultation (*shūrā*) that elected 'Uthman caliph as to whether or not he would follow the policies of Abu Bakr and 'Umar.

'Ali's gradual reemergence onto the stage of public life coincides with the coalescing of opposition forces against the policies of 'Uthman. When garrison rebels marched on Medina in 656, 'Ali attempted but failed to mitigate their grievances. After the caliph's assassination, many of the rebels, not all of whom had wished 'Uthman dead, rallied to 'Ali as their natural leader per the entreaties of the rebels. 'Ali swiftly stepped into the power vacuum left by 'Uthman's death, quelling the chaos that had upended Medina's peace. 'Ali's hastily convened *shūrā*, unlike 'Uthman's, incorporated not merely the emigrants, but also the helpers. Numerous prominent Meccan Quraysh fled the city—especially 'Uthman's Umayyad clansmen—to avoid yielding to 'Ali's authority, whereas others, such as the prominent Companions Zubayr b. 'Awwam and Talha b. 'Ubaydallah, offered their allegiance only under duress.

'Ali's relationship with the rebels on an ideological level is difficult to discern. His criticism of 'Uthman was markedly more public than his criticism toward Abu Bakr and 'Umar. However, it remains clear that the rebels, along with the *anṣār* whom 'Uthman severely alienated, quickly filled the ranks of his political and military base and 'Ali, perhaps out of necessity, readily acquiesced to a number of their demands: most famously the distribution of the funds of the treasury and the dismissal of 'Uthman's governors from the provinces.

The factions that took up arms against 'Ali universally decried his leniency with the rebels and even accused him as equally guilty of 'Uthman's murder. In Iraq, Zubayr and Talha, along with the Prophet's wife 'A'isha, formed a coalition that was swiftly crushed by 'Ali's forces at the Battle of the Camel in 656. 'Uthman's governor, Mu'awiya b. Abi Sufyan, led the Umayyad opposition to 'Ali in Syria. Mu'awiya demanded that 'Ali surrender 'Uthman's murderers to him so that he could determine the murderers' fate, a right he regarded as his by Qur'anic decree due to his status as 'Uthman's next of kin (*walī*; cf. Q. 17:33). After failing to successfully negotiate these demands at Siffin, the armies met in pitched battle. To prevent defeat, the Syrians signaled their desire for arbitration on the basis of the Qur'an by raising sheets (*maṣāḥif*) of the text on the tip of their lances in the midst of the battle. The Syrian and Iraqi factions each put forward a representative arbiter (*ḥakam*) to render a judgment on the dispute.

'Ali's consent to this agreement proved to be his ultimate undoing; the arbiters' decision proved untenable for 'Ali. Rejecting the rebels' claims of 'Uthman's guilt, it buttressed Mu'awiya's claims to pursue vengeance for 'Uthman's death and, therefore, also spurred the Syrians to pledge allegiance to Mu'awiya as caliph in 659. 'Ali's coalition, rather than being galvanized like the Syrians', disintegrated, with large numbers of his followers, later known as Kharijis, censuring the decision as abandoning Qur'anic authority in favor of the decisions of men. They regarded 'Ali's agreement as tantamount to disbelief (*kufr*), crying, "There is no judgment but God's [*lā ḥukma illā li-llāh*]!" After attempts at reconciliation, 'Ali eventually met, defeated, and massacred this group at Nahrawan in 658, though at a considerable cost to his coalition's morale. Mu'awiya could subsequently act aggressively as a rival caliph rather than a rebel governor, seizing swaths of territory in Egypt, Arabia, and even Iraq. A Khariji assassin, Ibn Muljam al-Muradi, murdered 'Ali as he plotted to remobilize his forces against Mu'awiya to avenge the deaths of his companions at Nahrawan.

Sharif al-Radi (d. 1015) collected the political orations, discourses, and letters of 'Ali in the *Nahj al-Balagha* (Peak of eloquence) that today serves as an authoritative text among Shi'is. It putatively contains many of 'Ali's views on sundry political and religious topics and has been published in numerous English translations.

See also Companions of the Prophet; imamate; Shi'ism; succession

Further Reading

Asma Afsaruddin, *Excellence and Precedence: Medieval Islamic Discourse on Legitimate Leadership*, 2002; Sean W. Anthony, *The Caliph and the Heretic: Ibn Saba' and the Origins of Shī'ism*, 2011; Martin Hinds, "The Siffin Arbitration Agreement," *JSS* 17, no. 1 (1972); I.K.A. Howard, trans., *Kitāb al-Irshād, or The Book of Guidance into the Lives of the Twelve Imams by al-Shaykh al-Mufīd*, 1981; Wilferd Madelung, *The Succession to Muḥammad*, 1996; Erling L. Petersen, *'Alī and Mu'āwiya in Early Arabic Tradition*, 1974; Abu Ja'far Muhammad b. Jarir al-Tabari, *The Community Divided (The History of al-Ṭabarī*, vol. 16), translated by Adrian Brockett,

1997; Idem, *The First Civil War* (*The History of al-Ṭabarī*, vol. 17), translated by G. R. Hawting, 1996; Maya Yazigi, "'Alī, Muḥammad, and the *Anṣār*: The Issue of Succession," *JSS* 53, no. 2 (2008).

SEAN W. ANTHONY

Aligarh

Located some 77 miles southeast of Delhi and 46 miles north of Agra, where the Taj Mahal stands, Aligarh underwent significant transformation after its conquest in 1801 by the British, who justified the conquest as the populace's liberation from an "intolerable yoke of oppression." In 1864, the British laid the railway line in Aligarh, dividing it into two: the old part, called *shahr* (town), and the new part, called the Civil Lines. Prior to the British conquest, the Civil Lines was largely uninhabited. When the British arrived, they built cantonments and bungalows there. The Civil Lines further developed when Sayyid Ahmad Khan founded the Muhammadan Anglo-Oriental (MAO) College, a "Muslim Cambridge," there in 1875. In 1920, the MAO College flowered into Aligarh Muslim University (AMU). The Civil Lines thus emerged as a small town with elites drawn from diverse locations. It symbolized colonial-aristocratic modernity. The district administrative buildings, court, railway station, post office, and so on were all in the Civil Lines. In the 20th century, the Civil Lines became famous worldwide for its university and the *shahr* for its locksmithing industry. With MAO College's foundation, Aligarh became a key network of what David Lelyveld has called "Muslim solidarity." For Indian Muslims under colonialism, Aligarh emerged as a crucial venue for multiple and diverse dialogues with their coreligionists, coinhabitants, the West, and the Muslim world. In particular, it became a vehicle for conversation with modern science and education. As the dialogues were diverse, so were the participants who belonged to many ideological shades.

Described by Fazlur Rahman (d. 1988) as the central figure of "Muslim modernism," Khan intended to orient Muslims toward a Western education. He sought to do this first by translating European knowledge into Indian languages. To this end, he formed the Scientific Society in 1866 and launched a journal called the *Aligarh Institute Gazette*. Later, he realized that Muslims could progress only when they directly acquired knowledge of the Western sciences. On his return in 1870 to India from a 17-month trip to Britain, Khan launched an Urdu journal called *Tahzibul Akhlaq* (Rectifying the morals). Its aim was to advocate social and educational reform of Muslims. It also issued a call to establish a college for Muslims. Khan hoped that the graduates of MAO College would "preach the gospel of free inquiry, of large-hearted toleration and of pure morality." The MAO College—its doors open to students of all faiths—began with four students, but enrollment increased every subsequent year. The first graduate was a Hindu, Ishvar Prasad. To attract more Muslim students to the college, in 1886 Khan established the pan-Indian Mohammadan Education Conference, held at a different place each year, where intellectuals such as Deputy (Dipti) Nazir Ahmad (1836–1912) delivered lectures and recited poems and representatives from all provinces passed resolutions.

Religion played an important role in the boarding houses of MAO College. Most students observed the daily prayers voluntarily. With Theodore Beck as the principal of MAO College, prayers were made mandatory, and punishments were introduced for not performing them. The annual ritual of Eid (the festival marking the end of Ramadan, the month when Muslims observe daylong fasting) was observed; so was the celebration of the Prophet's birthday (*mawlid*). The Turkish fez was part of the college uniform. These religious observances went hand in hand with the secular Western ones: observing the queen's birthday, participating in or attending debating clubs, and playing or watching cricket matches.

MAO College received both applause and criticisms at once. In a couplet, Akbar Allahbadi (1846–1921) worried that Khan's college would douse the students' Muslimness: "Thank God, they [students] attained much qualification / But alas they did not remain Muslim." In the novel *Ibnul Waqt* (Son of the moment/time), Nazir Ahmad satirized Khan's Westernism. In contrast, Altaf Husain Hali (1837–1914), who later wrote Khan's biography, applauded his mission and its outcome. He exhorted his readers to come to Aligarh College if they wanted to see a fine example of Hindu-Muslim friendship.

Notably, Aligarh became an important center of Urdu, which Muslims regarded not simply as a cosmopolitan language or literature but also as a rich, vibrant culture. But the dominant image of Aligarh—shared by the majority community (across ideological divides) as well as the enthusiasts for Pakistan—is as a center of "Muslim separatism" because, according to the popular assumption, it led and supported the movement for the creation of Pakistan in 1947. The established frameworks that construe Aligarh as a center of "separatism" (by Indian nationalists) or the birthplace of "Muslim nationalism" (by Pakistani enthusiasts) only show the extent to which our language is captive to nationalist sentiment. A different description is due—perhaps that of Rashid Ahmad Siddiqi, a noted Urdu litterateur: "Aligarh is neither a paradise nor a hell . . . it is a world where everyone has the freedom to make their own paradise or hell."

Although a trend in revisionist history within South Asian scholarship has questioned the discourse of "separatism," it continues to prevail. In postcolonial India, Aligarh became the symbol of the struggle for Muslim identity. The Indian state constantly sought to "nationalize" AMU by eradicating its Muslim minority character. Aligarh also became a site of activism to protect the Urdu language, which successive governments had tried to undermine. While the majoritarian nationalists rendered Urdu as a "foreign" language, for people such as Siddiqi, "Urdu's name is also Aligarh" (meaning how Aligarh and Urdu are inseparable from each other). Given the conjunction of such factors, Aligarh is seen, especially by the majoritarian nationalists, as a "mini-Pakistan" within the nation-space

of India: a place of "national infidelity" where Muslims supposedly nurse, secretly if not publicly, sympathy for Pakistan. In 1998, Mahmudur Rahman, then vice chancellor of AMU, said that AMU was "bristling with ISI [Pakistan's Inter-Services Intelligence] agents." Since September 11, 2001, this image only sharpened, partly because the president of the Student Islamic Movement of India (SIMI), an organization banned by the state on allegations of terrorism, was an AMU alumnus, and SIMI was headquartered in Aligarh until the early 1980s. However, such prejudiced images of Aligarh—abundant in popular media of all hues (print, visual, English, or vernacular)—seldom depict how Muslims in Aligarh experience their lives in their full complexity and diversity.

See also India; madrasa; modernism; Sayyid Ahmad Khan (1817–98)

Further Reading

Irfan Ahmad, *Islamism and Democracy in India: The Transformation of Jamaat-e-Islami*, 2009; David Lelyveld, *Aligarh's First Generation: Muslim Solidarity in British India*, 2003; Khaliq Ahmad Nizami, *Secular Tradition at Aligarh Muslim University*, 1991; Jamal Muhammad Siddiqi. *Aligarh District: A Historical Survey from Ancient Times to 1803 AD*, 1981; Rashid Ahmad Siddiqi, *Maghribi Ta'lim ka Tassawur aur uska Nifaz 'Aligarh men*, 1993.

IRFAN AHMAD

alliances

In tribal pre-Islamic Arabia, alliances (*ḥilf*) sometimes supplemented or even replaced common descent as a force holding groups together. Alliances were concluded through ceremonies and oaths. Three types may be discerned:

Cooperation between tribal groups for specific military or political purposes. Sometimes a group would act against its own tribe by forming an alliance with outsiders. Alliances also could be formed within the same tribe. The duration of such alliances varied, sometimes outlasting their original specific purpose; occasionally, the parties involved in the alliances took permanent oaths.

General cooperation. Pairs of tribal groups (or sometimes three groups) that were committed to cooperating with each other in a general way were known as "the [pair of] allies." Alliances of this kind sometimes led to a gradual merging of the parties involved.

Attachment of people to descent groups other than their original ones. A small tribal group would be accepted as "guest allies" by a larger, stronger group and sometimes would eventually merge with it. Such "hosting alliances" entailed specific rights and obligations, such as shared legal responsibility and mutual inheritance. Mutual assistance would be given in a variety of circumstances.

Alliances can hardly be considered an Islamic institution. In principle, Islamic solidarity was supposed to exclude groupings within the Muslim community (*umma*) because the whole of the *umma* is supposed to constitute one unified entity; yet historical sources reflect diverse attitudes. The Prophet Muhammad is reported to have been involved in pre-Islamic alliances. He also is reported to have said, "There are no alliances in Islam; but you should adhere to the pre-Islamic alliances." The two parts of this statement are sometimes recorded independently of one another, thus reflecting contradictory attitudes: one banning alliances and the other endorsing adherence at least to the pre-Islamic alliances. In any case, this statement bans new alliances. Some scholars claim that the ban applied only to specific alliances that contradicted Islamic rules and principles, such as the rules of inheritance (in the case of "hosting alliances") and the principle of unity among all Muslims. However, pre-Islamic alliances of all types continued to function in Islamic times, and new alliances were forged, too, regardless of whether they conformed to Islamic principles or not. Modifications of the pre-Islamic institution also occurred. For example, in Islamic times "guest allies" of a given descent group were counted as part of that group for administrative purposes.

The tribal political alliances typical of the Umayyad period (660–750) certainly infringed upon Islamic unity, as they reflected and further caused deep rifts within the community. This was one possible source of the widespread opposition to newly inaugurated alliances. Legal discussions of the subject remained vague. No attempt was made, for instance, to specify legal stipulations for new alliances that would make them conform to Islamic principles.

"Hosting alliances" continued to be established as late as the 13th century. Certain Muslim scholars rejected some or all of the legal effects of such alliances. Instead, they devised a substitute, though only for individuals and only for the purpose of attaching them to Arab groups. This substitute was the contractual relationships between nonagnates called *walā' al-muwālāt*, or *walā' bi-l-ḥilf* (contractual patronate, or patronate by alliance). Apart from that, political and military alliances in the later Middle Ages far exceeded the boundaries of the archaic *ḥilf*, and Muslim sources do not usually refer to them as such. The principle of Islamic unity was constantly violated by elite groups conspiring against governments and Muslim states forming alliances, sometimes with infidels, against other Muslim states. As this phenomenon was unacceptable in theory, Muslim scholars as a rule ignored it.

See also clients; tribalism

Further Reading

R. Amitai-Preiss, *Mongols and Mamluks: The Mamluk-Ilkhanid War 1260–1281*, 1995; J. A. Boyle, ed., *The Cambridge History of Iran*, vol. 5, *The Saljuq and Mongol Periods*, 1968; P. M. Holt, *The Age of the Crusades: The Near East from the Eleventh Century to 1517*, 1986; Idem, *Early Mamluk Diplomacy (1260–1290): Treaties of Baybars and Qalāwūn with Christian Rulers*, 1995; E. Landau-Tasseron, "Alliances among the Arabs," *Al-Qantara* 26 (2005); Idem, "Alliances in Islam," in *Patronate and Patronage in Early and Classical Islam: Origin, Legal Regulations and Social*

Practice, edited by M. Bernards and J. Nawas, 2005; Idem, "The Status of Allies in Pre-Islamic and Early Islamic Arabian Society," *Islamic Law and Society* 13, no. 1 (2006).

ELLA LANDAU-TASSERON

Almohads (1130–1269)

The Almohad (or Mu'minid) dynasty was the first to rule a unified Islamic West (North Africa, excluding Egypt and the Iberian Peninsula) from 1130 to 1269.

The dynasty's first ruler was 'Abd al-Mu'min (r. 1130–63), a Zanata Berber from the area of Tlemcen and the conqueror of what are now Morocco, Algeria, and Tunisia, as well as Andalus (Muslim Spain and Portugal). 'Abd al-Mu'min was a pupil of the Masmuda Berber Ibn Tumart (d. 1130), the founder of the Almohad (Arabic *al-muwaḥḥid*) movement, so-called because of the insistence on God's unity (*tawḥīd*) and the rejection of the anthropomorphist beliefs with which the previous dynasty, the Almoravids, were charged. Characterized as a Mahdi—meaning a messianic figure whose doctrine guaranteed religious certainty and truth—and as the inheritor of the station of prophecy and infallibility (*wārith maqām al-nubuwwa wa-l-'iṣma*), Ibn Tumart paved the way for 'Abd al-Mu'min's adoption of the caliphal title of "Commander of the Faithful" (*amīr al-mu'minīn*), first adopted in North Africa by the Fatimids. After defeating the Arab tribes (Qays 'Aylan) Banu Sulaym and Banu Hilal at Sétif in 1153, 'Abd al-Mu'min incorporated them into the Almohad army to free himself from the original Almohad (mostly Masmuda) tribes whose shaykhs constituted the backbone of the political and military organization. 'Abd al-Mu'min then adopted a Qaysi genealogy that included the Prophet Muhammad and the pre-Islamic Prophet Khalid b. Sinan, which—being a lineage of prophecy—was also a lineage entitled to the caliphate. In order to rule an extended empire, 'Abd al-Mu'min created new political and religious elites, the *ṭalaba* and the *ḥuffāẓ*, who, after having received religious, intellectual, and military training, were sent to all the districts of the empire, charged with teaching Ibn Tumart's creeds and implementing Almohad policies recorded in official epistles, some of which have been preserved. Jews and Christians were forced to convert in the same way that Muslims were obliged to adhere to Ibn Tumart's understanding of true Islam. Changes were introduced in the direction and architecture of the mosques, new formulas were pronounced in the call to prayer, and the square shape came to characterize Almohad coins; all of these signs of the new era were brought on by the Mahdi. The Almohad anti-*madhhab* stance (i.e., rejection of legal discrepancies and therefore of the existing legal schools) led to a rapprochement to Zahirism and Ibn Hazm's legal and doctrinal views. The Almohad caliph's rule was assimilated to God's order (*amr Allāh*).

Under 'Abd al-Mu'min's successors, Abu Ya'qub Yusuf (r. 1163–84) and Abu Yusuf Ya'qub al-Mansur (r. 1184–99), Sufism and philosophy flourished as possible developments of the Almohad reformulation of Islamic doctrinal and political thought, producing the important works of Ibn Tufayl (d. 1185), Ibn Rushd (d. 1198), and Ibn al-'Arabi (d. 1240). Sufis and philosophers, however, were also subject to charges of heresy, with most Sufis emigrating to the Islamic East, as their claims to God's friendship were seen as a threat to Almohad "totalism" (*tawḥīd*). The use of the Berber language declined as the original local focus (the Islamic West as a sort of "new Hijaz") was gradually abandoned in favor of more universalistic tendencies, as shown in Ibn Jubayr's (d. 1217) *Riḥla* (Travels).

Fights against the Christians in the Iberian Peninsula did not succeed in the permanent recovery of lost territories, and the victory at Alarcos (1195) was shortly followed by the defeat at Las Navas de Tolosa (1212) and the loss of Córdoba and Valencia (1236 and 1238) and later Jaén and Sevilla (1248). In North Africa, the Almoravid Banu Ghaniya posed a constant military threat, while internal opponents—sometimes with Mahdist claims—had to be fought. Internal divisions among the Mu'minids and the Almohad elites eventually led to civil strife and even rejection of Ibn Tumart's figure and doctrine. The disintegration of the empire manifested itself in autonomous Hafsid rule in Tunisia and Eastern Algeria (1229) and in the conquest of Marrakesh by the Marinids in 1269, after their occupation of northern Morocco, while the 'Abd al-Wadids carved out a kingdom of their own in western Algeria with their capital at Tlemcen.

See also Almoravids (1056–1147); Ibn Tumart (ca. 1080–1130); Spain and Portugal (Andalus)

Further Reading

P. Cressier, M. Fierro, and L. Molina, eds., *Los almohades: Problemas y perspectivas*, 2005; H. Ferhat, *Le Maghreb aux XIIème et XIIIème siècles: Les siècles de la foi*, 1993; J.F.P. Hopkins, *Medieval Muslim Government in Barbary until the Sixth Century of the Hijra*, 1958; R. Le Tourneau, *The Almohad Movement in North Africa in the Twelfth and Thirteenth Centuries*, 1969.

MARIBEL FIERRO

Almoravids (1056–1147)

The Almoravid dynasty was a Berber (Sanhaja) dynasty that ruled over the extreme Maghrib (now Morocco and part of Algeria) and Andalus (Muslim Spain and Portugal) from the 11th century to the first half of the 12th century. Their name derives from *murābiṭūn*, "performers of *ribāṭ*'," usually interpreted as indicating their links with a fortified convent on the frontiers of Islam, although most likely referring to a way of life that united both spiritual and military discipline.

The Almoravid movement began among Judala and Lamtuna nomads in Southern Morocco and the Sahara who were involved in the salt, gold, and slave trade with West Africa. According to the accepted story, after performing the pilgrimage, a Judala chief asked Abu 'Imran al-Fasi (d. 1039), a reputed Qayrawani Maliki jurist and Ash'ari theologian, to accompany him to the desert to teach his tribesmen. Abu 'Imran refused but recommended he contact his pupil Wajjaj b. Zallu, who lived closer to their settlements. It was Wajjaj's pupil, the Maliki scholar 'Abdallah b. Yasin al-Jazuli, who followed the Judala chief Yahya b. Ibrahim to what is now Mauritania. Ibn Yasin eventually became the politico-religious leader, while Yahya b. 'Umar—from the Lamtuna branch of the Sanhaja—commanded the army.

Under their joint leadership, the Almoravids became the masters of the Sahara and Southern Morocco. Yahya b. 'Umar died in 1056 and was succeeded by his brother Abu Bakr b. 'Umar. Ibn Yasin died in 1058 while fighting the heretical Barghawata Berbers. His successor in religious leadership died shortly after. Meanwhile, Abu Bakr left for the Sahara accompanied by the Qayrawani scholar Muradi (d. 1095–96)—later to become the Mauritanian saint al-Imam al-Hadrami—leaving his cousin Yusuf b. Tashfin (d. 1106) as commander of the army in Morocco. It was under Ibn Tashfin—responsible for the conquest of the rest of Morocco, part of Algeria, and Andalus—that the movement united under a single religious, political, and military leadership, with the capital of the empire established in the newly founded Marrakesh.

Treatment of the Almoravids in historical sources shares many features with that of the Seljuqs, Turkish tribesmen who became the actual rulers of the central Abbasid lands and who were presented as champions of Sunnism with strong links to Sufi shaykhs. Like the Seljuqs, the Almoravids were invited by the ruling powers of the time to take control of the state. In the case of the Almoravids, the Andalusi Taifa kings—unable to stop Christian military advances in the Iberian Peninsula—reportedly asked for Ibn Tashfin's intervention in the Iberian Peninsula. Ibn Tashfin won the battle of Zallaqa (1086) and eventually incorporated Andalus into the Almoravid Empire. The new rulers and their Berber troops were seen by the Andalusis as aliens who inverted the normal rules, with the men veiling their faces—like the Tuaregs—and the women enjoying a high degree of freedom and influence.

Ibn Tashfin and his successors, who claimed a Himyari (Southern Arab) genealogy, adopted the title of "Commander of the Muslims" (*amīr al-muslimīn*) and acknowledged the Abbasid caliphate. The Sevillan Maliki scholar Abu Bakr b. al-'Arabi (d. 1148) was highly influential in this political move, having brought from Baghdad letters from Ghazali, Turtushi (d. 1126), and the Abbasid caliph that legitimized Almoravid rule. According to Abu 'Ubayd al-Bakri (d. 1094), such rule aimed at "propagating truth, repressing injustice and abolishing illegal taxes" (*da'wat al-ḥaqq wa-radd al-maẓālim wa-qaṭ' al-maghārim*). The Maliki jurists played an important religious and political role, with the Almoravid rulers asking for their legal opinions (*fatāwā*) to back their policies. At the same time, interest in Ash'ari theology grew. The Mirrors for Princes genre found fertile ground: Muradi wrote *Kitab al-Ishara fi Tadbir al-Imara* and Turtushi—settled in Alexandria—wrote *Siraj al-Muluk*.

Sufism flourished under the Almoravids to such an extent that those who claimed to be in God's proximity became suspect. Ghazali's works were burned and Sufi leaders with a great following—such as Ibn Barrajan and Ibn al-'Arif—were eliminated. However, the late Almoravid rulers were inclined to portray themselves as "friends of God" (*awliyā' Allāh*).

The Almohads considered the Almoravids heretics because of their alleged anthropomorphism, and they fought the Almoravids in Morocco, conquering Marrakesh in 1147. In Andalus, the weakening of Almoravid power in the fight against the Christians led to the formation of independent polities led by charismatic leaders (such as the Sufi Ibn Qasi), military men, or urban notables (mostly judges). Almohad intervention in the Iberian Peninsula eventually put an end to those new political entities and to the surviving Almoravid rule, with only the Massufa Banu Ghaniya managing to preserve their independence, ruling first in the Balearic Islands and then in Ifriqiya (Tunisia and Algeria).

See also Almohads (1130–1269); Berbers; North Africa; Spain and Portugal (Andalus)

Further Reading

J. Bosch Vila, *Los almorávides*, 1956 (repr. 1990); V. Lagardère, *Les almoravides jusqu'au regne de Yusuf b. Tashfin (1039–1106)*, 1989; Idem, *Les almoravides: Le djihad andalou (1106–1143)*, 1998; N. Levtzion, "'Abd Allah b. Yasin and the Almoravids," in *Studies in West African Islamic History*, vol. 1, edited by J. R. Willis, 1977; H. T. Norris, "New Evidence on the Life of 'Abdullah b. Yasin and the Origins of the Almoravid Movement," *Journal of African History* 12, no. 2 (1971).

MARIBEL FIERRO

Amal

Amal—an acronym for Afwaj al-Muqawama al-Lubnaniyya (the Lebanese Resistance Brigades), which also means "hope" in Arabic—was initially founded as the militia branch of Harakat al-Mahrumin (the Movement of the Deprived) in 1975. The Movement of the Deprived was established in 1974 by the charismatic religious leader Sayyid Musa al-Sadr. Born to an Iranian father and a Lebanese mother in Qum and trained at Najaf, Sadr had come to Lebanon from Iran in 1958. During the 1960s, a rapidly growing urban population of mostly Shi'i poor in Lebanon was mobilized through leftist parties such as the Lebanese Communist Party and the Syrian Socialist Nationalist Party. Sadr began to challenge the leftist parties for the loyalty of Shi'i youth by offering in their stead a movement dedicated to attaining political rights for the underrepresented Shi'is within the structures of the Lebanese state. In 1969,

he founded the Islamic Shi'i Higher Council and later, in 1974, established the Movement of the Deprived.

Although the Movement of the Deprived initially called for greater rights for the politically and economically marginalized in Lebanon, it quickly became a Shi'i movement. Sadr drew on religious symbolism, and especially on the Battle of Karbala and the model of the Prophet Muhammad's grandson Imam Husayn, who was martyred at that battle in 680, to mobilize people and underscore the importance of resistance against oppression. In 1975, as the Lebanese civil war began, he formed Amal as the new movement's military branch.

In August 1978, while on a visit to Libya, Sadr mysteriously vanished, leading to a surge in his popularity. The unexplained nature of his disappearance suggested to many of his followers that he was still alive, and he was simultaneously catapulted into the Shi'i narrative of the Hidden Imam, such that some of his followers awaited his eventual return. That same year, to push back the Palestinian Liberation Organization (PLO) fighters then based in Lebanon, Israel invaded the south, displacing nearly 250,000 people. The initial consequence of these two events was Amal's revitalization, as Amal militiamen fought PLO guerrillas in south Lebanon. Amal's popularity was also fueled by increasing Shi'i perceptions that the Lebanese left had failed both in securing greater rights for the poor and in protecting the south from the fighting between the PLO and Israel.

Following the 1979 Islamic Revolution in Iran and the 1982 Israeli invasion of Lebanon and the siege of Beirut, many prominent members of Amal left the party, accusing it and its leader, Nabih Berri, of having become increasingly involved in patronage politics and detached from the larger struggles against poverty and Israeli occupation. Berri's decision to join the National Salvation Committee, led by Lebanese president Elias Sarkis, in 1982 during the Israeli siege was especially viewed as selling out the resistance. Many of those who left, including Sayyid Hasan Nasrallah, who became Hizbullah's secretary general in 1992, went on to join Hizbullah, the Shi'i militia that gained prominence in Lebanon in the mid-1980s and by the mid-1990s was the most popular Shi'i political party in Lebanon.

Amal, however, persisted and in 2010 was one of the two Lebanese Shi'i-specific political parties led by Berri. Although Amal did not highlight an Islamic ideology in the way that Hizbullah did and never called for the establishment of an Islamic state in Lebanon, a religious undercurrent existed in the party's official statements. Belief in God was highlighted in its founding charter, as was the trope of Karbala and Imam Husayn's martyrdom for the side of good in that battle as a model of resistance against oppression, Lebanese nationalism, and an anti-Zionist stance. Furthermore, Amal continued to highlight its heritage and cast its members as the rightful heirs to Sadr's original movement. In this, Amal competed not only with Hizbullah but also with other social welfare institutions originally founded by Sadr and then led by his sister, Rabab al-Sadr.

See also Hizbullah; Lebanon; Palestinian Liberation Organization (PLO); Shi'ism

Further Reading

Augustus Richard Norton, *Amal and the Shi'a: Struggle for the Soul of Lebanon*, 1987; Idem, *Hezbollah: A Short History*, 2007.

LARA DEEB

anarchism

Anarchism, the idea of abolishing government, has a long tradition in Muslim thinking. In part, the origins of Islamic anarchism can be found in the Qur'an, which is vague on issues of government and political succession. Islamic anarchism began when a large group seceded from the forces of the caliph 'Ali b. Abi Talib (r. 656–61) during the First Islamic Civil War. This group became the Kharijis, whose rallying cry was "judgment belongs only to God." Some of these Kharijis extended this idea to political anarchism. The Kharijis from Najd region, in particular, earned a reputation in early Islamic history for maintaining that the people were obligated and able to uphold God's law without the rule of an imam or other leaders.

The Najdis' rejectionist attitude was kept alive in Islamic discourse over the centuries. Ninth-century Basra was home to Mu'tazili thinkers and also some Zaydi Shi'is who were sympathetic to the Najdi view of government. Ja'far b. Harb (d. 850), a Mu'tazili writer, noted that a belief in anarchy was common among Mu'tazilis of the period. A popular Mu'tazili argument was that since the rulers continually set themselves and their kinsmen as kings, it was better to do away with government altogether. Prominent Mu'tazilis, including al-Asamm (d. ca. 817), Hisham al-Fuwati (d. ca. 833), al-Nazzam (d. between 835 and 845), and 'Abbad b. Sulayman (d. 874), articulated similar views.

The Sunni response was to concede that anarchism was possible in theory but impossible in practice. Later Islamic thinkers accepted this compromise. Ghazali (d. 1111) concluded that government was necessary, but he did not go on to characterize those who held dissenting views as infidels. Later, Ibn Khaldun (d. 1406) agreed with the Mu'tazilis that if people could live by God's law, then there was no need for an imam.

Another anarchist trend within Islam originated with Sufi groups, some of whom preached antiauthoritarian ideas. Their often intentionally vague declarations spoke of the unnecessary nature of state power. These Sufis may have inspired 20th-century Muslim anarchists as well. Sufi groups were often prominent in resistance to state control, as is evident in their involvement with the Chechen resistance to the Tsarist Empire or the North African Arab resistance to the French.

In the 19th century, the ideas of Western anarchists began to circulate in the Arab and Muslim world. The Lebanese writer Butrus al-Bustani, while critical of Western socialism, repeated the observation of previous Muslim thinkers that anarchism was a part

of the political tradition of Bedouin tribes. In the early 20th century, a number of European anarchists and adventurers converted to Islam. A prominent example is the Swiss-Russian adventurer Isabelle Burchart, who converted to Islam in Algeria and became involved with the Sufi resistance to the French occupation. Other examples include the Swedish painter Ivan Agueli and the French cartoonist Gustave-Henri Jossot, who both were part of anarchist circles and hostile to statist Christianity before their conversion. In 2005, Yakob Islam, a British Muslim convert, published the Muslim Anarchist Charter, which calls for the creation of communities in which "peaceful cultural evolution is uninhibited by power, greed, or ignorance." European anarchist converts to Islam found in Sufism a facet of Islam that was nonhierarchical, exemplified anarchist principles, and was a counterbalance to statist Christianity. They also found Islam compatible with the Western anarchist tradition, though they were largely unaware of the doctrines of the Kharijis and Mu'tazilis.

See also government; individualism; libertarianism; shari'a

Further Reading

Patricia Crone, *Medieval Islamic Political Thought*, 2004; Eadem, "Ninth-Century Muslim Anarchists," *Past & Present*, no. 167 (2000); Yakob Islam, *Muslim Anarchist Charter*, 2005; Cecily Mackworth, *The Destiny of Isabelle Eberhardt*, 1977; Elie Adib Salem, *Political Theory and Institution of the Khawarij*, 1956.

JOSEPH HAMMOND

apartheid

The word "apartheid" entered South African politics in the post–World War II years and became an official ideology upon the National Party's victory in the 1948 general elections. Until the first democratic elections of 1994, which brought majority rule to the country, the white National Party ruled the country on the basis of its philosophy of apartheid. "Apartheid" is Afrikaans (a creole language made by European settlers and slaves by the early 19th century) and translates as "separateness" or "apartness." Its defenders argued that blacks were inferior and found biblical justification for these views; thus whites, with a superior civilization, had the right and responsibility to govern over blacks. After the end of apartheid, apologists argued that it had simply expressed a badly implemented belief in cultural autonomy for the separate groups that made up the country.

The National Party of Prime Minister D. F. Malan, from 1948 until the end of apartheid rule, implemented policies of separate and unequal development that radically discriminated against the country's majority nonwhite population. Later administrations refined the legal and administrative practices by which apartheid was implemented. Apartheid entailed a series of laws such as the prohibition of marriage between whites and nonwhites, residential segregation and the appropriation of nonwhites' property by whites, a register that classified the population into "races," and other practices that seriously discriminated against the majority population. Apartheid also gave support to an exploitative economic system based on cheap labor, especially in the important mining sectors, and continued an extensive process of land dispossession in rural and urban areas. Although apartheid became the official ideology of the state only from the late 1940s, in many ways it had been the practice of the previous governments as well.

Given the cold war context in which it emerged, the major Western powers never condemned the apartheid state; instead, it was a Western ally in the sub-Saharan region. The apartheid state developed very close ties with Israel. Egypt and Lebanon were the only Arab states with representation in South Africa, but they cut ties with South Africa in the 1950s, and the Arab bloc countries came to be major supporters of the antiapartheid movement. *Al-niẓām al-'unṣuriyya*, which is how apartheid came to be translated into Arabic, was heavily attacked in the Arabic media, not least for its connection to Israel. However, the Shah's Iran maintained close ties to South Africa until the revolution of 1979, and Turkey never cut its ties with South Africa. Other Muslim states kept a safe distance from the apartheid state. Informal networks, however, existed with the country's Muslim population.

Apartheid was provided with significant legitimacy by the Dutch Reformed Church, and the country was conceived as a "Christian country" ruled by Christian values and led by believing Christians. Opposition to apartheid was routinely dismissed as communist inspired and anti-Christian in origin. The country's small Muslim population was largely classified as "Malay" or "Indian" and, in most cases, lived among the urban-based, nonwhite working class and small middle class. The Muslim religious leadership taught that, since Muslims were a minority and were allowed to practice their basic religious duties, they should not engage in antiapartheid political campaigns. Indeed, Muslims could build mosques, make the call to prayer, take days off for the religious festivals (*'īd*), perform the annual pilgrimage to Mecca, and so forth. However, there was a long history of Muslims articulating various forms of resistance to segregation policies.

Opposition to apartheid by the black majority became increasingly radical throughout the 1950s, and eventually an armed struggle was launched in the early 1960s. Muslims were involved in all the major campaigns. But a response against racial discrimination based in the teachings of Islam took root among the youth only in the later 1950s, becoming more radical and finding a larger following with the 1976 countrywide student uprising until the end of apartheid. Imam Abdullah Haron, a young activist imam at a Cape Town mosque, represented this opposition to apartheid on firmly Islamic grounds. He was ultimately killed by the police while in detention in 1969. After his death, a series of Islamic initiatives addressed the apartheid question as a necessary issue for South African Muslims on explicitly Islamic grounds. Political action was an integral part of the faith as prayer was.

Islamic views of social justice, explicated in English translations of works by Sayyid Qutb and Abul al-A'la Mawdudi, were popular in the 1980s. After the Iranian revolution, the ideas of 'Ali Shari'ati, the Iranian thinker who had produced a body of thought founded on Islam and Marxism, circulated in the country. These ideas went beyond a condemnation of racial discrimination and also comprised a critique of class inequality and, later, of gender-based discrimination.

See also South Africa

Further Reading

William Beinart, *Twentieth-Century South Africa*, 2001; Deborah Posel, *The Making of Apartheid, 1948–1961: Conflict and Compromise*, 1991; Muhammed Haron, *Muslims in South Africa: An Annotated Bibliography*, 1997; Abdul Kader Tayob, "Muslims' Discourse on Alliance against Apartheid," *Journal for the Study of Religion* 3, no. 2 (1990).

SHAMIL JEPPIE

apocalypse

Deriving from the New Testament's *Apocalypse* or *Book of Revelation*, the first work to bear such a generic designation, the term "apocalypse" refers to dire and violent happenings that presage the end of the world, and/or consummation of the divine plan, as well as to the end of the world itself. Scholarship in religious studies over the last 50 years suggests that apocalypse is a complex literary and social historical phenomenon that comprises three separate categories intimately related in history and individual religious experience: eschatology, social movement, and literary genre. The Islamic instance provides an instructive example of how these three modes or manifestations of apocalypse influence one another and then separate into self-contained categories once again.

Islamic eschatology is clearly apocalyptic in form and content, focusing as it does on ultimate judgment of the wicked and the good, another world, an end to time, and so on. In his trailblazing work *Muhammad et le fin du monde* (Muhammad and the end of the world), Paul Casanova recognized a distinct and characteristic eschatological vision in the Qur'an and identified in it two major relevant moments corresponding with the Meccan and Medinan phases of the Prophet's career. In the first, Muhammad expects the imminent end of the world and warns his audience about it, while in the second, the responsibilities of the newly formed Islamic community divert his attention from preoccupation with the world's end, which causes him to focus on the welfare of the community. The Qur'an nonetheless remains permeated with eschatological motifs and scenarios, and these are, perhaps somewhat unequally, spread over these two traditional periods of revelation. The end time of the world and the end time of the Muslim community or individual are somehow conflated. Individual salvation or damnation replaces concern with the actual end of the world. The apocalyptic vision frames Qur'anic eschatology and conditions the entire text, regardless of specific topic or subject otherwise at hand. Key Qur'anic terms such as the hereafter (*al-ākhira*), paradise (*al-janna*), and hell (*jahannam*) are pertinent markers of apocalypse as eschatology. Even more important is "the [approaching] Hour" (*al-sā'a*), or "the Appointed Time," a phrase that appears 48 times in the Qur'an. The hour is inevitable (Q. 40:59) and cannot be delayed or hastened (Q. 35:12). Its time is known only to God (Q. 43:85). Nonetheless, the heavens and the Earth are even now "heavy" with the hour (Q. 7:187). The approaching event, however designated, is a prominent topic in both Meccan and Medinan suras, where, together with descriptions of paradise and hell, it ranks as one of major themes of the Qur'an. Among the most dramatic events associated with the hour, synonymous with impending occurrences referred to as *al-amr* (the cause), *al-wāqi'a* (the event), *al-qiyāma* (the resurrection), and *al-qāri'ah* (the calamity), are the following: the splitting of the moon (Q. 54:1), a massive earthquake accompanied by mass terror (Q. 22:1–2), disbelievers surrounded by clouds of fire (Q. 39:16), mountains crushed and scattered "like carded wool" (Q. 20:105; 27:88; 52:10; 56:5; 70:9; 101:5), the Earth illuminated by divine light (Q. 39:69), the presence of all previous prophets (Q. 39:69), the broadcasting of the deeds of all humankind (Q. 39:69), universal judgment and dispensing of justice (Q. 39:69), believers' entrance into paradise, and polytheists' abandonment by their gods (Q. 30:12–16). In addition, many hadith reports attributed to the Prophet speak of the nearness of the hour in greater detail, sometimes including specific dates. Such a focus in Islam's scripture is naturally and inevitably linked to those numerous messianic or apocalyptic movements that have been a feature of Islamic history from the very beginning, eventually emerging also from Sunni, Shi'i, and Sufi traditions. The apocalyptic, messianic, and visionary-cum-experiential élan of the Qur'an and the hadith is such that numerous "Islamicate" individuals, groups, and movements continue to derive their identities and orientation in direct reference to it to the present day.

The early Islamic community has a remarkable affinity with the type of religious community (e.g., Qumran) classified in the literature as apocalyptic. The factions that emerged after the Prophet's death also employed and exploited the rhetoric of apocalypse: proto-Shi'is, with their multiple fissiparous developments, and their opponents. Muhammad's preaching was interpreted as involving the establishment of a saved community in an Islamic iteration of the Abrahamic theme of a divine remnant (*baqiyyat allāh*; Q. 11:86). Quite apart from the portents of the end found frequently in the short "hymnic" suras of the Qur'an, the hadith literature also portrays an urgent expectation of an end to history that must be faced by the community. A dramatic example of this is the "booth like the booth of Moses" hadith, which features the Prophet instructing two of the faithful not to bother making overly sturdy mosques of brick and wood but rather counseling them to use more convenient thatch structures because the apocalypse (*al-amr*) was

due to happen at any moment. In the history and development of subsequent apocalyptic social and military developments, there is remarkably scant concern with the Qur'an itself as a reflection or source of an apocalyptic ethos (see Cook).

A significant stratum of post-Qur'anic apocalyptic literature focuses on events in the five holy cities of Jerusalem, Alexandria, Antioch, Constantinople, and even Rome—something that may indicate a vision among early Muslim groups of the conquest of all Christendom in one triumphant gesture. Much apocalyptic and messianic lore is used as validation, sometimes post-eventum, for the major political dynasties of Islam, including the Umayyads, the Abbasids, the Fatimids, the Ottomans, the Safavids, and others. Likewise, groups and movements who disputed the authority of such triumphant religiopolitical powers all relied to one degree or another on a specific interpretation of Qur'anic *apocalyptica*, especially with regard to eschatology and the centerpiece of Islamicate religious authority: the institution known as *walāya*, a complex term that suggests numinous presence, devotion, and guardianship as well as political, moral, and spiritual authority simultaneously with allegiance to this same authority. Such apocalyptic historical movements include the Kharijis, the 'Uthmanis, the Kaysanis, the Qarmatians, the Khurramis, some of the activities of Hallaj (d. 922) and his followers, the Abbasid revolution (749–50), the Hurufis, the Nuqtawis, the Sarbadarids, the Ni'matullahis, the Shaykhis, the Babis, the Baha'is, the Mahdi of Sudan, the Ahmadis, the Iranian Revolution (1978–79), al-Qaeda, and others. So pronounced and pervasive is this feature of Islam that it stimulated various apocalyptic and messianic movements among Jews and Christians within the abode of Islam. It was not only the marginalized of Islamicate society who sought to calculate the precise time of the end of the world and to offer descriptions, based on the Qur'an and the hadith, of the events that will accompany it, but also such prominent figures, among others, as Kindi, Ghazali, Suhrawardi, Ibn al-'Arabi, Ibn Taymiyya, Ahmad Sirhindi, Sayyid Qutb, Mawdudi, and Ayatollah Khomeini. Of course, contemplation of such themes and imagery need not result in a political or historical vision, and many of the mystics of Islam offered a more purely existential and personal interpretation of such material.

There is almost a perfect fit between the contemporary theory of apocalypse (see Collins) and the Qur'an text (see Lawson, *Gnostic*). The Qur'an is as much about revelation as it is about God or His prophets, so it may be viewed as a kind of meta-apocalypse, one that is conscious of itself and in which it is, in fact, the main character of the revelatory communication. In the Qur'an, several interrelated subthemes are markers of the apocalypse as a literary genre. Perhaps the most important is the agency of the angel in the process of revelation. Some others include the interplay of duality and opposition (the *enantiodromia* of the church fathers), revelation, glory, justice, history and its periodization, story, otherworldly beings, and paradise. Typological figuration is a potent Qur'anic literary device by which the apocalyptic élan of the Qur'an is expressed, whether in relation to itself and its immediate audience or through taking account of previous religious history to demonstrate that Muhammad's mission is of the same order of authority and vision as previous messages. In this way, the Qur'an functions as a commentary on previous scripture in much the same way that the New Testament functions as a commentary on the Old Testament. Apocalypse also involves an overall atmosphere or voice of urgency and intensity that characterizes both the delivery and reception of the revelation (see Lawson, "Duality")—the sense of being on the verge of something, as if waking from a dream, when the supralogical device of typological figuration engages with the imagination of the audience. Time collapses, the voice of the Qur'an is heard as the message of all prophets, and the impending reckoning is yet another in a cycle. This cyclical pattern of apocalypse is demonstrated in the Qur'an through the stories of several previous prophets and their communities. An excellent example is in the Qur'an's narrative about the communities of 'Ad and Thamud and their prophet Salih. In this story, there occurs a great mysterious scream or cry that is heard by 'Ad and Thamud symbolizing the irruption of the divine into the world to call it to account (see Stetkevych). It dramatizes the nearness of the overwhelming, divine power that is "closer than the jugular vein" (Q. 50:16) yet simultaneously utterly remote: "its like is not comparable to anything" (Q. 42:11; 112:4). In a fine example of serene self-consciousness, the Qur'an calls this the divine presence (*sakīna*, e.g., 48:4, 26; 9:40), a complex notion involving tranquility and the occasional aid of invisible hosts. It descends, according to the tradition, with the chanting of the Qur'an, and it is seen to have much in common with the descent of other powers and energies, such as the angels and the spirit mentioned in connection with the Night of Power (*laylat al-qadr*; Q. 97). The Qur'an presents an articulation and dramatization of many, if not all, of the themes and phenomena associated with the genre of apocalypse, and this category of religious expression and action was not only an integral part of the mission of the Prophet and the life of his movement but also a formative feature of various historical Islamic societies' major forms of thought, social rhythms, and political and spiritual institutions.

See also messianism; Qur'an; utopia

Further Reading

Suliman Bashear, "Early Muslim Apocalyptic Materials," *Journal of the Royal Asiatic Society* 3, no. 1 (1991); Shahzad Bashir, *Messianic Hopes and Mystical Visions: The Nūrbakhshīya between Medieval and Modern Islam*, 2003; Norman O. Brown, "The Apocalypse of Islam," *Social Text*, no. 8. (1983–84); Paul Casanova, *Mohammed et la Fin du Monde: Étude critique sur l'Islam primitif*, 1911–24; John J. Collins, *The Apocalyptic Imagination: An Introduction to the Jewish Matrix of Christianity*, 1989; David L. Cook, *Studies in Muslim Apocalyptic*, 2002; Todd Lawson, "Duality, Opposition and Typology in the Qur'an: The Apocalyptic Substrate," *Journal of Qur'anic Studies* 10, no. 2 (2008); Idem, *Gnostic Apocalypse in Islam: The Literary Beginnings of the Babi Movement*, 2010; Jaroslav Stetkevych, *Muhammad and the Golden Bough: Reconstructing Arabian Myth*, 1996.

TODD LAWSON

apostasy

Apostasy is the abandonment of Islam either by a declared desertion in favor of another religion or by a clandestine rejection of Islam often combined with the secret practice of another religion. From the earliest period of Islamic law in the seventh century, Muslim jurists agreed that apostasy bears the death penalty. During the early period, however, jurists also developed legal institutions to circumvent this harsh punishment. These institutions set the standard for what counts as apostasy from Islam so high that before the 11th century practically no judgment of apostasy could be passed. This changed during the 11th century, when jurists lowered the criteria that prevented the death penalty from being applied. In the following centuries, judges could interpret the law in various ways, setting either high or low criteria for punishing apostates from Islam.

The Qur'an does not mention the case of explicit rejection of Islam after conversion. However, it does address the assumed clandestine apostasy of a group of people at Medina called *al-munāfiqūn* (the hypocrites). No worldly penalty is ordained for them so long as they refrain from rebellion, but harsh punishments are proclaimed for them in the afterlife. In the Qur'an (49:14), a group of Bedouins is described as Muslims but not believers. This led to lively discussions of the criteria for being a Muslim, understood in terms of legal membership in the Islamic community, versus being a believer (*mu'min*), understood as someone deserving otherworldly salvation.

The dispute about the meaning of "Muslim" and of "*mu'min*" is one of the subjects that led to the First Islamic Civil War (656–61). One party, the Kharijis, claimed that committing a capital sin (*kabīra*) reveals unbelief (*kufr*). A group of radical Kharijis felt justified in killing grave sinners as unbelievers and thus legitimated the killing of the third caliph, 'Uthman b. 'Affan (r. 644–56). At about the same time, Muslims agreed that the penalty for apostasy from Islam should be death. This judgment is based on the authority of a hadith of the Prophet that states, "Whoever changes his religion is to have his head cut off." After the Kharijis lost the civil war, the various groups of their enemies, who dominated the early development of Islamic law, were terrified by the prospect of Muslims killing each other over accusations of apostasy and worked to abate the harsh punishment prescribed in the hadith.

Early Muslim jurists agreed that actions other than the explicit rejection of belief in Islam could not constitute apostasy. To commit a sin could not be an act of apostasy. Apostasy was regarded as the declared rejection of Islam and could only be sufficiently established after a person accused of apostasy had rejected three offers to repent and return to Islam. The legal institution of the "invitation to repent" (*istitāba*) is mentioned neither in the Qur'an nor in the hadith. In early Islamic law, it nevertheless became a necessary condition for convicting an apostate. It safeguarded that an accused apostate had a chance to return to Islam, to fully avert punishment, and to be reinstated in all rights as a Muslim. Subsequently, only those Muslim apostates who openly declared their abandonment of Islam and who maintained their rejection in the face of capital punishment could be punished.

Most early jurists understood that the general application of *istitāba* effectively ruled out any penalty for apostasy. They allowed persons accused of apostasy to declare their return to Islam even when it was understood to be nominal. This became the accepted position in the early Hanafi and Shafi'i schools of law. Their views fitted well into a situation during the eighth and ninth centuries when conversion to Islam happened collectively and often only nominally. Malik b. Anas (d. 795), the founder of the Maliki school of law, ruled differently, saying that *zanādiqa* (which could be translated as "heretics") should not be given the right to repent and could thus be killed straightaway. What he meant by *zanādiqa* here is not entirely clear. Later Maliki jurists understood it to mean clandestine apostates—in other words, people who broke away from Islam but still paid lip service to it in order to avoid punishment. Some Maliki jurists went still further and applied this judgment even in cases when the apostasy was only implied—for example, when a person expressed opinions that were deemed contrary to Islam. This ruling meant that the Maliki school of jurisprudence was, in practice, less tolerant of heterodox Muslim views than others. It allowed Maliki jurists to apply the death penalty against accused apostates who had never explicitly abandoned Islam. In some cases, heterodox views were regarded as evidence of clandestine apostasy.

During the 11th century, the consensus of the Hanafi and Shafi'i jurists regarding the general application of the "invitation to repent" broke down. Hanbali jurists had already argued that some points of religious doctrine were so central to the Muslim creed that a violation should be regarded as apostasy from Islam and punished by death. During the mid-11th century, scholars from all schools argued that in the case of the political agents of the Isma'ili-Shi'i countercaliphate, no "invitation to repent" should be granted and the agents could be killed as apostates even if they repented. This view was shared by the influential Shafi'i jurist Ghazali (d. 1111), who wrote systematically about the criteria of apostasy and developed the judgment of apostasy into a legal tool that could be used to pass capital punishment on Muslims who held views that violated central elements of the Muslim creed.

After the 11th century, Muslim jurists had a choice between applying either the tolerant rules of the early Islamic period aimed at preventing the application of the judgment of apostasy or the rules established by Ghazali and others that allowed the application of the judgment even in cases where the apostasy was not openly declared. While the Hanafi school, for instance, generally maintained the early, tolerant principles, the other three schools of Sunni law were open to the stricter application.

In the modern period, Muslim fundamentalist thinkers like Mawdudi justified the death penalty for apostasy from Islam. Mawdudi compared it to the punishment of high treason in, for instance, the British legal system. The judgment of apostasy played an important role in the attempts of radical fundamentalist groups

such as the Egyptian al-Gama'a al-Islamiyya to legitimate violence against the state and its representatives. In the recent past, there have also been cases in which fundamentalist Muslims applied the judgment of apostasy in its stricter interpretation against secular or liberal thinkers in Islam.

See also excommunication; Faraj, Muhammad 'Abd al-Salam (1954–82); al-Gama'a al-Islamiyya; Ghazali (ca. 1058–1111); hadith; Mawdudi, Abu al-A'la (1903–79)

Further Reading

Frank Griffel, "Toleration and Exclusion: al-Shāfi'ī and al-Ghazālī on the Treatment of Apostates," *Bulletin of the School of Oriental and African Studies* 64, no. 3 (2001); Sherman A. Jackson, *On the Boundaries of Theological Tolerance in Islam: Abū Ḥāmid al-Ghazālī's Fayṣal al-Tafriqa bayna al-Islām wa al-zandaqa*, 2002; Abu al-A'la Mawdudi, *Punishment of the Apostate According to Islamic Law*, translated by Syed Silas Husain and Ernest Hahn, 1994; Rudolph Peters and Gert J. J. de Vries, "Apostasy in Islam," *Die Welt des Islams* 17, no. 1 (1976).

FRANK GRIFFEL

Arab nationalism

"Arab nationalism" (*al-qawmiyya al-'arabiyya*) conventionally refers to the belief that, by virtue of their common history, language, and culture, the Arabs constitute a single nation whose political destiny can only be realized by uniting their divided people into one single, sovereign, national state. The political doctrine of Arab nationalism is thought to have emerged in reaction to imperial despotism during the late Ottoman Empire before being confounded by British and French machinations at the time of World War I, when the region was carved up into separate subnational states. Arab nationalism experienced a revival during the 1940s and 1950s in the romantic nationalist ideologies of Sati' al-Husri (d. 1968) and the Ba'th Party and the anticolonial nationalism of Gamal Abdel Nasser. Yet following the collective failure of the Arab nations to prevent the territorial expansion of Israel in the Six Day War of 1967, Arab nationalism has largely been considered a spent force. National identities attached to local states seem to have superseded Pan-Arabism. When revanchist movements do exist, they are couched in the language of Islam, not secular nationalism. While Arab nationalism can be understood either as a consciously articulated political doctrine or as an objective expression of an essential and immutable sociocultural truth, these are not the only options, as recent sociological work has shown.

The first generation of Western scholars to study Arab nationalism was largely concerned with accounting for its origins as a cultural movement during the late Ottoman Empire and tracing its evolution into a fully fledged doctrine of nationalism by the 1940s. Historians such as Albert Hourani, Nikki R. Keddie, and Sylvia G. Haim adopted an implicitly idealist view of nationalism, which led them to focus on intellectual production in their search for the precursors of nationalist consciousness. Works by intellectuals, reformers, and literary writers in Syria and Lebanon during the cultural renaissance of the late 19th century provided the first hints of a distinctly Arab identity. Increased educational activity by Christian missionaries from the United States, France, and Russia sparked new interest in reinvigorating Arabic literature: belles-lettrists such as Butrus al-Bustani (d. 1883) and his contemporaries opened the door to innovation by editing dictionaries, compiling encyclopedias, and adapting the Arabic language to suit the demands of scientific discoveries made in Europe. Cultural salons and literary clubs, which sprang up in Beirut and other cities in the 1860s and 1870s, became a key channel for the dissemination of a revived Arab identity that became increasingly valuable as a way to mobilize against the despotic policies of Sultan Abdülhamid (d. 1909) and the trend toward the increasing Turkification of the Ottoman Empire. In addition to the secular, mostly Christian writers of the *Nahḍa* (Awakening), Islamic reformists such as Afghani and Muhammad 'Abduh were similarly identified as protonationalists. According to this narrative, nationalism was essentially an idea imported from Europe and then adapted to suit conditions local to the Arab world.

Arab nationalists writing in the 1940s and 1950s took a dim view of the notion that they had "borrowed" their political doctrine; to them, their Arab identity was so deeply rooted in their culture that it was almost biological. Husri is perhaps the most influential advocate of the thesis that the Arabic language formed the essence of the historical Arab nation. Husri argued strongly against the French theory of a voluntaristic, civic nationalism and espoused a romantic, organic view of the nation derived from German philosophers such as Johann Gottlieb Fichte and Johann Gottfried Herder. The appeal of German nationalist theories can partly be explained by the reaction against Britain and France following their dismemberment of the Arab body politic after World War I. Husri's writings did much to popularize the idea that nations were natural features of human society: unique groups united by ancient ties of blood and race. Such notions had a profound influence on Michel 'Aflaq, a founder of the Ba'th Party. Gamal Abdel Nasser, however, understood Arab nationalism in more pragmatic terms: for him it was less a cultural or spiritual entity than a political instrument to mobilize support for his position as head of state. The unification of Egypt and Syria (1958–61) proved to be a disastrous experiment, permanently dividing Nasser and the Ba'thists and splitting the Arab nationalist movement. The Arab defeat of 1967 and Nasser's death in 1970 seemed to mark the defeat of nationalist dreams of Arab unity by the harsh truths of real-world politics.

While earlier narratives of Arab nationalism were based on this idealist-materialist divide, since the 1980s this dichotomy has been rejected in favor of a more nuanced sociological approach. The revisionist narrative of Arab nationalism is inspired by works such as Ernest Gellner's *Nations and Nationalisms* (1983) and Benedict

Anderson's *Imagined Communities* (1991), which propose that nationalism is the product not of a particular intellectual genealogy but of a particular configuration of modern sociological processes. These processes include urbanization, modern education, industrialization, the conjunction of the printing press and capitalism, and the modern representational technologies of cartography and census-taking. Gellner and Anderson's "modernist" approach implies that a focus on elites is misplaced: Middle East scholars such as James Gelvin, Israel Gershoni, and Keith Watenpaugh show how the nation is instead produced through the everyday practices of the popular classes. This new wave of writing inscribes both subaltern agency and the oft-overlooked decade of the 1920s into the old narrative of Arab nationalism.

While much of this work focuses on the creation of local rather than Pan-Arab nationalisms (e.g., Joseph Massad's *Colonial Effects* [2001]), it also highlights that practices of nationalism can simultaneously serve apparently contradictory ends. Local state nationalism does not necessarily oppose broader, suprastate identities, whether religious or ethnonational. From this perspective, the consolidation of local national identities need not entail the retreat of Arab nationalism. Indeed, recent work on the proliferation of satellite and Internet communication across the Arab world argues that this new transnational space is giving rise to a revived (and considerably revised) understanding of the "Arab nation." Only by attending to what nationalism means to a given population—rather than applying 19th-century formulas—can we even begin to assess the state of contemporary Arab nationalism.

See also Ba'th Party; nationalism; Pan-Islamism

Further Reading

James L. Gelvin, "Modernity and Its Discontents: On the Durability of Nationalism in the Arab Middle East," *Nations and Nationalism* 5, no. 1 (1999); Albert Hourani, *Arabic Thought in the Liberal Age*, 1962; Israel Jankowski and Israel Gershoni, eds., *Rethinking Nationalism in the Arab Middle East*, 1997; Bassam Tibi, *Arab Nationalism: Between Islam and the Nation-State*, 1997.

DANIEL NEEP

Arafat, Yasir (1929–2004)

For four decades, Yasir Arafat served as a leader and a symbol of the Palestinian national cause. His rise to prominence paralleled the ascendancy of the Palestinian National Liberation Movement (Harakat al-Tahrir al-Watani al-Filastini), known commonly as Fatah. Arafat cofounded Fatah in 1959 with other Palestinian university students and activists, all of whom had become refugees during the war of 1948 to 1949. Arafat's significance lies in his legacy as leader of the Palestinian national movement. From 1968 to 1969, Fatah took control of the Palestinian Liberation Organization (PLO), a body originally established under the auspices of the Arab League and intended as a means to sublimate and thus control Palestinian nationalist sentiments. As a result of the takeover, Arafat became the chairman of the PLO and thereby acquired diplomatic recognition, at least initially among Arab states, as the leader of the Palestinian people. From this platform, Arafat projected a distinct interpretation of what it meant to be Palestinian and, in doing so, established the terms of political identity for all other competing movements, including Pan-Arab nationalists and Islamists.

In contrast to Pan-Arabists, Arafat insisted on the priority of independent action, particularly through armed struggle, to (1) catalyze a specifically Palestinian nationalist identity among the dispersed and fractured Palestinian communities and (2) provoke wider Arab involvement by capturing the imagination and sympathy of the Arab masses. Pragmatic to the core, Arafat worked with individuals and groups espousing diverging orientations—from Islamism to secular nationalism and Marxism. The sole criterion for cooperation was shared commitment to liberating the territories lost in 1948.

The Six Day War of June 1967 proved decisive in the definitive rise of Fatah and the approach it advocated. The war left Pan-Arabism and its state sponsors in disarray. Fatah, at Arafat's urging, stepped into the gap by organizing armed cells within the territories newly occupied by Israel. Although tactically ineffective, Fatah-led guerrilla attacks inspired a generation of Palestinian youths to align with the movement and its message of Palestinian self-assertion. Appearing consistently in military fatigues, with a pistol at his side and a scruffy beard on his face, Arafat quickly became the symbol of this newfound empowerment.

Exploiting its growing prominence, Fatah took control of the PLO from 1968 to 1969. Soon after, the Palestinian National Council (PNC), the PLO's governing body, elected Arafat chairman of the executive committee, the organization's main day-to-day decision-making unit. He held that position continuously and later assumed the presidency of the Palestinian National Authority (PNA) until his death in 2004.

Under Arafat, the PLO became a state-in-exile that worked to integrate the dispersed Palestinian constituencies. Arafat enticed political competitors into the organization, using a combination of patronage, allocation of seats in the PNC, and coercion to maintain cohesion. He also cultivated the backing of prominent families and personalities as well as religious groups. He reserved positions in the PLO for Christians and integrated Muslim Brotherhood activists by, for example, promoting "Islamic Fatah" (Fath al-Islam) in 1969.

Increasingly, Arafat moved to centralize decision-making authority, forging a "neopatrimonial" style of leadership that fused loyalty to the national cause with loyalty to the PLO chairman as father of the nation. This development accompanied Arafat's gradual embrace of diplomacy and a two-state solution. The shift coincided with key events—particularly, the first Intifada (1987–93), the mass uprising against the Israeli occupation that brought to prominence a new generation of PLO and Islamic movement activists within the Occupied Territories, and the Oslo Peace Process (1993–2000), a diplomatic initiative that rehabilitated the external PLO leadership

and created quasi-state structures for the Palestinians in the West Bank and Gaza Strip—leading to the creation of a PNA in circumscribed areas of the West Bank and Gaza Strip.

This same period saw the rise of the Islamic Resistance (Harakat al-Muqawama al-Islamiyya), also known as Hamas. Shunning absorption into the PLO, Hamas sought to return Palestinians to the original, uncompromising vision of total territorial liberation. In doing so, Hamas effectively subordinated global Islamic solidarity to national concerns: the liberation of Palestine was the necessary first step toward the *umma*'s revivification—an assertion that echoed Fatah's inversion of the Pan-Arabist hierarchy of solidarity three decades earlier. By the late 1980s, any movement seeking legitimacy among Palestinians had to justify its raison d'être in the terms set by Arafat and the Fatah-led PLO.

The PLO-Israel negotiations collapsed violently in 2000. In response, Israel systematically crippled PNA institutions and placed Arafat under extended siege in his Ramallah headquarters—a building, known as "*al-muqāṭa'a*," which once housed the local British Mandate administrative offices and prison and continued to serve the same purpose during the Jordanian annexation (1948–67) as well as during the period of direct Israeli occupation after 1967. On October 29, 2004, after contracting an unspecified illness, Arafat was flown to a French military hospital, where he gradually fell into a coma and never recovered. He was pronounced dead on November 11, 2004. Fatah's hold on Palestinian politics rapidly dissolved shortly thereafter. In January 2006, Hamas won Palestinian Legislative Council elections and 18 months later routed Fatah forces from the Gaza Strip entirely.

See also Hamas; Palestine; Palestinian Liberation Organization (PLO)

Further Reading

Yasser Arafat, "Palestine at the United Nations: The Speech of Yasser Arafat," *Journal of Palestine Studies* 4, no. 2 (1975); Idem, "Vision of Coexistence," *Presidents & Prime Ministers* 3, no. 4 (1994); Rex Brynen, "The Neopatrimonial Dimensions of Palestinian Politics," *Journal of Palestine Studies* 25, no. 1 (1995); Alain Hart, *Arafat: A Political Biography*, 1984, reprinted 1989; Barry M. Rubin and Judith Colp Rubin, *Yasir Arafat: A Political Biography*, 2003; Yezid Sayigh, *Armed Struggle and the Search for State: The Palestinian National Movement, 1949–1993*, 1997; Janet Wallach and John Wallach, *Arafat: In the Eyes of the Beholder*, 1990, reprinted 1997.

LOREN D. LYBARGER

arbitration

Arbitration, as a privatized system of justice, was virtually the only form of justice known to the pre-Islamic Arabs. Confirmed by the Qur'an, it continued to be recognized as a valid means of dispute resolution after the advent of Islam. The Prophet Muhammad's position at Medina was modeled at least in part on that of the pre-Islamic arbiter appointed to settle intertribal disputes. For Sunnis, arbitration was available even if a government-appointed judge was available to hear the dispute. For the Twelver Shi'is, arbitration could take place only if an imam was present. Upon the occurrence of his occultation (*ghayba*), arbitration was no longer possible.

The best-known incident involving arbitration in Islamic history occurred during the Battle of Siffin (657), when Mu'awiya sought to escape defeat at the hands of 'Ali b. Abi Talib by suggesting that the two warring parties submit their differences to binding arbitration for resolution. According to most reports, Mu'awiya appointed 'Amr b. al-'As as his arbitrator, while 'Ali appointed Abu Musa al-Ash'ari. The two arbitrators were charged with resolving the dispute between the two parties in accordance with the teachings of the Qur'an. Traditional accounts of the arbitration present a picture of a cunning 'Amr b. al-'As, who was able to take advantage of the less sophisticated Ash'ari to enhance substantially the prestige of Mu'awiya at the expense of 'Ali, even if the result of the arbitration was inconclusive. Perhaps because of the inconclusive nature of this early attempt to use arbitration to resolve political disputes within the Muslim community, it appears that later generations of Muslim rulers never again attempted to resolve political disputes using arbitration. According to Qalqashandi, later Muslim dynasts looked at the arbitration between 'Ali and Mu'awiya as providing the model for peace treaties between rival Muslim rulers. It was the practice of later Muslim rulers, in connection with the assumption of solemn obligations toward their political rivals, to secure their obligations by oaths of divorce, manumission, and other penalties against the ruler in the event he violated his undertaking. One such example is the succession of Amin and Ma'mun to the caliphate of their father, Harun al-Rashid. The terms of the succession agreement were enforceable by oaths of divorce, manumission, and even excommunication.

While all four surviving schools of Sunni law recognized arbitration as valid, they differed regarding the scope of an arbitrator's jurisdiction and the legal effect of an arbitrator's judgment. For the Hanafis, the Shafi'is, and the Malikis, the authority of an arbitrator in principle derived from the will of the private persons who had appointed him. Accordingly, the arbitrator's jurisdiction was generally limited to matters amenable to the private resolution of the disputing parties, in other words, disputes involving claims of money. For the same reason, the parties of the dispute could withdraw from the arbitration at any time prior to the arbitrator's judgment.

The Hanafis, however, did not recognize the finality of an arbitrator's judgment: if the enforcing court disagreed with the outcome, it could reverse the arbitrator's verdict. For the Malikis, Shafi'is, and Hanbalis, in contrast, an arbitrator's verdict—assuming it was otherwise legal—had the same force as a judgment issued by a state-appointed judge and consequently could not be reversed simply because the judge would have applied a different rule. Malikis, de facto, and Hanbalis, de jure, in contrast to the Hanafis and Shafi'is, were willing to give arbitrators powers that exceeded the powers of the parties to the dispute. According to the Hanbalis, an arbitrator

could hear all legal claims, including cases involving marriage, divorce, and canonical punishments (*ḥudūd*). While Malikis held that an arbitrator had no original jurisdiction to hear such claims, should an arbitrator exceed his jurisdiction and rule on those cases, his rulings would be enforced to the extent that they were substantively correct. If the arbitrator attempted to enforce such rulings, however, he could be criminally liable for exceeding his jurisdiction.

As a general rule, an arbitrator needed to have the same qualifications as a judge, but, as in the case of the arbitrator who exceeded his jurisdiction, the Malikis were willing to enforce the judgment of female arbitrators, arbitrators who were slaves, or arbitrators who were hostile to one of the disputing parties, on the condition in each case that the decision was substantively correct, even if in principle only free males who were neutral could serve as arbitrators. These relaxed procedural and jurisdictional principles were no doubt a reflection of the fact that the parties themselves chose the arbitrator, in contrast to the judge, whose jurisdiction was not subject to the parties' consent.

See also difference of opinion; succession

Further Reading

Fatima Muhammad al-'Awa, *'Aqd al-Tahkim fi al-Shari'a al-Qanun*, 2002.

MOHAMMAD FADEL

Ash'aris

Founded by Abu al-Hasan al-Ash'ari (d. 935), the Ash'ari tradition is considered one of the most influential theological schools of Sunni Islam. In his famous *Muqaddima* (Prolegomena), the historian Ibn Khaldun (d. 1406) gives a succinct sketch of how Ash'ari theology is generally viewed in Sunni Islam. According to him, the Ash'ari tradition represents the golden mean between extreme traditionalism and rationalism on one hand and determinism and free will on the other.

Ash'ari doctrine emerged against a background of debate between traditionalists, such as Ahmad b. Hanbal (d. 855), and rationalists, such as the Mu'tazilis and the early Hanafi legal scholars. One of their main disagreements was over the interpretation of ambiguous verses (*āyāt mutshābihāt*) in the Qur'an, such as those that attribute anthropomorphic characteristics to God. The traditionalists called for *tafwīḍ*, or the avoidance of interpreting these verses and of any attempt to tackle complex metaphysical problems, pointing to the example of the early Muslims (*al-salaf al-ṣāliḥ*), who had supposedly restricted themselves to the literal meaning of the Qur'an and traditions attributed to Muhammad. The rationalists held interpretation (*ta'wīl*) to be necessary, claiming that this method had been employed by Muhammad's Companions, especially in connection with textual ambiguities and the application of the Qur'an to problems without precedent in the Prophet's life. Ash'ari took a middle position, neither rejecting interpretation nor counseling the avoidance of it. Rather, he accepted it within the limits set by other verses of the Qur'an and the tradition of the Prophet, thereby ensuring that its result would be traditional.

Another problem between Mu'tazilis and the traditionalists concerned free will. The traditions credited to the Prophet are overwhelmingly determinist, or indeed predeterminist, and determinism was also represented in other theological schools, such as that of Jahm b. Safwan. Determinists (*jabriyya*) held that God was the creator of all acts and that His omnipotence was incompatible with the freedom of the human agent. By contrast, Mu'tazilis argued that the human being has both the capacity (*qudra*) and the will (*mashī'a*) to act and that determinism was incompatible with God's justice (*'adl*)—for, as all agreed, humans were responsible for their own actions and would be punished or rewarded for them in the hereafter. Ash'ari argued that actions are created by God and then acquired (*muktasab*) by the human agent; God creates them in an atomistic manner on the basis of a temporary will in the human agent, and the human agent acquires the result of these actions thanks to that will. God remains the ultimate cause of good and evil, but the ambiguity of the theory of acquisition (*kasb*) made a later thinker such as the famous theologian and heresiographer Shahrastani (d. 1153) classify Ash'ari as an intermediate determinist.

Ash'ari's position on dialectical reasoning (*kalām*) has been much debated. In two books (*Kitab al-Luma'* [Flashes of insight] and *Risala Istihsan al-Khawd fi 'Ilm al-Kalam* [The epistle on applying critical examination in theology]), he seems to endorse dialectical reasoning, but in another (*Kitab al-Ibana 'an Usul al-Diyana* [The book of elucidation on the principles of religion]) he seems to oppose it in full agreement with the traditionalist Ahmad b. Hanbal. Later Ash'aris held him to have endorsed the use of dialectical reasoning, sometimes arguing that his apparent rejection of it in the *Ibana* represents an early traditionalist phase that he later abandoned in favor of acceptance of his mature view—namely, that dialectical reasoning was valid and that interpretation could be practiced within the limits set by the tradition. Famous Ash'ari scholars such as Juwayni (d. 1085), Ghazali (d. 1111), and Fakhr al-Din al-Razi (d. 1208) all practiced the dialectical method.

The political position of the Ash'aris is that of the Sunnis at large: the first four caliphs are accepted as legitimate and exemplary, the law remains valid even under wrong-doing rulers, all rulers must be obeyed as long as this does not entail the violation of divine commands, and keeping the community together and rightly guided is more important than ensuring the rectitude of person in temporary control of it.

See also free will; Mu'tazilis; theology

Further Reading

Richard M. Frank and Dimitri Gutas, *Early Islamic Theology: The Mu'tazilis and the Ash'aris: Texts and Studies*, 2007; Daniel Gimaret, *La Doctrine de al-Ahs'arī*, 1990; George Makdisi, "The Ahs'arī and the Ash'arites in Islamic Religions History I," *Studia Islamica* 17 (1962); Idem, "The Ahs'arī and the Ash'arites in

Islamic Religions History I," *Studia Islamica* 18 (1963); Richard J. McCarthy, *The Theology of Al-Ahs'arī*, 1953; Harry Wolfson, *The Theology of the Kalam*, 1979.

AHMED ABDEL MEGUID

'Ashura'

'Ashura' refers to the tenth day of Muharram, the first month of the Islamic calendar, when Husayn b. 'Ali, the third Shi'i imam and the grandson of the Prophet Muhammad, was martyred at Karbala, Iraq, in 680. Husayn was on his way from Medina to Kufa, the former capital of 'Ali's caliphate, where local supporters had invited him to lead them as their imam. 'Ubaydallah b. Ziyad, the Umayyad governor of Kufa, feared a rebellion and sent troops to stop Husayn's caravan at Karbala before it reached Kufa. He ordered his commanders to make clear to Husayn that he had no choice other than to pledge allegiance to Yazid, the second Umayyad caliph (r. 680–83). Though his party was prevented from reaching water in the Karbala desert and his followers were so few in comparison with the Umayyad troops, Husayn rejected submission to the Umayyad caliph, whom he viewed as a usurper caliph and, consequently, an illegitimate ruler. After some days, on 'Ashura', 72 males (from Husayn's 6-month-old baby to a 75-year-old man) were killed by Umayyad troops. The women and children were taken as prisoners to Yazid's palace in Damascus, the capital of the Umayyad caliphate, where Zaynab, Husayn's sister, confronted and shamed Yazid in a memorable speech. She is therefore known as the messenger of 'Ashura'.

Shi'i devotees throughout the world mourn on 'Ashura' to commemorate and lament the martyrdom of Husayn and his companions at Karbala. The ceremonies, which often begin on the first day of Muharram, culminate on the 10th day, and continue until the 12th day, involve (with some differences from place to place) dramatic processions in which the participants chant "O Husayn!" and other slogans; beat their breasts; strike their backs with chains; carry massive devotional displays; perform other gestures associated with mourning, such as strewing the head or face with dust or mud; and stage elaborate passion plays, or reenactments of the events leading up to the martyrdom and the Battle of Karbala itself. The open, organized commemoration of 'Ashura' began under Mu'izz al-Dawla in Baghdad in 964, after the Shi'i Buyids had established dominance in Iraq (945–1055). Not long after, 'Ashura' rituals became popular in Cairo under the Fatimids (969–1171), and they have been popular ever since in areas where Shi'is form a significant part of the population. In some environments where the community includes large Sunni and Shi'i groups, 'Ashura' has often been a time when sectarian violence can flare up, leading to fights and riots. Buyid Baghdad, for example, witnessed scores of such riots on 'Ashura', some of which resulted in fires that burned large quarters of the city, and similar outbreaks of violence have taken place in modern Iraq and Pakistan. Some Sunni groups in some areas of the world, such as Syria and Egypt, have developed traditions of celebrating on 'Ashura' that include eating particular delicacies as a way to advertise Sunni identity and spite the Shi'is, whereas other Sunnis in other parts of the world, such as in Afghanistan, retain traditions of fasting, reading the Qur'an, or visiting cemeteries on 'Ashura'.

Husayn's martyrdom has retained a strong symbolic significance in Islamic history, especially for Shi'is, who have used it as a marker for their distinct identity within the Islamic world and as ideological grounds for their religiopolitical movements. The commemoration of 'Ashura' stresses the iniquity of tyrannical rule and Shi'i existence as an oppressed minority. In addition, it stresses the failure of Husayn's supporters from Kufa—the Shi'is—to come to his aid. Very soon after the Battle of Karbala, rebellions and resistance against the Umayyad caliphate emerged that adopted the memory of Karbala as a rallying cry, including the rebellion of the Penitents (*Tawwābūn*), led by Sulayman b. Surad al-Khuza'i in 684; the rebellion of Mukhtar al-Thaqafi in 685; and many other revolts in the name of descendants of 'Ali. 'Ashura' has therefore often lent itself to a contemporary political interpretation, supporting a potential uprising against any political system that is viewed as unjust.

See also Husayn b. 'Ali (626–80); Karbala; martyrdom

Further Reading

Mahmoud Ayoub, *Redemptive Suffering in Islam: A Study of the Devotional Aspects of 'Āshūrā in Twelver Shiism*, 1978; Gustave E. von Grunebaum, *Muhammadan Festivals*, 1951; Sayyid Jafar Shahidi, "The Significance of 'Āshūrā in Shī'ī History," in *Shī'īte Heritage: Essays on Classical and Modern Traditions*, edited and translated by L. Clarke, 2001.

ALI-AHMAD RASEKH

Asia. *See* Central Asia; Southeast Asia

astrology

Astrology deals with the observation of celestial phenomena for the purpose of explaining past, present, and future events on Earth. It is based on the assumption that the movement of the celestial bodies has an influence on the sublunar world and that this influence can be observed and used for prognostication. Such prognostications might be used for private purposes. In the context of politics

in Islam, they have helped in decision making and have been an important tool for propaganda.

The science of astronomy and astrology was highly developed in the medieval Islamic world. Astronomers, including Jews, Christians, and Muslims, drew extensively on the scientific traditions of both the Greeks and the Indians but made significant advances to the practice, including correcting the Ptolemaic model of the planet's orbits or proposing heliocentric models of the solar system. Major observatories were built in Baghdad, Maragha, Samarqand, Istanbul, and Jaipur, and extensive programs of astronomical observations were carried out and recorded in tabulations. The use of astronomy to determine the correct direction of prayer (*qibla*) and precise prayer times for different geographical regions caused it to gain acceptance with religious scholars, too.

Astronomy proper usually was not sharply distinguished from astrology. One of the main employment opportunities for the scientists who investigated the heavens was as astrological advisors to rulers, charged with predicting the outcomes of important decisions and determining propitious times for important undertakings. Astrological predictions were generally disapproved by Sunni scholars, while the Shi'i position toward astrology was more favorable.

Astrology is divided into two main branches: individual astrology and mundane astrology. Individual astrology deals with the fate of a single person, while mundane astrology focuses on the fate of the entire world, or at least the fate of a region or town. Changes of rulers and dynasties also fit under the rubric of mundane astrology. Individual astrology includes nativities, interrogations, and elections. Nativities are horoscopes cast at the moment of birth that are used to predict general aspects of a newborn's life. These predictions might be refined every year by birthday horoscopes. Astrologers also answer specific questions of their clients (interrogations/*masā'il*) regarding, for example, the fate of a missing husband or the whereabouts of a runaway slave. *Katarchai* (elections/*ikhtiyārāt*) serve to determine the best timing for undertaking or beginning such actions as marriage or travel. All three types of horoscopes were used not only by ordinary men but also by officials and rulers. Thousands of birth horoscopes for princes have been cast in the history of the Islamic world. Some of these horoscopes were collected in a kind of family album, while others constitute entire books, sometimes lavishly produced, with up to more than 350 pages. The birth horoscope of Iskandar Sultan, a Timurid ruler of Shiraz, even contains a circular miniature showing the zodiac and the planets at the moment of his birth. Such extensive birth horoscopes usually predict the future importance and glory of the prince. They were presumably produced long after the fact, following the accession of the prince in question. This was certainly the case not only with the birth horoscope of Iskandar Sultan but also with the four different birth horoscopes of the Mughal emperor Akbar the Great (r. 1556–1605) given in the *Akbarnama*. Predicting his religious and political reforms, they were completed only after the implementation of his reform program and therefore clearly served propagandistic aims.

Katarchai were often used in the context of political decision making. They helped to decide when to hold a coronation, when to set out for a campaign, when to enter a town, when to break ground for a construction project, and especially when to begin a battle. The events so determined varied in importance. Cairo owes its name (*al-Qāhira* in Arabic, meaning "the Conquering One") to the ascendant position of Mars, *qāhir al-aflāk* (Subduer of the Heavens), at the moment the city walls were raised at the order of Caliph Mu'izz (953–75) shortly after the Fatimid conquest of Egypt in 969. In contrast, many rulers did not even go on a hunt without consulting their astrologers. Some of a ruler's responsibility was thus delegated to the astrologer, who was to blame in case of failure. Under such dynasties as the Ottomans and the Safavids, the court astrologers, and particularly the chief astrologer (*munajjimbāshī*), were consulted constantly for propitious dates to begin campaigns, conclude treaties, make diplomatic overtures, and even receive guests. The standard procedure was for the chief astrologer, or a group of several court astrologers, to propose a couple of dates from which the sovereign would choose the most fitting. Some rulers shared the misgivings of the pious or religious scholars with regard to astrology. The Ottoman sultan Abdülhamid I (1774–89) refused to delay setting out on a military campaign when his astrologer cautioned him to wait for a more propitious time, remarking that his affairs were in the hands of God, not the stars. He was in the decided minority among the other members of the dynasty, as the chief astrologer was a trusted and influential advisor for many of them. His namesake, Sultan Abdülhamid II (r. 1870–1909), was so dependent on the advice of his chief astrologer, Ebu al-Huda, that he would not meet an ambassador or make any administrative decision without consulting him. Ebu al-Huda reportedly increased his influence with the assistance of an accomplice in the telegraph office who would reveal to him the messages from the provinces before delivering them to the sultan. Ebu al-Huda would immediately present predictions about affairs in the provinces to Abdülhamid II, and the telegrams would inevitably prove his "predictions" correct, reinforcing the sultan's belief in his abilities. The astrologer fell out of favor only when he failed to predict the revolution of the Young Turks in 1908 and, condemned for high treason, was incarcerated on an island in the Sea of Marmara.

In the field of mundane astrology, the annual return of the sun to the vernal equinox at the New Year underlies all calculations. The years are not equally important, however, but are grouped into so-called World Years. These World Years are fixed periods of time that divide history into cyclically returning segments of similar length. The beginning of each new World Year indicates an important event such as the ascension of a new dynasty, and the horoscope of the corresponding vernal equinox is of foremost importance for prognostication. The most common of these World Years depends on the conjunction of Saturn and Jupiter, which happens about every 20 years. Great conjunctions, which are time cycles of approximately 240 years, result from grouping together 12 to 13 of these conjunctions depending on their location in the zodiac. Great

conjunctions are the unit most frequently used in mundane astrology, although cycles (*dawr*, *adwār*) of 360 years and other time intervals were also taken into consideration. The political relevance of these cycles results from their association with specific regions, religions, and ethnic groups. According to this doctrine, the people, the religion, and the region of the actual cycle dominate politics and society during their interval of time. The fate of rulers and dynasties and especially their impending end was therefore predicted with the help of this theory, but as periods of 240 years are too long to be very useful for political propaganda, cycles of 360 years and 240 years and subdivisions of both were intermixed. By this combination, the number of potentially significant vernal equinoxes was considerably increased.

Mundane astrology, which was widespread in the Late Sasanid Empire, probably gained popularity in the Islamic world with the rise of Iranian influence after the Abbasid revolution. Astrological arguments were frequently used in the context of anti-Abbasid or anti-Arab propaganda and eschatological expectations. The need to confront such propaganda on equal footing might initially have been the strongest incentive on the Arab side for tackling the foundations of astrology. The discipline was more or less unknown in pre-Islamic Arabia, where the stars were observed mainly for information on the seasons and guidance in the desert. After the Arab conquest, pro-Iranian restoration movements referred to astrological arguments for claiming that the end of Arab dominance was near. In the *Kitab al-Dawr al-'Utaridi* (The book of the cycle of Mercury), a cyclic world history based on the theory of conjunctions and *adwār*, predictions of the final collapse of the Abbasid dynasty in the year 1001 went together with expectations of the end of Arab rule and a return of Iranian supremacy. Such ideas were especially popular with the Isma'ili, and they proved long-lived: in the 16th century, we still find speculations about the beginning of eschatological times, which were based on the approach of a Great Conjunction. The Safavid ruler Shah 'Abbas I took these predictions of an impending change so seriously that he resigned for three days at the ominous date and had himself replaced by a Nuqtawi shaykh, who was killed afterward. The title *ṣāḥib-qirān* (Lord of the Auspicious Conjunction), attributed to Tamerlane (r. 1370–1405) and later to Shah Jahan (r. 1627–58), as well as the tendency to correlate the birth date of important rulers with specific Saturn-Jupiter conjunctions also testify to the enduring importance of conjunctional astrology.

Political astrology lost its outright importance in the Islamic world only at the end of the 19th and the beginning of the 20th century. Its persistence in private context is unknown.

See also knowledge

Further Reading

Edward S. Kennedy and David Pingree, *The Astrological History of Masha'allah*, 1971; Fatemeh Keshavarz, "The Horoscope of Iskandar Sultan," *Journal of the Royal Asiatic Society of Great Britain & Ireland* 2 (1984); Eva Orthmann, "Circular Motions: Private Pleasure and Public Prognostication in the Nativities of the Mughal Emperor Akbar," in *Horoscopes and Public Spheres: Essays on the History of Astrology*, edited by Günther Oestmann, H. Darrel Rutkin, and Kocku von Stuckrad, 2005; George Saliba, "The Role of the Astrologer in Medieval Islamic Society," *Bulletin d'Etudes Orientales* 44 (1992); Sergei Tourkin, "The Horoscope of Shah Tahmasp," in *Hunt for Paradise: Court Arts of Safavid Iran 1501–1576*, edited by Jon Thompson and Sheila R. Canby, 2003; Keiji Yamamoto and Charles Burnett, *Abū Ma'šar on Historical Astrology: The Book of Religions and Dynasties (On the Great Conjunctions)*, 2 vols., 2000.

EVA ORTHMANN

asylum

The concepts of asylum and sanctuary go back to antiquity, especially among the Egyptians, Greeks, and Phoenicians. Migration, sanctuary, and asylum are perennial features of religion. Almost every prophet of the world's religious traditions experienced abandonment, displacement, or exile. Hospitality toward strangers was a deep source of pride in pre-Islamic Arab and Bedouin cultures, and solidarity with one's neighbors was necessary for survival in the harsh Arabian desert. According to the Qur'an, the Ka'ba (meaning "cube" in Arabic—a place of prestige and honor) in Mecca was built by the Prophet Abraham and his son Ishmael as the first house to be dedicated solely to the worship of God. The Ka'ba was a sanctuary because God established a sacred precinct (*ḥaram*) around it. Violation of a person's claim to immunity within the sacred confines of the Ka'ba was considered a sacrilegious act. The concept of asylum in Islamic thought developed out of earlier frameworks of sanctuary in Judaic, Christian, and Arab custom and practice and the specific experiences of the Prophet Muhammad himself.

Pre-Islamic Arab custom recognized various rights and duties related to asylum, as seen in the concepts of *istijāra*, which is the requesting of protection of a benefactor on the grounds of proximity (a form of territorial asylum), and *ijāra*, which is the granting of protection by the benefactor in such a case. This culture of granting asylum was built on the ideals of Arab morality, driven by honor, chivalry, bravery, and generosity—qualities celebrated in pre-Islamic Arabic poetry. The Prophet Muhammad preached in this cultural milieu, and despite the Meccans' disapproval of his message, Muhammad was, for many years, protected from danger by *'aṣabiyya* (clan solidarity); any harm to Muhammad against the wishes of his powerful uncle Abu Talib would have dishonored his entire clan, the Banu Hashim, and would have provoked serious reprisals.

Many verses in the Qur'an address the imperative of active resistance to oppression and advocate, when that is not possible, migration to more peaceful lands (4:97, 100; 16:41; 22:58–59). In addition, two significant events in early Islamic history led to the development and institutionalization of asylum within the precepts of Islamic law. Around 615, in response to early persecution of the

Muslims in Mecca, Muhammad instructed some of his followers to migrate (as *muhājirūn*, or migrants) to the lands of the Christian king, or Negus, of Abyssinia. Overwhelmed by the Negus's generosity, a group of Meccan ambassadors, bearing numerous gifts, attempted to convince him to extradite the Muslims to Mecca. The Negus's magnanimous response and his rejection of the ambassadors' request are thought to have had a profound impact on the development of the legal sanctity of asylum in the Constitution of Medina and subsequent Islamic law. Following the death of Abu Talib, the Meccans' hostility toward the prophetic mission could no longer be contained, and the Prophet Muhammad lost the protection of his own clan. When it became clear that the fledgling Muslim community would not be viable in Mecca, Muhammad and his followers emigrated to and sought refuge in the northern Arabian city of Yathrib (present-day Medina), where they were warmly received by the *anṣār*, faithful Islamic partisans who resided in that town. This migration, called the hijra, marks the beginning date of the Islamic calendar.

The institution of asylum in Islam is founded on two central principles: *amān* (safety), or a grant of protection, guarantee of safety, or pledge for safe passage, and *dhimma* (pact), an agreement extending temporary or permanent protection to those requesting it. Asylum is a legal right and duty in Islamic law. Any person within the territory of Islam (called *dār al-islām*, or the abode of Islam), and not just state elites as in modern times, was capable of offering protection to a *musta'min* (beneficiary of safeguard), rendering the *musta'min* sacred and inviolable for a minimum of a year. This action was considered part of the ethical obligation to honor a guest. The *musta'min* had full rights to protect life, family, religion, and property; to undertake economic activity; and to marry people of beneficiary status. A *musta'min* who wished to reside in *dār al-islām* after a year's time was transferred to the status of *dhimma* (permanent guest). *Dhimma* is often called perpetual *amān*, a duty of protection incumbent on all Muslims and the Muslim state. Within the spirit of Islamic law, the concept of *amān* and the sacred rights afforded to the *musta'min* mandated the rule of nonextradition. Islam was one of the first political and religious systems to adopt the principle of nonrefoulement (protection of refugees fearing for their lives) and the prohibition on extradition for all political émigrés.

Contemporary application of international law divides asylum seekers into various categories, including refugees, stateless persons, internally displaced persons, asylum seekers, returners, and persons at risk of displacement, and endows them with differing rights. While some migrants traverse borders freely under peaceful conditions, the "forced migrant" (*muhājir*) is the migrant displaced by war or strife (i.e., on account of violence, political or religious persecution, or instability). The universalist message of Islam facilitated the granting of equal rights to all migrants under Islamic law, with some provisions for those who had committed crimes in their former lands.

The development of the principles of *amān* and nonextradition were likely influenced by the early Muslim experience in Abyssinia. Islamic thought on the issue of asylum was also built on the general Islamic principle of respect for difference—toleration and generosity toward all people regardless of race, religion, nationality, and gender—expressed, for example, in the verse of the Qur'an that prohibits compulsion in religion (2:256) and in the final sermon of the Prophet Muhammad concerning the unwavering humanity of all people. Voluntary repatriation, or the breaking of *amān* before the end of a year, was only possible by the spontaneous decision of the *musta'min* or by proper and sufficient notice of the benefactor.

Islamic ideology and indeed the spirit that characterized the Islamic golden ages in Spain and India, for example, were premised on the sacredness of asylum and justice. The Mogul Emperor Akbar (r. 1556–1605) in India advanced progressive policies toward his disparate population through the ideals of unity and ecumenical spirit. A great deal of Islamic history was marked specifically by a lack of xenophobia; the political subject of Islam was, for the most part, comfortable with difference. One model of this respect for difference was the Constitution of Medina (622), which attempted to bridge the various Muslim and Jewish groups of Medina under a single community structure. Another model was the Convention of Najran (632), which ensured the Christians of Najran protection and freedom from humiliation. This spirit is quite unlike that of the modern-day nation-state, which attempts to regulate with mechanical precision the inflow and outflow of strangers. The 1981 Universal Islamic Declaration of Human Rights, especially article 9, was a contemporary attempt to mandate a rule consonant with the Islamic rule of asylum.

See also abodes of Islam, war, and truce; hijra

Further Reading

Muddathir Abd al-Rahim, "Asylum: A Moral and Legal Right in Islam," *Refugee Survey Quarterly* 27, no. 2 (2008); Ahmed Abou el-Wafa, *The Right to Asylum between Islamic Shari'ah and International Refugee Law: A Comparative Study*, 2009; Ghassan Maarouf Arnaout, *Asylum in the Arab-Islamic Tradition*, 1987; Khadija Elmadmad, "Asylum in Islam and in Modern Refugee Law," *Refugee Survey Quarterly* 27, no. 2 (2008); Volker Turk, "Reflections on Asylum and Islam," *Refugee Survey Quarterly* 27, no. 2 (2008).

MELISSA FINN

Atatürk, Mustafa Kemal (1881–1938)

Mustafa Kemal Atatürk was the founder and first president of the Republic of Turkey. Born in Salonica to a middle-class Muslim Ottoman family, he graduated from the Royal Military Academy in Istanbul in 1902 and from the Staff Officer College, also in the capital, in 1905. Like many cadets, he developed a sympathy for the Young Turk movement and participated in some clandestine activities.

After graduating from the Staff Officer College, he was briefly arrested in connection with a plot against the life of the sultan and was then assigned to serve in Damascus, far from the capital of Istanbul. There he made some attempts to establish an opposition society. He also participated in the work of Ottoman dissidents in his hometown of Salonica, where they founded the Ottoman Freedom Society, a major opposition organization, in 1906. A year later, the society merged with the Paris-based Ottoman Committee of Progress and Union and became its internal headquarters and power base within the Ottoman military. These organizations played a decisive role in carrying out the Young Turk Revolution of 1908.

Following the revolution, Mustafa Kemal became an important figure in the military ranks of the Ottoman Committee of Union and Progress (CUP) as a protégé of Major Cemal Bey (who later became a pasha, or general). Immediately after the revolution, the CUP dispatched him to Tripoli of Barbary to quell the disturbances there. In April 1909, he served on the staff officer committee of the Action Army that marched on to Istanbul to crush the counterrevolution. Despite these important contributions, his relationship with the CUP leadership was strained by statements he made against direct intervention by the military in politics. In 1911, he volunteered for service in Tripoli of Barbary to organize a local militia against the Italian invasion and served in Darnah, the capital of Cyrenaica, for less than a year. Upon his return to the capital, he participated in the later stages of the Balkan Wars and then assumed the post of military attaché in Sofia. The Ottoman Empire's entry into World War I prompted his return to active military service, where he gained fame for his successes at Gallipoli in 1915. He later served on the Ottoman eastern front and accompanied the Ottoman heir apparent during a visit to Germany in 1917–18.

At the time of the surrender in October 1918, Mustafa Kemal was in Aleppo trying to organize an orderly retreat of Ottoman forces. The harsh terms imposed by the Entente powers on the empire, followed by the Greek occupation of İzmir in May 1919, provoked a backlash of Turkish nationalist sentiment. The ensuing Turkish War of Independence lasted until 1922. Mustafa Kemal, sent to Samsun in May 1919 with orders to pacify central and eastern Anatolia and the Black Sea coast and to monitor the implementation of the Mudros armistice, instead assumed leadership of the national movement against the Entente's partition plans. In July 1919, he resigned from the military. He was the driving force behind the national congresses in Erzurum and Sivas, which rejected foreign mandates and pledged to fight for the independence and territorial integrity of the country. The British occupation of Istanbul in March 1920 and the prorogation of the Ottoman Chamber of Deputies drove the nationalists to convene the Grand National Assembly in Ankara in April. In addition to his political portfolio as speaker of this chamber, Mustafa Kemal also served as commander in chief of the nationalist troops, which defeated the Greeks in September 1922.

On the heels of victory and the subsequent Treaty of Lausanne (1923), Mustafa Kemal became the natural leader of the new Turkish State. Although the sultanate had already been abolished in November 1922, the republic was founded in October 1923. Mustafa Kemal became the first president of the republic, a capacity in which he served until his death. In September 1922, he announced the establishment of a political party called the People's Party (later Republican People's Party). This organization subsequently became his civilian basis of power and the only party of significance in the state. Following a Kurdish revolt with strong Islamist undertones in 1925 and an assassination attempt against Mustafa Kemal in 1926, the party cracked down on the opposition and tolerated little dissent.

Mustafa Kemal immediately launched an ambitious reform program aimed at the creation of a modern, secular state and the construction of a new identity for its citizens. His education and years of military service exposed him to many of the ideas shared by the educated elite of his generation. Among these ideas were popular scientism, based on the mid-19th-century German *Vulgärmaterialismus* (pseudoscientific elitism), based on Gustave Le Bon's theory of crowd behavior; Turkism and Turkish nationalism; and a view of modernization that privileged science as the engine of Western-style progress. Mustafa Kemal was broadly familiar with all of these ideas, but his reading was limited and he was no theorist. Although his reform program bears a remarkable resemblance to proposals drawn up in 1913 by Kiliçzâde Hakkı, a leading Westernist of the Second Constitutional Period of 1908–18, his personal touch was undeniable. It was especially evident in the radicalism of the reform program, which unflinchingly refused to countenance the persistence of dualism in Turkish society. Rejecting the Ottoman reform legacy, Mustafa Kemal aimed at eradicating old habits and institutions instead of allowing them to coexist alongside the new. At the same time, his pragmatism saved the program from excessive ideological rigidity. By the time of his death, Mustafa Kemal, who took the family name Atatürk (Father of Turks) in 1934, had transformed Turkish society. The secular republic he helped to build was a novelty in the Muslim world. The strict control of the state over religion, the banning of time-honored Islamic institutions such as religious orders and dervish lodges, the acceptance of European legal codes, the unabashed promotion of a European way of life, and the deification of the nation were all virtually unknown in Islam up to his time. Mustafa Kemal's decision in 1928 to adopt a modified Latin alphabet to replace the Arabo-Persian set of characters used for centuries demonstrated his desire to remove yet another traditional symbol that had gained religious connotation. To Mustafa Kemal, these changes were not only justified but also necessitated by science, "the most truthful guide in life."

Mustafa Kemal also promoted a new identity for the Turks, founded upon notions of a glorious historical and linguistic past that stretched back in time to the pre-Ottoman era. The state-sponsored Thesis of Turkish History sought to explain all major historical developments as Turkish achievements. Similarly, the Sun Language Theory maintained that Turkish is the main language of humankind

from which all other languages derive. Although these state-sponsored theories had some initial impact among Turkish intellectual and nationalist circles, they have long since been forgotten.

Mustafa Kemal Atatürk was one of the foremost leaders of the 20th century. Inside Turkey, his legacy has been revered by Kemalists, who have refined his ideas to produce a strictly secular state ideology. In the wider Muslim world, his work has been viewed by secularists as an exemplary reform project and by conservatives as one of the greatest heresies in the history of Islam.

See also Ottomans (1299–1924); Turkey; Westernization

Further Reading

Atatürk'ün Bütün Eserleri, 2008; Klaus Kreiser, *Atatürk: Eine Biographie*, 2008; Andrew Mango, *Ataturk*, 2000.

M. ŞÜKRÜ HANIOĞLU

Aurangzeb (1618–1707)

Aurangzeb ʻAlamgir, Muhyi al-Din Muhammad, sixth ruler of the Mughal Empire (India) and last of the "Great Mughals," was the third son of Emperor Shah Jahan and Mumtaz Mahal. Aurangzeb reigned for half a century, from 1658 until his death in 1707. During his reign, the empire reached its greatest territorial extent but also saw the rise of the internal weaknesses and external threats that brought about its decline.

After defeating his brothers in a bloody war of succession, Aurangzeb crowned himself emperor and took the regnal title of ʻAlamgir (*ʻĀlamgīr*, "conqueror of the world") on July 21, 1658. He was already a seasoned administrator and military commander, having served as governor of Gujarat for three years and of the Mughal territories in the Deccan for eight years. From the beginning of his reign, Aurangzeb pursued an expansionist policy and attempted to extend the empire's sway in Bengal and Assam in the northeast and in the Deccan in the south.

Aurangzeb's reign was repeatedly challenged by rebellions and insurrections from various quarters. The Pathan tribes on the western front of the empire rebelled: the Yusufza'is in 1667 and the Afridis and Khattaks in 1672. The latter rebellion was a more serious challenge, requiring Aurangzeb's personal intervention, and was not quelled until 1676. Beginning in 1678, an internal succession dispute among the Rajputs resulted in rebellion and provided the opportunity for Aurangzeb's son, Prince Akbar, to rebel against his father and attempt to claim the throne. Aurangzeb's defeat of both the Pathan and Rajput rebellions resulted from a successful combination of military might, diplomacy, bribery, and misinformation. Popular uprisings of the Jat peasantry in the region of Agra (1669, 1681, 1689) and the Satnami community (1672) were mercilessly crushed. In 1696, a revolt of the *zamīndārs* (landowners) in Bengal required both a military response and an administrative reorganization of the province.

During the latter half of his reign, Aurangzeb was occupied in continuous warfare in the Deccan. In order to crush the Maratha state and the Deccan sultanates, he brought the imperial army south and from 1681 onward made the military encampments his capital. By 1689, Bijapur, Golconda, and much of the Maratha territory had been conquered and annexed. However, Maratha resistance and raids continued and the war dragged on, causing great destruction and the impoverishment of both the populace and the imperial treasury.

Aurangzeb attempted to better regulate revenue collection and, during the early part of his reign, reduce the power of the nobility in relation to the royal household. However, by the end of his reign, the Mughal *jāgīrdārī* system, under which a military commander was paid with the revenue of an assigned area (or *jāgīr*), was in crisis. The policy of giving appointments to buy the loyalty of enemy commanders or conquered vassals resulted in a disproportionate number of appointments relative to *jāgīrs* available for assignment. At the same time, the power of the English, French, and Dutch East India Companies was rising. Aurangzeb was unable or, occupied with the Deccan War, unwilling to seize control of the autonomous fortified European trading centers at Bombay, Madras, Pondicherry, and Calcutta.

Many of Aurangzeb's policies, especially in religious matters, reflected his sober and pious personality and his commitment to a shariʻa-oriented Islam. In a departure from the practice of his predecessors, he disallowed wine drinking, opium use, music, and dance at court; forbade the building of new Hindu temples and the repair of existing ones; restricted tax-free grants to only Muslim recipients; and, most radically, imposed the *jizya* (poll tax) on non-Muslims in 1679. Aurangzeb was not the patron of the arts that his father and grandfather had been. Instead, he commissioned the important compendium of Hanafi law, *Fatawa-yi ʻAlamgiri* (The ʻAlamgir compendium of legal rulings), and personally occupied himself with copying the Qur'an. Aurangzeb's discriminatory policies toward his non-Muslim subjects have been seen by some scholars as a factor in the Rajput and Maratha rebellions and as a cause of general discontent and the ultimate destabilization of the empire.

See also Akbar the Great (1542–1605); Mughals (1526–1857)

Further Reading

Muzaffar Alam and Sanjay Subramanyam, eds., *The Mughal State 1526–1750*, 1998; Robert C. Hallissey, *The Rajput Rebellion against Aurangzeb: A Study of the Mughal Empire in Seventeenth-Century India*, 1977; John F. Richards, *The Mughal Empire*, 1993.

AMINA STEINFELS

authority

From the *laylat al-qadr*, the "night of power" in which the Qur'an symbolically "came down" from God, to the death of the Prophet, Muslim affairs were governed by the special authority of that

prophetic-revelatory event, and it remains the primary paradigm of political authority in Islam. Muhammad was a religious, political, and military leader who founded a new form of community, an *umma*, that was both spiritual and worldly in nature. The development of this new community, which defined itself in terms of faith rather than national or tribal boundaries, marked a transition from polytheism to monotheism, and was ultimately shaped by both Arab tribal bonds and Persian monarchic systems.

The Arab Bedouin were not anarchic. Their society was governed by what the 14th-century North African philosopher of history Ibn Khaldun referred to as solidarity (*'aṣabiyya*). *'Aṣabiyya* signifies internal cohesion, often brought about by the unity of blood or faith. Islam universalized this sense of belonging by replacing local, tribal customs with the sunna (the normative conduct of the Prophet) of the universal tribe called the *umma*, made concrete through the hadith (reports of the Prophet's sunna) and shari'a (sacred law). In understanding political authority in the Islamic world, this "post-tribal" element is essential, as authority does not rely necessarily on formal state structures. First and foremost, Muslims adhere to God and to the expression of God's commands through the medium of prophethood.

The Qur'an is composed in a rhythmic style that makes considerable use of symbolic and allegorical imagery. Its allusions and indirect explanations allow for a multitude of interpretations. Consequently, it is difficult to determine any firm principles of government within the text. The Qur'an provides examples of the proper use of authority, such as Muhammad's consultation with his Companions (3:159) or the imperative to abide by the principles of justice and kindness (e.g., 4:58, 65, 105, 135, and 16:90), but it is concerned more with general principles such as fairness, equity, and discipline than with specific details of government. Political theory in the Qur'an focuses on the status of Muhammad as Prophet and the authority he wielded as long as he was alive, although the Qur'an does suggest that his authority could be questioned and that his role was often one of arbiter among a federation of tribes rather than the possessor of absolute, unquestioned authority.

According to Sunni tradition, Muhammad did not specify a successor, while Shi'is believed that Muhammad had chosen his cousin and son-in-law 'Ali b. Abi Talib to succeed him. As a result of this conflict, a *fitna*, or civil war, divided the *umma* between 656 and 661. The title *khātam al-nabiyyīn* (usually translated as "seal of the prophets"), given to Muhammad in the Qur'an (33:40), has traditionally been interpreted to mean that there were to be no prophets after Muhammad, and so an important symbol of religious and political authority was lost after his death. Abu Bakr was selected as caliph (deputy) partly because he came from a relatively insignificant clan with no pretensions to power; it was a *falta*, an affair concluded with haste and without much reflection, to preserve the unity of the *umma* and avoid the very real danger of tribal conflict. In fact, Abu Bakr's status of successor to the messenger of God (*khalīfat rasūl Allāh*) did not come with great power. At the beginning of his reign he was only a part-time caliph, spending the rest of his time as a merchant. In his short reign of only two years, however, he maintained the Medinan regime, bringing the breakaway tribes back into the fold of the *umma* through the policy of wars of apostasy (*al-ridda*). Abu Bakr and the three caliphs that followed are known as the *Rāshidūn*, or the "Rightly Guided Caliphs," because they knew the Prophet personally and, it is believed, assimilated some of his charisma and values. As such, Muslims looked to the actions and words of the *Rāshidūn* as a source of authority.

Divisions within this new community nonetheless continued. The third caliph, 'Uthman b. 'Affan, was assassinated, and the *umma* was divided between those who supported and those who opposed 'Ali as the fourth caliph. 'Ali was subsequently assassinated by a puritan "seceder" (*khārijī*), and the majority of Muslims accepted his opponent, Mu'awiya b. Abi Sufyan (602–80), as the leader of the fledgling *umma*, thus beginning the reign of the Umayyads. The Sunnis eventually took the *Rāshidūn* as their model, stating that the leader should be elected by a council from within the Quraysh (the dominant tribe in Mecca), whereas Shi'is developed the notion of the imamate, in which leadership belonged to Muhammad's direct biological descendents.

The Umayyads and Abbasids

The period between 661 and 750 marks the era of two great Islamic dynasties: the Umayyad followed by the Abbasid. With the rapid spread of Islam, the *umma* came to include not only Arabs but also many other races and traditions, which affected its political makeup. As the religion spread, it encountered a patrimonial bureaucracy, prevalent in Iran. This absolutist notion of authority placed power in the hands of the monarch and his family, who ruled on behalf of the people. This model was in many respects adopted by both the Umayyad and Abbasid caliphs as the most efficient system to preserve order. Rule of law and stability trumped piety. A shift in title accompanied the shift in style of government: Umayyad and Abbasid caliphs preferred to be known as God's deputy (*khalīfat Allāh*) instead of successor or vicegerent of God's messenger (*khalīfat rasūl Allāh*). This claim to absolute authority was opposed not only by Shi'is but also by some Sunnis.

The Abbasids came to power following the Third Fitna (744–50) and claimed to represent justice, opposing themselves to the monarchical Umayyad regime and thus garnering support from Shi'is. Yet before long, they too became patrimonial, incorporating Iranian practices of government to an even greater extent than their predecessors. An early work on political thought was the *Risala fi al-Sahaba* (Epistle on the caliph's entourage, written 754–56) by Ibn al-Muqaffa', who served as secretary to Umayyad and Abbasid caliphs. In response, one suspects, to the views expressed by the Kharijis, he stated that all men are not, in fact, equal before God. Second, he stated that it was erroneous to obey a leader unconditionally, which seemed to reflect a Shi'i view. Ibn al-Muqaffa' argued for obedience to the caliph only so long as he acted according to the shari'a. This may at first suggest that the ultimate authority is Islamic law, with its basis in the Qur'an and the sunna of Muhammad especially, but Ibn al-Muqaffa' states that while

shari'a is dominant, it is the role of the caliph to not only administer the law but also *interpret* it. This effectively takes power out of the hands of the 'ulama' (the religious body) and places it firmly in those of the caliph as God's deputy. This conflict of authority between the 'ulama' and the political body, symbolized by the caliph, has been a concern throughout much of Islamic history, with the 'ulama', on the whole, remaining silent on political matters, especially in the Sunni tradition. The political theory of Ibn al-Muqaffa', though simply presented, was best reflected in the career of the Abbasid caliph Ma'mun (r. 813–33), who put into practice Ibn al-Muqaffa''s view that leadership must have a strong ideological basis. Ma'mun associated himself closely with the Shi'i view of the imam and encouraged the translation of Greek philosophical texts by founding the House of Wisdom (Bayt al-Hikma) in Baghdad. These respected Greek works helped to portray monarchical leadership as more enlightened and therefore legitimized the caliphate, although many within the 'ulama' were suspicious of appealing to a philosophy that they considered "un-Islamic." This presents another conflict that has existed throughout Islamic history: the authority of theological "Islamic" sources as opposed to philosophical "non-Islamic" sources or, put another way, faith versus reason. Ma'mun argued for leadership on rational rather than religious grounds and promoted Mu'tazili teachings on the subject. This led to a Platonic conception of authority with a pessimistic view of human nature, which called for the masses to be ruled by a rational and enlightened caliphate. These views are perhaps best expressed by the Mu'tazili philosopher Jahiz (d. 869).

Although the Abbasids continued to hold the office of caliph, real power was eventually exercised by the Shi'i Buyids (932–1075), followed by the Sunni Seljuqs (1075–1258). From this point, what had been understood as "caliphate authority" transferred to the 'ulama', who also came to be known as imams. In Sunni Islam, the head of state no longer had religious authority. In 1258, the Abbasid capital of Baghdad fell to Mongol rule and the Abbasid caliphate became extinct. Consequently, authority became more communal or neotribal in nature with the development of jurisprudence (*fiqh*). In time the four legal schools (*madhhab*) were recognized and the influence of the legal scholar Shafi'i (d. 820) redefined authority. Shafi'i effectively put religious authority back into the hands of the 'ulama' rather than the caliphate.

Shi'i Leadership

The Zaydi Shi'i Qasim b. Ibrahim (785–860) also argued for a largely Platonic conception of political authority: obedience to the leader is a necessity due to the imperfections of human nature. In Sunni Islam, this meant that the caliphs had to legitimize their power by proclaiming themselves to be less susceptible to desires and emotions than other human beings, while not going so far as to declare themselves prophets. For Shi'is, this claim to legitimacy was made somewhat easier due to the semidivine status accorded to their imams. In Twelver Shi'ism, the imams are considered essential to the existence of the universe, especially the twelfth, Hidden Imam. This doctrine of leadership was developed under the Buyids by such notable figures as Mufid (d. 1022), Murtada (d. 1044), and Tusi (d. 1067). It is the belief of the "Twelver," or Imami, Shi'is that the Twelfth Imam, Muhammad al-Mahdi, went into occultation (*ghayba*, a period of concealment) in 873. While the Mahdi is in occultation, guidance must be provided by the religious scholars who are essentially the Mahdi's representatives. Only when the Twelfth Imam returns are Shi'is obliged to take over the political reins. Until then, they remain politically quiet under illegitimate rulers. In contemporary times, this doctrine led many to believe that Ayatollah Khomeini (1902–89) was the Mahdi.

Imami quietism was countered by a much more politically active Isma'ili doctrine that consisted of a hierarchy of seven emanations of God, with the seventh being the human world, and seven major historical epochs, each having its own prophet and seven imams. Their political hierarchy corresponds with this metaphysical pattern. In 909, the Fatimids declared 'Ubaydallah al-Mahdi (d. 934) to be the Mahdi; he went on to conquer Sicily, North Africa, and Egypt and took control of Mecca and Medina. No longer in hiding, the Fatimid imams could claim much greater political and religious authority than the Sunni caliphs.

The Seljuqs and a New Doctrine of the Caliphate

The creation of the Isma'ili Fatimid caliphate in Cairo, together with the existence of the Umayyad caliphate now residing in Andalusia, raised the question of who was the legitimate caliph and whether more than one caliph could exist at the same time. In addition, a military dynasty called the Buyids had effectively seized power within Baghdad, retaining the Sunni Abbasid caliphate as a symbol of unity, despite the fact that the Buyids were Shi'i sympathizers. Further, another force was on the horizon: the Seljuq Turks, who conquered Baghdad in 1055.

With the rise of the Seljuqs from the 11th century, a new Sunni polity emerged that, to a great extent, rejected rational, philosophical speculation in favor of legalism and literalism. One key figure of this period was Mawardi (972–1058), whose main political work, *On the Principles of Power* (also often translated as *On the Ordinances of Government*, *Kitab al-Ahkam al-Sultaniyya*), was written between 1045 and 1058, during the Seljuq Turks' rise to power in Baghdad. In this treatise, he expresses his preference for a strong caliphate based on revelation. Mawardi criticized the view of philosophers that reason alone was sufficient for an understanding of how to rule a state. For Mawardi, reason—a human construct—has its limitations, whereas revelation is God's word. Like the Christian thinker St. Thomas Aquinas, Mawardi saw a direct link between divinely revealed order and political order.

Another important figure during the Seljuq ascendancy was the theologian, jurist, philosopher, and mystic Ghazali (ca. 1058–1111), universally known as the "proof of Islam" (*ḥujjat al-islām*) and the great "renewer" (*mujtahid*) of the faith. He attempted to synthesize the three main strands of Islamic rationality: theoretical and philosophical enquiry, juridical legislation, and mystical practice. His writings redirected and reinvigorated Sunni religious thought

in the aftermath of the Shi'i intellectual dominance of the previous century. In 1085, Ghazali went to Baghdad and joined the court of the celebrated Nizam al-Mulk (d. 1092), who, though merely a vizier, was effectively monarch in all but name and was at the height of his power. Ghazali's best-known work is *The Revival of the Religious Sciences* (*Ihya' 'Ulum al-Din*), in which he argues that the essence of the human being is the soul (*nafs*), which, in its original state—that is, before being attached to the body—is a pure, angelic, and eternal substance. Through reason, the soul has the potential to know the essence of things and acquire knowledge of God, but to achieve this potential it must attach itself to a body, for the body is the vehicle that carries the soul on its journey to God. The body, however, is a corrupting influence that succumbs to anger, desire, and evil. Consequently, the soul, though still possessing its divine elements, also has "animal" elements. To perfect the soul, the person must subordinate the animal qualities and pursue the virtues of temperance, courage, wisdom, and justice. This can be achieved through Sufi practices, which shut the gate to worldly desires. Ghazali points out, however, that it also is important to engage in the rituals associated with Islam, such as pilgrimage, prayer, ablutions, alms, fasting, reading the Qur'an, following the shari'a, and so on. Ghazali's views on religion and mysticism have political implications that are also Platonist in character, for only the few can truly manage to come close to perfecting their soul, and their knowledge of Islam gives them greater political authority. This was Ghazali's attempt to "revive" Islam by making knowledge of religion synonymous with political knowledge, for the religious and the worldly are interdependent.

Andalusian Politics

In the 11th and 12th centuries especially, efforts were made to determine a Sunni religious polity in opposition to the Christian Reconquista (the Spanish and Portuguese word for "reconquest," referring to the retaking of Andalus from the Muslims). Whereas the first major movement led by the Almoravid dynasty emphasized Hanbali literalism and even burned Ghazali's books, the second movement under the Almohads championed Islamic philosophy. This policy was supported by the Aristotelian philosopher Ibn Rushd (also known by the Latin name Averroes, 1126–98). For Ibn Rushd, the truth achieved through the study of philosophy does not differ from the truths of revelation as contained in the Qur'an. What may appear as difference is a matter of interpretation. Ibn Rushd argues that just as reason, through philosophy, can be used to reach truth, so can reason be used to interpret the Qur'anic text. The Qur'an contains many symbols, allegories, and analogies that can be instructive to the less learned, but, Ibn Rushd argues, those possessed of suitable intellect should determine their real meaning rather than treat them literally. It follows from this that the best qualified to interpret shari'a are philosophers, not the theologians. Ibn Rushd wrote commentaries on both Plato's and Aristotle's works, and the influence of these two Greek philosophers is evident in his political views, particularly his view that the leader should be a philosopher-king possessed of a rational intellect.

The Reign of the Mamluks

During the Mamluk regime (1250–1517), there were two great figures of Sunni Islamic political thought: Ibn Taymiyya (1263–1328) and Ibn Khaldun (1332–1406). Ibn Taymiyya was a jurist of the Hanbali school of law, a strict traditionalist who railed against what he saw as the "innovations" (*bid'a*) of such authorities in Islam as Ghazali, Ibn al-'Arabi, and the Sufis. He emphasized the need to return to what he perceived as the pristine ideals and practices of Islam at the time of the Prophet Muhammad. In his main political work, *Treatise on the Government of the Religious Law*, he argues that under the *Rāshidūn* the Islamic state achieved moral and political purity and that this should be the main aim of Islamic law. In Ibn Taymiyya's view, rulers since the *Rāshidūn* have failed to achieve such perfection. The ruler should follow rigorously the tenets of the shari'a, applying it firmly but fairly and relying on it for all legal opinions and rulings. Those who are ruled should obey the authority of the caliph provided he, in turn, obeys the shari'a. Ibn Taymiyya was dogmatic in his view that religion cannot be practiced without state power. The religious duty of "commanding right and forbidding wrong" (*ḥisba*), he argues, cannot be achieved without a central power and authority, and so there is a necessary link between state and religion. Controversial in his own lifetime, he had few followers and little influence until long after his death. A small number of Ottoman scholars studied him in the 16th century, but in the 18th century, Muhammad b. 'Abd al-Wahhab (d. 1792) drew on Ibn Taymiyya's ideas to create Wahhabism, which, together with his military endeavors, led to the creation of the first Saudi state in 1744. Since that time, Ibn Taymiyya has been seen as the champion of revivalism and the founder of many reform movements that look to the time of Muhammad and the principles inculcated in the Qur'an to counter what is perceived as the threat of modernism.

Ibn Taymiyya's idea that religion and government need each other was explored empirically by the great Muslim philosopher of history, Ibn Khaldun. His major work on history (*Kitab al-'Ibar*) is divided into three books. The famous first book, the *Prolegomena*, outlines his methodology and outlook on history as well as the dynamics of human society. The second book concerns the history of the Arabs, and the third deals with the history of the Berbers. Although the emphasis of the work is political and focuses on the rise and fall of dynasties, it also explores what politics tells us about human nature. Having studied philosophy, theology, and history, Ibn Khaldun noted that philosophical concepts and reasoning had been applied to theology but not to history. The central theme in the *Prolegomena* is the sociology of human society, which he called the science of civilization (*'ilm al-'umrān*). Studying *'ilm al-'umrān* would reveal the dynamics of human society, which in turn would enable the historian to sift through historical records and separate fact from fiction. Hence, historical facts are those that correspond to the logic of societies' dynamics and their rules of evolution. To Ibn Khaldun, the power base of each state depends on its *'aṣabiyya*, or group solidarity based on family ties and lineage, which is to be found mostly among nomadic people and savage

nations. Ibn Khaldun argues that the power of each *'aṣabiyya* extends basically to four generations. The first generation, driven by tribal expansionism or religious mission, would conquer the settled nations and establish a powerful state. The second generation would consolidate and expand the state, build its institutions, and still enjoy strong solidarity due to its close connection with a tribal ethos. The third generation would enjoy the prosperity of the state and provide support for arts, sciences, and culture but would have less solidarity as a result of its urban upbringing. The fourth generation would waste the achievements of its ancestors. Confined to a life of palace machinations and the pursuit of material gratification, members of this generation would concern themselves mostly with raising money to spend on their own welfare and the preservation of their thrones, which would lead to an intensified tax burden on the populace. The resulting injustices would lead to the dissolution of the state and the annihilation of its civilization, making it vulnerable to invasions from other nomadic or savage groups. The cycle then starts anew. Despite the originality of his thought, however, it seems that his principles were neither applied nor studied by his Muslim successors.

Muslim Rulers as "Masters of the Age"

Although little new political theory was produced during the period of the Ottoman dynasty, the ruler Süleiman "the Lawgiver" (*al-Qānūnī*, d. 1566), known in the West as "the Magnificent" due largely to his military conquests, oversaw the most detailed codification of Qur'anic and sultanic law that any Islamic state had ever experienced. Süleiman's update of the law codes that had been largely produced by the Ottoman sultan Mehmed II (d. 1481) later became known as "Süleiman's law-code." What came into existence was nonreligious law, known as *kanun*, which was the law of the sultan or Ottoman law (*kanuni osmani*). *Kanun* dealt with criminal infractions and was intended to supplement shari'a by specifying penalties, although the punishments actually tended to be harsher than those under shari'a. It also dealt with the collection of taxes, land tenure, and other matters. Finally, it was concerned with the form of government and the relationships between the various spheres of authority. Because of the integration of *kanun* and shari'a, the judges implemented secular as well as religious law in Islamic law courts. The justification for *kanun* was that shari'a simply could not cover everything required to maintain social order in such a huge empire with a diversity of cultures and beliefs, so, as shari'a law only applied to Muslims, another law was needed. Both systems of law, it was argued, were after the same thing, which was public order and justice. The problem was that *kanun* often conflicted with shari'a, although this raised less concern during Süleiman's reign than it did later, when the Ottoman Empire was in its decline. Süleiman, especially in his early years, considered himself the *ṣāḥib-qirān* (Lord of the Auspicious Conjunction), the very embodiment of human perfection, and thus a reflection of God Himself. The Mughal emperor Akbar (1542–1605) had likewise given himself such a title, for it also meant that the ruler saw himself as the *universal* ruler of Islam who was responsible for guiding Muslims along the right path. Süleiman also called himself "caliph of the whole world." The Ottomans had claimed the title of caliph for some time, especially when Sultan Selim I (d. 1520) brought Mecca and Medina into his realm. It was believed that the sultan-caliph had not only the responsibility to execute shari'a in all parts of the world but also the power to interpret the law, hence the creation of *kanun*, the product of a ruler guided by divine inspiration.

Responses to Modernity

Sir Sayyid Ahmad Khan (1817–98) was an influential modernist thinker who, rather than shun Western influence, adopted it wholeheartedly. His importance rests in his realization that Islam needed to reform if it was to survive, although he remained a controversial figure due to his collaboration with the British, who occupied India at the time. Khan was a great believer in the need for Islam to modernize, and he saw in Western thought, especially in the realm of science, a force that he did not regard as antithetical to Islam. Like his counterparts in the Middle East, he believed that the survival of Islam required the abandonment of blind imitation (*taqlīd*). He undertook the reinterpretation of the Qur'an, believing the more obscure passages had to be interpreted symbolically, allegorically, or analytically in order to reveal their true meaning. He believed that reason played an important part in this process and that the main principles in the Qur'an were in tune with scientific progress and reason in accordance with nature. Like Ibn Rushd, Khan believed Islam was the religion of reason and nature. Heavily influenced by 19th-century European rationalism and natural philosophy, he also drew heavily on both the reformism of Shah Waliullah as well as the rationalism of Mu'tazilis and the Ikhwan al-Safa' (the Isma'ili-influenced "Brothers of Purity").

Khan's fellow Indian Sir Muhammad Iqbal (1873–1938) remains an important influence not only in South Asia but also in the Middle East. He is renowned and admired for his passionate poetry, but he was also a philosopher, political thinker, and the spiritual father of Pakistan. He was aware of the problems faced by Islam when confronted with so-called modernity, in particular the failure to respond to Western encroachment not only in the political and social spheres but also in the technological and scientific arenas. His more philosophical works culminated in his *Secrets of the Self* (*Asrar-i-Khudi*), which speaks of the need for Muslims to reawaken their souls and act. His rejection of territorial nationalism was based on his belief in the *umma*: a community of like-minded individuals that existed beyond national boundaries. He saw in the Prophet Muhammad the exemplar of the Muslim community: a prophet-statesman who founded a society based on freedom, equality, and brotherhood reflected in the central tenet of "unity" (*tawḥīd*). In the practical sense, Iqbal believed that a requisite of being a good Muslim was to live under Islamic law, which acts as the blueprint for the perfect Islamic society as envisioned by the Prophet Muhammad. In 1937, Iqbal sent a letter to Muhammad 'Ali Jinnah, the leader of the Muslim League and future founder of Pakistan, in which he emphasized the importance of Islamic law if Islam was to remain a force in the region. Aside from the need for shari'a to exist in any Islamic

state, Iqbal also stressed the importance of absolute equality. He believed that democracy was the best form of government, whereas aristocracy suppressed human individuality. When Iqbal talked of democracy, however, he was not referring to Western forms of democracy, which give the franchise to any individual over a certain age regardless of educational level. In this sense, Iqbal shared a view of democracy not dissimilar from his compatriot Mawdudi (1903–79): democracy is only for those who are sufficiently learned to know what they are voting for.

Mawdudi was head and founder of the political movement Jama'at-i Islami, the Indo-Pakistan equivalent of the Muslim Brotherhood in Egypt, and was the most controversial and significant Islamic thinker and activist in the region until his death. In many respects, his views echo those of the modernist movement known as the Salafis. Mawdudi's writings and activities contributed greatly to the founding of Pakistan in 1947. His concentration on leaders rather than on the common man is reflected in his doctrine of *al-Jihad fi al-Islam*, in which the social order flows from the top down. This necessarily implies a form of authoritarianism: he believed that practical social change was impossible unless the views of the leadership changed first. On this point, he frequently makes reference to the authority of the Prophet, the caliphs, and the great jurists as prime examples of forces for change. Mawdudi considered an Islamic form of government to be a moral imperative: the system by which the laws of God are given form. Many Islamists, Mawdudi among them, make reference to a "golden era" of Islam, a period that is portrayed as a pure Islamic state, an age of unity between the religious and the secular with Muhammad as its head. In appealing to traditional hadith and histories, the Islamist sees ultimate authority resting with the *Rāshidūn*. Mawdudi does not detail exactly how much authority the rulings of past great jurists would have in his Islamic state, nor does he specify which rulings. In Mawdudi's Islamic state, authority—the power to make and enforce laws—would rest with a small number of individuals, acting as representatives of God. This conception of authority, which he calls "theo-democracy," is reminiscent of medieval European societies rather than any modern democratic system.

Together with his friend and colleague Afghani (1838–97), Muhammad 'Abduh (1849–1905) is the founder of the Salafis. Although considered modernist, this movement looks back to the time of Muhammad and his Companions as a guide to the right way to live. Together, these two figures were the most influential spokesmen for Egyptian Islamic modernism in the 19th century. 'Abduh's writings have had an immense and lasting influence on the Muslim world. His most distinguished follower was the Syrian Rashid Rida (1865–1935). 'Abduh and Rida are considered the great synthesizers of modern Islam. The general policy of the Salafis was to look to the "pious ancestors" (*al-salaf al-ṣāliḥ*, the Prophet Muhammad and his Companions primarily) for guidance but also to appeal to man's rational capacity. While those laws that governed worship, such as prayer, fasting, and pilgrimage, were unchangeable, the majority of legislation, such as regulation on family law and the penal codes, were open to change according to the social and cultural traditions of the time. In theory, then, a Salafi approach to Islam should allow for independent reasoning, although there is always the danger that interpreters would be unwilling to adopt anything other than a literal approach to the "pious ancestors" and the Qur'an, in the same way some Muslim scholars have been reluctant to contradict the rulings of traditional legal scholars.

The Tunisian Rachid al-Gannouchi (b. 1941) is a controversial political and social activist who represents the generation following that of the Salafis. While maintaining essential Islamic values, he sees no contradiction between a multiparty system, pluralism, or women's rights, for example, and Islam. Gannouchi argues that what is at fault with Islam, at least in his own society, is its failure to identify itself with the impoverished working classes and with women. In his view, Islam should be seen as a liberating force, not an oppressive one. In fact, he argues that democracy originates in Islam and that the Western concept was inherited from Islamic civilization during the Middle Ages. For Gannouchi, a state that upholds such values as human rights, the rule of law, a multiparty system, and freedom of speech is in effect a Muslim state, regardless of its secular credentials. He argues that he would rather live in a free secular state than any state that imposes an oppressive version of Islam. As his paradigm, he cites Andalusia (Muslim Spain) as a time when Islam embraced diversity and pluralism and thrived from it.

Recent Shi'i Political Thought

'Ali Shari'ati (1933–77) is regarded as the ideological father of the 1979 Iranian Revolution. His writings were certainly revolutionary, modern in style, and radical in approach, targeting the oppression and alienation experienced by Muslims under the Pahlavi regime in Iran. Shari'ati combined Islamic concepts with Western political philosophy. While acknowledging the popular appeal of Marxist ideology, he criticized it for treating people as mere units of production. Islam, he argued, was always inherently a mass movement but also possessed humanistic values that Marxism lacked. Shari'ati placed great emphasis on the role of man as God's vicegerent on Earth. In other words, God had given man the responsibility of ruling the Earth: "man" did not mean, for Shari'ati, a small minority or a caliph, but all people. Therefore, God's vicegerency was synonymous with the power of the masses, of *al-nās* (the people). To Shari'ati, the *umma* is a classless society over which only God's will can reign. While Shari'ati's ideas owe much to the revolutionary values of Karl Marx and the existential values of Jean-Paul Sartre, he also takes a great deal from the works of mystical Muslims such as Ibn Sina (commonly known by his Latinized name, Avicenna, 980–1037) and Sadr ad-Din Muhammad Shirazi (also called Mulla Sadra, 1571–1641). In his well-known work *The Sociology of Islam*, Shari'ati writes of the "theomorphic man": a "Perfect Man" who possesses the qualities of truth, goodness, and beauty, a rebellious spirit who combines the virtues of Jesus, Caesar, and Socrates. This vision of a "theomorphic being" owes much to the concept of the Perfect Man (*insān-i kāmil*) as promulgated by Ibn al-'Arabi and the Sufis, which was also developed by the Indian poet and

reformer Iqbal. In fact, Shari'ati's writings on science and nature are highly reminiscent of Iqbal, for he also regarded the Qur'anic view of nature as close to the scientific view of the world, and perhaps surprisingly, Shari'ati sees Iqbal, a Sunni Muslim, as typical of the Perfect Man.

If Shari'ati was the ideological father of the revolution, Khomeini was its living symbol and guide. In his writings and lectures, Khomeini argued that if Islam was to be rejuvenated, it needed to look toward the Perfect Man for guidance, and he sets out the qualities required. He argued that monarchy is incompatible with Islam and rejects Iranian nationalism in favor of an Islamic universalism, albeit of the Shi'i variety. By the 1970s, Khomeini was arguing that in the absence of the imam, the clergy should do more than simply advise the government; instead, the clergy should rule directly. This doctrine of "rule by the jurists" (*wilāyat al-faqīh*) had little Qur'anic support and was rejected by virtually all the Shi'i clergy. For Khomeini, however, the concept of rule by jurists was a logical conclusion to the much more widely held view that an Islamic state, if it were to be truly Islamic, must be governed by shari'a. It was believed that shari'a amounted to a complete social system, providing regulations for all aspects of life: if this was indeed the case, then all legislation has been provided for by God. The problem rests, however, in interpreting divine law so that it may adapt to changing circumstances. Shi'ism has a long tradition of *ijtihād* (independent reasoning), and Khomeini argued that those best qualified for *ijtihād* are the jurists. Khomeini presents a view of his Republic of Iran not unlike Plato's hypothetical *Republic*: a state governed by philosopher-kings who should rule because they have access to moral truths.

Counter to Khomeini is Abdolkarim Soroush (b. 1945), who has offended the traditional clergy by questioning the validity of the concept of *wilāyat al-faqīh*. Soroush argues that, as the knowledge of the jurists is human rather than sacred, they should not be allowed to claim infallible authority. Instead of obeying the dictates of the ayatollahs, or any person claiming a monopoly in religious knowledge, Soroush argues that the student of religion should struggle to determine his own understanding of the body of religious knowledge through dialogue and questioning. Soroush's democratic approach to knowledge encourages people not to imitate or obey previous rulings but to search for themselves; otherwise, jurists will become power hungry and hypocritical. He has championed the cause of democracy on the basis that Islam cannot thrive unless such a political system exists: people must be free to believe or not, and Islam, or any religion, cannot be imposed upon a people from above.

See also caliph, caliphate; traditional political thought

Further Reading

Aziz Ahmad, *An Intellectual History of Islam in India*, 1969; Hamid Algar, *Religion and State in Iran 1785–1906: The Role of the Ulema in the Qajar Period*, 1969; Joel Beinin and Joe Stork, eds., *Political Islam: Essays from Middle Eastern Reports*, 1997; Patricia Crone and Martin Hinds, *God's Caliph: Religious Authority in the First Centuries of Islam*, 1986; Hamid Enayat, *Modern Islamic Political Thought*, 1982; John Esposito, ed., *Voices of Resurgent Islam*, 1983; Marshall G. S. Hodgson, *The Venture of Islam: Conscience and History in a World Civilization*, 3 vols., 1974; Albert Hourani, *Arabic Thought in the Liberal Age, 1798–1939*, 1983; Roy Jackson, *Fifty Key Figures in Islam*, 2006; Idem, *Mawlana Mawdudi and Political Islam: Authority and the Islamic State*, 2011; Ira M. Lapidus, *A History of Islamic Societies*, 1988; W. Montgomery Watt, *Islamic Political Thought*, 1968.

ROY JACKSON

ayatollah

"Ayatollah" is an honorific title with political significance that emerged in Twelver Shi'i tradition during the late Qajar dynasty (1848–1925). The word "ayatollah" combines the Arabic words *āyah* (sign) and *Allāh* (God) and designates members in the uppermost tier of jurists capable of independent legal reasoning (*mujtahids*). The term is closely related to the highest clerical rank in Twelver Shi'ism, *marja' al-taqlīd* (source of emulation), now synonymous with the title "grand ayatollah" (*ayatollah 'uẓmā*), the holder of which may be adopted as an authority by lay Shi'is (*muqallids*) who have chosen him as the most accomplished living expert on Islamic law. Because the bearers of the title ayatollah have often played a pivotal role in the entrance of the traditionally quietist Shi'i clerical class into the contemporary political spheres, this entry focuses on the relationship between ayatollahs and Shi'i Islamic activism.

The consolidation of the Shi'i 'ulama' as an independent political class coincided with the decline of the Qajar monarchy under the long reign of Nasir al-Din Shah (r. 1848–96). The Qajars' demise was hastened not only by formidable military defeats but also by a set of modernizing reforms that destabilized the domestic economy and an increased Iranian reliance on foreign financial and technical assistance. In this context, Nasir al-Din Shah granted, in 1890, a 50-year concession over the production, distribution, and export of Iran's tobacco to a British firm. Encouraged by the anticolonial Pan-Islamist Afghani (d. 1897), Iraq's then leading religious authority, Grand Ayatollah Mirza Hasan al-Shirazi (d. 1896), issued a fatwa banning all forms of involvement in the production and sale of tobacco. The fatwa triggered the Tobacco Protest of 1891–92, which led to a halt of the tobacco industry, violent demonstrations across Iraq and Iran, and the eventual withdrawal of the concession.

The Iranian Constitutional Revolution of 1905–11 was the next major event in which the Shi'i religious hierarchy asserted its political will. Although the converging forces of the constitutional movement did not originate from a specific political act on the part of the clergy, many of the demands of the movement were carried by the Sayyids (descendants of the Prophet Muhammad) 'Abdallah Bihbihani (d. 1910) and Muhammad Tabatabai (d. 1918), who came to be called ayatollahs despite not belonging to the highest clerical orders of the time. The popular bestowal of the title upon them

marked an early precedent in which political credentials trumped traditional scholarly merit in the establishment of religious authority. The Constitutional Revolution also marked one of the first times in which nationalist political mobilization coincided with the Shi'i mourning rituals of 'Ashura' and employed the material resources of the religious establishment in direct opposition to the state, as in, for instance, the use of shrine complexes as asylums and seminaries as centers of protest mobilization. In this period, clerical groups in Iran also began to organize independent political associations and networks (*anjaman*) that paralleled those of other emerging groups in civil society. Other constitutionalist clerics of the period included Ayatollah Muhammad Kazim Khurasani (d. 1911) and his influential student Ayatollah Muhammad Husayn Na'ini (d. 1936).

By 1921, when Reza Khan's coup consolidated his control over the powers of state, the awkward alliance between the 'ulama' and liberals had sufficiently weakened. Furthermore, the leading traditional cleric of the period, Ayatollah 'Abd al-Karim al-Ha'iri (d. 1937), had withdrawn from political activity, focusing instead on strengthening Qum as a center of religious scholarship. The bulk of the Shi'i 'ulama' thus retained a conventional quietist posture. Out of fear of encroaching secularization and foreign domination (as had occurred in Turkey and Iraq, respectively), leading figures such as Ayatollahs Abu al-Hasan Isfahani (d. 1946) and Na'ini—who were expelled from Najaf after openly opposing British occupation—quietly consented to Reza Khan's rise to power, seeing him as the least of three evils.

This political arrangement came to an abrupt halt as Reza Shah instituted rapid modernizing reforms such as compulsory conscription, the emancipation of women, and the state administration of religious education. Qum, relatively immune from the reforms, became the de facto center of underground religious opposition and later fostered the rise of militant groups such as Navab Safavi's (d. 1955) Fida'iyyin-i Islam (sacrificers of Islam). Ayatollah Hossein Burujirdi (d. 1961), who succeeded Ha'iri as the sole *marja' al-taqlīd*, shunned political activism but endorsed a militant anti-Baha'i campaign and was particularly active in religious propagation (*da'wa*).

Shortly after Burujirdi's death, Ayatollah Khomeini (1902–89) began an outspoken campaign against the Pahlavi monarchy, which was catalyzed by the government's attack on the Fayziyah Madrasa in 1963. Khomeini also criticized quietist 'ulama' who did not confront the state. His efforts were supported by figures like Ayatollahs Muhammad Bihishti (d. 1981), Mahmud Taliqani (d. 1979), and Murtada Mutaharri (d. 1979), who promoted the success of the clerical movement headed by Khomeini. It is in this context that the influential doctrine of the rule of the jurist (*wilāyat al-faqīh*) was consolidated as a justification for modern governance by the 'ulama'.

In Iraq, Ayatollah Muhammad Baqir al-Sadr, along with Mahdi al-Hakim, the son of Grand Ayatollah Muhsin al-Hakim (1889 –1970), had already helped form the Da'wa Party in 1957, which advocated an Islamic alternative to Arab socialist nationalism. Meanwhile, Lebanese Shi'is' efforts to achieve greater communitarian recognition and civil rights were led by Imam Musa al-Sadr (disappeared in 1978), who, as the son of Ayatollah Sadr al-Din al-Sadr (d. 1954), was raised and educated in Qum's religious and political milieu.

When Khomeini's Islamic Republican Party emerged triumphant in the aftermath of the Iranian Revolution of 1979, the activist current among the Shi'i 'ulama' became militarized, and they forced their quietist opponents underground or out of power. Ayatollah Shari'atmadari (d. 1986) bore the brunt of this action when he was forcibly demoted from his rank as *marja' al-taqlīd*. The Islamic Republic then patronized and further militarized the preexisting Shi'i movements of Lebanon and Iraq, which had themselves splintered over related ideological differences. For example, Ayatollah Kho'i (d. 1992) of Najaf remained quietist and opposed to the doctrine of *wilāyat al-faqīh*, while members of the Hakim family who had survived assassination attempts established the Supreme Council for the Islamic Revolution in Iraq, sharing a Khomeinist program and receiving ample material support from the Islamic Republic of Iran.

In the 1990s and 2000s, both Lebanese and Iraqi Shi'i movements gravitated toward local interests. For example, Ayatollah Muhammad Husayn Fadlallah (1935–2010), regarded as the spiritual father of the Lebanese Shi'i movement Hizbullah, advocated a secular-based religious communitarian social order rather than a state governed in accordance with Islamic law in order to suit the interconfessional context of Lebanon. After the American invasion of Iraq in 2003, Ayatollah Kho'i's successor, Ayatollah Sistani (b. 1930), though not a supporter of the doctrine of *wilāyat al-faqīh*, nonetheless exerted his de facto political authority as *marja' al-taqlīd* to demand popular elections and thus ensure a Shi'i rise to power. Ayatollah 'Abd al-'Aziz al-Hakim's (d. 2009) revolutionary movement changed its name from the Supreme Council for the Islamic Revolution in Iraq to the Islamic Supreme Council of Iraq and began to operate within a secular constitutionalist framework. The power of Shi'i clerical-based Iraqi political parties directly influenced the formation of a rival Sunni organization, the Association of Muslim Scholars, in 2003.

In the Persian Gulf states of Saudi Arabia, Kuwait, and Bahrain, clerical authorities largely followed the quietist policies of Ayatollahs Kho'i and Sistani. Having for the most part shunned Khomeini's doctrine, they nonetheless mobilized to seek greater communitarian rights within existing political frameworks. In Iran, authorities such as Grand Ayatollahs Montazeri (d. 2009) and Sani'i (b. 1937), despite attempts to silence them, continued to oppose the supreme rule of the jurist, while the majority of Iranian ayatollahs remained either de facto or de jure supporters of the doctrine and operated within or in tandem with the state apparatus.

See also al-Afghani, Jamal al-Din (1838–97); Fadlallah, Muhammad Husayn (1935–2010); guardianship of the jurist; Iran; Khomeini, Ayatollah (1902–89); al-Sadr, Muhammad Baqir (1935–80); Shi'ism; source of emulation

Further Reading

Hamid Algar, *Religion and State in Iran, 1785–1906: The Role of the Ulama in the Qajar Period*, 1969; Hamid Dabashi, *Theology of Discontent: The Ideological Foundation of the Islamic Revolution in Iran*, 2006; Nikki R. Keddie, *Sayyid Jamal ad-Din "al-Afghani": A*

Political Biography, 1972; Ruhollah Khomeini, *Islam and Revolution*, translated by Hamid Algar, 1981; Laurence Louer, *Transnational Shia Politics: Religious and Political Networks in the Gulf*, 2008; Yitzhak Nakash, *Reaching for Power: The Shi'a in the Modern Arab World*, 2006; Vali Nasr, *The Shia Revival*, 2006.

ABBAS BARZEGAR

Ayyubids (1169–1250)

The Ayyubid dynasty was founded by Saladin (Salah al-Din b. Ayyub, d. 1193), a military commander of Kurdish descent, who deposed the Fatimids and assumed control over Egypt in 1171. The commitment to jihad, the abolition of taxes deemed illegal by Islamic law, and the patronage of religious learning and Sufism, all spearheaded by Saladin, were presented as part of the wider ideology of the revivification of the sunna (prophetic traditions). His victory over the army of the Latin kingdom of Jerusalem and reconquest of Jerusalem in 1187, the apex of his career, immortalized him in Arabic historiography and popular culture as a heroic prince of virtue.

Before his death in 1193, Saladin concluded a peace treaty with Richard the Lionheart, leader of the Third Crusade, and bequeathed his domain to 17 of his sons, brothers, and nephews, who formed a confederation of autonomous principalities of varied size and importance. It was a novel political organization for Syria and Egypt, reminiscent of the Buyid confederation (946–1012). Cohesion largely depended on the authority of the sultan—the reigning head of the clan, usually situated in Cairo. Prerogatives of sultans included the vow of allegiance from the lesser princes and the mention of their names on coins and in the Friday noon sermon (*khuṭba*). The sultan in turn recognized the authority of the Abbasid caliph and repeatedly sought his formal investiture. Conflicting interests, a mobile military elite, and shifting alliances—some forged with external enemies—undermined familial solidarity and the confederation's stability, yet most internal conflicts ended in agreements and territorial adjustments. Diplomacy and coexistence were also preferred to warfare with the Franks.

In 1250, Mamluk conspirators murdered the heir of the Ayyubid sultan who had made Turkish slaves the principal element in his army. By 1260, following the Mongol onslaught, only the principality of Hama in northern Syria remained in the hands of Ayyubid princes (until 1342).

Ayyubid rule brought economic renewal. Changes in the system of *iqṭā'* (grants of land to the military) and the reclamation of land led to greater agricultural production; cities and commerce expanded. Culturally, Syria assumed the leading position in the Arab-speaking lands, attracting immigrants and refugees.

The Ayyubids inherited most of their civil and military institutions from the Fatimids, Abbasids, and Seljuqs, including the division of the administration into three main offices: the chancellery (*dīwān al-inshā'*), the office of military affairs (*dīwān al-juyūsh*), and the treasury (*dīwān al-māl*). The armies had no clear system of ranks and command; the officer corps was by and large hereditary. Toward the end of Ayyubid rule, Syria and Egypt underwent a steady process of militarization, strikingly reflected in the appointment of the *mushidd*—a military official entrusted with the supervision of the civil administration.

The Ayyubid period does not seem to have produced political thinkers of great caliber, yet three contributors to the field of governance and administration deserve to be mentioned: 'Ali al-Harawi (d. 1215), better known as the author of the first pilgrims' guide to Syria, wrote his *Tadhkira Harawiyya fi al-Hiyal al-Harbiyya* (On the ruses of war) and *Wasiyya Harawiyya* (Last counsels) in the tradition of Mirrors for Princes for al-Malik al-Zahir (d. 1216) of Aleppo. He addresses warfare and governance, recommending piety, justice, sound fiscal and economic administration, surveillance of judges and officials, respect toward religious scholars and foreign ambassadors, wariness of bad counselors, secrecy and discreetness, and caution and patience. Above all, he calls for fidelity to the shari'a and military might, in light of Saladin's example.

Sibt b. al-Jawzi (d. 1257), Damascene historian and popular preacher, is considered author of another Mirrors for Princes, *Al-Jalis al-Salih wa-l-Anis al-Nasih* (The good counselor), composed for al-Malik al-Ashraf (d. 1239) of Damascus, in his praise. Sibt b. al-Jawzi lists trustworthiness, grace (*faḍl*), justice, piety, the patronage of scholars, and the love of beneficence and munificence as attributes of a good ruler. He ends his book with stories (*ḥikāyāt*) of exemplary rulers of the past.

As'ad b. al-Mammati (d. 1209), author of *Qawanin al-Dawawin* (Rules of administration), provides a detailed description of the administration of Egypt under the Fatimids and the Ayyubids, written as a guide for state officials (*kuttāb*) for the sultan al-'Aziz 'Uthman.

See also Mirrors for Princes; Saladin (1138–93)

Further Reading

R. Stephen Humphreys, *From Saladin to the Mongols*, 1977; Tryggve Kronholm, "Dedication and Devotion: The Introduction to the *Kitāb al-Jalīs as-Ṣāliḥ wa-l-Anīs an-Nāṣiḥ*, Ascribed to Sibṭ ibn al-Jawzī (d. 654/1257)," *Orientalia Suecana* 38–39 (1989–1990); Daniella Talmon-Heller, *Islamic Piety in Medieval Syria*, 2007.

DANIELLA TALMON-HELLER

Azhar University

The history of Azhar, a mosque and an institution of religious learning situated in Cairo, Egypt, has reflected shifts in political power since its foundation in 970 by the Fatimids. Historians have disagreed about the role of Azhar as a tool for political and religious propaganda under the Fatimids, and there is no consensus on when

Azhar became a central institution of learning. Under the Mamluks, it was a major institution for the transmission of knowledge, and this continued in the early Ottoman period, with the top positions within the institution occupied by Ottoman officials. Its influence and reach went beyond Egypt, and Azhar became a site where knowledge, religious authority, and politics were tightly linked. Its prominent ‘ulama’ (religious scholars) participated in a partnership with the rulers, but the ‘ulama’ rarely held the upper hand. They mediated between the rulers and the Egyptian populace, relaying the demands of the general public to the sovereign and vice versa and helping maintain social stability. Thus Azhar participated in politics through negotiation rather than overt opposition or strong political leadership. The ‘ulama’ would articulate political advice (*naṣīḥa*) to the ruler but rarely expressed overt opposition.

In the early 19th century, Azhar and its ‘ulama’ were politically marginalized by the emergence of a strong state that aimed at reforming its own administrative structures and transforming the domains of law and education. Through these reforms, Islam lost its preeminence in the two domains where the ‘ulama’ had previously been the main actors. New channels for educating the elites were created, and Azhar's scholars and the student body suffered from the competition with new schools (such as Dar al-‘Ulum, established in 1872). Muslim scholars and reformers in the 18th and 19th centuries also articulated strong critiques of Azhar and its ‘ulama’, who they said had become passive and were more interested in life in this world than in the defense of their religion. This economic and social marginalization did not mean that Azhar entirely lost its significance. Rather, its ‘ulama’ still had relevance in normative and political debates, at least as individuals if not as representatives of their institution. The political constraints around them changed, however, as the modern state's reach and regulatory power in society weakened Azhar's influence on Egyptians. This transformation of state power found its apex in postcolonial Egypt when President Gamal Abdel Nasser's regime nationalized the religious endowments (waqfs; 1952–53), put an end to the existence of shari‘a courts (1955), and introduced wide-ranging reforms at Azhar itself (1961). This series of changes circumscribed the power of Azhar further: its ‘ulama’ were deprived of their judicial domain, they lost their economic independence, and they became civil servants within a bureaucracy at the service of the state. They did not all accept this new set of circumstances; some prominent ‘ulama’ resigned in opposition. The curriculum of Azhari institutes and of the university was transformed with the introduction of new subjects, in particular faculties for secular knowledge that were added to the older faculties of theology (*uṣūl al-dīn*), law (*sharī‘a wa-qānūn*), and Arabic language (*lugha ‘arabiyya*). The Nasserist regime echoed many of the criticisms directed earlier at Azhar for its passivity, in particular the Muslim Brotherhood's criticisms of Azhar as a dormant institution, which had helped justify the state's reforms. The reinvigoration of Islam had become the task of the state.

Many ‘ulama’ from Azhar continued, however, to view themselves as the guardians of the tradition, and they resented Nasser's transformation of their institution. For instance, Azhar was forced to condemn the Muslim Brotherhood when the state fought them and to legitimate socialism from an Islamic point of view. During the presidency of Anwar Sadat, however, gaining greater space to maneuver and armed with the large state bureaucracy that Nasser had created, the ‘ulama’ attempted to reform politics through their own articulation of Islamic norms. They did this, for instance, by appealing to the state for the implementation of Islamic law in the 1970s and by providing their own draft of an "Islamic constitution" in 1979. Far from losing their ability to participate in political debates, the ‘ulama’ insisted on the necessity of implementing societal and political Islamic norms as they understood them. They also reinvigorated a classical political trope in the history of Sunni Islam: in a state whose religion is Islam and for which the shari‘a is the main source of legislation—as is stated in the Egyptian constitution of 1980—it is the duty of the ‘ulama’ to articulate the Islamic norms to be followed by the state. Hence it is the responsibility of the ‘ulama’ to lay down the Islamic norms—but certainly never to govern on their own—and it is the responsibility of the policy makers who are in power to implement them. This reinvigoration of the partnership between those who have the knowledge of the foundations of Islamic law and those who devise state policy did not always provide Azhar with more legitimacy, however. This very partnership with the authoritarian state, and the administrative status of Azhar as a state institution, put Azhar's officials at odds with members of Islamist movements. Within Azhar, this partnership paradoxically created resistance against state policies through the voice of some ‘ulama’ aligned with Islamist discourses on diverse subjects from the criteria for pious public behavior to international relations. Whereas Islamist movements in general have had a negative view of Azhar's ‘ulama’ as the scholars "of the state," Azhar's leadership has been able to show some autonomy at times to force its way into politics and to make its voice heard, especially through ‘ulama’ expressing themselves in the Egyptian public arena and beyond.

See also Egypt; madrasa; ‘ulama’

Further Reading

Rainer Brunner, *Islamic Ecumenism in the 20th Century: The Azhar and Shiism between Rapprochement and Restraint*, 2004; Chris Eccel, *Egypt, Islam, and Social Change: Al-Azhar in Conflict and Accommodation*, 1984; Afaf Lutfi al-Sayyid Marsot, "The Ulama of Cairo in the 18th and the 19th Centuries," in *Scholars, Saints, and Sufis: Muslim Religious Institutions in the Middle East since 1500*, edited by Nikki R. Keddie, 1972; Malika Zeghal, *Gardiens de l'Islam: Les oulémas d'Al Azhar dans l'Égypte contemporaine*, 1996

MALIKA ZEGHAL

B

Babur, Zahir al-Din (1483–1530)

Zahir al-Din Muhammad Babur is known for three achievements. First, he survived the internecine conflict in his Central Asian homeland of modern Uzbekistan (*mā warā' al-nahr*) in the 15th and early 16th centuries. Second, he founded a Timurid state in India in 1526 generally known as the Mughal Empire. Third, he wrote a memoir that has endured as one of the richest examples of that genre.

Babur, which is a Perso-Turkish name that means lion or tiger, was a patrilineal descendant of the Turkic conqueror Timur (d. 1405), or Tamerlane in European parlance, and a matrilineal descendant of the Mongol Chingiz Khan (d. 1227). Babur was born as a Muslim in the Ferghana Valley, east-southeast of Tashkent, at a time when the region was contested by three groups, who by the late 15th century were also Muslims: his own relatives, the Timurids; the Chaghatay branch of the Mongols; and the Uzbeks, a Mongol-led Turkic tribal confederation. After inheriting his father's small Ferghana appanage in 1494 at the age of 12, he spent the next decade struggling with members of all three groups to capture Samarqand, Timur's capital, and establish himself as the recognized heir of his ancestor. After twice occupying but failing to hold the city, Babur abandoned Transoxiana in 1504 and, with fewer than 300 supporters, seized Kabul, a former Timurid outpost.

During the next decade, he fought to survive in this desolate outpost while simultaneously struggling to recapture Samarqand and his homeland. After occupying Samarqand for a third time in 1511 with help from Shah Isma'il, the Uzbeks forced him to flee the city, and by 1514 he had abandoned his attempt to return to the Timurid homeland. Babur subsequently focused his self-described *mulkgirliq*, or "kingdom-seizing," ambitions on India. Timur had invaded India in 1398 and sacked Delhi and established a Timurid claim to rule Hindustan. Babur invoked his Timurid descent to legitimize the campaigns that he began in northwestern India in 1519. After conducting a series of probing actions in territories then ruled by members of the unstable Afghan Lodi dynasty, Babur marched from Kabul in December 1525 with no more than 12,000 men and camp followers. In April 1526, he defeated the Lodhis at Panipat, a small town about 50 miles north of Delhi. Following a subsequent victory over a formidable Hindu Rajput army the following year, he spent the next three years trying to consolidate his hold over the agriculturally rich regions of the Punjab, the Ganges-Jumna Duab, and the Gangetic Valley.

Babur modeled his fragile new regime on the city-state of Herat, the city where the last great Timurid ruler, Husayn Bayqara (d. 1506), had presided over a florescence of Perso-Islamic art and literature that Ottomans, Safavids, and Indian Muslims alike idealized as a cultural golden age. As Babur demonstrates in his remarkable autobiography, his political ideal was a sedentary state dominated by Timurid and Chingizid Hanafi Sunni Muslims, who patronized Perso-Islamic literary and artistic culture, and before his death in 1530, he welcomed to his capital at Agra political, religious, and cultural refugees from the former Timurid lands in Transoxiana and Afghanistan. These included Turco-Mongol warriors; Naqshbandi Sufis, who practiced a restrained form of Sunni piety; and artistic and literary representatives of late-Timurid high culture. While Babur's Indian state is usually called the Mughal Empire, Mughal (the Persian term for Mongol) is a misleading name for a state that represented a Timurid renaissance.

See also Delhi; India; Mughals (1526–1857)

Further Reading

Jean-Louis Bacqué-Grammont, trans., *Le Livre de Babur*, 1980; Annette Susanah Beveridge, *The Bâbur-nâma in English*, 1969; Stephen F. Dale, *The Garden of the Eight Paradises: Babur and the Culture of Empire in Central Asia, Afghanistan and India 1483–1530*, 2004; W. M. Thackston Jr., *The Baburnama: Memoirs of Babur, Prince and Emperor*, 2002.

STEPHEN F. DALE

Baghdad

Baghdad has been the principal city of Iraq since the eighth century. The origin and meaning of the city's name are unknown. At least one settlement by this name existed in ancient times. In 762, it was chosen by Abu Ja'far al-Mansur, second Abbasid caliph, as the site of the dynasty's new capital, evidently because of its arable land and its proximity to trade routes and because—unlike the other places where the Abbasids had tried to establish a capital—its inhabitants were not hostile or otherwise dangerous to the dynasty. Mansur's city-complex consisted of concentric circles formed by fortified walls. The space between the first and second walls was divided into lots distributed among his allies and clients. The inner circle contained Mansur's palace, the great mosque, and government

offices. The soldiery was housed outside the walls to the northwest, and the bulk of the population, along with many of the markets, was accommodated in Karkh to the south. The caliph's city was thus an extension of his private domain. It served both to seclude him and to emphasize his centrality. The doors of the main gates were brought from the Umayyad city of Wasit and a Pharaonic site in Syria, thus symbolizing both the appropriation of the land and of the past. The city's official name was "the city of peace" (*madīnat al-salām*), perhaps reflecting the doctrine that allegiance to the imam—in this case, the Abbasid caliph—guaranteed bliss in the hereafter. The division into quadrants, the central dome, and other features may have had cosmological implications, though modern arguments to this effect are circumstantial.

Also known as the Round City, Baghdad served only intermittently as the seat of government. Mansur's successors and their dependents built new residences outside it to the northeast as well as across the river in al-Rusafah. Later caliphs left the city altogether. From 813 to 819, 'Abdallah al-Ma'mun, who had overthrown his predecessor in a destructive civil war, governed the empire from distant Marv, in what is now Turkmenistan. In 836, the caliph Abu Ishaq al-Mu'tasim transferred the seat of government to Samarra in order to accommodate his army of mostly Central Asian slave soldiers. In 892, Abu al-Abbas al-Mu'tamid returned the government to Baghdad. Under the Buyid and Seljuq emirates, which governed Iran and Iraq in the 10th and 11th centuries, the caliphs continued to live there, often under virtual house arrest. Secluded from view, they became objects of popular veneration. Sunni rulers customarily affirmed their allegiance to the caliph in Baghdad even after the caliph had ceased to exercise real authority. This state of affairs constitutes the background to the theories of the sultanate espoused by Mawardi (d. 1058) and Abu Ya'la b. al-Farra' (d. 1066).

During the two centuries that followed its foundation, Baghdad was the center of commercial and intellectual life in southwest Asia. It inherited the traditions of Medina, Kufa, and Basra in such fields as Arabic grammar, hadith, theology, and law and attracted representatives of numerous sects and schools, including Jewish and Christian as well as Muslim sects. The city itself was the subject of at least two ethical debates: one on the legality of its capture by the Muslims and the other on the permissibility of pronouncing its name, which was thought to mean "gift of the idol" in Persian. It was the birthplace of activist Hanbalism (the rigorist Sunni movement led by admirers of the hadith scholar Ahmad b. Hanbal, d. 855) and the site of frequent altercations between Sunnis and Shi'is, especially in the tenth century.

In 1258, the Mongols sacked the city and massacred many of its inhabitants, including the caliph Abu Ahmad al-Musta'sim. The city was never again to house a caliph, though a nominal Abbasid line persisted in Cairo until 1517. After a century of Turkoman rule (1410–1508) and a brief period of Safavid control, the city came under the sovereignty of the Ottomans (1534). It remained in Ottoman hands until World War I, after which Iraq came under a British mandate.

Since 1932, Baghdad has served as the capital of the modern nation of Iraq. Although the early Islamic-period structures, built of perishable mud brick, have completely disappeared, modern Baghdad contains numerous memorials that recall the Islamic and pre-Islamic past. Many Muslims, especially Arab Muslims, associate the city with the golden age of Arab-Islamic culture. After the U.S.-led invasion and occupation of Iraq (2003) and the civil conflicts between Sunni and Shi'i factions that ensued, the city became an especially poignant symbol of tarnished glory.

See also city; Iraq

Further Reading

Amatzia Baram, *Culture, History, and Ideology in the Formation of Ba'thist Iraq, 1968–89*, 1991; K.A.C. Creswell, *A Short Account of Early Muslim Architecture*, revised by James W. Allan, 1989; Jacob Lassner, *The Shaping of Abbasid Rule*, 1980; Idem, *The Topography of Baghdad in the Early Middle Ages: Text and Studies*, 1970; Guy Le Strange, *Baghdad during the Abbasid Caliphate from Contemporary Arabic and Persian Sources*, 1900, repr. 1972.

MICHAEL COOPERSON

Bangladesh

Long considered the backwoods of Indian Islam, Bangladesh has become one of the largest Muslim countries in the world. Concentrated in an area approximately the size of Wisconsin, its total population as of 2010 exceeds 150 million, 87 percent of whom are Sunnis. Part of a larger political-linguistic entity called Bengal, the region was divided into two halves in 1947 when the British left India and handed over the eastern half (then known as East Bengal), with an overwhelming Muslim majority, to Pakistan and the other half (called West Bengal), with a Hindu majority, to India, even though both halves shared a common ethnic and linguistic tradition and history. East Bengal, renamed East Pakistan in 1947, soon came into conflict with the dominant Pakistani landowning military and bureaucratic elite based in West Pakistan, principally over the sharing of resources but also on the question of autonomy for the province and the status of the Bengali language.

The Language Movement of 1952, which demanded recognition of Bengali as one of the state languages, was the first political manifestation of this discontent. The killing of several university students on February 21 by police dramatically transformed the language issue into a resistance movement against the policies of the central government and brought it to the center of political and cultural discourse in Bangladesh. Widely celebrated as the Martyrs' Day through annual marches, cultural events, songs, and literature, the incident galvanized increasing popular support during the next few years. By 1969, this support developed into a mass movement for greater autonomy and finally, by 1970, into a

full-fledged war of liberation, resulting in the creation of Bangladesh on March 26, 1971, under the leadership of Shaykh Mujibur Rahman (d. 1975).

The region came under Muslim political control gradually under the Delhi Sultanate starting in the 13th century. Through a long process of Sufi propagation, acculturation, land reclamation, and immigration from outside Bengal, a greater part of the area ultimately became Muslim. However, the religious tradition that developed there was a unique mix of orthodoxy and Sufism, which, coupled with accretions from local popular cultural symbols and rituals, was unique to Bangladesh. Since the 19th century, a powerful purist trend initiated by a series of Islamic reform movements, notably the Faraizi and the Tariqah-i-Muhammadiya, seriously challenged the older traditions. This tension, manifested through conflicting ideologies and symbols, led to continued violence and dissension. The fundamentalist group Jama'at-i Islami, which opposed the Bangladesh Liberation War and collaborated with the Pakistani regime, became one of the most divisive forces in the country. Several other underground extremist Islamist organizations, such as the Harkat-ul-Jihad-i-Islami and the Jama'atul Mujahideen Bangladesh, kept the tension alive. Corruption at all levels of government, the lack of political will and determination, the politicization of the police force, and the growing ambition of the armed forces further complicated the situation.

Notwithstanding the tension, Bangladesh has made great strides in alleviating poverty in recent years under the leadership of several nongovernmental organizations (NGOs), notably the Grameen Bank, initiated by Muhammad Yunus in 1983. Designed to address the problems of those in extreme poverty, especially women, through a unique microcredit system, Yunus and his bank were awarded the Nobel Peace Prize in 2006. The initiative made Bangladesh a leader in empowering the poor despite being one of the poorest countries in the world.

See also India; Jama'at-i Islami; Pakistan

Further Reading

Rafiuddin Ahmed, ed., *Religion, Nationalism, and Politics in Bangladesh*, 1990; Richard M. Eaton, *The Rise of Islam and the Bengal Frontier 1204–1760*, 1993.

RAFIUDDIN AHMED

al-Banna, Hasan (1906–49)

Hasan al-Banna (1906–49) was the founder and lifetime leader of the Egyptian Muslim Brotherhood (al-Ikhwan al-Muslimun, MB), for decades the largest and most influential Islamic movement in the Arab Middle East. Formed in 1928, the MB was still active in Egypt and many other Muslim countries at the beginning of the 21st century. Information on Banna's life, career, and character derives mostly from his so-called memoirs (*Mudhakkirat al-Da'wa wa-l-Da'iya*), probably compiled in 1947–48, as well as sympathetic reports from his family and members of the MB. His own writings, which in addition to his "memoirs" include editorials, tracts, sermons, and fatwas (legal opinions), constitute functional prose, written almost exclusively for the Muslim Brothers and published by their press.

From an early age, Banna was influenced by Salafi reformism; "sober," shari'a-oriented popular Sufism; and Egyptian patriotism, as understood in his particular sociocultural milieu. Banna was born in the small town of Mahmudiyya in the western Nile Delta near Rosetta (Rashid). He was the eldest son of Shaykh Ahmad al-Banna al-Sa'ati (1882–1958), a clockmaker with a good religious education; his mother was the daughter of a local merchant, whose family included men of religious learning. It is worthy to note that Shaykh Ahmad, who represented the familiar type of the artisan-cum-scholar, published several works on Sufi texts and prophetic traditions, including Ahmad b. Hanbal's *Musnad*, which he rearranged according to subject matter, testifying to the enduring attraction of hadith studies in a Muslim milieu that was at the same time reform-minded and rooted in tradition.

Banna's education was a blend of Qur'anic schooling (*kuttāb*) and government schooling, where he specialized in the Arabic language. In this field, secular government education retained core elements of traditional religious learning, both in subject matter and methods of instruction. In 1919, he enrolled in the primary teachers' training school in Damanhur, a commercial center in the Nile Delta. From 1923 to 1927, he attended Dar al-'Ulum in Cairo, founded in 1872 to train teachers for the new government schools. This training college was a prime example of the educational crossover between the religious and the secular, the traditional and the modern. However, it was not his education that singled Banna out but his early commitment to an "Islamic morality" combining core concepts of Islamic reform with Sufi teachings. His efforts started with individual acts of vigilantism, undertaken as a schoolboy in Mahmudiyya. While still in primary school, he joined with friends in an association to "form" their character and manners (*takwīn al-akhlāq*) and to fulfill the Qur'anic injunction "to command right and forbid wrong" (*al-amr bi-l-ma'rūf wa-l-nahy 'an al-munkar*), which was to play a crucial role in Banna's career as an Islamic activist. Outside school, in a Sufi setting, he and his friends formed the Hasafi Benevolent Society to spread the call to Islam (*da'wa*). Banna had been attracted to the Hasafi Shadhili brotherhood when he was 12 years old, and his affiliation with them greatly eased his transition from country town to provincial city to capital.

In 1927, Banna was sent to Isma'iliyya on the Suez Canal to teach Arabic at a primary school. Although not yet 21, he had vowed to engage in *da'wa* to call his fellow Muslims to true Islam. There is no indication that Banna ever thought of proselytizing among non-Muslims or of engaging in interreligious dialogue. What the mission did include was the fight against Christian missionaries from Europe and America who were increasingly active in the Egyptian countryside at the time.

In March 1928, Banna joined with six young men from modest backgrounds to create the MB. The MB recruited mainly through personal contacts based on kinship, friendship, and worship; mosques and schools were their principal recruiting grounds. In contrast to the existing political parties in the country, their press effort was insignificant. Indoctrination played a crucial role in enhancing internal cohesion and public appeal, with instruction being based almost exclusively on Banna's speeches, articles, and tracts or treatises (*rasā'il*). Several of these tracts were required reading, ideally to be memorized by members; some were later supplemented with commentaries (*sharḥ*) by members of the MB. The journalistic style and format Banna employed places him in the tradition of modern Arab and Islamic reformism. His objective, however, was not to invite critical debate and reflection but to offer "guidance" and "correct instruction." It is no coincidence that his title as leader of the MB was "general" or "supreme guide" (*al-murshid al-'āmm*).

Banna and his associates built an organization with a solid structure and trained cadres that took Islamic education beyond the mosque, the school, and the press and linked it to larger social and political concerns, giving it a new shape and momentum. In just over a decade and a half, the MB changed from a charitable association with a strong Sufi touch into a nonelite mass movement. With its popular base, style, and agenda, it appealed mostly to the educated and semieducated urban middle class (*efendiyya*). Over the course of the 1930s, it spread to the Suez Canal, the Delta, and Upper Egypt, yet it was only during World War II that the MB emerged as a mass movement on par with the nationalist Wafd Party. In 1944, estimates ranged from 100,000 to 500,000 members (out of a population of some 19 million). By that time, the organization consisted of several units. The MB Organization and its Section of Welfare and Social Services as well as the Rover Scouts (*jawwāla*) and the Battalions (*katā'ib*) all operated in the open, whereas a Special Section, probably created around 1940, operated underground. The MB's military support of the Palestinian Arabs before and after the foundation of the State of Israel in May 1948 earned them respect; the terrorist activities of the Special Section raised widespread alarm. On December 8, 1948, the government declared the MB dissolved; on December 28, 1948, the prime minister was assassinated by a young member of the organization; and on February 12, 1949, Banna was shot by the secret police.

As a thinker, Banna was neither original nor sophisticated, nor did he wish to be so. He was an activist who essentially "put to work" what Muslim reformers had been advocating since the 1870s. His objective was to establish a moral order based on true Islam, which was to end all forms of foreign influence in the country and the Islamic world at large. From this perspective, Islam served as a source of empowerment with the potential to liberate Egypt and the Muslim community and indeed to save humanity. This required a program of individual and communal reform, struggle, and dedication, involving *da'wa* as well as jihad. The MB offered an Islamic education (*tarbiya*) and moral orientation (*tahdhīb*) to their fellow Muslims in order to make them "understand Islam correctly." Education and *da'wa* were thus intimately linked. But Banna also propagated jihad, covering the broad range of meanings from self-discipline to armed struggle, also described in the Islamic tradition as the "greater" and the "lesser" jihad. Thus he extolled the military spirit of the earliest generations of Muslims, *al-salaf al-ṣāliḥ*, and famously celebrated "the art of death" (*fann al-mawt*) to be cultivated by the Muslim activist. Yet his choice of words remained open to interpretation. On many occasions, he also advocated peace, and in contrast to later Islamists such as Sayyid Qutb (1906–66), he did not encourage *takfīr* (i.e., excluding believers from the Muslim community and declaring jihad against them licit).

Banna's "activist thinking" (*fikr ḥarakī*) was characteristic of modern Islamic discourse in that it integrated established terms and references in a new framework, subtly modifying their status and meaning. It was nothing new to state, as he did, that Islam provided the moral foundation of community and society. But it was decidedly modern to claim that Islam was a comprehensive "system" or "order" (*niẓām*) regulating individual life as well as public affairs. According to Banna, Islam was eternal, universal, and all encompassing; simple, easy, and practical; and comprised not just faith, dogma, and ritual obligations but also work and action (*'amal*). His aim was to create "a modern Islamic style" (*minhāj 'aṣrī islāmī*), a style that adapted to contemporary needs and aspirations while remaining firmly rooted in the Qur'an and sunna. In Islam, Banna asserted, religion and politics could not be separated. The state fulfilled crucial functions: namely, to implement the Islamic way of life, or the Islamic order, based on the shari'a; to defend Islam; to ensure social justice; and to exert moral control. The caliphate played no prominent role in Banna's vision; he thought in terms of the modern nation-state. With regard to the political system, Banna advocated "constitutional consultative rule" (*ḥukm dustūrī shūrawī*) based on consultation (*shūrā*) and a written constitution, but he rejected a multiparty system and party politics (*ḥizbiyya*). His position on the status of non-Muslims in the "Islamic order" was less clear: the terms he used in this context—*umma* (nation), *waṭan* (homeland), *muwāṭin* (citizen or compatriot), and *jinsiyya islāmiyya* (Islamic citizenship)—remained vague and ill-defined.

With regard to socioeconomic issues, Banna invoked the ideal of a community beyond race and class, building on the tradition of "Islamic egalitarianism" (as described by Louise Marlow). He denounced class struggle; anticommunism was a cornerstone of his worldview. To effect change, he encouraged individual thrift and industry and decried the pervading spirit of materialism and consumerism, while he simultaneously advocated state intervention to eradicate poverty, illiteracy, and disease. More specifically, he called for a ban on interest (*ribā*) and saw the Islamic alms tax (zakat) as an instrument to promote social justice.

Banna did not underrate the importance of material resources in achieving liberation from foreign domination. But he put even greater emphasis on interior strength or moral fiber and was

convinced that men could improve their lot through their own efforts. Banna thus thoroughly embraced 19th-century faith in self-help and moral improvement with an emphasis on individual responsibility, not individual freedom. His aim was not to foster individualism but to *form* the self and *reform* the community to render them capable of installing the "Islamic order." His concern with discipline, self-observation, and time management may have been influenced by Ghazali's *Ihya' 'Ulum al-Din* (The revival of the religious sciences), which Banna read with one of his Sufi shaykhs. The influence is there, but the differences must not be ignored: it is not introspection and self-purification that Banna sought to promote but an active involvement in the world with energies directed outward, not inward. Throughout, he espoused a decidedly masculine ethos, which he wished to instill in Muslim youths. With regard to women's rights, he opposed female liberation or emancipation and endorsed the principle of male guardianship over women (*qiwāma*, based on Q. 4:34), denying women access to leading positions in society, as well as in the MB, as not befitting their sex and nature.

Banna's death threw the MB into profound disarray, yet it survived and reemerged in the 1980s. Together with Sayyid Qutb, who joined the MB in the early 1950s, Banna remains one of the central figures of modern Sunni Islamism, whose legacy continues to be invoked by the MB and their critics alike.

See also Egypt; fundamentalism; jihad; Muslim Brotherhood; revival and reform

Further Reading

Gudrun Krämer, *Hasan al-Banna*, 2010; Brynjar Lia, *The Society of the Muslim Brothers in Egypt: The Rise of an Islamic Mass Movement 1928–1942*, 1998; Richard P. Mitchell, *The Society of the Muslim Brothers*, 1993; Gregory Starrett, *Putting Islam to Work: Education, Politics, and Religious Transformation in Egypt*, 1998; Charles Wendell, *Five Tracts of Hasan Al-Banna' (1906–1949): A Selection from Majmū'at Rasā'il al-Imām al-Shahīd Ḥasan al-Bannā'*, 1978.

GUDRUN KRÄMER

Barelwis

The Barelwi movement represents the devotional tradition of Sufi-related Sunni scholars and schools from South Asia, which has expanded to many countries hosting Muslim migrants from the region. It derived from the legacy of the religious scholar Ahmad Raza Khan Barelwi (1856–1921) in the town of Bareilly in North India. He gathered guardians of Sufi shrines (*pīrs*) and Muslim theologians (*mawlānā*) of devotional Islam around the turn of the 20th century to counter the critique of their beliefs and practice by puritan reformist scholars of the Deobandi tradition, which emanated from the Islamic school of Deoband (1866), not far from Bareilly. Their doctrinal differences were small, as both followed orthodox adherence (*taqlīd*) to the Hanafi school of law. But the Barelwis held on to Sufi-influenced rituals, such as the expression of special praise for the Prophet, public celebrations of his birthday (*mawlid*), and the worship of saints and their shrines with their associated powers of intercession, based on their reading of the Qur'an and the hadith (i.e., the prophetic traditions). The Barelwis are also linked to some of the Sufi brotherhoods (*tarīqa*), mostly branches of the Qadiri and the Naqshbandi orders. Their cultural style has been exuberant, and their politics were often marked by loyalty to the ruling powers during the colonial period and afterward to the independent states of South Asia. Unlike the Deobandis, they fully supported the Pakistan movement for the partition of British India.

The Barelwi network significantly expanded and emulated the Deobandi institutions with which they saw themselves in strong competition. In 1900, they created an umbrella group of theologians, the Jama'at-e Ahl-e Sunnat—that is, the party of the people following the traditions of the Prophet and his Companions (sunna), showing that they regard themselves as the only true Sunnis. From there they appropriated the label "Sunni" as their trademark designation in South Asian Islam. In 1920, they created the All-India Sunni Conference (AISC) to champion their religious and political interests during the late colonial era. The Barelwis formalized their system of religious education by establishing a large number of new madrasas and *dār-ul-'ulūms*. In Pakistan, they formed their own Board of Religious Education (Tanzim-ul-Madaris), working on parallel lines with the Deobandis. Across South Asia their relative influence among the Muslim population was estimated as being roughly on par with the Deobandis.

The Barelwis developed close links with the ruling families and political culture of Pakistan. They established their own political party, the Jam'iat-e 'Ulama'-e Pakistan (JUP, Party of Religious Scholars of Pakistan), which emerged in 1948 out of the AISC. Since the 1990s, Barelwi leaders in Pakistan increasingly cooperated with the Deobandis in public life. To push back sectarianism, they joined forces in 1995 in the National Reconciliation Council (Milli Yakjehti Council), led by the late Barelwi leader Maulana Shah Ahmad Noorani (1926–2003). He initiated a formal alliance of religious parties in Pakistan in 2001, the Muttahida Majlis-e-'Amal (MMA). During the Afghan war in the 1990s, the Barelwis also became part of the emerging mujahidin culture in Pakistan. Their own religious militias participated in the conflicts of Kashmir and Afghanistan. Barelwi representatives also sat on the coordinating body of the Afghan Jihad Council. Since the 1980s, militant sectarian groups confronted Deobandi radicals in deadly strife over the control of mosques and "un-Islamic" rituals and behavior. Sectarian beliefs were as influential among the Barelwis as among Deobandis. They denounced all dissenting sects as un-Islamic and joined forces against groups such as the Ahmadis, whom they saw as heretical. Arshad-ul-Qadri (1925–2002) was one of the most prominent Barelwi polemicists.

To compete with the rising influence of the Deobandi-dominated missionary movement of the Tablighi Jama'at (Preaching Movement), the Barelwis created the Da'wat-e Islami (Islamic Mission) in 1981, with affiliated groups in India under the name of the Sunni Da'wat-i Islami (Sunni Islamic Mission). The Barelwi doctrine also influenced followers of modern groups such as the political-educational movement of the Minhaj-ul-Qur'an (Quranic Path) and the Muttahida Qaumi Movement (MQM, United National Movement). The World Islamic Mission, based in Britain, is the oldest international Barelwi platform. The global Barelwi and related Sufi network serves the wider Pakistani diaspora and other South Asian migrant communities around the globe, although the Barelwi groups do not commonly attract followers beyond the limitations of their ethnic South Asian descent.

See also Deobandis; India; Pakistan

Further Reading

Arshad-ul Qadri, *Tableeghi Jamaat in the Light of Facts and Truth*, 1996; Dietrich Reetz, *Islam in the Public Sphere: Religious Groups in India, 1900–1947*, 2006; Usha Sanyal, *Devotional Islam and Politics in British India: Ahmad Riza Khan Barelwi and His Movement, 1870–1920*, 1996; Oskar Verkaaik, *Migrants and Militants: Fun and Urban Violence in Pakistan*, 2004.

DIETRICH REETZ

Ba'th Party

Hizb al-Ba'th al-'Arabi al-Ishtiraki (Party of Arab Socialist Resurrection) is a Pan-Arab nationalist party founded in the 1940s that exerted far-reaching political and cultural influence on the Arab world, particularly in Syria and Iraq. Though conceived as a secular nationalist movement, its ideology considered Islam a vital part of Arab heritage but not the basis for politics. In practice, Ba'thists have been antagonistic to members of the traditional Muslim elite as well as violent opponents of Salafism and Shi'i religious movements.

Party Origins

Upon their return to Damascus, Syria, from university studies in Europe, Michel 'Aflaq and Salah al-Din al-Bitar (1912–80) began a discussion circle among the city's educated young men that would form the nucleus of the Ba'th Party (1942). Both 'Aflaq, a Greek Orthodox Christian, and Bitar, a Sunni Muslim, were of solid middle-class origins and brought to the party their distrust of the elite and bourgeois nationalists of a previous generation who had failed to rid Syria of colonial rule. The party's ranks were swelled by the addition of the followers of an embittered 'Alawi refugee intellectual from the Sanjak of Alexandretta, Zaki al-Arsuzi (1901–68), who also brought to the party an emphasis on social justice, the cult of personality, and Arab chauvinism. The party's socialism and secularism held little appeal for Syria's Sunni elite or its middle class. Nevertheless, the party proved particularly attractive to non-Sunni landowners and rural smallholders, Arab Christians, and junior officers.

The Ba'th Party in Syria and Iraq

The party held its first congress in 1947. Branches of the party were founded in Iraq, Jordan, and Lebanon in the early 1950s. Gamal Abdel Nasser's rise to power and his advocacy of Arab unity gave a considerable boost to the party's program. In 1958, Syrian Ba'thists engineered the short-lived period of unity with Egypt (1958–61), creating the United Arab Republic (UAR). After the failure of the UAR, the center of gravity in the Syrian wing of the party shifted to military cadres dominated by 'Alawis and Sunnis of rural and peasant origin. This faction, led by Minister of Defense Hafiz al-Asad (1930–2000), took control of Syria (1970) following a bloodless coup. Asad rejected many of the more radical dimensions of Ba'thism and Pan-Arabism in favor of regionalism. An 'Alawi from the area of Latakia in northwestern Syria, Asad placed 'Alawis and Christians in positions of leadership in the state and party apparatus, further supplanting members of the Sunni middle class and elite in the process.

The Ba'th Party had a similar trajectory in Iraq. As in Syria, Ba'thism proved initially attractive to non-Sunni-Arab educated young men, in this case Shi'is. Shi'i leadership gave way in the years before the 1968 coup, which brought the Ba'thists to power, as 'Aflaq, then still party leader, appointed men from Iraq's Sunni minority, including a young Saddam Hussein (1937–2006), to key regional leadership positions. Throughout the 1970s, Hussein and his kinsmen from the city of Takrit methodically took control of the state and the party. The régime that emerged was authoritarian in nature and sought to control all aspects of culture, religion, and thought through a vast secret police network and the party's ideological domination of education, the arts, and media. Though weakened in the period following the Gulf War (1991), the Iraqi Ba'thists under Hussein remained in tight control of the majority of Iraq until 2003 when the U.S.-led occupation of Iraq and the systematic program of de-Ba'thification eliminated the party as a viable entity.

Ba'thism and Islam

Ba'thism is an amalgamation of leftist and ultranationalist ideas from 1930s and 1940s Europe. The basic tenets of the party are embodied in its slogan, "Freedom, Unity, and Socialism." The party is secular in its view of citizenship and political participation, seeing religious distinction as antimodern and an impediment to Arab unity. However, Ba'thism does reserve a special role for Islam in the formation of the "Arab spirit" and character and considers it, with language, as the essential element of Arab heritage (*turāth*). As the party's chief ideologue, 'Aflaq developed this idea first in his essay "Valediction for the Arab Prophet" (1943), in which he identifies Muhammad as the ideal prototype of the

fully realized Arab ("Muhammad was all the Arabs. May all the Arabs today be Muhammad") and sees Islam as the basis for a particular Arab humanism. Later essays explicitly identify Islam as the genius of the Arabs and argue that the manner in which Ba'thism incorporates Islam into its ideology prevents Arab nationalism from becoming a sterile copy of European nationalism and precludes the need to use Islam as the basis of a reactionary political movement. While 'Aflaq represents the dominant trend in Ba'thist thought, others in the party, including Arsuzi, were more reluctant to valorize Islam in such a way, preferring atheism. Nevertheless, mainstream Ba'thism secularized Islam, making it exterior to politics but seeking to capture it as a feature of Arab history and culture.

Throughout the 1980s and 1990s, both Ba'thist régimes suffered crises of legitimacy in part based on their lack of credible Muslim credentials. In response, the Syrian Ba'thist leadership sought greater accommodation with Islam by making changes to the constitution to guarantee that the head of state would be a Muslim, more closely identifying heterodox 'Alawism with Twelver Shi'ism, and assuring the president's attendance at Friday prayers at Damascus's Umayyad Mosque. In Iraq, the crisis emerged during the war with Iran (1980–88) and worsened with the Gulf War and its aftermath. Saddam Hussein responded with largely symbolic measures, including renouncing Ba'thist secularism, adding the *takbīr* ("God is great") in his own handwriting to the Iraqi flag, banning the sale of alcohol, rescinding some women's rights, encouraging veiling, and embarking on massive mosque-building programs.

To many mainstream Muslims, Ba'thism is inherently un-Islamic. This is, in part, based on the leading role Christians and heterodox Muslims have played—and continue to play—in the formulation of party ideology and leadership. It also derives from episodes like the massacre of members of the Muslim Brotherhood (an organization that was outlawed in Syria) and its supporters during an abortive uprising in Syria in 1983, the most violent moment of which occurred in the central Syrian city of Hama when Syrian forces killed an estimated 20,000 people and destroyed several of the city's important mosques and shrines. Systematic Ba'thist persecution of religious Shi'is took place in Iraq, the most noteworthy examples being the murder of Ayatollah Muhammad Baqir al-Sadr (1935–80) and members of his family and the mass killings and desecration of holy sites during the Shi'i uprising following the Gulf War.

See also 'Aflaq, Michel (1910–89); Arab nationalism; Iraq; Syria

Further Reading

Michel 'Aflaq, *al-Ba'th wa-l-Turath*, 1976; Eric Davis, *Memories of State: Politics, History, and Collective Identity in Modern Iraq*, 2005; Ray Hinnesbusch, *Syria: Revolution from Above*, 2002; Patrick Seale, *Asad: The Struggle for the Middle East*, 1990.

KEITH DAVID WATENPAUGH

bazaar

The word "bazaar" can refer to a periodic market such as a weekly farmers' market or a fair held at specific times of the year. But in modern Persian, it usually refers to a permanent and more abstract entity—namely, the sector of the economy comprising all levels of trade, from wholesale, brokerage, midlevel business, and distribution, to small-scale businesses and shops. It can also refer to the physical establishment in which trade is conducted or the underlying financial system.

In the cultural region roughly encompassing Iran, Afghanistan, northern India, and Central Asia, the term usually applies to an architectural complex that houses merchants, brokers, retailers, and craftsmen, divided into sections according to the commodity sold. These complexes usually comprise a row or several rows of two-story buildings. The buildings are connected by a brick ceiling consisting of small domes over the alleyways. There is an opening at the center of each minidome for light and ventilation. This design provides the alleyways with some light and keeps the complex cool in summer. In a typical bazaar, the top level of the buildings is usually used by wholesalers and brokers and sometimes for storage, while the lower level houses shopkeepers and craftsmen. Additionally, the bazaar complex may contain social institutions such as mosques and madrasas (Muslim schools). Sometimes there are also interior courtyards and smaller caravansaries adjacent to the bazaar. Caravansaries are hostel-like establishments for merchants from out of town. In larger cities, some caravansaries could be at the outskirts of the town and spatially separated from the bazaar.

The bazaar complex can have anywhere from two hundred shops to several thousand in major cities. The Friday mosque is sometimes next to or part of the bazaar complex, which adds a religious aspect to the otherwise mostly economical and social significance of the bazaar. In most major cities, the bazaar complex is in a central position in the city, which gives it prominence. A perfect example is the Safavid capital Isfahan, where the complex of Maydan-i Shah houses the palace, several mosques, and a new bazaar.

There are no (permanent) residences within the bazaar complex, so it can be locked at night or on holidays. It can also be closed for political protest. For instance, during the Iranian revolution of 1979, prolonged planned closure of the bazaar of Tehran was used as a means of protest.

See also capitalism; trade and commerce

Further Readings

P. W. English, *City and Village in Iran*, 1966; M. Scharabi, *Der Bazar*, 1985.

HADI JORATI

Beirut

Beirut, a port on the eastern shore of the Mediterranean Sea at the foot of Mount Lebanon and the capital of Lebanon, became a Roman colony town in 14 BCE and developed into an important center of commerce and learning in Roman times. Destroyed by an earthquake in 551, it was easily conquered by the Muslim Arabs in 635. The Umayyads and Fatimids transformed it into a fortified city, but it fell to the onslaught of the Crusaders in 1110. Retaken by Saladin in 1187, it was lost again to the Crusaders, who were finally driven out by the Mamluks in 1291. Under Mamluk rule, the defenses of Beirut were reinforced and its commerce with Italian cities flourished. From 1516 onward, the city passed under Ottoman rule and, in the 18th century, fell under the control of local feudal lords. Because of an influx of Christian refugees from Syria from 1860 onward, it acquired a growing Christian minority. During the French Mandate (1920–43), Beirut became the capital of an independent Lebanese Republic in 1926 in which Maronite and Orthodox Christians played an important role. It developed into an important intellectual center of the Middle East, with three universities (American, French, and Lebanese) and a National Library.

Since the late 19th century, Beirut has served as the gateway to the Middle East. Its port harbored early steam ships that carried passengers and freight, and it remains a regional center of shipping and trade. Its highways extend north and east over the Lebanon range of mountains to Syria. Beirut has a mercantile, cosmopolitan spirit that some Lebanese trace to their Phoenician origins. The mix of Christian and Muslim populations makes Beirut unique among the cities of the Arab Middle East.

At the end of the 19th century, the population of the city was mainly Sunni Muslim and Greek Orthodox, but the centrality of the city also drew in Maronites from the mountains and some Shi'is from the Biqaa valley. In 1948, Palestinian refugees were crowded into camps on the periphery of Beirut; In the 1970s, Israeli retaliation for attacks by the Palestine resistance drove Shi'is from their villages in the south to the suburbs of Beirut to form the southern suburbs (*ḍāḥiyya*). This completely changed the makeup of the city, which had traditionally consisted of Sunnis and Christians and now also included an increasing number of Shi'is.

In 1973, Israeli Defense Forces raided Palestinian targets in Beirut in retaliation for the Munich massacre of the previous year, in which militant Palestinians had kidnapped and executed Israeli Olympians. The general breakdown in order erupted into civil war in April 1975. The Palestinians living in camps on the outskirts of the city were able for a time to cut Beirut off completely from the rest of the country. After the civil war, Beirut was a divided city with Christians on the east and Muslims on the west. Another Israeli incursion in 1982, this time as far as Beirut, led to the emergence of Hizbullah, a Shi'i militant resistance movement that has evolved into an influential political party. Following the Ta'if Accords of 1989, peace was established and Beirut began the process of reunification. Prime Minister Rafiq al-Hariri is to be largely credited for the normalization following the civil war, a task he was unable to complete because of his assassination in 2005.

In spite of the trauma that Beirut has experienced in recent history, Lebanese publishing houses continue to publish literature from all corners of the Arab world and participate in book fairs. Bank secrecy laws have made Beirut the banking hub of the region. Centers of learning such as the American University of Beirut continue to attract international scholars. It appears that the city's cosmopolitanism combined with a Mediterranean climate will continue to provide the capital necessary for its place as a cultural hub in the modern Arab world.

See also Jordan; minorities; Palestine; Syria

Further Reading

Samir Khalaf, *Heart of Beirut: Reclaiming the Bourj*, 2006; Samir Khalaf and Philip Khoury, *Recovering Beirut,* 1993; Samir Kassir, *Beirut*, translated by M. B. Bebevoise, 2010.

JOHN DONOHUE

Berbers

The Berbers are the indigenous inhabitants of North Africa from the oasis of Siwa in Egypt to the Atlantic Ocean. Their distant origins are much contested, and their conceptualization as a single people rests primarily on the understanding that their languages belong to a single linguistic family, variously classified as Afro-Asian or Hamitic. At the time of the Arabo-Islamic conquest, the Arabs understood them to be one of the major non-Arab ('Ajam) peoples who accepted Islam. Over time, however, 'Ajam increasingly denoted the Persians, while *barābira*, a term probably derived from the perjorative Greek *barbaroi* or Latin *barbari*, came to be used for the "barbarian" tribes of the Islamic "wild west." There is little evidence that the Berbers considered themselves a united people prior to the 20th century, and they certainly did not believe that they had a single political destiny. However, their political history has largely been written by outsiders: first, the Arabs and subsequently the French, who did view them in this light and thus measured their political achievements by an external yardstick predicated on the desirability of national unity.

In particular, French colonial historiography, which has been highly influential in determining both indigenous and postcolonial understandings of the Berbers, posits a North African religiopolitical trajectory, according to which the Berbers repeatedly attempted to create a "national" state by means of the Fatimids, Almoravids, and Almohads, only to succumb to their inherent factional tendencies. These tendencies divided the Maghrib into

three political units, roughly coterminous with modern Morocco, Algeria, and Tunisia in the 13th century. At the same time, the Berbers lost control of significant portions of the countryside to Arab tribes migrating west who initiated rural linguistic Arabization. In the 15th century, "outsiders"—Arabs of sharifi descent (descent from the Prophet) in Morocco and Ottomans of various ethnic origins in Algeria and Tunisia—seized control of these political entities but failed to incorporate their restive Berber populations, many of whom had retreated to the mountain ranges and deserts as Arabic-speaking tribes came to dominate the lowlands. Berbers were finally integrated into the state only under the aegis of French colonialism.

From the imperial French perspective, this success reflected not only France's military and cultural superiority but also their ability to appeal to the true Berber spirit, liberate it from the bonds of Arab Islam, and return it to its supposed Christian European essence (a reference to the importance of Christianity in North Africa in the days of St. Augustine). The significance of this view may be seen in the factually accurate but implicitly negative historical sections of the article on the Berbers in the second edition of the *Encyclopaedia of Islam*. Conversely, the chimera of unity has inspired Berbers in the modern states of the Maghrib to reimagine their history as that of the Imazighen (sing. Amazigh), a term meaning free men comparable to the Arabic *aḥrār*, both of which originally encapsulated the pride of tribal peoples who were beholden to no political master due to their ability to evade taxation or co-optation except on their own terms.

Contemporary Maghribi political discourse incorporates the colonial concept of the Berbers as one people, albeit with the more positive aim of forcing the contemporary governments of Algeria and Morocco to accept the indigenous Berber component of national identity rather than continuing to impose a hegemonic Arabo-Islamic identity. Many Berbers were happy to subscribe to an Arabo-Islamic identity during the height of Pan-Arab nationalism and the struggle for independence in North Africa. But now many Berbers wish to see their own languages and cultures recognized within the national framework in the Maghrib and beyond it to diaspora Amazigh communities in France and the United States, who consider themselves Imazighen as much as Moroccans or Algerians.

Much of this would have made little sense to the premodern inhabitants of the Maghrib, whose main political objective seems to have been to negotiate a religiopolitical identity within Islam as distinct tribes or ethnolinguistic communities. It is apparent that from an early stage, the tribes of North Africa found the Islamic paradigm of a prophet and a book compelling but sought to disconnect it from Arab overlordship while also using it as a mode of differentiation within the supposed Berber world. Most famously, the Barghawata tribes of the Atlantic plains of Morocco identified Salih, one of their own ancestors, as their prophet and produced their own book apparently in the Barghawata dialect. Other groups showed sympathy for the oppositional discourses of mainstream Islam such as Kharijism and various 'Alid and Shi'i belief systems, which served to assert not a Berber identity writ large but rather more local ethnolinguistic identities. For example, Kharijism, an early Islamic sect, in its Ibadi form underpinned the development of the state of Tahart, which united sections of the Lawata, Nafusa, Nafzawa, and Hawwara, among others, while rival Sufri Kharijism was adopted by the Maknasa, who founded the city state of Sijilmasa. Farther north, the Awraba settled for 'Alid leadership in the form of the Idrisids, who established Fez.

The most famous Berber political endeavors are, however, the empire-building experiments of the 10th to 13th centuries, described in great detail in Ibn Khaldun's seminal *Kitab al-'Ibar* (The book on important events). Although this historical work is best known for its introduction, the *Muqaddima*, it is also one of the most complete compilations of information on the rise and fall of various Maghribi states led by an assortment of different Berber peoples. Ibn Khaldun superficially gives the Berbers a unitary identity but then deconstructs it by dividing them into two main groups descended from the eponymous ancestors Butr and Baranis, respectively. He then subdivides them further into large ethnolinguistic communities such as the Awraba and Masmuda, reckoned to be Baranis, and the Lawata, Nafusa, Nafzawa, and Zanata of the Butr, to name but a few. Additionally, Ibn Khaldun removes some groups from this genealogical schema completely, such as the Sanhaja, who claimed to be descendants of the Arabs of Himyar in Yemen and therefore not Berber at all.

Given the huge geographical expanse of the Maghrib, this diversity is not surprising. Ibn Khaldun's accounts of the Fatimid, Almoravid, and Almohad movements testify to Islam's powerful role in enabling larger political formations to coalesce. In the case of the Fatimid mission among the Kutama tribe of Ifriqiya (roughly, modern Tunisia) and the Almoravid appeal to the Lamtuna, Lamta, and Guddala peoples of the Sanhaja tribe in Saharan Africa, the initial supremacy of one Berber group was quickly elided by the Arabo-Islamic character of the message itself. Almohadism was, however, slightly different. Although the movement's founder, Muhammad b. Tumart, was inspired by various eastern Islamic religious trends, he reportedly taught his Masmuda followers in their own tongue and perhaps even prepared didactic materials in their language.

That said, Arabic quickly came to dominate at the level of government due to its already well-entrenched predominance in religious, governmental, and urban settings. This may have had something to do with the assumption of leadership by the lineage of 'Abd al-Mu'min, a member of the Kumiyya tribe, which was part of the Zanata who shared the Sanhaja's pretensions to Arab rather than indigenous lineage. While the Almohad successor states in the Maghrib—Marinid Fes, Zayyanid Tlemsen, and Hafsid Tunis—were ruled by lineages of Zanata or Masmuda Berber origin, their political self-conceptualization was similarly Arabo-Islamic. This tendency reached its apogee in Morocco with the rise of two successive sharifi dynasties, the Sa'dis (1525–1603) and the 'Alawis (1669–present), who claimed descent from the Prophet via the Hasani-Idrisi line but undoubtedly possessed Berber as well as Arab ancestors.

In the political discourse of the early modern Moroccan sultanate created by these dynasties, Arab and Berber identities were understood in linguistic and political terms and accordingly had considerable fluidity. The 19th-century Moroccan historian Ahmad b. Khalid al-Nasiri speaks of tribes as being variously "Arab," "Arabized," "Berber," or "Berberized" in terms of their language and sometimes appears to use "Arab" as shorthand for progovernment and "Berber" for rebel, which meant that tribes could be "Arab" and then "Berber" depending on their changing political affiliations. This more complex, multilayered discourse seems to best reflect the political experience of the Berber peoples in the Islamic era rather than the notion of either a Berber or Imazighen nation.

See also ethnicity; North Africa

Further Reading

Michael Brett and Elizabeth Fentress, *The Berbers*, 1996; Ibn Khaldun, *Histoire des Berbères et des dynasties musulmanes de l'Afrique septentrionale*, translated by William MacGuckin Baron de Slane, 1956; Ch. Pellat, G. Yver, and R. Basset, "Berbers." *Encyclopaedia of Islam*, 2nd ed., edited by P. Bearman, Th. Bianquis, C. E. Bosworth, E. van Donzel, and W. P. Heinrichs, 2010; Michael Willis, "The Politics of Berber (Amazigh) Identity," in *North Africa: Politics, Region and the Limits of Transformation*, edited by Yahia H. Zoubir and Haizam Amirah-Fernandez, 2007.

AMIRA K. BENNISON

Bin Laden, Osama (1957–2011)

Osama bin Laden (born March 10, 1957, in Riyadh, Saudi Arabia; died May 2, 2011, in Abbottabad, Pakistan) became the preeminent symbol of global terrorism in the wake of the attacks of September 11, 2001. Driven by a desire to avenge the many wrongs committed against the *umma* (worldwide community of believers) in what he viewed as a war on Islam, he supported the killing of innocents in the name of fair reciprocity (*al-mu'āmala bi-l-mithl*)—in other words, appropriate retribution for the loss of Muslim lives. Frustrated at what he saw as the failure of the modern nation-state to represent Islam and counter the forces that threaten it, he built up a nonstate organization, al-Qaeda (*al-Qā'ida*), to defend the honor of Islam worldwide. In so doing, he turned politics into a wholly religious affair: a battle not for international harmony or even the triumph of justice but for the victory of piety over idolatry.

Hailing from a wealthy family with close ties to the Saudi dynasty, Bin Laden proved an effective organizer of jihadist activity against the Soviets in Afghanistan in the 1980s and, subsequently, of terrorist activity around the globe, including the 1998 attacks against the U.S. embassies in Kenya and Tanzania and, most famously, the events of 9/11. In Afghanistan, he came under the tutelage of 'Abdallah 'Azzam (d. 1989), a Palestinian militant, with whom he broke ties in 1988 in order to consolidate his own jihadist stature under the banner of al-Qaeda. Following the 1989 Iraqi invasion of Kuwait, he unsuccessfully tried to convince the Saudi dynasty to entrust its security to his resources rather than the U.S. military. In his view, the presence of infidel soldiers in Arabia, the land of Islam's two holiest shrines in Mecca and Medina, was the ultimate humiliation for Islam. He relocated from Afghanistan to the Sudan in 1991, at the same time sponsoring the London-based Committee for Advice and Reform, through which he sought to undermine the religious legitimacy of the Saudi dynasty for its complicity in the U.S. "occupation" of Islam's holy land. He was stripped of his Saudi citizenship in 1994 and not long thereafter returned from the Sudan to Afghanistan. From there, he issued his 1996 declaration of war against the United States, targeting "the far enemy" as the ultimate cause of the *umma*'s corrupted and humiliated state.

Bin Laden cultivated close ties with the Taliban under Mulla 'Umar, whom he recognized as the "Commander of the Faithful" (a title by which Mulla 'Umar had been recognized within his own Taliban ranks). His willingness to join forces with the Taliban points to the parasitical nature of the relation. With a global vision, Bin Laden showed no interest in becoming master of national affairs in Afghanistan, the goal of the Taliban, but only to use it as a base from which to launch attacks against his enemies across the globe. His alliance with Ayman al-Zawahiri, leader of the Egyptian Islamic Jihad (Tanzim al-Jihad), led to the 1998 announcement of "The Global Islamic Front for Jihad against Jews and Crusaders." During the 2001 U.S. invasion of Afghanistan, Bin Laden allegedly went into hiding in the mountainous region along the northwestern border of Pakistan, but he turned out to have been residing for the last several years of his life in Abbottabad, Pakistan, a military center outside Islamabad. Al-Qaeda would mushroom into a worldwide network. Bin Laden continued to direct its activity while also serving as a figurehead of world jihadism. As such, he was able to inspire Muslim youths, even those with no formal connection to his organization, to engage in terrorist activity at both the local and global level.

Bin Laden saw the ultimate test of religious commitment as a willingness to kill and be killed—or to inspire others to do so—in the path of God (*fī sabīl Allāh*). His terrorism thus flowed from a religious vision wherein virtuous action on God's behalf is possible only in battle against infidel enemies. Thus, militancy becomes the sole option for believers wherever God's divine speech (i.e., the Qur'an) is not politically supreme. In this sense, his politics was decidedly utopian, ignoring a heritage of political thought in Islam that always balanced religious ideals against worldly realities. He opposed democracy and any form of governance that includes human decision-making in the legislative process. His conception of "the Islamic state," however, gave no details other than the sovereignty of God, as enshrined in the first part of the Muslim declaration of faith: *lā ilāha illā Allāh* (i.e., "there is no god but God"). In this view, all that is needed to govern human affairs is perfect monotheism, in which society responds completely to

God's sovereign voice as articulated by the recited Qur'an: injustice in this view results from human attempts to usurp the unique sovereignty of God by ruling without adequate recognition of the oneness of God.

Implicit in Bin Laden's outlook is a rejection of the nation-state, the emblem of secular (i.e., worldly) power, as intrinsically evil. The jihad he called for may speak of defending the *umma* but ends as a battle of eschatological proportions, destined to climax in a divinely promised victory over all forces that fail to conform to the way of God. The task of Muslims is therefore to separate themselves from and fight all that is not unequivocally subordinate to divine authority. The real risk for Muslims, according to this view, is to jeopardize their standing in the next world by compromising themselves through submitting to worldly interests in this one. In Islam, the concern for keeping one's religious integrity (piety) relatively untarnished is not normally accompanied by such a universal condemnation of the ways of the world. As a result, in Bin Laden's view, to display one's piety in a world where all that falls short of perfect religion is idolatrous; one must battle the forces of idolatry (*ṭāghūt*), whether those forces are infidel powers or apostate leaders who collaborate with them. In this sense, one is a Muslim (i.e., submissive to God) insofar as one risks one's life (*al-mukhāṭara bi-l-nafs*) in battle against God's enemies. Politics, as a result, is read through the lens of a religious narrative of conflict. God invites Muslims to sacrifice themselves to preserve His interests (one's life in exchange for paradise), fighting against the world even to the point of self-destruction. In this view, the true believer avoids being implicated in the ways of the world, which would compromise God's ways and contribute to the humiliation of His religion. Suicide attacks are thus meant to serve as a powerful witness (martyrdom) to the glory of Islam. Ultimately, then, Bin Laden's goal was to witness the power of Islam, a perverse sort of missionary who hopes to draw the world's attention to God through acts of violence. There are no clear political objectives, only the desire to demonstrate the might of God over the world and its tyrannical rulers who mistakenly believe that they have power over who lives and who dies.

The idea that the Muslim "abandonment" of religion has caused a state of "weakness" in relation to other nations is hardly new, but Bin Laden gave it a further spin, placing the blame on non-Muslims. Jews especially were singled out as scapegoats, somehow responsible for Muslim "sinfulness" before God. In this odd twist of logic, it was the Jews who seduced Muslims from religion, causing them to sell their religion for paltry recompense in this world. This, in turn, left the *umma* in a weakened state, unable to achieve the political success that serves as evidence of divine favor.

Bin Laden saw the *umma* to be in peril. Jews and Christians have taken control of the abode of Islam, either directly or through the agency of Muslim apostates who willingly compromise the supremacy of God's interests for worldly gain. The result is the humiliation of the *umma* at the hands of what he called Zionists and Crusaders who possess Muslim lands, plunder Muslim resources, and make light of Muslim lives; thus the action of the West today vis-à-vis the abode of Islam is no different from—but simply the ongoing extension of—the Crusades and colonial conquests of the past. Bin Laden believed the most heinous actions committed by these infidel forces is the pollution of Islam's holiest sites: the Aqsa mosque in Jerusalem (under Israeli control) and the two shrines of Arabia, Mecca and Medina (under the control of the apostate Saudi regime in alliance with the Crusader West). This wretched state prevails throughout the abode of Islam—Chechnya, Somalia, Kashmir—literally everywhere Muslims are ruled by worldly calculations rather than otherworldly governance.

As Bin Laden saw it, the only way to restore the integrity of the *umma* has been to fight for the cause of God rather than live in ignominious shame, subjugated to the forces of idolatry. Indeed, the divine punishment currently inflicted on the *umma* is the result of its neglect of jihad as a paramount religious duty. Only a renewed willingness to fight and die against the enemies of religion will liberate the *umma* from the forces of idolatry and restore its standing before God. Fortunately for Bin Laden, righteous Muslim youths who prefer death over life have responded to the call, sacrificing themselves in total war against infidels and apostates until Judgment Day. Fighting the agents of idolatry is cast as emulation of the first Muslims. Violence thus becomes ritualized—in other words, a way by which Muslims can please God by reenacting what the first Muslims did to please God. It is for this reason that religious education, especially the study of the Qur'an, is central to al-Qaeda military training, serving as a way to "purify" operatives of any stain of worldliness and making them worthy soldiers (and sacrificial victims through martyrdom) for God, just like the first Muslims before them.

Bin Laden was by no means the architect of jihadism, nor did his voice command uncontested scholarly respect within jihadist circles. 'Abd al-Qadir b. 'Abd al-'Aziz (better known as Sayyid Imam al-Sharif, the Egyptian doctor who helped found the Egyptian Islamic Jihad and went on to become a key ideological architect of al-Qaeda, imprisoned in Egypt) and 'Abd al-Mun'im Mustafa Halima (better known as Abu Basir al-Tartusi, a London-based Syrian scholar of a jihadist bent) have disagreed with Bin Laden on key issues, such as suicide attacks and the targeting of innocents. In contrast, Abu Jandal al-Azdi, Saudi jihadist scholar in prison since 2004, declared Bin Laden to be "the renewer of the age" (*mujaddid al-zamān*), an extraordinary title used to designate those understood to be Islam's saviors for ensuring the continued existence of the religion in pristine form. Indeed, jihadism itself is only a small segment of a larger development, the so-called Islamic awakening (*al-saḥwa al-islāmiyya*), a contemporary trend in which social and political activism—but not necessarily violence—is understood as essential to the valorization of Islam. The goal is not to wait for the judgment of God in the world to come but to execute it in this world, by force if necessary, in order to redeem the *umma* from its "disgraced" political state.

With no scholarly status of his own, Bin Laden nevertheless was able to manipulate key elements within this broader "Islamist" discourse to excite Muslim youths to partake in terrorist activity.

The religious prestige that Bin Laden sought to garner would not have been possible without the prior development of Salafism and its dismissal of traditional religious authority in favor of intense individual engagement with the Qur'an and sunna, apart from mediation of their meaning by traditional experts, as a way to inspire an activist response in believers rather than servile emulation of their religious elders. This religiosity was articulated in radical form by the likes of Sayyid Qutb (d. 1966), key figure in the Muslim Brotherhood after Egyptian independence, and 'Abd al-Salam Faraj (d. 1982), author of the text *The Neglected Duty* that inspired the assassins of President Anwar Sadat in 1981. Religion in this case is guaranteed not by the ability of scholarly masters to derive correct rulings from revealed texts but by the willingness to fight—hence the title Bin Laden bore (along with many others): *al-shaykh al-mujāhid* (the fighting shaykh). It is the jihadist, not the scholar, who ensures the integrity of religion; war against the enemies of religion becomes the key element of religious devotion, turning Islam in the view of such advocates into a singularly militaristic affair.

Bin Laden's quest for divine justice may have resonated not only with those who tie the validity of Islam to political success but also with those who have experienced marginalization in the world in one way or another. In the end, however, he was a terrorist with limited religious understanding. His enthusiasm for his own glory following the jihadist victory against the Soviets in Afghanistan (made possible by U.S., Saudi, and Pakistani support) gave him an exaggerated sense of invincibility. As a result, he underestimated the resolve of the international community in the face of the threat he posed. More tragically, his deficient religious knowledge left him ignorant of the well-established reasoning processes of shari'a that Muslim scholars carefully crafted over the centuries to limit, or even eliminate, violence in the name of religion. As a result, his jihad was motivated more by sentiments of tribal honor and revenge rather than by religious truth, bringing the *umma* not glory but intra-Muslim strife (*fitna*) and engendering a perplexing image of Islam for Muslims and non-Muslims alike. In the final analysis, Bin Laden is the true heir of early Kharijism, calling the *umma* to rise up (*khurūj*) against any force that would keep it from living in the shadow of the Qur'an alone. In an age in which injustices are immediately broadcast to international audiences, his defiance of the global powers that claim to be defenders of justice garnered him popularity in some circles, both Muslim and non-Muslim. Some have likened him to Che Guevara (d. 1967). His actions, however, brought no benefit to the *umma* or the world. His manner of struggling against tyranny deployed violence indiscriminately, targeting innocents (including fellow Muslims) while inflaming sectarian strife within the *umma* itself. It is for this reason that his brand of piety has been rejected by the vast majority of Muslims. Bin Laden was killed on May 2, 2011, by U.S. Navy Seals in a covert operation. After identification, his body was buried at sea according to Islamic ritual.

See also fundamentalism; Mulla 'Umar (b. 1959); al-Qaeda; Sayyid Qutb (1906–66); suicide; Taliban; terrorism; al-Zawahiri, Ayman (b. 1951)

Further Reading

'Abd al-Rahim 'Ali, *Tanzim al-Qa'ida, 'Ashrun 'Amman . . . wa-l-Ghazu Mustamirr, Markaz al-Mahrusa li-l-Nashr wa-l-Khadamat al-Suhufiyya wa-l-Ma'lumat*, 2007; Raymond Ibrahim, ed. and trans., *The Al Qaeda Reader*, 2007; Bruce Lawrence, ed., *Messages to the World: The Statements of Osama bin Laden*, translated by James Howarth, 2005.

PAUL L. HECK

blasphemy

Blasphemy is speech that insults or shows a lack of reverence for God, holy persons, or sacred things. In the Qur'an, one may identify several types of blasphemy. Blasphemy by denial (*takdhīb*, or "giving the lie") involves the willful rejection of essential religious truths, such as the existence and unity of God or the messages of His prophets. Blasphemy by invention (*al-iftirā' 'alā Allāh*, or "contrivance against God") involves the concoction of false doctrines regarding God and His prerogatives. Another Qur'anic term for blasphemy is *kalimat al-kufr* or "statement of unbelief," a direct statement that indicates the speaker is an unbeliever, used in reference to the disbelievers and hypocrites in Qur'an 9:74. A Qur'anic example of such a direct blasphemy is 79:24, where the pharaoh declares, "I am your Lord the Highest!" (*anā rabbukum al-a'lā*).

This last term is taken up in later legal and theological literature. Despite a common misunderstanding that Islam is defined by practice and not by doctrine, so that acts and not creeds matter, it is widely understood in both Sunni and Shi'i theology that it is one's thoughts and opinions more than one's acts that render one an unbeliever. When one sins or violates the law, one may do so as a consequence of weakness, addiction, or other afflictions, but what makes one a heretic is the belief that a legal obligation is actually unnecessary or that a legal prohibition is actually invalid.

Evidence of one's heresy or unbelief may be provided by deed, such as the desecration of the Ka'ba—the shrine or temple of God in Mecca that is the focus of the annual pilgrimage (hajj)—or adoration of idols, or by word, which is blasphemy. A genre of Islamic legal literature developed, termed *kalimāt al-kufr* or *alfāẓ al-kufr* (statements of unbelief), that attempts to define and catalogue blasphemies. The legal effect of uttering these words intentionally is to cause the apostasy of the speaker, and apostates merit capital punishment. One of the best known of these treatises, authored by Badr al-Rashid al-Hanafi (d. 1366–67), makes the point that blasphemies are based on one of three principles of infraction: "mockery" or "derision" (*istihzā'*), "making light of" or "considering trivial or unimportant" (*istikhfāf*), or "considering licit that which is forbidden" (*istiḥlāl*). Uttering blasphemy under duress, however, does not make one an apostate and has no legal consequences. These and other legal discussions of blasphemy define what are essentially

six categories of blasphemy: vilification of God; vilification of the Prophet; vilification of other prophets or holy personages; vilification of sacred texts, monuments, and so forth; denial of fundamental religions doctrines such as the existence of the Day of Judgment, paradise, hell, and so on; and vilification of the Prophet's Companions.

Vilification of the Prophet Muhammad acquired its own literature, and the infraction was held to require capital punishment not only for Muslims, on the ground that it made them apostates, but also for Jews, Christians, and others living under Muslim rule on the grounds that it detracted from the veneration due to Islam and the obligation to maintain public recognition of the dignity and superiority of Islam. This made it somewhat dangerous for Jews and Christians in Islamic societies to enter into religious polemics with Muslims, for in attempting to refute Islamic doctrines they might adopt a stance interpreted as a direct insult of the Prophet. The ruling, however, was more often ignored than enforced, and most of the cases brought before judges occurred in the course of angry altercations in the streets and markets rather than in elite, scholarly debates. Ibn Taymiyya (d. 1328) argued for a stricter application of the punishment in his treatise *al-Sarim al-Maslul 'ala Shatim al-Rasul* (The sword drawn against the insulter of the messenger). Some have argued against the enforcement of this law on non-Muslims on the grounds of the Qur'anic verse "Revile not those unto whom they pray beside God lest they wrongfully revile God through ignorance" (Q. 6:108), which suggests a circumspect approach to blasphemy by non-Muslims since it is assumed to result from ignorance.

Blasphemy against the Companions, often termed *sabb al-ṣaḥāba* (vilification of the Companions) or *sabb al-shaykhayn* (vilification of the two old men) referring to the first two caliphs, Abu Bakr (r. 632–34) and 'Umar b. al-Khattab (r. 634–44), was a standard subcategory of blasphemy and a frequent topic of Sunni-Shi'i polemics. The term *rafḍ*, or "rejection, refusal," was also used to denote blasphemy against the Companions specifically, and from this derives the most common term of opprobrium applied to Shi'is in the Islamic world: *rāfiḍa, rawāfiḍ*, or *rafaḍa*, which mean "rejecters." The most frequent charge of heresy brought against Shi'is in both premodern and modern times, insulting or cursing the Companions, has been the main reason behind the execution of Shi'is as heretics throughout Islamic history, though lesser punishments such as banishment, imprisonment, or flogging were often substituted. The historical polemic over the position of imam or caliph led the Shi'is to reject the legitimacy of the first three caliphs—Abu Bakr, 'Umar, and 'Uthman b. 'Affan—and also to reject the moral probity of many additional, prominent Companions, including the Prophet's wives 'A'isha and Hafsa. Comparison with 'Ali and arguments over the historic details of the Prophet's mission and the role played by his Companions in those events led to the development of a wide array of negative anecdotes, accounts, and descriptions of these figures. The Shi'is justified the insult and cursing of these figures, despite their closeness to the Prophet, on the grounds that they wronged Fatima or 'Ali and waged war against him, and the Shi'is consequently adopted the view that these figures were actually unbelieving hypocrites.

Disparagement of the Companions became a feature of various Shi'i societies so that, for example, saying that someone is "'Umar" in contemporary Iran means that he is irritable and irascible, and "going to 'Umar's house" means a visit to the bathroom. By the 16th century, a Shi'i holiday was developed to celebrate the assassination of 'Umar. Called *'Omar-Koshūn*, or "'Umar-Killing," this carnavalesque inversion of veneration for the Prophet or the imams involves the singing of disparaging ditties about the second caliph and the burning or stabbing of his effigy. Where Shi'is are a minority, these views of the Companions are suppressed, and the Iranian leaders Ayatollah Khomeini and Ayatollah Khamene'i both issued fatwas forbidding Shi'is to abuse the Companions for the sake of unity and solidarity in the Islamic world. The Kuwaiti Shi'i activist Yasir al-Habib (b. 1979) has taken the opposite view, arguing that it is necessary to voice Shi'i views openly, including the cursing of the Companions. He was arrested and imprisoned for blasphemy against the Prophet's Companions in 2003 but was subsequently released in a general amnesty in February 2004. After fleeing Kuwait, he now has an active following in England, where he continues to criticize Sunni doctrines, and has held celebrations on the occasion of 'A'isha's death. He had his Kuwaiti citizenship revoked in 2010 for calling 'A'isha "the enemy of God." He also has denounced accommodationist clerics such as Hasan al-Saffar (b. 1958), the leading Shi'i authority in Saudi Arabia, for publicly expressing approval of Abu Bakr, 'Umar, and 'Uthman, calling Saffar "the Samaritan of this Community," a reference to the character responsible for convincing the Hebrews to worship the golden calf in Moses' absence in the Qur'anic version of Exodus.

In 16th-century Spain, blasphemy became an issue for the Moriscos, Muslims who were forcibly converted to Christianity between 1501 and 1526. A well-known fatwa was issued in Fez in 1504 for the Moriscos in which the North African jurist Ahmad b. Abi Jum'a al-Maghrawi al-Wahrani (d. 1511) ruled that Muslims were allowed to utter Christian creeds under duress without committing apostasy as long as they kept the correct intention in their hearts. If possible, though, it was preferable to use a double entendre and other verbal ambiguities in uttering such creeds so that they would not in fact state the offensive creed explicitly while at the same time convincing the hostile audience that they had.

Blasphemy laws are part of the legal code in many contemporary Muslim-majority countries, though such laws also exist in Britain, Germany, Brazil, Denmark, Finland, and other countries. In five Muslim-majority nations, however, the penalty for blasphemy is capital punishment, and this has made the laws an issue of some controversy between Pakistan, Saudi Arabia, and the West, as the laws that focus mainly on the denigration of the Prophet Muhammad have been used primarily against Christians or Muslim converts to Christianity. In Pakistan, the blasphemy law was instituted as part of a legal Islamization reform by President Zia-ul-Haq in the 1970s and 1980s, among other measures such as the imposition of mandatory zakat (alms tax) deduction from bank accounts.

From then until the present, 1,000 people have been convicted, and while none have been executed, many have served long or life sentences in prison, and a number of defendants have been killed by public lynching. The law has been used to target Christian converts and also in attempts to win property and other disputes. On January 4, 2011, Salman Taseer, the governor of Punjab and a secularist member of the Pakistan People's Party, was assassinated by one of his own security guards in the capital Islamabad as punishment for his outspoken opposition to the blasphemy law and for his support of Aasia Bibi, a Pakistani Christian woman sentenced to death for allegedly insulting the Prophet Muhammad. Other recent cases in Afghanistan, Nigeria, Sudan, and elsewhere have drawn international concern.

Since 1999, the Organization of the Islamic Conference, now comprising 57 nations, has supported annual resolutions denouncing defamation of Islam or religions in general in the United Nations to support their own blasphemy laws in the international arena and to counter perceived defamation and ideological attacks on Islamic cultures. Opponents charge that such resolutions merely curtail the freedom to express one's views and opinions openly and risk not only stifling debate but also promoting violence. On February 14, 1989, Ayatollah Khomeini issued a fatwa proclaiming that Salman Rushdie was an apostate on the grounds that his book *The Satanic Verses* was blasphemous, and the Iranian government put a bounty on his head. The Danish newspaper *Jyllands-Posten*'s publication of cartoons that portrayed the Prophet Muhammad on September 30, 2005, resulted in widespread protests by Muslims in Europe and the Islamic world and death threats against the editors as well as the cartoonists. Concerns over violence related to accusations of blasphemy remain strong.

See also apostasy; Companions of the Prophet; faith; God; prophecy

Further Reading

David F. Forte, "Apostasy and Blasphemy in Pakistan," *Connecticut Journal of International Law* 27 (1994–95); Bernard Haykel, *Revival and Reform in Islam: The Legacy of Muḥammad al-Shawkānī*, 2003; Devin J. Stewart, *Islamic Legal Orthodoxy*, 1998; Lutz Wiederhold, "Blasphemy against the Prophet Muhammad and His Companions (Sabb al-Rasūl, Sabb al-Ṣaḥābah): The Introduction of the Topic into Shāfiʿī Legal Literature and Its Relevance for Legal Practice under Mamluk Rule," *Journal of Semitic Studies* 42, no. 1 (1997).

DEVIN J. STEWART

Brethren of Purity

The Brethren of Purity (or "Pure Brethren") is the pen name adopted by the otherwise anonymous authors of a compendium of 52 treatises on a wide variety of disciplines titled *Rasa'il Ikhwan al-Safa' wa-Khillan al-Wafa'* (The epistles of the pure brethren and the loyal companions). The date and authorship of the *Epistles* are not known with certainty. Attributions vary from a group of intellectuals in Basra in the mid-tenth century, whom Abu Hayyan al-Tawhidi names in his *Kitab al-Imta' wa-l-Mu'anasa*, to the ninth-century leaders of the Isma'ili movement in Syria, who organized the uprising that culminated in the establishment of the Fatimid caliphate.

The *Epistles* are divided into four parts, covering mathematical and logical sciences, the natural sciences, the sciences of the intellect and the soul, and lastly what one could call theological sciences. The work is presented as an instructional curriculum based on an eternal wisdom assumed to have been found in all cultures at all times. One of the main aims of the *Epistles* was to present an epistemological basis on which revealed scripture and prophetic teachings on the one hand and philosophical exertion and rational enquiry on the other could be accepted as true paths to knowledge of the human being, the universe, and divinity. Although no single epistle is devoted to political theory, the work repeatedly touches on the subject along four main lines.

Social and political reform. The *Epistles* regard the contemporary world as corrupt on all levels of society, from the marketplace to the court. They advocate moral reform according to a concept of humans based on prophetic lore and philosophical teachings, but they never explicitly propose social or political measures, let alone the overthrow of the Abbasid dynasty. They do give occasional hints that the contemporary regime is an evil that must be replaced by "the government of the good" (*dawlat ahl al-khayr*), if necessary by means of revolution and uprising. Given the climate of the time, it is possible, but by no means certain, that this should be understood as support for the Isma'ili underground movements. The *Epistles* see the succession of empires, dynasties, rulers, and even religions as a natural process regulated by astrological cycles. This view, which was widespread at the time, may play a role in formation of Ibn Khaldun's concept of the rise and fall of dynasties.

*A multilayered concept of governance (*siyāsa*).* The *Epistles* treat governance as an activity conducted at all levels of the world, from God's management of the universe by means of angels to the ruler's management of countries by means of soldiers and administrators to the family's management of the household and the individual's management of his own moral character by means of education, intellectual exertion, and purification of the soul.

The perfect society. Possibly building on ideas expounded by their older contemporary Abu Nasr al-Farabi in his work *The Virtuous City*, with which they seem to be intimately acquainted, the authors conceive the ideal society as a hierarchy in which people are ranked according to their knowledge and intellectual capacities and evaluated in terms of four faculties: the rational faculty, acquired at the age of 15; the intellectual or "wisdom" faculty, acquired at the age of 30; the nomic (related to the Law) faculty, acquired at the age of 40; and the angelic faculty, acquired at the age of 50. Their ideal society is not necessarily envisaged as a politically organized

society or state, as opposed to a perfect society or brotherhood within whatever state existed: it was a "spiritual virtuous city" (*madīna fāḍila rūḥāniyya*). This interpretation makes it difficult to see them as revolutionaries.

Leadership and community. Though the *Epistles* resonate with tenth-century Isma'ilism, their views differ from those of either the Fatimid caliphate in North Africa and Egypt or the Abu Sa'idis (usually called Qarmatians) in Bahrain and southern Iraq, the two main strains of Isma'ilism at the time. The *Epistles* seem to be more in line with the Neoplatonizing Isma'ilism pursued by some leaders inside the Isma'ili *da'wa* (mission) who had not accepted the leadership of the Fatimids and who continued working on their own.

The authors' views on the imamate and its relationship with the community remain unclear. At times, they intimate that the imams from the *ahl al-bayt* (the people of the house, i.e., the descendants from Muhammad and 'Ali) should be the leaders of the *umma* (the Muslim community), since they are the repositories of all virtues and the sources for the interpretation (*ta'wīl*) of revelation that must be applied to current times. At other times, it is clear that in the absence of the imam, all the qualities of leadership are subsumed in the community, especially in the brotherhood espoused by its members. The community organizes itself as an intellectual brotherhood knit together by two main characteristics—mutual cooperation (*ta'āwun*) and friendship (*ṣadāqa*)—and in this community, the use of the intellect could take the place of a ruling imam.

See also al-Farabi, Abu Nasr (ca. 878–950); Isma'ilis; philosophy

Further Reading

Butrus al-Bustani, ed., *Rasa'il Ikhwan al-Safa' wa-Khillan al-Wafa'*, 1957; Patricia Crone, *Medieval Islamic Political Thought*, 2004; Godefroy de Callataÿ, *A Brotherhood of Idealists on the Fringe of Orthodox Islam*, 2005; Ian R. Netton, *Muslim Neoplatonists: An Introduction to the Thought of the Brethren of Purity*, 1982.

OMAR ALÍ-DE-UNZAGA

brotherhoods

The Sufi brotherhoods (*ṭuruq*, sing. *ṭarīqa*; lit. "path") are the social and institutional face of Sufism (*al-taṣawwuf*), broadly construed as those doctrines and practices that seek to remove the mundane veils separating humanity from the divine and thereby render the transcendent immanent. The brotherhoods are often likened to Christian monastic orders, but this is misleading, for *ṭarīqa* refers to both the social organization of a particular group and the spiritual *path* that the Sufi traverses in his or her quest for the divine. In terms of social organization, Sufism can be divided into three major historical phases corresponding to three types of social organizations.

The eighth through tenth centuries mark the appearance of a group specifically identified as Sufis. This period is characterized by the predominance of individual Sufi masters and small circles of traveling disciples. Some of the most prominent teachers of this early period include Rabi'a (d. 801), Muhasibi (d. 857), Dhu al-Nun al-Misri (d. 860), Bistami (d. 874), Sahl al-Tustari (d. 896), and Junayd (d. 910). The Sufism of this period is further distinguished by the idiosyncratic nature of its literary production. At this point, there was not a highly systematized doctrine of Sufism that had been thoroughly reconciled with particularly Sunni modes of thought and piety, as would develop during the second phase.

The period from the 11th to the 13th centuries might be called the period of systemization and is marked by two developments. First, Sufis began congregating regularly in specifically Sufi sites, known variously as *zāwiya*, *ribāṭ*, *khānaqāh*, or *tekke*. The usage of these terms to refer to physical structures in which Sufis meet to practice their devotions was not systematic in the medieval literature, and they were often used interchangeably. The second development was the analyzing and reworking of Sufi doctrine into a Sunni (and particularly Ash'ari) discourse. Qushayri's (d. 1074) *Risala* (Principles of Sufism) and Ghazali's (d. 1111) *Ihya' 'Ulum al-Din* (The revival of the religious sciences) are prime examples of this genre. It was during this period that the first manuals of Sufi life were written, which provided a systematic basis for communal living. The most important of these manuals for the development of organized Sufism were Sulami's (d. 1021) *Adab al-Suhba* (The rules of companionship), Abu al-Najib al-Suhrawardi's (d. 1168) *Adab al-Muridin* (The rules for Sufi novices), and Abu Hafs 'Umar al-Suhrawardi's (d. 1234) *'Awarif al-Ma'arif* (The attainment of true understanding). The *Adab al-Muridin* is of particular importance because it was the first systematic exposition meant to detail the life and daily habits of the Sufi. The combination of written manuals of discipline and a specific location where like-minded Sufis could gather and spread the doctrines of a particular teacher provided fertile ground for the growth of organized Sufism.

The 14th century to the present marks the period of brotherhoods organized around the personality and doctrines of an eponymous "founder." Although scholars formerly assumed that each of the brotherhoods was founded deliberately by the eponymous shaykh, recent scholarship has shown that it was the second and third generation of the eponym's disciples who performed most of the work of institutionalizing the shaykh's doctrines and practices. Thus while most organized brotherhoods emerged in the 14th century, the eponyms of these brotherhoods were actually active during the 13th century. The most important are 'Abd al-Qadir al-Jilani (d. 1166), Ahmad b. Ibrahim al-Yasa (d. 1166), Ahmad b. 'Ali al-Rifa'i (d. 1182), Najm al-Din Kubra (d. 1221), Abu Hafs 'Umar al-Suhrawardi (d. 1234), Mu'in al-Din Chishti (d. 1236), Abu al-Hasan al-Shadhili (d. 1258), Jalal al-Din Rumi (d. 1273), and Baha' al-Din al-Naqshbandi (d. 1389). These represent the major *ṭarīqa* lines, or primary brotherhoods, which, according to Spencer Trimingham's *The Sufi Orders in Islam*, are to be distinguished from the later *ṭā'ifa* lines. The latter are smaller Sufi sublineages that often

trace their authority to one of those in the *ṭarīqa* lines. In the two or three generations after these teachers' deaths, and once the basic structures of the orders were in place, Sufism began to attract widespread adherents and gain popularity among the masses as well as the religious elites.

It is not entirely clear why the brotherhoods became so appealing in the 13th and 14th centuries. Most scholars have attributed this increase in popularity to the major social upheavals of the time—the Mongol invasions in the East, Crusader activities in Egypt and the Levant, and the Black Death of the 14th century—and a corresponding desire for social stability. Another factor contributing to Sufism's increasing social profile was undoubtedly royal patronage. The growing popularity of Sufi movements attracted notice from political powers beginning in the 11th century. The Seljuqs (1055–1194) instituted a policy of establishing and endowing *khānaqāh*s similar to the ways they patronized the madrasas (Muslim schools). The Abbasid caliph Nasir li-Din Allah (1180–1225) patronized Abu Hafs 'Umar al-Suhrawardi in what seems to have been an attempt to gain control of the burgeoning social movement. The Ayyubid sultan Saladin (r. 1171–93) endowed the first *khānaqāh* in Egypt in 1173, which began a policy that the Mamluks (1250–1517) would continue in Egypt and Syria. Whether this royal attention spurred the public's interest in Sufism or whether these were attempts to establish some state control over an already burgeoning movement is less important than the clear implication that by the 13th century the Sufi brotherhoods were beginning to be a political force in their own right. Sufism had taken political turns before—the early masters criticized the prevailing politics and culture of the Abbasid state—but this later development marks the beginning of a relationship between the state and Sufis that would last, in many cases, to the present day; for example, Rumi was an advisor to Seljuq rulers, Ahmad Sirhindi (d. 1624) advised the Mughal court, and the Naqshbandi-initiated Recep Tayyip Erdoğan became the prime minister of Turkey in March 2003.

The brotherhoods are, by their very nature, potentially influential political actors, as the average adherents look to a single master (shaykh) for guidance. The shaykh (*pīr* in Persian and Urdu) could effectively mobilize large numbers of the populace if needed, although this possibility was attenuated as it has become more acceptable after the 16th century to be affiliated with more than one *ṭarīqa* or *ṭā'ifa*, as was the case with the famous Egyptian 'Abd al-Wahhab al-Sha'rani (d. 1565), who belonged to every brotherhood in 16th-century Egypt. In any case, the relationship between Sufi brotherhoods and the political sphere has taken different forms over time and cannot be generalized in any way. No single *ṭarīqa* has a definitive teaching on political activity. The Chishtis, for example, were quite politically disengaged during the early years of the Delhi Sultanate (1206–1526) but became more politically active during the Lodi period (1451–1526). One can, however, outline a few broad trends in the ways Sufi brotherhoods have approached political leaders or organizations. The following, while not exhaustive, is a representative description of the ways Sufi brotherhoods have engaged with the political sphere with a few examples from the Muslim world.

Nonengagement

Rarely do Sufi groups choose to completely disengage from the political sphere. By refusing to engage with political rulers, these groups are making implicit statements about, in an extreme case, the illegitimacy of a political group or actor or, in a minimalist case, the incommensurate nature of the spiritual and political spheres. The Delhi Sultanate offers an instructive case here. Both the Chishti and Suhrawardi orders appeared very early in South Asia (13th century), but their relationships to the political rulers were quite different. The Suhrawardi order cultivated close relationships with rulers in Delhi and often held governmental positions, carried official titles, and participated in the land-grant system (*jāgīr*). The Chishti order, by contrast, was generally opposed to political involvement. They refused governmental positions, would not accept the titles offered them, did not participate in the *jāgīr* system, and even refused to allow the sultans to visit their *khānaqāh*s. The Suhrawardi Sufis seem to have been following the model of their founder, who had advised and represented the Abbasid caliph Nasir li-Din Allah. Likewise, the Chishti Sufis were following the advice of their founder, who was quite explicit about the proper relationship between the spiritual and political spheres.

The early Bektashi order of Anatolia is another example of political quietism, although in this case their political involvement was a consequence of their numbers. In the early stages of their development, they were politically quietist while they gained in numbers. But in the years following the rise of the Ottoman Empire, their increasing number became a valuable asset to Ottoman rule, and the Bektashi order worked closely with the Ottoman rulers. The Bektashis were associated with the Jannisaries (professional soldiers) of the Ottoman realm, and when the Jannisaries were officially abolished in 1826, the Bektashis suffered a decline as well.

In the Caucasus, the Qadiri order has been traditionally quietist for many years. During the Russian invasions of the 18th and 19th centuries, they did not participate with their Naqshbandi compatriots in the struggle for independence. Likewise, the Qadiri Sufis did not take an oppositional stance to the Bolshevik revolution and were allowed to retain their clerical positions, whereas the Naqshbandi order, having opposed the Bolsheviks, was generally outlawed.

Cooperation

In some cases, Sufi brotherhoods and political leaders have overlapping interests and participate in a mutually beneficial exchange. This seems to happen most often in situations when powerful rulers make strong claims to religious legitimacy: the Ayyubids, the Seljuqs, and the Ottomans, to name a few. Typically, influential Sufi leaders will lend their support—both human support in the form of followers and spiritual support in the form of legitimating the ruler—in exchange for royal or state patronage. This patronage is usually in the form of endowments, gifts, prestige, or a voice in governance. Sufi cooperation with the ruling powers was perhaps the most common form of political activity of the premodern

brotherhoods. As mentioned earlier, the Bektashi order supported the Ottoman state in exchange for royal patronage, and the Mevlevi Sufis were likewise quite close to the power structures; not only was Rumi an advisor to the Seljuq sultans but the Ottoman sultan Selim III (r. 1789–1807) was himself an initiated Mevlevi.

Sufis appeared in the Balkans in the 14th century, and it was primarily dervishes of Qalandari and Bektashi affiliation who took up residence in this area and were integral in Islamicizing the population. By the 16th century, the brotherhoods were a fixture of the urban landscape and critical members of Muslim military efforts to continue to convert the population. The Khalwati shaykh Bali Efendi (d. 1553) and his successor, Muslih al-Din Nur al-Din Zada (d. 1571), both worked closely with Ottoman officials and wrote extensive reports detailing the political and religious situation in the region. Nur al-Din Zada explicitly argued that Sufis, as the clients of God, have a duty to council politicians about their decisions in order to make governance more religiously correct. In Africa, the Tijanis worked closely with the French colonialist enterprise in Senegal. This situation has led to a strong backlash against the Sufis on the part of Islamic reformers in that country today. In Pakistan, Jama'at 'Ali Shah (d. 1951), a Naqshbandi shaykh from the Punjab who is said to have had over one million disciples, was briefly appointed as the *amīr-i-millat* (head of the Muslim community) in an early attempt to unite South Asian Muslims. He was a strong supporter of the "father of Pakistan," Muhammad 'Ali Jinnah (d. 1948), and was instrumental in gathering popular support for an independent Pakistan.

Co-optation

While the reasoning is different from case to case, some governments have found it advantageous to co-opt the brotherhoods under their jurisdiction in an attempt to control what they see as potentially antigovernmental social groups. In the case of post-1952 Egypt, the orders were co-opted by the government to some degree for their potential to offer an alternative to the Muslim Brotherhood. In order to do so, the government created the office of the *shaykh mashāyikh al-ṭuruq al-ṣūfiyya*—"the shaykh of shaykhs of the Sufi brotherhoods." This has allowed the Egyptian government to exert some control over how the various brotherhoods are overseen, the nature of their celebrations, and appropriate behavior at religious festivals. The office even publishes a journal. Similarly, the Syrian state has taken over responsibility for organized forms of Sufism. Here, however, the state did not create an office for the direct coordination of the brotherhoods but rather set up a ministry of endowments that oversees all the land used for Sufi activities.

Sudan offers an especially interesting case of the government attempting to co-opt Sufi groups. In an effort to bring Sufis into the political fold, the Sudanese government sponsored a large conference for Sufis in 1993 that included hundreds of participants from other African and North African countries. In 1995, the Sudanese government established an agency to supervise the brotherhoods and provide funding for the education, welfare, and pilgrimage of Sufis. The effect (probably intended) has been to polarize the brotherhoods in the Sudan between those who support the Islamist project and those who oppose it. This is most clearly seen in the splintering of the Sudanese branch of the Tijani brotherhood since the mid-1990s into a number of subgroups divided along political lines.

Resistance

In the modern era of colonial enterprises in the Islamic world, political Sufism has most often taken the form of resistance. Because they are not state actors but localized groups with overlapping interests, the Sufi brotherhoods have been in a unique position to resist colonialism. Sufi shaykhs are often able to mobilize their disciples in large numbers by portraying the struggle against colonial powers as a struggle between Islam and unbelievers.

The Portuguese incursions into Morocco in the 15th and 16th centuries led to their control of most of the Mediterranean ports of the region. It was the Jazulis (named for the rural saint Muhammad b. Sulayman al-Jazuli [d. 1465]) who were instrumental in driving them out. Muhammad Jazuli advocated a socially conscious form of Sufi activism that lent itself particularly well to resistance, and the Jazulis were instrumental in fighting the Portuguese encampments. By the mid-16th century, the jihad was successful and the Portuguese were driven out. Similarly, in Algeria, resistance against the French was led by the Sufi 'Abd al-Qadir al-Jaza'iri (d. 1883) and his followers. The Sanusi brotherhood consistently resisted colonial rule in Africa and was a major force of opposition in Chad, Libya, and the Sudan.

In the Caucasus, most of the Muslim population were Sufis by the 18th century. In the wake of Russian incursions in the 18th and 19th centuries, it was the Naqshbandi order that led the resistance. Between 1824 and 1859, Imam ('Ali) Shamil (d. 1871)—a Daghestani Naqshbandi—commanded an Islamic state in the area that was the center of anti-Russian struggle. While Shamil was not the Naqshbandi shaykh, his followers saw him as their temporal guide and would chant the *dhikr* (remembrance of God's name) in their marches into battle. The cumulative effect of this political involvement and agitation when the Russians eventually gained control of the area was the deportation of thousands of Naqshbandis to Siberia. Thousands more fled to Ottoman-controlled territories, and many of those remaining joined the Qadiri order, which had been politically quiet during the Caucasian War. Some Naqshbandis, however, by virtue of having gone underground, were able to infiltrate and occupy offices in the Soviet government and ensure the continuation of Islamic life in the North Caucasus. In the Russian invasions of the 18th and 19th centuries and the subsequent Bolshevik revolution, the Naqshbandis were visible antagonists, while the Qadiris, as mentioned, remained quietist.

Revolution

It is not often that Sufi resistance calls for the outright upheaval of the political realm and the installation of a new political order. The most salient example of a politicized Sufism with imperial designs is the Safavid order of Central Asia. Named for the shaykh

Safi al-Din Ardabili (d. 1334), the Safavids began as a Sufi (Sunni) brotherhood in Gilan (in the northwest of present-day Iran) and quickly expanded their interests to proselytizing in Azerbaijan and Anatolia. By the time of the fourth shaykh of the order, Isma'il Abu al-Muzaffar Safawi (d. 1524), they had become quite powerful. Isma'il declared that the Safavids were Ithna 'Ashari (Twelver) Shi'is, and in 1501 he was crowned king in Tabriz and declared Twelver Shi'ism the religion of the state. In a fascinating twist, fearing the power of other Sufi brotherhoods, Isma'il ordered the disbanding of all the brotherhoods under his geographical control. The only brotherhood spared was the Ni'matullahi, who had declared themselves Shi'i and aligned themselves with the Safavids. Such governmental suspicion of organized Sufi brotherhoods persists to the present day in Iran.

The Sammani order played a similar role in the founding of the Mahdist state in Sudan led by Muhammad Ahmad b. 'Abdallah (d. 1885). He was given authority in 1861 to initiate others into the Sammani brotherhood and began attracting followers. He declared himself the Mahdi (savior) in 1881 and launched a successful offensive against the Egyptian occupation of Sudan. The Khatmi brotherhood, by contrast, disavowed the claims of the Mahdi and his political aspirations, and their shaykh was forced into exile in Egypt.

It is clear that the relationship between Sufism and the political sphere is heterogeneous and unstable, even within the same brotherhood. These political relationships are determined less by the particular teachings of any certain brotherhood than by historical circumstances and charismatic individuals. It would be more accurate to describe the Sufi brotherhoods as a latent political force—complete with a hierarchical social organization—that can be deployed in certain circumstances by powerful personalities. Political rulers have often been aware of this latent potential and attempted to use the brotherhoods to their own advantage in a number of ways.

See also shaykh, *pīr*; Sufism

Further Reading

Jamil Abun-Nasr, *Muslim Communities of Grace: The Sufi Brotherhoods in Islamic Religious Life*, 2007; Paul L. Heck, *Sufism and Politics: The Power of Spirituality*, 2007; Annemarie Schimmel, *Mystical Dimensions of Islam*, 1978; Spencer Trimingham, *The Sufi Orders in Islam*, 1971.

NATHAN HOFER

bureaucracy

The term "bureaucracy" refers to a system of administrative departments known as bureaus (*dawāwīn*, sing. *dīwān*) that function as an extension of the ruler's political authority for managing the affairs of the realm. The bureaucratic concept is not elaborated in the Qur'an or sunna but was adopted by early Muslim rulers from Byzantine and Persian practices. A complex bureaucratic structure developed under the Umayyads (661–750) and Abbasids (750–1258) and became the administrative model for subsequent dynasties: a system of administrative norms, embodied in bureaucratic departments, for managing soldiers' salaries and rations, tax revenues, official correspondence, court attendants and provisions, subjects' complaints, lands possessed by the ruling dynasty and those parceled out as grants to military commanders, monies confiscated from disgraced officials, and a whole host of other governmental interests. Bureaucratic structures existed at the caliphal (or sultanic) center, and in the provinces, and in the borderlands (*thughūr*); at the summit of the bureaucratic hierarchy stood such offices as that of vizier and chief comptroller (*zimām al-azimma*), two posts created in the early Abbasid period.

Bureaucracy, at its heart, is the craft of writing (*kitāba*) in the service of governance (*siyāsa*), and the bureaucratic corps was known simply as "writers" or "scribes" (*kuttāb*, sing. *kātib*) or "people of the pen" (*ahl al-qalam*; *qalamiyya* in the Ottoman context) in contrast to the military corps, known as "people of the sword" (*ahl al-sayf*; *'askariyya* in the Ottoman context), which formed the second pillar of rule. Letters, registries, documents, and records—written material—constituted the professional substance and occupation of the bureaucratic corps of the various dynasties ruling in the name of Islam, whether Sunni or Shi'i. Writing, in this bureaucratic form, was understood to exist for the sake of political coherency. Bureaucratic manuals commonly warned against the political breakdown that would occur as a result of deficiencies in written communication, and bureaucratic circles saw administrative order as a product of written order, known as the art of writing (*ṣinā'at al-kitāba*). This association of writing with bureaucracy left its mark on Muslim intellectual life. For example, a tenth-century work on different methods of communication, *al-Burhan fi Wujuh al-Bayan* (Proof of the means of communication) by Abu al-Husayn b. Wahb, secretary in the employ of 'Ali b. 'Isa, celebrated vizier during the reign of the Abbasid caliph Muqtadir, identifies written communication wholly with the bureaucratic profession. Also, Ibn Khaldun (d. 1406) recognized the political significance of bureaucracy, suggesting that a dynasty that had lost its clan solidarity (*'aṣabiyya*), once it had become accustomed to the luxuries of settled life, could still hope to preserve its rule—and thus the political coherency of the realm—by maintaining a strong and well-run bureaucracy.

The *dīwān*—that is, the administrative bureau—was conceived as the written repository of information of import to the state. This information, recorded in official documents, embodied rules and regulations that, along with the ruler's edicts, set expectations of governance. In this sense, the *diwān* represented an authority in its own right to which recourse could be had for managing public affairs. In the Ottoman context, the *diwān* also referred to the cabinet of administrators who constituted the highest authorities of the realm both at the imperial center and in the provincial governorates. In this sense, the existence of a bureaucratic system as a

recognized feature of Islamic rule, as articulated in such works as *al-Ahkam al-Sultaniyya* (The ordinances of government) by Mawardi (d. 1058; an influential scholar in the employ of the Abbasid caliphs of his day), lent itself to a notion of "rational rule" in Islam—that is, governance by intelligible and predictable norms and not simply by personal decisions made in potentially whimsical fashion by a dynastic ruler or a coterie of figures close to him. The ruler's judgment (*ra'y*) was, to be sure, the origin of political authority, and dynasties—as well as leading bureaucratic departments and ministries—were not above nepotism. Still, the expansion of bureaucratic institutions set the expectation of regular administrative order against which the conduct of dynastic officials, such as tax collectors, could be measured.

Muslim appreciation for bureaucracy arose in the wake of the first conquests, when figures such as ʿUmar b. al-Khattab (r. 634–44), the second Rightly Guided Caliph in succession to Muhammad, recognized the necessity of bureaucratic organization for administering conquered lands and peoples. There was need for a repository (*dīwān*) of administrative information—a written record to preserve, for example, the fiscal terms of treaties made with the various towns and cities that fell to the Muslim conquerors, including the nature of capitulation (with or without fighting), which was a key criterion for determining the amount of money and goods to be extracted by the political center as a land tax (*kharāj*). Adjustments could be and were made in fiscal policies, but important precedents were set for the bureaucratic practice by the dynamic of conquest, as seen, for example, in the work of the historian Ahmad b. Yahya al-Baladhuri (d. ca. 892) on the first conquests (*Futuh al-Buldan*) and also in Ottoman taxation policies, which were ultimately grounded in the imperial edict (*qanun-nama*) issued at the time of conquest.

At the same time, bureaucratic structures and norms used by Muslims, even if legitimized by conquest, were generally based on customs used by previous rule. The Qur'an and sunna offered little guidance when it came to the constitution and details of bureaucratic administration, and dynastic servitors were quite aware that they were building on a past heritage. Not only did they tend to see the Islamic dispensation in light of the conquests and decisions of earlier Muslims, but they also idealized the Persian past, especially as a model of competent administration, as seen in a tenth-century work on bureaucratic history, *Kitab al-Wuzara' wa-l-Kuttab* (The book of ministers and secretaries) by Abu ʿAbdallah Muhammad al-Jahshiyari (d. 942), servitor to a number of viziers in the Abbasid dynasty of his day. Features unique to Muslim administration gradually disappeared, such as the Umayyad practice of registering soldiers by tribe, which, in the early Abbasid period, was changed to registration by village. Greek, Persian, and Coptic continued as bureaucratic languages until the fifth Umayyad caliph, ʿAbd al-Malik b. Marwan (r. 685–705), made Arabic the language of Islamic rule, as it was already the language of Islamic religion. This too did not last, and other languages, notably Persian and then Turkish (under the Ottomans), were used for bureaucratic purposes by later dynasties. However, ʿAbd al-Malik's cultural policy did play a role in encouraging the rise of Arabic prose, a development in which leading members of the bureaucratic establishment—namely, ʿAbd al-Hamid al-Katib and Ibn al-Muqaffaʿ—had a hand.

The bureaucratic corps embodied a distinct culture within Muslim society, identifiable not only in terms of standards of language and writing but also in dress, etiquette, and a sense of hierarchy and authority, symbolized in the governing seal (*khatam*; *tughra* in the Ottoman context) by which bureaucratic writing was imprinted (quite literally) with political authority. To this end, a genre of administrative literature arose, beginning in the early Abbasid period: manuals defining bureaucratic writing and procedures as well as the general ethos of bureaucratic culture. This literature, composed in Arabic at first, invariably drew on the language of the religious heritage for standards of communication, working to integrate rule and religion together in a singe cultural framework. Indeed, in some works, bureaucracy—that is, written communication—was classified as a branch of shariʿa. Bureaucracy would thus become something of an ideological battleground between those who would align it with the language and standards of eloquence of the first Muslims and those who would recognize its "linguistic autonomy"—that is, its own set of terms and nomenclature. However, it is best to see shariʿa and bureaucratic administration as symbiotic realms, mutually reinforcing each other in shaping the public order of Muslim society—a synthesis noticeable in many administrative works, such as the bureaucratic "encyclopedia" *Subh al-Aʿsha fi Sinaʿat al-Insha'* (Morning for the night-blind in the art of composition) of Abu l-ʿAbbas Ahmad al-Qalqashandi (d. 1418), an Egyptian scholar and administrative servitor during the reign of the Mamluks, and also in the Ottoman policy of integrating circles of the religiously learned (*ʿilmiyya*) into the bureaucratic ranks of the empire.

See also ʿAbd al-Hamid al-Katib b. Yahya al-ʿAmiri (d. 750); government; Ibn al-Muqaffaʿ (ca. 720–56)

Further Reading

Cornell Fleischer, *Bureaucrat and Intellectual in the Ottoman Empire: The Historian Mustafa Âli (1541–1600)*, 1986; Paul L. Heck, *The Construction of Knowledge in Islamic Civilization: Qudama b. Jaʿfar and His Kitāb al-kharāj wa-ṣināʿat al-kitāba*, 2002.

PAUL L. HECK

Buyids (945–1062)

The Buyids, named after their ancestor ʿAli b. Buyah, came from Daylam, the highlands south of the Caspian Sea. With the help of armed forces composed of Daylami footsoldiers and Turkish horsemen, from 935 onward they controlled an area that at the zenith of their power included modern-day Iraq, Oman, and Iran and reached as far as the borders of Baluchistan and Khurasan. The distribution

of the territory among the members of the Buyid family, with their leader holding the position of *amīr al-umarā'* (supreme commander) in Baghdad, brought about problems of unity and succession, which in the long run turned out to be unsolvable. Succumbing to the onslaught of the Seljuqs, Buyid rule came to an end in Baghdad in 1055 and in Fars in 1062.

According to the Sunni theory of state as formulated Mawardi, a leading contemporary authority, the caliph was supposed to be from among the Quraysh, the Prophet Muhammad's clan. In contrast, Shi'is of various denominations held the caliphate to be the prerogative of the 'Alids, the progeny of 'Ali's marriage with Fatima, the Prophet's daughter. The Buyids were Shi'is of the Zaydi branch, which prevailed in their homeland of Daylam. Mu'izz al-Dawla, the first Buyid to assume the office of supreme commander in Baghdad in 945, fearing a Zaydi imam might threaten his authority and considering the fact that the Samanids in the East were staunch supporters of the Abbasids, did not interfere with the caliphate in principle. His successors continued this policy. However, this did not prevent them from sympathizing with the Twelver (Imami) Shi'is, promoting Shi'i festivals, and choosing Shi'i sanctuaries for their burial. As for the leadership of the Islamic community, the Twelver Shi'is assumed an attitude of quietism, waiting for the return of the Twelfth Imam who had gone into hiding (*ghayba*) in 874. Eventually, Buyid amirs even had an eye for the Isma'ilism of the Fatimids, which propagated activism in going ahead with the 'Alid pretension to the caliphate.

The Buyids gave the supreme emirate, which had been established a decade before their takeover in Baghdad, a degree of stability after a period of unrest. The names of the leading amirs were mentioned together with that of the caliph in the Friday sermon (*khuṭba*) and put on coins according to their ranks. The Abbasids eventually transferred full powers to the Buyid leaders, confining their own rule to the administration of personal possessions, the enthronization of the supreme amir and the provincial rulers, and the settling of religious matters. In exchange, the Buyids assumed titles that expressed support of the Abbasid caliph (*dawla*), to which were later added titles that were meant to demonstrate protection of the community (*milla, umma*) and promotion of Islam (*dīn*). When the Buyids claimed descent from the Sasanids (224–642), the Zoroastrian rulers of Iran before the Arab conquest, the caliph found himself compelled to allow the Iranian title *shāhānshāh* (great king, *malik al-mulūk*), a title detestable to pious Muslims, to be mentioned in the *khuṭba* and put on the coins. Buyid power attained its apex under 'Adud al-Dawla, and subsequent to his death in 983, Buyid power was beginning to wane and the authority of the caliphs increased once again, earning them the place of arbiters in internal Buyid disputes.

Throughout the Buyid century, Iraq, the center of Shi'i activities since the early Islamic period, was stricken by unrest and riots, sometimes taking the shape of civil war, particularly in Baghdad. The Buyid army, composed of Shi'i Daylamis and Sunni Turks, experienced the same problem within their ranks. In addition, there were the difficulties of financing the soldiers. They were paid in cash or kind, which is the assigning of land (*iqṭā'*) in exchange for services rendered. Mismanagement, decay of the irrigation system in Mesopotamia, and the shift of the trade route from the Persian Gulf to the Red Sea contributed to the downfall of the Buyid commonwealth.

As for their cultural achievements, the Buyids did not promote New Persian literature but gave the Iranian fine arts a lasting impetus. Scholars, writers, and high officials excelled in Arabic literature, philosophy, and natural sciences. Theologians like Ibn Babuya laid the foundations of Imami theology. Whereas the Buyids were a foreign occupying power in the eyes of modern Iraqi historians, Iranian authors view them as the first power possessing the dynasty of the Shi'a. To define the place they deserve in history, one must take into account their achievements in various fields of culture. Depriving the caliph of his power without encroaching on his authority testifies to their sense of proportion in politics—a pattern that persisted under the subsequent and uncompromisingly Sunni Seljuqs.

See also Abbasids (750–1258); Baghdad; caliph, caliphate; coinage; Friday prayer; Ghaznavids (977–1086); holy places; Iraq; Mawardi (974–1058); Seljuqs (1055–1194); Shi'ism; Sunnism

Further Reading

Clifford Edmund Bosworth, "Military Organisation under the Būyids of Persia and Iraq," *Oriens* 18–19 (1967); Heribert Busse, *Chalif und Großkönig. Die Buyiden im Iraq (945–1055)*, 1969; John J. Donohue, *The Buwayhid Dynasty in Iraq 334/945 to 403/1012: Shaping Institutions for the Future*, 2003; Wilferd Madelung, "The Assumption of the Title Shāhānshāh by the Būyids and 'The Reign of the Daylam (Dawlat al-Daylam),'" *JNES* 28, no. 2 (1969); Luke Treadwell, *Buyid coinage. a die corpus (322–445* AH*)*, 2001.

HERIBERT BUSSE

C

Cairo

Cairo (*al-Qāhira*, "the Victorious"), the capital of Egypt, is a major cultural center in the Islamic world. The city developed from the camp established in 969 by General Jawhar al-Siqilli ("the Sicilian," d. 992) in the service of the Fatimid caliph Mu'izz (r. 953–75), on the east bank of the Nile several miles south of where the river divides into channels to form the Delta. An escarpment of cliffs known as the Muqattam approaches the river at this locale, assuring its strategic significance. Successive governments have constructed fortifications there since Pharaonic times, and following the Arab conquest in 641, a permanent settlement called *al-Fusṭāṭ* (Gr. *Phossatun*, or "tent") was established near a Byzantine garrison tower. Over the following three centuries, Fustat grew into a large port town, and successive ruling regimes built their residences and ceremonial mosques to the north. Jawhar plotted the parameters of Cairo partially on sightings of the planet Mars (*al-Qāhir*, hence the title *Miṣr al-Qāhira*, "Egypt the Victorious"). He designed a rectangle roughly one mile square and designated it as the seat of governance for the Fatimid caliphate and Isma'ili Shi'i missions (*da'wa*). Two large palaces, divided by a central avenue running south to north (*Bayn al-Qaṣrayn*, "between the two palaces"), and a cathedral mosque, al-Azhar, occupied most of this rectangle.

Habitation in al-Qahira was initially limited to the Fatimid elite. But after the Ayyubid termination of the Fatimid caliphate (1169) and restoration of Sunnism, Sultan Saladin (d. 1193) ordered the construction of a vast citadel (*al-Qal'a*) on a western spur of the Muqattam. Subsequently, the zones between the southern gate of al-Qahira (*Bāb Zuwayla*) and the citadel were urbanized. The town of Fustat, already diminished in population under the late Fatimids, was effectively abandoned after fires were ordered by the vizier Shawar (d. 1169) to empty the site during the Crusader period preceding the Ayyubid coup. From its foundation, the citadel replaced the former Fatimid palaces as the primary seat of governance and military power in Egypt and remained so until the onset of modernization following the reign of Muhammad 'Ali (1805–48). The Ayyubid sultans surrounded the urbanized zone with defensive walls extending from Fustat to the citadel and then north to al-Qahira. Aqueducts leading from the Nile to the citadel supplied water to the government center, and the population began to expand across the canal (*al-Khalīj*) to the Nile shore some miles west of the citadel and Fatimid al-Qahira.

After Mamluk soldiers who had served the last Ayyubid sultan, al-Malik al-Salih (d. 1250), seized control, the entire urban area became known as al-Qahira and underwent massive development. During the 267 years of independent Mamluk rule, Cairo attained its medieval apogee with a population of several hundred thousand. Following the fall of Baghdad to the Ilkhanids in 1258, Cairo became the leading center of literary and scholastic activity in the central Islamic lands, which it has subsequently remained. Under the Mamluks, Egypt experienced its final phase as a great power, and Cairo witnessed the construction of numerous mosques, colleges (madrasas), and Sufi hospices (*khānaqāhs*). Even in the aftermath of successive plague epidemics during the 14th and 15th centuries, Cairo persisted as the largest city in the Arabic-speaking world.

Following the Ottomans' defeat of the Mamluks in 1517, Cairo continued as the seat of government in Egypt, their most prominent Arab province. Direct Ottoman rule persisted for approximately 100 years and was followed by semiautonomous control at the hands of local military officers who belonged to an elite descended from indigenous Mamluks and Ottoman Janissaries (Muslim infantry soldiers of European Christian origin). Cairo maintained its significance as one of the primary cities of the Ottoman Empire and as a center of trade between northeast Africa, Southwest Asia, and Mediterranean Europe. This period of autonomy was abruptly terminated in 1798 by the invasion of Egypt by the French under Napoleon Bonaparte. Although the French occupation lasted only three years, the resultant interregnum was ultimately resolved by Muhammad 'Ali, an officer of Albanian descent sent by the Ottomans to restore their authority. Muhammad 'Ali entrenched himself as the effective autocrat in Egypt, founded a dynasty that lasted until 1952, and proceeded to launch programs for the modernization of Cairo and its integration into the emerging European-dominated global economy. From Muhammad 'Ali's reign, Cairo has been gradually transformed into a modern megalopolis with a population eventually exceeding 15 million. Yet Cairo has retained its character as the leading center of culture and intellectual vitality in the Arabic-speaking world, and much of its medieval architecture has been restored.

See also Ayyubids (1169–1250); Egypt; Fatimids (909–1171); Mamluks (1250–1517)

Further Reading

Janet L. Abu-Lughod, *Cairo: 1,001 Years of the City Victorious*, 1971; Marcel Clerget, *Le Caire, Étude de géographie urbaine et d'histoire économique*, 2 vols., 1934; K.A.C. Creswell, *The Muslim Architecture of Egypt*, vol. 1: *Ikhshids and Fatimids, A.D. 939–1171*, 1952; Idem, *The Muslim Architecture of Egypt*, vol. 2: *Ayyubids and Early*

Bahrite Mamluks, A.D. 1171–1326, 1959; Edward William Lane, *The Manners and Customs of the Modern Egyptians*, 1908; Nasser O. Rabbat, *The Citadel of Cairo, A New Interpretation of Royal Mamluk Architecture*, 1995.

CARL F. PETRY

caliph, caliphate

The caliphate (*al-khilāfa*) is the term denoting the form of government that came into existence in Islamic lands after the death of the Prophet Muhammad and is considered to have survived until the first decades of the 20th century. It derives from the title caliph (*khalīfa*, pl. *khulafā'* or *khalā'if*), referring to Muslim sovereigns who claimed authority over all Muslims. The caliphate refers not only to the office of the caliph but also to the period of his reign and to his dominion—in other words, the territory and peoples over whom he ruled. The office itself soon developed into a form of hereditary monarchy, although it lacked fixed rules on the order of succession and based its legitimacy on claims of political succession to Muhammad. The caliphate was constrained by neither any fixed geographical location or boundaries nor particular institutions; rather, it was coterminous with the reign of a monarch or a dynasty.

This entry discusses the political, historical, and institutional aspects of the caliphate but not the theological or judicial. Despite frequent overlap between the terms caliph/imam and caliphate/imamate, this article also does not deal with topics that are only relevant to imam/imamate, as in Shi'ism, for example.

The term "caliphate" is most commonly restricted to five periods or dynasties: the Rightly Guided Caliphate (632–61), the Umayyad caliphate (661–750), the Abbasid caliphate (750–1258 and 1261–1517), the Fatimid caliphate (909–1171), and the Umayyad caliphate of Córdoba (928–1031). Throughout the centuries, however, various other rulers have made claims to the caliphate or adopted the caliphal titulature—that is, one or more titles usually associated with caliphs. The first four successors of the Prophet Muhammad are usually called the Rightly Guided Caliphs (*al-khulafā' al-rāshidūn*). But those Muslims who do not accept the legitimacy of some of these rulers refrain from applying this expression to them.

Despite the ubiquitous use of the terms "caliphate" and "caliph" in modern scholarship, they were not the principal or exclusive terms used in official documents or in the writings of Muslim authors, nor were they adopted immediately following Muhammad's death. Many Muslim writers eschewed these two terms in favor of alternatives, especially imam and *imāma*, or (religious) leader and leadership. The two terms, "caliph" and "caliphate," were almost always employed in conjunction with other terms and expressions. They also hardly appear in official or unofficial documentary sources (papyri, coins, rock inscriptions, textiles, weights, and seals), and non-Muslim sources do not use them when referring to Muslim sovereigns or to Islamic political institutions, especially for the first Islamic centuries. The institution of the caliphate developed gradually with time and crystallized only at the beginning of the Abbasid period in the second half of the eighth century. Also, despite their claims to universal rule over all Muslims, few Muslim sovereigns actually did so; many provinces and regions controlled by Muslims did not acknowledge the suzerainty of any caliph. Furthermore, the caliphs possessed actual power for a relatively short period, as they became mostly puppets in the hands of military commanders and high-ranking officials.

The history of the development of the institution of the caliphate can be divided as follows:

632–945. This timespan covers three periods. The foundational period, beginning with the election of Abu Bakr as leader of the Muslim community after the Prophet's death in 632, continued until the end of the second *fitna* (civil war) in the second half of the seventh century. It was followed by the formative period and period of strength, from the reign of 'Abd al-Malik (r. 685–705) to about the middle of the ninth century. The subsequent period saw the decline of central caliphal authority and growth of independent and autonomous regions in the ninth and tenth centuries, when an increasing number of provinces were ruled by semiautonomous or autonomous dynasties. The gradual loss of power by the Abbasid caliphs culminated with the Buyids gaining control of Baghdad in 945.

945–1517. Two periods are included in this time frame. A period of multiple caliphates, which extended from the 10th to the 12th centuries, began with the establishment of the Fatimid caliphate in 909 in Ifriqiya, followed by that of the Umayyads in Córdoba in 928. The latter, a Sunni caliphate, lasted a century, while the former, a Shi'i Isma'ili one, extended its rule to Egypt and Syria and lasted until 1171. The period of the shadow caliphate ensued as the Muslim world became independent of any caliphal control between the 12th century and 1517. This period saw the demise of the Abbasid caliphate after the Mongols' sack of Baghdad in 1258 and the transfer to Cairo, then under Mamluk rule, of a scion of the dynasty in 1261. This caliphate, which had neither power nor symbols thereof, ended in 1517 with the Ottoman conquest of Egypt. Other dynasties, like the Hafsids (1229–1574) and the Marinids (1269–1465), appropriated the caliphal titulature, although they lacked the universalist ambitions of the original caliphates.

1517–1924. With the fall of the Abbasid caliphate, there arrived a period of multiple pretenders and competition for supremacy in the Muslim world. A greater number of Muslim rulers added the title *khalīfa* to their titulature, although for most rulers that did not correspond to any higher claims of authority over all Muslim lands, as was the case of the Mughal rulers from Akbar (r. 1556–1605) to Shah 'Alam II (r. 1759–1806). The title caliph was also given to Ottoman sultans, first unofficially from the end of the 14th century, and then officially in the 18th and 19th centuries. The end of the caliphate came about in February 1924, when the Grand National

Assembly of Ankara deposed the Ottoman sultan ʻAbd al-Majid II and abolished the caliphate. Some Muslim rulers attempted but failed to restore the institution, notably the Sharif of Mecca, al-Husayn b. ʻAli, in 1924, and King Farouk of Egypt in 1939.

Not all Muslims considered their rulers primarily as caliphs, nor did all Muslims interpret the title of *khalīfa* in the same way. Not only did the institution of the caliphate itself develop over time, but so did the terminology associated with it and the way that Muslims throughout the world viewed it.

Titulature of Pre-Islamic Arabian Monarchs

For centuries prior to the rise of Islam, sovereigns in the Arabian Peninsula adopted a titulature based on the title *m.l.k* (king, monarch). This is attested in documents written in the various North and South Arabian languages that were in use in the Arabian Peninsula and dating from approximately the seventh century BCE to the mid-sixth century CE. The title was also employed by Arabian dynasties at the northern limits of the Arabian Peninsula (like the Nabataeans and the Palmyrenes) that used non-Arabian languages (Aramaic and Greek) in their documents. The use of the title *m.l.k* occurs in rare pre-Islamic inscriptions in Arabic as well.

That *malik* was the title in Arabic given to the holder of the highest political office is further verified in subsequent literature in Arabic. In the Qur'an, the title appears 13 times in the singular and twice in the plural (*mulūk*) to denote a sovereign, with 5 of the 13 occurrences in the singular actually referring to God, who is described as the ultimate possessor of all sovereignty. In pre-Islamic Arabic poetry, an independent monarch's title is also *malik*. This is also the title given to sovereigns, both Arabian (from the pre-Islamic period) and non-Arabian (of all periods), in Islamic Arabic literary sources from the eighth century onward (e.g., *mulūk Kinda*, or kings of Kinda, and *mulūk al-Rūm*, or kings of the Romans).

The predominance of the title *malik* in the Arabian Peninsula over a 1,000-year period was broken when Muslim sovereigns did not adopt a titulature based on it. The reason for that may be the Qur'anic notion that God is the one and only king of all (creation). Indeed, kingship came to be considered synonymous with worldly rule from early Abbasid times, when a hadith (a Prophetic tradition) was circulated attributing to the Prophet Muhammad the statement, "*Khilāfa* after me will be thirty years; after that it will be kingship." Since the Rightly Guided Caliphs ruled for 30 years, they were given an especially elevated position by Sunni religious scholars, who called their rule the "vicarage of prophecy" (*khilāfat al-nubuwwa*), mostly considering the caliphs' order in succession as their order in merit.

Titulature of Early Muslim Sovereigns up to 750

According to Islamic literary sources, Abu Bakr, the first leader of the Muslim community after Muhammad's death, adopted the title of *khalīfat rasūl Allāh*, "the successor of the messenger of God." It is, however, unlikely that Abu Bakr held any official title, since the literary sources make this assertion for polemical reasons, to argue that the title *khalīfa*, which came into official use much later, is in reality short for *khalīfat rasūl Allāh*, not *khalīfat Allāh*. This debate over the meaning of the term *khalīfa* probably emerged during the early Abbasid period.

The literary sources also assert that ʻUmar b. al-Khattab, Abu Bakr's successor, coined for himself the title of *amīr al-mu'minīn*, "Commander of the Faithful," in part because the conquests gave him a military standing. Some reports state that this title was held before him by ʻAbdallah b. Jahsh during the Prophet's lifetime. Nonetheless, there is reason to accept that ʻUmar was the first sovereign to adopt the title of *amīr al-mu'minīn*, since there is evidence that his successor, ʻUthman b. ʻAffan, used it in diplomatic exchanges with foreign rulers. The first documentary attestations of this title to date come from the reign of Muʻawiya (r. 661–80). His full title in Arabic documents reads, "*ʻabd Allāh Muʻāwiya amīr al-mu'minīn*," or "God's servant, Muʻawiya, Commander of the Faithful"; in Greek documents, it is fully transliterated, and on a silver coin (*dirham*) the titulature is partially transliterated and partially translated into Pahlavi.

In fact, the official full titulature of the earliest Muslim sovereigns up to the end of the Umayyad period was the formula *ʻabd Allāh* (name of sovereign) *amīr al-mu'minīn*, which means "God's servant (name), Commander of the Faithful." This is found on a variety of official and unofficial documents (most commonly inscriptions, papyri, coins, seals, and weights) and in several languages. The sovereign is normally identified by his first name only, although sometimes the father's name is also included.

The only deviation from this titulature was the addition, on some coins from the reign of ʻAbd al-Malik, of the title *khalīfat Allāh*, although the first word of the title had a peculiar orthography *(kh.l.f.t)* that has been read differently by various scholars. The title *khalīfat Allāh* was, however, removed from coins during the reign of ʻAbd al-Malik himself, and it does not reappear in the surviving documents until the Abbasid period. Could this have been in response to early objections to the use of this title by the Muslim sovereign? The Umayyad caliphs, including ʻAbd al-Malik, did not object to being addressed by such a title by poets in panegyrics.

The term *khilāfa*—not *khalīfa*—appears even later in documentary sources, the earliest being an unofficial inscription dated 737–38 from the reign of Hisham (r. 724–43). It then appears officially near the end of the Umayyad dynasty in a lead seal and two lead bullae of Marwan b. Muhammad (r. 744–50). Such attestations indicate that the office or institution of the caliphate was indeed officially identified by a term derived from *khalīfa* by the end of Umayyad times, although the predominant title of Umayyad sovereigns until the end of their dynasty in 750 remained *amīr al-mu'minīn*.

Although the titulature of Muslim sovereigns in documentary sources presents a clear break with the titulature of pre-Islamic monarchs, the break was not as pronounced in Arabic poetry, where the vocabulary used to refer to politics and political institutions evolved gradually with time. In the poetry allegedly contemporaneous with the Prophet and his first successors, rulers are still mostly referred to with pre-Islamic terms and concepts interspersed with

some new Islamic terms. The latter grow steadily in importance and become more prevalent so that by the end of the Umayyad period, they dominate the political vocabulary of the poetry. Beginning with poetry from ʻUmar's reign, the titles imam and *amīr al-mu'minīn* are applied to Muslim sovereigns, while *khalīfat Allāh* is first attested from the reign of Muʻawiya. Some scholars have mistakenly assumed that the latter title was already in use during the reign of ʻUthman because it is applied to him in several verses. However, all these verses come from elegies, which means that they were posthumous to ʻUthman's reign. In addition, Muʻawiya and the later Umayyads built their legitimacy partly on their association with ʻUthman, and, therefore, a poet lamenting ʻUthman's death was not only expressing his sorrow for the slain sovereign but also presenting his allegiance to the Umayyads. This in turn means that such verses could have been composed any time during the Umayyad period. Poets with different political allegiances opted for different political vocabulary. Those who favored ʻAli b. Abi Talib and his descendants avoided using the title *khalīfa* for their political leaders, preferring to use imam or *amīr al-mu'minīn*. The latter term eventually became the sole prerogative of ʻAli in Shiʻi literature.

In the Islamic literary sources, the titulature applied to Muslim sovereigns varies from source to source. Most sovereigns are referred to just by their first names or by their full names when it is necessary to avoid ambiguity. If a titulature is given to the sovereign, then the choice of titles usually depends on the author himself, although there are trends depending on the religious affiliation of the author and/or the type of literature that is being composed. An author could favor the title *amīr al-mu'minīn*, or imam, or *khalīfa*, or might use all three interchangeably. However, in works of hadith or *fiqh*, the title of imam takes precedence over the others. Imam is also the title preferred by non-Sunni authors, such as the Zaydis, the Ibadis, and the Imami Shiʻis. On the other hand, Christian authors writing in Arabic apply the title *malik* to all sovereigns, whether Muslim or non-Muslim.

Non-Muslim authors writing in a language other than Arabic chose one of three ways to refer to Muslim sovereigns in their literary compositions: (1) through their given names only; (2) through a title in their native language that was commonly used to refer to other sovereigns; and (3) by applying the title *amīr al-mu'minīn* to them, in either a transliterated or translated form.

The Meaning of the Title *Khalīfat Allāh*

Most modern scholars have understood the title *khalīfat Allāh* to mean "vicegerent of God" or "deputy of God." However, this was not the original meaning of the expression.

The title itself appears rarely in pre-Abbasid documentary sources and never in papyri. But the term *khalīfa* itself does appear several times in papyri dated from the eighth to the tenth century, beginning with a bilingual, Arabic-Greek receipt dated 643. In most of these examples, the individuals referred to as *khalīfa*s are involved in some financial transaction, usually the collection of, or receipt for, a payment, without any associated political connotation.

For a better understanding of the meaning of the title, we must study pre-Islamic documents from Arabia. In South Arabian languages, words from the root *kh.l.f* have several meanings (e.g., "gate of a town" and "violating an oath"). But one meaning has a political/administrative connotation and occurs in two inscriptions by Abraha, the sixth-century South Arabian monarch of Abyssinian origin. The usage of the verb *s.t.kh.l.f* in these two texts is similar to the Arabic *istakhlafa*, which is a Qur'anic word and is often found in *Sīra* literature to describe the Prophet's appointment of individuals as overseers of Medina with limited authority during his absence from the town. The spelling of the term *kh.l.f.t*, which appears twice in one of these texts, is also identical with that of *khalīfa* as found on the coins of ʻAbd al-Malik. The exact meaning of these words remains unclear. Scholars have translated *kh.l.f.t* as "governor" and as "viceroy," but they have been influenced in this interpretation by later Arabic usage.

The most common occurrence of words from the root *kh.l.f* in pre-Islamic documents is in personal names found in North and South Arabian; in Nabataean and Palmyrene, the names are based on the root *ḥ.l.p*. Transliterated forms of these names are found in Greek documents as well. Scholars agree that the names based on the root *kh.l.f* are originally compound names, part of which is the name of a deity, although the latter is often omitted. In all instances where the name of the deity appears in full, the name is *l.h* or *'.l.h*. These compound names have equivalents in Arabic based on the root *kh.l.f* added to the name Allah. Understanding the meaning of these names can provide us with an insight on the meaning of the title *khalīfat Allāh*.

In bilingual inscriptions, names from the Semitic root *kh.l.f/ḥ.l.p* are equated with the Greek Antipatros and less frequently Antigonos. These names were given to newborns considered as replacements for a relative, most commonly the father, who had died. A number of scholars have argued that the belief was that a god had replaced the deceased person with the newborn baby. Equivalent names in Arabic from the root *kh.l.f* carry the same meaning and are attested from the earliest surviving documents in Arabic to the present day.

Scholars thus agree that the meaning of the names based on the root *kh.l.f* is "replacement or substitute (of a deceased person) *by* a god." It is the god that makes (*jaʻala*)—selects, assigns, designates, creates, places—the *khalīfa*. This is exactly the meaning and usage that we find in the Qur'an. It is also the same meaning that late Umayyad ideology used in order to legitimate Umayyad rule, making prophethood and the caliphate parallel institutions, both initiated and implemented by God.

Words derived from the root *kh.l.f* have various meanings in Arabic. But if we focus on the meaning "to substitute" or "to replace," we notice that in the Qur'an, these actions are always associated with God: it is God that is replacing or bringing forth substitutes for individuals or peoples. In other words, the making—selecting, assigning, designating, creating, placing—of *khalīfa*s in the Qur'an is the exclusive prerogative of God. The word *khalīfa* appears in the Qur'an twice (2:30 and 38:26), where God is explicitly said to make

or have made a *khalīfa*. The two plural forms *khalā'if* and *khulafā'* occur in similar situations seven times. In all these instances, the verb used is *ja'ala*. However, none of these Qur'anic terms possesses a specifically political connotation, nor did early Muslim scholars in the Umayyad period equate the Qur'anic *khalīfa* with the head of the Islamic community; this had to wait until the tenth century, well into Abbasid rule.

This clearly indicates that the original meaning of the expression *khalīfat Allāh* was "replacement or successor placed by (the agency of) God," and not "vicegerent or deputy *of* God." The title indicated God's approval of the sovereign and God's support of his legitimacy.

Succession to Rule after Muhammad

Soon after the Prophet Muhammad's death in 632, leading Medinan Muslims met to discuss the leadership of the community. Some Meccan Muslims rushed to the meeting and ended any attempts to divide rule over the Muslims. In the spur of the moment, Abu Bakr was given a pledge of allegiance (*bay'a*) as the leader of the Muslim community. His election was formalized at the mosque of Medina, where he received the general allegiance of all present Muslims.

Before his death in 634, Abu Bakr designated 'Umar b. al-Khattab as his successor. The Muslim community did not in this case select their ruler but only endorsed the choice of Abu Bakr by making a pledge of allegiance to 'Umar. After he was critically stabbed in 644, 'Umar appointed a consultative council (*shūrā*) of six members that was to select one of its own as his successor. They chose 'Uthman b. 'Affan. After 12 years of rule, 'Uthman was killed in 656 by a group of Muslims after he refused their demands to abdicate or to accept deposition.

Medinan Muslims subsequently selected 'Ali as 'Uthman's successor. 'Ali was immediately cast in an impossible situation, between arresting or protecting some of his supporters who were implicated in the killing of 'Uthman. He moved his base from Medina to Kufa in Iraq and faced continuous civil strife. 'Ali was victorious at the Battle of the Camel; however, the Battle of Siffin against the governor of Syria, Mu'awiya, ended with an arbitration that led to a stalemate. As a result, a group splintered from 'Ali's camp, the Kharijis, whom 'Ali was forced to fight. He was eventually killed by one of them in 661.

The Kufans immediately elected 'Ali's son, Hasan, to succeed his father. This was the first time that a son succeeded a father as head of the Muslim community. But the Syrians had already elected Mu'awiya as sovereign, and Hasan relinquished his position to Mu'awiya in 661. Then, for the first time in the history of the Muslim community, a sovereign, Mu'awiya, designated a successor, his son Yazid, as his heir apparent during his lifetime. This designation was controversial, but its limited success, followed by Yazid's accession to the caliphate in 680, laid the foundation for hereditary rule. A few years later, Marwan b. al-Hakam (r. 683–85) was able to set up his family as the first Islamic dynasty.

Overall, there were two main methods of succession in the caliphates: by designation, which was the most common method, or by election, when a successor had not been designated. Designation was normally done by a testament (*'ahd*), when the heir apparent, normally of the age of majority, was called *walī al-'ahd* ("one in charge of safeguarding the testament," equivalent to crown prince); his appointment was binding on him and on the community and could not, in principle, be repealed. In the case of the Marwanids, all their rulers were nominated by their predecessors, with the exception of Marwan, the founder, Yazid b. al-Walid (r. 744), and Marwan b. Muhammad. On some occasions during the Abbasid period, the caliph was elected by a group of dignitaries when the previous monarch died without having designated a successor. But in the case of the Fatimids, succession was accepted solely through an explicit designation (*naṣṣ*) from the previous caliph/imam.

Several times during the Marwanid and Abbasid periods, the ruling monarch designated two successors simultaneously. This usually caused tensions within the ruling family that occasionally escalated into full warfare. Succession in the various caliphates was agnatic (i.e., restricted to males in the male line) and did not follow rules of primogeniture. In fact, there were no fixed regulations for the succession as any member of the ruling family had a theoretical claim to the throne. Although sons were favored, succession could pass on to a brother, a cousin, an uncle, or a nephew.

Once selected, the new caliph was procedurally given the *bay'a*, or oath of allegiance of the community. This was done through a handshake by the dignitaries of the town or province in which the caliph resided. Those in distant lands gave their allegiance through the governors of their respective districts.

The caliph was considered the leader of the Muslim community, just like the Prophet without the function of prophecy. As such, he was the judge and temporal authority in the realm, who appointed the members of his government, maintained order in society, defended the community against its enemies, and collected and distributed its wealth. But above all, he was the Muslims' religious leader who ensured the obedience of the community to the divine law. Thus he led the Friday communal prayer, the Friday sermon was held in his name, he led the Muslim armies in jihad, and he led the annual pilgrimage to Mecca. Under the Abbasids, he protected religion from innovations that departed from established practice; wore in public the Prophet's insignia, his cloak (*burda*) and scepter (*qaḍīb*); took up titles that emphasized his relation to God, like *al-manṣūr* ("one made victorious by God"); and identified himself as "God's power (*sulṭān*) on His Earth." Whatever religious duty he could not fulfill, he delegated to others to fulfill in his name. Whether he was an interpreter of the law is a more complicated question. Certainly the early caliphs, including the Rightly Guided Caliphs and the early Umayyads, played an active role in shaping and adding to the corpus of Islamic law. In early Abbasid times, the intellectual Ibn al-Muqaffa' proposed to the caliph Mansur (r. 754–75) that the caliph start, supervise, and play an active part in the construction of a unified code of Islamic law. Mansur, however, did not implement his proposal, and the development of the law remained the domain of religious scholars. This situation was

confirmed further after Ma'mun's (r. 813–33) and his two successors' failure to impose their theological ideas on those scholars in the famous *miḥna*, or inquisition. The interpretation of the law since then remained outside the functions of the caliph.

Once a caliph acceded to power, there were no regulations in place that specified how he could be deposed. The issue is old, raised by the opponents of 'Uthman, as we have seen; both the Umayyads (except Yazid b. al-Walid) and the Abbasid caliphs implicitly believed that only God could remove them from power since it was He who placed them in power. But by the tenth century, it was legally stipulated that if the monarch lost his mental health or certain aspects of his physical fitness after his accession to power, then he should be deposed and replaced. Blindness in particular made one ineligible to accede to the throne. This rule existed already in the Roman and Sasanian empires as well as in the Latin-speaking kingdoms, and it led some political rivals to blind their opponents in order to make them ineligible to rule. Among Muslim caliphs, the first instances of this practice occurred in the tenth century, when several Abbasid monarchs were blinded by high-ranking officials in order to have them replaced: Qahir in 934, Muttaqi in 944, and Mustakfi in 946.

Theoretical Works on the Caliphate

Prior to the decline of the caliphal system in the tenth century, theoretical works on the caliphate were scarce, short, and almost accidental. During late Umayyad times, for example, the distinguished secretary 'Abd al-Hamid (d. 750), in defense of the Umayyads, expressed his vision of the caliphate as an institution parallel to, and succeeding, prophethood, with both institutions created by God and with the obligation of all Muslims to obey "God's caliphs" as they obey God and the Prophet. Under the Abbasids, the Hanafi jurist Abu Yusuf (d. 798) believed God to be the source of power but the imam is His vicegerent on Earth who must have sufficient resources to rule. And the Mu'tazili litterateur Jahiz (d. 869) believed the imamate was necessary due to the predatory nature of humans, but an impious ruler may be removed from power if the circumstances permitted that.

From the 11th century onward, theoretical works intensified among Sunnis with the resurgence of Sunnism under the Seljuqs and their successors. The most influential and authoritative of those works is Mawardi's (d. 1058) *al-Ahkam al-Sultaniyya* (The ordinances of government). There the author considers the caliphate necessary on the basis of divine law, not of reason, giving the caliph alone the mandate to rule from God; it is his prerogative to delegate authority and lend legitimacy to the other members of his government (the vizier, the judge, etc.). The author discusses the requirements for being caliph, vizier, or judge and considers, due to the de facto deterioration of caliphal power, allowing more than one caliph under specific circumstances, validating the rule of usurpers, limiting caliphal power, and even—albeit unclearly—removing him from office. Ghazali (d. 1111) goes further. Although he asserts that the caliph was the supreme symbol of the divine law, he considers the rule of whoever holds actual political power as valid provided he received nominal recognition by the caliph. Writing after the Mongol invasion and the de facto end of the classical caliphal system, Ibn Taymiyya (d. 1348) reaffirmed the legitimacy of those who have actual power and did not even believe that they required legitimation from the caliph.

In the modern era, debates about the political and social meanings of the term "caliph" turned into a platform for Muslim intellectuals to debate the ideas of reform, constitutionalism, and the need to rethink Islamic political theory according to the needs of the modern age. Shah Waliullah (1703–62) separated the social from the political and believed in the existence of two types of caliphate: an outward caliphate (*khilāfat al-ẓāhir*), the political authority in charge of the superficial order, and an inward caliphate (*khilāfat al-bāṭin*), guarded by religious scholars and responsible for the social order. Usman dan Fodio (1754–1817), championing a program for political and social change, declared a jihad that led to the establishment of the Sokoto caliphate (in modern Nigeria) in 1806. The reformist Rashid Rida, in his *al-Khilafa aw al-Imama al-'Uzma* (The caliphate or the supreme leadership, 1922) called for a renewed Arab caliphate, in which the caliph needed to adapt Islamic law to the needs of modern life. In 1925, 'Ali 'Abd al-Raziq, in his *al-Islam wa-Usul al-Hukm* (Islam and the principles of governance), caused great commotion with his call for the separation between temporal and religious power and his characterizing the Prophet's rule in Medina as being independent of his prophetic mission. The interest in the caliphate became a matter of urgent debate with its abolition under the secular regime established by Atatürk in Turkey in 1924, which resulted in the famous Caliphate Conference in Cairo in 1926 that attempted unsuccessfully to revive the caliphate.

In more recent times, some Muslim rulers took up the title *amīr al-mu'minīn*, not *khalīfa*, particularly the kings of Morocco and even the leader of the Taliban in Afghanistan. The use of the term *khalīfa* is nowadays rare, even among groups seeking the reunification of the Islamic community.

See also Abbasids (750–1258); imamate; Khilafat movement (1919–24); Mawardi (974–1058); Rida, Muhammad Rashid (1865–1935)

Further Reading

Khalil 'Athamina, "The Tribal Kings in Pre-Islamic Arabia: A Study of the Epithet *Malik* or *Dhu al-Taj* in Early Arabic Traditions," *al-Qanṭara* 19 (1998): 19–37; Aziz al-Azmeh, *Muslim Kingship: Power and the Sacred in Muslim, Christian, and Pagan Polities*, 1997; Patricia Crone and Martin Hinds, *God's Caliph: Religious Authority in the First Centuries of Islam*, 1986; Fred M. Donner, "The Formation of the Islamic State," *Journal of the American Oriental Society* 106, no. 2 (1986): 283–96; Hamilton A. R. Gibb, "The Evolution of Government in Early Islam," *Studia Islamica* 4 (1955): 5–17; Ignaz Goldziher, "Du sens propre des expressions Ombre de Dieu, Khalife de Dieu pour désigner les chefs dans l'Islam," *Revue de l'histoire des religions* 35 (1897): 331–38; Ann K. S. Lambton, *State and Government in Medieval Islam*, 1981; Bernard Lewis, *Political Words and Ideas in Islam*, 2008; Wilferd Madelung, *The Succession*

to Muḥammad: A Study of the Early Caliphate, 1997; Carlo Alfonso Nallino, *Appunti sulla natura del "califfato" in genere e sul presunto "califf ato ottomano*," 1917; Rudi Paret, "Signification coranique de *halīfa* et d'autres dérivés de la racine *halafa*," *Studia Islamica* 31 (1970): 211–17; Wadād al-Qāḍī, "The Term 'Khalīfa' in Early Exegetical Literature," *Die Welt des Islams* 28 (1988): 392–411; Émile Tyan, *Institutions du droit public musulman*, 1957; W. Montgomery Watt, *Islamic Political Thought: The Basic Concepts*, 1968.

WADAD KADI AND ARAM A. SHAHIN

capitalism

Capitalism has been a particular preoccupation for Muslim intellectuals concerned about the place of Islamic values in the modern world. They have focused both on the transformative economic power of capitalism and on the radical political changes associated with it. This is scarcely surprising: throughout Asia and Africa, Muslims first experienced capitalism under European imperialism and the unequal global power that it brought into being.

The response to these developments was visible initially among Muslims who admired the productive power of capitalist enterprise but tried to tie it more closely to Islamic values. Thus Talaat Harb (d. 1941) founded Banque Misr, the only bank in Egypt at the time that was owned and run by Egyptians, as well as other major financial and industrial companies, such as Misr Insurance and Misr Textiles. Harb believed that capitalism could be put to the service of Egypt and Islam if Egyptian Muslims, rather than Europeans, were to control its main enterprises. Similarly, in Java the "virtuous capitalists" of the Sarekat Islam—an organization that began as a grouping of batik traders but became a campaigning political force with wider ambitions in the first quarter of the 20th century—called for a capitalist system owned by and serving the local, mainly Muslim, population of the region. Increasingly prominent in the debate, however, were those intellectuals who feared the effects of capitalism on Islamic values, regardless of where the ownership lay. This concern centered chiefly on the principles it embodied and thus on the impact that such a powerful system of wealth creation had on social life and specifically on Islamic society and sociability. The approaches were various but can be grouped into three distinct, although sometimes overlapping, trends.

There were those who drew chiefly on the classical rulings of *fiqh* (Islamic jurisprudence) relating to financial and commercial transactions. For them, it was the charging of interest, equated with *ribā*, that lay at the heart of capitalist enterprise and that directly violated explicit Qur'anic prohibitions. The Syrian religious intellectual Rashid Rida (d. 1935) and others like him throughout the 20th and 21st centuries drew on a long chain of jurisprudential authority to argue that *ribā*, as a direct contravention of God's command, made capitalism fundamentally at odds with an Islamic ethos. Nevertheless, there were those like Rashid Rida's own mentor, Muhammad 'Abduh (d. 1905) in Egypt, who argued that *ribā* should be understood in the context in which it was being used—that is, the morally repugnant and socially harmful practice of pre-Islamic Arabia whereby interest on a loan was charged at such high rates that it could end in the enslavement of the debtor. It was the context, he asserted, that should determine whether it was a practice to be condemned. This opened up a debate about the term and its moral significance that continues to generate controversy, although the clerical consensus still leans heavily toward Rashid Rida's interpretation.

By the middle of the 20th century, distinctively Islamic critiques of capitalism had shifted their focus to embrace social criticism and political opposition. Writers like Mustafa al-Siba'i (d. 1964), Sayyid Qutb (d. 1966) in Egypt, Mawdudi (d. 1979) in Pakistan, Ayatollah Baqir al-Sadr (d. 1980) in Iraq, and Shaykh Muhammad al-Ghazali (d. 1996) not only criticized capitalism as a morally flawed economic system but also attacked it for the politics of inequality with which it was associated and the ideology of possessive individualism, which it promoted. By contrast, they championed a system that would encourage a return to Islamic values, represented not only by strict Islamic observance in all social and economic transactions but also by the primacy of public welfare and the values of "mutual social responsibility."

Thinkers like these helped to lay the groundwork for later debates as Muslims developed appropriate ways of responding not only to the doctrinal and moral repulsion of capitalism but also to its attractive material power. Thus a radical Islamist critique of capitalism developed, attacking those Muslims who had accepted the dominant global economy and the power it represented. Many of these writers and activists drew on the works of earlier thinkers such as Qutb, the Palestinian Taqi al-Din al-Nabhani (d. 1977), or 'Ali Shari'ati (d. 1977) in Iran, but they also developed their own vehement criticism of the inequality, injustice, and imbalance of world power that they saw in the capitalist system. This was taken up by those thinkers and activists linked to al-Qaeda, notably the Palestinian 'Abdallah 'Azzam (d. 1989), and the Egyptian Ayman al-Zawahiri, as well as by the radical Islamists Abu Bakar Ba'asyir in Indonesia and Maulana Abdul Aziz in Pakistan. Their condemnation of the United States has been combined with a vehement denunciation of all aspects of Western power, including the "world-devouring" power of capitalism. As the attack on the New York World Trade Center in 2001 demonstrated, if that power could not be defeated, it could be symbolically and violently challenged.

The latter part of the 20th century also witnessed efforts to create alternatives to capitalism intended eventually to generate equal power but grounded in Islamic principles. These took the form of the development of a field of "Islamic economics," which attempts to create models of economic growth and efficiency that draw heavily on the established field of positive economics but tries to infuse it with values and preferences compatible with Islamic principles. As an alternative system, it suffers from a lack of practical

application. Even those states that stress their Islamic identities run their national economies in conformity with the rules of the global market.

More visible and more successful has been the emergence of Islamic banking as a distinct financial sector in the global economy, tentatively at first and then, after about 1990, with increasing confidence and a growing market share. The Islamic banks define themselves with reference to a strict but imaginative application of Islamic principles to financial practices. These involve not simply the avoidance of all interest-bearing transactions but also measures such as *mushāraka* (joint capital ventures) and *muḍāraba* (joint ventures between capital and enterprise), which had long been sanctioned by Islamic jurisprudence as legitimate ways of using capital productively. Although scarcely a challenge to capitalism as a system, the Islamic banks seek to put into practice, within the confines of successful financial institutions, principles that demonstrate that Islamic values are wholly compatible with the pursuit of profit.

See also economic theory

Further Reading

Hamid Enayat, *Modern Islamic Political Thought*, 2004; Maxime Rodinson, *Islam and Capitalism*, 1977; Charles Tripp, *Islam and the Moral Economy: The Challenge of Capitalism*, 2006; Ibrahim Warde, *Islamic Finance in the Global Economy*, 2009.

CHARLES TRIPP

censorship

Most broadly conceived, censorship is any action that seeks to control human expression through the application of power. Typically, censorship is enacted by a state, and nearly every government in the contemporary world practices some form of censorship. While censorship is frequently thought of as erasing information or stopping certain kinds of expression, such a deletion is more the result of censorship; the purpose of censorship is to *control*, not only to erase, information and expression.

Generally, in premodern Islamic history, the state was far too weak to police the speech and literary production of its many subjects. However, publicly insulting the Prophet (*sabb al-rasūl*) seems to have been considered a crime early on. We also occasionally hear of book burnings (e.g., the Almoravids' burning of Ghazali's [d. 1111] works), but these were all seemingly ad hoc and directed at specific, usually famous, targets. The best-known episode of inquisitorial activity, the *miḥna* (inquisition) inaugurated by the caliph Ma'mun (r. 813–33), lasted for less than 30 years, revolved around a single issue, and targeted only men of religious learning or station.

This situation began to change with the advent of both stronger and more centralized state structures in the so-called gunpowder empires but especially in the Ottoman Empire and with the introduction of the printing press into the Muslim world. Presses for printing Hebrew, Armenian, and Greek books were active in the Ottoman Empire centuries before printing was permitted for books in Arabic or Turkish, which began fitfully in the mid-1700s. Newspapers began to appear in Turkish and Arabic in the early 1800s, and state censorship laws followed shortly thereafter. The first such act, the Printing Houses and Publications Act, was decreed in 1857 and established penalties for speech deemed seditious to the Ottoman state, morally contemptible, or slanderous. Censorship of printers went hand in hand with government subsidization, licensing of the presses, and the creation of official government censors. In Qajar Iran, a ministry of the press was formed in 1871 to oversee the censorship of the burgeoning Persian press. It was the 19th century that saw the beginning of censorship in the Muslim world as state surveillance and the control of all published speech.

This brief historical sketch contrasts markedly with the development of censorship in Europe. The printing press was adopted in the Muslim world much later than in Europe, and Islam never possessed a centralized, religious authority like the medieval office of the inquisitor in the Roman Catholic Church, which was charged with investigating and extirpating heretical writings. This is not to say that the premodern Muslim world enjoyed a unique freedom of expression but rather that the state was not the regulator of literary production. The limits of speech in the premodern Muslim world were determined more locally and informally by the reactions of an author's peer group and audience. In many cases, we might imagine that the punishment for transgressing social limits on speech was not exile or imprisonment but obscurity.

A case in point, the poems of Husayn b. al-Hajjaj (d. 1001) are not widely known today. Ibn al-Hajjaj's specialty was *sukhf*, poetry of the most obscene kind. A market inspector (*muḥtasib*) by day, he sometimes composed his scurrilous verses with some notable contemporary in mind and then proceeded to blackmail his victim, who would rather pay to keep the poem private than be made a laughingstock. Ibn al-Hajjaj reportedly made a fine living and never feared retaliation. In the modern period, however, the poetry of Ibn al-Hajjaj has never appeared in a published edition in the Muslim world due to censorship restrictions.

See also blasphemy; inquisition; media

Further Reading

Sinan Antoon, *The Poetics of the Obscene: Ibn al-Ḥajjāj and Sukhf* (PhD diss., Harvard University, 2006); Donald J. Cioeta, "Ottoman Censorship in Lebanon and Syria, 1876–1908," *International Journal of Middle East Studies* 10, no. 2 (1979); M. Şükrü Hanioğlu, *A Brief History of the Late Ottoman Empire*, 2008; Mona A. Nsouli, *Censorship in the Arab World: An Annotated Bibliography*, 2006; Amnon Raz-Krakotzkin, *The Censor, the Editor, and the Text*, 2007.

NICHOLAS G. HARRIS

Central Asia

Adjoining China, South Asia, the Middle East, and Russia, the region of Central Asia has throughout its history maintained extensive ties with its neighbors, and its political thought has developed in dialogue with them. The Mongol conquests of the 13th century integrated Central Asia into the neighboring world regions and left an enduring political legacy. For many centuries after Chingiz Khan (ca. 1160s–1227), descent from the Mongol ruler was the key to political legitimacy. Apart from showing military prowess and political acumen, leaders who aspired to head the khanate were expected also to observe Chingizid customs and legal norms (known as the Yasa) in addition to Islamic law. The Yasa validated the rights of ruling clans, rather than individuals, and gave greater weight to those claiming seniority. This mode of distributing authority contributed, in turn, to the consolidation of regional polities, a phenomenon reinforced by a physical geography that favored human settlement in a few oasis settings separated by stretches of desert. In the early 17th century, these centered on the towns of Balkh and Bukhara. Chingizid sources of legitimacy faltered during political crises in the early 18th century, and the rulers of small states based in Bukhara, Khiva, and Khoqand employed a variety of strategies to legitimize their autocracies. Celebrating their roles as conquerors, scholars, and Sufis, some did continue to highlight their descent from Chingiz Khan, but others presented themselves as pious defenders of Sunnism and the shari'a.

Russian conquest of the region between the 1860s and 1880s provoked a variety of political responses. Although some notables initially resisted or emigrated to China or Afghanistan (or were exiled by the tsarist military), most regional scholars, who were adherents of the Hanafi school of law, concluded that the tsarist regime's latitude toward Islamic rites, personnel, and institutions allowed Muslims to regard the territory of the governor-generalship of Turkestan as *dār al-islām* (the abode of Islam). Thus a great number of scholars arrived at various kinds of accommodation with the regime. Calls for jihad, for example, by a Sufi leader in 1898 in Andijan were short-lived and widely criticized by the majority of scholars. Focused on educational and cultural reforms, the modernist Jadid movement was an irritant to tsarist authorities, but it was only during World War I and the introduction of a plan to conscript Central Asian Muslims for labor battalions that communities began to abandon their quietist approach to politics and oppose state power on a broad scale.

The revolutions of 1917 in the Russian Empire and the civil war that ensued inaugurated new waves of migration and political fragmentation as locally based militias battled the Bolsheviks and the nascent Soviet state. Not all Muslim elites were hostile to the new regime, however, and a number of modernists saw in socialism and the state's commitment to national liberation aspirations that were compatible with their interpretations of Islam. For their part, the Bolsheviks sought out local partners to join the Communist Party and state apparatus. Central Asian elites participated in the delineation of the region into national republics (the Soviet socialist republics of Uzbekistan, Turkmenistan, Kyrgyzstan, Kazakhstan, and Tajikistan, which in turn belonged to the Union of Soviet Social Republics) and sought to shape policies aimed at consolidating national groups in the region. In the late 1920s and early 1930s, however, collectivization and antireligious campaigns, including an antiveiling campaign, mosque closures, censorship, and the arrest and assassination of clerics, spurred resistance and more emigration. Policies shifted again during World War II, opening up space for some kinds of Islamic practice. In 1943, the Soviets created the Central Asian Muslim Ecclesiastical Administration (Sredneaziatskoe dukhovnoe upravlenie musul'man). Staffed by clerics of the region and supported by voluntary donations, it encouraged obedience to Soviet authorities while calling for the reform of local ritual practices. Echoing the appeals of many modernist reformers, its fatwas (religious opinions) of the 1950s and 1960s condemned the veneration of local saints and shrines and the celebration of holidays such as the Prophet's birthday, insisting that these were contrary to the shari'a. They also targeted the payment of excessive bride-prices and dowries and criticized affiliation with Sufi groups or involvement in Sufi devotions.

In the late 1970s, some of these views overlapped with those of a group of young scholars known collectively as the Mujaddidi. Also hostile to many Sufi rituals, they criticized a number of influential but quietist Hanafi scholars who had taught clandestinely. Inspired in part by the Iranian Revolution (1978–79) and the Afghan jihad, they argued instead for the re-Islamization of society and the construction of an Islamic state. Some of these figures became politically active after Mikhail Gorbachev came to power in 1985 and supported an Islamic political party founded in 1989 in Russia: the Islamic Renaissance Party. Amid the chaotic collapse of the Soviet Union in 1991, young militants in the Ferghana Valley formed vigilante groups committed to administering Islamic justice, and in 1992 one of their leaders, Tohir Yo'ldoshev (1967–2009), openly challenged the authoritarian president of Uzbekistan, Islam Karimov (b. 1938), during a meeting in Namangan. When Tajikistan descended into civil war in 1992, a bloody conflict in which regional solidarity groups fought for control of the state and resources, a number of these activists, including Yo'ldoshev and Juma Namangoniy (1969–2001), escaped repression in Uzbekistan and joined the conflict in Tajikistan. In 1999, they founded the Islamic Movement of Uzbekistan (IMU) and issued publications from Taliban-ruled Afghanistan in which they lamented the oppression of the world's Muslims and faulted the United States and a global Jewish conspiracy for preventing the faithful from living in accord with Islamic law. The focus of IMU agitation was nonetheless on the government of Uzbekistan, which it accused of imprisoning and torturing the faithful. In rejecting the Karimov government as a despotic and infidel regime, Yo'ldoshev called for armed struggle under his close direction to overthrow the government and replace it with one based on Islamic law. Although the movement's leaders sought refuge in Afghanistan, they publically distanced themselves

from Taliban rule and its association with Osama bin Laden (1957–2011). After American forces targeted IMU camps following September 11, 2001, however, IMU propaganda shifted. Despite the apparent death of the head of the group's militant wing, Namangoniy, in 2001, IMU militants led by Yo'ldoshev continued to be active in Afghanistan and in the Federally Administered Tribal Areas of Pakistan. IMU videos and other communications claimed that they had pledged loyalty to the head of the Taliban, Mulla Muhammad 'Umar. The United States claimed to have killed Yo'ldoshev in an air strike in Pakistan in 2009. Nonetheless, other Uzbek militant groups, including the Islamic Jihad Union, which broke off from the IMU in 2002, continued to operate in the Afghanistan-Pakistan borderlands.

In addition to these jihadist groups, a transnational organization, Hizb ut-Tahrir, became active in Central Asia from the early to mid-1990s. Probably first established in Uzbekistan, the movement spread to neighboring states, recruiting young men and women, including students, though it largely operated underground. Though anti-Semitic and critical of existing states, its campaign for a single state to unify all Muslims did not use violence. Hostile state policies and propaganda apparently broadened its appeal, and prisons seemed to play a key role in the expansion of its membership. Despite severe repression in Uzbekistan as well as Tajikistan, Hizb ut-Tahrir attracted between 20 and 100,000 members in the region. Since 2001 authoritarianism throughout Central Asia has intensified, and there remain few legal venues for independent political activity.

See also Afghanistan; Shamil (1797–1871)

Further Reading

Nicola Di Cosmo, Allen J. Frank, and Peter B. Golden, eds., *The Cambridge History of Inner Asia: The Chinggisid Age*, 2009; Adrienne Lynn Edgar, *Tribal Nation: The Making of Soviet Turkmenistan*, 2004; Allen J. Frank and Jahangir Mamatov, *Uzbek Islamic Debates: Texts, Translations, and Commentary*, 2006; Emmanuel Karagiannis, *Political Islam in Central Asia: The Challenge of Hizb ut-Tahrir*, 2010; Adeeb Khalid, *Islam after Communism: Religion and Politics in Central Asia*, 2007; R. D. McChesney, *Central Asia: Foundations of Change*, 1996.

ROBERT D. CREWS

charity

Charity has been an integral part of Islam's doctrinal and social fabric from the inception of the religion. In fact, almsgiving, or zakat, constitutes one of the Five Pillars of Islam. As many scholars have pointed out, even a cursory examination of the Qur'an suggests that the social context of early Islam strongly resembles an "economy of poverty." Qur'an 93:10 instructs the Prophet never to turn away a beggar, and a hadith report attributed to the Prophet instructs believers not to turn away a beggar even if he shows up riding a horse. Concern for the poor dominated economic thought and behavior during Islam's formative years.

Traditionally, there are two main categories of charity in Islam: zakat and *ṣadaqa*. Zakat is an obligatory form of giving that is due annually provided one meets certain benchmarks of accumulated wealth, including cash, property, livestock, or crops. *Ṣadaqa* is a voluntary charitable offering, the rendering of which signifies a Muslim's moral excellence and is a highly valued demonstration of his or her faith and practice in Islam. The waqf, or religious endowment, represents another major type of charity in Islam. Throughout Islamic history, rulers, high officials, and other individuals have used charitable endowments to build and support a variety of social and religious institutions such as public fountains, elementary schools, colleges of Islamic law, hospitals, and Sufi lodges.

Zakat is a tax on accumulated wealth that is owned for a year, usually of 1/40th or 2.5 percent of the total. One pays only if one's property has reached the minimum amount, termed *niṣāb*, and one's home and items of personal use are exempted. For cash, property, or livestock, the standard rate is 2.5 percent, so an owner of 40 camels or cows, for example, should give one as zakat. The rules for crops differ: 10 percent is to be paid for crops that do not require irrigation and 5 percent is to be paid for those that do. Zakat must be paid to deserving recipients or causes. Recipients must be devout Muslims of good moral conduct (at least not openly committing major sins), and most Shi'i authorities require that the recipients be Shi'is as well. Descendants of the Prophet may not receive zakat, apparently on the logic that it would not be in keeping with their honor and dignity to do so and would be a shame for the Muslim community. Recipients cannot be relatives of the donor whom the donor would be otherwise required to help or support. Recipients must be destitute or in need, which is defined as having funds insufficient to meet their basic needs for the year. Debtors, slaves who are trying to buy their freedom, and stranded travelers are also legitimate recipients of zakat. Zakat may also be used for public welfare, such as repairing roads or bridges, building mosques, or facilitating the annual pilgrimage to Mecca. It may also be used for jihad or the support of border warriors. Most jurists allow an agent who collects zakat to take his fee from the property collected.

A second type of zakat, termed *zakāt al-fiṭr*, or "the zakat of breaking the fast," is paid at the end of the month of Ramadan. The head of each household pays the equivalent of a substantial meal to the poor for each member of the household. The purpose is to allow the poor to celebrate the end of fasting. A similar form of charity occurs on the most important holy day of the Islamic calendar, 'Id al-Adha, or the Feast of Sacrifice. On the 10th day of the 12th month of the Islamic calendar (Dhu al-Hijja), synchronized with the rituals of the pilgrimage to Mecca, Muslims sacrifice an animal—most frequently a sheep throughout the Islamic world—and give away all or part of the meat to poor Muslims.

Twelver Shi'i charity is funded not only by zakat but also by *khums*, or "the fifth," which according to Shi'i authorities is a

20 percent tax on all legitimate income, after deductions for expenses of the individual and dependents, that should be paid to one of the leading Shi'i jurists. The funds gathered in this manner are spent on religious education, especially the centers of learning in Najaf and Qum; support of the needy among the descendants of the Prophet, who are not allowed to receive zakat; and other public welfare projects, such as building hospitals, paying disaster relief, and so on.

Charity has always been a prominent means for rulers in the Islamic world to gain the good will of their subjects and to establish and bolster political legitimacy. The construction and repair of religious monuments in the major cities of their realms or in holy places such Mecca, Medina, and Jerusalem have served as highly visible and effective propaganda. Support of the pilgrimage caravans, providing the ornate covering (*kiswa*) for the Ka'ba, and outfitting and supporting border warriors were regular means for rulers to advertise their piety and devotion. Some efforts, often through the establishment of endowments, involved more direct provision of facilities to the local populace, such as the construction of mosques, water fountains (*sabīl*), elementary schools (*kuttāb*) for teaching the basics of reading and writing as well as memorization of the Qur'an, and soup kitchens, or the refurbishment of houses of worship or provision of other additions or amenities for worshippers, such as oil lamps, rugs, and facilities for washing. Examples abound, but in contemporary times the huge Hassan II Mosque in Casablanca, completed in 1993 and funded primarily by public conscription, stands as a massive tribute to the late Moroccan monarch's dedication to Islam. Other endowed institutions, such as colleges of Islamic law (madrasas) and Sufi lodges (*khānaqāh*s), catered to a smaller group of the population but nevertheless were viewed as important acts of generosity because of the esteem accorded to those adept in the Islamic religious sciences, and premodern rulers often provided banquets and largesse for the religious scholars or for the public during Ramadan or on other holy days.

Zakat was the most venerated and widespread source of charity in Islam in premodern and remains so in contemporary times. Annually, Muslims in different parts of the world donate millions of dollars to charitable causes by way of zakat, in addition to income tax owed to governments. In countries such as Pakistan, for example, the zakat of Sunni bank account holders is deducted from the accounts at the banks, while Shi'i account holders are exempted, since the Shi'is believe that zakat must be given to a spiritual leader, an imam or his representative, or in the contemporary period one of the leading Twelver Shi'i jurists in Najaf or Qum. These charities and acts of philanthropy are in many places an informal process. Monies are rendered to local mosques, schools, soup kitchens, nurseries, hospitals, and other socially beneficial causes.

As in many other domains of ethical importance in Islam, the onset of modernity and its accompanying technologies of organization have presented both daunting challenges and exciting opportunities for Islamic charity. The major challenge confronting Islamic charity in the contemporary world is that of reconfiguring premodern categories and taxonomies of giving in relation to contemporary technologies and practices of philanthropy in the global economy. There is no shortage of enthusiasm for religiously motivated charity among Muslims around the world. However, much remains to be done to establish a robust system for the collection, monitoring, and distribution of funds generated through charity in a formally structured, cost-efficient, and socially productive fashion. A major part of the problem has to do with the informal mechanisms of giving that continue to dominate the landscape of Muslim charity. While informal networks of collecting and distributing philanthropic funds, such as within families or through local mosques, are highly effective means of cultivating community ties and solidarity, they are less effective in consolidating a centralized, institutionally grounded culture of charity that might propel more macro-level projects of social justice such as poverty alleviation and sustainable development. In order to channel the outstanding potential for philanthropic activity into the work of sustaining long-term projects of social justice, practices of Islamic charity must be ensconced in and supported by modern institutions, organizational structures, and technologies of philanthropy.

See also economic theory; endowment; Pillars of Islam; taxation

Further Reading

Michael Bonner, Mine Ener, and Amy Singer, eds., *Poverty and Charity in Medieval Contexts*, 2003; Yaacov Lev, *Charity, Endowments, and Charitable Institutions in Medieval Islam*, 2005; Adam Sabra, *Poverty and Charity in Medieval Islam: Mamluk Egypt, 1250–1517*, 2000; Amy Singer, *Charity in Islamic Societies*, 2008.

SHERALI TAREEN

China

According to the 2000 national census of China, Muslims total 20.3 million, or 2 percent, of the population. Since the census registers people by nationality, not religious affiliation, their precise number is still unknown, and other estimates can be as high as 100 million. A 2009 Pew survey and the CIA Factbook, however, both agree with the lower estimate in conformity with the census data.

Spanning the border between Eurasia and Central Asia, the Muslims of China have strong ties to both the East and Middle East, which were resumed, after half a century of self-imposed isolation, with the death of Mao in 1976 and Deng Xiaoping's "open door" policy in the 1980s. Non-Uighur Muslims travel fairly freely on the hajj to Mecca and engage in cross-border trade with coreligionists in Central Asia, the Middle East, and increasingly, Southeast Asia. There are few Han converts to Islam in China, yet Muslim population numbers have continued to increase, and there are more mosques now than before 1949. Many of the challenges the Muslims of China confront remain the same as they have been for the

last 1,200 years of interaction with Chinese society, but others are new and reflect China's transformed and increasingly politicized society, especially the watershed events of the 9/11 terrorist attacks and the subsequent "war on terror."

Historically, most Muslims in China have been the people now known as "Hui." "Hui teaching" (*Hui jiao*) was the term once used in Chinese to indicate "Islam" in general and probably derives from an early Chinese rendering of the term for the modern Uighur people (*Hui he*). In 2000, their total number was given as 9.8 million. The other Muslim nationalities are Uighur (8.4 million); Kazakh (1.25 million); Dongxiang (513,805); Kyrgyz (160,823); Salar (104,503); Tajik (41,028); Uzbek (14,502); Bonan (16,505); and Tatar (4,890). The Hui speak mainly Sino-Tibetan languages. The Uighur, Kazakh, Kyrgyz, Uzbek, Salar, and Tatar are Turkic speakers, while combined Turkic-Mongolian speakers include the Dongxiang and Bonan, concentrated in Gansu's mountainous Hexi corridor. The Tajik speak a variety of Indo-Persian dialects.

With the exception of the Tajik minority, who follow Isma'ili Shi'ism, all Muslim nationalities in China are Sunnis, but they are divided by regional, linguistic, and ethnic differences. The Hui are generally the closest to the Han Chinese in terms of physical location and cultural accommodation, adapting many of their Islamic practices to Han ways of life, which often invited criticism from Muslim reformers. Because they speak a variety of Chinese dialects and have no common place of residence or ethnic history, the Hui are the only nationality in China for whom religion (Islam) is the primary marker of identity, but many secularized, or even Marxist, members of the Hui nationality may not actually practice Islam. Islamic factional struggles have begun to reemerge among China's Hui Muslims, however, dividing them internally, especially as increased travel to the Middle East prompts criticism of Muslim practices at home and exposes China's Muslims to new, often politically radical Islamic ideals.

The northwestern Muslim communities, especially the Uighur, were incorporated into Chinese society more recently as a result of Mongolian and Manchu expansion into Central Asia and were forced to reach social and political accommodations that have challenged their identities. The Uighur are perhaps the least integrated into Chinese society. Since 1980, the Chinese state has reported over 160 incidents of Uighur-related violence, mostly in the Xinjiang Uighur Autonomous Region. In July 2009, the largest and bloodiest civil riots in modern Chinese history took place in Urumqi, pitting Uighur Muslims against Han Chinese citizens.

It was not until 1760 that the Manchu Qing dynasty exerted full and formal control over the northwestern region, establishing it as their "new dominion" (*Xinjiang*), only to lose it barely 100 years later thanks to the Yakub Beg rebellion (1864–77) and growing Russian influence. The end of the Qing dynasty and the rise of Great Game rivalries between China, Russia, and Britain saw the region torn by competing loyalties and marked by two brief and drastically different attempts at independence: the short-lived proclamations of an "East Turkestan Republic" in Kashgar in 1933 and another in Yining (Ghulje) in 1944. Uighur sovereignty organizations are now based in many international cities, including Istanbul, Ankara, Almaty, Munich, Amsterdam, Melbourne, Toronto, London, and Washington, D.C. The independence of the former Soviet Central Asian Republics in 1991 has done much to encourage their hopes for an independent "East Turkestan," though the new, mainly Muslim Central Asian governments all signed protocols with China in the spring of 1996 that they would not harbor or support separatist groups. Despite their resistance to Chinese rule, the Uighur continue to be divided internally by religious conflicts (between Sufi and non-Sufi factions), territorial loyalties, linguistic discrepancies, commoner-elite alienation, and competing political loyalties. Islam is only one of several markers of Uighur identity, suggesting that Islamic fundamentalist groups such as the Taliban in Afghanistan (often glossed as "Wahhabiyya" in the region) will have only limited appeal among the Uighur. Few Hui support an independent Xinjiang, and the one million Kazakh in Xinjiang would have very little say in an independent "Uighuristan." Local support for separatist activities, particularly in Xinjiang and other border regions, is ambivalent at best given the economic disparity between these regions and their foreign neighbors, including Tadjikistan, Kygyzstan, Pakistan, and especially Afghanistan. Memories are still strong in the region of mass starvation and widespread destruction during the Sino-Japanese and civil war in the first half of the 20th century, including intra-Muslim and Muslim-Chinese bloody conflicts, not to mention the chaotic horrors of the Cultural Revolution. It is clear, however, that Uighur separatism and Muslim complaints regarding Chinese policy will have important consequences for China's economic development of the region.

See also Uighurs

Further Reading

Z. B. Benite, *The Dao of Muhammad: A Cultural History of Muslims in Late Imperial China*, Harvard East Asian Monographs, no. 248 (2005); J. Fletcher, *Studies on Chinese and Islamic Inner Asia*, edited by Beatrice Forbes Manz, 1995; D. C. Gladney, *Dislocating China: Muslims, Minorities, and Other Subaltern Subjects*, 2004; J. A. Millward, *Eurasian Crossroads: A History of Xinjiang*, 2007; S. Murata, *Chinese Gleams of Sufi Light*, 2000; F. S. Starr, ed., *Xinjiang: China's Muslim Borderland*, 2004.

DRU C. GLADNEY

chivalry

Chivalry is a medieval European phenomenon concerning the behavior of the chevaliers or knights that developed in feudal society. The ideal knight was not simply a mounted warrior but a warrior who had become a vassal to a monarch or lord. Through a ceremony of dubbing, the knight received equipment such as swords

and weapon-girdles, gained title to property, and paid homage and owed fealty for the same. A contract regulated the ties between lord and vassal. On the moral plane, the values expected from the knight included the virtues of courage, honor, gentleness, courtesy, and, by and large, chastity.

Sporadic and disjointed vestiges of the practices, customs, and sentiments of chivalry have been found in Islamic lands in various periods. While some scholars have claimed to find the Islamic equivalent of European chivalry in knighthood (*furūsiyya*), a somewhat closer analogue exists in the institution of *futuwwa* (manliness). It is true that medieval Muslim authors referred to the Frankish knight as a *fāris*, or "mounted warrior," and used the same term to apply to his Muslim counterpart, but while the term *fāris* could refer to the valiant, the champion, the intrepid warrior, or one ideally endowed with the noble features of chivalry, it was a personal chivalry, without any precise code, initiation ceremonies, investiture, or accolade. These missing aspects were found in the institution of *futuwwa*. Already in the 19th century, Joseph von Hammer-Purgstall termed *futuwwa*, as practiced by the Abbasid caliph Nasir, "*chevalerie arabe*" (Arab chivalry) and excitedly announced that he had found the source of all European knighthood.

Islamic chivalry, like its European counterpart, did not emerge in the world by fiat or official decree but came into being during Nasir's reign as caliph (r. 1180–1225), the longest in the history of the Abbasid dynasty, through an organic process. His success in spreading his influence far beyond Baghdad and in winning back some of the lost respect and glamor of the caliph's office have been attributed in part to his clever approach toward independent *futuwwa* associations, which he managed to unite, reform, and bring under his control.

Futuwwa, a noun derived from *fatā* (young man), in all likelihood translated the older Persian *jawānmardī* (young-manliness) and denoted a complex of moral virtues comprising courage, generosity, liberality, hospitality, unselfishness, and the spirit of sacrifice, generally attached to an elaborate ceremony observed in certain organizations. It emerged gradually in the Abbasid period as a canon of social and moral principles. Heterogeneous social organizations throughout the central Islamic lands at different epochs have claimed adherence to *futuwwa* and cultivated its tenets and the ceremonial connected with it. *Futuwwa* came to embody the corporate ideal and standard rules of conduct of aristocratic clubs of pleasure-seeking youths, urban militias (*'ayyārūn, aḥdāth*), Sufi brotherhoods, dervish orders, craft guilds, Persian gymnastic clubs, warriors for the faith (*ghāzī*s, *mujāhid*s, *murābiṭ*s), and certain brigands.

The divergent terms used in modern studies to designate the members of these organizations—vagabonds, drifters, stragglers, knights-errant, brigands, adventurers, bandits, scoundrels—show above all a failure to understand their true nature. *'Ayyār*, *shāṭir*, *fatā*, and *ẓarīf*, all terms for brave and troublesome youth, are often used as synonyms, both as positive appellations and as abusive epithets, with no apparent distinction among them. At times of disturbance, the *'ayyār*s are always ready to serve as auxiliary troops. They show group solidarity, are well organized, and enter the scene as an active arm of the popular masses in the city's quarters. When they act on the side of the central government, the official chronologists praise them as heroes and men of high morals, self-sacrifice, and valor; when they fight for opposing factions or defend local interests, they are disparaged as despicable and lawless bandits who show no respect for people's rights, honor, or property.

The presentation of the *'ayyār*s varies according to time, place, and historical source. Classical Persian literature celebrates the *'ayyār*s as national heroes who, in the mid-ninth century, brought the Saffarids to power, the first independent Iranian dynasty of the Islamic period, in a movement against social injustice. Arab and later Turkish governors in Iran, often foreign to their fiscal territories, only occasionally succeeded in manipulating and controlling the popular movements headed by the *'ayyār*s. They did not have a defined long-term program for the management of towns and villages given to them as *iqṭā'*, or fiefs, and left civic administration in the hands of the old civil servants. Their continual removal from office did not allow them to develop strong ties with the local residents. Tribal chiefs at the center of the empire often used their influence to determine the choice of governors and policies, and factionalism led to neglect of outlying cities and villages. The central government's weakness and lack of structure led organized bands of *'ayyār*s to take the affairs of their communities into their own hands and act as governors and militia commanders. During the siege of Baghdad in the civil war fought between the two brothers Amin and Ma'mun in 809 to 813, the *'ayyār*s defending the besieged city led a genuinely popular uprising. Because of their precarious situation as disorderly, antiestablishment militants who did not balk at plundering the property of the wealthy, the *'ayyār*s had to secure support among the populace by backing local sentiments, avoiding damage to the property of the weak and needy, supporting the deprived, and respecting local women. The enterprises of these social bandits provided the impetus for a rich folkloric literature in Persian that elaborated and idealized the *'ayyār*s' lifestyle and chivalrous values, including the 12th-century works *Samak-i 'Ayyar* (The exploits of Samak the bandit) of Faramarz b. Khudadad b. 'Abdallah Arrajani and *Darab-nama* or *Qissa-yi Firuz Shah* (The book of Darab, or the romance of Firuz Shah) of Muhammad b. Ahmad b. 'Ali Bighami. Here the *'ayyār* is a clever and resourceful fighter with an elaborate code of honor who accompanies the prince in his quest for the love of his life and whose main activity is to rescue repeatedly the more or less inept prince from numerous pitfalls. This literature sponsors and glorifies the deeds of rebel *'ayyār*s, keeping their gangs financially fit at the expense of the wealthy and terrorizing unpopular authorities at the same time.

A medieval Islamic type that overlaps both with the *'ayyār* or *fatā* and with the European knight is the border warrior for the faith, termed *mujāhid*, *murābiṭ*, or *ghāzī*. In the early Islamic centuries, jihad became associated primarily with the constant border warfare conducted against the Christian Byzantines in eastern Anatolia, northern Syria, and northern Iraq, but it was also used to describe border warfare in the Andalus, the Caucasus, Transoxiana,

and elsewhere. While the Abbasid caliphs had a duty to protect Muslim territories and to defend the frontiers from the assaults of non-Muslim invaders, in reality, their political and military power declined to such an extent that they left the pursuit of the jihad in the hands of local warlords. The *ghāzī*s—volunteer, freelance, and later organized warriors for whom the *futuwwa* code formed the ethical organizing principle—played a decisive role in the political expansion of Islam, conquering territories and establishing a number of small princely houses in Central Asia, Iran, and Anatolia prior to the foundation of the most successful of *ghāzī* states, the Ottoman Empire. Charged with religious zeal and the prospect of booty, numerous landless *ghāzī*s gathered together in massive military undertakings against the Byzantines. While the resemblance of the *ghāzī*s to Frankish knights is disputed, the existence of an organization and code of behavior among the *ghāzī*s led the historian Wilhelm Barthold to call them collectively "warrior guilds." Saladin, the Ayyubid sultan famed for his personal courage, resolution, generosity, and gallantry, is one *ghāzī* whose activity is of direct relevance to Muslim chivalry. According to European sources, Saladin actually entered the order of European knighthood, and his way of life was that of a true chevalier. He is often praised as a man of dignity and integrity whose oath was his bond and who followed a firm moral framework, and he is still considered a paragon of chivalry. Nevertheless, though he was a warrior for the faith par excellence, nowhere he is referred to as a *fatā* or in possession of *futuwwa*.

From the early ninth century onward, the *futuwwa* ideal is documented as a dominant form of ideological and ceremonial orientation in Sufi organizations as well. The affiliation of the two was probably most prevalent in border garrison towns, where *ghāzī*s and Sufis seeking salvation in holy war mixed. A theoretical distinction was made between *al-jihād al-aṣghar* (the lesser holy war, or war against the infidels and the enemies of the faith) and *al-jihād al-akbar* (the greater holy war, or the struggle against passion and worldly desires, considered to be the more difficult of the two). This marked the division between the mystic Sufi and the warrior *ghāzī*. Sufi authors began to formulate what they understood as "spiritual chivalry" in treatises titled *Kitab al-Futuwwa* (The book of chivalry), *Risala fi al-Futuwwa* (The epistle on chivalry), and so forth.

The conservative Hanbali jurist Ibn al-Jawzi (d. 1200), while decrying the widespread influence of the *'ayyār*s in Baghdad of his day, described them in some detail. Belonging to *futuwwa* organizations, they would steal people's property while hypocritically intoning that a true *fatā* does not lie, fornicate, or violate the privacy of women but rather strives to preserve their honor and reputation. They swore an oath to uphold the *futuwwa* code, abstained from excessive food and drink, and donned special trousers (*sarāwīl*), parallel to the patched garment (*muraqqa'a*) of the Sufis. If a rumor spread about the misconduct of a sister or wife of a *fatā,* they would kill her without verifying the truth of the matter. In August 1137, the terrorism of the *'ayyār*s under the leadership of Ibn Bukran and Ibn al-Bazzaz, who planned to issue coinage in their own name, assumed such proportions that the prefect of Baghdad, the sharif Abu al-Karam, had his nephew Abu al-Qasim infiltrate their association, being girded and granted *futuwwa* trousers by Ibn Bukran. Only the intervention of the vizier brought the disturbances to a halt, and Ibn Bukran and Ibn al-Bazzaz were killed.

Nasir's reform program sought to bring as many of these assorted fraternities as possible under his direct control and ended up unifying them, causing them to flourish and giving them a legitimacy that would live on for several centuries. Nasir was initiated into the *futuwwa* in 1182, three years after he had acceded to the caliphate, donning the *futuwwa* trousers in a ceremony conducted by the Hanbali 'Abd al-Jabbar b. Yusuf, the head of the *futuwwa* organization. 'Abd al-Jabbar drafted the official *futuwwa* code, and Abu 'Ali b. al-Dawami, the *naqīb*, or syndic, of the *futuwwa*, expounded the code further in terms of noble virtues and civil manners (*makārim al-akhlāq*) so that everybody could understand and follow them. 'Abd al-Jabbar also gave public lectures on the subject, promoting gallantry and courtesy. He preached that *futuwwa* was an ancient tradition limited neither to a particular time or place nor to a particular national, religious, or social group. Non-Muslims could enter the *futuwwa* organization, though they could not become full members without conversion to Islam. In 1207, Nasir abrogated the older *futuwwa* and placed himself as its *qibla* (the source of orientation and guidance), centralizing the organization and concentrating authority in himself. By adopting explicit regulations and an elaborate ceremony of initiation comparable with those of knighthood, recruiting the wealthy and powerful as well as the urban middle class, and encouraging Muslim princes far and near to make similar efforts under his aegis, Nasir transformed the *futuwwa* into an instrument of social cohesion. Some 15 princes from Egypt, Syria, Anatolia, Iran, and elsewhere, including Saladin's brother al-Malik al-'Adil and his son al-Malik al-Zahir Ghazi, responded to his call. The Rum Seljuq rulers of Anatolia remained members of the *futuwwa* order for generations after Kay Ka'us II (r. 1246–60) was initiated in Konya by Nasir's personal advisor, Abu Hafs 'Umar al-Suhrawardi, which led to the rapid spread of the Akhi brotherhoods in Anatolia. Nasir's reorganization of the *futuwwa* thus proved to be of enduring importance for the history of Islam.

The *futuwwa* continued to play a pivotal role in the internal politics of the central Islamic lands until the early 20th century. They were involved in countless social and political upheavals, incidents of factional or sectarian strife, and fighting between different city quarters. When the Mongols invaded Iran under Hulagu, the *'ayyār*s were the only unified armed bands that showed effective resistance and succeeded in influencing Mongol policies toward the conquered territories. They played a considerable role in the history of Syrian towns, in particular Damascus and Aleppo. They were the military spearheads of the urban artisan corporations, and their chief, termed *naqīb*, shaykh, or *ra'īs,* was often one of the most influential personages in the community, though the notables of the towns generally lacked the opportunity to take political initiative

against the central government. The *'ayyārs* and *fatās* of Iran and Baghdad and the Akhis of Anatolia played analogous roles in the politics of their communities.

See also Abbasids (750–1258); brotherhoods; *ghāzī*; Sufism

Further Reading

Gerard Salinger, "Was the Futūwa an Oriental Form of Chivalry?" *Proceedings of the American Philosophical Society* 94 (1950); Franz Taeschner, *Zünfte und Bruderschaften im Islam: Texte zur Geschichte der Futuwwa*, 1979; Mohsen Zakeri, *Sāsānid Soldiers in Early Muslim Society: The Origins of 'Ayyārān and Futuwwa*, 1995.

MOHSEN ZAKERI

Christian-Muslim relations

Narratives on both sides of Christian-Muslim relations traditionally emphasize distrust, fear, polemics, and military expansionism. Yet as historian Richard Bulliet has shown, this discourse of confrontation (popularized in the 1990s as "the clash of civilizations") obscures the reality of long periods of trade and cultural exchange. In fact, Bulliet coins the term "Islamo-Christian civilization," arguing that these "fraternal twins" expanded into new territories at about the same time, with Christians facing the more daunting challenge of evangelizing mostly polytheists in northern and eastern Europe and Muslim caliphs seizing lands previously Christian, Jewish, or Zoroastrian. Other parallels abound: they both experienced the emergence of a distinctively religious leadership in the ninth and tenth centuries; Sufi brotherhoods and the great Catholic orders like the Franciscans and the Dominicans began to expand in the 13th century; the great Christian theologians like Thomas Aquinas and the leading scientists of Europe were propelled forward in their work through the translations of countless Arabic manuscripts brought from Spain, Sicily, and elsewhere.

However, these observations by no means overlook the wounds in the Muslim psyche—namely, the Crusades and Western colonialism. Although the Crusades had limited military and geopolitical impact at the time, they remain etched in the Islamic imagination to the point that the word "crusade," used by U.S. president George W. Bush in connection with the 2001 military campaign in Afghanistan, instantly stirred up anger throughout the Muslim world. To many Muslims then and now, the brutal massacre of Muslims, Jews, and local Christians in the taking of Jerusalem in 1099 came to epitomize the Crusades as a whole. Then came the shock of the three great premodern empires of Islamdom in the 18th century—the Ottomans, Safavids, and Mughals—slowly run over by an aggressive Western military, technological, and cultural powerhouse. And finally, Muslims generally perceived that the flood of missionaries into their lands were part and parcel of the overall colonial strategy.

The postcolonial period has been marked by unprecedented efforts at dialogue in three phases. A monumental shift occurred in the Catholic Church in 1962 with the Vatican II document *Nostra Aetate*, which recognizes that Muslims share in the Abrahamic worship of the one God and mentions their rituals with great respect. In 1970, the World Council of Churches set up a vigorous program of Muslim-Christian dialogue. Finally, with the attacks of September 11, 2001, on U.S. soil and those that followed elsewhere, the initiative shifted to the Muslim side. Momentum for Islamic unity began to build with the Amman Message issued by King Abdullah II of Jordan and the following international conferences, resulting in 2006 in a far-reaching consensus on the issue of who is a Muslim, a condemnation of *takfīr* (declaring another Muslim an apostate), and clear guidelines as to who is authorized to issue fatwas (legal opinions). This movement then issued a document in October 2007 ("A Common Word," based on Q. 3:64) addressed to the Pope and all Christian leaders that stated that the core beliefs of Christians and Muslims are love for God and love for neighbor. World peace, it said, is predicated on Muslims and Christians committing to fraternal dialogue and bold cooperation. A climate of mistrust on both sides, however, fanned by regional conflicts and political considerations, has continued to challenge religious leaders' attempts to transmit this spirit of dialogue to the masses.

See also Crusades; minorities

Further Reading

Richard Bulliet, *The Case for Islamo-Christian Dialogue*, 2004; Hugh Goddard, *A History of Muslim-Christian Relations*, 2000; David L. Johnston, *Earth, Empire, and Sacred Text: Muslims and Christians as Trustees of Creation*, 2010; David A. Kerr and Stephen R. Goodwin, *World Christianity in Muslim Encounter: Essays in Memory of David A. Kerr*, 2009; Frederick Quinn, *The Sum of All Heresies: The Image of Islam in Western Thought*, 2008; Ataullah Saddiqi, *Christian-Muslim Dialogue in the Twentieth Century*, 1997; Miroslav Volf, Ghazi bin Muhammad, and Melissa Yerington, eds., *A Common Word: Muslims and Christians on Loving God and Neighbor*, 2010.

DAVID L. JOHNSTON

citizenship

Citizenship is a modern Western notion that does not fully fit into political interpretations of Islam. The modern perception of citizenship as a relationship between the state and the individual ignores the importance of group identity in both classical and modern notions of

citizenship in Islam. In classical Islam, one's rights and duties in relation to the state were defined by one's religious affiliation. A similar situation exists in many contemporary Muslim states that claim an Islamic government, such as Iran, Pakistan, and Saudi Arabia. Individuals relate to the state based on whether they are Muslim or non-Muslim. This emphasis on a corporate identity derives from the classical emphasis on the *umma*, or the Muslim community, and the notion of the *ahl al-kitāb* (People of the Book), or religious minorities recognized by Islam and often referred to as *dhimmīs*. The rights and duties of each of these groups were different, and usually only Muslims were allowed full participation in the state.

The role of nationalism in Islamic perceptions has been an important factor since the development of nationalism in Europe in the 18th century. However, for both classical Islam and many modern Muslim thinkers, such as Sayyid Qutb (1906–66) and Mawdudi (1903–79), the notion of citizenship does not necessarily depend on one's relationship to the state but rather to Islam itself. The focus on the *umma* allows for a transnational emphasis on Muslim citizenship. Mawdudi tried to emphasize this approach by claiming that in areas that are considered *dār al-islām* (abode of Islam), a Muslim is a citizen by virtue of the fact that he or she is part of the Muslim *umma* and not by birth in that country.

The notion of citizenship based on one's identity as a Muslim has an important impact on non-Muslims living in Muslim lands. Traditionally, the relationship of *dhimmīs* to the government is contractual; they are given rights and freedoms as citizens of the state based on their political submission to the Islamic state. While there is much debate over the status of *dhimmīs* in Islam, it is clear that their position as citizens is different from, and inferior to, that of Muslims. At times, this has led to a state of what might be called partial citizenship for non-Muslims. In Muslim countries that define themselves as Islamic states, the political rights of non-Muslims are shaped by their religious identity.

This view of citizenship as based on membership in the Muslim community also affects Muslims living in non-Muslim lands. In debates over how Muslims should relate to their country of residence and its government, some groups advocate complete separation from their non-Muslim host society, since the government is not based on shari'a (Islamic law). Others, such as the Swiss Muslim intellectual Tariq Ramadan (1962), have argued for full civic and political participation by Muslim citizens of Western countries.

See also civil society; democracy; individualism

Further Reading

Sayyid Abul A'la Mawdudi, *The Islamic Way of Life*, http://www.al-islamforall.org/books_Detail.aspx?book_Id=000073; Tariq Ramadan, *Western Muslims and the Future of Islam*, 2004; Nawaf A. Salam, "The Emergence of Citizenship in Islamdom," *Arab Law Quarterly* 12, no. 2 (1997); Eliz Sanasarian, *Religious Minorities in Iran*, 2000.

JENNIFER MITCHELL

city

The original model for the Islamic city is Medina, *Madīnat al-Nabī* (the City of the Prophet) or simply *al-madīnah* (the city), the name by which the city of Yathrib became known after the Prophet Muhammad and his followers settled there in 622, having fled Mecca, their hometown, in the hijra (emigration). At that point, the movement based on the Prophet's mission also acquired a political character. The term *madīna* implies a change in the sociopolitical structure of tribal society and the establishment of a multireligious and multiethnic society (*umma*) defined through a written legal document that has been called the Constitution of Medina. This document, drafted as a result of negotiations between the involved parties, was binding on all affected groups, thus ensuring political unity and social stability. Moreover, it defined the borderlines for the city, which it termed a *ḥaram* (inviolate precinct), ensuring the territorial integrity of the sociopolitical union. Thus the hijra and establishment of the *umma* marked a new phase in the sociopolitical life of Muslims and initiated a social project based on religious, cultural, and legal autonomy.

As the Islamic state expanded into an empire, it came to incorporate many major preexisting cities, but at the same time the garrison towns (*amṣār*), established in the wake of conquests, including Kufa and Basra in Iraq and Fustat in Egypt, provided another model for Islamic cities, which were developed after the urban model of the Arabian Peninsula. In general, these settlements were founded on the outskirts of major cities or settled areas and at the edge of the desert, where Arab armies had a decided advantage. They were organized on a grid, with specific quarters or neighborhoods assigned to military units based on tribe or clan. However, the *amṣār* rapidly transformed into principal cities of the main empire, which shows that establishing urban foundations was a state policy in the earliest phases of the conquests. Analytical studies of Islamic cities show that there are three Islamic factors that motivate processes that yield an "Islamic" city. First is a distinction between members of the *umma* and outsiders. Second, this distinction is reflected through the spatial organization of distinctive neighborhoods. The third factor, a result of the first two, is a legal system that does not enforce common regulations on the different neighborhoods. Rather, it is a flexible system in which legal decrees are a product of negotiations about the mutual rights of the involved parties. These characteristics actually reflect the organization of Medina, described earlier.

Perhaps the most salient distinctive feature of Islamic cities was the close connection between the commercial bourgeoisie (merchants, craftsmen, and landowners) and the 'ulama' (religious scholars), which in turn affected the relationship between the central government and settled urban society. The bourgeoisie and the 'ulama' provided an urban leadership that shared an interest in a peaceful, stable, and prosperous urban life. Their

relationship to the central government or ruler is not clearly defined because of the absence of formal political institutions; the city was not a legal entity, as it often was in medieval Europe. However, urban leaders could exercise independent power by mobilizing urban forces to put pressure on the ruler. Sometimes, a strong government would rule in close affiliation with the urban leadership, while other times, urban leaders and notables would protest or even rebel against a government that did not share their interests. In terms of spatial organization, a typical Islamic city was divided into roughly four parts. First was the citadel, often located on some natural defense work, such as the city of Aleppo, which has a natural tell, or archeological mound, dominating the countryside around it. Second was the royal city or quarter, usually in the form of a compound including the royal palace, administrative offices, and barracks for guard personnel. The royal quarter was established either by being implanted in an already existing urban gathering or by being founded on new soil around which an urban conglomeration later grows. In times of political instability, the compound was sometimes placed in the citadel itself for the sake of defense. Third was a "central urban complex," which included mosques; the central markets, the organization of which reflected strict professional specialization; and caravansaries, combinations of inns and warehouses that played a central role in international trade in the Islamic world. Another important feature of the urban complex was the educational institutions that started to flourish in the ninth century by the establishment of the House of Wisdom (Bayt al-Hikma) in Baghdad. The center was originally established by the caliph al-Ma'mun to translate *awā'il* sciences (pre-Islamic sciences such as Greek, Indian, and Persian sciences) into Arabic. With the flourishing of Islamic civilization, the center turned into a scientific academy that housed scholars and scientists from different parts of the globe. Later, other scientific academies were established in other cities such as Dar al-'Ilm in Cairo. The institutions of higher learning developed most in the second half of the 11th century with the establishment of a chain of colleges (madrasas), which integrated the study of natural, philosophic, and religious sciences, in Baghdad, Naishapur, and other cities. Rulers established and supported educational institutions as well as hospitals, which spread throughout different cities. Both education and hospitalization were funded by Muslim waqf (pious endowment) and thus they offered free services for the public, which transformed Islamic cities into a cosmopolitan haven. Islamic institutions acquired prestige and strength, which endowed urban life with a stable framework. Rulers' acts could be legitimated by the 'ulama', and communal action would take place through religious institutions. The royal foundation and patronage of such prominent urban institutions through the legal instrument of pious endowment thus played a central role in political propaganda and the establishment of legitimate rule. The proximity between religious and commercial buildings reflected the alliance between the 'ulama' and bourgeoisie and directly affected the urban life of the Islamic city. The last and fourth part of the Islamic city was a center of residential quarters, which comprised autonomous quarters of different ethnic and religious groups. Quarters were represented by local chiefs who acted as leaders when the government was weak and as subordinates under strong governments.

Muslim philosophers, inspired by Greek political philosophy and Islamic ethics, addressed the city in theoretical terms. Drawing on Plato's *Republic*, the tenth-century thinker Farabi (d. 950) described the city as a union of different communities whose various functions are integrated to fulfill the purpose of their union. The concept of the city is predominant in Farabi's political theory, for he considered it to represent the smallest form of a complete association and the basic unit of a perfect society. By "complete" association, Farabi meant one that was self-contained, unlike a household or a village, which is too small to fulfill that purpose. The perfect city is one whose people cooperate for the things by which true felicity can be attained. The structure of the perfect city is like that of the sound, healthy body whose different limbs and organs cooperate to make its life perfect and preserve it in that state. Through this analogy, Farabi implies that a single person cannot reach perfection and attain happiness without mutual cooperation within an organized community. Similar to the moral life of individuals, the fashioning of the city-state is not involuntary but dependent on whether will and choice are directed toward the true good.

In the modern period, the fates of traditional Islamic cities have varied. The French colonial practice of building their administrative center, termed *ville nouvelle*, outside the major cities and physically separated from them has led to the preservation of the old city, termed *madīna*, on the one hand and to a sharp social and economic division between the two on the other. In Fez, Morocco, for example, the walls surrounding the old city remain intact, along with the original gates, streets, and alleyways, and it is a car-free urban area within the city walls. This may be contrasted with Cairo, where in the late 19th century the old walls were torn down in many places, broad thoroughfares were run through entire old quarters, and little separation was maintained between the old and the new, after the fashion of Baron Haussmann's renovation of Paris. Especially in the 20th century, the Islamic world witnessed tremendous urban growth; immigration from rural areas rose sharply, while birth rates remained very high in most areas of the Islamic world and have only begun to decline in recent decades. The result has been sprawling, overcrowded metropolises such as Cairo and Tehran, in which both the infrastructure and the local economy have been severely strained. In many of the oil-producing nations such as Saudi Arabia and Kuwait, the tremendous returns on oil from World War II until the present have financed the construction of modern cities, either entirely dwarfing earlier settlements or building where nothing existed before, with limited roots in Islamic tradition. Capital cities remain primary sites of political propaganda in the Islamic world, often expressed in the construction of both secular monuments, such as Gamal Abdel Nasser's Cairo Tower, and religious monuments, such as

the Hassan II Mosque in Casablanca. In the year 2011, the capital cities were transformed into major sites of people's protests against oppressive regimes.

See also bureaucracy; city (philosophical)

Further Reading

Janet Abu-Lughod, "The Islamic City—Historic Myth, Islamic Essence, and Contemporary Relevance," *International Journal of Middle East Studies* 19, no. 2 (1987); C. E. Bosworth, *Historic Cities of the Islamic World*, 2008; A. H. Hourani and S. M. Stern, eds., *The Islamic City: Colloquium*, 1970; Seyyed Hossein Nasr, *Science and Civilization in Islam*, 1968.

KATRIN JOMAA

city (philosophical)

In the tenth century, Muslim philosophers introduced the concept of the excellent city (*al-madīna al-fāḍila*), a utopian perfect polity created for the purpose of guiding its inhabitants toward perfection and felicity (typically understood as a conjunction [*ittiṣāl*] with the Active Intellect [the active principle of understanding that is an emanation of God] and separation from matter) and ruled by a single philosopher (also known as a sage) or by a group of them. All descriptions of the excellent city found in Islamic thought are based on Plato's *Republic* (in particular, books V and VII–IX). The best known philosophers who discuss this issue are Farabi, the Brethren of Purity, and Ibn Rushd (Averroes). The description of the perfect city given by Farabi in his *Principles of the Opinions of the Inhabitants of the Excellent City* (*Mabadi' Ara' Ahl al-Madina al-Fadila*) is by far the most important. According to Farabi, the inhabitants of the excellent city assist each other to obtain true (i.e., intellectual) felicity. The city resembles a body whose parts assist each other in perfecting and protecting the life of the animal. The ruler of the city relates to the inhabitants as the heart relates to other bodily parts. The inhabitants of the city are ranked in accordance with the distance between them and the ruler. Those closest to the ruler possess qualities that allow them to pursue his objectives directly, while the lower ranks pursue the objectives of those above them and thus indirectly those of the ruler. While the inhabitants of the city differ from one another in their innate natures (*fiṭra*), which is why different kinds of people perform tasks that are suitable for them, they become perfected (within the limits of their own natures) through acquired voluntary habits (*al-malakāt al-irādiyya*) such as crafts and arts.

The ruler of the city must possess the acquired intellect (*al-'aql al-mustafād*) by means of which he communicates with the Active Intellect, and his imaginative faculty must also be perfect. When the Active Intellect infuses his passive intellect with the knowledge of universals, such a ruler becomes a philosopher and, owing to the infusion of his imaginative faculty with the knowledge of particulars, also a prophet and warner (*mundhir*; of the punishment in the hereafter). A ruler who possesses all the aforementioned qualities is called "the true king" (*al-malik fī al-ḥaqīqa*). If, however, at a certain time no one is qualified to be a true king, the city must be ruled by the traditional king (*al-malik bi-l-sunna*)—one who does not issue new laws but preserves those issued by the previous leader or leaders. Although all inhabitants of the city share the same beliefs, seeking happiness, only a tiny minority—the philosophers—can establish the veracity of these beliefs by demonstrative proofs (proofs that consist of a chain of syllogisms). The majority—the common believers—know them only through their likenesses (*muthul*)—namely, imitations (*muḥākāt*) of their intelligible forms. These likenesses that exist in their imagination differ from one another in their degree of perfection and particular characteristics, which leads to differences of opinions among the inhabitants of different excellent cities.

There are also nonexcellent cities. Philosophers discuss a variety of them, but there are two main types: the ignorant city (*al-madīna al-jāhila*) and the sinful city (*al-madīna al-fāsiqa*). The inhabitants of the ignorant city have incorrect conceptions of happiness and adhere to corrupt practices. The inhabitants of the sinful city share the sound beliefs of the inhabitants of the excellent city but engage in the corrupt actions of the inhabitants of the ignorant city.

The Brethren of Purity (*Ikhwān al Ṣafā'*, who wrote their treatises somewhere in the tenth century) discuss the issue of the philosophical city in the 48th epistle of their encyclopedia, titled "On the manner of mission on behalf of God" (*Fi Kayfiyyati Da'wat ila Allah*). As they address their epistles not to fellow philosophers (as Farabi did) but instead to a wider and less sophisticated audience, their account is simplified and more popular. They urge their followers to assist each other and to unite their bodily and spiritual powers in order to build an excellent and virtuous spiritual city (*madīna fāḍila rūḥāniyya*), "the refuge of spirits" (*ma'wāt al-arwāḥ*), in the country of the "Greatest Trusted One" (*al-nāmūs al-akbar*), in other words, the angel Gabriel. The inhabitants of this city must be a tribe of pious, wise, and virtuous men, discerning the affairs of the souls and their states. The city must rest on the foundations of sincerity (*ṣidq*) and the fear of God (*taqwā*) and must be supported by the pillars of fidelity (*wafā'*) and trust (*amāna*), the ultimate goal of its existence being eternal bliss (which consists of the separation from the world of generation and corruption).

The inhabitants of the city are divided into four ranks: craftsmen, chiefs (managers and administrators), rulers (those who command and forbid), and divines (the possessors of volition [*mashī'a*] and will [*irāda*]). The craftsmen must possess a purified soul, excellent receptivity, and a quick wit. These qualities are provided by the intellective faculty, which discerns the meanings of sensible affairs and typically develops by the age of 15. The possessors of this rank

are referred to as "the merciful [and the] righteous" (*al-abrār al-ruḥamā'*). The chiefs, in turn, must possess a generous soul and take care of the brethren with compassion and mercy, employing the philosophical faculty, which develops by the age of 30. The possessors of this rank are called "the virtuous [and] pious" (*al-akhyār al-fuḍalā'*). The rulers must possess authority of command and prohibition and be able to eliminate obstinacy and resistance in a subtle and friendly way. This ability is provided by the legislative faculty (*al-quwwa al-nāmūsiyya*), which develops by age 40. The possessors of this rank are called "the noble [and the] virtuous" (*al-fuḍalā' al-karrām*). Finally, the divines must embody a complete submission to God, receiving in return His support and the ability to witness Him. This ability is given by the angelic faculty, which develops by age 50. This division is based on the seventh book (537c–540c) of Plato's *Republic*.

Ibn Rushd deals with the issue of the philosophical city in his commentary on Plato's *Republic* (which survives only in Hebrew translation). He identifies the philosophical city with the perfect Islamic state based on the shari'a. The city is ruled by the philosopher, because happiness can be achieved only through theoretical knowledge (however, no mention of his conjunction with the Active Intellect is made). The ruler-philosopher, who is also king, legislator, and imam, presents the elite with demonstrative arguments but addresses the common people with persuasive and poetical ones. His duty is to create and maintain an administrative hierarchy that would perfectly reproduce the natural hierarchy among the moral virtues and practical arts, all of which exist for the sake of perfecting theoretical virtues.

See also Brethren of Purity; al-Farabi, Abu Nasr (ca. 878–950); Ibn Rushd (1126–98), Isma'ilis; philosopher-king; philosophy; utopia

Further Reading

Averroes, *Averroes on Plato's* Republic, edited and translated by Ralph Lerner, 1974; Charles E. Butterworth, *The Political Aspects of Islamic Philosophy*, 1992; Patricia Crone, *Medieval Islamic Political Thought* (*God's Rule*), 2004; Abu Nasr al-Farabi, *Mabadi' Ara' Ahl al-Madina al-Fadila*, 1989; Ralph Lerner and Muhsin S. Mahdi, eds., *Medieval Political Philosophy: A Source Book*, 1963; Richard Walzer, ed. and trans., *Al-Farabi on the Perfect State*, 1985.

YANIS ESHOTS

civil society

During the 1990s, civil society became a popular conceptual tool for studying democratic transformations within the Muslim world. Civil society was portrayed as the icon of democracy, where not only associations, unions, and parties but also clubs and less formal groups were formed and mediated the relations between citizens and state authorities. In the post–cold war era, civil society provided social scientists with an ecumenical paradigm of political development that could satisfy both the residual supporters of modernization theory and its opponents. A more sobering view of the concept requires exploring the extent to which the idea of civil society is the outcome not only of the specific modern history of the West but also of its relations with "the rest," first and foremost the Muslim world.

The perhaps too-optimistic use of the notion of civil society in the 1990s was shared by the social movements that brought about the collapse of the authoritarian regimes in Eastern Europe. This mood spilled over to the Muslim world and furthered hopes for democratization in face of the perpetuation of various types of autocratic and sometimes pseudodemocratic regimes variably associated with ongoing neoliberal globalization. In the process, Muslim responses to oppressive state systems took a more nuanced view of the relationship between the ideas and practices of civil society and democratic transformations. The original European model of civil society, as elaborated by the Scottish Enlightenment, laid a primary stress on the individual agent who knows his own interest and possesses a capacity to act autonomously while sharing a sense of affection and sympathy toward other individuals. Against this streamlined model, a more inclusive notion highlights the value-setting power of human beings' capacity to transcend the satisfaction of material necessities through dynamics of passionate interaction and interested cooperation.

In light of these developments, which occurred within continental social theory, civil society appears overstretched as a concept if it is mainly intended to cover the civil power of autonomous social ties. It also risks oversimplifying the dimensions of collective action, which are not rooted in trust and cooperation among self-interested individuals but are based on specifically collective mechanisms of protest and empowerment. This problem was highlighted by the early 19th-century French thinker Alexis de Tocqueville, who looked at the emerging non-European societies of the United States and Russia and stressed the importance of a "political society" as a necessary match to civil society. The idea of a political society extends the original notion of civil society to include the realm where individuals fight over notions of common good and implement collective welfare programs within smaller or bigger communities and municipalities, notably with the help of voluntary associations, including political parties.

Such collective endeavors can be considered the manifestation of a profound metamorphosis—but not the erasure—of traditions in the wake of modern transformations. Colonialism itself did not completely disrupt the way social groups and movements within non-European societies proved able to build distinctive versions of civil (or of civil-*cum*-political) society. As shown by leading social theorist Hannah Arendt, the impersonal and potentially totalitarian quality of the "social" as a marker of impersonal modernization cannot be entirely balanced out by the civil ties of trust and reciprocity. A collective dynamics not captured by the liberal notion of civil society reenacts key factors of the *koinonia politike* of Aristotle (in Latin, *societas civilis*—since the Greek *polis* corresponds

to the Latin *civitas*—that is, semantically, the antecedent to "civil society"). Politics within human society requires the articulation of practices supported by a deeper symbolic bond. Boundaries are continuously created and challenged, and the ongoing mediations and contestations can be accommodated only within a larger concept of civil society that incorporates key elements of more classic notions. To pinpoint this deeper dimension of the social bond, the consideration of the common good (e.g., as incorporated in religious traditions) contributes to rendering the idea of civil society more inclusive by creating a strong nexus between common sense–oriented praxis in human relationships and a disciplined "passion" for justice, which can be mediated and expressed through modern forms of collective mobilization.

The tension between a liberal, European, and largely colonial notion of civil society and a more inclusive idea of the social bond has provided the main framework for debates in various parts of the Muslim world since the 1990s. In Egypt and in other parts of the Arab world, the discussion focused on the distinction and competition between *al-mujtama' al-madanī*, an Arabic translation of "civil society," and *al-mujtama' al-ahlī*, which literally means "indigenous" or "communal society" and so captures the communal nature of the social bond. Comparable contentions between polar models occurred in other parts of the Muslim world, such as Southeast Asia, where the idea of a *masyarakat madani*, though meaning "civil society," reenacted the Medina paradigm of Muhammad's virtuous community while also attempting to reconcile the two rival understandings of civil versus "communal" society. While stressing the religious foundations of social solidarity, *masyarakat madani* evidences the more secular idea of a "moral sense," central to the original formulations of civil society, as the human engine facilitating the autonomy of action and the self-sufficiency of the civil bond.

Both the conceptual bifurcation and the attempts to restore a unitary meaning of civil society are a product not only of Western experiences and approaches but also of the German sociologist Ferdinand Tönnies's self-critical reflections on Western modernity. One major example is the distinction between *Gemeinschaft* and *Gesellschaft* (literally "community" and "[civil] society"), designating not a traditional versus a modern form of the social bond but two different types of will, agency, and voluntary action. Tönnies's arguments might be read as antecedents of the reasoning of many contemporary Islamic thinkers. He saw *Gemeinschaft* as expressing the agency that is oriented to a collective *telos*. Such social bonds, characteristic of smaller communities that are not necessarily archaic but live on trade and depend on some specialized division of labor, are quite different from the division of labor within *Gesellschaft*, which is premised on exploitation. Tönnies also stressed the richness of Roman law, which encompassed both a dimension of *communio* and one of *societas*—in other words, of collective and individual property versus the one-sided use of the principles of Roman law within modern codes, subjected as they are to the logic of capitalism and requiring the erasure of customary law. Such theorization helps us better situate the Islamic postcolonial critique of simplified and exclusive notions of civil society as not unique.

The diffuse concept of social agency incorporated in the liberal notion of civil society happened to be too dependent on legal underpinnings (civil law and more specifically the laws demarcating and often restricting associational rights) and so remained a partly unfulfilled "Western dream." This is most visible in the entrenched top-down bureaucratic steering necessary to the maintenance of modern polities that are based on ordered labor relationships. The leading anthropologist and social theorist Ernest Gellner provocatively described the "Western dream" of civil society as a "failed *umma*" in order to highlight that excessive expectations of mutual trust as the glue of civil society, supposedly replacing a communal bond of faith, fall back inevitably on some nonliberal and premodern idea of social harmony. A civil society eschewing any form of *waṣta* (authoritative mediation, or even intercession) is unthinkable even in Western historic models. This aspect was also recognized by Hegel, who argued that the condition for a *bürgerliche Gesellschaft* was a cluster of traditionally rooted intermediary institutions.

In conclusion, the hegemony of liberal notions of civil society has been seriously contested within the West itself for more than two centuries. In this sense, the Islamic critiques and reconstructions are not instances of an Islamic exceptionalism but rather reflections of the postcolonial predicament of contemporary Muslim-majority societies.

See also globalization; individualism; modernity; rights

Further Reading

Jonathan Benthall, "Civil Society's Need for De-deconstruction," *Anthropology Today* 16, no. 2 (2002); Simone Chambers and Will Kymlicka, eds., *Alternative Conceptions of Civil Society*, 2001; Ernst Gellner, "The Importance of Being Modular," in *Civil Society: Theory, History, Comparison*, edited by John A. Hall, 1995; Chris Hann and Elizabeth Dunn, eds., *Civil Society: Challenging Western Models*, 1996; Serif Mardin, "Power, Civil Society and Culture in the Ottoman Empire," *Comparative Studies in Society and History* 11, no. 3 (1969); Augustus R. Norton, ed., *Civil Society in the Middle East*, 2 vols., 1995, 1996; Adam B. Seligman, *The Idea of Civil Society*, 1992.

ARMANDO SALVATORE

civil war

The term "civil war" describes severe intrastate violence, as distinguished from lower-intensity violence, be it chronic or sporadic, in premodern societies, and interstate violence, such as invasion or conquest. What is at stake is the possession of ultimate political power, and the parties involved in the conflict are rival claimants (in dynastic polities, frequently brothers or cousins) supported by political, religious, and military factions.

The classical Arabic term that is frequently translated as civil war, *fitna*, has the root meaning of trial or affliction, and in historical and political prose, the term includes not only civil war among Muslims but also the related phenomena of social and economic disorder or strife that ruptures the community's unity and pits Muslim against fellow Muslim. In premodern usage, the same word is also used to describe the apocalyptic circumstances and battles at the end of history. To distinguish itself from the cultural and religious associations of the premodern tradition, modern Arabic has produced a neologism, *ḥarb ahlī*, which translates more precisely the conventional use of "civil war" in the European tradition.

The political history of Islam can be said to date from 622, when the Prophet Muhammad emigrated from his hometown of Mecca to Yathrib (Medina), where he established a political community and waged war against those who refused to acknowledge his claim to temporal and religious authority. After Muhammad, caliphs (God's deputies) ruled the Islamic polity in more-or-less unbroken succession until the middle of the ninth century. Throughout this period, civil wars were not uncommon, but the ruling dynasty itself proved robust by Byzantine standards: caliphs were invariably drawn from Muhammad's tribe of the Quraysh, sons or brothers typically acceding to the throne.

The early Islamic state was unitary in both conception and execution. Organized political violence was far more centripetal than centrifugal—in other words, civil war was far more common than was secession. The tribal warfare that broke out upon Muhammad's death was counted as the "Wars of Apostasy" (the tribes having renounced their loyalty to the religious movement that survived Muhammad's death) rather than as a *fitna*. What the tradition unequivocally regards as the greatest *fitna* of all took place in 656–61, in events that would come to be understood as the source and origin of Islamic sectarianism. In the eyes of Muslims and non-Muslims alike, the events marked the end of political unity and, with it, an orthodoxy ascribed to the first community.

In the explicit political discourse of the later Islamic tradition, at issue was the succession of the second caliph, ʻUmar b. al-Khattab (r. 634–44), and the claims of his successor, ʻUthman b. ʻAffan (r. 644–56), as compared to those of ʻAli b. Abi Talib, the son-in-law and cousin of the Prophet himself. The *fitna* involved the murder of ʻUthman; ʻAli's claim to the caliphate (including accusations that his supporters were complicit in ʻUthman's murder); the Battle of the Camel, which pitted two of the Prophet's most revered Companions, along with one of his wives (ʻA'isha), against ʻAli; the Battle of Siffin between ʻAli and Muʻawiya (including the secession of some of ʻAli's supporters, the Kharijis); and, finally, the killing of ʻAli himself. This was the greatest of all *fitnas* because it was the earliest and marked the end of what the tradition viewed as original unity and because it planted the seeds of Shiʻi sectarianism.

What have come to be called the second (683–92) and third (744–49) *fitnas* produced less sectarian identity than sustained violence. The second *fitna* ushered out one ruling branch of the Umayyads, the Sufyanids, in favor of another, the Marwanids. Regions fell under the authority of a variety of claimants, most notably Ibn al-Zubayr, who was defeated only by systematic campaigning, including a violent siege of Mecca carried out on behalf of the eventual victor, ʻAbd al-Malik (r. 685–705). ʻAbd al-Malik was followed in the caliphate by no fewer than four sons and two grandsons, but eventually the Marwanid dynasty imploded during the third *fitna*, which opened the door for eastern armies to rout what remained of the Umayyad support. It appears that the third *fitna* so fractured the Umayyad political and military elite that the century-old idea of Umayyad and Syrian rule was quickly discredited, and the new metropolitan capital of Baghdad was soon founded (in 762–63) in what had been a restive province, with all the resulting cultural reorientation to the east that this implied. The caliphs would still be drawn from Muhammad's tribe, but now they came from the Abbasid branch; civil war had led to political revolution.

The civil war of 809–13, which pitted one son of Harun al-Rashid (Amin) against another (Ma'mun), provides the most spectacular early Islamic case of a complicated succession arrangement gone horribly wrong: Harun stipulated that Ma'mun would follow Amin to the caliphate, but neither brother thought it workable. This civil war is sometimes said to mark the transition between the early and mid-Abbasid period, not least because Ma'mun's siege of Amin's Baghdad fatally undermined the military establishment that had brought the Abbasids to power and engineered early Abbasid success. In time, Harun's sons and grandsons effected a decisive change in military recruitment, which by the 860s placed de facto military and political power in the hands of Central Asian commanders. A protracted civil war that broke out in 866 between two rival claimants to the caliphate, Mustaʻin and Muʻtazz, reflected the militarized and factional Turkish politics of the period.

The Umayyad and Abbasid pattern—succession crisis triggers civil war, which leads, in turn, to structural changes in the state—is hardly unique to Islamic history. It might be said that the more unitary the state, the greater the potential for structural change. For example, when the Seljuq sultan Malikshah died in 1092, a civil war erupted among three sons; the unitary Seljuq state ended with that civil war, replaced by separate polities ruling Syria, Iraq, Iran, and Asia Minor. A better example is the civil war that broke out in Fatimid Egypt in the 1060s: it took the end of civilian rule and a fundamental reengineering of the state to squelch the violence the war had engendered. On the other hand, the effects of the civil war of the late 1020s and 1030s on the federated Buyid states of Iraq and Iran were relatively slight.

In Islamic states of the post-Abbasid period, sectarianism could emerge from civil war and secession, the best examples coming in the highly centripetal Fatimid state in Egypt (969–1171). The infusion of Turco-Mongol traditions into Islamic politics during the 13th and 14th centuries, especially an appanage system that institutionalized competition for succession among multiple contenders, marks a break in patterns of rulership, at least as inasmuch as it could lead to chronic and violent civil war, such as in the Mughal Empire in India. Another example is the civil war of 1600–1605, which pitted a father (Akbar) against a son named Salim (the future Jahangir).

To avoid succession disputes, formal and informal procedures intended to secure elite and military loyalty were put in place in the late seventh century; thus came the solemn and ceremonial giving of oaths of allegiance (*bay'as*) to acceding caliphs and their appointed heirs-apparent, along with other wills and testaments. As much as court practices attempted to regularize succession so as to preclude civil war, theory tended to legitimate the authority of Qurashi caliphs who possessed power, even if their rule was imperfect, and to prescribe political quietism. Muslim political thinkers throughout much of the pre-Mongol period were concerned with elaborating, updating, and otherwise exploring the view that government was to be ordered by a divinely favored leader who, occupying a sacral office (the caliphate) and providing the leadership necessary for salvation, was to be obeyed. Disobeying God's representatives meant breaking the oath of loyalty binding subject to sovereign, which was made before God Himself and therefore meant disobeying God Himself.

Rather than warring with each other, Muslims were to live in peace with each other; when they could not, they were accountable to God. The Qur'an stipulates that peace should be made between warring factions of believers (49:9), and according to one hadith, "When two Muslims encounter each other with swords, both the killer and the killed are in Hell." For virtually all Muslims of the early period, believing and belonging were one and the same, and communities were either errant or rightly guided. Although their legal discourse made some allowance for rebellion, for Sunnis especially, belonging meant remaining within the bounds of the community, even if under unjust or underqualified rulers.

Criticisms can be made of imprecise terms such as "activist" and "quietist," but the general tendency over the first five centuries of Islam is clear enough: revolutionary political activism for the sake of constructing just political communities, a tendency exemplified by many Shi'i movements especially, lost its appeal, eclipsed by the emergence of more individualistic and local pieties and loyalties. Cleaving to community, as opposed to rending it, is the defining feature of classical orthodoxy, be it Sunni or Shi'i.

See also 'Ali b. Abi Talib (ca. 599–661); Ma'mun (786–833)

Further Reading

K. Abou El Fadl, *Rebellion and Violence in Islamic Law*, 2001; Patricia Crone, *Medieval Islamic Political Thought*, 2004; H. Djaït, *La grande discorde: Religion et politique dans l'Islam des origines*, 1989; W. Madelung, *The Succession to Muhammad*, 1997.

CHASE F. ROBINSON

clients

"Clients" (*mawālī*) is a term used in early Islamic history, and in Islamic law thereafter, for a legal status originally bestowed on every non-Arab member of the Arab society established by conquest in the Middle East outside Arabia. The Arab conquerors were tribally organized, but their non-Arab subjects had "forgotten their genealogies," as the Arabs put it. Partly for this reason and partly because most converts in the first century were slaves (originally captives) who had been uprooted from their own families, non-Arab newcomers to Muslim society had to be attached to a kin group willing to pay blood money for any damage to life or property they might inflict. The group in question was that of the newcomer's patron (also called a *mawlā*). Freed slaves in principle always became clients of their manumitter, but a free person could choose his own patron by converting "at the hands of" a Muslim with whom he had reached an agreement. The reward for the patron, apart from a loyal follower, lay in his entitlement to a share in his client's estate. The tie survived the death of both parties, continuing among their descendants in perpetuity, but its relevance decreased as time passed. Clients rapidly acquired clients of their own. Whether the patron was an Arab or an assimilated client, the institution served to regulate the reception of newcomers and ensure both their subordination and their assimilation to the Arabs. The tie did not affect the newcomer's status in public law, however: the convert became a full "citizen," endowed with the same rights and duties as other Muslims. At some point, perhaps in the mid-eighth century, the jurists began to reject the institution of clientage for converts, but all jurists retained the institution for freedmen, and some retained it for free partners as long as conversion was not involved. The obligation to pay blood money on behalf of a kinless newcomer was shifted to other institutions, such as the treasury.

The term "clients" eventually came to be used in the loose sense of "non-Arab Muslims" (as in the expression *al-'arab wa-l-mawālī*), and it is in that sense that it tends to be used in the secondary literature, too. The sources never use the word in the sense of protegés and beneficiaries of patronage in general, and though the institution was of considerable social and political importance in the first centuries, its significance lies primarily in cultural history. The Arabs formed a privileged ruling elite imposed on the non-Arabian Middle East by conquest, and like most elites of this kind, they were both jealous of their privileges and contemptuous of the defeated natives. Non-Arab Muslims were derided as "slaves," paid less than their Arab peers in the army, deemed unfit for positions of authority or marriage with Arab women, and worth less than Arabs in terms of blood money. But even so, they rose with extreme rapidity in Muslim society, and they appear to have outnumbered Arab Muslims within two generations of the conquests, for the Arab conquest society had one characteristic unparalleled in other imperial expansions: the bar to membership was set extremely low. The Arabs had expanded in the name of a universalist religion, with the result that the community of believers happened also to be an imperial elite. The only requirement for membership of this elite was recitation of the confession of faith to a Muslim willing to act as one's patron. In practice, many migrated to the Muslim centers without even having patrons. Fearing the loss not only of their revenues but also of their very identity, the Arab authorities tried to stem the tide by imposing tests on converts, refusing to register them on the military roll, or

deporting them outright as illegal immigrants. But however much they pushed away converts with one hand, they continued to accept them in the form of freedmen with the other, so the privileged conquest elite disappeared with great speed. It was in that context that the jurists, often non-Arabs themselves, began to reject the institution of clientage for converts.

The fact that newcomers were granted what we would now call full citizenship meant that non-Arab Muslims accepted the legitimacy of the Muslim polity that had replaced their native states instead of clamoring for independence: what they sought to change was the dynasty that they saw as responsible for the prejudice against them. The Abbasid revolution, conducted from eastern Iran a mere century after the conquest of this region, would under other circumstances have been a war of independence. Instead it replaced the Umayyad dynasty with that of the Abbasids and put an end to what remained of the political hegemony of the Arabs. This did not of course put an end to the tense relationship between the original bearers of Islam and its new representatives. The century after the revolution was dominated by often acrimonious debates about the relative merits of Arabs and *mawālī* in the sense of non-Arabs, best known in the form of polemics for and against the so-called Shu'ubis. But the debates were about the terms of coexistence within the same political house, the desirability of which was taken for granted. A prominent item of debate was the relative value and prestige of the cultural traditions represented by the parties involved. This debate accompanied the formation of a synthesis of the beliefs and values brought by the conquerors and the legacy of the imperial civilizations they had defeated. In short, this was when classical Islamic civilization emerged.

See also conversion; patronage; Shu'ubis; tribalism; Umayyads (661–750)

Further Reading

M. Bernards and John Nawas, eds., *Patronate and Patronage in Early and Classical Islam*, 2005; P. Crone, "Post-Colonialism in Tenth-Century Islam," *Der Islam* 83, no. 1 (2006); Eadem, "Were the Qays and Yemen of the Umayyad Period Political Parties?" *Der Islam* 71 (1994).

PATRICIA CRONE

coinage

Before the spread of machine-struck coinage in the Islamic world in the 19th century, the coins of Muslim states were prepared by hand, as individual bits of metal were struck between two dies, resulting in the transfer of the design of those dies to the two faces of the coin. These coins, which varied tremendously in size and shape over the chronological span and geographical scope of the Muslim world, were usually prepared from gold, silver, or copper. While the main purpose of coins is economic, they are also intimately linked to matters of politics. The common words in Arabic for gold coin (*dīnār*) and silver coin (*dirham*) appear in the Qur'an, and Muslim jurists subsequently wrote treatises establishing Islamic principles of money and the need for those in authority to provide proper coinage. The two faces of coins, moreover, proved to be excellent vehicles for political messages.

It is thus not surprising that the right to mint coins (*sikka*) emerged as one of two major prerogatives of rulership in the premodern Islamic world. The other was the right to have one's name mentioned as ruler in the Friday sermon (*khuṭba*).

There was no tradition of coin minting in the early Islamic community of the Hijaz. Thus as the first Muslims expanded outside of the Arabian Peninsula, they simply adopted the coinage in use by the states they conquered. It was not until the year 696 that what may be called the first Islamic coinage was produced during the reign of the Umayyad caliph 'Abd al-Malik (r. 685–705). These were gold coins that bore only writing, in this case legends derived from Qur'anic verses and other pious phrases. Two years later, silver *dirhams* were struck bearing similar legends. Beginning in the reign of the Abbasid caliph Mu'tasim (r. 833–42), the names of the caliphs were added to the coin legends. While the subsequent breakup of the Abbasid state resulted in the emergence of several other styles and types of coins, from this point in the ninth century onward, coins became a major source of political history for the Muslim world. As local autonomy developed in the farther reaches of the Abbasid Empire, provincial governors began to add their names to the coins minted in the regions under their control. Changes in these names reflect either a change in the ruler or a change in the dynasty. With the rise of the competing caliphates of the Fatimids and the Spanish Umayyads, coins were struck in the names of those respective leaders as well. The Fatimids not only changed the layout and design of their coinage but also used Shi'i phrases in their coin legends. Changes in legends and titles often reflected immediate political circumstances. The Mamluk sultan Malik al-Zahir Baybars (r. 1260–77), for example, added the title "supporter of the Commander of the Faithful" (*qasīm amīr al-mu'minīn*) to some of his gold coins to reflect his establishment of a new Abbasid caliphate in Cairo after the Mongols had destroyed Baghdad in 1258.

While never as common as the purely scriptural coin designs, figural imagery and symbols appear on some coins minted by Muslim states, although the reason is not always clear. Baybars had a feline figure engraved on his gold and silver coins, possibly a reference to the fact that his name meant "panther" in his native tongue. In states as diverse as the Turkoman dynasties of northern Mesopotamia in the 12th century and Mughal India in the 17th century, images linked to astrological concepts were used on coins, although in the former case that astrological link is fiercely debated. Finally, while coins with images become slightly more prevalent with the spread of modern machine-struck coinage, some modern Muslim states such as Saudi Arabia continue in the long established pattern of epigraphic coinage established long ago by 'Abd al-Malik.

See also trade and commerce

Further Reading

Jere L. Bacharach, *Islamic History through Coins: An Analysis and Catalogue of Tenth-Century Ikhshidid Coinage*, 2006; Michael L. Bates, *Islamic Coins*, 1982; Andrew S. Ehrenkreutz and Gene W. Heck, "Additional Evidence of the Fatimid Use of Dinars for Propaganda Purposes," in *Studies in Islamic History and Civilization in Honor of David Ayalon*, edited by M. Sharon, 1986; Tayeb El-Hibri, "Coinage Reform under the 'Abbasid Caliph al-Ma'mun," *Journal of the Economic and Social History of the Orient* 36, no. 1 (1993); William F. Spengler and Wayne G. Sayles, *Turkoman Figural Bronze Coins and Their Iconography*, vol. 1, *The Artuqids*, 1992.

WARREN C. SCHULTZ

collective obligations

Collective obligation (*farḍ kifāya*), in contrast to individual obligation (*farḍ 'ayn*), is one of the two categories of moral obligation known to Islamic jurisprudence. The distinction between the two categories is at least as old as Shafi'i's *Risala* (the first work in theoretical jurisprudence, or *uṣūl al-fiqh*, in Islamic history), and it is accepted in both Sunni and Twelver Shi'i jurisprudence.

The basic distinction between a collective obligation and an individual one is that in the former, one may fail to perform the obligation but still escape moral blame if someone else fulfills the obligation, whereas in an individual obligation, only the individual performance of the command is sufficient to avoid moral censure. Collective obligations can generally be thought of as issues requiring collective action, but no one specific person is legally obliged to perform them. Accordingly, unless a person is the only one capable of discharging the legal requirement, such as when only one man in town is qualified to serve as a judge, a collective obligation translates into a supererogatory command (*nadb*) with respect to individual Muslims. Because collective duties are only supererogatory with respect to individuals and not absolutely obligatory, their performance entails a large degree of altruism, since the discharge of the obligation benefits third parties who were not responsible for discharging the duty.

Collective obligations are found in both Islamic ritual law and the Islamic law of civil obligations (*mu'āmalāt*). Examples of ritual law representing collective obligations would be such duties as performing the funeral prayer; washing, shrouding, and burying the dead; and memorizing the entirety of the Qur'an. Individual obligations, by contrast, include the familiar Five Pillars of Islam and also, for example, knowledge of al-Fatiha (the first chapter of the Qur'an) and one other short chapter of the Qur'an so that one could fulfill one's individual obligation to perform the ritual prayer. Examples of collective obligations in the realm of civil responsibility include the duty to take possession of lost property and protect it from loss, as well as teaching and practicing agriculture, medicine, trades, and crafts.

For Sunnis, engaging in politics is a collective obligation, including the obligation to appoint a caliph, organize a judicial system, and train specialists in the law. Commanding right and forbidding wrong (*al-amr bi-l-ma'rūf wa-l-nahy 'an al-munkar*) is also a collective obligation, as is the general obligation to preserve expertise in the religious sciences. Taking part in offensive military operations or manning the frontiers of the Islamic state, both considered part of the obligation of jihad, are also examples of collective duties. Jihad becomes an individual duty only in the circumstance of an enemy attack on Islamic territory.

Collective obligations of a secular character, such as engaging in agriculture or industry, can take on a religious character, but only if the individual subjectively intends to serve God through discharging the obligation.

See also jurisprudence; al-Shafi'i, Muhammad b. Idris (767–820)

Further Reading

Michael Cook, *Commanding Right and Forbidding Wrong in Islamic Thought*, 2000; Abu Ishaq Ibrahim al-Shatibi, *al-Muwafaqat fi Usul al-Shari'ah*, 1991.

MOHAMMAD FADEL

colonialism

The expansion of Europe into the heartlands of the Muslim world in the 19th and early 20th centuries not only posed a sustained political and military threat to native populations but also prompted an internal debate over how best to renew Muslim societies that were apparently in decline. Under colonial rule, Islamic reformism and, increasingly, nationalism were the main vehicles for this debate, which continued over subsequent decades once it became evident that the end of European occupation did not necessarily lead to political independence. To figures as diverse as Gamal Abdel Nasser, Ayatollah Khomeini, and Osama bin Laden, the insidious workings of neocolonialism still restrained the development of the Arab and Islamic worlds.

European colonialism typically encountered sporadic armed resistance as it spread across first North Africa and then the Near East. Anticolonial revolts often legitimized themselves by appealing to the concept of jihad, though in some cases the mythic paradigm of the Mahdi, or redeemer, was invoked to galvanize the local community's millenarian zeal. Such resistance was largely rural, rooted in Sufi networks and united by the extraordinary charisma of one individual leader. Traditional urban elites, in contrast, were more accustomed to the need for political agility and typically acquiesced to the new European rule. The rebellion of 'Abd al-Qadir al-Jaza'iri against the French in Algeria (1830–47) provides one of the earliest examples of this form of resistance. Taking advantage of the speed and mobility of his irregular troops, 'Abd al-Qadir

used guerrilla tactics to good effect against the slow, cumbersome, and heavily armored columns of France's Armée d'Afrique. His revolt ended only when General Bugeaud made the transition to lighter columns and the collective punishment of Algerian villagers the keystone of his military strategy. Just as the Qadiri Sufi order played an important role in this revolt, so too did the Sanusi brotherhood seek to counter Italy's invasion of Libya (1911) from their stronghold in Cyrenaica. The Sanusi also fought against the British in Egypt (1915) and the French in sub-Saharan Africa; their battle against the Italians in Libya did not end until 1931. In Sudan, Muhammad Ahmad (1844–85) was declared a Mahdi and led a revolt against Egyptian rule in 1881, resulting in the creation of an independent state until Britain's Lord Kitchener reconquered the region in 1898.

While this early resistance largely drew on religious attachments and rural networks, after World War I, local populations increasingly turned to nationalism to provide their desire for independence with a coherent ideological framework. This development paralleled the construction of modern state forms in the Middle East (most evident in the mandated territories of Iraq, Transjordan, Palestine, Syria, and Lebanon) and the reorientation of political life toward urban centers, which soon became the most important arena for politics. Rural revolts continued to erupt in reaction to the imposition of British and French rule, most notably in Iraq (1920) and Syria (1925–27), but in many countries, outright insurgencies were superseded by new forms of urban resistance, such as student demonstrations, strikes, and public protests. Elites who formerly had not been inclined to contest European rule while it supported their interests found their positions as compradors increasingly untenable. Admittedly, these elites were handed the reins of power by the colonial authorities upon their departure, but more often than not these "bourgeois nationalist" regimes were overthrown by a younger, more radical generation that sought to purge the traces of colonial complicity from their newly independent states.

The Muslim world's inability to withstand European penetration preoccupied social and religious thinkers in the 19th century who asked, first, how Muslims could modernize their societies without mimicking the West and, second, how they could secure independence from Europe. The two questions were intimately related. Afghani (1838–97) thought that Islam's essential vitality could be seen in the successful episodes of armed resistance against the Europeans; he advocated a deep sociocultural revival to wake the Muslim people from their slumber. This line of argument can be traced from Afghani to the writings of Muhammad 'Abduh (d. 1905) and his followers, who were also proponents of Islamic reformism. But it also carried through to the postindependence period, when political ideologues couched their appeals to the dormant nationalism of their people in remarkably similar terms. Mystified by the failure of the Egyptian masses to come out in support of the Free Officers coup of 1952, Nasser concluded that his nation's sleeping political will could be revived only through a profound social and political transformation. Bin Laden also expressed the belief that a moral awakening was the sole necessary condition for reasserting Muslim civilization against the West's ongoing occupation of Islamic lands. This focus on Muslim moral regeneration as a tool to cast off colonial domination was prevalent in popular Arab political discourse, and structural questions regarding the global system (such as economic dependency) were featured mostly as second-order issues.

Suspicion of Western domination remained alive in many developing countries, and the mere existence of the State of Israel rendered such concerns especially acute in the Middle East. To nationalists and Islamists alike, Israel represented the enduring success of colonialism in the region. For many Arabs and Muslims, the 2003 occupation of Iraq confirmed that colonialism could not yet be consigned to the history books.

See also al-Afghani, Jamal al-Din (1838–97); Bin Laden, Osama (1957–2011); Europe; modernity; nationalism; revival and reform; Westernization

Further Reading

Nikki R. Keddie, "The Revolt of Islam, 1700 to 1993: Comparative Considerations and Relations to Imperialism," *Comparative Studies in Society and History* 36, no. 3 (1994); Ruhallah Khomeini, *Islam and Revolution: Writings and Declarations of Imam Khomeini*, translated by Hamid Algar, 1985; Bruce B. Lawrence, *Messages to the World: The Statements of Osama bin Laden*, 2005; Robert J. C. Young, *Postcolonialism: An Historical Introduction*, 2001.

DANIEL NEEP

commanding right and forbidding wrong

"Commanding right and forbidding wrong" (*al-amr bi-l-ma'rūf wa-l-nahy 'an al-munkar*) is a pervasive Islamic doctrine with textual roots in the Qur'an and hadith, the recorded sayings and actions of Muhammad, that articulates a general moral duty incumbent upon all Muslims. Its interpretations and applications have varied significantly throughout the history of the Islamic tradition, depending on sectarian affiliation, scholastic tradition, and political context. For convenience, the doctrine is referred to here as "forbidding wrong." The most thorough treatment of the principle can be seen in Michael Cook's magisterial *Commanding Right and Forbidding Wrong in Islamic Thought*, which serves as the primary reference for the following summary.

While there are many Qur'anic sources for the obligation to forbid wrong, 3:104 resolutely describes the tenet as a principle constituting the Muslim community and Islamic identity writ large: "Let there be one community of you, calling to good, commanding right and forbidding wrong." As is often true in Qur'anic style, the details of the tenet are obscure, leaving only a broad ethical injunction,

and as is common in Islamic tradition more generally, such interpretive gaps are readily filled in by the hadith literature. The most common hadith report relevant to the doctrine appears in a number of both Sunni and Shi'i collections, canonical and otherwise. It relates that Muhammad said, "Whoever sees a wrong, and is able to put it right with his hand, let him do so; if he can't, then with his tongue; if he can't, then in his heart, and that is the bare minimum of faith." In Cook's words, this hadith "provided later generations with a fundamental building-block for their scholastic doctrines of forbidding wrong," because in its contradistinction to the opacity of the Qur'anic articulations, it "spells out a hierarchy of modes of response to wrong: deed, word, and thought." It is within this broad spectrum that the political possibilities of the tenet can range from activism to quietism.

Exemplifying the quietist approach to the practice, Ahmad b. Hanbal (d. 855), the famed scholar of hadith, was modest in describing the parameters of the duty to forbid wrong. He did not advocate the use of violence in the performance of the duty, though the destruction of forbidden objects (e.g., smashing musical instruments, overturning chessboards) was permissible. Verbal extortion and scolding were also considered appropriate measures. If an offender's repeated refusal to change his or her behavior might lead to an escalation or confrontation, it was deemed better to cease. Privacy of one's home was also considered an insurmountable barrier to implementation of the duty. Also, according to Ibn Hanbal and other quietists, one should refrain from the duty when one's safety is in question. Therefore, like other formative quietest Sunni thinkers, he discouraged its performance against the state and shunned political activism.

The activist manifestation of the doctrine, which does not necessarily imply political rebellion, would nonetheless find expression in the movement founded by Ibn Hanbal in later generations, most specifically in the activities of the infamous Baghdadi activist Hasan b. 'Ali al-Barbahari (d. 941) and other tenth-century populists who engaged in acts of public disturbance in targeting various figures who strayed from "proper" Islamic behavior. The duty was also regularly articulated in doctrinal terms and thus supported public attacks against competing theological and sectarian visions of Islam.

Activist interpretations also came from Mu'tazili theologians such as Sayyid Mankdim (d. 1034) and al-Hakim al-Jishumi (d. 1101), who, though grounded in the school of 'Abd al-Jabbar (d. 1025), may have varied on the place of arms in the performance of the duty but rejected the idea of restricting the duty to performance in the heart solely. The Zaydi Shi'is likewise were activist oriented, though expectedly more so in terms of rebellion against unjust rulers. Hadi ila al-Haqq (d. 911), founder of the Zaydi imamate of Yemen, considered it foundational to his religious leadership and political mission, making it a formal component of his followers' pledge of allegiance to him. Imami Shi'i positions on the quietist-activist spectrum centered on the need for the imam's permission to perform the duty. The majority of scholars endorsed a view restricting the responsibility of the duty to the imam or his deputy, while 'Allama Hilli (d. 1325) argued that a qualified jurist could enact it—a juridical theme later expounded on by Ayatollah Khomeini in his adaptation of the guardianship of the jurist (*wilāyat-i faqih*), the religious doctrine that justifies clerical Islamic rule in Iran.

Given the ambiguity of the term "Sufi," it may not be fruitful to search for the Sufi theory of forbidding wrong. Nonetheless, the influential mystical thinker Harith al-Muhasibi (d. 857) declared that the best method includes the sincere cultivation of the obligation to forbid wrong. A regular refrain in Sufi articulations of the duty is the need to sublimate the ego's passions and to turn to God for help in correcting the wrongdoer's actions.

Forbidding wrong has had an ambivalent place in the development of modern state institutions in Muslim majority countries. In the wake of colonialism, many nations adopted secular codes of civil law, thus rendering many of the provisions of the shari'a irrelevant, much less subject to enforcement. It was not uncommon for reform intellectuals in the early 20th century to read into the Qur'an (3:104), the political injunction of representative assembly or other liberal modes of governance. However, in polities seeking a reconstitution of Islamic law, forbidding wrong became a cornerstone principle of public order. Shortly after the consolidation of Ibn Saud's conquests across the Arabian Peninsula in the late 1920s, committees for commanding right and forbidding wrong were established in Mecca to regulate pilgrims during their visits to the holy sanctuaries. The function quickly spread to the regulation of moral behavior in society at large, and it has since been a prominent feature of the modern Saudi state. Ayatollah Khomeini and like-minded Shi'i activists took up the doctrine of forbidding wrong as a central justification for their revivalist aspirations. In line with their general political views, they sharply criticized religious scholars who subscribed to the traditional quietest approach of Twelver Shi'ism, which held that in the absence of the direct instructions of the imam, many such political obligations were suspended indefinitely. Instead, they argued that with the permission and guidance of a jurist, forbidding wrong could again be a duty incumbent upon Muslims. The tenet was adopted as the basis for an article of the constitution of the Islamic Republic, and as in Saudi Arabia, the doctrine has been entrusted to substate local committees and councils for implementation.

In conclusion, forbidding wrong in Islamic tradition is as all encompassing as it is ambivalent. Its manifestations can range from the attacks of the violent activist to the inner thoughts and passive resistance of the quietest; likewise, its interpretation can lead to either conservative or liberal political conclusions.

See also Iran; quietism and activism; Saudi Arabia; shari'a; Zaydis

Further Reading

Michael Cook, *Commanding Right and Forbidding Wrong in Islamic Thought*, 2000; Idem, *Forbidding Wrong in Islam*, 2003.

ABBAS BARZEGAR

communism

The contemporary Arabic word for communism—*shuyū'iyya*—is a neologism from the root *sh-i-'*, meaning to spread, to circulate, to diffuse, and by extension, to have in common. This usage has been accepted since the early 1920s. Before that time, with the Paris Commune of 1871, cognate words such as *kūmūnizm* were used. Other renditions were *ibāhiyyūn*, which denoted licentiousness and atheism, and *dahriyyūn*, meaning materialists or freethinkers.

Communism as social theory and practice historically has been relegated to minorities in the Middle East, if not the larger Islamic world, and has never entered into the political mainstream. Among such minorities have been Copts in Egypt, Kurds in the Fertile Crescent, Christians in the Levant, and Jews. The majority of the people classified as minorities have not been drawn to communism, yet appeals to communism in the Muslim world historically have come from minorities.

Although communism has been a marginal factor in the Muslim world, Marxist-Leninist regimes were established in South Yemen (1969–90) and Afghanistan (1978–89), as were relatively coherent and well-organized communist parties in Syria, Iraq, Sudan, and Iran. In Indonesia (with the largest Muslim population in the world), during the nationalist struggle against the Dutch and again in the late 1950s and early 1960s, communism was able to find a niche that it had not been able to establish in Middle Eastern Muslim societies. Altogether, however, the majority of Muslim societies have continuously expressed antipathy toward communism both as thought and practice because of its relegation of religion to a secondary plane, if not to total irrelevance, in the lives of the people.

With the creation of the Communist International (also known as the Comintern, or Third International) in 1919, headquartered in Moscow, Vladimir Lenin and his associates sought both to influence and to attract the people of the Third World by emphasizing the solidarity of communism with anticolonial nationalism. At the second congress of the Comintern in 1920, theoretical justifications were given for Marxists to appeal to the "bourgeois" nationalism of the populations of the colonial territories. At the Baku Conference of the Peoples of the East (July–August 1920), Soviet representatives revealed the contents of the secretly drafted Treaty of London, April 1915, and the secretly drafted Sykes Picot Treaty, May 1916, according to which Britain and France betrayed the Arabs by reversing promises they had made to them in exchange for their support against the Ottoman Empire in World War I. Meanwhile, the Soviets materially assisted the Turkish nationalist movement led by Mustafa Kemal to stymie British and French efforts to carve up Anatolia into spheres of influence.

Soviet attempts to promote provincial separatist movements in areas such as the Gilan province in Iran in 1919 and 1920 did not succeed, but local communist parties or factions did emerge between 1921 and 1925 in Tunisia and Algeria (where, until 1936, they were basically extensions of the French Communist Party), Egypt, Lebanon, and Palestine, and later in Syria (1933) and Iran (1941).

One of the difficulties in the diffusion of communism to the Muslim world was its association with the international Zionist movement and specifically its goals in Palestine. The Jewish *bund* (federation of Jewish workers) was active both in the development of Bolshevism, the Leninist variant of Communism, and mainstream and radical Zionism, and this was bound to conflict with Muslim sensibilities over the issue of Palestine. Later on, when Soviet leader Joseph Stalin supported the creation of the State of Israel (mainly as a means of ensuring the departure of the British from the Middle East), many Muslims felt that the identification of communism with Zionism was indubitably established.

It is routinely stated that communism's atheism is the key impediment to its spread in the Muslim world. This may be true, but also significant is the stress on proletarian internationalism—no matter that this emphasis might be tactically modified at historical junctures when it served the purpose of communist policy makers to relegate that principle to a secondary plane. For example, if Lenin and his successors perceived that anticolonialist nationalism could be a valuable asset at a specific historical point to communism's larger goals of defeating global capitalism, they would de-emphasize proletarian internationalism. However, Muslim thinkers were keen to maintain the solidarity of the *umma* (community of believers), which would be difficult to uphold in the face of arguments about class solidarity. Among the standard accusations made against communism by Muslim spokespersons was that it preached class warfare, and its adherence to this position was so uncompromising that it spawned social hatred and invited coercion and brutality.

In the 1950s and 1960s, when the postindependence leaders of Algeria, Egypt, Syria, Iraq, and Indonesia began to adopt socialist economic policies, communism in the Muslim world appeared poised to make widespread gains. Ironically, however, it was precisely at this time that these rulers suppressed the communist parties and jailed, tortured, and executed the leaders of these organizations. Even when Nikita Khrushchev (r. 1953–64), then first secretary of the Communist Party of the Soviet Union, came to Egypt in 1964 to participate in the inauguration of the first stage of the Aswan Dam, bitter recriminations—which had already surfaced around 1959 to 1960—intensified between him and Egyptian president Gamal Abdel Nasser (r. 1956–70). Similar developments transpired in Iraq. In Indonesia, around 1964 to 1965, a ferocious campaign was launched against the Communist Party of Indonesia, leading to the deaths of hundreds of thousands of actual and supposed cadres of that party.

Later, friendlier relations prevailed between Moscow and Cairo, and eventually thousands of Soviet military advisors were sent to Egypt. Despite the presence of these advisors, however, Egyptian leaders used the media to insulate their populations from communist ideas and doctrines. President Anwar Sadat's expulsion of these advisors in 1972 suggested how weak Moscow's strategic position in the Middle East really was.

The Organization of the Islamic Conference, established in 1969 to promote solidarity among Muslim majority states, condemned the Soviet invasion of Afghanistan in 1979, and individual Muslim leaders, such as Ayatollah Khomeini (r. 1979–89) of Iran, joined in this action. Muslim commentators saw the collapse of communism in eastern Europe in the late 1980s and of the Soviet Union in December 1991 as the fully justified end of totalitarian systems, although some expressed concern that the United States remained as the world's only superpower.

See also Afghanistan; Algeria; capitalism; Egypt; ideology; Indonesia; masses; public interest; socialism; Tunisia

Further Reading

Ervand Abrahamian, *Iran between Two Revolutions*, 1982; Joel Beinen and Zachary Lockman, *Workers on the Nile: Nationalism, Communism, Islam and the Egyptian Working Class, 1882–1954*, 1987; Selma Botman, *The Rise of Egyptian Communism, 1939–1970*, 1988; Walter Laqueur, *Communism and Nationalism in the Middle East*, 3rd ed., 1961; Maxime Rodinson, *Marxism and the Muslim World*, 1979; Gabriel Warburg, *Islam, Nationalism and Communism in a Traditional Society: The Case of the Sudan*, 1978.

SHAHROUGH AKHAVI

community

A term capable of accommodating a number of different social collectives and identities, "community" is useful in describing a vast array of overlapping yet sufficiently distinct groups that nevertheless might belong to and participate in a larger collective identity or "community." It is important to note, however, that communities are neither radically independent nor wholly discrete; rather, they form, overlap, intersect, and coalesce in ways that generate still more ways of conceptualizing community both as an abstract analytical category and as observable phenomena of social organization and identity construction. Different orders of criteria particularize, contextualize, and add greater complexity to the concept of community and its application. Thus age, gender, race, nationality, language, class, social status, and historical era—to name only a few—easily frustrate any notion of community as a single, simple, or static entity immune to change and lacking internal differentiation.

With regard to the concept of community as it pertains to Islam and Muslim identity, two Arabic terms are of particular importance: *umma* and *jamā'a*. Both are typically translated as "community," and although they share a number of semantic features, their respective usages have grown and differed in important ways.

The term *umma* is found in the Qur'an, where it signifies a number of different yet interconnected meanings. At its most basic, the term retains the sense of a community or a social collective of men and women. It is, however, a fairly elastic term and is also used in the Qur'an more specifically to connote a religiously defined community, with each *umma* being distinguished from the others by the degree and content of its collective beliefs or disbeliefs. The social and religious significance of the term *umma* is also found in the Constitution of Medina, documents that were drafted to define the nascent polity established by Muhammad and to detail the communal obligations shared by the various constituent kinship groups and religious communities of Yathrib (Medina). Its position at the nexus of the sociopolitical and religious spheres of the burgeoning Islamic empire helps to explain the strong religiopolitical value the concept of *umma* quickly came to assume. Indeed, already in the early centuries of Islamic social and political development, the term *umma* was used to describe a mutually affiliated community of believers populating numerous lands but unified as a group under the banner of the caliphate.

Two key features of the early conception of *umma* that distinguish it from the seemingly synonymous term *jamā'a* are its encompassing (or "global") range of inclusion and its ideological function. The *umma* was a vital concept in the expansion and maintenance of Muslim dominance. A prescriptive concept, the notion of the *umma* as a vast "global" Muslim community was formed through a confluence of political, social, and religious concerns. It emerged from scholarly elaborations of the social contract between leader and community and served to unite religious identity with political leadership. The insistence on the importance of the *umma* was not merely an assertion of the importance of social unity; it was also an endorsement of the very structures of social, political, and religious power and control that ostensibly served to construct and sustain social unity. Indeed, many political texts, no doubt written in part to justify caliphal power and forestall radical activism, prescribed acquiescence and quietism, arguing that the unity of an increasingly expansive and internally diverse Muslim community, which, ideally, should transcend factional and cultural differences, had to be preserved at all costs. Political and social agitation, it was argued, would only result in chaos, violence, and the disintegration of the idealized *umma*. When the Abbasid caliphate collapsed beneath the pressures of Mongol invasion in the 13th century, the symbolic value of the caliphate as the center and defining feature of the *umma* remained. However, with the conceptual status of the *umma* renegotiated in direct proportion to the shifting locus of caliphal power, the *umma* was reimagined and re-presented as a predominantly religious community with minimal political valence.

In the 19th and 20th centuries, among the reformist circles of the Islamic world, the term *umma* and its connotations of global community resonated once again with a political tone. Before the Ottoman caliphate was finally abolished in 1924, conceptions of a unified Muslim community had come to the foreground of 19th- and 20th-century anticolonial discourse. To this end, the concept of *umma* was appropriated and redeployed in Pan-Islamic rhetoric. Typically presented as an ideal yet realizable political entity, the *umma* was envisioned as a unified community that would transcend geographical, historical, sectarian, and political differences

and unite Muslims of the world into a network of mutual association. For Afghani (1838–97), one of the earliest reform-minded political activists of the modern period, this meant a newly constituted caliphate, and, indeed, his attempts at realizing this were subsidized and propagated by the Ottoman Empire, with the sultan Abdülhamid II styling himself as the caliph of the new, emerging *umma*. The caliphate failed, however, and following World War I, the Ottoman Empire was dismembered. Subsequently, Pan-Islamic ideologues found themselves contending with the fragmentary outlook and rather divisive rhetoric of nationalist discourse. As Sayyid Qutb (1906–66) noted, the term *umma* did not properly belong to the Islamist perspective, which focused largely on national identity, much to the exclusion of a larger, global Muslim polity. Indeed, as its use in nationalist and Islamist politics revealed, the term *jamā'a* served as a much better descriptor of the kinds of imagined community that proliferated in the latter half of the 20th century.

Jamā'a, unlike *umma*, is not found in the Qur'an; however, like *umma*, it is described in the hadith. While *umma* soon came to signify a broad social and political formation founded on religious and legal justifications and characterized by its authoritative center, the originally synonymous term *jamā'a* referred to a communal formation largely free of political entanglements and situated beyond the authoritative scope of human and terrestrial centers of power. In its simplest form, a *jamā'a* is a community defined by its members, who are joined to one another in and by a common set of beliefs. Whereas *umma* signifies a vast community whose unity is determined by a symbolic center—a caliph who speaks for and unites the believers into a cohesive, though variegated, global community—*jamā'a* is distinguished from *umma* by its connotation of localized forms of communal ties and identity.

As a descriptor of much smaller groupings of Muslims who form around a spiritual or religious leader, the term *jamā'a* has been used simply to refer to any group of Muslims that congregates at a mosque or follows a particular imam. Nevertheless, the term assumes much greater political import where it is used to describe and name the collective leadership for a community of Muslims. For example, in Timbuktu, at least up until the 19th century, the term *jamā'a* referred to an authoritative body of imams, scholars, and wealthy townsmen who acted as an unofficial representative body. From the 17th to the early 20th century in Morocco, two neighboring pastoral tribes, both the Dawi Mani' and the Ait Atta, employed the term *jamā'a* in a similar fashion, using the term to describe their council of tribal leaders. And yet, despite the close proximity of these two tribal groups, their respective conceptions of *jamā'a* remained specific to the particular needs and social formations of the two tribes. For the Dawi Mani', the *jamā'a* was an informal regulative and judicial body of important male members who implemented a combination of shari'a and tribal customary law. The *jamā'a* of the sedentary Ait Atta, however, was a formal, officially elected assembly charged with judicial and administrative responsibilities. In each example, *jamā'a* not only serves to describe a higher, more regulatory, and more socially involved form of organization than the simple notion of a religious congregation but also points to the formation of a particular body of collective leadership that responds to the social and political concerns most relevant to the localized communities that they represent and regulate. In a similar way, the term *jamā'a* was used to refer to the larger and more radical Islamist movements that emerged in the latter half of the 20th century in the Islamic world. In late 20th century Egypt, for example, the term *jamā'a* referred to political organizations motivated by Islamist sociopolitical aspirations. Radically politicized organizations such as the al-Gama'a al-Islamiyya and Jama'at al-Muslimin were, however, elitist and ultimately divisive, for, in articulating a specific vision of Muslim society and conceiving of themselves as models for its realization, these organizations produced communal organizations within shared national and local spaces, culminating in exclusive and contesting visions for an Islamic state.

Instantiations of *jamā'a* are diverse, entirely context-specific, and historically contingent. Whether the term connotes a congregational model or a model of leadership and increased sociopolitical involvement, it clearly pertains to local groupings of communal identity. In an increasingly globalized and globalizing world, however, the distinction between *umma* and *jamā'a* is blurred by diasporic activity, telecommunications, and international travel. The increasing globalization of the world has resulted in a vast and interconnected dispersal of diverse cultural identities and patterns resulting in "distanciated communities," translocal collectives of individuals for whom physical location is neither static nor prohibitively constraining. The vast and complex networks of international and translocal affiliation among seemingly disparate and distanced groups of Muslims calls into question the notion of local Muslim communities that are somehow not influenced and imbedded in a larger, more global context at the same time as it calls into question a global *umma* that is somehow not determined, at least in part, by the virtual presence and influence of more local communities. Technological progress alongside the increased frequency of intercommunal encounters, however, does not collapse the distinction between *umma* and *jamā'a*; rather, it highlights the perennial complexity, heterogeneity, and interpenetrating nature of community and communal identity.

See also brotherhoods; caliph, caliphate; fundamentalism; globalization; government; nationalism; nation-state; Pan-Islamism

Further Reading

Mohammed Ayoob, *The Many Faces of Political Islam: Religion and Politics in the Muslim World*, 2008; Nazih N. Ayubi, *Political Islam: Religion and Politics in the Arab World*, 1991; Patricia Crone, *God's Rule: Government and Islam*, 2004; Ross E. Dunn, *Resistance in the Desert: Moroccan Responses to French Imperialism 1881–1912*, 1977; Ahmet Karamustafa, "Community," in *Key Themes for the Study of Islam*, edited by Jamal J. Elias, 2010; Peter Mandaville, *Global Political Islam*, 2007; Idem, *Transnational Muslim Politics: Reimagining the Umma*, 2003; W. Montgomery Watt, *Muhammad at Medina*, 1981.

J. C. ARSENAULT

Companions of the Prophet

The Companions of the Prophet Muhammad have been a source of religious inspiration and divisive controversy in the Islamic community since its origins. The Arabic terms *aṣḥāb rasūl Allāh* and *ṣaḥāba*, meaning "companions," signify the collectivity of men and women who met the Prophet Muhammad during his mission (ca. 610–32), embraced Islam, and remained Muslim until they died. While there is widespread agreement among nearly all Muslims over the political activities of the Companions, Sunnis and Shi'is remain deeply split over the religious authority of these individuals.

The political activities of the Companions can be classified into four historical phases. The first phase lasted for the time of Muhammad's mission, when the Companions served as the Prophet's supporters, soldiers, and commanders of raids in which he was not present. The two great categories of Companions are the emigrants (*muhājirūn*), who converted to Islam in Mecca prior to the hijra (emigration) of 622, and the helpers (*anṣār*) of Yathrib (Medina), whose invitation to Muhammad and conversion to Islam led to the foundation of the Muslim political community (*umma*). Muslim historians have preserved the names and tribal affiliations of most of the emigrants and helpers, whereas information about the thousands of Companions who joined Islam in the later years of Muhammad's mission is far more circumscribed.

The second phase of the Companions' political activities dates from the death of Muhammad until the assassination of the third caliph, 'Uthman b. 'Affan (d. 656). This age witnessed the Muslim conquests of Syria, Palestine, Egypt, Iraq, and Persia. The caliphs Abu Bakr (r. 632–34), 'Umar b. al-Khattab (r. 634–44), and 'Uthman b. 'Affan (r. 644–56) all hailed from the prestigious class of emigrant Companions, as did some of their military commanders, such as Abu 'Ubayda b. al-Jarrah (d. 639) in Syria, Sa'd b. Abi Waqqas (d. 675) in central Iraq, and Abu Musa al-Ash'ari (d. 672) in southern Iraq. 'Umar and Abu 'Ubayda played a crucial role in securing Abu Bakr's political dominance over the helpers, a contingent of whom initially sought to elect a leader from among themselves to govern their affairs. Abu Bakr's firm insistence on there being only one supreme leader of the Muslim community from the tribe of Quraysh long remained a central principle of Sunni political theory. 'Umar's deathbed appointment of six emigrants to a consultative council (*shūrā*) to elect his successor has been seen by many Muslim reformers in the modern period as an early example of "democracy."

The third phase of the Companions' political activities dates from the assassination of 'Uthman in 656 until the assassination of 'Ali b. Abi Talib in 661. The first Muslim civil war (*fitna*) erupted in the wake of 'Uthman's death. Some Companions, such as Sa'd b. Abi Waqqas and 'Umar's son 'Abdallah (d. 693), remained neutral during this conflict, but most of the Companions who were living at this time supported either the caliph 'Ali (who was also an emigrant) or his adversaries. These adversaries included one of the Prophet's wives, 'A'isha (d. 678), who, along with the emigrants Talha b. 'Ubaydallah (d. 656) and Zubayr b. 'Awwam (d. 656), set out for Basra with an army and were vanquished by 'Ali and his allies at the Battle of the Camel. 'Ali's camp included his sons Hasan (d. 669) and Husayn (d. 680), his cousin 'Abdallah b. 'Abbas (d. ca. 686), and the venerable emigrant 'Ammar b. Yasir (d. 657). His primary rivals after the Battle of the Camel were Mu'awiya b. Abi Sufyan (d. 680), governor of Syria, and the latter's advisor, 'Amr b. al-'As (d. 671). Both men were Companions who had converted to Islam late in the Prophet's career, and Mu'awiya's father, Abu Sufyan (d. ca. 653), had actually led the Meccan opposition to Muhammad until he surrendered his city to the Muslim army in 630. According to the contemporary scholar Fu'ad Jabali, 'Ali had the allegiance of at least 120 Companions, Mu'awiya was supported by at least 31 Companions, and 7 Companions remained neutral during the conflict that lasted from the battle of Siffin (657) until 'Ali was killed by a Muslim rebel (661).

The final phase of the Companions' political activity lasted from the triumph of Mu'awiya until the end of the Second Civil War. Mu'awiya made peace with 'Ali's son (and the Prophet's grandson) Hasan shortly after 'Ali's assassination, and most Companions appear to have devoted their twilight years to teaching Islamic practices during Mu'awiya's largely peaceful reign (661–80). However, two Companions who were children during Muhammad's mission, Muhammad's grandson Husayn b. 'Ali and Zubayr's son, 'Abdallah, raised revolts as soon as Mu'awiya died and his son Yazid (r. 680–84) became caliph. Husayn's revolt was crushed in Karbala, Iraq, in 680, but 'Abdallah b. al-Zubayr managed, with the help of his brother Mus'ab in Iraq, to establish a caliphate from his base in Mecca that administered a significant portion of the Islamic empire. Ibn al-Zubayr's caliphate was terminated by the Umayyad caliph 'Abd al-Malik b. Marwan (r. 685–705) in 692. With the death of Abu al-Tufayl 'Amir b. Wathila, a strong supporter of the political claims of 'Ali and his descendants, around 718 in Mecca, the Companions as a class of Muslims ceased to exist.

From their inceptions, the two largest sects of Islam, Sunnis and Imami (or Twelver) Shi'is, have differed sharply over the religious authority of the Companions. Since the ninth century, Sunnis have insisted that all the Companions were authoritative and that none of the individuals involved in the civil wars was guilty of sin. They also professed that the historical order of the first four caliphs, to whom they affixed the honorific "Rightly Guided," reflects their respective merits. Thus Abu Bakr was the greatest Companion, followed by 'Umar, then 'Uthman, and in fourth place, 'Ali. According to one popular report attributed to the Prophet, ten Companions were promised paradise: the first four caliphs, Talha, Zubayr, Sa'd b. Abi Waqqas, Abu 'Ubayda, 'Abd al-Rahman b. 'Awf (d. 652), and Sa'id b. Zayd (d. ca. 670).

The Imami Shi'is believe that the Prophet Muhammad clearly designated 'Ali as his political successor after the "Farewell Pilgrimage" in the final year of his life at a location called Ghadir Khumm, a pool or marsh located midway between Mecca and Medina. Since

the overwhelming majority of the Companions immediately gave their oath of allegiance (*bay'a*) to Abu Bakr, the Imami Shi'is consider them to have disobeyed the messenger of God and, according to some books, to have become non-Muslims. Thus a tiny number of Companions—Salman al-Farisi (d. ca. 656), Abu Dharr al-Ghifari (d. ca. 652), al-Miqdad b. al-Aswad (d. 654), and 'Ali's sons Hasan and Husayn—were recognized by Imami Shi'is as pious Muslims, while all the remaining Companions, especially Abu Bakr, 'Umar, 'Uthman, Mu'awiya, and 'Amr b. al-'As, were subjected to derision and, occasionally, cursing. These contrasting views of the Companions' religious authority were the primary religious sources of friction between Sunnis and Shi'is in Pakistan, Iraq, Lebanon, Bahrain, and Saudi Arabia.

See also Abu Bakr (ca. 573–634); 'A'isha (ca. 614–78); 'Ali b. Abi Talib (ca. 599–661); caliph, caliphate; consultation; Hasan b. 'Ali (ca. 624–70); Husayn b. 'Ali (626–80); Karbala; Mu'awiya I (602–80); oath of allegiance; Rightly Guided Caliphate (632–61); Sunnism; 'Umar b. al-Khattab (ca. 580–644); 'Uthman b. 'Affan (ca. 579–656)

Further Reading

Fred McGraw Donner, *The Early Islamic Conquests*, 1981; Fu'ad Jabali, *The Companions of the Prophet: A Study of Geographical Distribution and Political Alignments*, 2003; Etan Kohlberg, "Some Imami Shi'i Views of the Sahaba," *Jerusalem Studies in Arabic and Islam* 5 (1984); Idem, "Some Zaydi Views on the Companions of the Prophet," *Bulletin of the School of Oriental and African Studies* 39, no. 1 (1976); Martin Lings, *Muhammad: His Life Based on the Earliest Sources*, 1983; Scott C. Lucas, *Constructive Critics, Hadith Literature, and the Articulation of Sunni Islam*, 2004.

SCOTT C. LUCAS

consensus

Consensus (*ijmā'*), a technical term of Islamic jurisprudence, refers to the unanimous agreement of qualified jurists on a particular legal issue, the third of the four principal "sources" of Islamic law after the Qur'an and the sunna and preceding either *qiyās* (legal analogy) or *ijtihād* (exhaustive investigation of the bases of a legal ruling), according to most Sunni authorities. Twelver and Zaydi Shi'is also accept the principle. Unlike the Qur'an and sunna, consensus is not a text from which law derives but a sanctioning device that guarantees the infallibility of the ruling subject to agreement, rendering it binding and theoretically removing it from the purview of subsequent challenge and review. Already by the early ninth century, legal theorists recognized consensus as a fundamental principle of legal hermeneutics: both Shafi'i (d. 820) and Abu 'Ubayd al-Qasim b. Sallam (d. 838–39) discussed it. The Mu'tazili theologian Nazzam (d. 835–45) defined consensus as any opinion of which the truth has been incontrovertibly established, a view that suggests a reaction to the argument that consensus is a binding proof (*ḥujja*). Ja'far b. Harb (d. 850), another Mu'tazili, wrote a monograph on consensus. Consensus became a standard chapter in manuals of jurisprudence (*uṣūl al-fiqh*) by the late ninth century, as is evident from the extant references to the manuals of Dawud b. 'Ali b. Khalaf al-Isfahani (d. 884), his son Muhammad b. Dawud (d. 910), and Muhammad b. Jarir al-Tabari (d. 923).

According to the classical theorists, the principle of consensus cannot be founded on reason because Jews, Christians, and other groups, despite their large numbers, agree on errors; mere agreement of a particular religious community, even other monotheists, does not guarantee truth. The probative nature of consensus is a special quality of the Muslim community conferred by divine grace, and proof of it must be provided by revelation. Among the most common texts cited as proof of the principle is the famous hadith report, "My community will never agree on an error." In theory, consensus must be based on evidence, and even if the evidence is not known, it is assumed to have existed in the past. Objections in the classical sources question the ability to know that a consensus exists, suggesting that some scholars might remain silent, withholding their opinions out of fear or intimidation, yet the majority of Sunni jurists do not admit that this invalidates the authority (*ḥujjīyya*) of consensus.

Consensus is an important locus for defining the limits of acceptable religious interpretation and the boundaries of the interpretive community. According to some theorists, including Shafi'i, consensus is of two main types: general consensus on matters such as the number of daily prayers or the obligation to perform the pilgrimage, in which the entire community participates, and scholarly consensus, or the agreement of jurists on more arcane legal issues. The latter is the type discussed in manuals of Islamic jurisprudence; this consensus is not the vox populi of Islamic societies but is more akin to scholarly consensus in a particular field of inquiry, such as astronomy or medicine.

Consensus, along with the institution of the legal *madhhab* (school of law), worked to control religious discourse and restrict religious authority to scholars who had been trained as jurists. Adherents of the Maliki legal *madhhab* held that *ijmā' ahl al-madīna*, the consensus of the scholars of Medina, was a binding authority, apparently on the grounds that the Medinan authorities preserved the traditions of the Prophet better than jurists elsewhere, but adherents of other Islamic legal traditions regularly rejected this position. The opinions of laymen were excluded from consideration, but so too were the opinions of authorities who were not trained jurists, including theologians, hadith experts, caliphs, and other rulers. The vehicle by which this act of exclusion was carried out was the institution of the legal *madhhabs*, which were established in the course of the ninth and tenth centuries. After that period, no scholar could voice opinions on Islamic law with authority unless he belonged to one of the accepted legal *madhhabs*. Tabari famously excluded Ahmad b. Hanbal (d. 855) from his historical survey of Islamic legal opinions, *Ikhtilaf al-Fuqaha'* (The differing legal opinions of the jurists), on the grounds that he was merely a

hadith scholar and not a jurist. The caliphs, who in an earlier period had been able to set precedent and change Islamic law of their own accord, were no longer granted the authority to do so. In addition, the theologians were denied consideration on the grounds that they lacked proper legal training. This effectively turned the table on the Mu'tazilis, who had, in concert with the Abbasid caliphs, conducted an inquisition in the early ninth century to impose their views, including the doctrine that the Qur'an is created instead of eternal, on all prominent scholars. The Sunni jurists also rejected participation of the Shi'is and Kharijis, arguing that their legal traditions were not historically valid. To work outside the legal *madhhabs* and to espouse opinions that were not represented within those traditions was to violate consensus (*mukhālafat al-ijmā'*) or to deviate therefrom (*al-khurūj 'an al-ijmā'*), and whoever did so willfully was denounced as an unbeliever. By the mid-tenth century, groups threatened with exclusion from the consensus of the jurists reacted to the pressure to conform by affiliating with a particular legal *madhhab*. Ash'ari theologians most often affiliated with the Shafi'is and Mu'tazili theologians with the Hanafis. Similarly, Shi'is and Kharijis sometimes chose affiliation with a Sunni legal *madhhab* in order to participate in authoritative religious discourse. The Twelver Shi'is affiliated first with the Zahiri *madhhab*, then with the Shafi'is, while the Zaydi Shi'is associated primarily with the Hanafis. Both the Twelvers and the Zaydis, however, would go on to claim that, since their legal traditions were as historically valid as those of the Sunnis and since the Sunnis' definitions of consensus and their proof texts logically referred to them, their opinions should be considered in consensus as well.

The question of whose opinions counted for consensus defined the structure of the interpretive community. Debate on legal issues is based on the content of fatwas, or legal responsa, rather than the verdicts of judges. Though jurists were theoretically independent and equal and consensus was described as the end result of free battle of fatwas, in many Islamic societies there was a recognized hierarchy of authority among the jurists. Sayf al-Din al-Amidi (d. 1233), for example, refers to the senior jurists, whose opinions carry authority and thus are able to establish consensus, as *ahl al-ḥall wa-l-'aqd* (the people of binding and loosing), borrowing a term that originally referred to those who chose a new caliph. Kamal al-Din Muhammad b. Humam (d. 1457) refers to "greater jurists" (*akābir*), who voice opinions on pressing issues, part of the process of reaching consensus, and "lesser jurists" (*aṣāghir*), who do not speak out on such issues but follow the greater jurists instead. The debate between these prominent jurists effectively settled new questions such as the legal status of opium, hashish, coffee, and tobacco or the legality of in vitro fertilization or cloning. Some theorists held that it was necessary for the entire generation of jurists who had formed a consensus to die out in order for the consensus to be recognized because one of them might change his mind before he died.

The establishment of a consensus on a particular point of law was usually negative and retroactive: consensus existed when there was an absence of conflicting opinion (*khilāf*), and many jurists would say that they knew of no dissenting opinion on an issue rather than claiming direct knowledge of a consensus. In addition, works on the disputed points of law were quite common, and the study of these issues formed the higher of two stages in advanced legal study, the first of which was devoted to the study of the standard legal positions (*madhhab*) of the tradition of legal study to which one adhered. Nevertheless, important works on the points of consensus included *al-Ijma'* (Consensus) by Abu Bakr Muhammad b. Ibrahim b. al-Naysaburi (d. 921), *Maratib al-Ijma'* (The degrees of consensus) by Ibn Hazm (d. 1064), and *Naqd Maratib al-Ijma'* (Refutation of the degrees of consensus) by Ibn Taymiyya (d. 1328). In a sense, *ijmā'* and *khilāf* are two sides of the same coin: the dissenting opinions of jurists whose opinions are taken into account in consensus are also considered valid contributions to legal debate. *Ijmā'* and *khilāf* together represent precedent: the historical record of opinions that must be taken into account by later jurists in arriving at an independent ruling. A description of the levels of consensus by Fakhr al-Islam al-Bazdawi (d. 1089) emphasizes this historical aspect. He distinguishes the consensus of the Prophet's Companions, claiming that it is as strong as the Qur'an or a report attested by multiple chains of transmission (*khabar mutawātir*); the consensus of those after the Companions, which is of the same level of reliability as a well-known hadith report (*ḥadith mashhūr*); and a consensus that comes into being after dispute, the validity of which is comparable to a hadith report attested through a solitary chain of transmission. For this reason, knowledge of the points of consensus and dissent is often cited in lists of the requirements for *ijtihād*, or the ability to derive legal rulings through independent effort.

Consensus has binding authority, and a ruling sanctioned by consensus is understood to be an infallible representation of the divine law. In addition, many theorists hold that, if historical debate reveals two authoritative conflicting opinions on an issue, it is not permissible to adopt a third opinion. This appears to limit inquiry severely and dictate strict adherence to a traditional corpus of legal rulings. In practice, however, it was possible for jurists to propose new rulings by distinguishing the issue at hand from that which had been debated earlier or by showing that the earlier claims of consensus were not actually valid. The claim of consensus has often been used as a rhetorical device in legal debate, sometimes by authorities on both sides of a question and even when the ruling championed is arguably an innovation outside the traditional array of possible opinions. In the modern period, reformers found consensus a hindrance, since classical jurisprudence seems to prevent the origination of new rulings for old questions. Reformers such as Muhammad 'Abduh (d. 1905) argued that consensus should be based on rational inquiry and therefore should be subject to revision and change with the changing circumstances of Islamic societies. Modern theorists have also argued that the circle of interpreters whose opinions should be taken into consideration should be widened to include experts in many fields, weakening the jurists' claimed monopoly on authoritative religious discourse.

See also *ijtihād* and *taqlīd*; jurisprudence; shari'a

Further Reading

Wael B. Hallaq, *Islamic Legal Theory: An Introduction to Sunni Uṣūl al-Fiqh*, 1998; George Makdisi, *The Rise of Colleges*, 1981; Devin J. Stewart, *Islamic Legal Orthodoxy*, 1998; Bernard Weiss, *The Spirit of Islamic Law*, 1998.

DEVIN J. STEWART

constitutionalism

In the most general sense, constitutionalism is the legal regulation of political power, which includes the delimitation of the rightful acquisition, use, and distribution of legitimate political authority and the regulation of relationships among holders of political power and authority and their subjects. Thus while in contemporary parlance to speak of "constitutionalism," Islamic or otherwise, may signify substantive commitments to limited political authority, the regular rotation of power, and the rights of citizens, in this entry the term refers more generally to all thought on public law.

In the pre-Ottoman tradition, constitutional ideas were expressed in debates over the (1) rightful claims to the caliphate; (2) classical rules on the status and qualifications of rulers, succession, rebellion, and political unity; and (3) the functions of government. These debates revealed classical Islamic views on the core issues of constitutionalism: rightful authority, the rightful use of authority, divisions of authority, and limitations on authority.

Doctrines of Rightful Claims to the Caliphate

The early consensus held the caliph (or imam) himself as crucial to salvation because he gave the community legal status and guided it. The Muslim community was thus regarded as a vehicle of salvation. The assassination of the third caliph ('Uthman b. 'Affan) in 656 raised for the first time the question of whether 'Uthman had been an imam of guidance or of error. If he had been an imam of guidance, then his successor, 'Ali b. Abi Talib (r. 656–61), would be a usurper, and the community following him would be considered unbelievers. If he was an imam of error, then he had forfeited the caliphate, rendering 'Ali a legitimate imam. These questions were never resolved to the satisfaction of all Muslims.

In the long run, the basic divide was between those who held doctrines of inheritance (legitimism) and those who held doctrines of merit. Hybrid doctrines involved restricting the election of the most meritorious to a particular family or tribe, whether the Prophet's tribe (the Quraysh) at large or his own descendants (*ahl al-bayt*).

The Umayyads (661–750) grounded their right to rule in the legitimacy of 'Uthman and their right to avenge their kin's death. Their rule represented a restoration of the practice of selection through tribal council (*shūrā*) of the best man among the Quraysh. They gave two justifications for their return to dynastic succession: (1) each ruler was asserted to be in fact a man of unsurpassed merit, indeed, the best man of his age, and (2) their successful acquisition and retention of power was said to suggest both this merit and God's will. Thus they were "God's vicegerents" (*khalīfat Allāh*), a politicization of the prevailing deterministic theology.

The Shi'is ('Alids) grounded right government in right lineage, specifically the house of the Prophet through 'Ali and his wife Fatima. That the 'Alids were to become *the* Shi'is and *the* party of opposition and protest emerged only after the Abbasids established themselves as a dynasty from a different branch of the Prophet's Hashimi clan. Under the Umayyads, "Hashimi Shi'ism" was the term for the general opposition based on the popularity of the Prophet's wider clan. After the Abbasid revolution (749–50), the opposition was known as 'Alid Shi'ism, which asserted that 'Ali was designated caliph already by the Prophet. This doctrine is called *rafḍ*, or "rejection" (i.e., of the first three caliphs as usurpers of 'Ali's right). Their line ended at 12 imams after the Abbasids successfully excluded them politically.

The Abbasids (750–1258) grounded right government in right lineage, specifically the house of the Prophet through his uncle 'Abbas. Early on in their reign they circulated stories of a designation from 'Ali to the Abbasids or, alternatively, of the bequeathal of the imamate from the Prophet to 'Abbas. This, incidentally, also implied a doctrine of *rafḍ* (rejection of the first three caliphs). They gradually reformulated a doctrine that recognized Abu Bakr and 'Umar al-Khattab and then even 'Uthman and 'Ali, resulting in the commonly known four Rightly Guided Caliphs thesis. The only stable position from beginning to end was that they were members of the Prophet's family (*ahl al-bayt*) who had rendered themselves deserving of the imamate over all other kinsmen of the Prophet by deposing the Umayyads.

The Kharijis were a group of 'Ali's supporters in the war against 'Uthman's kin who assassinated 'Ali for his willingness to subject the quarrel to arbitration. Their doctrine of legitimate rule was a radically meritocratic one. Anyone (famously, "even an Ethiopian [freed] slave") could be the imam, with no descent criterion whatsoever. They imposed strict election conditions, and some even held that the imam must be elected unanimously by all Muslims. However, the caliph was required to rule Islamically; otherwise he could be deposed and killed by the community. Some (the same group that insisted on unanimous election) claimed not only that the caliphate was not necessary but also that it had never existed.

From the beginning of the civil wars, there were those who stuck to communal unity and refused to form separatist communities under present or future imams even though they might regard the present caliph as sinful. Around the ninth and tenth centuries, they became "Sunnis." They declared the caliphate elective *within the Quraysh* to legitimate both the Umayyads and the Abbasids while distinguishing themselves from Shi'i hereditary succession. Communal unity, however, was more important to them than right government, and the community was formed by the guidance left by the Prophet (through the hadith), not by any imam of the day. Sinful imams were to be endured and passively resisted, not openly rebelled against.

The Classical Sunni Rules

Once the caliph was "the deputy of the Prophet" (not of God) and came to symbolize religious and political *unity*, not religious doctrinal authority, and the scholars appointed themselves as the guardians of religious truth, it was important to specify a set of rules (*aḥkām*) for legitimate political rule. This is the true "constitutional" heritage of classical Islam: that the Islamic polity was a community of law and that the determination of the law was in the hands of the scholars, not the rulers.

The caliph was supposed to be from the Quraysh, but this was flexible. He had to be free of physical and mental handicaps and had to be a man of probity (*'adāla*), piety (*wara'*), and significant religious legal knowledge (*ijtihād*), with a talent for governance and warfare. Ideally, he was supposed to be the most meritorious man of his time.

The Sunni scholars spoke of "election," but by this they meant simply that the caliph was selected by "the community" in some way, as opposed to the imamate having an inherent, transcendent personal quality, as the Shi'is believed. In the Sunni view, no one was born an imam; one had to be chosen by someone else (an existing caliph, a group of select notables ["the people who loosen and bind"], or later, from the tenth century on, even a "warlord" [*dhū al-shawka*]) and be recognized through the oath of allegiance (*bay'a*).

How imperfect could a caliph be and still be the caliph? He certainly could not leave Islam or suffer serious physical or mental disabilities. The real question related to when the caliph lost his "probity," both personally and as a ruler. The basic answer was that while immorality (*fisq*) disqualified a candidate for election, it did not automatically make him subject to removal. Removing him could be done only through civil war, which was a much worse source of disruption, disorder, bloodshed, and corruption for the "people of (the Prophet's) authoritative practice and communal unity" (*ahl al-sunna wa-l-jamā'a*). This, perhaps, was the single great lacuna in the basic Sunni "constitutionalism" described earlier and what prevented Sunnism from developing constitutionalism proper.

Of course, the diminished role and status of the caliph allowed this pragmatic view: he simply didn't matter enough to risk civil war. The idea that the community (in the form of religious scholars, perhaps) should take an active role in deposing an unjust ruler was hardly rare. Thus the following positions could all be found: (1) the ruler must be obeyed and tolerated; (2) rebels are to be fought but pardoned; (3) rulers can be deposed, but we do not have precise rules on how it is to be done and on what cost. On the other hand, there was a certain sympathy for rebels (*bughāt*) who revolted (*khurūj*) in great enough numbers (*shawka*) and with a religious "interpretation" (*ta'wīl*). They were to be treated leniently afterward and not held responsible for destroyed lives and property. "Bear the ruler but spare the rebel" encapsulates the position. The Sunni position was not Hobbesian (might makes right) or absolutist. In fact, though the Sunni scholars valued stability and legal order above all else, the state per se was not the highest object of loyalty, and the state had no monopoly on religious or moral interpretation. Both of these, loyalty and religious interpretation, belonged to the community. The community and the practice of Islamic interpretation was the essential, transcendent, necessary reality. Thus rebels could be pardoned both because the pardon contributed to reconciliation and unity and because the scholars might be able to understand the reasons for the rebellion. And, of course, rebels who won would then be accepted and obeyed. (The concept of "moral luck" is also at work here: rebels who won and imposed a more pious order could in fact be lionized.) This is evidence of tensions—but not outright contradictions—in Sunni thought between obedience, order, and stability on the one hand and piety, justice, and "commanding right and forbidding wrong" on the other.

Mawardi (d. 1058) began the trend of recognizing those who usurped power in the provinces (*imārat al-istīlā'*). The idea in doing so was to keep both the fictional unity of the *umma* or *jamā'a* and the continuity of legal order intact. These ideas were developed by Mawardi's contemporary Juwayni (d. 1085) who argued that the caliphate or imamate existed to keep the people together on a shared basis of Islamic law, which itself required not only legitimacy but also power and competence. Everything else, such as Qurashi descent, was dispensable. Juwayni's solution to the Sunni scholars' dilemma of prohibiting rebellion but also wanting actual coercive power to be in the hands of the caliph was to say that a warlord could not only usurp power but also take the next step of seizing the caliphate. In effect, he wanted to make the real power lie in the hands of the caliph, whether that was the "sultan" of the time or even the "minister" (*wazīr*; e.g., a figure like Nizam al-Mulk). This was a proposal to secularize the caliphate. If actual power was already in the hands of warlords, why keep a spare figure who has neither power nor religious authority? Juwayni thought it better to induce the actual power to assume religious and symbolic legitimacy. Juwayni's student, Ghazali (d. 1111), advocated the opposite solution. Whereas Juwayni seemed to want an effective ruler, Ghazali wanted a legitimate imam. For Ghazali, the legitimacy of the legal order and public sphere (judges, marriages, deputies) all depended on their being appointed by a legitimate imam. Perhaps in response to the Isma'ilis' claims to live under a true imam of guidance, Ghazali seems to have felt that the Sunnis needed a "real imam" who represented genuine Islamic learning or to argue that *ijtihād* was not a requirement of the imam, who existed solely to validate communal Islamic life. He thus seemed to believe that without somehow showing the present imam to be legitimate the community would lose its public sphere. What this involved is not finding the man who would be a legitimate imam, or giving the imamate to the sultan of the day, but to keep redefining the role and qualifications of the imam so that the existing one would be legitimate. Thus Ghazali preferred to recognize the secular power of the Turkish sultans to the extent that their power was what *identified* the caliph (by formally acknowledging him and symbolically offering him their allegiance), while his reciprocal recognition legitimated them. If the secular ruler supplied the power, the caliph supplied

the moral purpose for which power was to be used. One needed a ruler (power) to acquire a ruler (authority). The idea was thus to be realistic about the emergence of actual military power but also to not lose hope about the possibility of taming this power, of convincing it that it served a higher moral purpose.

The Functions of Government

The jurists expressed their views of the limits on the use of power largely through discussions of the ruler's obligations. Those obligations were divided into *Shar'ī duties* (those prescribed by the religious law) and *non-Shar'ī duties* (those tasks that were recommended or beneficial but not mandatory).

Shar'ī *Duties*

Validation of the community. Flexibility on this issue became the hallmark of Sunnism. Activist groups like the Zaydis and Kharijis did not flourish, while the Imami Shi'is became quietist.

Validation of public worship. The Muslim holy day of Friday was to be marked by a communal prayer that a just imam was supposed to validate. Thus groups that believe the present ruler was unjust would hold that there could be no Friday communal prayer. The Sunnis, however, held that Friday prayers (as well as the payment of the zakat and *ṣadaqa* religious alms taxes) could continue despite an immoral imam or later in the absence of any imam whatsoever. These matters were subject to sectarian disagreements.

Execution of the law. This was the essence of the imam's functions and the one from which all others derived. It consisted of establishing courts and appointing judges and local governors. With the weakening and then occasional absence of such an imam, the jurists debated whether the scholars themselves could establish and validate legal authority. It was Ghazali's position that the entire edifice of Muslim society required legitimate appointment by an imam, but this position did not withstand the events of history. The essence of Sunni constitutionalism was that the law that the imam or ruler was meant to implement was not his to determine. At most, the legal political order could tolerate the ruler's discretionary authority granted and circumscribed by the law.

Execution of the ḥudūd *punishments*. The *ḥudūd* were a set of limited punishments for the worst moral offenses, such as murder, adultery, false accusation, highway robbery, theft, wine-drinking, and (sometimes) apostasy and blasphemy. The corporal nature of the punishments involved lashing, amputation, or death. Originally, the application of these punishments was the monopoly of the imam, since they addressed violations of the "rights of God," not private or civil offenses. Some scholars (across various sects) argued that only jurists and judges could order the punishments; others argued that certain punishments, including those for adultery, could be administered in private. Such debates addressed various aims and imperatives: not only obeying God, upholding morality, and creating an Islamic order but also preserving social peace and stability, avoiding anarchism, and respecting the privacy and presumptive innocence of Muslims.

Jihad. There were two kinds of jihad: defensive and missionary. The protection of Islamic lands against an outside invasion did not require the presence or permission of an imam. The use of force to bring Islamic law to unbelievers, however, could be done only with the leadership of a rightful imam. Thus Shi'is who held the imam to be absent also held that the duty of jihad had been suspended. Among the Sunnis, missionary jihad was a collective duty (*farḍ kifāya*) that the community had to discharge. Thus Sunni scholars willing to see the legal life of the community continue in the absence of a just ruler had the resources to see jihad as something the community could validate; it could not be suspended merely by the lack of a just ruler.

Commanding right and forbidding wrong. There was a general duty in Islam to "command the right and forbid the wrong"—that is, to promote morality as revealed in the law. The institution of the *ḥisba* was the expression of this. The imam was supposed to appoint a person to supervise the market and public morals (office holder: *muḥtasib*). Like jihad, this was a collective duty, although, also like jihad, there could be individual duties in connection with it. The ability of individual Muslims to take the enforcement of morality into their own hands is a matter of debate. Some scholars, seeing the capacity for anarchy and the violation of privacy, insisted that only public officials could enforce morality. Others held that self-help was permissible in the enforcement of morality; all Muslims were their brother's keepers, so to speak. (Ghazali wrote famously on this, and the Hanbali school, the descendants of the hadith scholars, were known for this view.) Wine bottles could be smashed, house parties could be crashed, and people could be flogged for illicit activities. This is the "pious zealotry" strain in Islamic political thought, which is in perpetual conflict with the "stability and social order" strain. The latter strain, in which rulers were to be endured without rebellion and the state enforced law and morality, was not in principle more tolerant of moral vice: morality could be enforced in principle, including by physical means, but there was merely a caution about who could do so and when.

Preservation of religion. This included promoting both orthodoxy and orthopraxy and is thus part of "commanding right and forbidding wrong." The ruler was supposed to take both positive steps to make sure right religion was represented and taught in his area of rule and also negative steps to deal with heterodoxy. The *muḥtasib* could check on beliefs propagated in public, test religious teachers, and correct false interpretations of doctrine. When people failed to correct their views, he could turn them over to the ruler for punishment. Here, private action (self-help) also surfaced: people could report on others and scholars were known to single out people for heterodoxy and even to organize mobs. Targets included Mu'tazilis, dualists (Manicheans), materialists, philosophers, Sufis, Shi'is, false prophets, deviant Qur'an reciters, and blasphemers.

Fiscal services and taxation. The imam was supposed to collect only three taxes: the poll tax on non-Muslim residents (the *jizya*), the land tax (*kharāj*, *'ushr*), and the tithe (zakat, *ṣadaqa*). Muslim conquerors used the poll tax and land tax to deal with immovable

war spoils (*fay'*): they left the land in the hands of the conquered subjects but extracted taxes for it, which were then distributed to the conquerors in the form of stipends. Eventually the taxes would be regarded as the collective property of all Muslims to be spent in the public interest. The imam was also entitled to a fifth (*khums*) of movable war spoils (*ghanīma*), which he was to use for the public interest, including poverty relief.

Non-Shar'ī Duties

The imam or other rulers were also expected or entitled to use public power to protect internal security, improve infrastructure (roads, bridges, inns, walls, and mosques), promote charity and social welfare, provide public medical services, and sponsor religious education. Many of these were provided by nonruling notables and others in addition to the state. Their provision varied greatly according to time and place.

See also authority; caliph, caliphate; governance; government; imamate; nation-state; Quraysh; republicanism

Further Reading

Khaled Abou El Fadl, "Political Crime in Islamic Jurisprudence and Western Legal History," *UC Davis Journal of International Law and Policy* 4, no. 1 (1998); Asma Afsaruddin, "The 'Islamic State': Genealogy, Facts, Myths," *Journal of Church and State* 48, no. 1 (2006); Patricia Crone, *God's Rule: Government and Islam: Six Centuries of Medieval Islamic Political Thought*, 2005; Wael Hallaq, *The Origins and Evolution of Islamic Law*, 2005; Sherman A. Jackson, *Islamic Law and the State: The Constitutional Jurisprudence of Shihab al-Din al-Qarafi*, 1996; Wilferd Madelung, *The Succession to Muhammad: A Study of the Early Caliphate*, 1998; Abu al-Hasan al-Mawardi, *The Ordinances of Government: A Translation of al-Aḥkām al-Sulṭāniyya w'al-Wilāyāt al-Dīniyya*, translated by Wafaa H. Wahba, 1996; Bernard Weiss, *The Spirit of Islamic Law*, 1998; Muhammad Qasim Zaman, "The Caliphs, the 'Ulama', and the Law: Defining the Role and Function of the Caliph in the Early 'Abbasid Period," *Islamic Law and Society* 4, no. 1 (1997).

ANDREW F. MARCH

Constitution of Medina

The so-called Constitution of Medina is the most significant surviving document from the time of the Prophet Muhammad; it is Muhammad's first legal document. Its two main versions are found in Muhammad's biography and in several other sources. In Muhammad's biography, it is placed among the events of the first year after the hijra, or emigration, of 622. The emigration brought Muhammad from his hometown of Mecca to Medina, a cluster of towns that, in the document, was still called Yathrib, after a town at the northwestern edge of the cluster. The term "constitution" is a misnomer, since the document deals with tribal matters such as warfare, blood money, the ransoming of captives, and war expenditures. Some clauses are enigmatic, presumably because their terminology reflects the little-known legal vocabulary of Medina.

Close scrutiny of the document reveals that it is not made up of several distinct documents, as some have argued, but is rather one document divided into two clearly defined sections. The first section includes the rights and duties of the *mu'minūn* (literally, "believers"). The singular form *mu'min* and the plural form *mu'minūn* appear almost 30 times in this section, hence it can be called the Treaty of the *Mu'minūn*. Nine groups participated in this section: the *muhājirūn*, or emigrants who came with Muhammad from Mecca, and eight groups belonging to the two main tribes of Medina: the Aws and Khazraj. Five of the eight groups belonged to the Khazraj and three to the Aws.

The second section includes the rights and duties of the *yahūd*, or the Jews, and their clients and can hence be called the Treaty of the Jews; it is a treaty of nonbelligerency and cooperation. The shift from the first section to the second one is clearly discernible: the latter begins with a clause addressed to the Jews that stipulates, "The Jews share expenditure with the *mu'minūn* as long as they are at war." The treaty of the Jews includes almost 40 clauses, some of which relate to "the people of this document"—namely, all of those listed in both sections.

In addition to *mu'minūn* and *yahūd*, the document refers to an obscure group, the *muslimūn*. They appear in the opening clause as a main party to the document that was concluded "between the *mu'minūn* and *muslimūn* from Quraysh and Yathrib." But unlike the *mu'minūn*, who are mentioned frequently, the *muslimūn* appear in only two clauses, both in the Treaty of the Jews. The first clause is at the beginning of a list of Jewish participants and relates to the Yahud Bani 'Awf (the Jews of Banu 'Awf). It stipulates that the *yahūd* have their *dīn*, or religion, while the *muslimūn* have theirs. The *muslimūn* in question either were part of the Yahud Bani 'Awf or were associated with them in one way or another. Both *yahūd* and *muslimūn* probably were found among the other Jewish groups listed later in the document, which would account for the appearance of the *muslimūn* in the opening clause as a main party. The second clause that includes the *muslimūn* stipulates that the *yahūd* and the *muslimūn* bear their (war) expenses separately.

Six out of the nine groups listed in the treaty of the Jews had counterparts among the groups listed in the treaty of the *mu'minūn*—for example, Banu 'Awf and Yahud Bani 'Awf. This leaves three groups out of the nine that had no such counterparts. One of the three, Tha'laba, was Jewish and should be identified with a Jewish tribe of the same name. The other two, Jafna and Shutayba, were non-Jewish. The Jafna and Shutabya belonged to the Ghassan (an alliance of tribal groups from the tribe of Azd), and the same is probably true of the Jewish Tha'laba. The tribal alliance of Ghassan was for decades allied with Byzantium, but the political implications

of the Ghassani descent of these groups are as yet unknown. As for the three main Jewish tribes of Medina—Nadir, Qurayza, and Qaynuqa'—they do not appear in the document simply because they were not part of it. Muhammad's nonbelligerency treaties with them were far more basic than this document.

At the beginning of the document, the *mu'minūn* and *muslimūn* from the Quraysh and Yathrib are declared an *umma*, or a community: a group of mutual solidarity. This was not an empty declaration and had clear legal implications. For example, a *mu'min* must not kill another *mu'min* in retaliation for a kafir, or a nonbeliever. In other words, a *mu'min* could not exact vengeance for, say, his brother who was a nonbeliever and had been killed by another *mu'min*. The new *umma* superseded the old tribal solidarity and severed the links between those who had followed Muhammad and those who had not.

The term *umma* also occurs at the beginning of the treaty of the Jews: the earlier-mentioned Yahud Bani 'Awf—probably the leading Jewish group in this document—are declared an *umma* alongside the *umma* of the *mu'minūn*, or perhaps even part of that *umma*. Both possibilities seem to be unlikely—after all, the Treaty of the Jews was fundamentally different from the Treaty of the *Mu'minūn*. Hence an admittedly rare variant reading of the word *umma* has to be adopted, namely *a.m.n* (with the added character *nūn*; there are several possible vocalizations of *a.m.n*, but they do not affect the meaning). The previously mentioned Jewish group—and all the other groups in the Treaty of the Jews that were entitled to the same rights—received a guarantee of security from the *mu'minūn*.

The document severely destabilized the internal tribal system of Medina, as well as the intertribal alliances on which Medinan politics were founded. This allowed Muhammad to introduce a new political order that separated the *mu'minūn*, who had followed him, from the families and tribes that had not. When hostilities with the Jews broke out, they could no longer rely on their old alliances, since the tribes that were allied with them were split between tribe members that became *mu'minūn* and were loyal to Muhammad and other tribe members that were not yet *mu'minūn*.

In the premodern period, the Constitution of Medina became one of the bases—along with other episodes in the life of the Prophet and early Islamic history portrayed in hadith reports, biographical sources, and historical accounts—for the elaboration of *siyar* (the Islamic law governing war and relations with non-Muslim powers). Some modern Muslim thinkers have considered the document a precursor of modern state constitutions and have presented it as the ideal model for an Islamic state. In addition, it is often referred to as a historical landmark in modern discussions of international law and international treaties from an Islamic perspective. Nineteenth-century reformers such as Muhammad 'Abduh saw in the document an authentic precedent for modifying and removing some of the traditional Islamic legal restrictions placed on Jews and Christians living under Muslim rule, and it continues to be cited frequently in contemporary debates on tolerance, religious pluralism, and relations among Muslims, Christians, and Jews, both within the Muslim world and outside it.

See also alliances; Mecca and Medina; Muhammad (570–632)

Further Reading

Moshe Gil, "The Constitution of Medina: A Reconsideration," *Israel Oriental Studies* 4 (1974); Michael Lecker, *The Constitution of Medina: Muḥammad's First Legal Document*, 2004; R. B. Serjeant, "The *Sunnah Jāmi'ah*, Pacts with the Yathrib Jews, and the *Taḥrīm* of Yathrib: Analysis and Translation of the Documents Comprised in the So-Called 'Constitution of Medina,'" *Bulletin of the School of Oriental and African Studies* 41 (1978); Arent Jan Wensinck, *Muhammad and the Jews of Medina* [*Mohammed en de Joden te Medina*], 1908, with an excursus by Julius Wellhausen, translated and edited by W. H. Behn, 1975.

MICHAEL LECKER

consultation

The idea of mutual consultation, or *shūrā* (also *mushāwara, mashwara, tashāwur*, or *istishāra* in Arabic, i.e., conferring with other individuals or a group), which is referred to in the Qur'an (42:38; cf. 2:233, 3:159) and the sunna as an aid to decision making in both private and public affairs, has become the core value of a newly propagated Islamic system with the rise of Islamic fundamentalism. In Islamic history, the term *shūrā* is especially connected with the small council of prominent early Muslims, which selected 'Uthman b. 'Affan as the third caliph. In the following centuries, the notion of consultation remained attractive for dissidents (e.g., Kharijis), who used it to question the legitimacy of the reigning dynasty of the day. Likewise, the motif of advice appears in several obviously nonauthentic reports on the Rightly Guided Caliphs, who supposedly held councils frequently concerning important matters of the state. In Arabic-Islamic literature, particularly in books on etiquette, the merits of consultation were praised and arbitrary personal rule condemned. Nevertheless, *shūrā* neither played a central role in premodern Muslim reasoning on the Islamic state nor was ever institutionalized prior to the 19th century. Occasionally, judges or rulers applied *shūrā* in order to distribute responsibility in sensitive cases. As in pre-Islamic tribal society, however, the consultation circles in the premodern era remained ad hoc assemblies and exclusive bodies.

In the 19th century, reformers began to seize upon the ideal of consultative government as a way of arguing for the basic compatibility between Islam and constitutionalism. Intensive research on *shūrā* since the 1970s did not result in an innovative approach to deliberative democracy. Generally, the debate remained confined to a retrospective discourse of Islamic jurisprudence, focusing on the

same questions as centuries before: What is the meaning of *shūrā* and its derivatives? What is the scope and necessity of its application? Is consultation obligatory or only recommended? Are the results of the consultative process binding or nonbinding? Who are the councilors, and who should select or elect them? On which issues is consultation allowed? When a concrete political system had to be identified with *shūrā*, both religious and secular authors either adopted a conventional Western model or defined Islamic systems only in the negative (in other words, in contrast to autocracy or theocracy). As a result, theories of an Islamic democracy have offered reformulations of Western perceptions in an Islamic idiom rather than a real alternative.

Notwithstanding the great spectrum of theories, four tendencies can be distinguished in the contemporary debate on *shūrā* and democracy. Representatives of the first tendency, radical Islamists such as Sayyid Qutb and his adherents, see the superiority of an Islamic system based on shari'a and *shūrā*; democracy as well as political parties and the sovereign electorate are condemned as alien ideas, rooted in evil and unbelief. The opposite view, held by 'Allal al-Fasi and Khalid Muhammad Khalid, among others, equates *shūrā* with a kind of original or authentic Arabic-Islamic democracy. A third view is held by the majority of pragmatic or moderate Islamists. They have embraced the rhetoric and politics of democratization and have adopted several aspects of the reformist discourse. Apart from consultation, consensus and *ijtihād* (individual reasoning with particular reference to the so-called public benefit) are crucial concepts in their articulation of an Islamic democracy. *Shūrā* is often considered a comprehensive principle not limited to the political sphere but equally desirable in other realms, including familial matters. The specific political order should accord with the requirements of the times, provided it remains within a framework of Islamic principles. Critical issues in conceptions, such as those of the major ideologists of the Muslim Brotherhood, are the implications of this particular view for the legal status of both women and religious minorities and the degree to which tolerance and pluralism are accepted. Insisting on the centrality of a fixed shari'a without defining its exact meaning, maintaining a traditionalist gender discourse, restricting religious freedom to monotheist religions, and expressing disdain toward "alien" values such as individualism, secularism, materialism, and atheism call into question their adherence to the concept of liberal democracy. All in all, proponents of this tendency seem to envisage the Islamization and moralization of democracy.

The fourth tendency is represented by various secular scholars and intellectuals, among them Mohamed Talbi (b. 1921) or Mohammed 'Abed al-Jabri (1935–2010). Having realized the necessity of a culturally embedded democracy, they perceive *shūrā* as an essential principle derived from the Qur'an and sunna and consider it one of the universal principles that all humans know through their innate sense. The secular modernists discern in *shūrā* not an early democracy awaiting contemporary resurrection but rather some general human truth or, as Talbi puts it, an antityrannical ethos. Since human institutions and organizational forms are always time-bound and limited, the actual task is to work out a concept of government in the Islamic territory that would realize the higher ideal, whether one calls it democracy or *shūrā*.

Because of the Imami Shi'i doctrine of the imamate, *shūrā* has never played a key role in Shi'i political thought, not even in modern times.

In practice, the idea of consultation has proven to be compatible with various political systems, whether monarchical or republican, with nominated or selected members, and with assemblies of different kinds.

See also advice; caliph, caliphate; constitutionalism; democracy; human rights; pluralism and tolerance; representation; Rightly Guided Caliphate (632–61); succession

Further Reading

Roswitha Badry, "Marja'iyya and Shūrā," in *The Twelver Shia in Modern Times: Religious Culture & Political History*, edited by Rainer Brunner and Werner Ende, 2001; Eadem, "'Democracy' versus 'Shura-cracy': Failures and Chances of a Discourse and Its Counter-Discourse," in *30 Years of Arabic and Islamic Studies in Bulgaria*, edited by Tzvetan Theophanov, Penka Samsareva, Yordan Peev, and Pavel Pavlovitch, 2008; John Cooper, Ronald L. Nettler, and Mohamed Mahmoud, eds., *Islam and Modernity: Muslim Intellectuals Respond*, 1998; Larbi Sadiki, *The Search for Arab Democracy: Discourses and Counter-Discourses*, 2004.

ROSWITHA BADRY

contracts

'Aqd, conventionally understood as "contract," may be more precisely understood as the confirmation of an obligation or undertaking (*Lisan al-'Arab*, Ibn Manzur). The Qur'an refers to *'aqd* in numerous verses (e.g., see 5:1, *al-Ma'ida*), as well as the closely related term, *'ahd* (e.g., see 23:8, *al-Mu'minun*). The Qur'an describes faithfulness to such undertakings as a fundamental attribute of believers. Although it is generically used in Islamic jurisprudence to refer to all sorts of contracts, here we are specifically concerned with its usage in Islamic political thought. Not only is the concept of a contract foundational to the idea of the caliphate, but it is equally constitutive of other political offices within Islamic constitutional law. It also represents the basic framework by which Muslim jurists understand international law.

The contract of the imamate (unlike other generic contracts in Islamic law such as that of a sale or marriage, for example) is obligatory according to the vast majority of premodern Sunni authorities. Muslim theologians have disputed whether the obligatory character of the imamate is a rational obligation or one derived from

revelation. Mawardi (d. 1058), a prominent Shafi'i jurist and author of *al-Ahkam al-Sultaniyya* (The ordinances of government), reports both positions, and the prominent jurist, theologian, and mystic, Ghazali (d. 1111), even as he claims a revelatory source—consensus—as the origin of the obligation, nevertheless grounds that consensus in practical reason: human life, including religion, cannot flourish in the absence of a state (*al-Iqtisad fi al-I'tiqad*). Accordingly, despite the religious connotations of the imamate, the institution in the writings of the jurists takes on a largely functional character intended to further the secular welfare of the community. This functional character is reflected clearly (1) in the statement of the jurists that the caliphate, as an institution, involves the claims of man as well as the claims of God and (2) by the representational character of the caliphate.

Like any other contract, the contract of the caliphate involves two parties. On one side is the community of Muslims (*al-muslimīn* or *'āmmat al-muslimīn*), represented by a group of electors ("those who loosen and bind," *ahl al-ḥall wa-l-'aqd*), and on the other is the candidate(s). The electors are to select the fittest candidate as imam or caliph, considering both the legal requirements for the office and the wishes of the community. They then offer the office to the successful candidate who only becomes caliph upon his acceptance of the offer. Alternatively, the sitting caliph can designate a successor via the device of *'ahd*. This power is consistent with the representative character of the contract insofar as Islamic law treats the caliph, when appointing a successor, as one acting on behalf of the community, not for himself. Accordingly, although the caliph has the power to appoint a successor, he lacks the power to dismiss him without cause. Offices of the caliphate can be divided into those that are deemed to be mere delegates of the ruler, such as viziers—in which case their jurisdiction terminates upon the death or dismissal of the ruler—or offices whose incumbents enjoin tenure independent of the will of the ruler and can only be dismissed for legal cause, such as local rulers (*umarā'*), if they had been appointed by the caliph.

Just as the relationship between the Muslim community and its ruler is specified by the terms of a ruler's contract, so too is the relationship between the ruler and the other offices of the caliphate determined by a contract of appointment (*'aqd al-tawliya*, *'aqd al-taqlīd*). The contract of appointment would specify the extent of the office holder's powers and the jurisdiction over which the office holder could exercise that power.

The Islamic state's relationship with non-Muslims was also structured contractually. A non-Muslim could reside temporarily in an Islamic state pursuant to a temporary grant of security (*amān* or *'ahd*), or permanently pursuant to a grant of permanent protection (*dhimma*). The chief difference between the two was in the depth of solidarity created between the non-Muslim and the Islamic state as a result of the particular relationship. Because of the temporary nature of the residence of a non-Muslim in Islamic territory pursuant to an *amān* or an *'ahd*, he was not under an obligation to pay the *jizya* tax, a per capita levy payable by a non-Muslim permanently residing in Islamic territory. Conversely, the non-Muslim who was a permanent resident in an Islamic state was obliged to pay this tax as part of the relationship of permanent protection. In exchange, however, the Islamic state was obliged to afford him military protection against all aggressors, whereas it was obliged with respect to those non-Muslims only temporarily living in Islamic territory to protect them against aggression from Muslims. Likewise, a non-Muslim permanent resident of an Islamic state had a greater obligation to obey the substantive rules of Islamic law than did a non-Muslim only temporarily residing in the territory of an Islamic state. Although the contractual relationship between Muslims and non-Muslims permanently residing in an Islamic state is not described as involving claims of God, nevertheless the contract of *dhimma* must include certain mandatory provisions. Accordingly, a contract of *dhimma*, from the perspective of Islamic law, includes mandatory provisions as well as permissive provisions that are subject to negotiation between the Islamic state and the non-Muslim. A breach of one or more of the mandatory provisions of the contract of *dhimma* by a *dhimmī* constitutes a repudiation of the contract of protection. Mandatory provisions of the contract of *dhimma* include, for example, prohibitions against cursing the Prophet Muhammad, disparaging Islam, or fornicating with a Muslim woman. An example of a permissive provision would be the rule requiring non-Muslims to wear distinctive dress. Because such a term is not mandatory, as a matter of legal theory not all contracts of *dhimma* need include it.

Finally, the relationship of Muslims to non-Islamic states was also deemed to be contractual via the device of the *amān*. The question of the permissibility for a Muslim to take up permanent residence in a non-Islamic state was often considered in light of the terms of the *amān* that were being offered to the Muslim. If, for example, he would be permitted to manifest his religion freely, there would be a greater chance that Muslim jurists would deem such residence to be permissible.

Despite the ambiguities inherent in the notion of the manifestation of religion, the general rule was that Muslims are bound by their obligations and that if a Muslim wished to renounce protection granted to him by a non-Muslim power or its agent, he had to renounce it openly. Likewise, if a non-Muslim, whether temporarily or permanently in an Islamic state, repudiated his contract, he was not to be killed or fought merely for that repudiation; rather, he was to be deported safely to the frontier. Non-Muslims resident in the Islamic state could be killed or fought on the territory of the Islamic state only if they aided non-Muslim invaders in making war on the Muslims.

See also abodes of Islam, war, and truce; caliph, caliphate; government; imamate; minorities; taxation

Further Reading

Malcolm Kerr, *Islamic Reform: The Political and Legal Theories of Muhammad 'Abduh and Rashid Rida*, 1966; Andrew March, *Islam and Liberal Citizenship: The Search for an Overlapping Consensus*, 2009.

MOHAMMAD FADEL

conversion

"Conversion" is a word fraught with imprecision. The psychologist William James described the conversion experiences of Christian enthusiasts listening to evangelical preachers at camp meetings. Arthur Darby Nock recounted the conversion experiences of figures like the Christian St. Augustine and the Isis-worshipping protagonist of Apuleius's novel *The Golden Ass*. General histories of Europe attribute early conversion to Christianity to the underground activities of Roman slaves, persecution or forced conversion by rulers, the semilegendary activities of apostles and missionaries, and the outcomes of military campaigns.

The conceptual tools derived from these approaches do not greatly help the historian of Islamic conversion. Though revivalist preaching, which can inspire zealous commitments to the faith in certain individuals who are already Muslim, is currently common in some Muslim communities, this is not usually termed "conversion." The Arabic word *da'wa*, or "call," covers both revivalism and proselytization, but it is more strongly associated with the former activity. Nor does premodern Muslim literature contain much in the way of personal testimony about individual paths to Islam à la St. Augustine. Semilegendary missionaries do receive some attention after the 13th-century rise of Sufi brotherhoods, but rarely before. And evidence of conversions achieved by conquest or a ruler's fiat is similarly rare.

Within the Muslim tradition, the earliest history of the community yields conflicting paradigms: 'Umar b. al-Khattab, overcome with anger toward Muhammad, was instantly won over when he heard the recitation of verses from the Qur'an's *Surat Taha*. Conversion here is ecstatic. The Aws and Khazraj tribes of Medina proclaimed themselves Muslims in a treaty concluded before most of them had ever seen or heard the Prophet. Conversion here is collective without significant individual preparation. Tribes that had fallen away from allegiance to the Muslim leadership in Medina reentered the community, albeit under a cloud, after being defeated in war by a Muslim army after the Wars of Apostasy (*ḥurūb al-ridda*). Conversion here reflects coercion, though only from a state of apostasy. Outside of Arabia, individual conversion narratives are rare, and the verb *aslama* in histories of the early conquests is sometimes ambiguous since it can mean both "surrender" and "become Muslim."

Over time, conversion conventions of both a substantive and procedural nature arose. In the first two centuries, individuals are often described as converting "at the hands of" (*fī yaday*) another Muslim. But this usage wanes in the early Abbasid period. The *shahāda*, or the profession that there is no god but God and that Muhammad is the messenger of God, emerges in many written works as a verbal marker of conversion, though often with the untestable proviso that it be enunciated in the heart and not just with the lips. New Muslims often have religiously distinctive names conferred on them, and by the Mamluk period, they are commonly designated as "son of 'Abdallah." Occasional reports from the Abbasid period well into Ottoman times depict the convert being given religiously appropriate clothing or money for acquiring such clothing. Finally, a male convert may be required to undergo circumcision, though this is rarely mentioned in accounts of collective conversion.

However, none of these concomitants of conversion, including circumcision, has a strong evidentiary base dating back to the pre-Abbasid era. There is no regularly attested equivalent to Christian baptism as an indicator of conversion to Islam. Consequently, historians have speculated widely about the rate and causes of the spread of Islam. The main schools of thought on conversion have been the following: forced conversion following defeat in battle, or "conversion by the sword"; conversion to avoid paying the *jizya* tax imposed by Muslim rulers on "peoples of the book," the scripture-based faith communities also known as *dhimmī*s; conversion caused by information-based logarithmic growth following the pattern attested in many cases of technological diffusion; group or tribal conversion symbolized by the words or actions of a group or tribal leader; conversion for clear-cut economic advantage; conversion to escape from slavery; and conversion as a result of gradual growth in response to the preaching or pious example of Sufis, merchants, or both.

Central to all of these approaches has been the assumption that being a Muslim is clearly distinguishable from belonging to some other faith community. This has constrained discussion of middle positions between Islam and other faiths. Yet many groups generally classified, or self-classified, as Muslim have syncretic characteristics that link them closely to other religious traditions. In the early centuries, sects based in part on Muslim practices or scriptural example (e.g., the Barghawata and the followers of Ha-Mim in North Africa or the followers of Muqanna' in northeastern Iran) were clearly identified as threats to the true Muslim faith and forcefully suppressed. In later times, however, groups of questionable Muslim identity (e.g., the Druze in greater Syria, the Alevis and Bektashis in Anatolia, the Baha'is in Iran, the Ahmadis in Pakistan, the Nation of Islam in the United States) established themselves successfully. Sufism also became a way station between "normative" Islam and local spiritual traditions in many parts of the Muslim world to such a degree that the Dutch colonial administration in the Dutch East Indies (today Indonesia) designated most of the country's inhabitants as "nominal Muslims."

Substantive intellectual or behavioral reasons for individuals or groups converting to Islam are often advanced. These include the simplicity of Islamic monotheism, as opposed to Trinitarian Christianity; the practice of polygamy, which is alleged to appeal to societies that already indulge in plural marriages; an intrinsic superiority of monotheism over polytheism; a supposed fraternal Muslim blindness to distinctions of race and color; and a presumed Muslim opposition to global domination by modern Western political and cultural powers. These allegations are only rarely backed up with empirical evidence. Thus conversion to Islam, both generally and locally, remains hard to define, hard to measure, and hard to explain.

See also apostasy; *ijtihād* and *taqlīd*; minorities; patronage; People of the Book

Further Reading

W. Thomas Arnold, *The Preaching of Islam: A History of the Propagation of the Muslim Faith*, 1913; Monique Bernards and John Nawas, eds., *Patronate and Patronage in Early Classical Islam*, 2005; Richard W. Bulliet, *Conversion to Islam in the Medieval Period: An Essay in Quantitative History*, 1979; Idem, *Cotton, Climate, and Camels in Early Islamic Iran: A Moment in World History*, 2009; Daniel C. Dennett Jr., *Conversion and the Poll Tax in Early Islam*, 1950; Devin Deweese, *Islamization and Native Religion in the Golden Horde: Baba Tükles and Conversion to Islam in Historical and Epic Tradition*, 1994; Richard M. Eaton, *The Rise of Islam and the Bengal Frontier, 1204–1760*, 1993; Michael Gervers and Ramzi Jibran Bikhazi, eds., *Conversion and Continuity: Indigenous Christian Communities in Islamic Lands, Eighth to Eighteenth Centuries*, 1990; Nehemia Levtzion, ed., *Conversion to Islam*, 1979; Anton Minkov, *Conversion to Islam in the Balkans: Kisve Bahasi Petitions and Ottoman Social Life, 1670–1730*, 2004.

RICHARD W. BULLIET

coup d'état

During the 1950s and 1960s, numerous Muslim countries saw secret cliques of officers successfully conspire to overthrow the incumbent civilian government. In Egypt, for example, the Free Officers abrogated the monarchy after their 1952 coup. Gamal Abdel Nasser (1918–70) then advanced to the leadership position, replacing the original figurehead of the coup, General Muhammad Naguib. Nasser did not rely on the army simply to seize power; he inserted loyal military personnel at all levels of the state apparatus to consolidate his control. In contrast, military rule in Syria proved more difficult to institutionalize, with three successive coups in 1949 alone; civilian government was reestablished in 1954 when a military faction overthrew the authoritarian military ruler. Syrian officers opposed to Nasser later forced an end to Syria's political union with Egypt in 1961, while the Arab Socialist Ba'th Party installed itself as Syria's new ruler in the coup of March 8, 1963; factional struggles resulted in additional coups in 1966 and 1970. Iraq witnessed its first coup in 1936, but the monarchy was not permanently overthrown until July 14, 1958. A 1963 coup by the Iraqi Ba'th Party was reversed the same year; the Ba'th Party seized power more decisively in July 1968. In Iran, royalist forces supported by the United States overthrew nationalist prime minister Mohammad Mossadegh (1882–1967) in the coup of 1953. Coups also occurred in Libya (1969), Yemen (1955, 1962), Turkey (1960, 1971, and 1980), and Pakistan (1956, 1977, and 1999).

In the Arab Middle East, this wave of military coups is perhaps best understood as the reassertion of local political forces following a period of more or less direct European rule. Upon independence, political life was typically dominated by traditional elites whose positions were bound up in the distorted patterns of socioeconomic order inherited from colonialism. Unwilling to accommodate increasingly vocal demands from below and unable to respond effectively to the creation of the State of Israel in 1948, the old elites lost all credibility and were unable to contain the mounting pressure for change. As military service had long been disdained by these elites, the army provided a unique channel for the mobilization of political actors from traditionally marginalized social strata.

Western scholarship has passed through several stages in its efforts to explain what appears to be a recurrent tendency of Muslim countries to produce military rule. Early work highlights the long tradition of military government in Islam, as exemplified by the Mamluk dynasties. However, deterministic claims regarding political culture have difficulty explaining cases where civilian regimes remain in power. Other social scientists note the institutional fragility of postcolonial Muslim states and conclude that the army's political strength was positive. Military regimes generally advocated radical socioeconomic reform, leading some scholars to identify them as prime agents of modernization. The decline in military interventionism since the 1960s has been explained by the notion of "coup proofing," which proposes that the expanding size and complexity of the military apparatus has made it virtually impossible for conspirators to turn the whole organization against the chain of command.

While much academic attention has been devoted to military rule, far less has been given to the question of whether it is appropriate to call military seizures of power in the Arab-Muslim world "coups." The conceptual distinction between "coup" and "revolution" may be evident in English, but it is less clear-cut in Arabic. Since the radicalization of politics in the 1960s under the influence of Nasser, *thawra* has been used to imply the depth of social and political change associated with "revolution." (Prior to this, its meaning was closer to "revolt.") In contrast, the change of personnel involved in a coup is dismissed as a "mere" *inqilāb*. Yet in the 1940s and 1950s, the meaning of the words was almost the reverse. Officers who carried out Iraq's first military coup in 1936 called it an *inqilāb*; *thawra* still had a strong negative connotation in contemporary writings. Early Ba'thist texts describe the party as "revolutionary"—*inqilābī*, not *thawrī*. Not until 1963 did Ba'thists adopt the Nasserist tradition of calling their coups *thawra*.

The evolving lexicon of military politics highlights the extent to which social phenomena are constructed by linguistic convention. The distinction between coup and revolution hinges on the presence or absence of mass participation when the new regime comes to power but says little about the policies, programs, or practices of those regimes. Drawing a line between coup and revolution on these grounds arguably expresses a normative preference for popular participation in politics more than it determines a difference of sociological kind.

See also Ba'th Party; colonialism; dissent, opposition, resistance; military; quietism and activism; rebellion; revolutions

Further Reading

Ami Ayalon, "From *Fitna* to *Thawra*," *Studia Islamica* 66 (1987); Ofra Bengio, *Saddam's Word: Political Discourse in Iraq*, 1998; Manfred Halpern, *The Politics of Social Change in the Middle East and North Africa*, 1963; J. C. Hurewitz, *Middle East Politics: The Military Dimension*, 1969; James T. Quinlivan, "Coup-Proofing: Its Practice and Consequences in the Middle East," *International Security* 24, no. 2 (1999).

DANIEL NEEP

Crusades

The Crusades, as viewed by the West, were a series of at least eight military campaigns against the Muslims of Syria, Palestine, and Egypt. Their initial impetus was to protect the holy places of the Christian Near East, but especially Jerusalem. The Crusader presence in the Middle East lasted from 1098 to 1291.

In the 20th century, the Arab world "rediscovered" the Crusades, viewing them as symbols for current political problems. Some saw the medieval Crusading states as "protocolonies," the precursors of Napoleon in Egypt, the British Mandate for Palestine, and the state of Israel. The Crusades marked the initial phase of Western imperialism in the region (*isti'mār mubakkar*, or premature colonialism). Arab nationalist leaders reminded their people of the glorious Muslim victories over the Crusaders (the Franks), and although the most famous Muslim generals—Saladin (a Kurd) and Baybars (a Turk)—were not ethnically Arab, the rhetoric used in political speeches by Middle Eastern leaders allowed modern Arabs to claim these medieval military triumphs as their own. Several Arab leaders, such as Gamal Abdel Nasser, Hafez al-Assad, and Saddam Hussein, aspired to become "the second Saladin," the charismatic figure who would one day reunite the Middle East. Saladin's conquest of Jerusalem in 1187 has clear resonance for modern Palestinians.

For other Muslim spokesmen, the Crusades have been seen not in national but in religious terms, as part of a continuing conflict between Christianity and Islam. The leading figure of the Muslim Brotherhood, Sayyid Qutb (executed by Nasser in 1966), referred in his *Fi Zilal al-Qur'an* (In the shade of the Qur'an) to the perennial struggle between Muslims and "polytheists" and spoke of "international Crusaderism," arguing that the blood of the Crusaders flowed through the veins of all Westerners.

The core meaning of the word "crusade" is the Latin word "crux" (cross), and the modern Arabic phrase for crusade—*al-ḥurūb al-ṣalībiyya* (the cross wars)—reflects this inherent religious focus. Indeed, in contemporary times hostility toward American hegemony is often expressed in religious terms. As Osama bin Laden put it in an interview with Aljazeera, "This battle is not between al-Qaeda and the U.S. This is a battle of Muslims against global Crusaders"; his fatwa (religious opinion) of February 23, 1998, "Jihad against Jews and Crusaders," mentions a Crusader-Zionist alliance. He likened American military bases in Saudi Arabia, the birthplace of Islam, to Crusader armies spreading like locusts, and he said that their banner was the cross. The involvement of Jews in his anti-Crusader rhetoric is thus contradictory.

Thousands of miles from the geographical sites of the medieval Crusades, the concept of *Perang Salib* (The War of the Cross) is now used in Islamist circles in Indonesia, the world's most populous Islamic country, to denote what is perceived as wicked Christian aggression against Muslims, especially after 9/11. As in the speeches of Bin Laden found on the Internet, Indonesian Islamist discourse links the concept of "crusade" with the words "Zionists" and "Jews" and presents a global conspiracy of Christian Crusaders and Zionist Jews bent on destroying Islam. After President George W. Bush's visit to Indonesia in 2006, he was labeled "the Supreme Commander of the War of the Cross" by one of the leaders of the Islamist organization Ahl al-Sunna wa-l-Jama'a (The People of Tradition and the Community).

See also Ibn Taymiyya (1263–1328); Jerusalem; Mamluks (1250–1517); Mongols; Saladin (1138–1193)

Further Reading

Osama bin Laden, "Jihad against Jews and Crusaders," http://www.fas.org/irp/world/para/docs/980223-fatwa.htm; FBIS Report, *Compilation of Usama Bin Ladin Statements 1994–January 2004*, 2004, http://www.fas.org/irp/world/para/ubl-fbis.pdf; Carole Hillenbrand, *The Crusades: Islamic Perspectives*, 1999; Sayyid Qutb, "Crusaderism" in *Fi zilal al-Qur'an*, 1992; Mark Woodward, "Tropes of the Crusades in Indonesian Muslim Discourse," *Contemporary Islam* 4, no. 3 (2010).

CAROLE HILLENBRAND

culture

A term used in everyday speech as well as an ambiguous category of academic inquiry, "culture" has a history of contested meanings and usages. The term has been and continues to be used, in a humanistic sense, to refer to any complex of intellectual or aesthetic expression and learned behavior emerging from elite social circles as products of leisure and expressions of identity. Culture, in this sense, refers to a body of refined knowledge and cultivated education based largely on a sense of tradition and canon. Thus one can speak of the culture of the Abbasid court, for example, and intend by this phrase the generation, acquisition, cultivation, inheritance, and perpetuation of a system of learned behaviors (i.e., etiquette, ceremonies, hunting, protocol, patronage, etc.) as well as the products that participate

in providing material expression for the very identities constructed through these processes of behavioral cultivation (i.e., patronizing the arts—music, calligraphy, painting, poetry, prose, dance, architecture, fashion, etc.). Often implicit in this conception of culture is the assumption of refinement and progress or increasing excellence; culture, so understood, is an ascendant vector of elite intellectual and aesthetic improvement.

Expanding this rather narrow conception of culture to include a vertical or horizontally concentric spectrum, however, lends breadth and availability to the category. Instead of privileging the culture of the elite as the only "true" culture, a dichotomous model of culture—one that constructs and contrasts a spectrum of "high" and "low" cultures, elite and popular cultures, or cultures of the center and those of the periphery as analytical categories—permits a more socially inclusive and economically diverse model of that which constitutes culture and cultural activity. As a more inclusive approach, sensitive to the differences in the various sectors of a given society or social body, a dichotomous model provides a broader vantage point from which to observe the various expressions of cultural activity at the same time as it gives consideration to the way in which various communities and individuals interact within a larger social framework. Thus one can speak of cultural "contact" or "confluences" occurring between, among, and by means of the members of different social classes, people from unrelated language communities, or practitioners of contesting religious traditions, for example. The internal social divisions that separate high from low and elite from popular are typically intended, however, as value-free heuristic categories—helpful ways of providing a conceptual apparatus or framework for comparing what are actually porous, abstract categories.

More expansive, pluralistic, and relativistic models of culture(s) have emerged from the field of anthropology. Although the history of the culture concept in anthropology (and sociology) is long and complex, in general, anthropological models (i.e., those of Franz Boas, Leslie White, and Clifford Geertz) have tended to posit a holistic conception of culture. The practice in cultural anthropology is to observe distinct human societies and provide detailed descriptions of social phenomena. This is done in order to articulate the ways in which various social systems and networks of human communication and interaction form (and are reciprocally informed by) individual and communal identities. This holistic, pluralistic, and descriptive approach to human activity, while admitting the existence of multiple cultures and subcultures, employs the term "culture" to signify a total system of human action, interaction, and meaning. Thus the anthropological model acknowledges the wide array of different and diverse cultures in the world at the same time as it posits the total and holistic nature of each one. Conceptual categories such as tradition, custom, behavior, action, value, and symbol are important components in such anthropological approaches and have been employed differently in describing and defining cultures as complex, patterned wholes.

Due in part to the fact that the various social *processes* of human activity in the anthropological conception of culture can be articulated and objectified only in a descriptive and narrative language, the anthropological practice of carefully describing and interpreting each culture as a total system of human interaction necessarily reproduces that complex, patterned whole *as a text*. Moreover, in the work of White and Geertz, the entire anthropological enterprise is defined by a semiotic conception of culture. Culture is understood as a deeply symbolic and meaning-producing model of and for reality. As a corollary, culture is imagined and presented as a complete object possessing *meaning*. Consequently, culture, to be comprehensible, becomes that which is always in need of scholarly engagement and interpretation. The critical question then becomes, who has the authority to speak for and about a culture? Because the characteristics attributed to a cohesively identified and contoured culture are always presented by someone, to someone, and for someone, and always from a specific perspective not lacking in agenda or context, the authoritative position from which one can define and describe "culture" has come under scrutiny in postmodern and postcolonial studies of the culture concept.

Given the anthropological acknowledgment of global cultural diversity, the various cultures of the world can be thought of as complex wholes distinguished from one another by the differences observed from any positioned perspective. Deeply entrenched in, and defined by, the observation of differences, the category of culture has become an immediately available and instrumental category of identity construction. As such, it has been consciously employed to establish criteria of cultural inclusion and "purity" and to determine the boundaries of communal and nationalist affiliation. As a tool of identity politics and nationalist discourse, the culture concept has also been deployed as both a defensive and an offensive strategy in an effort to either justify the status quo or call it into question. These general observations describe just some of the political implications of the concept of culture in today's increasingly globalized world.

Finally, if culture is taken in an anthropological sense to mean a total complex of human activity and interaction, then recognizing religion as an integral element in the development of that total complex becomes a necessity. The historicist tendencies in some anthropological models of culture provide relevant insight into the study of Islam, especially as it relates to the concept of culture. Geertz's *Islam Observed*, for example, describes the differences and similarities between the Muslim cultures of Indonesia and Morocco and in so doing demonstrates how Islam, in a sense, is "mediated" differently in different locations and at different times. This serves to demonstrate how the radical diversity of the many particular local histories, customs, languages, cuisines, and family structures of nations or communities that are commonly identified as "Islamic" complicates any notion of a simple association or identification between religion and culture. Such a study calls into question the notion of a pristine or pure Islam that is somehow outside of temporal and terrestrial concerns and agency. At the same time, it places in relief the question of whether "Islam" is a useful organizing principle in the discussion of culture, especially where other more local or historically contingent and less abstract principles of

organizing observed phenomena might prove to be useful in the analysis of a culture.

See also Arab nationalism; community; custom; education; family; Ibn Khaldun (1332–1406); ideology; Mirrors for Princes; nationalism; Pan-Islamism; secularism; solidarity; tribalism; ʻulamaʼ; Westernization

Further Reading

Robert Borofsky et al., "When: A Conversation about Culture," *American Anthropologist* 103, no. 2 (2001); Michael Cooperson, "Culture," in *Key Themes for the Study of Islam*, edited by Jamal J. Elias, 2010; Clifford Geertz, *The Interpretation of Culture*, 1973; Idem, *Islam Observed*, 1971; Tomoko Masuzawa, "Culture," in *Critical Terms for Religious Studies*, edited by Mark C. Taylor, 1998; Marshall Sahlins, "Two or Three Things I Know about Culture," *The Journal of the Royal Anthropological Institute* 5, no. 3 (1999); Boaz Shoshan, "High Culture and Popular Culture in Medieval Islam," *Studia Islamica* 73 (1991); Bassam Tibi, *Islam between Culture and Politics*, 2nd ed., 2005; Raymond Williams, *Keywords: A Vocabulary of Culture and Society*, 1976.

J. C. ARSENAULT

custom

Custom served an important role as a social norm in pre-Islamic Arab society and thereafter in Muslim society, as it did in many ancient societies. Its application encompassed a wide variety of areas: economics, family, and ritual. In Islamic legal theory, formulated during the course of the eighth and ninth centuries, custom was recognized as a formal, valid source of law, as is the case in other legal systems, including Jewish and Roman law. Prominent questions concerning custom in the context of Islamic legal theory are the extent to which it conformed to the formal sources of Muslim law, the sources' proximity to a divine origin, and the means used to prove its existence.

In the Islamic legal tradition, sources of law are graded according to their degree of certainty and the weight given to the proofs of their divine origin. On the highest level stand the Qur'an and the sunna (oral reports concerning the words and deeds of the Prophet), officially recognized sources for scriptural proof texts (*naṣṣ*) with the status of divine revelation. On the next level are *ijmāʻ* (consensus) and *qiyās* (legal analogy), which do not have the same status as the written sources, being of a more technical nature and connected as they are with the exegesis of the jurists, yet they are still held to reflect divine will in determining human behavior. According to this theoretical model, custom lies outside the realm of divine revelation; recognition of custom (*ʻurf*) as an integral part of the legal system appears to contradict one of the mainstays of Islamic legal theory: the idea that law is of direct divine origin. Indeed, classical Islamic juridical theory does not recognize custom as a legal source, since it depended to a great extent on human social interaction, even though it was always ubiquitous in practice and deeply entrenched in all levels of society. Custom thus belongs to a number of supplemental sources of law or bases for legal interpretation that have been disputed and irregularly incorporated into Islamic jurisprudence, such as *istiḥsān* (juristic preference), *istiṣlāḥ* (consideration of a human interest), *sharʻ man qablanā* (the law of previous monotheistic religions), or *istiṣḥāb al-ḥāl* (presumed continuance of status quo ante). The decidedly textualist approach of Islamic jurisprudence militated against the uniform or easy acceptance of custom.

The jurists' exclusion of custom from the theoretical hermeneutics of Islamic law nevertheless did not affect its power in actuality. Custom was held to include both general custom (*ʻurf ʻāmm*) and local custom (*ʻurf khāṣṣ*), as well as customary definitions of words (*ʻurf qawlī*) and customary practices (*ʻurf fiʻlī*). Classical theoretical objections notwithstanding, custom was recognized by many jurists as important for the interpretation of specific terms, verbal agreements, and types and stipulations of transactions in particular local or social contexts. Customary rulings became extremely widespread, striking roots in various areas of the law and thereby threatening the integrity of theory. This development was not lost on legal thinkers who attempted to bridge the gap between theory and reality, where custom was widespread. These attempts, particularly those of the Hanafi legal scholars, are reflected in the juristic literature reflecting the efforts, at least from the early Middle Ages, to grant custom some sort of official status in the scale of legal sources. Striking testimony to this appears in the criticism regarding the definition of the sunna directed at the famous early figure Abu Yusuf (d. 798–99), a disciple of Abu Hanifa, by Sarakhsi (d. 1097) in his work *al-Mabsut* (The extensive treatise on law). With regard to the disputed permissibility of using weights and measures in commercial transactions, Abu Yusuf thought that in every case custom must be taken into consideration on its own merits. In other words, in a statement attributed to Abu Yusuf, "One should take custom into consideration in all things. For if it was [sold] by measure at a particular time or by weight at another time, [each particular situation] was in consideration of custom and not in consideration of a scriptural proof text from the Prophet." He thus holds that custom remains valid even when it contradicts a scriptural proof text—a position likewise affirmed by the Hanafi jurist Marghinani (d. 1192) in his work *al-Hidaya* (The guidance). Another testimony to the hermeneutical autonomy of custom is that of the judge Husayn al-Marwazi (d. 1070), who considered custom to be a fifth source of law along with the other four recognized legal sources. He wrote, "Resort to custom is one of the five foundations on which the law (*fiqh*) is built."

In accordance with modern legal theories, two elements underlie the rejection of custom, though they are not explicitly stated anywhere in Islamic legal literature. From the legal historical perspective, scholars recognize that the existence of custom per se is not sufficient reason for its integration into and enforcement as a legal norm. From the analytical perspective, the jurists and institutions such as courts lack the authority to grant certain customs the status

of validity. In classical Islamic legal theory, these two components exist alongside each other. The negation of the jurists' authority to recognize custom is indeed consistent with Islamic legal theory, which greatly restricts juristic involvement in the development of the law, limiting their authority to the role of interpreting or implementing the written sources—particularly of those laws incorporated in the Qur'an and the sunna.

The rejection of custom on the theoretical level, notwithstanding its acceptance in reality, was dealt with in four ways. First, during the formative period of Islamic law, the possibility still existed of incorporating custom into the sunna, which was in the process of crystallization into standard collections in the ninth and tenth centuries. At times, these incorporated legal norms, including customs, reflected current developments. Second, the widespread identification of custom with consensus (*ijmā'*), especially but not exclusively in Hanafi literature, at times obscured the boundary between these overlapping categories to such an extent that there was often no major difference between them. Third, custom was often seen as a dispositive condition whose legal validity was based on its acceptance by agreement of the parties involved. This view is found primarily in the literature of the Hanafi school and finds expression in the following formula and similar statements made in other contexts: "That which is known by custom is like that which is known by stipulation." Fourth, custom was often accepted in a substantive manner but by means of principles such as *maṣlaḥa* (public welfare) or *ḍarūra* (necessity or dire need), allowing rulings to be made in accordance with custom without recognizing it as an autonomous source. The latter three types belong to a later stage in legal history; they were adopted when the method of accepting custom by means of hadith reports had effectively closed with the canonization of the sunna and its organization into standard collections.

The absorption of custom by these means, which fit harmoniously into Islamic legal theory, worked as long as they existed as real options. Once these means were closed, however—particularly once the collections of the sunna had taken shape and when, later, it was no longer possible to identify custom with *ijmā'*—outstanding Hanafi legal theorists effected a dramatic hermeneutic turn with regard to custom. During the postclassical period, from the 16th century on, they came to present custom as an autonomous, formal legal source incorporated into the theoretical framework of Islamic jurisprudence (*uṣūl al-fiqh*). Thus, for example, Ibn Nujaym (d. 1563) admits the ubiquity of custom and its power to determine legal rules, writing, "Know that the consideration of custom and usage reappears frequently in law in many cases, so much so that the jurists have transformed it into a legal source, and they say in works devoted to jurisprudence, in the chapter on the abandonment of literal meaning: 'The literal meaning is abandoned on the basis of an indicator found through inferential methods of inquiry and in custom.'" Here, he was in effect following Abu Yusuf, the first jurist who attempted to view custom as an autonomous source. The same view was later taken up by Ibn 'Abidin (d. 1836), author of a brief work titled *Nashr al-'Arf fi Bina' Ba'd al-Ahkam 'ala al-'Urf* (The wafting of perfume, on some legal rulings based on custom), in which he states that custom has the power to overrule a scriptural text, thus establishing custom as a formal legal source.

At the end of this process, custom assumed a place even in the 19th-century Ottoman *Mecelle*, which recognized it in practice as a formal source. Even though the *Mecelle* was not a legal source, it reflected the change that had taken place in the status of custom in Islamic law, effectively putting an end to the explicit and implicit debates that had taken place among legal scholars regarding the status of custom as a source in Islamic legal hermeneutics.

See also consensus; *ijtihād* and *taqlīd*; jurisprudence; Ottomans (1299–1924); shari'a

Further Reading

Wael Hallaq, *Authority, Continuity and Change in Islamic Law*, 2001; G. Libson, "On the Development of Custom as a Source of Islamic Law," *ILS* 4 (1997); H. Toledano, *Judicial Practice and Family Law in Morocco*, 1981; A. L. Udovitch, "Islamic Law and the Social Context of Exchange in the Medieval Middle East," *History and Anthropology* 1 (1985).

GIDEON LIBSON

D

Dan Fodio, Usman (1754–1817)

'Uthman b. Muhammad b. 'Uthman b. Salih b. Fudi, known as Ibn Fudi, Usman dan Fodio, or the *shehu* (the Hausa term for shaykh), was a religious scholar and social reformer who led a jihad in Hausaland (northern Nigeria). His struggle led to the founding of the largest Islamic caliphate in 19th-century Africa, known as the Sokoto Caliphate or the Fulani Empire.

Born in Maratta in the Hausa city-state of Gobir in what is now northwestern Nigeria on December 15, 1754, dan Fodio belonged to a clan of Muslim Fulani scholars known as the Torodbe, who migrated in the 15th century from Futa Toro in the north to the town of Birni-N'Konni (on the border between Niger and Nigeria). The Fulani were an ethnic minority in Hausaland. Through their intellectual positions as teachers and scribes, Fulani scholars contributed to the spread of Islam in Hausaland. Although the authorities of Gobir officially accepted Islam, they remained uncommitted to strict Islamic rules, such as applying shari'a or condemning polytheism and pagan practices. Growing frustration among the Muslim community ultimately led to the emergence of an Islamic reform movement in the 18th century, which carried the support of revered Muslim scholars of the time.

When dan Fodio was a child, his family settled in Degel, where he would eventually start his activities. His early education included Arabic, memorization (*ḥifẓ*) of the Qur'an, Maliki jurisprudence, and Muslim traditions. His life was marked by the influence of his teacher, Jibril b. 'Umar, a prominent Sufi scholar who initiated dan Fodio into the Qadiri Sufi order. Sufism played a considerable role in dan Fodio's life and career. Mystic visions, such as the one dan Fodio experienced in 1794, convinced him of the mission he had been assigned and his duty to raise the sword against the enemies of Islam.

Dan Fodio started his activities in 1774 and 1775 as a wandering teacher and preacher, along with his son Muhammad Bello (d. 1837) and his brother 'Abdullahi dan Fodio (1766–1828). For a decade, dan Fodio's career would involve peaceful teachings about Islam and religious practices and the writing of poems calling people to Islam. At the time, his relationship with the Hausa authorities was amicable, and education was seen as the key instrument for a progressive and profound reform of society. His project had a distinctively practical dimension, which was not as prominent in previous local movements. A distinguishing feature of his approach was tolerance and nonconfrontation. Dan Fodio refused to declare apostates (pronounce *takfīr* against) people who failed to follow Islamic rulings out of ignorance. He denounced earlier reformers who condemned society, like his mentor, Jibril b. 'Umar, and strongly criticized the reformer 'Abd al-Mahalli, who took hasty recourse to armed confrontation with the Moroccan state.

Dan Fodio's writings dealt mostly with education until 1803, when the first mention of jihad was made in his work *Masa'il Muhimma* (Important matters). From 1803 to 1804, the resistance of the Hausa rulers to Muslim demands and their attacks on dan Fodio's community led to a change in method. Forced to emigrate, dan Fodio and his followers declared a jihad against the Hausa rulers in 1803.

In order to remain consistent with his earlier ideas, dan Fodio conceived of an original theory of *takfīr* by distinguishing between religious and political unbelief; political *takfīr* could be pronounced against rulers who did not follow the shari'a and against whom waging jihad was legitimate. These rulers were not accused of personal *takfīr* and remained within the realm of the Muslim community. After the fall of Gobir in 1808, conflict spread to the neighboring Hausa states. By 1808, all the Hausa states had been conquered, resulting in the establishment of a centralized Islamic state, the Sokoto Caliphate. Ruled by religious scholars and governed by shari'a, it took the Abbasid caliphate as a model. Dan Fodio was recognized as its first leader, with the title of Commander of the Faithful. In 1812, he divided the caliphate into two states to be ruled by his son Muhammad Bello and his brother 'Abdullahi. Dan Fodio retired from his political career in 1812 and devoted the rest of his life to writing and teaching Islam and Sufism. He died in Sokoto on April 20, 1817.

Dan Fodio wrote more than 100 scholarly works, which continue to be read and quoted today. He remains a respected figure in the history of West Africa. His successful jihad had a long-term impact on West African society and inspired a number of subsequent uprisings, including the jihad of Seku Amadu (1773–1845) and El-Hajj 'Umar ibn Sa'id Tall (1797–1864), who founded the Massina and Tukulor empires, respectively.

See also colonialism; Nigeria; revival and reform; shari'a; Sufism; West Africa

Further Reading

A.D.H. Bivar, "The Wathīqat Ahl Al-Sūdān: A Manifesto of the Fulani Jihād," *Journal of African History* 2, no. 2 (1961); Usman dan Fodio, *Bayān wujūb al-hijrah 'alā al-'ibād*, edited and translated by F. H. El-Masri, 1978; Idem, *Masā'il muhimma*. 180; Mervyn Hiskett, *The Sword of Truth: The Life and Times of the Shehu Usuman*

Dan Fodio, 1967, repr. 1973; H.A.S. Johnston, *The Fulani Empire of Sokoto*, 1967; Murray Last, *The Sokoto Caliphate*, 1967; Ibraheem Sulaiman, *A Revolution in History: The Jihad of Usman Dan Fodio*, 1986; Idem, *The Islamic State and the Challenge of History: Ideals, Policies, and Operation of the Sokoto Caliphate*, 1987.

NASSIMA NEGGAZ

Dawani, Jalal al-Din (1427–1502)

A major philosopher of the Timurid period, Jalal al-Din Dawani wrote a number of works on ethics and politics for his patrons, following the model of the *akhlāq* (ethics and statecraft) literature established by Nasir al-Din al-Tusi. Dawani studied with important philosophers in Shiraz, and early in his career he became a courtier to the Turkmen Qara Quyunlu rulers. Later he sought the patronage of various rulers in the turbulence of 15th-century Persia, writing books for the Aq Quyunlu ruler Uzun Hasan (d. 1478), the Timurid sultan Abu Sa'id (d. 1469), the Ottoman sultan Bayazid II (d. 1512), and Sultan Mahmud I of Gujarat (d. 1511). He served in major roles as the head of the religious establishment (*ṣadr*) under the Qara Quyunlu and as chief qadi (judge) of Fars under the Timurid sultan Ya'qub (d. 1490). Dawani engaged in polemics and scholarly debates with his major rivals in Shiraz, such as the philosophers Mir Sadr al-Din (d. 1497) and his son Mir Ghiyath al-Din Dashtaki (d. 1542); they were also rivals for patronage. The Dashtaki family later rose to prominence under the new Shi'i Safavid rulers, and the stigmatization and marginalization of Dawani might be due to their condemnation of him as a Sunni thinker. Dawani's views on the Safavids were ambiguous, and his death in 1502 before they conquered Shiraz prevented any disambiguation.

Dawani's political views are found primarily in the *Lawami' al-Ishraq fi Makarim al-Akhlaq* (Flashes of illumination on the excellence of conduct), popularly known as *Akhlaq-i Jalali* (The Jalalian ethics), written for Uzun Hasan, whom he describes in terms of the Sunni and Iranian consensus in medieval Islamic political thought as the "shadow of God on Earth" and as the caliph and successor to the Prophet. His Sunni political views are clear in the short work *'Arznama* (Testament), written for Uzun Hasan's son, Khalil, in 1478, and in his commentary on the creed of Muhammad b. Ahmad al-Nasafi and its supercommentary by 'Adud al-Din al-Iji written in 1499. However, before his death, and perhaps to prevent repercussions from the impending Safavid conquest of Shiraz, he wrote a short work, *Nur al-Hidaya* (The light of guidance), on a Shi'i conception of political authority while setting aside the more messianic claims of the Safavid shahs.

The *Akhlaq-i Jalali* was popular in the Safavid and Mughal periods and was the conduit for the dissemination of the ideas of Tusi in the *Akhlaq-i Nasiri* (*Nasirean Ethics*). The text differs little from Tusi's text: the section on moral psychology was omitted and more aphorisms were added in the final section from the Persian tradition as well as from Aristotle (including pseudo-Aristotelian sayings from works such as the *Liber de Pomo*, the alleged testament to Alexander). The main difference between his and Tusi's work (and this probably accounts for its greater dissemination and fame) is stylistic: Dawani's work became a model for Persian composition and was even used for training in epistolary writing in India and subsequently in Persia. Dawani also arguably practiced the role of the philosopher-ethicist-vizier in a more effective manner with a wider range of patrons than Tusi had done before him.

See also Timurids (1370–1506)

Further Reading

Muzaffar Alam, *The Languages of Political Islam in India*, 2004; Linda Darling, "Do Justice, Do Justice for That Is Paradise: Middle Eastern Advice for Indian Muslim Princes," *Comparative Studies of South Asia, Africa and the Middle East* 21, nos. 1–2 (2002); Jalal al-Din Dawani, *Akhlaq-i Jalali* [*The Practical Philosophy of the Muhammadan People*], 1839; Murtaza Yusufirad, *Andisha-yi Siyasi-yi Jalal al-Din Davānī*, 2008.

SAJJAD H. RIZVI

Delhi

Also known in the past as Dihli or Dilli and, in some medieval records, as Yoginipura, Delhi is the capital and third largest city of the Republic of India. It occupies a triangular area bounded on the west and south by a low-lying spur of the Aravalli mountains and on the east by the river Yamuna. The triangular riverine plain contains several settlements stretching from the prehistoric into the modern age.

Although the ancient history of Delhi is always linked with Indraprastha, the capital of the Pandavas in the Mahabharata epic (ca. 1500–1000 BCE), no archaeological trace of the city has been discovered. Instead a variety of smaller settlements attest to the occupation of the area from the fifth century BCE without leading to full scale urbanization until, at the earliest, the 11th and 12th centuries CE, when the Tomara and Chawhan chieftains established their relatively humble headquarters in the southern reaches of the Delhi plain.

It was not until the 1220s that Delhi emerged as the capital of a realm comprising much of North India. Its rise to political prominence coincided with Chingiz Khan's invasions of Transoxiana, eastern Iran, and Afghanistan and a vast influx of refugees into the subcontinent and Delhi. This conjuncture of events contributed to the reputation of the city as a sanctuary with a sacred aura, known by such names as *Qubbat al-Islam* (or *Quwwat al-Islam*, The stronghold of Islam) and *Hazrat-i Dehli* (Her Highness Delhi). It was not just the center of a political realm extending from Bengal in the east to Sindh in the west but also a refuge for aristocrats, literary luminaries, and the pious from the Persian-speaking world.

Delhi remained the paramount political power in North India during the 13th and 14th centuries with somewhat reduced fortune in the 15th. The Delhi Sultans constructed their cities in its riverine plain or on the foothills of the Aravalli spur, and by the 15th century "Delhi" contained several settlements of different sizes and population densities. In the 16th century the Lodi sultans (r. 1451–1526) shifted their capital to Agra. The Mughal emperors Zahir al-Din Babur (r. 1526–30), Jalal al-Din Akbar (r. 1556–1605), and Nur al-Din Jahangir (r. 1605–27) visited Delhi but did not choose it as their capital. Nasir al-Din Humayun (r. 1530–40 and 1555–56) briefly resided there, but it was not until 1648 and the construction of the new city in the northern part of the riverine plain by Shihab al-Din Shah Jahan that the imperial capital returned to Delhi. The new capital was named Shahjahanabad after its eponymous founder and was the largest, most complex and expensive city to be constructed in the Delhi region.

Although its morphology, architectural style, and decorations have been celebrated as the apogee of Mughal creative accomplishment, the life of its bazaars, its quarters, and a diffused cultural patronage developed slowly and only as the heavy hand of Mughal administration weakened. The city was looted twice in the 18th century but recovered quickly. It came under British administrative supervision in the early 19th century and the following half-century of peace provided for a great literary efflorescence. This ended abruptly with the 1857 uprising against the British under the nominal leadership of the Mughal emperor. The uprising was ruthlessly suppressed. The British exiled the Mughal emperor, mercilessly punished the "rebellious" residents of the city, denuded the city of its gardens, and carried out wide-scale demolitions and expulsion of residents, eventually shifting their capital to Calcutta.

The demise of Shahjahanabad as a center of culture, social life, and political authority was confirmed when the British started constructing New Delhi as their capital. The new colonial capital was modeled on architectural paradigms first tested in South Africa and Australia and, other than in its decorative aspects, retained little of the urban traditions of the Delhi Sultanate or Shahjahanabad. Independent India inherited this city as its capital in 1947, a transition that was disrupted by partition and communal clashes when large numbers of the city's Muslim population fled and were replaced by displaced Punjabi refugees from West Pakistan. The demographic change in the population brought new residents to the city who were far removed from its history and culture. *Hazrat-i Dehli* meant little to the new residents of the capital of independent India, a past of the city that resides uneasily with its present.

See also Delhi Sultanate (1206–1526); India; Mughals (1526–1857)

Further Reading

Stephen Blake, *Shahjahanabad: The Sovereign City in Mughal India, 1639–1739*, 1991; R. E. Frykenberg, *Delhi through the Ages: Essays in Urban History, Culture and Society*, 1986; Narayani Gupta, *Delhi between the Empires: 1803–1931*, 1999; Ebba Koch, *Mughal Art and Imperial Ideology*, 2001; Sunil Kumar, *The Present in Delhi's Pasts*, 2010; Upinder Singh, *Ancient Delhi*, 1999; Emma Tarlo, V. Dupont, and D. Vidal, eds., *Delhi: Urban Space and Human Destinies*, 2000.

SUNIL KUMAR

Delhi Sultanate (1206–1526)

The Delhi Sultanate consisted of five successive regimes that controlled large sections of North India and occasionally the South between the end of the 12th and the middle of the 16th centuries (ca. 1190–1556). With some brief exceptions, all the rulers of these regimes made Delhi their capital—hence their collective name, the Delhi Sultans, for the period of their rule. A chronological list of the successive dynasties includes the Mamluk (1206–96), Khalji (1296–1320), Tughluq (1320–1414), Sayyid (1414–51), and Lodi (1451–1526).

The Mamluk regime differed from the others in that its three lineages were each founded by a ruler of servile origin (Qutb al-Din Aybak, r. 1206–10; Shams al-Din Iltutmish, r. 1210–36; and Ghiyas al-Din Balban, r. 1266–87). The other regimes were established by freeborn men who had been commanders on the northwest marches of the Indus plain bordering modern-day Afghanistan. With the exception of the Lodis, who were chiefs of an Afghan tribe, all were of Turkish or Turkicized origin, and all were regarded as outsiders at the beginning of their reign.

All the regimes shared the feature of recruiting military slaves and groups of low social status, such as mahouts (elephant drivers), as well as Afghans, Mongols, and new converts to Islam, all of them sometimes described in the Persian chronicles as the "lowest and basest." Promoting social menials to high office allowed the rulers to centralize authority at the expense of existing elites while at the same time creating roots in local society by establishing influential households.

At its inception (ca. 1190s), the Delhi Sultanate was a collection of garrison towns commanded by the senior military commanders and former slaves (*bandagān*) of Mu'izz al-Din Ghuri (r. 1173–1206). It was not until 1228–29 and the reign of Iltutmish that Delhi's military supremacy was established. In the early 13th century, the Delhi Sultans had firm control of lands only around their cantonments, and in economic terms their regime was sustained largely by revenues from trade and plunder/tribute. In the years after Iltutmish's death, his military commanders marginalized the late monarch's successors and battled among themselves. They consolidated their respective governorships (*iqṭā'*), often with accommodative relationships with neighboring local chieftains, and resisted the intrusive efforts of Delhi to reassert its authority. For brief periods, especially during the reigns of Ghiyas al-Din Balban, 'Ala' al-Din Khalaji (r. 1296–1316), and Muhammad Tughluq (r. 1324–51), the Delhi Sultans energetically altered the balance of power in their own favor, but even then their ambit of influence

rarely extended beyond northern India into the Deccan. Provinces like Bengal, large parts of Gujarat, western Punjab, Sindh, and Rajasthan passed in and out of their control, and by Firuz Tughluq's reign (r. 1351–88), these provinces were well on their way to possessing independent sultanates. Accordingly, historians have tended to interpret the period from 1350 to 1550 as a period of decline. Although the territorial control (and thus revenues) of the sultanate diminished considerably, the period is notable for the increasing prominence of new political groups. Already from the 13th century onward, considerable migration and settlement had taken place—Persian scholars, jurists, Sufi teachers, and military adventurers from varied backgrounds were now a prominent part of the subcontinental landscape. These were years of great opportunity and a huge expansion of what Dirk Kolff called the "military labor market," where the courts of kings and princelings competed with each other to attract clients. A rough approximation of their geographical location in the subcontinent would include the Ganges plain, Gujarat, Rajasthan, Deccan, and Bengal.

Although military slaves, social menials, and frontiersmen (particularly Afghans) were important in the political and military organization of sultanates through its entire history, after 1351 a new idea of "service" (*nawkarī*) gained currency. This new idea of service carried the implication of free choice in the search for patrons, a politics of mutually supportive accommodative alliances with local chieftains, and recruitment of peasant warriors. War, service, and valorous conduct offered opportunities through which groups seized political initiative and reinvented their identities. It was during the 14th and 15th centuries, for example, that "Rajput" as a caste identity gained ground. Originally a title borne by a prince in an earlier period, the term "Rajput" now came to refer to a warrior caste, a status claimed by a variety of soldiers and commanders in Indian history.

All the sultanates, both before and after 1350, had complicated relationships with the Persian literati: scribes and chroniclers, jurists and Sufi masters. Some of them, notably the scribes and the chroniclers, had little compunction about receiving patronage from the state. For others, notably the jurists and the mystics, it was more problematic. By virtue of their learning and pietistic inclinations, they were deeply involved in the social and political affairs of the Muslim community. Some mystics were fairly direct about their close relationship with the regnant sultan and his courtiers, while others kept aloof from politics.

Two other developments were distinctive to the period. The first was the use of vernaculars (especially Hindawi) for the production of Sufi literature; the second was the emergence of Sufi gravesites as pilgrimage centers. The Malwa Sultanate in the 15th century developed the famous shrine of Mu'in al-Din Chishti in Ajmer and the Gujarat Sultanate built that of Shaikh Ahmad Khattu in Ahmadabad. By 1556, when the last of the Delhi Sultans was defeated by the adolescent Mughal emperor Jalal al-Din Akbar (r. 1556–1605), the sultanates of Jaunpur, Malwa, and Gujarat provided some of the templates that would be used to construct the Mughal Empire.

See also Delhi; India; Mughals (1526–1857)

Further Reading

Peter Hardy, *Historians of Medieval India: Studies in Indo-Muslim Historical Writing*, 1966; Peter Jackson, *The Delhi Sultanate: A Political and Military History*, 1999; Dirk A. Kolff, *Naukar, Rajput, and Sepoy*, 2002; Sunil Kumar, *The Emergence of the Delhi Sultanate*, 2007; Tapan Raychaudhuri and Irfan Habib, eds., *The Cambridge Economic History of India, vol. 1, c. 1200–1750*, 1982.

SUNIL KUMAR

democracy

Conceptions of Democracy

Conceptions of democracy generally accepted in the discipline of political science vary from the procedural to the substantive. While procedural conceptions are limited to electoral processes, substantive conceptions include civil liberties and individual rights, separation of powers with checks and balances, and the rule of law. Maximalist conceptions also consider the provision of social justice a requirement for democratic politics. Most conceptions of democracy by 20th-century Islamic thinkers concur with the electoral aspect of democracy but diverge on the question of civil liberties.

While minimalist/procedural definitions view democracy as little more than a competitive struggle for the people's vote, their proponents concede that such a struggle requires a certain amount of freedom of expression (in particular, freedom of the media). The requirement of civil liberties is formalized in Robert Dahl's more substantive conception of democracy, which consists of six institutional guarantees: free, fair, and frequent elections (political rights); elected representatives; the freedom to form and join organizations; the freedom of expression (civil liberties); alternative sources of information; and inclusive citizenship. Juan Linz and Alfred Stepan expand Dahl's notion by insisting on the existence of the state as a democratic precondition (the Palestinian territories therefore could not democratize until they form a state), as well as the existence of a vibrant civil society (consisting of guilds, trade unions, and professional and other associations), political society (mainly political parties), and economic society (a market-based economy with protected property rights). Established indexes of whether a country can be deemed democratic include Polity IV, the Bertelsmann Transformation Index, the World Bank Government Indicators, the Goteborg Quality of Government Index, and for civil liberties and political rights, indexes by Freedom House.

The Output of Democracy

Economist Amartya Sen has pointed to the intrinsic, instrumental, and constructive value of democracy. Democracy has *intrinsic* value insofar as political and social participation contribute to a

person's quality of life. Further, democracy has *instrumental* value in enhancing political attention to people's claims and (economic) needs. Finally, democracy has *constructive* importance in helping societies form their values and priorities.

Empirically, the notion of democratic citizenship, of those who enjoy the political rights and civil liberties to be safeguarded by the democratic state, has expanded over time as limits based on property (first in 1824–28 in the United States), race (in 1866 and 1965 in the United States), and gender (first in 1893 in New Zealand) have gradually been eliminated. Like other political regimes, democracies may break down. Similarly, the quality of democratic citizenship may decrease over time, for instance, due to rising economic inequality or the failure of the state to "monopolize the legitimate use of force."

The Place of Religion in Democracy

Democracy does not require a strictly secular order in institutional terms. Indeed, most long-standing democracies entertain relations of cooperation rather than strict separation between organized religion and the democratic state. Democracy in Muslim-majority societies can, and in the five Muslim-majority democracies mentioned later often does, involve religious instruction in public schools, state funding of private religious schools, state support for mosque construction, and tax breaks for religious organizations. Neutrality toward religious views, however, is a democratic precondition. A democratic state needs to guarantee both positive and negative religious freedom—that is, the freedom for its citizens to practice any religion as well as the choice not to practice any religion. Religious freedom also includes the freedom to change one's religious affiliation, to enter interreligious marriages, and to freely discuss religious views in public without needing to fear state sanction.

Democracy in the Muslim World

In 2007, about half of the world's Muslim population lived in democratic states and about a third enjoyed democratic citizenship. About 150 million lived as Muslim minorities in democratic societies, with the largest numbers in India, the United States, and Western Europe. Further, about 300 million lived in democratic Muslim-majority societies, in Indonesia, Turkey, Mali, Senegal, and Albania. None of the Arab states could be classified in 2007 as a democracy. Political scientists therefore speak of an "Arab-democracy gap." Identified causes for the Arab-democracy gap range from the prevalence of rentier economies among the gulf states to the Arab-Israeli conflict that allows authoritarian incumbents to suppress internal dissent in the name of security concerns. Other explanations highlight international support for authoritarian rulers (particularly by the United States and European Union) through commercial ties and military cooperation and few international incentives to democratize. Cultural and religious reasons to explain the Arab-democracy gap tend to be dismissed. In the words of Sen, "A country does not have to be deemed fit *for* democracy; rather, it has to become fit *through* democracy."

Islamic Law and Democracy

From the viewpoint of Islamic legal history, most of the core criteria of democracy delineated previously are acceptable: electoral politics are often juxtaposed to the Islamic principle of consultation and deliberation (*shūrā*). They are per se easily compatible with various traditions and interpretations of Islamic law (shari'a). The core conflict between 20th-century proponents of procedural notions of democracy and those of a substantive notion lies in the question about the scope of divine law. On the one end of the spectrum stand thinkers such as Mawdudi, with a maximalist view of divine law, in whose model a democratically elected parliament is commissioned only with "identifying God's law," not with making the law. Even to thinkers like Yusuf al-Qaradawi, who sees democracy as an effective antidote to despotism, a core element of democracy remains limited by the parallel basis of the polity on both God's and popular sovereignty. "There can only be voting on matters of human judgment," Qaradawi writes, without specifying who will determine what precisely lies beyond human judgment. At the other end of the spectrum are thinkers like Iranian philosopher Abdolkarim Soroush, who fully subscribe to the idea of popular sovereignty and view the place of religion in the polity as subject to public deliberation.

Three aspects of Islamic legal traditions in particular are often conceptualized as being irreconcilable with civil liberties: the legal inequality of men and women, the legal inequality of non-Muslims in relation to Muslims, and corporal (*ḥudūd*) punishments.

Attempts to engage with this normative conflict over the role of religious law in a modern polity chiefly involve one of three approaches. One focuses on international human rights standards and international covenants to which most Muslim-majority states are parties. Most Muslim-majority states have signed and ratified without reservation the International Covenant on Civil and Political Rights. Many have also signed and ratified the Convention against Torture as well as the Convention on Elimination of Discrimination against Women, the latter notably often with reservations that allow these states to abide only partially by the covenant's legal standards. Human rights lawyers and activists often try to press states to fully harmonize their legal systems with the standards of the covenants they have ratified and thereby eliminate inegalitarian legal provisions.

Other approaches concentrate on renewed engagements with religious sources and legal traditions, one to privilege established egalitarian over inegalitarian interpretations, the other to generate new legal maxims. Various jurists, theologians, and philosophers of the 20th century have reexamined the legal traditions, the Qur'an, and the hadith in order to derive interpretations that mitigate the legal inequality between men and women, as well as Muslims and non-Muslims, and limit the applicability of *ḥudūd* punishments. Some, like Pakistani philosopher Riffat Hassan and Iranian jurist Seyyed Mohsen Sa'idzadeh, argue for a methodological reorientation to emphasize the primacy of Qur'anic injunctions over more inegalitarian views in the hadith literature. Others focus on developing more contextual readings to "make Islam democratic"

(Bayat). For instance, Indonesian Islamic thinkers like Ahmad Siddiq, Nurcholish Madjid, and Abdurrahman Wahid have generated interpretations that necessitate religious tolerance from an Islamic perspective and, by extrapolation, the legal equality of Muslims and non-Muslims. Moroccan scholar Fatima Mernissi places Qur'anic verses of gender-inegalitarian content into their historical context and calls for the adjustment of such verses to today's socioeconomic conditions.

Those who do not subscribe to the view that legislation in the modern state needs to proceed within the framework of Islamic legal traditions do see religion as an important source of a political culture. They emphasize that democracies rely on the existence of a certain ethos for citizens to obey laws and for rulers to prioritize the public good over individual pursuits. In the words of Soroush, "Democracy cannot prosper without commitment to moral precepts. It is here that the great debt of democracy to religion is revealed: Religions, as bulwarks of morality, can serve as the best guarantors of democracy." While democracies need to be neutral toward worldviews, including religious views, they do rely on morality, of which religion may be a source, as well as constitutional and republican values.

See also civil society; constitutionalism; consultation; elections; government; human rights; minorities; public opinion; representation; republicanism

Further Reading

Asef Bayat, *Making Islam Democratic: Social Movements and the Post-Islamist Turn,* 2007; Robert Dahl, *On Democracy*, 1998; Yusuf al-Qaradawi, *Min fiqh al-dawlah fī al-Islām*, 1997; Amartya Sen, "Democracy as a Universal Value," *Journal of Democracy* 10, no. 3 (1999); Abdolkarim Soroush, *Reason, Freedom, and Democracy in Islam: Essential Writings of Abdolkarim Soroush*, 2000; Alfred Stepan and Graeme B. Robertson, "An 'Arab' More Than a 'Muslim' Democracy Gap," *Journal of Democracy* 14, no. 3 (2003); Max Weber, *Economy and Society: An Outline of Interpretive Sociology*, 1978.

MIRJAM KÜNKLER

demographics

According to a 2009 Pew survey, the worldwide population of Muslims is 1.57 billion, representing 23 percent of the estimated global population. The largest cultural block of Muslims is in South Asia (mainly Bangladesh, Pakistan, and India). Although India has a minority of Muslims, it has the third largest Muslim population of any nation, following Indonesia and then Pakistan. Over 85 percent of Muslims are Sunni, and the remaining are Shi'i. The largest population of Shi'is is in Iran, followed by Pakistan, India, Iraq, Turkey, and Yemen. Minority Shi'i populations, such as the international Isma'ilis or the 'Alawis of Syria, are significant less for their numbers than for their cultural or political influence. Of the world's Muslims, less than 20 percent live in the Arabic-speaking Middle East and North Africa.

Muslim populations have tended to have a higher growth rate, on average, than the global population. As a result, the overall proportion of Muslims in the world is on the rise, and an increasing number of Muslims are young. A combination of these two factors (growth and youth) sets the framework for contemporary discourses on Muslim demographics in light of heightened security concerns that prevail in Western nations. Islamic positions on abortion and contraception, however—necessary elements of population planning and control—are diverse. Recent attempts to stabilize growth, with the support of the religious elite, in countries such as Iran and Indonesia, have yielded success. Although the overall rate of growth of Muslims will continue to decline, the global Muslim population is expected to continue to grow faster than the world's non-Muslim population in the coming decades.

Islamist political thought tends to favor a high-growth-rate model, attributing the concern over rising Muslim populations to Western attempts at limiting Muslim power. On the other hand, segments in Western societies, particularly in Europe, have exhibited concern that the high growth rate of Muslims in Europe will result in a significant shift in Europe's ethnic and religious makeup. Evidence suggests, however, that the growth rate of Muslim populations in Europe follows the patterns of the countries of origin for the first generation but normalizes and aligns with the patterns of the host population in subsequent generations. Thus although the Muslims of Europe will continue to increase in number relative to native Europeans, extrapolations of future Muslim populations on the basis of the high birthrates of first generation Muslim immigrants do not yield accurate results.

A look at the countries of the Muslim world shows that no single political model or outlook unifies them all. There are secular democracies, Islamic republics, monarchies, and dictatorships. Over the course of the past century, Muslim majority countries have fought wars with each other, fallen into the spheres of influence of either the eastern or western blocs during the cold war, and also striven to be nonaligned. That any of these positions or alliances can be justified as "Islamic" indicates the pliability of political thought among Muslims according to pragmatic needs and immediate strategic, cultural, and historical contexts. It should be understood that political thought among Muslims is neither static nor monolithic, nor should it always be considered as normatively "Islamic."

There is no single authority that speaks for all Muslims. The standard reference for normative Islam, however, remains the text of the Qur'an, the mass of prophetic sayings, and the legacy of the intellectual and interpretive tradition across the centuries, which is collectively reappropriated and reapplied in changing historical contexts. The platforms of the Jama'at-i Islami in Pakistan and India, for example, differ on account of their unique contexts—one rooted in a Muslim majority country that was founded in the name

of Islam, the other in a Muslim minority democratic context. Political thought among Iranians stems from Shi'i historical and religious experiences and the interaction of these with a myriad of modern influences, including nationalism and imperialism. In contrast, Saudis draw on their Sunni Hanbali-Wahhabi background. Muslims in America reflect this contingency and diversity within the Muslim world and Islamic history. Unsurprisingly, the political thought and activism of American Muslims are increasingly in conformity with the sociology of American political culture.

See also authority; democracy; jurisprudence; minorities

Further Reading

John Esposito and Dalia Mogahed, *Who Speaks for Islam? What a Billion Muslims Really Think,* 2007; Gavin Jones and Mehtab Karim, eds., *Islam, the State, and Population*, 2005; Jonathan Lawrence, "European Islam in the Year 1451," in *Europe 2030*, edited by Daniel Benjamin, 2010; Pew Research Center, *The Future of the Global Muslim Population: Projections for 2010–2030*, 2010, http://features.pewforum.org/FutureGlobalMuslimPopulation-WebPDF.pdf; Idem, *Mapping the Global Muslim Population*, 2009, http://pewforum.org/Muslim/Mapping-the-Global-Muslim-Population.aspx; Katrina Riddell, *Islam and the Securitisation of Population Studies: Muslim States and Sustainability*, 2009.

MAHAN MIRZA

Deobandis

The Deobandi movement emerged from religious schools and institutions devoted to the purist religious tradition associated with an Islamic school, the Darul Uloom (*Dār al-'Ulūm*), founded in 1866 in the North Indian city of Deoband. While considered traditional and orthodox today, Deoband originally represented a modern approach, emulating British colleges with its fixed curriculum, salaried teachers, regular class schedules, and hostel facilities. Its founders, Muhammad Qasim Nanotawi (1832–79) and Rashid Ahmad Gangohi (1829–1905), wanted to continue the tradition of Shah Waliullah (1703–62), who had sought to cleanse South Asian Islam of local customs. In their view, British rule had undermined religious laws and learning. The return to the true Islam of the pious forebears (*al-salaf*) through the reform (*iṣlāḥ*) of religious practice and thought was the prime theological objective. The study and implementation of the prophetic traditions (hadiths) received special attention. However, this did not entail challenging traditional adherence (*taqlīd*) to the Hanafi law school or the guidance of teachers (shaykh). Sufi practice (*tasawwuf*) was condoned, even encouraged, if it proceeded within the limits of Islamic law (shari'a), as it helped to foster the morality, moderation, and stability of personality and mind. The Deobandis regarded their own approach as the only true Islam and were critical of other sects and law schools. In particular, they attacked Sufi shrine-based devotion common in South Asia as it detracted from the focus on Allah being the one and only God (*tawḥīd*). This critique led to particularly strong competition with the Barelwi sect, which defended traditional religious practices.

The defeat of the anticolonial revolt of 1857–58, in which a number of Muslim notables and scholars also were implicated, left a deep impact on the founding generation of the Deoband school. Its adherents came to emphasize religious learning and piety, joining other scholars of the time in renouncing jihad as a means of militant resistance against British rule. It was the abolition of the Muslim majority province of East Bengal in 1912 that spurred Muslim leaders across the theological spectrum into action. In Deoband, a new generation of scholars argued for a political role of the school. They included the Shaykh al-Hind Mahmud al-Hasan (1851–1920), Husain Ahmad Madani (1879–1957), and 'Ubaydallah Sindhi (1872–1944). Deobandi scholars traced their political philosophy back to Sayyid Ahmad Shahid (1786–1831), who was a puritan reformer and had led a movement of jihad against Sikh rulers in northwest India.

As British rule was regarded as an obstacle to proper Islamic practice and life, colonial India was viewed by many Deobandis as *dār al-ḥarb*, the land of war, as opposed to being the land of Islam, *dār al-islām*. This theological opposition led the Deobandis to cooperate with nationalists from the Indian National Congress under Mohandas Gandhi. The Silk Letter Conspiracy of 1916 revealed the extent to which Deobandi scholars had become involved in clandestine efforts against the British. Deobandis soon dominated the first public organization of Muslim religious scholars of India, Jamiat-Ulama-i Hind (JUH) after its foundation in 1919. The Khilafat movement (1919–24) turned into a mass campaign to mobilize Indian Muslims against the abolition of the Ottoman caliphate. The JUH aimed to create conditions in India under which Muslims could follow a religious life in accordance with the demands of Islam. For a future independent India, it envisaged a government commissioner of Islamic affairs who would be the highest arbiter in religious and social matters concerning Muslims. This position favored a united India, in contrast with demands for a separate Muslim state as advanced by the Muslim League.

Shortly before the partition of the subcontinent, a faction of the JUH broke away to form the Jamiat-Ulama-i Islam (JUI), which continued to operate in Pakistan. In India, the JUH avoided political activity. While the JUI was the largest religious party in Pakistan, its political influence remained limited to local pockets in the former Northwest Frontier Province and Baluchistan. During the reign of Pakistan's military dictator, General Zia-ul-Haq (r. 1977–88), with U.S. strategic support, selected Islamic schools (madrasas) in the Afghanistan border area following the Deobandi curriculum, were used to train tribal militias as mujahidin, or holy warriors, for intervention in the Soviet-Afghan War (1978–89). Simultaneously Pakistan directed the militias to the conflict in Kashmir, where they helped revive the civil war in the Indian-controlled

territory. These militias drew much of their motivation from sectarian doctrines striving to defend "true" Islam and uprooting un-Islamic practices, which led to sectarian strife with Shi'i groups as well as attacks on Christian, Hindu, and Ahmadi targets. After the Afghan mujahidin groups failed to control the country, a new movement of religious students, the Taliban, emerged from some Deobandi madrasas near the Afghan borderland in 1994 with active support of the Pakistani government. The new international war in Afghanistan in 2001 toppled the Taliban, who withdrew into Pakistan. There, they regrouped and reemerged as a major force, later forming an alliance of tribal religious groups, the Taliban Movement of Pakistan.

While the politicization of Deobandi militias owed much to political and ethnic factors, the vast majority of Deobandi madrasas remained committed to religious learning, offering educational opportunities to aspiring rural and suburban families. As the share of madrasa education did not exceed 3 percent in Pakistan in the early 21st century, their influence remained limited. Their religious education became more formalized with the introduction of degree courses for religious scholars. The more advanced schools also offered secular subjects and the national curriculum. The Darul Uloom madrasa in Deoband split in 1982 in a factional dispute, creating a rival institution, the Darul Uloom Waqf, in the same city. The old school was dominated by the descendants of Husain Ahmad Madani's family, while the new school was controlled by the offspring of Deoband founder Nanotawi. The regional and global expansion of Deobandi institutions relied on diaspora groups from the colonial era but also on traditional migrants from Muslim trading groups as well as other migrants. The global influence of Deobandi thought significantly expanded through the Deobandi-dominated missionary movement, the Tablighi Jama'at. Many observers believe it to be the largest transnational Islamic grassroots movement, operating in all countries where Muslims live.

See also Barelwis; India; madrasa; Pakistan; Taliban; Tablighi Jama'at

Further Reading

"Darul Uloom Deoband-India," http://www.darululoom-deoband.com; "Jamiat-Ulama-i-Hind," http://www.jamiatulama.org; Muhammad Khalid Masud, ed., *Travellers in Faith: Studies of the Tablighi Jama'at as a Transnational Islamic Movement for Faith Renewal*, 2000; Barbara Daly Metcalf, *Islamic Revival in British India: Deoband, 1860–1900*, 1982; Ahmed Rashid, *Taliban: Militant Islam, Oil, and Fundamentalism in Central Asia*, 2000; Dietrich Reetz, "The Deoband Universe: What Makes a Transcultural and Transnational Educational Movement of Islam?" *Contemporary Studies of South Asia, Africa and the Middle East* 27, no. 1 (2007); Idem, *Islam in the Public Sphere: Religious Groups in India, 1900–1947*, 2006; Sayyid Mahboob Rizvi, *History of the Daru'l-'ulum*, 1980; Yoginder Sikand, *Bastions of the Believers: Madrasas and Islamic Education in India*, 2005.

DIETRICH REETZ

difference of opinion

A difference of opinion (*ikhtilāf*) is a ubiquitous feature of Islamic law. More often than not, on any given issue a number of equally legitimate legal rules exist. Classical legal theory (*uṣūl al-fiqh*) tended to explain the legitimacy of differences of opinion as a result of the many ways in which the divine textual sources of the law (Qur'an and sunna) could be interpreted. Given that one of the main functions of a ruler or judge is to apply Islamic law, the legitimacy of a plurality of interpretations of the Divine Law (*ijtihād*) posed acute problems: Which law should the ruler implement? Which body of rules is the judge to apply? What makes the applied rule legitimate? In the classical period, Muslim legal theorists' justifications for the legitimacy of the applied rule vacillated between emphasizing the legitimacy of the institutional role of the applier of the rule (i.e., did the applier legitimately occupy the role of the ruler or judge?) and the scholarly competence of the individual applier (i.e., was the individual applier himself a *mujtahid* [expert jurist]?).

In the early classical period, the legitimacy of a judicial application of one opinion over another depended on whether the judge possessed the competence to derive the relevant legal rule from the textual sources of the Divine Law. In theory, this competence required the possession of knowledge of the divine textual sources, rules of textual construction and the accepted methods of legal reasoning, and moral probity. The scholar of the Shafi'i school Mawardi (d. 1058) regarded the absence of these qualifications as ground for invalidating a judge's appointment and his judicial decisions. Two generations later, Ghazali (d. 1111) upheld the necessity of these qualifications for judges but did not regard them as essential for the validity of the cases that the judge had decided. As long as the judge's appointment by the ruler was legitimate, he was willing to accept the validity of past decided cases even if the judge was not a *mujtahid* in his own right. Similarly, the Maliki scholar Abu al-'Abbas Ahmad b. Idris al-Qarafi (d. 1285) identified the validity of the judicial decision as resting not on the individual judge's expert competence but on "receipt (from an authorized authority) of a specific jurisdiction (*wilāya khāṣṣa*)" (Jackson, 1996, 160). Jackson interprets Qarafi's justification as motivated by the desire to protect the legitimacy of disagreement among the major Sunni legal traditions of his time. Qarafi held that a judge's decision according to the rule of any one of the established legal traditions (*madhāhib*) could not be challenged on the ground that the rule rested on an incorrect understanding of the sources of the Divine Law. Qarafi argued that a firm consensus had validated the legitimacy of the differences of opinion as enshrined in the four Sunni legal traditions. Any judicial decision based on a legal rule upheld by any one of these traditions was valid because of this consensus. This meant, for example, that a Hanafi jurist who had the ear of the sultan could not seek to invalidate a judicial decision based on the application of a Maliki rule by arguing that the Maliki rule is an incorrect

interpretation of the divine sources. Such an argument would be a violation of the consensus.

The Ottoman solution to the problem of which rules should be applied favored the Hanafi legal tradition over others. Hanafi doctrine, in contrast to the other Sunni legal traditions, permitted the ruler to restrict judges to the application of a specific legal tradition. Based on this legal doctrine, the Ottomans directed all judges, regardless of school affiliation, to apply only Hanafi legal rules in certain types of cases.

As a legacy of this older Ottoman prejudice and initial 19th-century Ottoman attempts at codifying Islamic law, much of the law constituting the legal codes to be applied by judges was heavily indebted to the Hanafi legal tradition, even in areas where the majority of a region's inhabitants belonged to another legal tradition. Between 1880 and 1955, for example, the Egyptian legislature directed judges of religious courts to construe family law statutes according to the Hanafi legal tradition. This changed shortly after the shari'a became explicitly identified as a constitutional source for the legal rules of the country (article 2 of the 1971 Constitution). The Supreme Constitutional Court started hearing cases in which the application of Hanafi rules had undesirable consequences. In many of the decisions in these cases, the justices asserted, much like Qarafi, that only laws that were unanimously agreed upon were binding from a shari'a perspective. Thus, in the absence of consensus, the Supreme Constitutional Court of Egypt ruled that political authorities were free to pursue legal rules that more faithfully fulfilled the objectives of the shari'a. Here the difference of opinion on an issue of legal controversy opened the possibility of weakening a legislative statute that had previously directed judges to follow the rules of one tradition.

For the contemporary Egyptian scholar Yusuf al-Qaradawi, a difference of opinion broadly indicates an area that the shari'a left open to discretionary human judgment (*al-umūr al-ijtihādiyya*). He argues further that where difference of opinion exists, ordinary Muslims can legitimately engage in deciding issues of the common good, such as the proper constitutional framework for their politics, setting policy, making law, and electing their leaders. When several competing options exist on an issue, Qaradawi insists that ground must be found for preferring one opinion to another and denies that the preference can be arbitrary. In his view, there must be some nonarbitrary way to tip the favor of one legal rule over others. Reasoning that the "opinion of two is more likely to be correct than the view of a single person," he attempts to justify the democratic practice of voting as one such way of deciding upon the constitutional framework and issues of policy that is, at the minimum, consistent with the shari'a.

See also consensus; *ijtihād* and *taqlīd*; jurisprudence; shari'a

Further Reading

Hamid Enayat, *Modern Islamic Political Thought*, 1982; Sherman A. Jackson, *Islamic Law and the State: The Constitutional Jurisprudence of Shihāb al-Dīn al-Qarāfī*, 1996; Baber Johansen, "The Constitution and the Principles of Islamic Normativity against the Rules of Fiqh: A Judgment of the Supreme Constitutional Court of Egypt," in *Dispensing Justice in Islam: Qadis and Their Judgments*, edited by Muhammad Khalid Masud, Rudolph Peters, and David Stephan Powers, 2006; Rudolph Peters, "What Does It Mean to Be an Official Madhhab?" in *The Islamic School of Law: Evolution, Devolution, and Progress*, edited by Peri Bearman, Rudolph Peters, and Frank E. Vogel, 2005; Yusuf al-Qaradawi, "Islam and Democracy," in *Princeton Readings in Islamist Thought*, edited by Roxanne L. Euben and Muhammad Qasim Zaman, 2009.

MAIRAJ SYED

diplomacy

Diplomacy is the art and practice of conducting external relations, as in the negotiating of treaties, alliances, and other agreements. Islamic history is replete with records of diplomatic activity of various sorts from the earliest period. Accordingly, classical Islamic political theory dealt with many different aspects of diplomacy, such as the negotiation of agreements relating to war and peace or to trade, limits on such agreements and rules relating to their observance, the qualifications of Muslim envoys, and the treatment of foreign ambassadors. These topics are discussed in a number of genres in classical historical (*tarīkh*), legal (*fiqh*), and ethical (*adab*) literature.

Examples of the Prophet Muhammad's diplomacy abound in classical historical literature, including the earliest known biographies of the Prophet, Ibn Ishaq's *Sirat Rasul Allah* (Life of the Messenger of God) and Waqidi's *Kitab al-Maghazi* (Book of military expeditions). Arbitration, negotiations for ransoming prisoners or for trade agreements, guarantees of security, and military alliances between tribes were all well-established pre-Islamic Arabian customs. Muhammad's statecraft, beginning in the early Meccan period of his prophethood and continuing until his death, used all of these practices in the interest of the developing Muslim community (*umma*) and later the state founded in Medina. The most important treaty concluded by Muhammad—the one most often cited as a precedent by subsequent Muslim theorists—was the treaty of Hudaybiyya in 628. This agreement, among other things, declared a truce between the Muslims and Quraysh (the Prophet's tribe) of Mecca, as well as their allied tribes, for ten years. The truce lasted less than two years, however. In 630, a tribe allied to the Quraysh violated the truce when they attacked and killed a member of a tribe allied to the Muslims, whereupon Muhammad ordered the Muslims to march on Mecca. The city fell without resistance.

Diplomacy was also a significant aspect of Muslim statecraft under the *Rāshidūn* caliphs and their Umayyad and Abbasid successors. The historical records of this period detail instances of negotiations between Muslim military commanders or envoys of the

caliph and non-Muslim leaders. An important principle governing jihad was that non-Muslims should receive the call to Islam and be given a chance to convert or become *dhimmīs* (protected communities) before any attack. As a result, histories of the early Islamic conquests contain numerous accounts of parlays between Muslim and non-Muslim commanders on the eve of battle. The early histories also record negotiations to resolve conflicts within the Muslim community. The most famous is the arbitration to resolve the conflicting claims to the caliphate of 'Ali b. Abi Talib and Mu'awiya in 658, which failed to resolve the dispute and led to the uprising of the Kharijis against both men.

In classical legal treatises dealing with the external affairs of the Islamic state, the main concern of the jurists was to outline the rules for conducting jihad. Since the majority of jurists viewed jihad as a permanent struggle between the Islamic state and non-Muslims, diplomacy had limited objectives. It could be conducted to convince non-Muslims to surrender without fighting and to open their territory to the preaching of Islam, or it could precede a truce (i.e., a suspension of jihad). Ibn Rushd (d. 1198) summarizes disagreements of the jurists over the permissibility, terms, and duration of such truces in *Bidayat al-Mujtahid* (Primer for jurists). He writes that although some scholars did not permit truces except under dire necessity, most scholars of the Maliki, Hanafi, and Shafi'i schools permitted the Muslim ruler to negotiate truces whenever he deemed it in the Muslims' interest. The Syrian jurist Awza'i (d. 774) permitted an agreement requiring Muslims to pay a tribute or some other compensation to the enemy, but other scholars, especially Shafi'i (d. 820), forbade such terms unless necessary to stave off catastrophe. The jurists also disagreed over the maximum length of a truce; some suggested three or four years, but the majority agreed on ten years based on the treaty of Hudaybiyya. Once a truce or other agreement was concluded, Islamic law required Muslims to observe it faithfully. As Shaybani (d. 805) writes in *Kitab al-Siyar* (Book of the rules of war), a treaty is akin to granting *amān* (assurance of safety) and as such cannot be violated. If the Islamic state wished to end a treaty before its term, such an intention had to be clearly conveyed to the other party before hostilities resumed. Similarly, in Islamic law, Muslim envoys were to act in good faith during their missions. The immunity of a foreign messenger (*rasūl*) or ambassador (*safīr*) was assured throughout the duration of his diplomatic mission.

In classical literature, *Kitab Rusul al-Muluk* (Book of envoys of kings) by Abu Ya'la b. al-Farra', is the most detailed treatment of diplomacy and diplomats. This short work describes the qualities of an envoy with illustrative vignettes from pre-Islamic and Islamic history up to the Abbasid period. The Mirrors for Princes genre, aimed at providing practical guidelines on statecraft to the ruler, also dealt to some degree with the qualifications, functions, and treatment of envoys.

The development of the European "law of nations," from which evolved public international law, along with new diplomatic norms and practices significantly influenced Islamic approaches to diplomacy. Ambassadors from the Italian city-states were resident in Istanbul from the 16th century. Although the Ottomans dispatched numerous diplomatic missions to European capitals, they did not establish embassies until the end of the 18th century. In the 20th century, as Muslim states gained independence, they invariably acceded to international law. Most have ratified the principal treaties governing diplomacy, including the Vienna conventions on diplomatic relations (1961) and consular relations (1963). State practice is largely endorsed in current Muslim scholarship, which argues for the essential compatibility between Islamic law and international diplomatic law. The Iranian seizure of the American embassy in Tehran in November 1979, and the subsequent hostage crisis, was one of the most serious breaches of diplomatic norms in recent history. The Iranian government defended its actions by claiming the embassy personnel were engaged in subverting the Islamic Republic, but Iran was subjected to heavy international criticism, including from Muslim governments and scholars.

See also abodes of Islam, war, and truce; alliances; international relations

Further Reading

M. Cherif Bassiouni, "Protection of Diplomats under Islamic Law," *American Journal of International Law* 74, no. 3 (1980); Muhammad Hamidullah, *The Muslim Conduct of State*, 1977; Afzal Iqbal, *Diplomacy in Islam*, 1962; Yasin Istanbuli, *Diplomacy and Diplomatic Practice in the Early Islamic Era*, 2001; Majid Khadduri, *War and Peace in the Law of Islam*, 1955.

SOHAIL H. HASHMI

dissent, opposition, resistance

Though dissent is often understood in negative terms, primarily as a means of expressing opposition, in the Islamic tradition dissent can also be construed in terms of a positive duty. The duty of commanding right and forbidding wrong has been emphasized as a primary obligation for Muslims throughout Islamic history. It has often been construed as a duty to dissent against unjust forms of government; a Prophetic tradition recorded by Ahmad b. Hanbal and others states that to be killed as a result of speaking up to an unjust ruler is the best form of holy war. Thus, Islam has a long tradition of political dissent; even the earliest caliphs faced some dissenters motivated to speak out against injustice or the un-Islamic comportment of the ruler.

Equally prevalent within the tradition, especially among Sunnis, has been a trend of limiting the conditions under which the exercise of this duty may be carried out. The Hanbali thinker Abu Ya'la b. al-Farra' (d. 1066) offers one set of restrictions on the duty that is mirrored by many other Sunni writers. Ibn al-Farra' argues that the obligation to command right and forbid wrong, even to political leaders, applies only when it can be carried out without a risk of

bodily harm to oneself, when it is likely to succeed, and when its exercise does not carry the risk of engendering a greater evil. Effectively, these restrictions serve to limit the extent to which this duty can be used to legitimate political rebellion. Many Sunni thinkers argued that because of these or similar restrictions, dissent against those in political power could be carried out only in the heart rather than through physical violence or even spoken opposition. These restrictions limited the likelihood that political dissent would turn into actual rebellion.

Even with these limitations, however, dissent has of course always been a characteristic of Islamic communities; furthermore, it has sometimes resulted in physical rebellion. Marshall Hodgson describes, for example, the widespread "piety-minded" opposition that eventually contributed to the success of the Abbasid revolution. Shi'ism has often been understood as a movement founded in part on the basis of political opposition, as early Shi'is saw the imam as an alternative to the injustices of the ruling caliph. Abdulaziz Sachedina, a scholar of Shi'ism, argues that early Shi'is' position as political resisters of the caliphate had a strong influence on some important aspects of Shi'i theology, including the eschatological nature of its doctrine of the Mahdi, who came to be understood as a redemptive figure of political resistance. In the contemporary context, Shi'ism continues to be the source of political resistance in many regions, especially in Muslim-majority countries in which Shi'is are a minority and seek greater political access and social privilege.

Two other contemporary Islamic dissent movements are Islamism and reformism. Individuals supporting these movements are likely to limit their resistance to the sphere of speech, in accordance with the restrictions described earlier. However, at particular moments each of these movements has manifested itself in a violent manner. Mohammed Hafez's study of resistance in Muslim-majority countries demonstrates that the move to rebellion or violence is precipitated by particular identifiable factors. Islamic resistance is much more likely to become violent if resisters are denied other means of expressing their dissent; thus, resisters in countries that lack institutional access and popular participation in the government are more likely to turn to violence. When governments provide the inclusive space in which dissenters can express their opposition in meaningful ways, they are more successful at preventing dissent from becoming violent rebellion.

See also commanding right and forbidding wrong; quietism and activism; rebellion; revolutions

Further Reading

Juan R. I. Cole and Nikki R. Keddie, eds., *Shi'ism and Social Protest*, 1986; Michael Cook, *Commanding Right and Forbidding Wrong in Islamic Thought*, 2000; Mohammed M. Hafez, *Why Muslims Rebel: Repression and Resistance in the Islamic World*, 2003; Marshall G. S. Hodgson, *The Venture of Islam*, 1974; Abdulaziz Abdulhussein Sachedina, *Islamic Messianism: The Idea of the Mahdi in Twelver Shi'ism*, 1981.

ROSEMARY B. KELLISON

dissimulation

Literally "caution" or "wariness," *taqiyya*, the technical term for dissimulation, is an Islamic legal dispensation that allows the believer to commit an act that would ordinarily be forbidden or to omit an act that would ordinarily be required in cases of danger from a hostile or potentially hostile audience. The term is related to but distinguished from other legal dispensations such as *ḍarūra* (dire need), which derives from a general, impersonal situation, and *ikrāh* (coercion), which, like *taqiyya*, is caused by a hostile party but is not necessarily related to questions of religious identity. Throughout Islamic history *taqiyya* has been most strongly associated with the Twelver Shi'i tradition, which has the most developed literature on the topic, but has been adopted in various historical contexts by members of other Shi'i sects as well as Kharijis, Sunnis, and various Islamic movements. The social use of *taqiyya* by persecuted groups such as the Moriscos of 16th-century Spain or Shi'is under the rule of the Ghaznavids, Seljuqs, Mamluks, Ottomans, and other oppressive Sunni regimes may be likened to a dramaturgical discipline that guided members of a minority group to manage their identities and adjust their behavior not only in cases of severe duress, such as at heresy trials, but also in their everyday encounters with the majority.

Jurists found the justification for *taqiyya* in the Qur'an and hadith. Verse 16:108 of the Qur'an reads, "Whoever expresses disbelief in God after having accepted belief [will suffer greatly]—except him who is forced while his heart is still at peace in belief." This verse is said to refer to the case of the Companion of the Prophet 'Ammar b. Yasir, who was compelled to worship pagan idols and deny the Prophet Muhammad by polytheists in Mecca. He witnessed his parents, Yasir b. 'Amir and Sumayya bt. Khabbat, being brutally killed for refusing to worship the gods of the polytheists, but 'Ammar said what was demanded of him and thus survived. Afterward, when 'Ammar reported to the Prophet what had happened, the Prophet asked him how he felt in his heart, and 'Ammar responded that his heart "was at ease in belief." The Prophet informed him that this was all that was necessary, and if the polytheists were to attack him in a similar fashion in the future, he should do the same thing. The term *taqiyya* likely derives from Qur'an 3:28, which reads, "Let not the believers take unbelievers for their allies in preference to believers. Whoever does this has no connection with God, unless it be that you but guard yourselves against them out of fear" (*illā 'an tattaqū minhum tuqātan*). Muhammad b. Jarir al-Tabari and other commentators report the recognized variant reading *taqiyyatan*, a verbal noun construed as a cognate accusative (fear), rather than *tuqātan*, a plural adjective construed as an accusative of condition (fearful, fearing). If the variant is accepted, one may say that the term *taqiyya* occurs in the Qur'an with its technical meaning; in either case, there is little doubt that the cognate verb *tattaqū* in this passage refers to dissimulation.

In one sense, *taqiyya* served as the regime of secrecy adopted by underground, revolutionary movements, the premodern term for which was *da'wa* (call). This form of *taqiyya* was used in the movement leading up to the Abbasid revolution, which involved the extensive participation of Shi'is, and in the various Isma'ili *da'was*, which led to the establishment of the Fatimid state, the Qarmati state in eastern Arabia, and the territories of the Nizari "Assassins" in Iran and Syria. Legacies of this revolutionary usage are seen in Twelver hadith reports that stress the centrality of *taqiyya* to one's religious obligations and impress on the believer the need above all else to keep the name and location of the imam—the leader of the movement—secret. The Abbasid revolution was conducted in the name of *al-riḍā min ahl al-bayt*, "the agreed-upon one from among the descendants of the Prophet," in part to avoid conflicts within the movement but also for the sake of secrecy. It is also in this sense that *taqiyya* has figured in the description of modern political movements, including various Islamist political parties whom detractors accuse of pretending to accept democratic principles while they actually intend to ignore them in the event that they attain political power.

In the most common sense, *taqiyya* is used by the Twelver Shi'is and other sectarian groups who live as stigmatized minorities and potential targets of discrimination or persecution. Whereas the legal literature refers to a limited number of behaviors, such as denying adherence to the sectarian group in question or refraining from highly visible obligations such as prayers, *taqiyya*, in order to be performed successfully, may extend to nonlegal matters and involve hiding, for example, one's town or region of origin. It is generally recognized that the person who is able to assess the need for *taqiyya*—the threat of danger in the case at hand—is the performer himself (*al-muttaqī*). It necessarily involves an audience before whom one performs it (*al-muttaqā minhu*), which may include government officials, judicial officials, or lay members of the majority group. It allows one to commit acts that are legally forbidden or omit acts that are legally obligatory without changing the underlying legal status of those acts; these matters are collectively the substance of *taqiyya* (*al-muttaqā fīhi*).

The most frequent practices subject to *taqiyya* are those that are most visible. For Shi'is living in Sunni societies, many of these have to do with prayer. Shi'is in many societies have often suppressed their distinctive form of the call to prayer—for example, the use of the phrase "come to the best of works" in the dawn prayer instead of *al-ṣalātu khayrun min al-nawm* ("Prayer is better than sleep"), as well as the addition of the creedal statement *ashhadu anna 'Aliyyan waliyyu llāh* ("I witness that 'Ali is the ward of God"). Shi'is have also suppressed their doctrinal position that praying behind a Sunni prayer leader or praying Friday prayer with the Sunnis is actually invalid, as refusal to do so would place them in danger as heretics. They often avoided the common Shi'i practice of combining the noon and afternoon prayers, or the sunset and evening prayers, even when not traveling. Likewise, touching the forehead to a *muhr*, or pellet of clay from Karbala, in prostration and holding the hands at the sides of the body rather than folded on one's chest or belly when in standing position would also reveal adherence to Shi'ism and so were avoided.

A curious consequence of the regular use of dissimulation to conceal Shi'i views on details of religious practice was the establishment of *taqiyya* as a principle of Shi'i hadith criticism. If several hadiths report that the imams voiced contradictory opinions on a legal issue, and if one of those opinions agreed with one upheld in Sunni law, Shi'is assumed it to be false, for it must have been uttered by the imam for the benefit of a Sunni audience. The correct opinion in such cases must be that which opposed the Sunni view.

Other matters subject to *taqiyya* have been Shi'i doctrines concerning the status of the imams and Companions of the Prophet, for a number of the latter, those who openly opposed 'Ali or usurped the position of leader of the community that rightly belonged to him, especially Abu Bakr, 'Umar b. al-Khattab, 'Uthman b. 'Affan, and 'A'isha, are technically unbelievers and should be cursed. Because of the tensions with Sunnis that curses and insults of such figures bring out, many Shi'i authorities, including Ayatollah Khomeini and Ayatollah Khamene'i, have ruled that Shi'is should avoid cursing them for the sake of creating unity in the Muslim community.

Other matters involve any distinctive Shi'i practice, such as the tradition for men to wear a signet ring on the right hand rather than the left hand or the celebration of the Prophet's birthday on a slightly different date. In addition, the modification of identity in an Islamic context led Shi'is to certain practices, including modifying one's name, particularly the *nisba* (filiation), in order to conceal one's exact place of origin, which might reveal one's sectarian identity. The most famous case of this is that of Afghani, who was not actually Afghani but an Iranian whose *nisba* was Asadabadi; he changed his name to hide the fact that he was a Shi'i. In a number of cases, Shi'is are known to have adopted a forged genealogy (*nasab*), as when Afghani claimed descent from the renowned hadith scholar Tirmidhi or Baha' al-Din al-'Amili claimed descent from the famous Sunni theologian Ghazali. Other practices connected with the performance of *taqiyya* are changing one's distinctive clothing in order to hide one's affiliation or to adopt an assumed identity, such as that of a merchant or dervish. Documents were also important props for the performance of *taqiyya*; these included *ijāzahs*, which are diplomas or certificates of study, as well as works dedicated to rulers or other potential patrons. In addition to establishing the scholarly credentials and accomplishments of the holder, they also suggested his doctrinal acceptability.

Taqiyya has also served as the broad rubric under which Shi'is have discussed all types of relation with the majority community, including ones that are framed in positive rather than negative terms. A hadith report attributed to the sixth imam, Ja'far al-Sadiq, urges Shi'is not only to tolerate the Sunni majority and patiently endure living among them but actually to show themselves exemplary members in the majority society, praying in the first row along with the Sunnis, visiting their sick, attending their funerals, and so on.

Although dissimulation is an accepted principle in Sunni Islamic law, some Sunni commoners and scholars alike have often denounced Shi'is for their constant resort to *taqiyya*, accusing them of making *taqiyya* the basis of their religion and comparing them to the hypocrites (*munāfiqūn*) of the Qur'an, contemporaries of the Prophet Muhammad who had outwardly adopted Islam but secretly worked to undermine his prophetic mission. Such critiques are often exaggerated by the fact that the Sunnis have been in most instances the majority and have felt little sympathy with members of minorities who suffer regular discrimination and persecution. Nonetheless, in historical contexts where Sunni Muslims were persecuted, most often by Christians, they regularly resorted to *taqiyya*. Muslims captured by the Byzantines, Muslim communities in Sicily and the Balkans, and, most famously, the Moriscos of Spain all resorted to dissimulation in order to maintain adherence to Islam while outwardly adopting Christianity. It is known that in Spain the Moriscos performed ablutions and prayed in secret and used various ruses to hide the fact that they fasted during Ramadan, abstained from eating pork and drinking wine, slaughtered animals according to Islamic law, and so on. They also performed double marriage ceremonies, once in church and once afterward with an Islamic marriage contract.

See also jurisprudence; shari'a; Shi'ism

Further Reading

Etan Kohlberg, "Taqiyya in Shī'ī Theology and Religion," in *Secrecy and Concealment*, edited by Hans G. Kippenberg and Guy G. Strousma, 1995; Devin J. Stewart, "*Taqiyyah* as Performance: The Travels of Bahā' al-Din al-'Āmilī in the Ottoman Empire (991–93/1583–85)," *Princeton Papers in Near Eastern Studies* 4, no. 1 (1996).

DEVIN J. STEWART

division of labor

The increased degree of division of labor and occupational specialization in the manufacturing and service sectors of medieval Islamic economies was essential to their economic performance. Classical economic theory demonstrates that a greater division of labor leads to greater output, better quality products, increased efficiency, and greater implementation of technical innovations in the manufacture of commodities.

The Arabic literary sources provide a great deal of information about individual trades and occupations, which permits a reliable statistical assessment but no theory of the division of labor. A quantitative study of Islamic occupations covering the period from 700 to 1500 reveals 1,853 unique trade names and occupations. This occupational classification permits us to measure the degree of specialization within each of the industries in the manufacturing and service sectors in comparison to earlier and contemporary societies; the relative distribution of manpower in the economy; and other related aspects such as gender and ethnic labor, Islamic labor organization, social and economic integration, and optimal economic performance. The numbers reveal a relatively limited specialization in the primary sectors of agriculture and mining, ranging between 29 and 49 occupational terms over the period, but a considerable expansion in the manufacturing sector in the early and later Middle Ages, ranging between 398 and 418 names, and numerous occupations in the tertiary or service sector, ranging between 522 and 883 trade names. The small number of occupations found in the primary sector points to less division of labor in this sector, although the bulk of the population lived and worked in rural areas. This finding is due to the simple nature of agricultural tasks and to the fact that that they were performed by all members of the family.

In contrast, the impact of an increased division of labor was very visible in urban centers. In the cities, the ratio of those employed in manufacturing ranged from 44 percent to 32 percent of the labor force and from 51 percent to 66 percent of those employed in services. Extensive division of labor occurred in key urban industries such as textiles, food preparation, building, metalworking, and leather. The textile industry showed the most intensive specialization, with trade names reflecting the manufacture of new items, the use of new raw materials, and the development of new techniques. This industry employed a commercially significant share of the full-time urban labor force, including both male and female workers. The textile industry was also unique in having a government manufacturing component in the form of the *ṭirāz* (textiles) factory. The manufacture of luxury items generated greater specialization and greater productivity. Studies of the Italian textile industry have indicated greater dependence on raw materials from the Middle East than on technical and organizational patterns derived from Islamicate models, such as the division of labor, specialization, or manufacturing techniques. Increased specialization in the building trades also corresponded to new building techniques and materials and increased demand for private and monumental buildings in the cities, as well as manufacturing installations such as presses and mills in specific urban and rural environments, an indication of growth in the economy in general.

The increased division of labor in the service sector was linked to an increased drive for commercialization demonstrated by the division of labor in the manufacturing sector, geared to greater volume and better products for local sale and export, as well as increased economic activity throughout. The correlation between the increased demand for manufactured items and population growth is reflected in diversification and occupational specialization in the service sector. Occupations in industrial services such as wholesale commerce, retail marketing, finance, and transport increased, as did the number of categories of professional service providers and skilled workers. Religious institutions provided service occupations in mosques, religious teaching, the police force, and the judiciary. In Mamluk Egypt and Syria, the effects of long subjection to an ethnic political and military regime are reflected in the number of military-cum-administrative

occupations and offices in the economy. In the Islamic city's division of labor, service occupations play a fundamental role in integrating manufacturing, legal, and economic functions.

Division of labor occurred also along gender and ethnic lines. In the textile industry, females monopolized spinning occupations and specialized in silk dyeing, sewing, and brocade making, while commercial weaving remained a male occupation. There were female brokers and sellers of agricultural products, but there is no evidence that women's guilds existed anywhere, even in the modern period. Ethnic and religious division of labor was manifested in trades exercised almost exclusively by Jews, Armenians, Berbers, and Copts over long periods and was prominent in the military and administrative occupations of the Turks and Persians. Strict ethnic division of labor mitigated against economic integration and technical innovation. Slave labor, in contrast, never developed an occupational specialization.

The quantitative analysis of occupational terms mapped the division of labor in the Islamic economic sectors, but the results should also be qualified according to historical circumstances. The results indicate that in comparison to previous and contemporary Roman, Byzantine, and European economies, the Islamic Middle East had much more diversified manufacturing and service sectors. Nonetheless, variations in regional patterns also occurred. For instance, North Africa and Spain had less sophisticated manufacturing industries and trade occupations than the Middle East. The division of labor varied according to the size and function of urban centers: cities that served as major administrative centers had scope for more occupational specialization and greater division of labor than others.

There is insufficient information about occupational structures and division of labor patterns to indicate a major change over the premodern period. Increased division of labor is sometimes seen as compensating for a lack of technical innovation with sheer manpower numbers, which in the long term provokes stagnation, conservatism, and social barriers to progress and integration. Despite the absence of innovation in methods of production, however, the Islamic occupational world remained closely involved with science and technology. Musicians, time keepers, astronomers, and writers of fiscal manuals consulted and made use of mathematics, while physicians, scribes, secretaries, calligraphers, binders, agriculturists, animal trainers, and veterinarians used written manuals to learn and instruct.

MAYA SHATZMILLER

Beginning in the 16th century, the discovery of the route around the Cape of Good Hope to the Indian Ocean, which allowed Portuguese, British, and other merchants direct access to East Africa, India, and eventually Indonesia and the Far East, drastically cut the revenues from long-distance trade in the Islamic world and the Middle East in particular, reducing the merchant sector of the economy. Increasingly direct contact with the international markets, culminating in the 19th and 20th centuries with the European colonization of most Muslim societies on the globe, led to the disruption or disintegration of long-established economic relations. As a result, an international division of labor developed in which the colonies in the Muslim world and elsewhere provided raw materials and cheap labor, while the citizens of industrialized nations provided skilled labor and administrators. Locally, foreign investors with access to capital and to the government were able to take advantage of cheap materials and labor, taking the place of local investors and employers. The manufacturing sectors of the economy in the Muslim world suffered, as traditional artisans were unable to compete or were forced into new sectors. Textile production and animal transport were especially hard hit. In agriculture, many regions in the Muslim world became increasingly dependent on a limited number of cash crops such as cotton or tobacco and thus more susceptible to international fluctuation in commodity prices. Privatization and the creation of large estates forced peasants to leave rural areas and migrate to the major cities.

While the Muslim world has been subject to many of the same trends found in the global economy, such as the reduction of the percentage of the population engaged in agriculture, the manufacturing sector remains relatively weak in most Islamic societies. Agriculture remains important, although it has become less labor-intensive, and the service and tourism sectors have grown rapidly in many nations of the Islamic world. In the oil-producing states, a new economic pattern based primary on oil revenues emerged in the 20th century. In Saudi Arabia, Kuwait, and the Gulf countries, little manufacturing or industry takes place unless it is directly connected with the oil industry. The service sector in these countries is very strong, but the majority of the labor is foreign, including workers from other Arab nations, Iran, Pakistan, India, the Philippines, and elsewhere. The division of labor along ethnic and gender lines remains strong in Islamic societies and is more pronounced than in other regions of the world. One of the legacies of colonialism is an important presence of foreign companies, experts, advisors, and skilled workers in many sectors, often from the former colonial powers or from other western European nations. Female education and labor force participation rates in the Middle East and North Africa and in other Islamic societies are among the lowest in the world as a consequence of conservative cultural norms and social values, and this remains a prominent cause of low productivity. The gender-segregated division of labor is also more pronounced than in other regions of the globe, with women working primarily in light manufacturing and service industries, clerical occupations, informal and domestic activities, and agriculture.

EDITOR

See also economic theory; guilds; trade and commerce; women

Further Reading

Eleanor Abdella Doumato and Marsha Pripstein Posusney, eds., *Women and Globalization in the Arab Middle East: Gender, Economy and Society*, 2003; Valentine M. Moghadam, *Women, Work, and Economic Reform in the Middle East and North Africa*, 1998; Maya Shatzmiller, *Labour in the Medieval Islamic World*, 1994.

Druze

The Druze religion is a faith that arose from within Fatimid Isma'ilism, one of the branches of Shi'ism. The faith appeared in Egypt during the last years of the reign of the sixth Fatimid caliph al-Hakim bi-Amr Allah (r. 996–1021), whom some extremist Isma'ili followers—and later all Druze followers—regarded as an incarnation of God. The Druze who survive as a small minority in Syria, Lebanon, Israel, and Jordan (their estimated number in these countries totaled around one million in the beginning of the 21st century) diverge substantially from Islam, both Sunni and Shi'i.

A number of Isma'ili preachers (*dā'īs*) who arrived in Cairo from Persia and Central Asia propagated radical doctrines concerning Hakim. Notable among them were Muhammad b. Isma'il al-Darazi (or Darzi), who gave his name to adherents of the Druze faith (*durūz*), and Hamza b. 'Ali al-Labbad (the feltmaker) of Zawzan in eastern Iran, who is viewed as the founder of the Druze religion. By dispatching delegations of individual *dā'īs*, Hamza attempted to spread the new religion as an internal preaching (*da'wa*) within the already existing Isma'ili missionary movement. In a series of epistles—a number of which were later incorporated into the *Epistles of Wisdom* (*Rasa'il al-Hikma*), constituting the Druze canon—Hamza preached the divinity not only of Hakim but also of the earlier Fatimid caliphs beginning with al-Qa'im (r. 934–46). Relying upon early extremist Isma'ili doctrine, Hamza also preached the abrogation (*naskh*) of the Muslim religion and its Isma'ili inner interpretation (*ta'wīl*). The old religion, and the existing political rule under which it had flourished, had to be replaced by a new one: that of the Druze. The main pillar of the new faith became the belief in God's unity as manifested in his incarnation, al-Hakim. Hamid al-Din al-Kirmani (d. ca. 1021), the great Isma'ili *dā'ī* and a witness to the emergence of the Druze religion, stated that according to Druze doctrine, Muslim tenets should be rejected as "superstitions [*khurāfāt*], husks [*qushūr*] and mere stuffing [*ḥashw*]. Salvation does not depend on them."

Hamza built up his preaching organization to spread the new religion throughout the world. The wide range of the Druze missionary system is reflected in the *Epistles of Wisdom*, which are addressed to a variety of peoples and include, inter alia, the treatment of doctrinal themes and organization of the new religion as well as polemics against such faiths as Sunni Islam, Isma'ilism, Nusayrism, Judaism, and Christianity. The active political phase of the Druze faith, however, did not last long. Hamza and the other prominent *dā'īs* supporting him in disseminating the new faith—primarily Muhammad b. Wahb al-Qurashi, Salama b. 'Abd al-Wahhab, and Baha' al-Din al-Muqtana—began their religiopolitical activity in 1017 (considered the first year of the Druze era) and ended it in 1035, the year of the closing of the *da'wa* and the beginning of an era of concealment (*dawr al-satr*), a period in which the Druze faith had to cease its proselytizing activity. In 1021, Hakim disappeared suddenly under mysterious circumstances. According to Druze doctrine, the era of concealment would come to an end only with the eschatological return of Hakim, which would mark the definitive victory of the Druze faith. Hakim's successor, Zahir (r. 1021–35), denied his predecessor's claim of divinity. The entire Druze community was subjected to persecution and forced to retreat to remote mountainous areas, chiefly in Lebanon and Syria. Under such circumstances, the Druze doctrine could not continue to develop. Druze religious writings were accessible to only a small minority of initiated scholars (*'uqqāl*, literally "learned"); they were entirely unavailable to the vast majority of the uninitiated (*juhhāl*, literally "ignorant"). The *'uqqāl* alone participated in weekly religious sessions, traditionally held on Thursday nights; the uninitiated were not committed to the performance of religious commandments, with a few exceptions. The Five Pillars of Islam were not observed, and one of the epistles of the Druze canon—*al-naqḍ al-khafī* (the hidden destruction)—was even dedicated to their systematic rejection.

In the remote areas of Lebanon and Syria, however, the Druze were able to return to the political arena. Druze leaders (amirs) gradually rose to power, maintaining a de facto autonomous semi-feudal rule. Fakhr al-Din II (1585–1653), of the Ma'n dynasty, ruled—formally under the sovereignty of the Ottomans—over most of Lebanon and parts of Syria and Palestine. In the 18th century, the house of Shihab gained ascendancy over rival feudal lords. The history of the Druze in Syria and Lebanon over the past four centuries has been marked by a continuing struggle for hegemony between themselves and their Christian-Maronite neighbors. The intercommunal rivalry led to periodic violent clashes, culminating in the civil war that broke out in 1860 and turned into a sweeping Druze massacre of Christians. In the 19th century, two Druze clans—the Junbalat and the Arslan—emerged as the chief rivals for leadership. French involvement on behalf of the Maronites ended in the creation of a self-governing Christian hegemony that became the basis of an enlarged Lebanon, first under the French Mandate in 1920 and then as an independent state in 1943 in which the Druze were also represented. The leading Druze political figure since independence, until his assassination in 1976, was Kamal Junbalat, who was succeeded by his son Walid. The political leadership of the Druze in Syria traditionally has been in the hands of the Atrash family. Traditional leadership in Israel has come from the Tarif clan from the village of Julis in Galilee.

Despite the Druze involvement in political activity during certain periods of their modern history, they were predominantly characterized as quiet and nonpolitical. This approach is deeply embedded in the principle of *taqiyya* (precautionary dissimulation), which in the Druze faith—as among other minority Muslim groups (mainly within Shi'ism)—is a fundamental doctrine. Relying upon this principle, the Druze were allowed in time of danger outwardly to adopt the faith of the dominant majority. Kais Firro, an Israeli scholar of the Druze community, rejects this explanation

of Druze political behavior, however, claiming that it is based on external, non-Druze, and even anti-Druze, sources.

See also Fatimids (909–1171); Hakim bi-Amr Allah (985–1021); Isma'ilis; Shi'ism

Further Reading

Nejla M. Abu-Izzeddin, *The Druzes: A New Study of Their History, Faith and Society*, 1993; David R. W. Bryer, *The Origins of the Druze Religion . . .* (PhD diss., University of Oxford), 1971; Kais M. Firro, *A History of the Druzes*, 1992; Hamid al-Din al-Kirmani, *al-Risala al-Wa'iza*, vol. 14, ed. Muhammad Kamil Husayn, 1952; Silvestre de Sacy, *Exposé de la religion des Druzes*, 2 vols., 1838; Daniel de Smet, ed. and trans., *Les épîtres sacrées des druzes* (*Rasa'il al-Hikma*), 2007.

MEIR M. BAR-ASHER

E

East Africa

The proximity of the cradle of Islam in the Arabian Peninsula to the East African coast led to the new religion's early arrival in East Africa and the absorption of Arabic influences. East African Islam was also influenced by the central position of the coast on the trade route between the Middle East and the Far East and by relations with Persia and Yemen. The geographical position of the East African coast contributed to the development of the Swahili culture and language, which combined external Islamic elements with local ethnic, religious, and linguistic features.

Archeological and numismatic evidence indicate the existence of a Muslim settlement at Shanga in the Lamu archipelago on the Kenyan coast as early as 780. Evidence of Muslim settlement between the 10th and 13th centuries has been found in Pemba, Zanzibar, and Kilwa, which are all in present-day Tanzania. In the course of the 14th century, Islam spread along the coastline up to the Comoro Islands and Madagascar and into the hinterland. It is estimated that by the 14th century, there were more than 30 Muslim communities. These communities were composed of Eastern Bantu, Sudanic and Southern Cushitic, and Northeast-Coastal Bantu speakers, together with communities of Arabic, Indian, Persian, and Yemenite immigrants, mostly traders and merchants.

The concept of a supreme God was found already in the pre-Islamic beliefs of the region, but it was associated with the worship of spirits and ancestors. Some of these pre-Islamic beliefs were assimilated into the new religion, as observed by later travelers, such as Abu 'Abdallah Muhammad b. Battuta in the 14th century. The existence of immigrants that came from the town of Shiraz in Persia suggests that Persian forms of Islam may have been present at an early stage, which may have led to the introduction of Shi'i elements. Yet the Fatimid dynasty's dominance in trade with India and the East Indies along the Red Sea since the 11th century resulted in the dominance of Sunni influences in the area. With the migration of *shurafā'* (plural of *sharīf*) families from Yemen and the Hadhramaut beginning in the 13th century, local Muslims adopted the Shafi'i *madhhab* (one of the four schools of law in Islam). It is in urban settlements such as Mombasa, Zanzibar, Kilwali, and Kilwa, which flourished between the 12th and 14th centuries, that these developments can be traced. Kilwa was the most powerful Islamic settlement on the coast, known for its Islamic architecture, governance, and center of learning, as well as its jihad against the "infidels" of the hinterland.

The Portuguese conquest of the East African coast, which occurred from 1498 to 1530, threatened to wipe out the age of Islamic prosperity. As part of their attempts to secure control of the maritime trade routes against the Ottomans, the Portuguese established Fort Jesus in Mombasa and subjugated most of the Muslim settlements along the coast. Powerful Islamic settlements such as Kilwa declined, and new centers, such as Lamu and Pate, emerged with new ruling elites, mostly from *shurafā'* families. Islamic scholarship began to flourish on the coast, including written literature in both Arabic and Swahili. Attempts to convert coastal Muslims to Christianity were rarely successful and led local Muslims to seek external aid in order to expel the Portuguese.

During the 17th century, the sultanate of Oman became a considerable force in the Indian Ocean. At the request of local Swahili leaders, such as the Mazru'i dynasty from Mombasa, the Omanis helped the latter expel the Portuguese from all areas north of Mozambique at the beginning of the 18th century. The Omanis gradually began to conquer areas along the coast, however, and during the 1820s they established the Zanzibar Sultanate. In 1837, Sa'id b. Sultan from the Al Bu Sa'idi dynasty made Zanzibar his main place of residence. Through the influence of the new sultanate, a more Arabized form of East African Islam flourished until the arrival of the Europeans.

European protectorates were established over Zanzibar, Tanganyika (both which are in present-day Tanzania), Kenya, Uganda, and other territories toward the end of the 19th century. European colonial rule was generally based on indirect rule, in other words, on collaboration with local Muslim rulers who continued their traditional ruling systems. Sufi *tarīqa*s (Sufi brotherhoods) such as the 'Alawis, Qadiris, and Shadhilis, which had flourished in the area in previous centuries, became the main basis for social organization and the spread of Islam over new communities during the colonial era. Many workers who emigrated from the hinterland to the coastal areas were also converted to Islam. Yet European colonialism also encouraged Christian missionary activity and colonization of European settlers, which resulted in a notable decrease in Islamic diffusion. Thus, with the rise of the East African secular nation-states in the early 1960s, Muslims were substantial minorities in the new states but not a dominant factor in the determination of political and ideological agendas.

Since the 1980s, feelings of marginalization of Muslims in states dominated by Christians elites such as Kenya and Uganda have resulted in an Islamic revival, accompanied by politicization and even radicalization. Influences from revolutionary Iran and Saudi Arabian Wahhabism have resulted in the establishment of educational

and welfare networks that in some cases have translated into a demand for active political representation.

See also Ethiopia and Eritrea; Sudan

Further Reading

Justo Lacunza-Balda, "Translations of the Quran into Swahili, and Contemporary Islamic Revival in East Africa," in *African Islam and Islam in Africa: Encounters between Sufis and Islamists*, edited by Eva Evers Rosander and David Westerlund, 1997; Ira M. Lapidus, *A History of Islamic Societies*, 2002; Randall L. Pouwels, "The East African Coast c. 780 to 1900 C.E.," in *The History of Islam in Africa*, edited by Nehemia Levtzion and Randall L. Pouwels, 2000; J. Spencer Trimingham, *Islam in East Africa*, 1964.

IRIT BACK

economic theory

Throughout its history, Islam has sought to regulate all aspects of life, including economics. Its holy book contains verses concerning such matters as credit, trade, resource allocation, taxation, redistribution, and inheritance. The Qur'an prohibits *ribā*, a pre-Islamic credit practice, which commonly led borrowers into enslavement (2:274–80, 3:130, 4:160–61). It prescribes an annual tax called zakat on certain forms of wealth and income in order to finance eight categories of public expenditure, including defense, the propagation of Islam, and poor relief (2:177, 2:215, 4:8, 9:60, 24:22). It entitles all surviving children of a deceased person to a share of his or her estate (4:11–12, 176). It requires individuals to be honest and fair in commercial transactions (55:7–9).

Intellectual Heritage

Over the ages, a wide variety of economic policies have been justified through these prescriptions and prohibitions, including ones that are mutually incompatible. Often the justifications in question have rested also on the sunna, the normative practice of the Prophet Muhammad. From the dawn of Islam to the present, the use of interest on loans has been treated as illegitimate through an expansive interpretation of the ban on *ribā*, understood as usury. The preindustrial guilds that regulated the activities of craftsmen were given monopolistic and monopsonistic privileges out of a sense of fairness defined in Islamic terms. In certain times and places, agricultural taxes were collected according to rules prescribed by the Qur'an.

In defining proper economic behavior and prescribing economic policies, the fundamental sources of Islam did not provide a methodology of economics, a theory of economics involving causal relationships, or empirical accounts of how incentives shape economic performance. Nowhere in the Qur'an or the sunna does one find what one might call an economic analysis of some phenomenon. For premodern theories based at least partly on Islam, one must look to great Muslim philosophers, most notably Ghazali (1058–1111), Ibn Taymiyya (1263–1328), Ibn Khaldun (1332–1406), and Taqi al-Din al-Maqrizi (1364–1442). Ghazali and Ibn Taymiyya drew also on the great Hellenic philosophers of antiquity. In line with Aristotle, they treated greed, avarice, deceit, corruption, and oppression as traits that could be overcome, to one degree or another, through moral education. As for Ibn Khaldun and Maqrizi, they were impressed by the immutability of human selfishness and hunger for power. They attributed recurrent patterns of overtaxation, poor governance, and expropriation primarily to ineradicable human drives and only secondarily to deficient socialization or education.

Yet, in writing about matters central to economics, the great Muslim thinkers of the Middle Ages did not forge a distinct or coherent approach to interpreting phenomena such as trade flows, inflation, public finance, productivity, and living standards. In short, they did not develop what we would recognize today as a discipline of economics. Hence, when the rise of western Europe became a threat to Muslim sovereignty in the Ottoman Empire, Safavid Iran, Mughal India, and elsewhere, Muslims who began to reflect on the underlying causes found little of economic relevance in the works of earlier Muslim thinkers. Unable to derive adequate guidance from their own intellectual heritage, they inferred, by and large, that their troubles stemmed from moral failings. Only in the 19th century did their successors begin to formulate coherent economic responses. By then the thinking of most economic reformers was divorced from identifiable Islamic concepts; insofar as they were guided by economic theory, their presumptions, concepts, and terminology were largely of foreign provenance. Upholding this pattern in the first half of the 20th century, Muslim leaders, including those committed to Islamic causes, formulated economic policies without reference to Islam's intellectual heritage. For their part, contributors to Islamic thought did not develop distinctly Islamic interpretations of economic problems or solutions to overcoming them. The half century leading up to World War II constituted a period of near-complete separation between religious and economic thought in the Muslim world.

Rise of Islamic Economics

These two spheres began to reunite in the 1940s with the emergence of a school of economic thought that claimed to draw inspiration primarily from Islam's traditional sources. Called "Islamic economics," it was initiated by Abu al-A'la Mawdudi (1903–79), an Indian whose goal was to preserve the religious identity and cultural heritage of India's Muslim minority rather than to solve its economic problems. Mawdudi set out to demonstrate the comprehensiveness of Islam as a source of guidance by proposing distinctly Islamic approaches in various areas, including economics. Promoting Islamic economics as a superior alternative to capitalism and socialism, the leading economic systems of his time, Mawdudi offered Islamic banking as a just system of finance respectful of Islam's ban on interest, zakat as the basis of a redistribution system meant

to eradicate poverty, and norms of economic behavior drawn from Islam's traditional sources as a remedy for corruption and mistrust in the marketplace.

Over the following two decades, other seminal contributions to Islamic economics were made by Sayyid Qutb (1906–66), an Egyptian, and Muhammad Baqir al-Sadr (1931–80), an Iraqi. Like Mawdudi, they invoked the economic performance of Islam's initial decades in seventh-century Arabia as proof of how Islamic principles can benefit societies economically. Though differing on certain details of the historical record, these pioneers took it for granted that Islamic principles were followed broadly in the days of Prophet Muhammad, that subsequent Muslim leaders invited economic troubles by skirting rules for personal gain, and that Islamic economic teachings are equally beneficial in a modern economy based on impersonal exchange as in a medieval economy whose exchanges are mostly among acquaintances.

None of the early contributors to Islamic economics attempted to explain why, once in place, the ideal economic policies proved unsustainable. Focusing on identifying exemplary behaviors by revered early Muslims, their writings attributed the behaviors to personal virtues rooted in piety. Echoing Ghazali and Ibn Taymiyya, they also emphasized the possibility of overcoming personal shortcomings through faith and education. From its inception, then, Islamic economics was in conflict with the theoretical framework of neoclassical economics, the dominant economic methodology since the mid-20th century. Under the assumption that in most contexts people are essentially selfish, neoclassical economics tries to identify the incentives that lead individuals and collectivities to particular outcomes and, in addition, the social mechanisms responsible for the incentives themselves. Islamic economists have by and large disregarded the incentives responsible for Muslim economic underdevelopment, rampant corruption in Muslim-governed societies, and huge inequalities both within and among Muslim countries, to cite just a few of the failures they attribute to the prevailing, un-Islamic economic systems of the Muslim world. This orientation has drastically limited the attention Islamic economics receives from scholars with formal training in economics. Most professional economists of the Muslim faith continue to treat economics as a secular domain at least implicitly by conducting their analyses within neoclassical theoretical frameworks divorced from religion.

Methodological Transformation

Islamic economics entered a new phase during the Middle East's oil boom of the mid-1970s, as political threats to the oil-rich monarchies made them increase their aid to various Islamist movements, including Islamic economics. Well-funded organizations began a campaign to raise the profile of Islamic economics within scholarly circles. Journals of Islamic economics were founded, international conferences were organized, and subfields of Islamic economics were defined to match those of the American Economic Association, the world's leading association of professional economists. Research presented under the rubric of Islamic economics began to use mathematics and to borrow concepts, terms, and methods from neoclassical economics and, to a lesser and declining extent, Marxian economics.

The resulting research output has continued to ascribe a key role to Islamic morality in enabling efficient resource allocation, ensuring fair trades, and providing a safety net to the disadvantaged. By the same token, it has incorporated incentives into its theoretical framework through such concepts as utility functions and offer curves. Islamic variants of neoclassical models have been developed, such as general equilibrium models of an economy without interest and aggregate consumption models with zakat-paying individuals. Contributions promote the view that markets work well provided the participants pass their choices through an Islamic moral filter. They thus depart from a central tenet of neoclassical economics, whose roots go back at least to Adam Smith (1723–90): the view that markets serve general welfare precisely when individuals and firms seek selfishly to maximize utility or profit.

Themes and Topics

Major differences have existed with regard to the specifics of the moral filter in question. For almost any widely condemned economic outcome or practice, Islamic economics offers writings that call on good Muslims to avoid it, if not also to take preventive steps. The use of child labor, income inequality, poor working conditions, industrial pollution, and disharmony in the workplace are among the generally troubling phenomena that the norms of Islam are expected to alleviate. However, there have also been writings that treat social patterns considered troubling by most Islamic economists as unavoidable and not necessarily problematic. A research center in Qum, Iran, has proposed sharp restrictions on regulations concerning workplace conditions and child labor.

Conspicuously missing from Islamic economics has been research aimed at explaining the operation of economies governed under Islamic law after the first few decades. Very few attempts have been made to understand the operation of the Abbasid, Mamluk, Ottoman, Safavid, or Mughal economies or to draw lessons from their records for modern economic development. In this respect, Islamic economics has maintained a pattern set by Mawdudi, who found little value in economic practices after the first few decades of Islam on the ground that Muslim economic life was corrupted. Research aimed at explaining the successes and failures of Islamic economic institutions has been conducted mainly outside the rubric of Islamic economics.

The theme that corruption spread among Muslims after Islam's "golden age" in the seventh century has coexisted in Islamic economics with the attribution of the Muslim world's current economic shortcomings to Western imperialism. Starting around the 18th century, many contributors hold, Europeans destroyed local crafts, monopolized natural resources, replaced Islamic institutions with Western institutions, and took over key aspects of economic governance. They also lowered Muslim standards of honesty and weakened adherence to Islam's ethic of brotherly cooperation.

By far the most popular topic in Islamic economics is Islamic finance, which constitutes its main practical achievement. The size of the global Islamic finance sector, estimated at $400 billion as of 2010, has prompted much empirical research aimed at evaluating its performance, as well as theorizing to explain the findings. Only some of this research takes place under the guise of Islamic economics. Its analytical tools are drawn mostly from secular schools of economic thought.

See also capitalism; communism; Islamization; socialism

Further Reading

Sohrab Behdad, "A Disputed Utopia: Islamic Economics in Revolutionary Iran," *Comparative Studies in Society and History* 36, no. 4 (1994); Umar Chapra, *Islam and the Economic Challenge*, 1992; Mahmoud A. El-Gamal, *Islamic Finance: Law, Economics, and Practice*, 2006; S. M. Ghazanfar, ed., *Medieval Islamic Economic Thought: Filling the "Great Gap" in European Economics*, 2003; Timur Kuran, *Islam and Mammon: The Economic Predicaments of Islamism*, 2004; Idem, *The Long Divergence: How Islamic Law Held Back the Middle East*, 2011; Mervyn K. Lewis and Latifa M. Algaoud, *Islamic Banking*, 2001; Sayyid Abul-Ala Mawdudi, *Islamic Way of Life*, 1950; Tim Niblock and Rodney Wilson, *The Political Economy of the Middle East, vol. 3: Islamic Economics*, 1999; Maxime Rodinson, *Islam and Capitalism*, translated by Brian Pearce, 1966; Abraham L. Udovitch, *Partnership and Profit in Medieval Islam*, 1970.

TIMUR KURAN

education

Islamic education should be viewed historically against the background of pre-Islamic times, which Muslims call the *jāhiliyya*, or "age of ignorance." Muslims equate the polytheistic state of affairs in Arabia before the mission of the Prophet Muhammad with paganism, savagery, and barbarism—the antithesis of civilization. In contrast, Islam means to understand and acknowledge that there is no god but God and to submit to His will. For Muslims, the Islamic religion and way of life thus perfectly represent the wholeness and holiness of education and are synonymous with enlightenment, culture, and civilization.

Islamic education builds on two major principles: acquiring knowledge is both a lifelong pursuit and a religious duty. A correlation exists between knowledge and action for the welfare of the Muslim community—and humanity in general. Hence, Islamic learning aspires to develop persons who acquired a solid general education and are well-grounded in, and shaped by, the virtues of Islam so that they can become productive members of society.

This inclusiveness of Islamic learning is evident in the Qur'an and the hadith; it is also expressed in proverbs, aphorisms, and wisdom sayings. Scholarly discussions of educational theories and practices are offered in a wide variety of medieval Arabic and Persian writings, particularly in classical Islamic philosophical, ethical, and didactic works. The transformations and challenges in contemporary Islamic societies resulting from postcolonial developments, interaction with the West, globalization, migration, and the reality of Muslim life in non-Islamic countries constitute the basis for discourses on education within an Islamic framework.

The Qur'an expressly prioritizes learning and education. God is humankind's undisputed supreme teacher, for God "taught humankind that which they knew not" (Q. 96:5). In the first revelation to the Prophet Muhammad, he was given the divine command to "read" or "recite" words of revelation and thus to proclaim and teach the Word of God to his people and to the world (Q. 96:1–5). Numerous other Qur'anic passages deal with the instruction of believers in the faith and their spiritual growth as individuals and members of the community. Some passages also demand the application of reason and understanding in matters of faith. Similarly, the Qur'an determines the ideal political and religious leaders as those whom God "endowed abundantly with knowledge and bodily perfection"; they will be the leaders on Earth, even if they have "not been given amplitude of wealth" (Q. 2:247).

The imperative to seek knowledge is clearly expressed in many well-known sayings and traditions attributed to the Prophet Muhammad. The command "Seek knowledge, even unto China" sanctifies the idea that the search for knowledge (*talab al-'ilm*) has no geographic or cultural boundaries. The Prophet's insistence that "the pursuit of knowledge is incumbent on every Muslim, male or female" highlights that learning is a religious duty, irrespective of gender. Another prophetic statement calls for well-educated leadership, as "the person with the best knowledge of the Book of God and most experience in reading [it] should lead the people [in prayer]."

In early Islam, instruction took place in teaching sessions and study circles in mosques or privately in the homes of scholars. Oral instruction was a predominant feature of learning, and personal contact between the teacher and students was considered the best guarantee for the authenticity of the transmitted knowledge. This idea of authoritative transmission has remained crucial to Islamic learning throughout history, especially in the religious disciplines. Nonetheless, as early as the seventh century, lectures and seminars regularly were based on written collections of notes used by scholars and students as memory aids. In the ninth century, "the book" emerged in Muslim society and was soon recognized as a powerful medium of education.

By the tenth century, the Muslim world extended from Spain to China. This religiopolitical development significantly stimulated Islamic learning, causing the Arabic-Islamic civilization to become a "knowledge society" characterized by a considerable degree of religious tolerance and intellectual open-mindedness. Baghdad (founded in 762), the capital of the Abbasid caliphate, was the vibrant commercial, cultural, and intellectual metropolis of the Muslim world. It witnessed dynamic activities in the humanities and

great advancements in the natural sciences. Significant achievements in mathematics, astronomy, chemistry and alchemy, medicine, pharmacology, optics, physics, engineering, architecture, irrigation, and agriculture attest to the industriousness of medieval Muslim scholarship and education. It is also evident in history and geography, in the codification of law, and in the development of philology and grammar. Classical Islamic philosophy demonstrates originality and brilliance in abstract thinking, while Islamic mysticism (Sufism) played a significant role in the transmission of knowledge (*'ilm*), as it was generally considered a prerequisite for gnosis (*ma'rifa*). Influential scholarly families played a decisive role in recruiting, funding, and controlling the intellectual elite of medieval Muslim society.

Academies remarkably free of cultural, ethnic, or confessional constraints were established. For example, Baghdad's famous translation academy and research center—Bayt al-Hikma, or House of Wisdom—was officially sponsored by the caliph Ma'mun (r. 813–33) and employed numerous Christian, Syriac-speaking scholars to prepare Arabic translations of philosophical and scientific works, particularly those in Greek. In Cairo, the Shi'i Fatimids (969–1171 in Egypt) founded academies to study Shi'i theological tenets, as well as much of the intellectual heritage of the Greeks, Iranians, and Indians. The Dar al-'Ilm, or House of Learning, founded in Baghdad in 993 by a Buyid vizier, was administered by two Shi'i notables and a judge; its director of studies, however, was a Sunni (Hanafi) professor.

Azhar ("the Radiant"), the famous mosque and university, was founded in 970 as a Shi'i institution. When the Sunni Ayyubids took power in Egypt (1171–1250), Azhar became a Sunni place of learning and eventually the principal religious university of the Islamic world. Major centers of Islamic learning also developed in cities such as Damascus, Aleppo, Basra, Kufa, Qum, Mashhad, Isfahan, and Farghana in the East; Qayrawan, Tunis (Zaytuna mosque-university from the eighth century), and Fez (the Qarawiyyin mosque and college was founded in 859) emerged in the West; and Córdoba, Toledo, and Granada represented Andalus (Islamic Spain). Famous medical schools existed in Gondeshapur (Iran), Alexandria (Egypt), and Harran (Iraq).

Colleges specializing in Sunni religious and legal instruction were established to meet the growing need for skilled personnel. In addition to mosque- and shrine-colleges, the most important type of college—the madrasa (lit. "a place to study")—flourished from the 11th to 14th centuries. Its most notable example, the Nizamiyya in Baghdad, was founded in 1057 by the vizier Nizam al-Mulk (d. 1092) in response to the Fatimid "threat" of spreading Shi'i doctrine and learning, best exemplified by the great Azhar mosque-university in Egypt. In the 13th century, many Shi'i madrasas were established in Iraq and Persia, especially in Hilla, Qum, Rayy, and Kashan. The madrasa—both Sunni and Shi'i—became a tangible feature of Islam's culture and civilization, often financed by a pious endowment (waqf) supporting both faculty and students. The madrasa combined living and teaching accommodations. It was usually built close to a large mosque and led by an imam-professor. The madrasa was largely concerned with Islamic jurisprudence (*fiqh*), Qur'anic exegesis (*tafsīr*), theology (*kalām* and *'aqīda*), tradition (the hadith), Arabic language, and logic (the latter two disciplines being considered essential for accurate expression and sound thinking).

Although this issue has been viewed controversially, some modern scholars suggest that with the rise of an extensive network of (predominantly Sunni) madrasas in the Eastern Islamic world, and given the constraints in the various subjects taught, the religious scholars ('ulama')—by then thoroughly professionalized under state patronage—came to influence the cohesiveness and unity of Islamic thought. To be sure, this decisive institutional victory of dogmatic thought over discursive scholarship resulted in conservatism and, among certain scholars, an opposition to "secular" learning. Traditional Islamic learning (both Sunni and Twelver Shi'i) became increasingly deductive and textually centripetal, particularly regarding the text of revelation itself. Inductive reasoning, required to deal scientifically with matters not yet fully established, was nearly excluded from the curriculum of the madrasa, although it was practiced to some extent in legal reasoning, philosophy, and the physical sciences as such.

Key appointments at madrasas were regularly made by the donor, who designated a prominent scholar for the chair he established. These appointments were monitored by the ruler, but imam-professors of the important "cathedral mosques" were appointed by the caliph himself. Through this web of indirect and direct governmental "patronage" and supervision, the military and political elites in medieval Muslim societies exercised a significant degree of control over the 'ulama' and ensured that scholars would provide the political regime with the religious legitimization it needed. However, despite the fact that madrasas in medieval times had a political dimension, the 'ulama' were free to supervise and regulate the transmission of knowledge without interference from the political elite.

In view of this complex situation, from the 8th through the 16th centuries, there was a continuous tradition of Islamic scholarship dealing with pedagogy and didactics. Farabi (d. 950), probably the most important Islamic political philosopher, made significant contributions to Islamic learning in the context of political and ethical thought, expressed in his books *The Perfect State*, *The Political Regime*, and *The Attainment of Happiness*. Living in Baghdad, Farabi insisted that virtuous societies must be based on a political order whose guiding principle is the realization of human excellence through virtue. Therefore, both rulers and citizens need a certain degree of education, and human societies attain perfection to the extent that their rulers organize their citizens' duties according to their knowledge and specialization, give them laws, and provide leadership in other aspects of communal life. Rulers must become philosopher-kings, perfect in their intellectual faculties and divinely inspired. Farabi claimed that philosophy was indispensable for the founding and survival of the "virtuous state," while prophecy was indispensable for the founding of a virtuous state but not for its survival.

Khatib al-Baghdadi (d. 1071), an intellectual historian from Baghdad, emphasized that the teacher must ensure equal learning opportunities for all his students, regardless of whether they are Muslims, Jews, or Christians—a statement clearly suggesting that the true spirit of learning does not know religious boundaries. Ghazali (d. 1111), one of the great architects of Islamic learning, affirmed in his monumental work *The Revival of Religious Studies* that orthodox belief, spirituality, and reason were the foundations of traditional Islamic learning. He shaped the theory and practice of Islamic education in a way that is still evident today.

The Tunisian historian and social philosopher Ibn Khaldun (d. 1406) determined in his famous *Muqaddima* (Prolegomena) three types of theoretical and practical knowledge. First, there is the knowledge of essences, which leads to understanding the realities behind phenomena. Second, there is the knowledge of the natural world and human culture, which enables humans to arrange their lives and control the world they live in. Such "knowledge of civilization" includes technology as well as social and political relationships. Third, there is moral knowledge, which refers to the human ability to think and gradually acquire experience so that ordinary citizens will deal reasonably with each other, rulers will govern in the best interest of society, and thus human life in general will improve. In this context, Ibn Khaldun stresses the role of experience, social skills, and the ability to cooperate. However, human intellect should not be overestimated in learning and human growth, for Ibn Khaldun states that religious knowledge, based on Muhammad's prophecy, was to be preferred and overrides reason and philosophical thought whenever it contradicts divine law (shari'a); this was particularly true in politics. Therefore, prophecy must be accepted as the unquestionable foundation of a sound political society in which humans, as naturally social and political beings, would actively build their existence.

Mulla Sadra Shirazi (d. 1641), a Twelver Shi'i thinker and important educator in Shiraz, insisted that scientific knowledge must be balanced with intuitive knowledge. He severely criticized the worldliness of the 'ulama' of his age and stressed the otherworldly aspect of learning—a view that significantly influenced the theory and practice of religious learning in later times. In contrast, other Shi'i clerics, like the Lebanese 'Ali al-Karaki (d. 1534) and the Iranian Muhammad Sabzavari (d. 1679), suggested that scholars take a more world-embracing attitude. They expressly encouraged religious scholars to become socially active and even to associate with the powerful in order to educate and guide them.

European colonial powers in the Middle East and Southeast Asia had a dramatic impact on Islamic society. They provided Muslim intellectuals and enlightened rulers with the grounds for educational reform in their attempt to raise the standard and widen the scope of learning. Muhammad 'Ali (d. 1849) in Egypt, Sultan 'Abdulmajid I (d. 1861) in Turkey, and Sayyid Ahmad Khan (d. 1898) in India are just a few examples.

In the Arab world, the intellectual reform movement of the Nahda (Awakening) made important steps in reconciling traditional and modern (Western) areas of knowledge in a spirit of openness while retaining the values of Islam and a Muslim identity. In Egypt, Muhammad 'Abduh (d. 1905) called for the reformulation of Islamic doctrine in the light of modern thought, while Qasim Amin (d. 1908) campaigned for the liberation of women. Educational reforms were carried out by Muhammad Bayram (d. 1889) in Tunisia, the Alusi family in Iraq, and by 'Abd al-Hamid b. Badis (d. 1940) in Algeria. In Turkey, Atatürk (d. 1938), founder and first president of the Turkish Republic, implemented the idea of secular nationhood in an Islamic country and secularized the country's educational system.

Throughout much of the 20th century, Islamic education was transformed not only by the struggle between secular and Islamic ideologies but also by a new politicization of Islam in large parts of the Muslim world. In Egypt, the situation of the 'ulama' changed radically in 1952 when the Nasserist regime nationalized the waqfs, thus depriving Azhar University of its financial basis. A 1961 reform aimed to integrate Azhar and their 'ulama' into what was considered "modern society." This reform successfully introduced secular fields of study into the traditionally religious Azhar curriculum. These changes had long-term effects on the 'ulama''s social and political identity: by creating a state-controlled religious monopoly, the regime forced the 'ulama' into complete political submission, but it also provided religious scholars with the space and instruments for their political emergence in the 1970s and 1980s.

In addition to reputable secular universities in the Muslim world, and the robust efforts of the Arab Gulf states to modernize their educational systems, institutionalized Islamic learning in the early 21st century was associated with the highly respected centers of religious scholarship in Cairo, Mecca, Medina, Najaf, and Qum, as well as Hyderabad, Lucknow, and Saharanpur in India, and Dar al-Ulum of Deoband (founded in 1867)—the most renowned Indian madrasa and the largest in Asia. New international Islamic universities were established in Islamabad, Pakistan (1980), and in Kuala Lumpur, Malaysia (1983); both admitted women as well as men. Muslim intellectuals and politicians demonstrated a growing awareness of the need to reform the madrasa program of study to enable students to deal with the challenges of modern society and to come to a more relevant understanding of their faith while upholding the identity and the industriousness of 1,400 years of Islamic learning.

See also jurisprudence; knowledge; philosophy; propaganda; Sufism; theology

Further Reading

Jonathan Berkey, *The Transmission of Knowledge in Medieval Cairo: A Social History of Islamic Education*, 1992; Sebastian Günther, "Be Masters in that You Teach and Continue to Learn: Medieval Muslim Thinkers on Educational Theory," *Islam and Education—Myths and Truths; Comparative Education Review* 50, no. 3 (2006); Robert W. Hefner and Muhammad Qasim Zaman, eds., *Schooling Islam: The Culture and Politics of Modern Muslim Education*, 2007; George Makdisi, *The Rise of Colleges: Institutions of Learning in Islam and the West*, 1981.

SEBASTIAN GÜNTHER

Egypt

Located in the northeastern corner of Africa, Egypt is the most populated Arab state, with a population of over 80 million and an area slightly more than three times the size of New Mexico (385,229 square miles). The Nile River cuts through the country, linking it to the Mediterranean Sea in the north and Africa in the south. Several great civilizations developed on the banks of the Nile: the most ancient is the Pharaonic, which thrived for more than 3,000 years. Egypt's strategic location as a trading center connecting Africa, Europe, and Asia made it attractive to invading foreign armies. It fell under the rule of the Persians, Greeks, Romans, Byzantines, Arabs, Mamluks, Ottomans, and British, finally to become an independent nation-state in 1954. Egypt has been part of the Muslim world since 641 and is predominantly Arab and Islamic in culture. Over 90 percent of Egypt's population is Sunni Muslim, and the rest are mostly Coptic Christians; there are also small numbers of Shi'is, Baha'is, Jews, and Christians of other denominations. Many Egyptians belong to Sufi orders.

Long recognized as a main cultural and Islamic center in the Arab and Muslim worlds, Egypt is home to the oldest Islamic educational institution, Azhar University, which was built by the Fatimids in 970 to propagate the Shi'i doctrine. Under the Ayyubids, Azhar University was converted to a Sunni institution and the four legal *madhhab*s (schools)—Maliki, Hanafi, Shafi', and Hanbali—have been taught side by side for centuries, attesting to the country's tradition of religious and cultural toleration. Egypt has produced scores of Muslim scholars that made prominent contributions to Islam such as al-Layth b. Sa'd (713–91), Badr al-Din al-Zarkashi (1344–73), Ibn Hajar al-Asqalani (1372–1448), Shams al-Din al-Sakhawi (1428–97), and Jalal al-Din al-Suyuti (ca. 1445–1505).

By the end of the 19th century, the movement of Islamic modernism emerged in Egypt, inspiring political and social reform in the Arab and Muslim worlds. Started by Afghani (1837–97) and Muhammad 'Abduh (1849–1905), Islamic modernism was a revival movement that sought to rescue Islam from further decline by adopting the positive aspects of Western civilization, reinterpreting the Qur'an along modern lines, exercising *ijtihād* (independent reasoning), restricting the powers of the government, and achieving Muslim unity. Afghani and 'Abduh's message bifurcated into Islamic reformism on the one hand and secular nationalism and liberalism on the other, with Muhammad Rashid Rida (1865–1935) as the foremost exponent of the former and Sa'd Zaghlul (1825–1927), Qasim Amin (1863–1908), Lutfi al-Sayyid (1872–1963), and Taha Hussein (1889–1973) as the main representatives of the latter. In 1928, one of Rida's disciples, Hasan al-Banna, started a grassroots movement, the Muslim Brotherhood, that eventually became a mainstream Islamic movement and the most important opposition force in Egypt, with branches all over the Arab and Muslim worlds.

The emergence of the Muslim Brotherhood has to some extent shaped the interaction between Islam and politics in Egypt. Having assimilated the reformist precepts of Afghani, 'Abduh, and Rida, Banna produced a reformist framework that presented Islam as a comprehensive way of life, the catalyst for social and political change, and the essential basis of the postcolonial state. Still inspired by the teachings of its founders, the Muslim Brotherhood continues to work at the individual and communal levels to reconstruct the social, political, economic, and cultural dimensions of society along Islamic lines in preparation for the eventual establishment of the Islamic state. This approach has set the organization in a collision course with various regimes. The most severe confrontation took place with Nasser's regime (1952–70), which brutally suppressed the organization. In this context, Sayyid Qutb, a prominent member of the Muslim Brotherhood, produced a polarizing ideology that constituted a clear deviation from the main orientation of the Muslim Brotherhood. Qutb viewed the incumbent regimes as *jāhilī* (un-Islamic) for not accepting the *ḥākimiyya*, or sovereignty, of God and for not implementing the shari'a (Islamic way of life). Qutb's ideas inspired future generations of young Islamic activists, particularly the al-Gama'a al-Islamiyya and al-Jihad groups that assassinated Anwar Sadat in 1981 and engaged in violent clashes with the Mubarak regime during the 1980s and mid-1990s.

Egyptian independent Islamic thinkers continue to influence Islamic political thought in the region. Religious scholars and intellectuals such as Shaykh Muhammad al-Ghazali (1917–96), Shaykh Yusuf al-Qaradawi (b. 1926), Muhammad Galal Keshk (1929–93), Tariq al-Bishri (b. 1933), and Muhammad Salim al-'Awwa (b. 1942) have attempted to synthesize Islam and modern civic concepts and institutions. Their writings address such issues as democracy, political participation, human rights, and citizenship.

EMAD EL-DIN SHAHIN

Inspired by protests against the regime in Tunisia in the fall of 2010, a revolutionary wave of demonstrations spread throughout 2011 into other regions of the Arab world, in particular Egypt, Yemen, Syria, and Bahrain. This wave of Arab awakening became known as "the Arab Spring" and received wide media attention in the Islamic world and the West. It began when thousands of Egyptians staged a peaceful demonstration on January 25, 2011, in Tahrir Square of Cairo, demanding the resignation of the Mubarak regime. (There were protests in other parts of Egypt as well, though less noticed by the media.) The movement relied on techniques of civil resistance, as well as cell phones, text messaging, and Internet technology (especially social media) for communication. It counted Muslims and Copts, as well as both men and women, among its participants, with copies of the Qur'an and Christian crosses held high in the hands of demonstrators. The uprising was spontaneous and drew its strength from the middle classes; it also was leaderless and organized on an ad hoc basis, which some observers saw as a weakness. The revolution garnered international support as it received round-the-clock coverage by the Qatar-based satellite news network Aljazeera.

The uprising, which came to be called "the Egyptian revolution," clearly targeted state corruption, the rule of emergency law, police

brutality, and the abuse of tens of thousands of political prisoners. On February 2, 2011, violent clashes occurred between anti-Mubarak and pro-Mubarak forces. The Muslim Brotherhood and the Salafi segments of the Islamists on the extreme right of Egyptian society were apparently taken by surprise and did not play a significant role in the organization of the uprising. The revolution proved successful in bringing down President Mubarak, who had ruled Egypt since 1981 and was forced to resign on February 11, 2011. (On August 3, 2011, he went on trial together with his two sons and top police officers.) In the wake of the Egyptian developments, the autocratic regimes of ʿAli ʿAbdallah Salih in Yemen and of Muʿammar Qaddafi in Libya were ousted as well, leading to the assassination of the latter (on October 20, 2011) and the exile of the former. In these two cases, tribal conflicts and outside involvement, including French-led NATO forces in Libya and American intelligence and drone bombing in Yemen, played a significant role—actions that were not required in Egypt, where the uprising remained both peaceful and powerful.

After Mubarak's resignation, the military elite of the Egyptian army, led by trusted generals appointed by Mubarak, held on to power. Egyptian society, however, remained restive into the fall of 2011, when first elections took place, awarding the majority of the vote to the Muslim Brotherhood (about 40 percent) and the Salafi party (about 20 percent) with no significant counterweight organization visible in the center or on the left of the political spectrum. The leadership of the Egyptian army discounted the significance of the vote and manifested its determination to remain in power. The Muslim Brotherhood and the Islamist Salafis did not find a common platform. The Coptic Church supported the popular sentiment and observed a guarded caution, fearing for its survival as a non-Islamic minority. In December 2011, Muslim women took to the street for the first time in great numbers, demanding an end to military rule. A presidential election was planned for July 2012.

The general mood in Egypt in early 2012 remained tense, oscillating between fear of chaos and religious strife on one side and hope for decisive change toward democracy and a new order of freedom on the other. The political response of America and Europe to the Arab Spring and the persistent Egyptian revolution reflected both sides of the dilemma. Americans and Europeans were also concerned about the repercussions of Egyptian developments on the security of Israel and the consequences for the entire Middle East. One concern was that a Shiʿi crescent would dominate the northern rim of the Arab world, stretching from Iran, via Iraq and Syria, into Lebanon, and enter into a struggle over control of Arab oil and the Sunni core of the Arabian peninsula, including a number of smaller states clustered around Saudi Arabia. Two political frontier lines seemed possible, one cutting through the waters in the Arab/Persian Gulf and the other running along the mountains of the Turkish border with Syria and Iraq. It seemed possible that Egypt in the south and Turkey in the north might develop systems of political order that combined Islam with the ideals of freedom and democracy. To achieve such a position of sovereignty and power, Egypt would need to maintain its peaceful process of restructuring and revolution.

GERHARD BOWERING

See also ʿAbduh, Muhammad (1849–1905); al-Afghani, Jamal al-Din (1838–97); al-Banna, Hasan (1906–49); Muslim Brotherhood; Rida, Muhammad Rashid (1865–1935); Sayyid Qutb (1906–66)

Further Reading

John Esposito, *Islam: The Straight Path*, 2004; Derek Hopwood, *Egypt: Politics and Society, 1945–1984*, 1985; Nadav Safran, *Egypt in Search of Political Community: An Analysis of the Intellectual and Political Evolution of Egypt, 1804–1952*, 1961.

elections

The concept that the public should participate in the selection of its political leaders and legislators became an important feature of Islamic reformist thought in the late 19th and early 20th centuries through the works of Khayr al-Din al-Tunisi (1822–90), Muhammad ʿAbduh (1849–1905), and Muhammad Rashid Rida (1865–1935). It was developed more fully by contemporary Islamic thinkers, including Yusuf al-Qaradawi, Muhammad Salim al-ʿAwwa, Tariq al-Bishri, and Ahmad Kamal Abu al-Majd. Their support for elections derived from the principle that political authority (*ṣulṭa*) lies with the community (*umma*). In their view, the Qur'an, the sunna, and the historical experiences of the Rightly Guided Caliphs (632–61) all confirm that the people are entitled to select their ruler. According to Qaradawi, this idea lies at the foundation of the faith. It is most clearly captured in the Prophet's statement that Muslims are empowered to choose who will lead them in prayer. ʿAwwa further argues that the public's right to choose the ruler can be traced back to the selection of Abu Bakr as the first successor to Muhammad. Abu Bakr ascended to power through a process by which two prominent members of the community (ʿUmar and Abu ʿUbayda) showed their support for him by pledging an oath of loyalty (*bayʿa*); the community in turn showed its support through its own *bayʿa*. ʿAwwa, who argues that the first *bayʿa* constituted a nomination and the second a referendum, concludes, "one of the most significant results of this event was the decision that a ruler can be chosen only through consultation with the community of Muslims." This principle was upheld by the Rightly Guided Caliphs and serves as the foundation for Islamic government.

These theorists further propose that the public should participate in day-to-day governance. ʿAwwa asserts that one of the central purposes of an Islamic state is to "serve the interests (*maṣāliḥ*) of the governed." These interests can be ascertained only through consultation (*shūrā*) with the community. The concept of *shūrā* has clear doctrinal support in both the Qur'an and the sunna, but the texts

are not clear regarding which members of the community should be consulted. Abu al-Majd observes that the classical texts sometimes refer to "the people of consultation" (*ahl al-shūrā*), which is understood to mean those members of the community with knowledge relevant to the issue at hand. At other times, the texts refer to the "people who loosen and bind" (*ahl al-ḥall wa-l-ʻaqd*), who are understood to be the most respected and influential members of the community. The reformist thinkers under discussion argue that the circle of persons involved in *shūrā* should expand to include the entire *umma*. Abu al-Majd develops this point by invoking an event as reported in prophetic tradition (hadith). The passage describes the Prophet consulting with his followers about how to treat prisoners captured in a recent battle. The Prophet not only consulted with the believers who were present but also told them to travel to their homes, consult with their relatives, and return to inform him of their opinions. Abu al-Majd argues that this proves *shūrā* was conceptualized from the earliest days of Islam to include the entire community and that this conception of *shūrā* should be revived in modern times. ʻAwwa agrees, concluding that *shūrā* "will have no meaning if the view of the majority [of the *umma*] is not adhered to."

The classical texts do not indicate the procedure for conducting *shūrā*. ʻAwwa observes that neither the Qur'an, the sunna, nor the experiences of the Rightly Guided Caliphs offer "any specific method for conducting this consultation or any fixed system for its application." Muslims are free to develop the specific mechanisms that are best suited to their time and circumstances. Qaradawi and other reformist thinkers argue that the most effective mechanism for *shūrā* under modern conditions is free and fair elections that produce a parliament. The deliberations of an elected parliament constitute a collective process of interpretation (*ijtihād*) that adapts the principles of shariʻa to the challenges of daily governance. These deliberations are also described as a form of *ijmā'*, or consensus building, in which the community gradually reaches agreement over the course of action that conforms with shariʻa and best serves the interests of the community. In this view, elections provide a transparent and reliable means for identifying those citizens who command the public's respect and thus can be entrusted with the responsibility of exercising *ijtihād* on behalf of the community. In order for elections to work effectively, every citizen must participate fully and seriously. Qaradawi makes a detailed case on this point. He writes that voting is analogous to testifying in a court of law, since it entails a personal witness to the moral and professional suitability of a candidate. He cites a Qur'anic passage to the effect that each believer is obligated to testify in court if he has information relevant to a case. Thus, by analogy, each Muslim has a religious obligation (*farḍ*) to vote, since he has a religious duty to convey his knowledge of the candidate for office. ʻAwwa holds a similar view and invokes the Qur'anic proclamation, "Do not conceal testimony, for he who conceals it has a sinful heart."

While these reformist thinkers support elections, they have reservations about unrestrained popular sovereignty. In their view, elections must produce legislative bodies that operate within predefined ethical boundaries. Unconstrained democracy can legalize vice, perpetuate injustice, and strengthen tyranny. All of these outcomes are at odds with Islam. In order to avoid them, an Islamic democracy requires that man-made law conform to the moral precepts of shariʻa. No law may violate shariʻa and allow what is forbidden in Islam (such as adultery or alcohol consumption) or prohibit what is required (such as prayer, charity, or pilgrimage). In practice, this means that the representatives of the people who draft man-made laws must have substantial knowledge of Islam. They need not be ʻulama', but they should be willing to consult with specialists on religious law when the topic under discussion requires it.

Some contemporary Islamic thinkers hold a more skeptical view of elections. Sayyid Qutb (d. 1966), for example, argues that sovereignty can lie only with God and that the only source of law is shariʻa. While he accepts the principle that a ruler should consult with his subjects, he rejects the premise that *shūrā* includes an elected parliament that issues legislation. Ayman al-Zawahiri, a leading ideologue of al-Qaeda, adopts an even more critical stance. He argues that the creation of an elected parliament that issues laws elevates human beings to the level of lawgivers, which usurps a power reserved only for God.

See also democracy; public opinion

Further Reading

Ahmad Kamal Abu al-Majd, *Nazarat Hawla al-Fiqh al-Dusturi fi al-Islam*, 1962; Muhammad Salim al-ʻAwwa, *Fi al-Nizam al-Siyasi li-l-Dawla al-Islamiyya*, 1989; Sayed Kotb (Sayyid Qutb), *Social Justice in Islam*, translated by John B. Hardie, 1953; Idem, *Hiwar la Muwajaha*, 1988; Yusuf al-Qaradawi, *Min Fiqh al-Dawla fi al-Islam*, 1997; Bruce K. Rutherford, *Egypt after Mubarak: Liberalism, Islam, and Democracy in the Arab World*, 2008.

BRUCE K. RUTHERFORD

endowment

Known in Arabic as waqf or in North Africa as *ḥabs*, the endowment was the preeminent socioeconomic institution of premodern Islamic society. Found extensively throughout the Muslim world, endowed property constituted, at times, upward of half of all useful land in a given vicinity. Modern legislation and state centralization subjected endowments to drastic reforms, however, and their importance has declined dramatically in contemporary times.

The origins of the institution have often been traced to analogous legal arrangements found in pre-Islamic cultures, most notably the concept of *piae causae* found in Roman Byzantine law. More recent scholarship, however, has cast doubt on this influence, finding significant discrepancies between the waqf and its pre-Islamic counterparts and arguing that the former should therefore be thought of as a distinctly Islamic institution. The earliest textual evidence of an endowment in the Islamic period is a tradition of the Prophet

encouraging one of his Companions to establish an endowment for the sake of charity.

The creation of an endowment, often recorded in an endowment deed known as a *waqfiyya*, involves the transfer of ownership of a given property from the erstwhile owner to God, rendering it inalienable thereafter in perpetuity—that is, ineligible to be given as a gift, sold, or inherited. Endowments paradigmatically took the form of real estate such as farmland or rented shops, residences, or other buildings, the proceeds of which would then be devoted to charitable causes or public utilities such as mosques, schools, hospitals, bridges, or fountains. It was not uncommon, however, to endow movable property such as books or weaponry for the sake of God, though there was some dispute about the legality of this.

The endowment's proliferation throughout Islamic societies has been attributed to its utility in fulfilling certain social and economic needs. In particular, the alienation of an estate was an effective way to protect it against confiscation by rulers or fragmentation through the precise rules of inheritance laid out in Islamic inheritance law. What came to be known as the family endowment (*waqf ahlī*), as distinct from the strictly charitable endowment (*waqf khayrī*), often served as a useful way to provide a regular income to one's relatives or descendants or perhaps a subset (e.g., the needy) among them. Administrators of the endowment were entitled to compensation from its proceeds, usually 10 percent of the endowment income, in exchange for maintaining the endowed property and ensuring the proper disbursement of funds to its beneficiaries.

Endowments were established by a wide range of individuals—both men and women—but the most prominent endowments were the exclusive domain of the upper classes, including rulers; their relatives; and high officials such as viziers, judges, and military commanders. In particular, the ruling elite often used the endowment of mosques and madrasas (Muslim schools) as a means of securing the favor of the scholarly class and thereby legitimacy among the masses—a necessary political strategy given that premodern governance was largely ill-equipped to wield the extensive power exercised by the modern, bureaucratic nation-state. The effect of endowments on the religious and scholarly landscape of major cities in the Islamic world was enormous, as through the law of endowment a plethora of institutions arose that supported intense scholarly, pious, and charitable aims, including mosques, elementary schools, madrasas, Sufi lodges, and hospitals.

The onset of modernity in the Muslim world signaled the decline of the endowments, which in turn threatened, particularly in the Sunni Islamic world, the viability of the 'ulama' (religious scholars) class, whose attachment to institutions of learning and worship, subsidized through endowments, rendered them financially dependent on the latter's success. In some places, the weakening and displacement of traditional religious leadership was one of the key goals of modernization; in others, colonial powers were simply interested in the revenues produced by endowed land, in the land itself, or in more efficient and productive use of resources. Relying on both religious arguments alleging the illegality of family endowments as well as Western theories of economic development, which disapproved of the exclusion of property from the economic cycle, these efforts largely met with success. Modern regimes throughout the Islamic world have simply confiscated endowed land and property or have brought it under direct government control through a ministry of endowments.

See also madrasa; mosque

Further Reading

Peter C. Hennigan, *The Birth of a Legal Institution: The Formation of the Waqf in Third-Century A.H. Hanafi Legal Discourse*, 2004; George Makdisi, *The Rise of Colleges: Institutions of Learning in Islam and the West*, 1981.

JUNAID QUADRI

environment

Islamic environmentalism generally finds its inspiration in three main theological concepts. First, the unity of God (*tawḥīd*) as Creator implies that all creation is one. All creatures are equal in this regard and worthy of protection, whether humans, animals, or the physical environment. Second, in the Qur'an humankind is called to be God's trustee (*khalīfa*) on Earth, and thus is accountable to manage equitably and responsibly the Earth's bountiful resources. Finally, a number of sayings (hadith) of the Prophet Muhammad enjoin kindness to animals, preservation of natural resources (especially water), and their fair distribution among all.

The environmental anxieties that gripped the Western world in the 1960s also sparked some soul-searching in religious circles. Just a few months before the publication of Lynn White's groundbreaking essay indicting monotheism—chiefly Christianity—as the cause of the ecological crisis, Seyyed Hossein Nasr published *Man and Nature: The Spiritual Crisis of Modern Man*. Nasr's adherence to the philosophy of Frithjof Schuon that all religions derive from the same absolute source limited his influence somewhat, and his concerns were more theoretical than practical.

Since the early 1990s, perhaps the two most influential Muslim environmentalists have been Mawil Izzi Dien and Fazlun Khalid, both British. Izzi Dien was one of six Muslim ecologists to be commissioned in 1983 by Saudi Arabia to write a short treatise on Islamic principles of environmental conservation. As he later noted with regret, little of that wisdom was ever implemented in government policy. Besides his participation in international forums, Izzi Dien wrote the first monograph—with the exception of Nasr—on Islam and ecology, *The Environmental Dimensions of Islam*. Khalid, for his part, is the first Muslim environmental activist with a global reach. In 1994, he founded the Islamic Foundation for Ecology and Environmental Sciences (IFEES), which launched projects in the United Kingdom and several Muslim-majority countries. Perhaps the best known of these was a successful 2005 wildlife

preservation campaign in the Zanzibar archipelago aiming to stop fishermen from using dynamite. The IFEES also developed a research center; a database to exchange information with other similar organizations; and an educational wing that publishes articles, books, and a biannual newsletter.

Many other Muslim scholars have weighed in since the 1990s, as Richard C. Foltz's bibliography on Islam and ecology indicates, and new local initiatives have continued to appear on the Internet. But as Foltz notes, although several Muslim countries have state-sponsored environmental programs, they are poorly implemented and take a back seat to the priorities of economic development and the alleviation of poverty.

Another challenge is how to educate the mostly pious masses about the urgency of environmental protection, renewable energy generation, and global warming mitigation. Much of the literature has focused on Islamic principles derived from the Qur'an and sunna, and scholar-activists like Khalid emphasize the shari'a-compliant nature of their initiatives. Indeed, some of the traditional provisions of Islamic law are being revived, like *ḥīma* (conservation zones) and *ḥārim* (inviolable zones, mostly for the protection of water). Yet the contemporary context is so vastly different from that of the medieval period that discourse on "shari'a" today is more about environmental ethics than classical Sunni or Shi'i law.

A last challenge concerns the framing of environmental priorities. The contemporary Islamic theology of creation, as in Christian and Jewish circles, is anthropocentric—that is, God mandates humankind to act as his trustees on Earth (the *khalīfa* principle). This clashes with the more biocentric forms of environmentalism, in which humans have no priority in their rights over animal and plant species.

See also caliph, caliphate

Further Reading

Richard C. Foltz, *Islam and Ecology Bibliography*, 2005, http://fore.research.yale.edu/religion/islam/islam.pdf; Richard C. Foltz, Frederick M. Denny, and Azizan Baharuddin, eds., *Islam and Ecology: A Bestowed Trust*, 2003; Mawil Izzi Dien, *The Environmental Dimensions of Islam*, 2000; David Johnston, *Earth, Empire, and Sacred Text: Muslims and Christians as Trustees of Creation*, 2010; Seyyed Hossein Nasr, *Religion and the Order of Nature*, 1996; Ibrahim Ozdemir, *The Ethical Dimension of Human Attitude towards Nature: A Muslim Perspective*, 2008; Lynn White, "The Historical Roots of Our Ecological Crisis," *Science* 155 (1967).

DAVID L. JOHNSTON

equality

Islam has often been described as an egalitarian religion that in principle does not recognize racial, ethnic, or hereditary distinctions. The nomadic egalitarianism of the Arabs, in which the Arab leader was first among equals, contributed to the ideal, found in the formative period of Islamic political thought from the mid-seventh to mid-ninth century, that all Muslims were equal in moral worth and had the right to speak out and advise others.

This egalitarianism, however, applied only to Arabs in the early formative period and was later subsumed by the ideal of benevolent absolutism that characterized the caliph's court. Early Muslims saw themselves as both Arabs and Muslims, and conversion was not encouraged until about the eighth century. Non-Arab Muslims were given a second-class status, and the sense of a multinational Islamic community did not develop until the early part of the Abbasid period (750–1250).

While classical Islamic jurisprudence insisted that all free Muslim men were on the same level before God, this did not necessarily extend to equality in everyday life, and class distinctions grew with the consolidation of the Abbasid Empire. The Islamic ideal of equality, however, depended upon being Muslim, free, and male: normative classical Sunni Islam accepted legal, political, and social inequalities between masters and slaves, men and women, and Muslims and non-Muslims. Slavery was recognized although its practice was moderated. Legally, slaves were persons with civil and criminal rights but also were the property of their owners.

The inequality between Muslims and non-Muslims was based on the concept of the *dhimma*, essentially a contract through which the Muslim community accorded protection to Jews, Christians, Zoroastrians, and in some cases other non-Muslims, on the condition that they paid the *jizya* (a poll tax), acknowledged the domination of Islam, and agreed to certain legal and social inequalities. Women were subject to unequal marital, divorce, and inheritance rights, although they could inherit and independently own property.

The extent of such inequalities and exclusion from the polity varied. Perhaps the most restricted were women, who by the Abbasid period were largely isolated from the public sphere. Military slaves (e.g., the Mamluks, 1250–1517), by contrast, frequently exercised power. While in theory non-Muslims had restricted political responsibility and were exempt from the duty put upon Muslims "to command right and forbid wrong," in practice non-Muslims were often employed in government service because of their administrative expertise.

The Ottoman reforms of the mid- to late 19th century partially resolved the legal inequality of non-Muslims and of slaves, but family law was left relatively untouched. The legal equality of slaves was established in 1887, although slavery was not abolished in most states of the Arabian Peninsula until as late as the second half of the 20th century. The Ottoman Constitution of 1876 affirmed equality among people of different faiths. The current constitutional commitment to equality between Muslims and non-Muslims and to men and women varies from one Muslim country to another.

The principle of equality (*musāwā*) features strongly in contemporary Islamic political thought. While the Arab socialism of many Arab countries in the 1950s and 1960s was largely secular,

socialism more recently has been a prominent theme within Islamic thought. The Egyptian Islamist theoretician Sayyid Qutb (1906–66) denounced unjustifiable social inequalities and immorally gained wealth. The Muslim Brotherhood member Muhammad al-Ghazali (1917–96) connected the lack of social justice in postwar Egyptian society with what he saw as a retreat from Islam, for which he partly blamed the 'ulama' (religious scholars) of Azhar University. Mustafa al-Siba'i (1915–64), former head of the Syrian branch of the Muslim Brotherhood, also wrote on Islamic socialism.

While some contemporary thinkers reject the principle of equality—either between Muslims and non-Muslims or between men and women—as a Western imported principle that is incompatible with classical normative Sunni Islam, the concept of equality figures prominently in contemporary Islamic political thought in part because Western polemic against Islam has given so much attention to these issues.

Many modernists argue that the Qur'an sanctions equality between men and women and between Muslims and non-Muslims and that such equality is an expression of the values of a "true" Islam. A common position is that the legal and political discrimination that non-Muslims received in the classical Islamic period was not necessarily a reflection of the true Islam. The so-called Constitution of Medina, an agreement (dating from about 622) between Muhammad and the Jews, who, as monotheists, were distinguished from other nonbelievers at the time, the Arab polytheists, is invoked as a precedent for establishing equality between Muslims and non-Muslims despite religious differences. This thinking has had considerable influence on political activists within the Islamic world. Notwithstanding skepticism concerning sincerity and details, the Egyptian Muslim Brotherhood has recently argued for the compatibility of Islamic law with the principle of Egyptian nationality whereby all citizens, Muslims and non-Muslims, enjoy equal rights.

Many contemporary feminists argue that the true values of Islam are compatible with gender equality and make a distinction between the egalitarian nature of Islam in terms of its ethical vision as stated in the Qur'an (e.g., in 33:35) and the discrimination against women sanctioned by classical Islamic jurisprudence. Taking a contextual approach to the Qur'an and building on the ideas of Fazlur Rahman (d. 1988), Amina Wadud argues that equality between men and women can be established through the notion that the Qur'an established a trajectory of reform and that while the restrictions against women were appropriate for the context of pre-Islamic Arabia, they were not meant to be interpreted as a timeless exposition of Islamic values. Few would, it is argued, state that because slavery is condoned by the Qur'an, it should be legal today. Many other discussions within contemporary Islamic thought on gender take the position that Islam sanctions an understanding that men and women are equal but different: equal in terms of their value before God and their spirituality but different in terms of the social roles that Islamic law stipulates.

See also minorities; women

Further Reading

Leila Ahmed, *Women and Gender in Islam: Historical Roots of the Modern Debate*, 1992; Nazih Ayubi, *Political Islam: Religion and Politics in the Arab World*, 1991; Antony Black, *The History of Islamic Political Thought*, 2001; Enayat Hamid, *Modern Islamic Political Thought*, 2005; Charles Kurzman, ed., *Liberal Islam: A Sourcebook*, 1998; Sayyid Qutb, *Social Justice in Islam*, translated by John Hardie, 1970; Amina Wadud, *Qur'an and Woman*, 1999.

RACHEL M. SCOTT

ethics

Broadly speaking, the concept of ethics refers to any normative evaluation of acts. While some make a conceptual distinction between morality and ethics based on a distinction between obligations of the "right" owed to other persons and the pursuit of the "good," this entry subsumes under the term "ethics" both theories of moral obligation (to others, to God) as well as theories of the good, of virtue, or of the cultivation of the self.

On this broad understanding of the concept, then, Islamic ethics can be found in a wide range of genres and discourses in addition to the revelatory texts of the Qur'an and hadith. They include exegesis and commentary on revelation (*tafsīr*, *sharḥ*, *ta'wīl*); investigation into the ontology of ethics in dialectical theology (*kalām*) and philosophy (*falsafa*); the epistemological investigation into the sources and conditions of moral knowledge in Islamic legal theory (*uṣūl al-fiqh*) and *falsafa*; the elaboration of substantive moral rules in positive law (*fiqh*, *furū' al-fiqh*); and the study of and the search for individual virtue, the perfection of motivations, and spiritual purification in Sufi mystical practices as well as some genres of philosophy. This entry will, of necessity, focus only on a select few of these sources of ethical thought.

Ethics in the Qur'an

The Qur'an presents itself as a universal ethical code for humankind, in sharp contrast to the tribal particularism of pre-Islamic Arab codes. It presents a conceptual scheme for both sociopolitical ethics and the duties and virtues of individual believers. The values, norms, and commands revealed in the Qur'an transform select pre-Islamic ones while introducing a normative revolution. Such pre-Islamic values as generosity, courage, loyalty, veracity, and forbearance are given Islamic validation as virtues that believers are commanded to cultivate in the service of Islam within the limits set down by God. For example, the Qur'an praises generosity in the giving of charity, while condemning both profligacy and spending of one's wealth out of vanity and the desire for praise. Similarly, the pre-Islamic value of absolute in-group loyalty (*wafā'*) was transformed by the more complex ethical terrain of the new religion. Loyalty to family and tribal kin was not only expanded to the

community of believers (which trumped more particular loyalties) but also constrained by other Islamic commitments. Believers were commanded to not violate oaths or transgress against divine commands, even in the service of communal interests. Loyalty within sociopolitical contexts thus becomes subsumed within the general obligation of loyalty to the covenant with one's Creator, which the Qur'an indicates is required by man's recognition that he is created by a sovereign, autonomous God.

However, the Qur'an views pre-Islamic Arab society predominantly in negative terms. It is characterized as *jāhiliyya*, a concept that refers to a state of moral recklessness arising from submission to human–social passions and whims. The normative revolution in Islam consists in its theocentricity. God Himself is referred to in ethical terms (many of the names of God refer to ethically salient features of God's essential nature), and man's attitude toward God is the primary criterion of moral evaluation. The *summum malum* for a created being is *kufr*, a state of being that alludes to unbelief, ingratitude, and the (public) denial of God's existence (*takdhīb*) and that results in acts of insolence, arrogance, presumptuousness, mockery of revelation, and the violation of divine limits. That the kafir goes astray by committing acts that are substantively unjust, criminal, sinful, forbidden, or tyrannical (referred to in the Qur'an variably as *ẓulm*, *jurm*, *fasād*, *munkar*, *sharr*, *sū'*, *faḥshā'*, *khabīth*, *ḥarām*, etc.) is not itself fully constitutive of the state of *kufr*; rather, it is the consciously held and affirmed beliefs in one's own independence and self-sufficiency in the formulation of judgments, moral and otherwise. The reliance on one's own judgment, which lies at the root of error and *kufr*, is often referred to as *hawā*, or (roughly) the lustful, whimsical, and passionate inclination of the human animal. Importantly, the reliance on reason to arrive at sound moral and practical judgments can fall under the scope of *hawā*.

The *summum bonum* for a created being is thus *īmān*, a state of being that includes belief in God and His revelation, performance of all mandated rituals, good works and observances, obedience to all commands and prohibitions, and, perhaps most centrally, the willingness to put all trust in God and to subordinate one's individual judgment to Him. The *mu'min* is the one who accepts God's guidance (*hudā*), fears God (*muttaqī*), is grateful to God (*shākir*), and is upright (*ṣāliḥ*) according to God's prescriptions.

The Qur'an also has much to say on the ethics of social relations among humans. While the specific norms and rules of social relations are elaborated within Islamic law, it is possible to generalize some of the broad principles and major themes of Islamic sociopolitical ethics. The Qur'an exhorts strong bonds of communal loyalty, extensive social solidarity, charity for the poor, and obedience to those in authority. The sociopolitical vision is a moderately egalitarian one. Rulership is just only when exercised in the interests of the ruled according to divine guidance. Extreme inequalities are condemned, the poor are said to have a claim on the property of the rich, and wealth is strictly detached from evaluations of virtue, desert, and piety. At the same time, the Qur'anic vision is less ascetic and unworldly than that of early Christianity. Wealth is not, per se, a sign of impiety, nor are other good things of this world. The Qur'anic emphasis is on remaining within the limits of enjoyment established by God and on purifying individual motivations. As such, it might be said that the Qur'an attends to considerations of moral psychology or a realistic attempt to take humans as they are according to an understanding of their motivations, capacities, and needs.

There are, however, limits to the Qur'an's egalitarian vision. In addition to some of the inegalitarian distributions of roles and rights within the Muslim community along gender lines, Qur'anic ethics distinguishes sharply between Muslims and non-Muslims. The primary solidarity community is the community of believers, at least from the Medinan period on. Muslims are enjoined not to value relationships of loyalty with non-Muslims at the expense of the Muslim community. Among other reasons, non-Muslim communities are seen as potential political and military rivals to Muslims. Similarly, while Muslims acquire rights by virtue of being Muslim (i.e., they do not need an explicit relationship to a state or ruler), non-Muslims may acquire rights only contractually. However, the Qur'an enjoins strict adherence to compacts with non-Muslims (particularly in the Medinan verses, with Jewish and Christian ones), and this forms a means of constructing relationships of mutual moral obligation.

Islamic Theories of Metaethics

Any systematic theory of ethics must address *ontological* and *epistemic* questions. First, do moral norms and values have an objective existence or are they created by some being subjectively? Second, how do humans know what morality requires? Can they arrive at true knowledge of morality through reason or intuition or do they require morality to be revealed to them authoritatively? Islamic investigations into metaethics have taken both (dialectic) theological and philosophical forms, and all possible combinations of answers have been given to the ontological and epistemic questions.

The Mu'tazili theologians asserted a doctrine of "ethical objectivism" and "rationalism." Their doctrine was "objectivist" because it held that norms exist independently of God's will. God cannot will or command what is immoral. The basic claim is that our description of certain acts as "good," "bad," "just," "unjust," and so on has some basis in objectivity yet not quite in the same way as our descriptions of the material world. These are "intuitions" that are extremely hard to flatly deny and can be discovered or made intelligible by certain intellectual and discursive acts. Their doctrine was "rationalist" because they held that reason gives independent knowledge of right and wrong and the status of revelation. Revelation helps and often fills in the gaps of reason but is not per se essential to *all* moral knowledge. Mu'tazilis do recognize that some acts are known to be good only by revelation in some select cases, like the good of prayer and worship, noting that reason alone might have found them worthless or optional. But even here, it is stressed that God reveals their goodness rather than makes them good.

These themes would be echoed later in the doctrines of the philosophers (*falāsifa*), who added a conception of a hierarchy between

rational philosophy and religion. While philosophy represents both the purest path to moral (and other) knowledge and (for some) the highest form of human flourishing (*sa'āda*, *eudaimonia*), thinkers such as Farabi (ca. 878–950), Ibn Sina (980–1037), and Ibn Rushd (1126–98) held that religion was strictly necessary for giving specific form to the general principles deducible through reason and for convincing and motivating the masses (who would not be able to comprehend complex rational proofs) through its inspirational, imaginative, and symbolic powers.

The eventual orthodox view, however, was the Ash'ari view, which defended a doctrine of "theistic subjectivism" or "voluntarism"—morality is something that is determined or willed by a certain agent (in this case God), not something that exists objectively and can thus be discovered. The doctrine was defended primarily on the grounds of God's omnipotence: if man could judge right from wrong, and thus presume to judge what God can and cannot prescribe for him, this would imply limits on God's power. So-called intuitions can be shown to be the product of circumstance and socialization, while judgments of "reason" are seen as arbitrary, mere statements of will, desire, or feeling. They contradict one another, cannot prove their premises, and render revelation useless. A person may think that some actions are good and others bad, but that person has no proof for this judgment without knowledge of their ontological status. God's omnipotence means that He can command things that seem to us immoral. The role of reason is to prove the truth of revelation and then to help with the interpretation of revelation and possibly to extend it to uncovered areas according to certain approved methods. Epistemically, thus, Ash'arism is "hermeneutic" or "traditionalist" rather than rationalist, and for this school, applied normative ethics thus largely manifests itself as law.

Beyond "Law"? Contemporary Political Ethics

By and large, Islamic law retains its traditional prestige in ethical matters. Almost all practical ethical questions admit of being treated as "jurisprudential" (*fiqhī*) questions. However, in addition to the traditional alternatives or supplements to law (particularly Sufism), some contemporary Islamic thinkers are developing approaches to ethical questions, particularly in the social and political realms, which are both indebted to and also unconstrained by traditional jurisprudential methods. Thus thinkers might draw from classical legal theory to emphasize religion's insistence on worldly welfare (*maṣlaḥa*) or the overall objectives of the law (*maqāṣid*), such as protecting religion, life, reason, progeny, and property.

However, with this foundation in the concepts and categories of "law" as traditionally understood, it is a short step to speaking about Islamic normativity almost entirely in these general terms or even to invoke a more abstract "spirit" of justice, equality, mercy, spirituality, or self-sacrifice, which ethical claims must embody. Many thinkers are also unwilling to exclude non-Muslims or lax Muslims from this ethical purview. At this point, a nonparticularist Islamic ethics emphasizing universal interests and a "spirit" of justice and mutual human concern might be regarded as fundamentally "postlegal." A particularly relevant exemplar of this trend is the European writer Tariq Ramadan, who expands the idea of the *maqāṣid* from five to dozens of human interests, speaks of "two revelations" (the Qur'an and the universe), and insists that "the real" is a source of law, all while refusing to exclude non-Muslims and their forms of reason from the realm of "Islamic ethics." Similar patterns of thought that are partially indebted to concepts and values of law but not recognizably jurisprudential can be found in Islamic theories of feminism, democracy, medical ethics, and the environment.

See also jurisprudence; rights; Sufism; theology

Further Reading

Richard M. Frank, "Moral Obligation in Classical Muslim Theology," *Journal of Religious Ethics* 11, no. 2 (1983): 204–23; George F. Hourani, *Reason and Tradition in Islamic Ethics*, 1985; Toshihiko Izutsu, *Ethico-Religious Concepts in the Qur'an*, 1966; Oliver Leaman, *An Introduction to Classical Islamic Philosophy*, 2001; Fazlur Rahman, "Some Key Ethical Concepts of the Qur'an," *Journal of Religious Ethics* 11, no. 2 (1983): 170–85; Tariq Ramadan, *Radical Reform: Islamic Ethics and Liberation*, 2009; Bernard G. Weiss, *The Spirit of Islamic Law*, 1998.

ANDREW F. MARCH

Ethiopia and Eritrea

The early phase of Muhammad's life was closely associated with the Axumite kingdom (first to tenth centuries) of Ethiopia. His own wet nurse, Umm Ayman, was Ethiopian, and one of his first followers, the Ethiopian Bilal b. Rabah, became the first *mu'adhdhin* (the person who calls the faithful to prayer in the mosque) of the emerging community. But the focal point of relations between Ethiopia and Muhammad came to be the tale of Najashi, the Christian "king of kings" of Ethiopia based at Axum. According to the story (not mentioned in the Qur'an but well-known from the *sīra* [life of the Prophet]), it was the Axumite ruler Ashama who provided refuge to Muhammad's followers when they were persecuted by the Quraysh of Mecca. As the Ethiopian king had been the only leader who responded to the Prophet's request, Muhammad reputedly later instructed his followers to "leave the Abyssinians as long as they leave you," meaning that they were not to initiate jihad against them even though they were Christians. This early seventh-century tale left a legacy of two contradictory interpretations: one that the existence of Christian Ethiopia could be tolerated because of its act of benevolence, the other that the Ethiopian ruler had actually converted to Islam even though the Ethiopians denied it, so that the existence of Christian Ethiopia was not legitimate after all.

In contrast to other Africans, the Ethiopians did not usually accept Islam as a divine revelation. The conversion of Ethiopia to

Christianity had begun already in the fourth century, and by the seventh century Ethiopian Christianity had come to be identified as the official religion, with well-established institutions and networks of churches and monasteries. Nonetheless, thanks to long-distance trade, Islam was adopted by local groups such as the 'Afar and the Somalis and in coastal towns such as Zeil'a and Massa'wa (in present-day Eritrea). The inland town of Harar was another important Muslim community, a center from the 13th century onward of the Qadiri Sufi order, which was active in the diffusion of Islam. Many Muslim communities also appeared in the Christian highlands, where they are known mainly as Jabarti and reputed to be descendants of the *ṣaḥāba* (Companions of the Prophet). In the 13th century, the Sidama Muslim principalities of 'Adal and 'Yifat in present-day Somalia gained power and threatened the southern boundaries of the Solomonic dynasty kingdom. Yet it was not until the 16th century that Islam in Ethiopia shed its image as peripheral and faction-ridden and started being perceived as a threat to Christian Ethiopia.

During the years 1529 to 1543, Imam Ahmad b. Ibrahim (known as Ahmad "Gran," or Ahmad the Left-Handed) of 'Adal led a holy war (jihad) during which he conquered most of Ethiopia, destroyed churches and monasteries, and converted many Ethiopians to Islam. Christian Ethiopia was saved by the arrival of the Portuguese and the Ethiopian perception of Islam as a unified political and military force, able to destroy Christianity dates from the Muslin occupation in the 16th century. During the 17th and 18th centuries, waves of Oromo migrations from the south, many of whom converted to Islam during this period, reinforced the Islamic hegemony over the southern boundaries of Ethiopia and shifted the demographic balance, only partly offset by the waves of Ethiopian expansion to the south toward the end of the 19th century.

Although Ethiopia proper was not occupied by a European power, the imperialist race for control of the Middle East and the Horn of Africa did affect its relations with the Muslims, both inside and outside Ethiopia. Islamic revival in neighboring countries occasionally aroused Ethiopian fear of Muslim invasions from countries such as Egypt, Sudan, and Somalia; Eritrea was occupied by Italy and thus separated from Ethiopia. The transfer of Eritrea to Ethiopia as part of the Ethiopian Federation in 1952 led to the emergence of the Eritrean Liberation Front (established in 1960). Islam was one of the main motivating forces of this movement, especially in the ideology and activities of the Eritrean Liberation Front. In the consolidation of 20th-century Ethiopia, on the other hand, Islam was usually marginalized by the increasing strength of Christianity, the state religion. After the revolution of 1991, a new dialogue emerged between the republican and secular Ethiopian state and its Muslim subjects, but although the Muslims gained more economic power and freedom of worship, they still claimed to be politically underrepresented. According to the 2007 census, Muslims constitute about 34 percent of the population in Ethiopia and less than half in Eritrea, but the leadership of both countries continues to debate whether to pursue policies of integration and equality or marginalization and deprivation.

See also East Africa

Further Reading

Hussein Ahmed, "The Historiography of Islam in Ethiopia," *Journal of Islamic Studies* 3, no. 1 (1992); Haggai Erlich, *Ethiopia and the Middle East*, 1994; Paul Henze, *Layers of Time: A History of Ethiopia*, 2000; Asafa Jalata, *Oromia and Ethiopia: State Formation and Ethnonational Conflict, 1868–1992*, 1993.

IRIT BACK

ethnicity

The relationship between Islam and ethnic identity has created dynamic forms of political expression in all Muslim cultures. The form of government adopted during the time of the Prophet Muhammad and the first four caliphs was largely in accordance with Arab tribal practice. The leader of the community was a tribal shaykh who acted as a mediator and arbitrator of conflicts within the community and also served in the expanded role of military leader during times of crisis. For much of Arab history, a tension has remained between the mobile and democratic values of the Bedouins and the more authoritarian tendencies of the Byzantine and Persian political traditions that were absorbed into the Umayyad and Abbasid caliphates. The dominant political discourse that emerged in Muslim culture was authoritarianism, which was seen as preferential to the threat of anarchy in society.

During the initial expansion of Islam in the century after the Prophet, Islam was brought to vast new territories by armies consisting of Arab tribal units, and an ethnic divide between the conquerors and the conquered influenced conceptions of both religion and rule. Islam was associated with being Arab, and non-Arab Muslims, both converts and their descendants, became known as *mawālī* (clients). In many cases, this term was literal: slaves who had been captured in the conquest converted and were subsequently liberated by their Arab masters, or converts who accepted Islam at the hands of an Arab Muslim became formal clients of Arab tribes and used the tribal gentilics as part of their own names. Especially under the Umayyad caliphate, the association of Arab identity with adherence to Islam had widespread effects on Islamic religion and culture, some of which changed and dissipated during the Abbasid era (750–1258), but lingering effects remained in Islamic law, theology, and culture. Arabs were granted rights or given privileges that other Muslim believers were not, and among the Arabs, certain tribes and clans were favored over others. The organization of the army and of stipends from the state treasury favored early converts and was biased against non-Arab Muslims. The majority view among Sunnis was that the caliph had to be a member of the Quraysh tribe in particular; the more egalitarian Kharijis rejected this rule and did not limit the caliphate to Arabs, whether Quraysh or not. According to Islamic law, while slavery was legal, Arabs could not be enslaved. The exclusion of Jews and Christians from

the Arabian Peninsula, a policy attributed to ʻUmar b. al-Khattab (586–644), may be seen in part as a demonstration of the ethnic superiority of Muslim Arabs to outsiders. Many legal works continued to suggest that Arabs should not marry their daughters to non-Arabs, as a woman should not be married to a husband of inferior status. Similar distinctions were sometimes made between the Quraysh or the clan of Hashim and other less reputable Arab tribes. Similarly, Sayyids, or descendants of the Prophet, gained enormous prestige in many Islamic societies. Early leaders expressed concern about increasing numbers of non-Arab converts and about children of Muslim men with non-Arab women (generally captured concubines). At the same time, the special status accorded to Arabs was in some sense made permanent by the sanctity attributed the Arabic language. While a careful reading of the Qur'an suggests that the Arabic language of that scripture was part of an exceptional attempt to make biblical monotheism easily comprehensible to the Arabs, these same verses were interpreted as indicating Arabic's superiority as sacred language. It came to be considered the language that God speaks and the language in which the inhabitants of paradise converse: the richest, most perfect language. Arabs therefore were considered superior to their *ʻajam* (mutes, speakers of barbaric or incomprehensible language)—most often taken to mean Persians. By the time of Shafiʻi (d. 820), the idea that native speakers of Arabic had privileged access to God's message as contained in the Qur'an and were therefore more reliable interpreters of the sacred text had become widespread.

These forms of discrimination angered the increasing numbers of non-Arab converts to Islam, who saw the discriminations as incompatible with the universality of Islam's message and the Qur'an's insistence on the inherent equality of believers' souls. Arabic, to them, was a language, not a racial designation—an international language of religion and scholarly discourse shared by many peoples. Some non-Arab Muslims expressed their dissatisfaction by adopting the views of the Kharijis, who did not privilege Arabs, which may explain the success of the Kharijis among the Berbers in North Africa, such as the Rustamid dynasty (777–909) with its capital Tahert in the central Maghrib. Others adopted Shiʻism; even though the Shiʻis granted authority exclusively to descendants of the Prophet, they generally discriminated less among the believers. The most prominent manifestation of this protest was the Shuʻubis, a term that derives from the word *shuʻūb* (nations), which occurred in Qur'an 49:13: "O people! We created you from one male and one female, and made you nations (*shuʻūb*) and tribes so that you may know each other." It was championed mostly by Persians who, while recognizing the accomplishments of the Arabs in conquest, the spread of the faith, bravery, and eloquent poetry, stressed superior achievements of the Persians in high civilization, refinement, administrative skills, and so on, claiming that they deserved at least as much recognition for their contributions to the Muslim community as the Arabs. The heyday of the controversy occurred in the ninth and tenth centuries, but aspects of it have resurfaced regularly in various contexts to the present day.

Arab dominance did not, however, continue in the political sphere, and one may describe the premodern history of Islam as falling into three periods of political regime. Until the tenth century, most regions of Islamdom were under the rule of Arabs; in the 10th and 11th centuries, many regions came under the rule of Persians; and from the 11th until the 19th century, almost all areas of the Muslim world were ruled by ethnic Turks or Mongols, whose dominance continued in the Middle East until World War I and the abolishment of the Ottoman Empire in 1924. For nearly a millennium in the Persianate world, the upper echelons of society were seen as divided along ethnic lines into Turks, who constituted the military and ruling class, and Tajiks, Persians, or non-Turks, who were the administrators, accountants, tax-collectors, and land owners. The division was viewed as natural and not unfair because Turks and Mongols were considered ethnically suited to military exploits because of their sturdiness, fierce nature, ability to endure hardship, and superior skills in horsemanship and archery. Even in contexts where Turks did not make up the bulk of the military, rulers often used troops belonging to foreign ethnic groups because of their military skills, internal solidarity, lack of attachment to the local populace, and direct allegiance to the ruler. The Fatimids in Egypt (969–1171) employed both troops who belonged to the Berber Kutama tribal confederation from North Africa and "Sudanese" troops from sub-Saharan Africa. The 14th-century historian Ibn Khaldun argued, reflecting primarily on the Berber dynasties of North Africa, that there was a strong relationship between the life of political regimes and ethnic groups. Tribal groups from outside settled regions have much stronger ethnic solidarity than settled peoples, and this enabled them to work as efficient military units, conquering territories and establishing new dynasties. The settled life of the conquerors, however, corrupted them and made them lose their ethnic solidarity in just a few generations, and this made them vulnerable to new tribal invaders.

Ethnic identity has overlapped with language and religion in the Muslim world in complex ways. In the modern period, Arabness is often established by speaking Arabic as one's mother tongue, regardless of one's ethnic background, so that Egyptians or Moroccans see themselves as Arabs even though very few of them are actually descendants of Arab tribesmen. Arab nationalism, the belief that the Arab nations should unite and form one nation, is based on the idea that the Arab nations for the most part share an ethnicity. In contrast, the individual nationalisms often emphasize the unique ethnic origins of their citizens, Lebanese claiming descent from the Phoenicians, Egyptians from Pharaonic ancestors, and so on. In other cases, ethnic identities are interpreted as overlapping entirely with religious sects, so that the Coptic Christians see themselves as true descendants of Pharaonic Egyptians, distinct from their Muslim compatriots, whom they view as the descendants of foreign invaders, even though the genetic makeup of the two groups is nearly identical. Similarly, Armenians, Greeks, and Assyrians in the Middle East are distinguished as much by their adherence to particular sects of Christianity as by language or ethnic background.

While authoritarianism has remained the dominant political system in Islamic societies in modern times, including the colonial and postcolonial periods, other systems have persevered. Some Islamic cultures have used and continue to use Islamic beliefs to strengthen decentralized forms of government: examples abound from the Bedouin to the Moros of Mindanao. Sometimes Islam has been embraced as the basis of political mobilization in reaction to the intrusion of an invading power. Examples include the Naqshbandi Sufis in the Caucasus region and various religious groups that organized in Africa in the 19th century to fight encroaching European powers, such as the followers of the Mahdi in Sudan. The first proclaimed secular state in the Muslim world was the Azerbaijan Democratic Republic of 1918–20. This brief experiment was followed by the revolution led by Atatürk (1923–38) that would end the Ottoman Empire and form a nation-state out of its ashes. Atatürk's revolutionary vision had foundations in Western political thought and also in Ottoman legal traditions. Despite his secular ideals, Atatürk nevertheless drew on religious imagery and Turkish history in his political discourse. In many ways, his reforms were not an attack on religion per se but rather an attack on the hegemony of the religious class over society.

For the next century, Muslims in Africa and Asia developed a sort of "confessional nationalism" in which religion distinguished the boundaries of linguistic, cultural, and political identity. In 20th-century India, Muslim political identity developed in reaction to the Hindu-dominated Indian independence movement. A clique of elites advocated wider Muslim political expression and rights, even though many of the early Pakistani elite were only nominal Muslims. These elites created Pakistan without fully delineating the meaning of an "Islamic Republic." In order to forge a nation-state, Pakistan's first leader, Muhammad Jinnah (r. 1947–48), advocated the use of Urdu as the national language at the expense of Bengali. This caused lasting tensions that led to the creation of Bangladesh in a bloody civil war in 1971. For South Asian Muslims, religious identity and ethnic identity were often synonymous. A similar phenomenon developed in the newly independent Arab world, where states also tried to co-opt Islam. In many new states in Africa, the transition was less successful. Precolonial elites were more substantially disrupted in Africa. Muslims form a large but not dominant community in many African states, such as Guinea-Bissau, Tanzania, Ivory Coast, Nigeria, Eritrea, and Ethiopia. Politics in these states is often, though not always, organized along confessional lines. The newly independent states of modern Central Asia have also tried to co-opt Islam as an official ideology—as a new ideological cement to hold together the Central Asian peoples of the region and as a replacement for Soviet communism. Across Central Asia, Islamic identity is on the rise while tribal identity continues to decline. Shared Islamic identity among warring factions helped end the Tajik Civil War (1992–97). Similar tensions exist in other areas of the globe, and Islam is used as a societal glue in other regions as well. In Southeast Asia, both the government and opposition groups use Islam for the political mobilization of the populace. The Malaysian state has embraced an Islamic identity in order to promote Malay unity and political leadership in a multiethnic society. Indonesia is home to Nahdatul Ulama, the largest Muslim organization by membership in the world. This traditional Sunni organization was founded in 1926 and was mobilized as a political movement by Abdurrahman Wahid, who was elected president in 1999.

In other instances, competition between religious and national identities has led to the submergence of one in the favor of the other. The Pan-Arabism of the 1960s and 1970s was promoted largely at the expense of traditional religious identity. Conversely, the rise of popular Muslim identity in the Arab world in the late 20th century occurred at the expense of Pan-Arabism. In Somalia, the inability of both Islamic and pan-Somali identity to gain sustainable traction resulted in decades of instability. Occasionally Muslims have sacrificed religious and ethnic identity in pursuit of political goals. During the Crusades, Muslim-Crusader coalitions often aligned against other Muslim-Crusader alliances. In the 18th century, Russian Tartars helped the Russian Empire expand into Central Asia at the expense of local Muslim elites. A more recent example is the Bedouin of Israel and the Sinai, who have often strived to maintain political independence by establishing a close relationship with the Israeli state rather than Arab centers of power.

The late 19th and early 20th centuries saw a revival of Pan-Islamic thinking. For the first time, advances in communication and transportation technology made it possible to imagine a global Muslim state. In the late 19th century, modernity made the concept of a Pan-Islamic community imaginable for the first time. Muslim thinkers from the Jadids of Central Asia to Afghani (1838–97) and Muhammad Iqbal (1877–1938) proposed a global community of Muslims. For some, the abolition of the Ottoman caliphate between 1923 and 1924 was a great setback for the ideal of Pan-Islamic unity. The Organization of the Islamic Conference (OIC), established in 1969, embodies ostensibly Pan-Islamic aspirations but has been handicapped by important rivalries between its most powerful states: Saudi Arabia and Iran. On occasion within the OIC, ethnic concerns trump Pan-Islamic sentiments. While most issues are decided nearly unanimously, regional voting blocs—Arab, African, Central Asian—form occasionally.

Ethnic-religious minorities continue to play an important role in the modern politics of many nations in the Muslim world. Before the U.S. invasion of Iraq and overthrow of Saddam Hussein's regime, Sunni Arabs controlled the military and administration of the nation. Syrian president Bashshar al-Assad belongs to the 'Alawis of Syria, who follow a religion that is an offshoot of Shi'i Islam. The 'Alawis are strongly represented in the military and government as well. In other nations, substantial populations of underrepresented minorities have presented a continuing political problem. The Shi'is of Lebanon, whom the constitution assigned a subordinate position in national politics, engaged in a civil movement under the leadership of Musa al-Sadr (d. 1978) in the 1960s and 1970s, claiming more political rights and a larger share of public works and services. Shi'i minorities in Saudi Arabia, long denied any official recognition, have suffered widespread discrimination

and have gained some ground only in recent years. In North Africa, the French tried to exploit the ethnic differences between Arabs and Berbers: with the Berber Dahir, a decree issued in 1930, the French Protectorate of Morocco sought to make the division a permanent feature of legal and political institutions. After independence from the French, Berbers in Algeria and Morocco have struggled for the rights to publish and broadcast in the Berber language and to educate their children in Berber. The Kurds have long represented one of the most difficult political problems for states in the region, as they are one of the largest ethnic groups in the world who remain stateless, divided as they are among Iran, Iraq, Syria, and Turkey. While the Treaty of Sèvres (1920) assigned to them a national territory, Atatürk's military successes, confirmed in the Treaty of Lausanne (1923), put an end to the project, and since then they have suffered various forms of discrimination and persecution, particularly in Turkey and Iraq, where thousands of Kurds were imprisoned, deported, and massacred under Hussein. One consequence of the U.S. overthrow of Hussein is that the Kurds now have something resembling an autonomous state in the north of Iraq. At the same time, the official treatment of Kurds in Turkey has improved since 2000: Turkey's bid for membership in the European Union has led the government to rescind the death penalty, partially repeal the ban on the Kurdish language, and allow limited broadcasts on radio and television in Kurdish. Nevertheless, these rights remain restricted; for example, the mayor of Diyarbekir was prosecuted in 2007 for sending a holiday card for the New Year written in Kurdish.

See also family; Quraysh; tribalism

Further Reading

Ian Almond, *Two Faiths, One Banner: When Muslims Marched with Christians across Europe's Battlegrounds*, 2009; Michael Brett and Elizabeth Fentress, *The Berbers*, 1997; Patricia Crone, *God's Rule—Government and Islam: Six Centuries of Medieval Islamic Political Thought*, 2005; Ignaz Goldziher, *Muslim Studies*, vol. 1, 1967; Jacob M. Landau, *The Politics of Pan-Islam: Ideology and Organization*, 1994; David McDowall, *A Modern History of the Kurds*, 2004; James T. Monroe, *The Shu'ūbiyya in al-Andalus: The Risāla of Ibn Garcia and Five Refutations*, 1970; Andrea Pacini, ed., *Christian Communities in the Arab Middle East: The Challenge of the Future*, 1999.

JOSEPH HAMMOND

Europe

Muslim presence in Europe has a long and varied history. Between the early 8th and late 15th centuries, parts of Spain (Andalus) and Southern Italy were under Muslim rule, and starting from the 15th century, the Ottoman Empire expanded into southeastern Europe and twice advanced as far as Vienna. Whereas Muslim rule of Andalus was ended by the Reconquista in 1492, the effects of the Ottoman presence continue to be strongly felt until today. The wars in former Yugoslavia during the 1990s, which also assumed traits of a religious strife, deeply disturbed the rest of Europe and had severe repercussions on the relations between the West and the Islamic world.

Contemporary discussions about Islam in Europe mostly refer to the more recent presence of Muslims in Western Europe. As of 2010, approximately 18.5 million Muslims are estimated to live in these countries, with the largest communities in France (outnumbering both Protestants and Jews), Germany, the United Kingdom, and Italy. The majority of Muslim migrants arrived in Europe after World War II either as refugees from former European colonies to the colonizing country (North Africans in France, South Asians in Great Britain) or as "guest workers," cheap labor hired by European states (Turks in Germany, Turks and Moroccans in the Netherlands since the 1960s). Later, they were joined by students from Muslim countries, refugees from various international crises, and also by a growing number of European converts to Islam.

Despite the highly diverse background of Muslims in Europe, discussions since the 1980s have increasingly focused on issues of "Muslim identity" and "European Islam." Previously, migrants had been perceived mainly in ethnic terms (as Turks, Arabs, etc.) and in a more regional context, but the religious angle came to predominate the association with migrants due to events on the global stage such as the Islamic Revolution in 1979 that "Islamized" public debates about these minorities. This development presented grave challenges to European states and societies, as well as to Muslim migrant communities and their second- or third-generation offspring (who were not automatically naturalized in all European states). The problems are further complicated by the fact that the Western approach to religion is far from homogeneous. Rather, the relationship between secular politics and religious communities ranges from the British combination of a state church and a liberal model of recognition of religious communities by the state to the German church laws that focus on corporative intermediate units to the rigorous French *laïcité* and its strict separation of religion and the public sphere. All these approaches, however, are tailored to the model of the Christian churches and often conflict with the far more amorphous structure of Islam.

For Muslims in Europe, on the other hand, the challenges are of two sorts. On the organizational level, the constant demand by most European states for a national representative body—if possible, single and uniform—to serve as interlocutor in legal issues (such as religious instruction in public schools) led to the emergence of several Muslim umbrella organizations. The most important of these include the Exécutif des Musulmans de Belgique (founded in 1996), the Muslim Council of Britain (1997), the Conseil Français du Culte Musulman (2003), the Dutch Contactorgaan Moslims en Overheid (2004), and the German Koordinierungsrat der Muslime (2007). They consist mostly of coalitions of local or regional associations but are far from unanimously acknowledged by the Muslim

community; in addition to inner rivalry, groups like the 'Alawis or the Ahmadis, which are deemed heterodox or even heretic in the Islamic world, are either excluded or refuse to be coerced under an all-encompassing Muslim umbrella.

The second challenge for Muslims in Europe consists of the relationship between Islamic law and secularism. Whereas in previous centuries Muslim scholars ruled out the possibility of Muslims living under non-Muslim rule in what they perceived as the "abode of war" (and instead demanded Muslims to emigrate to the "abode of Islam"), present-day Muslims are permitted to live as minorities under non-Muslim rule, although Islamic law (shari'a) is not formally acknowledged in any European country (only Greece concedes a special status to the Muslim minority in Thrace). Discussions about how to adapt the provisions of Islamic law to the European environment gave rise, in the early 21st century, to a new genre of legal literature, a so-called Muslim minority right (*fiqh al-aqalliyyāt al-muslima*), propelled both by Muslim scholars who settled in the West (such as Taha Jabir al-Alwani) and by some eminent experts from the Islamic world. In this regard, too, institutionalization is to be observed in the shape of the European Council for Fatwa and Research set up in Dublin in 1997. This committee, which comprises 38 Muslim scholars from 21 Middle Eastern and European countries, organizes regular international conferences and issues statements and fatwas on all kinds of legal problems confronting Muslims in Europe; its president is the Qatar-based Yusuf al-Qaradawi, one of the most potent representatives of contemporary Islam.

Apart from individual scholars such as Qaradawi, organizations from Islamic countries run or backed by the state also compete for authority over Muslims in Europe (such as the Mecca-based Muslim World League or the Turkish Presidency of Religious Affairs), as do transnational groups such as the Muslim Brotherhood or the Tablighi Jama'at. But there are also important individual Muslim voices even at the European level. While outspoken secular approaches (Soheib Bencheikh) have not caught on, Tariq Ramadan, a Swiss-born conservative reformer and grandson of Hasan al-Banna, the founder of the Egyptian Muslim Brotherhood, has established himself as one of the most influential, albeit highly controversial, contemporary Muslim intellectuals. However, the real influence both of European Muslim organizations and individual reformers on the bulk of Muslims in Europe is difficult to assess, given that, for example, in Germany the mosque associations and umbrella institutions represent less than 30 percent of Muslims living in the country.

Several organizations have attempted to comply with European expectations and emphasized the compatibility of Islam and Western political and social values: in 2002, the German Central Council of Muslims (Zentralrat der Muslime) issued an "Islamic Charter," which was intended as a declaration on the relationship between Muslims, the state, and society, and in January 2008 the Federation of Islamic Organizations in Europe in Brussels published a "Muslims in Europe Charter" to the same effect. These efforts (which aim at fundamental problems such as Islamic ethics, equality of the sexes, democracy, and human rights) notwithstanding, several more practical issues of contention persist: the question of the headscarf, Islamic religious instruction in public schools, the education of imams, the construction of mosques, and the practice of ritual slaughtering. More often than not, controversies in these areas are taken to court, and decisions vary greatly even within individual states.

An especially sensitive topic that affects the relations between Muslims and Western societies is Islamist terrorism and Islamism at large. Great Britain in particular served for a long time as a retreat for many activists from the Islamic world threatened by persecution in their countries of origin, among them also radical preachers of jihad, long before London itself was hit by (home-grown) Islamist terrorists in July 2005. Events such as the conflict over Salman Rushdie's novel *The Satanic Verses* (1989), the riots in the suburbs of Paris (2005), or the publication of the controversial Danish Muhammad cartoons (2006)—all of which had severe consequences far beyond their European context—show the potential of agitators to eclipse the peaceful majority of Muslims living in Europe and to provoke hostility among Europeans toward everything Islamic.

The debates about what has aptly been described as "globalized Islam" is determined by several important issues: the contest for legal and spiritual authority over Islam in Europe, the interaction between organizations in the Islamic world and European Muslim individuals and associations, the attempts to create a European Muslim identity, and the emergence of international terrorism. In the process of reaching common ground for coexistence, both sides have to redefine traditional stances with regard to the relation between religion and society.

See also abodes of Islam, war, and truce; minorities; Muslim Brotherhood; Muslim League; al-Qaradawi, Yusuf (b. 1926)

Further Reading

Aziz al-Azmeh and Effie Fokas, eds., *Islam in Europe: Diversity, Identity and Influence*, 2008; Christopher Caldwell, *Reflections on the Revolution in Europe: Can Europe Be the Same with Different People in It?*, 2009; Gilles Kepel, *Allah in the West: Islamic Movements in America and Europe*, 1997; Jytte Klausen, *The Islamic Challenge: Politics and Religion in Western Europe*, 2005; Yusuf al-Qaradawi, *Fiqh of Muslim Minorities. Contentious Issues and Recommended Solutions*, 2003; Tariq Ramadan, *Western Muslims and the Future of Islam*, 2004; Olivier Roy, *Globalized Islam: The Search for a New Ummah*, 2004.

RAINER BRUNNER

excommunication

In Islam, excommunication is the denial by some members of the Muslim community of the rights of other members whose religious beliefs or practices are deemed incompatible with Muslim status.

Unlike Roman Catholicism, Islam has no central institution or legal body authorized to engage in excommunication and also no generally accepted legal procedures whereby jurists or courts can reach such a verdict. The lack of these central institutions and common procedures, together with a general willingness to allow for differences in the ways Islam is practiced and understood, has led to a significant degree of tolerance among different Muslim denominations and groups. Still, the Islamic world has hardly ever been free of attempts to curb the religious freedom of Muslim groups regarded as heterodox. Certain legal judgments, chief among them the judgment of apostasy, are applied in ways that allow for the persecution of heterodoxy.

The parameters of Muslim debates about excommunication were set in the aftermath of the First Islamic Civil War (656–61). One party, the Kharijis, justified the murder of the third caliph, ʻUthman b. ʻAffan (r. 644–56), on the grounds that he had committed a capital sin (*kabīra*), which showed that he was an unbeliever and therefore deserved death. A group of radical Kharijis went further and felt justified to kill grave sinners as unbelievers. After the defeat of the Kharijis, their various enemies, who dominated the early development of Islamic law, rejected positions that would make a grave sinner lose his legal protection as a member of the Muslim community. Thereafter, however, discussions of excommunication in Islam focused less on the practices than on the convictions of the accused. When practices are considered grounds for excommunication, it is mostly because they are assumed to reveal a heterodox mindset or to lead to it. An exception is the view of the Hanbali school of law that neglecting the duty of prayer leads to unbelief and apostasy.

The Qur'an distinguishes between a Muslim and a polytheist (*mushrik*) and also between a believer (*mu'min*) and an unbeliever (kafir). From Qur'an 49:14, it is clear that there were Muslims in the days of Muhammad who were not considered believers. Muhammad, however, accepted these people, often referred to as "hypocrites" (*munāfiqūn*), as members of his community and thus set a standard for the toleration of heterodox opinions in Islam. This, together with a well-known hadith stating that the Muslim community would divide into 73 sects of which only one would be saved, facilitated the acceptance of heterodox groups in early Islam. Even so, scholars routinely accused one another of unbelief (*kufr*). This, however, rarely meant to deprive the accused of his rights as a Muslim but rather expressed that he had forfeited his prospect of otherworldly reward on account of his opinions. In Islam, a "declaration of unbelief" (*takfīr*) can be either a mere protest that a certain opinion is unorthodox or a formal, legal accusation or ruling that the holder of the opinion in question has forfeited his legal protection as a Muslim and should be killed. The legal means to do the latter is the judgment of apostasy in Islamic religious law (shariʻa).

One of the earliest attempts in Islam to use the judgment of apostasy to curb heterodox opinions was the so-called Qadiri creed, published by the caliph Qadir (r. 991–1031) in 1017. Expressing the convictions of a group of traditionalist jurists among the Sunni Muslims, Qadir declared that whoever held that the Qur'an was not eternal but created in time—as most Muʻtazilis indeed did—"is an unbeliever who can be killed (*kāfir ḥalāl al-dam*) after he had been given the opportunity to repent from this position." Muslim jurists unanimously accepted that an apostate from Islam could be killed, and most required that he must first be granted a "right to repent" (*istitāba*), enabling him to return to Islam unharmed. Heterodox groups who regarded themselves as members of the Muslim community were assumed to have committed apostasy clandestinely, or without realizing the full extent of their doctrinal deviation. In legal terms, this was regarded as *zandaqa*—in other words, clandestine apostasy in which the accused pretends to be a Muslim, though he has in fact abandoned his Muslim faith.

In the decades following the creed of al-Qadir, Muslim jurists focused on heterodox views disseminated by Ismaʻilis and philosophers. Among the latter, the followers of Ibn Sina raised the attention of the prominent Shafiʻi jurist Ghazali (d. 1111), who in 1095 published a fatwa (religious opinion) as part of his book *The Incoherence of the Philosophers*. Ghazali, however, did not dispense entirely with the earlier tolerant attitude toward heterodoxy in Islam; instead, he aimed to qualify it. He stressed that heterodox groups in Islam should all be tolerated by other Muslims as long as they did not teach a limited number of doctrinal offenses identified by him. In his *Decisive Criterion for Distinguishing Islam from Clandestine Apostasy,* he offers a systematic justification for religious tolerance in Islam as well as where the limits of tolerance should be set, in other words, which doctrinal positions lead to excommunication from Islam. For Ghazali, the Muslim community falls into two groups—the rightly guided and the heterodox—both to be protected as members of Islam. A third group of people (including Ibn Sina), who pretended to be Muslims but whose convictions showed them to be unbelievers, were subject to the death penalty for apostasy.

Muslim jurists after Ghazali had a variety of legal options regarding heterodox teachings in Islam. Many adopted a tolerant position toward heterodoxy. Others followed Ghazali. Ibn Taymiyya (d. 1328), for instance, issued several fatwas in condemnation of Ismaʻili Shiʻis, Druzes, and the Nusayri-ʻAlawi group in Syria and Lebanon. These and similar condemnations were formulated as judgments of apostasy. During the late 18th and 19th centuries, the Wahhabi movement in central Arabia advocated the excommunication of Muslims who prayed at graves and thus revealed convictions that the Wahhabis regarded as apostasy from Islam.

With the advent of Islamic fundamentalism in the 20th century, there was a surge of excommunications based on the judgment of apostasy, among them the execution of Mahmoud Mohamed Taha in 1985 in Sudan and the forced dissolution of Nasr Hamid Abu Zayd's marriage to a Muslim woman 1995 in Egypt. Khomeini's fatwa in 1989 against the British-Indian writer Salman Rushdie can also be seen as an excommunication along the lines of the legal reasoning of Ghazali, although the scant justification given by Khomeini also points to blasphemy as a ground for the death penalty. The law of apostasy has also been used to curb the religious

freedom of members of the Baha'i faith in Iran and of the Ahmadi movement in Pakistan.

See also Ahmadis; apostasy; commanding right and forbidding wrong; fundamentalism; Ghazali (ca. 1058–1111); heresy and innovation; Ibn Sina, Abu 'Ali (ca. 980–1037); inquisition; Kharijis; shari'a

Further Reading

Yaron Friedman, "Ibn Taymiyya's Fatāwā against the Nuṣayrī-'Alawī Sect," *Der Islam* 82, no. 2 (2005); Yohanan Friedmann, *Tolerance and Coercion in Islam: Interfaith Relations in the Muslim Tradition*, 2003; Frank Griffel, *Apostasie und Toleranz im Islam*, 2000; Sherman A. Jackson, *On the Boundaries of Theological Tolerance in Islam*, 2002.

FRANK GRIFFEL

exegesis

As a translation of the Arabic term *tafsīr*, exegesis signifies primarily the process and results of textual interpretation, particularly scriptural interpretation. While texts of various genres were the subject of systematic interpretation, the scope of this article is restricted to exegesis of the Qur'an. According to both classical and contemporary Muslim sources, the interpretation of the Qur'an began during the period of its revelation as the Prophet Muhammad sought to explain ambiguous or unfamiliar references to his earliest audiences.

Classical and Medieval Processes and Products

Such rudimentary glossing is captured as a stage in the more developed interpretive procedures that were eventually codified by medieval scholars like Ibn Taymiyya (d. 1328). According to this Hanbali scholar-activist, the Qur'an itself is its own best interpreter. A verse or verses in one part may clarify or elaborate what is expressed more elliptically in another part. When intra-Qur'anic exegesis proves insufficient, Ibn Taymiyya's four-step hermeneutical procedure seeks recourse in the sunna. By sunna, he means specifically those exegetical comments that Muslim tradition traces back to the Prophet Muhammad. Within collections of exegetical hadiths, the number of such statements is relatively small, which explains the need for steps three and four—that is, reference to the recorded statements of Muhammad's Companions and their Followers (*tābi'ūn*). Among the most noted names in the former category are 'Ali b. Abi Talib (d. 661), the Prophet's cousin and son-in-law; 'Abdallah b. 'Abbas (d. 687–88), another cousin; and the Kufan Companion 'Abdallah b. Mas'ud (d. 635). In the latter, prominent names include the Meccan Mujahid b. Jabr (d. ca. 720), the Transoxanian Dahhak b. Muzahim (d. 723), the Medinan 'Ikrima (d. 723), and the blind Basran Qatada b. Di'ama (d. 735). Taken in its entirety, this four-step process is traditionally known as *al-tafsīr bi-l-ma'thūr* (or *bi-l-riwāya*), interpretation according to the received tradition. Its counterpart in Muslim discussions of classical hermeneutical principles is *al-tafsīr bi-l-ra'y* (or *bi-l-dirāya*), interpretation by informed personal opinion. (A subset of this latter category, *al-tafsīr bi-l-ishāra*, refers to the esoteric and allegorical readings to be found in Sufi commentaries.) The thousands of volumes, in all major Islamic languages, that 14 centuries of Qur'anic commentary has generated are an admixture of these two forms of exegesis. Their basic structure is a linear, sequential, verse-by-verse exposition (*tafsīr musalsal*).

That exegetical library spans the full spectrum of intellectual, spiritual, and sectarian orientations within the Muslim tradition, such as Sunni, Shi'i, Sufi, Hanbali, Maliki, Ash'ari, and Mu'tazili. Among the most famous of these productions from the classical and medieval periods of Islam are those of Muqatil b. Sulayman (d. 767), *Tafsir al-Qur'an* (Exegesis of the Qur'an); Tabari (d. 923), *Jami' al-Bayan 'an Ta'wil ay al-Qur'an* (Clarifying the interpretation of Qur'anic verses); Abu 'Abd al-Rahman Muhammad b. al-Husayn al-Sulami (d. 1021), *Haqa'iq al-Tafsir* (Realities of interpretation); Abu Ishaq Ahmad b. Muhammad b. Ibrahim al-Tha'labi (d. 1035), *al-Kashf wa-l-Bayan 'an Tafsir al-Qur'an* (The unveiling and clarification of the interpretation of the Qur'an); Muhammad b. al-Hasan al-Tusi (d. 1067), *al-Tibyan fi Tafsir al-Qur'an* (Exposition of the interpretation of the Qur'an); Mahmud b. 'Umar al-Zamakhshari (d. 1144), *al-Kashshaf 'an Haqa'iq Ghawamid al-Tanzil wa-'Uyun al-Aqawil fi Wujuh al-Ta'wil* (The unveiler of the hidden realities of revelation and choicest opinions on interpretation); Fakhr al-Din al-Razi (d. 1210), *al-Tafsir al-Kabir (Mafatih al-Ghayb*; The major commentary, known as The keys of the unseen) Abu 'Abdallah al-Qurtubi (d. 1273), *al-Jami' li-Ahkam al-Qur'an* (Compendium of the rules of the Qur'an); 'Abdallah b. 'Umar al-Baydawi (d. ca. 1292), *Anwar al-Tanzil wa-Asrar al-Ta'wil* (The lights of revelation and secrets of interpretation); 'Imad al-Din Isma'il b. 'Umar b. Kathir (d. 1373), *Tafsir al-Qur'an al-'Azim* (Commentary on the mighty Qur'an); Jalal al-Din al-Mahalli (d. 1459) and Jalal al-Din al-Suyuti (d. 1505), *Tafsir al-Jalalayn* (Commentary of the two [scholars named] Jalal).

Modern Developments

This multifaceted tradition of classical commentary shapes and structures modern and contemporary interpretation of the Qur'an but does not control it. New directions and emphases have emerged, and their genesis is connected, either directly or indirectly, to the effects of migration, economic development and stagnation, colonialism, the European Enlightenment and political upheaval. Influential efforts to which the tag of "modernism" has been attached include those of Sir Sayyid Ahmad Khan (d. 1898) in South Asia, Muhammad 'Abduh (d. 1905) and his disciple Rashid Rida (d. 1935) in Egypt, and Hamka (Haji 'Abdul Malik Karim Amrullah, d. 1981) in Indonesia. The need to address the consequences of social, political, and cultural change prompted not a break with the enduring exegetical tradition, but an expansion of intellectual interests and

foci. Philosophical rationalism, the advances of scientific knowledge, historical-critical analyses of both secular and sacred literature, and the growing imperative to engage compelling social and political issues all have influenced the shape and scope of Qur'anic commentaries in the 20th century and beyond.

The attempt to find foreshadowing in the Qur'an of modern scientific advances (*tafsīr 'ilmī*), while not unknown in earlier periods, achieved particular popularity in the first half of the 20th century, stimulated especially by the Egyptian exegete Tantawi Jawhari (d. 1940) and his 26-volume *al-Jawahir fi Tafsir al-Qur'an al-Karim* (Jewels of the interpretation of the generous Qur'an). Such work found a European advocate in the French physician Maurice Bucaille, whose *The Bible, the Qur'an and Science* continues to enjoy popularity on proselytizing (*da'wa*) websites and in other forums of Muslim popular discourse. "Scientific" interpretation did not, however, garner wide support and has been continuously challenged on both exegetical and scientific grounds.

Exegesis in the Service of Political and Social Change

More successful, and certainly more broadly influential, has been the work of contemporary commentators who seek to use *tafsīr* as an instrument of political and social change. Two names dominate discussion of this phenomenon: the Pakistani journalist, ideologue, and politician Mawdudi (d. 1979) and the Egyptian scholar-activist Sayyid Qutb (d. 1966). Born in India in 1903 to a notable Delhi family, Mawdudi received a classical Muslim education that prepared him for the writing and translation projects to which he allocated time throughout his life. After the partition, Mawdudi moved to Lahore and assumed leadership of the Pakistani branch of the Jama'at-i Islami, the political party that he and others founded earlier in the 1940s. Mawdudi was a prolific author, but his most influential work was the multivolume translation and commentary on the Qur'an, *Tafhim al-Qur'an* (Understanding the Qur'an). A number of translations from Urdu to English have been completed, including one that is available on the Internet.

Qutb's *Fi Zilal al-Qur'an* (In the shade of the Qur'an) is significantly influenced by Mawdudi's earlier work. Both are unsparing in their critique of social and political behavior, whether by non-Muslims or Muslims, that contravenes Islamic norms, and their commentaries characterize such conduct as tantamount to a contemporary *jāhiliyya*, or a reversion to the moral and intellectual barbarism of the pre-Islamic "age of ignorance." Qutb was born only three years after Mawdudi, but his education and early professional life followed a quite different path. Yet he, too, moved from journalism to political activism, a move that eventually cost him his life: he was executed for sedition in 1966. Qutb's commentary follows an important trend of 20th-century interpretation, as it seeks to collapse the distance between the corrupt present and the pristine past, the latter understood as the period of the Prophet's life and the formation of the first Islamic community. This collapse quite deliberately expels the accumulated exegetical heritage of intervening centuries. Qutb expresses little confidence in the classical and postclassical commentaries that constitute that tradition. Rather, he reads the text of the Qur'an as a manifesto for a new political order or, more precisely, for a restoration of the divinely ordained social contract of the earliest Muslim society. Those who reject this reading and its underlying hermeneutics are dismissed as nonbelievers (*kuffār*), whether they call themselves non-Muslims or Muslims.

Genre Diversification

While Qutb's *Fi Zilal*, arguably the most influential commentary of the 20th century, follows the traditional structure of verse-by-verse analysis, much Qur'anic interpretation occurs in other forms and genres. Given the centrality of the Qur'an to Muslim thought and practice, it is not surprising that there is frequent reference to it, in all varieties of Islamic literature, to support arguments and to secure their authority. A 2006 article, for example, studied the exegetical judgments contained in Osama bin Laden's *Declaration of War* and his *Statement of the World Islamic Front Urging Jihad against Jews and Crusaders*. Countless other works, whether theological, philosophical, or mystical, can be mined for their exegetical insights. The many books, pamphlets, and tracts of thematic interpretation (*tafsīr mawḍū'ī*) are yet another source of sustained Qur'anic interpretation. These works gather passages relevant to a particular topic, such as marriage, God's oneness, or fasting, and treat them as a coherent collection. Their value as resources for pedagogy and preaching has assured the ever-growing number and popularity of this type of commentary.

A characterization as "thematic commentary" could also be applied to the writings of a newer generation of Muslim commentators: those whose intellectual formation has not taken place in the traditional centers of Islamic learning, but in European, North American, Australian, and South African universities. An earlier generation of such individuals would include figures like Mohammed Arkoun (b. 1928), the French-educated Algerian scholar whose pioneering work on a multidisciplinary approach to the understanding of the Qur'an makes a clear distinction between the dynamically understood *fait coranique*, the original prophetic proclamation, and the "Closed Official Corpus" created by the imposition of a dogmatic exegetical orthodoxy. It would also include Fazlur Rahman (d. 1988), the Pakistani scholar whose writings and whose years on the faculty of the University of Chicago shaped a dual legacy of doctoral graduates and engaged exegetical discourse. His *Major Themes of the Qur'an*, certainly a significant English-language example of *tafsīr mawḍū'ī*, introduced the Qur'an to countless American college students.

Some of the most interesting and challenging work to emerge from this Euro-American context concerns those verses of the Qur'an that treat the social and spiritual status of women. Both male and female scholars have contributed to this interpretive dialogue, and the conversation has been varied and frequently at variance. In the first decade of the 21st century, a younger generation of Muslim women scholars risked both academic and social censure by constituting themselves as qualified successors to the intellectual lineage of the classical and medieval *mufassirūn*—that is, commentators on the Qur'an. They have challenged earlier

interpretations of statements like "but their men have a degree above them" (Q. 2:228) or "men are the managers of the affairs of women" (Q. 4:34). They have focused particular attention on the threefold admonishment mandated by Qur'an 4:34. The command "to beat" rebellious or disobedient wives (*wa-ḍribūhunna*) has legal and social implications of concern to Muslims in many political contexts. Other exegetical investigations have focused on the significance of gendered language in the Qur'an and on the verses that address marriage, divorce, polygyny, child support, and the testimony of female witnesses.

A Contested Arena

The study and interpretation of the Qur'an has never been an uncontested activity or one devoid of political consequences. Traditional Muslim historiography credits the 'Alid–Umayyad split, a precursor to Sunni and Shi'i sectarianism, to a failed arbitration on the Qur'an. Ninth-century Baghdad was convulsed by the caliph Ma'mun's (r. 813–33) efforts to enforce his interpretation of the Qur'an's ontological status, an interpretation and enforcement rescinded by a subsequent caliph, Mutawakkil (r. 847–61). The 19th-century Indian reformer Sayyid Ahmad Khan used a rationalist hermeneutic to justify and promote cooperation between Indian Muslims and the British colonial government. The Sudanese leader of the reformist Republican Brothers, Mahmoud Mohamed Taha (d. 1985), who was executed during the military regime of Ja'far Nimeiri (r. 1969–85), espoused the exegetical preeminence of the Meccan verses and chapters (*sūras*), arguing that these transcend the chronological and cultural constraints of the Medinan *sūras* and provide a dynamic foundation for democratic social practices and values.

In the 20th century, innovative Muslim scholarship on the Qur'an has damaged academic careers, been subject to publication suppression, and even led to death threats. Although separated by a generation, two Egyptian academics offer examples of those who have felt the force of conservative opposition to their work. In 1947, Muhammad Ahmad Khalafallah (d. 1997), a student of the literary scholar Amin al-Kholi (d. 1967), submitted a thesis on Qur'anic narratives that stressed their function in forming the spiritual and ethical attitudes of their recipients rather than their historical accuracy. His thesis was rejected by its University of Cairo examiners, and he eventually lost his university position. About 40 years later, another faculty member at the University of Cairo, Nasr Hamid Abu Zayd (d. 2010), published a hermeneutical treatise, *Mafhum al-Nass* (Understanding of the text), built on contemporary linguistic theories of textual formation. For Abu Zayd, sensitivity to the cultural consciousness of both the Qur'an's initial recipients and its contemporary hearers stands as a fundamental exegetical principle. In the view of his critics, however, this stance challenges both the eternal truth of the divine revelation and the cumulative consensus of its commentators. Legal and professional actions taken against Abu Zayd became so dangerous that he sought self-exile in Europe.

The history of non-Muslim study and interpretation of the Qur'an has created another arena of contestation. Earlier forms of this exercise, such as Peter the Venerable's (d. 1156) translation project or the early modern publications of Theodor Bibliander (d. 1564), were largely in the service of Christian polemic. The 19th- and 20th-century efforts of scholars like Gustav Weil (d. 1889), Ignaz Goldziher (d. 1921), Theodor Nöldeke (d. 1930), Richard Bell (d. 1952), and John Wansbrough (d. 1992) that purport to be straightforward scholarly analyses have been criticized as covert proselytization, intellectual colonialization, or unabashed blasphemy.

See also Qur'an

Further Reading

J.M.S. Baljon, *Modern Muslim Koran Interpretation* (1880–1960), 1961; Asma Barlas, "Women's Readings of the Qur'ān," *The Cambridge Companion to the Qur'ān*, edited by Jane Dammen McAuliffe, 2006; Gerhard Böwering, "The Scriptural 'Senses' in Medieval Ṣūfī Qur'ān Exegesis," in *With Reverence for the Word: Medieval Scriptural Exegesis in Judaism, Christianity, and Islam*, edited by J. D. McAuliffe, B. D. Walfish, and J. W. Goering, 2003; Ignaz Goldziher, *Die Richtungen der islamischen Koranauslegung*, 2nd ed., 1952; J.J.G. Jansen, *The Interpretation of the Koran in Modern Egypt*, 1974; Jane Dammen McAuliffe, "An Introduction to Medieval Interpretation of the Qur'ān," in *With Reverence for the Word: Medieval Scriptural Exegesis in Judaism, Christianity, and Islam*, edited by J. D. McAuliffe, B. D. Walfish, and J. W. Goering, 2003; Angelika Neuwirth, "Structure and the Emergence of the Community," *The Blackwell Companion to the Qur'ān*, edited by Andrew Rippin, 2006; Walid Saleh, *The Formation of the Classical Tafsīr Tradition: The Qur'ān Commentary of Al-Tha'labī (d. 427/1035)*, 2004; Rotraud Wielandt, "Exegesis of the Qur'ān: Early Modern and Contemporary," *Encyclopaedia of the Qur'ān*, edited by Jane Dammen McAuliffe, 2001–6; Stefan Wild, ed., *The Qur'ān as Text*, 1996.

JANE DAMMEN MCAULIFFE

F

Fadlallah, Muhammad Husayn (1935–2010)

Muhammad Husayn Fadlallah, a leading Twelver Shi‘i religious authority in Lebanon, combined the training of a traditional Shi‘i jurist with the analysis and concerted activity of a political ideologue. He exerted a strong influence on the political aspirations and military activism of the Shi‘is of Lebanon, including Hizbullah (Hizb Allah) in particular; of Lebanese Sunnis; and of Shi‘is and Sunnis outside Lebanon. He was born in 1935 in Najaf, Iraq, the foremost center for Shi‘i legal education in the world, while his Lebanese father, ‘Abd al-Ra‘uf Fadlallah (1907–84), was studying and teaching there. The Sayyids claimed descent from the Prophet's grandson Hasan through his son Hasan al-Muthanna. Fadlallah's grandfather, Sayyid Najib (1863–1917), had been a scholar of some renown in Bint Jubayl, his hometown in southern Lebanon, where he taught at his personal madrasa (Muslim school). Fadlallah grew up in Najaf, studying first with his father and then under a number of other teachers, including Abu al-Qasim al-Kho'i (1899–1992), Muhsin al-Hakim (1889–1970), and Mahmud Shahrudi (1882–1974). He completed his education under Kho'i in 1965 and received from him a certificate recognizing him as a mujtahid or fully qualified jurist.

While in Najaf, Fadlallah showed a profound interest in literature, particularly Arabic poetry, and edited a journal titled *Majallat al-Adab* (Journal of literature). He also became involved in Iraqi politics, and his early debates with Marxists and secularists and his experience with the organization of leftist movements influenced his views concerning political action. He was inspired by the teachings and example of the prominent Iraqi Shi‘i authority Muhammad Baqir al-Sadr, who advocated the involvement of jurists in political and social spheres and, before being executed by Saddam Hussein's regime in 1980, played an important role in the Islamist political mobilization of Shi‘i youth through Iraq's Da‘wa Party.

In 1966, having completed his studies, Fadlallah moved back to Lebanon and settled in al-Nab‘a quarter, an eastern suburb of Beirut populated by poor Shi‘is, immediately establishing himself as an effective community leader and an excellent teacher. He founded the Islamic Legal Institute, a center where students could study teaching the traditional curriculum of Najaf, and also built mosques and centers for Shi‘i religious ceremonies. In 1976, in the course of the Lebanese Civil War, the Nab‘a quarter was bombarded and eventually occupied by the Maronite Christian Phalangists. The experience of bombardment and being driven out of his home in a Beirut suburb along with thousands of other Shi‘i residents radicalized Fadlallah. During this time, he wrote the book *al-Islam wa-Mantiq al-Quwwa* (Islam and the logic of power) under heavy shelling and working by candlelight. It shared with other modern Arabic works on political theory an emphasis on resistance and the right to resist drawn ultimately from French anticolonialist writings, but it had an innovative aspect aimed at critiquing the traditional quietist position adopted by Shi‘i jurists. He drew on Friedrich Nietzche's (1844–1900) 1887 work *On the Genealogy of Morality*, which critiqued the passive posture historically adopted by Christians, characterizing it as slave morality, and suggested that they should adopt noble morality instead, seeking to attain redress for grievances by taking revenge through action rather than through the imagined revenge traditionally adopted in Christian thought. Fadlallah applied this same argument to Shi‘i tradition, urging their jurists to adopt an activist stance and to become directly involved in social, economic, political, and military issues. The work describes two opposing groups, the *mustaḍ‘afūn* (the downtrodden), referring primarily to Shi‘is but also to Muslims in general, and the *mustakbirūn* (the arrogant), referring primarily to the United States and Israel, whom he held responsible for the crimes of the Phalangists. According to Fadlallah, following the examples of ‘Ali and Husayn, Muslims must oppose force with force; they have a duty to gain economic, political, and military power in order to resist these oppressive forces in an effective manner.

At this juncture, Fadlallah, newly ensconced in the Bi'r al-‘Abd quarter in southern Beirut, was named by Abu al-Qasim al-Kho'i, the leading jurist and religious authority in Najaf after the death of Hakim in 1970, as his representative in Lebanon. This gave Fadlallah access to *khums* funds—the 20 percent income tax collected from Shi‘i believers for religious purposes—which allowed him to undertake large charity projects such as the building of schools and hospitals. He, somewhat more than his quietist and learned rival Muhammad Mahdi Shams al-Din (d. 2001), filled the void left by the mysterious disappearance of Musa al-Sadr in Libya in 1978. *Islam and the Logic of Power*, published in 1976, had established him as a leading Islamist ideologue, and he continued to decry foreign influence in Lebanon and encroachments on Lebanese sovereignty, particularly in the journal of the Lebanese Muslim Students Organization, *al-Muntalaq* (The outbreak). Establishing himself in the role of mentor and guide to Islamist cadres throughout Lebanon,

he wrote against the Israeli invasions of 1978 and 1982, as well as the presence of the multinational UN peace-keeping force in Lebanon, whom he saw as supporting the illegitimate rule of Pierre Gemayel's government. For this reason, he endorsed the October 1983 attacks on U.S. Marines' and French troops' barracks. After the Israeli invasion of southern Lebanon in 1982, Israeli aggression became a constant focus of his writings, which urged sustained and tactical resistance. By 1983, Fadlallah had become a major public figure in Lebanon and beyond.

Assessments of Fadlallah's relationship with Hizbullah, the political and military Shi'i movement that originated in the early 1980s and was backed by the Islamic Republic of Iran, have varied. Some claim that he was the spiritual guide of the movement, that he had a major hand in directing it, and that he was directly responsible for planning its operations. Others deny this, clearing him of guilt for specific terrorist attacks. The CIA, taking the former view and holding him responsible for the deaths of 241 American servicemen in the Marine barracks bombing and also for kidnappings of U.S. and other European citizens in Lebanon in the early 1980s, attempted to assassinate him in 1985 with a car bomb outside the Imam Rida Mosque where he preached. An estimated 80 to 105 people were killed, but Fadlallah survived. Later, in 2006, during the war between Israel and Hizbullah, Israeli planes bombed his home, but he happened to be elsewhere. It is undeniable that he exerted an important influence over Hizbullah, inspired its leaders, and had close ties with the organization. His articles appeared regularly in *al-'Ahd* (The pledge), Hizbullah's official journal. His bodyguards were Hizbullah operatives, and they manned checkpoints on the way to his house and the Imam Rida Mosque. However, he did not accept an official role for both tactical and ideological reasons: he could deny responsibility for any specific actions taken by Hizbullah, and he did not want to have his opinion be hampered by an adherence to a particular political program.

Fadlallah was a radical yet pragmatic political ideologue. He was looked on with suspicion in the West because he condoned violence and strategic action against U.S. and Israeli interests. He insisted that Islamic resistance was not terrorism and that force must be met with force, and he urged armed resistance to the Israeli occupation of Lebanon, the West Bank, and the Gaza Strip. He wrote legal opinions justifying the use of suicide bombing against military targets and forbidding the normalization of ties with Israel, and he called for a boycott of American products. However, he often differed from hard-line ideologues in his pragmatism, for he showed himself willing to accept gradual, incremental changes and to work with other groups in Lebanese society, including the Christians. He also condemned the killing of civilians, and in particular denounced the 9/11 attacks as illegitimate. His approach differed from that of Musa al-Sadr, who had led a civil rights movement for Shi'is in the 1960s and 1970s, for he saw that important changes were best achieved not by widespread social movements but by select, indoctrinated cadres through organized, tactical work. Much of his rhetoric, however, including the constant opposition of *al-mustakbirūn* to *mustaḍ'afūn*, resembled that adopted by Musa al-Sadr and Ayatollah Khomeini. Fadlallah, at least by the late 1980s, did not endorse Khomeini's concept of *wilāyat al-faqīh*, the absolute rule of the leading Shi'i jurist, but rather supported a constitution that would allow wide participation of societal groups and would be controlled by a system of checks and balances. In 1988, he proposed a model he called *dawlat al-insān* (the human state), in an obvious reference to human rights guaranteed through regime change. In this he differed with the leadership of Hizbullah, who adopted the views of Khomeini and his successor in Iran, Khamene'i.

Fadlallah's views on the top jurists of the Shi'is also provide significant evidence of his independence of Hizbullah. Fadlallah, born in Najaf, had participated in the long tradition of study in the shrine cities of Iraq that was challenged by the rise of Qum as a major center of learning beginning in 1922. When Kho'i died in 1992, Hizbullah followed Iranian government circles in claiming that the leading Shi'i jurist was first the Sayyid Rida Gulpayegani, who died in 1993; then Muhammad 'Ali al-Araki, who died in 1994; and then the "leader" of the Islamic Republic of Iran, Ayatollah Khamane'i. Throughout, Fadlallah accepted 'Ali al-Sistani, who had acceded to the position of *marja' al-taqlīd* (source of emulation) in Najaf, as the leading authority. However, Fadlallah soon came to be recognized as a senior authority in his own right. In 1986, the Iranians had already recognized Fadlallah as an ayatollah and regional authority. Beginning in 1994, Fadlallah called for the *marja'iyya*, the position of supreme legal authority for the Twelver Shi'is, to be modified from a personal institution into an international organization, not unlike the Vatican, with specialized bureaus and functionaries; it should not be synonymous with the Islamic Republic of Iran. In 1995, Fadlallah's supporters published a manual of his legal rulings, a necessary step toward recognition as a senior, international Shi'i legal authority. His reputation continued to grow, in part because of his innovative legal positions, and before his death, some supporters even suggested that he should succeed Sistani as the next *marja' al-taqlīd* in Najaf. Fadlallah became known for his relatively liberal views on women, in keeping with his emphasis on resistance and mobilization. He encouraged women to participate in sports and to develop strength. He stressed that women had a social responsibility equal to that of men. He upheld the rights of women to resist violence and coercion of husbands or male relatives. He wrote fatwas (religious opinions) against honor killings and female circumcision and permitted abortion if the life of the mother was in danger. A number of jurists in Najaf and Qum accused him of violating consensus on some issues in which he rejected commonly accepted rulings in the Twelver legal tradition, including his qualified permission of cloning, his argument that Jews and Christians and indeed all people regardless of religious affiliation were not ritually impure, and the ruling that one may resort to astronomy to determine the beginning of the month of Ramadan, rather than relying on sighting the new moon with the naked eye.

See also Hizbullah; *ijtihād* and *taqlīd*; jurisprudence; Lebanon; al-Sadr, Muhammad Baqir (1935–80); shari'a

Further Reading

Talib Aziz, "Fadlallah and the Remaking of the Marja 'iya," in *The Most Learned of the Shia: The Institution of the Marja' Taqlid*, edited by Linda S. Walbridge, 2001; Jamal Sankari, *Fadlallah: The Making of a Radical Shiite Leader*, 2005.

DEVIN J. STEWART

faith

In the Qur'an, faith (*īmān*) and its antithesis, unbelief (*kufr*), denote two radically opposed moral categories. Faith leads the believer to perform good works continually in this world and to receive a blessed existence in paradise in the next, while its opposite leads the unbeliever to wreak continual havoc and corruption in this world and to suffer hellfire in the hereafter. In fact, the terms most frequently used in the Qur'an to designate the Muslim community, the followers of the Prophet Muhammad's mission, are *al-mu'minūn* (the faithful) and *alladhīna āmanū* (those who have faith) rather than "Muslims," while those who reject and oppose the Prophet's mission are kafirs (unbelievers). Faith is the basic condition for membership in the Muslim community, while lack of it excludes one from the community. This idea lies behind a number of key Islamic terms, such as *ummahāt al-mu'minīn* (the mothers of the believers), which is applied to the wives of the Prophet Muhammad in the Qur'an on the grounds that the Muslims essentially form one family, with the Prophet as their father and his wives as their mothers, the basis of which is faith. Another key term, *amīr al-mu'minīn* (Commander of the Faithful), a title adopted by the caliphs beginning with 'Umar b. al-Khattab (r. 634–44), similarly is based on the identification of faith as the central identifying characteristic of the community's members.

In Islamic tradition, a distinction is often made between having faith (*īmān*) and being Muslim (*islām*). In a famous hadith report, the angel Gabriel questions the Prophet about the meaning of the two terms and his response shows that *islām* is external (*ẓāhir*) and more general (*'āmm*), while faith is internal (*bāṭin*) and a more specific (*khāṣṣ*) matter. *Islām*, outward adherence to the Islamic faith, includes the performance of basic ritual obligations such as praying, fasting, almsgiving, making the pilgrimage, and uttering the creed that there is no god but God and that Muhammad is the messenger of God. *Īmān* refers to the inner belief in the one God, His angels, His scriptures, His messengers, the Day of Judgment, and fate, whether good or bad. However, the terms are nearly interchangeable in the Qur'an: "Then We evacuated those of the believers who were there, But We did not find any Muslims there except one house" (53:35–36). In other contexts, the distinction holds: "The desert Arabs say, 'We believe.' Say, 'You have no faith'; but say, 'We have submitted our wills to God,' for faith has not yet entered your hearts" (Q. 51:14). Islam, therefore, is the quality of outward adherence to the religion, whereas faith is a matter of complete inner conviction.

The Qur'an upholds the possibility that an apparent believer may lack internal faith. A group among the Prophet's community in Medina, termed *munāfiqūn* (hypocrites) or *alladhīna fī qulūbihim maraḍ* (those who have a disease in their hearts), are described as adhering to Islam outwardly but actively working to undermine it in secret. In later texts, the term *ahl al-qiblah* (those who pray toward Mecca) is used to designate all ostensible Muslims, including those who harbor concealed heresy or lack of faith. The accusation of unbelief, termed *takfīr*, is a grave matter in Islamic law, because the apostate is deemed deserving of capital punishment. The outward signs of lack of faith, or heretical beliefs, may be words or deeds. Uttering blasphemies against God, the Prophet Muhammad, other prophets, the sacred books, angels, the Companions of the Prophet, or Islamic doctrines or obligations that were conveyed by the Prophet or appear in the Qur'an and are subject to consensus may reveal that one is actually an unbeliever. Acts such as the desecration of sacred monuments or holy ground produce the same result. Various Muslim groups differed over other Muslims' status with regard to faith. The Kharijis, in particular the Azariqa and the Najdis, condemned grave sinners and all non-Kharijis as infidels who could be killed, enslaved, or robbed of their possessions with impunity. Other groups, such as the Murji'a, claimed that faith is not determined by deeds and that one could not condemn a grave sinner as an unbeliever, except one who has abandoned prayer altogether, a view that became generally accepted in Sunni Islam. Indeed, popular views held that faith alone, and particularly devotion to the Prophet—and for Shi'is, to the imams as well—can make up for sins and a poor record of devotions and, through intercession, gain one entrance to paradise.

Creeds detailing the beliefs required of Muslims have been written from the early Islamic centuries until the present, and one of their main functions was to correct or exclude groups considered to hold heretical beliefs. Most jurists required the believer to know the very basic elements of Islamic theology and nothing more, but many theologians required a stronger adherence to complex creeds and wrote long doxographies detailing the beliefs of many Islamic sects, arguing that only one of these was "the saved sect" (*al-firqa al-nājiya*). Between 833 and 848, the Abbasid caliphs Ma'mun (r. 813–33), Mu'tasim (r. 833–42), and Wathiq (r. 842–47), in league with Mu'tazili theologians, initiated the inquisition (*miḥna*), attempting to enforce public adherence to the doctrine that the Qur'an was created rather than eternal. The Qadiri Creed, publicly promulgated by the Abbasid caliph Qadir (r. 991–1031) and his son and successor Qa'im (r. 1031–75) in the early 11th century, was inspired by traditionalist theologians and condemned Mu'tazili and Shi'i views as heretical in an attempt to exclude them from public religious discourse. Other influential Sunni creeds were written by Abu Ja'far al-Tahawi (d. 933), Abu Hafs 'Umar b. Muḥammad al-Nasafi (d. 537), Ibn Taymiyya (d. 1328), and Muhammad b. Yusuf al-Sanunsi (d. 1486).

See also blasphemy; God; theology

Further Reading

Toshihiko Isutzu, *Ethico-Religious Concepts in the Qur'an*, 2002; W. Montgomery Watt, "Conditions of Membership of the Islamic Community," *Studia Islamica* 21, no. 1 (1964); A. J. Wensinck, *The Muslim Creed*, 1932.

DEVIN J. STEWART

family

The family is the building block of Islamic societies. Family structures, as well as ideas about the family, play crucial roles in the economic, social, and political life of Islamic communities. The text of the Qur'an presents a number of important ideas about family, including the idea that attachment to family and one's relatives are part of the human obsession with the material world. The audience of the Qur'an is berated for its obsession with the amassment of material wherewithal, succinctly represented by "property and sons." The new religious dispensation urges the audience to give up this obsession, even if it requires breaking with relatives: "If your fathers, your sons, your brothers, your wives, your clan, the wealth you have acquired, the merchandise for which you fear that there will be no sale, and dwellings that you desire are dearer to you than God and His messenger and jihad in His way, then wait until God causes his command to pass" (Q. 9:24). Islam requires a radical break with existing structures: "You will not find folk who believe in God and the Last Day loving those who oppose God and His messenger, even though they be their fathers, their sons, their brothers, or their clan" (Q. 58:22). Several passages stress that one's relatives and progeny cannot help one on Judgment Day (Q. 60:3). At the same time, though, obligations toward blood relatives are confirmed, and the believers are urged to help their relatives and maintain contact with them, as well as to honor their parents.

The Prophet is a blood relative of the primary audience to whom he was sent to preach God's word. Prophecy works in a predictable manner, in part because God has a customary way (*sunnat Allāh*) of dealing with humanity, but also because human nature is predictable and people tend to be recalcitrant and set in their ways, so that they most often reject the prophetic messages that reach them. Prophets are members of the nations to whom they have been sent, and in the cases of tribal societies, they are actually related by blood ties to the members of the society to whom they preach, literally their "brothers." For this reason, Noah is described as the brother of his people, Hud the brother of the tribe of 'Ad, Salih the brother of the tribe of Thamud, Lot the brother of his people, and Shu'ayb the brother of the tribe of Midian (Q. 7:65, 73, 85; 11:50, 61, 84; 26:106, 124, 142, 161; 27:45; 29:36; 46:21; 50:13). These examples all suggest an emphasis on the Prophet Muhammad's blood ties to the rest of the Quraysh tribe, his primary audience. The importance of this is twofold. A member of the tribe is understood to have the same cultural background as his audience and should therefore be able to convey God's message to them in the appropriate language and manner. In addition, the fact that he is a close relative of his audience and not an outsider should impress upon them that he has their best interests at heart and could not be trying to mislead them for surreptitious or ulterior motives. A hadith report depicts the Prophet gathering the tribe and asking them from a hilltop outside Mecca whether they would believe him if he told them that a neighboring tribe was going to raid them the next day. When they all assented, he told them that his divine message was exactly analogous, except that he was warning of a much more devastating impending event, the Day of Judgment. The point is that they would have no reason to doubt the truth of his first warning because he is a member of their group and would have no reason to lie or distort the truth.

The blood ties of the Prophet played a critical role in his biography and the political machinations of the Quraysh tribe in response to his mission. The Prophet was initially protected, even though his preaching was rejected and perceived as a threat by the majority of his own tribe, because he enjoyed the backing of his clan, Hashim, under the leadership of his uncle and foster father, Abu Talib. This gave him immunity from attack. The clan continued to protect him even when they were boycotted by the rest of Quraysh. The Prophet lost the protection of his clan when Abu Talib died and leadership of the clan passed to another uncle, Abu Lahab 'Abd al-'Uzza, an enemy of the Prophet who was cursed in the Qur'an itself—"May the hands of Abu Lahab perish, and may he perish!" (Q. 111:1)—and this ultimately forced Muhammad to leave his native town. The story of Joseph in the Qur'an portrays a betrayal of a charismatic figure by his brothers as well as his kind treatment of them, and it may be read as an indirect comment on the trials of the Prophet with the members of his own tribe and his efforts to treat them with clemency and forgiveness.

Historical prophecy runs in families. The Qur'an refers to the prophets among the progeny of Adam, Noah, or Abraham (Q. 6:84; 19:58; 29:27; 57:26) and clearly shares with the Hebrew Bible the notion of Abraham as the patriarch. It also refers to the Tribes of Israel, using the term *asbāṭ*, cognate with the Hebrew term *shevaṭim*, rather than the ordinary Arabic term for tribes, *qabā'il*. Aaron is repeatedly held up as the brother of Moses, his help and support in his prophetic mission.

A crucial idea in the Qur'an and the Prophet's mission was that the believers form a new spiritual family, which supersedes and replaces the original biological or genetic family. Salvation history provides a number of examples of the distinction between the two. Abraham rejects his father's beliefs and society. When a son of Noah is drowned in the flood, he remonstrates with God, who had promised to save his household. God responds, "O Noah! He is not of your household. He is of evil conduct, so ask not of Me that whereof you have no knowledge" (Q. 11:45–46). The point is not that the son was illegitimate, though some commentaries suggest this interpretation, but rather that, as an unbeliever, he did not

belong to Noah's true family, the basis of which was faith. Noah's wife and Lot's wife are presented in a similar fashion: unbelievers who do not literally belong to the families of their husbands even though they are married (Q. 66). The believers are brothers of one another, and their new family will be the basis of a future nation (Q. 3:103). Though literal adoption is no longer allowed, foster children are part of the spiritual family: "Call them by their fathers' names; that will be more equitable in the sight of God. If you know not their fathers, then they are your brothers in faith and your clients" (Q. 33:5). The Prophet put this new understanding of family into literal effect after the flight to Medina, when he made the *muhājirūn*, those Meccan Muslims who had fled with him to safety in Medina, "brothers" of the *anṣār* (Muslims from Medina) in an event termed "the Brothering" (*al-mu'ākhāh*). The Prophet, exceptionally, was not paired with one of the *anṣār* but with his cousin 'Ali. This was not a mere announcement of affection or goodwill: the paired brothers entered into a defined legal relationship. They were obligated to support each other and could inherit from each other.

Even though in the Arab tribal system, wives remained members of their fathers' rather than their husbands' tribes, the Prophet's wives are assigned a special status in the Qur'an. Tellingly, the believers are instructed that the Prophet's wives are like their mothers: "The Prophet is closer to the believers than themselves, and his wives are their mothers" (Q. 33:6). The implication of the verse is not only that the believers form a spiritual family but also that Prophet Muhammad actually stands in the place of their father. Indeed, historical variants of this verse preserved in medieval Islamic texts such as the famous commentary of Muhammad b. Jarir al-Tabari (d. 923) add the phrase, "and he [i.e., the Prophet Muhammad] is a father to them." The term *ahl al-bayt* (the people of the house) is used in the Qur'an as a term of respect for wives, referring to Abraham's wife Sarah (Q. 11:73), for example, and to the Prophet Muhammad's wives, who are declared to be purified by divine act: "God's wish is to remove uncleanness from you" (Q. 33:32–33).

The prophetic mission introduced modifications of pre-Islamic family arrangements and associated practices. Polygyny was limited to four women, and marriage to two sisters was forbidden. The institution of formal adoption was abolished; an adopted child would no longer acquire the lineage of his or her adoptive father. The Qur'an severely criticizes the favoring of daughters over sons in Arabian society, a result of the emphasis on increasing one's male progeny, the agnate group that was the basic military and economic unit of tribal society. The text denounces female infanticide and mocks men in the audience for being upset when they are informed of the birth of a daughter, claiming that God himself has daughter goddesses.

One pre-Islamic institution that survived was that of clientage, and the patron-client relationship became crucial in the early Islamic centuries in the spread of Islam. Slaves who had been captured in warfare and converted to Islam while serving their Muslim masters became freedmen (*mawālī*) formally attached to the tribe of their former masters. Other free individuals simply converted at the hands of the members of Arab tribes and adopted the tribal *nisba* or gentilic as part of their new name.

Islamic law recognizes as a fundamental unit not only the nuclear family but also the extended family, with some emphasis on the father's relatives over the mother's. A remnant of the Arab tribal system from pre-Islamic times, the *'aṣaba* or agnate group—a man, his brothers, his father, his sons, and his brother's sons—represent the fundamental tribal fighting unit. They are the ones who rush to take revenge for an injury or insult to any one of their members, and they are liable to be pursued for revenge if any one of their members causes such injury or insult. The *'aṣaba* appears, importantly, in inheritance law: according to the Sunni *madhhabs*, when the set fractions do not take up all the estate, the remainder is inherited by the *'aṣaba*. Shi'i law rejects this rule, merely granting increased proportional shares to the other more closely related heirs. They, or the clan or tribe, are also responsible for paying blood money for injury or death. Laws regarding child custody are based on the premise that the natural allegiance of a child is to the father's side of his or her family, and custody always reverts to the father even though young children may remain with their mothers temporarily. In addition, most Islamic languages preserve a strong distinction between the mother's and father's sides of the family, so instead of having one term each for uncle or aunt, there are (at least) two terms. In Arabic, for example, a father's brother is *'amm* and a father's sister is *'amma*, while a mother's brother is *khāl* and a mother's brother is *khāla*. In many Islamic societies, the paternal uncles are associated with the father's role as the formal face of the family and a strict disciplinarian, while maternal uncles are associated with the nurturing, informal, and affectionate role of the mother.

Some aspects of marriage law reflect the endogamic ideal of the pre-Islamic Arabs. Some law books contain rulings that Arab women may not be married off to non-Arab men or that female descendants of the Prophet should not be married to Arabs descended from tribes considered base. In most Islamic societies, endogamy became highly preferred, especially for females, and Islamic law confirms that a Muslim man may marry a Jewish or Christian woman, while a Muslim woman does not have the corresponding right to marry a Jewish or Christian man, despite the fact that they all believe in God. The preferred marriage is between a young man and his paternal cousin—his father's brother's daughter; marriage between first cousins is not prohibited but favored. The reasons for this are several, including that it keeps wealth within the agnate unit, something succinctly expressed in modern Egypt as "putting our oil in our flour." While the percentage of such marriages that occur is not extremely high in most contexts, the idea is so pervasive that *bint 'ammī* (my cousin) is a typical term of endearment for one's wife, an equivalent to "honeybunch" or "sugarplum." In addition, when a young woman receives a suitor, her cousin (*ibn 'amm*) is often asked to relinquish his prior right to her, even in a perfunctory manner, before a match is arranged. This is widely understood to be the traditional way, even though it is the opposite of some other traditional societies, such as that of the Mongols,

where exogamy was the ideal and was supposed to strengthen the individual tribe.

Closely associated with the family structure is the concept of honor, which regulated the behavior of family members and governed their interactions with society at large. There are two quite distinct types of honor, termed *sharaf* and *'irḍ* in Arabic: the first refers to oneself and the second refers to people under one's protection, including, especially, the women of one's household, but also other relatives, clients, and supplicants. One's reputation depends on one's ability to defend oneself and one's dependents and control their behavior.

Lineage has played crucial roles in Islamic political history. Despite the fact that the Prophet's mission seems to have instituted a radically new spiritual family and, along with it, a radically new form of political organization, governed not by a hereditary ruler or a tribal chieftain but by a religious authority, even the first caliphs, the Prophet's immediate successors, were related to him. Abu Bakr (r. 632–34) was the Prophet's father-in-law, father of his wife 'A'isha, and 'Umar b. al-Khattab (r. 634–44) was the Prophet's father-in-law as well, father of his wife Hafsa. 'Uthman b. 'Affan (r. 644–56) was the Prophet's son-in-law, having married two of the Prophet's daughters, Ruqayyah and Umm Kulthum, and 'Ali b. Abi Talib was the Prophet's son-in-law as well, having married his daughter Fatima, in addition to being his cousin. The leadership of the Islamic empire quickly changed, however, to dynastic succession with the caliphate of Mu'awiya, the establishment of the Umayyad dynasty, and the designation of Yazid as heir apparent.

Not only the caliphal dynasties of the Umayyads and the Abbasids but also the leadership of their opponents, the Shi'is, were based on the dynastic principle. Shi'is of all stripes, like the Abbasids, claimed authority on the grounds that they represented the descendants of the Prophet Muhammad, who had been granted by divine fiat the right and responsibility to shepherd the Islamic community. One of the Shi'is' main proof texts in support of this was a transmitted report in which the Prophet had said to 'Ali that he, with respect to Muhammad, was in the position of Aaron with respect to Moses, serving as the assistant or lieutenant of the prophet. The biblical analogy served to attach the authority of 'Ali and his descendants to that of the Prophet, with the subtext that the political and spiritual leadership of the imams was the natural and logical continuation of prophetic authority. The divisions of Shi'is into the major groups of Twelvers, Isma'ilis, and Zaydis, as well as most of the factional disputes within each group, likewise focused on the dynastic principle and succession within the family. The exceptions were the Kharijis, who rejected the dynastic principle and held that any capable Muslim would be the caliph or imam.

As the Abbasid caliphs lost control over the peripheral regions of the Islamic empire from their center in Iraq, the typical pattern was for local governors or military commanders to establish hereditary dynasties, and Islamic history is replete with polities ruled by dynastic families, though other systems existed in contexts such as the Mamluk Empire in Egypt and Syria. The famous historian Ibn Khaldun proposed an organic theory of states in which he argued, from his study of Maghribi history, that dynastic succession was a cyclical pattern. New dynasties were established by seminomadic, uncivilized tribes who invaded settled regions and by virtue of their strong group affiliation, which he terms *'aṣabīyya*, are able to dominate the less tribal inhabitants. Once settled, though, they inevitably become accustomed to the comforts of civilization, lose their tribal cohesion and rough nature, and are then subject to invasion by another tribal group.

Some provisions in Islamic law recognize that descendants of the Prophet, termed *sayyid*s or sharifs, have special status. They cannot receive alms, for this would be disparaging to the family of the Prophet, but they are entitled to receive part of the *khums* or "fifth" that is levied on war booty. Descent from the Prophet grants one high social status, something recognized as important in marriage law, not to mention other customary privileges accorded to *sayyid*s in regions of the Muslim world from Morocco to India. Some Shi'i legal works contain the rule that a man cannot marry two wives who are both *sayyida*s on the logic that they are like sisters, and Islamic law forbids him from marrying sisters.

Most Islamic societies were organized into corporate entities first, such as neighborhoods, villages, religious minority communities, and so on, and then into families. The family remained a crucial economic and social unit in society. Though medieval Islamic society was relatively mobile, and merchants and others could travel more or less freely from one Muslim polity to the next without applying for citizenship or satisfying other formal requirements, one's position in society was determined to a great extent by heredity. It was commonly understood that society was hierarchical not only by force of circumstances but also by divine design and that ranks had to be respected. Professions of all kinds were understood to run in families, and the same often held for government posts. Supervisors of endowments; professors of Islamic law; judges of towns, cities, and provinces; and so on were often succeeded by their sons or nephews, and such practices were usually questioned only when the successor was deemed utterly corrupt or incompetent.

Unsurprisingly, Islamic law assumes a patriarchal system in which the head of the family is male, paternity determines what family one belongs to, and men are generally dominant over women. While men and women are each held to believe in the same way and to have roughly equal religious obligations, one may argue that in a blunt, practical sense, a woman's value is half that of a man of similar status. According to the traditional system of blood money payments, which likely goes back to pre-Islamic customs in pagan Arabia, a free Muslim woman is worth 50 camels, exactly one-half the price of a free Muslim man and equal in value to a Jewish or Christian male or a male slave. Similarly, a daughter's share of inheritance from her parents is half that of a son, and the testimony of a woman in court is worth effectively one-half of the testimony of a man. Nevertheless, women have many rights under Islamic law, including the right to own and dispose of property without the interference of their husbands, something

that women in Western societies did not have until quite recently. Husbands are required to pay for the food, shelter, clothing, and upkeep of their wives and children, while wives are not required to use any of their own property or income, even if it is vast, to support the family.

Social hierarchy, or a system of class distinctions, may be detected—and was upheld—in various areas of the law, particularly in marriage law. The law of *kafā'a* (suitability) held that a husband had to be of appropriate status to marry a woman from a family of high status and could be used to annul marriages of an heiress who ran off with a servant or the local butcher. When a specific dower was not mentioned in the marriage contract, it was assumed that the bride was entitled to *mahr al-mithl* (the dower of a similar woman), meaning a woman of similar social standing, and it was determined in practical terms by referring to the dowers received by her sisters, or if she had no married sisters, her cousins on her father's side of the family. Many of the financial obligations of the husband toward his wife were determined not by universal rules but by judging what could be expected by a woman of similar social standing. For example, if it was not ordinary for a woman of the wife's status to breast-feed her children, the husband was obliged to provide a wet nurse as part of his normal marital obligations for her upkeep. If this was so and she nevertheless breast-fed the baby, she was entitled to the salary that would have been paid to the wet nurse.

In most contexts in the premodern Muslim world, the shari'a fit into a system that was based on a more or less rigid separation of the government or military class from the bureaucracy, judiciary, and functionaries and the merchants, craftsmen, tradesman, and the populace in general. These groups were often divided along ethnic lines, and the law served the smooth operation of the system by promoting public order, keeping crime in check, and limiting the potential abuses of the ruler and the military class. The goal of this system was order rather than equality. The material benefits of the realm were not to be distributed evenly but according to merit and rank, recognizing appropriate distinctions between the various groups that made up society.

The family in the Islamic world is undergoing many of the transformations observed in other areas of the world, and this is having a tremendous effect on the economics and politics of the region. Modernization and its associated changes are producing a move away from the extended family to the nuclear family as the fundamental unit of society, and the single household that includes multiple married couples—a patriarch and his wife and all his sons and their wives—is becoming a rarity. The birth rate in many regions in the Islamic world, despite being quite high, is decreasing, and the age at which people marry is increasing for both men and women, largely because of the number of years spent in education and training. Social mobility has increased, also because of education, and the youth are not as constrained as in the past to follow the professions of their forefathers. It is interesting, though, that in a country like Egypt it is common to see pharmacists marry pharmacists, doctors marry doctors, engineers marry engineers, and so on, in part because while they are studying in their university faculties, they are not as subject to the social strictures that limit free interaction between young men and women in other contexts. While there have been a number of attempts to reform or modify specific areas of Islamic law with regard to marital rights, access to divorce, and child custody, a strong commitment remains throughout the Islamic world to the legal framework that governs family life, and the family—more than the individual—is still seen as the corporate entity that reproduces the economic, social, and political categories of society.

See also authority; honor; shari'a; women

Further Reading

Khaled Abou El Fadl, *Speaking in God's Name: Islamic Law, Authority and Women*, 2001; Abdullahi An-Naim, *Islamic Family Law in a Changing World: A Global Resource Book*, 2002; Michael Cook, *Commanding Right and Forbidding Wrong in Islamic Thought*, 2010; Wael B. Hallaq, *Sharī'a: Theory, Practice, Transformations*, 2009; Devin J. Stewart, *Islamic Legal Orthodoxy: Twelver Shiite Responses to the Sunni Legal System*, 1998; Knut S. Vikør, *Between God and Sultan: A History of Islamic Law*, 2005.

DEVIN J. STEWART

al-Farabi, Abu Nasr (ca. 878–950)

Abu Nasr Muhammad al-Farabi was, along with Ibn Sina, the most important representative of Islamic Aristotelianism. Farabi played a crucial role in the transmission of Greek philosophical thought to the Muslim world. His synthetic philosophy became the point of departure for all major branches of Islamic philosophy, including political philosophy. At the heart of his political thought, which is a major component of his philosophical system, lies the doctrine of the excellent city ruled by a philosopher-king.

Named Avennasar or Alfarabius in the medieval West, Farabi became known among the Arabs as "the second teacher," the first being Aristotle. Born in Turkestan as the son of a Turkish officer in the caliph's palace guard, Farabi probably studied first under Yuhanna b. Haylan, a Christian teacher of philosophy in Marv (Khurasan) and in 908 followed him to Baghdad, where he lived as a private citizen rather than a man of the caliphal court. In Baghdad, Farabi was in close contact with Bishr Matta b. Yunus (d. 940), the Jacobite translator of Greek philosophical works, and Farabi became the teacher of the Jacobite Yahya b. 'Adi (d. 972), the chief representative of Christian Aristotelianism in Baghdad. In 942, Farabi accepted the invitation of the Shi'i Hamdanid ruler of Aleppo and spent the rest of his active life there at the court with other men of letters until his death.

Farabi argues that the goal of human existence is the attainment of happiness, which consists of conjunction (*ittiṣāl*) with the

Active Intellect (*al-ʻaql al-faʻʻāl*, the active principle of understanding that is an emanation of God) and the separation from matter. But the overwhelming majority of human beings are not able to achieve this goal on their own and need a guide to lead them. The governance of the city (*al-siyāsa al-madaniyya*) is thus necessary due to the majority's need for guidance toward true happiness.

The city governed by the ruler-sage, who possesses the acquired intellect (*al-ʻaql al-mustafād*; which allows him to communicate with the Active Intellect) and whose inhabitants assist each other in the affairs through which happiness is obtained, is called "the excellent city" (*al-madīna al-fāḍila*). Such a city resembles a perfectly sound body whose parts (i.e., different social and professional groups, formed by the inhabitants of the city) assist one another in perfecting and protecting the life of the whole body. The city's ruler relates to other inhabitants as the heart relates to other body parts and the First Cause (God, considered as the sustainer of the world) to other existents. The inhabitants of the excellent city have different ranks depending on their closeness to the ruler. Those closest to the ruler possess qualities and habits that allow them to pursue his objectives in their actions, while those ranking below them pursue the objectives of those above them and, through their intermediacy, the objectives of the ruler. Every rank is governed by the rank above it and governs the rank below it. The innate nature (*fiṭra*) of the city's inhabitants makes each of them suitable for performing a particular task. However, the inhabitants become parts of the city not only through their innate nature but also through acquired, voluntary habits (*al-malakāt al-irādiyya*) such as crafts and arts.

The ruler must have achieved intellectual perfection; his imaginative faculty must also be perfect, enabling him to receive revelations from the Active Intellect about particulars and universals (e.g., about humanity as a universal notion and about Peter or Mary as particular human beings). Thanks to what the Active Intellect bestows on his passive intellect, such a ruler becomes a sage and philosopher; thanks to what the Active Intellect bestows on his imaginative faculty, he becomes a prophet and forewarner (*mundhir*). Such a man belongs to the highest rank of humanity and enjoys the highest degree of happiness. In order to be an efficient ruler, he must be able to express his knowledge in words, to guide people toward happiness, and to rigorously perform the tasks that constitute the routine of king's office.

A ruler who possesses all the aforementioned qualities is called "the true king" (*al-malik fī al-ḥaqīqa*). Should no one qualify to be a true king at a certain time, however, the city must be ruled by the traditional king (*al-malik bi-l-sunna*): a sage who follows and preserves laws issued by previous leaders and city founders. He typically does not issue new laws but can do so concerning an unprecedented case.

Although all inhabitants of the excellent city seek happiness and share common beliefs and principles, only a tiny minority—the sages—know these beliefs and principles through concepts and demonstrations. The majority—the believers (*mu'minūn*)—know them through their likenesses (*muthul*), which appear in the imagination as imitations (*muḥākāt*) of the intelligible forms of these beliefs and principles. The intelligible realities of happiness and principles, known through demonstration, are perfect and immutable, so there is a complete harmony among all the sages. However, the likenesses through which these realities are presented to the believers differ from each other, which leads to differences in opinions among the inhabitants of different excellent cities. According to their treatment of these differences, the believers can be divided into several groups. When those seeking guidance (*mustarshidūn*) discover an inconsistency in one of the likenesses, they replace that likeness with another that is closer to the truth and free from that contradiction. If the likenesses of the principles become obstacles to those who pursue ignorant goals (like obtaining rank or wealth), then they attempt to falsify those likenesses. When yet another group discovers certain inconsistencies in some likenesses due to the weakness of their understanding, they rashly dismiss those likenesses as false.

The variety of nonexcellent cities can be reduced to two types: the ignorant city (*al-madīna al-jāhila*) and the sinful city (*al-madīna al-fāsiqa*). The inhabitants of the ignorant city have incorrect conceptions of happiness and adhere to corrupt practices. The inhabitants of the sinful city share the sound beliefs of the inhabitants of the excellent city but perform the corrupt actions of the inhabitants of the ignorant city.

Inhabitants of the ignorant city live in permanent conflict and struggle; everyone's goal is to subdue or destroy the other. Whoever is most dominant over others is the happiest. All relationships among people rest on need and necessity. Natural justice is nothing but the right of the strongest, whereas the conventional rules of justice are observed due to mutual fear and weakness of the involved parties or due to external force.

Farabi's political teachings appealed to a number of Muslims—mainly Shiʻi rulers such as Sayf al-Dawla in Aleppo (r. 944–67) and the Fatimids (909–1171) in Egypt and Syria. However, his teachings were never effectively implemented. The key merit of his political writings lies in introducing Muslim intellectuals to Greek (in particular, Plato's) theories of government and providing a set of distinctive principles well suited for the evaluation and assessment of contemporary critical regimes.

See also city (philosophical); government; philosopher-king; utopia

Further Reading

Charles E. Butterworth, *The Political Aspects of Islamic Philosophy*, 1992; Hans Daiber, *The Ruler as Philosopher: A New Interpretation of al-Fārābī's Views*, 1986; Miriam Galston, *Politics and Excellence: The Political Philosophy of Alfarabi*, 1990; Muhsin S. Mahdi, *Alfarabi and the Foundation of Islamic Political Philosophy: Essays on Interpretation*, 2001; Ian Netton, *Al-Fārābī and His School*, 1992; Richard Walzer, ed. and trans., *Al-Farabi on the Perfect State*, 1985.

YANIS ESHOTS

Faraj, Muhammad ʿAbd al-Salam (1954–82)

Muhammad ʿAbd al-Salam Faraj (1954–82) was an ideologue belonging to the group that assassinated Egyptian president Anwar Sadat during a parade on October 6, 1981, in Cairo.

Faraj worked as a maintenance electrician at the Faculty of Arts of the University of Cairo in Giza. According to people who met him there, he was a "kind, soft-spoken and quiet" man. He was hanged for his role in the assassination of Sadat on April 15, 1982, together with the actual assassins.

Faraj is the author of a small book, *The Neglected Duty*, which does not mention Sadat by name but presents a justification for the assassination of any Muslim ruler who does not rule by the prescripts of Islamic law. Faraj quotes Ibn Taymiyya (d. 1328) and Qur'an 5:48: "Whosoever does not rule (*yaḥkum*) by what God has sent down—they are the unbelievers." He concludes that a Muslim ruler who does not rule by the shariʿa becomes, by doing so, an apostate who has to be killed for his apostasy. This view had been similarly expressed in Sayyid Qutb's (d. 1966) Qur'an commentary *In the Shade of the Qur'an* and in the writings of the Pakistani activist and ideologue Mawdudi (d. 1979).

The neglected duty mentioned in the title of Faraj's book is the duty to wage jihad. This duty, according to Faraj, following traditional doctrine, is a collective duty that the state has to fulfill. When the state neglects to do so, however, it is no longer a collective duty but becomes an individual duty that is incumbent on every Muslim. In addition, not only individuals but also various types of Muslim nongovernmental organizations may see it as their duty to carry out the divine obligation to wage jihad if the government is in the hands of non-Muslims or Muslims perceived as apostates.

The group that assassinated Sadat had contacts with Shaykh ʿUmar ʿAbd al-Rahman, who worked at the time as a preacher in the Fayyum oasis. Early in 1981, these contacts were broken off for security or other reasons. When he was interrogated in the wake of the Sadat assassination, ʿAbd al-Rahman admitted believing that a Muslim who rules by laws other than the shariʿa had to be killed. He expressed doubts, however, about whether Sadat had been properly notified of this doctrine. These doubts saved his life: the authorities released him, and this gave ʿAbd al-Rahman the opportunity to continue his career in Pakistan and the United States.

About 500 copies of *The Neglected Duty* were printed in great haste, probably in 1980. The original edition contains many misprints, a result of the typesetter's carelessness and fear of discovery by the political police. Once a number of copies of the book had been distributed, the group that distributed the pamphlet and actually assassinated Sadat realized that the police would be able to trace the copies back to them. They decided to burn the remaining copies.

Nevertheless, a few copies survived, and in the trial of Sadat's assassination in the fall of 1981, the prosecution added one of these to the file. On December 8, 1981, the Cairo daily *Al-Ahram* (The pyramids) published parts of an official refutation of the contents of the book. This refutation was written by the mufti of the Republic, Shaykh Jad al-Haqq ʿAli Jad al-Haqq (mufti of Egypt from 1978–82). The newspaper article contained quotations from *The Neglected Duty*. This brought the open publication of the full text within the realm of possibility, and the weekly newspaper *Al-Ahrar* (The free) took this risk on December 14, 1981.

Al-Ahrar's version of the book contains even more misprints than the original and is hence occasionally unintelligible. Yet it is the basis of most current editions and reprints and remains one of the few uncensored documents originating with the *takfīr* (to brand someone as a kafir, or unbeliever) movement of the 1980s.

See also apostasy; Egypt; excommunication; fundamentalism; al-Gamaʿa al-Islamiyya

Further Reading

Muhammad ʿAbd al-Salam Faraj, *Al-Farida al-Gha'iba*, translated by Johannes J. G. Jansen as *The Neglected Duty: The Creed of Sadat's Assassins*, 1986; Johannes J. G. Jansen, *The Dual Nature of Islamic Fundamentalism*, 1997.

JOHANNES J. G. JANSEN

Fatimids (909–1171)

An Ismaʿili dynasty that ruled from North Africa and Egypt from 909 to 1171, the Fatimids represented the crowning success of the Ismaʿili movement. The Ismaʿilis had organized a far-flung revolutionary movement in the hope of replacing the Abbasid caliphs with their own imams, descendants of Jaʿfar al-Sadiq through his son Ismaʿil. The religiopolitical message of the movement, designated as *al-daʿwa al-hādiya* or "the rightly guiding mission," was propagated by a network of *dāʿīs* (missionaries) throughout the Muslim world and achieved particular success in North Africa. Here the *dāʿī* Abu ʿAbdallah al-Shiʿi (d. 911) was active among the Kutama Berbers of the lesser Kabylia from 893. Between 903 and 909, he conquered Ifriqiya, in what is now known as eastern Algeria and Tunisia, from the Sunni Aghlabids who ruled it as vassals of the Abbasids. ʿAbdallah al-Mahdi (d. 934), who had succeeded to the central leadership of the Ismaʿili movement in 899, left the secret headquarters of the *daʿwa* movement in Salamiyya and entered Qayrawan (Kairouan) on January 4, 910, to become the first Fatimid caliph. The new dynasty was designated as such (*Fāṭimiyya*) because Mahdi and his successors traced their genealogy to the Prophet Muhammad's daughter Fatima and her spouse, ʿAli b. Abi Talib, the first Shiʿi imam.

The early Fatimids did not control any region of the Maghrib beyond Ifriqiya proper for any extended period. Enemies of the Abbasids and the Umayyads of Spain, they also had numerous hostile encounters with the Byzantines in the Mediterranean, having inherited the island of Sicily as successors to the Aghlabids. Their

main problem, however, was the rebellious activities of the Khariji Berbers of the Zanata tribal confederation, especially the prolonged revolt of Abu Yazid (943–47), who also capitalized on the hostility of the Sunnis toward their new Shi'i overlords.

Fatimid rule was firmly established in North Africa only under Mu'izz li-Din Allah (953–75). This caliph also made detailed plans for the conquest of Egypt, then ruled by the Ikhshidids on behalf of the Abbasids. Jawhar, a long-serving commander of the dynasty, led the Fatimid expedition to Egypt in 969, and with the arrival of Mu'izz in Cairo in 973, the North African phase of the Fatimid caliphate came to an end.

After the Fatimid conquest, Egypt became a major commercial and cultural center, but the Fatimids' attempts to advance further east through Syria were checked by a resurgence of Byzantine power, by the armies of the Qarmatians (dissident Isma'ilis) in Bahrain, and later by the Seljuq Turks. The Fatimids did, however, supplant the Abbasids as protectors of the holy cities of Mecca and Medina.

The Fatimids continued their mission (*da'wa*) in Egypt, especially from the time of Mu'izz, with particular success outside the Fatimid state, especially in Yemen, Iraq, Persia, and Central Asia. In Egypt, the population continued to adhere mainly to Sunni Islam, insofar as it was not Christian. The Fatimids paid great attention to the education of their *dā'īs* and ordinary Isma'ilis, founding a number of distinctive traditions as well as institutions of learning in Cairo. The movement underwent several splits, however. In the reign of Hakim bi-Amr Allah (996–1021), some *dā'īs* preached extremist ideas leading to the formation of the Druze community. On the death of Mustansir bi-llah in 1094, the Isma'ilis divided into the Musta'li and Nizari factions, named after two of Mustansir's sons who claimed his heritage. The Musta'li Isma'ilis of Egypt and elsewhere acknowledged the caliph Musta'li (1094–1101) and the later Fatimid caliphs as their imams, while the Nizari Isma'ilis of Persia and Syria recognized a different line of imams held to descend from Nizar b. al-Mustansir (d. 1095), the original heir-designate of Mustansir. By 1132, in the aftermath of Amir bi-Ahkam Allah's assassination and the irregular succession of his cousin Hafiz, the Musta'li Isma'ilis themselves split into Hafizi and Tayyibi branches. Only the Hafizis, concentrated mainly in Fatimid Egypt, recognized Hafiz and his successors in the Fatimid dynasty as their imams.

The political decline of the Fatimid caliphate began during the long reign of Mustansir, who was eventually obliged to turn to the Armenian general Badr al-Jamali for help. In 1074, Badr arrived in Cairo with his Armenian troops, eventually to acquire all the highest positions of the Fatimid state. Henceforth, military men appointed as viziers, rather than the Fatimid caliphs themselves, exercised effective power in the state. Salah al-Din (Saladin) ended Fatimid rule on September 10, 1171, when he had the sermon at the Friday public prayers (*khuṭba*) read in Cairo in the name of the Abbasid caliph. A few days later, 'Adid, the 14th and last of the Fatimid caliphs, died while the new Ayyubid masters of Egypt had begun their systematic persecution of the Isma'ilis there.

See also Egypt; imamate; Isma'ilis; North Africa; Saladin (1138–93); Seljuqs (1055–1194)

Further Reading

Michael Brett, *The Rise of the Fatimids: The World of the Mediterranean and the Middle East in the Fourth Century of the Hijra, Tenth Century* CE, 2001; Farhad Daftary, *The Ismā'īlīs: Their History and Doctrines*, 2007; Heinz Halm, *The Empire of the Mahdi: The Rise of the Fatimids*, translated by M. Bonner, 1996; al-Qadi Abu Hanifa al-Nu'man b. Muhammad, *Founding the Fatimid State*, translated by Hamid Haji, 2006; Paul E. Walker, *Exploring an Islamic Empire: Fatimid History and Its Sources*, 2002.

FARHAD DAFTARY

fatwa

A fatwa (*fatwā*, pl. *fatāwā*) is a nonbinding legal opinion issued by a qualified Islamic scholar in response to a question posed by an individual, judge, or government. The Arabic root *f-t-y* appears in two of several Qur'anic verses that instruct the Prophet Muhammad in answering the early Muslims' questions (Q. 4:127 and 4:176). Following his death in 632, many of Muhammad's Companions acted as the first muftis (jurists who issue fatwas), basing their legal opinions on their knowledge of the Qur'an and of Muhammad's exemplary practices and guidance. From the first Islamic century to the present, the issuing of fatwas (*iftā'*) has been a central Islamic institution providing believers with legal and moral advice and contributing to the ongoing development of Islamic law.

Process, Form, and Function

The work of a mufti is distinct from that of a judge (qadi). Whereas a judge faces rival claimants, evaluates evidence, and reaches an enforceable decision, a mufti issues an advisory opinion on the basis of the information provided to him by a petitioner (*mustaftī*). In addition to those areas of law governed by the courts, the mufti must be prepared to answer queries regarding ritual practices, ethics, and religious tenets. Muftis may dispense fatwas privately or in the service of a court or government. In Muslim Spain, judges were required to solicit fatwas from court muftis; judges have also sought muftis' assistance with difficult cases or support for controversial judgments. Unlike most court decisions, the fatwas of prominent muftis have been preserved in collections as valuable precedents and for training new jurists. Although the need for judges trained in Islamic law has declined since the institution of secular courts in most modern Muslim states, the practice of *iftā'* has continued to thrive. This is especially true for questions related to ritual practice and worship and to Muslim life in majority non-Muslim countries.

Private muftis derive their legitimacy from public and peer recognition of their scholarly expertise, upright character, and sound judgment. Muftis may be women, but in practice, they have primarily been men who have achieved the necessary competence to issue

fatwas after a lengthy period of formal instruction in the religious and linguistic sciences. Initially, muftis were expected to be *mujtahid*s, those jurists capable of independently deriving a legal rule from the Qur'an and the sunna (normative example) of Muhammad. By the tenth century, most muftis practiced *taqlīd* (emulation) rather than *ijtihād* (independent reasoning) by affiliating with the interpretive tradition of one school of law (*madhhab*) and relying on opinions established by that school's earlier authorities. Theoretical treatises on *iftā'* rank muftis according to their level of expertise and assign them a corresponding degree of interpretive license; *mujtahid*s may respond to new and difficult issues, whereas lesser jurists may only apply existing school doctrines.

Most Sunni legal theorists allow the questioner (*mustaftī*) to approach more than one mufti with the same question, which must address a real rather than hypothetical situation. Adherents of the dominant Twelver branch of Shi'i Islam have in modern times been expected to designate one high-ranking *mujtahid* as their *marja' al-taqlīd*, or "source of emulation" in religious affairs. Unlike the fatwas of other jurists, those of a *marja'* are binding for his followers.

Fatwas may be written or oral and range from a simple "yes" or "no" to a lengthy treatise. A shorter, "minor" fatwa might communicate a well-established legal rule to a nonspecialist, while a "major" fatwa might detail the mufti's reasoning in deriving a new rule for an unprecedented case. Major fatwas are generally directed to educated audiences and are more likely to be preserved.

Political Fatwas

A political fatwa is one that either is issued by an official mufti or is political in content. Although less numerous than private and judicial fatwas, political fatwas have served as powerful instruments of religious legitimation, political criticism, doctrinal disputation, and popular mobilization.

Muftis operated independently prior to their gradual incorporation into government administration, first as advisors to the early caliphs and later as high-ranking officials, such as the Ottoman shaykh al-Islam, the Persian and Mughal Sadr, and the grand mufti of several modern states. Although state muftis have often been expected to legitimate governmental policies, they have also wielded considerable influence of their own. Ottoman sultans regularly sought the chief mufti's sanction for administrative and military initiatives, including justifications for jihad against Muslim states in Mamluk Egypt and Safavid Iran. Conversely, several Ottoman and Moroccan sultans were deposed by fatwas. Contemporary state muftis and fatwa-issuing institutions respond to government and private requests, ruling on such issues as regional conflicts, interest banking, and medical ethics. In the process, they help define a national Islamic identity.

Muftis have also used fatwas to dispute doctrinal points or identify individuals and groups for inclusion or exclusion from the Muslim community. *Takfīr*, or declaring Muslims to be unbelievers, has often been accomplished through fatwas, as have accusations of apostasy and blasphemy. In 1989, Iran's supreme leader Ayatollah Khomeini (1902–89) issued a statement calling for the execution of author Salman Rushdie for insulting Islam in his novel *The Satanic Verses*. Although not strictly a fatwa, this death sentence was quickly treated as such, gaining heightened prominence because of Khomeini's status as the head of state and a *marja' al-taqlīd*. The prevalent use of *takfīr* by militant Islamist groups to justify jihad against nominally Muslim rulers led to a unique form of counter-fatwa, the Amman Message, in 2005. Signed in Jordan by nearly 200 high-level jurists, the statement recognizes eight legitimate schools of Islamic law and prohibits declarations of apostasy within these schools. In reaction to the issuance of fatwas by militants lacking the requisite professional qualifications, the Message also restricts *iftā'* to properly trained jurists.

Osama bin Laden's coauthored 1998 fatwa calling on all Muslims to wage jihad against Americans is a prominent example of this trend, as Bin Laden is widely considered unqualified for either *iftā'* or declarations of war. Yet the fatwa garnered support, thus additionally exemplifying the use of fatwas for popular political mobilization. Colonial resistance movements in British India and French Algeria also included fatwas calling on Muslims to emigrate from foreign-occupied territory. In each case, rival interests secured fatwas urging accommodation rather than emigration.

The spread of new media technologies has placed more fatwas in the realm of public discourse. By the close of the 20th century, fatwas had become readily accessible through journals, radio and television programs, and Internet sites. Controversial fatwas are often circulated and debated by both specialists and lay Muslims worldwide.

See also *ijtihād* and *taqlīd*; judge; judicial courts; jurisprudence; shari'a; shaykh al-Islam; source of emulation; 'ulama'

Further Reading

Wael B. Hallaq, *A History of Islamic Legal Theories: An Introduction to Sunnī uṣūl al-fiqh*, 1997; Muhammad Khalid Masud, Brinkley Messick, and David S. Powers, eds., *Islamic Legal Interpretation: Muftis and Their Fatwas*, 1996; Jakob Skovgaard-Petersen, *Defining Islam for the Egyptian State: Muftis and Fatwas of the Dār al-Iftā*, 1997; Knut S. Vikør, *Between God and the Sultan: A History of Islamic Law*, 2005.

JOCELYN HENDRICKSON

freedom

The concept of freedom (*ḥurriyya*) was well-known to Islamic thought in all periods as the opposite of slavery. Although in premodern times there was no school of thought calling for the abolition of slavery, it was universally recognized that being a slave was an undesirable condition and being free a desirable one; at the same

time, to manumit a slave was an act of virtue. This valuation colors some of the secondary uses of the contrast between freedom and slavery discussed in the following paragraphs.

As in other societies familiar with the institution of slavery, there was a tendency to use the relationship between master and slave as a metaphor for unequal relationships. Thus a saying ascribed to a daughter of the first caliph, Asma' bt. Abi Bakr (d. 692), as well as to 'Umar b. al-Khattab, 'A'isha bt. Abi Bakr, and the Prophet, equates marriage with slavery; likewise, humans are thought of as slaves—or servants—of God in the sense that they are owned by Him. A well-attested strain in Sufi thought contrasts enslavement to the things of this world with the freedom that results from emancipating oneself from them.

In the political domain, premodern Islamic texts occasionally invoke the relationship between master and slave as a metaphor for oppression. Thus the Spanish Muslim Ibn Hafsun (d. 918), the leader of a rebellion against Umayyad rule supported mainly by Muslims of native Spanish descent, told his followers that the Arabs had enslaved them and that his wish was to deliver them from their slavery (*'ubūdiyya*). An earlier example is a speech attributed to Abu Hamza al-Mukhtar b. 'Awf, a Khariji rebel against the Umayyads in the later 740s. He says that Mu'awiya, followed by the Marwanid rulers, "made the servants of God slaves," and he ascribes to the Umayyads in general the sentiment that "the people are our slaves." A story set on the eve of the Battle of Qadisiyya, around 636, takes us closer to the time of the Prophet: two of the envoys sent by the Muslim commander to negotiate with the Persian general Rustam tell him that the Muslims have come to Iraq to deliver those who so wish from being slaves of men to being servants of God. This wording echoes a letter said to have been sent by the Prophet to the people of Najran.

Two points need to be made about such attestations. The first is that they employ only one side of the metaphor: while the notion of political slavery as an undesirable condition is explicit, any notion of political freedom as its contrary remains implicit. The second is that this notion of political slavery is not taken up in the Islamic tradition of systematic political thought. Thus antidespotic and antipatrimonial values often expressed in terms of political freedom in the European tradition are articulated in other ways in the premodern Islamic tradition.

Since the late 18th century, the European idea of political freedom has spread widely in the Islamic world. One of the earliest responses to the idea was that of the Egyptian chronicler Jabarti (d. 1824–25) in his *Ta'rikh Muddat al-Faransis bi-Misr* (The history of the French presence in Egypt), in a critical commentary on the proclamation issued by Napoleon on his invasion of Egypt in 1798. The way in which Jabarti explains the term suggests that he misunderstood it (whereas the egalitarianism of the French seems to have been immediately intelligible to him). Later authors had no trouble understanding the concept and saw it as central to European success; thus the Tunisian statesman Khayr al-Din Pasha (d. 1890) distinguished "personal freedom" from "political freedom" and described freedom as "the basis of the great development of knowledge and civilization in the European kingdoms." The idea of political freedom has thus become part of the standard vocabulary of political discussion in the Islamic world. In rendering the concept into Arabic, the metaphor at the root of the European concept was preserved: the word employed (*ḥurriyya*) is the same word that in premodern times denoted freedom as opposed to slavery (this contrasts with Chinese, where the term used to translate "freedom" originally meant "doing as one pleases," with much less favorable connotations).

Despite the fact that it lacks an explicit precedent in the Islamic tradition, the idea of political freedom has also found favor among Islamists. Thus Mawdudi (d. 1979) emphasized the complete freedom people enjoyed in expressing their opinions under the early caliphs. More generally, he saw the message of the Qur'an as having set people free of "the bonds of slavery" and given them "a real charter of liberty and freedom." Likewise Sayyid Qutb (d. 1966), who was entranced by the message delivered by the Muslim envoys to Rustam, frequently used a language of liberation (*taḥrīr*) in his presentation of one of his favorite themes: the elimination of the domination of men over men. This is not, of course, to say that Islamists have espoused the idea of political freedom in the spirit of European liberals; while taking a positive view of freedom as such, they often criticize the excessive freedom they see as prevalent in the West.

See also democracy; individualism; slavery

Further Reading

Michael Cook, "Is Political Freedom an Islamic Value?" in *Freedom and the Construction of Europe*, edited by Quentin Skinner and Martin van Gelderen, forthcoming; Patricia Crone, *Medieval Islamic Political Thought*, 2004; Bernard Lewis, *The Political Language of Islam*, 1988; Franz Rosenthal, *The Muslim Concept of Freedom Prior to the Nineteenth Century*, 1960.

MICHAEL COOK

free will

Islamic theologians addressed the problem of the freedom of human will as early as the eighth century, primarily in connection with destiny (*qadar*) and God's attributes, among the metaphysical questions delineated by Islam's six articles of faith: belief in God, the angels, the scriptures, the prophets, Judgment Day, and destiny. Overall, Muslim theologians may be grouped into three main categories with regard to this topic: those who denied free will and advocated determinism, those who advocated the free will of the human agent, and those who upheld an intermediate view, combining the stances of the first two groups.

The first category of theologians came to be known as the *jabriyya* or determinists, meaning those who believe that the action of

the human agent is preordained. Among the theological schools that advocated this position is that of Jahm b. Safwan (d. 745). According to the theologian and heresiographer Shahrastani (d. 1153), Jahm argued that "the human being is incapable of anything, and capacity cannot be attributed to him in any respect; all human actions are pre-determined (*majbūra*). The human being has no capacity, will or choice. God creates his actions as much as he does in all inanimate objects. Actions are then attributed to the human being metaphorically, just as they are to inanimate objects. We thus say that the tree bore fruit, the water flowed, the stone moved, the sun rose and set." Also considered among the *jabriyya* are the followers of Husayn b. Muhammad al-Najjar (d. 844). Shahrastani relates that Najjar said, "The Creator—Exalted be He—is the ultimate agent Who wills good and evil. . . . He creates the actions of His servants, the good and the evil, the beautiful and the ugly. The servants of God only acquire these actions." Among other key theologians who denied free will and argued that human actions are created by God are Dirar b. ʻAmr (d. early ninth century) and Ibn Ishaq al-Rawandi (d. 859).

The second category, those who argued for absolute human freedom, is best represented by the Muʻtazili school of theology. In his *Maqalat al-Islamiyyin* (The tenets of faith of the followers of Islam), Abu al-Hasan al-Ashʻari (d. 935) reports that according to Abu al-Hudhayl al-ʻAllaf (d. 850), one of the founding figures of the Muʻtazili tradition, capacity is necessary for any action to take place. This means that the capability to undertake actions precedes the actions themselves, which allows for free will. Similarly, Ibrahim al-Nazzam (d. ca. 846) argued that all human actions or motions (*ḥarakāt*) are caused by the human agent directly and that the will necessitates or brings about its object. Abu Hashim al-Jubba'i (d. 933) extended the Muʻtazili theory of free will to the problem of reward and punishment in the afterlife, arguing that they depend both on the actions one performs as well as on the actions one omits. Jubba'i argues that since one has the freedom to perform or refrain from the obligations God imposes, one accordingly merits reward for acting and deserves punishment for not acting. A more comprehensive outline of the Muʻtazili theory of free will may be traced in Qadi ʻAbd al-Jabbar's (d. 1025) magnum opus, *al-Mughni fi Abwab al-Tawhid wa-l-ʻAdl* (The chapters on God's oneness and justice), where he argues that all Muʻtazilis agreed that human acts are not created and that "whoever says that God . . . is their creator and cause has committed a grave error." He adds that the "will and the object willed are both acts by the servants of God . . . and whatever results from that will is due to the human act, whether such result is found in the agent of the act or in another object." In addition, the human being is capable not only of physical actions but also of "acts of the heart like thinking, willing and believing," or what might be called mental operations. Both will and the capability of fulfilling that will are human acts. Like other Muʻtazilis, Qadi ʻAbd al-Jabbar leaves room for involuntary acts that affect human will and capacity and may either hamper them or cause them to perform undesired acts. He argues that these should be neither praised nor blamed from either a moral or a religious perspective.

In the third category, those who held an intermediate position between arguing for free will and completely denying it are the Ashʻaris, members of a theological school founded by Ashʻari. Ashʻari argued that acts are created by God and then "acquired" by human agents. In his famous work *al-Lumaʻ* (Flashes of insight), Ashʻari argues, "If we find that infidelity is evil and corrupt compared to that which it opposes (i.e., faith), and if we find that faith is exhausting and involves pain. . . . But the infidel intends that his infidelity appear truly beautiful, even though the reality is at odds with his intention. . . . If this is the case, this means that infidelity has been caused to appear ugly by an agent that intends it to be so. This causing agent cannot be the infidel himself, who would want infidelity to be truly beautiful and true." Ashʻari believes that if the human being is the free cause of his own acts, his acts would always lead to a desirable result. Hence there must be another cause underlying human actions, and this cause is God. Shahrastani explains Ashʻari's concept of acquisition (*kasb*) as follows: God creates an act based on the temporary will and choice of the servant of God. Thus God is the actual cause of the act, while the human agent only acquires the act or attributes it to himself because he wills it temporarily. However, this explanation does not resolve the problem of making God the ultimate cause of both evil and good deeds. Later Ashʻaris such as Juwayni (d. 1085) tried to overcome this problem; he argued that there is an immediate connection between an act and the capacity of the human agent undertaking it. That capacity, however, is ultimately caused by another cause, and that other cause by another cause, in a chain that goes back to the ultimate cause of all causes, or God. This leaves a marginal yet nominal level of freedom for the human agent; for while it acknowledges that the human agent has true capacity to perform the act, it argues that the ultimate cause is still God.

Apart from theology, the problem of free will was addressed in both Islamic philosophy and mysticism. The Peripatetic orientation of Muslim philosophers makes the possibility of human free will as difficult to ascertain as it is in the Aristotelian system, because of the complex implications of Aristotle's *Physics*, *De Interpretatione*, and *Metaphysics*. Ibn Sina's (d. 1037) claim in the *Metaphysics* of *The Book of Healing* that every possible existent is possible in itself and necessary with respect to its ultimate cause, the necessary existent, leads him to a deterministic reading, as Catarina Belo has recently argued. Still, his position in the treatise on destiny, *Risala fi Sirr al-Qadar* (Epistle on the secret of destiny), along with his later critique of Aristotle's naturalistic metaphysics, creates room for human freedom and choice. The same holds for Ibn Rushd (d. 1198). The teleological structure of his *Physics* and *Metaphysics* and his restricted characterization of will in *Manahij al-Adilla fi ʻAqa'id al-Milla* (The methods of proof on the articles of faith) lead him to a deterministic reading. Nonetheless, in his *Commentary on Plato's Republic*, the emphasis he places on the role of individual imagination opens up the possibility of human freedom and choice, especially on the political level. Sufi thinkers such as Junayd (d. 910) and Qushayri (d. 1074) generally assert that trust in God's will and power (*tawakkul*) and contentment with

God's will and decree (*riḍā*) are an essential part of living as a true servant of God and hence conditions for attaining communion with Him. This view is bolstered by an emphasis on the need to renounce one's conscious desire to determine one's life (*tadbīr*). While Sufis have tended to take a deterministic position, it differs from the theological determinism discussed earlier. The latter is based on the ontological denial of free will, while the former is based on a subjective willingness to accept and harmonize oneself with God's decree. If this is taken into consideration along with the fundamental Sufi doctrine of the annihilation of the human will in the divine will, particularly as it was characterized by philosophical mystics such as Junayd and Ibn al-'Arabi (d. 1240), a new theory of the subjective origins of freedom in Islamic thought might be constructed.

See also Ash'aris; Mu'tazilis; theology

Further Reading

Abu al-Hasan al-Ash'ari, *Maqalat al-Islamiyyin wa-Ikhtilaf al-Musallin*, 1980; Catarina Belo, *Chance and Determinism in Avicenna and Averroes*, 2007; G. Gimaret, *Theories de l'acte humain en theologie musulmane*, 1980; J. van Ess, *The Flowering of Muslim Theology*, 2006; W. M. Watt, *The Formative Period of Islamic Thought*, 1973; Harry Wolfson, *The Theology of the Kalām*, 1979.

AHMED ABDEL MEGUID

Friday prayer

The Friday gathering at which Muslims listen to a sermon (*khuṭba*) and perform a set of ritual prostrations (*raka'āt*) is known as *ṣalāt al-jum'a* or *jumu'a* (congregational prayer) within the Muslim legal tradition. The *ṣalāt al-jum'a* is taken to be the reference of the Qur'anic verse, "When the call is proclaimed on the day of assembly (*yawm al-jum'a*), make haste to the remembrance of God, and abandon your selling" (62:9). There is some evidence to suggest that the congregational Friday prayer ritual was derived from and in part in a mimicry of the Jewish and Christian Sabbath traditions. The manuals of jurisprudence list various elements of and conditions for the validity of Friday prayer, some of which have obvious political implications, both theoretical and practical. Furthermore, in historical terms, the establishment of Friday prayer under the auspices of, and in the name of, an individual ruler was an outward symbol of the ruler's hegemony and, along with the minting of coinage in the ruler's name, the most important of such symbols.

The political importance of Friday prayer is underscored by reports relating to the Prophet Muhammad's institution of Friday prayer, indicating that it formed an element in the formation of the first Muslim community in Medina following the hijra in 622. Through the establishment of this political community, the Muslims were able to expand their empire throughout the Arabian Peninsula and beyond. A regularly cited hadith report found in the collection of Sulayman al-Tabarani (d. 970) underlines the role of Friday prayer in political community formation: "Whoever abandons *al-jum'a* when having either a just or an unjust Imam, will have no [valid] prayer, fasting, alms or pilgrimage." Failure to perform Friday prayer in a Muslim state context puts at risk the validity of all of one's other religious duties and ultimately excludes the individual from community membership.

The development of law concerning the legitimate and illegitimate performance of Friday prayer became a cipher for political theory among some jurists. That the leader of the Friday prayers, the *imām al-jum'a*, should be appointed by the ruler, termed variously sultan, imam, or *wālī* in the legal literature, is a widely accepted position. The view is based on the notion that one should not lead prayers in another's home without the owner's permission. It was particularly promoted within the Hanafi school, which was founded by the great eighth-century jurist Abu Hanifa (d. 767) and later dominated the Muslim world through its official standing in both the Mughal and Ottoman empires. Similarly, there was a prevalent view that there can only be a single Friday prayer in any city. In this way, this weekly occasion became an opportunity for creating and enforcing political cohesion, and there is plenty of evidence to suggest that caliphs and sultans used it for precisely this purpose.

Before the Friday prayer prostrations, there was a period reserved for a sermon, or rather two sermons, with a short break between them. The historical sources describe how it had become accepted practice for the preacher (*khaṭīb*) to mention the name of and utter a blessing for the current ruler as an element of the *khuṭba*. This element is not universally replicated in the works of Islamic law. When jurists do mention the blessing for the sultan, they do not make it obligatory for the valid performance of the prayer. This failure, or perhaps refusal, to stipulate, in an explicit manner, that the blessing for the sultan must be part of the Friday prayer should not be seen as an act of open rebellion by the jurists. Rather, it reflects the general juristic tendency, particularly in ritual law such as prayer, of the individual and the necessary conditions for his or her effective performance of a duty demanded by God. In any case, as some hadiths of the Prophet's Companions indicate, the blessing for the sultan was an innovation, introduced into the practice after the life of Muhammad: if the prayer for the preservation of the ruler was an essential element of the *khuṭba*, the Prophet would have had to pray for himself in the third person—a strange practice for which no evidence exists.

In the Imami Shi'i tradition, the legal status of the Friday prayer was the subject of great controversy. The common understanding among the jurists, both Sunni and Shi'i, was that a legitimate ruler had to give his permission before a valid Friday prayer could be held in a city, but Imami jurisprudence upheld a theoretical commitment to the idea that all governments other than that led by the rightful imam were illegitimate. The Twelfth Imam of the Imami Shi'is had been incognito since 870 and hence was unavailable to

provide the essential validating decree. For some Imami jurists, this meant that Friday prayer had lapsed during the period of the imam's concealment (*ghayba*), and holding Friday prayer was, therefore, forbidden until he revealed himself. The debate around the legitimacy of Friday prayer in later Imami jurisprudence became intricate and politically charged, particularly when the presence of a "just jurist" (*faqīh 'ādil*) was introduced by some jurists as a legitimating element. During the Safavid period, some jurists argued that Friday prayer could become "optionally" obligatory (*wājib takhyīrī*, i.e., one can perform it or one can perform the usual noon prayers instead, but one must perform one of the two) through the activating presence of the just jurist, who could substitute for the imam. The Safavid state officially supported this view, appointing an *imām-i jum'a* to each city as the Friday prayer leader. The move was controversial and provoked a series of rebuttals and counter-rebuttals in a debate that continued into the 21st century.

The importance of the Friday prayer event as a political tool within Muslim societies is obvious. Through the *khuṭba*, the objectives of the government's religious policy can be made known, as they have been in modern-day Saudi Arabia. The *khuṭba* can also function as a conduit for revolutionary propaganda as it did in the months leading up to the Islamic Revolution in 1979, when Ayatollah Khomeini's Friday sermons from Najaf in Iraq, and then later from Paris, were smuggled into Iran on cassette tapes. The holding of a communal congregational prayer has, unavoidably, proven to be of great political possibilities, both in terms of its formal requirements and in its potential as a vehicle for social mobilization.

See also Pillars of Islam

Further Reading

Norman Calder, "Friday Prayer and the Juristic Theory of Government: Sarakhsī, Shīrāzī, Māwardī," *Bulletin of the School of Oriental and African Studies*, 49, no. 1 (1986); Andrew J. Newman, "Fayd al-Kashani and the Rejection of the Clergy/State Alliance: Friday Prayer as Politics in the Safavid Period," in *The Most Learned of the Shi'a, The Institution of the Marja' Taqlid*, edited by Linda Walbridge, 2001; Haggay Ram, *Myth and Mobilization in Revolutionary Iran: The Use of the Friday Congregational Sermon*, 1994.

ROBERT GLEAVE

friendship

Friendship is an informal, voluntarily entered, and noncontingent social relationship. It is distinguished from kinship and servitude in that it is acquired by choice, not ascribed or inherited. According to the Qur'an, friendship—overwhelmingly but not exclusively rendered by words deriving from the root *w-l-y*—is to be sought with God, prophets, and other believers, in that order. Those who reject God—for example, Satan and his supporters, and unbelievers who actively oppose the believers—are not to be befriended. God is, because of the succor He provides, the best and most trustworthy friend. Cognizant of this, when Abraham experiences adversity, he rejects Gabriel's assistance in the expectation of God's help, which is in fact provided; this earns Abraham the title *khalīl Allāh*, "the bosom-friend" of God. As might be expected, only the elect attain this level of friendship. The very pious and the saintly do, however, benefit from a special relationship with God and are consequently called *awliyā' Allāh*, or "friends of God." The close relationships—ranging from discipleship to veneration—developed with such saintly figures, notably Sufi shaykhs, have been criticized by many reformist groups (e.g., the Salafi movement).

Friendship with the Prophet Muhammad is described by the term *ṣuḥba*, or companionship; thus both intimate friends of Muhammad, such as Abu Bakr, and those who had limited contact with him, are called *ṣaḥāba*, or "Companions," perhaps because this relationship implies discipleship. Later, in the scholarly context, a disciple, or an advanced student, would, along the same lines, come to be known as a *ṣāḥib* (literally, companion).

Companionship was the dominant form of friendship enjoined in manuals of guidance and counsel for rulers, so-called Mirrors for Princes, and was actively pursued by Muslim leaders. From Umayyad times, caliphs and rulers sought courtiers and boon companions (*nadīm*), some becoming favorites or lifelong friends. One courtier, Abu Hayyan al-Tawhidi (d. 1023), after decades of mixed fortunes at court, wrote a treatise on the subject, titled *Kitab al-Sadaqa wa-l-Sadiq* (On friendship and friends). The *Kitab Fadl al-Kilab 'ala Kathir min man Labisa al-Thiyab* (The superiority of dogs over many who wear clothes) of Ibn al-Marzuban (tenth century) also treats friendship, but, as the title suggests, using humor and satire.

By virtue of the inevitable asymmetry, friendship with God, the Prophet, saintly figures, caliphs, and other high officials, even teachers, resembles patronage; indeed, the term frequently used to describe God, Muhammad, a religious leader, or a ruler, is *mawlā* (Lord, master, protector). Additionally, *mawlā* is the term used to describe non-Arabs who were affiliated to Arabs. This clientage (*walāya*) was an important feature of early Islam, socially and politically.

Walāya is also the term used to describe political alliance; its antithesis, *barā'a*, means dissociation or disavowal. These are both variously discussed in historical, religiopolitical and juridical Sunni texts, even latter-day tracts produced by the likes of Mulla 'Umar, the spiritual leader of the Taliban and, from 1996 to 2001, de facto head of state in Afghanistan. For Shi'is, these concepts appear as two of their fundamental principles of belief, *tawallā* and *tabarru'* (also *tabarrī* and Persian *tabarrā*). These doctrines developed in connection with early theological discussions about dissociation (*barā'a*) from the first two caliphs, Abu Bakr and 'Umar b. al-Khattab, regarded as usurpers of 'Ali b. Abi Talib's rightful succession to Muhammad, and about the consequently implied allegiance

(*walāya*) to ʿAli. Paradoxically, it appears to have been the Kharijis who first developed theories of dissociation in connection with their unhappiness with this same ʿAli. Dissociation (*barāʾa*) formed the basis for the elaboration of theories of excommunication, either of the historical individuals to be denigrated or of contemporaries to be shunned.

Muslims are bound together as friends by the ultimate communal norm—namely, the adherence to Islam. This makes the Muslims an *umma*, or a community, one that transcends tribal or kinship relations, though Muhammad also frequently described Muslims as brothers (*ikhwa*), suggesting that kinship, even metaphorically, remains the most potent and valorized social relation. Clientage, by obligating shared sympathies and antipathies, in many respects resembled (and was meant to resemble) kinship, and even Muhammad cemented his ties to his closest Companions through marriage (and the ensuing kinship).

See also abodes of Islam, war, and truce; Pillars of Islam

Further Reading

Antony Black, *The History of Islamic Political Thought*, 2001; Patricia Crone, *Medieval Islamic Political Thought*, 2005; Ibn al-Marzuban, *The Book of Superiority of Dogs over Many of Those Who Wear Clothes*, translated and edited by G. R. Smith and M.A.S. Abdel Haleem, 1978; Tawhidi, *De l'amitié*, translated by Eveyne Larguèche and Françoise Neyrod, 2006.

SHAWKAT M. TOORAWA

fundamentalism

Fundamentalism refers to contemporary religiopolitical movements that aim to establish the primacy of scriptural authority as a defense against the moral, political, and social decay that supposedly defines the modern world. It is also often used in everyday language to designate inflexible and dogmatic beliefs of any kind, religious or otherwise. Such common connotations tend to obscure the specific cultural and historical circumstances that produced both the term and the movement it originally described. The term "fundamentalism" was coined in 1920 by Protestant Evangelicals eager to rescue American Christianity and culture from what they characterized as the degeneration inaugurated by "modernism in theology," "rationalism in philosophy," and "materialism in life." Committed to "do battle royal for the Fundamentals," such warriors for God launched an offensive against liberalism, Darwinism, and secularism in particular, declaring the Bible the authoritative moral compass for American life, infallible not only in regard to theological issues but also in regard to matters of historical, geographical, and scientific fact.

The broadened understanding of fundamentalism presumes that there is sufficient commonality and overlap among Christian, Muslim, Jewish, Hindu, Buddhist, and other kinds of religious revivalism to warrant a single rubric despite significant cultural, historical, and linguistic differences. There are some good reasons for this assumption. In general, these are historically contemporaneous, distinctively religious movements that assert the authority of transcendent truths and timeless traditions in response to a perceived crisis precipitated by rapid cultural, social, and economic transformations. As urbanization, industrialization, and the crises they are said to engender are distinctive to the contemporary epoch, fundamentalism has, as Bruce Lawrence writes in *Defenders of God*, "historical antecedents, but no ideological precursors." Fundamentalists may well see themselves as custodians of continuity, yet it is precisely this self-description that distinguishes them from believers for whom tradition was simply lived rather than justified. Tradition becomes a conscious commitment in need of systematic justification when longtime rituals, beliefs, and practices can no longer be taken for granted. Paradoxically, then, defenders of tradition are actually reconstructing it in response to challenge and change.

Fundamentalism and Modernity

This means that efforts to restore the primacy of supposedly timeless truths and traditions inadvertently reveal how thoroughly intertwined contemporary religiopolitical movements are with the conditions, ideas, and processes fundamentalists oppose. This is evident in fundamentalist depictions of modernity as a condition of decay or disease evinced by pervasive corruption, disorder, relativism, and immorality. Fundamentalists contend that such ills are the wages of human hubris, by-products of the misguided assumption that the ever-enlarging scope of human mastery evinced by rapid scientific and technological advances demonstrates the irrelevance of metaphysical sources of knowledge about the world. Such an assumption transfigures sins into natural urges, recasts selfishness as the wellspring of collective life, and reduces the divine plan for the universe and all things in it to a system of physical causality just waiting to be mastered by human ingenuity. Stripped of the moral compass only faith in God provides and bereft of the religious scaffolding that endows life with meaning and purpose, humans are portrayed as lurching toward an abyss we no longer have the ability to recognize, let alone navigate. At this critical juncture, we are told, only the righteous attuned to God's will are capable of charting the path to redemption. Like the prophesies of Cassandra, however, their warnings and guidance are largely destined to fall upon deaf ears.

To the degree that this perspective characterizes a wide range of contemporary religiopolitical movements, fundamentalists can be said to share an ambivalence toward modernity and the rationalist epistemology, or human-centered theory of knowledge, that in part constitutes it. Scholars have interpreted this ambivalence in quite different ways, however. Some portray fundamentalism as the last gasp of atavistic impulses and archaic commitments, the residue of premodern beliefs and practices rendered obsolete by scientific advances, technological innovations, and the globalization of

capital. Others argue that fundamentalists' restorative aspirations are less exhortations to re-create the past than rhetorical techniques designed to indict the present. In this view, fundamentalists are antimodern rather than premodern, committed to fighting modern pluralism, secularism, relativism, and rationalism in the name of divinely ordained truth and the sociomoral order it authorizes.

Still other scholars contend that fundamentalism is simultaneously a reaction to and an expression of modernity, its existence and purpose predicated on the socioeconomic processes, philosophical arguments, and political arrangements fundamentalists vociferously oppose and with which they are deeply engaged. This argument in particular has much to recommend it. These religious revivalists are not, for example, Luddites who object to technology on principle. On the contrary, fundamentalists from Jerry Falwell to Osama bin Laden have proven themselves quite fluent in the visual rhetoric made possible by modern techniques of communication and propaganda, deftly deploying various media to lambaste many of the epistemological premises and methods that made such technology possible in the first place.

In addition, comparisons among contemporary religiopolitical movements reveal some striking patterns in education and social class that belie characterizations of fundamentalists as predominantly rural, impoverished, uneducated, or too backward to heed the call of reason and the authority of science. Many Christian fundamentalists are middle-class, college-educated urban children of rural parents. Similarly, Muslim fundamentalists are frequently the progeny of rural migrants to the city, beneficiaries of an expanded higher education system initiated by modernizing elites, and recipients of advanced training in the natural and applied sciences. Unlike the largely impoverished and uneducated Afghan Taliban, for example, a significant contingent of al-Qaeda is comprised of middle-class, somewhat cosmopolitan young men with university educations in engineering, architecture, medicine, agricultural science, technical military science, or pharmacy. One case in point is Muhammad 'Ata, the alleged ringleader of the 9/11 attack on the United States, who was a student at the Technical University of Hamburg-Harburg and had a degree in architectural engineering. Khalid Shaikh Muhammad, said to be crucial to planning both the 9/11 attacks and the murder of the journalist Daniel Pearl, is an engineer, and Ayman al-Zawahiri, Bin Laden's second-in-command, is a doctor.

Conceptualizing fundamentalists as simultaneously children of modernity and among its fiercest critics suggests that they are, among other things, interlocutors in a debate not only about the state of the modern world but also about what modernity itself means. This conclusion does little, however, to differentiate fundamentalism from a succession of movements, thinkers, and arguments, religious and otherwise, that have criticized the processes and presuppositions associated with modernity from its inception. Moreover, given scholarly disagreements about when, precisely, the modern period begins, if or when it ended, and what it consists of, predicating definitions of fundamentalism on modernity may seem a bit like building on quicksand. Finally, inasmuch as fundamentalists themselves seek to challenge prevailing assumptions about what it does or should mean to live in the contemporary world, such arguments beg questions both about what modernity is and whether fundamentalism is usefully understood in terms of it.

These questions are posed sharply by shifting the theoretical perspective from the Euro-American "center" to the "periphery" inhabited by what are often called postcolonial peoples. Many scholars suggest that, at the other end of the colonial project, modernity registers less as an objective index of historical and intellectual maturation than a deracinated account of the ways Europe has ordered its past in relation to its present. Indeed, the content and contours of modernity are rooted in a persistent—albeit contested—narrative in which the rise of capitalism, the consolidation of the nation-state, the discoveries of the scientific revolution, and the development of Enlightenment philosophy are depicted as both cause and consequence of Europe's emergence from the Middle Ages in which "a Great Chain of Being" issuing from God was thought to hold sway.

This vision of civilizational maturation is double edged. On the one hand, it implicitly positions the West as (in Marx's words) the beacon that "shows to the less developed the image of its own future" by deriving modernity tout court from the universalization of historically and culturally specific experiences, assumptions, and standards. On the other hand, it explicitly offers to all peoples the promise of mastery, of control not only over recalcitrant facts and things but also over human suffering through the application of increasingly effective scientific and technical solutions. As the European colonial enterprise gathered scope and speed, this double-edged vision of modernity would spread to other shores by way of territorial incursions, cultural domination, and noblesse oblige. For many colonized peoples, then, modernity and the mastery it promised came to be understood as a prerogative of conquest rather than an index of freedom.

Fundamentalism, Islamism, and the Politics of Terminology

Does the terminology of fundamentalism, like the category of modernity with which it is so closely intertwined, obscure rather than illuminate critical differences among the specific political contexts, cultural idioms, and historical experiences informing contemporary religiopolitical movements? Many scholars of colonial and postcolonial societies explicitly reject fundamentalism on precisely these grounds. In this view, fundamentalism says too little by encompassing too much. For how can a single term derived from a specific moment in American Christianity say anything of substance about the assassins of Egyptian president Anwar Sadat, Hindus who attacked the mosque at Ayodhya, Christian militants who bomb abortion clinics, and Israeli settlers who justify violence in the occupied territories as sanctioned by God?

Many contend that if fundamentalism is empty at best, at worst it deepens longstanding prejudices and generates new distortions by remaking what is unfamiliar in familiar terms. This problem is particularly acute in the case of the contemporary Islamic

religiopolitical movement, not least because Islam itself has so often been obscured by a haze of ignorance, prejudice, and polemic, both in the past and in the present. As a result, the term "Islamic fundamentalism" is nearly as controversial as the phenomenon it purports to describe.

At first glance, many objections to it appear to hinge on its origins: fundamentalism was born in a time and place equally distant from the seventh-century Arabia of the Prophet Muhammad and the maelstrom of contemporary Muslim politics. Yet terms originating in one place and language frequently become part of a transcultural political lexicon used widely, if not always consistently, to capture recognizably common phenomena. Both nationalism and socialism are often cited as two cases in point. Another such example is "the West," a category of relatively recent provenance through which Euro-American history and geography have been retroactively organized. Scholars from diverse disciplines routinely argue that what is called the West is an amalgamation of multiple traditions—including Greek, Roman, Judaic, and Christian—and owes myriad debts to diverse civilizations past and present. They further argue that while it has always been difficult to pinpoint exactly where the West begins and ends, this is particularly true now that peoples, information, and material goods crisscross cultural and national borders at will, creating hybrid and multiple identities that shift and reconstitute themselves in unpredictable ways. Such scholarly arguments nothwithstanding, "the West" continues to be invoked by people throughout the globe, evoking powerful allegiances and enmities.

What is ultimately at stake in most objections to Islamic fundamentalism, however, is power rather than etymology or geography. As philosophers, linguists, and translators have demonstrated, language not only reflects but produces our understandings of the world. Disputes about terminology often raise critical questions about who is using what words to describe whom and for what purposes. In a postcolonial world characterized by rapid globalization, any discussion of Islam operates within a web of social relations in which power—both actual and perceived—has already been apportioned unequally among various peoples, classes, regions, genders, and cultures. Given this context, many argue that the universalization of terms and categories derived from specifically European and American experiences reflects and reinforces the cultural hegemony of West over non-West, center over periphery. Scholarship organized around such categories and background assumptions may thus reveal less about Muslim practices and cultures than about the ability of those who already have power to produce, disseminate, and control a series of descriptions and images about themselves and the rest of the world.

Given this politics of terminology, it is instructive that there was no equivalent for fundamentalism in Arabic, the language of the Qur'an, until the need to approximate the English term called for one. *Uṣūliyya*, derived from the word for fundamentals or roots (*uṣūlī*), has emerged as an Arabic name for Islamic fundamentalism, but its currency is due to the way it approximates the English fundamentalism rather than any correspondence with aspects of the Islamic tradition. (On the contrary, *uṣūlī* is associated with scholarship on the roots and genesis of Islamic jurisprudence, and experts in this discipline are often referred to as *al-uṣūliyyūn*.) In a 1995 interview, the spiritual leader of Hizbullah in Lebanon, Shaykh Muhammad Husayn Fadlallah, rejected the terminology of fundamentalism as more revealing of Western projections than Muslim revivalism:

> We Islamists are not fundamentalists in the way the Westerners see us. We refuse to be called fundamentalists. We are Islamic activists. As for the etymological sense of *uṣūliyya*, meaning returning to one's roots and origins [*uṣūl*], our roots are the Qur'an and the true *sunna* or way of the Prophet, not the historical period in which the Prophet lived or the periods that followed—we are not fundamentalists [*uṣūliyyīn*] in the sense of wanting to live like people at the time of the Prophet or the first Caliphs or the time of the Umayyads.

Some scholars regard the debate about appropriate terminology as concluded, yet alternatives to the term "Islamic fundamentalism" in use range from "radical Islam" to "Islamic extremism" and "Islamic terrorism" to "political Islam." Indeed, new names for the phenomenon continually arise. A case in point is "jihadism," a neologism derived from the Arabic "jihad" (to struggle or strive) that is frequently used in the press to denote the most violent strands of Islamism, and those associated with what are alternatively called "suicide bombings" or "martyrdom operations" in particular. Older terms put to new uses occasionally gain wide currency as well. Such is the case with "Salafism," which refers to contemporary Muslims who generally eschew the interpretive methods and norms of the classical Islamic schools and take as a guide for proper behavior only the word of God, the teachings of the Prophet Muhammad, and the example set by the *salaf*, the earliest and most pious of Muslims. Perhaps the most widely used term among scholars of Muslim societies is "Islamism," although it is not universally accepted and is frequently invoked with caution and caveats. As some observers argue, for example, Islamism wrongly implies that those who claim the name have captured the essence of Islam; thus it is no more appropriate than calling the former Branch Davidian leader David Koresh a Christianist.

Scholars' apparent preference for the term "Islamism" has not, however, yielded agreement about how to best define or identify it, let alone understand or explain it. Some emphasize the socioeconomic characteristics of the Islamist movement; others identify certain patterns in recruitment, organization, and mobilization; still others foreground the theological and philosophical tendencies of Islamist thought; and some home in on the regional and sectarian dynamics of various Islamist groups. Such disunity is, in part, a function of the disciplinary and methodological differences among historians, anthropologists, political scientists, and scholars of religion, all of whom regard Islamism as within their academic jurisdiction. The best scholarship on Islamism is substantively interdisciplinary and methodologically plural, attending

closely to the complex interplay among Islamist ideas and objectives, the specific public spheres in which they operate, and the material conditions that inform and are in turn transformed by them. Yet ultimately, even the most careful scholarship suggests that the kaleidoscopic literature on the subject is less a reflection of academic balkanization than the irreducible diversity of contexts and concerns animating a powerful yet rapidly changing Islamist movement.

Islamism: Origins and General Characteristics

In contrast to the confusion swirling around matters of terminology and definition, the advent of Islamism is almost universally traced to 1928, the year Hasan al-Banna (1906–49) founded the Egyptian Society of Muslim Brothers (al-Ikhwan al-Muslimun). By all reports, Banna was gifted with great personal charisma, rhetorical skill, and organizational acumen; by the time of his assassination in 1949, he had already built a formidable organization with deep roots in Egyptian society and a broad base of membership, ranging from civil servants to soldiers, urban laborers to rural peasants, and village elders to university students. As Banna was more activist than theologian, however, the task of developing an Islamist theoretical framework would largely fall to thinkers who came to prominence in the decades after his death. The most important among them include Sayyid Qutb from Egypt (1906–66), Abul al-A'la Mawdudi from Pakistan (1903–79), and Ruhollah Khomeini from Iran (1902–89). Under the tutelage of these and other Islamist thinkers and activists, the organization Banna founded would inspire a movement that now stretches throughout the Middle East, North Africa, South Asia, and beyond, continuously adapting and transforming itself to divergent political exigencies and changing historical circumstances.

While the Muslim Brotherhood continues to be a formidable presence in places like Egypt and Jordan, its profile and political purchase in contemporary Muslim-majority societies have frequently been eclipsed by what are often dubbed "radical" Islamist groups. Such groups include Egypt's al-Gama'a al-Islamiyya, the Pakistan-based Lashkar-e-Taiba (Army of the Pure), the Islamic Salvation Front in Algeria, and al-Qaeda, the fluid Islamist network linked to violent operations from the Philippines to Kashmir, including the assault on the U.S. embassies in Kenya and Tanzania in 1998, the attack on the World Trade Center and Pentagon in 2001, and the bombings of a Bali nightclub in 2002 and Madrid commuter trains in 2004. Whereas Banna had largely sought to coax action out of quiescence without acceding to the demands of those he described as "overzealous and hasty," these organizations tend to eschew the gradualist path of grassroots sociomoral transformation in favor of immediate, direct, and often violent challenges to the legitimacy of Muslim governments and the power of "infidel" regimes.

This distinction must not be overdrawn, however. Despite significant differences in emphasis and strategy, there is also a fair amount of continuity and overlap between the Muslim Brotherhood and such "radical" groups. Hamas, for example, was founded in 1987 to serve as the "strong arm" of the Muslim Brotherhood by several members convinced that the organization's strategy of "Islamization without confrontation" had been outpaced by events in the Israeli-occupied territories. Conversely, many radical groups share the commitment to charitable endeavors that had been central to Banna's strategy of recruitment and sociomoral transformation. Islamists from Morocco to Pakistan are well known for building schools, mosques, and health clinics, as well as for raising funds to support impoverished Muslims who have been abandoned by ineffective or corrupt state bureaucracies.

Islamism is thus a 20th- and 21st-century phenomenon, its history deeply intertwined with the local, regional, and geopolitical dynamics of the contemporary world. As the present always builds on the past, however, Islamism must also be located within a long and complex tradition of religious reform, revivalism, and even insurrectionism in the history of Muslim-majority societies. The activism and intransigence of many contemporary Islamists, for example, has been likened to the Kharijis, a seventh-century group of Muslims known for an uncompromising emphasis on righteous deeds and the unadulterated authority of the Qur'an. While Islamists often object to such a comparison, they do depict themselves as disciples of Ibn Taymiyya (1263–1328), the 14th-century jurist who argued that Mongol rulers who mixed Islamic prescriptions with tribal law (the Yasa) had contravened shari'a and could therefore be forcibly removed from power.

Finally, Islamist ideas and preoccupations must be understood as a continuation of 19th-century Muslim political thought rather than a radical break from the concerns and dilemmas that characterized it. For example, Banna's insistence on Islam as a comprehensive way of life and a set of religiopolitical imperatives distorted by corruption, sectarianism, and indifference is, in many ways, an extension of the work of such Muslim reformists as Jamal al-Din al-Afghani (1839–97), Rifa'a Rafi' al-Tahtawi (1801–73), and Muhammad 'Abduh (1849–1905). Like Banna, these thinkers had sought, in different ways, to revive and reinterpret the foundations of Islam as a bulwark against the rise of European power and the internal weakening of the Ottoman Empire.

The preceding discussion only hints at the scope and depth of persistent disagreements about how to best name, define, and delimit this complex and diverse movement. Given such disagreement, it is particularly useful to approach Islamism as an interpretive framework rather than a set of propositions and strategies to which every Islamist subscribes in the same way or to the same degree. Understood as an interpretive framework, Islamism does not simply reflect or obscure a set of material conditions and socioeconomic grievances but instead constitutes a lens on the world that determines how and in what terms such conditions and constraints are understood. Such an approach enables observers to attend to the differences and diversity of what travels under the rubric of "Islamism" without losing sight of it as a complex system of representation that articulates and defines a range of identities,

categories, and norms; organizes human experience into narratives that assemble past, present, and future into a compelling interpretive frame; and specifies the range and meaning of acceptable and desirable practices. In short, this approach makes it possible to define Islamism without essentializing or instrumentalizing it.

Islamism refers to those 20th- and 21st-century Muslim groups and thinkers that seek to recuperate the scriptural foundations of the Islamic community, excavating and reinterpreting them for application to the contemporary social and political world. Such foundations consist of the Qur'an and the normative example of the Prophet Muhammad (sunna, hadith), which constitute the sources of God's guidance, in matters pertaining to both worship and human relations. In general, Islamists aim at restoring the primacy of the norms derived from these foundational texts in collective life, regarding them not only as an expression of God's will but also as an antidote to the moral bankruptcy inaugurated by Western cultural dominance from abroad, aided and abetted by corrupt Muslim rulers from within the *umma* (the Islamic community).

Against this backdrop, Islamists conceptualize their work in terms of diagnosis and cure. Muslims must first recognize that the modern world is diseased, its inhabitants corrupted by a condition that Qutb, borrowing from the South Asian Islamist scholar Abul Hasan Nadwi (d. 1999), calls *jāhiliyya*. *Jāhiliyya* derives from the Arabic verb meaning "to be ignorant" and, in Muslim tradition, refers specifically to the epoch in Arabia before Islam had been revealed to the Prophet Muhammad. As used by contemporary Islamists, however, *jāhiliyya* signals a pathology into which a society descends when it willfully turns away from the truths Allah has already made manifest. The new *jāhiliyya* is thus distinguished from the old by sheer human arrogance. More specifically, it is defined by an unwarranted confidence in human beings' ability to know, govern, and master the world without divine guidance along with the presumption that human beings have the right and wisdom to legislate rules for collective behavior. Within an Islamist framework, this presumption is not only a symptom of human hubris but a transgression against Allah's sovereignty (*ḥākimiyya*), the scope of which encompasses both public and private domains of human affairs as well as both visible and unseen dimensions of the universe. For many Islamists, such transgression is at the root of all human sovereignty in the modern epoch—nationalist, democratic, communist, and monarchical alike. It is equally evident in a long history of Euro-American aggression against Islam in which the Christian Crusades, European colonialism, Israeli treatment of Palestinians, ethnic cleansing in Bosnia, German anti-Turkish violence, the American invasion of Iraq, and Dutch cartoons of Muhammad are but a few examples.

While the roots of the new *jāhiliyya* are usually traced to the West, Islamists also contend that it is no longer an exclusively foreign pathology. In their view, Muslim rulers who claim for themselves the legislative authority that belongs only to Allah represent a metastasizing cancer within the *umma*, inaugurating an internal crisis of unprecedented scope and scale. Given such a diagnosis, the cure is clear and its implementation urgent: divine sovereignty must be restored over all domains of collective life, an imperative that entails establishing the primacy of Islamic law through the agency of the state. This in turn requires righteous action, for while shari'a is an expression of divine wisdom and will, it is only realized on Earth by human struggle in the path of God (*jihād fī sabīl Allāh*). Actualization of *ḥākimiyya* thus requires a vanguard of Muslims who have penetrated the miasma of *jāhiliyya* and its false gods of materialism, science, and rationalism. These are the true believers who are capable of not only recognizing the scope of Islam as a way of life but also cultivating the discipline, faith, and courage to reshape the world in its image.

As the following discussion makes clear, there is a great deal of disagreement among Islamists about what, precisely, the establishment of Islamic law entails and what practices are appropriate or justifiable in pursuit of it. Yet even this preliminary sketch makes visible several common features that are, again, better understood as broad tendencies rather than fixed attributes—that is, characteristics of an Islamist framework that not every Islamist endorses in the same way all the time. In contrast to those Muslims who primarily seek to cultivate a mystical understanding of the divine through study or ascetic contemplation, for example, Islamist aspirations may be characterized as explicitly and intentionally political. Using German sociologist Max Weber's terminology from *The Sociology of Religion*, Islamism is not defined by an "other-worldly" orientation in which salvation requires withdrawal from worldly affairs. It is, rather, a movement in which salvation is possible only through participation in the world, or more precisely "within the institutions of the world, but in opposition to them." As Islamist exhortations to change collective life require words and deeds, they may be further defined not only as political but also as activist, thus distinguishing them from the quietism characteristic of some Saudi Salafis, whose acquiescence to established power is no less political than Islamist intransigence.

Islamism and the Politics of Authenticity

Islamist aspirations to restore foundations located in a mythical past are far from unique. Nor are Islamists alone in their conviction that scriptural authority is guaranteed by its divine author—for in that all Muslims agree. Rather, what distinguishes Islamists from many other Muslims is the claim to recuperate an "authentic Islam" comprised of self-evident truths purged of alien and corrupting influences, along with an insistence on remaking the foundations of the state in accordance with such purified prescriptions. Islamists depict such fidelity to the unadulterated word of God as the ultimate expression of deference to divine omniscience. Indeed, humility is not only a proper expression of faith but also a constitutive feature of the human condition, in contradistinction to the nature of Allah. From this vantage point, aspirations to fully know and master the natural and social worlds reflect a human hubris deaf to the Qur'anic admonition that "Allah knows, but/and you do not know" (Q. 3:66).

The Islamist emphasis on the limits of human knowledge, however, requires humility only in relation to Allah. What it rarely yields is humility in regard to their own claims to speak in His

name or forbearance toward Muslims who disagree with Islamist claims about what the divine Will requires. This suggests that while Islamist challenges to state power are obviously political, the Islamist claim to authenticity is also political in the coercive power it routinely enacts and justifies, most notably by way of the silences it imposes and the debates it forecloses. As Aziz al-Azmeh points out in *Islams and Modernities*, "The notion of authenticity is not so much a determinate concept as it is a node of associations and interpellations, a trope by means of which the historical world is reduced to a particular order, and a token which marks off social and political groups and forges and reconstitutes historical identities." Whether in the service of Arab nationalism, Christian fundamentalism, European romanticism, or 19th-century Muslim modernism, the claim of authenticity is an act of power that functions not just to reflect the world but to construct it by determining who is included and excluded, who may and may not speak authoritatively, what is the proper realm of debate, and what is beyond contestation.

It is certainly the case that a single "Islam" captures and organizes the perspectives of millions who self-identify as Muslim (among other things), yet what travels under the name "Islam" is inescapably diverse, multiethnic, and defined as much by disagreement as by consensus. Just as the Torah and Bible sometimes lend themselves to radically divergent interpretations of what it means to be Jewish or Christian, the Qur'an and hadith are complex and susceptible to many different, and at times contradictory, enactments. This means that Islam is not a fixed essence but rather, as Talal Asad points out in "The Idea of an Anthropology of Islam," a discursive tradition that captures what is imagined as continuous and unitary in dialectical relationship to those concrete articulations and practices by which it is transformed and adapted in different contexts for plural purposes. It is precisely this understanding of religion that is anathema to Islamists who seek to fix the parameters of Islamic authenticity once and for all. Doing so enables them to arrogate for themselves the right to determine who qualifies as a good Muslim; discredit those 'ulama' (Muslim scholars) unable or unwilling to purge Islam of purported impieties; declare nominally Muslim rulers apostates unfit to govern; and characterize all who disagree as corrupt, heretical, guilty of unbelief, or victims of false consciousness.

In Sunni Islamism, such arguments frequently entail the claim that ordinary, untrained Muslims have the right and obligation to engage the sacred texts directly, without the mediation of those religious scholars who have traditionally served as gatekeepers of the Islamic tradition. Given this claim, it is unsurprising that many prominent Sunni Islamists—from Banna to Zaynab al-Ghazali and from Qutb to Bin Laden—are autodidacts rather than formally trained or credentialed 'ulama'. As the sacred texts contain the rules and regulations meant to govern both public and private affairs, this insistence on unmediated access to the texts can be understood as the grounds on which such self-taught Islamists claim for themselves the stature of religious experts who have penetrated the moral bankruptcy of *jāhiliyya* to clearly see what others cannot. Indeed, despite Islamists' tendency to characterize the "real Islam" as self-evident, many actually assume that only a small vanguard of believers will have the ability to recognize it and act decisively to remake the world in its image. In this way, Islamists position themselves as purveyors of God's will who, like Plato's philosopher-king in *The Republic*, are no longer enthralled by dark shadows cast on cave walls but capable of beholding the truth in direct light.

On the one hand, then, Islamists are committed to establishing a religiopolitical order that simultaneously presumes the supremacy of the few capable of true knowledge and promises a world in which dissent itself will become both unnecessary and illegitimate. On the other hand, this emphasis on the potential wisdom of untrained believers entails a kind of democratization of access to the authority conferred by knowledge of the sacred texts. This claim that religious knowledge depends on commitment rather than training or expertise can be seen as part of a broader challenge to elite power evident in Islamist arguments that Muslims have the right and obligation to determine when rulers are illegitimate and that those who prefer order to justice, security to freedom, and money to piety have forfeited any claim to authority.

This particular aspect of Islamism evokes the Protestant Reformation and, as Ellis Goldberg argues in his article "Smashing Idols and the State: The Protestant Ethic and Egyptian Sunni Radicalism," echoes Calvinists' attempts to transfer "religious authority away from officially sanctioned individuals who interpret texts to ordinary citizens." Such a comparison has sparked a great deal of speculation regarding a possible "Islamic Reformation," along with a range of arguments about whether and how Islamism might facilitate the democratization of Muslim societies, much as the Protestant Reformation is said to have heralded the emergence of European "liberal democracy." While such parallels are evocative, they are frequently overdrawn. A fuller understanding of Islamism requires first situating it in relation to a historical shift in the nature and locus of religious authority in Islam beginning in the 19th century. As scholars such as Muhammad Qasim Zaman have shown, mass higher education and a variety of new technologies enabling broad dissemination of information and knowledge have made available to amateurs what had previously been the purview of religious experts. At the same time, such processes have inaugurated a fragmentation of authority within the very ranks of the 'ulama' that continues to the present day. In this context, the ascendance and influence of autodidacts such as Qutb, Banna, 'Abd al-Salam Faraj, and Bin Laden simultaneously express and accelerate an ongoing renegotiation of authority over who may speak for Islam and on what basis.

This discussion requires an additional qualification, as the prevalence of autodidacts among prominent Sunni Islamists contrasts sharply with recent developments in Shi'i Islamism, particularly as articulated by one of its best known figures, Ruhollah Khomeini. A jurist and learned *mujtahid* (legist), Khomeini is most widely known as a spiritual leader of the revolutionary movement that overthrew the Shah of Iran in 1979, as well as expositor of the "guardianship of the jurist" (in Arabic, *wilāyat al-faqīh*; in Persian, *velāyat-i*

faqīh), the doctrine that would become the foundation of rule in the Islamic Republic of Iran. Like many Sunni Islamists, Khomeini understands the legitimacy of sovereignty in terms of Allah's exclusive right of legislation and defines justice as the rule of revealed law. Yet Khomeini also argues that, as law requires both institutions and executors, the best guarantor of legitimate sovereignty is rule by those jurists (*fuqahā'*; sing. *faqīh*) most knowledgeable in matters of shari'a. As Islamic law encompasses both matters of worship and human relations, Khomeini reasons, so must the authority of those with the expertise required to implement Islamic law extend to political as well as religious domains.

Here Khomeini augments the already formidable authority of the Shi'i *fuqahā'*, who had previously been designated custodians of Shi'i religious belief and practice in the absence of the Hidden Imam (the legitimate leader of the Muslim community believed to have disappeared into occultation in the late ninth century). Such justifications for institutionalizing clerical authority and broadening its scope bear little resemblance to the arguments of Sunni Islamists such as Qutb, Banna, and Faraj, whose writings often exhibit a palpable frustration with religious scholars who they contend have a greater stake in stability than justice. At the same time, several prominent Sunni Islamists are also religious scholars, from Yusuf al-Qaradawi (b. 1926), the founder of the influential website Islam Online, to 'Umar 'Abd al-Rahman (b. 1938), the Egyptian cleric linked to the assassins of Sadat, now serving a life sentence in an American federal penitentiary for "seditious conspiracy" in connection with the 1993 World Trade Center bombing. Both Qaradawi and Abd al-Rahman are credentialed scholars in Islamic law from Azhar, Egypt's preeminent university and mosque. These and other trained Islamist scholars exemplify the political coming of age of what Malika Zeghal has called peripheral 'ulama': products of Azhar whose sympathies and affiliations with Islamists undermine conventional wisdom about a sharp divide between establishment Sunni 'ulama' and untrained, anticlerical Islamist upstarts.

Islamism and the Politics of Gender

Gender is frequently considered tangential to the knotty problems of defining Islamism and charting its central dynamics. Yet scholars from a variety of disciplines have shown that gender is consistently the terrain over which battles for political control and cultural identity are fought. In times of internal crises and external threats, women's bodies and behavior are frequently transformed into symbols of moral purity or vessels of cultural corruption. This is especially true of contemporary fundamentalists who, as Martin Riesebrodt argues in *Pious Passion*, tend to "idealize patriarchal structures of authority and morality," endorse gender dualism as God-given or natural, and vigorously condemn recent changes in gender relations as a symptom and symbol of secularist moral bankruptcy. Islamists are a case in point. Their concerns with the place and purity of Muslim women reveal the unwritten gender norms—in other words, standards of masculinity and femininity that organize human beings into political, social, and reproductive roles and reflect and reinforce prevalent assumptions about the "nature" of men and women—arguably at the heart of Islamist politics and political thought.

Despite important differences among Islamist thinkers, many explicitly or implicitly endorse gender norms in which female nature is inextricably tied to the domestic realm, and women are symbolically transformed into an index of moral and cultural virtue. This view is built on the premise that men and women are equal in belief but perform fundamentally different and complementary functions in society. While men are naturally made to rule in both the public and private domain, a woman's primary role is to be a wife and mother as well as to ensure the integrity of the family, the first school of moral education. As such functions are rooted in an inescapable human nature expressive of divine will, a woman's inability or unwillingness to perform her duties signals a disobedience to God and presages the corruption of the Muslim family from within. From this vantage, the Western insistence on full equality between the sexes only liberates women from moral constraint, enslaving them to mutually reinforcing sexual and capitalist exploitation. As women are responsible for producing the next generation of Muslim men destined to restore Islam to its former glory, it is not only the virtue of women or the integrity of the family that hangs in the balance but also the future of Islamic civilization itself.

Several Islamist thinkers make these arguments explicitly and in detail, but in much of Islamist thought and rhetoric, the nature and significance of women are established indirectly and symbolically and through three recurrent images in particular. The first of the three images is of women as silent symbols of cultural, moral, and sexual vulnerability—voiceless figures in need of masculine protection or defiled bodies that mutely demand vengeance. So, for example, 'Abdallah 'Azzam, one of Bin Laden's mentors, graphically details the agonizing humiliation of young men unable to act when the Afghan woman is "crying out for help, her children are being slaughtered, her women are being raped, the innocent are killed and their corpses scattered." In the second image, women function as a chorus that speaks in permitted cadences to ratify masculine endeavors. Such is the case, for example, in Bin Laden's 1996 "Declaration of War against the American Occupying the Land of the Two Holy Places," where the women exhort men to jihad in the following way:

> Prepare yourself like a struggler, the matter is bigger than words! Are you going to leave us . . . for the wolves of Kufr [unbelief] eating our wings?! . . . Where are the freemen defending free women by arms?! Death is better than life in humiliation! Some scandals and shames will never be otherwise eradicated.

In the third image, women are creatures not of this world but of another: they are virginal rewards for the courageous martyr in the afterlife. This is evident in the final instructions for the 9/11 hijackers, for example, in which Muslim "brothers" are urged to

purify their carnal impulses, sharpen their knives for the slaughter (*dhabḥ*), and heed the call of the *ḥūr 'ayn* (the black-eyed ones) awaiting them in paradise.

Such rhetoric primarily registers women as an extension, mirror, or measure of masculinity and, in tandem with explicit Islamist arguments about the proper nature and purpose of men and women, embeds gender within a divinely ordained social hierarchy. So understood, deviance from this gendered script tends to signal disruption of a much broader religiopolitical order it both presumes and seeks to bring into existence. When precipitated by foreign aggression, such disruption exacerbates a predisposition to translate conflict into an assault on Muslim masculinity and to conceptualize women as potential conduits for Western corruption in need of guiding, guarding, and covering. Such a gendered script has posed a significant challenge to Muslim women who have sought a place and voice within the Islamist movement. Despite significant differences among them, such women have had to navigate carefully between Islamist characterizations of women's visibility and agency as symptomatic of *jāhiliyya* on the one hand and essentializing arguments that equate Islam with veiling, female genital mutilation, and honor killings on the other.

Zaynab al-Ghazali (1917–2005) and Nadia Yassine (b. 1958), two of the few women who have risen to positions of leadership in the Islamist movement, have negotiated such constraints and pressures quite differently. Ghazali founded Jama'at al-Sayyidat al-Muslimat (the Muslim Women's Association, or the MWA), an organization devoted to educating women in the Islamic tradition and training them in the practice of *da'wa* (call to greater piety), in the 1930s. She even stepped in to help reconstitute the Muslim Brotherhood in the 1950s, after the Egyptian state formally dissolved the organization and executed or incarcerated virtually all of its ideological leadership in response to a member's alleged attempt to assassinate President Gamal Abdel Nasser. Ghazali was in many ways a pioneer whose own life demonstrated a fierce resistance to conventional norms of domesticity, even as much of her early work articulated an Islamist gender ideology that defines women as wives, mothers, and "builders of men." Yassine, by contrast, has come to prominence as the daughter of the founder of Morocco's Justice and Spirituality Association (JSA) and its unofficial spokeswoman. Unlike Ghazali, Yassine has positioned herself as a dedicated wife and mother who embraces an "Islamic feminism" that urges women to engage the sacred texts directly through *ijtihād* (independent reasoning, judgment, or interpretation). If women and men do, in fact, have distinct perspectives on the world, Yassine suggests, women have a special obligation to recuperate what they see as the gender parity of the Qur'an buried beneath those "macho interpretations" of Islam on which men have built their privilege and power.

Importantly, Yassine and Ghazali are only among the most visible examples of a larger trend: the increasing participation of women from diverse social backgrounds in *da'wa* (practices and arguments meant to exhort, invite, and guide Muslims to what is regarded as proper conduct and moral devotion). Women's participation in *da'wa* is not a brand new phenomenon, as is evident in Ghazali's work with the MWA. Yet scholars have shown that the number of *dā'iyyāt* (those engaged in *da'wa*) is significantly increasing in places such as Egypt, Pakistan, Saudi Arabia, and the United States. This reflects, in part, current doctrinal emphases on *da'wa* as incumbent on both men and women and less dependent on technical knowledge than moral virtue and practical familiarity with Islamic tradition. This increase is also tied to a number of political and socioeconomic transformations in Muslim-majority societies. Crucial among them is the expansion of mass education that has simultaneously increased women's literacy and social mobility and made Islamic texts more accessible. Also crucial are the proliferation of technologies—from the tape cassette to the Internet—that facilitate the circulation of religious knowledge even among those who cannot read or travel, the precedent set by the vigorous participation of Iranian women in postrevolution debates about Islam, and the model of legal activism evident in the Islamist movement's own challenge to the status of the 'ulama' as gatekeepers of religious knowledge.

If Ghazali and Yassine exemplify the feminization of *da'wa* among elites, the mosque movement in Egypt illustrates the growing participation of women from diverse social backgrounds in religious classes devoted to studying and debating what Islam requires for a woman to be virtuous in the contemporary world. As Saba Mahmood shows in *The Politics of Piety*, participants in the mosque movement conceptualize piety in terms of a deep and holistic commitment to self-transformation. Consequently, they are concerned less with matters of sovereignty and politics conventionally understood and more with the "moral cultivation" of those daily practices seen as crucial to becoming closer to God. Some Islamists have criticized this focus on practices of worship as apolitical and overly privatized, yet such criticism misses the force of Islamists' own insistence on religion (*dīn*) as a way of life in which the domains of public and private are inextricably linked. As Mahmood argues, these women's intense efforts at "retraining ethical sensibilities" have a "sociopolitical force" that extends well beyond matters of governance, facilitating no less than the emergence of a "new social and moral order." Evidence of its transformative power may be found not only in the sheer numbers and variety of women—wealthy and poor, literate and illiterate—participating in the mosque movement but also in the rhetorical and political efforts by the state and some Islamists to curtail, control, or discredit it.

Taken together, these examples show how Muslim women from different perspectives and social classes are increasingly insisting on engaging the sacred texts directly for and with one another without the mediating authority of men, who have traditionally held the monopoly on such activities. Despite the proliferation of voices intent on claiming for themselves the authority to demarcate what is authentically Islamic and un-Islamic once and for all, contestation over Islam's scope and meaning proceeds apace, facilitated at least in part by women formerly excluded from the conversation. This is true despite the fact that Islamist women's agency and claims to

authority are frequently still predicated on a willingness to follow fairly patriarchal rules about where, how, and with whom they may practice their vocation.

Islamism, Political Action, and Violence

If gender is frequently an implicit preoccupation among Islamists, jihad is arguably Islamists' most consistently explicit concern. Jihad is derived from the Arabic verb that means "to struggle" or "to strive," yet it is a particular kind of struggle of concern to many of the most prominent Islamists: the often violent struggle against apostates and infidels both at home and abroad to which every individual Muslim must contribute. Many (though not all) Islamists represent this understanding of struggle as jihad tout court, yet it is a historically specific interpretation derived from a selective use of texts and precedents, foremost among them the claim by Ibn Taymiyya that Muslim rulers who had violated Islamic law could be subject to forcible removal. It is, moreover, an interpretation that breaks with much of antecedent doctrine and practice. The claim that fighting unbelievers is the preeminent enactment of individual Muslim piety, for example, is a departure from the distinction Muslim exegetes had developed between a "collective obligation" (*farḍ kifāya*, a duty a group of people within the community may perform on behalf of the rest) operative in jihad against foreign enemies and an individual duty (*farḍ 'ayn*) that must be fulfilled by every Muslim in the event that the *umma* is under attack. This interpretation also explicitly rejects Muslim modernists who emphasized the largely defensive character of jihad and sought to show that relations between Muslims and non-Muslims were normally peaceful rather than antagonistic.

Within Islamist terms, jihad is a means and an end rolled into one: it is a form of action necessary to eradicate obstacles to restoring a just community on Earth that simultaneously brings human action into accord with God's plans and purposes. While the Qur'an states (2:256) that "there is no compulsion in religion," for many Islamists, it is only in a state in which Islamic law reigns supreme that human beings are free from enslavement to one another's rule and all are equal by virtue of their common submission to God. From this perspective, the realization of justice, liberty, equality, and choice itself necessitates the forcible removal of the constraints imposed by *jāhiliyya*, along with those who aid and abet it. This entails action on two distinct yet interrelated fronts: domestic and global. Within the *umma*, jihad is in the service of challenging the legitimacy of Muslim rulers who claim for themselves the sovereignty that belongs only to Allah. By rereading Qur'an 5:44 (conventionally rendered as "He who does not judge by what God has revealed is an unbeliever") as "Those who do not *govern* by what God has revealed are unbelievers," Islamists contend that rulers who have abandoned the prescriptions of Islamic law have forfeited any claims to obedience and are lawful targets of jihad. In this way, revolt becomes an act of restoration rather than destruction. Much as the 17th-century English philosopher John Locke sought to legitimize revolution by characterizing a government that violates the purposes for which it was created as unlawful, Islamists depict the ruler who violates shari'a as the outlaw rather than those who justifiably rise up to depose him.

At the same time, jihad is regarded as a necessary response to the pervasive power—both actual and perceived—of those outside the *umma* who have demonstrated hostility to Muslim lives, lands, pieties, and sensibilities. This view of jihad reframes it as a matter of self-defense, in language that subsumes individuals into archetypes of "infidels" and "believers" and vitiates more conventional distinctions between, for example, soldier and civilian or collective and individual responsibility. Indeed, for many Islamists, the scope and depth of this physical as well as symbolic assault ultimately renders fine distinctions between offensive and defensive jihad irrelevant. As Qutb famously argued in *Ma'alim fi al-Tariq* (*Signposts along the Road*), jihad must be regarded as a "permanent condition, not an occasional concern," one that in current circumstances requires deeds rather than words, struggle rather than contemplation, and revolution at home as well as resistance abroad. Muhammad 'Abd al-Salam Faraj, author of the pamphlet justifying the assassination of President Sadat, argues along similar lines that the nature of the attack makes political authorization by a legitimate caliph (deputy, referring to a legitimate successor to the Prophet's leadership) unnecessary. As Faraj writes, leadership "over the Muslims is (always) in their own hands if only they make this manifest. . . . If there is something lacking in the leadership, well, there is nothing that cannot be acquired."

These arguments about jihad may be said to constitute a common grammar and framework of analysis, yet, as in so many other matters, Islamists disagree with one another not only about strategy but about substance. Challenges to the equation of jihad with violence against infidels have come not only from non-Islamist exegetes but also from within the ranks of Islamists themselves. A case in point is Yassine of Morocco's JSA, who insists that jihad is the dedicated struggle against arrogance (*istikbār*), particularly in its common form as the lust for power and domination. As jihad against *istikbār* is both a final goal and a prescription for action, Yassine contends, it is antithetical to violent practices that aim at domination. For Yassine, the primary instruments of jihad are not bombs but words, particularly those deployed in the art of persuasion. When Islamists seek to legitimize violent revolution by recourse to Islamic texts, they contravene the true meaning of jihad to serve their own arrogant ends. By the same token, Yassine argues, Bin Laden's decision to "fight evil with evil and barbarity with barbarity" not only violates specific Islamic prohibitions against harming civilians, women, and children but also betrays the ethical imperative to embody the message of a merciful God who cautions believers that "you have no power over them" (Q. 88:22).

Even Islamists who endorse the more radical view of jihad adapt this framework and grammar to suit the distinct public spheres in which they operate and to which they carefully calibrate their political commitments. In his justification for the assassination of Sadat, for example, Faraj depicts the struggle to reclaim the moral foundations of the Egyptian state as a fight against *jāhiliyya* from within and further argues that the jihad against a corrupt nationalist regime

at home must take precedence over fighting enemies elsewhere. The charter of Hamas welds Islamist rhetoric to that of nationalist resistance in an effort to both fight Israeli occupation and compete for adherents with the Palestinian Liberation Organization, yet simultaneously insists that all Muslims recognize the primacy of the jihad for Jerusalem. In contrast to both Faraj and Hamas, Bin Laden embraced a global jihad that essentially collapses distinctions between national and international, offensive and defensive fighting, and enemies at home and those from afar.

Here as elsewhere, these Islamists claim to speak for an unchanging authentic Islam that exists outside of time and space. Far from transcending history and local circumstances, however, this understanding of jihad mirrors the very state-sanctioned violence against which Islamists have struggled for almost a century. Indeed, along with thousands of Muslims caught in the machinery of 20th-century state violence, prominent Islamists from Qutb to Ghazali to Zawahiri are well known to have been radicalized by extended and often brutal terms of incarceration. It is thus unsurprising that Islamists forged by interrogation torture in prison camps would conclude that the preeminent enactment of Muslim piety is violent struggle. In this context, as scholar of Middle Eastern politics Timothy Mitchell argues, Islamist views of the world can be characterized as both a mode of resistance to state mechanisms of coercion and an expression of them. This is powerfully illustrated in Ghazali's memoirs *Ayyam min Hayati* (Days of my life), where she describes how the "darkness of prisons, the blades of torture and the vicious beatings only increase the endurance and resolve of the faithful."

Conclusion

The example of jihad shows why any definition—let alone understanding or explanation—of Islamism requires attending not only to the multiple and various ways Islamist thinkers reinterpret Islam but also to the specific conditions and cultures in which they are embedded and the partisans and audiences they seek to address. These conditions and contexts determine the extent to which an Islamist framework resonates with Muslims who live in a wide range of cultural contexts and geographic locations. Such resonances are, in turn, facilitated by a concatenation of forces that mark this particular moment in history. These include the ways in which contemporary global inequalities compound the legacy of European colonialism to reproduce a sense of Muslim powerlessness relative to the West; ongoing Euro-American political and financial support of corrupt autocrats, many of whom preside over nation-states stitched together by Western fiat; the persistence of authoritarian regimes eager to control domestic unrest by catalyzing "Muslim rage" toward external targets; the sense of emasculation produced by decades of political repression and economic frustration; and the flow of images of bloodied Muslim bodies delivered by a burgeoning array of video, satellite, and electronic media. Islamism is thus constituted by a complex dialectic between the selective appropriation of texts and precedents by Islamist thinkers and leaders, and the ways such ideas are enacted and reworked by Islamist activists forged in the crucible of Egyptian prisons, Pakistani villages, Gazan refugee camps, Saudi schools, French housing projects, British mosques, and the battlefields of Afghanistan, Bosnia, Chechnya, and Iraq.

See also ʻAbd al-Rahman, ʻUmar (b. 1938); authority; al-Banna, Hasan (1906–49); Bin Laden, Osama (1957–2011); Egypt; Faraj, Muhammad ʻAbd al-Salam (1954–82); al-Gamaʻa al-Islamiyya; guardianship of the jurist; jihad; Khomeini, Ayatollah (1902–89); knowledge; Mawdudi, Abu al-Aʻla (1903–79); modernity; Muslim Brotherhood; al-Qaeda; Sayyid Qutb (1906–66); shariʻa; Shiʻism; sovereignty; Sunnism; ʻulamaʼ; West, the; women

Further Reading

Talal Asad, "The Idea of an Anthropology of Islam," Center for Contemporary Arab Studies Occasional Paper Series, March 1986; Aziz al-Azmeh, *Islams and Modernities*, 1993; James Barr, *Fundamentalism*, 1978; Osama bin Laden, "Declaration of War against the Americans Occupying the Land of the Two Holy Places," 1996; Norman J. Cohen, *The Fundamentalist Phenomenon*, 1991; Roxanne L. Euben, *Enemy in the Mirror: Islamic Fundamentalism and the Limits of Modern Rationalism*, 1999; Roxanne L. Euben and Muhammad Qasim Zaman, *Princeton Readings in Islamist Thought: Texts and Contexts from al-Banna to Bin Laden*, 2009; Muhammad Husayn Fadlallah, "Islamic Unity and Political Change: Interview with Shaykh Muhammad Hussayn Fadlallah," *Journal of Palestine Studies* (1995); Zaynab al-Ghazali, *Ayyam min Hayati* [*Days of My Life*], 1978; Yvonne Haddad, "The Qur'anic Justification for an Islamic Revolution: The View of Sayyid Qutb," *The Middle East Journal* 37, no. 1 (Winter 1983): 14–29; Johannes J. G. Jansen, *The Neglected Duty: The Creed of Sadat's Assassins and Islamic Resurgence in the Middle East*, 1986; Bruce Lawrence, *Defenders of God*, 1989; Saba Mahmood, *Politics of Piety: The Islamic Revival and the Feminist Subject*, 2005; George M. Marsden, *Fundamentalism and American Culture: The Shaping of Twentieth-Century Evangelicalism, 1870–1925*, 1980; Sayyid Qutb, *Maʻalim fi al-Tariq* [*Signposts along the Road*], 1964; Martin Riesebrodt, *Pious Passion: The Emergence of Modern Fundamentalism in the United States and Iran*, translated by Don Reneau, 1990; Max Weber, *The Sociology of Religion*, 1964; Nadia Yassine, "Inside Bin Laden's Head," 2005; Muhammad Qasim Zaman, *The ʻUlama of Contemporary Islam: Custodians of Change*, 2002; Malika Zeghal, "Religion and Politics in Egypt: The Ulema of al-Azhar, Radical Islam, and the State (1952–94)," *International Journal of Middle East Studies* (1999).

ROXANNE L. EUBEN

G

al-Gama'a al-Islamiyya

Al-Gama'a al-Islamiyya, or The Islamic Group (hereafter, Gama'a), appeared in Egypt as a distinct organization in the early 1980s, but its core membership, ideology, and tactics emerged in the mid-1970s, primarily on university campuses, when a changing political climate favored appeals to religious ideals. After demonstrating a capacity for successful mobilization by repeatedly winning elections that gave it control over the General Union of Egyptian Students, the Gama'a launched multiple initiatives aimed at gaining wider exposure and advancing its agenda, which drew inspiration from a radical interpretation of the social and political vision of the Muslim Brothers.

Beginning by sponsoring religious conferences, organizing daily prayers, distributing literature, appropriating bulletin boards, and offering classes, the group soon progressed to providing occasional services, such as inexpensive meals and low-cost copying, and selling articles of clothing identified with the movement. At the same time, it urged strict compliance with its view of proper Islamic morals, which often resulted in attempts to police gender relations, prevent the sale of alcohol, impose a dress code, and censor the presentation of films and theatrical performances. Such unauthorized vigilante assertions inevitably led to conflicts that were not always easily contained, as they threatened to stir up latent friction between political rivals, clan groups, social classes, and sectarian communities.

With its strength initially concentrated in the urban centers of Upper Egypt (e.g., Asyut, Minya, and Sohag), the attitudes and behaviors characteristic of the organization tended to reflect features of a regional subculture emphasizing traditional rural values such as honor, strength, and loyalty. These qualities surfaced with increasing force and frequency after the organization's leaders sought out and designated the blind Shaykh 'Umar 'Abd al-Rahman as their spiritual guide. At their request, evoking the Qur'anic verse that became the group's motto ("Fight against them till all opposition ends, and obedience is wholly God's" [Q. 8:39]), this Azhar-trained jurist-scholar (mufti) issued legal opinions consistent with the extremist doctrine of *takfīr*—that is, the legitimating of violence against people deemed to have become infidels.

Uncompromising opposition to President Anwar Sadat's peace initiative toward Israel served to increase the militancy of the Gama'a, as their protests moved from the campus onto the streets. A series of confrontations, arrests, incarcerations, and escapes into a clandestine underground followed, reaching a climax in the mass crackdown on Islamist activists in September 1981 and shortly thereafter the assassination of Sadat by assailants who belonged to a different but allied organization known as Jihad.

Throughout the 1980s, the Gama'a remained active although contained by extensive government surveillance, while some members managed to flee to Afghanistan to join the struggle against the Soviet invasion. But in the early 1990s, the Gama'a once again staged an aggressive campaign to challenge the regime of Husni Mubarak both by promoting popular opposition and by targeting prominent secular intellectuals, foreign tourists, or state officials. Then, in the late 1990s, Karam Zuhdi and several other Gama'a leaders announced from prison their renunciation of violence and a revision of their religious thinking, leading to their release in 2003 and an apparent moderate direction for the movement.

See also Egypt; fundamentalism; jihad; terrorism

Further Reading

Gilles Kepel, *Jihad: The Trial of Political Islam*, 2002; Carrie Rosefsky Wickham, *Mobilizing Islam: Religion, Activism, and Political Change in Egypt*, 2002.

PATRICK D. GAFFNEY

genealogy

In English usage, "genealogy" refers to (1) a blood relationship in the form of a lineage, pedigree, or family stock; (2) an account or representation of a blood relationship; and (3) a discipline for the study of blood relationships. The Arabic term *nasab* relates to the first and second senses. *'Ilm al-nasab* (or *'ilm al-ansāb*) refers to genealogy in the third sense, as a discipline, or simply the knowledge of blood relationships. The term *nasab* has passed into several other languages used by Muslims, where it carries similar meanings.

In Muslim societies, an individual's genealogy is almost always traced through male ancestors with a man named as his father's son (*ibn*, written here as b.) and a woman named as her father's daughter

(*bint*, here bt.). As elsewhere, certain bloodlines are remembered, whereas others are forgotten, and the ancestor originating a lineage is critical. Classical Islamic sources refer to the Prophet himself—who was from the tribe of Quraysh and the clan of Hashim—as Muhammad b. ʻAbdallah b. ʻAbd al-Muttalib and trace his genealogy to Adam and the origins of humanity, including among his ancestors major Arab tribal figures and, in addition to Adam, the prophets Noah, Abraham, and Ishmael.

Many families trace their genealogies to the Prophet Muhammad, his Companions, or other famous early Muslims. In Muslim societies, descendants of the Prophet are often called *sayyid*s, although sometimes the term *sayyid* is reserved for descendants of Muhammad's grandson Husayn, compared to a sharif, a descendant of his grandson Hasan (yet confusingly, sometimes the term "sharif" refers either to a descendant of Hasan or Husayn). Muhammad left no sons; Hasan and Husayn were the sons of Muhammad's cousin, ʻAli b. Abi Talib, who married Muhammad's daughter, Fatima. Ruling dynasties in Jordan (the Hashimites) and in Morocco (the ʻAlawis) trace their ancestries to Hasan. Families who are descendants of Abu Bakr bear the ancestral appellation al-Siddiqi, those of ʻUmar b. al-Khattab al-ʻUmari, those of the Shiʻite Imam Musa al-Kazim al-Musawi, and so on.

From early on in Islamic history, the value of a prestigious genealogy was debated by Muslims. Traditions attributed to the Prophet on this matter are as numerous as they are contradictory. Muhammad reportedly instructed his Companions to remember their genealogies and praised his own family and ancestry. He is also reported to have said, "When a people's nobleman comes to you, honor him." At the same time, in many hadith reports, Muhammad rejects the significance of noble birth and restates Qur'an 49:13: "The noblest among you before God is the most righteous among you." Muhammad is also thought to have referred to *ʻilm al-nasab* as a useless discipline, the ignorance of which does one no harm. One solution to these apparent contradictions has been to state that genealogy matters for this world but not the next.

Genealogies, real and fictitious, have played a major role in national traditions that explain the origins of Islam outside of its earliest boundaries. In these traditions, Islam is often remembered to have been brought by noble Arabs, descendants of ʻAli, or Sufi masters. The merchant-prince conqueror of Darfur, Zubayr Rahma Mansur, for example, reportedly bore the *nisba*, or filiation, ʻAbbasi, indicating his descent from the Prophet's uncle. Besides providing explanations for the arrival of Islam, such blood ties strengthen communities' bonds with the wider Muslim community.

Historically, genealogical claims have played a significant role in legitimating dynasties. Dynasties that emerged in Umayyad (661–750) and Abbasid (750–1258) times and onward claimed descent from Muhammad's family or from his Companions, other early Muslims, or aristocratic Arab tribes. In Iran, dynasties also attached themselves to the Iranian epic or Sasanian past. The arrival of Turco-Mongolian rule in Muslim lands initiated new lines of noble ancestry. Babur (d. 1530), the founder of the Mughal dynasty in India, claimed to be a direct descendant of Timur (d. 1405) on his father's side and of Chingiz Khan (d. 1227) on his mother's side. Several dynasties have also claimed descent from ʻAli, in some cases through one of his descendants recognized as an imam, in other words, the rightful leader of the Muslim community. The Fatimids (909–1171), who ruled first in North Africa and then in Egypt and southern Syria, claimed descent from the Shiʻi imams through Ismaʻil, son of the sixth imam, Jaʻfar al-Sadiq. In Iran, the Safavids (1501–1722)—who originated as leaders of a Sufi order in Persian Kurdistan and were Kurds, not Arabs—claimed descent from ʻAli through the seventh imam Musa al-Kazim and were responsible for the conversion of Iran to Twelver Shiʻism. Across the Islamic world, many a failed rebellion has also advanced genealogical claims, especially for descendants of ʻAli.

The families of *sayyid*s and sharifs have been accorded enormous prestige in various Muslim societies, such as Iran and Morocco, and claims of such noble ancestry have played important roles in certain families' gaining not only preferential treatment in society but also access to patronage in the form of royal stipends and hereditary judgeships, positions as shrine superintendents and endowment supervisors, and other sinecures. Their prestige has also frequently allowed them to act as power brokers and mediators between central governments and provincial rebels, urban populaces and conquering forces, or disputing urban factions.

Ideas about genealogy continue to play significant roles in the defense, formation, and reformation of communal and national identities. Scholarship here is new but highly suggestive. Andrew Shryock has discussed "genealogical nationalism" and the role such a phenomenon has played in the transformation of popular conceptions of tribe and state in modern Jordan.

See also Abbasids (750–1258); ʻAli b. Abi Talib (ca. 599–661); Hasan b. ʻAli (ca. 624–70); Husayn b. ʻAli (626–80); imamate; kinship; Shiʻism

Further Reading

Clifford Edmund Bosworth, "The Heritage of Rulership in Early Islamic Iran and the Search for Dynastic Connections with the Past," *Iran* 11 (1973); Idem, *The New Islamic Dynasties: A Chronological and Genealogical Manual*, 1996; Devin DeWeese, "The Politics of Sacred Lineages in 19th-Century Central Asia: Descent Groups Linked to Khwaja Ahmad Yasavi in Shrine Documents and Genealogical Charters," *International Journal of Middle East Studies* 31, no. 4 (1999); Louise Marlow, *Hierarchy and Egalitarianism in Islamic Thought*, 1997; Andrew J. Shryock, *Nationalism and the Genealogical Imagination: Oral History and Textual Authority in Tribal Jordan*, 1997; Idem, "Popular Genealogical Nationalism: History Writing and Identity among the Balqa Tribes of Jordan," *Comparative Studies in Society and History* 37, no. 2 (1995); Zoltan Szombathy, *The Roots of Arabic Genealogy: A Study in Historical Anthropology*, 2003; Daniel Martin Varisco, "Metaphors and Sacred History: The Genealogy of Muhammad and the Arab 'Tribe,'" *Anthropological Quarterly* 68, no. 3 (1995).

SARAH BOWEN SAVANT

Ghazali (ca. 1058–1111)

Abu Hamid Muhammad b. Muhammad al-Ghazali al-Tusi (the "Proof of Islam") is the most renowned Sunni theologian of the Seljuq period (1038–1194). He was born in Tus, in what is now northeastern Iran in 1058 (or, as recently argued by the Yale-based scholar Frank Griffel, ca. 1056). After his initial education in law in Jurjan, he moved to Nishapur, where he became a student of the leading Ash'ari theologian Juwayni (d. 1085) and the Sufi Abu 'Ali al-Farmadhi (d. 1084–85). Ghazali's alliance with the Seljuq court led to his 1091 appointment as a professor of Shafi'i law at the Nizamiyya college in Baghdad at the invitation of the powerful Seljuq vizier Nizam al-Mulk (d. 1092). Ghazali taught in Baghdad until 1095. During this period, he composed a number of polemical and dogmatic treatises in which he defended official Sunni theology against internal and external ideological threats, particularly the Isma'ilis and the philosophers.

In 1095, following a profound spiritual crisis described in his autobiographical and apologetic work *al-Munqidh min al-Dalal* (*The Deliverer from Error*), Ghazali resigned from his teaching post and left Baghdad. He traveled to Damascus, Jerusalem, Hebron, and the Holy Places in Mecca and Medina, performing the pilgrimage in 1096. It was during his travels that Ghazali wrote his most influential work, *Ihya' 'Ulum al-Din* (*The Revival of the Religious Sciences*).

In *The Revival*, Ghazali laid out his program for a far-reaching religious reform. His underlying assumption was that, due to the disproportionate influence of jurisprudence (*fiqh*) and dogmatic theology (*kalām*) on Islamic religious life, the Islamic spiritual tradition had become moribund, and the spiritual "science of the path to the hereafter" (*'ilm ṭarīq al-ākhira*), taught by the Prophet and the first generations of Muslims, had been forgotten. In Ghazali's view, the map of Islamic religious sciences needed to be redrawn and this spiritual science (allegedly revived but in fact largely developed by Ghazali himself from philosophical and Sufi sources) was to take on central importance. The remaining religious disciplines, including jurisprudence, hadith, Qur'anic exegesis, and dogmatic theology, were to be demoted to a subsidiary status.

Following his return to Tus in 1097, Ghazali gradually enlisted the support of the Seljuq ruling elite to promote the ideals of *The Revival*. This led to his 1106 appointment as a professor at the Nizamiyya college in Nishapur—a position analogous to the one he had held in Baghdad—by one of Nizam al-Mulk's nine sons, Fakhr al-Mulk (d. 1106). Ghazali accepted this position with the belief that he was the divinely appointed renewer (*mujaddid*) of Islam at the beginning of the sixth Islamic century (beginning 1107). However, as shown by Kenneth Garden in *al-Ghazali's Contested Revival*, Ghazali's appointment met with significant opposition among religious scholars and jurists in Nishapur, not least due to *The Revival*'s assault on the traditional religious disciplines and the controversial nature of the science of the hereafter, especially in view of its pronounced philosophical component. Ghazali's enemies appealed to Sanjar b. Malikshah (the Seljuq king of Khurasan in 1097–1118, then the supreme sultan until 1157), who summoned Ghazali to court. Although Sanjar acquitted him of all charges, Ghazali eventually retired from public teaching and returned to Tus, where he died in 1111. Despite powerful political patronage, Ghazali's religious reform did not have the broad social resonance for which he had hoped, and its influence was limited to intellectual and Sufi circles.

Ghazali's political theory was shaped by the political realities of his time (the power struggle between the Seljuqs, who effectively controlled the Abbasid caliphate, and the Isma'ilis of Alamut), his theological and teaching activity at the service of the Seljuqs in Baghdad and Nishapur, and his agenda as a religious reformer. Despite the unwillingness he declared in *The Deliverer from Error* to serve political authorities (as expressed in his vow at the tomb of Abraham in Hebron never again to serve rulers), Ghazali remained involved in politics throughout his life.

In his anti-Isma'ili treatise *Fada'ih al-Batiniyya* (*The Infamies of the Batinites*, ca. 1094), commissioned by the Abbasid caliph Mustazhir (r. 1094–1118), Ghazali sought to establish the caliph's legitimacy, countering the rival Isma'ili claims in favor of the Fatimid caliphate in Cairo. While concurring with the Isma'ilis that the Muslim polity must be governed by a divinely appointed leader (imam), Ghazali maintained that this leader must be elected (*ikhtiyār*) rather than designated (*naṣṣ*) by his predecessor—the practice followed by the Isma'ilis. Ghazali argued that the election need not have a wide basis (a broad consensus of religious scholars) and could be accomplished through the oath of allegiance (*bay'a*) of a single individual if that individual possessed uncontested military supremacy (*shawka*) and could provide a power base for the elected leader. Such an elected leader was, for Ghazali, the Abbasid caliph Mustazhir, who was supported by the military power of the Seljuq sultan. In effect, Ghazali legitimized the political status quo, in which the Seljuq sultans pledged allegiance to and effectively appointed the caliph, thereby validating their own authority. He represented this symbiotic system of government as a warrant of peace, unity, and stability for the Muslim polity.

Ghazali also rejected the Isma'ili view that the imam must be a divinely inspired religious scholar uniquely qualified to interpret the shari'a. He argued that in the same way the imam (i.e., in Ghazali's view, the Abbasid caliph) relied on the sultan for military support, so also he could rely on religious scholars ('ulama') for support in matters of religion. Therefore, the imam himself need not be an expert religious scholar.

In his dogmatic treatise *al-Iqtisad fi al-I'tiqad* (*The Golden Mean in Belief*, ca. 1095) and in the brief political section (book 14, chapter 5) of *The Revival*, Ghazali reiterated his views on the relation between the imamate and the sultanate and emphasized that obedience to the sultan, who has military supremacy, is obligatory, even if he is ignorant and unjust. This is because any attempt to depose him would result in unendurable civil strife (*fitna*), which must be prevented at all costs.

Ghazali's concept of the ideal ruler is reflected in the ethical advice offered to rulers in his Mirrors for Princes: chapter 10 of *The Infamies of the Batinites*; book 2, chapter 10 of *Kimiya-yi Sa'adat* (*The Alchemy of Happiness*); *Nasihat al-Muluk* (*The Counsel for Kings*), of which only the first part is authentic; and some of his Persian letters. (*The Alchemy*, *The Counsel*, and the letters were all composed in Persian, as they were addressed to the non-Arabic-speaking Seljuq ruling elite.) In these works, Ghazali urged rulers to be mindful of their impending death and the Day of Judgment, when they will be held accountable for any injustice done to their subjects. These Mirrors for Princes are to be understood in the context of Ghazali's religious reform laid out in *The Revival*. Their primary focus is ethical and religious rather than political.

See also Abbasids (750–1258); madrasa; Nizam al-Mulk (1018–92); philosophy; Seljuqs (1055–1194); Sufism

Further Reading

Leonard Binder, "Al-Ghazālī's Theory of Islamic Government," *Muslim World* 45, no. 3 (1955); Gerhard Böwering et al., "Ġazālī," *Encyclopaedia Iranica*, vol. 10, 2001; Kenneth Garden, *al-Ghazālī's Contested Revival: Iḥyā' 'ulūm al-dīn and Its Critics in Khorasan and the Maghrib* (PhD diss., University of Chicago, 2005); Idem, "al-Māzarī al-dhakī: al-Ghazālī's Maghribi Adversary in Nishapur," *Journal of Islamic Studies* 21, no. 1 (2010); Frank Griffel, *Al-Ghazālī's Philosophical Theology*, 2009; Carole Hillenbrand, "A Little-Known Mirror for Princes by al-Ghazālī," in *Words, Texts and Concepts Cruising the Mediterranean Sea*, edited by R. Arnzen and J. Thielmann, 2004; Idem, "Islamic Orthodoxy or Realpolitik? Al-Ghazālī's Views on Government," *Iran* 26 (1988); Ann K. S. Lambton, *State and Government in Medieval Islam*, 1981; Henri Laoust, *La Politique de Ġazālī*, 1970; Erwin I. J. Rosenthal, *Political Thought in Medieval Islam: An Introductory Outline*, 1958; William Montgomery Watt, "Reflections on al-Ghazālī's Political Theory," *Glasgow University Oriental Society Transactions* 21 (1966).

ALEXANDER TREIGER

ghāzī

Derived from the earliest traditions of the Prophet Muhammad's raids against the infidels, the term *ghāzī* denotes one who fights the enemies of God, whether non-Muslims outside the borders of the Islamic lands or religious dissidents within the lands under Islamic rule. The *ghazw* differs from the jihad (struggle in the cause of Islam) in that it refers to a campaign that is limited in either scope or duration.

During the age of the original Islamic Conquests (from 634 until 717), the term *ghāzī* was rarely used. From the 720s and 730s, however, the first famous *ghāzīs* of Islamic history began to appear, many of them no longer under government sponsorship or control. Some of these *ghāzīs*, such as the famous Sayyid Battal, about whom epics were written, became legendary figures and religio-political models. Due to the influence of such figures, prominent personal engagement in *ghazwas* also became de facto government policy under the early Abbasid caliphs, the so-called *ghāzī*-caliphs, who both sponsored and occasionally led summer raids on Byzantium.

Due to the political breakup of the universal caliphate in the ninth century, the best way for the founder of a polity to gain political legitimacy for his rule was to be a *ghāzī*. Thus most of the founding figures of the great medieval and early modern Islamic kingdoms—including such major ones as the Samanid, Ghaznavid, Seljuq, Ghurid, Mamluk, Mughal, and Ottoman governments—cultivated careers as *ghāzīs* and also incorporated *ghāzīs* into their armies. The members of modern Islamist groups view themselves as the heirs and preservers of the *ghāzī* tradition.

See also Ghaznavids (977–1086); Ghurids (1009–1215); jihad; Mamluks (1250–1517); Mughals (1526–1857); Ottomans (1299–1924); Samanids (819–1005); Seljuqs (1055–1194)

Further Reading

Ali Anooshahr, *The Ghāzī Sultans and the Frontiers of Islam: A Comparative Study of the Late Medieval and Early Modern Period*, 2009; Khalid Yahya Blankenship, *The End of the Jihād State: The Reign of Hishām Ibn 'Abd al-Malik and the Collapse of the Umayyads*, 1994; Michael Bonner, *Aristocratic Violence and Holy War: Studies in the Jihad and the Arab-Byzantine Frontier*, 1996; Jürgen Paul, *The State and the Military: The Samanid Case*, 1994; D. G. Tor, *Violent Order: Religious Warfare, Chivalry, and the 'Ayyar Phenomenon in the Medieval Islamic World*, 2007; Paul Wittek, *The Rise of the Ottoman Empire*, 1938.

D. G. TOR

Ghaznavids (977–1086)

The Ghaznavids were founded in 977 by Sebuktegin b. Qara Bechkem, a Turkish military slave, in the town of Ghazna in eastern Afghanistan. In 999, Sebuktegin's son and successor, Mahmud b. Sebuktegin, in cooperation with the Qarakhanid Turkic nomads, overthrew the Ghaznavids' nominal overlords, the Samanids, which were, at the time, the most important political power of the eastern Islamic world. Under Mahmud, who ruled from 998 until his death in 1030, the dynasty reached its apogee, controlling most of Iran, Afghanistan, and much of northern India. Mahmud based his right to rule on fierce dedication to holy warfare against the infidels and heretics of India, Iran, and adjacent areas of Central Asia; because of this he is known to history as "Mahmud Ghazi." It was during

his reign that the Muslim conquest of the Indian subcontinent began in earnest.

In 1040, Mahmud's son and successor, Mas'ud, lost all the dynasty's Western possessions to the Turkish Seljuqs and the nomadic Turkmen whom they led. Henceforth, from 1040 until the fall of the Ghaznavids in 1186, the Ghaznavid realm was limited to eastern Afghanistan, Baluchistan, and northwest India, while the Seljuqs inherited the Ghaznavids' former position as the leading dynasty of the Islamic east.

The Ghaznavids had a significant impact on the history of Islamic political thought in several key areas. First, the Ghaznavid era marks an important stage in the political acceptance of the de facto divorce of the governing power from the caliphate, a process that had begun with the establishment of the Ghaznavids' Persian predecessors, the Saffarids and Samanids. The Ghaznavid achievement of a new level of religious and political legitimacy is demonstrated by the fact, emphasized in the medieval sources, that Mahmud of Ghazna was the first person other than the caliph to be called by the title sultan, a term that at that time denoted the embodiment of legitimate authority, as opposed to a mere wielder of power.

Second, the Ghaznavids were the first major ruling dynasty in the history of the central and eastern Islamic lands to be founded by a Turkish slave. Moreover, in contrast to their Saffarid and Samanid predecessors, who derived their political and military support from the various armed elements of the free, indigenous Muslim population, the Ghaznavids relied heavily on Turkish slave soldiery. The Ghaznavids thus inaugurated the Turkic political dominance of the ethnically Arab and Iranian Islamic heartlands that was to last until the 20th century.

Perhaps as a result of their reliance upon an alien political class, the Ghaznavids came to be seen as the embodiment of political despotism. Authors who espoused this absolutist ideal, therefore, most notably the Seljuq minister Nizam al-Mulk, regarded Mahmud as a paragon of Islamic sovereignty, admiring in particular the elaborate internal spy system that Mahmud established.

Finally, the Ghaznavids bequeathed a militant Sunni holy warrior legacy to Muslim India, which became a salient feature of its political tradition; Mahmud of Ghazna was the declared political ideal of Islamic successor states such as the Ghurids, the Delhi Sultanate, and the Mughals, which eventually conquered virtually the whole of the Indian subcontinent and continued to rule much of it until the advent of British rule.

See also Afghanistan; Central Asia

Further Reading

W. Barthold, *Turkestan down to the Mongol Invasion*, 1968; C. E. Bosworth, *The Ghaznavids: Their Empire in Afghanistan and Eastern Iran, 994–1040*, 1973; Idem, *The Later Ghaznavids: Splendour and Decay*, 1977; Julie Meisami, *Persian Historiography to the End of the Twelfth Century*, 1999; Nizam al-Mulk, *The Book of Government or Rules for Kings: The Siyasat-nama or Siyar al-Muluk of Nizam al-Mulk*, 1960; Muhammad Nazim, *The Life and Times of Sultān Maḥmūd of Ghazna*, 1971; André Wink, *Al-Hind: The Making of the Indo-Islamic World. Vol. 2: The Slave Kings and the Islamic Conquest 11th–13th Centuries*, 2002.

D. G. TOR

Ghurids (1009–1215)

The chiefs (*maliks*) of Ghur, an obscure mountainous region in central Afghanistan, came to prominence after 1150, when the armies of 'Ala' al-Din Husayn (r. ca. 1149–61), chief of the dominant Shansabanid clan, sacked and burned Ghazni, the capital of the Ghaznavid sultanate. Formerly subject to both the Seljuqs and Ghaznavids, over the following decades the Ghurids rapidly expanded the territories under their control. The apogee of their dominion was reached during the reign of the brothers Ghiyath al-Din (r. 1163–1203) and Mu'izz al-Din (r. 1173–1206), the former overseeing the westward expansion of the sultanate from Firuzkuh in west-central Afghanistan and the latter expanding its dominion eastward from Ghazni. A third line, based in Bamiyan, was celebrated for its patronage of Persian literati. This unusual arrangement reflects clan-based structures within which rights of succession were horizontal rather than strictly vertical, fostering a system of appanages consolidated by intermarriage and affinal ties.

By the end of the 12th century, the Ghurids and their agents ruled over an area extending from Khurasan and eastern Iran in the west to the Ganges in the east. The changing fortunes of the sultanate are reflected in the construction of an elaborate genealogy linking the Shansabanids both to the heroic past of pre-Islamic Iran and to the early caliphs. Shifts in the names (*laqab*s) of the sultans and their adoption of increasingly bombastic titles, including those formerly held by the Seljuq and Ghaznavid sultans, also reflect the transition from a rural emirate to a transregional sultanate.

The dynamic self-fashioning of the Ghurids extended to their pietistic affiliations and patronage. During their rise, the Ghurids patronized the Karramis, a Sunni pietistic sect whose founder, Muhammad b. Karram (d. 869), helped convert the recalcitrant Ghur from paganism to Islam. A spectacular four-volume leather-bound Qur'an produced for sultan Ghiyath al-Din in 1189, the sole manuscript that can be associated with Ghurid patronage, may have been commissioned as a bequest to a Karrami madrasa. In addition, it seems likely that the complex epigraphic program of the most spectacular example of Ghurid architectural patronage, the roughly 220-foot-high brick minaret at Jam in central Afghanistan, was chosen to rebut contemporary criticisms that the Karramis were anthropomorphists. Dated 1174 to 1175 according to recent research, the minaret is generally believed to mark the site of Firuzkuh, sultan Ghiyath al-Din's summer capital.

In 1199, at the zenith of their political power, the Ghurid sultans broke with the Karramis, aligning themselves with the more transregional Hanafi and Shafi'i law schools of Islam instead. The realignment can be correlated with increased cultural and diplomatic contacts with the Baghdad caliphate, especially during the lengthy reign of the Abbasid caliph Nasir (r. 1180–1225). This "international turn" was also reflected in the introduction of new coin types in the Ghazni mint in 1200, which linked the Ghurids more directly with their Sunni contemporaries in the wider Islamic world.

Architecture was equally instrumental to these developments, and the last decade of the 12th century saw a major architectural program undertaken in the name of the Ghurid elite (male and female) in both Afghanistan and India. In 1201, for example, the Friday Mosque of Herat was rebuilt, some of the funds deriving from Ghiyath al-Din's share of the golden booty taken from Ajmir, the capital of the Chawhan rulers of Rajasthan. The Indian victories were useful for bolstering the orthodox credentials of the Ghurid sultans in the wider Islamic world. Yet, despite the rhetoric of idolatry and orthodoxy by which they were framed, in several cases, scions of defeated Rajput dynasties were reinstated as tributary subjects of the Ghurids, a practice that conforms (perhaps serendipitously) to the normative ideals of Indic kingship. In addition, the administrative *iqṭā'*, a type of land or revenue assignment that carried with it military or financial obligations to the state, was introduced to India, with administration devolving to the sultan's mamluks or manumitted Turkic soldiery. The last decade of the 12th century thus saw sultan Mu'izz al-Din ruling over an eclectic combination of subordinate Turks and vassal Hindu princelings, resulting in what the historian Khaliq Ahmad Nizami memorably called "a type of polity, half-Ghurid, half-Indian."

After Ghiyath al-Din's death in 1203, Mu'izz al-Din assumed the role of paramount sovereign; his demise three years later effectively marked the end of Ghurid sovereignty. In its aftermath, the neighboring Khwarazmshahs of Central Asia incorporated the western Ghurid territories into their domains, while in the east, the Turkish slave generals on whom the Ghurids had relied during their Indian campaigns vied for power, creating the conditions for the emergence of an independent sultanate based in Delhi.

See also Abbasids (750–1258); Delhi Sultanate (1206–1526); Ghaznavids (977–1086); Seljuqs (1055–1194)

Further Reading

C. E. Bosworth, "The Early Islamic History of Ghur," in *The Medieval History of Iran, Afghanistan, and Central Asia*, 1977; Finbar Barry Flood, *Objects of Translation: Material Culture and Medieval "Hindu-Muslim" Encounter*, 2009; K. A. Nizami, *On History and Historians of Medieval India*, 1983; J. Sourdel-Thomine, *Le Minaret Ghouride de Jam: Un chef d'oeuvre du XIIe siècle*, 2004.

FINBARR BARRY FLOOD

globalization

Globalization is the process of formation of multiple interdependent ties among various locales in the world, facilitated by the emerging common vision of one interconnected world. Historical literature notes earlier processes of globalization, but contemporary globalization is primarily centered on the continual opening of national economies and their mutual integration via free trade agreements and domestic reform policies.

The vision of "one world" is largely the inheritance from a European hegemony imposed on the world at the highest stage of colonial domination, achieved prior to World War I. A convergent dimension of the present-day globalization is therefore geopolitical, since the program of economic integration often reflects Western priorities of supporting pro-Western governments, resulting in the erosion of welfare regimes and, more generally, weakening the autonomy of the states and the sovereignty of their jurisdictions within industrial and developing countries.

Islamic politics has been deeply enmeshed in this global dynamic, both in the colonial and the postcolonial eras. Islamic movements and groups that oppose pro-Western governments within Muslim majority societies often hold these governments responsible for disregarding the needs of their populations, particularly those of the middle classes, and for neglecting the basic tenets of the "common good" (*al-maṣlaḥa al-'āmma* in Islamic jurisprudential parlance). Another close affinity of Islamic politics to globalization rests on the fact that the premodern configuration of Islamic civilization reflects a form of globalization sui generis, occurring prior to the current wave of Western-centered globalization and building on extensive transnational connections. In Islamic history, notably in the epoch that Marshall Hodgson called the Middle Periods (between the 10th and the 15th centuries, roughly corresponding to the European Low Middle Ages), such ties encompassed traders and scholars, Sufis and pilgrims alike. Islamic civilization was located, geographically and socially, at the center of a medieval world system that did not require centralized governance, either nationally or transnationally based, but fostered long-distance exchange, connectedness, and solidarity while keeping fluid the distinction between insiders and outsiders. This type of transnational and civilizational solidarity and governance was further cultivated in early modern Muslim empires, like the Ottoman and Mughal (rather more than in the Safavid, with its sectarian Shi'i identity). Contemporary sociopolitical movements with an Islamic orientation integrate subnational locales into transnational networks of solidarity and mobilization that can create new bonds or confirm old divides, as between Sunnis and Shi'is. From this perspective, globalization relativizes the centrality of any rooting of human communities in territorially and corporately defined communities, like nation-states. It therefore resonates with a historic Islamic approach privileging ties between locales, groups, and cities more than stressing the autonomy of cities or the sovereignty

of national and corporate communities. This affinity is strengthened by the erosion of the legitimacy and institutional ossification of postindependence states within Muslim majority societies.

This specifically Islamic articulation of a global vision is also nurtured by the evolving cultural and communicative dimensions of globalization. It is particularly well supported by the growth, since the late 1990s, of satellite channels and websites with an explicitly Islamic orientation (e.g., Iqraa and islamonline.net). Such new media are often linked to intellectual authorities, opinion leaders, and "directors of consciences" whose activities are qualified as global, like in the case of Yusuf al-Qaradawi and ʻAmr Khalid. Here the movement aspect of globalization meets and sometimes clashes with the fact that the investments necessary to support such global media enterprises, be they public or private, tie them closely to sectors of the establishment, be they financially strong states (like those of the Gulf) or corporate investors.

A hybrid, emerging character of Islamic globalism, trying to bring a common denominator to the movement aspect and the interests and support of the establishment, is the figure of the "new *dāʻiya*," in other words, practitioner of *daʻwa* (the call to Islamic belief and practice). Often devoid of the scholarly credentials traditionally ascribed to the ʻulama', this character aggregates audiences and creates potential constituencies across national borders, often via a combined use of satellite television, websites, and even cooperation with international organizations. This is the case with ʻAmr Khalid, for instance, who, banned from Egypt in 2003, resettled in England and intensified his presence on a variety of Arab satellite channels while also working with the World Health Organization on an antismoking campaign, which he saw as part of his larger efforts to promote a moral conduct—oriented both to individual success and to the pursuit of the common good—among the Muslim youth in Muslim majority countries and in Western diasporas alike.

The latest manifestations of this type of Islamic globalism highlight the prevalence of common standards of globalization especially at the level of culture and communication. Yet this standardization is matched by a pluralization of the political signifiers legitimizing the various messages, which the international state system is no longer able to contain within conventional views of participation, citizenship, and rights. For example, while the human rights framework has gained ground in tandem with globalization, its articulation according to particular civilizational perspectives (like the campaign for "Islamic human rights") has become widely accepted, if not fully legitimate. Islamic politics in this sense reflects the search for a balance between universal globalism and civilizational particularism. At a deeper level, easily traced in the message of emerging media leaders, the juridification of economic and political ties, which is part of the inheritance of the international state system, is often matched by a growing awareness of the centrality of lifestyles and modes of expression. These are influenced by global standards but rearticulate specific identities (e.g., Muslim hip-hop).

It is uncertain whether this emerging Islamic globalism (also dubbed "Islamic transnationalism" or even "cosmopolitanism," terms that accentuate different aspects of the global connectedness) is more of a challenge to the international state system and in particular to the postcolonial states in the Muslim majority world itself than it is to the hegemonic forms of Western-centered globalization. Generally speaking, and in the long term, "integrationist" tendencies seem to prevail within Islamic movements and groups over "isolationist" temptations (a contrast exemplified by the urban puritan versus tribal articulation of the movements). Yet even within the integrationist approach, the idea of an integration of Muslim interests and lifestyles into the wider dynamics of the world system is subordinated to the possibility of preserving the autonomy of key Islamic notions of solidarity and good life vis-à-vis the process of global standardization linked to consumerist models. Therefore, voicing fears of globalization in an Islamic idiom is often the expression of a will to negotiate a fair insertion into the world system in ways that avoid a civilizational sellout. It also reflects a will to support the subinstitutional impetus of globalization processes without accepting rootlessness and homogenization.

Even if Islamic approaches to globalization do not easily fit into standardized forms of political and cultural expressions, they often work as a catalyst of their growing differentiation and complexity. They enhance the importance of voluntary interventions within more informal communicative forms and political spaces than those anchored within conventional—and increasingly weakened—state jurisdictions. Such spaces and practices appear to be strongly connected both to larger civilizational programs and to methodical approaches to personal conduct. A certain primacy of moral self-steering is one notable result of their convergence, with its increasing avoidance of institutional power rituals and strategies. A leader like Qaradawi has become since the 1980s the representative of such a convergence by generating a public attention whose intensity can be compared to the popularity of postcolonial leaders of the 1950s and 1960s, like the Egyptian president Gamal Abdel Nasser.

See also international relations; modernity; Nasser, Gamal Abdel (1918–70)

Further Reading

Mohammed A. Bamyeh, *The Ends of Globalization*, 2000; Miriam Cooke and Bruce B. Lawrence, eds., *Muslim Networks from Hajj to Hip Hop*, 2005; Heba Raouf Ezzat, "Beyond Methodological Modernism: Towards a Multicultural Paradigm Shift in the Social Sciences," in *Global Civil Society 2004/5*, edited by Helmut Anheier, Marlies Glasius, and Mary Kaldor, 2004; Armando Salvatore, "Qaradawi's *Maslaha*: From Ideologue of the Islamic Awakening to Sponsor of Transnational Public Islam," in *Global Mufti: The Phenomenon of Yusuf al-Qaradawi*, edited by Jakob Skovgaard-Petersen and Bettina Gräf, 2009; Jakob Skovgaard-Petersen, "In Defense of Muhammad: 'Ulama', Da'iya and the New Islamic Internationalism," in *Guardians of Faith in Modern Times: 'Ulama' in the Middle East*, edited by Meir Hatina, 2009.

ARMANDO SALVATORE

God

The Arabic word *Allāh*, probably a contraction of *al-ilāh* (the god), is used in the Qur'an and Islamic tradition to refer to the biblical God, the same God who spoke to Moses from the burning bush and caused Mary to conceive and bear Jesus Christ without the intervention of a human father. The god Allah already existed as a high god in the pagan pantheon of the pre-Islamic period and was held to have daughter goddesses (al-Lat, al-'Uzza, and Manat), but the Prophet Muhammad's mission reinterpreted the deity Allah within the framework of biblical history and theology, decidedly rejecting the pagan view.

The Qur'an uses a number of metaphorical frames, all of which can be found in the Hebrew Bible, to describe God. In one set of descriptions, God is a master or lord (*rabb*). Every human is God's servant or slave (*'abd*) and owes God service or worship (*'ibāda*) as well as gratitude for his favor (*ni'ma*). Each is rewarded for obedience (*ṭā'a*) and punished for disobedience (*'iṣyān*, *ma'ṣiya*). God is also portrayed as a king. God watches over the heavens and the Earth from His throne. He is attended by a council (*mala'*). He resides in a fortress equipped with magnificent ascending staircases and defended by ramparts and towers. Guards on the ramparts fire projectiles at invasive genies, who attempt to eavesdrop on the celestial court, the attack of which produces shooting stars. God will also judge all people on the Day of Judgment after they have been physically resurrected and gathered together. The accused will be confronted in His presence with the records of their deeds, which they will receive in their right hands if the record is good but in their left hands if it is not. On the basis of this trial, God will issue a verdict, sending the innocent to paradise and the guilty to hell.

Several categories of signs (*āyāt*) convey important messages about God to those who are observant of the world around them. Islam is thus the religion of innate human understanding (*fiṭra*), being inscribed in nature, and one understands from the Qur'an that someone who grows up in isolation should be able to derive the main precepts of the faith independently from careful observation. The wonders of the natural world, including the sky, mountains, seas, and those things that are evidently impossible for humans to produce point to the existence of a divine power. The regularities of the natural world, such as the rotations of the planets, the alternation of night and day, and the rotation of the seasons, indicate the unity of the divine power. One knows that there is one God and not multiple gods because the universe is regular and not chaotic. The sustenance provided in the world for humankind, including rain, vegetation, crops, livestock, shelter, and so on, form another category of signs, and these show humans that they owe gratitude to God, on whose providence they depend utterly. Yet another class of signs are the ruins and relics of earlier civilizations, including Noah's ark; Iram, the great city or temple of the 'Ad tribe; the deserted dwellings of Thamud, which are carved into the rock walls of their valley; the pyramids of the pharaohs; and the ruins of "the Overturned Cities" (*al-Mu'tafikāt*) of Sodom and Gomorrah. Examination of such ruins conveys to the observer that God has destroyed earlier peoples and nations, despite their strength, prosperity, and accomplishments, presumably for disobedience and the rejection of earlier prophetic missions. The final category of signs—miracles that accompany prophetic missions, such as that of Moses' staff, which turned into a snake before Pharaoh—attests to the validity of the messages of God's prophets.

The Qur'an and Islam emphasize God's transcendence. The Qur'an pointedly alters several biblical portrayals, such as the statement that God rested on the seventh day after creating the universe in six, instead reporting that God settled on the throne to direct the universe. The point is obviously to avoid the implication that God gets tired or needs to rest and is thus subject to an anthropomorphic imperfection. No equivalent of the biblical statement that God created man in His own image appears in the Qur'an. Other passages argue against the Holy Trinity on the grounds that God has no need of a son, since He can create whatever He wishes simply by uttering a command. Nevertheless, some passages in the Qur'an and the hadith describe God in anthropomorphic terms, referring, for example, to God's hand or face, and these passages became the subject of much controversy. On the one hand, the Mu'tazilis generally held that such anthropomorphic descriptions should be interpreted in a figurative sense, so that God's hand should not be understood as a hand but as a reference to His power. On the other hand, Hanbalis and other traditionalist theologians argued for a literal interpretation. If the text of the Qur'an refers to God's hand, then the divinity has an actual hand. The intermediate Ash'ari position, which came to dominate Islamic discourse, states that one is supposed to accept these descriptive statements as fact but without probing into their particular implications—succinctly characterized as the *bi-lā kayf* ("without 'how'") position.

God has divine epithets, termed *al-asmā' al-ḥusnā* (the very beautiful names) in the Qur'an and in later Islamic tradition. They are generally single adjectives, such as *al-Karīm* (the Generous), *al-Mu'īn* (the Helping), *al-Ghafūr* (the Forgiving), and so on, and appear frequently in Islamic theophoric names with the masculine *'abd* and the feminine *ama* (both translate to "servant"), such as 'Abd al-Karim (Servant of the Generous One) or Amat al-Rahman (Servant of the Beneficent). The divine epithets are used primarily in the context of prayer, and they stress particular aspects of his power. As a category of speech, these epithets probably predate the Qur'an, and they were presumably used for other pagan gods in the pre-Islamic period. Islamic tradition came to stress that there are 99 such names, and the tradition includes a number of lists that are based primarily on the Qur'an but do not entirely agree. God also has, it is said, the exceedingly powerful "Greatest Name" (*al-ism al-a'ẓam*), which remains a secret.

Related to the divine epithets are God's attributes, the seven essential qualities of action, volition, knowledge, life, speech, sight, and hearing. These attributes created a problem of interpretation for theologians because admitting a plurality of attributes risked

describing God as composite or possessed of a plural nature. The Ash'ari solution to this was to affirm that God knows through His knowledge, is able to act through His power, and sees through His sight, but they argue that explaining exactly how this is so is beyond human capacity.

God is the supreme ruler, legislator, and guarantor of social order. Sovereignty belongs, theoretically, to God, and both political and religious authorities are dependent on Him. According to the Qur'an, He appointed Adam, David, and other early nations' *khalīfa*s (successors or viceroys) on Earth, signifying that He has delegated dominion over the world, of sorts, to them. In Islamic history, this status was extended first to the caliphs or successors of the Prophet and then to other rulers, such as sultan and kings. Muslim rulers thus claimed to rule by divine right—otherwise, God, who is omnipotent, would not have allowed them to gain power—and were styled *ẓill Allāh 'alā al-arḍ* (the shadow of God on Earth). God is also the ultimate source of law, and through prophecy He has imposed successive legal regimes on human communities, including those associated with Judaism, Christianity, and Islam. God is also the architect of political and social order and the guarantor of public morality, for moral behavior is presumably promoted by the fear of God above all. The biblical prohibition of using God's name in vain has not been stressed in Islamic cultures, where frequent invocation of God permeates all levels of discourse. God is understood to control all contingent matters, and one scarcely ever utters a statement in the future tense without the expression *in shā' allāh* ("if God wills"). God is invoked in many formulas of politeness, suggesting that the regular exchanges of social life occur under divine sanction and control. The word "God" is also used in a metonymic sense for the community, so that an expression such as *'aduww allāh* (the enemy of God), used to refer to a dangerous heretic, has the sense of "public enemy number one." Similarly, *khayl allāh* (the army of God) denotes the army of the Muslim state, and so on.

See also caliph, caliphate; faith; prophecy

Further Reading

Toshihiko Izutsu, *God and Man in the Qur'an*, 1980; Josef van Ess, *The Flowering of Muslim Theology*, 2006; W. Montgomery Watt, *Islamic Philosophy and Theology*, 1985; Idem, *Islamic Political Thought: The Basic Concepts*, 1968.

DEVIN J. STEWART

governance

Governance (*al-siyāsa al-shar'iyya*) refers to political and administrative policies regulating matters of public law and the public interest (*maṣlaḥa*) in classical Islamic thought. The term *siyāsa* refers broadly to executive matters associated with governance and statecraft. *Shar'iyya* is the adjectival form for divine law (shari'a), articulated by the jurists in a body of legal doctrine, called *fiqh*, which are rules resulting from applying particular methodologies for interpreting Islamic legal texts. For this reason, the phrase *al-siyāsa al-shar'iyya* has been translated as "governance in accordance with the shari'a." It may also be viewed as the exposition of classical Islamic political theory, as jurists systematized doctrines of politico-legal theory primarily through writings on this topic.

After Muhammad's death, the fledgling Muslim community needed a new leader. A portion of the community supported the leadership of the first four caliphs—Abu Bakr, 'Umar b. al-Khattab, 'Uthman b. 'Affan, and 'Ali b. Abi Talib. Later, Sunnis argued that this order reflected the caliph's rank in excellence, for which the entire Muslim community owed them respect and reverence. (The argument was clearly in response to the Shi'i refrain that 'Ali was the best and most excellent candidate to assume leadership over the community immediately after the Prophet.) For support of their position, Sunnis pointed to the Qur'an's instructions for Muslims to "obey God and his Messenger and those in authority over you" (4:59). A separate portion of the community maintained that Muhammad had designated his first cousin and son-in-law 'Ali to lead the community, to be followed by a series of his descendants (called imams). This group came to be known as the Shi'is, who argued that only the imams were divinely guided and thus qualified to lead the community in religious affairs. Both groups argued early on that community leaders were necessary—indeed divinely sanctioned—to carry out God's will on behalf of the entire community. The important questions were, Who was authorized to guide the community, and what was their scope of political and religious authority?

An initially wide scope of authority narrowed over time. The first four caliphs asserted broad political and religious authority, issuing decrees on matters of governance as well as Islamic law. But this stance did not go unchallenged during the reigns of the first two dynasties, the Umayyads (661–750) and Abbasids (750–1258). From the start, the proto-Shi'is challenged Umayyad political legitimacy and law-making authority. Many retreated to the scholarly circles of Muhammad's family members and Companions, who increasingly taught and issued legal decisions quite independently of the circles close to the reigning caliph. Discussions in these circles intensified, and political developments fostered an enduring split between the agents of government and these scholars, who dissociated themselves from government ties, forming a "pious opposition" to Umayyad and early Abbasid rule. The scholars resisted a proposal by the Abbasid litterateur 'Abd Allah b. al-Muqaffa' to permit the ruler to exercise unlimited political and legal authority. This proposal failed, and the scholars ('ulama') gradually formed the class of jurists (*fuqahā'*) that came to enjoy virtually exclusive interpretive authority over matters of law. In this context, *al-siyāsa al-shar'iyya* meant political governance in accordance with Islamic law, which could not always be determined by the ruler. The ruler therefore was to consult with the jurists on many matters.

Mawardi (d. 1058) is credited as the first to propound a developed theory of *al-siyāsa al-shar'iyya* in his book *Al-Ahkam al-Sultaniyya* (which means roughly "Ordinances of governance"). In his conception, only jurists who had received the requisite training were qualified to interpret Islamic law. However, the ruler enjoys considerable discretion over ostensibly legal issues by virtue of his duties to uphold and execute the law, ensure the continued existence of the Muslim community, and preserve the sanctity of the public sphere. Mawardi discussed these duties in terms of a ruler's overarching obligation to vindicate "God's claims" (*ḥuqūq Allāh*), which were public duties involving the public sphere. In contrast, private claims (*ḥuqūq al-nās* or *ḥuqūq al-'ibād*) were readily pursued by individuals in courts or before private jurists. Mawardi outlined ten public duties for which the ruler was responsible; these included such matters as providing for public works through tax collection, ensuring public safety through policing and imposing criminal sanctions, and making appointments to public offices. In this context, the term *siyāsa* was used synonymously with criminal law and tax-collecting jurisdiction, among other areas of public duties.

Most jurists including Mawardi had maintained the supremacy of shari'a by insisting that the operation and scope of political governance were restricted to the appropriate confines of government administration, as designated by the jurists. In other words, these jurists maintained that the ruler had authority only over areas that fell under the legal doctrine permitting expedient decisions in the public interest. However, jurists of the various legal schools differed regarding the definition of the public interest and its relation to shari'a. The Maliki jurist Qarafi (d. 1285), for example, maintained that expedience is an essential part of Islamic law in line with its broad aims to ensure the well-being of the community, avert corruption, and uphold the public interest. Thus law was not to be suspended when a ruler acted expediently, giving the ruler significant discretion, nor was the ruler bound to juristic definitions of expedience. Moreover, jurists of various legal schools also differed about the qualifications of the ruler. While some, such as Juwayni (d. 1078), argued that the ruler should ideally be an expert in Islamic law (*mujtahid*), others, such as Ibn Taymiyya (d. 1328), rejected that requirement, insisting that it was enough that the ruler cooperate with the jurists. Ibn Khaldun (d. 1406) noted that such cooperation between the ruler and the jurists was necessary only in religious matters, not in political or economic matters. In sum, all maintained that political legitimacy extended from the shari'a, which came from God, and some, such as Abu Bakr al-Baqillani (d. 1013), suggested that legitimacy also extended from the Muslim community at large through electors or "those who loosen and bind" (*ahl al-ḥall wa-l-'aqd*) the ties between the community and their leaders. These electors were respected leaders and elders who pledged allegiance to the rulers on behalf of their local communities. This, along with the Qur'anic verse 4:59, set up arguments that modern-day jurists would use to find bases in the Islamic historical traditions of governance for democracy.

See also Ibn Taymiyya (1263–1328); jurisprudence; Mawardi (974–1058); shari'a

Further Reading

L. Carl Brown, *Religion and State: The Muslim Approach to Politics*, 2000; Patricia Crone, *God's Rule: Government and Islam*, 2004; H.A.R. Gibb, "Constitutional Organization," in *Law in the Middle East*, edited by M. Khadduri and H. Liebesny, 1955; A.K.S. Lambton, *State and Government in Islam—An Introduction to the Study of Islamic Political Theory*, 1981; Mawardi, *The Ordinances of Government*, translated by Wafaa H. Wahba, 1995; Muhammad Qasim Zaman, *Religion and Politics under the Early 'Abbasids*, 1997.

INTISAR A. RABB

government

The term commonly used to refer to "government" in Arabic is *ḥukūma*; the term in Turkish is *ḥükümet*; and the term in Persian is *ḥukūmat*. They all refer to the holders of authority, the members of the cabinet, and more generally to the authoritative structures of the state. These specific meanings were acquired only in the 19th century. Traditionally, Muslim jurists used a variety of terms, sometimes interchangeably, to refer to the acts of government in Islam, including *amr*, *imāra*, *wilāya*, *khilāfa*, *imāma*, *dawla*, *mulk*, *ḥukm*, *tadbīr*, *siyāsa*, and *sulṭān*. The historian Ibn Khaldun (1332–1406) considered *al-khilāfa*, *al-imāma*, *al-ri'āsa*, and *al-sulṭān* to mean the same thing: the succession to the political authority of the Prophet. Following the same tradition, a prominent 20th-century Muslim scholar, Muhammad Rashid Rida (1865–1935), used *al-khilāfa, al-imāma al-'uẓmā*, and *imārat al-mu'minīn* as synonymous terms that refer to the leadership of the Islamic government in religious and worldly matters. The Egyptian constitutional jurist 'Abd al-Razzaq al-Sanhuri (1895–1971) used *al-khilāfa* and "Islamic government" interchangeably.

The traditional usage of the term *ḥukūma* refers to the act of arbitration between disputing parties and of deterring others from transgression. The word *ḥukūma* derives from the root *ḥ-k-m*, which in classical Arabic generally means "judgment, knowledge, and wisdom." *Ḥukm* is an ancient Arabic word and is mentioned in the Qur'an, as a root or its derivatives, 192 times with a wide range of meanings, including wisdom, judgment, perfection, deterrence, knowledge, and arbitration. Traditionally associated with the acts of adjudication and arbitration, the word gradually acquired broader meanings and entered into a variety of fields such as jurisprudence, logic, philosophy, linguistics, literature, and politics. In politics, *ḥukūma* denotes a binding authority that dispenses justice, deters people from wrongdoing, and directs them to fulfilling their welfare (*maṣlaḥa*).

In Islamic history, the word *ḥukm* has had a critical association with authority and justice. The Qur'an 4:59 commands believers to "obey Allah and obey the Messenger and those in authority (*ulū al-amr*) from among you; then if you quarrel about anything, refer it to Allah and the Messenger." The term *ulū al-amr* was interpreted in various ways and covered different groups that include political authority. 'Abdallah b. 'Abbas (619–87), a prominent interpreter of the Qur'an, explained "those in authority" as referring to the learned scholars. It also denotes "those who unbind and bind" in society. The term was then commonly used to refer to the "rulers." Ghazali (ca. 1058–1111) used the term for those with military authority (*aṣḥāb al-shawka*). The Egyptian reformer Muhammad 'Abduh (1849–1905) expanded the meaning of the term to include the rulers, the scholars, the army commanders, and all the heads and leaders to whom the people refer for their needs and public interests.

The question of who rules, or the qualities of the head of the Islamic government, has been critical in Islamic history. The first political conflict between the members of the early Muslim community took place immediately after the death of the Prophet (632) over the issue of *ḥukm*, or rule. The disagreement was not over the necessity of the establishment and continuation of political authority after the death of the Prophet but instead over who should succeed the Prophet as ruler of the Muslim community. Early Muslims also believed in the necessity of establishing one government under a single leader. This was indeed the source of the second conflict that took place between the fourth caliph, 'Ali b. Abi Talib, and Mu'awiya b. Abi Sufyan, the governor of Damascus, over who had the right to select the caliph and the source of the political legitimacy of the head of state.

Constitutional Theory of Government

Classical Muslim writings on government were drawn from the fundamental sources of Islam: the Qur'an and the sunna of the Prophet and the practices and consensus of the members of the early Muslim community, particularly of the Companions of the Prophet and the Rightly Guided Caliphate. The early views on government and rule were often dispersed along the various sections of the classical jurisprudential sources. The classical manuals of Islamic jurisprudence included discussions of government and administration as separate sections of *imāra* or *wilāya* or under sections dealing with zakat (alms giving), jihad, *kharāj* (revenues), and obedience. In the Muslim worldview, politics was viewed primarily in terms of welfare (*ṣalāḥ*), justice, avoiding corruption, and leading people to fulfill their religious obligations. Several prominent jurists discussed issues of government and administration, such as Ibn al-Muqaffa' (ca. 720–56), Abu Yusuf (ca. 731–98), Ibn Abi al-Rabi' (d. 864), Jahiz (d. 868), Baqillani (d. 1013), and Baghdadi (d. 1037). However, it was not before the 11th century that a comprehensive and systematic juridical theory of government and administration developed. This was marked by the writing of Mawardi's (974–1058) influential book *al-Ahkam al-Sultaniyya* (The ordinances of government), which laid down many of the tenets of the classical political theory of government and became an influential reference for later generations of political theorists.

The classical constitutional theory of government revolved around six essential principles: (1) the establishment of authority is a religious and rational necessity; (2) the leader of the community is selected by *ahl al-ḥall wa-l-'aqd* (those who unbind and bind, i.e., the influential elites in the community) or by testamentary designation; (3) the leader combines political and religious functions and has jurisdiction over the legislature (in cases where there is no ruling from the Qur'an or the traditions of the Prophet [sunna] or preexisting consensus) and the judiciary; (4) the leader is a successor to the Prophet and is obliged to implement the rules of Islam; (5) the leader has authority over the entire Muslim territories; and (6) as long as the ruler performs his functions, he is entitled to the obedience and support of the *umma*.

The Principles of Government

Muslim jurists, classical and modern, agree that the Qur'an does not stipulate a specific form or system of government. The Prophet died without designating a successor or delineating certain structures of government. Shi'is differ on this issue and believe that 'Ali was designated as a successor. Juwayni (1028–1105) asserts that there is no point trying to find a text in the Qur'an that addresses the details of the imamate. The Prophet's act has been interpreted to mean that as a primarily worldly issue he wanted the Muslims to devise the form of government they found suitable for the needs of the time and circumstances. The jurists concur, however, that the Qur'an sets forth several guiding principles for government. These principles are open to a variety of interpretations. Modern Muslim thinkers expand the scope of these principles to include up to 12 social and political values that guide the government of Islam, of which the most common in classical and modern writings on government are justice, equality, and *shūrā* (consultation).

Justice

The value of justice is a central principle in Islam and an essential source for legitimizing the government. The Qur'an contains about 300 verses that directly relate to justice and a similar number dealing with injustice, attesting to the centrality of this concept. The injunctions to adhere to justice take a variety of forms ranging from establishing justice—in the best of ways—to pursuing this value with those one disagrees with or even hates. The Qur'an sets a universal rule: "God enjoins justice, doing good, and giving to kinsfolk, whilst He forbids indecent conduct, disreputable deeds, and insolence. He admonishes you so that you may be reminded" (Q. 16:90). According to Fakhr al-Din al-Razi (1149–1209), a prominent commentator on the Qur'an, the entire Qur'an is an elucidation of this principle. With those that may hold different, even hostile positions, the Qur'an urges Muslims, "O you who believe, be steadfast for God, bearing witness with equity. Let not the hatred of any people induce you to act injustly. Act justly—that is nearer to fear of God—and fear God" (Q. 5:8). The impartial delivery of justice is a fundamental value for government in Islam.

The traditions of the Prophet list the "just" imam among those whom God protects in His shade on the Day of Judgment. It is part of the Islamic tradition that justice is the basis of rule and government and that God supports the just state even if it is not Muslim. The jurists have considered justice as one of the qualities of the imam and a requisite for his selection. According to Ghazali, the true sultan was he who acted with justice and refrained from tyranny and corruption. This condition is also required for the appointment of judges, the people (*ahl al-ikhtiyār*) who have the right to select the ruler, and government officials. Justice as a value is central in defining the relationship among the members of the community as well as between them and other communities.

Equality

The concept of equality rests on the belief in One Creator and in the equal nature of all human beings: men and women, Muslims and non-Muslims. Human beings have rights and responsibilities regardless of their color, religion, or social status. Of course, Islam considers the inevitability of distinctions between people based on knowledge, reason, faith, and functions. However, the Qur'an asserts the principle of the equal nature of humanity, "O people, fear your Lord, who created you from a single soul and who created from it its fellow and who spread many men and women from the two of them; and fear God, through whom you seek rights from one another and from the ties of relationship. God is a watcher over you" (Q. 4:1). No one could lay claim to superiority over others, for all people are equal in origin and in creation or nature. In his farewell address, the Prophet emphasized the equality of all people and the criteria for distinction: "O people, your Lord is One, and your father is one: all of you are from Adam, and Adam was from the ground. The noblest of you in Allah's sight is the most god-fearing: Arab has no merit over non-Arab other than god-fearingness." The concept of equality was perhaps one of the reasons for the appeal of Islam among the poor and slaves, as it stressed the human equality of everyone, regardless of wealth or status.

The confirmation of the principle of equality has clear and direct implications for government. The equal membership of the community necessitates equality of rights and duties and the supremacy of the shari'a over everyone. As equals, Muslims have the same political rights in assuming public positions, running for an office, and voting. Muslim political theorists often refer to the incidents of Muslims rulers, particularly some of the Rightly Guided Caliphate, who were subject to the rule of law and obligated to carry out judgments made against them.

Shūrā

Muslim political theorists agree on the principle of *shūrā* (consultation) as an essential component of government in Islam. Modern thinkers consider the *shūrā* the most important constitutional principle of the Islamic system of government. The Qur'an refers to this principle of *shūrā* twice. In verses 3:159 and 42:38, *shūrā* is associated with two important pillars of Islam, ritual praying and almsgiving, or salat and zakat, attesting to the fundamental significance of the concept. The sunna of the Prophet stresses the value of *shūrā*. It is reported that the Prophet frequently consulted with his Companions on various important issues that pertained to the affairs of the community. The Maliki scholar Abu 'Abdallah al-Qurtubi (1214–73) asserts, "When [a ruler] does not consult with the learned scholars, then it becomes necessary to depose him. There is no disagreement among the scholars on this [issue]." 'Abduh argues for the necessity of the *shūrā* on the basis of a third verse that states, "Let there be [one] community from you, summoning [people] to good and enjoining what is reputable and forbidding what is disreputable. Those will be the ones who prosper" (Q. 3:104). He relates this verse to the need for a group of people with the authority to encourage the rulers to do good and forbid them from wrongdoing. 'Abduh equates good with justice and wrongdoing with tyranny.

While acknowledging the importance of *shūrā* as a fundamental concept of government, scholars debated its nature and implementation. They differed on whether the *shūrā* was of an obligatory or advisory nature; whether or not it was binding; its scope; and which people (*ahl al-shūrā*) the ruler ought to consult. Classical scholars did not devise a structure or an institution for regulating the practice of the *shūrā*; such developments arose only many centuries later. The conventional views and practice established that while the rulers needed to consult with advisors and experts, the *shūrā* was neither compulsory nor binding. Highlighting the importance of *shūrā*, some jurists reduced the whole issue of government to an imam and his council of advisors (*imām wa-ahl mashūrātihi*).

The Islamic views of government are anchored in the premise that God has revealed the necessary principles, laws, and rules and has obligated Muslims to follow them in their relations with Him, among themselves, and with others. These principles, laws, and rules are contained explicitly or implicitly in the shari'a, which should be the guiding frame of reference and the source of legitimacy for an Islamic government. It is exactly this point that captures the essence of an Islamic government and distinguishes it from other types of government. The Islamic government draws its principles, laws, and practices from the shari'a. Classical jurists realized fully the implications of this orientation and placed the shari'a and God as the sovereign supermen, not the government, the state, or the people. Many attribute the development of this concept to the contemporary Muslim thinkers Mawdudi and Sayyid Qutb, but, in fact, classical jurists underscored this principle as well. Ghazali stated, "*Ḥukm* (rule, judgment, or sovereignty) belongs only to Allah; there is no sovereignty for the Messenger, or for a master over his slave, or a creature over another. All of that falls under God's jurisdiction and his stipulations; there is no ruler except him." Sayf al-Din al-Amidi (d. 1233) made a similar argument: "Know that there is no ruler except Allah and that there is no law except what he has revealed." Based on this concept, the classical scholars understood, first, that the shari'a

preceded the government and the state. Second, God and the shari'a have legislative sovereignty in the Islamic government. Third, the shari'a, or the legislature, is independent of the authority of the government. Fourth, the government and the ruler are not above the law, but their main function is to uphold the shari'a and implement the law.

The classical theory of government has had a formative and lasting impact on the formulations of political theory in Islam. The early writings on government concentrated on several fundamental issues: the necessity of establishing a government, the qualities and source of the authority of the right imam (i.e., the qualifications of the head of the state), those who have the right to select the imam (*ahl al-ikhtiyār*), the qualifications of the people who unbind and bind (*ahl al-ḥall wa-l-'aqd*), the transfer of rule or succession, obedience and rebellion, the unity of the authority, and usurpation of power. The jurists tried to devise the legal frameworks that would preserve the general order and unity of the Muslims. In many cases, they had to extend the juridical principles to accommodate the changes in the forms and practices of government. In these early formulations, the caliphate was central to the discussion of the ordinances of government among Sunni theorists, and the imamate was central to the Shi'i jurists. A major concern was to provide juridical arguments for accepting the existing institutions and the continuation of the religious and social life of the community as preferable to anarchy or civil disorder.

The Necessity of Government

Muslim political theorists considered government or the caliphate or imamate a necessary institution for fulfilling certain religious and temporal functions. They differed, however, on the justification for this principle and whether it was provided by divine law (*shar'*), reason (*'aql*), or both. Sunni theorists base the necessity of an authoritative entity on the concept of *ijmā'*, the consensus of the Prophet's Companions, who realized the need for political authority to continue managing the affairs of the Muslims after the death of the Prophet. The consensus of the early community of learned scholars is one of the fundamental sources of legislation, and, accordingly, the establishment of government becomes obligatory. Ayatollah Murtada al-'Askari (d. 2007) explains that the *amr* has always been understood as the issue of the imamate and government for the Muslims, Shi'i and Sunni alike. The Qur'an refers to the necessity of obeying those with authority. It also mentions that the Prophet stressed the need for the establishment of a ruling authority: "People are bound to have a just or unjust authority (*imāra*). They also need a ruler (imam)." According to another hadith, "The imam is a shield behind which people fight and defend themselves." The law therefore requires the establishment of an authority.

The Mu'tazilis and the philosophers justify the necessity of government based primarily on reason. Government is necessary for the welfare of the community, which consists of individuals who need to interact in an orderly fashion to ensure their welfare and prosperity. Government therefore is a natural form of social association, because individuals are incapable of living alone and tend to transgress against each other. An authority is necessary to keep order and promote the well-being of the members of the community.

Shi'is consider the imamate, the leadership of the Muslim community, a fundamental pillar of religion that should not be left to the discretion of the *umma* but instead must be designated by God and the Prophet. According to the Shi'i jurist Nasir al-Din al-Tusi (1201–74), the imam is *luṭf* (divine bounty) and therefore should be designated by God. In Shi'i political theory, the Prophet has designated an imam, 'Ali b. Abi Talib, who in turn has designated a successor. Therefore, government for Shi'is is necessary because of the *naṣṣ* (or designation) and is a *farḍ 'ayn* (an obligation on every Muslim).

The Kharijis, particularly the Najadat sect, and some Mu'tazilis do not consider government to be necessary. For them, the main purpose of government is to establish justice and implement the rules of the shari'a. If the people can achieve these objectives on their own, then an established authority or government becomes unnecessary. A few contemporary thinkers like 'Ali 'Abd al-Raziq (1887–1966) and other secular Muslim intellectuals hold similar views and do not consider the government a fundamental part of Islam.

The Prophet's Model

Muslim political theorists believe that Islam, unlike Christianity, was born to develop a state and a government. They concur that the Prophet established a form of political authority that reflected the basic components of a government. The state of Medina included a territory, a community, and a form of authority and sovereignty entrusted with managing the affairs of that community. The Prophet maintained dual functions and exercised both religious and temporal authority. He performed many of the functions of a government. He acted as a ruler, judge, and military commander and appointed *'ummāl* (officials) to represent him to the far regions under his control. This model represented a clear intertwining of religious and political authorities.

The Rightly Guided Caliphate (632–61)

Following the footsteps of the Prophet, the government of the Rightly Guided Caliphate continued, in the eyes of many Muslims, to merge the ideals with the practices. This government, however, was viewed as civic and not divine. The caliphs had religious functions, but they did not rule by divine authority or assume the religious nature of the Prophet. The members of the community were the main source for the selection of the caliph, the leadership of the community was based on a contract and consensus, the supremacy of the shari'a was closely observed, and the members of the community had the right to depose the rulers if they violated the essential principles of Islam. This "ideal" or idealized form of government lasted for about 30 years and was followed by a dynastic or imperial model that shaped the forms and functions of government in Islam for centuries to come.

The Dynastic or Imperial Model

Government in the imperial or dynastic model during the reigns of the Umayyad caliphate (661–750) and Abbasid caliphate (750–1258) rested on different principles and practices. This model reflected a clear separation between the Islamic ideals of government and the actual practices. It witnessed significant political developments such as the rise of the political sects or parties, increasing political rivalries and disputes, the formulations of systematic and comprehensive writings on political jurisprudence, and the establishment of elaborate administrative and legal institutions. The classical political writings tended to perceive the government as a functional post. The most important of its functions were to protect and defend religion, to establish an organized authority, and to maintain order to enable people to fulfill their religious and social life. As long as the government was able to achieve these objectives, it was considered legitimate, or at least acceptable. To consolidate power and prevent the disintegration of political authority, the dynastic model instituted the practice of the designation of a successor that presumably possessed the qualities of leadership. As usurpers and less-deserving rulers took over power, however, these qualities were overlooked and the theory allowed for the rule of the less competent (*imāmat al-mafḍūl*) as long as they possessed the requirements of leadership (i.e., controlling and maintaining order). The prominent jurist Shafi'i (767–820) was the first to sanction the leadership of the less competent. This became known historically as the "imamate of necessity."

The imamate of necessity became an accepted form, though viewed as irregular, and eventually replaced the rightful government. It was sanctioned by the jurists who were concerned for the continuation of the religious and social life of the community. In the 11th to 12th centuries Ghazali admits to this development and necessity: "There are those who hold the imamate is dead, lacking as it does the required qualifications. But no substitute can be found for it. What then? Are we to give up obeying the law? Shall we dismiss the qadis, declare all authority to be valueless, cease marrying and pronounce the acts of those in high places to be invalid at all points, leaving the population to live in sinfulness? Or shall we continue as we are, recognizing that the imamate really exists and that all acts of the administration are valid, given the circumstances of the case and the necessities of the actual moment? The concessions made by us are not spontaneous, but necessity makes lawful what is forbidden." The imperial model disintegrated in the tenth century and was replaced with empire states, the last of which was the Ottoman caliphate that was abolished in 1924.

Institutions and Structures of Government

The traditional theories of government centered on the institution of the caliphate and on the caliph. The issue of the caliphate of the Prophet is critical in Islamic history. It was a main cause for the emergence of political parties. Shi'is and Kharijis had different views on who should rule and on the authorities of the leader of the Muslim community. They often questioned the legitimacy of the existing authority. Sunni jurists formulated their theories on government largely in response to these views and in an attempt to accommodate the growing disparity between the Islamic ideals of government and the actual practices. They were concerned about maintaining the unity of government and the existing political institutions. Their discussions of the sources of legitimacy and political authority focused on the qualities of the ruler, the qualities of those who select him, and the main functions of government.

The Caliphate and the Caliph

Muslim jurists have provided various definitions for the caliphate, all focused on the nature and functions of this institution or on the position and the caliph himself, his qualities, and jurisdictions. Mawardi refers to the caliphate as the succession of the Prophet in the protection of religion and the management of earthly affairs. Ibn Khaldun considers the caliphate to be associated not with kingship but with religion and prophethood, as the Islamic government is a vicegerent to the Prophet in protecting religion and managing worldly affairs on its basis (*ḥirāsat al-dīn wa-siyāsat al-dunyā bihi*). Ibn Khaldun's definition qualified Mawardi's by stressing the role of religion in government. Both, however, rejected the notion that the caliph was the successor of God on Earth, a title that was used during the later days of the Abbasid caliphate. Stressing the importance of this post, Ghazali contends that the "shari'a is the basis of rule and authority (*mulk*) is its guardian. Whatever has no basis is bound to collapse and whatever has no guard is bound to disappear."

Based on the example of the Prophet and the Rightly Guided Caliphate, political theorists drew an idealistic image of the caliph and required certain qualifications that gradually became difficult to uphold. Mawardi specified seven qualifications: justice or moral probity, knowledge and the ability to exercise independent legal reasoning (*ijtihād*), the soundness of the senses, physical soundness, prudence, bravery, and descent from the Prophet's tribe of Quraysh. As less-competent or even unqualified rulers assumed power, however, the conditions of knowledge and *ijtihād*, prudence, or even moral probity were overlooked under the argument that the ruler could use the *ijtihād* and the knowledge of expert advisors. Similarly, as non-Qurashi and even non-Arab usurpers assumed actual control of the caliphate, the condition of lineage was reinterpreted primarily as an issue of solidarity and the capacity to exercise influence and power. The Kharijis rejected the condition of descent and reasserted the right of every Muslim to assume the caliphate.

The issue of the election or selection of the caliph and those who exercised this privilege was problematic. The caliph could not be duly invested and his authority could not be legitimate until he secured an oath of allegiance (*bay'a*) from the *umma* through its representatives, *ahl al-ḥall wa-l-'aqd* (those who unbind and bind), or the elites who exercised influence over their constituencies and who also had to possess certain qualities, such as moral probity, knowledge, and prudence. With the changes in actual practices, the number of the people who could make the selection was reduced to less than five, thus depriving the *umma* from a true voice in the selection

process. At some point, the actual seizure of power became a sufficient condition for the existence and acceptance of authority. Ibn Taymiya tried to redress this and considered the selection of *ahl al-ḥall wa-l-ʻaqd* an act of nomination that did not replace the general *bay'a* of the members of the community, the decisive process for the election of the caliph.

Another process for the investiture of the caliph was by testamentary designation, or *istikhlāf*. The jurists used the precedent of the first caliph, Abu Bakr, and his designation of 'Umar as his successor to sanction the later practice of hereditary rule as incumbent imams designated their heirs as successors. Shi'is acknowledged designation and not selection as the proper process for the selection of the imam. They bestowed on the imam innate and extraordinary qualities.

Jurists did not set limits for the term of the caliph. He could stay in power as long as he was capable of carrying out his functions and did not commit a violation that required his removal from power. Practically, however, the term of the caliph ended with his death, abdication, or an usurpation of his power. The classical political writings do not elaborate on the means by which the caliph could be removed peacefully from power, and in fact removals often involved armed takeovers (*istīlā'* or *taghallub*), which were then sanctioned as de facto situations that ensured the continuation of authority and order. The seizure of power gave de facto authority to the government.

When the caliphs were strong, they exercised expansive powers. The early writings on the caliphate did not refer to any separation of powers and gave the head of the government expansive authorities. The caliph by definition was the successor of the Prophet in defending religion and managing the earthly affairs of Muslims. As the head of the Islamic state, the caliph was expected to perform religious and political functions. He had to defend religion, launch jihad, uphold the main pillars of Islam, collect and distribute the revenues, manage public affairs, defend the state, maintain public order, dispense justice, and appoint the governors and officials. The caliph was not expected to perform all of these functions personally. He could appoint whomever he wished to help him carry out these tasks. The caliph had the right to appoint (and dismiss) governors (*walīs*), officials (*'ummāl*), ministers, and judges. As long as the caliph performed his functions and did not commit clear infractions, he was entitled to the obedience and assistance of the members of the community. While enjoying broad executive powers, the head of the government was in theory subordinate to the shari'a and was not free to contravene its rules.

The Legislative Functions of Government

Legislation in Islam is divided into two types: divine and human. The divine legislation is revealed in the Qur'an as general principles or explicit rulings and is stipulated in the sunna of the Prophet. The human legislation is driven from the understanding of the fundamental sources of Islam (the Qur'an and sunna) and through the independent reasoning (*ijtihād*) of the scholars and jurists to come up with rulings to address new issues. During the time of the Prophet and the Rightly Guided Caliphate, the Prophet, his Companions, and learned scholars performed the legislative functions. As a messenger and ruler, the Prophet combined the executive and legislative functions. The Rightly Guided Caliphate addressed worldly issues based on the Qur'an, the sunna, and their own judgment. As mentioned earlier, it is reported that the Prophet and the Rightly Guided Caliphate consulted regularly with learned Companions on developments for which the Qur'an had not provided a specific stipulation.

With the flourishing of the sciences of jurisprudence over the first three centuries of Islam, the functions of legislation were performed by the jurists (learned scholars) who were not elected or appointed by rulers but recognized in society for their knowledge of the fundamental sources of Islam, their integrity, and their capacity to deduce new rulings to address societal changes. The caliphs, governors, and political elites exercised legislative authorities for administrative and temporal matters. The gap between the two authorities, scholars and rulers, increasingly widened. Another significant development in the legislative process was the limited exercise of *ijtihād* by the tenth century and the stagnation of legislation in general. Scholars tended to follow the footsteps of preceding jurists, and the gap between legislation and reality grew. Most contemporary Muslim countries adopted modern, Western-inspired structures of government and established legislative institutions (elected or appointed parliaments, assemblies, or consultative councils) to carry out the legislative functions. With the adoption of foreign-inspired laws, many of these parliaments did not fully follow a system of codified shari'a laws and even contradicted the shari'a in their legislation, thus creating a state of tension and a problem of legitimacy.

The Judicial Functions

Islam has required the establishment of justice, equity, and fair adjudication among people. The early Islamic system of government did not distinguish between the structures of authority. The rulers combined executive and judicial functions. The Prophet assumed the judicial functions and also appointed judges to the far regions under his jurisdiction. The early caliphs followed this practice. With the expansion of the Islamic state and the responsibilities of the rulers, the position of judge was created. The second caliph, 'Umar, appointed judges to the different provinces to represent him in his judicial authority. Later, governors delegated by the caliph had the authority to appoint judges to look into legal and civic issues. The implementation of rulings and penalties (*ḥudūd* and *qiṣāṣ*), however, remained the responsibility of the executive authority (the caliphs and governors). During the Abbasid caliphate, the judicial system became more elaborate. The caliph Harun al-Rashid (r. 786–809) established the position of the head judge (*qāḍī al-quḍāt*), who was given the authority to appoint other judges. The first to assume this position was the famous jurist Abu Yusuf, the student of Abu Hanifa (699–767). The appointed judges assumed their judicial responsibilities in or outside the mosques or in specially designated places, like *dār al-qaḍā'* (court). Though

the jurists produced elaborate literature on the judiciary, the judges, their qualification, and best practices, the rulings and the judicial process at large were left up to the judge and often went unrecorded. In fact, the Islamic law was known as "the judges' law." The judges based their sentences on the shari'a, when applicable, and on customary laws. This created inconsistencies and contradictory rulings in many cases. The failure to delineate the judicial and the political establishment (rulers) created problems with regard to the jurisdictions of each and the implementation of sentences, which were left up to the authorities to carry out. The courts' structure was simple and did not allow for an appeal process.

Two institutions were associated with judicial functions: the *ḥisba* and the Court of Grievances. The system of *ḥisba* is directly drawn from the principle of enjoining good and forbidding wrongdoing. As a concept, the main purpose of the *ḥisba* was to safeguard the implementation of Islamic principles and protect society against their violations. The *ḥisba* official's, or *muḥtasib*'s, main functions combined those of a qadi and a policeman. The *muḥtasib* was expected to maintain public order and prevent public acts of immorality. In many cases, judges assumed this function, which focused on preserving public virtues and upright social standards; overseeing the marketplaces; inspecting the scales and commodities; making sure roads were open; forcing people to make house repairs; and protecting Muslims from fraud, extortion, and exploitation.

The Umayyad caliph 'Abd al-Malik b. Marwan (r. 685–705) established the Court of the Redress of Grievances as a separate institution. It resembled an administrative court and fell directly under the jurisdiction of the caliph, who appointed deputies or judges to address grievances against state officials (e.g., governors and tax collectors) and to arbitrate administrative disputes. In some cases, the caliph assumed this task himself. The jurisdictions of the Court of Grievances addressed the use of public funds, endowments, and complaints from public or state employees. This system continues to exist in several Muslim states.

The Administrative System

With the expansion of the Islamic state and functions of government, rulers needed to expand their administrative machinery. They appointed governors and officials to help them in the administration of the provinces. The administrative unit in the Islamic state was the *wilāya* or *iqlīm*, which was governed by a *walī* or amir. 'Umar organized the territories under his control into 8 main provinces. These were expanded into 14 under the Umayyad caliphate and 24 under the Abbasid caliphate. The governor of the province performed administrative, judicial, military, and religious functions on behalf of the caliph. The Umayyad and Abbasid caliphates followed a centralized system of government, and as the caliphate began to weaken, some provinces became practically autonomous or pledged nominal allegiance to the caliph. The revenues that were collected from the provinces were spent first to meet the needs of the province, and then any surplus was sent over to the central authority.

The system of government adopted some Sasanid and Byzantine administrative structures. The *dīwan* system was among the first to be adopted. The *dīwāns* were administrative departments with specialized tasks for facilitating government business and transactions. Their functions covered the collection of revenues and taxes and the distribution of financial benefits. They evolved from a main *dīwān* for the revenues during the reign of 'Umar to many other *dīwāns* for the military, correspondences, records and archives, postal service, grievances, and the police during the Umayyad and Abbasid dynasties. To manage the vast Islamic state, the central *dīwāns* had branches in the various provinces of the empire.

The *wizāra*, or ministry, was the second most important structure after the caliphate. The term "vizier" (*wazīr*) was mentioned in the Qur'an to mean supporter or assistant. The Arabs considered Abu Bakr as Prophet Muhammad's *wazīr*. As an institution, however, the position of the minister became important during the Abbasid caliphate. Gradually, some *wazīrs* assumed extensive powers as they took charge of the administrative structures, the *dīwāns*, and even the army. In some cases, the position became hereditary and was monopolized by certain families. The early political writings focused on the *wizāra*, its different types, the qualities and functions of the *wazīr*, and efficient administration. To keep up with the actual developments of the position, Mawardi and others classified the ministry into execution and delegation. The functions of the former were mainly to carry out the directives of the caliph, while the minister of delegation exercised almost similar executive and administrative authorities as the caliph, except for designating a successor, resigning without the consent of the caliph, or deposing the caliph. The power and authority of the *wazīr* vis-à-vis the caliph fluctuated depending on the qualifications and skills of either. Some *wazīrs* became more influential than the caliphs and exercised full control over the government.

Additional institutions of significance for the management of the state affairs included the *ḥājib* (court chamberlain) and the *kātib* (scribe, secretary, or counselor). All of these institutions, including that of the caliphate, were historical and administrative institutions for government that had no stipulations in the fundamental texts. They were adopted out of the need for expediency in order to govern and administer the rapidly growing Muslim state. The caliphate, however, acquired a symbolic significance. It was the product of the consensus of the early Muslim community and was a uniquely Islamic institution. The caliphate represented for centuries the symbolic unity of the vast Muslim *umma* and combined both religious and political functions, which made the position more in tune with the Islamic frameworks and set it apart from the modern positions and titles of heads of state.

Modern Formulations of Government

The early jurists addressed the issues that concerned their time and circumstances. They concentrated on the functions of the government and on the fulfillment of specific functions that were necessary for considering a government legitimate, even if it committed

injustice. These formulations preserved the continuation of the institutions of Islamic government for centuries. In retrospect, several elements were clearly absent in the classical formulations of government: the mechanism for exercising the principles of *shūrā* (consensus) or *ḥisba* (enjoining good and forbidding evil), the mechanisms necessary to rectify the government when it abuses its authority or deviates from the fundamental principles of Islam, and the practical role of the members of the *umma* in the political process. All of these issues became significant in the modern formulations of government.

Rida raised these concerns. He attributed the gradual disintegration of the system of government in Islam to the practice of hereditary rule, the failure of Muslims to devise a system of accountability to obligate the government to work for the welfare of the community and in accordance with the principles of Islam, and the ability of despots to undermine the control of *ahl al-ḥall wa-l-ʿaqd*. He also lamented the deterioration of the qualifications of the caliphs—namely, knowledge, moral probity, and *shūrā*—that led to the weakness of both the state and the Muslim *umma*.

The formulations of the modern theory of government were influenced to a large extent by classical theory, modern Western political theory, and developments in Muslim societies. The collapse of the Ottoman caliphate in 1924 caused vigorous debate among Muslim thinkers. Secularist intellectuals, like the Egyptian ʿAli ʿAbd al-Raziq and the Kemalists in Turkey, denied that government and political authority were an integral part of Islam. Abd al-Raziq maintained that the essence of the Prophet's message was religious and spiritual and that Islam, understood properly, never intended to establish a state and a political authority. Therefore, the restoration of the caliphate or the establishment of an Islamic government was neither necessary nor a religious obligation. Abd al-Raziq's views stirred up heated debates. Scores of books on the caliphate and government in Islam were produced during the 1920s and 1930s to refute his ideas.

A few political writings on government followed the classical theory and continued to focus on the head of the state, his qualifications, and his functions. They discussed the requirement of the Qurashi descent as a condition for the imamate or gave the head of the state the same idealized status and extraordinary powers. Certain intellectuals and parties proposed modern Islamic constitutions that gave the head of the Islamic state and the executive extraordinary powers at the expense of the *umma* and the modern principles of an accountable and representative government.

Several Muslim reformers, on the other hand, tried to reconstruct a modern theoretical basis for government in Islam. The modern reformulations often concentrated on the sovereignty of the people and the assertion that the people were the source of the government's authority. They also focused on restricting the power of the government either by the constitutional checks of the shariʿa or by the people. They revisited the classical Islamic principles of government and early political theory through the prism of the modern Western structures of government (the executive, legislative, and judiciary) and deduced "Islamic stands" on the separation of powers and the system of checks and balances. Many modern thinkers stressed the civic nature of the government and authority (in response to Western criticisms and to a fresh reading of the principles) and advocated term limits for the ruler. In their view, the Islamic government rested on three main constitutional principles: *shūrā*, accountability of the rulers, and the general will of the people (expressed in the *bayʿa*) as the source of authority. They reinterpreted the Qur'anic verse "Obey Allah, obey the Messenger, and those in authority from among you" as *ahl al-ḥall wa-l-ʿaqd*, who derive their authority from the *umma* and act as its representatives. They referred to the hadith "my community does not concur on error" and to the concept of consensus to reassert the authority—and, for some, the sovereignty—of the people. The reformist intellectuals expanded the principles of government to include, in addition to justice, equality, and *shūrā*, such principles as freedom, the accountability of the ruler, and the monitoring right of the *umma*. In most cases, they remained vague on the specifics and instruments of a modern Islamic government.

Rida attempted to synthesize the Islamic and modern principles of government. He described the Islamic government as the government of the caliphate and at the same time a civic government. In this government, the authority lies in the hands of the *umma*, the management of the state affairs is conducted by consultation, and the ruler assumes power through election or the *bayʿa* of the representatives of the *umma*. Acknowledging the difficulty of restoring the traditional type of government, Rida accepted "the caliphate of necessity" as a temporary phase that, after serious preparations, would eventually lead to the establishment of a legitimate caliphate. In this temporary caliphate, the caliph would not assume actual responsibilities but would act as a symbolic figure and represent some sort of a religious legitimacy for an assembly of local Muslim governments.

Writing during the collapse of the caliphate and almost at the same time as Abd al-Raziq, the Egyptian legalist ʿAbd al-Razzaq al-Sanhuri (1895–1971) considered the restoration of a proper Islamic government necessary to the unity of Muslims and the preservation of the law. He proposed a systematic and practical framework for a modern government in Islam. Sanhuri drew on the standard sources of Islam (Qur'an, sunna, and *ijmāʿ* of the members of early the community) to formulate a constitutional theory of government. He considered *ijmāʿ* as the basis of a parliamentary and representative system in Islam. Sanhuri listed several fundamental principles for the Islamic government that included popular sovereignty, the necessity of the *shūrā*, and the accountability of the rulers. For him, the democratic republican system was the closest to the Islamic type of government. He considered the abuse of power as an act of *fisq* (transgression) that led to the removal of the ruler. He also viewed foreign domination and influence as signs that the leader must end his *wilāya* (authority) and remove himself from power. The true Islamic government for Sanhuri performed three main functions: it combined religious and temporal authorities, defended the unity of the Muslim people, and adhered to the shariʿa. Sanhuri advocated the establishment of a league of Muslim governments to replace

the abolished caliphate until the Muslims were able to establish a rightful and proper one.

The Algerian Muslim reformer ʻAbd al-Hamid b. Badis (1889–1940) welcomed the collapse of the Ottoman caliphate, which for him had deviated from the true Islamic principles of government. He used the accession speech of Abu Bakr and reformulated a modernist perspective of government. Written in 1938, these principles emphasized the consensual nature of government, equality before the law, the shared responsibility of state and society, the accountability of the government, conditional obedience and loyalty, and public participation in policy making. While considering these principles as intrinsic to Islam, Ibn Badis recognized the West for enabling contemporary Muslims to reformulate these principles and read them along modern perspectives.

In his formulations of the government in Islam, the influential Pakistani Muslim thinker Mawdudi emphasized the concept of *ḥākimiyya* as the main criterion for the legitimacy of an Islamic government. For him, society and state should be subordinate to the authority of Islamic law as revealed in the Qur'an and the sunna of the Prophet. If a government discarded the revealed laws, it became illegitimate, and its authority ceased to be binding. He defined the proper Islamic government as a "theo-democracy" or a "democratic caliphate," which was based on the sovereignty of God and the vicegerency of men (i.e., man as God's caliph). This government conducts the affairs of its citizens on the basis of consultation. Many criticize Mawdudi for his adoption of contradictory terms inspired by a particular Western political experience—namely, theocracy and democracy. But his formulation demonstrates the reformers' struggle to synthesize modern and Islamic principles.

Ayatollah Khomeini (1902–89) is credited with infusing the doctrine of *wilāyat al-faqīh*, or the guardianship of the jurist, into modern Islamic government in Iran. In a series of lectures delivered in Najaf in 1969, under the title of "The Guardianship of the Jurists: The Islamic Government," Khomeini presented the main tenets of his thoughts on government. According to him, Islam necessitated the establishment of a government to uphold the principles and laws of the shariʻa and implement its injunctions. In this government, the jurists should play a major role as the most knowledgeable about Islamic law and as representatives of the imam. Since the *faqīh* is the source of emulation and represents the imam in religious matters, he can assume his "worldly authority" and preside over an Islamic government. Following the success of the revolution in Iran, the 1979 Constitution of the Islamic Republic carved a prominent role for the *faqīh* and entrusted Khomeini with overseeing the general policies of the republic. The new constitution adopted the modern structures of government and the system of checks and balances, but it also ensured the control of religious authorities over political processes.

The contemporary Iranian Islamic scholar Abdolkarim Soroush (b. 1945) has written against this tendency to "ideologize" religion. Such views have put him in disfavor with the Iranian government. Soroush is critical of the monopoly of the clergy over the interpretation of religious texts and the institutions of government. He stands against an a priori right of rule and the imposition of the government's will on the people. While the government may draw on religious values, it should be based on rational methods and the recognition of pluralism in society and the freedom of the individual.

The prominent Sudanese Islamic thinker and politician Hasan al-Turabi (b. 1932) bases his views on government on both the doctrine of *tawḥīd* (monotheism) and the consent of the people. This makes the government accountable to the higher authority of the shariʻa in the first place. However, the government for Turabi is not an absolute or sovereign entity because it is subjected to the constitutional checks of the shariʻa and to popular consent. It is a form of a representative democracy. Though the Islamic government is a government of the shariʻa, it is in a substantial sense a popular government since the shariʻa represents the dominant value system of the people. Turabi advocates limited government. He considers the *umma* the primary institution in the state and claims that not every aspect of Islam is entrusted to the government to enforce.

In his book *Public Freedoms in the Islamic State*, Rachid al-Gannouchi (b. 1941) elaborates on the specific structures and the institutions of the Islamic government. He acknowledges that several political concepts in Islam, such as *shūrā* and political parties, have not been turned successfully into stable institutions for administering differences in society. The West, by contrast, established various mechanisms for popular representation and controlled government. This realization affects Gannouchi's perception of the Islamic government as he attempts to devise a systematic and institutionalized design. Gannouchi underscores the centrality of the human being as the basis of government and highlights the concept of freedom. He considers political authority necessary to achieve justice and uphold religion. The nature of this authority is civic, however, not divine; its source of authority is not God but the people. The *shūrā*, which represents for Gannouchi the real empowerment of the members of society, can take place at various levels: a direct form (referendum and public elections), through parliamentary representation, and through councils of scholars and experts specialized in their fields.

With regard to the modern institutions, form, or specifics of government, modern Muslim intellectuals tend to adopt an instrumentalist approach that allows for the emulation of modern Western political institutions while preserving the fundamental Islamic principles of government. They justify this position on the basis of necessity and historical precedent. In their view, the efficient running of government requires the adoption of modern institutions that the West had already developed, such as constitutions, parliaments, separate structures for government, political parties, and a free press. This requirement makes the adoption of these institutions an obligation (*mā lā yatimm al-wājib illā bihi fa-huwa wājib*). They also argue that historically the early Muslims did not shy away from adopting Sasanid and Byzantine institutions of government to manage the affairs of the Muslim state. Therefore, the adoption of modern political institutions is beneficial to Muslims as long as they do not infringe on the general principles of the shariʻa. Hasan al-Banna,

the founder of the Egyptian Muslim Brotherhood, accepted the parliamentary/constitutional form of government as the closest to an Islamic system, which stands on the accountability of the ruler, the unity of the *umma*, and the respect of its will.

Government as a concept, a set of principles, and a structure is an evolving notion within modern Islamic political thought. Contemporary Muslim intellectuals struggle to devise a coherent and systematic modern theory of Islamic government, a modern and at the same time indigenous framework of government that enjoys wide acceptance.

See also ʻAbduh, Muhammad (1849–1905); authority; al-Banna, Hasan (1906–49); caliph, caliphate; consensus; consultation; democracy; guardianship of the jurist; imamate; leadership; Mawardi (974–1058); Mawdudi, Abu al-Aʻla (1903–79); obedience; parliament; public interest; Rida, Muhammad Rashid (1865–1935); Rightly Guided Caliphate (632–61); shariʻa; Shiʻism; sovereignty; succession; sultan; Sunnism; taxation; al-Turabi, Hasan (b. 1932); usurper

Further Reading

Charles Butterworth, "State and Authority in Arabic Political Thought," in *The Foundations of the Arab State*, edited by Ghassan Salame, 1987; Patricia Crone, *God's Rule: Government and Islam*, 2004; Rashid al-Ghannoushi, *Al-Huriyat al-Amma fi al-Dawala al-Islamiya*, 1993; Ruhollah Khomeini, *Islam and Revolution*, translated by Hamid Algar, 1981; Ann K. S. Lambton, *State and Government in Medieval Islam: An Introduction to the Study of Islamic Political Theory: The Jurists*, 1981; Bernard Lewis, *The Political Language of Islam*, 1988; Idem, *Political Words and Ideas in Islam*, 2008; Ali b. Muhammad al-Mawardi, *The Ordinances of Government*, translated by Wafaa H. Wahba, 2006; Muhammad Rashid Rida, *Al-Khilafa aw al-Imama al-ʻUzma*, 1922; Abd al-Razzaq al-Sanhuri, *Fiqh al-Khilafa wa-Tatawwuruha li-Tasbah ʻUsbat Umam Sharqiyya*, 1993; Hasan al-Turabi, *Al-Siyasa wa-l-Hukm: Al-Nuzum al-Sultaniyya Bayna al-Usul wa-Sunan al-Waqiʻ*, 2003.

EMAD EL-DIN SHAHIN

grievance

A grievance is a wrong or hardship, real or supposed, that is considered legitimate grounds for complaint or dispute, possibly expressed through formal legal action by the state or one of its citizens. In Islamic traditions, this concept generally has been rendered by the Arabic noun *maẓlima* (pl. *maẓālim*), meaning an unjust or oppressive action. In early Islamic history, *dīwān al-maẓālim* (board of grievances) came to denote a court through which governing authorities took direct responsibility for the dispensation of justice; it was an extrajudicial tribunal that accepted claims on behalf of the caliph, presumably for the purpose of correcting wrongs committed by state officials. More generally, however, grievance corresponds with the term *daʻwā* (claim, lawsuit), which signifies the action by which a person claims his right against another person and which may be submitted to an official court of Islamic law, to a board of grievances, or through the institution that inspects markets and monitors public morality (*ḥisba*).

According to Islamic law, anyone who is sane and rational can bring a lawsuit against another in four types of cases. The first of these is a claim for the application of the law of retaliation equivalent to an offense (*qiṣāṣ*) or the payment of compensation (*diyya*) by a victim or his kin. The second is a case of prosecution for offenses sanctioned by criminal penalties (*ḥudūd*) when brought in the exclusive or partial interest of a victim, such as for theft or fornication (*zinā*). The third category includes official criminal prosecutions in which the victim intervenes as plaintiff, as well as in every case of the exercise of *ḥisba*. Finally, the fourth includes actions brought in accordance with the extraordinary procedure of the *maẓālim* court.

Islamic law distinguishes between individual and collective rights, the latter arising from legal acts and instruments involving a class of persons, not an individual or a number of specific persons. A collective suit may be brought by any person or persons, since the claimant or plaintiff represents the class of beneficiaries or community at large. This is known as *daʻwa al-ḥisba*, and it is related to the position of the *muḥtasib* (market inspector and censor of morals). Historically, in matters of public interest, the judge (qadi) and the *muḥtasib* fulfilled some of the functions associated in modern law with public prosecution.

To be sound, a suit must be issued from a concerned party who is consistent in his or her claims; these must specify the characteristics and location of the matter or object under dispute and the identity of the parties involved. In dealing with any valid, sound suit, the judge must first determine who the plaintiff is in order to apply the correct evidential procedure; burden of proof falls on the plaintiff, and the defendant's innocence is presumed. The method of establishing legal proof is oral, in the form of acknowledgment or confession, oath, legal presumptions, and testimony, which is the quintessential proof. Writing is a valid mode of proof only insofar as it is orally confirmed by a duly qualified witness.

Once proof has been established according to the dictates of law and it is in conformity with the facts alleged, it binds the judge, regardless of his own inner conviction. Advocacy was rejected in theory and discouraged in historical practice; the task of legal specialists (*fuqahā*, muftis) is to aid the judge, providing him with scholarly council, although voluntary resort to a learned arbitrator (*ḥakam*) may initially be chosen by the plaintiff in lieu of a trial. The trial terminates with the judge's verdict, which is not subject to appeal before a superior jurisdiction. Once pronounced, a judgment cannot be changed by the same judge, and another judge can only repeal it if there was an egregious fault in the law. However, the suit may be determined anew before another judge, and in periods or areas where there exists an organized procedure of *maẓālim*, any person who feels he or she is a victim of public services may demand redress by petitioning the sovereign authority.

Scholars agree that the *maẓālim* court was theoretically sanctioned by Islamic law but that in reality it sometimes represented the rulers' absolutist governance and interference in the shari'a. Debate exists, however, as to the exact nature and extent of this jurisdiction in Islamic history. Earlier works assert the wide scope of *maẓālim* justice and its "secular" characteristics, while recent revisionist scholarship claims its limited and sporadic jurisdiction, the predominance of shari'a courts, and the essentially supplemental and overlapping role of the *maẓālim*.

The institution of *ḥisba* is explicitly characterized in juristic sources as supplementing the jurisdiction of the judge's court, sanctioning intervention without complaint for violations of the shari'a based on obvious and incontestable facts. On the one hand, it represents the individual duty of "commanding right and forbidding wrong," which is incumbent upon all Muslims. On the other hand, the majority of scholars simultaneously classify it as a collective duty, with a state-sanctioned officer assuming control over admonition by force; the *muḥtasib* supervised public moral behavior, particularly with respect to the markets.

Since the 19th-century legal reforms of the Ottoman Empire, the system of bringing a lawsuit has undergone far-reaching changes. The intrinsic probative value of writing was recognized, the principle of *res judicata* accepted, and procedure in default of appearance was introduced, along with representation by lawyers. These innovations ran parallel to the emergence of the nation-state and the modernization of judicial systems in accordance with European models of law. This resulted in the radical transformation or disappearance of shari'a courts, *maẓālim* courts, and *ḥisba* in most Muslim countries, with a few exceptions, such as the Kingdom of Saudi Arabia. The controversy over the jurisdictional relationship between *maẓālim* and shari'a is reflected in the disagreement over the nature of modernization, either as an expression of the evolution of an ever-present "secular" jurisdiction or as drastically uncharacteristic of Islamic law.

See also governance; justice; punishment; shari'a

Further Reading

Wael B. Hallaq, *Origins and Evolution of Islamic Law*, 2005; Idem, *Sharī'a: Theory, Practice, Transformations*, 2009; Jørgen S. Nielsen, *Secular Justice in an Islamic State: Maẓālim under the Baḥrī Mamlūks*, 1985; Émile Tyan, *Histoire de l'organisation judiciare en pays d'Islam*, 1960.

GREGORY MACK

guardianship of the jurist

The Twelver Shi'i legal doctrine known as "the guardianship of the jurist" (*wilāyat al-faqīh*; in Persian, *vilāyat-i faqīh*) is best known from the works of Ayatollah Khomeini (1902–89), who formulated his views on the topic around 1970. The doctrine is relatively recent and seems to date to no earlier than the writings of Mulla Ahmad al-Naraqi (d. 1829). One may view the guardianship of the jurist as the culmination of a trend to concentrate the prerogatives of the imam in the hands of jurists as a group, and the leading jurist in particular, that began in the 10th century and proceeded by stages until the 20th century.

Wilāya refers to the authority of a religious leader or official, and the term has been used to describe the religious authority of the Prophet Muhammad. Shi'i Muslims rallied around the argument that the Prophet's *wilāya* devolved on their imams, who were the Prophet's descendants. According to the Twelver, or Imami, Shi'is, the first imam was 'Ali b. Abi Talib (d. 661), the Prophet's paternal first cousin and then son-in-law. The Twelfth Imam, Muhammad al-Mahdi, born around 870 and a direct descendant of 'Ali through his son Husayn, is believed to have gone into concealment in the year 873 or 874 upon God's instruction. This Hidden Imam's return will occur prior to the end of time, but until then, his incognito existence apparently deprives the faithful of the only figure entitled to legitimate rule. Since *wilāya* is such a critical prerogative, and since it was believed to reside in the imams, the occultation (*ghayba*) of the Twelfth Imam created a crisis of religious authority: the question was whether that authority had devolved, or could devolve, on others. Eventually, by the 16th century at the latest, the Twelver jurists concluded that a relative form of it had devolved on them collectively as the "general representatives" of the imams.

The concept of the guardianship of the jurist is to a large degree implicit in Naraqi's writings. The expression appears explicitly, however, in the writings of two of his illustrious successors, Muhammad Hasan al-Najafi (d. 1849) and especially Murtada al-Ansari (d. 1864). However, Ansari's doctrine of *wilāyat al-faqīh* was firmly ensconced within the tradition that interpreted the authority that the jurists could exercise in the name of the imams to lie within the narrow compass of relative (*i'tibārī*) *wilāya*. In other words, their authority was limited to taking over a limited number of the prerogatives of the imam, a small subset of the whole. This *wilāya* of the jurists, Ansari stressed, was limited to the authority to make decisions on behalf of persons who, for various reasons, were either incapable of making their own decisions or incompetent to do so. Among those who fell under this category were widows, orphans, the mentally infirm, children, and the like.

In a series of lectures given in Najaf, Iraq, in January 1970, Khomeini altered the scope of the jurists' *wilāya* by expanding it to include political rule—indeed, nearly all the general functions of the imam. This was a drastic change from the classical understanding of the concept, though Khomeini did not present it as such, instead claiming that it was a widely held view. It is not surprising that most Twelver jurists rejected his interpretation. He sanctioned the idea that a single jurist, rather than the collectivity of the jurists, might be identified who could exercise this greatly broadened understanding of the concept, being careful to try to

vindicate this expanded version by seeking scriptural justifications for it. Khomeini's role in the Iranian Revolution of 1978–79 and its aftermath was so critical that his interpretation of the doctrine became the official line of the Islamic Republic of Iran, established in 1979. His sobriquet of *walī al-faqīh*—the supreme jurist—indicated that indeed it was he who would exercise political rule.

Shortly before his death in June 1989, Khomeini again broadened the conceptualization of this doctrine in a fatwa (legal opinion) that he issued in early January 1988 that made the *wilāya* of the jurist absolute. It now became *wilāyat al-faqīh al-muṭlaqa*. He argued that not only did the top jurist have the right to exercise political rule but he also had the power to suspend some of the secondary ordinances of the faith if he believed that such suspension was essential to rescue "Islam" from destruction. Among the secondary ordinances that he specifically mentioned were ritual prayer and the hajj (annual pilgrimage to Mecca). He apparently saw fit to elevate the already robust version of the doctrine to this even more categorical form because he believed that the Islamic Republic of Iran was the true warden of Islam and that enemies were conspiring to bring about its collapse, which would be tantamount to the collapse of Islam itself.

Khomeini's interpretations of 1970 and 1988 remained heterodox in the world of Shi'i Islam. However, his interpretations have become part of the discourse of high-ranking Shi'i legal authorities and cannot easily be dismissed. Yet it seems unlikely that his view of *wilāyat al-faqīh* will triumph altogether. Withal, Khomeini's death in 1989 left no one of his stature to champion the doctrine; the next *faqīh* (jurist) and "leader" (*rahbar*) of the Islamic Republic, 'Ali Khamene'i, was considered, by most top-ranking Shi'i clerics in Iraq, Lebanon, and even in Iran itself, too inferior to inherit Khomeini's mantle. Under such circumstances, most observers feel that the majority of Twelver jurists will revert to the pre-1970 interpretation of Ansari, especially if the Islamic Republic of Iran continues to experience normalization of relations with the outside world.

See also Iran; Khomeini, Ayatollah (1902–89); Shi'ism

Further Reading

Shahrough Akhavi, "Contending Discourses in Shi'ite Law on the Doctrine of *Wilayat al-Faqih*," *Iranian Studies* 29, nos. 3–4 (1996); Norman Calder, "Accommodation and Revolution in Imami Shi'i Jurisprudence: Khomeini and the Classical Tradition," *Middle Eastern Studies* 18, no. 1 (1982); Ruhollah Khomeini, *Ḥukūmat-i Islāmī* [*Islamic Government*], translated by Hamid Algar, 1981; Hossein Modarressi, "The Just Ruler or the Guardian Jurist: An Attempt to Link Two Different Shi'ite Concepts," *Journal of the American Oriental Society* 111, no. 3 (1991); Abdulaziz Abdulhossein Sachedina, *The Just Ruler in Shi'ite Islam: The Comprehensive Authority of the Jurist in Imamite Jurisprudence*, 1988.

SHAHROUGH AKHAVI

guilds

Guilds were so widespread in premodern Islamic societies that most of the urban population, including women who were connected to these informally, belonged to at least one. Although crafts and craftspeople existed during the late classical period of Islam, guilds (*ṭā'ifa*) began to appear as professionally organized and socially identifiable groups in the 16th century in the Ottoman lands and its Arab provinces. There were structural, ceremonial, and ritualistic continuities between the guilds that appeared during this time and the 13th and 14th century trade guilds known as Akhis of Anatolia. For example, the *futuwwa* literature (*javānmardī* in Persian, meaning a code of conduct for the members of a guild) of the Akhis was widely translated and incorporated into the guild systems and employed as a constitution for these guilds. The *futuwwa*'s moral code demanded from the members of the professional group the virtuous characteristics of a perfect youth (*fatā*). The virtues consisted of honor, courage, generosity, and loyal brotherhood. The Sufi influence and association of Akhis is widely known. They borrowed the hierarchical structure of the Sufi orders and brotherhoods, called their meeting places *zāwiya* (usually a gathering place of Sufi members of an order), and had initiation practices akin to those of Sufis, going back to the initiation of the Abbasid caliph Nasir (d. 1225) by the famous Sufi master Shaykh Abu Hafs 'Umar al-Suhrawardi (d. 1234). Furthermore, the strong cult of 'Ali b. Abi Talib, whom *futuwwa* literature presents as the artisans' patron saint, suggests Shi'i influence that bypassed the Sunni-Shi'i divide. These practices, hierarchies, and moral codes remained central to the institutional structure of the guilds down to the 20th century. The membership of these guilds generally cut across religious and ethnic boundaries: in Syria, for example, Jewish, Christian, and Muslim artisans and craftsmen worked alongside one another and held important positions in the guild hierarchy. However, the ceremonial rites were conducted according to the religious beliefs of the apprentices involved. From the beginning, guilds had a complex relationship with the ruling authorities. In his failed attempts to consolidate and restore the Abbasid power in the 13th century, Nasir, for example, conjoined urban guilds with Sufism, introducing organizational hierarchies and ritual practices that mirrored those of Sufi orders. Also, where close to the seat of the empire, guilds' hierarchical structure ensured more direct influence and control by the state. For example, through price regulation, court officials, and judges Ottoman rulers, employed their services for its ongoing military campaigns. In distant provinces, the state's control was relatively minimal and insignificant, allowing guilds to exercise great social and political influence. Overall, the guilds' economic activity reflected a careful accommodation of the demands imposed by the state, the interests of the guild masters, and the interests of their customers. Guild members showed ambivalence toward the state: they needed the state's help to resolve internal disputes but

also resisted state intervention in their affairs. In the early modern period, changing market circumstances such as the appearance of local industries, mass migration of nonskilled villagers to urban centers, and pressures of the capitalist European economy led to the marginalization of the guilds, forcing them to adopt stricter measures to ensure their survival, such as seeking legal and hereditary rights to exercise a craft. Sometimes their marginalization led to public riots (e.g., 1850 in Aleppo and 1860 in Damascus) and revolts within the guild's hierarchy due to decreases in wages or loss of jobs. Merchants and guildsmen also played an active role in the 1906 Iranian Constitutional Revolution. Though they have not disappeared entirely, guilds diminished in numbers and in sociopolitical significance during the 20th century.

See also Sufism; trade and commerce

Further Reading

Gabriel Baer, *Fellah and Townsman in the Middle East*, 1982; Suraiya Faroqhi, *Artisans of Empire: Crafts and Craftspeople under the Ottomans*, 2009; Willem M. Floor, *Guilds, Merchants, & Ulama in Nineteenth-Century Iran*, 2009.

SYED RIZWAN ZAMIR

H

hadith

A hadith (pl. *aḥādīth*) is a report of the words and deeds of the Prophet Muhammad. These reports include commands or legal edicts given by the Prophet, descriptions of his behavior, actions that took place in his presence and of which he implicitly approved, and his predictions of future events. Hadiths have served as the main sources for Muslim scholars studying the teachings and precedent (sunna) of the Prophet. As such, hadiths have been central to understanding the message of the Qur'an and providing Muslims with supplemental material on the legal, dogmatic, ethical, and political issues dealt with in Islamic thought but not found explicitly in the Qur'an.

Each hadith consists of two components: the *matn* and the *isnād*. The *matn* is the text of the report (e.g., the Prophet said, "Deeds are judged by their intentions"), and the *isnād* is the chain of transmitters who narrated the report from the Prophet to the scholar who wrote the hadith in a book or transmitted it to others (e.g., "Malik reported from Nafi', who reported from Ibn 'Umar, that the Prophet said . . .").

The Sunni Hadith Tradition

During the lifetime of the Prophet, his followers (known as Companions) preserved his teachings either by recounting orally what they had heard him say or by recording their observations in primitive notebooks composed of papyrus, parchment, or even more basic materials. An early private collection like this was known as a *ṣaḥīfa*.

There was a great deal of debate during the Prophet's life and after his death over whether it was appropriate to preserve his words in writing, with some Muslims insisting that he had forbidden the recording of any words except the Qur'an and others stating that he had permitted his followers to record his teachings and even ordered the compilation of his rulings on taxation issues. This debate reflects a tension in the Islamic intellectual tradition, which values highly the oral transmission of knowledge, encourages the reading aloud of a written text, and is suspicious of reading books privately without having their contents explained by one's teacher. This focus on orality was due partly to the primitive nature of the Arabic alphabet and the real possibility for misreading a written text, as well as to the importance of oral recitation in Islamic religious culture.

Under the Umayyad dynasty, leading Muslim scholars like Ibn Shihab al-Zuhri (d. 742) compiled collections of hadiths on specific topics, with the state encouraging the collection of *ṣaḥīfa*s into more comprehensive forms on issues such as taxation and administrative law. Soon, senior scholars like Malik b. Anas (d. 795) in Medina collected hadiths from the Prophet, the rulings of Companions, and the opinions of other early scholars into topically organized books of law known as *muṣannaf*s, the most famous of which is Malik's *The Well-Trodden Path* (*al-Muwatta'*).

Within a few decades of the compilation of *muṣannaf*s, Sunni scholars limiting their collections to hadiths from the Prophet instead of a variety of reports from later scholars organized their material according to *isnād*s—that is, they ordered them according to the Companion who narrated the hadith from the Prophet. Such works were called *musnad*s, the most famous of which is the *Musnad* of Ibn Hanbal (d. 855). The organization of such works allowed hadith scholars to engage in criticism of the authenticity of hadiths more easily. By this time, inexpensive paper had replaced rare papyrus in the Middle East, and scholars could afford to record many different transmissions of the same hadith in a *musnad*.

*Musnad*s were limited to hadiths from the Prophet, but they were difficult to use as reference works. Soon scholars began producing books known as *sunan*, which were organized like *muṣannaf*s but included only reports from the Prophet. Five *sunan* works in particular became widely read: those of Bukhari (d. 870), Muslim (d. 875), Abu Dawud (d. 889), Nasa'i (d. 915), and Tirmidhi (d. 892). By the mid-11th century, these hadith collections had become the heart of the Sunni hadith corpus. Although the last three included some hadiths that Muslims considered unreliable, these five books were taken as an acceptable representation of the body of hadiths commonly used by Sunnis. Some scholars included the *Sunan* of Ibn Majah (d. 887) as well, and together this canon became known as the "Six Books." Bukhari's and Muslim's works were specifically limited to hadiths that the two authors felt were the authentic sayings of Muhammad and are thus called the "Two Authentic Collections" (*al-Sahihayn*). They are the most revered books in Sunni Islam after the Qur'an.

Muslim Hadith Criticism

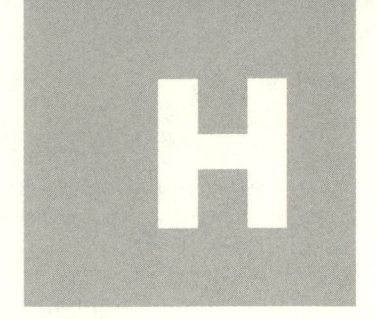

The religious and political authority of the Prophet was peerless in the community he founded. This meant that even within Muhammad's lifetime, people abused his authority by misquoting or misrepresenting his words for their own purposes. The widespread forgery of hadiths emerged in the decades after the Prophet's death

as a major challenge to Muslim scholars seeking to understand Muhammad's authentic legacy. The major engines for the forgery of hadiths were as follows.

The production of political propaganda. During the Sunni and Shi'i split, supporters of the Umayyads circulated hadiths equating Mu'awiya with a prophetic figure, while supporters of 'Ali circulated hadiths such as "If you see Mu'awiya mount my pulpit, then kill him." One hadith forged during the Abbasid revolution (749–50) relates that 'Abbas's descendants would be as numerous as the Pleiades and would rule the world. Fewer hadiths were forged in later political contests.

Theological and legal debates. Proponents of Sunnism, for example, forged hadiths supporting predestinarian beliefs, while Muslim rationalists forged hadiths advocating free will and the ultimate authority of reason.

Pietistic concerns. Pietistic concerns led Muslim preachers of all varieties to forge hadiths predicting the imminent end of the world and the Day of Judgment or providing graphic descriptions of the punishments inflicted on sinners in hell and the ample rewards provided to the righteous in paradise.

Chauvinisms. Chauvinisms such as racism, local pride, or partisanship prompted the forgery of hadiths characterizing black Africans as lascivious, Turks as warlike, or certain cities as particularly pleasing to God.

In an attempt to distinguish between authentic and forged hadiths, Sunni scholars of the eighth and ninth centuries developed a method of criticism based on three steps. First, any report attributed to the Prophet required a chain of transmission (*isnād*). Second, the individuals making up the *isnād* were examined to determine their accuracy in transmission, their character, and whether they realistically could have heard the hadith from their supposed source. Accuracy in transmission was determined by collecting all the hadiths transmitted by a person and checking for corroboration. Character examination centered primarily on determining whether a person was known to have lied or forged hadiths. Although many Sunni hadith critics sought to exclude transmitters belonging to other sects, non-Sunnis played an important role in transmitting the hadiths found in the canonical Six Books. Third, a transmission attributed to the Prophet was checked for corroboration against other reports.

This intense focus on the *isnād* as opposed to the contents of supposed hadiths was designed to prevent bias and personal opinion from influencing the preservation of the Prophet's sunna. In reality, however, if Sunni hadith critics came across reports whose contents they found suspicious or contrary to their worldview, they would assume that this error was due to a flawed *isnād* and reject the hadith.

Hadiths that had a reliable chain of transmission and were corroborated were considered "sound" (*ṣaḥīḥ*), while those that had minor flaws in the *isnād* but were nonetheless corroborated were deemed "fair" (*ḥasan*). Hadiths with unreliable *isnād*s and no corroboration were considered "weak" (*ḍa'īf*). Both *ṣaḥīḥ* and *ḥasan* hadiths were considered admissible as evidence in deriving Islamic law, with some Sunni scholars resorting to *ḍa'īf* hadiths as well when no other evidence was available.

In addition to these three categories established by Sunni hadith critics of the ninth century, later Sunni legal theorists of the 11th century also divided hadiths into *mutawātir* reports (those so massively transmitted that they could not possibly be forged) and *āḥād* reports (anything less than the level of *mutawātir*). Because these categories were so vague, however, Muslim scholars cannot agree on exactly which hadiths are in fact *mutawātir*. The term is thus regularly manipulated by scholars hoping to bolster hadiths useful to their legal or doctrinal arguments.

Western Academic Criticism of Hadiths

As a result of the serious problem of forgery, Muslim scholars from the early period of Islam onward adopted a critical stance toward hadiths. However, if there was no reason to doubt the reliability of a hadith, Muslim scholars treated it as a reliable saying of the Prophet. The default stance of Muslim scholars toward hadiths was not skepticism. More important, as believers in Muhammad's prophethood, Muslim scholars did not think it unusual for hadiths to predict future events or describe things that a typical person could not know.

Western scholars who began to evaluate the historical reliability of the hadith corpus in the 19th century did not share these assumptions. Because there are no surviving records of hadiths from the actual time of the Prophet, Western scholars reasoned that the hadith tradition was elaborated as part of the growth of Islam and not as its original foundation. Western scholars assumed as a matter of historical criticism that any report attributed to Muhammad that tells the future was naturally a later forgery concocted by Muslims involved in the events that the hadith describes. Moreover, Western scholars held that hadiths that seemed to uphold Sunni orthodoxy were almost certainly forged for that purpose. Scholars like William Muir (d. 1905) concluded that many hadiths that Muslims considered authentic were forged by Muslims to glorify the Prophet. Based on his study of the contents of hadiths, the Hungarian Ignaz Goldziher (d. 1921) introduced the theory that hadiths were generally forged by different Muslim groups to meet their needs as the Muslim community matured: the Umayyads forged hadiths supporting their rule, Shi'is forged hadiths glorifying 'Ali, and Sunni jurists forged hadiths to provide the raw material for elaborating Islamic law and dogma. The German scholar Joseph Schacht (d. 1969) and his disciples explored the *isnād*s of hadiths and concluded that many hadiths that appear in the canonical Sunni collections were originally the rulings of early Muslim scholars to which later Muslim scholars in the eighth and ninth centuries had added false *isnād*s leading all the way back to the Prophet so that these sayings would enjoy more authority. Some Western scholars have argued that no hadiths are reliable and that, in fact, the entire narrative of the Prophet's life and the early Muslim community was crafted a century later by Muslims eager to provide a stable basis for their faith.

Since the 1990s, some Western scholars have revaluated this radical skepticism, arguing that it would have been impossible for the decentralized and deeply divided Muslim community of the eighth and ninth centuries to weave a conspiracy in which the whole hadith tradition was concocted. In addition, many hadiths have so many chains of transmission from so many diverse regions and individuals that they must date back to at least the generation of the Prophet's Companions. Some scholars in the United States and Europe have set aside the study of the historical reliability of hadiths in the early Islamic period, a time when a scarcity of historical sources makes speculation inevitable, and instead study the role of hadiths in the expression of authority and the shaping of communal identity in later Islamic civilization.

The Imami Shi'i Hadith Tradition

Unlike Sunni Islam, Imami Shi'i Islam considers the religious and political authority of the Prophet to have been passed on through a line of 12 imams descended from him. As a result, Imami Shi'is defined hadiths as both reports transmitted from the Prophet, usually by the imams, and the reports of the imams themselves. The imams who served as both the most active transmitters of Prophetic hadiths and the largest source of "imam" hadiths are the sixth imam Ja'far al-Sadiq (d. 765) and his son Musa al-Kazim (d. 799). Students collected the teachings of the imams into notebooks called *uṣūl* (sing. *aṣl*).

At approximately the same time that Sunni Muslims were composing *muṣannaf*s in the late eighth century, Shi'i scholars began arranging the hadiths in these *uṣūl* into topical collection as well, known as *mubawwab*s. In the early tenth century, the Imami Shi'i community lost contact with the last of its imams, and its scholars produced comprehensive hadith references designed to provide all the information that pious Muslims needed to live according to the imams' teachings. Two of these books, the *Usul al-Kafi* (The sufficient foundations) of Muhammad al-Kulayni (d. 939) and *Man la Yahduruhu al-Faqih* (He who has no legal scholar at hand) of Ibn Babuya (d. 991), became the most famous Imami Shi'i hadith collections and the basis for the Imami Shi'i hadith canon. The later scholar Muhammad b. Hasan al-Tusi (d. 1067) wrote two works on hadiths as well: *Tahdhib al-Ahkam* (Refining the legal rulings) and *al-Istibsar fi ma Ikhtalaf min al-Akhbar* (Clarifying the differences in the prophetic traditions), which constituted the remaining two books of the four-book Imami Shi'i hadith canon.

Imami Shi'i hadith criticism strongly resembled the Sunni method of hadith criticism discussed previously. Imami Shi'is composed books of criticism identifying reliable narrators of hadiths who espoused the correct Shi'i beliefs. With the Imami Shi'i adoption of the rationalist (Mu'tazili) approach to legal theory and theology in the late tenth century, however, the criticism of the contents of hadiths became much more prominent in Imami Shi'ism than in Sunnism.

The hadith tradition of Zaydi (Fiver) Shi'ism closely resembles the Sunni tradition, with the exception of the Zaydis' rationalist leanings. Zaydis produced few of their own hadith collections, drawing instead on Sunni or Imami Shi'i hadiths that they considered appropriate and reliable.

The Role of Hadith in Sunni Political Thought

Hadiths have played two important roles in Islamic political history. First, as discussed previously, they have served as a major medium for propaganda. Second, as the Qur'an does not provide extensive discussions of ideal Islamic governance or the appropriate rulers of the Muslim community, important components of Islamic political thought have been drawn from the hadith corpus.

A core principle of Sunni political thought, the preeminence of the Prophet's tribe (the Quraysh) and the restriction of the caliphate to a member of that family, was derived from *ṣaḥīḥ* hadiths such as "This matter [of rule] will remain in the hands of the Quraysh as long as there are two people in this world."

The proper conduct of rulers and the relationship between ruler and ruled is also laid out in hadiths, which go beyond the Qur'anic injunction to "obey those in charge amongst you" (Q. 4:59). One *ṣaḥīḥ* hadith, which applies to husbands and fathers as well as to rulers, establishes the responsibility of authority: "Each of you is a shepherd, and each of you is responsible for his herd." Muslims are told in clear terms to obey their rulers and not to rebel regardless of unjust treatment or the ruler's impiety in *ṣaḥīḥ* hadiths such as "Whoever obeys me obeys God, and whoever disobeys me disobeys God, and whoever obeys the ruler [*amīr*] obeys me, and whoever disobeys the ruler disobeys me." Hadiths also place limitations on this submission, however: "Listen and obey in hardship and ease, in that which you are willing and unwilling, even if you are treated unfairly . . . do not contest those in power unless you see evident proof from God of their obvious disbelief [in Islam]," and "No obedience to the ruler in disobeying God." Such hadiths are the basis for the widely held Sunni tenet that rebellion is never justified unless the ruler renounces Islam or stops implementing the basic elements of Islamic rule, such as establishing the practice of daily prayer.

Other hadiths universally accepted by Sunni scholars affirm the collective infallibility of the Muslim community and the absolute necessity of solidarity: "God will never bring my community together on an error, so stay with the collective, for whoever strays from it strays into error."

The Qur'an states repeatedly that "fighting in God's path" is a righteous act and a duty expected of Muslims, but hadiths elaborate on the duties and rewards of jihad. "Indeed the gates of Paradise are beneath the shade of swords," states one *ṣaḥīḥ* hadith. Another clarifies that "fighting in God's path" is to struggle "so that the word of God might be supreme." Many hadiths testify to the rewards given a martyr in the afterlife, while others add that a martyr is not just one who dies in battle but also a Muslim who dies of disease, from drowning, in a fire, during a robbery, in a building collapse, or (in the case of women) in childbirth.

Hadiths also chart the general political trajectory of Muslim and world history: after the reign of the Prophet's four "Rightly Guided" successors (Abu Bakr, 'Umar, 'Uthman, and 'Ali), there will be a time of "intransigent kings." Hadiths tell that "there will not come upon you an age except that the age after it will be worse." As the world slides into moral entropy, "knowledge will be snatched up" and "holding on to one's faith will be like holding on to a hot coal." One famous hadith, however, assures Muslims that "there will remain a party from amongst my community, standing by the truth, not harmed by those who forsake them until the command of God comes"—a group that Sunnis have understood to be themselves. Finally, hadiths provide the only scriptural source for the coming of an Antichrist (*dajjāl*), who will be defeated by the combined forces of a messianic figure descended from the Prophet (*mahdī*) and the returned Jesus.

The Role of Hadiths in Shi'i Political Thought

Since the Qur'an makes no explicit mention of the centrality of 'Ali or Muhammad's descendents in the rule of the Muslim community, in Imami Shi'i political thought the hadiths of the Prophet and the imams have been essential as evidence. Imami Shi'i hadiths make it clear that 'Ali was both the foremost Companion and the chosen successor of Muhammad: "'Ali b. Abi Talib is the earliest to embrace Islam in my community, the most knowledgeable of them, the most correct in his religion, the most virtuous in his certainty, the most prudent, generous and brave of heart, and he is the imam and caliph after me." Other hadiths of Imam Ja'far clarify that the evident lack of mention of the Prophet's family in the Qur'an is not representative of the Prophet's teachings, for "hardly anything of the Qur'an was revealed without the Prophet explaining how it concerned the Family of the [Prophet's] House." Finally, hadiths from the Prophet and the imams specify each of the 12 imams as successors of one another and the impending occultation of the Hidden Imam and his eventual return as the messiah.

See also Muhammad (570–632) Shi'ism; Sunnism; theology

Further Reading

Shah 'Abd al-'Aziz, *The Gardens of Hadith Scholars*, translated by Aisha Bewley, 2007; Malik b. Anas, *Al-Muwatta of Imam Malik ibn Anas*, translated by Aisha Bewley, 1989; Jonathan Brown, *Hadith: Muhammad's Legacy in the Medieval and Modern World*, 2009; 'Abd al-Hadi al-Fadli and al-Shahid al-Thani, *Introduction to Hadīth, Including Dirāyat al-Hadīth*, 2002; William Graham, "Traditionalism in Islam: An Essay in Interpretation," *Journal of Interdisciplinary History* 23, no. 3 (1993); Ibn al-Salah, *An Introduction to the Science of Hadith*, translated by Eerik Dickinson, 2005; Scott Lucas, *Constructive Critics: Ḥadīth Literature and the Articulation of Sunnī Islam*, 2004; Al-Nawawi, *Forty Hadith*, translated by Ezzeddin Ibrahim and Denys Johnson-Davies, 1997; Andrew Newman, *The Formative Period of Twelver Shī'ism: Hadīth as Discourse between Qum and Baghdad*, 2000.

JONATHAN A. C. BROWN

Hakim bi-Amr Allah (985–1021)

Born in Cairo in 985, Hakim bi-Amr Allah ascended to the Fatimid caliphate at the age of 11 after the early death of his father in 996. He was then under the watchful supervision of Barjawan, a palace eunuch with unusual power and political skill. Soon enough, however, Hakim resolved to rid himself of his guardian by assassination and to rule alone. Thereafter, until the end of his reign, he governed his empire with an unusually resolute hand, acting both as caliph for a widely diverse population of Muslim and non-Muslim religious communities and as imam—the supreme authority—for the Isma'ilis, who were devoted to him with total and unreserved allegiance. His position therefore resembled a combination of king and pope. The Fatimids then governed a vast domain, comprising the vassal states of North Africa, Sicily, the Islamic holy cities of Mecca and Medina, Syria, plus Egypt and Palestine. In addition, missions (*da'was*) of his adherents reached clandestinely deep into the realm of the other Islamic lands. Significantly, the Fatimid state lost none of its territory or its status under him.

Nevertheless, in marked contrast to his father, who had become well known for tolerance and clemency, Hakim applied harsh and uncompromising policies that resulted in a large number of executions, particularly of members of the bureaucracy and the elite. Commencing about 1005, he issued a series of laws designed to closely regulate the habits, practices, and morals of the people in his domain. One edict ordered the public denouncing of those of the Prophet's Companions who had failed to support the direct succession of 'Ali b. Abi Talib. Others forbade the sale and consumption of foods such as *turmus* (lupine), *jirjir* (rocket, or arugula), scaleless fish, and *mulūkhiyya* (jute, whose leaves were used to make soup), as well as all kinds of intoxicating beverages, among them various beers, wine, and *zabīb* (raisin liquor). He likewise severely restricted the movements of women, eventually decreeing that shoemakers not produce footwear for them to ensure that they could not venture outside their homes. He also sought to control his Christian and Jewish subjects in an increasingly onerous fashion, commanding them to wear distinctive badges and clothing and to observe restrictions on interactions with Muslims and finally instituting a deliberate policy of destroying houses of worship, including, most notably, the destruction of the Church of the Holy Sepulcher in Jerusalem.

Of these measures, the denouncing of the Prophet's Companions lasted barely two years and was replaced by a decidedly tolerant policy. Consequently, the fomenting of religious strife, including speaking ill of those connected to the Prophet, became anathema. The other initiatives, however, not only persisted but were often strengthened, becoming more of a burden on the people. Yet after a decade, Hakim began to relent by granting Christians and Jews who wanted to leave his lands permission to do so. Near the end of his reign, he also permitted those who had converted to Islam as a response to his repressive policies to reclaim their original religions

and allowed the rebuilding of many of the churches and synagogues he had destroyed.

Despite his reputation for cruelty and repression and for an unpredictable and paradoxical style of rule, he remained uncommonly popular. Until the day of his disappearance in 1021, by that time having ruled for 25 years, he could ride through the streets and districts of the capital unaccompanied by an armed guard. His supporters boasted that he was courageous to appear regularly in public and that his seemingly untouchable, almost hallowed persona miraculously protected him from the harmful designs of his many enemies. A small group of especially fervent followers, who were later to be called the Druze, carried their enthusiasm for him further. They insisted that he was not really human but divine and that he was in fact an incarnation of God, come to instill in mankind a new and truer religion that superseded all others, including Islam.

See also Druze; Fatimids (909–1171); Isma'ilis

Further Reading

H. Halm, *Die Kalifen von Kairo: Die Fatimiden in Ägypten, 973–1074*, 2003; Paul E. Walker, *Caliph of Cairo: Al-Hakim bi-Amr Allah 996–1021*, 2009.

PAUL E. WALKER

Hamas

Hamas (zeal) is the acronym for Harakat al-Muqawama al-Islamiyya, the Palestinian Islamic Resistance Movement. Founded weeks after the start of the Intifada, the "uprising" of 1987–93, Hamas quickly emerged as the institutional and ideological anchor of *al-tayyār al-islāmī*, "the Islamic tendency," a phrase referring to all political movements bearing an Islamist orientation. The Intifada began as a spontaneous outbreak of protest and street violence following an incident occuring on December 6, 1987, in which an Israeli truck driver crashed into and killed four Palestinian laborers. Secular-nationalist political organizations quickly asserted control over the protests, issuing weekly leaflets in the name of the United National Command (UNC) of the Intifada. The goal of the UNC was to end Israel's 20-year-old military rule over the Gaza Strip, West Bank, East Jerusalem, and Golan Heights. Israel initiated its occupation, which entailed massive land expropriations and settlement building, following its defeat of Egyptian, Jordanian, and Syrian forces during the Six Day War in June 1967. Responding quickly to the UNC's assertion of leadership, the Muslim Brotherhood, at the behest largely of younger Islamist activists, announced the establishment of Hamas. Combining strategic use of violence, including devastating suicide bombings in Israeli cities, with pragmatic participation within existing political processes, such as local and national elections, the movement eventually became the main challenger of Fatah, the secular-nationalist faction that had dominated Palestinian nationalism since the late 1960s. In June 2007, 18 months after it won Palestinian Legislative Council elections, Hamas, seeking to consolidate its power, forcibly expelled Fatah-associated militias from the Gaza Strip. The Palestinian political field thereafter cleaved geographically and institutionally between the Islamists in Gaza and the Fatah-controlled Palestinian National Authority in the West Bank.

The origins of Hamas lie in the Islamic Collective (al-Mujamma' al-Islami). Founded by Shaykh Ahmad Yasin in 1973, the collective sought to revive moribund Muslim Brotherhood groups in the aftermath of the Six Day War. Ironically, the Israeli occupation that ensued provided circumstances favorable to Islamist mobilization. Perceiving a chance to divide Palestinians politically, Israel initially provided Yasin and the collective space to organize. For its part, the collective strategically avoided Israeli repression by choosing to make the spread of secularism among Palestinians, not the occupation, its primary enemy. Reorient Palestinian hearts and minds toward Islam first, so the thinking went, and all else would follow. To achieve its objective, the movement engaged in *da'wa* (calling to the straight path), charity work, network formation, and assertion of control over associational life (such as unions, universities, mosques, and professional societies). It also clandestinely collected weapons in anticipation of an eventual transition to an armed struggle. These initiatives brought the collective into violent conflict with Palestinian Liberation Organization (PLO) factions throughout the period leading up to the first Intifada.

At the heart of the alternative offered by the collective was a political theodicy that explained Palestinian suffering as a direct result of the failure of Muslims to uphold *taqwā* (the "fear of God" evidenced through acts of personal piety as prescribed in the Qur'an and sunna). This failure had led God to favor other nations, principally "the Jews." Israel's success, then, was a sign of God's displeasure with the Arabs and Muslims and with the Palestinians in particular. Implicit in this formulation was the idea that rectification of the current state of inverted affairs required a turning away from error (e.g., secularist ideologies) and a return to piety. The Islamic Collective justified its apolitical "culturalist" activism precisely in these terms: Palestine would return to the Muslims only after Muslims had returned to Islam. An authentic jihad demanded this type of deep individual and collective conversion. The explosion of the Intifada forced a reevaluation, however, of the sequence envisioned by the collective. Confronted by the demands of a younger generation of activists to engage the occupation directly, Islamic Collective leaders revised their ideology, stressing the immediate necessity of jihad. Through jihad the nation would return to *taqwā*, and thereby Israel would be overcome and an Islamic state would arise in Palestine. The return of Palestine would mark the first stage in the revival of the global Islamic religiopolitical community (*umma*). Palestine, indeed, was the key to an Islamic awakening (*saḥwa*). In this move, Hamas

essentially articulated an Islamic analogue of the PLO's vision that saw the liberation of Palestine as the first step toward uniting the transnational Arab nation.

The ideological flexibility shown by the collective in adapting to the new realities of the Intifada by creating Hamas has remained a defining characteristic of Islamist politics in Palestine. Hamas has repeatedly shown itself capable of adapting its ideological positions to new political realities in the interest of survival. Perhaps the best example of its flexibility is its proposal to agree to an indefinite "truce" with Israel, an idea that effectively recognizes the reality of Israel and provides a path toward achieving some form of peaceful coexistence even if the movement continues to assert its commitment to achieving an Islamic state within the entirety of pre-1948 Palestine. At the same time, however, Hamas has maintained its armed wing as well as its control over the police forces in the Gaza Strip. It has also allowed proxies, such as Islamic Jihad units, to fire rockets across the boundary fence into Israel proper or has initiated such actions on its own, directly, in response to the continuing Israeli blockade. In a bid to crush Hamas's military capacity, Israel launched a three-week armed invasion of Gaza in the winter of 2008–9. Named "Operation Cast Lead," the invasion inflicted heavy damage to infrastructure and, according to an Amnesty International report, caused more than 1,400 civilian deaths and 5,000 civilian injuries. Hamas, however, remained intact, organizationally, and arguably strengthened its control in the Gaza Strip in the aftermath of Israel's tactical withdrawal. Hamas continues to confront a total Israeli blockade and refusal by the United States, European Union, United Nations, and Arab states to accord it any official diplomatic recognition. Syria and Iran, however, provide financial and political support for the movement, and Islamist movements globally have maintained solidarity with it. Attempts to restart Palestinian-Israeli peace negotiations have repeatedly floundered due not only to Israel's continuing efforts to expropriate land and build settlements but also to the persisting Palestinian political disunity and Hamas's undeniable capacity to use violence to counter its diplomatic isolation.

See also Islamic Jihad; Muslim Brotherhood; Palestine; Palestinian Liberation Organization (PLO)

Further Reading

Amnesty International, *Israel/Gaza: Operation "Cast Lead": 22 days of death and destruction*, 2009; Jeroen Gunning, *Hamas in Politics: Democracy, Religion, Violence*, 2008; Khaled Hroub, *Hamas: Political Thought and Practice*, 2000; Loren D. Lybarger, *Identity and Religion in Palestine: The Struggle between Islamism and Secularism in the Occupied Territories*, 2007; Shaul Mishal and Avraham Sela, *The Palestinian Hamas: Vision, Violence, and Coexistence*, 2006; Sara Roy, *Hamas and Civil Society in Gaza: Engaging the Islamist Social Sector,* 2011; Azzam Tamimi, *Hamas: A History from Within*, 2007.

LOREN D. LYBARGER

Hasan b. ʻAli (ca. 624–70)

Revered as the eldest surviving grandson of the Prophet and the second imam by Shiʻis, Hasan b. ʻAli was unexpectedly thrust into political life by the assassination of his father, ʻAli b. Abi Talib, in 661 at the hands of the Khariji ʻAbd al-Rahman b. Muljam. Before this event, Hasan's political activity had not been significant (he was present but not prominent at the battles of the Camel in 656 and Siffin in 657), though he is credited with views at variance with those of his father (e.g., in his refusal of ʻAli's command to flog an alcohol-drinking governor of Kufa, his defense of ʻUthman b. ʻAffan's home from rebels, and his criticism of ʻAli's inaction during the affair). Although ʻAli himself had not designated Hasan as his political successor, the fact that he was his eldest son, and thus the eldest grandson of the Prophet, and that ʻAli bequeathed to him his land endowments (*ṣadaqāt*) in Arabia made him the natural candidate for leadership.

Hasan is depicted as modifying ʻAli's bellicose policy toward the Syrians, then under the leadership of Muʻawiya b. Abi Sufyan (r. 661–80). In the oath of allegiance (*bayʻa*) that he required of his followers, he not only included the words "make war against those he is at war with" but also "make peace with those he is at peace with," which displeased those unwilling to embrace peace with Muʻawiya. When Muʻawiya rejected his invitation to submit to his leadership and invited Hasan to submit to his authority instead, citing his superior experience, Hasan withheld his reply, apparently wishing to avoid further bloodshed. Hasan eventually consented to suspend his political rights until Muʻawiya's death in return for a handsome sum (a reported million *dirhams* per annum). Thereafter, Hasan retired to Medina and refused further political involvement, preferring quietist opposition to Muʻawiya's leadership. Hasan's hopes to succeed Muʻawiya as caliph were never realized, for on April 2, 670, he died (numerous accounts claim he was poisoned by one of his wives at Muʻawiya's instigation), thus freeing the line of succession for Muʻawiya's own son Yazid I.

Many of Hasan's followers perceived his first declaration of his pacifist inclinations as a betrayal of his father's legacy and reviled Hasan as "the humiliator of the believers" (*mudhill al-muʼminīn*). Hostile accusations after his abdication claim that during his time in Medina, he maintained a harem of 300 concubines and earned the title "the divorcer" (*al-miṭlāq*) for marrying and divorcing as many as 70 to 90 women. But both Sunnis and Shiʻis classically cast his abdication as a noble rather than self-serving deed. Sunnis see him as abdicating to restore peace for the divided community: as a widely disseminated Prophetic hadith claims, "Perhaps through [Hasan] God will cause peace to arise between two mighty factions of Muslims" (*laʻalla Allāha an yuṣliḥa bihi bayna fiʼatayni ʻaẓīmatayni min al-muslimīn*). Sunnis also often count the period after ʻAli's murder and before Hasan's apparent abdication as

completing the Rightly Guided Caliphate. Shi'is, revering Hasan as the second imam, see his abdication as rooted in the imam's denunciation of worldly ambition and a model of Shi'i noninvolvement in politics.

Although the Imamis eventually focused their loyalties on the descendents of his younger brother Husayn, the Zaydis also recognized imams to have descended from Hasan. The last two major revolts to be led by descendents of 'Ali during the Abbasid period in the Muslim heartlands were both led by descendents of the Hasanid line: Muhammad al-Nafs al-Zakiya (d. 762) and al-Husayn Sahib al-Fakhkh (d. 786). In Morocco, the Idrisid dynasty (eighth to tenth century) and the Sharifs of Morocco (1510 to present day; represented since 1999 by King Muhammad VI of Morocco) both legitimized their rule by appealing to Hasanid descent.

See also 'Ali b. Abi Talib (ca. 599–661); Husayn b. 'Ali (626–80); imamate; Mu'awiya (602–80); Rightly Guided Caliphate (632–61); Shi'ism

Further Reading

Dwight M. Donaldson, *The Shi'ite Religion*, 1933; S. Husain M. Jafri, *Origins and Early Development of Shi'a Islam*, 1979; Wilferd Madelung, *The Succession of Muḥammad*, 1997; Michael G. Morony, *Between Civil Wars: The Caliphate of Mu'āwiyah* (*The History of al-Ṭabarī*, vol. 7), 1987.

SEAN W. ANTHONY

heresiography

"Heresiography" is the term used in Islamic studies for a body of literature classifying, in a highly schematic way, religious sects, parties, and heresies. The genre was well established in early Christianity; it is also attested in both Karaite and Rabbinic Judaism, although lightly so and only after the tenth century, when it may have developed under Islamic influence. The earliest Muslim books seem to have been composed in the second half of the eighth century to support the practice of rationalizing theology (*kalām*), whose polemical purposes it served by identifying and categorizing doctrinal error. All Muslim groups that produced theologians also produced heresiography. Mu'tazilis, Ash'aris, Maturidis, Imami and Isma'ili Shi'is, and Ibadis all at one time or another used heresiography to defend their exclusive claims to the "true" Islam. Examples can also be found in Traditionalist circles unfriendly to theology.

As a rule, heresiographers take a schematic and ahistorical approach to the doctrines they describe. They do not see their particular versions of "orthodoxy" as, at base, historically contingent; instead, they understand themselves to represent an unchanging, original orthodoxy from which rival ("heterodox") groups have broken away. Accordingly, an Imami Shi'i writer will portray his own line of imams as having been the only legitimate one from the start and will treat the teachings of eighth-century Gnostic groups that surrounded some of those imams as heretical departures from—or exaggerations of (*ghulūw*)—an original Shi'i orthodoxy. An Ibadi writer, similarly, will present Kharijism as an originally moderate teaching perverted by extremists who called for an immediate and total break with non-Khariji Muslims. In neither case does the writer allow for the possibility of historical development but instead projects his own teachings back into the earliest period. Sunni writers will do the same thing in order to establish the priority of their own orthodoxy. This ahistorical perspective is embodied in a famous hadith cited by many heresiographers, in which the Prophet refers to the fragmentation of the Jews and Christians into 71 and 72 sects, respectively, and predicts that his own community will divide into 73 sects, one of which—the saved sect, or *firqa nājiya*—will be in paradise while the rest will end up in hell. Although the report appears in slightly different versions (including one in which 72 are in paradise and only one in hell), it always takes for granted orthodoxy's temporal priority over heresy. The teachings of the saved sect are not seen to have evolved over time from a pool of doctrines only later deemed heterodox but instead are understood to have been in place from the very beginning.

Although the categories of "orthodoxy" and "heresy" are frequently employed by scholars, some have questioned their aptness in an Islamic context. Islamic history has seen moments where rulers sought to impose or proscribe certain religious teachings (the latter especially when they were seen as linked to a political threat), but premodern Muslim societies did not possess the machinery for regularly delineating and enforcing correct doctrine, and in any case Islam itself has generally emphasized legal practice over doctrinal beliefs. Accordingly, Islamic heresiographical literature may be best seen as representing the efforts of Muslims of every stripe to depict their own particular teachings as normative while acknowledging the diverse array of doctrines and groups that possessed some claim to legitimacy within their societies.

See also Ibadis; Isma'ilis; Karramis; Kharijis; Qarmatians; theology

Further Reading

John Henderson, *The Construction of Orthodoxy and Heresy*, 1998; Keith Lewinstein, "Notes on Eastern Ḥanafite Heresiography," *Journal of the American Oriental Society* 114, no. 4 (1994); Wilferd Madelung, "Bemerkungen zur imamitischen Firaq-Literatur," *Der Islam* 43 (1967); Wilferd Madelung and Paul Walker, *An Ismaili Heresiography*, 1998; 'Abd al-Karim al-Shahrastani, *Livre des religions et des sects*, vol. 1, translated by Daniel Gimaret and Guy Monnot, 1986; J. van Ess, *Der Eine und das Andere*, 2011; W. Montgomery Watt, *The Formative Period of Islamic Thought*, 1973.

KEITH LEWINSTEIN

heresy and innovation

In Islamic texts, innovation (*bid'a*) refers to practices or doctrines considered to lack a precedent in the Qur'an and the sunna of the Prophet. A prophetic hadith (tradition) states that every novelty is an innovation and every innovation is an erroneous deviation (*ḍalāl*) leading to hell. According to the hadith, innovations are both the product and the cause of the progressive corruption of the community after the Prophet's death (*fasād al-zamān*); they are brought about by Jewish and Christian influences, by uncontrolled and inappropriately trained preachers and storytellers (*quṣṣāṣ*), by women, and more generally by those who are led by their passions (*ahwā'*). The spread of innovations can be halted by their condemnation by properly trained religious scholars ('ulama') and by the social isolation and physical punishment of innovators. (However, physical punishment usually falls short of the death penalty, as innovators are still considered by many to be believers, even if sinful and misled.)

Nonetheless, some scholars held certain innovations to be not only acceptable but also obligatory, such as the celebration of the Prophet's birthday (*mawlid*) and the establishment of Muslim schools (madrasas) and hospitals. The possibility of "good innovations" was backed by Shafi'i (d. 820), who stated that not every novelty (*muḥdath*) was a reprehensible *bid'a*, thus opening the way for the eventual incorporation of the concept of *bid'a* into the five legal categories (obligatory, recommended, indifferent, reprehensible, forbidden), which was effected by the Shafi'i Ibn 'Abd al-Salam (d. 1262) and the Maliki Qarafi (d. 1285).

Treatises against *bid'a* usually concentrated on innovations introduced in the field of ritual practices (*'ibādāt*), such as the celebration of non-Muslim festivals, the visiting of saints' graves, the performance of certain prayers at certain times or places, and certain funerary customs. These were practices subject to intense debates in the Islamic community, and the scholars were divided into two extremes: those who were afraid of widening the scope of Muslim ritual beyond the contents of the Five Pillars (e.g., by allowing the celebration of 'Arafat outside Mecca) and those willing to accommodate local practices and customs often followed by a majority of Muslims. Many such practices are still discussed in the early 21st century, with the Wahhabis the most vociferous opponents of innovations.

Deviants from correct belief are often labeled "those who indulge in innovations and follow their passions" (*ahl al-bidā', wa-l-ahwā'*) and condemned as such in Sunni heresiographical treatises (*al-firaq, al-milal wa-l-niḥal*) dealing with the sectarian doctrines of, among others, the Kharijis, the Qadaris and Mu'tazilis, and the Shi'is. The emergence and consolidation of the doctrines and practices that came to constitute Sunnism—with its internal varieties—constituted a process that lasted more than three centuries and that cannot be considered closed. Alexander Knysh, in his article "Orthodoxy and Heresy in Medieval Islam: An Essay in Reassessment," has shown how the construction of orthodoxy in Islamic societies involves "a perpetual collision of individual opinions over an invariant set of theological problems that eventually leads to a transient consensus that already contains the seeds of future disagreement."

Intellectual criticism and social disapproval could be accompanied by persecution and repression when rulers concluded that those who supported certain beliefs or practices (such as some activist Sufis) constituted a threat to their power or when the fight against "heresy" could provide legitimacy to their rule (such as the fight of Almoravids and Almohads against the Barghawata). Even so, the wars of religion that counted so many victims in Latin Christendom have largely been absent from Islamic societies. The nonexistence of persecuting institutions such as the inquisition went together with a prevalent Sunni pattern of coexistence with "deviant" groups, even in the case of such centralized states as the Ottoman Empire, where sectarians such as the Alevis—in spite of periods of persecution—were able to survive through the centuries.

In the early centuries of Islam, dualists were subject to repression and persecution to such an extent that the name given to them (*zindīq*, pl. *zanādiqa*) became the technical legal term for the heretic considered to be a "hidden apostate"—in other words, someone who claimed to be a Muslim while holding views that put him outside the Islamic community. The *zindīq* had to be sentenced to death because of his hidden apostasy (*ridda*). The Hanafis thought the *zindīq* should be granted the possibility of repentance (*istitāba*), whereas the Malikis rejected this possibility because they felt a *zindīq* could not be trusted. Accusations of *zandaqa* became a common resource for discrediting certain views or individuals, and many examples can be found in the biographies of 'ulama'. Those accusations seldom led to a trial. Scholars who had accused others of religious deviation (*zandaqa*, *ilḥād*, *zaygh*) often attended the funeral of the accused and even pronounced the death's prayer over him or her, thereby attesting to the general Sunni reluctance categorically to stigmatize others as unbelievers (*takfīr*).

See also Kharijis; Mu'tazilis; al-Shafi'i, Muhammad b. Idris (767–820); sunna

Further Reading

N. Calder, "The Limits of Islamic Orthodoxy," in *Intellectual Traditions in Islam*, edited by F. Daftary, 2000; M. Chamberlain, *Knowledge and Social Practice in Medieval Damascus, 1190–1350*, 1994; M. Chokr, *Zandaqa et zindiqs en Islam au second siècle de l'hégire*, 1993; M. Fierro, "The Treatises against Innovations (*kutub al-bida'*)," *Der Islam* 69 (1992); J. Karolewski, "What Is Heterodox about Alevism? The Development of Anti-Alevi Discrimination and Resentment," *Die Welt des Islams* 48, nos. 3–4 (2008); A. Knysh, "Orthodoxy and Heresy in Medieval Islam: An Essay in Reassessment," *The Muslim World* 83, no. 1 (1993); H. Laoust, *Les schismes dans l'Islam*, 1977; B. Lewis, "Some Observations on the Significance of Heresy in the History of Islam," *Studia Islamica* 1 (1953); G. Makdisi, "*Tabaqat*-Biography: Law and Orthodoxy in Classical Islam," *Islamic Studies* 32 (1993); V. Rispler-Chaim, "Toward a New Understanding of the Term *Bid'a*," *Der Islam* 68 (1992); A. El-Shamsy, "The Social Construction of Orthodoxy," in

The Cambridge Companion to Classical Islamic Theology, 2008; D. Stewart, *Islamic Legal Orthodoxy: Twelver Shiite Responses to the Sunni Legal System*, 1998; J. van Ess, *Theologie und Gesellschaft im 2. und 3. Jahrhundert Hidschra. Eine Geschichte des religiösen Denkens im frühen Islam*, 6 vols., 1991–98.

MARIBEL FIERRO

hijra

The Arabic term *hijra*, Latinized as *hegira*, refers primarily to the Prophet Muhammad's emigration from Mecca to Medina in 622 (the Hijra) and secondarily to an Islamic doctrinal obligation (hijra).

Establishment of the Community

When Muhammad began to preach publicly in about 613, he encountered strong opposition from Mecca's ruling tribe, the Quraysh. Although the earliest Muslims were few in number, they represented a challenge to the prevailing order; Arab identity was rooted in kinship rather than religion, and Mecca's prosperity was linked to its polytheist shrines. In 615, Muhammad responded to mounting persecution of Muslims by sending a group of his followers to seek refuge in Christian Abyssinia. The Prophet remained in Mecca but began to seek a more hospitable base of operations in 619 after the deaths of his wife Khadija and his uncle and primary guarantor of protection, Abu Talib.

In 620, Muhammad gained several converts from Yathrib, the agricultural oasis north of Mecca that would later be known as Medina. The following year, 12 representatives from Medina's two feuding tribes, the Aws and the Khazraj, converted to Islam and swore allegiance to Muhammad. In 622, over 70 members of Medina's Arab clans negotiated with Muhammad, pledging to protect him and his followers if he settled in Medina; this is known as the Pledge of War (*bay'at al-ḥarb*). That year, Muhammad sent most of his followers ahead to Medina in small groups. He and his Companion Abu Bakr (ca. 573–634) made the journey together in secret, arriving in Medina in September 622.

This emigration, the hijra, is one of the most significant events in early Islamic history. The event marks the establishment of the Muslim community (*umma*) as an autonomous religious and political entity, with Muhammad as both Prophet and political leader. The Islamic calendar dates from the beginning of the lunar year in which the hijra took place, and Islamic dates are indicated by "AH" (*Anno Hegirae*, in the year of the hijra).

Those Muslims who left Mecca for Medina are known as the *muhājirūn*, or emigrants, while the earliest Medinan converts who aided the community's establishment are known as the *anṣār*, or helpers. Although *hijra* is often translated as "flight," the Arabic root *h-j-r* primarily signifies a severing of friendly relations, withdrawal, or emigration. For many of the *muhājirūn*, emigration meant relinquishing their property, livelihoods, and association with polytheist friends and family; Muslims were expected to make a complete break with Mecca's *jāhiliyya* (pre-Islamic, "ignorant") society.

The Obligation to Emigrate

After the hijra, emigration became an essential Islamic obligation for all but the most vulnerable Meccan Muslims. By joining the Prophet in Medina, these emigrants strengthened the nascent Islamic polity, weakened polytheist Mecca, resolutely affirmed their faith, and refused persecution. Those who failed to migrate compromised their religious commitment and risked aiding Meccan enemies. Several Qur'anic injunctions address hijra, and two of these passages are frequently cited in legal discussions of this obligation. Qur'an 4:97–100 warns of divine punishment for those who suffer oppression rather than emigrate, unless they are truly too weak to do so, and promises both worldly refuge and divine rewards for those who emigrate. Qur'an 8:72 designates believers who emigrate and fight (perform jihad) in the path of God, along with those who offer them aid, as the allies and protectors of each other; these allies are not obligated to protect nonemigrant believers until they too perform hijra. These verses are interpreted as referring to the *muhājirūn*, the *anṣār*, and the state of enmity between Medina and Mecca that made the continued presence of Muslims in Mecca problematic. Although Bedouin converts to Islam were permitted to remain with their tribes, Meccan Muslims who failed to emigrate were initially disinherited from their emigrant relatives.

Medina's Muslims conquered Mecca in 630, after which hijra out of that city ceased to be obligatory. According to an oft-cited hadith, Muhammad declared there to be no hijra after the *fatḥ*, taken to mean the conquest of Mecca. However, other hadiths characterize emigration as an obligation that will continue until the Day of Judgment or as long as infidels are fought. Later Muslim jurists reconciled these traditions by concluding that although the obligation to emigrate to Medina lapsed in 630, hijra from *dār al-ḥarb* (the abode of war, non-Muslim territory) to *dār al-islām* (the abode of Islam; Muslim territory) remained obligatory.

Early Islam

During the first Islamic century, the significance of hijra shifted in two ways. First, the connection between hijra and jihad was strengthened as the expanding Islamic state conscripted Arab soldiers willing to emigrate to garrison towns in Egypt, Syria, and Iraq. These soldiers, often referred to as *muhājirūn*, fulfilled the communal religious duty of jihad through the defense and expansion of *dār al-islām*.

Second, hijra began to play a role in sectarian disputes. The Kharijis (or *khawārij*), which formed under 'Ali b. Abi Talib (r. 656–61) and became a prominent opposition group in the Umayyad period (661–750), considered all other Muslims to be infidels and their territory to be *dār al-kufr*, the land of unbelief. Members were required to perform hijra to Khariji camps in order to conduct jihad against the caliphate.

Later Interpretations

Interpretations of hijra in the medieval through contemporary periods have also reinforced religiopolitical divisions between Muslims and non-Muslims as well as among Muslims. Following the reconquest of Spain, jurists required Spanish Muslims who found themselves under Christian rule to emigrate to *dār al-islām*. Leaders resisting colonial rule in French Algeria and British India similarly declared these territories *dār al-ḥarb* and urged hijra as a means of weakening foreign control.

In the 18th and 19th centuries, several West African jihadist leaders, most notably Usman dan Fodio (1754–1817), paired hijra with jihad in the service of their reformist campaigns against nominally Muslim rulers. The Khariji pattern of *takfīr* (declaring Muslims to be infidels) and hijra in preparation for jihad against illegitimate rulers has also been reformulated by several Islamist movements, particularly in Egypt. One such group that arose in the 1970s was referred to by outsiders as al-Takfir wa-l-Hijra (Excommunication and Withdrawal) for its violent condemnation of Egyptian society as a new *jāhiliyya*.

The obligation to emigrate from non-Muslim to Muslim territory has also been the subject of renewed debate in the 20th and 21st centuries, as an increasing number of Muslims has settled or converted to Islam in the West and other regions with non-Muslim majorities. There is a wide spectrum of Islamic scholarly opinions, ranging from prohibition to obligation, regarding citizenship in non-Muslim countries and hijra in pursuit of work, education, religious freedom, or other goals.

See also abodes of Islam, war, and truce; Dan Fodio, Usman (1754–1817); excommunication; *jāhiliyya*; jihad; Kharijis; Khilafat movement (1919–24); minorities; Muhammad (570–632)

Further Reading

Khaled Abou El Fadl, "Islamic Law and Muslim Minorities: The Juristic Discourse on Muslim Minorities from the Second/Eighth to the Eleventh/Seventeenth Centuries," *Islamic Law and Society* 1, no. 2 (1994); Gilles Kepel, *Muslim Extremism in Egypt: The Prophet and Pharaoh*, 2nd ed., 2003; Ira M. Lapidus, *A History of Islamic Societies*, 2nd ed., 2002; Muhammad Khalid Masud, "The Obligation to Migrate: The Doctrine of *Hijra* in Islamic Law," in *Muslim Travellers: Pilgrimage, Migration, and the Religious Imagination*, edited by Dale F. Eickelman and James Piscatori, 1990.

JOCELYN HENDRICKSON

Hizbullah

Hizbullah (Party of God) is a Lebanese Shi'i political party that incorporates not only a political wing, including members of the parliament and the Lebanese cabinet, but also a military resistance wing and a broad social welfare apparatus. The party's complex and multifaceted organization has emerged gradually since its formation in the mid-1980s.

The 1970s saw a number of political, social, and economic changes in the Lebanese Shi'i community. Factors contributing to the origins of Hizbullah include the 1978 disappearance of Shi'i leader Musa al-Sadr while on a visit to Libya and the subsequent disaffection of many Amal members with the organization, the 1979 Islamic Revolution in Iran, and the 1982 Israeli invasion of Lebanon and siege of Beirut. In the wake of these events, and especially the Israeli invasion—during which tens of thousands of Lebanese were killed and nearly half a million people displaced—small, armed groups of young men organized under the banner of Islam and emerged in the south, the Beqaa Valley, and the suburbs of Beirut. Dedicated to fighting the Israeli occupation troops and trained by Iran, over time these groups coalesced into Hizbullah.

Although anti-occupation resistance operations began in 1982, it was not until February 16, 1985, that the formal existence of Hizbullah and its armed wing, the Islamic Resistance, was announced in an "Open Letter to the Downtrodden in Lebanon and the World." It is this initial statement that many point to as evidence of the party's Islamic ideology. The nature of that ideology, however, must be understood in light of the party's pragmatic actions and political program as well as changes in its relationship to Lebanon and its constituency. For example, while the "Open Letter" states, "We recognize no treaty with [Israel], no ceasefire and no peace agreements, whether separate or consolidated," the party's practices have indicated otherwise. This language reflects a time when the Israeli invasion of Lebanon had just given rise to the Islamic Resistance. As Augustus R. Norton notes, "While Hizballah's enmity for Israel is not to be dismissed, the simple fact is that it has been tacitly negotiating with Israel for years."

The party's ideological platform includes a commitment to Shi'i Islam and the imamate; support for the doctrine of *wilāyat al-faqīh* (guardianship of the jurist) as articulated by Ayatollah Khomeini during and following the Islamic Revolution in Iran; jihad in the spiritual and social as well as military senses; solidarity with oppressed peoples and support for resistance to oppression; and opposition to the Israeli occupation of Lebanon, Zionism, and U.S. imperialism. The party draws on Islamic history and especially the Battle of Karbala in 680 and the martyrdom of the Prophet Muhammad's grandson Imam Husayn at that battle, as models for resistance against oppression. It also draws on Islam by way of asserting moral claims in its anticorruption stances on Lebanese politics.

The 1985 "Open Letter" notes the party's desire to establish an Islamic state, but only through the will of the people, stating explicitly, "We do not want Islam to reign in Lebanon by force." While the party continues to be led by a seven-member religious council of prominent leaders first established in the 1980s Majlis al-Shura, two other decision-making bodies—an executive council and a politburo—were established as Hizbullah began to enter Lebanese

politics toward the end of the civil war. In addition, by deciding to participate first in Lebanese elections in 1992 and later in the government itself in 2005, the party signaled its commitment to working within the existing structures of the state. In keeping with this, since 1992 Hizbullah leaders have frequently acknowledged the contingencies of Lebanon's multiconfessional society of 18 officially recognized religious and ethnic groups and the importance of sectarian coexistence and pluralism within the country. And indeed, in November 2009, Hizbullah released a new "manifesto" (the English translation the party itself used for the "*Wathiqa Siyasiyya*" [literally, political document]), which highlighted coexistence within the Lebanese state and working toward the abolition of sectarianism within that state system.

Hizbullah and its Majlis al-Shura initially followed the teachings of Ayatollah Khomeini and since his death officially follows his successor Ayatollah 'Ali Khamene'i, the supreme leader of the Islamic Republic of Iran. However, individual supporters or party members are free to choose their source of emulation (*marja' al-taqlīd*) in personal and religious matters. Many Hizbullah supporters or party members have chosen to follow the late and prominent Lebanese *marja'* Muhammad Hussein Fadlallah since the late 1990s, and some have chosen to follow the Iraqi Ayatollah 'Ali Sistani in Iraq.

Fadlallah is often described as "the spiritual leader" of Hizbullah. Both Fadlallah and the party have always denied that relationship. For a time, there was a rift between them over the nature of the Shi'i Islamic institution of emulation. Fadlallah believed that religious scholars should work through multiple institutions and should not affiliate with a single political party or be involved in the affairs of a worldly government. In these views, he was closer to traditional Shi'i jurisprudence and to the schools of Najaf, Iraq, where he studied, and more distant from the concept of *wilāyat al-faqīh* promulgated by Khomeini. Fadlallah's own writings evolved over time, paralleling the changing contingencies of war and politics in Lebanon. Calls for developing Islamism in Lebanon in the 1980s gave way to calls for dialogue among and coexistence of multiple religious confessional groups in Lebanon in the 1990s. Fadlallah was also known for his relatively progressive teachings on gender, which sometimes contrast with those of Khomeini and Khamene'i. As of 1992, the political leader of Hizbullah is Sayyid Hasan Nasrallah. While he is also a religious scholar, he does not rank highly enough to be a *marja'* and instead remains a follower of Khamene'i and his powerful deputy in Lebanon.

See also Amal; Lebanon; Palestinian Liberation Organization (PLO); Shi'ism

Further Reading

Joseph Elie Alagha, *The Shifts in Hizbullah's Ideology: Religious Ideology, Political Ideology, and Political Program*, 2006; Augustus Richard Norton, *Hezbollah: A Short History*, 2007; Naim Qassem, *Hizbullah: The Story from Within*, translated by Dalia Khalil, 2005.

LARA DEEB

holy places

Holy places, as sites of pilgrimage and the loci of sacred narrative and prestige, are important to political concerns and discourses in Islamic traditions. The holy city of Mecca, located in the Hijaz region of the Arabian Peninsula, plays a central role in Islamic sacred geography and ritual practice; other sites considered holy include the cities of Medina, Jerusalem, and Karbala, the last of particular importance to Shi'i Muslims. Mecca is the site of the annual hajj, an extensive pilgrimage to a cluster of holy places in Mecca and the surrounding area, that is counted among the Five Pillars of Islam. Its performance is required of all Muslims at least once in a person's life if that person is not otherwise impeded by extenuating circumstances, such as finances or health. According to Islamic tradition, pilgrims follow the actions of earlier prophets and events in their lives during the pilgrimage procedures. Probably the most widely known of these rituals is the circumambulation of the Ka'ba, the Meccan sanctuary believed to have been constructed by Abraham. The pilgrimage and its rituals in the holy city of Mecca constitute a powerful expression of the sacred narrative of the religion of Islam as well as its basic principles.

Because of their ritual importance, the holy cities of Mecca and Medina and in particular the shrine of the Ka'ba have formed an important locus of political prestige throughout Islamic history. Many rulers have considered possession of the holy places to be both a sacred duty and a crucial component of their political legitimacy. Early caliphs such as 'Umar b. al-Khattab and 'Uthman b. 'Affan made improvements to the sacred area surrounding the Ka'ba, recognizing the site's sacred status early in the history of Islam. Whether their capital existed in Istanbul or Cairo, Sunni dynasts who ruled over the Hijaz drew enormous political prestige from their custodianship of Islam's holiest sites. Throughout the medieval period, the Umayyads, Abbasids, Fatimids, Ayyubids, Mamluks, and Ottomans invested heavily in maintaining the pilgrimage and building charitable foundations and amenities at its holy destinations. The production of the *kiswa*, for example, the ornamental cloth that covers the Ka'ba, was considered an important marker of caliphal authority and right of guardianship over the holy sites.

In the 19th century, the Ottoman sultans also claimed the title of caliph, their sovereignty over the Hijaz and its holy places forming a crucial component of their right to claim this religious authority. The Ottomans favored the region with light taxation and a low level of regulation and oversight by the central government in Istanbul, while at the same time supporting the annual pilgrimage to Mecca. Despite the relative poverty and small size of Mecca and Medina, their political fortunes under the Ottomans were determined largely by their status as holy sites. In the modern and contemporary periods, this relationship became an international issue with the rise of the Organization of the Islamic Conference, an organization that provided Saudi Arabia the opportunity to reform its regulation

of pilgrims during the hajj. The system of national quotas implemented by the Saudi government has given considerable power to national pilgrimage agencies that oversee the sending of pilgrims from nations across the Islamic world. As a consequence, the local agencies managing the annual hajj expeditions have had to interact with local politics in nations such as Indonesia, Malaysia, Nigeria, Pakistan, and Turkey.

As an undeniable religious obligation of great importance, the pilgrimage has given political dissidents, defectors, and scholars unhappy with their current royal patrons a good excuse to leave. Permission to perform the pilgrimage allowed such figures as Ghazali (d. 1111) and others to exit what may have been difficult political situations and seek their fortunes elsewhere. In addition, the tradition of pious residence (*jiwār*) in Mecca and the international networks to which the city was tied made Mecca a suitable place to spend time while contemplating a change in career or avoiding the wrath of a distant ruler.

As symbols of sacred ideals in Islam, holy cities have also played an important role in political discourse throughout Islamic history. Mecca's association in classical Arabic discourse with the construction of human civilization after expulsion from the Garden of Eden implies the necessity of the caliphal state as the rightful guardian and patron of human civilization. In this discourse, control over the holy sites and associated relics reinforces the caliphal state's claim to the patronage of both religious law and secular political authority.

Possibly the most notable example of the intersection of political discourse and discourse on the holy places is the use of Karbala's sacred narrative in Iranian politics in the late 20th century. According to Kamran Scot Aghaie's analysis, the traditional narrative of the death of Husayn b. 'Ali at Karbala in 680 was reinterpreted in different ways to express revolutionary political agendas in the 1960s and 1970s in Iran. While the Qajars in Iran, for example, had used the sacred narrative of Karbala to legitimize their own political authority, Iranian political thinkers in the 1960s and 1970s such as 'Ali Shari'ati manipulated its traditional elements to construct a narrative of resistance to the tyranny of the Shah and the Western imperialism his government represented. The sacred narrative at Karbala became the prototype of heroic resistance to tyranny and political injustice.

Finally, these political discourses on holy places have also interacted with other concerns in Islamic societies such as gender. In the Iranian context discussed earlier, for example, the female figures in the Karbala narrative were used to define the proper role of women in opposing the Shah's government. According to these dissident narratives of Karbala, women were expected to resist the political tyranny of the Shah's government by resisting the changes in gender roles it propagated. Within this framework, women were expected to emulate the "traditional" female roles exemplified by such figures as Fatima and Zaynab. Here, the discourse on Islamic sacred space becomes not only a medium for political protest but for formulations of gender as well.

See also Jerusalem; Karbala; Mecca and Medina; pilgrimage

Further Reading

Kamran Scot Aghaie, *The Martyrs of Karbala: Shi'i Symbols and Rituals in Modern Iran*, 2004; Robert R. Bianchi, *Guests of God: Pilgrimage and Politics in the Islamic World*, 2004; Michael Dumper, *The Politics of Sacred Space: The Old City of Jerusalem in the Middle East Conflict*, 2002; William Ochsenwald, *Religion, Society and the State in Arabia: The Hijaz under Ottoman Control, 1840–1908*, 1984; F. E. Peters, *Mecca: A Literary History of the Muslim Holy Land*, 1994; Brannon Wheeler, *Mecca and Eden: Ritual, Relics, and Territory in Islam*, 2006.

PHIL DORROLL

honor

The Middle East is often considered to be part of a circum-Mediterranean "honor-shame" cultural complex in which a desire for respect and a fear of humiliation guide public behavior. However, unlike the pursuit of personal honor and the avoidance of personal disgrace that prevails in Europe, Middle Eastern honor is collective and inheres in a group of close patrilineal kin. Under this system, all members of a kin group are tainted by the dishonor of any one of them. For example, if a man of the kin group has been murdered all male members of the group are responsible for cleansing the stain of dishonor. Conversely, all members equally share liability for tarnishing the honor of another group. Thus, if a man of another group has been murdered and compensation must be paid, all the kinsmen of the murderer should contribute. When blood revenge is taken by the murdered man's patrilineal clan, the victim can be anyone in the murderer's group, not necessarily the guilty party. This kinship-based honor system extends far beyond the Mediterranean basin into Iraq, Iran, Afghanistan, Pakistan, Morocco, and Somalia—in other words, precisely into those regions historically influenced by conquering Arabs and their Bedouin values.

Among the Bedouin, honor (*'irḍ*—often conjoined with *wajh*, or face) can be impugned in a number of ways. The primary and archetypical insult against *'irḍ* is a sexual offense against a woman of the lineage. This affront usually calls for blood revenge—not only against the offender but also sometimes against the woman as well, if she is thought to have been at fault. Another attack on *'irḍ* is the killing or injuring of a member of one's lineage or an attack on one's property, such as stealing one's cattle or appropriating one's land. These offenses can generally be wiped clean by payment of a fine and symbolic acts of contrition mediated by a *manshad*, or a judge who specifically decides such cases. A third, less direct affront is blackening a man's reputation by publicly accusing him of acting dishonorably or failing to meet an obligation. Thus, while robbery is not in itself dishonorable (it may well be a very honorable act of aggression against one's traditional enemies), it is dishonorable to

steal goods that are held in trust. Other dishonorable acts include neglecting one's duties as guardian and failing to give hospitality to guests or to provide safe refuge to those who are under one's protection. Cowardly acts also can lead to a loss of honor, as can breaches in etiquette and decorum. In fact, to maintain his honor, a man must display his upright personality in all his public presentations. In contrast to the unreliable man who hesitates or rushes heedlessly, the steady gait of the man of honor visibly demonstrates that he knows where he is going and that he will arrive on time. The honorable man stands straight and looks at others directly; he is alert and lets nothing escape him, unlike those who foolishly gaze at the clouds or stare at the ground. The women of the collective must also live up to the contrasting female standards of honor by showing proper restraint and diffidence in dress and demeanor.

The pursuit of what Pierre Bourdieu has called the "symbolic capital" of honor is the daily mode of political action in the Middle East. At stake is a man's ability to inspire respect and mobilize his allies in a world where his most important resources are his kin, networks, alliances, and other relationships. The accumulation of honor is the most valuable means of maintaining the web of personal ties necessary for success in a severe and competitive environment. The game of honor itself consists of the serious and continuous improvisation of challenges and counterattacks among equals who are constantly competing for public approval. Those who refuse to play are unworthy of respect. As a common proverb states, "A man without enemies is a donkey." Contestants can follow many strategies to achieve victory (or, more likely, a stalemate), but they must be careful not to accept challenges from the weak and shameless (which lead only to humiliation), not to delay a response to a challenge for too long (which demonstrates fear or indecision), and not to press advantages too far (which reveals immoderation).

Throughout the Middle East, when a man fails in the game, no punishment is meted out to him. A casual observer will notice no evident difference between the treatment of a dishonored man and one who is respected. But in fact a man without honor has become a nonperson, still living in the community but only as a shadow. He will not be asked to offer guarantees, his word is disregarded, his lineage is disgraced, and his children are shamed. Not respected by others, he can have no respect for himself. No wonder, then, that a man will sacrifice a great deal to avoid such a fate.

While everyone has at least the potential of possessing *'irḍ*, in classical Arabic, *'irḍ* and *sharaf* (nobility) are often used interchangeably, indicating the ancient association of honor with rank, an association marked by the contrasting but overlapping categories of *nasab* (pedigree) and *ḥasab* (honor acquired through deeds). Within the genealogically oriented value system of the Middle East, those of good pedigree are assumed to have inherited an honorable character from their ancestors. Furthermore, different professions and populations are thought to have varying degrees of honor inherent in them. Rural tribesmen claim the highest degree for themselves, whereas tradesmen, workers, and dependent farmers rank lower, since they lack autonomy and cannot live up to the highly valued warrior ethic of the tribal world. The elderly also deserve honor, as do descendants of the Prophet or members of the Quraysh (the Prophet's clan). Individual piety is also affirmed by the devout as the only lasting *ḥasab*.

The priority of lineage in the assignment of honor means that men who wish to be accepted as leaders often point to their genealogies as proof of their present virtues. The supposed correlation between *ḥasab* and *nasab* allows others to guess at the capacities of their fellows in fluid situations where leadership is never secure and where character is crucial. However, dishonorable behavior in the present can offset the credit established in the past, while honorable behavior today can raise the status of the lowly. As one poor Arab famously responded after being taunted by one of his betters, "My *nasab* begins with me, while yours ends with you." The notion that a man can become honorable by his own efforts reflects the deep traditions of individualism and the active pursuit of status that is characteristic of the Middle East throughout history. In principle, this open ideology of achievement permits upward mobility through the expression of character and punishes those who lack honorable qualities. Ideally, the great value placed on honorable behavior inspires leaders to give alms to the poor, protect the weak, and act with rectitude for the sake of their own self-respect and the reputation of their lineage. The pursuit and display of honor therefore serves as a mechanism for maintaining a degree of social order and equity in a highly egalitarian and competitive society.

See also chivalry; Ibn Khaldun (1332–1406); kinship; solidarity; tribalism

Further Reading

Pierre Bourdieu, *Outline of a Theory of Practice*, 1977; Ibn Khaldun, *The Muqaddimah*, 1967; Roy Mottahedeh, *Loyalty and Leadership in an Early Islamic Society*, 1980; Frank Henderson Stewart, *Honor*, 1994.

CHARLES LINDHOLM

household

In the Middle East, the military-administrative household may be defined as a conglomeration of kinship and patron-client ties in which administrative functions have been concentrated. Such households date at least to the Neo-Assyrian Empire (ca. 911–612 BCE), in which the ruler's palace was referred to as "our house" (*bitenu*), with the monumental palace gate (*babenu*, or "our doorway") demarcating the boundary between the household and the outside world. This basic paradigm informed later administrative households, up to and including those of the major Islamic empires. In such a structure, household membership and concomitant loyalty to the ruler who headed the household determined one's position. The more trusted

a household member was, the higher he rose in the hierarchy, and the more likely he was to have access to the inner sanctum where the ruler and his family resided.

Among Islamic regimes, the first well-documented example of a household-based administration is that of the Abbasid caliphate (750–1258). In the Abbasid capital of Baghdad, constructed in 762, the caliph's palace was surrounded by the residences of his sons and his African eunuchs, as well as the offices of the still-modest government, which was itself conceived as part of the caliph's household. Indeed, the office of vizier (*wazīr*), first documented under the Abbasids, originated within the caliph's household, since the original viziers were his trusted clients. In the ninth century, the Abbasids began systematically to recruit elite slaves, or mamluks, from among the Turkic and Iranian peoples of Central Asia, removing them from their homelands so as to ensure their exclusive loyalty to the caliph. In the Abbasid and all subsequent Islamic empires, mamluks were a key component of the ruler's household and armies. Eunuchs, who were also imported from outside the Islamic domains, achieved the closest proximity to the ruler and his immediate family, for they had no family ties that might divide their loyalty. The ruler was not the only household head in a given Islamic society, however; viziers, provincial governors, and even religious scholar officials ('ulama') founded their own households, modeled to varying degrees on that of the ruler.

Women played a pivotal role in these households, as they had in households of the ancient Near East. The wife or favorite concubine of a household head presided over what amounted to a parallel female household, usually based in the harem of the palace or mansion and consisting largely of the wife's or concubine's slaves or former slaves. In a ruler's palace, the "female household" was the site of dynastic reproduction. In the households of ministers and provincial notables, wives and concubines helped to generate and preserve household wealth since, under Islamic law, a woman retained her property after marriage and could acquire more in her own right.

As the most recent empire to dominate the Islamic heartland, the Ottoman Empire has left the most extensive record of how a regime based on administrative households functioned. A hierarchy extended from the sultan's household in Istanbul's Topkapi Palace through the households of the highest-ranking government ministers to those of provincial governors and provincial grandees. Though often based in palatial mansions, lower-ranking households might take shape in military barracks or ordinary houses. They could have an impact on the cities and neighborhoods where they were located if, for example, the household head established charitable works in the vicinity. A key turning point occurred late in the 17th century, when the grand vizier moved his household permanently out of the palace. This century also saw the rise of households led by provincial governors that were independent of, and occasionally antagonistic toward, the imperial palace; they relied on private armies of mercenaries and mamluks. During the following century, notables in the Ottoman provinces were able to parlay control of life-tenure tax farms into formidable households that dominated the provincial administration and proved indispensable to Ottoman military efforts. The Tanzimat reforms, undertaken between 1839 and 1876, aimed in part to reduce the influence of these provincial households.

See also Abbasids (750–1258); clients; family; Mamluks (1250–1517); tribalism

Further Reading

Jane Hathaway, *The Politics of Households in Ottoman Egypt: The Rise of the Qazdağlı*, 1997; Albert Hourani, "Ottoman Reform and the Politics of Notables," in *The Modern Middle East: A Reader*, edited by Albert Hourani, Philip S. Khoury, and Mary C. Wilson, 1993; Hugh Kennedy, *The Early Abbasid Caliphate*, 1981; Metin Kunt, *The Sultan's Servants: The Transformation of Ottoman Provincial Government, 1550–1650*, 1983; Leslie Peirce, *The Imperial Harem: Women and Sovereignty in the Ottoman Empire*, 1993; John Malcolm Russell, *Sennacherib's Palace without Rival at Nineveh*, 1991.

JANE HATHAWAY

human nature

In the history of Islamic thought, there are two main approaches to the question of human nature and the self: moralistic and ontological. The moralistic approach was based on the ethical discourse of the Qur'an, especially in connection with the problems of defining evil, self-purification, and the true experience of monotheism. The framework for the ontological approach was furnished by Aristotelian, Neoplatonic, and Hermetic psychology, but Muslim thinkers used it to address key questions evident in the Qur'an and the tradition of Prophet Muhammad, in discussions that parallel those of St. Augustine and other Christian theologians. The two approaches were often combined, especially in the works of mystics and philosophers, a development that arguably reaches its apex in the existential concept of "the perfect human" (*al-insān al-kāmil*) proposed by the Andalusian mystic and philosopher Ibn al-'Arabi (d. 1240).

The Qur'an argues that the human being has a natural inclination toward good; however, while the notion of original sin does not exist in Islam, it asserts that the human self or psyche tempts a person to do evil. In this respect, the Qur'an defines three levels of the human self or three existential modes. The lowest of these levels or modes is *al-nafs al-ammāra bi-l-sū'*, or "the self that tempts to evil." This self, as the famous theologian Ghazali (d. 1111) argues in *Ma'arij al-Quds fi Madarij Ma'rifat al-Nafs* (The ladder to God in the plains of knowing one's soul), describes the state in which a person completely gives in to animalistic, sensual drives. The second level or existential mode is *al-nafs al-lawwāma*, or the "blaming self." This mode describes the state of the person who is torn between sensual lusts and attaining peace through mental and spiritual education. The third and highest level or existential mode is *al-nafs al-muṭma'inna*, or the "tranquil or

peaceful self." According to Ghazali, this self describes the state when a person reaches tranquility and peace by aligning with reason and rejecting the turbulence caused by sensual drives. Ghazali's interpretation of the three levels of the self in the Qur'an resembles Plato's tripartite division of the soul in the *Republic* into appetitive, desiring, and rational parts. Like Plato, Ghazali argues that desires must be aligned with reason in order to reach the level of tranquility and peace; otherwise, if sensual appetites and drives dominate desires, the human being could descend to an animal level.

This struggle to achieve tranquility was addressed differently in Sufism, Islam's mystical tradition. Many Sufi treatises, like those of Junayd (d. 910), hold that the primordial covenant (*mīthāq*) between humankind and God mentioned in Qur'an 7:172 represents the essence of human existence: according to this covenant, all humans attested to the unity of God before being created. However, through societal associations and distractions with the material world, humans become oblivious to this perennial truth. The retrieval of this essence and thus the achievement of the ultimate form of monotheistic experience is the *telos* or purpose of human life. Such retrieval is possible through a process of intellectual abstraction (*tajrīd*), as Junayd and his teacher Muhasibi (d. 857) argued, guided by existential and spiritual exercises. This process aims at achieving the annihilation (*fanā'*) of the false ego that is constructed through societal influence, false reasoning, and the blind pursuit of sensual desires.

The physical and metaphysical framework of the classical Islamic view of human nature was inspired by Platonic, Aristotelian, and Neoplatonic philosophy, along with the Hermetic tradition. This is easily discernible in the work of the philosophers Farabi (d. 950), Ibn Sina (d. 1037), Ibn Rushd (d. 1198), and the Brethren of Purity (fl. tenth century). It is also evident in the work of theologians like Ghazali, mystical philosophers like Ibn al-'Arabi, and Hermetic mystics like Ibn Sab'in (d. 1269). Following the Aristotelian line of argument in the *De Anima*, Ibn Sina argues in his psychological work *Compendium on the Faculties of the Soul* (*Mabhath 'an al-Quwwa al-Nafsaniyya*) that the soul is the essence or form of living substances or beings that are capable of moving themselves, including plants, animals, and humans. The powers of the soul are accordingly divided into the vegetative, sensitive or animal, and rational powers. Following books II and III of the *De Anima*, Ibn Sina argues that the rational soul (*al-nafs al-nāṭiqa*), which is the highest power of the soul humans possess and therefore defines the human species, is separate from the body. Thinking, or the life of contemplation, is what allows humans to become Godlike and thus realize Him as the essence of everything. This view is Neoplatonic as much as it is Aristotelian. Since everything proceeds from God, the soul can return to Him through the life of contemplation. Because they adopted this Greek model, most Muslim philosophers faced the same challenges that Plato, Aristotle, Plotinus, and the long tradition of their commentators did, including the relation between the potential and active intellects and the eternity of the soul. However, Muslim philosophers, particularly Ibn Sina and Ibn Rushd, in contrast with the Greeks, placed more emphasis on the inner senses, especially imagination, and their role in mediating between rational, universal ideas and sense-perceived, substantial forms. This is particularly evident in the later works of Ibn Sina where he criticized Aristotle's theories and embraced a more mystical and Gnostic view, gravitating toward Platonism and Neoplatonism.

Despite his criticism of Ibn Sina's metaphysics in general, Ghazali presents an almost identical theory of the self in *Ma'arij al-Quds fi Madarij Ma'rifat al-Nafs*. He continues to analyze the self from an essentialist perspective as a substance that is fully actualized through thinking. However, he maps his analysis against the Qur'an. For instance, Ghazali argues that since several discourses in the Qur'an address the self directly, the self must be a substance that exists. He also adduces a number of traditions attributed to Muhammad to demonstrate that the intellect or the rational soul is the highest and most Godlike power of the soul. In other words, as a theologian, Ghazali uses dialectical arguments based on the Qur'an and the tradition of the Prophet alongside the demonstrative rational proofs Ibn Sina and other philosophers deployed. These proofs were ultimately intended to reconcile the psychological system of the Greeks with the main statements about the self and human nature in Islam's scriptural sources: the Qur'an and the tradition of Muhammad.

Ibn al-'Arabi is arguably the first thinker who combined the moralistic approach to human nature and Ibn Sina's Aristotelian psychology and metaphysics to form a creative vision of human nature focused on the human-divine relationship. In *The Bezels of Wisdom* (*Fusus al-Hikam*), Ibn al-'Arabi argued that the human and the divine are essentially connected because the divinity of God cannot be recognized without a being who *willfully* recognizes it, and this is the human being. The human being has two epistemological and ontological dimensions. The first is a rational, transcendent dimension that allows it to recognize the fixed essences (*al-a'yān al-thābita*), Platonic forms, or the realm of universal ideas. These ideas are the rational manifestation of the divine names that underlie and characterize the essences of all beings and the entire range of possible relations among them. The human being is also embedded in the physical world of spatial–temporal experience (*'ālam al-shahāda*), to which he or she has access through sense perception. Between these two dimensions exists the imaginal world (*'ālam al-mithāl*). Imagination functions to interpret the world of sense perception teleologically in terms of the forms or names of God. The more a human being is capable of interpreting worldly phenomena in terms of the universal ideas representing the divine names, the more perfectly he or she actualizes his or her humanity. Ibn al-'Arabi thus calls the perfect human (*al-insān al-kāmil*) the all-embracing cosmos (*al-kawn al-jāmi'*), because only through the capacity of his imagination to recognize the manifestation (*tajallī*) of God in every worldly phenomenon does God see a mirror image of Himself. The full actualization of the human being is thus achieved through the faculty of imagination and not reason, in contrast with the view found in Aristotelian philosophy. Moreover, the hermeneutical aspect of imagination allows for a more existentially fluid

view of human nature than the essentialist perspective underlying Aristotle's theory in the *De Anima*.

See also Ghazali (ca. 1058–1111); Ibn Rushd (1126–98); Ibn Sina, Abu 'Ali (ca. 980–1037); philosophy; Sufism

Further Reading

Abu al-'Ila Afifi, *The Mystical Philosophy of Muhyid-Din Ibnul-'Arabi*, 1974; Muhyi al-Din b. al-'Arabi, *Bezels of Wisdom*, translated by R.W.J. Austin, 1980; William Chittick, *The Sufi Path of Knowledge: Ibn al-'Arabī's Metaphysics of Imagination*, 1989; Herbert Davidson, *Alfarabi, Avicenna, and Averroes on Intellect: Their Cosmologies, Theories of the Active Intellect, and Theories of Human Intellect*, 1992; Ibn Rushd, *Middle Commentary on Aristotle's De Anima*, translated by Alfred L. Ivry, 1994; Ibn Sina, *Avicenna's De Anima, Being the Psychological Part of Kitāb al-Shifā'*, translated by Fazlur Rahman, 1959; Idem, *A Compendium on the Soul*, translated by Edward Abbott Van Dyck, 1906.

AHMED ABDEL MEGUID

human rights

As a contemporary political issue related to Islam, human rights is often invoked as an international legal yardstick to which some states with Muslim majorities, particularly in the Middle East, are seen, particularly by Westerners, to fall short. Related to this, some Muslims and their governments argue that aspects of contemporary human rights law reflect a Western neoimperialist political slant. Tensions along these lines usually center on political liberties, religious freedom, and women's rights.

Looking mostly at real or alleged shortfalls in Middle Eastern governments' enforcement of contemporary rights law, however, obscures both the fact that perceived violations may have little to do with Islam per se and the historical importance of Islam's role in bringing varied issues of equality and justice to the fore of many premodern societies. Given Islam's strong foundational and doctrinal strains of social and economic justice, religion has been and can be linked with providing greater equality or addressing severe poverty in Muslim-majority societies.

Early Muslim texts and legal scholars did not use the modern Western political term "human rights" (*ḥuqūq al-insān*), nor did they envision current core concepts of human rights, which generally are specific privileges that individuals enjoy in relation to nation-states in which they are citizens or residents. In classical Islam, individual rights came about as the duty of a divinely sanctioned ruler of a transnational community of Muslims, and of protected non-Muslims, to realize God's will through justice, fairness, and enhanced economic equality.

Islam, as a social system that has combined belief, political order, and flexible mechanisms for growth and evolution, represented a progressive social force in its early history for its ability to enhance women's status, institutionalize charity, and allow for separate, if unequal, privileges for some religious minority communities within its midst; these are all also central issues in contemporary human rights discourse. Indeed, believers assert that the shari'a need not enact specific provisions that institutionalize injustice, as justice is at the very core of Islam and its sociopolitical system.

Of course, such a principle could often produce idealized discourse among legal scholars based on the assumption that rulers would not needlessly do injustice to their subjects. Moreover, the rationalist, individualist foundations of contemporary rights language were not an obvious centerpiece of Islamic jurisprudence, or any other premodern religious system for that matter. In addition, the basic governing norms of the diverse historical empires ruling in the name of Islam, such as the Abbasids, Ottomans, Mughals, and Safavids, varied with respect to individual rights. Thus historical context and changes in the connection of human rights to Islam must be part of any analysis of this subject.

In the contemporary era of postcolonial states, the implementation of codified international legal standards of universal human rights is affected by four primary factors. First, many states with Muslim majority populations have explicitly endorsed, in their constitutions or otherwise, Islam as the prime source of legislation, including in regard to laws that involve rights. Ironically, however, this endorsement has been accompanied in most Islamic countries by the relegation of actual shari'a to the sphere of family law, if even there. Yet, Islam as a source of legal ideals and a tradition of diverse thinking about rights and justice is perhaps even more significant and potent in spurring debate on these issues because it typically lacks substantive realization in many areas of contemporary legal practice.

A second factor affecting human rights is dominant social customs that are often associated with Islam by native Muslims and outsiders but that generally are not required by the religion. Issues surrounding women's status are the most frequent way in which this factor plays out with respect to contemporary rights. Oftentimes, creative solutions within Islamic legal traditions and methods allow for social practices prevalent in Islamic history, especially issues surrounding the status of women, such as polygyny and unequal divorce rights, to be reformulated in relative conformity to human rights law.

Third, global tensions around the politics of Islamic states or social movements, particularly between the West and Arab and other Southwest Asian Islamic areas, encourages miscommunication and exaggeration with respect to human rights standards. Such tensions include concerns about the rights of Muslims in Western states around issues such as national security law in the United States or women's headscarves in Europe.

Fourth, and perhaps of greatest importance, the relatively unaccountable and frequently repressive political systems of many Arab and some other Muslim states, which affect and constrain the rule of law more broadly, are often the real reason for human rights

violations and impoverished rights discourse rather than anything connected to Islam. Taken together, these four factors help make sense of the general and specific political disputes around human rights and Islam and also amplify that Islam as a broad, global religion is not per se in clear tension with international rights. This helps make sense of the importance of rights claims as part of the discourse of Muslim Arabs who took to the streets in 2011 to challenge repressive political systems.

This is not to deny real tensions between the interpretation or textual formulations of some human rights law and contemporary Islam. If areas of alleged Islamic difficulty with women's rights are often, in fact, contestable and broadly reconcilable within Islam's emphasis on social justice and equality, some particular provisions of international rights law with respect to religious freedom are more problematic. Specifically, Islamic law has not allowed conversion out of Islam or for Muslim women to marry non-Muslim men, both of which are recognized as freedoms individuals enjoy under human rights law (e.g., Universal Declaration of Human Rights articles 16 and 18 and International Covenant on Civil and Political Rights articles 18 and 27). More generally, and given the four factors previously noted, tensions between Islam and contemporary international rights law may exist based on questions about the moral or pragmatic authority of a nonreligious, non-Islamic positivist legal process to determine rights. Additionally, it may seem inappropriate to ground rights in politics and institutions rather than as a consequence of religious obligation. Of course, such broad tensions are scarcely unique to Islam.

Thus, navigating the terrain of Islam and contemporary international human rights challenges Muslims themselves to negotiate the specific relation of global rights law standards to particular local contexts and practices and also challenges non-Muslims and Muslims alike to recognize how domestic, regional, and global politics can magnify or create disputes and misunderstandings that are not inherent in Islam's diverse historical experiences of seeking fairness and justice for individuals. The increasing diversification of Muslim societies and communities throughout traditional Islamic heartlands and the West increases opportunities for lively, sophisticated, and varied debates about the rapport between Islam and human rights.

See also modernity; shariʻa

Further Reading

Abdullahi An-Na'im and Mashood A. Baderin, eds., *Islam and Human Rights: Selected Essays of Abdullahi An-Na'im*, 2010; Jack Donnelly, *International Human Rights*, 2006; Chibli Mallat, *Introduction to Middle Eastern Law*, 2007; Ann Mayer, *Islam and Human Rights: Tradition and Politics*, 2006; Irene Oh, *The Rights of God: Islam, Human Rights, and Comparative Ethics*, 2007; "Universal Declaration of Human Rights," http://www.un.org/en/documents/udhr.

DAVID MEDNICOFF

Husayn b. ʻAli (626–80)

Husayn b. ʻAli was the Prophet Muhammad's grandson through his daughter Fatima and his cousin ʻAli b. Abi Talib. Considered imam by Shiʻis after his father ʻAli and his brother Hasan, Husayn is loved and remembered as the martyr of Karbala, the righteous man who sacrificed his life and family "in the path of God." Husayn's death, the ensuing deep mourning of his sympathizers, and their rallying around the call for retribution for his killing became the nexus for emotions and identity in Shiʻism.

Husayn was born in Medina in 626. He was six when his grandfather Muhammad and then his mother Fatima died. Historical works chronicle several anecdotes about his birth and childhood, most of them related to his grandfather Muhammad's affectionate regard. Hadith compilations record the Prophet's extolling of the two brothers, such as "Hasan and Husayn are the leaders of the youth of Paradise." The wide dissemination of this and other similar hadith indicates Husayn's high standing among the early Muslim community at large; Shiʻis interpret them as proof of his imamate.

When ʻAli became caliph in 656 and left Medina for Iraq to put down the rebellion that resulted in the Battle of the Camel, Hasan and Husayn accompanied him. Shortly after ʻAli's death in 661, Hasan ceded the caliphate to Muʻawiya, and the family returned to Medina. When Hasan died in 670, Husayn became the Hashimi patriarch, and he continued (like Hasan before him) to live quietly as a Qurashi elder in Medina.

In April 680, the Umayyad caliph Muʻawiya died after having appointed his son Yazid as his successor. Husayn (along with another Qurashi, ʻAbdallah b. al-Zubayr) refused to pledge allegiance to Yazid and left Medina for the safe haven of Mecca. In Mecca, he received repeated missives from Kufan leaders, imploring him to assert his own legitimate leadership and promising support if he did; as ʻAli's former capital, Kufa was home to widespread ʻAlid sympathies. Despite misgivings expressed by some of his Qurashi well-wishers unsure of Kufan support, Husayn sent his cousin Muslim b. ʻAqil to receive the Kufans' pledge of allegiance on his behalf and shortly thereafter himself set out toward Iraq.

On October 2, 680, Umayyad forces (which ironically included many of Husayn's former Kufan supporters) surrounded Husayn's small band on the desert plain of Karbala. On the 7th, they posted military units to block his access to water. On the 10th, the day named ʻAshura,' the Umayyads killed the 72 men from his company, including his sons and brothers, and finally killed Husayn himself. Husayn's son ʻAli Zayn al-'Abidin was the only adult ʻAlid male who survived; according to the Twelver and Ismaʻili traditions, he became the next Shiʻi imam. The Umayyads imprisoned him and the women of the family and carried them to Kufa and then Damascus, releasing them after some months to return home to Medina.

The killing of Husayn at Karbala shocked the Muslim community, especially the Kufan Shi'is, who were roused to grief for their role in his death. Four thousand Kufans came together as the "Penitents" to pledge "revenge for the blood of Husayn." En masse, they mourned at Husayn's tomb in Karbala, then advanced toward Damascus. The Umayyads engaged them with a large force at 'Ayn Warda near the Syrian border and killed all but a few. Soon thereafter, another Kufan leader named Mukhtar al-Thaqafi (who claimed to represent Husayn's half-brother Muhammad b. al-Hanafiyya) constructed a domed mausoleum over Husayn's grave and built a mosque at the site. He reportedly executed thousands of men implicated in the Karbala incident before he himself was besieged and killed. These early mobilizations and collective lamentations in Husayn's name were the catalyst for the crystallization of formal Shi'ism, which had developed nebulously up to that time.

Retribution for Husayn's killing continued to be cited in religiopolitical uprisings of the next few centuries, as in revolts of the Abbasids and the Fatimids. But after the occultation of the Twelver Shi'i imam and the concealment of the Fatimid-Tayyibi imam, it was reconstituted as a pledge that would be fulfilled at the hands of the Mahdi at the end of time.

Through the centuries, Husayn's legacy—his name, his shrine, and the commemoration of his martyrdom—became a keystone of Shi'i piety. Husayn's shrine in Karbala developed into an important geographical locus of Shi'i religious sentiment; successive Shi'i rulers, including the Buyids in the 10th century and the Safavids in the 17th century, expanded it on a magnificent scale, and devotees flocked there, considering a visit to Karbala second only to the pilgrimage to Mecca. The Buyids also built the city of Karbala around the site, and in time along with Najaf (the site of 'Ali's shrine), Karbala became a major center of Shi'i scholarship and activism in Iraq. Husayn's death anniversary at 'Ashura' became a significant temporal locus of Shi'i devotion, as a time for the performance of stirring lamentations and moving sermons. The Fatimids in the 10th and 11th centuries sponsored such assemblies of mourning in Egypt, and later the Safavids instituted in Persia rites such as passion plays (*ta'ziya*), breast-beating, and flagellation. The memorials for Husayn continue to play a key role in the manifestation of Shi'i identity in 21st-century Iran, Iraq, and Lebanon, as well as countries in South and Central Asia and other places where Shi'i Muslims reside in large numbers. Husayn's memory as the "Grandson of the Prophet," the imam who "courageously endured oppression at Karbala," and the "Prince of Martyrs" continues to permeate Shi'i consciousness and to underpin their outlook on life and death.

See also 'Ali b. Abi Talib (ca. 599–661); Hasan b. 'Ali (ca. 624–70); imamate; Karbala; martyrdom; Shi'ism

Further Reading

Kamran Aghaie, *The Martyrs of Karbala: Shi'i Symbols and Rituals in Modern Iran*, 2004; Mahmoud Ayoub, *Redemptive Suffering in Islām*, 1978; Heinz Halm, *Shi'a Islam: From Religion to Revolution*, translated by Allison Brown, 1997; Syed Akbar Hyder, *Reliving Karbala: Martyrdom in South Asian Memory*, 2006; Yitzhak Nakash, *The Shi'is of Iraq*, 1994; Abu Ja'far Muhammad b. Jarir al-Tabari, *The History of al-Ṭabarī*, vol. 19, *The Caliphate of Yazīd b. Mu'āwiyah*, translated by I.K.A. Howard, 1990; Idem, *The History of al-Ṭabarī*, vol. 20, *The Collapse of Sufyānid Authority*, translated by G. R. Hawting, 1989.

TAHERA QUTBUDDIN

hypocrisy

Hypocrisy (*nifāq*) and hypocrites (*munāfiqūn*) are referred to repeatedly in the Qur'an. In the early days of Islam, the hypocrites were people in Muhammad's community who were held to be insufficiently committed to his message, and they were depicted as reluctant to support him financially or to join his fight against his enemies (e.g., Q. 33:12–21 and 57:13–17). A typical example reports "that the hypocrites too may know. For it had been said to them: 'Come and fight in the cause of God, or else pay.' They had answered: 'Had we known fighting was to occur we would have followed you'"; the Qur'an adds, "that day they were nearer to unbelief than they were to belief" and "they would utter with their mouths what was not in their hearts—and God knows best what they conceal" (Q. 3:167). An entire chapter in the Qur'an is named after the hypocrites (63, al-Munafiqun), and Muhammad is ordered to fight them: "O Prophet, exert yourself against the unbelievers and hypocrites, and deal harshly with them" (Q. 9:73 and 66:9). They would end up "in the lowest reaches of the Fire" (Q. 4:145).

The Qur'an does not identify these hypocrites, but the Islamic tradition, especially the narratives of the life of Muhammad, has much to say about them. Ibn Ishaq (d. 767), the celebrated authority on Muhammad, identifies the Medinan notable 'Abdallah b. Ubayy (d. 631) as the leader of the hypocrites. 'Abdallah b. Ubayy is said to have accepted Islam grudgingly and with ill intent and to have deserted the Prophet when the Muslims marched to meet the army of the Meccans at Uhud. Ibn Ishaq also lists as hypocrites a number of Jews from Medina who accepted Islam but then recanted.

The concept of hypocrisy played a major role in early Islamic history because it supplied a rubric under which one could accept people with opposing views as coreligionists. For example, moderate Kharijis such as the Ibadis legitimated peaceful coexistence with non-Khariji Muslims (whom they did not recognize as Muslims) at times when revolt was impossible by classifying the latter as hypocrites as opposed to outright idolaters and polytheists: all were infidels, but the Prophet had accepted hypocrites as members of the Muslim community on the basis of their external conformance. Likewise, the Zaydis held their opponents to be guilty of grave sins,

which they counted as unbelief in the sense of hypocrisy. In the same vein, several early Sunni exegetes are cited by the scholar Muhammad b. Jarir al-Tabari (d. 923) as having interpreted the order to "exert yourself against the unbelievers and hypocrites, and deal harshly with them" in Q. 9:73 to mean that infidels should be fought with the sword, but hypocrites only with the tongue (i.e., by reprimands and preaching). Tabari himself held in the interpretation that infidels and hypocrites should be fought in the same way, but the "fighting" he recommended for both is that of "commanding right and forbidding wrong," with the hand when one can—that is, by forcibly correcting open wrongdoing. This interpretation also rests on the assumption that the hypocrites were coreligionists (the duty to command right and forbid wrong pertained only to coreligionists). The Prophet, Tabari explained, had accepted people as members of the Muslim community on the basis of what they said and did, not on the basis of their inner convictions, even when he knew their inner beliefs to be at odds with their external conformance, since God had prohibited people from speculating about others' inner convictions. The jurist Shafi'i (d. 820) said that Muslim rulers must heed the example of Muhammad in dealing with hypocrites and judge them by what they publicly profess, not what they conceal. What God says about them in the Qur'an is irrelevant, for that foretells their fate rather than ordains how they are to be treated in this world. By contrast, Ibn Taymiyya (1263–1328) deemed the threat of the hypocrites to Islam and Muslims to surpass the threat of the infidels and so recommended that they be put to the sword.

Ibn Taymiyya's position has become popular among some Muslims in modern times, as the loss of Islam's hegemonic position has forced many into a position of defensive intransigence. Sayyid Qutb (1906–66), author of the influential exegesis of the Qur'an *In the Shadow of the Qur'an*, argued that hypocrites must be fought as harshly as infidels, meaning that violent action had to be taken against the secularist regimes that dominated the Middle East, including his own Egypt. Several militant Muslim groups have adopted such harsh views to justify attacks on Muslim coreligionists.

See also commanding right and forbidding wrong; Ibn Taymiyya (1263–1328); jihad; Sayyid Qutb (1906–66)

Further Reading

M. Cook, *Forbidding Wrong in Islam*, 2003; P. Crone and F. W. Zimmermann, *The Epistle of Salim b. Dhakwan*, 2000; Gilles Kepel, *Jihad: The Trail of Political Islam*, 2002; Rudolph Peters, *Jihad in Classical and Modern Islam*, 1996; Sayyid Qutb, *Social Justice in Islam*, translated by John B. Hardie, 2000.

SULEIMAN ALI MOURAD

I

Ibadis

The only Khariji sect to survive into the modern period, in Oman and North Africa, the Ibadis (Ibadiyya) first emerged as a distinct sectarian group in the late Umayyad Basra. At that time, the broader Khariji movement was split between those favoring immediate separation from other Muslims (hijra) and open hostilities against the state and those looking for at least a tactical accommodation with the political authorities until the time was ripe for open rebellion. What would come to be called the Ibadi sect emerged from the latter group. Having begun to systematize their principles and quietly organize themselves in the early eighth century, they sent out teams of missionaries known as "bearers of knowledge" to propagate Ibadi teachings and organize rebellions in distant regions. By the end of the Umayyad period, they could appeal to disaffected groups in several provinces—in particular, Berber tribesmen in North Africa and Arab tribesmen in the Arabian Peninsula, more specifically Oman and South Arabia. Imamates were established in both areas, beginning with the short-lived state founded in the Hadhramawt region during the 740s by the Ibadi rebel known as Talib al-Haqq, who for a short time also extended his control to the holy cities of Mecca and Medina. In Oman and the Hadhramawt, there were imamates on and off over the course of several centuries, a pattern that lasted (in highland Oman, at least) into the 1950s. In North Africa, a dynasty of imams (the Rustamids) held sway from Tahert (central Algeria) between 778 and 909, when they were overthrown by the Fatimids.

This history is reflected in Ibadi political thought. The literature of the sect describes several different ideal types of imamates clearly intended to rationalize different stages in its history and changing political fortunes. Unlike the extremist Kharijis, the Ibadis distinguished between a state of secrecy (*kitmān*), when weakness forced the true believers to live quietly under the rule of their oppressors, as in Basra, and the open proclamation of an imamate (*ẓuhūr*), such as what occured in North Africa and Oman. The state of secrecy could be modified in various ways, including by the rebellion of at least 40 men who decide to fight to the death in order to establish proper Muslim (Ibadi) rule, even absent realistic hope of proclaiming an effective imamate. This last category, the activist or heroic imamate known as *shirā'* (selling oneself to God), appears to reflect an effort by the later Ibadis to maintain an association with venerated Khariji martyrs (*shurāt*) from the earliest days; at the same time, restrictions such as the 40-man requirement (modeled on the rebellion of the early Khariji figure Abu Bilal Mirdas b. Udayya [d. ca. 680]) were clearly intended to put limits around militant activity. Although the Ibadis grew increasingly uncomfortable with the label "Khariji" (ultimately reserving it in their own literature for the extremists while adopting for themselves labels such as "the people of rectitude"), their literary heritage shows that they shared the basic Khariji tenets. Merit (understood as piety and knowledge) rather than descent was deemed to be the principal qualification for the imamate (though the imamate in North Africa was dynastic and the imams in ninth-century Oman were drawn exclusively from one tribal grouping). The legitimacy of the first two caliphs is accepted in Ibadi thought, but both 'Uthman b. 'Affan and 'Ali b. Abi Talib are regarded as having been rightfully deposed after proving themselves unworthy of the office. Ordinary Muslims are deemed to be infidels from whom dissociation (*barā'a*) is required. What distinguished the Ibadis from their now extinct extremist brethren was a willingness to regard non-Khariji Muslims as infidels of a special, limited sort: in the earliest terminology, they were "hypocrites" (*munāfiqūn*) such as those in the Prophet's own day; later, they were "those ungrateful for God's blessings" (*kuffār ni'ma*). Because such people were not classed as outright idolaters, practical coexistence with them was deemed possible even while a posture of internal or spiritual dissociation was maintained. Intermarriage and mutual inheritance were permissible; emigration (hijra)—signifying a complete rupture with non-Khariji Muslims—was not. Rebellion itself was permitted when circumstances allowed, but in no way was it to involve the permanent and devastating break with the ordinary Muslims demanded by the extremists. Accordingly, indiscriminate killing of such people (*isti'rāḍ*) was out of the question, nor could they be enslaved or their property taken as booty.

Unlike Shi'is, the Ibadis do not seem to have adjusted their doctrines for political use in the modern world, and circumstances have not compelled Ibadi thinkers to produce a distinctive vision of a modern Ibadi state. At the same time, Ibadi thought has never been immune to broader currents within the Muslim world, including 20th-century Salafism.

See also heresiography; Kharijis; theology

Further Reading

Patricia Crone, *God's Rule: Government and Islam*, 2004; Patricia Crone and F. W. Zimmerman, *The Epistle of Sālim ibn Dhakwan*, 2001; 'Amr K. Ennami, *Studies in Ibāḍism*, 1972; Adam Gaiser, *Muslims, Scholars, Soldiers: The Origin and Elaboration of the Ibāḍī Imāmate*

Traditions, 2010; Wilferd Madelung, "ʿAbd Allāh b. Ibāḍ and the Origins of the Ibāḍiyya," in *Authority, Privacy, and Public Order in Islam*, edited by B. Michalak-Pikulska and A. Pikulski, 2004; Idem, *Religious Trends in Early Islamic Iran*, 1988; W. Schwartz, *Die Anfänge der Ibaditen in Nordafrika*, 1983; John Wilkinson, *Ibadism: Origins and Early Development in Oman*, 2010.

KEITH LEWINSTEIN

Ibn ʿAbd al-Wahhab, Muhammad (1703–92)

Founder of a revivalist and reformist religious movement centered in Najd in central Arabia and commonly referred to as the Wahhabiyya or Wahhabis, Muhammad b. ʿAbd al-Wahhab belonged to a prominent family of Hanbali scholars, the Al Musharraf of Ushayqir. He studied in his birthplace, al-ʿUyayna, as well as in Medina, al-Ahsaʾ, and Basra before settling back in Najd, where he began to preach an uncompromising message of strict monotheism that shunned many popular religious practices. The core of Ibn ʿAbd al-Wahhab's teachings and writings center on the theological doctrine of divine unity (*tawḥīd*), which he declared, like Ibn Taymiyya (d. 1328) before him, to consist of three elements of belief and action: the unity of lordship (*tawḥīd al-rubūbiyya*), the unity of godship (*tawḥīd al-ulūhiyya*), and the unity of the divine names and attributes (*tawḥīd al-asmāʾ wa-l-ṣifāt*). In accordance with this, to associate with any being or thing a power that is God's exclusively or to direct any form of worship to any being other than God constitutes unbelief.

Other than the Qurʾan and the hadith, his principal sources of inspiration were the writings of Ibn Taymiyya and Ibn Qayyim al-Jawziyya (d. 1350). Ibn ʿAbd al-Wahhab, by his own admission, was not a highly trained or qualified theologian or jurist with a noted pedigree of teachers, and he was criticized by his many opponents for this deficiency. He is best considered a missionary and leader of a revivalist and purificatory religious movement. In terms of the law, Ibn ʿAbd al-Wahhab and most Wahhabis remained loyal followers of the Hanbali school and not advocates of a radical form of independent judgment (*ijtihād*) that would deny the authority of the established *madhhab*s (schools of law), as some of their opponents claimed they were.

Ibn ʿAbd al-Wahhab's writings have no discernible political vision or template nor a specific political end. He was concerned with eradicating what he deemed to be reprehensible innovations (*bidaʿ*) and returning the community of Muslims to the original teachings of the Prophet Muhammad and his Companions, collectively known as the pious ancestors (*al-salaf al-ṣāliḥ*). He wished to institute what might be termed a regime of godliness, but not the historical caliphate nor a particular political formation.

Ibn ʿAbd al-Wahhab wrote more than 20 short works and many epistles, of which the most famous books are *Kitab al-Tawhid* (The book of divine unity) and *Kashf al-Shubuhat ʿan al-Tawhid* (Dispelling doubts about divine unity). None of his writings evinces a high degree of scholarship or originality; rather, they were written as primers and have since been extensively commented on and widely read and distributed. Their popularity owes more to the political success of his movement and the promotion of these works by its adepts and by the Saudi state than to any intrinsic quality in the writing or the organization of the information therein.

In one of his letters, Ibn ʿAbd al-Wahhab asserted that he became known for four positions: (1) the clear exposition of the affirmation of Divine Unity, (2) the elucidation of the concept of polytheism (*shirk*) and associated practices, (3) the declaration that those who derogate from monotheism are unbelievers (*takfīr*), and (4) the engagement in the divine commandment to fight the unbelievers. According to Ibn ʿAbd al-Wahhab, to be considered a Muslim, it is not sufficient to declare oneself a believer by, for instance, uttering the creedal statement (*shahāda*); one must also actively deny, in both speech and acts, all beliefs and forms of polytheistic worship. Not to share activist Wahhabi beliefs and praxis or to plead ignorance of the requirements of the faith will result in one being considered an infidel. Furthermore, Ibn ʿAbd al-Wahhab, as well as a number of his descendants, such as Sulayman b. ʿAbdallah (d. 1818), insisted that a Muslim show loyalty and friendship to fellow believers and evince animosity and hatred toward unbelievers. This doctrine, known as *al-walāʾ wa-l-barāʾ*, has embedded in it the potential for political activism, even violence, against individuals or a political order that is deemed un-Islamic. The Wahhabis are noted for not recognizing the Ottoman state as Islamic and therefore legitimate; instead, they considered it and the lands it controlled the abode of unbelief. The Wahhabi practice of *takfīr* and waging war (*qitāl*) on other self-described Muslims led many scholars, including some Hanbalis and members of Ibn ʿAbd al-Wahhab's immediate family, to condemn the movement and its teachings. These same muscular doctrines and practices, however, enabled Wahhabism to galvanize the military potential of the settled and Bedouin tribes of central Arabia and allowed its mission to spread alongside the expansion of the political entity to which it gave its allegiance.

The Wahhabi mission received considerable impetus when Ibn ʿAbd al-Wahhab received the support and protection of Muhammad b. Saʿud (d. 1765), the amir of the small town of al-Dirʿiyya, near present-day Riyadh. The relationship between the Saʿud family and Ibn ʿAbd al-Wahhab and his descendants, otherwise known as the Al al-Shaykh, endured and centered on a compact forged around 1744. Its terms, in effect, stated that the Saudi royal family would promote and defend Wahhabi doctrines and, in return, the Al al-Shaykh, with their students and followers, would accord legitimacy to Saudi rule.

There have been three successive Saudi states, the last being the Kingdom of Saudi Arabia (est. 1932), all of which have promoted Wahhabi teachings. In each of these states, the religious establishment was dominated, although not always exclusively, by the scholarly descendants of Ibn ʿAbd al-Wahhab. In the early 21st century,

the grand mufti of Saudi Arabia is a scion of the Al al-Shaykh. These religious leaders have invariably proffered their loyalty to the Al Sa'ud, although there have been periods of tension in the relationship, especially when the political leadership has sought to compromise or even undermine Wahhabi doctrines for reasons of realpolitik. The Al al-Shaykh have invariably accommodated the Al Sa'ud by restricting the application of Wahhabi teachings, and this has drawn criticism from a segment of the religious scholars and activists within and outside Saudi Arabia. These critics, among whom are the ideologues of al-Qaeda, invariably hark back to the more radical and militant elements of the movement's doctrines and accuse the accommodationists of betrayal. As such, the legacy of Muhammad b. 'Abd al-Wahhab remains hotly contested and subject to constant reformulation.

See also fundamentalism; Salafis; Saudi Arabia

Further Reading

David Commins, *The Wahhabi Mission and Saudi Arabia*, 2006; Michael Cook, "On the Origins of Wahhabism," *Journal of the Royal Asiatic Society*, 3rd series, 2 (1992); Mohammed Nabil Mouline, *Les Clercs de l'islam*, 2011; Esther Peskes, *Muḥammad b. 'Abdalwahhāb im Widerstreit*, 1993; Abd Allah Salih al-'Uthaymin, *Muhammad ibn 'Abd al-Wahhab*, 2009.

BERNARD HAYKEL

Ibn al-Muqaffa' (ca. 720–56)

Born in Fars, 'Abdallah b. al-Muqaffa' served as secretary to Umayyad officials in Kirman and, after the coming of the Abbasids (750–1258), to 'Isa b. 'Ali, uncle of the caliph Mansur (r. 754–75). He converted to Islam during this latter period of his life. A master of Arabic, he made essential contributions to the new Islamic culture as a writer and translator from the Middle Persian.

While several of his works, such as *Kalila wa-Dimna* (Kalila and Dimna) or the *Kitab al-Adab al-Kabir* (roughly, The greater essay on right conduct), aim to instruct rulers and courtiers on matters ranging from shrewdness to wisdom (e.g., how to guard against slander, when is it smart to make common cause with an enemy, how to control the passions), his *Risala fi al-Sahaba* (Epistle on the caliph's entourage), addressed to Mansur after 754, contains his thinking about issues particular to the Islamic state and his advice to the head of that state on how to best deal with them.

Ibn al-Muqaffa' draws attention to the divergence among judicial rulings, even in the same city, in important legal cases of various kinds (involving bloodshed as well as sexual and financial matters). He argues that the caliph should collect and examine these judgments and dispositions, along with arguments from tradition or analogy offered in their support, and then issue his personal determination through the use of reason (*ra'y*), thereby producing a code from which judges would not be allowed to deviate. Successive caliphs would do likewise. According to Ibn al-Muqaffa', judges' claims of support from tradition are often unreliable and analogy can be perilously subjective. Had the caliphs followed Ibn al-Muqaffa''s advice, the history of the Islamic world might have taken a different course.

Concerning the role of religion in stabilizing the state, Ibn al-Muqaffa' echoes Sasanian ideas in the *Kitab al-Adab al-Kabir*: "If a ruler enforces correct religion among his people [*aqāma li-ahlihi dīnahum*], and it is their religion that authorizes their expectations from him and imposes on them their obligations towards him, the people will be content; even the disaffected among them will be like the contented in their acquiescence in word and deed." In the *Risala fi al-Sahaba*, he offers similar counsel to the Abbasids, a dynasty whose ascension had been aided by religious enthusiasts. According to Ibn al-Muqaffa', the Khurasanian army should be sent a handbook of correct religious belief as fixed by the caliph because its chiefs hold extravagant notions and their subordinates are muddled, resulting in dangerous discord.

Ibn al-Muqaffa' proposed a certain policing of thought as salutary for the entire state: loyal men, experts in religion and law, must be sent to each city, military district, and border region to draw people's attention to error, prevent harmful innovation, and warn against sedition. These cultural commissars were to scrutinize the affairs of the people among whom they lived, noting deviant individual opinion when it first appeared and rooting it out before it gained a hold on people's minds. He also emphasized the importance of surveillance by trusted agents so that "if anyone makes a move in a matter that concerns the commonalty of the people a loyal eye will be watching him."

The question of whether there are limits to the obedience owed to the ruler is also raised in the *Risala fi al-Sahaba*. Misinterpretation of the maxim "No obedience [is due] to a creature who rebels against the creator" has led some men, Ibn al-Muqaffa' writes, to the false idea that anyone can decide what it means to obey the creator. But the view that the ruler is owed absolute obedience is, according to Ibn al-Muqaffa', also incorrect. The ruler has no discretionary power over the religious duties and punishments laid down in the Qur'an, but his word is supreme in such matters of state as war, the collection and allocation of revenues, the appointment and dismissal of government servants, and the issuance of legal rulings based on personal opinion in cases where there is no precedent from the practice of the Prophet or (probably) previous caliphs approved by the Abbasids.

To improve the administration of the empire, Ibn al-Muqaffa' argued for a predictable land tax that did not penalize increased production, for keeping soldiers out of the financial administration, and for a bureaucracy of competent, well-educated men.

See also Abbasids (750–1258)

Further Reading

Ihsan 'Abbas, "Naẓra jadīda fī al-kutub al-mansūba ilā ibn al-Muqaffa'," *Bulletin of the Arab Academy of Damascus* 52 (1977);

M. Cassarino, *L'aspetto morale e religioso nell'opera di ibn al-Muqaffa'*, 2000; P. Crone and M. Hinds, *God's Caliph*, 1986; S. D. Goitein, "A Turning Point in the History of the Muslim State," in *Studies in Islamic History and Institutions*, 1968; J. D. Latham, "Ibn al-Muqaffa' and Early 'Abbasid Prose," in *'Abbasid Belles-Lettres*, edited by J. Ashtiany et al., 1990; Ibn al-Muqaffa', *Conseilleur du calife* (edition and French translation of the *Risala fi al-Sahaba* by C. Pellat), 1976.

ANDRAS HAMORI

Ibn Bajja (d. 1139)

Abu Bakr Muhammad b. Bajja joins Ibn Rushd (1126–98) in the West and Farabi (ca. 878–950) and Ibn Sina (980–1037) in the East as one of the most renowned philosophers within the classical Islamic tradition. Although he left his mark on Islamic civilization as a philosopher, Ibn Bajja was also well known throughout Spain and North Africa for his accomplishments in medicine, poetry, music, and astronomy. Owing to his talents and acclaim, he was quick to impress those in power and rose to a high office in their courts. At the same time, however, Ibn Bajja was just as quick to acquire enemies and provoke rivals, which twice resulted in his imprisonment (first for treason, then for heresy) and possibly in his being poisoned at the beckoning of a rival courtier.

His political philosophy comes primarily from his *Governance of the Solitary*. In this work, Ibn Bajja makes explicit references to Plato, Aristotle, and Farabi, and the influence of these thinkers comes through clearly in his argumentation. Like Plato, Ibn Bajja contends that the city is properly called "virtuous and perfect" when it is ruled by the philosopher. Ibn Bajja's conception of the faculties through which the philosopher rules follows Farabi's treatment of the active intellect, which, in turn, has its origin in Aristotle's remarks on the soul. The active intellect is an intermediary between God and humanity often associated within the Islamic tradition with the angel Gabriel or the "faithful spirit" of the Qur'an. At times, it is described along the lines of the Platonic realm of forms as a kind of unified constellation of paradigmatic spiritual realities from which all things in the material world receive their being. At other times, it is depicted as supplying rational agents with principles of reason. It is also the means by which the philosopher receives prophetic and revelatory visions from God. Through earnest philosophical investigation and training, the accomplished philosopher is united with the active intellect. At this stage, the philosopher realizes his "universal spiritual form," which entails unsurpassed understanding of the cosmos and the workings of the terrestrial realm. When the philosopher takes his rightful place as ruler, he puts his theoretical knowledge into practice and governs in such a way that the character of each citizen is maximized according to its capacity. There is no false opinion in his city. All citizens are united in friendship so there are no disputes, making the office of judge irrelevant. Nor is there a need for physicians, since each citizen maintains a good state of health by eating proper foods and exercising regularly.

The philosopher's perfect city stands in contrast to four types of corrupt governance that Ibn Bajja characterizes in accordance with divisions established by Plato in the *Republic*: the timocratic, oligarchic, democratic, and despotic. The unique and defining feature of Ibn Bajja's political philosophy is inspired by the idea that the perfect city has not been realized and that the philosopher is forced to live in one of the four types of corrupt cities or a mixture thereof. Ibn Bajja's prescription for a healthy philosophic life, therefore, is withdrawal from sociopolitical affairs. In order to maintain his own spiritual health and union with the active intellect, the philosopher must isolate himself, shunning the affairs of the imperfect city and thereby protecting himself from its corrupting influences. This is not ideal, for Ibn Bajja recognizes with Aristotle that the human being is a political animal and concedes that there is something rather unnatural about withdrawing from political life. Nevertheless, the prescription of withdrawal is a necessary evil in the context of the corrupt state. Ibn Bajja likens it to opium, which is harmful to the healthy body yet beneficial to the diseased. In this regard, Ibn Bajja writes of the philosopher's sociopolitical isolation as "medicine for the soul."

Questions have been raised regarding the consistency of Ibn Bajja's prescription of withdrawal with his self-professed fidelity to Plato, Aristotle, and Farabi. Such withdrawal is out of the question for Aristotle, and although there is a seminal notion of withdrawal from the corrupt city in the work of Plato and Farabi, it is not clear that their political philosophies accommodate the radical isolation that Ibn Bajja recommends. Concern has also been voiced about Ibn Bajja's attitude toward the shari'a, which seems to be made obsolete in the life of the socially isolated philosopher and in the context of the perfect state, where the right action of its citizens is interpreted as an outgrowth of their well-formed character and true opinion rather than as obedience to religious law.

See also Almoravids (1056–1147); al-Farabi, Abu Nasr (ca. 878–950); government; Ibn Rushd (1126–98); individualism; North Africa; philosopher-king; philosophy; Spain and Portugal (Andalus)

Further Reading

Lenn E. Goodman, "Ibn Bajjah," in *History of Islamic Philosophy*, edited by Seyyed Hossein Nasr and Oliver Leaman, 1996; Ibn Bajja, "Governance of the Solitary,"in *Medieval Political Philosophy: A Sourcebook*, edited by Ralph Lerner and Mushin Mahdi, translated by Lawrence Berman, 1963; Oliver Leaman, "Ibn Bajja on Society and Philosophy," *Der Islam Zeitchrit für Geschichte und Kultur des islamischen Orients* 57, no. 1 (1980); E.I.J. Rosenthal, "Ibn Bajja: The Individualist Deviation," in *Political Thought in Medieval Islam*, 1962.

W. CRAIG STREETMAN

Ibn Hazm (994–1064)

The life of the man of letters and religious scholar Abu Muhammad ʻAli b. Hazm coincided with one of the most traumatic periods in the history of Andalus (Islamic Iberia). The Western branch of the Umayyad dynasty had lost its splendor with the death of Caliph Hakam II al-Mustansir in 976, in which time his young son Hisham II al-Mu'ayyad fell under the influence of his chamberlain Muhammad b. Abi ʻAmir al-Mansur, who claimed to rule in his name. Ibn Hazm's father had served Mansur as vizier, and Ibn Hazm himself briefly acted as vizier to at least two of the Umayyad caliphs that followed each other in rapid succession and with much bloodshed after the demise of Mansur's second son in 1009. The ensuing civil war between different Muslim factions profoundly affected Ibn Hazm, as is clear from autobiographical passages in his best-known work, *Tawq al-Hamama* (*The Ring of the Dove*). After twice suffering imprisonment for his political activities, Ibn Hazm turned to scholarship, producing an immense oeuvre spanning numerous disciplines.

His political views are expressed in several works, most notably *al-Fasl fi al-Milal wa-l-Ahwa' wa-l-Nihal* (The decision concerning religions, heresies, and sects), *al-Muhalla bi-l-Athar* (The book adorned with traditions), and *al-Radd ʻala Ibn al-Naghrila al-Yahudi* (The refutation of Ibn al-Naghrila the Jew), which reflect his literalist (*ẓāhirī*) reading of the Qur'an and the hadith and his opposition to the state-sponsored Maliki school of law. They can be summarized as follows: the Muslim community is in need of a supreme leader (imam or caliph) to whom obedience is owed; there can only be one imam at any given time; he must be an adult male from the tribe of Quraysh, though not necessarily closely related to the Prophet Muhammad; and he must be in possession of his full mental faculties on his accession. Physical defects do not constitute an impediment, nor need he be the most virtuous person available. The imam should be pious, promote the application of God's law, and see to it that justice is done. The imam is to show himself regularly to the public. He should refrain from openly committing major sins, and he should hide any minor ones.

An imam may legitimately come to power in one of the following ways: (1) the ruling imam himself appoints his successor, not necessarily his own son or relative; (2) if the imam dies without having appointed a successor, someone may stake a claim, which was how ʻAli b. Abi Talib obtained the leadership of the Muslim community; or (3) the incumbent imam appoints a person or a number of persons to elect the new leader, as was done by the second caliph, ʻUmar b. al-Khattab. The first option is preferable to Ibn Hazm. His predilection for the Umayyad house, to which he claimed to be linked by clientage, is reflected in his statement that Muʻawiya b. Abi Sufyan was not guilty of *bidʻa* (un-Islamic innovations) when he designated his son Yazid as his successor, for it was similar to the way that the Prophet Muhammad chose Abu Bakr, who in turn designated ʻUmar as his successor. Although the Andalusian Umayyads were ruling an increasingly shrinking part of the Muslim world, they were the sole legitimate heirs of the first Umayyad caliphate for Ibn Hazm, not the Persianate Abbasids and certainly not the Shiʻi Fatimids (whom he dismissively calls "Banu ʻUbayd") or the Hammudids, an ʻAlid dynasty that briefly supplanted the Umayyads in Andalus.

The imam will delegate several of his original functions, but he must be personally involved in the selection of his representatives, making sure they are pious as well as capable. He will surround himself with advisors, such as judges and military commanders, who are experts in their respective fields and with whom he meets regularly. Governors in remote provinces, especially rich and strategically important ones, are to be appointed for brief periods only so that they cannot create a power base; by moving them about, other areas, too, get to benefit from their skills. Soldiers are to be paid well, so as to minimize the danger of rebellions. By the time Ibn Hazm wrote these lines, it was already too late for Andalus.

In the absence of an imam—which was practically the case in the Iberian Peninsula under the so-called party-kings, who ruled the petty states created after the final collapse of the caliphate in 1031—the believers should follow the person who takes the initiative to promote God's law and fight the unbelievers. In Ibn Hazm's view, none of the new, self-styled kings qualified. With characteristic bluntness he scolds them for flouting the laws of the shariʻa, relying on non-Muslim functionaries and soldiers, raising illegitimate taxes, and otherwise oppressing the believers, all of which constitute acceptable grounds for deposing the ruler, whether he is the imam or someone of minor stature. It is no surprise, then, that Ibn Hazm became persona non grata at several local courts and that the king of Seville ordered the public burning of his books.

See also caliph, caliphate; Spain and Portugal (Andalus); Umayyads (661–750)

Further Reading

Ibn Hazm, *The Ring of the Dove*, translated by A. J. Arberry, 1994; Janina M. Safran, *The Second Umayyad Caliphate: The Articulation of Caliphal Legitimacy in al-Andalus*, 2000; Abdel Magid Turki, "L'engagement politique et la théorie du califat d'Ibn Hazm (384/994–456/1064)," *Bulletin d'études orientales* 30, no. 2 (1978); David J. Wasserstein, *The Caliphate in the West: An Islamic Political Institution in the Iberian Peninsula*, 1993; Idem, *The Rise and Fall of the Party Kings: Politics and Society in Islamic Spain, 1002–1086*, 1985.

CAMILLA ADANG

Ibn Jamaʻa (1241–1333)

The Banu Jamaʻa were one of the native Arab families that formed the new judicial and religious aristocracy that rose with the establishment of Mamluk rule in Egypt in 1250 and virtually

monopolized its Islamic learning system and judicial administration. The Banu Jama'a were originally an obscure Shafi'i family from Hamat (in northern Syria) who traced their descent to the Arab tribe of Kinana. They became the dominant Shafi'i family in the Mamluk state within a relatively short time. They were active in Damascus, Cairo, and Jerusalem between 1291 and 1383, during which three generations of the Ibn Jama'a family intermittently held the position of chief judge (*qaḍī al-quḍāt*) in Egypt and occasionally also in Damascus. The rise of the Banu Jama'a as one of the wealthy and leading religious families was due mainly to the achievement of one member of the family, Badr al-Din Muhammad b. Jama'a, the grandson of a provincial jurist, Burhan al-Din Sa'd Allah b. Jama'a (1200–1277).

Badr al-Din Muhammad was born in Hamat in 1241 and was educated in the traditional branches of Islamic learning. The early public positions he held were of professor (*mudarris*) in Damascus and preacher (*khaṭīb*) and prayer leader (imam) of the al-Aqsa Mosque in Jerusalem. In 1288, he was appointed as the Shafi'i judge of Jerusalem, and in 1291 he was summoned to Cairo by the Mamluk sultan Ashraf Khalil to serve as the Shafi'i chief judge in Egypt. In the wake of Ashraf Khalil's assassination, he was dismissed and transferred to Damascus, where he served as head of the Sufi orders (*shaykh al-shuyūkh*), chief judge, and professor. He was reinstated as the Shafi'i *qāḍī al-quḍāt* in Egypt in 1302. In 1310, he was dismissed by Sultan al-Nasir Muhammad, who disliked him, but his appointment was renewed the following year. He served in this position and in teaching positions in prestigious madrasas, or colleges, in Cairo until 1327, when he retired. He devoted himself to writing and teaching until he died in Cairo in 1333.

The Banu Jama'a maintained their position of distinction in Cairo after Badr al-Din Muhammad's death, thanks to the careers of his son 'Izz al-Din 'Abd al-'Aziz (1294–1366) and his nephew Burhan al-Din Ibrahim b. 'Abd al-Rahim (1325–88). The family enjoyed an established position in Jerusalem until the Ottoman conquest, probably because of the remoteness of the city from the political centers of the Mamluk state.

Badr al-Din Muhammad b. Jama'a was one of the most erudite and prolific scholars of his age. His 33 known works deal with a wide range of topics of Islamic traditional sciences, such as Qur'an commentary, hadith, jurisprudence, education, and Arabic language and literature. Ibn Jama'a left his mark on Islamic political thought mainly through his book *Tahrir al-Ahkam fi Tadbir Ahl al-Islam* (Summary of the rules to govern the people of Islam), which reflects the political circumstances of his time. After the destruction of the Abbasid caliphate by the Mongols in 1258, a new political order was created in the Muslim world: the Mamluk regime emerged as a great power and became the new guardian of orthodox Islam. The Mamluk sultan Zahir Baybars set up an Abbasid shadow caliphate in Cairo in 1261. Devoid of any ruling power, the caliph nevertheless played an important ceremonial role in legitimizing Mamluk rule by delegating his authority to the sultan. Much like their predecessors during the Buyid and Seljuq eras, the jurists of the time had to define the sultans' political and religious authority. Ibn Jama'a's restatement of the theory of rulership, which in general mirrors the prevailing view at the time, is that the seizure of government itself accords authority and that oppressive power is preferable to anarchy and therefore must be obeyed. This view justified the assumption of caliphal powers by sultans and laid the theoretical basis for their acceptance by the orthodox 'ulama'. The legitimacy of usurpation of power had already been addressed in the Islamic constitutional theories worked out by earlier jurists. Mawardi (d. 1058) had recognized the de facto provincial rulers (*imārat al-istīlā'*) who attained power by military force, and the caliph was under obligation to delegate authority to them in the interests of peace and order. Ghazali (d. 1111) viewed the sultanate, normally supported by military power, as a necessary element in the caliphate itself. Like his contemporary Ibn Taymiyya (d. 1328), Ibn Jama'a took a further step and avoided the distinction between the sultanate and the imamate. That is, he acknowledged the possibility that the caliphate is absorbed by the sultanate and that the functions formerly ascribed to the caliph (or imam) are performed by the sultan. In the absence of an imam, Ibn Jama'a also permitted the rule of an unqualified person who usurped power and ruled by force without pledging an oath of allegiance (*bay'a*) and held that it is in the interest of Muslims to obey him for the sake of unity and general well-being. For the same reasons, he argued, sins committed by the imam or sultan should be forgiven and should not lead to their removal.

Ibn Jama'a's theory is in line with classical Islamic political thought. He affirms that the appointment of an imam or sultan is necessary to protect religion (to "command the right and forbid the wrong"), to defend Islam from its enemies (jihad), and to conduct the affairs of the community with justice. He emphasizes the sultan's need to consult with the 'ulama' and their obligation not to withhold advice from him. In fulfilling his duties the ruler has the right to expect obedience from his subjects.

See also Mamluks (1250–1517)

Further Reading

Antony Black, *The History of Islamic Political Thought*, 2001; Ann K. S. Lambton, *State and Government in Medieval Islam*, 1981; K. S. Salibi, "The Banū Jamā'a, a Dynasty of Shafiite Jurists in the Mamlūk Period," *Studia Islamica* 9 (1958).

AMALIA LEVANONI

Ibn Khaldun (1332–1406)

Ibn Khaldun (1332–1406) was a historian, philosopher, sociologist, and official during a period that scholars sometimes refer to as the decline of the Muslim Arab regimes of North Africa and the Middle East. Born in Tunis to a family of Andalusian Muslim politicians and scholars, his youth was spent learning the traditional Islamic

sciences of Qur'an, hadith, Arabic, and law (*fiqh*). During the first 20 years of his life, he remained in Tunisia, where he witnessed political upheavals and experienced the intellectual stagnation beginning to affect North Africa. A plague also swept through the region, and his parents were among the many lives it claimed. These events greatly influenced his thinking and understanding of the world, as his later writings would demonstrate.

Ibn Khaldun spent the next 30 years of his life moving from place to place, balancing his interest in politics with teaching and writing. He spent years roaming before settling in Fez, Morocco, where he remained for eight years, occupying various government positions. He then spent many years traveling back and forth across North Africa, including visits to Bougie and Biskra, and going to Muslim-controlled areas of Spain, particularly Granada. All the while, he strove to dedicate himself to scholarship, but in all instances he could not resist the lure of government work. The constant shifting in his allegiance that his lifestyle dictated is what many scholars believe was the cause of his dismissal from official positions, as well as the catalyst for his engagement in constant traveling. He did succeed in settling in Algeria for a number of years at the castle of Salama. It was there that he began to write his magnum opus, the *Muqaddima* (Prolegomena).

In the remaining 20 years of his life, Ibn Khaldun curtailed his political career and focused on scholarly activities. He took up residence in Cairo and was appointed to a number of positions, including those of teacher and judge (qadi) of Maliki *fiqh*, an Islamic legal school (*madhhab*) based on the legal interpretations of Imam Malik, at one point becoming the head judge of Maliki rite in Egypt. In 1401, he was appointed an envoy and sent on a special mission to Damascus, which placed him in contact with the Mongol leader Timur (Tamerlane). Ibn Khaldun took part in the negotiations with Timur, an incident about which he wrote in detail. He spent the remaining years of his life teaching and compiling his works.

Ibn Khaldun did not produce a large number of books, but the *Muqaddima*, the introduction he wrote to his universal history, *Kitab al-'Ibar* (The book on important events), would have an impact on social scientists in an array of fields the world over. In this work, he defines history as the study of the entire human past, including its social, economic, and cultural facets. His primary emphasis is on social events. This concern led him to develop an innovative sociological concept he termed *'aṣabiyya*, which he defined as the bond that all humans share and that leads human beings to establish communities with one another. The *Muqaddima*, praised as a historical and sociological masterpiece, laid the foundation for other social sciences, such as economics and psychology.

See also Berbers; North Africa; Tamerlane (1336–1405)

Further Reading

Ibn Khaldun, *The Muqaddimah: An Introduction to History*, translated by Franz Rosenthal, 1967; Yves Lacoste, *Ibn Khaldun: The Birth of History and the Past of the Third World*, 1984; Bruce Lawrence, ed., *Ibn Khaldun and Islamic Ideology*, 1984; Nathaniel Schmidt, *Ibn Khaldun: Historian, Sociologist, and Philosopher*, 1967; Róbert Simon, *Ibn Khaldun: History as Science and the Patrimonial Empire*, translated by Klara Pogatsa, 2002.

MATTHEW LONG

Ibn Rushd (1126–98)

Abu al-Walid Muhammad b. Ahmad b. Rushd, whose name was Latinized to Averroes, was born in Córdoba into a politically active family of prominent religious jurists of the Maliki school. He studied Arabic grammar and literature, Qur'anic sciences, hadith, jurisprudence, theology, philosophy, natural sciences, and medicine. Following in the footsteps of his father and grandfather, he served as a judge, first in Seville (1169–72) and then as a chief judge in Córdoba (1172–82), a position that presumably was the highest civil authority in the city. After that, he became chief physician at the court of the Almohads in Marrakesh. Ibn Tufayl introduced him to the prince Abu Ya'qub Yusuf b. Tashufin, who asked him to comment on the books of Aristotle. He wrote short commentaries (*jawāmi'*), middle commentaries (*mukhtaṣar*), and long commentaries (*tafsīr*) on them in Arabic, some of which have survived only in Hebrew or Latin translations. It was due to their influence in Latin Europe that Ibn Rushd was called "The Commentator." Ibn Rushd also wrote important theological-philosophical, juridical, and medical books. He enjoyed the favor of the caliph Ya'qub al-Mansur until 1195, when he was tried and banished to Lucena, near Córdoba, and his philosophical books were burned. Biographers give different reasons for his fall from favor, all of which are of a political nature. Although Ibn Rushd was brought back to honor, he did not live long after those degrading events.

Ibn Rushd surpasses other Muslim philosophers in his awareness of the political character of religious law. Arguing against Muslim theologians, he states that prophecy is not to be proved by performing miracles but by its rational character, which consists of the empowerment of the sociopolitical function of religion in order to create and maintain order. The laws established by the prophets are essential for man's well-being, and they are derived from both reason and revelation. Their rational character is a commonality between them, and they surpass civil laws by being revealed. According to Ibn Rushd, philosophers acknowledge that religion aims at addressing the general public by using methods other than philosophical demonstration. Religious prescriptions that enhance virtuous conduct are, therefore, indispensable for a political community so that individuals can attain a life of virtue in this world and eternal happiness in the next.

Based on his belief in the unity of truth equally borne by religion and philosophy, Ibn Rushd argued, drawing on the Qur'an, that Qur'anic statements that apparently contradict reason should be interpreted allegorically by the philosophers. However, he also

argued that the true meaning of the ambiguous verses should not be announced to the masses in order to protect the community from friction and division. Aware of the political dimensions of Qur'anic exegesis, he considers the harmony of philosophy and religion to correspond to the harmony within the community. Some of his attitudes reflect his agreement with the Almohad doctrine established by Ibn Tumart.

Ibn Rushd summarized Plato's *Republic* instead of Aristotle's *Politics*, which was not available to him. Drawing on his knowledge of Aristotle and Islam, he used the *Republic* to display his ideas on the best governance. In essence, he considered the ideal Islamic state, which is basically led by the revealed law, as one that reflects Plato's ideal city. He applied Plato's political ideas as generally valid principles to Muslim concepts and institutions in past and present. However, he read Plato's political philosophy with the eyes of an orthodox Muslim who acknowledges the supremacy of the revealed and comprehensive shari'a.

Following Aristotle, Ibn Rushd considers politics to be, along with ethics, the second part of the practical science, which differs from the theoretical sciences in that its subject is the deeds people commit willfully and out of choice. Ethics addresses individuals; it deals with dispositions, volitional actions, and habits in general, explaining how they are related and how they affect each other. Politics addresses the community, examining how dispositions can be established in the souls and enhanced to become perfect.

Like Plato, Ibn Rushd saw an analogy between the just order of the soul and the just order of the city. The inhabitants of the virtuous city do the work assigned to them according to their natural capabilities. The rulers and the state can implant virtue in the souls of citizens by persuasion and coercion; persuasion takes place by means of rhetoric, coercion by war. Ibn Rushd observes that both ways have been practiced in Islam.

In liberal statements that are not in agreement with traditional Islamic teaching and practice, Ibn Rushd assigns to women an equal share in the management of state affairs as well as in warfare. Indeed, according to him, women could become philosophers and rulers. Furthermore, the fact that women, in his society, are confined to the rearing of children and not allowed to work other than a few lower jobs like spinning and weaving is for him one cause of the poverty of Andalusian society. However, when dealing with delicate matters that involved the community of women and children, he reports Plato's opinion in a narrative fashion and refrains from adopting it.

Like Farabi, Ibn Rushd states that the ruler of the virtuous city has to be a philosopher, lawgiver, king, and imam, giving a linguistic explanation of the last word as "he who is followed in his actions." As a political realist, he declares prophetic revelation to be useful but not necessary for virtuous governance, which is primarily based on reason and aims ultimately at bringing about happiness and providing the conditions necessary for people to pursue the good life. Ibn Rushd acknowledges the possibility that persons who are qualified to be virtuous rulers could exist in his time and under Islam, and if they rule for a long, uninterrupted period, the virtuous city could come into being. He states in a pragmatic way that, although Plato gave the best manner for its emergence, the virtuous city could emerge in a different manner and that already existing states could achieve the ideal status. This takes a long time to happen and is accomplished through both the beliefs and the deeds of virtuous rulers.

Considering the ideal Platonic state and the early Islamic state under Muhammad and the Rightly Guided Caliphate to be two paradigms for perfect governance, Ibn Rushd compares them with later Muslim states, giving examples from Islamic history that show the degeneration of virtuous governance. Evaluating the contemporary political situation in general, he pessimistically states that the rulers who remain virtuous according to the prescriptions of the Qur'an are rare. He criticizes the dynasties of many of the Muslim kings in his day for preserving the laws merely to keep their family privileges and usurp public property.

Ibn Rushd's teachings on the separation of reason and faith as well as the autonomy and universality of the intellect contributed widely to the development of European political thought, especially concerning the separation of church and state and the establishment of political rule on the basis of reason instead of religious authority. These secular ideas were adopted by several intellectuals in the 20th century, who strove to modernize the religious discourse in Islam and establish freedom of thought and expression in the Arab world. Despite their different political colors, their secularism is uniquely linked to Ibn Rushd.

See also al-Farabi, Abu Nasr (ca. 878–950); Ghazali (ca.1058–1111); Ibn Sina, Abu 'Ali (980–1037); philosophy

Further Reading

Averroes, *On the Harmony of Religion and Philosophy*, translated by George F. Hourani, 1976; Charles Butterworth, *Philosophy, Ethics and Virtuous Rule: A Study of Averroes' Commentary on Plato's "Republic,"* 1986; Majid Fakhry, *Averroes (Ibn Rushd): His Life, Works and Influence*, 2001; Ibn Rushd, *The Incoherence of the Incoherence*, translated by Simon van den Bergh, 1954; Oliver Leaman, *Averroes and His Philosophy*, 1988; Ralph Lerner, trans., *Averroes on Plato's Republic*, 1974; E.I.J. Rosenthal, ed., *Averroes' Commentary on Plato's Republic*, 1956; Dominique Urvoy, *Ibn Rushd (Averroes)*, 1991.

GEORGES TAMER

Ibn Sina, Abu 'Ali (980–1037)

Known as Avicenna in the Christian West, Abu 'Ali b. Sina is probably the most influential Muslim philosopher and the key figure of Islamic Aristotelianism. Political philosophy as part of practical wisdom (*al-ḥikma al-'amaliyya*) appears to be a minor constituent of his thought, which is dominated by metaphysical issues. The final chapters (10:2–5) of his *Kitab al-Shifa'* (The book of the cure) provide a summary account of his political teaching.

According to Ibn Sina, a human being cannot exist without companions and helpers who assist him in satisfying his needs. Human beings thus need to establish cities and live in communities. Companionship, in turn, leads to transactions (*mu'āmalāt*), which must be conducted in accordance with the tradition of justice (*sunnat al-'adl*). Such a tradition can be established only by a prophet, who is recognized through his miracles. The inhabitants of cities comprise three groups: governors (*mudabbirūn*), artisans (*ṣunnā'*), and guardians (*ḥafaẓa*). Each group has its own hierarchy. Every man occupies a specific station and brings some particular benefit to the city. No one should exploit another or receive his subsistence without labor, except the sick and weak, who should be placed together with an appointed guardian.

The city should have at its disposal public funds raised by collecting a certain portion of the profit made through transactions and by confiscating the property of those who desert the tradition. These funds should be used for the common good and maintenance of guardians. Occupations that imply a transfer of property without mutual benefit (such as gambling), harm somebody (such as theft and solicitation), or intrude on public benefit (such as usury) should be forbidden. Likewise, pursuing objectives that contradict the fundamental principles of the city is forbidden. Examples are fornication and sodomy: they undermine the principle of marriage and family, upon which the survival of humankind depends.

The prophet, who founds the tradition, is succeeded by a vicegerent (*khalīfa*). Direct appointment of the vicegerent by his predecessor is preferable to his appointment by the unanimous decision of a group of elders, because such an appointment will prevent disagreement, division, and dissent among citizens. The vicegerent must be independent in his decisions; possess an innate intellect and noble character traits, such as courage and purity in act and thought; and have proper governing skills. Hence whoever has a more powerful intellect and nobler character traits and is better at governing is more deserving to be a vicegerent. The vicegerent also must know the law (shari'a) better than anyone else. However, people must obey the vicegerent even if he has only some of the required qualifications (namely, if he does not possess an exceptionally powerful intellect, or if he possesses only few—but not all—noble character traits); in this case, he can be regarded as vicegerent only in some aspects. Those who refuse to recognize the vicegerent should be persuaded to do so by force or wealth (i.e., gifts). If this does not work, other citizens should fight and kill them; if they can fight these renegades but do not, they disobey God. After faith in the Prophet, allegiance to the victorious vicegerent by defending his right by every possible means is the next best way to be close to God.

The vicegerent's duty is to perform the acts of worship (*'ibādāt*), such as public prayers and festivals; perform transactions that support the pillars of the city; and create and lead public enterprises that prevent injustice and treachery (e.g., public executions of criminals). He also must prevent dangerous or risky transactions, thus defending the inhabitants of the city and their property. The vicegerent must be moderate in his appetites, temperament, and the way he governs, choosing the golden mean (the medium between extremes) whenever possible. He must achieve happiness by theoretical wisdom. If he possesses the aforementioned qualities and habits, then he truly can be regarded as the human lord (*rabb insānī*), the ruler of the Earth, and God's vicegerent.

Ibn Sina's political teaching, evidently influenced by Plato's *Republic* and the Shi'i doctrine of the imamate, has come down to us as a set of brief remarks on three interconnected issues: government of the city, prophecy, and vicegerency. Although Ibn Sina was deeply involved in practical politics, he never developed his seminal political ideas into an elaborate system, or if he did, he never put it into writing.

See also city (philosophical); al-Farabi, Abu Nasr (ca. 878–950); philosophy

Further Reading

Charles E. Butterworth, *The Political Aspects of Islamic Philosophy*, 1992; Dimitri Gutas, *Avicenna and the Aristotelian Tradition*, 1988; Abu Ali Ibn Sina, *The Metaphysics of Avicenna*, edited and translated by Michael Marmura, 2004; Tony Street, *Avicenna*, 2005.

YANIS ESHOTS

Ibn Taymiyya (1263–1328)

The writings of this major independent Sunni mufti, theologian, and activist of the Mamluk period influenced various reformist and puritanical developments in later Muslim societies. Often misinterpreted, they remain central in modern Islamist ideology and Muslim recourse to violence.

Taqi al-Din Ahmad b. 'Abd al-Halim b. Taymiyya was born in Harran (in present-day southeastern Turkey) on January 22, 1263, to a family of Hanbali scholars and, fleeing the Mongol threat, settled in Damascus in 1269. He spent his life in the Mamluk sultanate—Syria, Egypt, Palestine, and the Hijaz—and died in prison in Damascus on September 26, 1328.

Autobiographical statements and abundant contemporaneous corroboration by witnesses and historians make Ibn Taymiyya one of the most widely documented figures of classical Islam. Many sources nevertheless remain to be systematically examined to further shed light on his ideas and life, keeping in mind that Taymiyyan studies often suffer from uncritical editions, poor translations, and the absence of a precise chronology and proper contextualization.

Ibn Taymiyya's education and lifelong quest for knowledge made him a formidable champion of Prophetic tradition (hadith) and an expert not only in traditional religious sciences—Qur'anic exegesis, jurisprudence, theology (*kalām*), and heresiography—but also in Sufism, comparative religion, logic, and philosophy

(*falsafa*). He already was considered qualified to give fatwas at the age of 17 (1279) and actually began to teach hadith in Damascus in 1284 and Qur'anic exegesis one year later at the Umayyad Mosque. He would remain a teacher and a mufti until his death, working sometimes under very difficult circumstances. A prolific writer, Ibn Taymiyya authored, besides innumerable fatwas, various creeds (*'aqīda*) and treatises on the most diverse religious questions, long works that have become seminal references in their fields: in theology, *Dar' al-Ta'arrud* (Rejecting contradictions between reason and tradition); in Shi'itology, *Minhaj al-Sunna* (The way of the Prophet's Sunna) refuting *Minhaj al-Karama* (The way of charisma) by the Imami theologian Mutahhar al-Hilli (d. 1325); in polemics against Christians, *al-Jawab al-Sahih* (The correct response); in philosophy, *al-Radd 'ala al-Mantiqiyyin* (The refutation of the logicians); in economics, *al-Hisba fi al-Islam* (The Hisba in Islam); and in politics, *al-Siyasa al-Shar'iyya* (The book of governance according to the shari'a).

Ibn Taymiyya was often involved in public affairs. He had his first problems with the authorities in 1294, when he publicly demanded the death penalty for a Christian accused of insulting the Prophet. Actively taking it upon himself to implement the religious duty to command right and forbid wrong, he is said to have, among other things, shaved children's heads, led an antidebauchery campaign in brothels and taverns, struck an atheist with his hand before his public execution, destroyed a supposedly sacred rock in a mosque, conducted attacks on astrologers, and obliged deviant Sufi shaykhs to make public acts of contrition and to adhere to the sunna. He not only exhorted to jihad on various occasions but also personally took part in some expeditions and battles. During the Mongol invasion of Syria in 1299–1300, he was one of the leaders of the resistance in Damascus and, through direct discussions with the Ilkhan Mahmud Ghazan, his vizier Rashid al-Din Fadl Allah, and Tatar commanders, obtained the release of a number of Syrian prisoners, both Muslim and *dhimmī*.

Ghazan's defeat at Shaqhab in 1303, after that of Kitbuga at 'Ayn Jalut in 1260 and the fall of Acre, the last stronghold of the crusaders in Palestine in 1290, confirmed Ibn Taymiyya in his conviction that the Mamluks were the champions of Islam, although the internal stability of the sultanate was often mired in rivalries between the great amirs, which he sometimes personally experienced. In 1306–7, for example, when a theological controversy led to his trial and imprisonment in Cairo, the amir Baybars al-Jashnikir sided with his opponents and had him detained in a dungeon, whereas the amir Salar strived for his release and eventually obtained it. The young sultan al-Nasir Muhammad b. Qalawun himself was forced to contend with such powerful amirs. He was deposed twice and did not really rule before his third reign started in 1310. Ibn Taymiyya was nevertheless loyal to Nasir Muhammad, to the point of calling him the promised renewer of the religion for his age. In 1310, as a sort of *éminence grise*, or minister without portfolio, he advised the sultan on various religious affairs and policies and composed his *al-Siyasa al-Shar'iyya* with him in mind.

Ibn Taymiyya's sometimes close relations with the highest powers in the Mamluk sultanate did not protect him from detention on six different occasions, for a total of more than six years, between 1306 and 1328. The pretexts invoked related mainly to his theological views on the divine attributes and the oneness of existence, and later on to his jurisprudential positions on repudiation and on the visitation of graves. The real reasons were more trivial and had to do with his noncompliance with doctrines and practices prevalent among powerful religious and Sufi establishments of his time, an overly outspoken personality, the jealousy of his peers, the risks to public order due to his popular appeal, and political intrigues. He was supported both materially and spiritually until the end by his brothers, a group of companions and disciples like Ibn Qayyim al-Jawziyya (d. 1350). In fact, he called prison "a divine blessing" and he had "no motive to be afraid of people: no school (madrasa), no land grant (*iqṭā'*), no wealth, no leading position (*ri'āsa*), nothing!" In another, clearly autobiographical text, probably written during his last detention, he explains that "when a scholar forsakes what he knows of the Book of God and of the sunna of His Messenger, and follows the ruling of a ruler which contravenes a ruling of God and His Messenger, he is a renegade, an unbeliever who deserves to be punished in this world and in the hereafter."

Ibn Taymiyya's political thought is generally derived from his two books, *al-Siyasa al-Shar'iyya* and the *Hisba*, and even more so from his anti-Mongol fatwas. Many modern scholars and activists alike trace three central Islamist theses back to him: a clear-cut division of the world into the abode of Islam (*dār al-islām*) and the abode of unbelief (*dār al-kufr*) or war (*dār al-ḥarb*); the anathematization (*takfīr*) of any Muslim who disobeys religion; and the duty to oppose and kill Muslim rulers who do not implement the revealed Law (shari'a). He has thus become a sort of forefather of al-Qaeda. The Taymiyyan paternity of these three theses, however, can be disputed. Asked, for example, about Mardin—in his time, a little Mongol protectorate with a Muslim ruler and a religiously mixed population—Ibn Taymiyya places it neither in *dār al-islām* nor *dār al-kufr*, but rather gives it a third, "composite" (*murakkab*) status. In a fatwa on the Qalandars, he sees faith as a quality defined by God and the Prophet, which people are not allowed to question according to their whims, and it is not enough to have reasons to anathematize someone: all the objections against doing so must also be refuted. Rather than being condemned, ignorant sinners, such as new converts, should be educated into the religion. Finally, it is in his anti-Mongol fatwas that Ibn Taymiyya used the application of alien laws in lieu of the shari'a as a stepping stone to declare Muslim rulers to be apostates and thus justify the duty to fight them. It was an argument aiming at mobilizing Syria's resistance against an invader, especially when the Ilkhan Oljaytu, Ghazan's successor, threatened once again to invade it, after converting to Shi'ism in 1313. It was a theology of war against an external enemy, not merely a call to, or the legitimation of, rebellion against the political power in place. Ibn Taymiyya's relations to his own rulers, the Mamluks, whose digressions from the revealed law must also have been manifest to him, were a via media between passive quietism

and insurrection. They were determined by three fundamentals modeled on the commitments undertaken by the Companions when they pledged allegiance to the Prophet: "to obey within obedience to God, even if the one giving the order is unjust; to abstain from disputing the authority of those who exert it; and to speak out the Truth—or take up its cause—without fear, in respect of God, of blame from anyone."

For Ibn Taymiyya, the type of submission imposed by the Tatars—absolute obedience—is of a pre-Islamic, ignorant (*jāhilī*) nature. Although there is in the Great Law (Yasa) of Chingiz Khan followed by the Ilkhans a paradigmatic type of "rational" (*'aqlī*) "royal regime" (*siyāsa malakiyya*), neither Pharaoh, nor the Mongol conquerer, nor any other human power deserves unconditional obedience. Rather than being compatible with Islam and providing an acceptable alternative to Mamluk rule as claimed by some of its advocates, Mongol absolutism is an abomination. As for the political ideas of Muslim philosophers, Ibn Taymiyya ridicules the Platonizing utopia of a philosopher-king propounded by Farabi but appreciates the praise that Ibn Sina heaps on the shari'a as an ideal law (*nāmūs*).

Both faith and reason, as represented by Ibn Sina and his like, concur in convincing Ibn Taymiyya of the value of Islam as a model for the governance of society. This model was implemented perfectly under Muhammad and the first generations of Muslims, before innovations started creeping in. After the sealing of prophethood, the community (*umma*) of believers, in its consensus (*ijmā'*), became the "guardian of the Law" and is divinely invested with prophetic infallibility (*'iṣma*). Indeed, as asserted in the hadiths, "the hand of God is with the communion (*jamā'a*) [of the believers]" and "there will be no consensus of the community on something that would lead it astray." For Ibn Taymiyya, "what the Muslims agree on is [the equivalent of] a truth brought by the Prophet." This empowerment of the community relieves it from all kinds of central, self-imposing authority, be it a Shi'i imamate or a Christian church. In this popular theocracy where God's sovereignty, as known from the Qur'an and the Prophetic tradition, is now exerted through the Muslims themselves, the norms are the equality of all, the respect of diversity in unity, tolerance, moderation, and ponderation. Justice (*'adl*) is, of course, also essential: "the Law (*shar'*) is justice and justice is the Law." As explained by Ibn al-Qayyim, this means that societal guidance (*siyāsa*) should not be based exclusively on scriptural sources; rather, "whatever the ways by which justice and equity (*qisṭ*) obtain, they are a part of the religion and do not go against it." As for commanding right and forbidding wrong, it is the responsibility of everyone, each in accordance with his capacity and place in society, and it is achieved through mutual consultation (*shūrā*), sincere advice (*naṣīḥa*), and mutual support (*ta'āwun*). Rather than delegation, direct involvement is encouraged, as everyone is always, in some way, a shepherd (*rā'in*) entrusted with a flock.

Ibn Taymiyya, thus, feels no nostalgia for the caliphate suppressed by the Mongols in 1258, especially for its autocratic type exemplified by Ma'mun's reign with its inquisition (*miḥna*), and can easily accommodate the political reality of his age in his vision of the Muslim commonwealth. A religion without the power (*sulṭān*) to assert itself, unable or unwilling to wage jihad, and devoid of resources (*māl*) would be threatened in its existence and remains imperfect, hence the usefulness of the Mamluks. On the other hand, the pursuit of power, wealth, and war for any purpose other than establishing the religion (*iqāmat al-dīn*) is obviously to be condemned—hence the necessity for 'ulama' to educate not only the people but also their rulers. Amirs and other authorities should notably learn to "render the trusts to those to whom they are due," as commanded in Qur'an 4:58. This means that they must share power and appoint the most qualified in the appropriate offices (*wilāya*) at all administrative levels, be they military or civil, religious or judicial. Those in command (*ulū al-amr*) have the right to be obeyed but must consult advisers and have no authority over people's consciences. Just as they are obliged to protect *dhimmīs* from injustice and forced conversion, they have the duty to preserve doctrinal diversity within the Muslim community. All the more certainly, in debated matters, they are prohibited from abusing their power to compel anyone to follow specific opinions. It is indeed not up to them nor to 'ulama' or other scholars, dead or alive, but up to "the entire community of Muhammad . . . to speak out about this." An empowerment of individual consciences with pure intentions goes hand in hand with Ibn Taymiyya's magisterial empowerment of the community and doctrinal disempowerment of its rulers. When no decision can be derived from the Qur'an and the sunna, "Muslims must be allowed to hold to their opinions, each of them worshipping God according to his *ijtihād*, and no judge can force anyone to accept the sayings of another." "When a mufti, a soldier (*jundī*), or a commoner (*'āmmī*), speaks of something, by *ijtihād* or *taqlīd*, with the aim of following the Messenger, each in accordance with his level of knowledge, they do not deserve chastisement . . . even if they make mistakes."

Ibn Taymiyya is as much a Sunni radical liberal as he is a populist puritan. Influenced by circumstances, the opinions of a mufti are not to be expected to constitute a comprehensive, integrated system of thought—all the more certainly a political philosophy—and many more elements will surely have to be added to the picture drawn here. Much work also remains to be done to understand the rationale behind some of Ibn Taymiyya's toughest actions in relation to his commitment to a religion of the middle way. What is certain at this stage, however, is that the Taymiyyan *siyāsa shar'iyya* has little in common with modern political Islam, with its Westernized insistence on the necessity of a strong state, indiscriminate use of violence, or recourse to terror. It can, in fact, be seen as an antiextremist approach to societal self-governance with a strong emphasis on ethics, both communitarian and individual, rather than on politics.

Ibn Taymiyya's influence has not yet been systematically explored. That his views were often caricatured or misused during the 20th century is obvious. To quote his anti-Mongol fatwas in order to anathematize, fight, or kill Anwar Sadat, the Algerian junta, or other Muslims leaders, for example, is to forget that Ibn Taymiyya wrote these fatwas against an invader and that he always remained loyal

to the Mamluk sultan Nasir. Moreover, to use these same fatwas to question the Islamic status of a country following laws other than the shari'a is to ignore that, for Ibn Taymiyya, the status of a country varies according to "the states of the hearts of its inhabitants," not according to the nature of its regime, and that every law contributing to more justice, whatever its origin, scriptural or not, is per se a part of the shari'a. Before the 20th century, Muhammad b. 'Abd al-Wahhab (d. 1792) is generally considered as the greatest and most faithful disciple of Ibn Taymiyya since Ibn al-Qayyim. Such a view shall almost certainly have to be revised, once the confirmed influence of the Mamluk theologian on Ottoman puritanical reformists like Birgivi Mehmed Efendi (d. 1573), Ahmad al-Rumi al-Aqhisari (d. ca. 1631), and Kadızade Mehmed (d. 1635) has been properly investigated.

See also Ahmad b. Hanbal (780–855); governance; Mamluks (1250–1517)

Further Reading

'Umar A. Farrukh, *Ibn Taymiyya on Public and Private Law in Islam*, 1966; Y. Michot, *Ibn Taymiyya: Against Extremisms*, 2011; Idem, *Muslims under Non-Muslim Rule: Ibn Taymiyya on Fleeing from Sin, Kinds of Emigration, the Status of Mardin (Domain of Peace/War, Domain Composite), the Conditions for Challenging Power*, 2006; Y. Rapoport and S. Ahmed, eds., *Ibn Taymiyya and His Times*, 2010.

YAHYA M. MICHOT

Ibn Tufayl (ca. 1105–85)

Abu Bakr Muhammad b. 'Abd al-Malik b. Muhammad b. Tufayl was born in Wadi Ash/Guadix, northeast of Granada, sometime at the beginning of the 12th century. His writings reveal that he had an extensive education in jurisprudence, surgery and medicine, and astronomy. He was also widely read in poetry and philosophy and knew the works of Hallaj, Ibn Sina, Farabi, Ibn Bajja, and Ghazali. Two centuries after Ibn Tufayl's death, Ibn al-Khatib wrote that he was "versatile in many arts."

In 1148, the Almohad dynasty seized control of the Maghrib and Andalusia, and six years later, Ibn Tufayl became secretary and physician to the governor of Granada. Upon the accession of Abu Ya'qub Yusuf to the Almohad caliphate (r. 1163–84), Ibn Tufayl joined his court in Cordoba as his physician and dearly cherished confidant. In 1182, he retired and was replaced by Ibn Rushd (d. 1198), whom he had earlier introduced to the intellectually inquisitive and learned caliph. Ibn Tufayl died in Marrakesh in 1185, having become so admired that Abu Ya'qub's son and successor presided at his funeral.

It was under the aegis of Abu Ya'qub that Ibn Rushd produced some of his greatest philosophical works, at the same time that Ibn Tufayl wrote on astronomy, medicine, and philosophy. Ibn Tufayl's writings on astronomy have not survived, but after his death, he was praised by Nur al-Din al-Bitruji (d. ca. 1204) in his *Principles of Astronomy* for having developed a cosmological theory that ran counter to Ptolemy's. As a physician, Ibn Tufayl was remembered by Abu 'Abdallah Muhammad b. al-Abbar (d. 1260), Ibn al-Khatib (d. 1374), and as late as Maqqari (d. 1631), although only his long poem on medicine (*Urjuza fi al-Tibb*) summarizing his findings survived; the manuscript was preserved at the Qarawiyyin Library in Fez, Morocco. Ibn Tufayl was also one of the great "philosophers of the Muslims" (*falāsifat al-Muslimīn*) according to 'Abd al-Wahid al-Marrakushi (1185–ca. 1262). He wrote extensively on physics and metaphysics, ever seeking to harmonize philosophy (*ḥikma*) and theology (shari'a) and Greek thought with Islamic law. Chiefly ascetical, a few samples of his poetry have survived in biographical accounts about him.

Marrakushi and Ibn al-Khatib, along with Maqqari, mentioned specifically *Risalat Hayy ibn Yaqzan* (Epistle of Hayy b. Yaqzan), on which Ibn Tufayl's reputation rests. This short novella was probably written between 1177 and 1182 in response to a query by a "dear brother" or friend about the nature of the mystical experience that characterized "Eastern Wisdom." Aimed against the formidable jurist Ghazali (d. 1111) and using a storyline from the Persian philosopher-physician Ibn Sina (d. 1037), Ibn Tufayl demonstrated that the human mind—represented by his protagonist Hayy b. Yaqzan, "Alive son of Awake"—without any theological or intellectual instruction, can attain the truth of enlightenment. At the same time, Ibn Tufayl emphasized that the same truth was available to those who sought it by religious revelation, either through interpretation (*bāṭin*) or through obedience to its apparent (*ẓāhir*) laws. Importantly for Ibn Tufayl, the mystical truth of enlightenment was similar in its origin and destination to the Qur'anic experience, thus explaining the harmony between "wisdom and the Islamic sciences," as Marrakushi wrote.

Judging by the number of manuscripts of *Hayy ibn Yaqzan* that have survived, it was widely read throughout the medieval and early modern periods, not only in Arabic but also in various translations: in Hebrew (13th and 15th centuries), Latin (15th century), English (17th and 18th centuries), Dutch (17th century), and German (18th century). Other translations followed in the modern period. It was thanks to its Latin translation and publication in Oxford in 1671 by the English Orientalist Edward Pococke the Younger that it entered into Western thought—most famously through Daniel Defoe's *Robinson Crusoe*. From regions extending from Spain to New England, and from Oxford to Florence to Aleppo, *Hayy ibn Yaqzan* was the first literary Arabic text to leave its mark on early modern non-Muslim thinkers. By the beginning of the 21st century, it had been translated frequently into English and into various European and Asiatic languages.

See also Ibn Rushd (1126–98); philosophy; Spain and Portugal (Andalus)

Further Reading

Ibrahim al-Abyari, ed., *Al-Muqtadab Min Kitab Tuhfat al-Qadim*, 1957; Muhammad Sa'id al-'Aryan and Muhammad al-'Arabi al-'Alami, eds.,

Al-Mu'jib fi Talkhis Akhbar al-Maghrib, 1949; Avner Ben-Zaken, *Reading Ḥayy ibn-Yaqẓan*, 2011; Lawrence I. Conrad, *The World of Ibn Tufayl: Interdisciplinary Perspectives on Hayy ibn Yaqzan*, 1996; Henri Corbin, *Avicenna and the Visionary Recital*, 1988; Amélie Marie Goichon, *Le récit de Ḥayy b. Yaqẓān commenté par des textes d'Avicenne*, 1959; Bernard R. Goldstein, ed., Al-Bitruji: *On the Principles of Astronomy*, 2 vols., 1971; Lisan al-Din b. al-Khatib, *Al-Ihata fi Akhbar Gharnata*, 2 vols., 1974; Ahmad b. Muhammad al-Maqqari, *Nafh al-Tib Min Ghusn al-Andalus al-Ratib*, 1968; A. I. Sabra, "The Andalusian Revolt against Ptolemaic Astronomy: Averroes and al-Bitruji," in *Transformation and Tradition in the Sciences*, edited by Everett Mendelsohn, 1984.

NABIL MATAR

Ibn Tumart (ca. 1080–1130)

The Masmuda Berber Ibn Tumart was the founder of the Almohad movement that led to the establishment of the Mu'minid dynasty in the Islamic West (1130–1248). He is representative of the charismatic reformer whose preaching among tribesmen leads to the emergence of an army and of a state. His status as "the impeccable religious and political leader and the well-known Rightly Guided one" (*al-imām al-ma'ṣūm al-mahdī al-ma'lūm*) influenced the way his biography was written such that it is difficult to disentangle legend from actual facts. What follows is a summary of his standard biography, in which his relationship with Ghazali (1058–1111) is generally considered by Western scholars to have been invented. Some Arabic sources tend to apply the Prophet Muhammad's biographical model to Ibn Tumart, even presenting him as the Prophet's descendant.

Ibn Tumart was born in Igilliz, a village in the mountainous area of the Sus (in Southern Morocco), between 1078 and 1081 within the Harga tribe. Around 1106, he started his travel in search of religious knowledge, first visiting Andalus in 1107 and then the East, where he studied in Baghdad with scholars connected with the Nizamiyya madrasa (an institution of higher learning). Ibn Tumart then started his journey back to the Maghrib. In Alexandria, he met the Andalusi scholar Muhammad b. al-Walid al-Turtushi (d. 1126) and was forced to leave town after his performance of the precept of commanding good and forbidding evil. He continued his censoring activities on the ship that brought him to Tripoli around 1116 or 1117. From there, he proceeded to Mahdiyya, Monastir, Tunis, Constantine, and Bougie, where he arrived in 1117. In Mallala, near Bougie, he met 'Abd al-Mu'min b. 'Ali (r. 1133–63), a Zanata Berber of the Kumya tribe (in the region of Tlemcen), later to become the first Almohad caliph. Ibn Tumart, aware of 'Abd al-Mu'min's destiny, called him "the lamp of the Almohads." For his part, 'Abd al-Mu'min abandoned his intention to travel to the East, as he had already found in the West the religious knowledge (*'ilm*) he was looking for.

Ibn Tumart continued his journey in the company of 'Abd al-Mu'min and other pupils of his from different origins and backgrounds, stopping at Tlemcen, Agarsif, Fez, Meknes, and Salé. He continued censoring reprehensible practices such as men dressing like women, the use of musical instruments, the consumption of wine, and the crucifixion of living persons. He also engaged in debates with local scholars. The same pattern repeated itself in Marrakesh, the capital of the Almoravid Empire, where Ibn Tumart arrived in 1120. He censored the Almoravid custom of men using veils to cover their faces while women appeared in public unveiled. Having started teaching theology in the mosque, he was brought to debate in the presence of the Almoravid amir. Local scholars advised the amir to kill him, but Ibn Tumart—always accompanied by his disciples—managed to escape, seeking refuge first in Aghmat and then in his native town in 1121. There he continued his preaching, using the Berber language, and after retreating into a cave, he announced the appearance of the Mahdi, the one responsible for the suppression of error and the maintenance of truth, with whom he was eventually identified and acknowledged as such. The Almoravids had to be fought, he believed, because of their departure from correct belief, which was manifested in their anthropomorphism. In 1123 or 1124, Ibn Tumart and some of his followers emigrated to Tinmal in the Great Atlas, where the original settlers were massacred. Local tribal leaders became his followers, among them Abu Hafs 'Umar Inti from the Hintata Berbers, the forefather from which the later Hafsid dynasty (1229–1526) descended. A new political and military organization—grounded in Berber traditions—was developed to engage in the fight against the Almoravids and against those tribes, such as the Haskura, who refused to acknowledge the Almohad creed (*tawḥīd*). The close circle of the Mahdi's relatives and servants were called *ahl al-dār*. The Council of Ten (*al-jamā'a*) consisted of Ibn Tumart's first followers. The shaykhs of the tribes incorporated into the movement (Harga, Hintata, Gadmiwa, Ganfisa) constituted the Council of Fifty. A purge (*tamyīz*) that eliminated disaffected tribal elements took place in 1128, and one of Ibn Tumart's first followers, Bashir al-Wansharisi, was placed in charge of distinguishing between sincere believers and hypocrites.

In 1130, the Almohads besieged Marrakesh for six weeks but were eventually defeated in the Battle of Buhayra. Marrakesh did not fall into Almohad hands until many years later, in 1147, after the Almohad conquest of the north of Morocco and part of Algeria. Three months after the Battle of Buhayra, Ibn Tumart died, but his death, about which almost nothing is known, was hidden for some three years. In 1132, 'Abd al-Mu'min became the leader of the movement. Tinmal, the place where the Mahdi and the Almohad caliphs were buried, became a center of pilgrimage, and a mosque was built (which still stands).

Ibn Tumart was credited with several works, among them his creed (*'aqīda*) and his *Kitab*—also known by the title of the first treatise, "*A'azz ma Yutlab*" (The most precious that is sought after)—of which only a few copies are extant. Its contents still await a thorough analysis. Ibn Tumart's doctrine has been variously

explained, usually pointing to an Ash'ari background close to Mu'tazilism in terms of divine attributes. Its connections to Sufism and philosophy have been explored by Dominique Urvoy and Tilman Nagel, among others.

See also Almohads (1130–1269); Almoravids (1056–1147); commanding right and forbidding wrong; Ghazali (ca. 1058–1111); Mahdi; Spain and Portugal (Andalus)

Further Reading

R. Bourouiba, *Ibn Tumart*, 1974; M. Fierro, "Le *mahdi* Ibn Tumart et al-Andalus: l'élaboration de la légitimité almohade," *Revue d'Etudes sur le Monde Musulman et la Méditerranée* 91, no. 4 (2001); M. Fletcher, "The Almohad *Tawhid*: Theology Which Relies on Logic," *Numen* 38, no. 1 (1991); M. García Arenal, *Messianism and Puritanical Reform: Mahdis of the Muslim West*, translated by Martin Beagles, 2006; I. Goldziher, "Ibn Toumert et la théologie de l'Islam dans le Maghreb au XIe siécle," in *Le Livre de Mohammed Ibn Toumert*, edited by D. Luciani, 1903; M. Kisaichi, "The Almohad Social-Political System or Hierarchy in the Reign of Ibn Tumart," *Memoirs of the Research Department of the Tokyo Bunko* 48 (1990); E. Lévi-Provençal, "Ibn Toumert et 'Abd al-Mumin; le 'fakih du Sus' et le 'flambeau des Almohades,'" *Memorial Henri Basset* 2 (1928); H. Massé, "La profession de foi (*'aqida*) et les guides spirituels (*morchida*) du Mahdi ibn Toumert," *Mémorial Henri Basset* 2 (1928); T. Nagel, *Im Offenkundigen das Verborgene. Die Heilszusage des Sunnitischen Islams*, 2002; D. Urvoy, "La pensée d' Ibn Tumart," *Bulletin des Études Orientales* 27 (1974).

MARIBEL FIERRO

ideology

An ideology may be defined as a system of ideas and convictions that seeks to stimulate and guide or to resist major social and political change. Muslim political thinking has always been ideological in some respect, but modern ideologies are more consciously and systematically elaborated. They also have a more this-worldly orientation and involve a greater expectation that fundamental social change can be wrought by human effort. Modern Muslim ideologies have arisen mainly in response to Western domination and have been facilitated by the modern, Western-derived education that makes people receptive to them. They may be broadly divided into secularist ideologies, which take their cue from some Western ideologies, and Islamist (or fundamentalist) ideologies, which call for the full implementation of the shari'a in society. Islamic modernism is an intermediate category.

The most extreme secularists have been the Marxists, who, though antireligious in principle, have usually made some effort to co-opt Islamic institutions and ideas. Far more popular has been nationalism, usually in combination with other ideologies, such as socialism, capitalism, liberalism, or statism. These combine the prestige of the West with, in the case of nationalism, a claim to local authenticity. In most nationalist thinking, sovereignty resides in the nation (not God); Islam may be the religion of state, but the shari'a is to be replaced by human laws except in matters of "personal status"; and religious institutions are to be brought under state control. Both Iran and Egypt in the 1920s adopted this model, while Turkey under Atatürk (d. 1938) was more radical. The book, *Islam and the Principles of Governance,* published in 1925 by the Egyptian scholar 'Ali Abd al-Raziq (1888–1966), was a controversial but influential effort to provide an Islamic justification for secularism. Most of the Muslim countries that became independent after World War II followed a similar line. Particularly notable is the radically nationalist Ba'th Party that came to power in Syria and Iraq in the 1960s. A more moderate secularism is that of Indonesia's Five Principles (Pancasila), which include belief in God but not specifically Islam. Secularists may be personally pious and usually give value to Islam as a part of their national heritage.

"Islamic modernists," the intermediary ideological group, want a society guided by the shari'a interpreted flexibly and consistently with Western ideas. This was the position of the reformers Afghani (1838–97) and Muhammad 'Abduh (1842–1905) and of many others since their time, including the poet-philosopher Muhammad Iqbal (1876–1938), though rarely of those in political power. The writings of Fazlur Rahman (1909–88) probably best articulate the theory behind modernist thinking. Islamic modernism is well illustrated by the Pakistani constitution of 1973, which affirms the sovereignty of God and "the principles of democracy, freedom, equality, tolerance and social justice as enunciated by Islam" (Preamble).

Islamists call for "the application of the shari'a" without the Westernizing interpretations of the modernists, but they manifest many characteristics of modern ideology, such as systematic thinking about society and a conscious desire to make fundamental changes, and so appeal to people who have been exposed to ideology. The first Islamist movement was the Muslim Brotherhood, founded in Egypt in 1928 by Hasan al-Banna (1906–49). The second group was the Jama'at-i Islami, founded in India in 1941 by Mawdudi (1903–79), whose writings spread Islamist ideas worldwide. The Egyptian Brotherhood came to be a mass movement that suffered repression from 1954 to 1970. Out of this repression came the radical writings of Sayyid Qutb (1906–66), which have had wide influence, particularly among the extremists of the following decades. Among other Islamist groups was the Islamic Liberation Party, founded in East Jerusalem in 1952 and influential among students worldwide into the early 21st century. The "resurgence of Islam," beginning about 1970, fueled by a perceived failure of secularism and a decrease in Western moral authority, included increased support for Islamism and the appearance of many Islamist groups. Islamists came to power by revolution in Iran (1979), with the distinctively Shi'i doctrine of *wilāyat al-faqīh* (guardianship of the jurist), and by military coup in the Sudan (1989). Islamists along with others struggled against the Communists in Afghanistan and then were ousted by the

Taliban, an extremely traditionalist group, in 1996, who in turn were removed by direct Western intervention in 2001. Elsewhere, secularist governments have resisted Islamist takeovers but have become more "Islamic" in the process. While groups such as the Muslim Brotherhood and the Jama'at-i Islami have sought to work within the existing system, often facing government pressure and restriction, others have responded with violence. Among these are offshoots of the Muslim Brotherhood in Egypt, such as the al-Gama'a al-Islamiyya and the Egyptian Islamic Jihad. Particularly notorious are the "martyrdom operations" or "suicide attacks" mounted by al-Qaeda, by Hizbullah in Lebanon, by Hamas in Palestine, and by others (including some secularist groups), mainly against Western targets including Israel. An alternate direction, however, is suggested by the Justice and Development Party, which came to power in Turkey in 2002. Its background is Islamist, but it accepts the official secularism of Turkey while retaining some of its Islamic orientation. Those most prominent in the "Arab Spring" demonstrations for democracy in 2011 appear to have a similar ideological position, though some Islamists have supported these movements.

See also fundamentalism; liberalism; nationalism; Pan-Islamism; revival and reform; socialism; Westernization

Further Reading

Jason Burke, *Al-Qaeda: Casting a Shadow of Terror*, 2003; Hamid Enayat, *Modern Islamic Political Thought*, 1982; William E. Shepard, "The Diversity of Islamic Thought: Towards a Typology," in *Islamic Thought in the Twentieth Century*, edited by Suha Taji-Farouki and Basheer Nafi, 2004; John Obert Voll, *Islam: Continuity and Change in the Modern World*, 1994.

WILLIAM E. SHEPARD

ijtihād and *taqlīd*

In general, *ijtihād* means the exertion of effort, and in Islamic legal thought, it refers to the effort to determine God's will—the correct ruling—regarding a legal matter. One who practices *ijtihād* is termed a *mujtahid*. *Taqlīd* means "following, imitation." In Islamic legal discourse, *taqlīd* means adopting the opinion a *mujtahid* or other legal authority has reached, accepting it as authoritative. The one who adheres to such an authority is a *muqallid*, or performer of imitation. It is practically impossible to discuss *ijtihād* and *taqlīd* independently of each other.

Ijtihād is a process through which experts in the religious sciences explore and define the parameters of Islam. The sacred law of Islam establishes values, mores, and boundaries of Islamic society, and since not every Muslim is so situated that he can devote himself to religious and legal study, common sense dictates that such believers regularly practice *taqlīd*, following the guidance of a *mujtahid*. Some jurists associated *ijtihād* with *ra'y*, which in early Islamic legal literature meant a jurist's considered opinion. *Ijtihād* was the process through which *ra'y* was formed. If the considered opinion of a given jurist met widespread approval, it might come to be seen as properly authoritative, regardless of its basis in the Qur'an and sunna. Another concept often associated with *ijtihād* is *qiyās*, or reasoning by analogy. *Qiyās*, like *ra'y*, is a device one uses to answer questions that the Qur'an and sunna leave open. One uses *ijtihād* to apply *qiyās* to particular questions. Both *ijtihād* and *taqlīd* can take on negative senses: *ijtihād* can be taken to mean "interpreting law to fit one's individual needs," and *taqlīd* can be understood as "blind imitation."

Ijtihād is also used to mean the ability to found a new Islamic legal tradition. It has often been said that in Sunni Islam, the gate or door of *ijtihād* was closed in the distant past—ca. 900 or 1000—and remained so until the 19th century, at which time modernist, progressive thought provoked an intellectual reawakening and a return to a freer, more independent investigation of legal and other questions. Such statements must be understood as referring to the legal *madhhabs*—legal schools or traditions of legal study—which came to be limited to four Sunni schools in the 11th century, though the number had been somewhat larger in the previous century, including the Zahiri *madhhab*, founded by Dawud b. 'Ali b. Khalaf al-Isfahani (d. 884), and the Jariri *madhhab*, founded by Muhammad b. Jarir al-Tabari (d. 923). By the early tenth century, the nascent schools of law had coalesced around traditions of study that were claimed to represent the legacies of Abu Hanifa (d. 767), Malik b. Anas (d. 796), Muhammad b. Idris Shafi'i (d. 820), and Ahmad b. Hanbal (d. 855), as well as Dawud and Tabari. By the mid-tenth century, one may add the Twelver Shi'i, Zaydi Shi'i, and Ibadi Khariji *madhhabs*. After ca. 1000, it became recognized as unacceptable to begin a new tradition. It was already something of an embarrassment that the eponyms of the *madhhabs*, such as Shafi'i and Ibn Hanbal, were removed from the Companions of the Prophet by several generations, so it was difficult to argue that the legal system went back in an unbroken tradition to the Prophet himself. It was no longer possible to claim that the opinions one espoused could be connected with an authoritative tradition of opinions that had been passed down intact from the early generations of the pious forefathers, so establishing a new tradition became impossible. Muslim scholars did not stop practicing *ijtihād* at the end of the tenth century but rather changed their emphasis from examination of the Qur'an and sunna to further articulation of the shari'a as defined by the major schools of law. In this regard, the term *taqlīd* came to refer to adherence to one of these schools. That did not mean, however, that independent legal thought ceased in favor of the blind acceptance of traditional legal positions.

Recent scholarship has emphasized that, according to the works on legal theory and even according to the evidence of practice, *ijtihād* in the sense of the independent investigation of legal questions did not simply come to an end at any point in the premodern period. *Ijtihād* is required of a jurist who sets out to answer a legal question, and attainment of the rank of *mujtahid* is based on

a thorough education in the law, legal interpretation, and the sciences that are ancillary to it, such as Arabic grammar and rhetoric. Manuals of *uṣūl al-fiqh* or legal hermeneutics consistently require of the mufti (one who is qualified to offer a religious opinion or fatwa) that he be a *mujtahid* before he can answer legal questions. Other evidence suggests that this was often not the case and that muftis merely reported the standard views of their legal tradition, the opinion of other jurists, or legal rulings recorded in standard legal compendia. Nevertheless, even muftis who did not claim to be fully qualified *mujtahids* treated new questions that had not arisen earlier in history and so, by definition, required new legal research and the proposal of new rulings. Obvious examples are fatwas (religious opinions) having to do with the legality of coffee, tobacco, the printing press, telegraphs, photography, and many other technical inventions and imports to the Islamic world.

Ijtihād has also been used to refer to the degree of freedom a jurist enjoyed in formulating and propagating his opinions. It is clear that while *ijtihād* in the sense of expending an exhaustive effort in order to answer a legal question did not come to a halt, it is evidently true that jurists in the 13th and later centuries understood that they were not as free. Later jurists such as Jalal al-Din al-Suyuti (d. 1505), who claimed to be a *mujtahid* on a level with the eponyms of the legal traditions and capable of reaching opinions at variance with those of Shafi'i, the founder of the legal tradition to which he belonged, were roundly rebuked. Even Suyuti stated that while he arrived at a number of opinions in which he disagreed with Shafi'i, he did not give fatwas according to these opinions but gave the opinion generally accepted within the *madhhab*. His polemical work arguing for his own attainment of the rank of *mujtahid* rebukes his contemporaries for claiming that the status is no longer possible. In addition, legal theorists including Hasuna al-Nawawi (d. 1277) and later authors developed ranked schemes of jurists, including *mujtahid muṭlaq* (*mujtahid* at large), *mujtahid muntasib* (*mujtahid* affiliated with a particular *madhhab*), and so on; such schemes were almost always predicated on the idea that one or more ranks at the top of the scale were empty in the present generation. Many sources from the later period reveal that lower-level jurists often gave legal opinions simply by consulting the standard works of their traditions, even though the works of legal theory generally rejected this as invalid.

In the modern period, *ijtihād,* along with the term *tajdīd*, or "renewal," has taken on the meaning of searching or sweeping reform (*iṣlāḥ*) of traditional religious doctrines and societal practices in the Islamic world, generally equated with a rejection of *taqlīd*, here the unthinking adherence to ossified, traditional opinions. Its opposite, *taqlīd*, here means blind adherence to tradition. This use of the two terms departs considerably from their technical usage in premodern Islamic legal scholarship. *Ijtihād* in this sense has been used by a large number of modern Islamic thinkers belonging to a variety of distinct trends, including modernist reformers like Muhammad 'Abduh (d. 1905) and Rashid Rida (d. 1935), religious liberalists, utilitarians, and even fundamentalist thinkers. *Ijtihād* in this sense has been used as a means to reject certain traditional legal rules through rational arguments and appeals to utility, social benefits, or the necessity for legal change along with social transformations. A prominent example of the application of this type of *ijtihād* is a law made in Tunisia in 1956 that rejected polygyny on the grounds that the Qur'anic verse 4:3—which, ironically, had served as the legal basis for the practice—suggested that no husband would be able to treat cowives equally as required by the verse. Modern suggested reforms of Islamic legal hermeneutics have been quite varied, including the rejection of hadith (prophetic tradition) as foundational textual material for the derivation of law, the restriction of consideration to the principles found in the portion of the Qur'an revealed in Mecca, the rejection or restriction of the role of consensus in the law, the reevaluation of laws as conditioned by historical context, and the reinterpretation of *ijtihād* to include the opinions of scientists and scholars in fields other than jurisprudence. An important aspect of many of these reform efforts has been the emphasis on *maṣlaḥa*, or "public interest," as a central principle for the elaboration of the law.

Imami or Twelver Shi'is originally had no need for *ijtihād* because pressing questions could be referred to the present imam, whose opinions were infallible. Even when the Twelfth Imam went into the Greater Occultation in 941 (a period of concealment that continues to the present) and all ordinary contact with him was cut off, Twelver jurists traditionally rejected *ijtihād* on the grounds that it was based on personal opinion or legal analogy, neither of which was sufficient to answer legal questions. In their view, legal rules needed to have a scriptural basis in the Qur'an or the *akhbār*, the oral reports of the 12 imams. Nevertheless, in the 10th and 11th centuries, Twelver theorists admitted that the jurists of the community could in effect act as legal authorities, granting legal responses to petitioners, drawing in part on reason (*'aql*). By the 13th century, 'Allama al-Hilli (d. 1325) used the term *ijtihād* in his works on legal hermeneutics to describe the interpretive activity of Twelver jurists in a departure from earlier Twelver legal doctrine, and his view became standard. The application of *ijtihād* and the clear division of the believing populace into *mujtahid*s and *muqallid*s that it entailed were strongly challenged in the 17th century by Muhammad Amin al-Astarabadi (d. 1635), who argued that authority lay in the *akhbār* of the imams alone and not in the ratiocinations of the jurists. His work *al-Fawa'id al-Madaniyya* (Medinan moral lessons) touched off what would become known as the conflict between Akhbaris, who upheld Astarabadi's views, and Usulis, who held the view that an education in legal hermeneutics (*uṣūl al-fiqh*) was what granted one religious authority. The Akhbaris remained influential for over a century and a half but were defeated, for the most part, by Muhammad Baqir al-Bihbihani (d. 1791), whose work *Risalat al-Akhbar wa-l-Ijtihad* (Treatise on traditions and legal reasoning) was a major statement in justification of the Usuli position. Perhaps as a direct consequence of the Akhbari-Usuli conflict, the Twelvers stressed the necessity for all muftis to be endowed with *ijtihād* much more than contemporary Sunnis, and a diploma termed *ijāzat al-ijtihād* (diploma of *ijtihād*) recognizing the recipient's ability to derive legal opinions independently became a standard part of the

Twelver system of legal education in the course of the 19th century. In the Sunni system, the parallel diploma, which had existed at least since the 13th century, was termed *ijāzat al-iftā' wa-l-tadrīs*, or "the license to grant legal opinions and teach law"; it did not mention *ijtihād* explicitly, and recipients were not automatically termed *mujtahids*. Also in the 19th century, beginning with Muhammad Hasan Najafi (d. 1849–50), a single high-ranking jurist held to be the most learned in the law was recognized as *marja' al-taqlīd*, or "the model of emulation." Shi'i laymen were obligated to follow the rulings of this greatest living authority or, if more than one were recognized, one of them. The hierarchical authority of the jurists was enhanced yet again with Ayatullah Khomeini's (d. 1989) theory of *wilāyat al-faqīh* (guardianship of the jurist), which claimed for the most learned jurist the right to carry out most of the functions of the imam, including those that had fallen into abeyance, such as the ability to govern and to organize jihad. After the Iranian Revolution (1978–79) and the establishment of the Islamic Republic in 1981, his principle was enshrined in the Islamic Republic's constitution, which assigned to the leading jurist the position of "leader" (*rahbar*) and granted him sweeping powers of control and oversight.

See also consensus; jurisprudence; al-Shafi'i, Muhammad b. Idris (767–820); shari'a

Further Reading

Norman Calder, "Doubt and Prerogative: The Emergence of an Imāmī Shī'ī Theory of *Ijtihād*," *Studia Islamica* 70 (1989); Robert Gleave, "Conceptions of Authority in Iraqi Shi'ism: Baqir al-Hakim, Ha'iri and Sistani on Ijtihād, Taqlīd and Marja'iyya," *Theory, Culture, and Society* 24, no. 2 (2007); Wael B. Hallaq, *The Origins and Evolution of Islamic Law*, 2005; Idem, "Was the Gate of Ijtihād Closed?" *International Journal of Middle East Studies* 16, no. 1 (1984); Joseph Schacht, *The Origins of Muhammadan Jurisprudence*, 1967; Devin J. Stewart, *Islamic Legal Orthodoxy: Twelver Shiite Responses to the Sunni Legal System*, 1998.

DEVIN J. STEWART

Ilkhwan al-Safa'. *See* Brethren of Purity

Ilkhanids (1256–1336)

The descendants of Chingiz Khan, founder of the Mongol Empire (d. 1227), ruled in Iran as the Ilkhanid dynasty, the term "Il-khan" denoting "subject" or "subservient" khan—that is, acknowledging the sovereignty of the Great Qa'an (Khan). The first Il-Khan was Hulagu (r. 1256–65), grandson of Chingiz Khan and brother of the Great Qa'an, Mongke (r. 1251–59), who had dispatched Hulagu to complete the conquest of Iran in 1256. Mongke was the last Qa'an to rule from the Mongol capital at Qara Qorum, in the steppes; he was succeeded by another brother, Qubilay Khan (d. 1294), who established the imperial capital in China. The Ilkhanid dynasty was thus part of the Mongol Empire, which derived its legitimacy from the conquests and political dispensation of Chingizs Khan and owed nothing to Islamic political traditions. The chief aim of Hulagu's invasion was the subjugation of the Abbasid caliphate, and this was achieved by the conquest of Baghdad and the death of the caliph in 1258. Hulagu was a shamanist with a Christian wife; his successors in Iran maintained more or less close connections with their cousins in China and a sense of Mongol solidarity, as witnessed both by their coinage and also by their continuing rule according to Mongol tradition, the khan being served by a closely regulated household of loyal officers who acted both as bodyguards and government agents.

The political theorists of the Ilkhanid period, therefore, were confronted with the total collapse of Islamic norms and the need to dispense with the previous formulation of "usurped" coercive rule being exercised by authority delegated from the caliph. The establishment of a "shadow" Abbasid caliphate in Cairo allowed the jurists to maintain the fiction of caliphal authority in the Mamluk Sultanate for a time, but in Iran this theoretical construct was never to return, even once the Mongols officially converted to Islam under Ghazan Khan (r. 1295–1304). Instead, the political advisers of the Ilkhans, such as the philosopher Nasir al-Din al-Tusi, emphasized the practical aspects of good government, expressed largely in terms of encouraging sound economic and fiscal policies following the destruction of the Mongol conquests, and a glorification of the person of the monarch, modeled on the image of the legendary rulers of pre-Islamic Iran, particularly the Sasanians (224–642). Although the new vision of rule was both Iranian and secular, the Ilkhanate was still conceived as a dispensation sanctioned by God, and the promotion of Islamic ideals and the religious law was upheld as an important kingly virtue, especially under the Muslim Ilkhans. The most important royal quality, however, was justice. The ideal of just rule was not dependent on godliness but required the strength to maintain the stability of society and the protection of the weak from the tyranny of oppression. The exercise of justice was also assisted by the advice of wise counselors or the service of experienced ministers (especially the vizier), a formulation expressed in numerous historical works, including those written by prominent Persian bureaucrats such as 'Ata-Malik al-Juwayni (d. 1283) and Rashid al-Din al-Hamadani (d. 1318), whose chronicles sought to portray the Mongol rulers as conforming to the norms of Perso-Islamic political traditions. The didactic element of these works essentially provided a model of political thought close to the exemplary Mirrors for Princes, or handbooks of advice to kings, that had such a long history in Indo-Persian "wisdom literature." The fact that the acculturation of the Ilkhanid regime to Iranian conditions was still not achieved by the death of the last recognized

ruler, Abu Sa'id (r. 1317–35), is shown by the events of the next 20 years, during which a series of would-be Ilkhans struggled unsuccessfully to win the throne in a manner reminiscent of the tribal politics of the Inner Asian steppe. The last Chingizid ruler was murdered in 1353, by which time descent from the conqueror was also devalued as a source of legitimacy, and the sword remained the ultimate sanction for political authority.

See also caliph, caliphate; household; Mamluks (1250–1517); al-Tusi, Nasir al-Din (1201–74)

Further Reading

Thomas T. Allsen, "Changing Forms of Legitimation in Mongol Iran," in *Rulers from the Steppe: State Formation on the Eurasian Periphery*, edited by Gary Seaman and Daniel Marks, 1991; Anne F. Broadbridge, *Kingship and Ideology in the Islamic and Mongol Worlds*, 2008; Charles Melville, "From Adam to Abaqa: Qāḍī Baiḍāwī's Re-arrangement of History," *Studia Iranica* 30, no. 1 (2001); Idem, "From Adam to Abaqa: Qāḍī Baiḍāwī's Re-arrangement of History (Part II)," *Studia Iranica* 36, no. 1 (2007); Idem, "The *Keshig* in Iran: The Survival of the Royal Mongol Household," in *Beyond the Legacy of Genghis Khan*, edited by Linda Komaroff, 2006; I. P. Petrushevsky, "Rashid al-Din's Conception of the State," *Central Asiatic Journal* 14, no. 1–3 (1970).

CHARLES MELVILLE

imamate

Although the word "imamate" may be used to denote leadership in prayer and prominence in a specific branch of knowledge or profession, it was more widely used in juristic, theological, and exegetical literature and hadith to describe a particular political, frequently religiopolitical, leadership and, in modern jargon, a government or state. The scholarly tradition across a wide Islamic spectrum referred to the imamate as supreme leadership (*al-imāma al-'uẓmā*). At the core of the idea of the imamate lay the assumption that the Muslim community must have a legitimate leader who would be responsible for, as Mawardi noted, "upholding the faith and managing the affairs of the world," including such duties as implementing laws, defending borders, leading the army, maintaining social peace, collecting and distributing revenues, and appointing administrators to undertake such responsibilities. Whether the imam also guides his subjects to salvation (as in the case of the Shi'i imam) was a highly controversial question among various Muslim sects. Medieval Muslims discussed the imamate as the best form of leadership, although it is unclear if this meant the imamate was the only legitimate form of government. The views this entry addresses represent a consciously "religious" take on politics. This is particularly true compared to not only ideas expounded by Muslim philosophers, secretaries, and belles lettres but also dynastic laws derived from non-Islamic traditions that flourished under various Muslim dynasties as laws governing political domain.

It is fair to state that the theory of the imamate owes its development in a substantial way to intellectual responses to the caliphate, especially the patriarchal caliphate; to competing sectarian positions on politics and other doctrinal questions; to the political views of secretaries and philosophers; and finally to the existing political customs and conventions in the Near East. A wealth of opinions about the imamate was put forth in the books of theology, jurisprudence, exegesis, and hadith. Opinions reflect variations not only across different sects (Shi'is, Sunnis, Kharijis, etc.) but also within a particular sect (e.g., Shi'ism) for a range of doctrinal and historical reasons.

The Emergence of the Debate on the Imamate

Like the Roman Empire, the caliphate shaped how people thought about politics and statecraft. The caliphate emerged with the election of Abu Bakr (r. 632–34), a senior Companion of the Prophet Muhammad (ca. 570–632), to lead the Muslim community after the Prophet's death. Having been elected the first caliph, Abu Bakr adopted the title "Successor of the Prophet of God." His successor, 'Umar b. al-Khattab (r. 634–44), is said to have used the title "Successor of the Successor of the Prophet of God," but noticing how cumbersome this title would become in a few generations, he abbreviated the title to "caliph." He also adopted the apparently more mundane-sounding title of "Commander of the Faithful." The caliphs after 'Umar followed the usage he preferred, but many did not shy away from adopting pompous new titles such as "God's Caliph."

Although the first three caliphs were elected by peaceful means, the period afterward was anything but peaceful. The assassination of the third caliph, 'Uthman b. 'Affan (r. 644–56), and the controversial reign of 'Ali b. Abi Talib (r. 656–61) led to a civil war between the caliph and the governor of Damascus, the Umayyad Mu'awiya, a member of the Meccan nobility and a junior Companion of the Prophet. This civil war ended with the assassination of 'Ali (by a disillusioned supporter) and the transfer of the caliphate to Mu'awiya (r. 661–80) and the Umayyad family (661–750). The civil war of 656–61 split the Muslim community into factions (Kharijis, 'Uthmanis, and Shi'at 'Ali), which were the first to articulate views on the imamate. The supporters of 'Ali (Shi'at 'Ali) repudiated 'Uthman as illegitimate for having failed to uphold the laws and Mu'awiya as a usurper for contesting 'Ali. The supporters of 'Uthman and Mu'awiya repudiated 'Ali as illegitimate and incompetent. The Kharijis, who initially supported 'Ali against Mu'awiya, rejected 'Ali, Mu'awiya, and 'Uthman as illegitimate for various reasons. They withdrew from the broader society to establish their own righteous community. Growing controversies over the legitimacy of the successive Umayyad caliphs led to another civil war between 684 and 692. This civil war ended with the elimination of the non-Umayyad contenders, particularly the powerful 'Abdallah b. al-Zubayr, and shifted the caliphate from the Sufyanid to the Marwanid branch of the Umayyad family.

Under the Umayyads, election gave way to succession, which became even more regular under the Abbasids (750–1258). Only a very few of the Abbasid caliphs had fathers who had not been caliphs. The procedure of ascending to the rule followed either some sort of election (e.g., under the first four caliphs), designation by the ruling caliph (the most common practice under the Umayyads and Abbasids), or simple force. The caliph was nonetheless expected to have certain qualifications, including Qurashi descent, intelligence, physical ability, military prowess, and moral standing, although there was no constitutional or institutional oversight to verify their fulfillment. Often, political expediency and circumstances on the ground dictated the appointment of a particular individual to the office. There was no duration to the caliph's rule. As long as he was able, he could rule for life. In the absence of constitutional law outlining his responsibilities and privileges clearly, cultural norms, customs, and religious law, along with the power of social and political forces, provided some guidance to and restrictions on his authority.

The initial debates on the imamate came in the wake of the civil war and involved the identity, familial and social affiliation, qualifications (in particular, individual merit and seniority in Islam, prominence in a particular house, even age), and legitimacy of the caliph. The Umayyad period witnessed, alongside a more complex factional development, substantial doctrinal elaborations on the imamate, particularly on questions concerning the legitimacy and the nature of caliph's authority. In the Umayyad period, competing groups debated such concepts as consultation versus succession and divine appointment versus communal choice. Theological arguments such as free will and predestination, nature and definition of faith, and the status of the sinner also acquired substantial political implications. During the Abbasid period, sectarian views expanded and matured thanks to the proliferating paper industry and the articulate and socially engaged scholars. By the 13th century, all major sects and groups had produced substantial literature on the subject of the imamate in a scope far wider than the initial debates.

Necessity of Imamate

Scholars made a great deal of effort to show why and for which reason the imamate was necessary. Except for a small but articulate and intellectually rigorous group of scholars among the Mu'tazilis and the Kharijis, the great majority of Muslim sects asserted that instituting an imam was necessary. According to those scholars, the imamate was neither rationally necessary nor religiously obligatory. They reasoned that an ultimately perfect imamate was not possible. Even if it were possible it might not always be practical, and a less-than-perfect imamate might not be conducive to peaceful life. It was better for the community to have either multiple imams or no imam at all. Those who saw the imamate as necessary could not agree if it was necessary rationally by virtue of a human being's need for social life, which requires political organization (this was the view of the Mu'tazilis), or by virtue of God's command. The Shi'i theorists saw the imamate as both rationally necessary and a grace of God. They argued that reason alone could arrive at its necessity since the welfare and salvation of human beings depended on it, but nevertheless its institution and maintenance was incumbent upon God and not human beings. God simply could not leave his creatures without guidance. By and large Sunni scholars argued for the necessity of the imamate from the perspective of divine command, but they saw it as a communal duty and denied the imam the privilege of being a guide to salvation. Many jurists and theologians also tried to explain the rational need for an imam and rationalize religious arguments.

Appointing the Imam

The Sunnis, Mu'tazilis, and Kharijis emphasized election as the sole medium of appointing the imam. They meant that the process of instituting the imam was a mundane and voluntary task that could be fulfilled only by the community's preference for one candidate or another. While the principle of election opposed the Shi'i concept of divine appointment (that the imam should be singled out by the previous imam upon specific and binding instructions from God), it also shaped how the non-Shi'is thought about the nature of the imam's authority in relation to the Muslim community. The idea of election manifested itself in the actual practice of choosing the caliph. The views about election varied widely and could range from popular consensus to nomination by a single well-qualified individual, as well as any number of practices in between: majority opinion and decision by a specific group of qualified electors, whose number fluctuated depending on circumstances. As stipulated by Ghazali (d. 1111) in the age of the sultanates, election could also take the form of acknowledgement by the holders of coercive power (i.e., sultans). The imam could also be appointed by his predecessor or could win the seat for himself through a successful military coup. In all cases, however, the consent and approval of the community was sought, even if it was merely symbolic. The Sunnis made the point that the imamate was by election and that the community was the source of legitimacy; the imamate was neither a dynastic right nor a divine appointment. Furthermore, election required a mechanism to function. The idea of an "electoral body" arose as a palpable way to represent the will of the community at large. The Sunnis therefore needed to seek certain qualifications from the members of the electoral body, such as probity, knowledge, prudence, and wisdom. It was also accepted that qualified individuals might be more available in the capital, although there was no requirement to reside in a particular region. Despite acknowledging the Umayyad and Abbasid dynastic succession practices as legitimate, the Sunnis made sure that, at least theoretically, elections remained a part of the succession process. For the Shi'is divine appointment rather than election was the rule.

Qualification of the Imam

Whether the imam must be the most excellent of his generation reveals a fascinating debate about the historical caliphate. By the

tenth century, the Sunnis believed that the first four caliphs were the most excellent of their generations and the order of their caliphate reflected their order in merit. Part of this debate was, of course, about the legitimacy of the first four caliphs, but another part was about elaborating an ideal model to be pursued by the historical caliphate. The Sunnis required that the caliph should be the most excellent in the true imamate, but they allowed the inferior or the less excellent to be appointed to office under kingship. The Zaydis advocated the imamate of the most excellent from the family of the Prophet, while the Mu'tazilis, though arguing for the appointment of the most excellent, allowed the imamate of a less-qualified person for practical reasons (i.e., to prevent dissention). For the Imami (Twelver) Shi'is, no one could tell who was the most excellent except the current imam, who alone was entitled to identify and designate his successor. The Shi'is required family affiliation for the imam, the Imamis being more restrictive than the Zaydis. The Shi'is restricted the imamate to the descendants of 'Ali from the line of Husayn (Imamis) or to any meritorious and politically active member of the 'Alid house (Zaydis). Generally the Sunnis required that the candidate belong to the tribe of Quraysh, although there were strong voices (Ibn Khaldun, Ibn Jama'a) for opening the candidacy to individuals outside Quraysh, including non-Arabic speaking people. The majority of the Kharijis and the Mu'tazilis did not see tribal and ethnic affiliation as a condition for the imamate. They even rejected such an argument as unfair, biased, and entirely impractical.

The Sunnis added some qualifying conditions to Qurashi lineage: like the members of the electoral body, the candidate should have probity and knowledge. He should have sound vision, hearing, and speech as well as physical fitness. He should be prudent and courageous to undertake the task of governing and leading the military. Military juntas used some of these conditions as an excuse to depose the ruling caliphs in the late ninth and early tenth centuries: they blinded the caliph first, then asked the chief judge to declare him unfit for rule so that they could install another one of their liking.

One of the fundamental differences between Shi'i and non-Shi'i views on qualifications was the presence and absence of the imam. The Sunnis (as well as the Kharijis and the Mu'tazilis) required that the imam must be alive, present, in charge of affairs, and reachable, while the Shi'is allowed him to be absent and not ruling a state. In fact, only one of the Twelver Shi'i imams ruled ('Ali).

Religious Authority versus Temporal Authority

One of the fundamental questions about the imamate in political thought was whether the imam's authority extended over both religious and temporal matters. In general, Sunni, Khariji, and Mu'tazili views did not allow the imam any authority over doctrinal matters, while most of the Shi'is (except for the Zaydis) attributed religious authority (not only as a law giver but also as a guide to salvation) to the imam regardless of whether he held an actual political office. Many modern scholars have argued that the caliphs inherited only Muhammad's temporal authority, as prophecy ended with Muhammad while religious authority rested within the corporeal body of the community. The question of who would legitimately represent and articulate this authority led to a two-century-long competition between the caliphs (who adopted for themselves titles suggesting this prerogative, such as "God's Caliph") and scholars specializing in jurisprudence and hadith ('ulama'). Other arguments suggest that the caliphate was instituted from the beginning for leadership not only in temporal governance but also in matters of salvation: the caliph was both king and priest, so to speak, following the prophetic model exercised by Muhammad. It was only with the rise of the 'ulama' that the caliph's authority became a subject of contestation. In the ninth century, the caliphs had to recognize the power of the 'ulama' and relinquish their claims on religious authority.

True Imamate versus Kingship

Regardless of sectarian affiliation, medieval thinkers generally made a distinction between the true imamate and kingship. For the majority of the Imami Shi'is, the true imamate existed only during the reign of 'Ali. For the Zaydis, both the Umayyads and the Abbasids were certainly kings and, although legitimate, the first three caliphs after Muhammad were of lesser merit than 'Ali, the true imam. The true imamate afterward existed only in isolated regions where Zaydi imams ruled. The Kharijis rejected all the caliphs after 'Umar as illegitimate tyrants. For the Sunnis, the true imamate was the period of the first four caliphs, followed by kingship. They did not, however, mean by this that kingship was unlawful and that the Umayyads and Abbasids were illegitimate. On the one hand, the Sunni theorists wanted to make clear that the true imamate was possible and in fact existed under the first four caliphs, although it could not continue in perpetuity. On the other hand, the Umayyads and Abbasids were legitimate, though not ideal, caliphs since they complied with the minimum requirements of the law, keeping the Muslim community united, the transactions lawful, and the borders safe. Many of the Sunnis reasoned that, for the common good, working with the system was better than going against it. In medieval jargon, two fundamental concepts explained the Sunni attitude of acknowledging the legitimacy of the caliphate without fully endorsing it theoretically: welfare or utility and necessity.

One or Multiple Imams

Medieval scholars have generally argued for one imam at a time, except for some Mu'tazilis and anarchists, who allowed and even advocated the appointment of more than one imam. The singularity of the imam was true also for the majority of Sunni theologians and jurists, although after the demise of the Abbasid caliphate, this argument was no longer sustainable. Even before that, the community was ruled by three competing imamates despite theoretical rejection of multiple imams: the Abbasid caliphate, the Fatimid

caliphate in North Africa and Egypt, and the Spanish Umayyad caliphate in Spain. The Sunni ʿAbd al-Qahir al-Baghdadi (d. 1037) was one such theologian who read the situation pragmatically and accommodated the practice as legitimate. He stipulated that it was possible to have more than one imam if the imams ruled over regions separated from each other by a significant barrier, such as a large body of water. The Shiʿis also argued for the singularity of the imam, although they allowed the imam to be hidden.

Duties of the Imam

Generally the Sunnis, the Muʿtazilis, and the Kharijis restricted the duties of the imam to the administration of mundane matters and to the promotion and protection of the faith. His duties comprised the guardianship of the faith, enforcing the laws, leading public acts of worship, protecting the community from outside and inside threats, dispensing legal criminal punishments, maintaining and leading the army in military activities, collecting revenues and distributing them to their appropriate places, building and maintaining public amenities and spaces, and appointing and overseeing lesser administrators. Sunni scholars guarded religious authority from the encroachment of the caliph, but they bestowed holiness on the caliph and advocated obedience to his authority as long as he did not confront the fundamental tenets of the faith. Another reason they advocated obedience was for the unity and welfare of the community. They feared that any dissention and violence would disturb order, prevent the application of law, lead to the demise of religion, and the loss of this world as well as the next. Yet the Sunnis were far from a pacifist crowd, as exemplified in a widespread norm that one should not obey anyone in matters against God's ordinances. They did emphasize the right to remove the caliph from office for reasons of apostasy, loss of freedom or sanity, and even consistent acts of injustice. Yet they did not elaborate on how the caliph would be removed from office, nor did they propose any institutional framework to assure peaceful removal. For the Kharijis and the Muʿtazilis, violation of the law by the caliph was a valid reason for removal by either peaceful means or force. They did not share the same sentiments with the Sunnis that one should endure injustice, oppression, and violation of the law for the sake of community's welfare. Such actions were crimes significant enough to disturb the order itself.

See also caliph, caliphate; leadership; Shiʿism

Further Reading

Antony Black, *The History of Islamic Political Thought: From the Prophet to the Present*, 2001; Patricia Crone, *God's Rule: Government and Islam*, 2004; Ann K. S. Lambton, *State and Government in Medieval Islam: An Introduction to the Study of Islamic Political Theory: The Jurists*, 1981; Mawardi, *The Ordinances of Government: Al-Aḥkām al-Sulṭāniyya wa al-Wilāyāt al-Dīniyya*, translated by Wafaa H. Wahba, 1996; W. M. Watt, *Islamic Political Thought*, 1998.

HAYRETTIN YÜCESOY

imperialism

Imperialism refers to the varied practices associated with constructing and maintaining an empire. Found throughout the globe and in every period, empires are large, complex political entities that project power over heterogeneous populations and territories and rule them in ways that preserve hierarchies and distinctions among the various units that make up a given polity. Muslim societies have produced diverse imperial states from West Africa to Southeast Asia. Beginning with the era of Mongol conquests in the 13th century, Muslims have also been the subjects of empires ruled by non-Muslims. With the rise of European empires in the 15th century, even Muslim societies that did not come under direct imperial control began to confront the challenge of European expansion.

For Muslim political thinkers, this type of political form has posed varied dilemmas and opportunities. Most closely resembling empires elsewhere, the Ottoman, Safavid, and Mughal states were territorially sprawling, multiethnic, multilingual, and multiconfessional polities whose management involved an eclectic range of political ideas. The Ottomans interpreted their armies' capture of Constantinople in 1453 as confirmation that they had become the inheritors of an imperial tradition dating back to the Romans. Similarly, the Safavid dynasty would draw on pre-Islamic Iranian imperial institutions and ideas, while the Mughals would seek to enhance their legitimacy by highlighting their ties to Mongol imperial precedents. Each of these dynasties would act as patrons of an imperial aesthetic in architecture, painting, and poetry to dramatize the grandeur of their power and would devise various administrative and other mechanisms to incorporate a variety of constituencies. At the same time, imperial policies toward religious institutions as well as toward heterodox and non-Muslim groups frequently sparked controversies in learned circles about balancing pragmatic accommodation in the service of imperial stability with dynastic support for Islamic norms.

The problems of empire became far more pronounced for Muslim thinkers in the late 18th and early 19th centuries, when European armies began to gain the upper hand in confrontations with Muslim-led states, for example, in the Russian victory in the Russo-Ottoman War of 1768–74 and Napoleon's occupation of Egypt in 1798. European pressure may have had no direct impact on many of the revivalist movements in West and North Africa, the Arabian Peninsula, and South Asia during this period, but from Egypt to the North Caucasus and Southeast Asia, disparate Muslim thinkers began to appropriate European technologies and agitate for religious change as well as social, administrative, and military reform. Despite these measures, the British, Russians, French, and Dutch all expanded their territories at the expense of Muslim rulers.

The imposition of European rule, in turn, provoked widely divergent responses. Muslim scholars' debates centered on controversies

surrounding the status of conquered lands. For a number of thinkers, conquest transformed the territory of Islam (*dār al-islām*) to one ruled by unbelievers (*dār al-ḥarb*), thereby obligating the faithful either to wage war (jihad) or, in the view of some, to migrate (hijra) in emulation of the Prophet Muhammad. Determining when a given territory became *dār al-ḥarb* proved contentious, however. Many jurists, especially Sunni Muslims who followed the Hanafi school of law, drew attention to various conditions, like possession of the means to migrate, that further qualified such judgments. Indeed, for the majority of Hanafis, including most of the vast Muslim populations of British India and the Russian Empire, such states merited the status of *dār al-islām* because Muslims were able to gather for Friday prayers and other rites and because many elements of Islamic law were integrated into their legal systems. Such an outlook often provided the basis for accommodation with imperial authorities and institutions, as in French West Africa, and imperial states tended to reciprocate by offering patronage to religious scholars and notables. These views were not unanimous, however, and in different political contexts, charismatic leaders rallied followers around calls for jihad against imperial authorities. In 1827, for instance, Sayyid Ahmad Barelwi (1785–1831) launched a war among the Pathans on the North-West frontier of India to purify the faith and expel the British, and in the following decade, ʻAbd al-Qadir (1808–83) led a Sufi-based resistance movement in Algeria against the French. As in the 19th-century jihads among the mountain peoples of the North Caucasus, many of these campaigns simultaneously aimed at effecting religious change and building institutions rooted in Islamic law. In 1857, by contrast, many Muslims joined other subjects of the British in India in a massive revolt that articulated the most heterogeneous visions. The actors involved in these movements were frequently tied together through Sufi or scholarly networks, but local conditions tended to determine their varied trajectories.

In the late 19th century, a small group of activists critical of the state of Muslim societies and outraged, in particular, by the French seizure of Tunisia in 1881 and the British occupation of Egypt in 1882, formed a transnational network committed to disseminating critiques of European imperialism and calling on Muslims to unite in liberating themselves from foreign rule. At the head of this movement, Afghani (1838–97), the itinerant thinker and agitator, called on Muslims to strengthen Islamic civilization against the European—especially British—threat by arriving at a proper understanding of the faith and by seeking unity. This vision inspired followers in Egypt, Iran, and elsewhere and briefly earned him the patronage of the Ottoman sultan Abdülhamid II (r. 1876–1909), who sought to bolster his own authority among Muslims in Ottoman lands as well as in rival European empires by adopting the title of caliph and acting as the defender of the faithful everywhere. In the first decades of the 20th century these Pan-Islamic ideas proved less attractive to critics of empire who increasingly elaborated visions of the future around the idea of the nation.

Yet just as empires have persisted despite waves of collapse during and after World War I and of decolonization following World War II, critiques of imperialism have endured, sustained in part by the anticolonial rhetoric of the Soviet Union and the United States, as well as by international organizations such as the United Nations. These criticisms have, in turn, influenced Islamist discourse. The restoration of sovereignty to the Muslim community was central to the program of the founder of the Muslim Brotherhood, Hasan al-Banna (1906–49); while in Iran, Ayatollah Khomeini (1902–89) would repeatedly point to the dangers of American imperialism, mobilizing popular memory of 19th-century grievances as well as the U.S.-led coup of 1953. From the 1980s, wars in a number of theaters—Afghanistan, Lebanon, Palestine, Iraq, Bosnia, Chechnya, and Somalia—have focused Islamist thinkers on the problems of political sovereignty and military occupation. Although substantive ideological differences divide groups such as Hizbullah, the Taliban, al-Qaeda, and others, the global reach of American power in the early 21st century looms as the central preoccupation of their political thought.

See also colonialism; fundamentalism; modernity; revival and reform

Further Reading

Cemil Aydin, *The Politics of Anti-Westernism in Asia: Visions of World Order in Pan-Islamic and Pan-Asian Thought*, 2007; Jane Burbank and Frederick Cooper, *Empires in World History: Power and the Politics of Difference*, 2010; Stephen F. Dale, *The Muslim Empires of the Ottomans, Safavids, and Mughals*, 2010; Michael Francis Laffan, *Islamic Nationhood and Colonial Indonesia: The Umma Below the Winds*, 2003; Rudolph Peters, *Islam and Colonialism: The Doctrine of Jihad in Modern History*, 1979; David Robinson, *Paths of Accommodation: Muslim Societies and French Colonial Authorities in Senegal and Mauritania, 1880–1920*, 2000.

ROBERT D. CREWS

India

As in other parts of the Muslim world outside the Arabian Peninsula (but perhaps even more so because of its distinct socioreligious setting), Muslim political thought in the Indian subcontinent seems to have oscillated between uncompromisingly implementing the ordinances of the shariʻa and pragmatically adjusting Muslim politics to the social reality.

Little compromise was sought when in 705 the Umayyad commander Muhammad b. Qasim al-Thaqafi (d. 715) led a military expedition, identified as a jihad against the infidels, into Sindh and southern Punjab. Even the Arab Muslim traders who settled around the same time along the Indian coast appear to have maintained a sharp distinction from their Hindu neighbors, although pragmatics increasingly demanded social interaction.

It was not until 1206, however, that a more or less autonomous Muslim power was established in India. At its zenith in the

14th century, the so-called Delhi Sultanate, in reality a succession of various slave dynasties of mainly Turkish and Afghan descent, encompassed almost the entire subcontinent. Political theory during the Delhi Sultanate period clearly reveals the tension between an Arabic tradition revolving around the shari'a and a Persianized appropriation of kingship that left more room for pragmatic adjustments to the Indian conditions. Politically, this tension is epitomized by the fact that the sultans, although actually ruling independently, sought formal investiture by the Abbasid caliph who, by then, had been reduced to leading only a shadowy existence at the Mamluk court of Cairo. Intellectually, the two poles are represented by the 13th century *Adab al-Harb wa-l-Shaja'a* (The manners of war and of fortitude) of Muhammad b. Mansur "Fakhr-i Mudabbir" ("Glory of the State"), which echoes the uncompromising stand of the Arab conquerors, and the later *Fatawa-yi Jahandari* (The imperial fatwas) of Ziya' al-Din Barani (d. ca. 1357), which pleads for a compromise between religious normativeness (*dīndārī*) and worldly pragmatics (*jahāndārī*), including the incorporation of a limited number of non-Muslims into the administration of the sultanate. According to Barani, the implementation of the shari'a constituted the ideal of governance, but given the prevailing conditions, it could only be approximated by more secular state regulations (*ḍawābiṭ*).

The tendency evident in Barani's *Fatawa* gained strength during Mughal rule between the 16th and 19th centuries. Important in this respect was the reception of Iranian scientist-philosopher Nasir al-Din al-Tusi's (d. 1274) ethical thought as outlined in *Akhlaq-i Nasiri* (*The Nasirean Ethics*), which was repeatedly remodeled in later works, most importantly *Akhlaq-i Humayuni* (The Humayunian ethics) of Ikhtiyar al-Din al-Husayni (d. after 1556). The shift from politics to ethics is highly significant; political prudence became measured by the degree to which the ruler was able to promote and maintain social harmony instead of uncompromisingly enforcing the shari'a. The political maxim of checks and balances (*sulḥ-i kull*), vividly outlined in the *A'in-i Akbari* (The Akbarian institutions) of Abu al-Fadl "'Allami" ("the Learned One"; d. 1602), became the heart of Mughal political practice.

This rather liberal stance was adopted primarily because of the practical quest to govern a large and diverse polity effectively, but from the beginning it was fervently opposed by various influential 'ulama' and also shari'a-minded Sufis. The arguments invoked were almost exclusively derived from the authoritative texts of Islam, awarding the revelation of God's words in the Qur'an a higher degree of reality that overruled the need to adjust government to the circumstances of the moment. This growing opposition to rulers' acculturalistic politics was not unique to the Muslims, and it contributed to the disintegration of Mughal imperial organization and the emergence of increasingly autonomous rule in various parts of the empire. In this situation the Sufi scholar Shah Waliullah (d. 1762) proposed a reconciliation of ethics-based rational pragmatics and shari'a-based transmitted normativeness. But events had cast a shadow over such attempt: Persian and Afghan military interventions twice interrupted universalistic Mughal rule and paved the way for British colonial domination, which became direct in 1857 and lasted for almost a century.

The beginning of direct colonial rule forcibly confronted the Muslims with Western ideas and caused perhaps the most radical change in the history of Indo-Muslim political thought. It also drove a wedge between those who held firm to a hermetic understanding of Islam and those who borrowed creatively from Western thought to deal with the abolition of even nominal Muslim rule in the subcontinent.

The debate ignited the ideas of Sayyid Ahmad Khan (d. 1898), a descendant of a Mughal notable who had collaborated with the British colonial judiciary. Analyzing the reasons for the Sepoy uprising of 1857 in a treatise titled *Asbab-i Baghawat-i Hind* (The causes of the Indian revolt; 1858), Khan blamed both the British for suspecting general disloyalty on the part of the Muslims and the Muslims for rigidly maintaining a traditional and rather solipsistic outlook. As a way out of what was felt to be a social, political, and economic crisis, Khan strongly advocated a reform of Muslim education by incorporation of modern Western subjects, based on a new theology that aimed to prove there was no conflict between Western scientific thought and the Qur'anic revelation. Although Khan was vehemently refuted by more traditional Indian 'ulama' and accused of being a "materialist" by Afghani (1838–97), it was his religious thought that paved the way for later thinkers whose strong engagement with Western thought brought about radically new political ideas.

Important in this regard was Muhammad Shah Iqbal (d. 1938), whose studies of Western philosophy led ultimately to the formulation of an innovative anthropology "from a pragmatic point of view." It combined the Sufi idea of self-perfection with the dynamism of European life-philosophy and transferred this in a Hegelian way to the entire Muslim community as a collective subject. This seemingly abstract thinking had far-reaching practical consequences: it resulted in the idea of a distinct Indo-Muslim nation that would naturally require a distinct territory, epitomized in the idea of Pakistan.

Others, like Mawdudi (d. 1979), refused to accept the distinctiveness of the Indian Muslims or their demand for a separate state within the subcontinent. Mawdudi's systemic conception of Islam, culminating in an idealized Muslim polity, was clearly universalist in scope. At the core of this conception, which Mawdudi claimed to have solely deduced from the Qur'an, stood the distinction between God's absolute and unlimited sovereignty (*ḥākimiyyat-i ilāhī*) and man's limited power as God's trustee on Earth (*khilāfat allāh*). This "doctrine of the two kingdoms" led Mawdudi to his formulation of the Islamic state as a "theo-democracy" (*jumhūriyyat-i ilāhī*). The religiopolitical movement Jama'at-i Islami, founded in 1942 and long headed by Mawdudi himself, epitomizes the search for this idealized state.

Explicitly inspired by the works of Ernst Haeckel (d. 1919) and Herbert Spencer (d. 1903), the intellectual 'Inayatallah Khan "al-Mashriqi" (d. 1963) developed a biologistic reading of the Qur'an

and reduced its message to the theme of constant warfare and survival of the fittest. Among the requirements for the survival of the Muslims, Mashriqi stressed the importance of bodily fitness and military training. His paramilitary organization Khaksar, founded in 1930, resembled to a large extent the Fascist and National Socialist storm troopers; Benito Mussolini and, to an even larger extent, Adolf Hitler were indeed explicit points of reference and inspirations for Mashriqi. While the movement played a considerable role in communalist encounters in the 1930s, it collapsed with the establishment of Pakistan in 1947.

While the thoughts of Iqbal, Mawdudi, Mashriqi, and others considerably dominated the political discourse in a young independent Pakistan, the Muslims who remained in India found themselves as a religious minority within a secularist constitutional framework. For a long time, this framework was positively perceived by Muslim leaders, as it was seen as an effective tool to prevent privileging the Hindu religious majority. Personalities such as Abu al-Kalam Azad (d. 1958) associated themselves with the Indian National Congress as the flag bearer of secularism. However, this attitude changed during the "patrimonial democracy" of Indira Gandhi (assassinated 1984) in the 1960s and even more during her second term as prime minister between 1980 and 1984, when communalism increasingly became part of the political rhetoric and practice. Muslims were forced to find a separate political lobby to advocate their interests. Due to internal disputes, such a lobby was never very successful within the parliamentary realm, but a number of religiopolitical issues helped transform the political factions of the Muslims into a variety of nonparliamentary pressure groups. The most important are the All-India Muslim Majlis-i Mushawarat, founded in 1964, and the All-India Muslim Personal Law Board, established in 1972. The debates fostered by these groups revolve around the primacy of revealed law over man-made law, which implies that whenever a conflict occurs between the two, a Muslim has no choice but to remain loyal to the divine ordinances.

See also Bangladesh; colonialism; Pakistan

Further Reading

Muzaffar Alam, *The Languages of Political Islam: India, 1200–1800*, 2004; Markus Daechsel, 'Scienticism and Its Discontent: The Indo-Muslim "Fascism" of Inayatullah Khan Mashriqi', *Modern Intellectual History* 3, no. 3 (2006); Jan-Peter Hartung, "The Land, the Mosque, the Temple: More than 145 Years of Dispute over Ayodhya," in *Ayodhya 1992–2003: The Assertion of Cultural and Religious Hegemony*, edited by Richard Bonney, 2003; Nikki R. Keddie, *An Islamic Response to Imperialism: Political and Religious Writings of Sayyid Jamāl al-Dīn "al-Afghānī,"* 1968; Syed Ahmad Khan, *The Causes of the Indian Revolt*, edited by Francis Robinson, 2000; Seyyed Vali Reza Nasr, *The Vanguard of the Islamic Revolution. The Jama'at-i Islami of Pakistan*, 1994; Annemarie Schimmel, *Gabriel's Wing: A Study into the Religious Ideas of Sir Muhammad Iqbal*, 1963.

JAN-PETER HARTUNG

individualism

If individualism is understood narrowly as a component of liberal political theory, where the central concern is the protection of negative or positive liberties of individuals against the coercive powers of the state, the effort to mine the main genres of premodern Islamic political writing in Arabic, Persian, and Turkish for individualism will yield only slim pickings. After all, liberalism, like the modern scientific method, was a specifically early modern European development, and it would be naïve to look for its counterparts in earlier eras, in Europe itself, or in other cultures. If, however, individualism is viewed more generally as a cluster of ideas and social practices that collectively characterize Euro-American modernity, then one can find elements of individualistic thinking in premodern Islamic intellectual traditions.

Religious scholarship contained a robust notion of the individual. In *kalām* (theology), even though the metaphysical dimensions of individuality (namely, the issue of the nature of the human soul) remained contested, there was consensus on the personal nature of salvation/damnation. On the thorny question of human agency, however, the postclassical mainstream divided into the minimalist Ash'aris (nominal agency) and the maximalist Maturidis as well as Twelver Shi'is (real ownership of actions), with plenty of room for individual accountability for human actions. In *fiqh* (Islamic jurisprudence), the language of moral and legal obligation was regnant over any discourse of rights and liberties, but Muslim jurists built elaborate protections around "civil rights"—such as the rights to life, dignity, property, and personal relationships—that were often individual in nature. These protections were not conceptualized as "rights" of individuals against the state but as "claims" of private individuals against other private people; nevertheless, they did act as barriers against governmental encroachment on the private lives of individuals. The jurists displayed their individualist moral leanings also in the emphasis they placed on intention in ethical assessment of human actions, as well as on personal conviction in matters of faith. On balance, the edifice of *fiqh* was built on an assumption of personal accountability and entitlement, and in this connection, the refusal of jurists to recognize corporate bodies as legal entities was a natural consequence of the foundations of *fiqh* in human individuality. In Sufism (*taṣawwuf*), the early discovery of, and preoccupation with, the self led to intense scrutiny of inner motivations, emotions, and states as well as to development of such methods of cultivating the self as spiritual invocation (*dhikr*) and retreats (*khalwa*). Mystics debated the relative merits of inwardness and self-consciousness versus social action, which are all integral parts of modern discussions of subjectivity in the context of individualism. Regardless of many mystics' final assessment of the salvific worth of individuality, the emphasis they placed on "personal experiential verification" of religious truths was probably the most individualistic element of Sufism: godliness could

only be "realized" (*taḥqīq*) through personal experience, which necessitated direct and sustained efforts of self-cultivation on the part of each human individual.

Outside the world of religious scholarship, views and approaches that placed a high premium on the individual also abounded. In *falsafa* (philosophy), the nature of the human soul was hotly debated early on, but after Ibn Sina, it became normal to accept the immortality of individual souls (*pace* Ibn Rushd, who believed that individual souls would be submerged into the world soul after physical death) and to render the happiness of individuals contingent on proper cultivation and care of the self through the exercise of the rational faculty. In the careers and intellectual output of natural philosophers and scientists, individualistic tendencies in the form of skepticism toward received truths and a predilection for personal verification of knowledge claims are palpable, albeit understudied from the perspective of cultural history. Other cultural elites, including secretaries, administrators, writers, poets, artists, and even secular rulers themselves, displayed even more striking forms of individualistic tendencies. The intensely personal nature of the poetic voices of practically all the major poets of the many Islamic literary traditions (from Abu Nuwas and Abu al-ʿAla' al-Maʿarri in Arabic to Saʿdi and Hafiz in Persian, from Baki and Galib in Ottoman Turkish to Ghalib and Mir Dard in Urdu), the highly developed genre of autobiographical narrative among Mughal emperors, the unmistakable personal virtuosity of Timurid and Safavid visual artists like Bihzad, the long career of the Ottoman architect Sinan, the independence of spirit shining through the works of Ibn Khaldun and Ibn Battuta, and the ever playful but uncompromisingly personal narrative of the maverick Ottoman traveler Evliya Çelebi stand as randomly listed yet meaningful testimony for the individualistic riches that can be mined on these fronts.

It is, therefore, no exaggeration to state that premodern Islamic cultures provided ample venues for expression and development of individualistic tendencies at the personal level, and awareness of one's own worth as affirmation of individuality was not uncommon among the cultural elites. Yet before the colonial era, such avenues for construction of individuality were not directed toward the formation of overtly political ideologies of individualism. It may be speculated that since religious authorities had succeeded early on in Islamic history in erecting relatively secure legal and moral foundations for the exercise of personal freedoms at the level of civil society, there was little acute need to defend individual liberties either against the government, whose regular breach of such civil claims were already viewed as illegitimate, or against any corporate entities like cities or business corporations, which did not exist. It is only in the colonial and postcolonial eras, with the rapid erosion of the vibrant civil societies of the premodern period in the face of the growing power of the modern interventionist state, that new calls are heard for individual liberties in the form of citizens' and human rights.

See also freedom; modernity; rights

Further Reading

Amin Banani and Speros Vryonis, eds., *Individualism and Conformity in Classical Islam*, 1977; Michael Cook, *Commanding Right and Forbidding Wrong in Islamic Thought*, 2000; Mohammad Hashim Kamali, *Freedom of Expression in Islam*, 1997; Bernd Radtke, "How Can Man Reach the Mystical Union: Ibn Ṭufayl and the Divine Spark," in *The World of Ibn Ṭufayl*, edited by Lawrence I. Conrad, 1996; Dwight F. Reynolds, ed., *Interpreting the Self: Autobiography in the Arabic Literary Tradition*, 2001; Tzvetan Teofanov, "Canon and Individuality in Old Arabic Poetry," *Proceedings of the 17th-Congress of the UAAI*, 1997, 256–71.

AHMET T. KARAMUSTAFA

Indonesia

With 240 million citizens, the Southeast Asian nation of Indonesia is the most populous Muslim-majority country in the world. As of 2005, some 88.7 percent of the population were Muslim, most of them Sunnis of the Shafiʿi school of jurisprudence. With 300 ethnic groups dispersed over 12,000 islands, a central preoccupation of modern Indonesian political thought has been to devise a framework for holding the nation together.

Islam provided the symbols around which the first mass-based political organization took shape in the early 20th century. Founded in central Java in 1912, the Islamic Association (Sarikat Islam) used Islamic appeals to rally the population against Dutch colonialism and Chinese businesses. As the movement grew, it became polarized between proponents of an Islamic state and advocates of multiconfessional nationalism.

In the months leading up to the declaration of Indonesian independence in August 1945, Muslims and nationalists clashed over the role of Islam in the new constitution. The independence movement's main leaders, Sukarno and Mohammad Hatta (both nationalists committed to the establishment of a state based on equality among Indonesia's recognized religions), prevailed against Muslims under the leadership of Mohammed Natsir, who advocated what Natsir referred to as a "theocratic democracy." In a concession to the Muslim camp, the nationalists introduced a doctrine known as the "Five Principles" (Pancasila), the first of which affirms that the state is based on the belief in a unitary God. Sukarno invoked this principle to justify the deletion of an Islamist-supported preamble to the constitution known as the Jakarta charter, which would have obliged the government to implement shariʿa for Muslim citizens.

Over the next half century, demands for the restoration of the Jakarta charter were a recurring theme of Islamist politics. The stronger current in Muslim political thought, however, remained a multiconfessional nationalism that combined nonsectarian citizenship with state support for Islam and four other religions (Hinduism,

Buddhism, Protestantism, and Catholicism). Neither secular nor theocratic, this hybrid polity remained a pillar of Indonesian politics in part because it was supported by mass-based Muslim organizations like the traditionalist Nahdatul Ulama (established 1926, with about 35 million followers) and the reformist Muhammadiyah (established 1912, with about 20 million followers).

In the aftermath of a failed leftist coup, a military-dominated "New Order" government came to power in 1965–66. The regime placed strict limits on Muslim politics and promoted an authoritarian nationalism. Islamic learning nonetheless thrived under the New Order government, and the 1970s and 1980s saw a renaissance in Muslim thought. State-supported Islamic universities developed new curricula that were among the most forward-looking in the Muslim world. In the 1980s, prominent Muslim intellectuals like Nurcholish Madjid, Abdurrahman Wahid, and Syafi'i Maarif promoted the idea that pluralism and democracy were compatible with Muslim political ideals.

In the 1990s, Indonesia developed the largest Muslim-dominated prodemocracy movement in the world. Conservative Muslims in groups like the Saudi-funded Indonesian Council of Islamic Appeal (Dewan Dakwah Islamiyah Indonesia) condemned the democracy movement as anti-Islamic, but their views remained the minority. With the onset of the Asian economic crisis in late 1997, support for the New Order regime waned, and its leader, President Suharto, was forced from power in May 1998.

Elections held in 1999 and 2004 demonstrated that the majority of Muslims remained committed to the ideals of a democratic and multiconfessional Indonesia. Many Muslim intellectuals, however, as well as other citizens, also subscribed to the idea that Islam should play a role in public life. In 2001 and 2002, the National Assembly rebuffed efforts by Islamist legislators to require implementation of Islamic law. Islamist groups responded to the setback by successfully pressing for the implementation of portions of Islamic law in more than 50 districts and towns. The constitutional standing of these regional shari'a regulations remained unclear.

Although the post-Suharto period was marked by a conservative turn in matters of gender and public morality, the country continued to make progress toward the consolidation of a democratic electoral system. Survey data show that the majority of Muslims see democracy and human rights as compatible with Islam, even as a smaller but sizable minority support implementation of Islamic law. Efforts to balance democracy and shari'a are likely to remain a key feature of Muslim politics and thought in Indonesia for years to come.

See also Malaysia; Southeast Asia

Further Reading

Masykuri Abdillah, *Responses of Indonesian Muslim Intellectuals to the Concept of Democracy (1966–1993)*, 1997; Robert W. Hefner, *Civil Islam: Muslims and Democratization in Indonesia*, 2000; M. B. Hooker, *Indonesian Islam: Social Change through Contemporary Fatawa*, 2003; Michael Francis Laffan, *Islamic Nationhood and Colonial Indonesia: The Umma below the Winds*, 2003; Fauzan Saleh, *Modern Trends in Islamic Theological Discourse in Twentieth Century Indonesia: A Critical Survey*, 2001; Arskal Salim and Azyumardi Azra, eds., *Sharî'a and Politics in Modern Indonesia*, 2003; Martin van Bruinessen, "Genealogies of Islamic radicalism in post-Suharto Indonesia," *South East Asia Research* 10, no. 2 (2002).

ROBERT W. HEFNER

inquisition

Inquisition is the English rendering of the Arabic word *miḥna*, literally trial or tribulation, which refers to a caliphal attempt to impose a theological doctrine in the first half of the ninth century. In 827, the seventh Abbasid caliph Ma'mun (r. 813–33) declared the doctrine of the createdness (giving the text a temporal aspect that is otherwise lacking in the opposite doctrine) of the Qur'an to be correct. Six years later, in 833, he ordered a number of governors to test judges on this issue, while at the same time arranging for the interrogation of notable jurists and other religious scholars in Baghdad. According to surviving documents that appear to be verbatim reports of this state-led investigation, written for the caliph (who was then leading an attack against the Byzantine Empire), the religious scholars who acquiesced to the doctrine were left alone. The few who opposed it, the most famous being Ahmad b. Hanbal, the well-known jurist and traditionist, eponym of the Hanbali school of law, were jailed and later flogged or even executed. The caliph who initiated these steps died suddenly four months later, still on the Byzantine front. His successors, Mu'tasim (r. 833–42) and Wathiq (r. 842–47), continued his policies, but the next incumbent of the caliphal seat, Mutawakkil (r. 847–61), abolished them shortly after his accession. After some 15 years, the caliphal institution gave in to the religious scholars and endorsed their doctrine—namely, that the Qur'an was eternal rather than created in time.

Three theories have been advanced to explain Ma'mun's policy. The oldest is that he was moved by his personal convictions, but this does not explain why it was maintained by his successors (the first of whom had no interest in theological issues). The second theory invokes personal convictions as well, Shi'i in this case, but it also postulates a political aim: Ma'mun was trying to overcome the rift between Sunnis and Shi'is. The third and most recent theory postulates that, whatever Ma'mun's rationalist and Shi'i leanings, what was really at stake was the issue of religious authority: does it belong to the state or to the religious scholars ('ulama')? According to this theory, the *miḥna* was a defining moment in the religiopolitical development of Islam, since its failure meant that the caliphs conceded religious authority to their rivals, the religious scholars who remain the bearers of religious authority in Sunni Islam to the present day. They were to assume the same position in Shi'i Islam as well.

See also Abbasids (750–1258); Ahmad b. Hanbal (780–855); Ma'mun (786–833)

Further Reading

Patricia Crone and Martin Hinds, *God's Caliph: Religious Authority in the First Centuries of Islam*, 1983; Ira Lapidus, "The Separation of State and Religion in the Development of Early Islamic Society," *International Journal of Middle East Studies* 6 (1975); John Nawas, "A Reexamination of Three Current Explanations for al-Ma'mun's Introduction of the Mihna," *International Journal of Middle East Studies* 26 (1994); Dominique Sourdel, "La politique religieuse du calife 'abbaside al-Ma'mun," *Revue des études islamiques* 30 (1962); Muhammad Qasim Zaman, *Religion and Politics under the Early 'Abbasids: The Emergence of the Proto-Sunni Elite*, 1997.

JOHN A. NAWAS

intercession

Intercession (*shafā'a*) is pleading, petitioning, making requests, intervening, or mediating on behalf of others. In the Qur'an, deciding to grant intercession is God's prerogative alone. Only the righteous are permitted intercession at the final judgment because they have entered into a covenant (*'ahd*) with God (19:87). God also allows others to intercede if they "bear witness to the truth" (Q. 43:86). Later, Muhammad appears as intercessor before God on behalf of the believers, both in the hadith (prophetic tradition) and on a mosaic inscription inside the Dome of the Rock in Jerusalem dating to 691–92 that reads, "Muhammad is the messenger of God. May God bless him and accept his intercession on the day of resurrection on behalf of his community (*umma*)." Other hadith reports recognize the importance and praiseworthiness of intercession among human beings, as in the statement that "the best alms (*ṣadaqa*) is to use one's social prestige (*jāh*) to aid one who has no *jāh*." Intercession is also called "the alms of the tongue," according to the prophet a means of "freeing the prisoner, sparing lives, and bringing benefit to one's brother and protecting him from calamity."

For the Marwanid line of the Umayyads, the most direct path to salvation and justice led not through the prophet but through the caliph, and for the Shi'is, through the imam. Echoes of this attitude persist well into the Abbasid period. The implication is that ritual acts and the observance of Islamic law gained meaning only in relation to the caliphs and that the caliphs were the protectors of the community. In practice, then, intercession came to mean direct justice or setting things aright, not only divine or eschatological intervention, although both meanings persisted.

The implications of this in the sociopolitical realm were that those either permanently or temporarily lower in the hierarchy sought intercession from rulers or private patrons through written and oral petitions (*qiṣaṣ*), including subjects of the realm, paupers, prisoners, relatives of the missing and the deceased, courtiers fallen from grace, and anyone else considered to be in need of special protection. Both public and private petitions have survived, from the earliest Arabic papyri onward. Private petitions attest to the centrality of patronage as a social glue in rural and urban contexts alike. In petitions to rulers, the premise was that victims of injustices (*maẓālim*) should have access to justice (*'adl*) as directly as possible. When direct access was impracticable, appeal to rulers via intermediaries became the norm, with increasing regimentation and ceremony associated with the process of appeal and *maẓālim* justice in general, especially under the Mamluks.

The *maẓālim* system of providing intercession introduced a realm of administrative justice that competed directly with the courts of ordinary judges. In the early Abbasid period, judges controlled the *maẓālim* process, but by the late ninth century, it had come fully under the control of the viziers, with a brief reversal under the Buyids, when descendants of the Shi'i imams oversaw it. As a means of rule, the Fatimid caliphs relied heavily on the process of issuing rescripts in response to petitions, and the Ayyubids and Mamluks followed suit.

A curious feature of requests for intercession to both the state and private patrons is that petitions are generally written by others. Sometimes this had a practical reason, as when petitioners were illiterate. But even literate petitioners often had requests lodged by a friend, a supporter, a scribe, or some other professional versed in the writing of such documents. This feature seems to be central to the etiquette of *shafā'a*.

Some, though not all, chancery scribes took their role as intercessors seriously. Abu al-Qasim 'Ali b. al-Sayrafi, head of the Fatimid chancery in the mid-12th century, explains in his *Description of Chancery Practice* that "rescripts and decrees in response to petitions concerning grievances" are particularly important since they involve "a man obtaining his right from another and the establishment of justice in the realm. Also, most of those with a grievance are powerless people, paupers and retiring women, most of whom arrive from distant parts of the realm, believing that they are approaching someone who will help them and redress their grievances and assist them against their adversaries." At the same time, corruption, neglect, and sheer grudges could lead chancery officials to ignore petitions completely, as Ibn al-Sayrafi goes on to complain. In practice, connections to courtiers resulted in the prompt and effective handling of petitions, as is evident from documents preserved in the Geniza (storage chamber) of the Syro-Palestinian Rabbanite (now Ben Ezra) synagogue in Cairo.

See also patronage; vizier

Further Reading

Walther Björkman, *Beiträge zur Geschichte der Staatskanzlei im islamischen Ägypten*, 1928; A. Fu'ad Sayyid, ed., *al-Qanun fi Diwan al-Rasa'il wa-al-Ishara ila man Nala al-Wizara*, 1990; Christel Kessler, "'Abd al-Malik's Inscription in the Dome of the Rock: A Reconsideration," *Journal of the Royal Asiatic Society of Great Britain and Ireland* 1 (1970); Geoffrey Khan, *Arabic Legal and Administrative Documents in the Cambridge Genizah Collections*, 1993; Shaun E. Marmon, "The Quality of Mercy: Intercession

in Mamluk Society," *Studia Islamica* 87 (1998); Jørgen Nielsen, *Secular Justice in an Islamic State: Mazalim under the Bahri Mamluks, 662/1264–789/1387*, 1985; Marina Rustow, "A Petition to a Woman at the Fatimid Court (413–414 A.H./1022–23 C.E.)," *Bulletin of the School of Oriental and African Studies* 73 (2010); Samuel M. Stern, *Fāṭimid Decrees: Original Documents from the Fāṭimid Chancery*, 1964.

MARINA RUSTOW

international Islamic organizations

As of 2010, some 33 Islamic organizations were accredited as nongovernmental organizations by the United Nations (UN) Department for Economic and Social Affairs. Of these, five had general consultative status and seven had a narrow or technical focus. Most of them were accredited between 1995 and 2003. The most prominent organizations that had a general status were the World Muslim Congress, the Muslim World League (MWL), and the Islamic Call Society. The World Assembly of Muslim Youth, the Islamic Council of Europe, and 11 other Islamic organizations were, furthermore, associated with the UN Department of Public Information. Two Islamic organizations were considered by the UN as regional intergovernmental organizations according to the law of nations: the Organization of the Islamic Conference (OIC) and the Islamic Development Bank (IDB).

Most of these organizations claim international membership, scope, or presence. In part, they act as representatives of an Islamic identity in relation to a specific global objective (e.g., the environment, drugs, or relief work), and in part, they promote Islam. International Islamic organizations generally follow the pattern of international institutions that have emerged since the middle of the 19th century. In many ways, they look like Islamic versions of the UN; the United Nations Educational, Scientific, and Cultural Organization (UNESCO); the World Bank; the World Council of Churches; and the YMCA. They often emerged from congresses or assemblies modeled on the congregational practices of 19th- and 20th-century international politics.

The institutionalization of international Muslim "congregational" practice became notable after World War I. Wilfrid Scawen Blunt (1840–1922), the self-declared Byron of Arabia, is often portrayed as having given the decisive impetus for popularizing the idea of a nongovernmental congregation of Muslim public figures. Still, the congress idea was intrinsically tied to the question of the legitimacy of the Ottoman caliphate, which had become the subject of public debate since the early 1880s. It was in this context that, until 1924, various proposals for holding an Islamic congress were brought forward; they were sometimes criticized by Muslim reformers but at times they became part of the reformers' project. This early idea of a congress created a virtual framework for a transnational Islamic polity that Western observers linked to the notion of Pan-Islamism. In fact, the idea of the congress reflected the reformers' conception of a transnational Islamic *umma* (community of believers) that was to help transform local Islamic cultures according to the patterns of a universalistic system of Islamic norms and values and for which the reformers themselves were to act as political representatives. Consequently, they increasingly depersonalized the symbolic caliphal representation of the *umma* and substituted for the caliph a public normative discourse institutionalized by congresses or congregations. This tendency was further radicalized after the failure of the so-called Caliphate Congress of Cairo (May 1926), when the new king of Hijaz and amir of Najd, Ibn Sa'ud, convened the first congress of the Islamic world during the hajj (pilgrimage) season in June to July 1926. Though not yet established as a fixed organization, this congress became the progenitor of later congregations (Jerusalem 1931 and Karachi 1949, 1952), resulting in the formal foundation of the Islamic World Congress (IWC). Due to this history, the IWC regarded itself as an umbrella organization of many international organizations established after 1960.

Though Muslim elites who assembled as representatives of the Islamic *umma* tried to place their international activities within an Islamic public sphere independent of any government, the process of institutionalizing transnational Islamic discourses was mostly in alliance with local regimes. An exception is the General Islamic Congress of Jerusalem (founded in 1952), which was part of the Muslim Brotherhood's policy to transnationalize their claims to legitimacy. It continued to play a role until 1964. The IWC was attached to the new state of Pakistan, while the MWL, founded in 1962, was part of Saudi king Faisal's policy of transnational Islamic solidarity. The Egyptian High Council for Islamic Affairs was founded in 1954 as a transnational body to promote Islam in alliance with Gamal Abdel Nasser's (1918–70) regime. The tendency to seek international support for newly established regimes through the creation of international Islamic institutions also became apparent when the Libyan leader Mu'ammar Qaddafi (1942–2011) initiated the World Islamic Call Society in 1972 and when Iranian politicians formed an International Islamic Information Office in 1980.

In 1969, with the fading of the Egyptian-Saudi conflict that had influenced the foundation of the MWL, a new approach to intergovernmental Islamic organizations became possible. In several steps, the OIC was created with 25 states. Of these, 11 Arab states signed the OIC charter in 1972, and it was registered with the UN in 1974. Headquartered in Jeddah in Saudi Arabia, the OIC, with 57 member states as of 2010, considered itself to be the second largest intergovernmental organization after the UN. It consisted of four specialized institutions: the IDB (founded in 1975); the Islamic Educational, Scientific and Cultural Organization (founded in 1982); the Islamic Broadcasting Union (founded in 1975); and the International Islamic News Agency (founded in 1972), as well as other subsidiary and affiliated organizations and several standing committees. The internal power position among the member states may be deduced from the list of the main shareholders of the IDB, which are from Saudi Arabia, Libya, Iran, Egypt, Turkey, the United Arab Emirates,

and Kuwait. The OIC and its framework adapted the UN structures to the regional context of the member states. In placing the regional intergovernmental cooperation in an Islamic frame of reference, they interpret Islam as a system of values, modifying those derived from the UN charter where appropriate.

Almost all international Islamic organizations have advocated for what may be called a moral world order. "Islamic unity" and "Islamic solidarity" legitimate the transnational claim of these organizations. In reality, they have essentially translated local expressions of Islamicity into an emerging transnational Islamic public sphere (*da'wa*). This common feature, however, has remained abstract, and when it comes to practical policy, national or regional interests have clearly dominated. In this respect, intergovernmental or international nongovernmental Islamic organizations have rarely acted as representative of an independent transnational Islamic public, which had been the original ideal of Muslim reformers of the early 20th century. In certain respects, these organizations still reflect a state-centered approach to Islamic internationalism, which echoes the ideas of a new world order while assuming the possibility of directing and controlling the globalization of Islam "from above." Yet international Islamic institutions have slowly accommodated themselves to the complex character of transnational Muslim politics, which has created a rather different normative global framework with Islamic points of reference.

See also globalization; Pan-Islamism

Further Reading

Martin Kramer, *Islam Assembled: The Advent of the Muslim Congresses*, 1986; Kelly-Kate S. Pease, *International Organizations: Perspectives on Governance in the Twenty-First Century*, 2008; Reinhard Schulze, *Islamischer Internationalismus im 20. Jahrhundert. Untersuchungen zur Geschichte der Islamischen Weltliga*, 1990.

REINHARD SCHULZE

international relations

Islamic views on the nature of relations between political communities have varied considerably throughout history. Well before the rise of the modern system of nation-states at the core of contemporary international relations, Muslim political thinkers engaged in debates on matters of sovereignty, diplomacy, war, and peace. Central to these discussions was a tension between the theoretical precept of the *umma* (world community of believers) as a universal polity under divine law (shari'a) and the considerable territorial pluralism that has constituted the historical reality of Muslim societies. Another focal point in these debates was an apparent conflict between classical doctrines that seem to urge the expansion of Islam—by war, if necessary—into non-Muslim lands and other Islamic teachings that stress the permissibility, even the desirability, of peaceful and mutually profitable relations with non-Muslim polities.

The Qur'an contains several references to key concepts and themes in international relations, among which can be found the observation that humankind has been made "into nations and tribes, so that you might come to know one another" (49:13). Elsewhere are passages that refer to practices of treaty making, some of which seem implicitly to accept and respect distinctions between sovereign communities (Q. 8:72). But the Qur'an and sunna are also replete with injunctions to fight against unbelievers and polytheists—albeit with special accommodations for fellow monotheists (e.g., Jews and Christians). The complexity of these issues crystallized in practice as Islam began its rapid expansion from the mid-seventh century and particularly with the fragmentation of the Muslim world into separate dynastic polities from the tenth century. While the office of the caliph continued to serve as the nominal religiopolitical center of the Muslim world, by this time it had lost all meaningful claims to centralized political authority. Muslim scholars and statesmen were forced to come to terms with the presence of sovereign cleavages within the *umma* itself, not to mention the presence of significant numbers of non-Muslim "protected peoples" (*dhimmīs*) in territories under the rule of Islam. Beginning with the Abbasid period (750–1258), Islamic political thought divided the world into two domains: *dār al-islām* (the abode of Islam), describing those lands under Islamic rule, and *dār al-ḥarb* (the abode of war), referring to territories outside Muslim rule and potentially subject to conquest.

The apparent dualism at the heart of this worldview has, however, shifted considerably with history. Some schools of Islamic jurisprudence, for example, began to recognize a third category, that of *dār al-'ahd* (the abode of truce), to express tributary arrangements between states or even mutual recognition as sovereign equals. This latter category was frequently invoked by Ottoman jurists to describe that empire's relations with emerging European powers from the 16th century. The terminology of *dār al-ḥarb* also should not be taken to imply that offensive expansion constituted the core imperative of Islamic international relations. Mainstream legal thinking on jihad continued to stress a primarily defensive conception of armed conflict in the name of religion, with decision making by Muslim statesmen in this arena continuing to be guided primarily by sovereign interest and the *maṣlaḥa* (public good) of the political community. Moreover, the ethics of jihad came to resemble a code bearing striking similarities to the Christian just war doctrine, with clear distinctions between combatants and noncombatants and a heavy emphasis on the proportionate use of force.

With the exception of an aborted effort in the latter part of the 19th century to establish an anticolonial movement centered on ideals of "Pan-Islamism," the international relations of the Muslim world after the dissolution of the Ottoman Empire and in the wake of 20th-century decolonization tended to embrace territorial

sovereignty and the political form of the nation-state. Some reformers, such as Rashid Rida (1865–1935), regarded the abolition of the Ottoman caliphate in 1924 as a crisis for Islamic political thought and postulated the need for new forms of religious polity. Likewise, some early formulations of modern Islamism, such as that of Mawdudi (1903–79), founder of the Jama'at-i Islami in Pakistan, rejected the doctrine of nationalism as repugnant to Islamic teaching. Others, however, such as 'Ali 'Abd al-Raziq (1888–1966), a leading Egyptian religious scholar and judge, saw no intrinsic incompatibility between Islam and the modern system of nation-states. The world affairs of Muslim-majority countries in the contemporary period have hence generally proceeded in line with the norms of modern international relations. This does not mean, however, that Islamic considerations in foreign policy have disappeared altogether. Those countries claiming to be "Islamic states" (such as Saudi Arabia, Pakistan, and Iran) have, at various times, sought to define or explain their international affairs in terms of religion. In 1948, for example, Saudi Arabia registered concern with certain aspects of the Universal Declaration of Human Rights, claiming that the document relied too heavily on Western liberal values. For the most part, however, the diplomatic activity of these states mirrors mainstream international political behavior, even when Islamic rhetoric is invoked in the pursuit of statecraft. An intergovernmental organization, the Organization of the Islamic Conference (OIC), was established in 1969 to foster greater unity among the peoples of Muslim countries. Deliberations within the OIC, however, tended to highlight the diverse national interests of member states rather than a unified Muslim worldview. The latter part of the 20th century saw the establishment of a number of very small but highly visible transnational nongovernmental Islamic groups—such as Hizb-ut-Tahrir and al-Qaeda—that rejected the legitimacy of the international state system and sought the reestablishment of the caliphate.

See also abodes of Islam, war, and truce; diplomacy; international Islamic organizations; jihad; Pan-Islamism

Further Reading

Sohail Hashmi, ed., *Islamic Political Ethics*, 2002; Majid Khadduri, *War and Peace in the Law of Islam*, 1955; James Piscatori, *Islam in a World of Nation-States*, 1986.

PETER MANDAVILLE

Iqbal, Muhammad (1877–1938)

Iqbal's political thought represents a significant development in both the history of Indian Muslim political thought and the history of Islamic political thought in general. In his prose and poetical writings, Iqbal offers analytical reflections on aspects of Islamic political history as well as proposals for reforming Islamic political institutions. His political thought was formed by his critical study of doctrinal and historical Islam, his close observation of European politics during his stay in England from 1905 to 1908, and the political developments in British India, especially those pertaining to Hindu-Muslim communal relations.

Religion and Politics

While highly critical of ecclesiastical political dominance in European history, Iqbal believed that the Western divorce of religion from politics in modern times had, by lifting all ethical constraints from politics, led to disastrous conflicts between narrowly conceived national interests. "Divorced from religion, politics becomes the savage conduct of Chingiz Khan," runs a famous line in Iqbal's poetry. At the same time, religion's program of societal reform—Iqbal had the egalitarian Islamic political ideals in mind—requires, for its implementation, the support of state power. "Without a rod, the mission of Moses lacks all substance," reads another famous line in Iqbal's poetry. Iqbal seems to make a distinction between a nationalism that begins and ends with sanctifying territory and a nationalism that uses territory only as an instrument in the pursuit of universally valid ethical and humanity-oriented objectives, which, in his view, are embodied in Islam. Iqbal believed that European territorial nationalism arose against a particular background. Christianity, initially monastic and completely otherworldly, became, without warrant, a church organization, against which Martin Luther rightly protested. In Islam, however, Iqbal argued that religion and politics are organically related; no "metaphysical dualism of spirit and matter" separates them, and any division between them is purely functional. In Islam, the state exists only to translate the spiritual and ethical ideals of "equality, solidarity, and freedom" into the temporal world. Only in this sense may Islam be called a theocracy, and not in the sense that a supposedly infallible human despot can rule in God's name.

Democracy

Some of Iqbal's poetry contains a scathing critique of democracy, which Iqbal, quoting the French writer Marie-Henri Beyle, known as Stendhal (d. 1842), calls a mode of government in which people are counted, not weighed. But while his grounds for criticizing democracy were both philosophical (democracy has some inherent limitations) and practical (the European practice of the system in the first decades of the 20th century did not generate much optimism), Iqbal was a strong supporter of the democratic principle and considered democracy an essential part of Islamic government. In Islam, sovereignty belongs to God, and "authority, except as an interpreter of the law, has no place in the social structure of Islam. Islam has a horror of personal authority." Nevertheless, he wrote, "Political Sovereignty de facto resides in the people." Sovereignty is best exercised through democracy, democracy being "the most important aspect of Islam regarded as a political ideal," and election being, in turn, the principal form of democracy.

Muslim Commonwealth

Iqbal admired the modern Muslim thinker-activist Afghani (d. 1897) for his efforts to unify Muslims, but Afghani's so-called Pan-Islamism was conceived as an anti-imperialist instrument. Iqbal's view of worldwide Muslim unity had a philosophical-religious basis but also allowed for the complexities of practical reality: "The political ideal of Islam consists in the creation of a people born of a free fusion of all races and nationalities." The spiritual basis of Muslim unity itself obviates the need for a universal Muslim state under a single caliph or ruler; in Iqbal's view, it is much more practical to have a Muslim commonwealth, of which each country, having developed its individual potential, would freely choose to become a member. With "the absolute equality of all Muslims in the eyes of the law" as its cornerstone, the Muslim commonwealth "is not incompatible with the sovereignty of individual States, since its structure will be determined not by physical force, but by the spiritual force of a common ideal." Iqbal's Pan-Islamism, if one must use the term to describe his thought, is fundamentally different from Afghani's.

Homeland for India's Muslims

Iqbal's reputation as the spiritual founder of Pakistan is based on his vision of a homeland for the Muslims of India. After suppressing the allegedly Muslim-led 1857 revolt against their formal occupation of the country, the British made a systematic attempt to eliminate or weaken the Muslim political, economic, religious, and intellectual centers of power and influence, at the same time extending and bolstering their control over the country by replacing indigenous institutional structures with British or European ones. The hardest hit in the British colonial dispensation were the Muslims, who had supplied the country's former ruling class. For a while, the Muslims sought refuge in traditionalism, rejecting the aggressively introduced European cultural norms and practices in society. They also sought to collaborate with the Hindus, the country's other large religious and cultural community, in an anticolonial struggle; but such cooperation, as Iqbal eventually realized and expressed eloquently, was well-nigh impossible in view of the sharply divergent religious and cultural identities of Hindus and Muslims. In his presidential address at the 1930 meeting of the Muslim League in Lahore, Iqbal outlined his conviction that India's Hindus and Muslims were two fundamentally distinct religious and cultural communities and that, in the particular situation of India, the Muslims' collective survival depended on the creation of an autonomous or independent Muslim region: "Self-government within the British Empire or without the British Empire, the formation of a consolidated North-West Indian Muslim state appears to me to be the final destiny of the Muslims, at least of North-West India." This statement, which Iqbal later amplified by including India's eastern Muslim-majority areas in his proposal for the creation of "a separate federation of Muslim provinces," became the basis for the later development of the "two-nation theory," which, in turn, propelled the movement for the creation of Pakistan.

Of all the Muslim political theorists of post-1857 India, Iqbal perceived most clearly the distinctive character of Indian Muslim religious and political identities and articulated most forcefully the final political destiny of the Muslims of India. But Iqbal was interested in and concerned about the political situation of Muslims worldwide. He commented on the intellectual and political developments taking place in modern Turkey after the abolition of the caliphate, wrote about Italy's 1912 invasion of Libya, and analyzed the causes of the 1930 Muslim rebellion, led by a young boy, in Chinese Turkestan. The many strands of Iqbal's political thought, however, all derive from a cohesive religious outlook. The relationship between Iqbal's religious vision and his political thought needs a more detailed study.

See also al-Afghani, Jamal al-Din (1838–97); India; Pakistan

Further Reading

Aziz Ahmad, *Islamic Modernism in India and Pakistan 1857–1964*, 1967; Muhammad Iqbal, *The Reconstruction of Religious Thought in Islam*, edited by Saeed Sheikh, 1996; Mustansir Mir, *Iqbal*, 2006; Syed Abdul Vahid, *Studies in Iqbal*, 1967; Syed Abdul Vahid, ed., *Thoughts and Reflections of Iqbal*, 1992.

MUSTANSIR MIR

Iran

The most notable concept to have entered the Iranian political discourse since 1979 has been the guardianship of the jurist (*vilāyat-i faqīh*, Ar. *wilāyat al-faqīh*). Enshrined in the 1979 Iranian Constitution, it stipulates broad supervision of the entire political process by an Islamic jurist of the highest rank. It has become the pivotal institution of the Islamic Republic's system of governance, in which theocratic and republican ideas have uneasily coexisted. Associated with Ayatollah Khomeini, who published a tract titled *Vilayat-i Faqih* in 1970, the idea was barely known before 1979. An "absolute" version of it was incorporated in a constitutional amendment in 1989, but emphasis regarding the definition of the jurist shifted from recognized preeminence in religious learning to political-administrative competence coupled with adequate juristic knowledge.

As the chief instrument for sustaining and legitimizing Islamic governance, the guardianship of the jurist implies that clerical rule represents the authoritative Shi'i vision of both governance and faith, connoting that overt dissent verges on unbelief. Yet the clerical state eventually failed to conflate the roles of the jurist-guardian and the *marja'* (source of emulation) and encountered opposition both from within the Shi'i religious establishment and from the broader public. The enduring democratic-republican impulses of the Iranian Revolution (1978–79), coupled with the Islamic republic's waning ideological power, gradually opened up the public

sphere to competing interpretations of Islam, in which the clerics no longer exerted a monopolistic role. This involved broaching issues officially regarded as beyond discussion, including the officially sanctioned version of Shi'ism.

Combining modern analytical and exegetical approaches with indigenous intellectual traditions, thinkers embedded in Shi'i religious traditions who supported the emergence of an Islamic polity have engaged in reconstructing religious thought. Probing the genealogy of the ruling religious ideology, they have contested the official reading of Shi'i intellectual political traditions, emphasizing that other, historically more grounded readings are not only possible but also desirable.

Relying on hermeneutics, Mohammad Mojtahed-Shabestari (b. 1936), a professor of theology until his retirement in 2006, maintains that there is no single correct reading of the Qur'an and the sunna, and that the official version of Islam, purporting to be the only valid version, has been used to facilitate the state's control of society and culture. He argues that political legitimacy should rest on political rationality and the popular vote, and religious values and secular realities should be separated.

Similarly, for the influential lay thinker Abdolkarim Soroush (b. 1945), who sees himself as a neo-Mu'tazili, Islam lends itself to a variety of interpretations. Combining modern philosophical perspectives and Iranian-Islamic mysticism, he emphasizes the fallibility and historicity of religious knowledge and the contingency and historical specificity of prophetic revelation. For him, there is more than one approach to understanding scripture and therefore more than one path to salvation. Religious pluralism as advocated by Soroush requires the absence of an officially sanctioned interpretation and official interpreters; concomitantly, a pluralist society must be democratic and prioritize rights over duties.

Firmly basing his beliefs on Shi'i traditions of learning, the Islamic jurist Mohsen Kadivar (b. 1959) furnishes a wide-ranging critique of Khomeini's theory of governance and a forceful refutation of the theocratic cornerstone of Islamic rule in Iran. Kadivar maintains that rather than representing the only Shi'i view of governance, Khomeini provided one among many traditions. For Kadivar, the principle of the guardianship of the jurist is neither rationally necessary nor a requirement of faith or any of its cardinal principles.

The emphasis of critics on the absence of a single, authoritative interpretation of Shi'ism contrasts sharply with the official creed and its underlying premise. Hermeneutics and other historically grounded investigations have challenged the theocratic state and have helped transform the Shi'i modernist discourse. Criticisms of the official religious ideology have also been voiced by various ayatollahs, including Hosein-Ali Montazeri (1922–2009), Khomeini's successor designate, who was relieved of his position in 1989. Montazeri played an important role in developing the idea of the guardianship of the jurist but gradually turned against its prevailing form. Similar reservations have been expressed by many clerical and lay intellectuals and activists associated with the reform movement that culminated in the presidency of Mohammad Khatami in May 1997.

Countering or containing religiously grounded arguments against a state that bases its legitimacy chiefly on religion proved difficult, and the ruling clerics were not able to mount intellectually vigorous counterarguments. Unlike the ranks of their critics, those in power were unable to produce outstanding intellectual exponents of the ruling ideology or to compensate for the desertion of its erstwhile exponents. The reformist segments of the Islamic Republic proposed specifically Islamic forms of democracy and civil society but did not furnish coherent blueprints or formulas for their realization.

See also guardianship of the jurist; Khomeini, Ayatollah (1902–89)

Further Reading

Behrooz Ghamari-Tabrizi, *Islam and Dissent in Postrevolutionary Iran: Abdolkarim Soroush, Religious Politics and Democratic Reform*, 2008; Yasuyuki Matsunaga, "Mohsen Kadivar, an Advocate of Postrevivalist Islam in Iran," *British Journal of Middle Eastern Studies* 34, no. 3 (2007); Ahmad Sadri and Mahmoud Sadri, *Reason, Freedom, and Democracy in Islam: Essential Writings of Abdolkarim Soroush*, 2002; Mahmoud Sadri, "Sacral Defense of Secularism: The Political Theologies of Soroush, Shabestari, and Kadivar," *International Journal of Politics, Culture and Society* 15, no. 2 (2001); Abdolkarim Soroush, *The Expansion of Prophetic Experience: Essays on Historicity, Contingency and Plurality in Religion*, translated by Nilou Mobasser and edited by Forough Jahanbakhsh, 2009; Farzin Vahdat, "Post-Revolutionary Islamic Modernity in Iran: The Intersubjective Hermeneutics of Mohamad Mojtahed Shabestari," in *Modern Muslim Intellectuals and the Qur'an*, edited by Suha Taji-Farouki, 2004.

FAKHREDDIN AZIMI

Iraq

Some of the central ideas in modern Islamic political thought—notably, constitutionalism, just government, and the role of clerics in politics—were conceived or elaborated in Iraq during the 20th century and in the years following the 2003 U.S. invasion of the country. Shi'i clerics have taken the lead in developing ideas, overshadowing their Sunni counterparts. This is not simply a reflection of the majority share of Shi'is within the population but rather a consequence of the financial and intellectual independence of Shi'i clerics in relation to the Sunni government. Also, until 2003, Sunni clerics were part of the bureaucracy of the state and therefore had little control over the curriculum of their religious schools and the content of sermons delivered in mosques.

The Iranian Constitutional Revolution of 1905 to 1911 and the Young Turk Constitutional Revolution of 1908 had an impact in Najaf and Karbala. Both revolutions, and the Ottoman removal of the ban on publications and political association, enabled Shi'i

clerics to articulate their vision of constitutionalism and develop a political theory of a just government. Muhammad Husayn Na'ini's (d. 1936) *Tanbih al-Umma wa-Tanzih al-Milla* (The awakening of the community and the purification of religion) is the most famous theoretical and systematic work written by a Shi'i jurist in support of the Iranian constitution, defining government accountability in the eye of clerics and setting principles for their resistance to the ruler and their participation in state affairs.

Na'ini's work influenced later generations of Shi'i jurists and had an impact on the events surrounding the British establishment of Iraq. Thus, in the course of the 1919 plebiscite, Shi'i clerics and other religious functionaries in Karbala, inspired by the jurist Muhammad Taqi Shirazi (d. 1920), signed a petition calling for an Arab Islamic government in Iraq led by a king whose acts would be supervised by a national assembly elected by the people to enact the rules approved by the clerics.

The 1921 establishment of Iraq as a state dominated by a Sunni minority elite was a setback to Shi'i Islam, forcing Shi'i clerics to withdraw from politics in the country. While the revival of Islamic ideology may be traced to the late 1950s, it became pronounced only under the Ba'th Party (1968–2003) and following the 1978 to 1979 Iranian Islamic revolution. Muhammad Baqir al-Sadr was the moving figure behind Shi'i Islamic resurgence in Iraq and the establishment of the Da'wa Party in 1959. He gained reputation through his works *Falsafatuna* (Our philosophy), *Iqtisaduna* (Our economy), and *al-Islam Yaqud al-Hayah* (Islam leads life). Sadr developed a vision of Islamic government and distinguished between two types of religious leaders: the preeminent cleric who gains recognition by consensus, or a majority, among followers in the Shi'i world and the one who is not necessarily the most learned cleric but who springs from within his milieu and responds to the needs of his local constituency.

Sadr's activism was a threat to the Ba'th Party and led to his execution in 1980. Yet his legacy inspired followers, including Muhammad Sadiq al-Sadr (a cousin of Baqir al-Sadr and known as Sadr II). During the 1990s, Sadr II succeeded in reconnecting the Najaf world of clerics and seminaries with the rural communities of southern Iraq and the Shi'i urban poor in Baghdad. His strategy built on grassroots politics and on the function of the religious leader as a field commander. Sadr II's path to becoming a cleric commanding popular support was cut short, however, when gunmen shot him to death in 1999. His movement would reemerge under his son Muqtada al-Sadr following the collapse of the Ba'th Party.

The U.S. invasion reenergized Shi'i clerics and led Grand Ayatollah 'Ali al-Sistani (b. 1930) to adapt Islamic political thought to an Iraq led by Shi'is with significant Sunni and Kurdish minorities. From 2003 to 2009, Sistani insisted on direct elections to parliament, objected to the appointment of drafters to write the constitution, and advocated a government representing all social groups. Although Sistani had a vision of what an Islamic government should be, he was not inspired by Khomeini (d. 1989), who allowed the idea that clerics should rule to be implemented in the Islamic Republic of Iran. Sistani's ideas were more in tune with those of Na'ini and emphasized government accountability. Moreover, Sistani accepted the political reality of a modern nation-state led by lay politicians and tacitly acknowledged that there should be limits on clerical participation in state affairs.

Meanwhile, amid the collapse of the Ba'th Party, Sunni clerics emerged as community leaders. The period between 2003 and 2009 also saw the establishment of Sunni organizations such as the Association of Muslim Scholars (AMS), which attempted to position itself as a counter to the Shi'i religious leadership and sought to rethink the role of Sunni clerics and Sunni religious institutions in a Shi'i-led state—a novelty in the modern Arab world.

See also ayatollah; Ba'th Party; constitutionalism; Shi'ism

Further Reading

Faleh Jabar, *The Shiite Movement in Iraq*, 2003; Meir Litvak, *Shi'i Scholars of Nineteenth-Century Iraq*, 1998; Yitzhak Nakash, *Reaching for Power: The Shi'a in the Modern Arab World*, 2006; Linda Walbridge, ed., *The Most Learned of the Shi'a: The Institution of the Marja' al-Taqlid*, 2001.

EDITOR

Islamic Jihad

The organization known as Egyptian Islamic Jihad (Jihad al-Islami al-Misri, hereafter EIJ), also frequently referred to as the Jihad Organization (Tanzim al-Jihad), is a militant Islamist group. At least until 2007, its objective was to engage in offensive jihad (lit. struggle; here, military action) against the Egyptian state to weaken the regime and ultimately to initiate an Islamic revolution. The group draws its ideology from 'Abd al-Salam Faraj's work *al-Farida al-Gha'iba* (*The Neglected Duty*), which further develops ideas set out by Sayyid Qutb's *Ma'alim fi al-Tariq* (*Milestones*). EIJ was involved in the assassination of President Anwar Sadat in October 1981 and was a leading participant in the jihad in Afghanistan during the 1980s. It was also involved in several attempts on the life of high-ranking Egyptian politicians, among them an attempt against President Husni Mubarak in June 1995. EIJ carried out a series of bomb strikes on military and civilian installations in Egypt and abroad during the 1980s and 1990s. Throughout the 1990s, the group was affiliated with Ayman al-Zawahiri and subsequently constituted a subgroup of al-Qaeda.

The beginnings of the group go back to the late 1970s, when a number of loosely organized militant networks in Cairo came together under the leadership of Faraj. One of the networks feeding into the early EIJ was the circle of Zawahiri, which included his brother Muhammad al-Zawahiri, Ulwi Mustafa Ulaywah and his brother Muhammad Mustafa Ulaywah, 'Isam al-Qamari, and Sayyid Imam al-Sharif. The ranks of the early EIJ extended to the military; Qamari

and Muhammad Ulaywah were members of the armed forces, and Lieutenant Colonel ʻAbbud al-Zumur was a high-ranking officer who then organized the military wing of the group. In June 1980, Faraj managed to convince the Saidi (Upper Egyptian) network of Karam Zuhdi—which included smaller groups centered around Najih Ibrahim, ʻAbdallah Sayyid, Muhammad al-Islambuli, and Hamdi ʻAbd al-Rahman and which formed the nucleus of the later al-Gamaʻa al-Islamiyya (Islamic Group)—to coordinate their activities and join forces. The groups, which remained locally distinct, formed a *shūrā* (consultation) council of 12 and nominated ʻUmar ʻAbd al-Rahman as their mufti (interpreter of Islamic law).

On October 6, 1981, an EIJ military action unit under the command of Khalid al-Islambuli assassinated Sadat during a military parade in commemoration of the 1973 Arab-Israeli War. Following the event, a military trial sentenced Faraj, Khalid al-Islambuli, and the latter's three accomplices to death. The court cases against another 302 EIJ members resulted in 58 prison sentences and, except for a few senior members, most members of the organization were released within 3 years. The prison years revealed underlying tensions between the Saidi and the Cairene factions of the organization on questions of leadership, strategy, and the future of the organization. The differences led to the establishment of al-Gamaʻa al-Islamiyya under ʻAbd al-Rahman as a group distinct from EIJ, which chose Zumur as its leader.

In order to escape prosecution in Egypt and because of the prospect of engaging in combat, many EIJ members left to participate in the Afghan jihad against Russian troops. Since Zumur remained imprisoned in Egypt, Sayyid Imam al-Sharif (also known as Dr. Fadl) took charge of EIJ's operations. Following ʻAbdallah ʻAzzam's call to join the jihad in Afghanistan, EIJ adhered to the concept of the "near enemy," which draws on traditional concepts of Muslim warfare to stress the obligation to directly confront a force occupying what is perceived to be Muslim land.

With the withdrawal of Russia from Afghanistan, EIJ members reviewed their strategy and ideology, particularly their definition of jihad. Zawahiri and the remaining EIJ combatants favored the concept of warfare against the "far enemy," stressing their view that it was obligatory to fight against the United States and its allies, which they perceived as enabling the continuance of governments such as the Egyptian regime under Mubarak. Zawahiri thus gradually increased his influence on the Egyptian mujahidin (fighters engaging in jihad) and, with the beginning of the Gulf War in 1991, took charge of EIJ. EIJ then effectively merged with al-Qaeda under Osama bin Laden. Evidence of the correlation between EIJ and al-Qaeda is the fact that six of nine seats of al-Qaeda's leadership council belong to former EIJ members. Furthermore, a number of terrorist attacks, such as the 1995 bombing of the Egyptian embassy in Islamabad and the 1995 attempts on President Mubarak's life, were financed, planned, and executed through al-Qaeda.

Zawahiri's leadership and the strategy of international terrorism did not go unchallenged. In the late 1990s, ideological disputes emerged on the question of engaging in combat on a national or an international level; however, a clear rift took place in 2007, when Sayyid Imam al-Sharif published a statement that called for a review of the idea of militant jihad. This revision led EIJ members to distance themselves from international terrorism, al-Qaeda, and Zawahiri. It is still too early to say whether EIJ thus reinvented itself as an organization separate from al-Qaeda and opted to give up its militant opposition to the Egyptian state.

See also Egypt; al-Qaeda; terrorism; al-Zawahiri, Ayman (b. 1951)

Further Reading

Omar Ashour, *The De-Radicalization of Jihadists: Transforming Armed Islamist Movements*, 2009; Lisa Blaydes and Rawrence Rubin, "Ideological Reorientation and Counterterrorism: Confronting Militant Islam in Egypt," *Terrorism and Political Violence* 20 (2008); Johannes J. G. Jansen, *The Neglected Duty: The Creed of Sadat's Assassins and Islamic Resurgence in the Middle East*, 1986; Laura Mansfield, *His Own Words: A Translation of the Writings of Dr. Ayman al Zawahiri*, 2006; Marc Sageman, *Understanding Terror Networks*, 2004; Montasser al-Zayyat, *The Road to al-Qa'ida. The Story of Bin Laden's Right Hand Man*, 2004.

BARBARA ZOLLNER

Islamization

Islamization is the process by which practices, laws, knowledge, meaning, or peoples convert, conform, or adapt to Islam. It can describe (1) the redefinition of various pagan, Abrahamic, or native practices against the backdrop of conversion and expansion and (2) the integration of cultural, political, legal, or scientific systems with Islamic doctrines, language, and ethics, or their production from an Islamic perspective. In addition to reassessing conversion itself, appreciation of Islamization as a process has allowed scholars to show formal and substantive continuities during and after conversion; to pursue synchronic comparisons of Islamic cultures; and to capture the specific transformations facilitated by the adaptation of social phenomena and categories into Islam's normative and semiotic structures. An example of the last is the transformation during early Islam of various literary genres such as the metered Arabic lyric poem, called the *qaṣīda,* through the introduction of Islamic terms and themes. The significance and extent to which Islam is the product of the Islamization of pagan, Hellenistic, Christian, and Jewish thought and practice remains contested. Scholars on one side assume that all similarities between early Islam and its predecessors indicate "borrowing" or "influence"; those on the other side see Islam as a complete and total break with the past. More recent scholarship has shown how non-Islamic knowledge, myths, and histories were adapted, reorganized, and elaborated in Islamic milieus in areas as diverse as history, theology, philosophy, and zoology. "Islamization" has some baggage, particularly where "Islam"

is reified or where one assumes that the designation of something as Islamic or non-Islamic by nature is self-evident. Similarly, the term not infrequently carries polemical undertones. For example, self-described Islamizing agendas assert an authentic Islamic identity and cast their opposition or their objects of conversion as non- or un-Islamic, while non-Muslim descriptions of a place as "Islamizing" tend to cast the place as vulnerable and Islamization as a threat.

Scholarship on contemporary politics and society has drawn attention to the performative, spectacular, and relational dimensions of attempts to "Islamize" the public, public space, or oneself. For instance, Farha Ghannam, an anthropologist specializing in Egypt and Jordan, uses the term in her *Remaking the Modern* to describe Islamic groups' increasing displays of religious signs in homes, shops, and vehicles; the increasing numbers of educational and health services in their mosques; and their interactions with the general populace. Others have also highlighted the importance of visibility, where Islamization describes overtly religious practices and mosque construction projects. Finally, "Islamization of knowledge" describes a contemporary project to harmonize Islam with the modern sciences and anchor them in Islamic ethics. This enterprise can be traced to the writings of the Palestinian-American philosopher of Islam, Arabism, and comparative religion Isma'il al-Faruqi, starting in the 1960s. Organizations that grew out of this project include the International Institute of Islamic Thought. As the anthropologist of science Christopher Furlow suggests in his article "The Islamization of Knowledge: Philosophy, Legitimation, and Politics," such projects should be understood "within the broad context of decolonization and development and within the intellectual milieu of post-colonial negotiation between 'nativizing' cultural traditions and 'transnational' modernisms."

See also conversion; knowledge; political ritual

Further Reading

Devin DeWeese, *Islamization and Native Religion in the Golden Horde*, 1994; Isma'il al-Faruqi, "Science and Traditional Values in Islamic Society," *Zygon* 2, no. 1 (1967); Christopher A. Furlow, "The Islamization of Knowledge: Philosophy, Legitimation, and Politics," *Social Epistemology* 10, nos. 3–4 (1996); Farha Ghannam, *Remaking the Modern*, 2002.

MURAD IDRIS

Isma'il I (1487–1524)

Isma'il, born 1487, ruled as shah of the Safavid Empire between 1501 and 1524. He succeeded in conquering the lands of modern-day Iran, Iraq, and Afghanistan with his Qizilbash (Turkmen) disciples, who venerated him as God's incarnation on Earth. The first spiritual guide of the Safavid mystical order to assume temporal rule, Shah Isma'il claimed he was the reincarnation of Abrahamic prophets and heroic kings from Iran's cultural past. At a time marked by millenarian beliefs, Shah Isma'il appropriated the role of the long-awaited Mahdi (messiah), who intercedes with God on behalf of the common believers. To help validate this identity, he claimed membership, through 'Ali b. Abi Talib, to Muhammad's family, from which the messiah was expected to emerge at the end of time.

In his collection of poetry, the *Diwan-i Khata'i* (Book of the sinner), which is the closest historical depiction of his persona, Shah Isma'il represented himself as a penitent pilgrim, willing to sacrifice his soul for the benefit of all. He appropriated the conventional voice of the *ghazal* (love poem), depicting himself as a mournful sinner and the bedazzled lover of 'Ali, presenting a pious persona to the world while inaugurating a new era in the history of Iran and beyond and carving out his Shi'i dominion. His poetry announced his messianic mission both as an invitation to his followers and as a warning to those infidels who would resist his call. Believing that his personal path to salvation would be in the company of 'Ali, Isma'il imagined himself as a pilgrim circumambulating the Ka'ba, there confessing and publicly repenting in order to achieve his desired union with 'Ali, who not only disclosed universal mysteries to him but whose persona had actually been reincarnated in Isma'il. Recognizing 'Ali as the gate of Islam, in fact as God himself ("Know [him] to be God"), Isma'il invited the audience of his poetry to emulate him by converting to Islam and joining the Safavid cause. Within a decade, Isma'il had marshaled the support of Persian- and Turkish-speaking devotees who were ready to sacrifice their lives.

Isma'il's revolution could not have succeeded, however, without his corps of Turkmen devotees—that is, westward-moving Turks who his grandfather, Shaykh Junayd (d. 1460), had recruited from Ottoman domains in Asia Minor. Well before Isma'il's own revolution, Shaykh Junayd altered the character of the Safavid order from a Sufi brotherhood to a messianic movement with far-reaching political aspirations when he was banished to Anatolia and Syria in 1448. There he engaged in missionary activities and recruited Turkmen adepts known as Qizilbash, or Redheads (because of the color of their skull caps), who contributed military might and later aided Isma'il in conquering lands and amassing his empire. The Qizilbash Turkmen viewed Junayd as God's reincarnation—"the Living One, there is no God but he"—and his son Haydar as the son of God. In 1456 Junayd fought a holy war (*ghazw*) against the Byzantines at Trabezond, and he died in another battle in the Caucasus in 1460.

Isma'il not only merged divine justice and worldly kingship but also exercised their functions, as would be expected from a messiah-king. In his role of divinely just ruler, he shared war booty with his Qizilbash disciples and divided the conquered territories into appanages administered by governors and tutors of Safavid princes. This generosity confirmed his image as God on Earth to his subjects. Although some of Muhammad's descendants (*sayyids*) were awarded privileges, including some tax exemptions, a kind of overall social welfare was instituted: craftsmen and merchants were exempt from commercial taxes, and soup kitchens were set up for the poor and needy. Not surprisingly, Isma'il's treasuries were often empty.

The "Shi'ification" and "Iranization" of the Safavid Empire over a period of 100 years prepared the landscape for a regional split into distinct Sunni Ottoman and Shi'i Safavid dominions. Having publicly embraced Shi'ism, Shah Isma'il invited Arab Imami Shi'i scholars to emigrate from Ottoman to Safavid domains, including those in greater Syria. Many subjects, however, disapproving of his messianic claims, refused his patronage. The Ottoman-Safavid hostilities checked the fluidity that the Irano-Turkish world had known and created sectarian boundaries of religious identity, which remain strongly demarcated in the region's present-day rivalries.

Once Isma'il had conquered the Safavid domains, new regional groups, such as Persian bureaucrats and local notables, were incorporated into the system of rule and administration of the dominions, and they brought their own cultural ideas and attitudes. During Isma'il's lifetime, different historical versions of his rise to power and spiritual status as the Mahdi emerged, some circulated by the king himself and several by his court historians. But an official, master history of Isma'il's and the Safavids' ascendance was yet to be determined, reflecting the decentralized nature of power in this period. His son, Tahmasp, emerged from a 13-year civil war (1524–36) that had erupted over the issue of succession at Isma'il's death. These struggles over power eventually determined which version of Isma'il's story would be adopted as the Safavids' "official" history of ascendance. In the final, official version, Isma'il did not hold the messiah's role but was his humble precursor who, by establishing the "right order"—namely, Imami Shi'ism—would prepare the way for the advent of the messiah or Hidden Imam.

See also Mahdi; Ottomans (1299–1924); Safavids (1501–1722)

Further Reading

Aubin Jean, "L'Avenement des Safavides Reconsidere," *Moyen Orient & Ocean Indien* 5 (1988): 67–126; Fazl Allah b. Ruzbihan Kunji-Isfahani, *Tarikh-i Alam Ara-yi Amini*, edited and translated by John E. Woods, 1993; Michele Membré, *Mission to the Lord Sophy of Persia*, translated and introduced by A. H. Morton, 1993; Vladimir Minorsky, "The Poetry of Shah Ismail I," *Bulletin of the School of Oriental and African Studies* 10 (1942): 1006–53; Idem, *Tazkirat al-Muluk: A Manual of Safavid Administration*, translated and commentary by Vladimir Minorsky, reprint, 1989; Wheeler Thackston, "The Divan of Khata'i: Pictures for the Poetry of Shah Isma'il," *Asian Art* (Fall 1988): 37–63.

KATHRYN BABAYAN

Isma'ilis

Isma'ilism is a branch of Shi'ism best known for postulating a hidden, interior sense of the law and emphasizing it over the plain, exterior meaning. First attested in the late ninth century as a collection of cells spread throughout the Islamic lands and directed by leaders in Syria, the political thought of the first Isma'ilis was reduced to messianism. The last imam was to return from hiding as the Mahdi expected to usher in the end of days and abrogate the law (i.e., ritual worship). There would then be no need for conventional religion; believers would worship God directly, as Adam had done in paradise.

In 899, the leader in Syria had declared himself to be the Mahdi, thereby splitting the movement into two: Old Isma'ilis (often known as Qarmatis) and Fatimid Isma'ilis, so called because their leader fled to North Africa, where, in 909, he founded the Fatimid caliphate, which moved to Egypt in 969. In the writings of Isma'ili missionaries working for the Fatimid caliphs (r. 909–1171), the imam was no longer an absent figure expected to return to usher in the end of days but rather a religiopolitical leader in the here and now, as among non-Isma'ilis. The imam—that is, the Fatimid caliph—was God's representative on Earth, the political and religious leader for all humankind. As a political leader, his duties were identical to those that non-Isma'ilis ascribed to the imam: he was charged with executing the law, collecting and distributing alms and taxes, protecting the weak, defending the borders, and eventually bringing all humankind under God's rule. As a religious leader, he was divinely guided, sinless, and infallible; his example was a source for law. The imam alone possessed perfect knowledge necessary for salvation and was thus the supreme teacher, the gate of salvation for humankind. He alone was thought to know the true, inner sense of scripture and religion, and he disclosed these truths to high-ranking believers in his mission, who, in turn, distributed them to the community.

Just as the Fatimids transformed the role of the imam, so too did they modify his identity and devise explanations for the shifts. Early Isma'ilis believed the last imam and future Mahdi to be Muhammad b. Isma'il, a descendant of the Prophet's cousin 'Ali b. Abi Talib. In 899, the future Fatimid caliph announced to the missionary in Iraq that the awaited redeemer was not Muhammad b. Isma'il but himself. "Muhammad b. Isma'il" had been a cover name for a series of seven Hidden Imams. It was over this that the movement split. Fatimid missionaries explained that the end of days would unfold in stages. Now, with the rise of the Fatimid caliphs, the end of days had moved from a cycle of Hidden Imams to a "cycle of disclosure," in which the imams would fight their tyrannical enemies openly until the entire world was subdued.

Most Isma'ilis lived outside Egypt, where many of them remained faithful to the old doctrine. Some proceeded to prepare for the end of days, and in the 930s the so-called Qarmatis in Bahrain put an extreme form of antinomianism into practice. In 930, they attacked Mecca, slaughtered pilgrims, and abducted the black stone as a sign that conventional Islam had come to an end. In 931, they accepted a young Iranian captive as the Mahdi, apparently seeing him as a manifestation of God, and engaged in ritual violation of the law under his leadership. Non-Isma'ilis came invariably to associate Isma'ilism with the behavior seen in Bahrain, but in fact antinomianism is quite rare in Isma'ili history, and it never took so violent a form again.

Other Isma'ilis, including those in Iran and Transoxiana, taught that the present was an "interim" period—a period between imams. During such interims in which the imam was absent, the mission would be led by lieutenants of the imam. To appease these communities, the Fatimid caliph Mu'izz (r. 953–75) reinstated Muhammad b. Isma'il as the awaited redeemer and claimed that the Fatimid imams were his spiritual representatives who would rule until the final phase of the end of days.

Several authors unaffiliated with the Fatimids combined Isma'ili doctrine and Neoplatonic philosophy to develop highly original syntheses that would later be incorporated by Fatimid missionaries such as Hamid al-Din al-Kirmani (d. ca. 1021).

Fatimid-Isma'ili missionaries also debated with non-Isma'ilis over the identity of the imam. They claimed that their arguments rested on authoritative transmitted knowledge and logic. Proof from transmitted knowledge consisted of verses of the Qur'an that they believed referred to the authority of the family of the Prophet and traditions in which the Prophet explicitly designated 'Ali as his successor at a pond in Khumm. Proof from logic came, for example, in an attack on the Sunni notion that the first caliph, Abu Bakr, was nominated by "consultation" (*shūrā*) of the early Companions. How could the inferior have the capacity to identify and elect the superior? Through the Prophet, God Himself appointed 'Ali as His representative. Against the claims of the Twelver Shi'is, who argued that it was impossible for the imam Ja'far al-Sadiq's son Isma'il to be imam, since he had predeceased his father, Isma'ili missionaries produced traditions that showed that Ja'far had explicitly claimed Isma'il as his successor, claiming that he, in turn, had appointed his son Muhammad b. Isma'il. For the Fatimid missionary Abu al-Fawaris, the truth of all this was demonstrated by the fact that the current imam, the caliph Hakim (996–1021), was unparalleled in descent, knowledge, and generosity.

Expectations of the (spiritual) resurrection nonetheless resurfaced in the wake of the disappearance of Hakim in 1021, when a number of missionaries declared this caliph to have been a manifestation of God and the law to have been abolished, founding a community of breakaways in Syria known as the Druzes. In 1164 another breakaway community abolished ritual worship, this time at Alamut in northwestern Iran, but they restored it some 50 years later. After the fall of the Fatimids and the eclipse of small Isma'ili principalities in mountainous regions of Iran and Syria in the 13th century, Isma'ilism has persisted through quietist, minority subsects in Western China, South Asia, Syria, Yemen, and East Africa as well as Europe and North America.

See also Abbasids (750–1258); Brethren of Purity; Buyids (945–1062); Druze; Fatimids (909–1171); imamate; Qarmatians; Shi'ism; al-Tusi, Nasir al-Din (1201–74)

Further Reading

Patricia Crone, *Medieval Islamic Political Thought (God's Rule)*, 2004; Farhad Daftary, *The Ismāʿīlīs: Their History and Doctrines*, 1990; Heinz Halm, *The Empire of the Mahdī: The Rise of the Fāṭimids*, 1977; Sumaiya A. Hamdani, *Between Revolution and State: The Path to Fatimid Statehood*, 2006; Wilferd Madelung, "A Treatise on the Imamate of the Fatimid Caliph al-Manṣūr bi-Allāh," in *Texts, Documents and Artefacts: Islamic Studies in Honour of D. S. Richards*, edited by Chase F. Robinson, 1993; Paul Walker, *Master of the Age: An Islamic Treatise on the Necessity of the Imamate*, 2007.

DAVID HOLLENBERG

Istanbul

Istanbul is one of the oldest and most populated cities in Europe and the largest city in Turkey. Located on the Bosporus, spreading along the Sea of Marmara and connecting Thrace and Anatolia, Istanbul consists of four parts: the Golden Horn and Old Istanbul extending to the Eyyub district in the west; Galata to the north of Golden Horn; Üsküdar to the east on the Asian side; and Boğazıcı on the Black Sea side of the Bosporus, extending into Asia and Europe. The greater Istanbul region extends almost 30 miles east to west and 10 miles north to south. The Boğaz Bridge and the Fatih Bridge across the Bosporus connect the European and Asian parts. Its location at the meeting point of Asia and Europe has given it strategic importance, and placed it naturally on major modern and ancient trade routes.

The name Istanbul is from a Greek phrase that means "in the city." The ancient city was founded by Greek settlers in the seventh century BCE and called Byzantion. Later it fell under Persian rule, then reverted to Greek or independent rule, until in 73 it fell to the Romans. In 330, the emperor Constantine made it the eastern capital of the Roman Empire, calling it "New Rome" (*Nea Roma*), and it remained the capital of the Byzantine Empire under the name of Constantinople. The city withstood two sieges by the Arabs in late seventh and early eighth centuries. Other than the brief period when it was ruled by the Crusaders (1204–61), it stayed under Byzantine rule. But the expanding Ottoman principalities in Asia Minor gradually confined this empire to the Constantinople area. After several unsuccessful Ottoman attacks, the city fell to the Ottoman sultan Mehmed II the Conquerer in 1453. Under his rule, the city grew much bigger and was completely restructured as an Islamic city and the capital of the Muslim Ottoman Empire. The Hagia Sophia Cathedral was turned into a great mosque, today the Ayasofya, where the Friday prayer was held and the sultan received petitions, giving it a completely Islamic function. The sultan then started repopulating the city with Muslim, Christian, and Jewish immigrants from across his empire, with Muslims constituting the majority by design. The expansion and Islamization of Istanbul continued under Sultan Süleiman the Magnificent, making a full transformation from old Constantinople to the Islamic Istanbul, which was envisaged by the sultan as the true capital of the Muslim world, with the sultan as the rightful

leader of the Islamic community in general. The sultan's claim as the legitimate successor to the original caliphate, and hence worthy of the title "Commander of the Faithful," was on firm ground after the 1517 Ottoman takeover of Egypt, ruled by the Mamluks, who themselves had laid claim to the title after some Abbasid princes took refuge in Egypt following the 1258 sack of Baghdad by the Mongols and the murder of the last Abbasid caliph. Hence, during the next few centuries, Istanbul remained the capital and the seat of the Ottoman sultan and grew considerably, despite the gradual decline of the Ottoman Empire.

In the late 19th century, European railways reached Istanbul, and the city started to modernize. In World War I, the Ottomans joined the axis powers, and in 1919 Istanbul was occupied by the British and remained under their control until 1923, when the Ottoman Empire was abolished and the modern state of Turkey was founded. In the early 21st century, Istanbul is a center of culture and commerce, although no longer the capital.

See also Ottomans (1299–1924); Süleiman the Magnificent (1494–1566); Turkey

Further Reading

S. Faroqhi, *Geschichte des Osmanischen Reiches*, 2006; J. Harris, *Constantinople, Capital of Byzantium*, 2007; H. İnalcık *An Economic and Social History of the Ottoman Empire*, 1997.

HADI JORATI

J

Ja'far al-Sadiq (702–65)

Ja'far al-Sadiq, more formally named al-Sadiq Ja'far b. Muhammad b. 'Ali b. al-Husayn and regarded by the Imami Shi'is as the sixth of their 12 imams, was born in Medina and spent virtually his entire life there. His father, Muhammad al-Baqir (d. 735), was a great-grandson of 'Ali b. Abi Talib (d. 661), descended from Husayn b. 'Ali (d. 680), while his mother was a descendant in the male line of the first caliph, Abu Bakr (d. 634). Ja'far took no part in the political upheavals of his day. When his paternal uncle Zayd b. 'Ali (d. 740) rose against the Umayyads in 740, Ja'far refused to join him, and when Ja'far was offered the leadership of the Muslim community at the time of the Abbasid victory, he reportedly declined. In 762, he refrained from participating in the revolt against the Abbasid caliph Abu Ja'far al-Mansur (d. 775) that was led by another prominent 'Alid, Muhammad al-Nafs al-Zakiyya (d. 762). Following the suppression of this revolt, Ja'far was summoned to the caliph's court but was not harmed. He died three years later in Medina. Reports that he had been poisoned by order of Mansur are probably false. Disagreements as to who was to succeed him led to splits among his followers and marked the beginning of the Isma'ili sect.

As a scholar and traditionalist, Ja'far in his own lifetime was already held in high esteem and not only by Shi'is; both Abu Hanifa (d. 767) and Malik b. Anas (d. 795), the eponymous founders of the Hanafi and Maliki legal schools respectively, are said to have studied with him, and he often appears in chains of transmission in Sunni works of hadith. Non-Shi'is do not, however, regard him as an imam, but only as a distinguished jurist and transmitter. Deeply learned in religious law, Ja'far also is said to have been well versed in occult sciences such as astrology and alchemy. Various writings are ascribed to him, including a commentary on the Qur'an, though they are of dubious authenticity. Many of his Shi'i followers were residents of the city of Kufa, who would visit him during the pilgrimage.

Ja'far is often portrayed as playing a leading role in the growth of Imami law, known as "the Ja'fari legal school (*madhhab*)." Much of Imami law is based on countless utterances, directives, and decisions attributed to him (and in part to his father). These were set down by his disciples in written form.

The major components of the Imami doctrine of the imamate are said to have been in place by Ja'far's time, and Ja'far (or some of his disciples) may well have been instrumental in giving them shape. At the center of the doctrine stands the principle of loyalty (*walāya*) to an imam who is a descendant of 'Ali and his wife Fatima (the Prophet's daughter). Adherence to this principle is considered a foundation of faith, and the Imami credo includes, in addition to the Sunni formula "There is no deity but God, and Muhammad is His messenger," the declaration "'*Alī walī Allāh*" ('Ali is the beloved of God). The universe cannot exist without an imam. He is the axis of creation and the gate to God; recognition of the imam is a prerequisite for salvation. At a given moment, there can only be one active imam, though his successor may be at his side as a silent (*ṣāmit*) imam. 'Ali's appointment as the Prophet's successor was announced on various occasions, most significantly at Ghadir Khumm, during Muhammad's return to Medina from his last pilgrimage. 'Ali's rights were usurped by the first three caliphs, who are therefore regarded as sinners; so too are those among the Prophet's companions who supported these caliphs. The imamate passed from 'Ali via his son Hasan to Hasan's younger brother Husayn and is handed down among descendants of the latter. The identity of the imams is divinely determined and is confirmed by both explicit designation (*naṣṣ*) and the testament (*waṣiyya*) of the previous imam (or, in 'Ali's case, of the Prophet). The imams' position of leadership is also based on their unique characteristics, notably their possession of special knowledge (*'ilm*). This knowledge derives from four major sources: oral transmission from one imam to the next, transmission by heredity, transmission by inspiration, and sacred books that are unknown to ordinary mortals. The sources offer differing descriptions of the nature and extent of the imam's knowledge: according to some accounts, the imam has perfect mastery of the Qur'an and hadith. Elsewhere, he is also said to be endowed with supernatural knowledge (such as knowledge of the future and of all languages) and an understanding of the esoteric meaning of the Prophet's teaching. There is general agreement that the imam is divinely protected against error (*ma'ṣūm*) and is thus an infallible guide to Islamic law and doctrine.

The belief that Muhammad was the seal (i.e., the last) of the prophets is common to Imamis and Sunnis; but in contrast to the latter, the Imamis in their law give the imam a status identical to that of the Prophet. In other words, while both Sunnis and Imamis regard the Prophet's utterances and actions as the second source of Islamic law (after the Qur'an), the Imamis add to this source the utterances and actions of the imams. In fact, the number of sayings in Imami literature attributed to the various imams, and especially to Ja'far, exceeds by far the number of sayings attributed to the Prophet.

In line with Ja'far's policy of quietism, he advocated the principle of *taqiyya* (concealment of one's beliefs in times of danger), making it an article of Imami faith. This principle helped to preserve the Imami community in a hostile environment. Ja'far kept in check the messianic aspirations of some of his adherents and reportedly dissociated from the religious beliefs of the extremist Shi'is (*ghulāt*), which included veneration of the imams to the point of deification. He is credited with a decisive role in transforming the figure of the imam from an activist political leader to an apolitical spiritual authority.

See also Abbasids (750–1258); Abu Hanifa (699–767); 'Ali b. Abi Talib (ca. 599–661); dissimulation; hadith; imamate; Isma'ilis; quietism and activism; Shi'ism

Further Reading

Mohammad Ali Amir-Moezzi, *The Divine Guide in Early Shi'ism*, 1994; Patricia Crone, *Medieval Islamic Political Thought*, 2004; Farhad Daftary, *The Ismā'īlīs: Their History and Doctrines*, 2nd ed., 2007; Heinz Halm, *Shi'a Islam: From Religion to Revolution*, 1997; Etan Kohlberg, *Belief and Law in Imāmī Shī'ism*, 1991; Hossein Modarressi, *Crisis and Consolidation in the Formative Period of Shi'ite Islam*, 1993; Moojan Momen, *An Introduction to Shi'i Islam*, 1985; Muhammad Qasim Zaman, *Religion and Politics under the Early 'Abbāsids*, 1997.

ETAN KOHLBERG

jāhiliyya

The word *jāhiliyya* is commonly translated as "age of ignorance" and applied to the century or so in west-central Arabian history prior to the mission of the Prophet Muhammad. The primary meaning of the root *j-h-l* (from which *jāhiliyya* is derived) at that time, however, was not usually mere ignorance but the tendency to go to extremes of behavior, whether in violence, revenge, boasting, drinking, or even generosity, and was sometimes considered a virtue. In the Qur'an, the root *j-h-l* may mean either excessive behavior or simple ignorance, and it is never a virtue. The word *jāhiliyya* appears four times in the Qur'an and involves opposition to God arising apparently from moral excess. In Qur'an 48:26, we read of the "fierce arrogance of *jāhiliyya*" in contrast to the "self-restraint (*taqwā*)" imposed on the Muslims and in 3:154 of people "wrongly suspicious of God with a *jāhiliyya* suspicion," while 33:33 admonishes the wives of the Prophet not to "make a display of yourselves in the manner of the first *jāhiliyya*." In 5:50, we read, "Do they seek a *jāhiliyya* judgment but who can give better judgment than God?" Here the reference appears to be a refusal to follow God's commands.

These passages illustrate some of the main contrasts between the values of *jāhiliyya* and those of the Qur'an. Also, the *jāhilī* Arabs recognized Allah as a remote creator but usually turned to other deities closer at hand, something the Qur'an calls *shirk*, association of other beings with God, and treats as the worst of sins, since only God is to be obeyed and worshipped. The pagan Arabs were marked by a spirit of independence and self-sufficiency in relation both to gods and other humans, rejecting the idea of an afterlife and seeing themselves as subject only to a rather impersonal fate, while the Qur'an inculcates an attitude of submission to God and dependence on Him and promises a heavenly reward. The Qur'an calls for moderation and removes the excessive element from *jāhilī* values such as nobility, loyalty, courage, fortitude, revenge, and generosity, and it moderates discriminations relating to class and gender.

While the word *jāhiliyya* in the Qur'an refers primarily to a moral condition, it has come to refer to an epoch in history, probably because pagan Arab society soon ceased to exist although some of its traits persisted. In the hadith collection of Bukhari (d. 870), *jāhiliyya* is almost always a past epoch, as, for example, "The best people in the *jāhiliyya* are the best in Islam, if they have understanding." *Jāhiliyya* has sometimes been extended to include the time before earlier prophets or the period between the lives of Jesus and Muhammad.

In spite of this, Muslims have always been aware that *jāhiliyya* characteristics can be found among them, even after the coming of Islam. Muhammad in a hadith says to one his followers, "Within you is *jāhiliyya*." Even more forcefully in a Shi'i hadith, he says, "Whosoever of my community dies and does not have an imam from among my successors, has died the death of the *jāhiliyya*." Indeed, the early centuries of Islamic cultural history can be interpreted in terms of a struggle between the older *jāhiliyya* orientation, which did not disappear immediately, and the newer Islamic orientation.

In later times, Ibn Taymiyya (1263–1328) viewed, in effect, the pre-Islamic customs continuing among Muslims of his time as a kind of *jāhiliyya*. Ibn 'Abd al-Wahhab (1703–92) and his followers perceived many of their fellow Muslims as living in *jāhiliyya*.

In modern times, Muhammad 'Abduh (1849–1905) and Rashid Rida (1865–1935) have compared aspects of their societies with aspects of *jāhilī* society. Commenting on Qur'an 5:50, they state that some nominal Muslims of their time are "more corrupt in their religion and morals than those concerning whom these verses were revealed." A. Yusuf 'Ali (d. 1953), whose English translation of the Qur'an is one of the best known, says in his commentary on the same verse in his translation of the Qur'an, "The Days of Ignorance were the days of tribalism, feuds, and selfish accentuation of differences in man. Those days are not really yet over. It is the mission of Islam to take us away from that false mental attitude."

In a more forceful vein, Mawdudi (1903–79) in India and then Pakistan and Abul Hasan Nadwi (1914–99) in India have argued that *jāhiliyya* is found in the West and has infected Muslim societies, though without making them completely *jāhilī*. Mawdudi defined *jāhiliyya* as any conduct that goes against Islamic thinking, culture, or morality and claimed that Muslim society has long been a mixture of *jāhiliyya* and Islam.

Most radical has been the Egyptian Sayyid Qutb (1906–66) in some of his later writings. For him, a *jāhilī* society is any society that does not follow God's guidance in all areas of its life. Such societies worship human beings instead of God and are inevitably unjust, inhumane, and uncivilized. *Jāhiliyya* is not just a moral stance but a dynamic and organic power always fighting against Islam, as strong in modern times as in Muhammad's time, if not stronger. There is no room for compromise, and society cannot be partly *jāhilī* and partly Muslim. He considered all societies in the world at his time *jāhilī*, including all so-called Muslim societies. Given the violent nature of *jāhiliyya* and its all-encompassing hold on the world, it can only be replaced by revolutionary violence. These ideas contributed to his execution by the Egyptian government in 1966 and have inspired militants since his death, although for them the concept of *takfīr* (declaring someone an unbeliever and therefore liable to be killed) appears to have been more important than that of *jāhiliyya*.

In any case, Qutb and others have clearly updated the concept of *jāhiliyya* so that it now refers in the first instance less to the excessive behavior of the old pagan Arabs than to the materialism and secularism of modern societies.

See also ʿAbduh, Muhammad (1849–1905); fundamentalism; Ibn ʿAbd al-Wahhab, Muhammad (1703–92); Ibn Taymiyya (1263–1328); Qur'an; revolutions; Salafis; Sayyid Qutb (1906–66)

Further Reading

Ignaz Goldziher, *Muslim Studies*, vol. 1. Halle 1889–90, trans. C. R. Barber and S. M. Stern, 1967; Toshihiko Izutsu, *Ethico-Religious Concepts in the Quran*, 1966; Reynold A. Nicholson, *A Literary History of the Arabs*, 1907 (repr. 1969); Sayyid Qutb, *Milestones* (*Maʿalim fi al-Tariq*), translated by S. Badrul Hasan, 1978; Idem, *Milestones*, translated by M. M. Siddiqui, 1990; William E. Shepard, "Sayyid Qutb's Doctrine of *Jahiliyya*," *International Journal of Middle East Studies* 35, no. 4 (2003).

WILLIAM E. SHEPARD

Jalal Al-i Ahmad (1923–69)

Jalal Al-i Ahmad is an intellectual and novelist famed for his pioneering role in the formulation of ideas that culminated in the Islamic Revolution in Iran. Born in Tehran into a clerical family and originally destined for a clerical career, he studied Persian literature but abandoned his studies to work for the Tudeh (communist) Party. After three or four years, he left the Tudeh Party because of its dependence on the Soviet Union and took to writing novels and short stories, translating French literature and philosophy into Persian, and creating ethnographic descriptions of the remote, rural regions of Iran. In the last years of his life, he developed a nativist ideology, which was influenced by the German philosopher Martin Heidegger, German romanticism, French existentialism, engagé literature (socially responsible or engaged writing), and anticolonialist writers such as Frantz Fanon. A reaction to government policies, which had weakened the clergy and traditional institutions, his nativism went hand in hand with a return to Islamic ideals, which were not so much religious as political and social.

Al-i Ahmad's most important book is *Gharbzadagi* (*Weststruckness*), a highly influential work in which he picks up an expression originally coined as a philosophical term by Ahmad Fardid, a follower of Heidegger, as a name for the destructive influence of the West, which has reduced the East to servitude and disorder by means of machines. Combative and rhetorical in tone, *Gharbzadagi* traces the roots of the West's attack and alleged conspiracies to the period of the Crusades and even earlier, claiming that the Christian West conspired with the Turks of Transoxiana and again with the Mongols to bring about their attack on the Islamic world. *Gharbzadagi* interprets the travels of Marco Polo and the visits of European travelers to the Safavid court in Isfahan in the same manner. He saw the West as having repeatedly broken up "the Islamic collectivity," most recently by the partition of the Ottoman state: Muslim/Eastern man would remain "West-struck" as long as he was a consumer of Western products and an imitator of Western culture and politics. According to Al-i Ahmad, the Muslims must try to build machines for themselves, adapting them to their indigenous, native circumstances, without becoming like the machine-dependent Westerners. Instead, they should pay attention to India, Japan, or Israel, which he briefly visited and saw as a good example of how tradition and religion could be used to build a new society. He changed his view in response to clerical criticism and the 1967 Six Day War.

Al-i Ahmad developed the same idea in *On the Services and Treasons of the Intellectuals*, in which he attacked Iranian and other Muslim intellectuals for their Western orientation and prepared the ground for the legitimization of Islamic discourse by charging them with estrangement from their own society. In *Lost in the Crowd*, an account of his pilgrimage, he also affirmed his connection with traditional Islamic religion.

Despite his emphasis on Islam, Al-i Ahmad's language and expressions have an intellectual and nonreligious character, and thus one cannot compare him with the modern Muslim reformists and renewers in the Islamic world. He was more critical of the West and Westernization but was himself influenced by the West and Western thinkers. His concern is with inauthenticity, identity, and autonomy; this was why he turned to tradition, the better part of which naturally had a religious character. In practice, he became a link between the secular and the religious intellectuals.

The expression *gharbzādagī* quickly caught on among opponents of the Iranian regime, and copies of the book, which had been outlawed, passed from hand to hand. Ayatollah Ruhollah Khomeini, whom Al-i Ahmad visited in Qum, had a copy of the book and used the expression *gharbzādagī* in the revolutionary and postrevolutionary phase to condemn the situation in Iran in the period of the shah. Al-i Ahmad also visited ʿAli Shariʿati in Mashhad, and Shariʿati

mixed his ideas with Shi'i history and Islamic concepts after his death, turning them into a revolutionary ideology. Al-i Ahmad's premature death, which some of his friends wrongly pinned on the state by way of antigovernment propaganda, transformed him into the intellectual hero of Iran. After the victory of the Islamic Revolution, his popularity among secular intellectuals waned in proportion to the esteem he gained among the clerical leaders.

See also Iran; Shari'ati, 'Ali (1933–77)

Further Reading

M. Boroujerdi, *Iranian Intellectuals and the West*, 1996; H. Dabashi, *Theology of Discontent: The Ideological Foundation of the Islamic Revolution in Iran*, 2006; A. Gheissari, *Iranian Intellectuals in the Twentieth Century*, 1998; M. C. Hillman, trans., *Iranian Society: An Anthology of Writings by Jalal Al-e Ahmad*, 1982; Jalal Al-e Ahmad, *Gharbzadegi: Weststruckness*, translated by J. Green and A. Alizadeh, 1982; Idem, *Lost in the Crowd*, translated by J. Green et al., 1985; Idem, "The Mobilization of Iran," *Literature, East and West* 20 (1976); Idem, *Occidentosis*, translated by R. Campbell, 1984; A. Mirsepassi, *Intellectual Discourse and the Politics of Modernization: Negotiating Modernity in Iran, 2000*.

MASOUD JAFARI JAZI

Jama'at-i Islami

Jama'at-i Islami is a political party formed by Mawdudi in India in 1941. Mawdudi had outlined the need for "a pious party" (*ṣāliḥ jamā'at*) in the context of the struggle for independence from British colonial rule in India. He made his move because he believed none of the existing parties in the prevailing political landscape were truly Islamic. For him, pure Islam entailed establishing a state based on the shari'a. The constitution of the Jama'at-i Islami (Islamic Party) described its objective as the establishment of *ḥukūmat-i ilāhiyya* (divine government). In the 1950s, the terminology was changed to *iqāmat-i dīn* (the establishment of religion). Mawdudi ruled that a person could become a member (*rukn*) of the Jama'at only if he understood the "full meaning" of *tawḥīd*, the doctrine that there is only one God. Muslims would not be admitted into the party simply because they were born as Muslim. Mawdudi believed that the Jama'at was the only party to have grasped the full meaning of the Muslim profession of faith ("There is no god but God and Muhammad is His messenger"). He argued that a "proper Muslim" (*aṣlī musalmān*) had no option but to join the Jama'at or stand condemned as the Jews who had rejected Islam at the time of the Prophet Muhammad. In Mawdudi's view, there was no third way. Indeed, he argued that it would be akin to apostasy for someone to leave the Jama'at. The constitution of the Jama'at made it obligatory for its members to boycott nearly every key institution of the secular state: the legislative assembly, the judiciary assembly, the army, the banking industry, and so on. To participate in the affairs of such a state was forbidden (*ḥarām*), because its foundation was human rather than divine sovereignty. Mawdudi also urged his party members to sever social ties with "transgressors" (*fāsiqīn*), including those associated with Muslim institutions such as the Aligarh Muslim University. Yet the Jama'at sometimes invited non-Muslims to its open sessions. The Hindu Indian leader Mohandas Gandhi, for instance, is known to have participated in its regional meeting in Patna, the capital of the state of Bihar, in April 1947.

Mawdudi and the Jama'at were ambivalent about the formation of an independent Muslim state, making it their goal to establish Islam in a united India after the departure of the British. After the partition of India and the formation of Pakistan in 1947, however, Mawdudi shifted his headquarters to Pakistan and embarked on a program to shape the newly founded state into an Islamic state. The branches of the Jama'at in India and later in Bangladesh have developed independently of each other over the years.

According to Mawdudi, it was not simply its goal that set the Jama'at apart from other Muslim parties. He claimed that its structure and workings were "exactly like those of the party Muhammad had established in the beginning." He described processions, flags, sloganeering, uniforms, resolutions, addresses, emotional writings, and so on—mobilizing tools central to most parties—as poison. Notwithstanding his self-image and claims, however, his party was modeled on a Leninist approach, with the Jama'at conceived as a vanguard of pious Muslims leading to the inauguration of an Islamic revolution. Mawdudi was perhaps the first thinker in South Asia to open the membership of his party to women on the basis of the Qur'an and hadith. The Jama'at's constitution even urged women to "disobey the commands of their husbands and guardians if such commands were sins against Allah." But granting membership to women did not mean that women enjoyed the same rights as men. He held that it would be catastrophic if a woman became a ruler; initially, he did not allow women to vote in the elections.

The Jama'at eventually revised many of its positions. Mawdudi even came to support the candidacy of a woman, Fatimah Jinnah, in the Pakistani presidential elections in the mid-1960s. In Pakistan, Jama'at women now not only vote but also occasionally contest elections. In India, the Jama'at's consultative assembly, the *shūrā*, discussed in 1999 the problem of the absence of women in Jama'at leadership (in 2000, out of 4,776 members, only 303 were women). It proposed that the Jama'at president be empowered to nominate women to assume key roles. As of 2011, there still was no woman in the *shūrā*, but the proposal itself was significant. Similarly, the Jama'at has considerably toned down its general criteria for membership. Even so, the number of core members (*arkān*) in the Jama'at has not reached six digits in Bangladesh, India, or Pakistan, nor has the party won elections that would enable it to form its own government. In Bangladesh and Pakistan, the Jama'at has contested elections but is still far from a mainstream political force. In Bangladesh's parliamentary elections of 1991, 1996, and 2001,

the Jama'at won 18, 3, and 17 seats, respectively. In Pakistan's national elections of 1988, 1990, 1993, the Jama'at won 7, 8, and 3 seats, respectively (it boycotted the elections of 1997 and 2008). Electorally, student wings of the Jama'at on college campuses have performed better than the parent party. In Pakistan and Bangladesh, the Jama'at's student wings exercise considerable influence and are known to have resorted to force and violence to meet their objectives. In contrast, the Jama'at enjoys a rather less tarnished image. Compared to mainstream parties, the Jama'at members and leaders are often seen, even by their opponents, as less corrupt and more dedicated to their cause.

The 1990 national elections in Pakistan were remarkable in many ways. Seeking to transform itself into a popular party, the Jama'at-i Islami under the leadership of Qazi Hussain Ahmad tried for the first time to use the repertoire of mass mobilization: posters, billboards, sloganeering, mass rallies, processions, music videos, and in some accounts, even dances to the tunes of popular numbers. It also floated a sister organization, Pasban (protector), the membership of which was open to a broad range of Muslims, including those who did not strictly adhere to the provisions of the shari'a. Yet as in the past, the Jama'at won only a few seats. The 1990 elections demonstrated nonetheless that the Jama'at was no longer exclusively the party of the pious Muslims or averse to using the modern repertoire of politics—things it had previously condemned as pagan ignorance (*jāhiliyya*).

See also fundamentalism; India; Mawdudi, Abul al-A'la (1903–79); Pakistan

Further Reading

Irfan Ahmad, "Cracks in the 'Mightiest Fortress': Jamaat-e-Islami's Changing Discourse on Women," *Modern Asian Studies* 42, nos. 2 and 3 (2008): 549–75; Idem, *Islamism and Democracy in India: The Transformation of the Jamaat-e-Islami in India*, 2009; Syed Vali Reza Nasr, *The Vanguard of Islamic Revolution: The Jamaat-e-Islami of Pakistan*, 1994; Elora Shehabuddin, "Jamaat-i-Islami in Bangladesh: Women, Democracy and the Transformation of Islamist Politics," *Modern Asian Studies* 42, nos. 2 and 3 (2008): 577–603.

IRFAN AHMAD

Jerusalem

The city of Jerusalem (in Arabic *al-Quds*, or "the Holy") is often ranked third, after Mecca and Medina, among the holiest sites in Islam. Early Islamic sources call Jerusalem the "navel of the Earth" (*surrat al-arḍ*), a reference to its cosmological centrality, and the final "place of congregation and resurrection" (*arḍ al-maḥshar wa-l-manshar*) on Judgment Day. The Rock of Jerusalem at the summit of Mount Moriah is portrayed as a portal to paradise. One of the earliest Arabic names for Jerusalem, *Bayt al-Maqdis*, or "House of Holiness," is often interpreted as a reference to the temple built by Solomon at the site of the Rock of Jerusalem, associating Muslim reverence for Jerusalem with that of Jews and Christians. Jerusalem is known to Muslims as the first of the two *qibla*s, or prayer directions, referring to the tradition that Muhammad directed his followers in Medina to pray toward Jerusalem before changing the *qibla* to Mecca. It is also celebrated as the destination of the Prophet's "night journey," referring to the tradition that God transported Muhammad in his sleep from Mecca to Jerusalem and then to heaven to meet with earlier prophets, including Abraham, Moses, and Jesus.

Jerusalem was brought under Muslim control ca. 638. The Umayyad caliphs developed Jerusalem as a center of Muslim worship, most notably with the construction of the Dome of the Rock in 691 during the reign of 'Abd al-Malik b. Marwan. The reasons for the erection of this unprecedented example of Islamic monumental architecture have been debated extensively. A minority has argued that it was a bid to shift the pilgrimage (hajj) from Mecca to Jerusalem in response to 'Abdallah b. al-Zubayr's Hijaz-based rebellion against Umayyad rule. While Umayyad architectural patronage in Jerusalem may have had political motivations, it seems unlikely that Jerusalem was ever intended to supersede Mecca as a destination for pilgrimage. Others have seen the Dome of the Rock as a symbolic assertion of the righteousness of Islam in a city still dominated by Christian places of worship. Still others have interpreted 'Abd al-Malik's construction project as a pious attempt to restore a house of worship to the site of Solomon's temple.

Even though Jerusalem never acted as a seat of government under Muslim rule, the maintenance of its religious sites by political leaders was generally expected. Islamic sources from the 11th century through the Ottoman period include "pilgrimage guides" to the city and suggest that the practice of combining a visit to Jerusalem with the hajj to Mecca was widespread. When Jerusalem was lost to the Crusaders in 1099, demands for the restoration of Muslim rule in the city and the access to holy places it ensured were directed to the Abbasid caliph in Baghdad. The prestige gained by Muslim military commander Salah al-Din (Saladin) after his reconquest of Jerusalem in 1187 is reflected in the reams of panegyric composed in his honor and the legitimacy conferred upon the Ayyubid dynasty he founded in Egypt and Syria. The Mamluk and later Ottoman rulers of Jerusalem continued the practice of investing in the city's infrastructure and patronizing its religious architecture.

Jerusalem remained under Ottoman rule until the end of World War I, when it was made the capital of the British Mandate for Palestine. In the aftermath of the 1948 Arab-Israeli War, Jerusalem was divided in half; West Jerusalem was claimed as the capital of the new state of Israel, and East Jerusalem, along with the rest of the West Bank, was controlled by the Jordanian monarch. With its military occupation of the West Bank in the Six Day War of 1967, Israel annexed East Jerusalem. Since then, the question of control over and access to the area known to Muslims as "the Noble Sanctuary" (*al-ḥaram al-sharīf*)—which contains the Dome of the Rock, the

Aqsa Mosque, and a number of other Islamic holy sites but is also revered by Jews as the site of Solomon's temple—has been highly charged. Although Palestinians seek to make East Jerusalem the capital of an independent Palestinian state, it remains under Israeli sovereignty.

See also Crusades; Muhammad (570–632); pilgrimage; Umayyads (661–750)

Further Reading

Kamil J. Asali, ed., *Jerusalem in History,* 1989; Sylvia Auld and Robert Hillenbrand, eds., *Ottoman Jerusalem: The Living City, 1517–1917,* 2000; Michael Burgoyne and D. S. Richards, *Mamluk Jerusalem,* 1987; Amikam Elad, *Medieval Jerusalem and Islamic Worship,* 1995; Oleg Grabar, *The Dome of the Rock,* 2006; F. E. Peters, *Jerusalem,* 1985.

ZAYDE ANTRIM

jihad

Literally meaning "struggle," jihad may be associated with almost any activity by which Muslims attempt to bring personal and social life into a pattern of conformity with the guidance of God. Nevertheless, early in the development of Islam, jihad came to be associated particularly with fighting or making war "in the path of God." In thinking about jihad, then, we may learn a great deal through a focus on war.

Muslims have written about war in a variety of genres. A.K.S. Lambton once remarked that philosophical treatises, the Mirrors for Princes compiled by court officials such as Nizam al-Mulk (d. 1092) who were interested in communicating the lessons of statecraft, and the compendia of juridical opinions collected in the schools devoted to shari'a reasoning constitute three distinctive and important styles of Muslim political writing. One could speak similarly about war. For political thought, legitimation is the great issue: what form of order best coheres with the good, with practical wisdom, or with the guidance of God? And because experience indicates that establishing and maintaining political order often involves the use of military force, discussions of war ordinarily follow. A comparison of world civilizations shows that questions like "When is war justified?" "Who decides?" and "How is war to be conducted?" are typically tied to notions about the purpose of politics and the distribution of power: both are related to ideas about the nature and destiny of human beings, so religion comes into the mix as well.

In tying religion, politics, and war together, Muslims are hardly unique. They continue to speak and write in the distinctive ways previously mentioned. Indeed, Lambton's list of three types of writing is probably too short. For the fullest possible exposition of Muslim thought about war, one would need to consult the treatises (*adab*) of men of letters like Jahiz (d. 868 or 869) or the histories compiled by Tabari (d. 923) and others. Works of fiction would have their place in such a survey, as would poetic texts.

Nevertheless, one can speak of the relative importance of certain forms. The compendia of opinions or responses to questions by experts in the practice of shari'a reasoning constitute a source of inestimable importance for understanding the Islamic experience of war. This is true because the shari'a (i.e., the "path" or way of living most conducive to human happiness in this world and the next) suggests a focus on the questions of when, who, and how outlined earlier. In addition, the practice of shari'a reasoning, in the sense of a transgenerational argument about the guidance of God, goes to the heart of what it means to submit or to bring oneself and one's world into a pattern of behavior consistent with the purposes of the Creator. The attempt to relate the "sources of comprehension" (i.e., the Qur'an, the sunna of the Prophet, and the consensual precedents set by recognized experts) to contemporary situations (by means of reasoning, especially analogy) is perhaps the most characteristic attempt to think about war in an Islamic "voice." As such, changes in *aḥkām al-jihād* (the judgments pertaining to armed struggle) across the generations reflect the changing fortunes and political conditions of Muslims, thus opening the door to wider areas of Muslim experience.

Foundational Motifs

In speaking about shari'a discourse about war, it is useful to be aware of the following issues: (1) the story of Muhammad and his Companions, (2) theological ideas, and (3) accounts of the development of Islam across the centuries.

The Story of Muhammad

While the historical accuracy of traditional biographies of Muhammad may be in question, the outline of the story Muslims tell about the struggles of the Prophet and his Companions are not. Once the Prophet began his public ministry, the primary response in Mecca was resistance. The small community that gathered around Muhammad experienced discrimination and persecution. When this rose to the level of physical abuse, some of the Prophet's Companions urged retaliation. According to the story told by Muslims through the centuries, Muhammad refused, saying that he had been given an order only to preach.

This was not the final word, of course. Sometime during the negotiations by which Muhammad and his community moved to Medina, God sent the verses recorded in Qur'an 22:39–40: "Those who have been attacked are permitted to take up arms because they have been wronged. God has the power to help them; those who have been driven unjustly from their homes only for saying 'Our Lord is God.' If God did not repel some people by means of others, many monasteries, churches, synagogues, and mosques, where God's name is much invoked, would have been destroyed." The clear import of this text is that the Muslims now had different orders. In Medina, Muhammad added the roles of military commander and statesman to his preaching in the effort to achieve security for the believers.

As the story continues, we understand that the "permission" of Qur'an 22:39–40 evolves into the "destined" or "ordained" of Qur'an 2:216 ("Warfare is a thing written for you, though you do not like it") and the direct command of Qur'an 2:190–94 ("Fight those who are fighting you, but do not become aggressors"). In Qur'an 4:75, God challenges the believing community: "And why should you not fight in God's cause and for those oppressed . . . ?" In Qur'an 8:39, the order is to fight until God's cause succeeds, and in chapter 9, fighting against those who violate treaties or otherwise prove dishonorable is authorized "wherever you find them." The order of the verses is given in the story so that the intensity and expansiveness of the order to fight mirrors developments in the military and political struggle with unbelievers. When in the end the Muslims prevail, Muhammad proclaims that "Arabia is solidly for Islam." The narrative of struggle thus ends on a note of hope.

It also ends by reinforcing the message that runs throughout: from the Muslim point of view, the question is not whether the Muslims should go to war or not. Rather, the issue from beginning to end is obedience. When the Companions in Mecca urge retaliation as a means of justice against mistreatment, the response is negative, not because of any direct rebuttal or refutation of their appeal, but because of God's order. Similarly, when fighting is justified in connection with the migration to Medina, the decisive factor is the command of God. The emphasis on obedience suggests the ongoing importance of ascertaining God's directives. The development of the shari'a discourse on judgments pertaining to armed struggle provide a noteworthy attempt to address this issue.

The Natural Religion

This emphasis on obedience has its corollary in the notion that Muhammad's entire career constitutes a divine summons—a "calling" of humanity to the condition signified by *islam*, or "submission" to God. Whether by the "beautiful words" of preaching or the strong persuasion of military force, the point is to bring human behavior, both personal and social, into a pattern consistent with the guidance of God.

In this, the story of Muhammad and his Companions suggests a certain view of the nature and destiny of human beings. Qur'an 7:172–73 describes the primordial encounter between God and humanity: "When your Lord took out the offspring from the loins of the Children of Adam and made them bear witness about themselves, He said: 'Am I not your Lord?' And they replied, 'Yes, we bear witness.'" The text goes on to say that the establishment of this covenant means that, on the Day of the Resurrection, no human being will have an excuse. All are bound by the fact that human beings are creatures of God whose very purpose is to serve the divine will. In accepting this—that is, in submitting themselves to their Maker—human beings find happiness, purpose, and dignity. Those who reject the divine calling do harm to themselves. Their fights with one another mirror conflicts within themselves. They suffer in this life, and if they do not make things right, they will also suffer eternal punishment in the next.

The point here is that nothing in Muhammad's approach to unbelievers is an imposition on or violation of their rights. He is God's messenger, calling human beings to act in accordance with their true nature and thus their best interests. Like other messengers before him (most importantly, Moses and Jesus), Muhammad summons people to submit to, or obey, God. Even the strong persuasion of war should be seen in this light, with one important proviso. War may create a sphere of security for the practice of true religion. It may be used to enhance such security by bringing non-Muslims under the protection (*dhimma*) or "superintendence" of Muslims. But it should not be used to bring about faith in the sense of heartfelt acceptance of God's service. It should not because it cannot—in Islam, as in other faith traditions, unwilling faith is a contradiction in terms. The Prophet and his Companions are a blessing to humanity because they call everyone to live as God intended, according to the "natural" religion. And they give particular groups, with their individual members, as much of the blessing as possible. For those who believe, full participation in the community of Muslims leads to rewards in this world and the next. For those who cannot believe but are willing to accept Muslim governance, the protection of Muslims keeps them secure from the disobedience of others and limits their own errors.

Historical Development

The Prophet died in 632. According to tradition, he sent letters to the Byzantine, Sasanid, and Abyssinian rulers prior to his death and invited them to accept Islam. In this account, acceptance could mean profession of faith or the payment of tribute indicative of the kind of protection or superintendence already mentioned. Failing this, the Prophet's letter promised to put these rulers and their armies to the test of war.

Muslim accounts take this report to indicate Muhammad's plan to enlarge his ministry beyond the confines of the Arabian Peninsula. Whether or not such letters were sent, in the generations following the Prophet's death, Muslim armies conducted campaigns to establish Islam in most of the Middle East and North Africa. Eventually, Islam became the driving force behind a world civilization, with adherents in every part of the globe and with special influence in North Africa, Asia, and central and southern Europe.

Muslim tradition attributes many of that civilization's most characteristic patterns of political and military organization to the earliest period (632–61) and especially to the leadership of 'Umar b. al-Khattab (r. 634–44). Again, it matters little whether tradition matches historical fact on this point. Later generations would cite early practice as precedent for a form of governance dedicated to the notion that human beings should administer their affairs according to the guidance of God. In order to fulfill this ideal, Islam should be established as the religion of state. The ruler should be a Muslim and should consult with recognized specialists in the Qur'an and other approved sources in the formation of policy. There should be a clear distinction between those who profess Islam as a faith and those non-Muslims living under the protection of Islam. While both should enjoy basic rights, the former should

be viewed as citizens of the first rank, and the latter should pay additional taxes, observe limits on the public expression of religion, and in general behave or be regulated in ways suggestive of the priority of Islam.

We have already noted the theological motifs suggestive of the view that the imposition of such patterns of governance ought to be considered a blessing. Limits on Jewish or Christian religious expression, for example, were construed as a way of "reminding" or "recalling" members of these communities to the true or natural religion. According to this line of thinking, Moses had not founded a religion called "Judaism" any more than Jesus founded "Christianity." Both had proclaimed Islam. Where contradictions between the practice of Jews or Christians and that of Muslims became manifest, the judgment of Muslim tradition would be that the former had corrupted the preaching of the prophets. Muslim protection thus provided a kind of oversight or superintendence by which corruption could be contained.

It is in connection with these theological views that we may understand the insistence of Muslim tradition that the expansion brought about by Muslim armies was not precisely a matter of "conquest." Muslim thinking about war proceeded on the assumption that this expansion was a matter of "opening" or "liberating" territory in order to create opportunities for human beings to hear the call to practice Islam. A state led by a Jewish or Christian (or some other non-Muslim) establishment could be viewed as tyrannical by definition or, at the very least, not the best for human welfare. Given this assumption, experts in shari'a reasoning would develop their teaching on war in connection with a concern for the relations between the "territory of war" and the "territory of Islam."

Expansion of Islamic governance and of the Islamic profession of faith were not the same thing, although the establishment of a Muslim state did create incentives for conversion. Expansion into more established centers of trade and culture led to disputes and redistributions of power. Thus it was not long before Muslims located in Egypt complained of unjust treatment to the caliph 'Uthman b. 'Affan, who had succeeded 'Umar. 'Uthman's assassination in 656 led to the great intra-Muslim conflict known as the first *fitna*, or "test" of the community. When 'Ali b. Abi Talib, son-in-law of Muhammad and one of the earliest to profess Islam, pursued reconciliation with those accused of conspiracy against 'Uthman, the latter's relative Mu'awiya used his position as governor of Syria to mount a challenge to 'Ali's leadership. The resulting impasse led to further divisions—accounts speak not only of the partisans of 'Ali and Mu'awiya but also of a third party, the Kharijis, whose name indicates that they seceded or separated themselves from either side. 'Ali's death in 661 at the hands of members of this latter group did not resolve the issues of leadership. The dominance of Mu'awiya and his family—and thus the hegemony of Damascus in the territories now under Muslim rule—would not be set until the partisans of 'Ali, now under the leadership of his son Husayn, were defeated at Karbala in Iraq in 680 and opposition in the holy cities of Mecca and Medina quelled by forces under the command of 'Abd al-Malik in 692.

But matters did not remain settled for long. By the 740s, a disparate yet growing opposition to the Umayyads united under the banner of the Abbasids, whose victory moved the imperial capital once again, this time to Baghdad. The extent of religious difference in Islam can be shown by any number of developments in the period of Abbasid rule, but none made a greater impact on Muslim memory than the *miḥna*, or the test of scholars with respect to the nature of the Qur'an. Ma'mun (r. 813–33) and his successor determined that all recognized experts in religious matters should publicly adhere to the judgment that the Qur'an is God's "created" speech. The political import of the test was considerable. Resistance to Abbasid authority on this matter, and the subsequent change of policy so that the contrary view became the official norm, exemplifies the intense competition between adherents of distinctive notions of Muslim practice. Abbasid authorities coveted the legitimacy associated with Islam. But this would be a long time coming; the Abbasids never really obtained control over significant sectors of the population, particularly portions of Egypt and Syro-Palestine. The resulting divisions, in which a consensus associated with "the people of the sunna and of the community" held sway in the Abbasid regions, while Shi'ism, particularly in its Fatimid/Isma'ili forms did so elsewhere, would be reflected in Muslim accounts of the progress of the faith for centuries to come.

Thus one might speak of a Sunni version of the expansion of Islam in which the story recounted thus far constitutes the gradual progress of a community elected by God to bring the world into a condition of submission to God's will. The *fitna* involving Mu'awiya and 'Ali, the Abbasid revolt, the *miḥna*, and other instances of conflict constitute a series of tests by which God refined the community. The story of Islamic expansion is a story of God's providential care, in which the believers may for a time become unsettled, but the saying of the Prophet eventually proves true: "My community shall never agree on an error."

By contrast, one may speak of a minority point of view in which claims of progress are offset by Muslim disobedience. Mu'awiya's challenge to 'Ali was wrong, and the subsequent defeat of Husayn at Karbala was an act of betrayal. In the generations following, Abbasid authorities ignored the claims of those designated by 'Ali's successors to lead the community of Muslims. In doing so, they preferred might to right, and their marginalizing or even conspiratorial policies constituted a kind of theft by which the Muslim community was deprived of the wisdom of persons possessing extraordinary piety and knowledge of the esoteric, as well as the exoteric, dimensions of religious practice. While the expansion of Islam throughout the world indicates that God has not rejected the believers, they will not enjoy the success for which they are destined until the family of 'Ali takes its rightful place at the head of the *umma*.

The Sunni-Shi'i divide has had enormous implications for the practice of Islam, not least in connection with the conduct of war. These distinctive modes of Muslim practice achieved political instantiation during the middle periods of Islamic development. The Ottoman and, in a somewhat different way, the Mughal empires

reflected the Sunni consensus, while the Safavids constituted a Shi'i state. The latter in particular allowed for a considerable elaboration of the Twelver or Imami form of Shi'ism, with its distinctive eschatological emphasis. According to the doctrine of this school, the 12th in the series of imams or designated successors to the Prophet went into hiding in 874. He did so by the will of God and in response to the disobedience of the majority of the Muslims; this served to protect the imam from the fate of his predecessors, almost all of whom became victims at the hands of hypocrites. Imam Mahdi (i.e., the rightly guided leader) remains somewhere "in the Earth" and will do so until God decides that the time is right for his appearance. In his absence, a number of appointed "deputies" serve as guardians of the Shi'is. By the time of the Safavids (1501–1722), this role largely belonged to the experts in shari'a reasoning, whose view of the state was similar to that of their Sunni counterparts: an Islamic establishment in the service of adherence to the shari'a, a Muslim ruler with settled modes for consultation with the religious class, and distinctions between Muslim and non-Muslim citizens reflective of the primacy of Islam. The authority of the Hidden Imam served to relativize the authority of the ruler, however, with important consequences for the justification and conduct of war.

In the modern period (beginning ca. 1750), the decline and ultimate demise of the great empires altered the political standing of Islam. That these changes occurred largely as a result of the advance of European powers, followed in the second half of the 20th century by the United States, only served to reinforce the judgment: the political and military precedents associated with the early expansion of Islam no longer held. Muslim thinking about war reflected the changed situation. Some authors wrote as apologists, arguing that Muslim approaches to war were consistent with the norms of civilization, as defined by the norms of Europe and the United States. Others wrote polemical tracts arguing that Muslim approaches constituted the measure of truly civilized warfare and that Europe and the United States should learn from Islam and thus add a spiritual and moral dimension to their obvious prowess in science and technology. Other interpreters of Islam used their position as diplomats to bring precedents from the history of Islam to bear on international law. In particular, the protocols added to the Geneva Conventions in the 1970s showed the influence of Muslim interlocutors, especially the provisions respecting the status of resistance movements. In this, the diplomatic contributions of Muslims mirrored the strongest trend in 20th-century Muslim thinking about war. Proponents of armed resistance attempted to stretch premodern precedents to fit circumstances in which believers found it possible to ask whether any established state actually constituted a Muslim, and therefore legitimate, form of political order.

Warfare and the Norms of Islam

The earliest compendia of scholarly opinions related to the rules of war seem to be those associated with the Iraqi jurists who styled themselves as working in the tradition of Abu Hanifa (d. 767). A collection of opinions related to jihad and *jizya* (i.e., to questions about military affairs and taxation in the regions that came under Muslim rule during the postprophetic expansion) is associated with the work of Abu Yusuf (d. 798). Even more significant is the collection associated with Muhammad b. al-Hasan al-Shaybani (d. 804), which later generations knew by the title *Kitab al-Siyar*, or the "book of movements." As the contents indicate, the movements in question are those between the territory in which Islam is established (*dār al-islām*) and the territory where it is not (*dār al-ḥarb*). As the Arabic suggests, the latter is, under certain conditions, the object of war intended to expand the dominion of Islam.

Given this interest, the text is preoccupied with the rules of engagement for Muslim forces: how they should approach the foe, what targets and tactics are appropriate, what is to be done with enemy persons, and how war prizes are to be distributed or managed. The opinions collected in the text are presented as responses to particular questions: Must the Muslim forces issue an invitation to the opposition so that its people have an opportunity to submit voluntarily and thus avoid war? What if the Muslim forces find themselves in a situation in which they must employ tactics that will result in the death of children? Are enemy captives to be killed, or must they be transported to the territory of Islam? May the Muslim fighters keep prizes (horses, money, etc.) they capture, or must they place these at the disposal of their commander?

In these and other cases, the text reports the opinions of Abu Hanifa, Abu Yusuf, or Shaybani—and sometimes of all three. Answers are crafted in consultation with verses of the Qur'an, reports of Muhammad's words and deeds, and the practice of the early Muslims, but these scholars also appeal to the notion of "that which is salutary," meaning (at least in part) "that which works, in order for the Muslim community to carry out its mission." Here, their interest is in the ability of the Muslim forces to attain victory. Thus, when faced with questions regarding tactics that will result in the death of children, the responses grant considerable latitude in the interests of the Muslims' ability to carry out their mission. Looking at the text as a whole, we may reconstruct the argument as follows:

1. The Prophet forbade the killing of children (along with a number of other categories of persons whose noninvolvement in fighting classifies them as noncombatants).
2. There are cases in which Muslim armies must employ tactics that would result in the death of children or else stop fighting. These include siege warfare, in which the use of hurling machines does not allow for precise targeting, and cases in which an enemy tries to deter the Muslims by tying children to the city walls, so that archers firing into the city are likely to hit at least some of the children.
3. In cases like those previously mentioned, the Muslim armies should do their best to avoid harming children and other noncombatants. But they cannot be prohibited from doing what is necessary to win. As Shaybani puts it, "If the Muslims stopped attacking the inhabitants of the territory of war

> for any of the reasons that you have stated, they would be unable to go to war at all, for there is no city in the territory of war in which there is no one at all of these you have mentioned."

The overriding imperative is the expansion of the dominion of Islam. To drive the point home, the text mentions questions that focus on the possibility that the residents of a besieged city or the children tied to the city walls may be Muslims and then asks whether Muslim fighters deploying tactics that may lead to the death of these innocents should be required to pay blood money or to otherwise make up for the damage. The answer is an unequivocal no.

If such answers suggest the importance of the Muslim mission, others point to a concern that armies conduct themselves in an orderly fashion. Thus the responses make clear that war is authorized by a public authority and follows on an invitation to voluntarily submit. Enemy captives who might pose a threat to Islam—for example, adult males whose physical capacity suggests their ability to fight—should be killed, unless their capture occurs in territory that is already under Muslim control. Women, children, the old, the lame, and other noncombatants must be transported to the territory of Islam, even if this is expensive or dangerous for the Muslim forces. Part of the rationale for this restriction is the concern that fighters abstain from taking "private" booty. All prizes, including potential wives and slaves, must be placed under the administration of the authorities, who will (upon return to Muslim territory) distribute them according to rules governing the shares of various fighters.

Such concerns for regulation suggest the placement of the text in the early Abbasid drive to develop a standing professional fighting force. Tabari's history relates stories indicative of the way Abu Yusuf, Shaybani, and others crafted some of their opinions in response to questions from the caliph, and biographies compiled by later generations of Hanafi scholars report that these early scholars served in official capacities. Coupled with the fact that Shaybani's text appends a number of judgments related to the conduct of fighting within Muslim territory (e.g., against rebels or against *ahl al-dhimma*, "the people of protection," meaning Jews, Christians, and others living under Muslim rule, when these communities violate their agreement with the Muslims), the evidence suggests a set of opinions that draw on and reflect the condition of an imperial state. The rules of engagement bear comparison with those of Imperial Rome and other states governing an extended territory. The caliph's authorization makes war a public act, and the rules of engagement crafted by the scholarly community serve as norms for commanders in the field.

The condition of the empire changed, however, and the formulation of norms for the conduct of war shows similar alterations. Mawardi (d. 1058) is famous for his discussion of the ways the caliph can designate "lesser" rulers as his deputies. The powers assumed by those deputized include the authority to initiate war. In this respect, as in the more general question of public authority, Mawardi's opinion is crafted to serve the cause of continuity, even as it responds to a situation in which the notion of power centralized in Baghdad is at best a useful fiction. Particularly with respect to norms governing war, the idea that the caliph designates a deputy to serve as sultan preserves the idea that war is a public act fought in accord with standing notions of the mission of the Muslim community and for the benefit of humanity.

Mawardi's contributions do not end with his judgment about authority, however. In response to questions familiar from Shaybani's *Kitab al-Siyar*, Mawardi provides judgments that are quite distinct. For example, regarding the questions dealing with tactics that may bring about the death of children and others, Mawardi argues that if the Muslim forces cannot attain victory without killing large numbers of innocents, then they should cease fighting and offer the enemy a chance to surrender. If this does not work, then the Muslim forces should withdraw and wait for a more favorable opportunity. There is no appeal to the overriding importance of victory here. Mawardi maintains the authority of those reports in which the Prophet condemns the killing of noncombatants and thus the notion that Muslim forces should occupy the moral high ground. Given that Mawardi is usually presented as a follower of Shafi'i (d. 820) rather than of Abu Hanifa, one might suppose this is a difference between schools. However, Shafi'i is usually more aggressive than Shaybani on questions related to the issuing of an invitation to voluntarily submit and avoid war. For example, Shafi'i holds that the knowledge of Islam is universal and thus that the Muslim forces need not repeat the summons issued by the Prophet. On questions about the disposition of prisoners taken in the territory of war, Shafi'i says that all may be killed at the discretion of the commander. Mawardi's distinctive opinion may thus simply reflect a sensibility that the means employed by fighters must allow Muslim fighters to maintain the moral superiority of the Muslim community.

In any case, it is clear that judgments pertaining to military force are subject to interpretation. In this, the development of norms related to war is consistent with other areas in which scholars issued opinions developed in conjunction with shari'a reasoning. Finding a "fit" between textual precedents and the particular conditions of one's age is more an art than a science. Muslim reasoning about war, while indicating the outlines of a set of criteria or touchstones for believers in different times and places, nevertheless provides evidence of various opinions.

A move forward to the time of Ibn Taymiyya (1263–1328) points to serious debate on a number of questions addressed by Shaybani and Mawardi. Ibn Taymiyya stands at the end of the period in which the imperial model represented by the Abbasids was fading. Not only did the notion of central authority suffer from the rising power of lesser (Muslim) rulers, as suggested by Mawardi's development of the notion of "designated" authority, but by the 14th century the Crusades and the Mongol invasions posed new military and political challenges. With respect to the Crusades, the Book of Jihad, attributed to Sulami of Damascus (d. 1106), adapted the device of fighting as an "individual duty" to encourage Muslim rulers outside

the province of Syro-Palestine to aid those bearing the brunt of the Christian advance. The leadership provided by the Kurdish military leader Saladin (d. 1193) seems in some ways to be a response to this, while in other ways he fits the model outlined by Mawardi. While Sulami's appeal to individual duty does not seem to be entirely original, it does mark a development by which later figures would discuss the norms of war in relation to conditions of emergency: if the opinions outlined by Shaybani and Mawardi related to conditions in which Muslims held power, what is their purchase in times when Muslim power is threatened or even overcome by foreign invaders?

Ibn Taymiyya issued his opinions in response to questions raised by the Mongol sacking of Baghdad (1258) and subsequent incursions into Syro-Palestine. Working primarily from Damascus, Ibn Taymiyya discussed issues posed when non-Muslim invaders came to dominate the territory of Islam but then converted. He argued that the Mongols continued to rule by a "mixed regime" of Muslim and Mongol law and should thus be regarded as illegitimate. In such a case, the notion of fighting as an individual duty authorized any Muslim authority able to mount resistance to do so. Ibn Taymiyya's primary appeal was to the Mamluk sultan in Cairo, although his own troubles with that ruler (Ibn Taymiyya served time in a Cairo prison at the order of the sultan) suggest that relationship was not entirely satisfactory. In any case, the collections of Ibn Taymiyya's opinions show a serious engagement with the set of precedents provided by the Qur'an, the sunna of the Prophet, and the rulings of outstanding scholars like Shaybani and Mawardi. Styling himself as a follower of Ahmad b. Hanbal (780–855), Ibn Taymiyya clearly does not feel bound to simply imitate earlier scholars. He does relate his opinions to theirs, however, and thus discusses a number of standard cases. Who may authorize fighting? Who should serve in the Muslim army? What targets are legitimate? What tactics may the Muslim armies employ? In these and other cases, Ibn Taymiyya's judgments reflect the quest for a fit between precedent and present circumstance characteristic of the practice of shari'a reasoning. Thus authority for war rests with an established leader so that fighting is a public act. However, the emergency presented by the advance of the Mongols means that "establishment" may not follow the most obvious lines. The Mamluk sultan's historic interest in Syro-Palestine suggests he should organize the resistance, but if he fails to do so, nothing in Ibn Taymiyya's texts suggests that another, more distant leader should not rise to the occasion. As to who should serve in the Muslim army, Ibn Taymiyya cites the standard norms about believers who are physically able and can provide their own weapons, horses, and other equipment. He notes that in ordinary circumstances, those who do not wish to fight may fulfill their duty by providing money or equipment for those who do. But the emergency condition is different. In this case, everyone able should fight—and this could include women and children, at the leader's discretion. Necessity makes the forbidden things permitted in the sense that every believer can and should support the leader's efforts at resisting invasion.

Necessity does not affect the question of means, however. Ibn Taymiyya follows established precedents regarding the restrictions on targets, with one exception: he says that women who support the enemy by means of propaganda may be viewed as combatants. That is, they need not actually take up arms, although the opinion does not specify the nature of "propaganda." Overall, however, Ibn Taymiyya suggests that the standard rules of engagement apply even in an emergency.

New Conditions and Alternative Views

Ibn Taymiyya's rulings draw on and point to striking changes in the political structure of the areas dominated by Islam. In the centuries that followed, these would include, first, the growth and expansion of the three great dynasties of the middle period of Muslim history and, second, the modern expansion of European power, with its legacy of colonialism.

With respect to the first, the Ottoman and Mughal empires represent the continuation of the standard majoritarian or Sunni discussions of the norms of war. Scholarly discourse sought to build on the opinions formulated by Shaybani, Mawardi, Ibn Taymiyya, and others like them.

The Safavid dynasty and its successor (the Qajar dynasty) represent something a bit different, however. As noted earlier, the Safavids ruled in conjunction with an establishment of Twelver Shi'ism. They sponsored a discussion of judgments pertaining to war that bears the imprint of the sect's characteristic doctrines. Particularly with respect to the authorization of war, the Shi'i view that God appoints one ruler for every generation, coupled with the Twelver notion that all of those so appointed were, from the death of the Prophet forward, prohibited from carrying out his mandate by the unbelief of the Muslim majority, meant that authority for jihad belonged only with the Imam of the Age. According to the compendium associated with Muhaqqiq al-Hilli (d. 1277), for example, mature men who are physically able and are not slaves are obligated to fight in the cause of expanding the hegemony of Islam. This obligation only holds, however, when the imam or his deputy is present. Since God responded to the unbelief of the majority by taking the Twelfth Imam into hiding, the conditions for jihad seem not to hold. Assuming that the reference to the imam's "deputy" indicates one of those who, according to Twelver tradition, served as intermediaries during the period of "lesser" occultation (roughly from 874–914), even this authorization may be in question.

The fighting authorized in the absence of the imam or his deputy is defensive in nature. That is, if an enemy attacks, the ruler is authorized to organize a resistance; indeed, in certain cases, any individual may defend himself or herself or even other victims from aggression. In the ordinary case, though, Hilli's text indicates that the ruler organizes forces in order to deter or preemptively attack a potential enemy.

With respect to other matters, Hilli follows standard precedents in that the Muslim fighters are required to avoid direct attacks on noncombatants. In the case of siege warfare or an enemy's use of children as shields, his opinion is closer to that of Mawardi than

that of Shaybani. In a judgment that runs contrary to one of Ibn Taymiyya's views, Hilli says that even women or children who provide support to the enemy should be regarded as noncombatants, except in cases of emergency.

The consensus represented by Hilli becomes important in considering the effects of European expansion on Muslim judgments about war. In the early 19th century, Russia's advance to great power included increasing influence in the affairs of Iran. Shi'i scholars issued opinions advising the Qajar ruler of his authority as defender of the Shi'i faith and distinguished between an imposed war (*al-difā'*, a war of defense) and the jihad for which authority belongs only to the imam or his deputy. The distinction would appear again following the Iranian Revolution and the establishment of the Islamic Republic of Iran. The argument of Ayatollah Khomeini (1902–89) that the Shi'i scholars as a whole, or one of them having the requisite learning and piety, fill the office of deputy is enshrined in the Iranian Constitution. The notion that the scholar or scholars filling this role may authorize active resistance to an established ruler provides important background to the 1979 revolution. With respect to war, Khomeini called on the notion of defense, as well as of resistance to rebels, when he spoke about the war with Iraq (1981–88). Ongoing debates in Iran regarding the state's role in world affairs, its sponsorship of groups like Hizbullah and Hamas, and its nuclear program all show the import of traditional judgments like those collected in Hilli's compendium.

On the Sunni side, the erosion of Ottoman and Mughal power set off debates that similarly reflect the attempt to articulate a fit between historic precedents and changing circumstances. When a well-known Sunni scholar ('Abd al-'Aziz, grandson of the famous Shah Waliullah of Delhi) declared that the advance of British power rendered India a part of the territory of war rather than of Islam, he may or may not have meant to authorize popular resistance. Some groups in India thought it so, however, and organized the series of uprisings that led to the Sepoy Mutiny in 1857. Britain's brutal suppression of this rebellion suggested to many Muslims that a different strategy would be necessary, and Sayyid Ahmad Khan (d. 1897) advanced his well-known argument that jihad (at least in the sense of armed struggle) is obligatory when the Muslims are strong and not when they are weak. Post-Sepoy India would yield some of the most interesting examples of apologetic and polemical writing regarding jihad, with Syed Ameer Ali's (d. 1928) best-selling *Spirit of Islam* presenting the military campaigns of Muhammad as consistent with the highest standard of "humanity," while Mawdudi's (1903–79) treatise on jihad argued that fighting to establish a political order in which Islam is established is a duty for Muslims and a boon to an otherwise disorganized and heedless world community. For Mawdudi, the jihad is not only a necessary aspect of Muslim practice; it is also a feature of justice, because polities that are not organized around the norms of Islam tend to fight wars as they conduct domestic affairs—that is, by way of oppression, indiscriminate killing, and genocide.

Analogues to the apologetics of Ameer Ali and the polemics of Mawdudi appeared in other regions of the historic territory of Islam. In Egypt, for example, Mahmud Shaltut's (d. 1963) treatise on the "fighting verses" of the Qur'an combined a novel reading of the text with an account of the early Muslim expansion that rendered it a campaign of humanitarian intervention. For Shaltut, the account of the "occasions" connected with the revelation of the verses on fighting outlined in traditional biographies of Muhammad does not provide an adequate guide. Instead of reading the verses in relation to an escalating set of tensions between Muslims and their Qurashi rivals, one should read the text as a whole and thereby understand that the Qur'an meant only to authorize wars of defense. Similarly, Shaltut's understanding of the facts of the early expansion, by which for example the Christians living in Palestine petitioned 'Umar b. al-Khattab to defend them against their Jewish neighbors, presents a paradigm of one nation coming to the aid of another. In a modern context, Shaltut's point was that Muslim norms are fully consistent with those of the emergent tradition of international law.

More akin to Mawdudi is the essay on jihad by Hasan al-Banna (1906–49), the founder of the Muslim Brotherhood movement. Here, jihad is a duty laid upon Muslims for the benefit of humankind: the goal of jihad is the establishment of a state governed by Islamic values. As such values are consistent with the true nature of humanity, the jihad is a beneficent act. Left to their own devices, human beings will prove tyrannical and foolish, as the Qur'an indicates. Governed by Islam, human beings can live with dignity in the context of a political order that makes peace and justice possible.

Apologetic and polemical writing on jihad continued to develop throughout the 20th century and into the 21st. In the work of Sayyid Qutb (1906–66), this type of writing took a new turn, as the Egyptian writer and activist fused the style and arguments of the authors mentioned with arguments pertaining to resistance. In *Milestones*, *Social Justice in Islam*, and especially in his commentary on the Qur'an, Qutb argued that Muslims criticized global trends associated with the dominance of Europe and the United States and asserted that Islam alone provides a way of ordering life that accords with true human nature. In this sense, Muslims are always in a condition of resistance, because the way of submission is always opposed to *jāhiliyya*, that "heedlessness" to which, the Qur'an teaches, humanity is prone.

For Qutb, the notion of resistance becomes a characteristic trait of the Muslim life. Jihad, in the broad sense of struggle to bring oneself and the world into conformity with the path of God, is the principal theme of Muslim ethics. According to Qutb this struggle should focus on building communities of character, small groups of Muslims whose association would encourage personal discipline. These would be the seed from which a Muslim social movement might grow, with the aim of transforming the world. The use of military force would likely be a part of this aim, just as it was in the time of Muhammad. For the most part, however, Qutb focused on the need for these communities of character; as he put it in several places, if tyranny is overthrown and there is no group ready to assume leadership so that a truly Islamic social

order might be put in place, the result will only be a new form of tyranny. Muslim devotees must thus undergo a time of purification and preparation, not unlike the Prophet and his Companions during the Meccan period.

Qutb is thus an important transitional figure for modern discussions of war, and many surveys point to his work as a foundation for later discussions of resistance, from the apologia of the assassins of Anwar Sadat (*The Neglected Duty*, 1981) to the *Hamas Charter* of Hamas (1988) and the World Islamic Front's *Declaration Concerning Armed Struggle against Jews and Crusaders* (1998). Such documents contain echoes of Qutb's ideas, but their authors also typically cite earlier precedents such as the Qur'an, the sunna of the Prophet, Islamic history, and standard contributors to the discussion of the judgments pertaining to jihad. In the end, texts like those mentioned attempt to develop a rationale for a certain kind of fighting, in conjunction with the establishment of political goals. As such, they make a series of claims and are the subject of much debate among Muslims engaged in shari'a reasoning.

Thus *The Neglected Duty* speaks of the duty to struggle for the purpose of establishing an Islamic state, meaning one in which public law is derived according to the sources and procedures characteristic of shari'a reasoning. Such "government by divine law" is distinguished from other forms, in which "human law" is the measure of political and personal behavior. In the current circumstance, the author writes, such a government does not exist in Egypt. He believes this judgment holds elsewhere in the territory of Islam, but his particular concern is with Egypt. In such a circumstance, Muslims are called to exert themselves to bring about change, and their efforts can include armed force. This is especially so if the ruler fails to heed numerous calls for change. Appealing to the time and judgments of Ibn Taymiyya, the idea is that Egypt, like the territory governed by the Mongols, is governed by a "mixed" legal regime. A truly devoted leader would institute a program of reform and move the state toward fidelity to Islam. But, according to the author, the Egyptian leader has not; he is thus an apostate and deserves punishment by death.

Herein lies the problem of resistance, and the author understands it clearly: who can carry out the punishment when the criminals are in power? Ultimately, says the text, the authority to punish belongs to God, who gives it to the Muslim community as a whole. The recognition of a ruler is a kind of "vesting" of this communal duty and right in a particular person or group. If these become corrupt, however, responsibility devolves to the community as a whole, or to those who understand the situation. Jihad thus becomes an "individual duty" incumbent on every Muslim able to fulfill it. As the author writes, in this case, jihad is like prayer and fasting: everyone must perform as he or she is able or else be complicit in injustice.

In this way, the text calls on Ibn Taymiyya and other historic figures. As described earlier, however, Ibn Taymiyya's appeal to individual duty was actually aimed at neighboring Muslim rulers. The author of *The Neglected Duty* thinks more of a mass appeal and of a kind of popular uprising. Not surprisingly, his argument has been controversial, so authorities like Shaykh al-Azhar suggest that the theory of resistance developed in the text is an invitation to anarchic violence. This fear stems not only from the possibility that the argument of *The Neglected Duty* comes close to suggesting that every Muslim serves as his or her own commander. It is also fostered by the author's claim that any Muslim who fails to support the uprising is prima facie complicit in injustice and may be killed with impunity. The text does admit that some supporters of a corrupt government may be innocent, or at least affected by factors that mitigate guilt (e.g., coercion or ignorance). In the event some of these supporters die in a military action, however, the author suggests that the "sorting" between innocent and guilty will be done by God. The calling of the faithful is to struggle for justice, and the killing of Sadat, in particular, is understood as an execution or an administering of just punishment.

The *Charter* of Hamas makes a similar appeal to emergency and argues that in a circumstance where an enemy has occupied territory belonging to the Muslims, jihad becomes an individual duty, akin to prayer and fasting. The focus in this case is Palestine, and the text asserts that Muslim claims to the land are not simply a matter of history or of property wrongly taken from individuals. Rather, it argues that Palestine (and with it, Jerusalem) was given to the Muslims as a trust. Defending this territory, or struggling to restore it to the territory of Islam, is thus a religious duty. Similarly, the enemy is defined in religious rather than ethnic or national terms: "the Jews" are an individual and collective target of resistance, and the struggle is part of a long-term, even eschatological, contest between faith and disobedience.

The *Charter* does not discuss the details of fighting, so one does not find arguments about combatants and noncombatants or about various tactics or weapons. Hamas has of course used techniques that suggest a lack of concern with traditional shari'a judgments regarding the distinction between combatants and noncombatants (e.g., the firing of rockets into Israeli villages), and "martyrdom operations" (also known as "suicide bombings") raise many questions for Muslims. Shaykh al-Azhar, for example, allows that martyrdom operations may be an appropriate tactic, but only if the direct target is military. By contrast, the popular scholar Yusuf al-Qaradawi seems to suggest that there are no civilians in Israel, since all men and women between the ages of 18 and 60 are at least eligible for military service.

The clearest example of a Muslim argument that justifies resistance and also connects it with something close to a strategy of total (i.e., indiscriminate) fighting is the World Islamic Front's *Declaration*. Published in a London-based Arabic language newspaper in February 1998, the *Declaration* quickly attracted attention as an attempt by the leaders of a number of resistance movements to advance an argument in the form of traditional shari'a reasoning. After the September 11, 2001, attacks on New York and Washington, D.C., the text became known as "Bin Laden's fatwa or normative opinion." Muslim critics of the document complained that neither Osama bin Laden nor any of the other signatories actually

had standing to issue legal opinions. Bin Laden's subsequent replies make clear that he believed such criticism reinforced one of the basic claims of the *Declaration*, which is that the contemporary Muslim community, while numerous, is dominated by leaders whose faith is superficial. As with *The Neglected Duty* and the *Charter* of Hamas, the *Declaration* interprets current circumstances in the language of emergency. By way of analogy, rulings offered by historic scholars indicate that such circumstances render fighting a duty incumbent upon "any Muslim able . . . in any country where it is possible." In this interpretation, one need not wait for authorization from an established ruler; the corruption and/or impotence of those holding power in the territory of Islam renders this point moot.

The *Declaration* also declares total war on a specified enemy. Fighting as an individual duty targets Americans and their allies, civilians and soldiers alike. This point has proven highly controversial among Muslims, and Bin Laden and other resistance leaders have attempted to respond. The duty to avoid direct harm to noncombatants is a well-established precedent, according to Bin Laden, but it is not absolute. To indicate the possibility of exceptions, he cited rulings that allow the Muslim forces to continue fighting an enemy that hangs children on the walls of a besieged city. The fighters know their tactics are likely to kill at least some of the children, but the children's blood is on the enemy's hands. Then, too, Bin Laden and others insisted that killing American and allied civilians is reciprocal justice or repayment in kind for the death of Muslim innocents. Finally, in a document published in November 2002, Bin Laden advanced the claim that the citizens of democratic states cannot claim innocence, since they have the ability to change governments and thus to alter objectionable policies. When Bin Laden released a video aimed at the American people just before the November 2004 presidential election, he reiterated this point, indicating that peace was at hand if the U.S. electorate would just choose the right candidate.

The issue of distinguishing civilian and military targets continues to trouble Muslims, however. Since 2005, this question has divided advocates of resistance: the indiscriminate killing of Muslim civilians by fighters associated with the late Abu Mus'ab al-Zarqawi, commander of al-Qaeda in Iraq, brought warnings from several advocates of resistance, including Bin Laden's associate Ayman al-Zawahiri. In 2009, Mulla 'Umar, leader of the most important Taliban group involved in fighting in Afghanistan, issued orders that fighters associated with him should avoid the direct killing of noncombatants. It seems that the weight of precedent and the weight of Muslim public opinion complement one another in this matter; at least with respect to fighting in areas inhabited by a majority Muslim population, one might expect fighters to alter the strategy articulated in the *Declaration*.

The debate over resistance is perhaps the strongest trend in contemporary Muslim argument about the rules of war. Resistance is also the topic of what is generally considered the most significant contribution of diplomats representing Muslim states in international forums.

The record of those agreements constituting the modern law of war shows that Muslim states, and particularly representatives of the Ottoman court, took part as early as the 1856 Paris Declaration Respecting Maritime Law. The various Hague Conventions also indicate Muslim participation, as does the Geneva Accord. More recently, Muslim diplomats played a part in the development of the 1993 Chemical Weapons Convention.

With respect to resistance, the most important contribution of Muslim states may be seen in the 1977 Geneva Protocol I. Together with a second protocol, this agreement responds to changes in the character of armed conflict since World War II. In particular, Geneva Protocol I expands the application of the law of war so that it includes conflicts in which "peoples are fighting against colonial domination and alien occupation and against racist regimes in the exercise of their right of self-determination." The text also eases the requirement imposed by earlier agreements that combatants "distinguish themselves from the civilian population." For example, the fourth Hague Convention specified that combatants should fulfill this requirement by wearing a "fixed distinctive emblem recognizable at a distance"; the Geneva Accord reiterates this directive. Geneva Protocol I recognizes that there are times when a combatant cannot do this, "owing to the nature of the hostilities." Combatants are still required to carry their arms openly. The relaxation of the requirement of emblems, together with the expansion of the scope of application of the laws of war, seems clearly designed to take account of the activities of guerrillas and other irregular or nonstate forces. From the perspective of Muslim states, support for these changes correlates with sympathy for Palestinian resistance to Israel. Such sympathy does not transfer to other conflicts involving Muslim resistance groups, however. Diplomats representing historically Muslim states during a term on the United Nations Security Council have consistently supported the sanctions and other counterterrorism measures adopted since 1999 by the council in its effort to deal with al-Qaeda and the Taliban.

Conclusion

The centrality of resistance in contemporary Muslim argument about war reflects the larger debate about political authority in which Muslims have engaged since the passing of the imperial states of the middle period (from ca. 1258 until the modern era). In particular, the abolition of the Ottoman caliphate or sultanate set off a great debate over the proper form of government in an Islamic state.

This lack of consensus certainly has an impact on the attempt to regulate war. Historically, Muslims in positions of leadership appealed to shari'a norms in order to harness war to appropriate ends and to ensure that the harms associated with war (death, destruction of property, etc.) might be proportionate to the goods at which it aimed. Without an agreement over the location of authority, regulation of ends and means alike comes into question. "Who decides?" is always a relevant question, not least with respect to war.

At the same time, one must note the persistence of a number of historic features of Muslim thought about war. Even in a situation characterized by disagreement, some of it deadly, respect for precedent seems very strong. When resistance groups are criticized for violations—for example, in controversies over martyrdom operations and al-Qaeda's doctrine of total war—the responses point to the enduring appeal of the notions enshrined in tradition: that the means of war should be proportionate to its ends and that fighters claiming to engage in a just war should not themselves engage in injustice.

In all this, Muslim thinking about war bears a strong resemblance to that developed by Christians, Jews, and other groups. This does not minimize the objectionable nature of certain judgments, such as al-Qaeda's doctrine of total war. But the question of war is present for every historic and contemporary group, and the attempt to regulate it, to see war as a tool that is sometimes appropriate for attaining or defending justice, is difficult. In the end, the question of war for Muslims is this: in what ways, or under what conditions, is war an appropriate means of jihad, in that it is consistent with the guidance of God? And a second question quickly follows: how do human beings comprehend this guidance?

See also dissent, opposition, resistance; fundamentalism; military; nonviolence; rebellion; violence

Further Reading

Khaled Abou El Fadl, *Rebellion and Violence in Islamic Law*, 2001; James Turner Johnson and John Kelsay, eds., *Cross, Crescent, and Sword*, 1990; John Kelsay, *Arguing the Just War in Islam*, 2007; John Kelsay and James Turner Johnson, eds., *Just War and Jihad*, 1991; Rudolph Peters, *Jihad in Classical and Modern Islam*, 1996.

JOHN KELSAY

Jinnah, Mohammad ʻAli (1876–1948)

Mohammad ʻAli Jinnah was the leader of the All-India Muslim League, which successfully demanded the creation of Pakistan following India's independence from British rule. After Pakistan gained its independence from India, he was the country's first governor-general until his death on September 11, 1948.

Jinnah was born in Karachi on December 25, 1876. His father was a wealthy Ismaʻili merchant. He was sent to London in 1892 to work with Graham's Shipping and Trading Company, which had extensive dealings with his father's firm. He abandoned this career for the legal profession and successfully qualified as a barrister at Lincoln's Inn, the oldest of the four Inns of Court in London where lawyers are called to the bar. Upon his return to Bombay, Jinnah quickly established himself as the leading Muslim advocate in the high court. He moved in elite Indian circles, and in 1896 he joined the Indian National Congress, becoming a prominent figure in its so-called moderate wing. The Muslim League was founded in 1906 at the annual session of the All-India Muhammadan Educational Conference, but it was not until 1913 that Jinnah joined the organization while maintaining his congress membership. His burgeoning wealth as a result of careful investment of his earnings was further augmented by his marriage to Rattanbai Petit, the daughter of the wealthy Parsi magnate Sir Dinshaw Petit. Jinnah was considered a future leader of the congress and was instrumental in bringing about the 1916 Lucknow Pact between congress and the Muslim League. This agreement marked the high watermark of cooperation between the two parties.

Four years later, Jinnah resigned from the congress because of his disillusionment with the violence and communal passions that followed Mohandas Gandhi's (1869–1948) introduction of religion into politics. It was only in 1928, however, that the division further widened between him and the congress when the Nehru Report, the first nationalist draft of a constitution for an independent India, rejected his famous "Fourteen Points" constitutional proposals. These had been drawn up to protect the interests of the Muslim minority community. At their heart lay devolution of power to the provinces and separate electorates. For Jinnah, it was essential to maintain the latter as a safeguard for Muslim interests.

Shortly after parting ways with the congress in 1928, Jinnah abandoned Indian politics. He had become estranged from his young wife. His personal unhappiness increased as a result of her illness and later death in 1929. He thereafter increasingly turned to his sister Fatima both as a confidant and to help bring up his daughter, Dina. Between 1930 and 1935, Jinnah forged a lucrative legal career in London. The new political situation following the 1935 Government of India Act encouraged him to return to the fray. The All-India Muslim League fared poorly, however, in the 1937 elections in the provinces where Muslims were in the majority. The league was rescued from oblivion both by Jinnah's attempts to reorganize it and by the way in which the seven congress provincial governments insensitively handled Muslim interests. Following this episode, the Muslim League publicly committed itself in 1940 to the demand for a Muslim homeland.

Jinnah's espousal of the two-nation theory as the basis for Pakistan effectively provided a rallying cry for the Indian Muslim community, which previously had been divided by the conflicting political interests and demands of politicians from the Muslim majority and minority provinces. The disadvantage of the elevation of a minority rights discourse into demands for political sovereignty was the deterioration of community relations in the future "Pakistan" areas. This formed the backdrop to the constitutional negotiations at the end of the raj.

Jinnah's political skills as a negotiator were crucial to his success. He was also able to bring unity and discipline to the fractious Muslim League movement, in part through his strong personality. He could also stand aloof, because of his personal wealth, from the landed magnates who formed a key element in the party.

World War II also assisted Jinnah's rise to prominence. The British saw the Muslim League as a useful counterbalance to the

noncooperating congress, and Jinnah was elevated to a position of equality with Jawaharlal Nehru (1889–1964) and Gandhi. The key turning point was the July 1945 Simla Conference, which was designed to establish an expanded Viceroy's Council in which only the viceroy and the commander-in-chief would be British. The creation of a politically representative executive council was seen as a major step toward eventual independence. Jinnah blocked its formation by successfully demanding that all Muslim representatives be members of the Muslim League. He maintained that the proposals were a stopgap and could in no way affect the Muslim League's demand for Pakistan.

Pakistan did not, however, become an inevitability until after the collapse of the Cabinet Mission proposal and the first major outbreak of communal violence on August 16–18, 1946, known as the Great Calcutta Killing. This followed Jinnah's call for direct action in response to the British formation of an interim government without the league. While Indian unity was impossible thereafter, the circumstances were created in which the Muslim majority provinces of Punjab and Bengal were divided. Mass migrations and massacres accompanied the Punjab's partition. This meant that Pakistan faced an unprecedented refugee crisis at birth.

Jinnah held the two offices of Pakistan governor-general and president of the Constituent Assembly. On August 11, the eve of independence, in a famous speech to the Constituent Assembly, he laid the basis for a liberal and tolerant conception of Pakistan. By then, however, he had become increasingly ill with tuberculosis. The burden of state construction became an impossible task, and in the final months of his life, he spent much time at his official retreat in Ziarat.

See also India; Muslim League; Pakistan

Further Reading

Akbar S. Ahmed, *Jinnah, Pakistan and Islamic Identity: The Search for Saladin*, 1997; Hector Bolitho, *Jinnah: Creator of Pakistan*, new ed., 2006; S. M. Burke and Salim Al-Din Quraishi, *Quaid-i-Azam Mohammad Ali Jinnah: His Personalities and Politics*, 2004; Sikander Hayat, *The Charismatic Leader: Quaid-i-Azam M. A. Jinnah and the Creation of Pakistan*, 2008; Ayesha Jalal, *The Sole Spokesman: Jinnah, the Muslim League and the Demand for Pakistan*, 1985; M. R. Kazimi, ed., *M. A. Jinnah: Views and Reviews*, 2006; Stanley Wolpert, *Jinnah of Pakistan*, 1998.

IAN TALBOT

jizya

The *jizya* was a poll tax that all non-Muslim, adult males living in territories controlled by Islamic governments were required to pay. It was the substantive proof of a people's or region's subjugation to Islamic rule. The term appears once in the Qur'an (9:29), meaning tax or tribute, and refers to the tribute owed by "the People of the Book" (*ahl al-kitāb*), specifically Jews and Christians. The *jizya* became one of the most public stipulations of a pact between the People of the Book and the Muslim ruler, under which they were accorded the protection of the state and the freedom to practice their religion in return for abiding by public Islamic law and adhering to a number of restrictions regulating their behavior. In recognition of their protection under this pact, they became termed *dhimmīs*. Followers of other religions, such as Zoroastrians and Hindus, were later incorporated into the category of *dhimmīs* and were required to pay the *jizya*.

The Persian and Byzantine empires and pre-Islamic Arab tribes had already established systems of taxation and tribute. As Islam spread, previous structures of taxation were replaced by the Islamic system, but Muslim leaders often adopted practices of the previous regimes in the application and collection of taxes. Examples of the application of the *jizya* are found in a number of the hadith.

Prior to the Abbasid epoch, the *jizya* was not strictly defined or applied, which frustrated the efforts of later scholars attempting to understand the early Islamic tax system. The *jizya* during the early centuries of Islam was used interchangeably with another term for tax, *kharāj*. Lack of clarity regarding the categories of people to which *jizya* was applied further convoluted matters. In some instances *jizya* was applied to individuals; in other cases *jizya* was applied to entire communities or provinces. Sometimes the *jizya* meant a land tax. Under the Abbasids, the *jizya* was delineated as a poll tax all *dhimmīs* were required to pay. Rules for the application of the *jizya* were devised. Free, adult males who were not afflicted by any physical or mental illness were required to pay the *jizya*. Women, children, handicapped, the mentally ill, the elderly, and slaves were exempt, as were all travelers and foreigners who did not settle in Muslim lands. In exchange for paying the *jizya*, *dhimmīs* were permitted to practice their religion, were not obligated to serve in the military, and were offered protection by Muslim rulers. Collected yearly, the *jizya* was used to pay salaries, pensions, and charities.

The *jizya* remained in place for centuries and was applied by various Muslim regimes. The Ottoman Empire applied the *jizya* to its Jewish and Christian subjects for centuries. While adhering to traditional parameters of the *jizya*, the Ottomans allowed religious clerics and people of certain provinces, such as Serbia and Bosnia, exemption from or lower rates of taxation. A form of *jizya* was instituted in India near the 14th century, but the practice was eradicated by the early 18th century. Following the Mongol invasion, many regions of the Middle East saw the disappearance of the *jizya*. However, the *jizya* continued into the 19th century in many North African countries and Persia. With the disappearance of Islamic states and the spread of religious tolerance, the *jizya* nearly vanished in the 20th century. Reports of religious minorities being forced to pay *jizya* have occasionally surfaced in countries plagued by war and political instability, such as Pakistan, Afghanistan, and Iraq during the early 21st century. The imposition is seen to be at odds with modern secular conceptions of

citizenship in the nation-state, which entail the equality of citizens who adhere to different religions.

See also jurisprudence; minorities; taxation

Further Reading

Satish Chandra, "Jizyah and the State in India during the 17th Century," *Journal of the Economic and Social History of the Orient* 12, no. 3 (1969); Daniel C. Dennett Jr., *Conversion and the Poll Tax in Early Islam*, 1950; S. D. Goitein, "Evidence on the Muslim Poll Tax from Non-Muslim Sources," *Journal of the Economic and Social History of the Orient* 6 (1963); Norman Stillman, *The Jews of Arab Lands: A History and Source Book*, 1979.

MATTHEW LONG

Jordan

The present-day Kingdom of Jordan began as the Emirate of Transjordan when Winston Churchill, then Britain's colonial secretary, announced at the Cairo Conference of 1921 that the area east of the Jordan River (76 percent of the total) would be exempt from Jewish immigration and would be governed by Emir 'Abdallah, son of Sharif Husayn of Mecca. In 1946, the British granted independence to the Emirate of Transjordan, and, following the creation of Israel in 1948, 'Abdallah renamed his territory the Hashemite Kingdom of Jordan.

In the war that followed the proclamation of the state of Israel, which Israel's Arab neighbors did not recognize, Jordan gained East Jerusalem and parts of the West Bank, along with 700,000 Palestinians who fled from Israel. Fearing that Abdallah would compromise with Israel in order to claim a part of Palestine for himself, Palestinian militants assassinated him in 1951. He was succeeded by his grandson Husayn in 1952 after the abdication of Husayn's father, Talal. King Husayn ruled until his death in 1999, during which period he signed a peace treaty with Israel in 1994.

Amman, the capital of Jordan, was a small Circassian settlement until it became a stop on the Hijaz railroad in the early 1900s. It developed into the political and cultural center of Jordan, a metropolis of two million people.

Jordan's natural resources are limited to phosphates and uranium. Projected plans to rely solely on nuclear energy have been thwarted because of Israeli pressure in the name of security. Although the country remains heavily dependent on remittances from workers in the Gulf and foreign subsidies, recently construction has been flourishing, and the ongoing conflict in Iraq under the umbrella of the "war on terror" has transformed Amman into the gateway to Iraq and the Palestinian territories. A well-educated, technologically literate workforce makes Amman a rival of Beirut as the business center for the Levant.

Jordan is a constitutional monarchy with a bicameral national assembly. The legal system combines Islamic law and French codes. Tribal law was outlawed in 1976, but an editorial in the *Jordan Times* in October 2010 complained that it was still in practice. The present electoral law—"one person, one vote"—favors constituencies that support the regime. Politically, Jordan has had to maneuver astutely through the narrows of Arab politics. In order to fend off lingering colonial influence, actual or perceived, King Husayn was forced by Arab nationalist pressure to dismiss Glubb Pasha (1897–1986), a British officer who was head of the Arab Legion, in 1956. Two years later, the Arab Federation of Jordan and Iraq, formed as a shield against the ambitions of Egypt's Nasser, was cut short by the Iraqi revolution in July of the same year. In May 1967 Jordan entered into a military alliance with Egypt, which drew it into the war of June 1967 against Israel, resulting in the occupation of the West Bank and East Jerusalem by Israel. In the wake of this defeat, the Palestinian militants (*fedāyeen* or *fidā'iyyūn*, "those who sacrifice") arose and slowly formed a "government within the government" in Jordan. In September 1970, these militants landed three hijacked planes in Jordan and, after releasing the passengers, attempted to take control of the country. The showdown with the Jordanian army, known as Black September, led to the expulsion of the *fedāyeen* to Lebanon and Syria. Following the Arab–Israeli war of 1973, the Arab Summit at Rabat named the Palestine Liberation Organization as the sole representative of the Palestinian people. In 1988, Husayn would finally renounce all claims to the West Bank.

He supported Iraq in its war with Iran (1980–88), opening the port of Aqaba to supplies for Iraq. This led to the formation of the Arab Cooperation Council of 1989, embracing Jordan, Iraq, Yemen, and Egypt. When Iraq attacked Kuwait in the following year, Jordan was accordingly excluded, along with Yemen and Egypt, from the American coalition that liberated Kuwait. Nonetheless, Jordan was allowed to participate in the Madrid Conference (hosted by Spain and cosponsored by the United States and the Soviet Union to initiate peace talks between the Israelis and the Palestinians), which followed, and in October 1994 signed a peace treaty with Israel. King Husayn died in February 1999, ending a reign of 46 years. His crown passed to his son, 'Abdallah II, who has continued on the trajectory set by his father by maintaining peace with Israel. Educated in England and the United States, 'Abdallah II has made successful initiatives to liberalize the economy, but movement toward an open, free, and fair democracy has been slow. At present, the recent waves of protests in the Middle East seem to have arrived at the doorstep of Jordan. The path into the future is difficult to determine, but it is clear that Jordan, along with the rest of the Arab world, stands at the threshold of a new era at the dawn of 2012.

See also Beirut; Palestine; Syria

Further Reading

Beverly Milton-Edwards and Peter Hinchcliffe, *Jordan: A Hashemite Legacy*, 2009; Philip Robbins, *A History of Jordan*, 2004; Avi

Shlaim, *Collusion across the Jordan: King Abdallah, the Zionist Movement and the Partition of Palestine*, 1988; Idem, *Lion of Jordan: The Life of King Hussein in War and Peace*, 2008.

JOHN DONOHUE

judge

A judge is an appointed official (qadi) who presides over Islamic judicial courts. A judge is responsible for determining the application of Islamic law in individual cases brought to the courts of Islamic law.

The office of the qadi was first institutionalized during the Umayyad dynasty. An Arab-Islamic precursor to this office, however, can be found in the role of arbitrator (*ḥakam*). In pre-Islamic Arabian society, disputes between two parties were often settled by a mutually appointed *ḥakam*—a role the Prophet Muhammad filled during his time in Medina. Muhammad and his immediate successors in the early and mid-seventh century seem to have appointed *ḥakam*s to arbitrate on the leader's behalf. By the late seventh century, the Islamic Empire had expanded considerably, and Umayyad rulers introduced an array of bureaucratic innovations designed to facilitate the administration of justice. Among them was the systematic appointment of judges (though the precise dates of the first appointments are difficult to determine). Umayyad caliphs directly appointed a judge to each province to adjudicate court cases in that area. The judge was a delegate of the state and subject to removal at any time. Islamic jurisprudence was still in its infancy, and judges of that period ruled at their discretion, though informed by Qur'anic injunctions and Arab and local customs. As legal scholarship flourished and became more methodologically systematized in the eighth and ninth centuries, ruling authorities regularly began to appoint judges who were trained in jurisprudence.

Abbasid caliphs regularly chose judges from among an emerging class of jurists or legal specialists (*fuqahā'*). Such scholars often hesitated or even refused to accept such an appointment, as many jurists were uncomfortable with executing judgment on an individual—a role said to belong to God—and particularly with doing so as an instrument of the state, not to mention the moral dangers involved in the temptation to take bribes or to make decisions in favor of the caliph or other powerful and influential members of the government or society. The position of judge was often understood to be a corrupting influence for both political and economic motives. During the Abbasid era, a formal theoretical framework for legal decisions began to take shape, but the judge remained answerable to the political authority and ran the risk of losing his position if he made decisions counter to the ruler's political program. Although theoretically in an independent position as representative of the law, in practice the judge was appointed and could be dismissed by the caliph or sultan and so was beholden directly to the ruler and indirectly to other influential members of the government. This tension between holding a state-appointed office and following the guidelines of an independent scholarly discipline continued into the modern era. Accusations of injustice leveled against judges are not uncommon in the historical record, but occasionally judges skillfully managed the complexities of the office. The sources refer to a good judge as *maḥmūd al-sīrah*, or "of praiseworthy behavior," and some of the most esteemed scholars of Islamic history also served as judges of the state, such as Ibn Rushd, known in the West as Averroes (d. 1198), and al-Asqalani (d. 1449).

In most premodern contexts, the authority of the judge was solely vested in his personage, and judges heard cases in diverse places, including marketplaces and private homes, rather than in a building reserved for the purposes of adjudication. The judge's authority was not only reserved to the jurisdiction to which he was appointed but also limited with regard to types of cases. A judge had no power to initiate an investigation or to bring an individual to trial, unlike the police (*shurṭa*), who had their own courts. Instead, the judge arbitrated cases brought before him by two or more willing parties seeking resolution of a question or dispute. Such cases were almost entirely related to civil and religious law. Criminal law cases typically fell to the police or, when deemed a more serious threat to public order, the caliph's court.

In the Umayyad and Abbasid eras, a judge often held other positions simultaneously, such as that of a professor of law, treasurer, tax official, or even chief of police (*ṣāḥib al-shurṭa*). As government officials, judges typically worked in tandem with other public offices to preserve public order. Various assistants facilitated the judge's work, particularly a notary-witness (*shāhid 'adl*), who was responsible for legally verifying admitted testimonies or documents, and a scribe (*kātib*), who kept official court records. Occasionally, a judge would enlist the assistance of other specialists to give their legal opinions (fatwas) on a given matter. Such fatwas, however, were neither decisive nor binding from a legal standpoint since the judge retained full authority to issue the final verdict (*ḥukm*). In addition to adjudication, the judge oversaw pious endowments and the inheritance of estates and saw to the well-being of orphans and other disadvantaged persons in his jurisdiction.

Legal scholars of the early and classical period debated what qualifications a judge should have and urged caliphs to make appointments based on certain criteria. It was almost universally agreed that a judge should be a free, male Muslim known to be just, intelligent, and knowledgeable of the law. Notably, some Hanafi legal scholars believed women were eligible to serve as judges in some types of cases. Other qualifications occasionally mentioned include being wise, modest, and free of certain physical disabilities that might impede performance, such as deafness or blindness.

In theory, the classical Islamic judiciary contained neither a judicial hierarchy nor appellate courts, though the Abbasid caliph Harun al-Rashid (r. 786–809) established an enduring custom of

appointing a chief judge (*qāḍī al-quḍāt* or, as it came to be known in Muslim Spain and North Africa, *qāḍī al-jamā'a*) for the capital city. The chief judge functioned on the level of a vizier and was responsible for appointing judges to the provinces, yet he did not represent a higher court to which appeals could be made. The decision of any judge was final. In practice, however, several avenues existed for rulings to be overturned; the most obvious among them was the *maẓālim* (injustices) court. Established in the Abbasid era, the *maẓālim* court was a venue in which complaints of injustice or corruption (be it against a vizier, judge, or otherwise) were presented directly to the caliph. Islamic law was not necessarily authoritative in a *maẓālim* court—though the latter's existence was often justified in terms of the shari'a. In the court's early days, the caliph himself judged cases in which the interests of the state were paramount. In later centuries, caliphs often appointed a vizier or judge to act as judge of the *maẓālim* court. David Powers, in his article "On Judicial Review in Islamic Law," has shown that other means also existed by which rulings could be overturned. In addition to the right of a judge to overturn his own rulings, a process of "successor review" existed among the judges. Upon taking office, a newly appointed judge would review the court records of the previous incumbent. Any prior rulings on record could be overturned by the incoming judge.

See also arbitration; endowment; *ijtihād* and *taqlīd*; judicial courts; jurisprudence; justice; police

Further Reading

Irit Bligh-Abramski, "The Judiciary (*Qāḍīs*) as a Governmental-Administrative Tool in Early Islam," *Journal of the Economic and Social History of the Orient* 35, no. 1 (1992); Muhammad Khalid Masud, Rudolph Peters, and David S. Powers, eds., *Dispensing Justice in Islam: Qadis and Their Judgments*, 2006; Al-Mawardi, *The Ordinances of Government, al-Aḥkām al-Sulṭāniyya wa'l-Wilāyāt al-Dīniyya*, translated by Wafaa H. Wahba, 1996; David S. Powers, "On Judicial Review in Islamic Law," *Law and Society Review* 26, no. 2 (1992); Émile Tyan, "Judicial Organization," in *Law in the Middle East: Volume I, Origin and Development of Islamic Law*, edited by Majid Khadduri and Herbert J. Liebesny, 1955.

MATTHEW PIERCE

judicial courts

Medieval Sunni Islamic law recognized numerous judicial or quasi-judicial institutions that had the power to resolve disputes and whose decisions were subject to enforcement by the state. The most basic institution was that of the qadi (also called *ḥākim*). Both terms (or derivatives of each) are found in the Qur'an and the hadith to indicate some dispute-resolution mechanism, although in those instances, given the historical context, they may refer to mechanisms that were more arbitral in nature rather than courts of law established by a state. Upon the Abbasid institutionalization of the Islamic state, other judicial institutions were established alongside that of the qadi, such as the *nāẓir al-maẓālim*, the *wālī al-jarā'im*, and the *muḥtasib*. The *nāẓir al-maẓālim* was primarily a forum for the vindication of claims against government officials as well as disputes within the government bureaucracy, the *wālī al-jarā'im* was responsible for the punishment of criminals, and the *muḥtasib* was largely responsible for maintaining the good order of public spaces (in particular, the market). Ordinary civil disputes, however, were almost entirely the province of the qadi, and for that reason, the qadi has been traditionally viewed as the exemplar of the Muslim judge.

The Ideals of Judging: From Taboo to Learning and Impartiality

For Sunni writers on judging, the position of judge posed a dilemma. On the one hand, it was an office of immense political significance in the practical life of the Muslim community. In addition, giving judgment in accordance with Islamic law was also a collective obligation of the community, and therefore it could not be ignored. On the other hand, judging was a morally risky activity. A judge might be unjust as a result of either ignorance or venality. Even a just judge faced the constant temptation to abuse his position to enrich either himself or his friends. This ambivalence toward judges and judging is reflected in numerous cautionary tales regarding early scholars who, out of piety, not only refused the post but also were willing to endure the ruler's punishment for their refusal. It is also reflected in hadiths such as the one attributed to the Prophet Muhammad in which he is reported to have said, "Two judges in Hell, one judge in Paradise." Nevertheless, it would be a mistake to assume such stories represent a universal attitude among religious scholars, even in the early community. After all, Abu Yusuf Ya'qub b. Ibrahim and Muhammad b. al-Hasan al-Shaybani, Abu Hanifa's two most prominent disciples, and even Shafi'i were all reported to have served as judges at some point in their lives. Instead, Muslim scholars developed an ethic for judges based on two principal ideals: learning and impartiality. A judge who lacked legal knowledge was by definition unjust, unless he took advice from the learned and applied their counsel in resolving disputes. More important (at least in the sense that scholars spent more time thinking about it) was the requirement of impartiality. This placed all sorts of limitations on the judge and how the court should be organized. Scholars debated whether the impartiality ideal meant that only strangers should be appointed judges; it certainly meant that a judge could not engage in private business ventures with persons in his jurisdiction. It also meant that a judge could not hear cases in which his impartiality could be doubted, such as a case involving his friends, enemies, or close family members. By the 11th century, the extreme fear of judging that appears in narratives in the early centuries of Islam seems to have disappeared, replaced by the ethic of learning and impartiality. As a consequence, leading jurists by this time were able to accept the position of judge without fear of censure.

The Court's Jurisdiction

A qadi, in addition to being individually qualified by way of specialized learning in Islamic law (*'ilm*) and his exemplary ethical character (*'adāla*), must be appointed to his office by the ruler (caliph) or his representative (*nā'ib*). The scope of a judge's jurisdiction, whether in terms of the cases he is allowed to hear or the persons who can be brought before him, is determined exclusively by the terms of his appointment. If a judge exceeds the jurisdictional limits included in the terms of his appointment, whether by ruling on a matter for which he lacks jurisdictional competence or by ruling against a person not falling within the geographical limitations of his jurisdiction, his judgment is void.

The power to determine the judge's jurisdiction became a very important tool in legal reform, not only during the 19th century period of reforms known as the Tanzimat, but also in prior periods of Ottoman history. Pre-19th-century jurists, for example, stated that where a judge, pursuant to the jurisdictional terms of his appointment, is required to render judgment according to specified legal doctrines, he lacks power to rule according to other legal doctrines—despite their Islamic validity—and if he does, his judgment is void. This doctrine was reaffirmed in the *Majalla* and was also used by modernizing states such as Egypt in connection with family law reforms—for example, by prohibiting courts from hearing claims arising out of contested marriages that had not been registered with the civil authorities.

A judge obtained his office only through a valid appointment from the ruler and could be dismissed at the ruler's will. (Muslims living outside the jurisdiction of an Islamic state, however, could appoint, and indeed were required to appoint, a judge for themselves.) Even so, Muslim jurists understood the judge to be a representative of the community generally rather than of the ruler who appointed him. For this reason, a qadi's jurisdiction did not lapse with the death or dismissal of the official who appointed him, unlike, for example, the ruler's minister (vizier), who was understood to be the ruler's personal lieutenant.

The Judge's Relationship to Islamic Law

Until the 12th century, Muslim judges in theory were *mujtahid*s, meaning that they were required to render judgment directly from revelation in light of the Islamic foundational texts (the Qur'an and the reported teachings of the Prophet) or to use some valid method of interpretation to arrive at the applicable rule of law. In this period of Islamic legal history, attempts by the appointing authority to restrict a judge's right to independent legal interpretation were resisted by Muslim jurists, some holding that any stipulation in the appointment of a judge that purported to restrict the judge's right to engage in *ijtihād*—the independent search by a competent expert for God's rule as derived from revelation using the accepted interpretive methods set forth in works of theoretical jurisprudence (*uṣūl al-fiqh*)—was void; others went so far as to hold that inclusion of such a provision rendered the appointment invalid in its entirety. It should be noted, however, that the famous ninth-century Maliki jurist and judge of Ifriqiya, Sahnun, was reported to have required all judges in his jurisdiction to rule exclusively according to the doctrine of Malik b. Anas (d. 795), even if they were followers of Abu Hanifa.

Regardless of jurists' insistence on the right of judges to engage in *ijtihād*, the desire to ensure some predictability in legal outcomes, which was famously manifested as early as the eighth century in Ibn al-Muqaffa''s *Risala fi al-Sahaba* (Epistle on the caliph's entourage), as well as the increasing availability of a relatively stable and sophisticated body of jurisprudence, meant that by the end of the 11th century, resistance to the idea that a judge could be a *muqallid* (a legal official who defers to the legal opinion of a *mujtahid*) had substantially declined. Accordingly, Muslim jurists began to organize the doctrines of the various schools into a form (*mukhtaṣar*) that would be easier for judges to use based on a theory that an authoritative rule—described as the *mashhūr* in the Maliki school and the *ẓāhir al-riwāya* in the Hanafi school—exists within each legal school and that judges, insofar as they were *muqallid*s, were obliged to judge on the basis of that rule. These two developments—the convention that all judges were *muqallid*s and the convention that the *muqallid* judge was obliged to rule in accordance with the authoritative doctrine of his school—provided a doctrinal justification for a system of judicial review to ensure that judges complied with the rules of their particular school.

By the Ottoman period, qadis no longer applied Islamic law exclusively—at least if that term is understood to apply to the rules of *fiqh* alone. The rules of *fiqh* were those rules that could be traced to the interpretive activity of Muslim legal scholars as distinguished from the rule-making activity of the state and its agents. The Ottomans, for example, had issued numerous positive laws, known as *kanun*, that found their way into an ordinary judge's court. For example, the Ottomans placed a ceiling on the amount of interest that could be charged in connection with a popular *ḥīla* (legal fiction) used to circumvent the prohibition against interest-bearing loans, and Ottoman-era jurists applied that rule in disputes arising out of such transactions. In addition, Ottoman-era qadis increasingly took over responsibilities for administration of the criminal law, which in substance usually derived at least in part from *kanun*s.

The Religious Dimension of a Judge's Decision

Just as the corruption or ignorance of an individual judge could subvert the ends of the legal system, so too could the corruption of the litigants. Both the Qur'an and the hadith warn individuals against the temptation of manipulating the judicial system in order to deprive others of their rights. In addition to the risk that parties might manipulate the system for their own ends, there was also the question of a judicial ruling based on a controversial rule of law: did the judge's ruling in such a case effectively resolve the moral controversy for the purposes of the next life before God, or were its effects limited to the secular world?

As a general matter, Muslim jurists distinguished between the purely legal consequences of a judicial ruling in this life, which they referred to as *ẓāhir*, and its religious consequences, which they referred to as *bāṭin*. If the prevailing party intentionally corrupted the

court's decision by, for example, conspiring with the witnesses to submit a false claim (with certain exceptions to this rule among the Hanafi jurists in the area of family law), then, as a general rule, the judge's decision lacked any moral weight. If a judge were to learn subsequently that the initial judgment had been obtained fraudulently, it could be reversed. Where the prevailing party did not win as the result of intentionally false evidence but did prevail based on a controversial rule of law (e.g., a judge ruling that an adult woman did not need her father's consent to marry), jurists disagreed over whether the judge's ruling in fact changed the moral rule governing the conduct at issue. It appears that during the first centuries of Islamic history, jurists believed that the judge's decision in controversial areas of law did not resolve the underlying moral controversy. In later centuries, particularly after the 13th-century Maliki jurist Shihab al-din al-Qarafi strongly supported the view that a valid judicial decision based on a controversial legal rule conclusively resolved the moral as well as legal controversy involved in the dispute, Muslim jurists generally accepted the proposition that a judge's decision, untainted by fraud, resolved the moral as well as the legal controversy, but on the condition that the prevailing plaintiff did not assert a claim based on a controversial rule that he or she subjectively rejected. An example of such a case would be a Maliki who obtained a right of first refusal from a Hanafi judge based solely on his status as a neighbor of the seller, even though as a Maliki he rejected the validity of that rule.

Courts in the Post-Ottoman Era

As part of the legal reforms initiated by the Ottoman Empire in the 19th and 20th centuries, state-promulgated civil codes gradually began to displace the role of uncodified *fiqh* in the Ottoman legal system and in the legal systems of the successor states to the Ottoman Empire. The main impetus for replacing uncodified Islamic law with civil law codes modeled on European codes was a desire not so much to abandon Islamic law as such but rather to recast it in a manner that would make it more amenable to the needs of a centralizing and modernizing state. Whereas premodern Islamic jurists attempted to minimize the state's control over substantive law, post-Ottoman states, largely with the support of the modern legal class, asserted their control over courts (usually through the state's control of a court's jurisdiction) to further modernization projects. In this context, the Egyptian model of a civil code, derived at least in part from substantive Islamic law but applied by a secularly trained class of judges, has proven to be particularly influential throughout the Arab world.

See also *ijtihād* and *taqlīd*; jurisprudence

Further Reading

Nathan J. Brown, *The Rule of Law in the Arab World*, 1997; Mohammad Fadel, "The Social Logic of Taqlîd and the Rise of the *Mukhtasar*," *Islamic Law and Society* 3, no. 2 (1996); Sherman Jackson, *Islamic Law and the State: The Constitutional Jurisprudence of Shihāb al-Dīn al-Qarāfī*, 1996; Baber Johansen, "Truth and Validity of the Qadi's Judgment: A Legal Debate Among Muslim Sunnite Jurists from the Ninth to the Thirteenth Centuries," *Recht van de Islam* 14 (1997).

MOHAMMAD FADEL

jurisprudence

Jurisprudence in an Islamic context refers on the one hand to the corpus of laws or legal rulings and knowledge of the law, both termed *fiqh*. A jurist is therefore termed a *faqīh*, one endowed with knowledge of the law. On the other hand, jurisprudence also refers to the principles on which individual laws are based, or the hermeneutical system by which legal rulings on particular cases are derived, in which case it corresponds to the term *uṣūl al-fiqh*, literally "the roots of the law" but technically the science of legal hermeneutics. Already by the second Islamic century, *fiqh* had become a technical term signifying the academic discussion of Islamic law (shari'a). The term *fiqh* designates human activity and the specific legal rulings jurists reach; it cannot be ascribed to God or to the Prophet Muhammad. The shari'a, imposed on humankind by God's revelation and embodied in the foundational texts of the Qur'an and hadith, is explained and elaborated by the interpretive activity of jurists. Since this is the only access to the law in practice, shari'a and *fiqh* often overlap in usage, though the former retains the connotation of the divine (the law as God wills it) and the latter retains the connotation of the human (the law as an approximation of God's will as determined by jurists).

In its widest sense, *fiqh* covers many aspects of religious, political, and civil life, including both practical and theoretical regulation and justification. The two most important genres of juristic literature are *furū' al-fiqh* (the branches of the law) and *uṣūl al-fiqh* (the roots of the law). *Furū' al-fiqh* works are compendia that set out the rulings on specific areas of the law in chapters that follow a recognized order, in greater or lesser detail and with varying amounts of justificatory argument. *Uṣūl al-fiqh* works identify and classify the sources of law and the methods adopted to derive legal rules and assessments from the evidence of revelation. These works also present a structure of authority that distinguishes the qualified jurist (mufti, *mujtahid*) from the layman (*muqallid*), excluding the caliphs and scholars who are not trained specifically as jurists, such as theologians and hadith experts, in the interpretation and elaboration of the law. Ideally, *uṣūl al-fiqh* may be seen as a pure science in comparison with the applied science of *furū' al-fiqh*.

Most major works of *furū' al-fiqh* discuss the points of law under three main divisions: *'ibādāt* (acts of worship), *mu'āmalāt* (civil transactions), and *qaḍāyā* (court cases) or *ḥudūd* (prescribed criminal punishments). The *'ibādāt* section focuses on acts of religious devotion that are one's individual obligation toward God and comprises rulings on ritual purity, prayer, alms, fasting, pilgrimage,

and sometimes jihad, in that order, ostensibly corresponding to the frequency with which performance of the act of devotion in question is required. *Mu'āmalāt*, for the most part treating private law or obligations between people, is more loosely ordered and includes family law; mercantile law; and laws relating to agency, land ownership, compensation for injury, murder, and so on. The third section includes the set penalties (*ḥudūd*) for seven specific crimes: theft or robbery, highway banditry, apostasy, rebellion, adultery or fornication, false accusation of adultery, and drinking wine. It also includes judicial procedure. Islamic jurisprudence thus leaves relatively undefined two areas of the law that are of tremendous importance for politics: criminal law for infractions other than the ones set by the *ḥudūd* and public law addressing the relationship of subjects to the government, including such topics as the payment of taxes. Historically, a compromise of sorts developed between the jurists and the rulers whereby the jurists recognized the legitimacy of the ruler and relinquished the right to control a great deal of public law in return for the monarch's public commitment to the shari'a, recognition of the jurists' authority, and recognition of the jurists' control over private law—the law between individuals. These gaps opened up the possibility for the prosecution of many crimes not treated in the foundational texts and the application of various punishments to those convicted of committing them—termed *ta'zīr* in the legal tradition. It also opened up space for the relatively free elaboration of public law. The best-known and most developed of these systems is the *kanun* of the Ottoman Empire, which governed large areas of public law and procedure in government institutions.

Books on the points of law display literary formalism and casuistry but also attention to practical concerns and hardheaded realism. The four major Sunni schools of law or traditions of legal study—the Hanafi, Maliki, Shafi'i, and Hanbali *madhhab*s—as well as the Shi'i tradition show a broadly similar approach to the genre in this sense. There is a dual hermeneutical aspect to works in this genre: an interpretive relationship to the school tradition and a further interpretive relationship to the Qur'an and sunna. As loyal members of a legal school, jurists are committed to a discursive engagement with their past, the creative dimension of which is termed *ijtihād*, and the duty of submission, *taqlīd*. These legal schools functioned as authorizing institutions whose interrelations were governed by normative pluralism.

The standard content of a work of Sunni *uṣūl al-fiqh* may be exemplified by the *al-Mustasfa min 'Ilm al-Usul* (Methods of jurisprudence) of Ghazali (d. 1111), which represents a high point in the development of the genre. The position of *uṣūl al-fiqh* in relation to the other Islamic sciences is explained therein; the *uṣūlī*, or legal theorist, accepts the results of theology and hadith criticism and then explicates the way in which Islam's foundational texts indicate juristic norms, whether by explicit or implied meaning or through deduction and logical derivation. There are four broad areas of discussion: categories of the legal assessment of acts (mandatory, preferred, permitted, disliked, and forbidden); sources of the law (Qur'an, hadith, consensus, and analogy or independent reasoning); hermeneutical rules that permit extrapolation of norms from sources (analogical reasoning, a fortiori argument, reductio ad absurdum, etc.); and elaboration of the theory of *ijtihād* or independent reasoning.

The origins of Islamic jurisprudence are contested. Modern scholarship has rejected the traditional view that Islamic law began as a more or less mature system during or immediately after the lifetime of the Prophet. According to conventional understanding, *fiqh* came into being toward the end of the eighth century, created by jurists endorsing, modifying, or rejecting the popular and administrative practice of the Umayyad period. Revisionist scholarship has instead emphasized the emergence of *fiqh* from ancient Near Eastern legal cultures, Arabian customary law, or independent development. The *Risala* (Treatise) of Shafi'i (d. 820) was previously considered to be the first treatise in *uṣūl al-fiqh*, the work that established the genre, but it has been judged by contemporary scholars to be either a late work or a work the implications of which it took time to discover.

Since their emergence in classical Islamic history, the genres of *furū'* and *uṣūl al-fiqh* have been produced continually until the present day, finding their most important social realization in the Islamic legal educational system. With the emergence of the madrasa, or college of Islamic law, in the 11th century, *fiqh* was recognized as the main purpose of education and retained this position until the decline of the traditional system in the 19th and 20th centuries. In modern times, three major factors have radically affected *fiqh*, mostly as a result of Western influence: the gradual emergence of secular educational systems; the appearance of independent nation-states and their associated legal forms, including law codes, constitutions, and statute law; and the ideological dissociation of political opposition from the tradition of *fiqh*.

Scholarly debate on Islamic jurisprudence has been cast in relation to modern legal reforms, especially concerning the possibility of change in the law and the challenge to a number of standard rules of interpretation. The "closure of the gate of *ijtihād*" was previously understood to have contributed to the rigidity of Islamic law and the decline of Muslim societies. Recent scholarship has challenged this theory and presented Islamic legal hermeneutics as a method for the discovery and development of legal rules, implying a capacity for change and evolution. Some maintain that Islamic legal theory is not developmental but rather concerned with the discovery of the law as an eternal and enduring truth, while others claim that Islamic theory is either largely divorced from the practical content of the law or used arbitrarily to justify legal assessments predetermined by tradition or various biases. The interplay of legal theory and practice has thus become an important object of scholarly study and debate. Beginning in the 19th century, Muslim reformers, including Muhammad 'Abduh (d. 1905) and Rashid Rida (d. 1935), decried the rigid boundaries that had formed between the various *madhhab* traditions of Islamic law. They argued not only for modern jurists' freedom to choose from all the legal positions found in the sources (*takhayyur*) and to borrow from other Islamic legal traditions—termed *talfīq* (piecing together)—but also for recognition that laws can and should change according to historical

circumstances. A new field came into being, that of *fiqh muqāran* (comparative law), which involved studying similar issues across the *madhhabs*. One famous example of *talfīq* put into practice was the reform in the Anglo-Muhammadan legal system of the Hanafi law of divorce in order to facilitate the wife's access to divorce by using a principle borrowed from Maliki law. Other modernists, such as 'Ali 'Abd al-Raziq (d. 1966), argued for the rejection or limitation of consensus, the unanimous agreement of the jurists that acts as a sanctifying authority and makes a particular legal position historically unassailable, according to classical legal theory. Many thinkers have sought to limit the application of consensus, analogy, and other principles, emphasizing instead public interest (*maṣlaḥa*) or textually unregulated benefits (*al-maṣāliḥ al-mursala*) as a guiding principle in the reform and elaboration of the law. Still others have argued for the rejection of the hadith as a foundational source of law, restricting that role to the Qur'an, or even to the portion of the Qur'an that was revealed at Mecca. These radical efforts at reform have met with very limited success and in many cases have been vehemently rejected. Fundamentalists and others have argued for the development of an Islamic law that is not limited by or restricted to one *madhhab*; in practice, however, because the vast majority of the medieval texts they consult were written within the epistemological system of the *madhhabs*, they have tended to fall back on positions that resemble those of one or another *madhhab*.

Since the late 20th century, in reaction to the encroachment in Muslim nations of secular law, which often entirely replaced Islamic law except in matters of marriage, divorce, and inheritance, many religiopolitical movements have clamored for application of the shari'a. In many cases, a vague concept of shari'a is promoted with a utopian understanding of Islamic law's ability to bring order and social justice to the nations involved by curbing corruption, fending off Western influence, and promoting public morality. Such optimism is neatly captured in the slogan popularized by the Muslim Brotherhood in Egypt and others: *al-Islām huwa al-ḥall* ("Islam is the solution"). In Saudi Arabia, Iran under the Islamic Republic, Afghanistan under the Taliban, and the Sudan, various forms of Islamic law have been instituted. Hamas in Palestine, the Front Islamique du Salut in Algeria, and many other political parties and movements in the Islamic world have made vocal calls for doing the same in their nations.

See also minorities, jurisprudence of; shari'a; 'ulama'

Further Reading

Norman Calder, *Studies in Early Muslim Jurisprudence*, 1993; Wael B. Hallaq, *A History of Islamic Legal Theories: An Introduction to Sunnī Uṣūl al-Fiqh*, 1997; Idem, *The Origins and Evolution of Islamic Law*, 2005; Baber Johansen, "Legal Literature and the Problem of Change: The Case of the Land Rent," in *Islam and Public Law*, edited by Chibli Mallat, 1993; Joseph Schacht, *The Origins of Muhammadan Jurisprudence*, 1959; Bernard Weiss, *The Spirit of Islamic Law*, 1998.

GREGORY MACK

justice

The most common terms for justice in the Qur'an are *'adl* and *qisṭ*; its opposite, oppression, is *ẓulm*. The foundational text of Islam exhorts believers to be just, standing with the marginalized—the orphans, the needy, and the destitute (2:177; 90:8–18)—and speaking out against oppression, even if it entails going against one's own family (4:135). The Qur'an describes a deity who is thoroughly committed to justice. Indeed, as the famous Qur'anic metaphor testifies, God will not commit any amount of injustice, even if it be the weight of a mote or speck (4:40; 99:6–8). Moreover, because God is just, righteousness according to the Qur'an is ascertained not by tribal lineage or gender affiliation—a radical departure from pre-Islamic Arabian society—but solely on the basis of *taqwā*, one's level of piety (49:13). Whereas God does not wrong anyone (4:40; 45:22), human beings are fully capable of either upholding justice or committing oppression.

The obligation to promote justice and curb oppression was viewed as a central function of the ruler in premodern Islamic political theory and a major feature of the social contract between the ruler and the ruled. According to the medieval scholar Mawardi (d. 1058), the subjects of the ruler owe him obedience and support and, in return, he has ten public duties: (1) guarding the faith against heresy; (2) maintaining the rule of law; (3) ensuring public safety; (4) punishing criminals; (5) defending the Muslim territory; (6) supporting the expansion of Islam and recognition of its superiority; (7) collecting taxes; (8) making payments from the treasury; (9) appointing responsible and effective officials; (10) watching over the realm personally, without delegating or shirking responsibility. Justice is stressed particularly with regard to maintaining the rule of law—the point of this is regularly described as preventing the oppression of the weak by the strong. The ruler is therefore viewed as the champion of the oppressed, even when the oppressors are government officials. For this reason, Islamic regimes instituted special courts for the redressing of injustices, termed *maẓālim*. Instructional manuals on political leadership and court chronicles stress the ruler's obligation to facilitate the settlement of disputes and claims and to allow unrestricted access to the ruler, such as the ability of a commoner to submit a petition directly to him or to attend an audience before him. Justice is also stressed with regard to the imposition of taxes: they should be limited to legal taxes and should not be extremely burdensome or oppressive. Injustice, however, was viewed by most Sunni theorists as insufficient cause for rebellion or removing a ruler from office. While the legality of rebellion against an unjust ruler was disputed, the majority opinion was that rebellion should be discouraged and rebels subdued through negotiation if possible and by force if not.

Justice is a key theme in modern political Islamic thought. The Egyptian writer Sayyid Qutb (d. 1966) called for the creation of an Islamic state with justice as its core principle. Imprisoned and eventually executed by a regime that was clamping down on Islamic

activists, Qutb wrote in a context of oppression. In *Social Justice in Islam* (1949) and later *Milestones* (1964), Qutb argued that only a government based on the sovereignty of God (*ḥākimiyyat Allāh*)—in other words, a distinctly "Islamic" system—could ensure both socioeconomic justice and religious harmony. During the popular upheavals against the shah of Iran in 1978–79, Ayatollah Khomeini (d. 1989) condemned the regime as an oppressive monarchy that had sold Iran to American interests. That Khomeini's alternative, fleshed out in *The Guardianship of the Jurist* (1971), was a state supervised by religious jurists underscores a core, and often unquestioned, assumption of political Islamic thinking: that only an "Islamic" government will translate into a truly just Muslim order.

Some of the most profound articulations of justice in Islamic religious terms have taken place outside the historic heartlands of Islam. The African American activist Malcolm X (d. 1965) saw in Islam a radical message of liberation from white supremacy. He converted to Islam while in prison and, upon his release, became the most influential minister in the Nation of Islam, transforming the then fledgling black Muslim group into a powerful voice of racial equality. African American Muslims have also played a leading role in the struggle for gender justice, most notably the feminist scholar Amina Wadud (b. 1952). By undertaking a gendered reading of the Qur'an, she has challenged the historical monopoly that men have exercised over exegesis. Using the concept of *tawḥīd* (the central Islamic tenet of the absolute unity of God), Wadud has argued that equality constitutes a fundamental component of gender justice in Islam. Any practice that undermines the sacrosanct equality of women and men therefore violates the very unity of God. Questions of religious pluralism have also taken center stage in the Islamic quest for justice. During the collective struggle against Apartheid, the South African Islamic scholar Farid Esack (b. 1956) articulated a Qur'anic theology of liberation committed to socioeconomic, racial, and gender justice through a framework of religious pluralism. This understanding of Islam relinquished any claim of Muslim exclusivism—that adherence to Islam constituted the only possible path toward the transcendent—in favor of interreligious solidarity against oppression.

See also equality; ethics; human rights; pluralism and tolerance; rebellion; revolutions; solidarity; tyranny

Further Reading

Nimat H. Barazangi, M. Raquibuz Zaman, and Omar Afzal, eds., *Islamic Identity and the Struggle for Justice*, 1996; Hamid Dabashi, *Theology of Discontent: The Ideological Foundation of the Islamic Revolution in Iran*, 2006; Farid Esack, *Qur'an, Liberation and Pluralism: An Islamic Perspective of Interreligious Solidarity against Oppression*, 1997; Toshihiko Izutsu, *Ethico-Religious Concepts in the Qur'an*, 2002; William E. Shepard, *Sayyid Qutb and Islamic Activism: A Translation and Critical Analysis of Social Justice in Islam*, 1996; Amina Wadud, *Qur'an and Woman: Rereading the Sacred Text from a Woman's Perspective*, 1999.

SHADAAB RAHEMTULLA

K

Kadızadeli

"Kadızadeli" is a Turkish term that literally means "a supporter of Kadızade" and refers to a 17th-century revivalist movement, arguably rooted in the socioeconomic change in the Ottoman Empire. The movement was named after Kadızade Mehmed (d. 1635), a popular preacher in Istanbul. The history of the movement is usually divided into three periods, each of which revolves around a charismatic preacher.

Kadızade's intellectual inspiration was Birgili Mehmed (1523–73), a scholar of ethics and law who was originally from Balıkesir (in northwestern Anatolia) and eventually settled in Birgi (in western Anatolia). Birgili is known for his legal challenge against the practice of cash waqf (religious endowments) sanctioned by the Ottoman grand mufti Abu al-Su'ud (d. 1574). Birgili's *al-Tariqa al-Muhammadiyya (The Muhammadan Path,* 1572) became one of the most popular manuals of practical ethics in the 17th and 18th centuries. In this work, Birgili placed special emphasis on "commanding right and forbidding wrong," a principle that Kadızadelis took to heart.

Kadızade Mehmed was born in Balıkesir and studied with some of the former students of Birgili before he moved to Istanbul, where he eventually became a preacher, quickly moving up in the hierarchy of mosques and reaching the peak of this career preaching at Ayasofya (Hagia Sophia). The Kadızadeli movement emerged within the context of the disagreements he had with another famous preacher at the time, Shaykh Abdülmecid Sivasi (d. 1639).

Sivasi had followed his father and uncle in the Halveti Sufi order and came to lead it in Sivas in eastern Anatolia. His fame reached the ears of Sultan Mehmed III (r. 1595–1603), who invited him to Istanbul. In Istanbul, Sivasi became the shaykh of a Halveti convent and a well-known preacher, eventually becoming the Friday preacher at the Mosque of Sultan Ahmed.

While Kadızade and Sivasi were preaching in two almost adjacent mosques in the 1630s, they came to disagree on several issues, ranging from the permissibility of coffee and tobacco to Sufi practices, including music and whirling, which is a Sufi ritual meditational dance, and the teachings of Ibn al-'Arabi (d. 1240). Their disagreements did not remain confined to the intellectual realm, as the Kadızadelis, who included both preachers and laymen, embraced his strong emphasis on the principle of "commanding right and forbidding wrong" and eventually took some of the issues to the streets. At times, their agenda converged with that of the sultan, as in the case of the closure of coffee houses by Sultan Murad IV (r. 1623–40).

After the death of Kadızade in 1635, the Kadızadelis returned to the Ottoman public space, led by Muhammad al-Ustuwani (d. 1661), who was originally from Damascus. In Istanbul he first held study circles at Ayasofya and soon received preaching appointments; he was even invited to preach in the palace. After a confrontation between the Kadızadelis and Sufis at the Fatih Mosque in 1656, Ustuwani was exiled to Cyprus. Köprülü Mehmed Pasha (d. 1661), a grand vizier with extraordinary powers, had no tolerance for public disturbances.

It was Köprülü's son, Fazıl Ahmed, who brought the next leader of the Kadızadelis, Vani Mehmed (d. 1685), to the capital after having been impressed by him in a meeting in Erzurum, and Vani arrived in Istanbul when Fazıl Ahmed had already become the grand vizier. His sermons brought him many admirers, including Sultan Mehmed IV (r. 1648–87), who chose Vani as his sons' tutor and his own mentor. In this capacity, he persuaded the sultan to prohibit certain Sufi practices, such as whirling, in the late 1660s—a decision that was reversed after the gradual disappearance of the Kadızadeli movement.

Studies focused on the Kadızadeli movement have pointed out several factors, such as the tension between the privileged members of the Ottoman 'ulama', who were at times targeted by the Kadızadelis, and the Ottoman preachers, as well as the tension between preachers who belonged to Sufi orders and those who did not. The common provincial origins of all Kadızadeli leaders and the lack of knowledge about their family backgrounds suggest that they were all of modest means in comparison with the higher-ranking members of the Ottoman 'ulama' and Sufi shaykhs who mostly belonged to well-established families.

There are also some indications that the Kadızadelis might well have been targeting certain privileged socioeconomic groups, such as the Janissaries, many of whom in that period were merchants. A better understanding of this group also requires comparative studies that would take into account the impact of the thought of Ahmad Sirhindi (1564–1624) in the Ottoman Empire.

See also Ottomans (1299–1924)

Further Reading

Marc David Baer, *Honored by the Glory of Islam: Conversion and Conquest in Ottoman Europe*, 2008; Necati Öztürk, *Islamic Orthodoxy among the Ottomans in the Seventeenth Century with Special Reference to the Qadi-Zade Movement* (PhD diss., University of

Edinburgh, 1981); Derin Terzioğlu, *Sufi and Dissident in the Ottoman Empire: Niyazi-i Mısri (1618–1694)* (PhD diss., Harvard University, 1999); Madeline Zilfi, *The Politics of Piety: The Ottoman Ulema in the Postclassical Age (1600–1800)*, 1988.

BAKI TEZCAN

Karbala

Karbala is a town in Iraq, approximately 80 kilometers southwest of Baghdad. It is one of the most important shrine-cities (*'atabāt*) of Shi'i Islam. After the death of the caliph Mu'awiya b. Abi Sufyan (d. 680), Husayn b. 'Ali, the Prophet's grandson and third Shi'i imam, had agreed to lead the revolt of the "party of 'Ali" (Shi'at 'Ali), which considered the succession of Yazid I, designated by his father, to be unlawful. On October 10, 680, Husayn was killed in Karbala in a battle against Umayyad forces, allegedly together with 72 companions. Husayn's tragic end made 'Ashura', as the day is commonly called, the central reference point of Imami Shi'i cultural memory.

Imamis viewed Husayn's martyrdom in cosmic dimensions as predestined: God had revealed it to Adam, all pre-Islamic prophets, and Muhammad. Husayn was believed to have been aware of his destiny and to have consented to it, as it would achieve ultimate victory for his followers on the Day of Judgment, an idea that makes Husayn a Christlike figure undergoing what seems to be redemptive suffering. In other forms of Shi'ism, this idea is less prominent or wholly absent, and it is also wholly unknown in Sunni Islam. To the Imamis, however, Husayn was the Prince of the Martyrs (*sayyid al-shuhadā'*), and visiting his grave was sometimes considered more meritorious than making the pilgrimage to Mecca.

The only way for the Imamis to partake in this promised salvation was by engaging in constant remembrance of the tragedy of Karbala. From early on, therefore, a number of rituals evolved that emphasized mourning and weeping over the fate of Husayn. The earliest reports stem from the tenth century, when the Buyids (a Persian dynasty that controlled the Abbasid caliphate between 945 and 1055) allowed public memorial services in Baghdad, but the tradition as such is clearly older and seems to have started shortly after the events. Processions incorporating breast beating and other expressions of grief were part of these gatherings and from the beginning had the potential to spark sectarian clashes. Gradually, a literary genre commemorating Karbala developed; its most prominent work was *Rawdat al-Shuhada'* (The garden of the martyrs) by the Persian preacher Husayn al-Wa'iz al-Kashifi (d. 1504–5). During the Safavid (1501–1722) and especially Qajar (1794–1925) periods, these works evolved into stage presentations (*ta'ziya*), which took on the form of a Persian national theater over time. Eventually, self-flagellation rituals were introduced (originating probably in the Caucasus and Azerbaijan regions and possibly under Christian influence), which comprised the use of chains and swords.

The mourning rituals always aimed at linking Husayn's fate to that of the believer in his lifetime, but until the 20th century, the interpretation focused on salvation in the hereafter. In the 20th century, it was transformed into a revolutionary ideology that placed active resistance against any oppressor in this world at the center. The Iranian writer 'Ali Shari'ati (1933–77) had the most lasting influence in this regard. He blended 'Ashura' with a Marxist view of history, and his sentence "Every day is 'Ashura', every place is Karbala" became a central slogan in the Iranian Revolution in 1979, when the shah was equated with the caliph Yazid. Since then, the politicization of Karbala has been used in other contexts in Iran (e.g., during the war against Iraq in the 1980s) and also in India and Lebanon (where the label "Yazid" was attached to the Israeli occupying forces in the 1990s). In Iraq, the significance of Karbala itself dramatically increased since the shrine became accessible again for pilgrims after the fall of Saddam Hussein (d. 2006) in 2003.

The rituals of self-flagellation have been rejected by many Shi'i scholars (mainly on the grounds that they were unlawful innovations and harmed the image of Shi'ism worldwide) and even formally forbidden by Ayatollah Khamene'i in 1994. Nevertheless, they remain an integral part of the Muharram rites outside Iran as well as a major issue in anti-Shi'i polemical literature.

See also India; Iran; Lebanon; Shi'ism; Umayyads (661–750)

Further Reading

Kamran Scot Aghaie, *The Martyrs of Karbala: Shi'i Symbols and Rituals in Modern Iran*, 2004; Mahmoud Ayoub, *Redemptive Suffering in Islām: A Study of the Devotional Aspects of 'Āshūrā' in Twelver Shī'ism*, 1978; Werner Ende, "The Flagellations of Muharram and the Shi'ite 'Ulama'", *Der Islam* 55, no. 1 (1978); Jan Hjärpe, "The Ta'ziya Ecstacy as Political Expression," in *Religious Ecstasy*, edited by N. G. Holm, 1982; Wayne R. Husted, "Karbalā' Made Immediate: The Martyr as Model in Imāmī Shī'ism," *The Muslim World* 83, nos. 3–4 (1993); Yitzhak Nakash, "An Attempt to Trace the Origin of the Rituals of *'Āshūrā'*," *Die Welt des Islams* 33 (1993).

RAINER BRUNNER

Karramis

The Karramis (*Karrāmiyya*) were a theological group that flourished in the Iranian province of Khurasan between the 9th and 12th centuries. Their founder, Abu 'Abdallah Muhammad b. Karram (d. 869), achieved fame as an ascetic and fiery preacher. He began preaching his doctrines in his home province of Sistan but was expelled by the local authorities on charges of heresy. Ibn Karram was

eventually accepted in the city of Nishapur, where he gained many converts, most of whom were from the lower classes. Eventually, the school was adopted and patronized by the Ghaznavid dynasty, which built a few madrasas and Sufi lodges (*khānaqāhs*) for the Karramis.

Theologically, the school was very close to the traditionalist Hanbali school (Ibn Karram had been a pupil of Ahmad b. Hanbal [d. 855]). Ibn Karram's teachings have been described by opponent groups as "anthropomorphic," and the group achieved notoriety for their harsh polemics and tactics against more rationalist trends in Islam. They reached the pinnacle of their power in Nishapur in the tenth century but were eventually expelled to the neighboring province of Ghur, where it appears they dwindled into nonexistence.

The Karramis, due to their attitudes toward other groups and their anthropomorphic tendencies, were anathematized by all later authors who mentioned them. It was the Karramis who, during one of their power surges, accused the famous Ash'ari Ibn Furak (d. 1015) of heresy, and it is alleged that they eventually poisoned him. They were also at the forefront of instigating the notorious expulsion of the Ash'aris from Nishapur in 1053. Perhaps the most famous opponent of the Karramis was the Ash'ari theologian Fakhr al-Din al-Razi (d. 1210), who engaged in many public debates with the group and wrote extensively against them.

The Karramis adopted many elements of Hanafi jurisprudence, although it appears they had some unique legal opinions of their own. They stressed a simple lifestyle, shunned excessive worldly pleasures, and prohibited certain forms of economic gain. Despite their prominence, they were unable to leave a lasting intellectual legacy, and only a handful of their works exist in manuscript form in contemporary times.

See also heresiography

Further Reading

Edmund Bosworth, "The Rise of the Karāmiyyah in Khurasan," *The Muslim World* 50, no. 1 (1960); Wilferd Madelung, *Religious Trends in Early Islamic Iran*, 1988; Margaret Malamud, "The Politics of Heresy in Medieval Khurasan: The Karramiyya in Nishapur," *Iranian Studies* 27, nos. 1–4 (1994); Aron Zysow, "Two Unrecognized Karrāmī Texts," *Journal of the American Oriental Society* 108, no. 4 (1988).

YASIR QADHI

Kharijis

The origins of this dissident sect of the Umayyad and early Abbasid periods are generally traced to the First Islamic Civil War (656–61) and in particular to the divisions within 'Ali b. Abi Talib's camp following his acceptance of the Syrian call for arbitration at the Battle of Siffin (657). The name of the sect (those who go out) is frequently associated with the secession of pious elements at Kufa opposed to 'Ali's decision; nevertheless, precisely what was at issue between those first "Kharijis" and 'Ali is hard to pinpoint, and their famous slogan "Judgment belongs only to God" (the so-called *taḥkīm*, from which is derived another name for the sect) may have been born out of wider concerns than merely the arbitration episode. Recent scholarship has understood the name "Khariji" not as deriving from a particular foundational event during 'Ali's caliphate but as a self-designation, possibly drawn from Qur'an 4:100, intended to underscore the link between emigration and militant activism. During the decades that followed the First Civil War, the Khariji movement established itself as one of the principal streams of opposition to Umayyad authority in Iraq, Iran, Jazira, parts of the Arabian Peninsula, and the Maghrib.

Khariji resistance can be found as early as the 660s and 670s among small groups of militants around Kufa and Basra who shared a similar rejectionist stance toward the political establishment in Iraq. Many of these men had a reputation for ascetic piety (excessive prayer, fasting, and night vigils), as well as a particular attachment to scripture. The most fundamental Khariji political ideas were first incubated in this milieu of small, face-to-face groups sharply dissociating from their enemies while convinced of their own exclusive status as the true "People of Paradise." By the 680s, the center of Khariji activity had shifted to Basra, and under the pressure of the Second Civil War, their doctrines were debated and systematized as the movement itself broke into competing subsects.

Two key doctrines distinguished the Kharijis from other Muslims of the time. First, they saw the imamate as an office held on the basis of merit (variously understood as piety, knowledge, or militancy) rather than descent; should an imam lose his superior merit, he must also lose his office. The membership in the tribe of Quraysh shared by the first caliphs of Medina as well as the Umayyads was held to be irrelevant: Abu Bakr and 'Umar b. al-Khattab were both seen as legitimate on the basis of merit; 'Uthman b. 'Affan and 'Ali were both seen to have gone wrong and thus were lawfully removed from office (i.e., assassinated). The Umayyads were seen as illegitimate "imams of error" from the start, and it was up to the believers to take action in order to replace them with more suitable leadership. They held that the community retained the ultimate right to remove its imam. Accordingly, while the Kharijis ascribed both religious and political authority to their imams, they nevertheless granted them unquestioned obedience only insofar as they retained their superior merit. This does something to explain the fissiparous nature of the Khariji movement, which generated numerous subsects. Merit also superseded Arab ethnicity: the imam could be (and in practice sometimes was) a non-Arab, an expression of the ethnic egalitarianism that attracted non-Arabs to the movement from a relatively early period.

Second, all Kharijis judged ordinary Muslims to be infidels, a doctrinal stance known as *takfīr*. Believers were to join up with the true community by leaving the company of infidels in the garrison towns (i.e., performing hijra, or emigration) and actively

establishing their own imamates. When engaging ordinary Muslims in battle, they were to treat them in every respect as the infidels they were: such people could be despoiled of their property, enslaved, and killed indiscriminately (*isti'rāḍ*).

It was the second of these two key doctrines, *takfīr*, that generated differences of opinion and doctrinal systematization among the Kharijis of Basra during the 680s and afterward. Extremists such as the Azariqa and Najadat, active in western Iran and Arabia, maintained the original Khariji insistence on total separation from infidels. They tolerated no intermarriage or inheritance between themselves and ordinary Muslims and insisted on emigration and holy war. (Armchair Kharijis who did not actively seek to establish an imamate were to be considered unbelievers, while those who made hijra would retain their status as "People of Paradise," even if they sinned on occasion.) Others took a more moderate path. Without denying the infidel status of ordinary Muslims, they considered them infidels of a different sort. "Hypocrites" (*munāfiqūn*) was the usual term, or alternatively (and much later) "those who are ungrateful for God's blessings" (*kuffār ni'ma*). Either way, a complete severance of relations was no longer obligatory in all circumstances. The point was to justify coexistence until a resumption of political and military activity was practical. This moderate tendency came to be embodied in the Ibadi sect, the only surviving Khariji group. The more extreme wings of the Khariji movement met with suppression and flared out or, in one notable case, survived for a time by denying the very obligation to have an imam (and hence the need for emigration and holy war by which an imamate could be established). Extremist Kharijism can be found in contemporary times only in the political discourse surrounding certain radical Islamist groups, such as the one called Takfir and Hijra by the Egyptian authorities in the 1970s.

See also 'Ali b. Abi Talib (ca. 599–661); civil war; heresiography; Ibadis; theology

Further Reading

Patricia Crone, *God's Rule: Government and Islam*, 2004; Jeffrey Kenney, *Muslim Rebels: Kharijites and the Politics of Extremism in Egypt*, 2006; Keith Lewinstein, "The Azāriqa in Islamic Heresiography," *Bulletin of the School of Oriental and African Studies* no. 54 (1991); Wilferd Madelung, *Religious Trends in Early Islamic Iran*, 1988; Chase Robinson, *Empire and Elites after the Muslim Conquest*, 2000.

KEITH LEWINSTEIN

Khilafat movement (1919–24)

The short-lived Khilafat movement (from the term *khilāfat*—caliphate) was an agitation by Indian Muslims, allied with the Indian nationalist movement, during the years following World War I. Its purpose was to pressure the British government to preserve the authority of the Ottoman sultan as caliph of Islam. Integral to this was the Muslims' desire to influence the treaty-making process following the war in such a way as to restore the 1914 boundaries of the Ottoman Empire. The British government treated the Indian Khilafat delegation of 1920 as quixotic Pan-Islamists and did not change its policy toward Turkey. The Indian Muslims' attempt to influence the treaty provisions failed, and the European powers went ahead with territorial adjustments, including the institution of mandates over formerly Ottoman Arab territories.

The significance of the Khilafat movement, however, lies less in its supposed Pan-Islamism than in its impact on the Indian nationalist movement. The leaders of the Khilafat movement forged the first political alliance among Western-educated Indian Muslims and 'ulama' (Muslim clerics) over the religious symbol of the caliphate. This leadership included the 'Ali brothers, Muhammad 'Ali (1878–1931) and Shaukat 'Ali (1872–1936), two newspaper editors from Delhi; their spiritual guide Mawlana 'Abd al-Bari (1878–1926) of Firangi Mahal, Lucknow; the Calcutta journalist and Islamic scholar Abu al-Kalam Azad (1888–1958); and Mawlana Mahmud Hasan (1851–1920), head of the madrasa at Deoband, in northern India. These publicist-politicians and 'ulama' viewed European attacks on the authority of the caliph as an attack on Islam and thus as a threat to the religious freedom of Muslims under British rule.

The Khilafat movement crystallized anti-British sentiments among Indian Muslims that had been increasing since the British declaration of war against the Ottomans in 1914. The Khilafat leaders, most of whom had been imprisoned during the war, were already active in the nationalist movement. Upon the release of these leaders in 1919, the Khilafat issue provided a means to achieve pan-Indian Muslim political solidarity in the anti-British cause. The Khilafat movement also benefited from Hindu-Muslim cooperation in the nationalist cause that had grown during the war, beginning with the Lucknow Pact of 1916 between the Indian National Congress and the Muslim League and culminating in the protest against the Rowlatt antisedition bills in 1919. The congress, then led by Mohandas Gandhi (1869–1948), called for nonviolent noncooperation against the British. Gandhi espoused the Khilafat cause, as he saw in it the opportunity to rally Muslim support for the congress. The 'Ali brothers and their allies, in turn, provided the noncooperation movement with some of its most enthusiastic followers. For a time, these Khilafatists supplanted the politics of the Muslim League and its leader, Muhammad 'Ali Jinnah (1876–1948), who opposed the movement.

The combined Khilafat–Noncooperation movement was the first all-India agitation against British rule. It saw an unprecedented degree of Hindu-Muslim cooperation, and it established Gandhi and his technique of nonviolent protest (*satyagraha*) at the center of the Indian nationalist movement. Mass mobilization using religious symbols was remarkably successful, and the British Indian government was shaken. In late 1921, the government moved to suppress the movement and arrested, tried, and imprisoned its leaders.

Gandhi suspended the Noncooperation movement in early 1922. The Turks dealt the final blow to the movement by abolishing the Ottoman sultanate in 1922 and the caliphate in 1924.

See also caliph, caliphate; India; Ottomans (1299–1924); Pan-Islamism

Further Reading

P. C. Bamford, *Histories of the Non-Cooperation and Khilafat Movements*, 1974; Mushirul Hasan, *Nationalism and Communal Politics in India*, 1991; Gail Minault, *The Khilafat Movement: Religious Symbolism and Political Mobilization in India*, 1982; M. Naeem Qureshi, *Pan-Islam in British Indian Politics: A Study of the Khilafat Movement*, 1999.

GAIL MINAULT

Khomeini, Ayatollah (1902–89)

Ruhallah (Ruhollah) Musavi Khumayni (1902–89), usually referred to as Ayatollah or Imam Khomeini, was the leader of the Iranian Revolution of 1979 and an influential theoretician of the Islamic shari'a. He was born to a clerical family in Khumayn, in central Iran. Khomeini's great-grandfather lived in Kashmir, but his family was from Nishapur, in the northeastern province of Khurasan. When Khomeini's father was killed in 1903 in a dispute about irrigation rights with two provincial notables, members of his family, led by his widowed mother and paternal aunt, traveled to Tehran, and after a lengthy and relentless pursuit of the case, the influential culprit was brought to justice in 1905. Resilience and determination in the face of adversity and injustice appeared ingrained in the family.

Khomeini studied jurisprudence in Qum with the leading religious authority of the time, Shaykh 'Abd al-Karim al-Ha'iri (d. 1937), and *'irfān* (Islamic philosophy and mysticism) with Mirza Muhammad 'Ali Shahabadi (d. 1950), a staunch opponent of the Pahlavi dynasty (1925–79). The celebrated encyclopedist and historian Sayyid Muhsin al-Amin (d. 1952) was also one of his teachers.

Unrelenting opposition to the widespread American presence in Iran and the secularizing and state-building efforts of Muhammad Reza Shah Pahlavi (r. 1941–79) led to Khomeini's arrest in 1963. He was sent into exile in 1964, first to Turkey, soon thereafter to Iraq, and finally, in the last months of the Pahlavi dynasty, to France. He returned to Iran on February 12, 1979, having mobilized vast political demonstrations, masterminded the first religious revolution in modern times, and challenged the hegemony of the United States and the Soviet Union and their respective ideologies in the Muslim world and beyond.

With the possible exception of the first ruler of the Safavid dynasty (1501–1722), Isma'il I (r. 1501–24), Khomeini's tenure as leader of the Iranian Revolution marked the single most significant instance of the fusion of political with religious leadership in the country's history. Khomeini's contributions to Islamic political thought as a scholar and politician are conventionally considered in the context of his performance as *rahbar* (leader of the Iranian Revolution) and as the *walī al-faqīh* (guardian-jurist), which tends to subjugate his achievements in political thought to excesses committed by the Iranian government during his tenure in office. Most of his writings, and especially those written after 1979, are prescriptions for problems that he associated with Iran's immediate political malaise. He applied Islamic political precepts to radically modern situations and minimized opposition to his many innovations by adopting a clear-cut populist language and by appearing as an exemplar of austere, unflappable determination, whether in exile or at the helm of power. By resorting to Islamic precepts rooted in the Qur'an itself, in contradistinction to the abject and morally corrupt mayhem that he saw in the country's recent past, he succeeded in establishing his own novel and effective political vocabulary, with which many Iranians found themselves in some sympathy despite their avowed secularism.

Although opposed to the separation of religion from politics, which in his view was a colonialist import and not the sole gateway to good governance, he explicitly exploited the malleability of religious law when politically expedient and proved capable of adopting radical interpretations that went against the grain of centuries of jurisprudential received opinion, thereby substantially broadening the scope of interpretation to exigencies of time and place. In subordinating religious law to national priorities by resorting to the traditional concept of *maṣlaḥa* (in this context loosely defined as national interest), Khomeini transformed modern political discourse in Iran.

The Islamization of public life was an important concern of his after 1979, expressed and enforced through the pivotal concept of *wilāyat al-faqīh* (the guardianship of the jurist), first articulated by him in the 1950s. On the one hand, the principle reaffirms the clergy's claim to the authority of popular sentiment, and on the other hand, it makes Islamic rule and social order impossible outside the tutelage of the clerical profession. According to one of his students, 'Abbas Zaryab Khuyi (1919–95), it was the philosopher-king of Plato's *Republic* that inspired Khomeini's formulation of the *walī al-faqīh*. As legatees of the Prophet through his heir, the Twelfth Imam, in his role as the Mahdi (messiah), the clergy in Khomeini's view represented popular will and exercised just rule in the Imam's absence. Although many Iranians within the country and abroad regard the separation of religion from politics as essential to the welfare of the state and denounce the very concept of *wilāyat al-faqīh* as a self-serving ploy by the clerical establishment, the concept has gained further credence in the early years of the 21st century, as some of its erstwhile detractors now admit to a grudging acceptance of its utility as a necessary bulwark against an increasingly feasible emergence of a military dictatorship. Robust clerical presence in the public sphere, Khomeini warned, was alone capable of curbing Islamic radicalism, terrorism, and the militarization of civilian life. In his testament, Khomeini wrote, "My emphatic counsel to the armed forces is to observe and abide

by the military rule of non-involvement in politics. Stay away from politics and you'll be able to preserve and maintain your military prowess and be immune to internal division and dispute."

Cognizant of the perils of lay Islamism, as exemplified in the teachings of ʿAli Shariʿati (d. 1977), the Egyptian Sayyid Qutb (d. 1966), or more recently Osama bin Laden, Khomeini relied on *wilāyat al-faqīh* to curb the influence of scientistic religiosity and the possibilities it afforded to nonclerics to interpret the shariʿa. Presciently, as early as the 1960s, he warned his Sunni counterparts to occupy a more central role in Islamist politics in the Arab world. This plea for greater involvement was accompanied by his insistence on Muslim solidarity and the need to maintain unity in confronting the non-Muslim world, a view reflected in his fatwa (religious opinion) in 1979, which declared Friday prayers a religiopolitical obligation and, on that line of reasoning, permitted Shiʿis to participate in Friday congregational prayers alongside Sunni Muslims. This was a precursor to the 2008 fatwa by Ayatollah ʿAli Sistani, Iraq's highest-ranking jurist, allowing Shiʿis to participate in all congregational prayers led by Sunni imams and an example of the many ways in which, two decades after his death, Khomeini still retains a towering presence in contemporary religious and political debates.

In line with the plurality of authority that defines the nonhierarchical essence of Islamic religious infrastructure, and in a similar manner to constitutions of the United States and many European nations, Khomeini established a political system based on power sharing and exchange between the exigencies of governance and ideology. The supreme leader is selected by the 86 elected members of the Assembly of Experts, who serve for eight-year terms and have the authority to remove him from power. The Council of Guardians, whose six clerical members and six lay jurists are appointed by the supreme leader and parliament (*majlis*), respectively, has the authority to veto any legislation deemed contrary to Iran's constitution and the dictates of Islam and to screen all candidates for the Assembly of Experts, presidency, and parliament. Resolving the disputes between Iran's parliament and the Council of Guardians is left to the Expediency Council, the main venue for the resolution of potential conflicts between religious and secular legislation. The Expediency Council is also the institutional articulation of Iran's national priorities that will trump both the precepts of religious law and the partisanship along party lines that has defined the country's elected legislature.

A degree of pragmatism can be detected in Khomeini's views on the participation of women in public life, at least in the postrevolutionary period. While women were forced to conform to Islamic norms by covering their hair and donning *manteaux* (long coats), their rights to vote, run for parliament, and serve as cabinet ministers and lawyers were not taken away from them. In time, they were also allowed to serve as "advisors" to judges, circumventing the shariʿa's ban on women judges. By the first decade of the 21st century, women students outnumbered men in Iran's institutions of higher education.

See also ayatollah; guardianship of the jurist; Iran; revolutions

Further Reading

Hamid Algar, *Roots of the Islamic Revolution in Iran*, 2001; Ruhollah Khomeini, *Clarification of Questions: An Unabridged Translation of "Resaleh Towzih al-Masael,"* translated by J. Borujerdi, 1984; Idem, *Islam and Revolution, Vol. I, Writings and Declarations of Imam Khomeini, 1941–1980*, translated and annotated by Hamid Algar, 1981; ʿAbbas Zaryab Khuyi, *Maqalat-i Zaryab: 32 Justar dar Mawduʿat-i Gunagun bi-Damima-yi Zindiginama-yi Khudnivisht*, 2010; Parvin Paidar, *Women and the Political Process in Twentieth-Century Iran*, 1997; Larry Ray, "'Fundamentalism,' Modernity and the New Jacobins," *Economy and Society* 28, no. 2 (1999); Asghar Schirazi, *Constitution of Iran: Politics and the State in the Islamic Republic*, 1997; Richard Tapper, ed., *Ayatollah Khomeini and the Modernization of Islamic Political Thought*, 2000.

NEGUIN YAVARI

Khunji, Fazl Allah b. Ruzbihan (1455–1521)

Commonly called Khwaja Mawlana Isfahani and a member of the famous Ruzbihan family, Khunji was a prominent hadith authority, Shafiʿi jurist, litterateur, and historian at the Aq Quyunlu and Uzbek courts; he is also the author of works on theology and Sufism, as well as the *Suluk al-Muluk* (The conduct of kings), an important work on political theory. He is primarily known as an ardent and outspoken Sunni; the defining event of his life was the usurpation of Iran by Shah Ismaʿil I (r. 1501–24) and its transformation into a Shiʿi state. Khunji fled to Transoxiana and spent the remainder of his career urging his Uzbek and Ottoman patrons to purge his homeland of Ismaʿil, whom he viewed as a heretic, and Ismaʿil's extremist Turkmen horde, called the Qizilbash, or Redheads, because of their distinctive red headgear.

Apart from an invariably polemical posture in his writings, Khunji is responsible for the well-known refutation of the *Nahj al-Haqq wa-Kashf al-Sidq* (The path of truth and the exposition of righteousness) of ʿAllama Hilli (d. 1325), the preeminent Shiʿi theologian of the Ilkhanid period, titled *Ibtal Nahj al-Batil wa-Ihmal Kashf al-ʿAtil* (Refutation of the path of falsehood and deflection of the exposition of the specious). His central argument here and elsewhere is that the impeccable members of the House of the Prophet (*ahl al-bayt*) cannot be truly revered when one is consumed with hatred of the Companions of the Prophet, and he includes verses in praise of the imams to demonstrate his own veneration for them. His *Refutation* was refuted in turn a century later by Qadi Nur Allah Shushtari (d. 1610), judge of Lahore under Emperor Akbar, as well as, more recently, by Imam al-Hasan al-Muzaffar (d. 1955) in his work *Dala'il al-Sidq li-Nahj al-Haqq* (Proof of the correctness of the path of truth). Khunji's strident anti-Shiʿi views became somewhat tempered toward the end of his life, when it was evident that the Safavid state (1501–1722) would be no transitory phenomenon.

Khunji's status as one of the most important voices in Sunni-Shi'i polemics has tended to obscure the general erudition and breadth of his scholarship, including his political thought as formulated in the *Suluk al-Muluk*. Written in Persian in 1514 at the request of 'Ubaydallah Khan (r. 1535–39), his Uzbek patron after the death of Muhammad Shaybani Khan (r. 1500–10), the *Suluk* is a practical manual of government synthesizing two genres, that of jurisprudential (*fiqh*) works focused on the shari'a-state relationship and the hortative and sapiential style of Mirrors for Princes. It addresses the standard legal concerns from both Shafi'i and Hanafi perspectives and draws extensively on Mawardi (d. 1058), chief judge of Baghdad, and Ghazali (d. 1111), author of the seminal *Ihya' 'Ulum al-Din* (The revival of the religious sciences); it also shows the influence of the rational political philosophy of Jalal al-Din Dawani (d. 1502), author of the *Akhlaq-i Jalali* (The Jalalian ethics), with whom Khunji studied in his native Shiraz.

The *Suluk al-Muluk* reflects the author's central concern to protect the shari'a and restore orthodoxy, and it is clearly conceived as an updated and impassioned Sunni response to the fledgling Safavid Imami system of government. It contests the Shi'i position that religiolegal authority derives solely from the spiritual stature and lineage of the ruler by reasserting the standard Sunni position (held by, for example, Badr al-Din Muhammad b. Jama'a [d. 1333], the chief judge of Egypt under the Mamluks) that military force alone qualifies one to act as ruler, termed here as imam and sultan-caliph. Indeed, even a tyrannical usurper enjoys legitimate authority if he is able to consolidate his power through violent means. In the postcaliphal period inaugurated by the Mongol sack of Baghdad in 1258, Khunji, following Dawani and Fakhr al-Din al-Razi (d. 1209), considered any ruler of a Sunni polity to be caliph, or deputy of the Prophet. To achieve righteous government, Khunji held that the ruler should ideally be an administrator (*mudabbir*) whose main function is to apply the shari'a, while his authority should derive solely from his ability to enforce obedience; all members of government are considered his deputies.

As a prominent reformulation of Sunni political thought, Khunji's manual of government represents a sophisticated attempt to harmonize the norms of the shari'a with the prevailing non-Islamic realities of Turco-Mongol nomadic tribal confederations. His specific contributions to the development of Sunni political theory include his strong reassertion that all political power is centered in the sultan-caliph, regardless of personal character and lineage, and his recognition of the legality of taxes not provided for by the shari'a (such as the Mongol *ṭamghā* or customs impost), since they are necessary to ensure the functioning of the state—a stance that counters the common pietistic position that condemned latter-day rulers to permanent illegality. Khunji's works were widely studied in Central Asia and perhaps in Mughal India, but due to the increasing isolation of Transoxiana it appears they had little influence in the central Sunni lands.

See also caliph, caliphate; Dawani, Jalal al-Din (1427–1502); Ghazali (ca. 1058–1111); imamate; Isma'il I (1487–1524); Mawardi (974–1058); Mirrors for Princes; al-Razi, Fakhr al-Din (1149–1209); Safavids (1501–1722); shari'a; Shi'ism; sultan; Sunnism

Further Reading

Muhammad Aslam, trans., *Muslim Conduct of State: Based upon the Sulūk-ul-Mulūk of Faḍl-ullah bin Rūzbihān Iṣfahāni*, 1974; Anthony Black, "The Decline of Classical Islamic Political Thought," in *The History of Islamic Political Thought*, 2001; Ulrich Haarmann, "Yeomanly Arrogance and Righteous Rule: Fażl Allāh ibn Rūzbihān Khunjī and the Mamluks of Egypt," in *Iran and Iranian Studies: Essays in Honor of Iraj Afshar*, edited by Kambiz Eslami, 1998; Ann K. S. Lambton, "The *Imām*/Sultan: Faḍl Allāh b. Rūzbihān Khunjī," in *State and Government in Medieval Islam: An Introduction to the Study of Islamic Political Theory: The Jurists*, 1981.

MATTHEW MELVIN-KOUSHKI

kinship

It is impossible to overestimate the importance of kinship and ancestry to the history and culture of the Middle East. The traditional social order throughout the region was based directly on kinship, which remains the predominant mode for understanding and ordering the world. Only some of the implications of kinship for the evolution and organization of political life can be covered here.

With one exception (the matrilineal Tuareg people, who trace their descent through female ancestors), lineage in the Middle East is strictly patrilineal: individuals trace their genealogies solely through the male line. Patrilineages vary in size and in the degree of commitment they demand from their members, but in general they are collectives that retain and protect group rights to farmland, grazing land, or other entitlements. Even private property can be restricted by family ties; for instance, a man may be obliged to give his close relatives first bid if he wishes to sell his land. In cities, too, guilds, street gangs, and Sufis use the idiom of kinship (both real and fictive) to bind themselves together in self-contained and almost self-governing groups of putative "brothers."

Patrilineality in the Middle East is expressed in kinship terms that systematically differentiate between paternal and maternal lines. A mother's brothers are distinguished from the father's brothers, as are cousins on the father's side and the mother's side. There is also a strong tendency toward patrilocality: men are expected to remain in the village, quarter, camp, or house of their patrilineage: wives move to be with their husbands and not the other way around. Brides are kept near home by the common preference for men to marry the daughters of their father's brothers. This is referred to as marriage "close to the bone." Another typical feature of most of the kinship systems of the Middle East is the absence of any

terminological recognition of ranking of siblings, so that there is no linguistic differentiation of elder and younger. This coincides with an egalitarian system of inheritance and the absence of primogeniture, where the first-born son holds the place of privilege. As a result, when a ruler dies, he usually is succeeded by one of his brothers, not by his eldest son.

Traditionally, tribal political rivalries and alliances were based on a flexible pattern of complementary opposition among patrilateral kin, varying according to genealogical distance. Men were expected to side with their closer blood relatives against those more distant and to share the responsibilities and obligations of blood revenge according to the degree of "closeness." Thus, in the oft-quoted axiom "I against my brothers; my brothers and I against our cousins; my brothers, my cousins, and I against the world," the cousins in question were patrilateral. This neat picture of lineage-based segmentation was complicated by strategic alliances based on the ancient principle that "the enemy of my enemy is my friend," which led to a dual system of opportunistic factional blocs, such as the *liff* of the Berbers, that cut across lineage units. However, these blocs, while politically important in ordinary life, did not supersede blood ties or obligations.

The first theorist to analyze the pervasive political significance of kinship in the Middle East was the 14th-century North African scribe, judge, and scholar Ibn Khaldun (1332–1406), who argued that Bedouin tribesmen were characterized by their strong ties of *'aṣabiyya*, or "group feeling," a result of their common patrilineal descent. According to Ibn Khaldun, tribal leaders were "first among equals," chosen by consultation among their peers. United by their group feeling, the Bedouin could conquer centralized regimes, but inevitably the new ruler would then be tempted to marginalize and subdue his previously equal lineage mates, replacing them with compliant slaves and clients. Over four generations, this policy, while increasing the authority of the center, undermined tribal *'aṣabiyya*, leaving the state susceptible to conquest by a new wave of warriors bound together by their empowering ideology of shared blood.

The relationships and attitudes promoted by the kin-based ideology of *'aṣabiyya* thus coincided with a moral environment where authority was *achieved* by competition among coequal kinsmen, not *ascribed* to supposedly innate superiors, and where rulers were treated with no great awe or obeisance. Such a debunking ethic delegitimated relations of hierarchy and command and coincided with the relatively rapid rise and fall of dynasties in the Middle East, where no lineage had any intrinsic right to authority. To overcome factionalism, religious leaders often sought to supersede lineage allegiances under the flag of the faith. In this, they were inspired by the example of Muhammad, who proclaimed that piety, not blood, would determine authority in the encompassing womb of Islam. However, this ideal was not realized even in Muhammad's own time, when some of the elite members of Muhammad's own lineage (the Quraysh) jealously opposed diminution of their prestige.

The typical Arabic patterns of inheritance and terminology contrast with the Central Asian and Turkic kinship systems in which seniority among siblings is always terminologically marked so that lineages descended from the eldest son are ranked above those descended from younger sons in a ramifying hierarchical array. This system was imported into the Middle East by the Seljuqs, the Qajars, and, most importantly, the Ottomans, whose long-lived regime repudiates Ibn Khaldun's portrait of rapidly eroding imperiums. There are many reasons for Ottoman longevity, but one is the legitimation of authority implicit within its ranked kinship structure. As a result, the right of the Osmanli line (the lineage of the sultans) to rule was rarely challenged by lesser lineages. Rather, the sons of the sultan contested violently for the throne among themselves, with the victor putting his brothers to death or blinding them. But despite internal struggles over succession, it was nonetheless taken for granted that sovereignty was the natural prerogative of the Osmanli lineage. This assumption was at odds with the prevalent pattern in the Arabic world, where rivals unwilling to ascribe innate superiority to any sultan contested secular authority. Unstinting submission, in this system, could only be granted to those whose loyalty was solely to God. The family system of Arabia, it seems, favored the rise of prophets, while that of Central Asia favored the coronation of kings.

See also genealogy; honor; Ibn Khaldun (1332–1406); solidarity; tribalism

Further Reading

Jean Cuisenier, *Economie et Parente: Leurs affinites de structure dans le domaine turc et dans le domaine arabe*, 1975; Ibn Khaldun, *The Muqaddimah*, translated by F. Rosenthal, 1967; Charles Lindholm, "Kinship Structure and Political Authority: The Middle East and Central Asia," *Comparative Studies in Society and History* 28, no. 3 (1986).

CHARLES LINDHOLM

knowledge

Knowledge is information about the nature of existence, and such information, when true, provides guidance for human decision making in both private and public matters. Decision making, in principle, is led by true knowledge, and in Islam this means religious knowledge as derived from divine guidance, communicated in God's speech (the Qur'an) and embodied in the precedent (sunna) of the Prophet Muhammad. In addition, since these sources do not speak to every aspect of life, Muslim scholars have devised other means by which to issue rulings for emergent situations. These include communal consensus on an issue, possible comparison of a new situation to a past ruling, local custom if deemed good, and a host of principles that scholars have culled from the religious heritage over the centuries. The recognition of multiple sources of knowledge has given Islam a healthy degree of flexibility by which to adapt to changing patterns of history.

The worth of religious knowledge to the well-being of human society, however, has always been contested in some form. Its truth depends in part on its relevance alongside other kinds of knowledge, including not only secular knowledge obtained by human efforts, such as philosophical and scientific claims, but also "spiritual knowledge" that saintly figures claim to receive from the other world via special inspiration. Such alternatives often work in tandem with religious knowledge but can also challenge it. Central to the politics of religious knowledge is the effort to defend its value as divine guidance for the world. This can happen by a willingness to die in defense of it, skill in persuading others of it by reasoned argument, the use of force to enthrone it as emblem of national sovereignty, or the personal struggle to display a noble character as evidence of its impact on one's soul.

A number of studies call attention to the role of religious knowledge as an organizing agent of Muslim society, the corresponding social prestige of those who possess it, and the loss of this prestige when secular knowledge overtakes religious knowledge as the predominant agent of decision making. Knowledge is vital to public order, and the acquisition of culturally valued knowledge can bring status, but for knowledge to be acted upon, it must hold true. The impact of religious knowledge on public life is therefore a question not only of its prestige and power but also of its credibility as source of moral guidance for society. Is it demonstrably true?

Traditionally, for example, a statement of the Prophet is considered true if it can be reliably traced back via a sound chain of transmitters to its prophetic origin. In contrast, the truth of other kinds of knowledge, such as knowledge of geometry or politics, does not depend on a chain of transmission; its truth does not depend on a prophetic origin but on its rationality. Thus the force of religious knowledge for Muslim society is not simply a function of the prestige of those who have mastered it but because it is understood to be demonstrably true by examination of its transmission from the Messenger of God. The prophetic origins of knowledge verify its status as divine truth, making it a worthy guide. It is therefore essential to transmit religious knowledge from one generation to the next to ensure that society is in proper relation with God's will. Within this traditional conceptualization of religious knowledge, those who memorize and reproduce it are notable in society as guarantors of a life in conformity to truth as communicated by God.

This role, however, is considerably diminished when the truth claims of religious knowledge lose credibility in the face of other forms of knowledge that do not require a prophetic origin for their credibility. Religious knowledge in Islam has always had its competitors, but the advent of European rule in Muslim lands brought a profound and pervasive challenge to the truths of Islam. Not only did the ascendancy of European forms of knowledge marginalize the prestige of religious learning, but it also introduced critical analysis—apart from sound transmission—as the ultimate arbiter of truth claims, including those of religion. To be credible, religious knowledge had to hold up to human methods of verification. Thus the increasing irrelevancy of religious knowledge in its traditional form is a question not primarily of the loss of power and prestige on the part of religious authorities but rather of the acceptance of new standards for determining true and useful knoweldge.

This development did not spell the end of religious knowledge (and its ascendancy today in some circles is partly due to the failure of secular knowledge to live up to its own quasi-utopian claims) but rather its transference to epistemological terrain where demonstrable worth to human society, not sound transmission, has become the leading criterion of true knowledge. This has had the effect of greatly expanding the scope of religious knowledge. In traditional form, it is limited to select domains of life, notably ritual and moral affairs that correspond to the information transmitted from the Prophet. Since, however, the veracity of knowledge now depends largely on its demonstrable worth to society, it has become necessary to show that religious knowledge applies to all aspects of human society, including economic and political affairs. Only then, it is thought, can it continue to enjoy the status of truth.

The traditional conceptualization of religious knowledge continues to hold strong, but an alternative form, unbounded by a chain of transmission, now exists alongside it. Religious knowledge is therefore not limited to a traditional sphere but competes in all spheres of life. Indeed, some see it as source of solutions for all questions, political and economic no less then ritual and moral. The association of religious knowledge with secular criteria for determining truth has led reformists, seeking to maintain the veracity of religious knowledge in a secular age, to turn traditionally nonreligious branches of knowledge into religious knowledge, notably economics and politics. Religious knowledge is now presented as a total system of life (economics and politics as well as rituals and morals), requiring the Islamization of all knowledge. As a result, the testing ground for religious knowledge is not only the scholarly domain but also the political one.

Defining the Scope of Religious Knowledge

This "modernist" trend can result in the loss of the sacred whereby religious knowledge is judged according to its secular comprehensibility rather than as divine decree. One example is the Iranian intellectual Abdolkarim Soroush (b. 1945). Soroush challenges the political claims of Shi'i authorities as custodians of religious knowledge. By arguing for the ever-changing nature of religious knowledge, Soroush is able to contend that those trained in traditional forms of religious knowledge have no monopoly over religious knowledge and thus no special privilege to rule. This casts considerable ambiguity on the nature of religious knowledge, however, making it difficult to distinguish it from secular knowledge. A second example is Sayyid Qutb (d. 1966), the revolutionary voice of Egypt's Muslim Brotherhood. He, like Soroush, views religious and secular knowledge through a single lens. The difference is that Qutb makes the Qur'an a litmus test for all knowledge, whereas Soroush subjects all knowledge, including religious knowledge, to historical (i.e., secular) processes. Qutb thus makes God's voice the exclusive agent of political life no less than ritual life. These modernist trends, whether secularizing or

Islamizing, have had enormous impact on Muslim views of religious knowledge, but traditional approaches continue to be re-created. For example, Mohammed Shabestari (b. 1936) of Iran rejects a secular conceptualization of religious knowledge, as implied by Soroush, in order to preserve its sacred character, but in contrast to Qutb, he acknowledges the traditional limits of religious knowledge. Religious knowledge, as revealed by God, is necessary for humans to be "in relation" with God, but it is not the ideal material from which to build a political system.

A range of terms in Islam refer to knowledge and the varied methods of accessing it, but *'ilm* has its widest scope in signifiying the concept of "knowledge." The Qur'an is clear that all knowledge comes from God (e.g., 2:32), but this does not make knowledge a simple phenomenon, since God's signs are apparent in creation as well as in revealed verses. Indeed, God bestows knowledge by both scripture and wisdom (e.g., Q. 2:251, 4:113, 5:110). The Qur'anic term for "wisdom" (*ḥikma*) would eventually be identified with philosophy, making it possible to integrate nonrevealed forms of knowledge into the arena of religion. Indeed, the intimate relation of secular and religious knowledge has arguably been the driver of Islam as a civilization, both past and present. As a well-known saying of the Prophet puts it, wisdom is the lost possession of the believer, who can claim it wherever he finds it.

Traditionally, religious knowledge is silent on the constitution of rule. While Islam deals with matters related to both religion (*dīn*) and the world (*dunyā*), its knowledge does not extend to the state (*dawla*). The idea that Islam refers to both religion and state (*dīn wa-dawla*) is a new construction. Traditionally, rule, even if necessary to the purposes of religion, was not seen as essential to religion (although for the Shi'a, communal leadership, *imāma*, which has sometimes been conceived in terms of political power, is essential to religion). Thus even if Islam has much to say about public behavior, the structures and methods of governance have not been determined in advance by God.

Still, the political sphere is often the site for the intersection of religious and secular knowledge. The Qur'an calls for justice and prosperity as opposed to corruption on Earth but does not specify the means for achieving righteous rule in this world. The Prophet Muhammad acted not only as messenger of God and lawgiver but also as a governor in Medina who arbitrated local disputes, offering a precedent for rule in Islam (and perhaps even for rule by Islam). But the decision to develop institutions of governance under a central authority came from communal consensus and not revealed decree.

However, some, such as Farid al-Ansari (1960–2009) of Morocco, argued that while Islam never defined the state, its well-being does depend on the existence of a political system to enforce its teachings. That is, God's decrees as set out in shari'a in relation to certain crimes (e.g., adultery, alcohol consumption, slander, theft, and brigandage), family affairs (e.g., marriage, divorce, and inheritance), or commercial and financial matters (e.g., prohibition of usury and deceptive business practices) assume the backing of a state. Rule, even if not essentially religious, is still necessary to bring about a society in which God's decrees prevail.

In contrast to this traditional outlook, some (but by no means all) intellectuals associated with Islamism do make rule on Earth a part of the revealed order. For example, Mawdudi (d. 1979), a pioneer of Islamism, conflated God's rulings (*aḥkām*, i.e., a legal phenomenon) with the executive branch of government (*ḥukūma*, i.e., a political phenomenon) in a formula known as divine sovereignty (*ḥākimiyya*). Others, such as Qutb and Ayatollah Khomeini (d. 1989), inspired in part by Mawdudi, offered their own versions of religious rule. To define rule as a specifically religious entity, figures such as Hasan al-Turabi (b. 1932) of the Sudan, building on Mawdudi's concept of theodemocracy, associated shari'a procedures (i.e., jurisprudential concepts) such as interpretation (*ijtihād*) and consensus (*ijmā'*) with the democratic concepts of voting and popular will, respectively.

In general, however, Islam does not classify rule as part of religious knowledge. Those in power, rulers, are expected to be politically astute, using human wisdom and secular means (e.g., tax collection, security forces, public works, military organization, and diplomatic relations with foreign powers) to preserve the worldly interests of Muslims. While not religious authorities themselves, rulers are expected to support the religious institutions that help Muslims achieve their heavenly interests by teaching them the ritual and moral obligations owed to God and to others—and exhorting them to undertake them. In turn, this ethical formation of individuals and communities is seen to contribute to the well-being of the polity, making religion a pillar of prosperous rule, as argued by Mawardi (d. 1058) in his various ethical treatises. Thus rule in Islam is seen as a worldly entity that is dependent on secular knowledge for its proper functioning while indirectly supporting the goals of religious knowledge insofar as it establishes the sociopolitical conditions necessary for them to be lived out. The well-known adage that rule and religion are twins epitomizes this. That is, even if they are not the same, they go together, working in complementary fashion for the well-being of the *umma* (community of believers).

Traditional recognition of the limited nature of religious knowledge has meant that secular forms of knowledge have a place in the political heritage of Islam. This is not to suggest religious affirmation of secularism as a total way of life but rather religious appreciation of worldly wisdom in securing just and prosperous rule. A tenth-century work by Qudama b. Ja'far (d. 948), a high-ranking servitor in the administrative corps of the Abbasid caliphate, shows the range of knowledge that informed Islam's views of governance: Muslims did not hesitate to adopt standards of rule from their imperial predecessors, both Sasanian (r. 3rd to 7th century) and Byzantine (r. 4th to 15th century). Indeed, in this work, governance (*siyāsa*) constitutes its own branch of knowledge, weaving together Persian notions of strong rule, Greco-Hellenistic theories of a political community and philosophical-based ideas about the ethics of the ruler (*akhlāq al-malik*), and a system of bureaucratic institutions consciously built on the Sasanian and Byzantine past as well as the

historical experiences of Muslims as rulers of vast domains stretching from Andalusia to Central Asia. This hardly implies dynastic neglect of shari'a. Qudama not only assumes it in general but also mentions it as a source of knowledge for determining some matters of governmental importance—for example, penalties for certain crimes and principles for assessing the land tax (based in theory on the manner in which land was conquered by the first Muslims, i.e., by force or by peaceful capitulation).

This "religio-secular" character of rule in Islam, blurring the lines between religious and secular knowledge, marks the thinking of a major figure of classical Islam, Mawardi. In the diverse genres in which he wrote—jurisprudence, rule and public administration, and political advice—he combines religious and secular sources of knowledge into a single framework of rule. Indeed, for Mawardi, three sets of "rules" are at work in the formation of Muslim society: divine law, public law, and natural law. Divine law refers to the revealed rules of shari'a that regulate the moral life of Muslim society; public law refers to the administrative rules that regulate its governing institutions and the relations between rulers and ruled; and natural law refers to the rules that explain why political communities naturally come into existence in the first place. All are needed to fulfill the Qur'anic exhortation to pursue prosperity (*salāḥ*) over corruption (*fasād*).

Appreciation for the complex nature of rule in Islam, based on multiple sources of knowledge, continues in diverse ways in contemporary Islam. Morocco's Party of Justice and Development (PJD), for example, considers the common good to be a divine mandate but also believes that the means to achieve it cannot be gleaned from specific religious knowledge. Rather, a just and prosperous administration requires careful policy planning based on exact study of the country's actual conditions: The party's 2007 electoral program contained no religious sloganeering whatsoever, in contrast to the well-known motto of the Muslim Brotherhood that "Islam is the solution." Rather, the PJD limited itself to technical proposals aimed at developing national prosperity.

The PJD emerged from a leading Islamist movement in Morocco, Monotheism and Reform (Harakat al-Tawhid wa-l-Islah), a group that has periodically reassessed its place in a nation marked by diversity of religious sentiment even if officially committed to Malikism, a single branch of Sunni Islam. The king is known as the Commander of the Faithful and has final authority over the nation's religious arena, which he manages through a ministry of religious affairs. Extending from this ministry is a network of councils of religious knowledge (*majālis al-'ilm*) that handle the administrative documentation of such personal affairs as marriage and divorce. Monotheism and Reform, along with its political wing (PJD), recognizes the religious authority of the king (although one of its leading figures, Ahmad al-Raysuni, challenged the monarchy's monopoly over issuing fatwas [religious opinions]). Thus, in contrast to the Muslim Brotherhood in Egypt, this group has no need to seek to establish a religious polity, which is fulfilled in the person of the king who is both head of state and, as descendant of the Prophet, head of the religion. However, Monotheism and Reform works to fill a gap in society left by the transformation of traditional religious authorities into state bureaucrats. Its declared aim is to preserve the religious and moral character of Moroccan society in the face of secularizing forces.

The goal, then, is to establish religion (*iqāmat al-dīn*) in society in the sense of civilization (and not simply doctrines, etc.). At the same time, Monotheism and Reform acknowledges that a simple appeal to tradition is ineffective in today's world. Thus, as articulated by a leading member, Muhammad al-Hamdawi (b. 1957), its message is one of service (*khidma*) to society. It does work through various channels, missionary and educational (*da'wa wa-tarbiya*) as well as electoral politics, but it is hardly totalitarian. Religious knowledge is to be represented on all levels of society. It has moral import, giving it worth to society. The touchstone of its worth, however, is not a predetermined set of rulings traceable to a prophetic origin but rather its ability to be of service to society in the face of the many challenges of modern life. Islam in this sense is as much about a national future as a national past. Here, religious knowledge anchors the ethical reform of society as the key element of its overall health as a civilization.

Another nuance on Islam's view of secular power is found in Yusuf al-Qaradawi (b. 1926), a leading Sunni authority in both the Arab and European contexts. He is unfavorably disposed to secularism but, in contrast to al-Qaeda, refuses to condemn rule that does not fully implement what God has revealed as shari'a. This is signaled in his willingness to refer to kings and presidents, in other words, secular rulers, not as agents of idolatry (*ṭawāghīt*), which is how al-Qaeda defines them, but as sultans, a traditional category defining potentates whose rule is not religiously perfect in its application of shari'a but who do not "wage war" against Muslim society, for example by preventing believers from performing their duties to God. Such rulers would be subject to removal as obstacle to the *umma*'s fulfillment of its covenant with God.

A final example involves the shape of law in many Arab nations that were once part of the Ottoman Empire, such as Egypt, Jordan, and Syria. The laws of these nations have developed in response to colonial and postcolonial realities, but they also retain considerable material from the Hanafi branch of Islam once dominant under Ottoman rule. The figure who made this possible is 'Abd al-Razzaq al-Sanhuri (d. 1971), architect of the 1949 Egyptian Civil Code (as well as other Arab constitutions), who worked to harmonize Egyptian laws with both Islam and international standards of justice. Indeed, many countries in the contemporary Middle East have constitutions that recognize both secular norms of rule (e.g., parliamentarianism) and shari'a as source of national legislation. In Egypt, which is governed by a presidential system, shari'a is enshrined in the nation's constitution as the chief source of legislation, and a high constitutional court has the task of ensuring that no law is made that contradicts shari'a.

The Religious Value of Secular Reality

Key to the relation of Islam to modern society is the religious evaluation of secular knowledge. Is it, too, part of God's plan? One can

speak of two trends here: one that sees religious knowledge as the singular source of communal identity, setting Islam apart from the world, and another that sees religious knowledge as the platform for positive religious engagement with the world. The first case is illustrated by ascendant forms of Islam in South Asia such as Deobandism and Tablighism (as well as the Taliban, a more militant brand of Deobandism).

These trends are by no means the sole representatives of Islam in South Asia, where devotion to past saints as intercessory figures continues to feature alongside devotion to living saints as spiritual guides and even mediators of divine favor. However, partly in response to British rule that categorized its Indian subjects according to religion, powerful reformist movements emerged in the 19th and 20th centuries that elevated the importance of religious identity in opposition to secularism, associated first with British rule and then with the nascent Indian nation-state, which, even if independent, would be dominated by the Hindu majority. In both cases, Islam's way of life was left without rule to back it.

Loss of political power thus contributed to a Muslim sense of being strangers in Indian society, leading them to dismiss the worth of secular ways that were not identifiable with rule by Islam. If a clear identity was not spelled out for Muslim life, the cultural ways of India, it was felt, would adulterate the pristine body of religious knowledge defining true religion. Indeed, the appearance of innovations (*bidā'*) would jeopardize the purity of religious knowledge that specified actions pleasing to God. Mawdudi was a key player here. He had deep anxieties about secularism and felt the only way to defend Islam against it was through some type of political autonomy for Muslims to establish shari'a. As a first step, he founded in 1941, already before the partition of British India in 1947, a group for the purposes of religious activism, called Jama'at-i Islami (The Islamic Group). The goal was to restore the status of Islam that in his view had been humiliated by secular powers. His group worked to animate the religious consciousness of Muslims, but with the establishment of Pakistan, it turned its attention to politics, advancing its view of Pakistan as a nation under divine sovereignty. Its success at the polls was limited, but it exerted considerable influence behind the scenes and did much to create expectations of rule in the image of God. This contributed to the blurring of lines in Pakistan between religion and power, indeed military power. Mawdudi's group was closely associated with the dictatorship of Zia-ul-Haq (r. 1977–88) and his Islamizing policies. The presence of Jama'at-i Islami throughout South Asia has varied from one country to the next. In Pakistan it has oscillated between political participation as means to power and withdrawal from democratic processes to preserve its religious integrity from being compromised by secular ways. It strongly condemned the nation's failure to implement shari'a fully as an offense to religion.

Other groups also tend to think of religious knowledge in terms of communal identity but do not concern themselves with politics. Deobandism, with a network of madrasas (Muslim schools) across South Asia, does recognize traditional religious authorities as keepers of shari'a but looks askance at political power that does not outwardly conform to Islam, seeking instead to form alternative societies circumscribed by religious knowledge. Deobandism is locked in a polemical discourse with another reformist movement, Barelwism, which also operates a network of madrasas (rooted, like Deobandism, in the Hanafi branch of Sunni Islam) but diverges from Deobandism in its commitment to saints, both living and dead, without whom the ordinary believer would not enjoy full access to God. For Deobandism, divine favor is earned not by the mediation of human figures, no matter how saintly, but by a body of knowledge set apart from the tarnish of secular thought—namely, the corpus of reports that describe the life of the Prophet, who was undeniably pleasing to God. By modeling their actions after his, believers at large can also be assured of leading lives pleasing to God. Deobandism does acknowledge saintly figures, whose example can be ethically edifying for others, but rejects the idea that devotion to a saint is necessary to maintain one's religious integrity.

By emphasizing a closed corpus of religious knowledge as singular source of communal identity, Deobandism illustrates how Islam can assume a hostile stance toward local culture. The Taliban, after all, represent one of its offshoots. In its desire to protect a religious identity against "secularizing" influences, Deobandism encouraged communal identity through the study of prophetic reports, reducing Islam to a separate culture based exclusively on shari'a. This can also be seen in the devotional movement associated with Deobandism, known as Tablighi Jama'at (TJ), with a global mission dedicated to the revival of religious identity at a popular level. It is "modern" in the sense of encouraging all believers to take responsibility for Islam but "antimodern" in its disdain for secular reality. Spiritual charisma is embodied in the devotional group as a whole rather than a single saintly individual. TJ thus democratizes spiritual authority but adheres to the teachings of traditional religious authorities when it comes to shari'a rulings. It encourages devotion to the ritual practices of Islam while cultivating an inward-looking ethical character focused on the particulars of the Muslim way of life. Its central activity is collective reading of common texts that focus on the lives of the first Muslims. As a result, the virtues it cultivates in believers make sense only when manifestly conforming to the reported behavior of the Companions of the Prophet. TJ does not look to a chain of saints that extends the narrative of Islam to subsequent generations. As a result, its religious narrative is historically limited to the time of the Prophet and his Companions. This fosters a sense of existential separation from the contemporary world. The goal of religion, according to TJ, is not to serve the world but rather to promote religious identity. For this reason, conduct that imitates the minute details of the first Muslims—how they ate, laughed, bathed—is greatly esteemed. Islam is restored to the world not by political but by ritual means (i.e., by imitation of a sacred past, not by the establishment of a religious state). The goal is to accumulate heavenly merit through religiously identifiable acts, not sociopolitical ones.

TJ's negative view of this world recalls jihadism, but TJ aspires to the rule of God in the next world and does not seek to inaugurate

it in this one. The intense focus on heavenly reward is not always satisfying: TJ-inspired experience can lead to jihadist activity when individuals seek a more political expression of TJ-inspired otherworldliness. But the official TJ view of jihad is missionary activity, not fighting. Its members go on tours, locally and globally, with no concern for concepts of nationhood, using the world's mosques as entry points into the ritual lives of Muslims. While the world's secular identity has made it displeasing to God, attacking it is not the way to restore Islam and assert its supremacy over the world. The goal, rather, is to separate from it through a group experience that allows one to live in a time, the time of the Prophet, when religion prevailed over worldliness, in order to ensure a favorable place in the hereafter. Having turned its back on the political heritage of Islam, TJ shares al-Qaeda's antipolitical stance but rejects the idea of religious action for worldly objectives. It aims to revive Islam by enlivening the religious identity of Muslim youth, not by sending them to death in battle against infidels.

TJ's disinterest in the world can indirectly encourage secularism, since it holds that the world is essentially worthless and can therefore be left to its own devices without the need to Islamize it. However, TJ still has concerns for ethical character, even if formulated in narrowly religious categories. It is passively supportive of shari'a-based politics, as is true of Deobandism from which it derives. The literature of Deobandism indicates favorable attitudes to shari'a-based politics as the best form of rule but does not identify politics as essentially religious. It therefore eschews the label of party, defining itself simply as the people of the sunna (*ahl al-sunna*), but this does not mean it has no position on the political struggles of the age, even if it does not actively participate in them. Its literature recalls the movement's support for India's drive to independence and also for the caliphate in Istanbul. It is partial to causes that call for the defense of Muslims against hostile forces—such as the West or Hinduism—but it also appreciates the political rights of all peoples. Islam here, in general, is not a political project but a shari'a-oriented life exclusive of "popular" customs. Thus, under certain conditions, it can indirectly play into shari'a-exclusive rule, as the Taliban demonstrates. Still, by refusing to make politics essential to Islam, Deobandism, Tablighism, and Barelwism diverge fundamentally from the Islamism of Jama'at-i Islami. As a result, the many millions of Muslims who look to these groups for piety have extraordinarily diverse views on politics and non-Muslim life. Some may have Islamist associations, but the belief system is more reflective of traditional Islam, where scholarly, devotional, and spiritual networks make up the way to God.

In contrast, the movement led by Fethullah Gülen of Turkey seeks to engage the world and serve human society whether identifiably Muslim or not. Its members are socially diverse and morally conservative, and they have played a key role in the renewal of civil society in Turkey by creating networks of relations based on the ethics of Islam rather than the secular ideology of the state. They adhere to the particulars of Islam, but religion here is a means to cultivate universal virtues (honesty, humility, generosity, kindness) that allow for engagement with the wider world while implicitly witnessing to the ethical efficacy of Islam. This Turkish-based global movement, numbering in the millions, has interests in education, business, and the mass media. Its activities are international in scope, with top schools in Central Asia and interfaith initiatives in the West. Indeed, the Gülen movement has become the face of Turkey to the world as much as the Turkish state. Gülen has not always been successful in his attempts to accommodate the Kemalist state whose secularist ideology has dominated the Turkish Republic since its founding by Atatürk (1881–1938). He is a deeply spiritual figure heavily immersed in the heritage of Sufism, although his movement is not structured according to its traditional hierarchies. He is committed to the secular state but also to the teachings of Islam, working to create a new framework for Turkish society that does not threaten the secular constitution of the state but does marginalize its ideology as partisan interest of the state elite.

The fact that the Turkish state has control of official religious institutions is not inconsistent with the Ottoman past. The difference, of course, is that the modern state defines itself in secular categories, leading it to refashion Islam in the image of its secularizing policies. For example, the religious curriculum of state schools is much more geared to the glorification of the Turkish nation than to the beliefs and practices of Islam alone. However, since the founding of the republic in 1923, Sufi orders that continue to exist on the ground even if banned by law have nurtured forms of Islam apart from state supervision. A key group has been the Naqshbandis, a group whose affiliates have pursued diverse approaches to state and society in Kemalist Turkey. For example, some rebelled against the secularizing policies of the nascent Turkish state, founded on the materialist ideology of Kemalism that rejected the public legitimacy of spiritual authority and viewed religion as essentially backward. But others actually executed the state's decision to eliminate Sufism as a social institution by closing down its centers. Later, some affiliates of the Naqshbandis struck an Islamist tone, such as the poet Necip Fazil Kisakürek (d. 1983), who supported the idea of a national system under divine sovereignty. Others made alliances with secular parties, entering government ministries and even the military, the bastion of Kemalism. Still others combined Islam with notions of political liberty, creating an intellectual framework for Muslim democracy, and many have been employed in the state-controlled ministry of religion while still looking to the Naqshabandi spiritual heritage as ultimate authority.

Sufi brotherhoods in contemporary Turkey exist ambiguously as cultural or charitable foundations, not as religious institutions, but nevertheless do not seek to overturn the official ban on Sufism. Sufism is a religiosity that does not depend on state recognition or even social visibility—in contrast to shari'a, which defines the externals of people's lives (e.g., what they wear and how they act). As such, Sufism can exist in climates highly antagonistic to Islam, operating through spiritual networks that climax in a shaykh who, as spiritual successor to the Prophet, is ultimate guarantor of the religious integrity of the *umma* (or at least the part that acknowledges his authority).

A common theme marks the varied expressions of the Naqshbandis in Turkey: Islam as alternative to Kemalism, not in the sense of political challenge but rather in the sense of a spiritual life that Kemalism cannot control. This heritage has offered pious Turks a way to live the spiritual realities of Islam apart from state definitions of religious knowledge (e.g., in the national religious curriculum as noted earlier) but still within a public order defined by Kemalism. Eventually, this alternative vision would have political consequences. A key leader of the Naqshbandis was Mehmet Zahit Kotku (d. 1980), who encouraged his followers to engage the political arena first by allying with non-Kemalist secular parties and then by creating religious-oriented parties. Three prime ministers were all influenced by him in one way or another: Turgut Özal (d. 1993), Necmettin Erbakan (leader of the Islamist movement in Turkey known as Milli Görüş), and Recep Tayyip Erdoğan (leader of the Justice and Development Party, or AK Party, now at the head of Turkey's government). The speeches of Kotku's successor, Esad Coşan (d. 2001), sometimes castigated the West as source of the antireligious secularism he associated with Kemalism. He would call for greater freedom for Islam but not for all (e.g., religious minorities, atheists, gays). And yet he was a great proponent of free markets, seeing economic vitality as a way to protect the nation from foreign influence. Still, despite the variety, it has been this form of Islam, articulated chiefly by the Naqshbandis, that has offered a counternarrative to Kemalism, depicting spiritual and not solely material realities as shapers of the nation's character. Not only pious believers but also nonobservant Muslims appreciate this counternarrative, even if religiously framed, as a more effective guarantor of freedom than Kemalism. This is not to say that the Kemalist state is unthinkingly authoritarian. It did permit a democratic process that brought the AK Party to power, but it has vigorously sought to program the nation to believe that secular modernization is the purpose of life.

It is from this background that the Gülen movement emerged not as a spiritual brotherhood but as a socioreligious force that helped pave the way for the transformation of Turkish politics, a transformation symbolized in a religiously oriented party ruling a Muslim nation on behalf of a secularist state. This is not to suggest a formal relation between the movement and the party, but Gülen set the conditions for the AK Party to navigate between the hammer of Kemalism and the anvil of Islamism as represented by Erbakan. The stage was set in 1997 when the state removed Erbakan as prime minister. Islam in Turkey had been a force for economic liberalization, but 1997 marked a turning point that would make Islam a force for political liberalization, too—human rights, democracy, civil liberties, things that had previously been viewed negatively as products of the West. Kemalist repression of alternative expressions of Islam helped create the link between Islam and freedom. Long before 1997, the nation as a whole aspired to greater freedom from the state, but the chances of realizing it became greater when the forces of Islam assumed it as a necessary precondition for the well-being of Islam.

The emergence of Islam as proponent of civil society in Turkey cannot be explained wholly as a response to state action. Political liberalization, to make religious sense, would have to be captured in religious language, including the liberalization of religious attitudes toward nonreligious life: a religious message of tolerance and love for all without undermining the uniqueness of Islam. Gülen symbolizes this vision of Islam, articulating national harmony through a religious lens—not as a state policy but as an independent shaper of the character of society. His followers in general turned away from Erbakan's antagonistic style but enthusiastically support the AK Party, especially its goal of freeing society from state ideology. The leadership of the AK Party actually drew on Gülen's ideas to forge its approach to national politics: religiosity that is dynamically Muslim but also positively engaged with secular realities that are themselves worthy of reverence as part of God's created order. The aim of Islam, then, is primarily ethical, not political: to restore the character of a nation disfigured by the materialist ideology of the state. However, renewal of national character is not reducible to philosophical abstracts but depends on a message that speaks to the cultural particularities and ethical loyalties of the people, including Islam, while also resonating with the national and global whole. Gülen is not so much in dialogue with Kemalism as he is with Turkish society at large (and indeed the entire world), defining a new framework for the nation in which a dynamic concept of religious knowledge is freely at play.

Gülen was a disciple of Sa'id Nursi (d. 1960), once affiliated with the Naqshbandis, who broke with institutional Sufism but drew on its intellectual heritage to defend faith in the face of the highly secularizing trends of modern Turkish history. His voluminous commentary on the Qur'an, *Risale-yi Nur* (Epistle of light), widely studied in Turkey and widely available on the Internet in multiple languages, weaves together questions of modern science with a spiritual vision of the cosmos, leaving the impression that secularism is itself part of the sacred narrative of Islam. Gülen in turn added civic activism to Nursi's legacy, inspiring his followers to bring piety to life in the form of service to the nation. Indeed, the movement refers to itself as "service" (*hizmet*). Its promotion of piety operates not by preaching (*teblig*) for the sake of a religious identity but by representing (*temsil*) the ethics of Islam in the service of the common good: a panoply of virtues that others would recognize as part of human civilization but that here is identified with Islam. Islam still has its particular norms, and Gülen is committed to them, but more profoundly he represents a belief system that encourages not only harmonious coexistence with secular life and its various branches of knowledge but also constructive interaction with it.

The Political Demands of Religious Knowledge

Religious knowledge does make demands on society, but the nature of these demands depends on a number of factors, including the way in which the relation of religious to political authority is envisioned. In general, in echo of the Qur'anic depiction of the prophets, who did not rule but counseled rulers to fear God, the role of religious authorities has traditionally been that of advice givers (*naṣīḥa*). Those who are learned in religion do engage

rule—and thus give it a measure of religious legitimacy—but from a distance, where they can advise or admonish, depending on the circumstances. One sees this in contemporary Morocco, where the leader of the Butshishiyya, Sidi Hamza, has supported the monarchy, counseling the nation to support it as protector of national harmony, while ʿAbd al-Salam Yasin, leader of the banned Jamaʿat al-ʿAdl wa-l-Ihsan (Group of Justice and Charity), drawing from the same spiritual heritage as Hamza, denounces it as source of political injustice. Neither figure, however, is a force for democracy per se. Both affirm the hierarchical nature of religious and political authority but diverge in their assessment of whether the monarchy in place, holder of worldly power in Morocco, adequately preserves the interests of the country's citizen-subjects. Today, as in the past, religious authority can affirm or deny the legitimacy of rule.

For others, religious knowledge demands more than counseling rulers or even the nation as a whole. Instead, it holds out hope of a perfect society free of the tarnish of sin, making the subordination of God's decrees to worldly considerations a threat to the community's standing before God. In early Islam, the movement known as Kharijism took shape in response to the Battle of Siffin in the year 657, exactly 25 years after the death of the Prophet. At the head of the opposing armies were two of the Prophet's Companions: ʿAli b. Abi Talib and Muʿawiyya. When no clear victor emerged, the two sides agreed to resolve the dispute through arbitration by the book of God, but the process was soon manipulated in favor of Muʿawiyya, whereupon the proto-Kharijis denounced the worldliness of the process with the declaration of "no rule but God's rule." What exactly upset them is unclear. The earliest reports suggest that it involved the use of writing in the arbitration process (perhaps as a way to "authorize" the results), which would imply that "a book" (*kitāb*) other than the book of God might "govern" the affairs of the community. Indeed, in its earliest form, Kharijism identified the leader (*imām*) of the *umma* as the book of God exclusively.

Thus, particular cultural attitudes about the power of writing as a source of authoritative knowledge were at play in early Kharijism: religious knowledge, revealed by divine communiqué, had been "polluted" by human rule, which in this case implied a humanly composed rather than divinely revealed form of writing. At the same time, worldly considerations and tribal loyalties also featured prominently. A number of the partisans of Kharijism belonged to the tribe of Tamim, and others were warriors who had participated in the battles to spread Islam, known as "the conquests" (*al-futūḥāt*), with the expectation of a full share in the spoils. The decision by ʿUmar b. al-Khattab (r. 634–44) to put conquered lands under central control, to be taxed with the revenue going to the public treasury, did not provoke a hostile reaction, but the partisan way in which ʿUthman b. ʿAffan (r. 644–56) distributed communal sources of wealth in favor of his Umayyad tribal relations did. This led to his assassination at the hands of forerunners to Kharijism, who claimed that he had deviated from the Prophet's way of governing, introducing innovations into the religion and sowing corruption on Earth. Kharijism, its destructiveness notwithstanding, did much to stimulate Muslim thinking about the ambiguous relation of religious knowledge to the exercise of power and, indeed, about the religious status of "politics" in general.

The basic conviction of Kharijism—that secular considerations are not to prevail over God's decrees—still exists. One example is jihadism, which differs from Kharijism in many respects but shares its strong resistance to rule that is religiously ambiguous even if politically effective. Al-Qaeda adjudicates political realities wholly through a scripturally informed narrative where the forces of God do battle against the agents of idolatry (*ṭawāghīt*). Qutb especially gave shape to this narrative, overturning centuries of Muslim appreciation of secular processes in the workings of governance. His dismissal of nonrevealed explanations of human existence (such as sociological ones) was partly an overreaction to the increasingly secularizing character of his age when national authorities no longer were merely to govern society, as their dynastic forebears, but also came to claim jurisdiction over its moral character, traditionally the preserve of those learned in religious knowledge. The resulting narrative now inspiring jihadist groups ignores long-standing reservations about demanding religious perfection from rulers. In the mentality of al-Qaeda, the failure to incarnate religious knowledge as rule casts suspicion on its veracity. And this, in turn, makes it necessary to "stage" the truth of revelation by enacting the divinely revealed victory of belief over unbelief on the global stage, pitting a righteous remnant against worldly powers (now redefined as God's enemies in accordance with the jihadist script).

According to this outlook, there can be no compromise between divine sovereignty and worldly powers that place secular considerations above the literal wordings of divine speech. Thus the preference for secular systems, such as capitalism or socialism, raises questions about the veracity of religious knowledge. Its truth is suspect if it is not effectively guiding the entire globe. In an odd twist of logic, al-Qaeda makes divine speech the sole criterion of action in the world. Claims of tyranny do feature in its rhetoric, but the rulers of the world are judged not so much for their political shortcomings but for "humiliating" the religious integrity of the *umma* by leading it away from the clear knowledge of divine speech in favor of interpretations of it that only serve to mask knowledge that is actually worldly in nature and not heavenly. The jihadist reading of politics through the lens of a revealed narrative makes it necessary to "save" Islam from the political ambiguities that religiously imperfect rule casts on the certainty of religious knowledge. Jihadism is not merely a religious form of violent protest against global and local injustices but more so a battle for the supremacy of religious knowledge over secular processes. By linking the efficacy of religious knowledge to political supremacy, al-Qaeda limits the expression of piety to fighting until victory (i.e., God's word prevails over the world) or death in the way of God (i.e., martyrdom) as a noble way of exiting from a wayward world.

However, in both past and present, Muslims generally have been wary of calls for religiously perfect rule. Perfection (*kamāl*) is the affair of the hidden realm, a spiritual quest that ennobles one's

character but is not achievable by political means. Figures claiming to be the Mahdi, the figure who will deliver the world from injustice at the end of time, occasionally appear, especially when Islam is seen to be in peril, holding out the hope of quasi-divine rule. But Mahdism has limited effectiveness and often causes more harm than good. The deeper reason behind Muslim wariness of religious rule is that governance has no revealed status. Those learned in religion, such as Mawardi, discussed earlier, did write on governance (*siyāsa*), but they never made it integral to shari'a (i.e., as a recognized branch of *fiqh* literature). This did not mean that there were no standards for rule. The preservation of the worldly interests of the *umma* (e.g., protection of life and property, suppression of rebels and brigands) were foremost among the expectations of rule in Islam. A genre known as "counsel-for-rulers" served as a premodern form of political constitution, but this genre, as noted earlier, drew on multiple sources of knowledge. Because governance was never a recognized part of religious knowledge, Muslims, in general, suspend (or postpone) judgment when faced with rule that fails to conform fully to God's decrees. The exercise of power is judged against worldly standards (i.e., preservation of public order), and this may include the promotion of religious knowledge as a public good, but rule, in the end, is not evaluated in terms of religious knowledge exclusively.

This position, long held in Sunni Islam, is partly traceable to the so-called people of postponement (*al-murji'a*), who refused to judge the religious status of 'Ali or Mu'awiya on the basis of their governance of the *umma*. The Shi'a, too, while making leadership integral to religion, would also adopt a position of political accommodation. Following the Battle of Siffin, the proto-Shi'a responded to Kharijism by awarding religious authority (*wilāya*) to 'Ali as leader of the community. This idea, that a specially endowed human figure had a privileged role in ensuring the religious integrity of the community, eventually translated into the expectation that in the presence of the imam, religious knowledge is not limited, making all things, including politics, religiously legitimate or illegitimate depending on the extent of its conformity to the command of the infallible leader. He could issue religious rulings for all affairs, including those in flux (economics, politics, warfare) as they arose with the confidence that it represented God's will and not only an approximation of it.

The absence of the imam (at least for the main branch of Shi'ism), beginning in the ninth century, did not mean that the Shi'a were bereft of religious knowledge but only that its scope was limited to those areas, such as rituals and morals, where God's rulings do not change, in contrast to politics, which is always in flux. As a result, political affairs cannot be religiously determined in the absence of the imam. This encouraged Shi'i authorities, like their Sunni counterparts, to refrain from making decisive judgments about political action in the name of Islam, since religious knowledge in the imam's absence was limited and offered no clear indications for the ever-changing affairs of governance. For this reason the rise of constitutionalism in Muslim lands, beginning in the late 19th century, caused a good deal of confusion. Was it religiously legitimate? The traditional indifference to the nature of rule, so long as it served its purpose (i.e., the preservation of order), meant that Sunni and Shi'i authorities would take a wide range of positions on democracy, provided it did not threaten the integrity of religious knowledge as guidance for society.

However, modernity's challenge to the truth of religious knowledge, even in its limited domains, made it necessary to rethink the relation of religious knowledge to politics. In the past, the political order, sultans and shahs, posed no essential threat to religious knowledge. Dynasts were happy to patronize religion in exchange for recognition. Islam has generally respected the autonomy of secular knowledge in its own spheres, such as astronomy, geography, and medicine (i.e., outside the realm of rituals and morals; there has also been a long heritage of humanistic ethics alongside shari'a rulings). Leading scholars, notably Ghazali (d. 1111), sought to harmonize the philosophical life of the mind with the otherworldly orientation of religion. But the modernist claim that only secular knowledge has a claim on truth posed a profound challenge to Islam in public life. In reaction, some religious figures claimed that religious knowledge had relevance for all areas of life, including those not traditionally included within the scope of religious knowledge, such as economics and politics.

There have been many attempts to extend religious knowledge more assertively into the political domain. One way has been via "the goals of religion" (*maqāṣid al-dīn*). This approach, which seeks to cull the overall purpose of shari'a from amid its voluminous and sometimes contradictory precedents, works to bring a religious perspective to areas of life for which no explicit ruling, based on a clear precedent, exists. In this fashion, religious authorities are able to extend their voices to emergent domains not previously treated in shari'a. For example, Qaradawi takes this position, leaving it to the judgment of the leader (*ra'y al-imām*) to determine the public interest in areas where religious knowledge is silent but requiring him to do so in light of *maqāṣid al-dīn* that only religious scholars can verify. Abu Yusuf (d. 798), one of the early shari'a masters, also recognized the authority of the leader's judgment, but he did not qualify it as Qaradawi does, simply leaving it to the ruler to do what he sees best for Muslims so long as his command does not contradict the clear rulings of God.

It is true that past scholars, such as Ghazali and also his teacher, Juwayni (d. 1085), would define public interest (*maṣlaḥa*) in terms of shari'a considerations. In contrast to Qaradawi, however, this emerged not from a desire to link political affairs wholly to religious knowledge (or at least its broader intentions) but rather out of a concern for the corruption of religious learning. The perception that few could claim mastery of religious knowledge in all its details caused profound concern for the likes of Ghazali and Juwayni. How could one be certain that the *umma* is still guided by truth? The two figures realized that for religious knowledge to be preserved intact, one could no longer count on religious scholars. It would be necessary to construct a "rational" system where the essence of shari'a, defined as

"the universal interests" (*al-maṣāliḥ al-kulliyya*) of Muslim society, could be known and preserved in spite of the decline of religious expertise. The point, then, is that such premodern attempts to define public interests in terms of *maqāṣid al-dīn* were motivated by scholarly anxieties and not the desire to construct a political system out of religious knowledge as in the modern context.

The Politics of Religious Diversity

The fact that premodern scholars had different motives than those of today is not to suggest that Muslim thinkers of the past did not think systematically about the relation of religious knowledge to politics, only that they did so for different reasons than those motivating Islamism today. There has always been tension between the truths of religious knowledge and the political realities that are ideally to embody these truths but fail to do so. This tension can be compounded by competing definitions of Islam, a confessional pluralism that sometimes lends itself to communal conflict and even political strife. How are doubts about religious knowledge to be repelled when not all believers have the same understanding of religious knowledge? One way is violent attack against those who do not espouse one's own understanding of religious knowledge. Another is to reconsider the demands of religious knowledge within wider philosophical and theological categories.

The philosopher Farabi (d. 950) was one of the first to move in this direction. His political works should not be seen simply as Greek thought in Arabic but rather as cogent response to the sectarian fragmentation of Islam. He formulated a metacommunal conception of truth that can embrace multiple confessions. In this way, political legitimacy is not based on a simple implementation of religious knowledge in literal form. The particular wordings of religion, in other words, the specific beliefs and laws of a community (*milla*), while important for day-to-day life, are only the imitation of higher truths of a philosophical kind. They are not true in themselves since truth is determinable only by demonstrable proof via philosophical method. Religion cannot be so defended since it is composed of images (e.g., fires of hell, rivers of paradise) that are rhetorical and so cannot attain the rank of certain knowledge. Thus the particular wordings of religion are true insofar as they are consistent with demonstrably proven truths (e.g., happiness as the ultimate goal of life). Thus community-specific knowledge, such as shari'a, while valuable for its role in holding the *milla* together, is relative next to allegedly higher forms of knowledge that only the philosophical elite can attain, making it futile to fight and spill blood on behalf of religiocommunal knowledge, which, again, is not truth but only the imitation of it.

Another philosopher of the period, Abu al-Hasan al-'Amiri (d. 992), argued for the priority of religiocommunal knowledge (*milla*) over philosophical knowledge (*ḥikma*). Because *milla* provides norms for the details of human life, it effectively holds a polity together more so than *ḥikma*, which offers only abstract truths. Still, even if revealed knowledge stands above its nonrevealed counterpart, the former still exists for a rational goal—namely, the political good. Thus the particular wordings of *milla* are to be applied only in light of the greater interests of the polity. Thus, in the words of 'Amiri, the intellect is God's caliph on Earth. The idea that the law of God exists for a rationally identifiable purpose—namely, for the common good of Muslim society—rather than simply as a test of the believer's obedience would climax in the thought of Abu Ishaq al-Shatibi (d. 1388), a jurist of the Maliki branch of Islam, who would draw on the various intellectual streams of Islam in advancing a rational understanding of shari'a at the service of the human needs of Muslim society.

Contrast this, for example, with the Muslim Brotherhood, a transnational group that in Egypt is known to set the religiocommunal specifics of Islam above national harmony. 'Amiri places religiocommunal knowledge, at least as far as its public role is concerned, at the service of political ends, whereas the Muslim Brotherhood reverses this, identifying political ends more closely with religiocommunal knowledge. The Muslim Brotherhood sees political empowerment (*tamkīn*) as the logical consequence of the religious mission (*da'wa*). The Muslim Brotherhood, it should be added, does not see violence as a means to power. Its approach to power is gradualist through political mobilization, not warfare, but unlike 'Amiri, it would identify the constitution of the polity with shari'a rather than a secular good in which Muslims can enact their religiocommunal obligations.

A final example in this regard is Ghazali, who sought to systematize all branches of knowledge, both religious and secular, by orienting them to a common goal—namely, awareness of the other world (*ākhira*, i.e., the world beyond this one). He also sought to defend the truth of religious knowledge in a confessionally divided community where various groups with different interpretations of religious knowledge competed for social dominance. Ghazali was less sanguine about a political solution for the religious dilemma than his teacher, Juwayni, who proposed in his political treatise, *Ghiyath al-Umam* (Salvation of the nations), that Nizam al-Mulk (d. 1092), the celebrated Seljuq vizier, enforce public conformity to the truths of religious knowledge by the sword if necessary. In this, Juwayni hoped to eliminate the doctrinal contradictions from one Muslim group to another that confounded all claims to truth.

Despite his misgivings about the political defense of religious truth, Ghazali was no esotericist. He refused to reduce religiocommunal knowledge to philosophical categories. He was committed to the particular wordings of religious knowledge as well as political interests that the intellect might determine. He shared his teacher's concern that religious knowledge be visibly represented even if worldly powers could not be counted on to do so. In turning to the idea of brotherhood (*ukhuwwa*)—in other words, spiritual brotherhood—he did not intend to uproot Muslims from the realities of the world but to create a space apart where they could live as a brotherhood in God and, in turn, more perfectly witness the life of Islam to the world around them. The idea of religious brotherhood is Qur'anic (e.g., 3:103), and spiritual companionship (*ṣuḥba*) was prominent in Islam before Ghazali, but he deployed such concepts as a way to show the efficacy of religious knowledge in Islam when it was no longer unambiguously effective in the political domain.

Rather than seeking "proof" of the truth of Islam in a strongman who would back it, Ghazali looked to religious brotherhood as a way to present the truth of Islam to society, as suggested by his inclusion of a section in his magnum opus (*The Revivification of the Religious Sciences*) on "The Ethics of Harmony, Brotherhood, Companionship, and Affection." In his view, religious brotherhood demonstrates that the religious integrity of the *umma*—and thus the efficacy of its religiocommunal knowledge—remained intact even amid the corruption of the age and shortcomings of Islam's political and religious leadership.

Religious Knowledge and the Modern State

The battle for the enduring relevance of religious knowledge marks every age of Islam. In the modern context, it is as much a political endeavor as a scholarly one. In this sense, it is no longer clear where religious knowledge begins and political authority ends. One example is the work of Muhammad Baqir al-Sadr (executed by Saddam Hussein in 1980). Faced with a political context that assumed secular knowledge as the exclusive guide to life, Sadr countered with the claim that religion could define all aspects of life, including those areas that religious life traditionally does not define. Sadr referred to those areas as "the empty region" (*manṭiqat al-farāgh*)—that is, the legislative void that results from the imam's absence.

He first made reference to the idea of filling the void in a work on Islamic economics published in 1961, *Our Economics*. But the idea continued to occupy his attention and was featured in *Islam Leads Life*, a treatise he wrote shortly after the Iranian Revolution of 1979 that would leave its mark on the constitution of the Islamic Republic. His thinking differs from that of the Muslim Brotherhood. He does not view rule as a simple means to safeguard religion. Rather, knowledge in Islam consists not only of specific rulings (*aḥkām*; e.g., no interest, no deceptive business practices) but also of concepts (*mafāhīm*) that inform all areas of Muslim life, even those that pertain to society as a whole.

For example, in addition to rulings that forbid interest and deception, Islam also contains a narrative: God created the world and entrusted it to humans, who are to care for it and make it prosper, justly and righteously. The Qur'an encourages humans to enjoy the fruit of God's creation but discourages the hoarding of wealth. For Sadr, this worldview embodies principles that can be applied to economic matters: consumption, production, capital, labor, and so on. Indeed, the religious heritage—both revealed texts and scholarly treatises—contains a wealth of principles applicable to contemporary life. The void (again, the legislative void that results from the imam's absence) could thus be filled and the Shi'a could once again live Islam to its full as if the imam were present. They would not have to succumb to Western systems of life simply for want of a total system of knowledge of their own making.

It is left to those in command (*ulū al-amr*, a highly exploited Qur'anic phrase) to issue rulings pertinent to the governance of society. These rulings are not fixed and permanent, as if revealed by God, since new situations arise, but they could not be left to the interests of the elite. For Sadr, the gross shortcomings of worldly systems, capitalism and communism, only demonstrated the need for a divinely ordained system of governance to ensure justice and brotherly relations based on devotion to God. Islam has a philosophy of its own, embedded in the religious heritage; its concepts—equity and liberation from exploitation, ignorance, and tyranny—could dynamically engage the nation's affairs entirely. In other words, Islam could engender a religious polity.

Such a polity, governed by the principles of Islam, requires not merely rule by Islam but the involvement of the jurist (*faqīh*), who alone possesses the qualifications to guarantee the process. The exact role that the *faqīh* is to play in the polity is a matter of tremendous debate. Khomeini, for his part, claimed that the *faqīh* is to hold the reins of power, but how is such a figure to be checked when he is the imam's representative? Such concerns were less compelling to Sadr than the need to restore society on the basis of monotheism, where people would be free of oppression, harmonious, and productive. But he also acknowledged that such a project did not depend on legislation alone. The citizens needed to be educated in the virtues of Islam in order to be willingly ruled by its principles. Sadr was favorably disposed to democracy but cautioned against its manipulation by partisan interests; democracy needed to be "corrected" by Islam. The parliament would thus need the oversight of the *faqīh*.

Sadr sought to bring ethical standards to areas of life that in the modern age were the cause of great concern, especially economics and politics. By greatly expanding the boundaries of religious knowledge, however, Sadr unintentionally opened the door to the politics of religious supremacy. In his view, since Islam was a total system, Muslims could only be Muslim if ruled by Islam. Religiously undetermined areas of life could now become religiously determined by virtue of the concepts alongside the precedents of the religious heritage.

All of this has created a troubled legacy for Shi'ism, and various figures have tried to nuance or deflate Khomeini's idea of governance by the *faqīh*. However, while this idea has been significantly undermined, Sadr's notion of filling the legislative void in Islam in the absence of the imam has had lasting influence on such groups as Hizbullah. One can debate whether the supreme leader in Iran is fully qualified to fill the void, but it is more difficult to argue that life in all its aspects should not be guided by some measure of truth. Is it all relative? Are the world's resources simply up for grabs for the powerful to take all? Intense discussions on the nature of truth in Iran have important political implications. Those who say that heaven should rule can look to Sadr for inspiration: if not addressed, the void will be exploited by the powerful, and society will be governed by the law of the jungle, where might is right. Truth must be brought to bear on the void, and where else to find truth than in God's revelation, and only the *faqīh* fully comprehends what God has revealed. In this sense, politics becomes quasi-apocalyptic, as was the case with Khomeini. It was also the case with President Mahmoud Ahmedinejad, who was not a shari'a scholar but claimed to implement the truths of Islam, obviating the voice of the people. Long the preserve of scholarly circles, religious authority is now also a function of worldly criteria, political

astuteness and the willingness to use force to bring about rule by religion. Religion is unbound, making economics and politics, and ultimately power, integral to divine favor since religion now applies to those areas no less than to rituals and morals.

Religious Knowledge as Guidance for Society

Despite the ascendancy of Islamism, many Muslims, even within Islamist circles, no longer define the state in terms of divine sovereignty but rather as "the civil state" (*al-dawla al-madaniyya*), where religious and secular knowledge are equally at play (religio-secular knowledge) in determining what is best for the polity. This shift in terminology comes from the conclusion—reached after a sometimes painful learning process—that the notion of a religious state is actually contrary to the teachings of Islam (and can justify the abuse of power in the name of religion): no individual can pretend to represent divine sovereignty.

If religious knowledge is, then, a question not only of prestige and power but also of truth, it is worth asking what this truth is in a secular age. The response will vary according to sociopolitical circumstances, but the truth of religious knowledge is not simply a matter of historical contingency. The knowledge that Islam offers to society can be described as a tightly regulated economy of rights (*ḥuqūq*) owed to others, both to God and to fellow humans, and even to oneself. God has the right to be worshipped, as embodied in various ritual duties, but has also revealed sanctions against theft, adultery (and false accusation of adultery), alcohol consumption, and pillaging. Believers who commit such crimes will have to pay the penalty either in this world or the next. There is also the possibility that God will "cover over" (*satr*) people's sins in His mercy (*raḥma*). The Prophet Muhammad is thought to have embodied this "godly" character as a model ruler. He ensured justice and righteousness but was also known for a willingness to forgo retribution for a greater moral purpose—namely, peace in society. Members of society also have duties to one another, and God has forbidden Muslims from transgressing the life, property, and dignity of others unless there is just cause (e.g., if the person is a murderer and is judged to deserve death or is an unrepentant blasphemer who wages war against religion). Spouses have duties to one another and to their children. Society as a whole has a duty to care for the weak and poor, and relations between individuals are to be guided by justice; in other words, everyone gets his or her due, especially when it comes to commercial relations. Islam therefore places great emphasis on keeping promises and fulfilling contracts. When obligations are not met, justice can be sought, but there is also the possibility of acting mercifully toward others in imitation of the Prophet. Rulers are to be obeyed so long as they do not transgress the rights of God and of His slaves (i.e., humans). This could imply just rule or rule that does not offend the morality of Islam or, at a minimum, rule that does not prevent believers from performing their ritual duties (i.e., praying or fasting).

How, then, is such religious knowledge relevant to modern society? The case of Syria is illustrative. Few concepts have greater resonance in Syria—and throughout Arab society—than *ḥaqq*, a complex term meaning "right" in the sense of something owed to others (in the plural, it can refer to human rights, or *ḥuqūq al-insān*). In Syria, it features especially in commerce and, in principle, is the measure of virtually all relations. Syria has its poor, but it is acknowledged that they have their *ḥaqq* (i.e., a morsel of food is owed to them). To be sure, *ḥaqq* is not always realized and can be ignored, for example, by some entrepreneurs who exploit the dismal job market by arbitrarily deciding how much to pay employees at the end of the month.

Still, it is always a point of reference: "the *ḥaqq* is on you" (*al-ḥaqq 'alayka*, i.e., you owe something); "it's her *ḥaqq* to do so" (*haqqhā ta'mal hayk*); "he has no *ḥaqq* in the matter" (*mā ilhu ḥaqq fil-amr*). It is sometimes defined as just treatment of others. An entire segment of a talk show might be devoted to the *ḥaqq* of the wife in marriage. As a concept, it guides all commercial activity. Someone may have to pay a bribe to achieve an objective but can preserve his or her moral integrity by declaring it to be without *ḥaqq*. Some associate the concept with democracy, but it is not a precise match. It is not about everyone having an equal say in policy making (although it is not opposed to the idea) but about preserving a just balance in society. People make decisions in accordance with their interests (as well as their hope for familial and societal acceptance) but are limited by the framework of *ḥaqq*—what is owed to them and what they owe others. They may forgo what is owed them, but this must be by choice and not forced, as an act of magnanimity, generosity, charity, or simply a desire to please God. This is commonly called forbearance (*tasāmuḥ*). Those who have offended others might ask for this forbearance.

The point is that moral life in Syria (and elsewhere) is still guided by a framework that is ultimately based on religious knowledge, despite the ascendancy of secular politics. The point is not to enthrone the voice of God as national sovereign, although that remains a goal of some Islamists in Syria. Religion works with or without the state. That is, Islam need not be politically supreme, but beliefs are not suspended outside the mosque. They are present in the public sphere, not necessarily in explicitly religious categories but as universal values, justice and mercy, which in Syria (and elsewhere) are channeled by religious knowledge. Religious knowledge, encoding ethical standards, thus remains vital for the moral coherency of society, especially but not only when the state and its institutions show little commitment to these standards.

In this sense, those with traditional expertise in religious knowledge continue to play a central role in the dissemination of values that hold society together, but the means of doing so differ from one community to another. For example, residents in a district of Damascus known as Rukn al-Din show appreciation for religious figures who are not only learned in shari'a but also graced with a holy character. The devotion to them is not a slight on the monotheism of Islam but comes from the realization that these figures make piety and morality available to others by modeling it in their own persons. They are key agents in the process of making the community pleasing to God. Some may look to them in this sense as intercessional figures, caring for the community on behalf of the Prophet. This type of piety is noticeable in religious ceremonies that combine *dhikr* (i.e., group

recollection of the names of God), public readings of hadiths, and collective chanting in praise of the Prophet. Such ceremonies are often "sponsored" by one of these revered figures, to whom obeisance, such as hand kissing, is sometimes shown. His presence grants the ceremony its aura, making him focal point and agent of ethical solidarity and communal harmony as well as piety. This kind of religiosity, partly classifiable as Sufism, is integral to Syrian piety in particular and to Islam in general. Damascenes are proud of their "saints," which the heritage refers to as God's confederates (*awliyā' Allāh*). They, not the state, guarantee the religion and mediate its ethically productive knowledge, even long-dead figures such as Shaykh Arslan, the 12th-century holy man and patron saint of Damascus who continues to be remembered as "the protector of piety in Syria" (*ḥāmī al-birr bi-l-shām*).

In another section of Damascus, Maydan, there is similar appreciation for traditional religion, although with less emphasis on saintly intercessors and more on the preservation of the values of Islam against the encroachment of secularism. The custodians of religious knowledge in Maydan are known for a highly conservative piety unaffected by the ways of the world. They may harbor greater hostility toward the secular state than their counterparts in Rukn al-Din, but they too do not expect the state to be the guarantor of religion. What disturbs them is the spread of immorality and irreligion, which they attribute to the state as the prime seller of vice. This may make them more favorable toward Islamism, but it does not lead them to tie the validity of religious knowledge to its political implementation: The "rights of God" can be respected within communities of piety apart from state enforcement of them. Rather, they feel that the preservation of public decency requires greater acknowledgment of Islam as guide of the nation, and they would like the state to provide this acknowledgment. In particular, in addition to justice, they would like to see greater support of a public morality associated with the rulings of shari'a, such as a ban on alcohol consumption, punishment for sexual crime (i.e., adultery), and strict regulation of gender relations.

Mediators of traditional religious knowledge, whether in Rukn al-Din, Maydan, or elsewhere, also play a role at "secular" ceremonies, such as weddings and funerals, where their presence is seen as a blessing and a reminder of the higher purpose of life. This role, along with teaching and preaching (and also counseling troubled marriages), is seen as part of the work of reforming society (*iṣlāḥ al-mujtami'*), which proceeds irrespective of the character or policies of the state. Here, then, the religiomoral character of society is guaranteed by the traditional custodians of religious knowledge, not the state.

At the same time, it should not be thought that such "traditional" figures are against Islamism. Islamist and non-Islamist sentiment can and does overlap within a single religious milieu. Purveyors of traditional forms of piety, the shaykhs are united with Islamists against secularism. They too are not happy with rule by 'Alawi "heretics," but the shaykhs are able to coexist with an authoritarian and ideologically secular state in a way Islamism cannot. Moreover, as promoters of a religiosity that does not depend on political power for its success, the shaykhs also temper the "urgency" of the Islamist call. True to traditional Islam, the shaykhs offer the state passive support in exchange for freedom to promulgate religious knowledge on their own terms (in contrast to the state-defined version of Islam as taught in the national schools that tends to feed into a glorification of Pan-Arabism). They are confident that the morals of Islam will prevail over state ideology, and so they prefer teaching, preaching, and guiding to political confrontation, which, they maintain, only hurts the cause of Islam.

The shaykhs generally agree that Islam can effectively pursue its ends apart from party politics—and may be better off by avoiding it. They would support the Muslim Brotherhood if it came to power through free and fair elections but not if it took the power by force. This posture is not simply political caution. It comes from the widely recognized belief that piety is worthless if coerced and that such top-down attempts to coerce piety inevitably lead to strife (*fitna*), producing more harm than good for Muslim society. Their commitment to Islam as a guide to society is not simplistic but is qualified by the means used to pursue the goal: teaching and preaching that seeks to refine both individual souls and society as a whole in the virtues of religion. A state also guided by Islam, in their view, will help achieve the purpose of politics (i.e., the common good) but rule by Islam cannot be pursued at the cost of the common good itself, and, moreover, care must be taken to protect the religion itself from too close an association with worldly power.

There is, then, a broad consensus in this multipolar religious milieu that religious knowledge has a role in society. This, however, does not necessarily translate into a call for a political party to represent Islam. Sunni authorities in parliament have called occasionally and discretely for Islam-based but not Islamist political parties. This is not for the sake of Islamist ends but rather to preserve the moral integrity of Islam that, these members of parliament argue, is at risk when political actors, untrained in Islam, call for the overthrow of the state in the name of religion, reducing Islam to militancy. Religious knowledge is represented in public as a moral voice, not as a political party, since allowing parties to form in the name of Islam would only lead to its fragmentation into partisan interests. The Ba'thist state, amid its own crisis of legitimacy, is encouraging this type of religiosity: a vibrant Sunnism, active in educational and cultural spheres, teaching Islam for the sake of morals but not as a political project.

Religion has flourished in early 21st-century Syria. People are familiar with the writings of respected scholars, such as Muhammad Sa'id Ramadan al-Buti and Wahba al-Zuhayli, who defend traditional religious knowledge in terms that are understandable to all and not only to religious specialists. Pious literature exists in many forms—from scholarly treatises to popular stories of the prophets—and is the most widely read genre of literature in Syria. Modernist voices, such as Ratib al-Nablusi and Muhammad al-Habash, promote an "updated" version of Islam in harmony with science, pluralism, and human rights. The shari'a faculty at the University of Damascus trains the future religious establishment, and virtually all students there are taught that Sufism is an integral part of religious knowledge. Religious personalities from outside Syria, such as Qaradawi

and Yemeni spiritual entrepreneur Habib ʻAli al-Jafri, have visited Syria. Some shaykhs have websites, from the more Sufi-oriented site of ʻAbd al-Hadi Kharsa, an eloquent defender of Sufism against Wahhabism, to that of ʻAla al-Din al-Zaʻtari, a member of the state ministry of religious affairs who has brought a religious viewpoint to a wide range of ethical issues, from economics to hypocrisy.

But is this religious knowledge any more than a way to preserve the prestige of the traditional religious establishment? In the early 2000s, Damascus, to focus on one city, was known, among many things, as a regional center for sex tourism. Employment opportunities were limited. Prices were on the rise, partly due to the influx of Iraqi refugees but also as a result of immigration from Syrian villages. The state sought to extract revenues from all economic activity, and its institutions were hives of corruption, which state leaders tried to combat, at least rhetorically, to defend themselves from being implicated in it. The economic woes heightened concern for self-preservation, and urbanization encouraged the erosion of clan ties and neighborly solidarity (although social relations remained strong in principle). Caution, if not mistrust, was increasingly the norm in interpersonal relations. There is a creeping individualism, not in the sense of people doing as they please in public but in reduced expectations of support from others in society. Many religious leaders privately blamed the rampant vice they observed on the state's introduction of secular ways, which they saw as a pollutant to the city's reputation for piety and honesty—"honorable Damascus," long known for attracting both religious scholars and merchants. They concluded that the economic misery was due to the loss of morality that followed the abandonment of "the dear principles of Islam."

In such a context, where the state is clearly not the moral leader and nongovernmental organizations do not exist, the values of religion become all the more important for the sake of moral coherence in society. Despite the realities, religion was alive and well, maintaining standards of ethics that allowed society to function and, indeed, to exist. For example, a sandwich shop in the Halbuni section of Damascus displayed a hadith in full view of its clients that speaks of God's protection and provision, making the point that one should be satisfied and respond gratefully by fulfilling duties to God. Across from the main entrance to the University of Damascus, recitation of the Qur'an resounded from a newspaper kiosk, offering perspective, and perhaps a moral reminder, at a highly congested intersection. Down the road a bit, beyond the Baramika traffic circle, a motor-oil store displayed a banner referring to the Prophet as a mercy for the universe. A 15-minute walk from there, in a mosque named after ʻAmmar b. Yasir, Companion of the Prophet, in a middle-class neighborhood called Bikhtiyar, children sat in groups at the feet of middle-aged volunteer mentors, memorizing the Qur'an and imbibing the values of Islam. Just a bit farther, at a mosque at the Kafarsusa Circle, children were dropped off throughout the day for religious instruction.

The Sunni community in Damascus, then, and throughout Syria, as well as other communities in their own way, have cultivated something of a parallel society, alongside and in interaction with state institutions and categories. Allegiance to the nation is not undermined by religious commitments (and Baʻthists, members of the state party, are not necessarily atheists). There is, however, a concern to preserve the Sunni identity of Damascus through the deployment of religious symbols in the urban setting along with religious instruction in mosques. The prestige of the Sunni community in the face of the Baʻthist challenge is at stake, and this can spill over into politics. More significant than control of "politics" (in the sense of state institutions—including national legislation), however, is the claim to moral custodianship of urban life, in Damascus and elsewhere. Alongside the communal interests of Sunnism, then, there is aspiration, particularly acute in the current conditions described earlier, for righteousness in society.

This is the point; the place of religious knowledge in society is not simply about prestige and power. The details given from the particular example of Syria illustrate a deeper trend in Muslim society that modern scholarship has tended to explain in terms of structures of control. Religious knowledge exists to ensure a moral life that is traceable to prophetic origins and has demonstrable worth for the well-being of society; it is this twofold nature of religious knowledge that makes it a credible source of true information for guiding life. The truth of religious knowledge today may be less oriented to its sound transmission and more to its demonstrable worth for society, but even by this "modern" criterion, the facts on the ground suggest that religious knowledge remains a strong contender for the mantle of truth.

See also authority; education; shariʻa; traditional political thought

Further Reading

Farid al-Ansari, *al-Bayan al-Daʻwi wa-Zahirat al-Tadakhkhum al-Siyasi*, 2003; Dale F. Eickelman, *Knowledge and Power in Morocco: The Education of a Twentieth-Century Notable*, 1985; Wael Hallaq, "Caliphs, Jurists, and the Saljuqs in the Political Thought of Juwayni," *Muslim World* 74, no. 1 (1984); Muhammad Al-Hamdawi, *al-Risaliyya fi al-ʻAmal al-Islami*, 2008; Paul L. Heck, "Doubts about the Religious Community (*Milla*) in al-Farabi and the Brethren of Purity," in *In the Age of al-Farabi: Arabic Philosophy in the 4th/10th Century*, edited by P. Adamson, 2008; Idem, "Eschatological Scripturalism and the End of Community: The Case of Early Kharijism," *Archiv für Religionswissenschaft* 7 (2005); Kai Kress, *Philosophizing in Mombasa: Knowledge, Islam, and Intellectual Practice on the Swahili Coast*, 2007; Brinkley Messick, *The Calligraphic State: Textual Domination and History in a Muslim Society*, 1993; Barbara Daly Metcalf, *Islamic Revival in British India: Deoband, 1860–1900*, 1982; Felicitas Opwis, "*Maslaha* in Contemporary Legal Theory," *Islamic Law and Society* 12, no. 2 (2005); Paulo Pinto, "Sufism and the Political Economy of Morality in Syria," in *Sufism and Politics: The Power of Spirituality*, edited by Paul L. Heck, 2006; Franz Rosenthal, *Knowledge Triumphant: The Concept of Knowledge in Medieval Islam*, 1970; Yoginder Singh Sikand, *The Origins and Development of Tablighi Jamaʻat (1920–2000): A Cross-Country Comparative Study*, 2002; Thierry Zarcone, *La Turquie moderne et l'islam*, 2004.

PAUL L. HECK

L

leadership

Leadership in Islamic societies is firmly tied to two concepts, *imāma* and *khilāfa*. *Imāma* indicates the religious guidance a leader is expected to provide the Muslim community, deriving first and foremost from his ability to lead the community in prayer. *Khilāfa* refers broadly to the temporal aspects of leadership, central to which is maintaining the unity and internal harmony of the community. Implicit in both terms is the recognition that leadership in Islamic societies is subordinate to the dictates of the shari'a. The standard exposition of leadership is found in the *Ahkam al-Sultaniyya* (The ordinances of government) of Mawardi (d. 1058). This well-known treatise on governance provides the locus classicus for the Sunni doctrine of leadership, a principal feature of which is the obligation to establish a single leader of the Muslim community. Views that allow for more than one claimant to the position of supreme leadership over the Muslim community, or that would authorize more than one leader of the community on the basis of extreme distance or separation by sea, are characterized as heterodox.

Qualifications for leadership of the Muslim community include descent from the tribe of the Prophet Muhammad (*nasab*), knowledge of the law (*'ilm*), moral probity (*'adāla*), majority (*rushd*), and ability to carry out the duties of the office (*qudra*). This latter qualification encompasses such responsibilities as enforcing the law and settling disputes; dispensing legal punishments; maintaining peace in the lands under Islamic rule; conducting jihad to expand the realm of the faith; receiving alms, taxes, and war booty; and appointing trustworthy men (*'udūl*) to positions of authority and administration. Of equal importance is the duty of the leader to command the right and forbid the wrong and to protect the Muslim community from errant belief, a point that has proved particularly contentious in Islamic history and has at several turns placed the unity of Muslims in jeopardy.

Attaining leadership of the community is carried out through either designation by a predecessor (*'ahd*) or selection by a group of electors (*ikhtiyār*). The body of electors is commonly referred to as *ahl al-ḥall wa-l-'aqd* (those who loosen and bind), a designation with origins in early Arabian rituals accompanying the conclusion of pacts, truces, and agreements, and is typically composed of the prominent members of the community (*'ayān*) considered fit to choose a leader by virtue of their discernment and moral integrity. The number of electors that constitute this body varies, but it is widely held that their decision is binding on the community as a whole. The choice made by these notables results in the "most virtuous" figure (*al-afḍal*) assuming leadership; it has been conceded, however, that a "lesser" individual (*al-mafḍūl*) may be chosen if qualified. This distinction corresponds historically with the changing nature of leadership of the Muslim community from the time of the Prophet and the Rightly Guided Caliphs (632–61), held up as exemplary leaders beyond reproach, and their successors, the character of whose rule more closely approximated worldly kingship (*mulk*) and was often despotic in practice.

Notables took an oath of enduring loyalty (*bay'a*) in support of the newly chosen leader. Considerable importance was attached to public ceremonies surrounding the pledging of the oath, and this tradition survives in Morocco, where the pledging of loyalty to the monarch is attended with great pomp and ceremony. This act of near indissoluble fealty to the leader of the Muslim community can in theory be rescinded only if the leader suffers mental or physical incapacitation or, in the opinion of certain groups (the Kharijis most notably), if he is found guilty of immorality, oppressive rule, or errant belief. There is general agreement concerning the obligation of the community to remove an unjust leader, but the precise mechanism for doing so has never been fully articulated, and it is commonly held that the oath pledged to a leader is forfeit only upon death.

The *khilāfa* was effectively dismantled in 1924, and much thinking since then has centered on the means for restoring and adapting the institution to the modern world. The institution of *shūrā*, or a government run by consultation modeled on the pattern of the Rightly Guided Caliphs, has also been set forth as an acceptable form of leadership in the absence of the *khilāfa*.

See also authority; caliph, caliphate

Further Reading

Thomas Arnold, *The Caliphate*, 1924; Patricia Crone, *God's Rule*, 2004; Patricia Crone and Martin Hinds, *God's Caliph*, 1986; Hamilton A. R. Gibb, "Some Considerations on the Sunni Theory of the Caliphate," in *Archives du Droit Oriental* 3 (1939); Abu al-Hasan al-Mawardi, *The Ordinances of Government*, 1996; E. A. Salem, *Political Theory and Institutions of the Khawārij*, 1956; Émile Tyan, *Institutions du droit public musulman*, 1956.

RUSSELL HOPLEY

Lebanon

Lebanon is an Arab country on the eastern shore of the Mediterranean, bordering on Syria to the north and east and Israel to the south. The etymology of the name is a matter of dispute, like almost every other aspect of Lebanon's history and culture: it is usually linked to the color white in reference to the snowy mountains of Lebanon. The country is a modern creation, although ultra-Lebanese nationalists insist that the country extends far back in history to the times of the Phoenicians. The founding myth of Lebanon was devised early in the 20th century by Lebanese Maronite intellectuals with close ties to the French government and to the Maronite patriarchate, which wanted to separate its constituency from its Arab/Muslim surroundings after the demise of the Ottoman Empire. The country was created as an attempt to replicate the Jewish state in Palestine, but the French (the rulers of the area after World War I) decided that the viability of Lebanon as a political entity required the addition of territories outside of Mount Lebanon (the historic "homeland" of the Maronites). Those territories (including the greater Beirut area, the south, the north, and the Beqaa Valley) increased the number of Muslims in the new political entity and prevented the creation of an outright Christian republic—which was the demand of the Maronite patriarch at the peace conference in Paris. Thus the French created the Republic of Lebanon after World War I, putting an end to four centuries of Ottoman control over the Levant.

From the inception, the Lebanese split along sectarian and political lines over the identity and foreign policy of the new country: many Muslim Lebanese wanted unity with Syria (and later with other Arab countries during the heyday of Arab nationalism), and many Christians wanted a distinct entity with Western links. The constitution of Lebanon in 1926 recognized that sectarianism was at the heart of the Lebanese political system and society, and the state recognized citizens on the basis of their membership in the juridically recognized sects.

During the era of the French Mandate, when France ruled over Lebanon in association with a reliable political elite, a census was arranged to ensure the political dominance of the Maronites: other sects in the country were treated as secondary in public offices and posts. The political elite produced the unwritten "National Pact" in 1943 to achieve a modicum of understanding between the Sunni and Maronite elites. It reserved the top posts of government for the Maronites, and the prime ministership was awarded to the Sunnis (while the weaker post of speaker of parliament was given to the Shi'is, who would become the largest single sect in the country by 1975).

The arrival of Palestinian refugees into Lebanon after 1948 added an important factor that would radicalize the Lebanese body politic. Furthermore, tensions increased after Lebanon's independence in 1943. Many Muslims resented the National Pact, especially as their percentage in the population increased substantially, while secular Lebanese resented the sectarian basis of the political system and the domineering role of the clerics of all sects. The civil war of 1958 was a rehearsal for the major, protracted civil war that erupted in 1975 and continued until 1989, when Lebanese politicians produced the Ta'if Accords, which redistributed political power in the country in favor of the Council of Ministers, limiting the powers of the Maronite president. It took into consideration the new demographics and the military results of the civil war, which were not in favor of Christian militias. Lebanon entered an era of relative calm in the 1990s, but the assassination of Sunni prime minister Rafiq Hariri in 2005 and the Israeli war on Lebanon in 2006 increased tensions, even among the Muslims themselves.

In its contemporary history, Lebanon has suffered from Syrian political and military intervention and from successive Israeli invasions and occupations of Lebanese territories. Lebanon has a relatively open press and political system compared to those of neighboring Arab countries. It has survived a century of existence as a political entity, but its future remains uncertain.

See also colonialism; Hizbullah

Further Reading

Michael Hudson, *The Precarious Republic*, 1968; As'ad AbuKhalil, *Historical Dictionary of Lebanon*, 1998; Usamah Maqdisi, *The Culture of Sectarianism*, 2000; Augustus Richard Norton, *Hezbollah: A Short History*, 2007; Kamal Salibi, *A House of Many Mansions*, 1990; Fawwaz Traboulsi, *A History of Modern Lebanon*, 2007.

AS'AD ABUKHALIL

liberalism

Islamic liberalism grew out of the Islamic modernist movement of the 19th century. While modernism claimed that Islamic faith was compatible with a wide variety of European institutions, including technologies and administrative apparatuses, liberalism focused on a narrower set of norms relating to the Western liberal tradition, especially democracy, human rights, gender equality, and intercommunal harmony. Not every Muslim liberal adopted the entire package of Western liberalism, and many resented the term "liberal," which they associated with the hypocrisies of European imperialism. Nonetheless, the label of liberalism encapsulates a coherent and ongoing segment of Islamic political thought.

The first phase of liberal Islamic thought, from the middle of the 19th century to the first decades of the 20th century, treated liberal ideals as divinely revealed requirements. One of the most common liberal Islamic justifications for democratic reforms, the Qur'anic verse "and seek their counsel in the matter" (3:159) was pioneered at this time by Ottoman reformer Namık Kemal (1840–88). Early victories of these movements included constitutional documents in Egypt (1860, 1882), Tunisia (1861), and the Ottoman Empire (1876). These constitutional structures offered limited avenues for

democratic political participation, even by the standards of restricted suffrage then in force in Western Europe. Only in the early 20th century did liberal Islamic movements manage to institute more meaningful democratic reforms. Tatar and Turkish modernists participated in the Russian revolution of 1905, which led to the first parliamentary elections in the Russian empire. Iranians followed with the Mashrutiyyat, or Constitutional Revolution, of 1906, and Ottomans with the İkinci Meşrütiyet, or Second Constitutional Revolution, in 1908. In each of these cases, the prerogatives of the monarch were circumscribed by elected representatives, though suffrage was still strictly limited. Parallel movements arose but failed to take power in several other Muslim-majority states, including Afghanistan, Bukhara, and Khiva. Like the earlier constitutional experiments, these semidemocratic interludes were soon undermined. However, their legacy of political institutions and aspirations was adopted by authoritarian modernizing elites, as well as by anticolonial movements with modernist ideals.

Beginning in the 1920s, as Islamic modernism splintered into hostile camps, Islamic liberalism took shape as an independent movement seeking to reconcile Islamic faith and modern liberal norms such as democracy and human rights. This decolonization phase pioneered a new form of liberal Islamic reasoning, exemplified by the Egyptian ʿAli ʿAbd al-Raziq (1888–1966), who argued in the 1920s that Islamic sources left methods of governance for humans to devise. The Prophet Muhammad "was not a king nor the founder of a state, nor did he seek to rule," wrote ʿAbd al-Raziq, and by extension no other Muslims could claim an Islamic mandate for their form of government. Over the following decades, liberal Islamic movements engaged in similar arguments during the constitutional debates following decolonization. Liberal Islamic movements succeeded in creating partially democratic postcolonial states in several countries, including Indonesia and Pakistan, where competitive elections were held and civil legal systems were instituted. By the end of the 1970s, however, liberal Islamic politics had been suppressed by authoritarian governments in many Muslim societies. In Indonesia and Pakistan, for example, democratic experiments were overturned by military coups d'état.

In the 1980s, even as Islamic revivalism captured headlines, liberal Islamic movements began to revive as well, with a new liberal Islamic approach emerging simultaneously and independently in numerous Muslim societies at this time. According to this reasoning, all interpretations of the sacred sources, including one's own, are viewed as partial and fallible. In the words of Abdolkarim Soroush, a leading Iranian intellectual, "Religion is divine, but its interpretation is thoroughly human and this-worldly." Soroush's writings were among the inspirations for the Iranian reform movement, which won landslides in Iran's 1997 presidential election, as well as parliamentary elections in 1998 and elections for city councils in 1999, before being suppressed by illiberal factions. Elsewhere, too, liberal Islamic thought was linked with democratic and social reform. In Turkey, the Welfare Party reorganized itself as a liberal Islamic movement, committing itself to democratic procedures and pressing for membership in the European Union, recognition of Kurdish minority identities, and human rights limitations on the military. In Indonesia, liberal Islamic movements actively engaged in democratic political competition after the return of democracy in 1999, criticizing other Islamic parties for their failure to stand up to communal violence. In Malaysia, former fans of the Iranian revolution such as Anwar Ibrahim, a leading Islamic politician, helped to organize the Reformasi movement, the first Internet campaign for civil liberties in a Muslim society, which drew hundreds of thousands of hits from the well-wired Malay middle classes. In Egypt and several other Arab countries, the Muslim Brotherhood and its offshoots embraced pluralistic norms with more or less clarity and force.

Liberalism's opponents have long denounced it as un-Islamic. Derviş Vahdeti (1870–1909), founder of an Islamist movement in the Ottoman Empire, denounced liberals in 1909 as "cucumber people": "To expect religion from those who don't know their religion and have no Islamic training is like extracting oil from a cucumber." Almost a century later, in 2005, the Indonesian Ulama Council declared "liberal Islam" to be *ḥarām* (religiously impermissible), and Salih al-Fawzan, a senior Islamic scholar in Saudi Arabia, issued a fatwa against liberal Islam in 2007: "He who says, 'I am a liberal Muslim,' contradicts himself." Those who advocate such a position "should repent unto God in order to become truly Muslim." Notwithstanding these critiques, Muslims frequently view Islamic piety as consistent with liberal ideals. Surveys in the early 21st century consistently found large majorities of Muslims favoring democracy. Where a variety of Islamic movements have been permitted to contest elections, as in Indonesia and Kuwait, liberal Islamic candidates consistently outpolled more militant Islamists. Calls for revolutionary violence as a duty incumbent upon every individual Muslim have fallen on deaf ears, hence the minuscule portion of the world's billion Muslims who have engaged in such acts.

See also freedom; modernism; modernity

Further Reading

Michaelle L. Browers, *Democracy and Civil Society in Arab Political Thought*, 2006; Mehran Kamrava, ed., *The New Voices of Islam: Rethinking Politics and Modernity: A Reader*, 2006; Charles Kurzman, ed., *Liberal Islam: A Sourcebook*, 1998; Abdolkarim Soroush, *Reason, Freedom, and Democracy in Islam: Essential Writings of Abdolkarim Soroush*, translated by Mahmoud Sadri and Ahmad Sadri, 2000.

CHARLES KURZMAN

liberation theology

Liberation theology privileges the perspective of the poor and considers transformation of social orders the central theological task. It stresses human liberation from all forms of oppression: social,

political, economic, religious, racial, and environmental. Latin American liberation theology focuses on social, political, and economic oppression; South African liberation theology focuses on racism; and Asian liberation theology focuses on issues surrounding religious pluralism. According to Gustavo Gutiérrez (b. 1928), a key theorist, theology is a second act; praxis and contemplation are the first. Liberation theology is a new method of theology that transcends mere exposition and emerges from a context of lived oppression.

Vatican II (1962 onward) and the 1968 Medellin Conference in Colombia formalized liberation theology, reflecting a trend in Catholic social teaching that began with *Rerum Novarum*, an encyclical issued by Leo XIII in 1891 on the "Condition of Labour," and continued with landmark papal encyclicals in the 1960s. These encyclicals emphasized social justice, church and state as liberating forces for the poor and the oppressed, and workers' rights. They also affirmed the responsibilities of richer nations for the welfare of poorer ones and denounced unbridled capitalism. In 1967, a group of bishops from Latin America, Asia, and Africa wrote "A Letter to the Peoples of the Third World," which declared that revolution was a legitimate means to combat injustice and pointed fingers at the wealthy as instigators of violence. The Medellin Conference focused squarely on the church's role in the sociopolitics of Latin America and gave birth to the central tenet of liberation theology: "a preferential option for the poor." "The poor" was a broad term that included races and ethnicities suffering racism and women doubly exploited for being poor and for being women. Christian Base Communities appeared in the 1970s as the base of grassroots political action for faith as a liberating force. Since the 1990s, new perspectives have moved the discourse beyond economics and sociology. Women, indigenous peoples, and blacks speak of the broader "option for the excluded" and address topics of racism, culture, indigenous non-Christian spirituality, and nonpatriarchal ecclesiology. Other nontraditional subjects include ecology and interreligious dialogue.

Muslim theologians have only recently adopted the explicit terminology of liberation theology developed in Christian contexts. However, theologians like Shabbir Akhtar (b. 1960) and Asghar Ali Engineer (b. 1939) argue that the Qur'anic approach is fundamentally one of liberation, and they take inspiration from the Prophet Muhammad and his community as exemplifying struggle against injustice. Akhtar declares liberation theology an "Islamization of Christianity." Arguing the necessity for political religion, he claims that the political dimension of Islam was present from the inception of Muhammad's career. Akhtar argues that religion must engage with political power because of a moral responsibility to do so and because it is a natural human pursuit that should be regulated rather than wished away. He contrasts the "effective passivity [of Christianity] in the face of gross injustice" to the Qur'an's "morally constrained political action." He criticizes Christian thinkers for acknowledging the social dimensions of individual evil while proposing solutions only at the individual level, in contrast to Muslim thinkers, who address evil at a structural level. Engineer argues that Muhammad's movement stressed liberation from ignorance, superstition, and injustice through the power of reason and the pursuit of knowledge but that the Qur'anic spirit was lost once these ideas became merely subjects for theological reflection. Engineer emphasizes compassion as a central Qur'anic value and argues that warfare is legitimate only if fought on compassionate grounds to protect the rights of the oppressed and exploited. He identifies Sufi theology, with its focus on spiritual praxis, as closer to the heart of the people.

Irfan Omar argues that 19th- and 20th-century Muslim revivalist movements, which began as anticolonial struggles for economic and political liberation and self-determination, can be viewed through the lens of liberation theology. For example, Afghani (d. 1897), like many contemporary liberation theologians, divided the world into two categories: oppressor and oppressed. While anticolonial movements attempted to revive the political authority of Islam, postcolonial movements call for liberation from dependency on the West and resist Western military hegemony and adventurism, nationalism, cultural globalization, and economic liberalism. In an essay in Miguel A. De La Torre's *The Hope of Liberation in World Religions,* Omar argues that many of these movements can be counted as theologies because they "acknowledge the divine dispensation in how and what they set out to achieve." They include Palestinian theologies of liberation in the nonviolent intifada of the 1980s, as well as the more recent stand taken by African and Asian Muslims against globalization. They can also include the "Islamization of knowledge" movement, which integrates Qur'anically based epistemologies and ethical constraints into secular Western intellectual tools, categories, and modes of analysis.

These same movements also seek the liberation of Muslims from within by using Qur'an-based reasoning to analyze Muslim societies. 'Ali Shari'ati (1933–77) embraced socialist trends within the Qur'anic message and posited *tawḥīd* (unity of God) as a perfect means to implement this, while Hizbullah's Muhammad Husayn Fadlallah (1935–2010) criticized metaphysical discussions of justice that ignored realities like unjust rulers. Transnational groups include the Abu Dharr Collective, which articulates a theology of social justice, and the Muslim Peace Fellowship, which is devoted to the theory and practice of Islamic nonviolence. Akin to the Christian tradition, the insights of liberation theology have been applied much more broadly to issues of race, gender, and religious pluralism, equally influenced by Muhammad's example. The South African Farid Esack (b. 1959) seeks an Islam committed to contemporary progressive values and, more particularly, a South African Islam committed to the disempowered. His theology is founded on an alternative hermeneutical approach to the Qur'an that emphasizes praxis as the ultimate source of doctrinal orientation and stresses the historicity of and human experience behind the text while maintaining its universality and relevance for contemporary Muslims. Esack infuses his "horizon" as a South African Muslim under apartheid into the "Qur'anic horizon" to rediscover the text's identification with the oppressed and its embrace of pluralism. Hamid Dabashi argues for a postcivilizational period in global

conflict and explores post-Islamist responses to these new configurations of power. He articulates liberation theology as an attempt by those who have been denied a say in politics to democratize their voice, and he explores alternative resources for a politics of liberation, which include artistic movements like Iranian cinema and the *ta'ziya*, a Shi'i passion play, as a central performance of Islam as protest religion. Inspired by Malcolm X (1925–65), Dabashi stresses that an effective Islamic liberation theodicy must offer a solution to the disenfranchised in the heart of the "empire" (the United States) beyond an offer of conversion to Islam. Sherman Jackson, professor and scholar of law and Afro-American studies and a leading theological voice among American Muslims, addresses racial dimensions by seeking Qur'anic foundations for the protest agenda of black religion. Critiquing scholarship on the black American experience that denies the oppressor-oppressed paradigm, he explores the theological debate on black suffering through the lens of the Sunni tradition and argues that this tradition grants human beings agency in improving their condition. The Muslim feminist scholar Amina Wadud argues that women can be liberated through the Qur'anic text itself; though the prior texts of predominantly male Qur'an interpreters excluded women's experience, revisiting the text from a woman's perspective opens vast possibilities for nuanced approaches to gender. Another Muslim feminist scholar, Kecia Ali, rethinks Islamic sexual ethics to accommodate values of meaningful consent and mutuality, which she posits as crucial for a just ethics of sexuality, and gives precedence to wider Qur'anic principles of justice rather than specific "time-bound" commands.

See also apartheid; Malcolm X (1925–65); nonviolence

Further Reading

Shabbir Akhtar, *The Final Imperative: An Islamic Theology of Liberation*, 1991; Kecia Ali, *Sexual Ethics and Islam*, 2006; Hamid Dabashi, *Islamic Liberation Theology: Resisting the Empire*, 2008; Miguel A. De La Torre, *The Hope of Liberation in World Religions*, 2008; Asghar Ali Engineer, *Islam and Liberation Theology: Essays on Liberative Elements in Islam*, 1990; Farid Esack, *Quran, Liberation and Pluralism: An Islamic Perspective of Interreligious Solidarity against Oppression*, 1997; Sherman Jackson, *Islam and the Problem of Black Suffering*, 2009; Amina Wadud, *Quran and Woman: Rereading the Sacred Text from a Woman's Perspective*, 1999.

HOMAYRA ZIAD

libertarianism

Libertarianism is a tradition in Western political philosophy that emphasizes choice and political freedom from state coercion over other values such as equality. In one variant, libertarian thought approaches anarcho-syndicalism, promoting social organization that eliminates the state altogether. Another variant, minarchism, emphasizes a necessary minimal role for the state, such as the protection of basic rights and collective defense. Minarchist libertarianism, defined as the idea that the political authority of the central state apparatus should be constrained to certain necessary functions for preserving social choice, has notable parallels in Islamic tradition.

Minarchism and libertarianism are not labels that are widely associated with Islamic political thought. The word "libertarianism" evokes acceptance of social behaviors unfettered by common standards of decency or morality. Yet minarchist libertarianism's resonance with Islamic tradition comes from its emphasis on preserving the moral autonomy of the individual and collective grouping and protecting society from tyrannies and coercion by the state as well as nonstate actors.

A key Qur'anic injunction regarding religious choice reads, "Let there be no compulsion in religion" (Q. 2:256), which suggests that individuals cannot be coerced into religious observance. Choosing Islam, or submitting to the will of God, requires the opportunity to choose otherwise. State coercion can remove that choice and thus reduce the possibility of genuine submission by those in society. Numerous injunctions against spying, and a high bar for proving guilt in serious infractions of religious law, provide significant scope for individual choice without state interference.

Islamic law arguably developed in conscious opposition to the state as prominent scholarly authorities cultivated distance from political power. This is encapsulated in the failed Abbasid attempt to impose a Mu'tazili hegemony on Islamic interpretation. Furthermore, *fiqh*, the attempt to understand shari'a (Islamic law), has produced often-divergent rulings. The plurality of Islamic *fiqh* positions suggests that no single approach can be codified into public law without detracting from other approaches. This is represented by the traditional closing line in the fatwa (religious opinion) literature, "And God knows best," suggesting that the author does not presume to speak for God but rather offers a fallible opinion on an interpretative matter.

Particular claims to what constitutes an "Islamic" approach to state-society relations, despite the hegemonic aspirations of advocates, have been unsuccessful in gaining unanimous or high-majority support. There is no equivalent of the Roman Catholic pope (and the institutional structure provided by bishops), who can claim to definitively pronounce judgment on religious matters in most Islamic communities. The universal clerisy assumed in the Islamic context, as well as the normative practice that represents juristic legal opinions as fallible, suggests that respect for plural interpretation is built into Islamic tradition. Minarchist libertarianism offers a vision of a state that tries to safeguard such plurality through nonendorsement of specific doctrines. Ironically, the effort to assert a pluralism-respecting central state can itself be a totalizing claim about what state-society relations are most "Islamic."

Much of contemporary Islamic political activism seems inclined toward the statist direction, in which the Islamic state is presumed to endorse a comprehensive doctrinal position codifying Islamic

guidance into public law. This is notable in the platforms of Hizb ut Tahrir al-Islami (Islamic Liberation Party), the Jama'at-i Islami of Pakistan, and some branches of the Muslim Brotherhood. The opposite position—that the role of the central state should be restricted as much as possible—appears to have few takers, and there are relatively few self-proclaimed Islamic libertarians.

In practice, some approaches carrying the libertarian label are difficult to distinguish from liberal perspectives. One element that separates the two is that libertarian polities can potentially incorporate large numbers of illiberal constituents. This is partly because the libertarian approach is better placed to recognize the rights of plural social groupings as well as the rights of individuals. While a neat solution to the problem of reconciling individual and collective rights has not emerged, traditional norms of respect for interpretative choice suggest that plural groupings may coexist in an Islamic context.

See also collective obligations; freedom; jurisprudence; pluralism and tolerance

Further Reading

Saba Mahmood, "Is Liberalism Islam's Only Answer?" in *Islam and the Challenge to Democracy*, edited by J. Cohen and D. Chasman, 2004; Anas Malik, "Challenging Dominance: Symbols, Institutions, and Vulnerabilities in Minarchist Political Islam," *The Muslim World* 98, no. 4 (2008).

ANAS MALIK

loyalty

Loyalty is sustaining one's obligations toward friends, allies, patrons, clients, rulers, and groups. Various Arabic terms translate to "loyalty" or "fealty," reflecting a range of possible objects: God; other human beings; political and religious groups; and those higher, lower, or equal in the social hierarchy.

One such term is *walāya* (allegiance), from the verb *wālā* (also *tawallā*), meaning to affiliate with or declare loyalty to someone. In early Islamic sources, the implications of allegiance to an imam (e.g., Ibn al-Zubayr's allegiance to 'Uthman's party) are not merely political but eschatological. Early Islamic *walāya* thus differs from the *walā'* or *ḥilf* (covenant or alliance, frequently by oath) of pre-Islamic Arabia. One of the hallmarks of the early Islamic polity was the redirection of loyalty from individuals or kin groups toward the community of believers (the *umma*): people whom one might not know personally but with whom one nonetheless shared ties that transcended blood or politics. The *muhājirūn* of the early Islamic period or the supporters of 'Ali b. Abi Talib (Shi'at 'Ali) similarly shared this kind of ideologically based group solidarity; this was later famously described by Ibn Khaldun as *'aṣabiyya* (loyalty to the group).

Classical Islamic sources refer to both formal and informal loyalties, and the difference between the two is historically significant. Eighth-century jurists theorized *walā'*, which means patronage or clientele (the term itself being Janus-faced, literally meaning "proximity"), to be a formal, legal relationship that allowed non-Arabs to become Muslim by attaching themselves to an Arab-Muslim patron. This became the main mechanism of conversion and manumission during the Umayyad period. In principle, *walā'* was contracted between the individual who had converted and the Muslim patron who had converted him, but in practice, it entailed loyalty to the entire community of believers; as a social instrument, it thus staked out a middle ground between group solidarity (and its corollary, separatism) and reciprocity, making new social alliances possible and enabling increasing numbers of people to join the *umma*.

But one of the main effects of the Abbasid revolution was to extend the privileges formerly reserved for Arabs to non-Arab Muslims. Those privileges included a role in politics and at court. *Walā'* thus became unnecessary as a legal arrangement, and in the early Abbasid era, its legal obligations and prerogatives metamorphosed into a loose arrangement of patronage instead. The Abbasid house came to rely on its own clients—in the formal sense (those whom they had personally manumitted) and in the informal sense (those whose careers they had fostered through favors and benefactions)—for administration (the imperial bureaucracy), security (the palace guard and other military), and ideological legitimacy (supporters throughout the realm, often styled as *mawlā amīr al-mu'minīn*, or "client of the Commander of the Faithful," though it is difficult to know at what point this was no longer meant in the technical legal sense). In the ninth century, clients of the caliphal household came to hold governorships and other high-ranking positions and to form a distinct group at court, and eventually, entire armies came into being through *walā'*—the origins of the slave-soldier institution that dominated the Near East until the 19th century.

Uses of the terms *walā'* and *mawlā*, and the loyalties they represented, ramified as court culture, trade, and commerce burgeoned. The sources reflect the kinds of reciprocal exchanges that constituted political loyalty but also a pervasive consciousness of the obligatory nature of loyalty; its component parts were spelled out clearly only in moments when it risked severance. (Severance of ties of loyalty is often indicated with the noun *barā'a*, meaning "disavowal," or the verb *tabarra'a min*, meaning "declaring oneself free of.")

Another term related to loyalty is *birr,* which in the Qur'an means piety or devotion to God (2:177). In later sources, it comes to mean benefaction or reverence and thus to indicate two separate sides of human relationships of loyalty. Terms such as *'ahd* (pact, covenant, obligation, commitment) and *dhimām* (patronage), in literary and documentary texts from the post-Qur'anic period, likewise reflect the pervasiveness of loyalty and breaches of loyalty in politics and social relations. One also finds covenantal imagery invoked by *'ahd* (also *'aqd*, or contract) applied to people nearly equal in station, while *dhimām* reflects hierarchical

relations. Similarly, *ni'ma* in the Qur'an is a divine benefaction for which thanks and loyalty are due but later expands its semantic range to human relationships, in which it describes a favor granted by a patron. As God requires thanks and piety for benefactions, so, too, is loyalty to human benefactors an obligation understood to be imposed through *ni'ma*.

Formal and informal or individual and group loyalty were not, in practice, always separately conceived. The Mamluks, for instance, were procured, educated, and emancipated by an *ustādh* (master) to whom they remained affectively loyal and to whom they were also formally attached via *walā'*, and the Mamluks' individual bonds of loyalty produced group solidarity, described as *khushdāshiyya*.

See also civil war; family; obedience; tribalism

Further Reading

Patricia Crone, *Medieval Islamic Political Thought (God's Rule)*, 2004; Eadem, *Roman, Provincial and Islamic Law: The Origins of the Islamic Patronate*, 1987; Roy Mottahedeh, *Loyalty and Leadership in an Early Islamic Society*, [1980] 2001.

MARINA RUSTOW

M

madrasa

The term "madrasa" derives from an Arabic verb meaning "to learn" or "to study." In modern Arabic, *madrasa* means simply "school," although in Muslim communities throughout the world, it has recently been used to indicate institutions often established and run by revivalist and politicized organizations and offering a religious curriculum distinct from and in competition with those associated with government schools. In classical usage, however, The term "madrasa" had a more precise meaning, indicating schools devoted to instruction in the Islamic religious sciences, especially *fiqh*, or Islamic law.

The madrasa was a specifically Islamic institution and had no direct relationship with pre-Islamic religious or educational establishments in the Middle East (although one theory has suggested that the earliest madrasas in Khurasan and Central Asia may have been modeled on the Buddhist *vihara* [monastery]). Consequently, the madrasa was a product of, rather than a contributor to, the fully formed Islamic tradition.

Education in Early Islam

Two developments in particular were preconditions to the appearance of the madrasa. The first was the emergence of the 'ulama', the self-conscious community of scholars devoted both personally and, in some sense, professionally to the transmission of the Islamic religious sciences. Like Judaism, Islam is a religion of the book and of learning, and the 'ulama' function within Islam in a manner not dissimilar to that of the Jewish rabbis. Religious knowledge in Islam is known as *'ilm* and consists of interlocking discursive traditions preserving and interpreting the scriptural foundations of the faith, specifically the Qur'an and the hadith (accounts of the words and deeds of the Prophet Muhammad and his Companions). The emergence of the 'ulama' and of the intellectual traditions that lie at the root of their identity have not yet been systematically traced but had begun to develop by the end of the seventh century at the latest. By the ninth century, those traditions were firmly in place, and the 'ulama' had emerged as a prominent social group. The second development was the coalescence of the principal schools (*madhāhib*, sing. *madhhab*) of Sunni law between the eighth and tenth centuries—"school" here designating a community of intellectual discourse rather than an institution. With this development, law emerged as the most important of the Islamic religious sciences.

The premadrasa history of Islamic education has not yet been fully documented. Preliminary study of the Qur'an and the Arabic language took place either in the home or in primary schools (*maktab*, *kuttab*). At more advanced levels, instruction generally occurred in mosques, where scholars sat with their students for lectures, directed reading, and structured discussions and disputations of academic questions. In some mosques, particularly larger and more prominent ones and especially in Baghdad, the capital of the Islamic empire from the mid-eighth century, scholars might receive formal teaching appointments from the caliphs. Individual mosques might also benefit from endowments established by individuals as acts of charity, the income from which might be used to support instruction and learning. But absent a formal structure of educational institutions, the transmission of religious knowledge remained a fundamentally informal affair, regulated by personal relationships between teachers and pupils and networks of scholars in the various religious disciplines. That personal and informal character remained a hallmark of Islamic religious and legal education even after the advent of the madrasa.

Emergence and Development of the Madrasa

The madrasa as a distinctive institution, supported by endowments and devoted to instruction in Islamic law, first appeared in Khurasan in the tenth century. During the following centuries, the madrasa spread westward into Iran, Iraq, and Syria and became one of the most common institutions in the cities of the medieval Islamic world. Many madrasas, and virtually all the largest and most famous, were built and endowed by sultans or other leading political figures. Nizam al-Mulk (d. 1092), for example, the vizier to several Seljuq sultans, established madrasas that bore his name in Nishapur and other cities, including the particularly large Nizamiyya Madrasa in Baghdad, which was completed in 1067. Sultans Nur al-Din b. Zangi (d. 1174) and Salah al-Din Yusuf al-Ayyubi (Saladin, d. 1193) subsequently constructed many madrasas in the territories under their control as a part of their campaign to revitalize the Sunni world in the face of threats from militant Shi'ism and European Crusaders. Under the Mamluks, who ruled over Egypt and Syria from the mid-13th to the early 16th century, the spread of madrasas continued. By the 15th century, for example, the city of Cairo had more than 100 such institutions. Timur Lang (commonly known as Tamerlane; d. 1405) and his successors in Central Asia, the Ottomans in Anatolia and the Balkans, and the various Muslim dynasties that ruled over North India from the 13th century on also built and endowed madrasas to support instruction in the Islamic religious sciences.

There was considerable variety in the physical and institutional form of the madrasa. The term "madrasa" has been translated as "college," but that is a bit misleading, as madrasas were nothing like the medieval European institutions that evolved into modern universities. The madrasa itself was simply a building providing space for lessons, as well as accommodations for students and sometimes also for their professors. More important was the endowment (waqf) that supported the madrasa's activities. Typically, the endowment would fund salaries for one or more professors and stipends for students, as well as funds to support a diverse array of support staff, including cooks, cleaners, and guards, among others. Since many madrasas also functioned as mosques and were, in fact, often indistinguishable from them, the staff hired through the madrasa's endowment might also include prayer leaders, preachers, muezzins, and Qu'ran readers who served the spiritual needs of students as well as of others who used it as a place of worship. The classical madrasa was devoted to the study of law according to one of the four *madhhab*s: the Hanafi, Maliki, Shafi'i, and Hanbali schools of law. However, in 1234, the caliph al-Mustansir (r. 1226–42) founded a madrasa in Baghdad that provided support for professors and students in all four *madhhab*s, as well as classes in the Qur'an and hadith, and this became a common pattern, at least among the larger madrasas founded thereafter. As Sufism spread among the 'ulama' during the later Middle Ages, mystical devotions also became routine in the madrasas of the Middle East, and Sufi convents (variously known as *khānaqāh*s, *ribāṭ*s, or *zāwiya*s) began to offer courses in subjects such as law—in other words, to function as madrasas.

As George Makdisi, the pioneering modern historian of the madrasa, has pointed out, the madrasa was fundamentally a private institution. A madrasa was created as the result of an individual act of charity; it was not in any sense a public or "official" institution. Nonetheless, most madrasas were founded by sultans and other members of the ruling elite, if only because they had greater access to the large concentrations of wealth necessary to build and endow a school. Consequently, the spread of madrasas in the Middle Ages had important political dimensions. For example, the Ghazanvid sultans who ruled over the area of modern Afghanistan founded a series of madrasas as part of their campaign to Islamize the mountainous region of Ghur, the population of which resisted conversion into the tenth century. More generally, the foundation of institutions devoted to the transmission of Islamic religious knowledge offered rulers an opportunity to cultivate better relations with the 'ulama'. This was important, since most of the regimes that dominated much of the Middle East and South Asia in the medieval period were suspect according to the terms of Islamic law. The various sultans exercised authority that rightfully belonged to the caliph, and many of them came to power by violent means. Moreover, the predominantly Turkish warriors who formed the ruling elites in Egypt, Syria, India, and elsewhere frequently behaved in decidedly un-Islamic ways. The construction of madrasas offered these soldiers and sultans a chance to legitimate their rule in the eyes of the principal guardians of the Islamic tradition.

At first, the spread of madrasas had little impact on the curriculum or the procedures of Islamic education. The personal model, in which individual scholars supervised, evaluated, and attested to the accomplishments of their students, remained in place. Student mastery of a text or subject was guaranteed by the *ijāza*, the personal certification of an individual teacher, rather than by any system of institutional degrees. The proliferation of endowed institutions of education did, however, have major consequences for the social organization and authority of the 'ulama'. By providing stipends for students, the madrasa may have expanded the social reach of education by making it possible for larger pools of students to devote themselves to the transmission of Islamic learning. The increased number of paid professorships also solidified the social power of the leading religious scholars. An individual scholar might acquire appointments to several professorial "chairs" at the same time and appoint his friends, students, or relatives to substitute for him; he might also ensure that his own sons inherited the positions once he had died. Consequently, competition for these posts was often intense.

Modern Developments

Eventually, with the rise of more centralized governments in the early modern period, the madrasa was drawn more fully into the nexus of state power. Under the Ottomans, while madrasas were still created as acts of individual charity, they came to be controlled more tightly by political authorities. Professors and others became, in fact, employees of the Ottoman state, the institutions in which they taught were arranged in a hierarchical structure, and appointment to them was systematized and supervised by the sultan rather than left to the will of the individual founder or his heirs. Under the Ottomans, too, there was some regularization of the curriculum of the madrasas. That development was extended further by developments in India in the 18th and 19th centuries. Scholars at a center of learning in Lucknow (the Farangi Mahall) developed a clearly defined curriculum known as the Dars-i Nizami, and its prestige led it to be widely adopted by madrasas throughout India. Indeed, it had a broader influence throughout the Sunni Muslim world.

Later developments have separated modern madrasas even more from their medieval predecessors. Scholars at a madrasa at Deoband in India deliberately rejected the informal and personal model of classical Islamic education and developed a tightly defined organization and curriculum focusing especially on hadith. The Deoband madrasa became the model for thousands of others that were established throughout South Asia. Scholars belonging to the Deobandi network have seen themselves as playing a role in regularizing and homogenizing the religious life of Muslims. They include many teachers in madrasas that, in the late 20th and early 21st centuries, proliferated in Pakistan and elsewhere and have allegedly become a recruiting ground for radical Islamists—although it would be a serious mistake to see the Deobandi network as a whole as radical and politicized. The spread of Deobandi madrasas occurred at a moment of sharp decline of Muslim political power in India. Consequently, the Deobandi organization has been largely independent of the state. As such it stands in contrast to institutions

of religious education in territories that formerly formed part of the Ottoman Empire—for example, Azhar University in Cairo—where the legacy of state control of the religious establishment has been more persistent.

See also Azhar University; Deobandis; education; endowment; jurisprudence; knowledge; mosque; Nizamiyya; ‘ulama’

Further Reading

Jonathan Berkey, "Madrasas Medieval and Modern: Politics, Education, and the Problem of Muslim Identity," in *Schooling Islam: The Culture and Politics of Modern Muslim Education*, ed. Robert W. Hefner and Muhammad Qasim Zaman, 2006; Idem, *The Transmission of Knowledge in Medieval Cairo: A Social History of Islamic Education*, 1992; Michael Chamberlain, *Knowledge and Social Practice in Damascus, 1190–1350*, 1994; Daphna Ephrat, *A Learned Society in Transition: The Sunni ‘Ulama’ of Eleventh-Century Baghdad*, 2000; George Makdisi, *The Rise of Colleges: Institutions of Learning in Islam and the West*, 1981; Barbara Daly Metcalf, *Islamic Revival in British India: Deoband, 1860–1900*, 1982.

JONATHAN P. BERKEY

Mahdi

The Mahdi, also known as Qa'im (mainly among Shi‘is), is the Muslim messianic figure, and his title means "the one who is guided (rightly)." Although the title does not appear in the Qur'an and most of the traditions (hadith) concerning the Mahdi do not appear in the major canonical Sunni collections, there is no doubt of his significance for both Sunnis and Shi‘is from the middle seventh century, when the title first appeared. There are, in effect, two Mahdis: (1) the idealized figure described in the hadith and apocalyptic traditions and (2) the political and historical figure who is usually the leader of a revolutionary group or sect.

Apocalyptic traditions concerning the Mahdi usually start out with the basis for his appeal, which is the idea that he will "fill the Earth with justice and righteousness, just as it has been filled with injustice and unrighteousness." Other qualities associated with the Mahdi are—in addition to justice—generosity, eloquence, ability to judge between non-Muslim groups by means of their own holy books, and military conquest.

Early in Islamic history, questions concerning the Mahdi essentially grew out of the struggle between various branches of the Quraysh for supremacy (including the Umayyads, the Abbasids, and the ‘Alids). All these families emphasized or debated their relationship to the Prophet Muhammad as the basis for their legitimacy. Much of this discussion was projected into the question of who would be the Mahdi. In the end, the winners were the ‘Alids, who had the best genealogical claim, although it was contested strongly by the Abbasids, and ultimately either Sunni or Shi‘i Muslims came to see the former family as the rulers in the messianic future. There was a divide, however, between the Prophet's two grandsons, Hasan (d. 669) and Husayn (d. 680). Those who would ultimately become Shi‘is (either Twelvers or Isma‘ilis) held to Husayn's descendents, while by default the family of Hasan (eventually becoming the hereditary Sharifs of Mecca) were supported by the Sunnis. The Twelver Shi‘i candidate for the role of the Mahdi disappeared into occultation in 873, and it is said that he will reveal himself at the end of the world and establish the messianic kingdom.

A minority strand of Sunni opinion held to the Mahdi not as a genealogical descendent of the Prophet Muhammad but as the best possible Muslim. This more egalitarian trend contributes to the appearance of Mahdi claimants throughout the non-Arab Muslim world even in the 21st century. The Mahdi claimants that have garnered the broadest support, however, have usually been Arab.

Most of the traditions concerning the Mahdi center on two further problems: his personal appearance, or how to identify him, and the location of his emergence as Mahdi. Both Sunni and Shi‘i literature contain numerous detailed descriptions of the Mahdi. Naturally, that of the Sunnis is more varied and raises the question of whether the descriptions were of actual people. Presumably in order to weed out undesirable candidates, a series of portents, including heavenly communications, were added to these descriptions.

As for the location of his appearance, there are two irreconcilable families of traditions: Meccan-Medinan and Khurasan. The Meccan-Medinan family is probably dependent on the historical appearance of ‘Abdallah b. al-Zubayr—though he did not claim to be a Mahdi—in 683 and also probably on the revolt of Muhammad al-Nafs al-Zakiyya in 762. In both cases, the messianic figure is made to take refuge in Mecca from an invading army, usually Syrian, and during this utter extremity God intervenes, leads the army to be swallowed up in the desert, and causes the Mahdi to be proclaimed. In other versions, the Mahdi simply proclaims himself from Mecca, usually at the Ka‘ba, and then gathers an army with which he defeats all of his enemies.

The Khurasan family of traditions date to the Abbasid revolution (742–47) in which the Abbasid family used their support in the distant region of Khurasan—now eastern Iran, adjacent parts of Central Asia, and Afghanistan—to foment a revolution against the Umayyad dynasty ruling in Syria. As actually occurred in the revolution, the Mahdi's army is said to originate from this region, but it will not meet the messianic figure until the army has conquered the East and has arrived in Iraq.

A great many Muslim rulers or dynasties have either claimed as their founder a messianic figure or have used messianic titles and propaganda to strengthen the legitimacy of the dynasty. The earliest known "messianic figure" was apparently Muhammad b. al-Hanafiyya (a son of ‘Ali b. Abi Talib [d. 661] whose mother was not Fatima, the Prophet Muhammad's daughter), who was proclaimed by al-Mukhtar b. Abi ‘Ubayd al-Thaqafi, a proto-Shi‘i rebel in Kufa in 683 to 685. Ibn al-Hanafiyya did not necessarily push his own

claims; they were made in his name, and there is no way of knowing what precisely the term *madhī* meant at this early date.

The Abbasids (747–1258) were apparently the first successful dynasty to use messianic titles (Mansur, Mahdi, etc.) for its rulers, at least for the first 50 years of the dynasty. As a result of this development, the founders of many other dynasties also took titles such as Mahdi, or if they were Shi'is, Qa'im. Examples include the Fatimids in North Africa (910–1171) and the founder of the Mahdawis (Almohads), Ibn Tumart (ca. 1080–1130). In India, the Mahdawiyya, founded by Sayyid Muhammad Jaunpuri (d. 1505), was an attempt to create a mass movement prior to 1591, and it survives to this day.

Many Mahdi figures are associated with purification movements in the Muslim world during the 18th and 19th centuries or with anticolonialist jihads. The best example of this type of Mahdi was the Sudanese Muhammad Ahmad al-Mahdi, who revealed himself in 1881 and conquered Khartoum in 1885, founding a state that lasted until 1898. Some of these Mahdis were directed at Christian missionaries such as Ghulam Ahmad of India (d. 1908), who used messianic credentials to bolster his authority in anti-Christian polemic. Ultimately, Ghulam Ahmad's claims led to the Ahmadis being declared beyond the pale of Islam.

Shi'ism has had comparatively fewer claimants to be the Mahdi or Twelfth Imam, if for the reason that this figure is generally assumed to be in occultation. The Babi movement of the 1840s, however, resulted from messianic agitation at the 1,000-year anniversary of the Twelfth Imam's occultation and, as with the Ahmadis, led to the Babis (or Baha'is) leaving Islam altogether (Amanat, 1989).

Mahdi traditions have not been a major focus of contemporary Sunni apocalyptic literature. Since the Islamic revolution in Iran in 1979, however, Shi'is have increasingly highlighted the Mahdi (the Twelfth Imam), especially through his shrine located at Jamkaran, outside the holy city of Qum. Recently, Jamkaran and the foundations associated with it have generated a large number of publications detailing the messianic state and defending the belief that the Mahdi will soon appear. On the Sunni side, in order to avoid the political issues that stem from the Mahdi traditions, contemporary Sunnis have often focused on traditions that state that Jesus is the Mahdi.

Contemporary Mahdi claimants have usually been local rebels and have not generated much outside attention with the exception of the occupation of the Holy Mosque in Mecca in 1979 by the Saudi radical Juhayman al-'Utaybi and the somewhat mysterious Maitaisine movement in northern Nigeria the same year. The messianic impulse, however, stands behind a great deal of contemporary radical Muslim rhetoric.

See also messianism; revival and reform

Further Reading

Abbas Amanat, *Resurrection and Renewal: The Making of the Babi Movement in Iran 1844–50*, 1989; David Cook, *Contemporary Muslim Apocalyptic Literature*, 2005; Idem, *Studies in Muslim Apocalyptic*, 2002; Mercedes Garcia-Arenal, *Messianism and Puritanical Reform: Mahdis of the Muslim West*, 2006; J. Ketchichan, "Islamic Revivalism in Saudi Arabia," *Muslim World* 80 (1990).

DAVID COOK

Mahdi of the Sudan (1844–85)

Muhammad Ahmad al-Mahdi (1844–85) was a Sudanese holy man who led a successful revolt from 1882 to 1885 against the Turco-Egyptian forces that had been occupying the Nilotic Sudan since 1821.

Muhammad Ahmad was born in the northern Sudanese province of Dongola in 1844 to parents who both claimed to be *ashrāf*, or descendants of the Prophet Muhammad. At a young age, he studied the Qur'an, followed by Islamic jurisprudence, then Islamic mysticism, or Sufism, under the grandson of the founder of the Sammani order, Shaykh Muhammad Sharif Nur al-Da'im. In 1861, he requested the shaykh's permission to become one of his disciples and, his request granted, devoted himself to prayer and asceticism for seven years, after which the shaykh gave his disciple the license of shaykh of the Sammani order. This license gave him the opportunity to travel and engage in missionary work for the order and to return to his family in Khartoum and marry.

In 1871, Muhammad Ahmad emigrated to Aba Island in the White Nile and built a mosque and a school for the study of the Qur'an. His reputation for piety and asceticism became widespread, and many of the inhabitants of the island pledged allegiance to him and became his disciples. His former shaykh, Muhammad Sharif, visited Aba Island and ultimately settled in a village near the island. Shortly thereafter, however, the cordial relationship between the two men turned to one of animosity. As a result, Muhammad Ahmad professed allegiance to another important shaykh of the Sammani, Shaykh al-Qurashi b. al-Zayn. Qurashi's religious authority was at least on par with and perhaps even surpassed that of Muhammad Sharif. Meanwhile, the reputation of Muhammad Ahmad for piety and asceticism grew to such an extent that people from throughout the country traveled to Aba Island to seek his blessings and to request permission to join the ranks of his disciples.

Upon Qurashi's death in 1880, a majority of the adherents of the order agreed that Muhammad Ahmad should succeed the shaykh as leader. Muhammad Ahmad began traveling with his disciples to the western provinces of the Sudan, calling the people to remain steadfast in their adherence to the Qur'an and sunna of the Prophet Muhammad. During these travels he witnessed firsthand the discontent of the Sudanese masses with the Egyptian occupation, a discontent so great that many people asked Muhammad Ahmad if he was indeed *al-mahdī al-muntaẓar* (the anticipated deliverer) that would deliver them from the oppression of the Turco-Egyptian rule.

This rule, in the view of many Sudanese at the time, posed an economic threat because of the taxes levied against the populace

as well as the abolition of the slave trade. The Mahdi, however, viewed the Turco-Egyptian occupation as a threat to the very sanctity of Islam in the Sudan. He was angered by what he viewed as a regression into unbelief and the preponderance of *bid'a*, innovations that he believed were brought by the Turco-Egyptian occupation to Islam. He called for a revivification of the faith and the expulsion of the occupying forces from the Sudan.

On August 12, 1881, the Turco-Egyptian administration in Khartoum dispatched a steamer with two companies of troops to Aba Island to arrest Muhammad Ahmad, but a battle ensued that set the stage for the Mahdist Revolt. Muhammad Ahmad succeeded in defeating the Turco-Egyptian forces in this battle, and by December 9, 1881, he had defeated all the Turco-Egyptian forces sent to apprehend him. Thereafter, he no longer hesitated to refer to himself as the Mahdi and took up the title *khalīfat rasūl Allāh*, "the Successor of God's Messenger." Furthermore, Muhammad Ahmad dispatched letters to several tribal shaykhs, summoning them to join him, proclaiming his victories and identifying the purpose of his mission as ending the Turkish occupation and establishing an Islamic state modeled after the nascent state in Medina during the time of the Prophet Muhammad. By early June 1883, the Mahdi had consolidated his power over all of southern Kordofan, defeating the Turco-Egyptian forces, and on January 26, 1885, his forces conquered Khartoum, the capital, spelling the end of Turco-Egyptian imperial presence in the Sudan. The Mahdi, however, did not live to see his vision of an Islamic state come to fruition: he died of typhus on June 22, 1885. Nonetheless, his vision of an Islamic state manifested itself under the leadership of his second-in-command and eventual successor, the Khalifa Abdallah al-Ta'ayishi.

The Mahdist state, founded in 1885, ended in 1898, when the British conquered the Sudan and established the Anglo-Egyptian condominium.

See also Mahdi; Sudan

Further Reading

Peter M. Holt, *Mahdist State in the Sudan: A Study of its Origins, Development and Overthrow*, 1958; Kim Searcy, *The Formation of the Sudanese Mahdist State: Ceremony and Symbols of Authority, 1882–1898*, 2010; A. B. Theobold, *The Mahdiyya: A History of the Anglo-Egyptian Sudan, 1881–1899*, 1965; Francis R. Wingate, *Ten Years in the Mahdi's Camp: 1882–1892*, 1895.

KIM SEARCY

Malaysia

Muslim political thought in Malaysia bears the unmistakable imprint of the country's turbulent ethnic politics. The Pangkor Treaty, signed in 1874, gave responsibility for the colony's foreign and political-economic affairs to the British but left control of "Malay religion and custom" to Muslim sultans. The colonial policy of noninterference in native cultural affairs greatly expanded the Malay sultans' religious authority and provided a strong precedent for the native administration's extensive intervention in Islamic affairs. Since Malaysian independence in 1957, that intervention included efforts to deepen the practice of Islam among Muslims and to convert nearly half of the country's non-Muslim population.

Until independence, Malay society remained largely rural and traditionalist. To provide labor for the colony's mines and plantations, the British imported tens of thousands of Indian and Chinese workers. By 1920, Malays accounted for just 50 percent of the colony's population and only 10 percent of its urban population. Ethnic competition, the neotraditionalist authority of the sultans, and the agrarian nature of Malay society all insured that Muslim political thought in the colonial period was more conservative and deferential to native elites than its Indonesian counterpart.

In postwar Malaysia, ethnic competition between Malays and non-Malays shaped Muslim political thought even further. Although in 1946 the British proposed to extend full citizenship rights to Chinese and Indian immigrants, the Malay leadership objected and successfully presented an alternative plan that maintained the authority of Malay rulers, made Malay the national language, and recognized Islam as the religion of state, albeit while granting formal religious freedoms to all citizens. The agreement also reserved the largest portion of civil service posts for Malays.

The United Malays National Organisation (UMNO), which remained the dominant party in the ruling coalition, emerged from these circumstances as the champion of Malay-Muslim interests. During its first years, the party leadership was dominated by British-educated aristocrats who had little interest in religious affairs. The first prime minister, Tunku Abdul Rahman, stated openly that Islam could not solve the country's problems. However, the rivalry between UMNO and its main Malay opponent, the Pan-Malaysian Islamic Party (PAS, Parti Islam Se-Malaysia), gradually forced the UMNO leadership to change course and develop programs for state-supported Islamization. The administration of Mahathir Mohamed (r. 1981–2003) launched ambitious Islamization programs in law, banking, and higher education.

Founded in 1951, PAS long presented UMNO with its most serious challenge. During its early years, the PAS leadership pursued a largely ethnonationalist program. In 1963, however, the party called for the establishment of an Islamic state. The tension in the party between Islamic and ethnic appeals continued until 1982, when a young faction, dominated by Malay graduates of Middle Eastern colleges, ousted the senior PAS leadership. The new leadership spoke warmly of the Iranian Revolution and introduced policies to insure 'ulama' dominance in party affairs.

In 1982, Mahathir also responded to the PAS challenge by recruiting the most prominent of the student Islamists, Anwar Ibrahim (b. 1947), and assigning him responsibility for the government's Islamization initiatives. By the late 1990s, the charismatic Anwar had modified his views and become a spokesperson for a pluralist Muslim politics; he also seemed poised to succeed Mahathir as prime

minister. However, during 1997–98, Anwar fell out with Mahathir and was imprisoned. The displeasure of Malay citizens at Anwar's harsh treatment led to significant electoral gains by the PAS-led opposition in December 1999 and March 2008.

In 2004 the new prime minister, Abdullah Ahmad Badawi (b. 1939), assumed the UMNO helm. The Badawi government made what it called "civilizational Islam" (*Islām haḍārī*) a central element in its domestic and international platform. Borrowing a phrase from the medieval Arab historian Ibn Khaldun, Badawi's concept emphasized the need for Muslim moderation and forward-mindedness; it also underscored the necessity of collaboration across cultures rather than a clash of civilizations.

Islamic political thought in Malaysia long tended to display a more staid face than its Indonesian counterpart. But the country also suffered little of the paramilitarism or sectarian violence of its unsteady neighbor. Although theologically conservative, the PAS opposition abided by the rules of constitutional politics. In the early 21st century, there were signs that a new generation of Malaysian Muslim intellectuals was poised to play a more prominent role in global Muslim affairs.

See also Indonesia; Pan-Malaysian Islamic Party (PAS); Southeast Asia

Further Reading

Mona Abaza, *Debates on Islam and Knowledge in Malaysia and Egypt*, 2002; Virginia Hooker and Norani Othman, eds., *Malaysia: Islam, Society and Politics*, 2003; Hussin Mutalib, *Islam and Ethnicity in Malay Politics*, 1990; Farish A. Noor, *Islam Embedded: The Historical Development of the Pan-Malaysian Islamic Party PAS (1951–2003)*, 2004; Michael G. Peletz, *Islamic Modern: Religious Courts and Cultural Politics in Malaysia*, 2002; William R. Roff, *The Origins of Malay Nationalism*, 1994.

ROBERT W. HEFNER

Malcolm X (1925–65)

Malcolm X, born Malcolm Little on May 19, 1925, in Omaha, Nebraska, was the fourth child of Earl and Louise Norton Little. Both of his parents were ardent supporters of the Pan-African leader Marcus Garvey (1887–1940). Although Malcolm was probably too young to understand the deeper nuances and implications of Garvey's message, its major themes—African unity and liberation, commitment to the African "fatherland," and black economic self-sufficiency—would dominate Malcolm's career as both a religious leader and a political activist.

Assessing the public career of Malcolm X requires an examination of his segregationist, Nation of Islam period and his post-hajj period from April 1964 until his assassination a year later. Certain themes appear in both periods, such as his perception of a pervasive white supremacy that defined American race relations and caused the injustices faced by African Americans and his unwavering commitment to black liberation and self-sufficiency. His advocacy of black separatism and his demonizing of all whites as inherently evil "devils" are unique to the Nation of Islam period. His expressed humanism, symbolized by his reframing the race problem in America as a human rights problem, is unique to the post-hajj period.

The post-hajj period of Malcolm's life, from April 1964 to February 1965, was characterized by a dynamic interaction of ideas, leading many groups, ranging from socialists to black nationalists, to justifiably claim him as an embodiment of their particular ideas and agendas. The role that Islam played in defining his political thought in this period is neglected in scholarship. We know that Malcolm was devout and that a good portion of his second trip to the Middle East and Africa, from July to November 1964, was spent studying Islam at Egypt's Azhar University. Malcolm's evolving commitment to Sunni orthodoxy was expressed in the shaping of his Islamic organization Muslim Mosque Incorporated, founded a few days after his departure from Nation of Islam in March 1964, to advance the cause of Sunni Islam among African Americans.

Although Malcolm's orthodoxy did not affect his commitment to black liberation, it appears to have played a part in broadening his liberationist paradigm and his cooperation with a wide array of groups, many of which he had stridently condemned during his Nation of Islam phase. This development is evident in the attention he gave to building the secular Organization of Afro-American Unity in June 1964, shortly after his return from his pilgrimage to Mecca and travels in Africa. Islamic orthodoxy also led Malcolm to begin substantiating his political ideas with arguments rooted in the Qur'an. This empowered Malcolm against both his Nation of Islam adversaries and his new circle of assimilationist Sunni Muslim acquaintances, many of whom viewed Malcolm as a potential ambassador to white America. During this last period of his life, Malcolm would often situate his advocacy for African Americans and his militancy in the context of Islamic teachings. He would emphasize, for example, that the Qur'an calls for "fighting those that fight against you" (Q. 2:190).

Malcolm understood the importance of spirituality as a basis for social action, and in Islam he felt he had found the strong spiritual foundation necessary to overcome the abuses of power he vehemently critiqued. He would remark that Islam had solved his personal problem but also that his personal solution was inadequate as long as the problem of his people's oppression was unresolved.

At the end of his life, Malcolm had an identifiable political philosophy. It was a liberationist philosophy that emphasized justice, fairness, and equality in human relations. It also called for active struggle, even armed struggle if necessary, to achieve its ends. This philosophy was influenced by Marcus Garvey's movement, a life among the struggling African American masses, his longtime involvement in the black liberation struggle, his exposure to the ideas and key personalities of an emerging "Third World" anti-imperialist movement, and his deepening Islamic orthodoxy. Malcolm did not live long enough, however, to translate that philosophy into a

detailed political program, so it would not be accurate to affix to that philosophy a particular label—nationalist, socialist, Islamic, or otherwise.

See also liberation theology; Muhammad, Elijah (1897–1975); Nation of Islam

Further Reading

George Breitman, *The Last Year of Malcolm X: The Evolution of a Revolutionary*, 1984; Jan Carew, *Ghosts in Our Blood: With Malcolm X in Africa, England, and the Caribbean*, 1994; Louis A. Decaro Jr., *On the Side of My People: A Religious Life of Malcolm X*, 1997; Benjamin Karim, *Remembering Malcolm*, 1992; Y. N. Kly, *The Black Book: The True Political Philosophy of Malcolm X*, 4th ed., 1990; Malcolm X, *The Autobiography of Malcolm X: As Told to Alex Haley*, 1965.

ZAID SHAKIR

Malik b. Anas (712–95)

Malik b. Anas is the founder and eponym of the Maliki school of law in Islam and the compiler and organizer of the earliest Muslim legal text, *al-Muwatta'* (The trodden path), the oldest surviving large collection of traditions from the Prophet Muhammad (hadith). Because of the scantiness of contemporary biographical information about him and because of his importance as a foundational figure in Islam, there is considerable scholarly controversy about his history, despite the great mass of material about him.

Malik lived his entire life in his native city of Medina, which had been a political backwater since the beginning of the Umayyad dynasty in 661, but nevertheless remained a center for normative Muslim practice as the city of the Prophet Muhammad. Because of the pilgrimage requirement, important Muslims passed through the city on their way to Mecca at some point. While at Medina, they took the opportunity to learn more about Islam in the city of its original and authentic practice. For their part, the Medinans, including Malik, could take comfort from the fact that, despite their lack of political power, their city remained the center of Muslim traditional religious authority.

Malik strove to stay politically neutral during his life. There is no information about his relations with the Umayyads. After the new and insecure Abbasid dynasty came to power in 750, however, he received from the caliph Abu Ja'far al-Mansur (r. 754–75) in 761 some financial benefit confiscated from the property of a suspected opponent of the dynasty, 'Abdallah b. al-Hasan, a descendant of the fourth caliph 'Ali b. Abi Talib (d. 661). This may indicate that Malik was thought to be unfavorable to 'Alid political claims, which then greatly threatened the Abbasids' legitimacy, and therefore the Abbasids sought to gain his favor. Nevertheless, in 762, when 'Abdallah's son Muhammad al-Nafs al-Zakiyya (d. 762) proclaimed his revolt against Mansur in Medina, Malik issued a fatwa invalidating the oath of allegiance to Mansur on the grounds that it was coerced. By so doing, Malik freed the Medinans to join the revolt, but instead of actively participating in it like his fellow scholar 'Abdallah b. Yazid b. Hurmuz (d. 765), Malik himself stayed in his house. After the failure of the revolt, Malik was severely beaten for his defection in 763 by the governor of Medina and possibly also was put under house arrest.

Malik's passive attitude eventually made possible a later reconciliation with the Abbasid dynasty, when in 777 Mansur's son Muhammad al-Mahdi (ruled 775–85) consulted him about making alterations to the Ka'ba. When Malik expressed his opposition to that idea, Mahdi heeded his advice. Much later, during the pilgrimage of 795 near the end of Malik's life, Mahdi's son Harun al-Rashid (r. 786–809) paid his respects to him when he passed through Medina and even visited him, although Malik had turned down a summons to come to the caliph. This is all that is known about Malik's direct relations with political authorities. Other stories told about his dissuading either Mansur or Mahdi from promulgating his book, *al-Muwatta'*, as the law of the land appear to be apocryphal.

Malik's relatively few overt contacts with the Abbasid political authorities do not clearly describe his political stances. His general avoidance of them, however, demonstrates the orientation of the rising class of religious scholars that helped to set the tone for them through the centuries. Malik's own views are believed to be represented by the two Maliki law books, *al-Muwatta'* and *al-Mudawwana* (The compendium). *Al-Muwatta'* is entirely attributed to Malik but exists in various recensions, while *al-Mudawwana*, a larger compilation by the Tunisian Maliki scholar Sahnun (777–854), contains the reports of others beside Malik. Despite some uncertainty about the extent to which these works represent Malik himself, they clearly draw a specific image of him that has been received by the Muslims and that probably describes his views in general. Both works display an aversion to politics and, in particular, to the rulers of the time. Malik's aversion emerges not so much from direct statements as from silence: the state and its officials are infrequently mentioned, usually with vague terms such as imam, sultan, *wālī*, amir, without specification of particular offices or institutions. The individual rulers in office, the Abbasid caliphs, and their dynasty never receive a single mention, nor do the defunct Umayyads and their latter-day successors in Spain. The audience for these works can hardly have been the rulers, and indeed their continued transmission and cultivation by scholars make it clear that they were addressed mainly to scholars.

By their general lack of reference to government, the works may be seen as demonstrating that Islam can be established and practiced almost without reference to the state. Thus, for example, rather than being asked whether rulers have the right to organize, regulate, and lead public worship, Malik is asked whether it is permissible to perform public worship with "these rulers" (*hā'ulā' al-wulāt*)—a somewhat disparaging way to refer to the Abbasids. He replies in the affirmative, as long as the rulers do not display heresy.

One of the few areas where the state seems definitely to be necessary is war. Yet, even here, there is very little mention of the state or any chain of command, apart from the commander's power to give orders, including his power to allot the spoils, for example. In one of the few instances where rulers are mentioned, Malik is said to have been asked whether it was permissible to participate in a military campaign against the Byzantines with "these rulers." Malik is said originally to have regarded such participation as not permissible, but he changed his mind because of the notorious Byzantine attack on the Muslim city of Mar'ash in 778—an event that shook the caliph Mahdi himself. The reason Malik gave for his change of view was that not to allow participation in military campaigns, even if under "these rulers," would cause harm to the people of Islam in general. Such discourses show little regard for caliphs, match Malik's other history, and foreshadow the tendency of the 'ulama' to avoid close contact with the rulers that became standard through most of Islamic history down to the present.

On the other hand, Malik does assign to rulers the collection of mandatory alms (zakat) and the administration of *ḥudūd* punishments, which are major punishments mentioned or implied in the Qur'an, thus showing that he accepts the necessity of a ruler for some purposes. He also draws an important contrast between just and unjust rulers: while the former must be obeyed, the latter should not be obeyed when they issue unjust commands.

See also Abbasids (750–1258); jurisprudence; Mecca and Medina; shari'a

Further Reading

Malik b. Anas, *al-Mudawwana al-Kubra*, edited by Ahmad 'Abd al-Salam, 1994; Idem, *al-Muwatta*, translated by 'A'isha 'Abdarahman at-Tarjumana [Bewley] and Ya'qub Johnson, 1982; Yasin Dutton, *The Origins of Islamic Law: The Qur'ān, the Muwaṭṭa', and the Medinan 'Amal,* 2nd ed., 2002; Mansour H. Mansour, *The Maliki School of Law: Spread and Domination in North and West Africa 8th to 14th Centuries* C.E., 1995; Joseph Schacht, "Mālik b. Anas," *Encyclopedia of Islam*, 2nd ed., 1954–2005.

KHALID YAHYA BLANKINSHIP

Mamluks (1250–1517)

The Mamluk dynasty ruled in Egypt from 1250 to 1517. The term "mamluk" means "owned"; the Mamluk rulers were slaves by origin. The employment of slave soldiers in Muslim armies began with the Turkic guard regiment of slaves in Samarra under the Abbasid caliph Mu'tasim (r. 833–42) and lasted until the massacre of the last mamluks by Muhammad 'Ali, the reform-minded governor of Egypt, in 1811. The Mamluk regime is the only example of a state in which slaves ruled on their own instead of merely serving their masters.

Sources commonly divide Mamluk history into two phases: the Bahri phase, in which rulers were drawn from the corps garrisoned on the Nile (*al-baḥr*, also known as the Turkic phase, because the mamluks in question came from the Qipchaq steppe in Central Asia), and the Burji phase, in which the rulers were drawn from those stationed in the Citadel (*al-burj*, also known as the Circassian phase, because the mamluks were by then drawn from the Caucasus).

The Mamluk period produced a considerable amount of literature on political theory. Ibn Taymiyya's *al-Siyasa al-Shar'iyya fi Islah al-Ra'i wa al-Ra'iyya* (The book of governance according to the shari'a) focuses on public policy, while Ibn Jama'a's *Tahrir al-Ahkam fi Tadbir Ahl al-Islam* (Summary of the rules to govern the people of Islam) and Ibn Qayyim al-Jawziyya's *al-Turuq al-Hukmiyya fi al-Siyasa al-Shar'iyya* (Ways of governing and policy making) articulate the concept of the "Islamic state." Various authors offered advice on running the state's affairs or tried to justify the Mamluks' rejection of dynastic rule by referring to Islamic jurisprudence regarding the right to govern. Such writings deal with issues of governance under the shari'a, placing political thought within the framework of Sunni discourse on rules and administrative matters. The truly distinct political principles behind the Mamluk regime, however, may be gleaned from the reality of the Mamluks' pragmatic approach to governing.

In theory, the Mamluk sultanate was an oligarchy in which the assembled amirs would elect the most powerful person as ruler. In practice, however, once elected, many a sultan installed his son as successor, either by direct appointment or by an "election" by his own faction. Insofar as hereditary rule never gained consensus, it was always threatened by factional maneuvering. The resulting succession crises throughout Mamluk history underscore the tensions between the principle of hereditary monarchy, inherited from the Ayyubids, and the rival view of the Mamluk state as a crowned republic in which the throne was passed by election or usurpation.

The crisis of political legitimation began with the state's inception, which was itself the outcome of a rebellion in which the mamluks of Salih Ayyub fought to preserve their position as a faction. The assassination of the sultan Qutuz (r. 1259–60) crystallized the "law of the Turks" in the maxim "he who kills the ruler will be ruler himself." Baybars (r. 1260–77), the regicide, was declared sultan. The restoration of the Abbasid caliphate in Cairo and the shadow caliph's bestowal of powers on Baybars not only enhanced his claims to rule but also bolstered the Mamluks' legitimacy vis-à-vis the Ayyubids, their former lords. A combination of residual dynasticism and the political convenience of the oligarchy would become a recurrent theme in Mamluk history.

Baybars nominated his sons as joint sultans, but the last son was installed on behalf of Qalawun, a fellow amir, allowing him to usurp the throne. The prolonged rule of the Qalawunids (1279–1382)—Mansur Qalawun, his sons Ashraf Khalil and Nasir Muhammad, and Nasir's sons and grandsons—illustrates the Mamluks' perennial fluctuation between dynastic rule and military oligarchy. After Nasir's death, the system that had supported factional

integration collapsed. Ultimately a consultative council was established whose members agreed to recognize the supremacy of one among them (*al-amīr al-kabīr*) who would act as ruler, while the sultan was stripped of real power. All but one of Nasir's sons and grandsons were "elected" when they were teenagers, and they were governed by Nasiri amirs who served as mentors (*atābak*), viceroys, and viziers. When the Qalawunid dynasty was eventually removed at the hands of Barquq, a Circassian *atābak*, the elective principle was reenforced so that the throne was once again awarded to the victorious faction.

Zahir Barquq's (r. 1382–92) usurpation ushered in the Burji period, which saw continuous factionalism and dynastic/elective maneuvering, with some new features. Nearly every sultan endeavored to will the sultanate to his son, fully aware that his wishes would certainly be violated. Some mutual understanding seems to have existed between the sultan and his faction whereby the sultan's will created an interregnum after his death, during which his mamluks could elect one of their own to the throne. Gradually, the motto "kingship has no progeny" gained currency. By the end of the 15th century, the succession of a son, instead of a genuine first-generation mamluk, was generally regarded as illegitimate. Succession was passed along the line of the household, composed of both the heirs and the mamluks of the group's founder. The household founded by Qaytbay (r. 1468–96) produced six sultans—his son and five mamluks—and reigned until the coming of the Ottomans.

See also Ayyubids (1160–1250); Ibn Jama'a (1241–1333); military; slavery

Further Reading

David Ayalon, *The Mamlūk Military Society*, 1979; Idem, *Studies on the Mamlūks of Egypt (1250–1517)*, 1977; Patricia Crone, *Slaves on Horses: The Evolution of the Islamic Polity*, 1980; P. M. Holt, "The Position and Power of the Mamlūk Sultan," *Bulletin of the School of Oriental and African Studies* 38 (1975); Idem, "The Structure of Government in the Mamluk Sultanate," in *The Eastern Mediterranean Lands in the Period of the Crusades*, edited by P. M. Holt, 1977; Idem, "The Sultan as Ideal Ruler: Ayyubid and Mamluk Prototypes," in *Süleyman the Magnificent and His Age: The Ottoman Empire in the Early Modern World*, 1995; Carl Petry, *Protectors or Praetorians? The Last Mamlūk Sultans and Egypt's Waning as a Great Power*, 1994.

LI GUO

Ma'mun (786–833)

The seventh caliph of the Abbasid dynasty, 'Abdallah al-Ma'mun was appointed governor of the province of Khurasan by his father, Harun al-Rashid (d. 809). He led a successful revolt against the reigning caliph, his half-brother Muhammad al-Amin (r. 809–13), who was killed in the siege of Baghdad. To justify the coup d'état, Ma'mun claimed for himself the title of Imam al-Huda, the "rightly guided (and rightly guiding) leader." This designation implied that he had privileged insight into matters of faith and practice and was therefore best qualified to head the Muslim community. He described his movement as "the second call to allegiance," suggesting legitimate descent from the first "call": the Abbasid revolution of 749–50.

In 817, he named as his successor 'Ali b. Musa, a prominent member of the rival house of 'Ali b. Abi Talib. He gave him the title al-Rida, or "the one acceptable to all," a title that the original Abbasid revolutionaries had used to refer to the descendant of the Prophet whom they hoped to bring to power. Ma'mun's choice may have been motivated by a desire to placate the 'Alids, who had risen in Yemen and in Kufa. It may also have been motivated by messianic expectations associated with his being the seventh caliph and with the passing of the second Islamic century (816). Perhaps, too, he had no choice but to appoint an 'Alid, having severed his ties with his Abbasid relatives. In any event, the new heir apparent died soon after being appointed, giving rise to speculation that he was murdered to pave the way for reconciliation with the Abbasids. Today, Rida is revered as the eighth imam by Twelver Shi'is, who generally hold Ma'mun responsible for killing him.

During the latter part of his reign, Ma'mun adopted a series of measures intended to enforce general recognition of his authority in matters of belief and practice. His most powerful opponents were the Sunnis, who sought guidance from the hadith rather than from the Abbasid caliphs, whom they regarded as usurpers. In 827, Ma'mun proclaimed that 'Ali (r. 656–61) was the greatest of the caliphs and that the Qur'an was created (i.e., produced by God), as opposed to being a part of Him and therefore eternal. These proclamations were a deliberate affront to Sunnis, who believed that Mu'awiya, who declared himself caliph in 661 upon the death of 'Ali, was justified in doing so and that the Qur'an, being God's speech, was uncreated (or that the subject should not be discussed at all). Shortly before his death in 833, Ma'mun asked judges, teachers of hadith, and others suspected of Sunni sympathies to affirm that the Qur'an was created. Threatened with death, nearly all did as they were told, the most famous exception being the hadith scholar Ahmad b. Hanbal (d. 855). The so-called inquisition (*miḥna*) was pursued halfheartedly by Ma'mun's successor, Abu Ishaq al-Mu'tasim (r. 833–42), but revived with gusto by Abu Ja'far al-Wathiq (r. 842–47). It was brought to an end by Abu al-Fadl al-Mutawakkil (r. 847–61), who banned theological disputation and extended official patronage to Sunni scholars of hadith.

Ma'mun's claim to authority in matters of faith and practice may have been a deliberate revival of the archaic caliphate, which appears to have been a religious office. His designation of himself as an instrument of divine guidance manifested itself in his vigorous campaigns against the Byzantines and perhaps also in his interest in the so-called ancient sciences. His sponsorship of translations from Greek and Middle Persian, seemingly undertaken to strengthen the rationalists against the literalist hadith scholars, left an indelible mark on Arabic literature and science. Beginning in the 19th

century, his patronage of science and his encouragement of debate between representatives of different schools of thought have served reformers and apologists as evidence that free and rational inquiry is compatible with Islam. Historically, however, the most important part of his legacy may be his inadvertent contribution to the development of Sunnism. Despite his claim to be an "imam of right guidance," he failed to curb the power of the literalist hadith scholars, who emerged from their confrontation with the state stronger than ever before.

See also Abbasids (750–1258); inquisition

Further Reading

Michael Cooperson, *Al-Ma'mun*, 2005; Patricia Crone, *God's Rule: Government and Islam: Six Centuries of Medieval Islamic Political Thought*, 2004; Patricia Crone and Martin Hinds, *God's Caliph: Religious Authority in the First Centuries of Islam*, 1986.

MICHAEL COOPERSON

martyrdom

The term *shahīd*, used almost exclusively in later literature to refer to a martyr, military or otherwise, does not have the same meaning in the Qur'an. *Shahīd* and its cognate *shāhid* refer in the Qur'an only to a legal witness or eyewitness and are applied both to God and to humans in appropriate contexts (e.g., Q. 3:98; 6:19; 41:53). Qur'anic locutions commonly understood to refer to the military martyr include "those who are slain in the path of God" (*man qutila fī sabīl allāh/alladhīna qutilū fī sabīl allāh*: Q. 2:154; 3:169) and variations thereof. Only in later, extra-Qur'anic literature, including *sīra* (life of the Prophet), *tafsīr* (Qur'anic exegesis), and the hadith (prophetic tradition), does *shahīd*—and its plural *shuhadā'*—acquire the specific meaning of "one who bears witness for the faith," particularly by laying down his or her life. Some scholars attribute the semantic transformation of these terms to extraneous, particularly Christian, influence. Another concept of selling or bartering one's self or the life of this world for the hereafter (Q. 4:74; 9:111) has been connected to the notion of martyrdom.

In the exegetical literature, however, these Qur'anic locutions have been predominantly understood as endorsing the concept of earning martyrdom by dying on the battlefield, even if the terms *shahīd* or *shuhadā'* are not always used in these contexts. Some exegetes indicate that debates concerning the more meritorious manner of dying—dying naturally or being slain in the path of God—were robust and persistent in scholarly circles. Thus the 13th-century Andalusian commentator Abu 'Abdallah al-Qurtubi (d. 1273) affirms that Qur'an 22:58 clearly states that both types of death are equally meritorious in the case of a pious believer and earn the same reward in the hereafter, but certain jurists nevertheless came to advocate a superior status for the military martyr.

A number of early hadith compilations preserve reports that assign a broad range of meanings to the term *shahīd*. One such report, related by Masruq b. al-Ajda', declares that there are four types of martyrdom: dying from the plague, by giving birth, by drowning, and from a stomach ailment. Hadiths and other reports that preserve these early expansive meanings of martyrdom are also contained in early treatises on jihad (broadly, struggle, striving for the sake of God and, more narrowly, fighting for the sake of God), such as in Ibn al-Mubarak's *Kitab al-Jihad* (The book of warfare). In comparison with these earlier works, certain hadiths recorded in the *Sahih* (The sound collection) of Muhammad b. Isma'il al-Bukhari clearly assign a more privileged status to military martyrs, with special rewards in the hereafter reserved for them alone. A hadith on the authority of Samura b. Jundub states that "the abode of martyrs" (*dār al-shuhadā'*) is the best abode in the hereafter. Some hadiths warn, however, that the exalted status of the warrior should not lead to the deliberate courting of martyrdom on the part of the faithful by seeking to confront the enemy. The progressively higher valuation of military martyrdom becomes more blatant and pervasive in later popular *faḍā'il al-jihād* (excellences of jihad) works, especially those composed during the Mamluk period. One such work is the *Mashari' al-Ashwaq ila Masari' al-'Ushshaq fi al-Jihad wa-Fada'ilih* (The wellsprings of longing), composed by the anti-Crusader warrior Ahmad b. Ibrahim b. al-Nahhas (d. 1411), which promises exaggerated posthumous rewards to the military martyr.

The juridical literature came to reflect this evolving greater reverence for the military martyr, primarily in connection with preparation of his corpse for burial. Against the procedure followed in normal burials, the body of the martyr was not to be washed, following the precedent said to have been set by Muhammad after the Battle of Uhud in 625. If the martyr was wounded on the battlefield and died later in his home, then his body was to be washed. Martyrs were to be buried in the clothes they fought in, but their weapons were to be removed. Most jurists were of the opinion that there was no need to say the funerary prayers over the martyr's body, the assumption being that all his sins had been forgiven and that he would ascend to heaven right away.

Because of the trajectory of Shi'i history, "redemptive suffering" and martyrdom loom large in Shi'i consciousness and find ample reflection in their literature. Twelver Shi'is maintain that 11 of their 12 imams were martyred. The events at Karbala (680) led to enhanced reverence for martyrdom among Shi'is, especially the martyrdom of members of the Prophet's family (*ahl al-bayt*) and more broadly that of believers who were oppressed and killed unjustly. During the Occultation of the Twelfth Imam, however, military jihad fell into abeyance for the majority of Twelver Shi'is. After the Islamic Revolution in Iran in 1979 and during the Iran-Iraq War in the 1980s, the notion of military martyrdom was revived and used to mobilize populations on both sides against the national enemy.

In the context of European colonization of a broad swath of the Muslim world starting in the 18th century, jihad as a defensive war against foreign aggressors made a dramatic revival among Muslim

scholars and jurists. Nevertheless, death and the attainment of martyrdom were usually not glorified in such colonial discourses. In the colonial and postcolonial periods, the South Asian Islamist Abul al-A'la Mawdudi (d. 1979) and the fiery Egyptian activist Sayyid Qutb (d. 1966) wrote about waging revolutionary jihad against "illegitimate" governments in Muslim-majority societies, but they did not exhort believers to seek death through this kind of relentless military activity.

Contemporary suicide bombers in the Palestinian Occupied Territories, Lebanon, Afghanistan, Iraq, and elsewhere, who consider their actions "martyrdom operations" (*'amaliyyāt istishhādiyya*) and who legitimate their targeting of noncombatants under the rubric of jihad, have considerably deviated from premodern legal constructions of martyrdom. Mainstream scholars, such as the Syrian hadith scholar Nasir al-Din al-Albani (d. 1999), the Saudi jurist Muhammad b. Salih al-'Uthaymin (d. 2001), and Muhammad Tahir-ul Qadri of Pakistan, have criticized their positions as morally and legally indefensible.

See also fundamentalism; jihad; military; suicide

Further Reading

Asma Afsaruddin, *Jihad and Martyrdom in Islamic Thought and Praxis*, 2012, forthcoming; Talal Asad, *On Suicide Bombing*, 2007; Michael Bonner, *Jihad in Islam: Doctrines and Practice*, 2006; David Cook, *Martyrdom in Islam*, 2007; Robert Pape, *Dying to Win: The Strategic Logic of Suicide Terrorism*, 2005; Rudolph Peters, *Islam and Colonialism: The Doctrine of Jihad in Modern History*, 1979.

ASMA AFSARUDDIN

masses

A number of Arabic words may be translated as "masses," especially *al-'āmma* (commoners, general populace), *al-jumhūr* (public, multitude), and *al-sha'b* (folk, populace). More pejorative examples, usually translated as the rabble, riffraff, or mob, include *dahmā'*, *ra'ā'*, *ghawghā'*, and *ṭaghām*. The term unmistakably and consistently evokes class and hierarchy. The masses are the lower classes and the great majority of people, the common folk, usually workers and peasants, and sometimes soldiers and bureaucrats as well. The opposite of these terms is *al-khāṣṣa*, the elite, which was sometimes limited to the highest ranking political figures such as the sultan or amirs, and at others included their retinues and other important officials, judges, and religious leaders. The literal meaning of the two words is telling: *al-'āmma* is "the general, undifferentiated, or common," while *al-khāṣṣa* is "the distinguished, particular, or with distinction." It is in this sense that Ira M. Lapidus describes the indistinct masses in negative terms in his book *Muslim Cities in the Later Middle Ages*: *al-'āmma* did not hold office, have an education, or possess wealth. Other groups tend to be distinguished in between these two classes, such as *al-a'yān* or notables, the 'ulama' or scholars, and local leaders who acted as intermediaries between the elite and the masses.

Philosophers, theologians, and mystics of various political and sectarian commitments generally agreed on the proper value and role of the masses in Islamic societies: the masses were sharply distinguished from the elite by their ignorance; they were decidedly inferior to the elite; and the masses were intended to be led, guided, and controlled by them. Although Imamism is a complex and variegated system of belief, one of its key features is the gulf between the imam and his followers. The divinely inspired imam has knowledge that no ordinary human being can possess, and in turn, the gulf between the imam and the Imamis is replayed between the Imamis and other Muslims. In the words of Muhammad b. 'Ali al-Baqir (d. 743), as reported by Imami scholar Muhhammad b. al-Hasan al-Tusi (d. 1067) in *al-Amali*, the non-Imami masses were "created from the stinking mud of Hell."

Muslim philosophers also maintained a distinction inherited from Neoplatonism between the erudite elite and the ignorant masses. This division, which intertwined piety with epistemological, moral, and political rank, suggested that the many were deficient by nature. Unlike the prophet-philosopher figure and the privileged classes under him who know esoteric (*baṭin*) truths, the many lack reason and revelation. They can only comprehend representations of the truth transmitted in parables. Because of their lower placement along the spectrum of reason, they can only recognize the exoteric (*ẓāhir*) or surface meanings. With this distinction and along similar lines to those found in Islamic mystical thought, philosophers like Farabi (d. 950) suggested that religion imitates philosophy; it is instruction for the masses while philosophy is instruction for the elite. Law is necessary for the masses; members of the rational elite do not need this form of regulation. Likewise, Ghazali (d. 1111) also maintains the distinction between the elite and the masses. The masses are furthest from true knowledge and lack perception and understanding of God, as opposed to elites, who are marked by keen sight. The masses' level of understanding prevents them from benefiting from what rulers and scholars know. Their beliefs are determined by preachers. Ghazali casts them in typical fashion as the objects of instruction, to be taught restraint and good manners.

Nevertheless, it would be incorrect to say that the medieval Islamic view of the masses was utterly derogatory. While Ghazali maintains the masses-elite opposition, he derides others for casting themselves as elites on illegitimate grounds. When he lists the eight types of people who are mistakenly attracted to *bāṭiniyya* or esoteric doctrines, they include the stupid, the domineering, and, most relevant here, "those who seek to be part of an elite so as to distinguish themselves from the masses." Although Ghazali is not defending the masses, he calls attention to the falseness of such self-aggrandizing differentiations. In his analysis of metaphors, the literary theorist 'Abd al-Qahir al-Jurjani (d. 1078) notes that the aphorism "Food is not right without salt" signifies that the goodness and well-being of the masses, as represented by food, requires the elite, as represented

by salt. Jurjani's explanation reflects the elites' ideological position, for he overlooks that salt (the elite) is in some sense dependent on—and at its base even less necessary than—food (the masses).

Overall, these visions of the masses took their status and deficiencies for granted. The vast majority of Muslim political thinkers in the medieval period, like their Western counterparts, treated the hierarchy as proper, rigid, and ordained by both God and nature, taking the people's position in it as a given and then maneuvering from within it.

Sawsan El-Messiri notes in her study of Egyptian urban masses or folk (*awlād al-balad*) that the term encompasses a wide range of types, from shopkeepers and artisans to outlaws and mobs, and that the general category may be divided based on ethnicity, religion, and occupation. In his book *Mass Culture and Modernism in Egypt*, Walter Armbrust shows how the figure of *ibn al-balad* (son of the country) was used to represent the masses. The term does not appear often in pre-19th-century sources but thereafter signifies both the buffoon's idiocy and the worker's culturally authentic machismo. In the 20th century, this "diamond in the rough" was placed in a highly conventional model of the pedagogical state, wherein social reformism would educate and raise *ibn al-balad* from his ignorance, maintaining his better characteristics while removing the bad. The term is opposed to *ibn al-dhawāt*, or the aristocrat, linked to cultural inauthenticity and effeminacy. *Ibn al-balad*, like the term *sha'bī* (popular), has nationalist overtones, and generally designates those who stand in staunch opposition to inauthentic cultural practices, foreign political agendas, exploitation, and bad character. While the modern position maintains the opposition between the elite and the masses, a key difference is the belief in the common people's capacity to change, which lends them a different role in legitimating the political order. Typical of this modernist sentiment are proclamations that the elite would polish the masses' language, sometimes coupled with the claim that the elite would also adapt the commoners' sincerity and flexibility. An intermediary role is played by the intellectual, who serves to bridge the gap between the elite and the masses. Such a transformation should be understood in the context of the forces of nationalism and postcolonialism, the emergence of modern populism, the modern state's reliance on the concept of the masses, and its attendant construction of national culture. Indeed, it is typical for modern governments to invest in projects, centers, and ministries aimed at making the common people a source of their cultural and political authenticity.

See also Ghazali (ca. 1058–1111); government; modernism; philosophy; socialism

Further Reading

Walter Armbrust, *Mass Culture and Modernism in Egypt*, 1996; Patricia Crone, *God's Rule*, 2003; Abu Nasr al-Farabi, *Mabādi' ārā' ahl al-madīnat al-fāḍīlah (On the Perfect State)*, translated by Richard Walzer, 1998; Ira Marvin Lapidus, *Muslim Cities in the Later Middle Ages*, 1984; Sawsan El-Messiri, *Ibn Al-Balad*, 1998.

MURAD IDRIS

Mawardi (974–1058)

Abu al-Hasan 'Ali b. Muhammad b. Habib Mawardi was a Shafi'i jurist, chief judge, political theorist, and political advisor to two Abbasid caliphs: Qadir bi-llah (r. 991–1031) and Qa'im bi-Amr Allah (r. 1031–74). Born in Basra, he later moved to Baghdad but studied in both cities, after which he was appointed as a judge in various localities of the empire, including in Ustawa, near Nishapur, and in Baghdad. In Baghdad he was able to rise within the ranks of the judiciary and became the chief judge (*qāḍī al-quḍāt*) during Qadir's reign. When Qadir requested a manual on Islamic law (*fiqh*) from each of the representatives of the four Sunni schools of law, Mawardi wrote *al-Iqna'* (The conviction) on behalf of the Shafi'i school, which put him at the highest level of authority in Islamic jurisprudence. During Qa'im's reign, Mawardi gained more prominence in the political realm and carried out diplomatic missions on behalf of the caliph, traveling to the Buyid amirs (in 1032 and 1037) and to the Seljuq ruler Tugril Bey (in 1043). In 1038 Qa'im elevated him to an unprecedented position and gave him the title *aqḍā al-quḍāt* (the best judge among the judges). After decades of active presence at the caliphal court, Mawardi's involvement in politics diminished during the influential vizierate of Abu al-Qasim 'Ali b. al-Husayn, who is better known as Ibn al-Muslima (r. 1045–58). Mawardi spent the last years of his life engaged primarily in scholarly activities. He died in Baghdad in 1058.

Mawardi is best known for his seminal work *al-Ahkam al-Sultaniyya wa-l-Wilayat al-Diniyya* (The ordinances of government and religious positions). The *Ahkam* is one of the earliest examples of its kind in Islamic law, which systematically delineates the functions, rights, and duties of various government offices; defines their relationships to one another; and lays out the conditions of appointment and removal of individuals to and from these offices. Thus the main topics of inquiry in the *Ahkam* are the contract of the caliphate; the requirements and procedures of conferral to the caliphal office; the duties of the caliph; the appointment of viziers and amirs; the jurisdiction of judges and the office of complaints (*maẓālim*); the status and rules of the chancery (*dīwān*); and the distribution of booty, taxation, land grants, and market supervision. As Mawardi states in the introduction to the *Ahkam*, all of these topics are systematically examined from a juridical perspective so that the caliph could "familiarize himself with the views of the jurists (*fuqahā'*) regarding his rights . . . and duties."

The *Ahkam* received considerable attention immediately upon the publication of its critical edition by Max Enger in 1853 and since the mid-19th century became one of the foundational texts for the study of Islamic political thought in scholarly literature in the West. The comprehensive nature of the work, the systematic treatment of its subject matter, and its early date of composition within the Islamic legal tradition gave it an exceptional, if controversial, status in scholarly debate. A number of scholars of the early Orientalist tradition considered the *Ahkam* the most authoritative

work on the Sunni theory of the caliphate, emphasizing its theoretical nature and considering it as the earliest and most prominent example of public law, in particular constitutional law, in Islamic political thought.

Two articles written in the late 1930s by the renowned orientalist H.A.R. Gibb (1895–1971) expressed a different opinion of the *Ahkam,* which became the prevailing perspective in recent scholarship. Challenging the other approach, Gibb and a group of scholars who followed his perspective emphasized the importance of the book's historical context, asserting that the political concerns of the time played a significant role in the construction of Mawardi's theory. Gibb stated, in his article titled "Some Considerations on the Sunni Theory of the Caliphate," that the *Ahkam* did not seek to "codif[y] the orthodox Sunni doctrine on the subject of the caliphate" but rather attempted to rationalize and justify the authority of the Abbasid caliphate, which had become repressed under the Buyid amirs. In short, the *Ahkam* was meant to reassert and restore the power of the Abbasids, and thus it served as an apologia within the contemporary political situation. For example, Mawardi's acceptance of emirate by usurpation (*istīlā'*) legitimized the status of the amirs who came to power by force, as long as they acknowledged the authority of the caliphs and the supremacy of Islamic law. To this view, this indicated Mawardi's chief interest in effecting political change in the environment of his time.

Despite its usefulness for understanding the *Ahkam*, this prevailing view in effect reduces Mawardi's role as a jurist to a level at which the juridical enterprise serves only to legitimize emerging power groups and thus plays down the motivation that lies behind Mawardi's juridical writing. Mawardi, as a sensible jurist, is conscious of the paradigms that exist in his society, but he also depicts a more comprehensive and systematic order that defines power relationships from a legal perspective and attempts to limit any arbitrary exercise of power. The *Ahkam* thus indeed offers a legal remedy for the political system at a time of crisis. But in it, too, Mawardi draws up one of the earliest examples of a political legal text of its kind, is consistent in following methods of Islamic jurisprudence, and demonstrates a sense of contractual logic commonly applied in legal deduction.

In the Islamic sphere, the *Ahkam* quickly became a model for legal works on governance, as is clear from Ibn Jama'a's (d. 1333) *Tahrir al-Ahkam* (Amendment of "The Ordinances"). An earlier scholar and a contemporary of Mawardi, Abu Ya'la b. al-Farra' (d. 1066), in fact composed a book on Islamic governance and gave it the same basic title as Mawardi's work: *al-Ahkam al-Sultaniyya* (The ordinances of government). The book significantly resembles Mawardi's book in organization, structure, and content, as was profusely demonstrated by Muhammad 'Abd al-Qadir Abu Faris in his doctoral work published in 1980. Being a Hanbali, though, Abu Ya'la expresses in his *Ahkam* opinions on governance that agree with positions of the Hanbali school of law.

Mawardi wrote other important, surviving works on politics and governance that have not received as much attention in Western scholarship, such as his *Qawanin al-Wizara wa-Siyasat al-Mulk* (The laws of the vizierate and the management of rule) and *Tashil al-Nazar wa-Ta'jil al-Zafar* (Aiding examination and quickening success). Two other political works, *Nasihat al-Muluk* (Advice to kings) and *al-Tuhfa al-Mulukiyya fi al-Adab al-Siyasiyya* (The royal gem regarding political decorum), are ascribed to Mawardi, but their authorship has been called into question. Mawardi's other important work, *Adab al-Dunya wa-l-Din* (Good behavior in this world and religion), focuses on religious ethics and has become popular over the centuries.

See also Sunnism; traditional political thought

Further Reading

Muhammad 'Abd al-Qadir Abu Faris, *Al-Qadi Abu Ya'la al-Farra' wa Kitabuhu al-Ahkam al-Sultaniyya*, 1980; H.A.R. Gibb, "Al-Māwardī's Theory of the Caliphate," *Islamic Culture* 11, no. 3 (1937), reprinted in *Studies on the Civilization of Islam*, edited by S. J. Shaw and W. R. Polk, 1962; Idem, "Some Considerations on the Sunni Theory of the Caliphate," *Archives d'Histoire du Droit Oriental* 3 (1939), reprinted in *Studies on the Civilization of Islam*, edited by S. J. Shaw and W. R. Polk, 1962; D. P. Little, "A New Look at *al-Aḥkām al-Sulṭāniyya*," *The Muslim World* 64, no. 1 (1974); Mawardi, *Al-Ahkam as-Sultaniyyah: The Laws of Islamic Governance*, translated by Asadullah Yate, 2005; Idem, *The Ordinances of Government: A Translation of Al-Aḥkām al-Sulṭāniyya wa al-Wilāyāt al-Dīniyya*, translated by Wafaa Hassan Wahba, 1996.

MEHMETCAN AKPINAR

Mawdudi, Abu al-A'la (1903–79)

On July 14, 2003, the British magazine *New Statesman* published a list of "12 great thinkers of our time." Abu al-A'la Mawdudi was the only Muslim thinker on the list because, according to the publishers, "so influential are Mawdudi's ideas, and so profound has been his impact on Osama bin Laden and al-Qaeda as well as moderate Muslims, that we included him even though he died in 1979." This judgment, it seems, is heavily informed by the momentous events of September 11, 2001. Mawdudi's salience is much more complex and varied.

Mawdudi was a key ideologue of Islamism during the interwar period, and his legacy goes far beyond the putative divide, exemplified in most mainstream journalistic accounts in the West as well as in the Muslim world, between "radical" and "moderate." Of his several contributions, which stemmed from the vagaries of colonial Indian social formations but later transcended the frontiers of South Asia to affect collective actions in the Middle East and beyond, two stand out as the most important. The first is that he is, arguably, the first modern Islamic thinker to define Islam as a comprehensive,

all-encompassing "system" (*niẓām*). The second is that the state is theologically indispensible to Islam. To this end, Mawdudi cast Islam in a modern language, a language distinctively inspired by Western philosophy, to which most "traditional" 'ulama' (people of knowledge) were nonreceptive, if not hostile. His initial appeal was greater among the young, modern-educated, urban Muslims than among those schooled in traditional Islamic centers of learning and residing in villages. It was this modern, politicized (re)presentation of Islam by Mawdudi—in writings, speeches, and activism alike—that became the source of inspiration for a significant number of Muslims.

Early Life

Mawdudi was born in a Sayyid family in 1903 at Aurangabad in colonial India. His forefathers had association with Mughal royalty in Delhi, as well as with the princely state of Hyderabad, the Nizams. Mawdudi's paternal grandmother was related to Sayyid Ahmad Khan (d. 1898), founder of the Muhammadan Anglo-Oriental (MAO) College, which later became the Aligarh Muslim University (AMU), in Aligarh. Against the wishes of Mawdudi's grandfather, Khan persuaded Mawdudi's father, Ahmad Hasan (d. 1920), to study at MAO College. However, Mawdudi's grandfather recalled Hasan from the college because he was "wearing kafir dress and playing cricket" there. Indeed, his father was, to quote Mawdudi, overwhelmed by "Western thought and life style." Hasan later renounced "Westernism" (*firangiyat*) and turned to religion. Given this newfound religiosity, he resolved not to give his son a Western education, but he did not want him to study in a madrasa either. Until the age of nine, Mawdudi received his education in Urdu, Persian, Arabic, law, and hadith through private tutors. At the age of 11, he went to study at Aurangabad's Madrasa Fawqaniyya Mashriqiyya (Oriental High School), an institution founded specifically to synthesize Islam and modernity. Shibli Nomani (d. 1914), a key figure among 'ulama' and founder of the Islamic academy, Darul-Musannifin, in Azamgarh, and his disciple Hamiduddin Farahi (d. 1930) had designed its curriculum, and both men had been influenced by Sayyid Ahmad Khan's modernism and had learned Western philosophy at AMU, particularly from Thomas Arnold. The school's curriculum thus included natural sciences, English, and mathematics—subjects that Mawdudi learned and later acknowledged as having broadened his intellectual horizon. Meanwhile, Mawdudi's father moved to Hyderabad, where Mawdudi enrolled in Darul Uloom, an Islamic college inspired by the modern philosophy of education whose principal was Farahi. He could not continue his formal education thereafter as he had to rush to Bhopal, where his father was getting medical treatment. There, Mawdudi became friends with Niaz Fatehpuri, an Urdu litterateur known for his heretical views. Fatehpuri encouraged Mawdudi to pursue a career in writing.

In 1919, Mawdudi left for Delhi, where he read the works of Sayyid Ahmad Khan. He learned English and studied German. According to Abdul Haq Ansari, an ideologue of the Indian Jama'at, he "turned to Western thought, and devoted a full five years to the study of major works in philosophy, political science, history and sociology." He wondered why 'ulama' in the past did not endeavor to discover the causes of Europe's rise, and he offered a long list of philosophers whose scholarship had made Europe a world power: Fichte, Hegel, Comte, Mill, Turgot, Adam Smith, Malthus, Rousseau, Voltaire, Montesquieu, Darwin, Goethe, and Herder, among others. Comparing their contribution to that of Muslims, he concluded that the latter's did not reach even 1 percent. Mawdudi's call to Muslims became, thus, to master the Western sciences. In many ways, he admired the Turkish writer Halide Edip (a judgment he later revised), who visited India in the mid-1930s. He criticized the Turkish 'ulama' for their indifference to Western sciences and stressed the need for independent legal reasoning (*ijtihād*). Mawdudi was also drawn to Marxist intellectuals such as Abdul Sattar Khairi, and in Hyderabad he became close to Josh Malihabadi, "the poet of revolution."

Such associations informed not only Mawdudi's ideas but also his quotidian life. Until 1936, he remained clean-shaven. Later, when he grew a beard, it was so short that it appeared more fashionable than religious. In 1938, when Manzoor Nomani (1905–97), a Deobandi scholar (*'ālim*), first met Mawdudi in Delhi, he was jolted to see that Mawdudi had too short a beard. He was also surprised at his "Western (*angrēzī*) hair." During the early 1930s, Mawdudi also watched films and attended a program of music and singing. Notably, he married Mahmuda Begum, who was educated in Delhi's Queen Mary's School. She was quite a modern woman; she rode a bicycle and barely observed the purdah (veil).

Colonial Formations and Politics of Islamism

Early in his career, Mawdudi became attracted to the Jam'iat Ulama-i Hind (JUH), an organization of 'ulama' founded in 1919. At the young age of 23, he became the editor of its newspaper, *Muslim* (later *Al-Jam'iyat*), which he edited until 1928. Mawdudi participated in the Khilafat and Non-Cooperation movements led by Mohandas Gandhi (d. 1948), worked to involve Muslims in the Indian National Congress, and wrote favorable biographies of Gandhi and Pundit Madanmohan Malaviya (1861–1946), a key leader of the congress and well-known for his contribution to Hindu nationalist ideology. Mawdudi grew disenchanted, however, with the congress's nationalism that led to the marginalization of Muslims. Another reason for his distrust of nationalism stemmed from the breakup of the Ottoman Empire along nationalist lines. Dismayed, Mawdudi quit the JUH–congress alliance. In 1928, he left Delhi for Hyderabad, where he devoted himself to studying Islam. From his reading of Islam and his witnessing of the precarious fate of the Nizams, Mawdudi concluded that the reason for Muslims' decline lay in the corruption of "pure" Islam. To recover and propagate pure Islam, he launched in 1932 an Urdu journal, *Tarjumanul Qur'an*. His early writings in *Tarjuman* were published under the title *Tanqihat* (Inquiries).

The major turning points in Mawdudi's career were the elections of 1937 and the subsequent formation of provincial ministries by the congress. It was then that Mawdudi's Islamism fully evolved.

He equated the policy of the ministries (1937–39) with heralding a "Hindu raj." He criticized the congress ministries not only for marginalizing Muslims and their culture but also for gradually making them Hindu. After the elections of 1937, both Mawdudi and the Muslim League, a party of the landed magnates founded in 1906 to protect Muslim interests, thus opposed the congress. This did not make them friends, however. Indeed, as the possibility of Pakistan's creation intensified, so did Mawdudi's critique of the League. He saw no difference between the congress and the League; both desired a secular state. He called the League a "party of the pagans." Since the League had no agenda for a shari'a state, Mawdudi described the future Pakistan as an "infidel state of Muslims." It was for this reason that in 1941 he formed the Jama'at-i Islami and set its goal as *ḥukūmat-i ilāhiyya*, "Allah's Government" or "Islamic State." To this end, Mawdudi argued that a state based on shari'a was not only desirable but also central to Muslims' very belief in monotheism. In *Qur'an ki Char Bunyadi Istelahen* (Four fundamental concepts of the Qur'an), he reinterpreted words such as *ilāh* (God), *rabb* (Lord), *'ibādat* (worship), and *dīn* (religion) to argue that the Qur'an obliged Muslims to establish a state based on divine sovereignty and simultaneously reject, or rather dethrone, *jāhiliyyat*, the embodiment of human sovereignty. This approach also informs Mawdudi's multivolume commentary on the Qur'an, *Tafhimul Qur'an* (begun in 1942 and completed in 1972), which finds a coveted space on the bookshelves of many Muslims who are not Islamists.

Mawdudi used the metaphor of the inseparability of the organs of human body from each other to define Islam as a complete system. The soul of the organic system was the state. Like Islam, *jāhiliyyat* was an indivisible organic system as well, and both could never coexist. Under the influence of Hegel and Marx, he also offered a new approach to read history as a perennial battle between *ḥaqq* (truth) and *bāṭil* (falsehood), or Islam and *jāhiliyyat*. For Mawdudi, secular democracy was the ultimate expression of *jāhiliyyat*. He argued that it was forbidden (*ḥarām*) to vote for or contest the elections for a secular, democratic state. He also did not appreciate modern colleges established by Muslims. He described institutions such as AMU as "slaughterhouses."

The Nascent State of Pakistan and Mawdudi

After the partition of India in 1947, Mawdudi moved to Pakistan. Until 1949, he regarded the Pakistani state as a sign of *jāhiliyyat* because it based itself on popular, as opposed to divine, sovereignty. In 1948, the Punjab government made it mandatory for its employees to pledge an oath to the state. Mawdudi forbade his party members to take this oath until the state became Islamic. In March 1949, Pakistan's Constituent Assembly passed the Objectives Resolution acknowledging the sovereignty of God, after which Mawdudi no longer regarded contesting elections or joining the Pakistani army as *ḥarām*. In line with Mawdudi's ideology, his followers in India continued to boycott elections until mid-1980s and all key institutions of the state, including the AMU (until late 1950s).

Mawdudi's career in the nascent state of Pakistan began in the midst of controversies. Because of his refusal to endorse the war (in 1948) against India by the Pakistani state as jihad, he was charged with sedition and put in jail. That did not deter him from participating in politics. In the 1951 Punjab provincial elections, only one candidate he supported won. However, in 1953, he was sentenced to death (later annulled) for his role in the anti-Ahmadi agitation. Such measures by the state only enhanced his stature domestically as well as internationally. The regime under General Ayub Khan (1958–69) regarded Mawdudi's Islamism as a nuisance to its modernist goals. In the 1960s, he was imprisoned twice. So opposed was Mawdudi to the regime that he supported a woman (justified on the Islamic logic of necessity, or *ḍarūra*), Fatimah Jinnah, against Ayub Khan for the presidency of Pakistan. The result, however, went against Mawdudi. The outcome of the national elections of 1970 was not favorable to Mawdudi either: only four of his comrades managed to win. In the war of 1971, Mawdudi's sympathy clearly lay with the army as he stood against the independence of Bangladesh. Following the dismemberment of Pakistan, Mawdudi battled against Zulfikar Ali Bhutto's (d. 1979) socialist populism, including his land reforms. As an alternative, Mawdudi intensified the movement for the installation of *niẓām-i muṣṭafā* (Prophetic Order). So effective did the slogan of *niẓām-i muṣṭafā* become that, after the 1977 military coup, General Zia-ul-Haq (d. 1988) made it the cornerstone of his regime. General Zia's endorsement of *niẓām-i muṣṭafā* was perhaps the pinnacle of Mawdudi's political life, which ended in the United States in 1979. More than a million people participated in his funeral. He was buried in Lahore.

Mawdudi left behind a contested, varied, and complex legacy. Translated into nearly every influential language, his writings and public life have had an impact on Muslims the world over. While many in South Asia and elsewhere use his ideas to mobilize for militant-radical politics, for others the figure of Mawdudi has a significantly different valence. As an example of the latter, one may mention the rereading of Mawdudi by the Indian Jama'at and the group of scholars led by Javed Ghamidi in Pakistan. Indeed, there is not a single Mawdudi. There are several Mawdudis.

See also fundamentalism; India; Jama'at-i Islami; Pakistan; revival and reform

Further Reading

Irfan Ahmad, *Islamism and Democracy in India: The Transformation of Jamaat-e-Islami*, 2009; M. Abdul Haq Ansari, "Mawdudi's Contribution to Theology," *The Muslim World* 93, nos. 3–4 (2003); Muhammad Khalid Masud, "Rethinking Sharia: Javed Ahmad Ghamidi on *Hudūd*," *Die Welt des Islams* 47, no. 3–4 (2007); Syed Vali Reza Nasr, *Mawdudi and the Making of Islamic Revivalism*, 1996.

IRFAN AHMAD

mawlid

The term *mawlid*, literally birthday, is used to denote the celebrations Muslims hold in remembrance of the Prophet Muhammad's birthday, which Sunnis generally believe was a Monday on the 12th of the Islamic month of Rabi' al-Awwal. (Shi'is believe it was on the 17th.) Parts of the Muslim world additionally use the term to signify any festival honoring a saint, but many regions of the Muslim world assign saintly festivals a separate name. In addition to sermons and feasts, the Prophetic *mawlid* is characterized by the recitation of poems extolling the Prophet Muhammad and prayer formulas blessing him. The *mawlid* holds no intrinsic political significance but may, like any religious act, be used to further the agendas of those interested in power.

There is no explicit command in the Qur'an or hadith establishing Muhammad's birthday as a day for celebration. The first reports documenting the sanctification of Muhammad's birth, whether its place or time, occur during the eighth century, when the house of his birth in Mecca was converted into an area for prayer (*masjid*). A ninth-century historian notes that performance of the ritual prayer (salat) at that location is commendable, and a tenth-century exegete relates that supplications (*du'ā'*) made there just after midday on Mondays will be answered. The traveler Ibn Jubayr (d. 1217), who visited Mecca in 1183, records that Muhammad's birthday was commemorated every Monday of Rabi' al-Awwal by keeping open his birthplace, which is visited by all for its blessings, and other holy sites of the city.

While these accounts from Mecca illustrate the veneration of Muhammad's birth, they do not appear to be official public celebrations. The earliest instance of such celebrations can be traced to Egypt in 1123, during the rule of the Isma'ili Shi'i dynasty of the Fatimids. The Fatimids did not limit the *mawlid* only to Muhammad but also marked the birthdays of other members of the Prophet's family (*ahl al-bayt*). All of these *mawlids* were commemorated in the same manner and apparently did not involve the general populace. Sweets, and possibly money, were distributed to the Fatimid ruling and religious elite, which included the stewards of tombs holding Muhammad's descendants. This was followed by Qur'an recitals and sermons in the presence of the Fatimid ruler. The Fatimids' claim to leadership was their connection to Muhammad's lineage, and these *mawlids* emphasized this tie.

It is not known whether the Sunni Prophetic *mawlid* was an outgrowth of the Fatimid one, and the first records of the Sunni *mawlid* occur during the mid-12th century in Syria and northern Iraq. These observances were promoted by both Sunni rulers and Sufis and quickly grew in popularity. A report from 1207 describes a *mawlid* in northern Iraq as a renowned festival attracting attendees from as far south as Baghdad. In addition to official sermons, poetry was recited and banquets held for the poor. Soon thereafter, the celebration of the *mawlid* became commonplace throughout the Muslim world. These Sunni *mawlids* were endorsed by rulers to bolster their standing with the populace, win the support of influential families who claimed Prophetic ancestry, and emphasize the nobility of their own lineage if connected to Muhammad.

The *mawlid* was not accepted by all scholars, and prominent debates over its legitimacy occurred during the 13th and 14th centuries. Scholars who opposed the *mawlid* did so for a number of reasons: they found no explicit textual command for it; they did not find the earliest Muslims commemorating it; and they found aspects of the popular celebration, such as the use of wind instruments, to be un-Islamic. Scholars who supported the *mawlid*, while acknowledging these criticisms, saw it is as praiseworthy provided that the actions undertaken as part of the festivities remained within legal boundaries.

In the 19th century, the *mawlid* continued to be commemorated, even with the growth of conservative and reformist thinkers who opposed it, such as the Deobandis and Rashid Rida (d. 1935). Objections to the *mawlid* remained, with detractors adding that the excessive veneration of Muhammad transformed him into a demigod and encouraged superstitious beliefs among common people. The *mawlid* was banned by the conservative Wahhabis in Saudi Arabia by the late 1930s, though it presumably continued to be observed privately, and the late 20th century produced a flurry of writings revisiting the debate over its validity. In the early 21st century, the *mawlid* enjoys state recognition in almost all Muslim countries and remains an essential expression of Muslim piety.

See also Muhammad (570–632); Sufism

Further Reading

Nico Kaptein, "Materials for the History of the Prophet Muḥammad's Birthday Celebration in Mecca," *Der Islam* 69, no. 2 (1992); Idem, *Muhammad's Birthday Festival: Early History in the Central Muslim Lands and Development in the Muslim West until the 10th/16th Century*, 1993; Marion Katz, *The Birth of the Prophet Muḥammad: Devotional Piety in Sunni Islam*, 2007; Aviva Schussman, "The Legitimacy and Nature of Mawlid al-Nabī (Analysis of a Fatwā)," *Islamic Law and Society* 5, no. 2 (1998); Mark Sedgwick, "Saudi Sufis: Compromise in the Hijaz, 1925–40," *Die Welt des Islams* 37, no. 3 (1997).

SAYEED S. RAHMAN

Mecca and Medina

The cities of Mecca and Medina, located in western Saudi Arabia, are the most ritually significant sites in Islam. Both cities appear in Islamic cosmological legends as centers or origins of God's creation, and one of the epithets for Mecca, "Mother of Towns" (*umm al-qurā*), celebrates this precedence.

Mecca was the birthplace of the Prophet Muhammad, and according to Islamic tradition, he received his first revelations from

God in its environs in 610. Mecca was also home to the Ka'ba, a black, cubic structure believed by Muslims to be the earliest *bayt*, or house of worship, first built by Adam and then rebuilt by Abraham and his son Ishmael. At the time of Muhammad's birth, it housed a set of idols and attracted pilgrims from among the largely polytheistic peoples of the Arabian Peninsula. Mecca also seems to have been a commercial center of at least local importance, though its role in longer distance trade has been debated. When Muhammad took control of the city in 630, he maintained its status as a pilgrimage destination, although he destroyed the idols at the Ka'ba and dedicated it to the one true God. In the following year, he performed a series of rituals at the Ka'ba and sites in its vicinity that became the blueprint for the hajj, the annual pilgrimage to Mecca.

Medina, known in pre-Islamic times by the name Yathrib, was an oasis settlement of farmers and pastoralists some 200 miles north of Mecca. The Prophet Muhammad emigrated to Yathrib with a group of his followers in 622 to escape persecution from Meccan elites. This event, known as the hijra, marks the beginning of the Islamic calendar. Yathrib, which is referred to simply as *al-madīna* (the city) in the Qur'an, would remain the residence of the Prophet until his death in 632. His tomb, located in the Prophet's Mosque of Medina, is a site of pious visitation for Muslims.

According to Islamic tradition, Muhammad established a paradigm for religious and political authority during his career in Medina. One of the earliest political documents in Islamic history, known as the Constitution of Medina, establishes the Prophet as the leader of "believers" and "Muslims" who compose an *umma*, the term now used for the worldwide community of Muslims. Its text combines the language of tribal confederations, kinship-based mutual aid pacts well-established on the Arabian Peninsula, with a language of religious belonging and identity. Muslims date the revelation of those chapters of the Qur'an that contain the most explicit guidance for ritual practice and ethical standards of behavior to the Medinan period. Thus while Mecca figures more prominently in pre-Islamic sacred history, Muslims regard Medina as the crucible of a self-conscious religious community with a tradition of political and legal discourse.

Despite this, after Muhammad's death, Medina acted as a seat of political authority only during the reigns of the first four caliphs, or "successors" to the Prophet, up to the year 661, when a new dynasty of caliphs, the Umayyads, was established in Damascus. During the Umayyad and later Abbasid periods, caliphal involvement in Mecca and Medina was largely limited to the erection or renovation of ritual structures and patronage of the wives of the Prophet, who lived in Medina after his death. However, from time to time both cities were known or suspected to host politically fractious elements, which resulted in retribution or periods of relative neglect from the authorities. The most famous of these episodes was the rebellion of 'Abdallah b. al-Zubayr against the Umayyads, which culminated in the partial destruction and subsequent rebuilding of the Ka'ba in the late seventh century. Nonetheless, the expectation that the caliphs would be patrons and protectors of the annual pilgrimage meant that appearances and investments in Mecca and Medina were frequent and well documented. Successor regimes, including the Shi'i Fatimids based in Cairo as well as the Sunni Mamluks and later the Ottomans, also sought legitimacy through their control of Mecca and Medina. Today much of Saudi Arabia's prestige in the Islamic world stems from its role as regulator and protector of pilgrimages to the two holy cities.

See also Muhammad (570–632); pilgrimage; Umayyads (661–750)

Further Reading

Albert Arazi, "Matériaux pour l'étude du conflit du préséance entre la Mekke et Médine," *Jerusalem Studies in Arabic and Islam* 5 (1984); Michael Lecker, *The "Constitution of Medina": Muhammad's First Legal Document*, 2004; F. E. Peters, *Mecca*, 1994; W. Montgomery Watt, *Muhammad at Mecca*, 1953; Idem, *Muhammad at Medina*, 1956.

ZAYDE ANTRIM

media

Traditional Islamic political thought never dealt with media, or more accurately mass media, since its corpus predates the technological revolution. Anything that is "new," whether it is ideas or technology, tends to be viewed with suspicion by "tradition" because it represents a departure from the prophetic paradigm. The prevailing position is that the various media, such as radio, television, and the Internet, are to be treated as tools and are therefore inherently neutral. It is what one decides to do with them that matters. In other words, if the media are used to spread vices, lies, or corruption, then the one who has chosen to use them for these purposes, and not the tool itself, is blameworthy.

The spread of mass media across the globe has been met with tacit approval by the class of religious scholars of Islam, who themselves propagate their ideas through all the means of mass communication at their disposal. The majority of Muslims also have embraced modern media and social networking online, powerful impacts of which were felt in the "Arab Spring" of 2011.

In spite of this prevailing situation, an inherent tension exists between Islamic religious thought and much of what is considered as "normal" programming in the entertainment industry of the West or "acceptable" forms of speech in journalism. Tensions between Islam and technology, particularly the media, have been manifest historically, for example, with the hesitant adoption of the printing press on the one hand and more recently with the publication of caricatures of the Prophet Muhammad in Denmark in 2005, which sparked outrage among devout Muslims but was defended under the principle of freedom of speech among journalists. In everyday life devout Muslims experience unease with a variety of situations occasioned by mass media, from seeing the name of God in

a newspaper that has been trampled on the street to explicit sexual content or suggestive images in advertising and entertainment. Although Shi'is have a long tradition of the dramatic reenactment of the martyrdom of Husayn, this does not necessarily translate into more relaxed attitudes when it comes to the mass media.

It is noteworthy that the science of hadith, used by Muslims to authenticate Prophetic traditions since the classical age of Islam, has been compared to the principles of modern journalism that include the necessity of having a source, a check on the reliability of the source, and means to corroborate the report independent of the source. The science of hadith is a sacred endeavor in Islam whose principal aim is authenticating reports for the purpose of ascertaining God's will for humanity. One could say that, in some essential way, the methods of modern journalism are in harmony with, instead of in contradiction with, this sacred science. The difference is that modern journalism exists for the purpose of ascertaining truth in contemporary worldly events. Tensions arise between Islamic thought and the media in cases where news becomes entertainment or entertainment becomes news, the line between the two being subjectively drawn in the first place.

What is news or newsworthy? Few scholars have paid attention to this question in considering the potential contradictions between traditional Islamic values and the modern mass media. A core idea of modern journalism is that the public has the right to know. Traditional Muslim scholars, and by extension rulers, may take a more patriarchal view toward society, considering what they determine are people's *needs* in order to best worship God rather than their *rights* as autonomous subjects. In its most libertarian mode, the right to know justifies the invasion of privacy, the appeal to idle curiosity, and the appeal to a sovereign "public opinion," however unqualified from a traditional Islamic political perspective. It also can mean the circulation of intrinsically nonpolitical but morally discomforting news that exposes the vices of others, which is contrary to Islamic teachings. The Prophet is reported to have said that the better Muslim is "the one from whose tongue and hand the Muslims are safe." Nawawi, one of the great collectors and commentators on hadith, explains that this means to refrain from whatever hurts the Muslims in speech or deed and to restrain from scorning them. Contrast this attitude to that of modern tabloid journalism, which seeks to investigate and expose faults, if not to find ways to invent them for the sake of gossip, which is also forbidden in Islam.

In some Muslim countries, such as the United Arab Emirates (UAE), content is censored online and on video to avoid explicit images, although it is impossible to eliminate suggestive themes and innuendo altogether. The incarceration of political bloggers in the UAE is an example of the relationship between political power, which desires to maintain "stability," and political activists, who follow the principle of peoples' right to know. During the "Arab Spring" of 2011, the various reactions of religious scholars depended on their own particular circumstances and context, which is a clear indication of the positional nature of the issue in Islamic religious and political thought. On the other hand, in some Muslim countries such as Turkey, the media are as open and permissive as in most Western countries.

See also democracy; rights

Further Reading

Akbar S. Ahmed, *Islam under Siege*, 2003; Jonathan Brown, *Hadith: Muhammad's Legacy in the Modern World*, 2011; D. F. Eickelmann and J. W. Anderson, *New Media in the Muslim World*, 1999; Elizabeth L. Eisenstein, *The Printing Press as an Agent of Change*, 1979; K. Hafez, *Islam and the West in the Mass Media*, 2000; E. Said, *Covering Islam*, 1997; S. Abdallah Schleifer, "Islam and Information: Need, Feasibility and Limitations of an Independent Islamic News Agency," *American Journal of Islamic Social Sciences* 3, no. 1 (1986); Idem, "Mass Communication and the Technicalization of Muslim Society," *Muslim Education Quarterly* 4, no. 3 (1987); A. L. Tibawi, *Arabic and Islamic Themes: Historical, Educational and Literary Studies*, 1974.

S. ABDALLAH SCHLEIFER

messianism

Messianic ideas have played significant roles in Islamic political history in different forms. The traditional account of Muhammad's life represents him as a preordained messianic deliverer leading a community to political and military triumph. From early on in Islamic history, Muslim groups evolved distinctive doctrines of future messianic figures known under such terms as *mahdī* (rightly guided), *qā'im* (one who rises up), and *mujaddid* (renewer). Over the centuries, Muslims of many different persuasions have claimed messianic functions for themselves and led widespread movements, and messianic ideas have formed part of the imperial visions of major Islamic dynasties. In the modern period, messianic claimants have advocated activist struggles as well as political and socioreligious reform in the face of Western hegemony over Muslim communities.

The Qur'an does not evoke the notion of a future messianic deliverer. This is understandable since in its internal perspective, the scripture is the fulfillment of prior messianic prophecies through the figure of Muhammad. The traditional story of Muhammad's life, which acquired its contours in the first Islamic century, can be read as the first fully articulated messianic narrative in Islam. Muslims in this period were caught in a paradox: their great worldly successes, built on the foundations of Muhammad's religious message, had also precipitated severe internal dissension that included numerous wars and shocking massacres such as that of Muhammad's grandson Husayn at Karbala in 680. This situation generated new messianic paradigms in which the careers of Muhammad and some of his early Companions, regarded as heroes, became models for the hope of future messiahs.

Islamic messianism has from its origins consisted of a variety of doctrines. Among Sunni Muslims, views vary between complete denial of the idea of a future messiah, to the notion that the messiah is simply Jesus in his future Second Coming, to the expectation of a man who would lead Muslims to a worldwide religiopolitical triumph shortly before the world undergoes its final apocalypse and destruction. Among Shi'is, the messiah is a particular descendant of Muhammad, and he is either expected to be born in the future or is one of the imams of the past. The doctrinal structure of Twelver Shi'ism combines these two possibilities since it is centrally focused on the Twelfth Imam, Muhammad al-Mahdi, who, it is believed, was born in 869 and went into occultation (*ghayba*) in 874. He is expected to come back and, together with Jesus, lead the Twelver community to a triumph shortly before the end of time.

Throughout history, individuals from Sunni as well as Shi'i backgrounds have attempted to enact theological doctrines by proclaiming themselves messiahs. Generally speaking, messiahs rising from Sunni backgrounds tend to highlight the notion of renewal of Islamic law and the reestablishment of a righteous Muslim community in the image of the time of Muhammad and his early successors, the Rightly Guided Caliphs. Prominent examples include Muhammad b. Tumart (d. 1130) in North Africa, Sayyid Muhammad of Jawnpur in India (d. 1505), Muhammad Ahmad b. 'Abdallah of the Sudan (d. 1885), Mirza Ghulam Ahmad (d. 1908) in British India, Shehu Usman dan Fodio (d. 1817) in northern Nigeria, and a number of later West African figures. In contrast, Shi'i messiahs are likely to see themselves as harbingers of altogether new religious dispensations since, from a Shi'i perspective, early Islamic history is not a golden era but a tragedy marked by the usurpation of the rights of 'Ali b. Abi Talib and his descendants. Prominent examples of Shi'i messiahs include 'Abdallah (or 'Ubaydallah) al-Mahdi (d. 934), the founder of the Fatimid caliphate in North Africa, who presented himself as a messianic savior and was justified as such in later Isma'ili scholarship. Among the later Nizari Isma'ilis was the imam Hasan 'ala dhikrihi al-salam (d. 1166), who enacted a dramatic festival meant to represent the raising of the dead after the cosmic apocalypse (*qiyāma*) at the fortress of Alamut in Iran in 1164 and saw himself as fulfilling messianic expectations. In a Twelver Shi'i context, the fact that a particular person from the past, the Twelfth Imam, is seen as the messiah requires a claimant to the mantle to justify a seeming impossibility. Messiahs who have risen from Twelver contexts—for example, Muhammad b. Falah Musha'sha' (d. 1462), Muhammad Nurbakhsh (d. 1464), and Sayyid 'Ali Muhammad Bab (d. 1850)—have done so through innovative doctrines in which they claim themselves to be messiahs based on the idea that the Twelfth Imam's spirit has been transferred to their own bodies.

In the central Islamic lands from 1200 onward, Sufi ideas have overlapped with messianic doctrines of various provenances. This amalgamation stems from some Sufis' investment in a paramount living human figure—called the pole (*quṭb*), the perfect human being (*insān kāmil*), or the seal of God's friendship (*khātam al-walāya*)—who is supposed to mediate between earthly and heavenly realms. Over the past eight centuries, concrete messianic claims have very often been justified through a combination of sectarian and Sufi doctrines. While messianism is a political doctrine by definition, Muslim claimants are split between activists and quietists. Some have seen themselves as divinely appointed agents charged with reforming society by force, while others have espoused a religiously revolutionary function accompanied by a shunning of the political sphere.

The earliest connection between messianism and Islamic imperial doctrines can be seen in the origins of the Abbasid caliphate (750–1258). As a group opposed to the ruling Umayyads, Abbasid propagandists relied on nascent messianic doctrines to lead a revolutionary movement. Once triumphant, they co-opted the political potential of messianic ideas through acts such as the caliph Abu Ja'far al-Mansur (d. 775) giving his successor Muhammad b. al-Mansur (d. 785) the title Mahdi, which had acquired a distinctly messianic connotation by this time. In later history, ruling houses that wished to portray themselves as direct religious agents (instead of solely being supporters and protectors of law and religious scholars) appealed to messianic ideas. An example is the imperial myth surrounding Tamerlane (d. 1405) in which the conqueror is referred to by the messianic title the *ṣāḥib-qirān* (Lord of the Auspicious Conjunction). The Safavid dynasty of Iran (1501–1722) rose to power and ruled on the basis of a messianic claim that interweaves Twelver Shi'i and Sufi ideas. The Ottomans and the Mughals, contemporaries to the Safavids in their origins, also incorporated messianic functions in their imperial self-presentations.

In the modern period, the three most prominent movements stemming from messianic claims are Babism in Iran (which later evolved into a new religion, the Baha'í Faith), the Ahmadiyya led by Mirza Ghulam Ahmad of Qadiyan in South Asia, and the Nation of Islam led by Elijah Muhammad in the United States. All three reflect the evolution of Islamic messianic doctrines in the face of modern intellectual and sociopolitical challenges and the imperative to respond to European Christianity. Adherents of these movements have often faced repression and persecution by ruling authorities as well as the societies in which they have been influential.

See also Mahdi; revival and reform; utopia

Further Reading

Kathryn Babayan, *Mystics, Monarchs, and Messiahs: Cultural Landscapes of Early Modern Iran*, 2002; Shahzad Bashir, *Messianic Hopes and Mystical Visions: The Nūrbakhshīya between Medieval and Modern Islam*, 2003; Claude Andrew Clegg, *An Original Man: The Life and Times of Elijah Muhammad*, 1998; Yohanan Friedmann, *Prophecy Continuous: Aspects of Ahmadi Religious Thought and Its Medieval Background*, 2003; Mercedes Garcia-Arenal, *Messianism and Puritanical Reform: Mahdīs of the Muslim West*, 2006; Mervyn Hiskett, *The Sword of Truth: The Life and Times of the Shehu Usuman dan Fodio*, 1994; Abdulaziz Sachedina, *Islamic*

Messianism, 1981; Hayrettin Yücesoy, *Messianic Beliefs and Imperial Politics in Medieval Islam: The Abbasid Caliphate in the Early Ninth Century*, 2009.

SHAHZAD BASHIR

military

Military activity has been an important part of Islamic history since the Prophet. In the earliest decades of the Islamic community, under the leadership of both Muhammad and the early caliphs, the organized use of force continued to follow patterns typical of pre-Islamic Arabian society, in which fighting was confined to particular months of each year and took place primarily in the form of raids intended to acquire loot and livestock from rival tribes. In the early Islamic context, the men who carried out these campaigns were not career soldiers but instead were paid for their efforts in booty before returning to their usual occupations—often as herders—for the rest of the year. Aside from the elite, specially trained forces guarding the caliph, most of the individuals fighting in the name of Islam were minimally trained and came from each of the diverse tribes that had come under the protection of the Islamic caliphate.

As these early armed forces rapidly expanded the borders of the Islamic territory, the nature of the military in Islamic thought changed in several respects. First, strategists encouraged the use of more organized, line-formation military strategies on account of their greater efficacy. Second, there developed a greater concern for the distinctly Islamic character of military operations, attained through careful imitation of the Prophet in matters as precise as the day of the week on which operations should begin. Third, the military was professionalized, so that soldiers were paid a fixed salary for their work, which could now take up their entire year rather than only selected months. According to works on rule written from a theological or legal point of view, the military was dependent on the imam or caliph, who was the supreme leader of the Islamic state. It was his duty to keep public order, uphold the rule of law, subdue rebels within Islamic territory, suppress heretical movements, defend the borders against invasion, and support the superiority of Islam in the world, and so the military was essential in enabling him to fulfill his obligations. At the same time, the military was not allowed to act on its own, except in defense; it required the order of the imam to engage in offensive jihad, fighting in order to expand the abode of Islam. Later works delegated these same powers to sultans or other rulers of Muslim states.

The organization of the military also changed over time. While the early caliphs were leaders of a single Islamic military force, during the Abbasid caliphate military forces began to decentralize. Several different armies and navies existed simultaneously, associated with various smaller Islamic governments, including, for example, those of the Fatimids, the Zengids, and the Seljuq Turks, in the 11th and 12th centuries, as well as under the leadership of regional amirs. Slave soldiers (*mamlūk*, pl. *mamālīk*) came to play a pivotal role in these various forces. Mamluks were light-skinned slaves, often of Turkish origin, who were purchased, brought into Muslim territories, educated in Islam, and trained as soldiers. By 200 years after the Prophet's death, mamluks made up the majority of the soldiers in Muslim armies. Sometimes, as in the case of the Seljuqs in the 11th century, they gained power and became ruling sultans on their own. The Seljuqs instituted a new military organization in which soldiers were divided into different classes, each further subdivided into ranks. Enlisted soldiers and slaves received fixed salaries, while the more elite class of soldiers were paid with land grants for limited periods (*iqṭā'*).

The history of the military in the Islamic world thus went through what may be described as three ethnic phases. In the early expansion of the empire, the forces were primarily Arabs. From the 9th to 11th centuries, Daylamis—from the southern Caspian region—dominated the central Islamic lands, and from the 11th to the 20th centuries, Turks and Mongols dominated. Each ethnic group had a characteristic form of warfare. The Arabs were mounted swordsmen, who also used long spears. The Daylamis, accustomed to mountainous terrain, were primarily heavy infantry armed with stout javelins, axes, and short swords. Turks and Mongols were most effective as mounted archers and used composite bows that were short but extremely strong. Military command usually led to direct political rule, as commanders of mercenary forces or slave troops either controlled the rulers who were supposedly their masters, as occurred in the Abbasid caliphate already in the ninth and tenth centuries, or simply assumed rule. For example, the Ghaznavids (977–1186) and the Simjurids began as Turkish mercenaries for the Persian Samanid dynasty (819–999), then served as governors in Khurasan, and then carved their own states out of Samanid territory in the mid-tenth century. In Egypt and Syria, the Mamluks (1250–1517), former Turkish slave troops for the Ayyubids (1171–1250), established a new regime in which the top echelons of the military and the rulers were all Turkish slaves. In this unique system, sultans often passed on rule to their former protégés, slave troops that they had acquired and trained in their own barracks. The descendants of this elite group, termed *awlād al-nās*, were excluded from top military command. Turkish military rule therefore became a stable feature of politics in the Islamic world for nearly a millennium. It was viewed as natural by many theorists on the grounds that different ethnic groups had particular strengths and propensities: those of the Turks included horsemanship, archery, hunting, and warfare in general, while other ethnic groups were more suited to various civilian occupations.

Mirrors for Princes or instructive manuals on political rule from the premodern period gave Muslim rulers a variety of advice on their bodyguards and their armies. The bodyguard should be of mixed ethnic origins in order to avoid a coup. The army should also be comprised of units recruited from diverse ethnic groups so that they may be played against each other. In addition, spies

should be used to inform on matters within the army as well as in the populace. It is crucial that the military be paid promptly and well: the works lauded the ancient Persian kings for their acumen in realizing that wealth was the basis of long rule because it enabled the ruler to support his army properly. Some Mirrors for Princes also held that the populace at large should avoid military matters. Mahmud b. Sebuktigin of Ghazna supposedly castigated the people of Balkh for taking up arms against Qarakhanid invaders: the result, he argued, was the destruction of the city, which was to his own disadvantage, and he threatened to make them pay him for the damage.

In the modern context, national armies are the norm, and the authoritarian nature of many governments in the Muslim world has ensured that the military forms a relatively large part of the government, using a large percentage of national income. In fact, one might argue that the military—as much as or even more than the president or the executive branch of government—controls the nation-state and grants it stability and continuity over time, particularly in Pakistan, Turkey, Syria, Egypt, and Iraq before the fall of Saddam Hussein. In recent years, however, the rise of activist Islamist movements such as Hamas in Palestine and Hizbullah in Lebanon has led to the establishment of trained military groups outside of state control.

See also abodes of Islam, war, and truce; jihad; Mirrors for Princes; slavery

Further Reading

David Ayalon, "The Mamluks: The Mainstay of Islam's Military Might," in *Slavery in the Islamic Middle East*, edited by Shaun E. Marmon, 1999; Anthony H. Cordesman, *After the Storm: The Changing Military Balance in the Middle East*, 1993; Patricia Crone, *God's Rule—Government and Islam*, 2005; Eadem, *Slaves on Horses: The Evolution of the Islamic Polity*, 2003; Reuben Levy, *The Social Structure of Islam*, 1957.

ROSEMARY B. KELLISON
DEVIN J. STEWART

minorities

This entry treats both Muslim minorities under non-Muslim rule and non-Muslim minorities under Muslim rule. Due to the limitations of space, it includes only the most significant minorities.

Muslim Minorities under Non-Muslim Rule

The question of the majority-minority relationship has been relevant to Muslims since the emergence of Islam. Muslims began their history in Mecca as a minority persecuted by the polytheistic establishment of the city (610–30). This situation, however, did not last long. Following the conquests of the seventh century, the Muslims became an elite ruling over non-Muslim majorities in the vast expanses of the emerging empire. The process of conversion to Islam was much slower than the conquests themselves; scholars disagree on when Muslims became a majority in the Middle East and North Africa. It is clear that this transformation did not take place before the 11th century, but some argue that it did not occur until the beginning of the Mamluk period in the 13th century. In the Indian subcontinent, the Muslims never exceeded a quarter of the population, although various Muslim dynasties ruled substantial parts of India from the 13th to the 19th century. Historians of Indonesia—where Islam spread by slow penetration of traders and divines rather than by conquest—have not been able to chart demographic developments with great confidence, but Islamization apparently started there (probably in the 15th century) with the ruling elite so that Muslim rulers initially controlled a mainly non-Muslim population. It is not possible to say when exactly Muslims became a majority in Indonesia, which at the time of writing is the state with the largest Muslim population. Similar difficulties face the historians of sub-Saharan Africa. The coastal region of East Africa became a Muslim majority area between 1200 and 1500, while comparable development in West Africa differed from region to region. The Chinese Muslim minority developed during the Tang dynasty (618–907); its growth accelerated during the period of the Mongol invasions, and in 2006 it numbered 20 million, according to government estimates.

In the formative centuries of Islamic history, when Islam was constantly expanding, Muslims who lived as minorities under non-Muslim rule were rare. Early tradition (hadith) considered living under such conditions undesirable, and a tradition makes the Prophet denounce Muslims who live among polytheists. Later jurists do not distinguish between situations in which the Muslims formed a majority or a minority of the population: what matters is the religious affiliation of the ruler.

When the Muslims were forced for the first time to abandon significant areas previously under their control, the legal thinking on the permissibility of living under non-Muslim rule began to change. While some schools of law continued to reject the legality of living under non-Muslim rule, others weighed such issues as the ability to practice Islam freely in a non-Muslim area and the possibility that Muslims living there would bring about the conversion of the non-Muslims to Islam. In Spain, the process started with the fall of Toledo into Christian hands in 1085. Further Christian advances in the 12th and 13th centuries left substantial numbers of Muslims, known as Mudejars (those who were allowed to stay), under Christian rule, but the Muslim population eventually would vanish from Spain completely. In Syria and Palestine, on the other hand, the Crusaders' takeover at the end of the 11th century was followed by a Muslim restoration at the end of the 13th century. Nevertheless, for almost two centuries, the Muslims of Syria and Palestine lived under Frankish-Christian rule. In some areas they were a subjugated majority, while in others they were reduced to minority status. In the 12th century, the non-Muslim Central Asian empire of the Qara Khitay treated the Muslim population with tolerance and won the

general appreciation of their subjects. The 13th century, on the other hand, saw the destructive Mongol invasion of Persia and Central Asia, although this episode of non-Muslim rule over a Muslim population came to an end with the conversion of the Mongol Ghazan Khan to Islam in 1295.

During the era of the three great Muslim empires—the Ottoman, the Safavid, and the Mughal—barely any Muslim minorities lived under non-Muslim rule. This situation began to change in 1774 when the Ottomans were forced to surrender Crimea and its Muslim population to Russia in the Treaty of Küçük Kaynarca. A substantial Muslim minority came into being when the Ottomans ceded Bosnia and Herzegovina to the Habsburg Empire in 1878. The Muslims of India were a minority, but since the government of most areas of the Indian subcontinent was in their hands, they experienced few problems until 1858, when the gradual takeover of India by the British was formalized. India was incorporated into the British Empire, and the Muslims of India were transformed from a ruling elite to a subjected minority. After the partition of the Indian subcontinent and the establishment of Pakistan in 1947, a substantial Muslim minority came into being in the newly established independent and professedly secular Republic of India. The difficulties initially experienced by this minority because of its connections with the rival and professedly Islamic state of Pakistan were brilliantly analyzed by W. C. Smith in his *Islam in Modern History* (chapter 6). The question of living Islamically in a non-Muslim environment has long been the subject of public debate among Indian Muslims in terms of Islamic law: is India the abode of Islam (*dār al-islām*) or the abode of war (*dār al-ḥarb*)? How should this question be answered in a region that had been under Muslim rule in the past and in a situation in which the sovereign is non-Muslim but where Muslims enjoy unrestricted freedom of worship? A comparable analysis could be attempted concerning the Muslim minority in Israel.

The 20th century—and especially the years after World War II—saw the development of significant Muslim minorities in Europe and the Americas. In the medieval period, very few Muslims were ruled by others or lived in a non-Muslim environment, but in contemporary times millions of Muslims find themselves under non-Muslim rule. This has become a significant issue of debate among Muslims themselves and in the scholarly literature. The Muslim minorities that emerged in the West are diverse. They differ in their countries of origin, their mode of integration into the local society, and their vision of life in their adoptive countries. In England, most Muslim immigrants originated from Pakistan and Bangladesh, in France from North Africa, and in Germany from Turkey. The Russian Muslim minority has been estimated at 15 to 20 million. The Muslim minority in the United States, now estimated at about 4 million, is also of diverse origins. The first substantial number of Muslims entered the United States as slaves brought from Africa between the 17th and 19th centuries. In late 19th century, Muslims started immigrating to the United States from the Arab provinces of the Ottoman Empire. Beginning in the 1970s, the number of North American Muslim institutions and organizations increased dramatically. The Islamic Society of North America (ISNA), an umbrella association of a few hundred mosques and Islamic centers; the Muslim Public Affairs Council (MPAC); and the Council on American-Islamic Relations (CAIR) brought the problems of the American Muslims to the attention of the government and into public awareness. The debate concerning the Muslim minority in the United States grew in intensity and gained importance in the wake of the terrorist attacks on New York City and Washington, DC, perpetrated by radical Muslims on September 11, 2001.

Among the most important issues in the relationship between these minorities and their adopted countries are their involvement in politics, their economic integration, their mosques, their educational institutions, and their relations with the other religions. As of 2003, there were Muslim members of Parliament in England, the Netherlands, Denmark, and Sweden. All were elected in the framework of existing political parties; attempts to organize specifically Muslim parties in Belgium, England, France, and Germany were not successful. Muslim participation in local governing bodies was substantially greater than on the national level. Organizations that claimed to represent the generality of Muslims in various countries were established; prominent among them were the Muslim Council of Britain, Union des Organizations Islamiques de France, and Zentralrat der Muslime in Deutschland. Radical Muslim organizations with small memberships but considerable visibility also developed: among them, the Jama'at-i Islami (The Islamic Group) was active among Muslims of Indian and Pakistani extraction and the Hizb al-Tahrir (The Party of Liberation) promoted a radical Muslim agenda in several European countries.

In the early 21st century most Muslim children in Europe and America studied in state schools; additional instruction in Islam frequently was given in mosques or prayer rooms after school or on weekends. In recent years, Western Europe experienced a remarkable increase in the construction of mosques, estimated at 212 in 2003, and prayer rooms, of which several thousand were in operation. Countries with the largest number of mosques were England (80), Germany (66), and France (8). Hundreds of mosques from the Ottoman period survived in Bulgaria, Western Thrace, and Romania.

Since the 1990s, the emergence of significant Muslim minorities in non-Muslim countries provided the impetus for the development of a new branch in Islamic thinking called "legal theory for Muslim minorities" (*fiqh al-aqalliyyāt*). *Fiqh al-aqalliyyāt* addresses the problems encountered by Muslims who want to live according to Islamic precepts in a non-Muslim environment. The most prominent figures in the development of this branch of Muslim thought are Yusuf al-Qaradawi and Taha Jabir al-Alwani. Alwani was born in Iraq, studied at Azhar, taught in Saudi Arabia, and then became the president of the School of Islamic Social Sciences in Ashburn, Virginia. Qaradawi, a prominent public figure in contemporary Muslim thought, was born in Egypt, also studied at Azhar, and moved to the emirate of Qatar in 1961. Among the matters discussed in the framework of this legal theory are the nature of the Western countries when analyzed according to the classical

division of the world into *dār al-islām* (abode of Islam), *dār al-ḥarb* (abode of war), and *dār al-'ahd* (abode of covenant); the question of jihad; economic questions such as the permissibility of trading in stocks and bonds (i.e., if doing so violates the Muslim law that prohibits paying or receiving interest); the problems of child adoption (which is prohibited in classical Muslim law); and, in general, the permissibility of deriving new rulings from the sacred sources of the shari'a (*ijtihād*). Qaradawi maintains that since Muslims are a community with a global mission, they must have a presence in the West since the West is a leading force in the world and they must influence its policies. He devotes considerable attention to the question of marriages between Muslim men and non-Muslim women. Classical Muslim law allowed Muslim men to wed Jewish or Christian women, though many jurisprudents expressed reservations concerning this practice. The Qur'an permits marriage to scriptuary women, and while, in principle, Qaradawi accepts this rule, he considerably restricts its applicability. The Christian woman must be a real believer (being born of Christian parents is not sufficient proof of this—she herself must not be an atheist, an apostate, a communist, or a member of the Baha'i faith), and it is forbidden to marry a Jewish woman as long as there is war between the Muslims and Israel. Another interesting ruling by Qaradawi concerns what happens when a non-Muslim woman married to a non-Muslim man embraces Islam while her husband retains his original religion. After surveying the views of classical jurists—most of whom believed the woman must leave her husband—Qaradawi rules that in the West such a woman should stay with her husband. The purpose of this rule is to encourage married women to embrace Islam, to spare them the hardships facing women without husbands, and to give the husband an incentive to follow his wife into Islam.

The growing importance of Muslim minorities in Europe and America in the second half of the 20th century gave rise to a growing interest in public debate, academic study of interfaith relations, and interfaith dialogue. Numerous conferences, along with journals dedicated to this field (*Islamo-Christiana*; *Islam and Christian-Muslim Relations*; *Studies in Muslim-Jewish Relations*; *Journal of the Institute of Muslim Minority Affairs*; *Encounters: A Journal of Intercultural Perspectives*), have served as significant venues for adherents of diverse faiths to share their sensibilities and points of view.

Non-Muslims under Muslim Rule

This section focuses on non-Muslims living under Muslim rule, whether the non-Muslims constitute a majority or a minority in a given area. Medieval Muslim law initially distinguished among Jews and Christians ("People of the Book" or scriptuaries [*ahl al-kitāb*]), Zoroastrians, and polytheists. According to the Qur'an, the Muslims are obliged to fight the scriptuaries "until they pay the poll tax (*jizya*) out of hand while being humbled" (9:29). This has been taken to mean that the purpose of the war against the scriptuaries is not their conversion to Islam but rather their submission to Islamic rule. The scriptuaries who submitted to Islamic rule were described as "protected communities" (*ahl al-dhimma, dhimmī*s). Their rights and obligations were defined in a series of documents referred to as the Treaty of 'Umar (*al-shurūṭ al-'umariyya*), which probably date from the eighth century, despite being attributed to 'Umar b. al-Khattab, the second caliph (r. 634–44). These "conditions" promised the *dhimmī*s the right to retain their religion and perform their rituals, though various restrictions were placed on religious observance in public. The granting of this right was conditioned on the payment of the poll tax (*jizya*) and on the acceptance of a lowly status reflected in numerous rules relating to the construction and maintenance of places of worship and behavior in the public sphere.

The *dhimma* concept, which initially included only Jews and Christians, was broadened as a result of the huge expansion of the areas under Muslim control. The first religious group to be added to the *dhimma* category was the Zoroastrians, adherents of a dualistic religion that had been dominant in Iran before the Muslim conquest. Though the Zoroastrians are not mentioned in Qur'an 9:29, and though most schools of law do not consider them scriptuaries, they were included in the *dhimmī* category on the basis of a Prophetic tradition. As for polytheists, two of the four schools of law (the Hanafi and the Maliki) were willing to bestow *dhimmī* status on non-Arab polytheists. Only Arab polytheists were excluded from this category and therefore forced to choose between conversion to Islam and the sword; however, according to the perception of most jurists, all Arabs embraced Islam during the Prophet's lifetime. The exclusion of Arab polytheists from the *dhimmī* status therefore had little practical significance after the Prophet's death in 632. Hence, according to the Hanafi and Maliki schools of law, all non-Muslims living under Muslim rule—except for the apparently nonexistent Arab polytheists—are eligible for the *dhimmī* status; whereas, according to the Shafi'is and the Hanbalis, only Jews, Christians, and Zoroastrians are eligible.

The question of the relationship between Islam and the non-Muslims under its rule developed in the earliest period of Muslim history as a result of the major conquests in the first century. The non-Muslim communities of the Middle East, which was the first area conquered by Muslims, included Christians, Jews, Zoroastrians, and Manicheans (the latter were persecuted and never attained the status of *ahl al-dhimma*). In some regions of the Indian subcontinent, adherents of Indian religions lived under Muslim rule from the eighth century; this phenomenon grew dramatically in the 12th century and lasted until the 19th. Since the Hanafi school of law was predominant in India, the Hindus of the subcontinent were treated in most periods as *dhimmī*s; the few attempts to change their status and consider them unprotected polytheists came to naught. The Ottoman Empire had substantial Christian and Jewish minorities and developed the *millet* (from Arabic *milla* or "community") system for their governance. This system brought the non-Muslim communities (mainly the Greeks, the Armenians, and the Jews) into the framework of Ottoman law while giving them a substantial measure of religious and cultural freedom. The Iranian Safavid Empire had Armenian, Zoroastrian, and Jewish minorities

whose situation was, in general terms, worse than that of the minorities of the Ottoman Empire. In the 19th century, the Babi and Baha'i religions came into being in Iran; as religions founded after the revelation of the Qur'an, their adherents never received the *dhimmī* status and have been persecuted by successive Iranian governments. In Egypt, muftis have repeatedly declared the tiny Baha'i minority as apostates who are not entitled to the free exercise of their religion.

During the medieval period, several groups that began as Muslim sects developed beliefs so remote from Islam as to constitute distinct religions and therefore are considered minorities. The Druze community originated in the 11th century, developing out of the Isma'ili movement and named for Muhammad b. Isma'il al-Darazi, one of the early supporters of the Fatimid caliph Hakim (r. 996–1021) in his quest for recognition of his supernatural status. After Darazi's death in 1019, the leadership of these supporters passed to Hamza b. 'Ali, who is considered the founder of the Druze faith. The Druze call their faith "the Unitarian Way" (*madhhab al-tawḥīd*) and call themselves the "Unitarians" (*muwaḥḥidūn*). God is one, incomprehensible and undefinable by humans. The intricate cosmogony of the Druze faith cannot be discussed here. The faith has major ethical components, including truthfulness and solidarity within the community. The community is divided into the "learned," initiated into the secrets of the religion (*'uqqāl*) and the "ignorant" (*juhhāl*), who are not initiated but are nevertheless members of the faith. Of the principal commandments of Islam, only the Feast of Sacrifice ('Id al-Adha) is observed. Polygamy as well as divorce against the wife's will are forbidden. The Druze live in Syria, Lebanon, Israel, and Jordan. Their number is estimated at slightly above one million.

The Nusayris (or 'Alawis), whose main concentrations are in Syria and Turkey, are a syncretistic group that originated in ninth-century Syria among radical Shi'is. They are named after Muhammad b. Nusayr, who proclaimed the divine nature of the Shi'i imams and supported the transmigration of souls and antinomianism. They believe in the divine nature of 'Ali b. Abi Talib, as well as in the trinity of 'Ali, Muhammad, and Salman al-Farisi. They celebrate some Muslim and some Christian festivals, but the way in which these festivals are performed and the meaning given to them by the Nusayris are not the same as in Christianity and in Islam. It is noteworthy that despite their minority status, the Nusayris have held power in Syria since the early 1970s.

Mention should also be made of the Yazidis, a Kurdish-speaking group. They believe in one God who created the world and entrusted it to seven archangels, whose leader is the Peacock Angel (*Ṭāwūs-i malak*). This angel has been identified by outside observers with the devil; this identification has not yet been satisfactorily explained, but it resulted in the description of the Yazidis as "devil worshipers" and has increased the scholarly interest in their history and system of belief. The Yazidis were not considered as *dhimmīs* and their religion was not protected in any way until the period of the Tanzimat (Reforms) in the Ottoman Empire. Their origins can be traced to the activities of 'Adi b. Musafir, a Sufi shaykh who was born in Biqa' (now in Lebanon) in 1073 or 1078 and moved to Kurdistan at the beginning of the 11th century, where he established the 'Adawi order and acquired a considerable following. According to Maqrizi's (1364–1442) account, the order was transformed after 'Adi's death: his followers engaged in excessive veneration of their founder, claimed that he sits together with God, refused to accept any livelihood that is not from him, disregarded sexual taboos, and abolished the ritual prayers, saying that 'Adi prayed on their behalf. Consequently, 'Adi's tomb was destroyed in 1414–15; his bones were exhumed and burned. Since the 17th century, the Yazidis have experienced several waves of persecution and were even forced to convert to Islam. At the present time, most Yazidis (estimated by Kreyenbroek at about 120,000) live in Northern Iraq; in Syria they number about 15,000. In the 1980s, most Yazidis who lived in Turkey found refuge from religious persecution in Germany, where they number between 20,000 and 40,000. Modern Yazidis deny any relationship with Islam, but their religious vocabulary is still influenced by Sufism.

An important minority in the Indian subcontinent are the Sikhs. Their religion was founded in the Punjab province by Nanak (1469–1539). His creed centered on a preference for devotion as opposed to ritual and on a fierce criticism of the Hindu caste system. His followers in the leadership of the community were known as gurus, or teachers. They affirmed the existence of one God and rejected both Hindu and Muslim rituals. The Sikhs started as a peaceful religious group bent on bridging the gap between Hinduism and Islam but transformed themselves, since the 17th century, into a militant movement. This development was caused mainly by the change in the policies of the Mughal Empire from toleration during the reign of Akbar (r. 1556–1605) to persecution, which started during the reign of Jahangir (r. 1605–27), who executed Arjun, the third Sikh guru, in 1606. In the modern period, the number of Sikhs is estimated at 23 million, of whom more than 19 million live in India (according to the census of 2001).

In the medieval period, the *dhimma* system was the legal framework for the treatment of non-Muslims by the various Muslim governments. It seems to have been changed for a limited period only by the Mughal emperor Akbar, who abolished the *jizya* in 1581; the tax was restored in the framework of orthodox measures carried out by Emperor Aurangzeb (r. 1659–1707) in 1679. Though the exact nature of the *jizya* in India is open to debate, the symbolic significance of both its abolition and its restoration is not in any doubt. A much more significant change that heralded the end of the *dhimma* system took place during the Tanzimat period in the Ottoman Empire. The Hatt-ı Sherif of Gülhane (1839) proclaimed the equality of all Ottoman subjects, regardless of religion. In 1855 the *jizya* was abolished and the principle of equality of all subjects reaffirmed.

The question of non-Muslim minorities in Muslim majority countries entered a new phase in the 20th century with the emergence of numerous new states in the Middle East, Asia, and Africa. There are Hindu and Sikh minorities in Pakistan and a Hindu

minority in Bangladesh. The Jewish minorities in Egypt, Syria, Iraq, and North Africa practically disappeared when most of the Jews emigrated to the newly established state of Israel and elsewhere. Significant Christian minorities exist in Egypt (the Copts), Syria, Iraq, and Jordan.

The Shi'is

The minority with the most ancient roots in Islam are the Shi'is. In general, Shi'is have not been denounced as non-Muslims by mainstream Islam, and they are therefore different from the other minorities discussed in this entry. The term "Shi'i" is derived from the expression "Shi'at 'Ali," the party of 'Ali. Shi'is support the principle that the leadership of the Muslim community after Muhammad's death must be retained by the Prophet's descendants (*ahl al-bayt*) and that religious authority must be derived from the same source. Several attempts to implement these principles and place the Shi'is in positions of leadership were foiled during the Umayyad period. There is no way to estimate the size of the Shi'i community during this period, but its minority status does not seem to be in doubt. Similarly, in the premodern period it is not possible to estimate the size of the Shi'i population in any given region.

Despite being a minority, Shi'is succeeded in establishing major political units in the medieval period. The Buyid dynasty, which ruled from Baghdad between 945 and 1055, was significant for the development of the Twelver Shi'a. During Buyid rule, important developments took place in the development of Shi'i thought and ritual. Shi'i luminaries such as Ibn Babuya (d. 991), Mufid (d. 1022), Murtada (d. 1044), and Muhammad al-Tusi (d. 1067) flourished during the Buyid period. The lamentations of the Day of Ashura on Muharram 10 (the first month of the Islamic calendar), commemorating the killing of Muhammad's grandson Husayn and his supporters in Karbala on October 10, 680, as well as the festival of Ghadir Khumm, commemorating the alleged appointment of 'Ali b. Abi Talib as the Prophet's successor, were granted recognition during this period.

The main political achievement of the Isma'ili branch of Shi'is in the medieval period is the Fatimid state. Established by 'Ubaydallah al-Mahdi in the early tenth century, it progressively extended its power throughout North Africa; during the reign of Mu'izz it conquered Fustat in 969 and established the city of Cairo in 970. Thus began two centuries of Shi'i domination in Egypt, ending with the Ayyubid takeover in 1171 and the restoration of Sunnism. It is noteworthy that the Fatimid period does not seem to have brought about a substantial increase in the number of Shi'is in Egypt.

The political achievement of Shi'is that had the most durable results is the establishment of the Safavid state in Iran in the 16th century. In contrast to the Fatimid case, the establishment in Iran of the Twelver Shi'a as the official religion of the Safavid state by Shah Isma'il in 1501 launched the process by which Iran became, in the modern period, the most important concentration of Shi'i population.

Reliable statistics on the size of the Shi'i community are hard to come by, but it is estimated to constitute 10–15 percent of Muslims. Despite their minority status in the Muslim world in general, the Shi'is constitute a majority in Iran, Iraq, and Bahrain. In Iraq until 2003, the Shi'is were dominated by the Sunni minority. Since the establishment of the Iraqi monarchy in 1921, the government strove to marginalize the Shi'i majority. This was done by using citizenship criteria, such as holding Ottoman citizenship before the collapse of the Ottoman Empire, to restrict the civil rights of the Shi'is. In the late 1960s, the Ba'th government used the nationality law, first introduced in 1924 and amended several times in the 1970s, in order to deny the Iraqi nationality to a large number of Shi'is. During the Iran-Iraq War of 1980–88, according to Yitzhak Nakash's *Reaching for Power*, about 300,000 Iraqi Shi'is were forced to leave the country.

The Shi'is are the largest community in Lebanon. Substantial Shi'i minorities exist in Pakistan, India, Saudi Arabia, Yemen, the Gulf states, Afghanistan, Syria, and Turkey.

The Shi'is are not proponents of a single political attitude. In contradistinction to the idea propagated by Ayatollah Khomeini and his successors in Iran, according to whom scholars of religious law should rule (*wilāyat al-faqīh*), Ayatollah 'Ali Sistani, the most prominent religious leader of Iraqi Shi'is, has been reluctant to be drawn directly into worldly affairs.

Other Minorities under Muslim Rule

Minorities that adhere to religions known to the classical Muslim tradition (Judaism, Christianity, Zoroastrianism, polytheism) have their place in the scheme developed by Muslim jurisprudents. However, other types of minorities also developed during Muslim history. The Ahmadi movement emerged in the last decade of the 19th century in British India. The Ahmadis maintain that they are Muslims in the fullest sense of the word but are not recognized as such by many mainstream Muslim organizations and were declared a non-Muslim minority by the Pakistani parliament in 1974. This happened because their prophetology can be interpreted as contradicting the doctrine claiming Muhammad as the last prophet (*khatm al-nubuwwa*). Since then, and especially since the introduction of the Islamization policy of the Pakistani president Zia-ul-Haq in the 1980s, the Ahmadis suffered serious persecution in Pakistan, and the headquarters of their movement was relocated to London in 1984.

On the other hand, there are groups whose status as Muslims is not disputed but who are considered minorities because of their ethnic affiliation. A prominent example is the Kurds. The Kurds are a people who speak various Iranian languages and whose territory is divided between Turkey and Iraq; significant Kurdish minorities live also in Syria and Iran. Most Kurds are Sunni Muslims of the Shafi'i *madhhab*. In modern times, the Kurdish minority of Turkey rebelled several times in order to achieve the independence that was envisaged in the Treaty of Sèvres (1920) but abandoned in the Treaty of Lausanne (1923). The Turkish government suppressed these rebellions and went as far as denying

the very existence of a Kurdish people, officially calling the Kurds "mountainous Turks." As recently as 1967, a presidential decree prohibited the import into Turkey of any written or recorded material in Kurdish. In northern Iraq, the secessionist tendency was also in evidence in the wake of World War I, and several Kurdish revolts were suppressed both during the monarchy and after its fall in 1958. The most brutal suppression of the Iraqi Kurdish minority was committed during the so-called Anfal ("spoils," after the name of sura 8 in the Qur'an) campaign in 1987–88 when the Iraqi army massacred tens of thousands of civilians. In Iran, the most important event for the Iranian Kurds in the 20th century was the establishment of the ephemeral Kurdish republic of Mahabad (January to November 1946).

Concluding Observations

The issue of minorities in the Islamic world is complex. The minorities are not restricted to Jews and Christians, who are frequently given exclusive attention when the issue is addressed. Some minorities belong to religious communities that existed before the emergence of Islam (Jews, Christians, Zoroastrians, Hindus, Buddhists); among these can be included the Manicheans, who were not tolerated and are now extinct. Others were related to Islam when they came into being but developed into distinct religions (Yazidis, Nusayris, Druzes, Babis, and Baha'is). Another group considers itself Muslim but has been placed beyond the pale of Islam by the Muslim mainstream (Ahmadis). It is important to note that whatever tolerance was practiced in most historical periods in relation to the Jews, the Christians, the Zoroastrians, and even the non-Arab polytheists was not accorded to adherents of religions that came into being after the emergence of Islam. The prime examples of such minorities are the Baha'is in Iran and the Ahmadis in Pakistan. There are also minorities that are not religious but ethnic, such as the Kurds in Turkey, Syria, and Iraq and the Arabs in the Iranian province of Khuzistan.

The Muslims were a ruling minority for at least four centuries in the Middle East and for more than six centuries in various parts of India. The Arabian Peninsula, the birthplace of Islam, is an area with special rules: it was declared a region in which there would be no two religions, though there is evidence that Christians lived in Najran for some period after the Prophet's death. There was also a substantial Jewish community in Yemen, an area that was considered distinct from the rest of the peninsula according to most early jurists. The Yemeni Jews fared reasonably well until the 17th century, which brought a series of intermittent persecutions and oppressive policies. After 1948, most Yemeni Jews emigrated to the newly established state of Israel. In modern times, a considerable number of foreigners work in Saudi Arabia, but citizenship is conferred on Muslims alone: according to the "Saudi Arabian Citizenship System" (para 14.1), applications for citizenship must include "a certificate signed by the imam of the mosque at the applicant's area." This seems to preclude any non-Muslim from submitting an application.

In practical terms, the fortunes of the non-Muslims living under medieval Muslim rulers varied. Modern historians generally agree that non-Muslims under medieval Muslim rule fared better than non-Christians or heretical Christians under medieval Christendom. The prominent historian Bernard Lewis aptly observed that "there is nothing in Islamic history to compare with the massacres and expulsions, the inquisitions and persecutions that Christians habitually inflicted on non-Christians and still more on each other. In the lands of Islam, persecution was the exception; in Christendom, sadly, it was the norm." This must not be taken to mean that freedom of religion was unrestricted in the Islamic world or that the non-Muslims minorities also enjoyed equality. Nor was the relationship between the Muslims and their non-Muslim subjects as idyllic as it is sometimes described. Various disabilities were imposed on the non-Muslims and they were at times persecuted. The Abbasid caliph Mutawakkil (r. 847–61), for example, ordered his officials to destroy newly built churches, to confiscate parts of non-Muslim homes, to prevent the public performance of some Christian and Jewish rituals, and to impose distinctive clothing on the non-Muslims. It is not clear to what extent these instructions were carried out. The Fatimid caliph Hakim (996–1021) ordered the demolition of churches, the dismissal of non-Muslim officials, and the prohibition of various non-Muslim religious rituals, though he reversed this policy toward the end of his reign. The Almohad dynasty of North Africa and Spain (12th century) denied any tolerance to the Christian and Jewish communities and even engaged in forced conversions. This was also the policy of some Safavid rulers in 17th century Iran. Nevertheless, it seems that the treatment of non-Muslims under various Muslim governments in the Middle Ages was, overall, better than that of non-Christians or "deviant" Christians under medieval Christian rule. Modern Muslims frequently take pride in this comparison and draw from it conclusions concerning the tolerance inherent in the Islamic civilization.

In the modern period, the above-mentioned comparison is no longer tenable. Since the Enlightenment, there has been a marked increase in religious tolerance in the West. With the glaring exceptions of Nazi Germany and some communist regimes, countries whose population is predominantly Christian generally have shown more tolerance than countries whose population is predominantly Muslim. Massacres of Assyrians and Armenians in the late Ottoman Empire and the massacre of the Assyrians in Iraq in 1933 are significant examples of the harsh treatment of minorities in the modern Muslim world. Likewise, the growing strength of radical Islam in recent decades and the persecution of minorities such as the Baha'is in Iran and the Ahmadis in Pakistan and elsewhere go a long way to undermine the argument for the inherent toleration of religious minorities in Islam.

See also democracy; equality; minorities, jurisprudence of

Further Reading

Meir Bar Asher and Aryeh Kofsky, *The Nuṣayrī–'Alawī Religion: An Inquiry into Its Theology and Liturgy*, 2002; Allan D. Austin,

African Muslims in Antebellum America, 1997; Robert Brenton Betts, *The Druze*, 1988; Rainer Brunner and Werner Ende, *The Twelver Shia in Modern Times*, 2001; Michael Dillon, *China's Muslim Hui Community: Migration, Settlement and Sects*, 1999; Shammai Fishman, *Fiqh al-aqalliyyāt: A Legal Theory for Muslim Minorities*, 2006; Yohanan Friedmann, *Prophecy Continuous: Aspects of Aḥmadī Religious Thought and Its Medieval Background*, 2003; Idem, *Tolerance and Coercion in Islam: Interfaith Relations in the Muslim Tradition*, 2003; John S. Guest, *Survival among the Kurds: A History of the Yezidis*, 1993; Heinz Halm, *Shi'a Islam*, 1997; Idem, *Shi'ism*, 2004; M. Ali Kettani, *Muslim Minorities in the World Today*, 1986; Philip G. Kreyenbroek, *Yezidism—Its Background, Observances and Textual Tradition*, 1995; Philip G. Kreyenbroek and Stefan Sperl, eds., *The Kurds: A Contemporary Overview*, 1992; Donald Leslie, *Islam in Traditional China: A Short History to 1800*, 1986; Milka Levy-Rubin, "Shurut 'Umar and Its Alternatives: The Legal Debate on the Status of the Dhimmis," *Jerusalem Studies in Arabic and Islam* 30, 2005; Bernard Lewis, *The Jews of Islam*, 1984; Otto F. A. Meinardus, *Christians in Egypt*, 2006; Matti Moosa, *Extremist Shiites: The Ghulat Sects*, 1987; Yitzhak Nakash, *Reaching for Power: The Shi'a in the Modern Arab World*, 2006; Vali Nasr, *The Shi'a Revival: How Conflicts within Islam Will Shape the Future*, 2007; Jørgen Nielsen, *Muslims in Western Europe*, 2004; Wilfred Cantwell Smith, *Islam in Modern History*, 1957; Yosef Tobi, *The Jews of Yemen: Studies in Their History and Culture*, 1999; Raquel Ukeles, *The Evolving Muslim Community in America: The Impact of 9/11*, 2003.

YOHANAN FRIEDMANN

minorities, jurisprudence of

The jurisprudence of Muslim minorities (*fiqh al-aqalliyyāt*) has emerged as a distinct field of Islamic legal research in the wake of the establishment of sizable Muslim populations in Western Europe and North America since World War II. Although Muslims have lived as minorities throughout history, premodern Muslim jurists devoted little systematic reflection to the minority condition as potentially experienced by Muslims, although they addressed in a sustained manner the minority condition of Jews and Christians living under Muslim rule. Historically, one might contend that instances of *fiqh al-aqalliyyāt* have occurred whenever Muslim minorities have sought guidance under the shari'a. The problems they have faced and the juristic opinions these problems have elicited constitute *fiqh al-aqalliyyāt* in a descriptive sense. This entry is concerned with the normative usages of *fiqh al-aqalliyyāt* related to the calls voiced by a range of Muslims for construction of a new system of Islamic normativity (*fiqh*) that addresses the specific concerns of Muslim minorities. These calls represent a thoroughly modern phenomenon, engaging a number of contemporary Muslim scholars and intellectuals.

The debate on a new Islamic law for minorities, and even whether the project is a legitimate one, is transnational. It takes place in print, via satellite television, in Internet forums, as well as in mosques and Islamic centers of the Islamic diaspora in the West, and the proliferation of mass media has been crucial in facilitating it. Contemporary minority *fiqh* advocates are based in France, Britain, and the United States as well as in Egypt, Morocco, and Saudi Arabia. Like minority *fiqh* critics, proponents of *fiqh al-aqalliyyāt* operate in a global space of normative *fiqh* debate. Unlike their critical interlocutors, however, they have to work through the disjuncture arising out of their far-flung geographical locations on the one hand and their commitment to setting symbolic boundaries on the other. Minority *fiqh* advocates based in Muslim majority countries face an even more specific predicament: if their call for the creation of a new law for Muslim minorities by integrating knowledge of the reality of Muslim communities in the West works to disqualify competing voices in the Muslim world, it also undermines their own authority to speak on these issues, not least in the eyes of Muslims in the West, the audience they hope to reach.

The first attempts to theorize a *fiqh* for Muslim minorities appeared in the 1990s in Arabic theses submitted to the shari'a faculties of universities in Morocco, Saudi Arabia, Lebanon, and elsewhere by students who had come from, or had a special interest in, Europe. In addition to works in European languages, they drew on the research on Muslim minorities undertaken in Arab universities since the late 1970s—notably at the Institute for Muslim Minority Affairs at King 'Abd al-'Aziz University in Jeddah—and on a steady flow of accounts published by Muslim scholars and diplomats who had studied or worked in the West. Interest in the questions of Muslims in the West increased significantly in the post–cold war period, when "Islam" and the "West" became related and opposed with a new intensity. This wave of interest in law for Muslim minorities illustrates the effects of geopolitics on the production of knowledge in contemporary Islam. Although the discussion is framed in the language and categories of traditional Islamic law, the debate has attracted a wide range of participants, including Muslim social scientists. The journal *Islamiyyat al-Ma'rifa* (The Islamization of knowledge), edited by the International Institute of Islamic Thought in the United States, published the first major piece on *fiqh al-aqalliyyāt* in the late 1990s. In the following decade, and following the shock of the attacks in New York and Washington, many other texts followed.

Yusuf al-Qaradawi's 2001 book *Fi Fiqh al-Aqalliyyat al-Muslima: Hayat al-Muslimin fi al-Mujtama'at al-Ukhra* (On the law of Muslim minorities: The lives of Muslims in other societies) is perhaps the most widely read and taught treatise on the subject. By the turn of the millennium, Qaradawi had a long-standing audience in the West. His books were read in Arabic and translated into the major European languages, and his program on Aljazeera titled *Al-Shari'a wa-l-Hayat* (Islamic law and life), aired since 1997 and

regularly devoted to Muslim minority issues, had become a favorite of Arabic-speaking Muslims. Qaradawi was also a regular visitor to the United States until 1999 and to Europe until 2004. Since then, his traditionalist positions on gender and sexuality and his support for Hamas in Palestine have reduced his prominence, but he continues to be viewed as a high religious authority and still chairs the Dublin-based European Council for Fatwa and Research, which he helped found in 1997. His book carefully places *fiqh al-aqalliyyāt* within the discursive tradition of the shari'a, in keeping with his calls for *ijtihād* in the Muslim world. Taha Jabir al-'Alwani's (b. 1935) treatise on minority *fiqh*, first published in 1999, circulates widely in Arabic and English versions. This Iraqi scholar, who lived in the United States for two decades, links his understanding of minority *fiqh* to a larger project of reform not limited to Muslim minorities. In the English version of the text, he relates the need to construct Islamic law for Muslim minorities to the post-9/11 struggle against terrorism. His approach draws on the *Islamiyyat al-Ma'rifa* project and is grounded in an attempt to develop a new discourse of Islamic ethics drawing primarily on the Qur'an. Alwani's exclusion of the prophetic sunna—embodied in the canonical collections of hadith reports—from serving as a basis for the law is underscored by his understanding that the sunna is intolerant, a view that many of his peers have hotly contested. In 2007 'Abdallah bin Bayyah, a Mauritanian expert in Maliki law who now teaches in Saudi Arabia, wrote *Sina'at al-Fatwa wa-Fiqh al-Aqalliyyat* (The derivation of legal opinions and the Islamic law of minorities). He perceives in liberalism's claims to fairness and neutrality a real challenge to the Islamic legal tradition's understanding of justice. After elaborating his own method for issuing fatwas, he dedicates a large part of the text to a discussion of the opinions issued by the European Council for Fatwa and Research (of which he is also a member). His commitment to the traditional *madhhab* or juridical school gives Bin Bayyah's text a specific orientation. While Qaradawi and 'Alwani seem to start from general principles and draw rulings from these, Bin Bayyah proceeds by seeking to recapture the rich detail of traditional *fiqh*. These three texts highlight minority *fiqh* advocates' diverse views and raise the question of how to characterize minority *fiqh* as a project. Advocates of minority *fiqh* share a commitment to the Islamic legal tradition, the terrain where solutions to Muslims' problems continue to be sought, and a perception that the minority status poses a problem for that tradition. These two general ideas differentiate scholars calling for a new *fiqh* for Muslims in the West from many of their interlocutors. The level of commitment to the Islamic tradition and understanding of the kinds of problems posed by life in the West vary significantly from one theorist to another, and the minority *fiqh* project shares a certain indeterminacy with current calls for *ijtihād* (independent reasoning), *tajdīd* (renewal, reform), and the elaboration of Islamic law according to *maqāṣid al-sharī'a* (the fundamental goals of the law).

Islamic law for Muslim minorities is also embodied in a number of institutions, including the European Council for Fatwa and Research (ECFR) and the Fiqh Council of North America (FCNA), as well as the efforts of websites such as Islam Online (islamonline.net) and On Islam (onislam.net) to adapt religious rulings for Muslims living in the West. In general the fatwas of minority *fiqh* institutions seek to reconcile the impetus of the Islamic Revival with the problematics of integration. They oscillate between emphasizing the perceived powerlessness of Western Muslims and stressing their individual moral responsibility. The former founds a regime of exceptions that suspend traditional Islamic norms through legal dispensations such as "dire need" (*ḍarūra*) and stresses the need to abide by European laws. The latter purposefully ignores the context in order to consolidate a shared Muslim identity rendered fragile—in the eyes of the muftis—by strong pressures toward assimilation.

Criticisms of *fiqh al-aqalliyyāt* have been wide-ranging. Like its advocates, critics of minority *fiqh* cannot be easily categorized. They include 'ulama', public intellectuals, and secular Muslims with different intellectual commitments and disparate political agendas. Some of the critiques they have voiced include condemnations of minority *fiqh* as an attempt to secularize Islam, divide and weaken Muslims, and sell out to the West. Others have argued that the emphasis on the "minority" condition is a syndrome that prevents Muslims from realizing their rights and duties as citizens of liberal democracies. In a 2005 statement, the International Islamic Fiqh Council rejected the idea of a minority *fiqh* because it is based on an assumed minority–majority antagonism, deemed incompatible with an Islamic vision of pluralism and coexistence, and because it seems to deny Muslim agency.

The debate on whether minority *fiqh* is legitimate is partly a debate about how to understand the viability of the Islamic legal tradition (What continuities and changes are necessary for it to remain a living and coherent tradition in a diasporic context?) and how to conceptualize the political space that constitutes the West (What kinds of constraints are placed upon Muslims in European secular regimes, and what freedoms do they have?). Very often, however, the texts arguing for or against minority *fiqh* are more situated engagements with particular legal positions adopted by the scholars and institutions associated with the minority *fiqh* project. Critics of minority *fiqh* have targeted in particular the fatwas allowing Muslims to participate in elections in non-Muslim countries, allowing married women who convert to Islam to remain with their non-Muslim husband, and allowing Muslims to have recourse to interest-bearing mortgages to buy a house.

Since the aim of *fiqh al-aqalliyyāt* is to provide an authoritative reading of the Islamic tradition in a context of migration and social change, its success depends perhaps first and foremost on the recognition of Muslim audiences. This recognition has been ambivalent. The success of minority *fiqh* should also be related to the way the project resonates, or fails to do so, with wider public debates about the integration of Islam in the West. State policies and debates in the public sphere may contribute to authorize or undermine the idea of a *fiqh* for Muslim minorities. Both focus on the notion of "integration"—although what they mean by that often varies significantly. Minority *fiqh* advocates appear to assume that Muslims must "adapt" to Western societies. The muftis thus seem to

share with many European and North American policy makers and public intellectuals a common diagnosis of the current situation as a failure on the part of Muslims to integrate properly, an understanding that Muslims are morally responsible for this failure as a consequence of "extremist" interpretations of Islam, and a vision of the conditions under which community cohesion becomes possible and social conflict is eliminated, envisioning Islam as a "civil" religion contributing to the common good.

See also *ijtihād* and *taqlīd*; jurisprudence; al-Qaradawi, Yusuf (b. 1926); shari'a

Further Reading

Khaled Abou El Fadl, "Islamic Law and Muslim Minorities: The Juristic Discourse on Muslim Minorities from the Second/Eighth to the Eleventh/Seventeenth Centuries," *Islamic Law and Society* 1, no. 2 (1994): 141–87; Taha Jaber al-Alwani, *Toward a Fiqh for Minorities—Some Basic Reflections*, 2003; Alexandre Caeiro, "The Power of European Fatwas: The Minority Fiqh Project and the Making of an Islamic Counterpublic," *International Journal of Middle East Studies* 42, no. 3 (2010): 435–49; European Council for Fatwa and Research, *First and Second Collections of Fatwas*, 2002; Bettina Gräf and Jakob Skovgaard-Petersen, ed., *The Global Mufti: The Phenomenon of Yusuf al-Qaradawi*, 2009; Asif Khan, *The Fiqh of Minorities: The New Fiqh to Subvert Islam*, 2004; Peter Mandaville, "Globalization and the Politics of Religious Knowledge: Pluralizing Authority in the Muslim World," *Theory, Culture and Society* 24, no. 2 (2007): 101–15; Andrew March, *Islam and Liberal Citizenship: The Search for an Overlapping Consensus*, 2009.

ALEXANDRE CAEIRO

Mir Damad (1561–1631)

Mir Damad, grandson of the highest ranking jurist and head of the religious establishment in Safavid Iran, Shaykh 'Ali al-Karaki (d. 1534), was a scion of Persian nobility from Astarabad who were descendants of the Prophet. Trained as a jurist and philosopher in Mashhad and Isfahan, where he studied with leading students of Shaykh Zayn al-Din al-'Amili (d. 1558) such as Shaykh Husayn b. 'Abd al-Samad, as well as with leading philosophers of Shiraz such as Mir Fakhr al-Din al-Sammaki, he became a prominent figure at the Safavid court of Shah 'Abbas I. His skill in philosophy led him to be dubbed the "Third Teacher" after Aristotle and Farabi. While his writings primarily concern jurisprudence and philosophical theology more than political thought, he was a major political figure. He defended the Safavid polity; trained students in philosophy, including the important figure of Safavid thought, Mulla Sadra Shirazi (1572–1640); and served as a prayer leader and jurist for the capital, Isfahan, most notably conducting the coronation of Shah Safi in 1629 and leading the prayer in Isfahan. On a visit to the Shi'i shrine cities in Iraq with Shah Safi, he died in Najaf and was buried in the courtyard of the shrine.

His contributions to political thought and defense of the Safavid polity lie in three areas. First, he wrote glosses on major works in Shi'i jurisprudence and tradition to bolster the official status of Shi'i Islam in the empire and to further the Safavid project of reviving and disseminating Shi'i teachings as the official theory underlying the empire. He therefore wrote marginalia and commentaries on the four main collections of Shi'i hadiths as well as on *al-Sahifa al-Sajjadiyya* (The scroll of Sajjad), the famous collection of the supplications of the fourth imam, 'Ali Zayn al-'Abidin, that was widely disseminated and popularized in the period.

Second, in the field of jurisprudence, he wrote works on the necessity of establishing the Friday congregational prayers under the authority of the jurist and in the name of the just authority (*al-sulṭān al-'ādil*), which was either the Hidden Imam or the jurist as his general representative. He also wrote works on legitimate claims to the rights for declaring jihad and on the need for the polity and religious establishment to assume the guardianship of those unable to take care of themselves. These works, which represent some of the strongest claims to clerical authority in the Safavid period, argue clearly for the legitimacy of the Safavids as rulers with divine favor and for the jurists as figures whose authority underpins the polity of which they are guardians.

Third, as a leading courtier, Mir Damad was also involved in official embassies and wrote correspondence for the shah defending the dynasty, and his elite mysticism favored the imperial conception of authority.

See also Mulla Sadra (ca. 1572–1640); Safavids (1501–1722); al-Tusi, Nasir al-Din (1201–74)

Further Reading

Rula Abisaab, *Converting Persia: Religion and Power in the Safavid Empire*, 2004; Saïd Amir Arjomand, *The Shadow of God and the Hidden Imam: Religion, Political Order, and Societal Change in Shi'ite Iran from the Beginning to 1890*, 1984; Seyyed Hossein Nasr, "Spiritual Movements, Philosophy and Theology in the Safavid Period," in *The Cambridge History of Iran*, edited by Peter Jackson and Laurence Lockhart, 1986; Andrew J. Newman, "Towards a Reconsideration of the 'Esfahan School of Philosophy: Shaikh Bahā'ī and the Role of the Safawid 'Ulamā'," *Studia Iranica* 15, no. 2 (1986).

SAJJAD H. RIZVI

Mirrors for Princes

The term "Mirrors for Princes," following European practice, is given to works of literature that impart advice to rulers and high-ranking administrators; such writings are abundant in Arabic,

Persian, and Turkish. The designaton "Mirrors for Princes" has often been used as a synonym for the more general category of advice literature and applied to a variety of written texts as long as they serve an advisory purpose and address a royal recipient; in this sense, the term has been applied to works of *ḥikma* (wisdom), *maw'iẓa* (moral exhortation), *akhlāq* (ethics, characteristically in the personal, domestic, and political settings), and *waṣiyya* ("testament," usually of a father to his son[s] and successor[s]). In other usages, the term "Mirrors for Princes" has been restricted to a particular literary genre, understood as a branch of *adab* (belles lettres). According to this more limited definition, the designation is usually reserved for independent book-length works (sometimes known as *adab* or *ādāb al-mulūk* ["the manners of kings"], *naṣīḥat al-mulūk* ["counsel for kings"], or *siyar al-mulūk* ["the conduct of kings"]) subdivided into thematic chapters or sections, in which materials from varied sources (such as Qur'anic verses, hadith, proverbs, bons mots, poetry, anecdotes, historical narratives) feature prominently. Whether the broader or the more restrictive definition is taken, the author's choice of a distinct literary form played a major role in shaping his work and its reception.

Advisory works were among the compositions that facilitated the accommodation of late antique political-cultural ideas and ideals, and their literary expressions, into the medium of Arabic and later Persian. They incorporated and adapted materials that dealt in significant measure with matters pertaining to (or considered relevant to) courts and courtiers, drawn from texts such as the pseudo-Aristotelian *Sirr al-Asrar* (known in the Latin West under the title *Secretum secretorum*, or *Secret of Secrets*), the romance of Alexander, and the collection of animal fables titled *Kalila and Dimna*, all of which circulated in several languages and versions in the Mediterranean and West Asian regions in the late antique and early Islamic periods. In the context of later Muslim-majority societies, the best-known examples of Mirrors for Princes are a trio of celebrated late-11th-century works written in Persian in the shadow of the rise of the Seljuqs or during their rule in Iran: the *Qabusnama* (Book of Qabus) of Kay Ka'us, the *Nasihat al-Muluk* (Counsel for kings) of Ghazali, and the *Siyar al-Muluk* (Conduct of kings) or *Siyasatnama* (Book of governance) of the vizier Nizam al-Mulk. It is perhaps on account of the lasting popularity and familiarity of these highly individual works that Mirrors for Princes have sometimes been associated particularly with the Persian language and with "Iranian" political-cultural ideas. While the Persian language has indeed produced a remarkably rich moralizing literature, these associations should not be overstated: the Mirrors for Princes literature, richly represented in Arabic and Turkish as well as Persian, is extremely varied, and the meanings and significance of particular ideas and motifs, even where they can be traced to "translations" from Pahlavi or Greek, were shaped according to the exigencies of the specific environments in which they were articulated.

Modern scholarship has firmly established the importance of Mirrors for Princes in the context of medieval political thought, the category of which, otherwise construed so as to assign a preponderant role to juristic sources, has been greatly enriched by attention to the literature of the courts. Like their counterparts writing in Latin and the European vernacular languages, the authors of Arabic and Persian Mirrors for Princes did not necessarily, or even frequently, set out to expound a comprehensive political vision. At first glance, Mirrors for Princes often appear to be somewhat conventional in that certain themes (justice and injustice, the virtues of patience and clemency, the importance of consultation and heeding good advice, the need for the king to refrain from making hasty judgments, and so on) as well as certain sayings, citations, and formulae (such as the "circle of justice") recur with marked regularity. Despite these common elements, the Mirrors for Princes literature cannot be said to represent a remotely uniform outlook, style, or mode of expression. The form has proven highly flexible and has been employed to accommodate a wide range of authorial purposes and dispositions. From the 12th century onward, it becomes possible to identify a number of variants: some Mirrors for Princes emphasized matters of administration, some concentrated on the ruler's cultivation of personal virtue, some were encyclopedic in scope, some were homiletic, and some combined several approaches and tones appropriate to particular sections of the book. These choices depended on, among other factors, the background, professional training, and occupation of the author; the period and region in which he lived; the specific circumstances under which he wrote; the language he decided to use; and the interests of his royal patron. An author's reasons for writing might include the consolidation of ties with particular members of the courtly elite, aspirations for professional advancement, and a desire to instruct and entertain. What is clear is that every author wrote under and in response to specific conditions, political and otherwise; indeed, several Mirrors for Princes may be regarded as occasional in character.

A number of scholars, among them Cornell Fleischer and Julie Scott Meisami, have explored the meanings of the ideas and materials relayed in Mirrors for Princes when applied to the particular historical contexts in and for which they were written. If portions of the materials that appear in Mirrors for Princes can often be traced through a large number of earlier texts, their deployment in any given literary context carries its own significance. Situated in its full historical context, a book of counsel may convey a particular vein of commentary on, and criticism of, prevailing political and cultural trends; it may also represent the participation in political discourse of a specific group or faction in response to contemporary conditions and circumstances.

Recent scholarship has placed importance on the literary strategies pursued by authors of Mirrors for Princes in response to the constraints imposed by the relationship between counselor-writer and ruler-addressee. To read Mirrors for Princes in the light of the author's dependence on the recipient provides a necessary perspective, and, although relations between counselors and kings were sometimes quite complicated, it is important to acknowledge the effects of the differential in power. Following the conventions of the literary genre decreased the risks involved in offering advice to the ruler. In addition to addressing an established repertoire of themes and adducing expected quotations from recognized authorities,

authors sometimes cast their advice in the framework of paradigmatic embodiments of the wise sage and receptive monarch, such as Aristotle and Alexander or Buzurgmihr and Anushirvan: figures distant in time and context from the author and his addressee. Such techniques allowed the writer to present himself as an intermediary rather than a direct critic.

See also Nizam al-Mulk (1018–92)

Further Reading

F. R. C. Bagley, *Ghazālī's Book of Counsel for Kings (Naṣīḥat al-mulūk)*, 1964; Robert Dankoff, *Wisdom of Royal Glory (Kutadgu bilig)*, 1983; Cornell H. Fleischer, *Bureaucrat and Intellectual in the Ottoman Empire: The Historian Mustafa Âli (1541–1600)*, 1986; Ann K. S. Lambton, "Islamic Mirrors for Princes," in *La Persia nel Medioevo*, 1971; Reuben Levy, *A Mirror for Princes: The Qābūs Nāma by Kai Kā'ūs ibn Iskandar*, 1951; Julie Scott Meisami, *The Sea of Precious Virtues*, 1991; G. M. Wickens, *The Nasirean Ethics*, 1964.

L. MARLOW

modernism

Modernist Islamic political thought emerged in the middle of the 19th century as a response to European imperial expansion. Muslim scholars such as Rifa'a Rafi' al-Tahtawi (Egypt, 1801–73), Sayyid Ahmad Khan (India, 1817–98), and Shihabuddin Marjani (Tatarstan-Bukhara, 1818–89)—themselves trained in traditional Islamic settings—urged Muslim societies to adopt certain elements of European civilization in order to forestall further European encroachments. Fortunately, in their view, the institutions most associated with Europe's military and industrial power happened to coincide with the original principles of Islam. By adopting these institutions, according to modernists, Muslims would simultaneously join the "civilized world" and return to the proper practice of Islam. In the words of Albanian scholar Shemseddin Sami Frasheri (Ottoman Empire, 1850–1904), "Therefore, saving the Muslim peoples from ignorance and once again bringing them to civilization"—in the singular, by which he means European civilization—"are among the most important priorities of any zealous person who loves his religious community and fatherland, since the survival and glory of Islam are contingent upon this alone."

From the beginning, political institutions were among the modernist movement's most important targets for reform. Tahtawi, for instance, translated the French Charter of 1814 into Arabic and commented that it offered a model for Muslim societies: "What they [the French] hold dear and call liberty is what we call equity and justice, for to rule according to liberty means to establish equality through judgments and laws, so that the ruler cannot wrong anybody, the law being the reference and the guide." Muhammad Rashid Rida (Syria-Egypt, 1865–1935), one of the leading Arab modernists of the early 20th century, stated clearly that these political principles derived primarily from observation of European models: "The greatest benefit that the peoples of the Orient have derived from the Europeans was to learn how real government ought to be, as well as the assimilation of this knowledge." Muslims could not have developed this independently, he continued. Muhammad Iqbal (India, 1877–1938), the preeminent Islamic modernist of early 20th-century South Asia, went so far as to hail European imperialism as a progressive political force: "Democracy has been the great mission of England in modern times, and English statesmen have boldly carried this principle to countries which have been, for centuries, groaning under the most atrocious forms of despotism."

At the same time, many Muslim modernists rejected European imperialism. Afghani (Iran, 1838–97) and Muhammad 'Abduh (Egypt, 1849–1905), among the most influential Islamic modernists, railed against imperialism in their influential but short-lived journal *al-'Urwa al-Wuthqa* (The firmest bond), which was published in Arabic in Paris in 1884: "Are [Muslims] satisfied to live under the yoke of foreigners, after having enjoyed supreme power?"

To fend off European imperialism, as well as to reshape society and forestall secessionist movements, modernists sought to strengthen Muslim-led governments. "Can this state be saved?" the Young Turks asked of the Ottoman Empire. For more than half a century, from the Crimean War through World War I, they and other modernists answered in the affirmative, urging state-building through the spread of government-run education, the development of transportation and communication infrastructure, and the modernization of the military, among other reforms. Some of these plans were adopted by certain modernizing Muslim rulers, such as the long-ruling monarchs of the late 19th century, Sultan Abdülhamid II of the Ottoman Empire, Nasir al-Din Shah (r. 1848–96) of Iran, 'Abd al-Rahman Khan (r. 1880–1901) in Afghanistan, and Sultan Abu Bakar (r. 1862–95) of Johore in Malaya. In the view of these rulers and the Muslim thinkers who supported them, Western technologies could be imported to shore up the authority of traditional Muslim states.

Other modernists considered Western democratic institutions necessary as well. In keeping with contemporary European social science, these Muslim thinkers argued that such institutions would strengthen the state by generating popular commitment in the form of increased payment of taxes, obedience to the law, and participation in national defense. In addition to this secular reasoning, many Muslim modernists also marshaled Islamic justifications. For some, these justifications appear to have been strategic: "ideas which were by no means accepted when coming from your agents in Europe," Mirza Malkum Khan (Iran, 1833–1908) told a British audience, "were accepted with great delight when it was proved that they were latent in Islam." Even those who were sincere in their adoption of Islamic reasoning acknowledged the strategic advantage of this use. Iqbal, for example, urged modernists "not to shock the naturally suspicious conservatism of their people by appearing as prophets of a new culture. They would certainly impress them more

if they could show that their seemingly borrowed ideal of political freedom is really the ideal of Islam, and is, as such, the rightful demand of free Muslim conscience."

Among the most influential Islamic justifications for democracy was the Qur'anic concept of *shūrā*, or consultation, which modernists beginning with Namık Kemal (Ottoman Empire, 1840–88) associated with Western parliamentary institutions. Another Qur'anic justification for democracy appeared in a tract by Muhammad Husayn Na'ini (Iran, 1860–1936): "He [God] cannot be questioned about what He does, but they will be questioned" (21:23). Na'ini concluded from this and similar passages that "Absolute power belongs only to God, yet [reactionaries] declared it un-Islamic to struggle against the absolute power of earthly tyrants." Other modernists noted the protodemocratic selection and conduct of early Muslim leaders. Chiragh 'Ali (India, 1844–95), for example, argued that the "first four or five caliphates were purely republican in all their features. The law, when originally framed, did not recognize the existence of a king, of a nobility, or even of a gentry."

These and other Islamic arguments accompanied constitutionalist movements in many countries. Egypt promulgated a constitutionalist document in 1860 and a fuller constitution in 1882; Tunisia did so briefly in 1861 and then after the colonial interlude, in 1959; the Ottoman Empire issued a constitution briefly in 1876, then again in 1908; Iran did so as well briefly in 1906, then again in 1909; and so on. These constitutions did not enact democracy as it came to be understood later in the 20th century: universal adult suffrage, reduction of monarchs to symbolic offices, and constitutional protection of a growing list of rights. Rather, in keeping with most of Europe, most Muslim modernists sought constitutional monarchies with limited suffrage. Many modernists did not believe that illiterates—who comprised the great majority of Muslim populations at the time—or literate women were capable of exercising electoral rights responsibly. According to a demeaning joke told by modernists in Iran, a lower-class demonstrator supposedly thought constitutionalism was some sort of food, complaining, "I've been waiting for two days and I haven't gotten even a single piece of constitutionalism." Western observers noted that the terms that Muslims frequently used for constitutionalism at this time, such as *meşrütiyet* in Turkish and *mashrūṭiyyat* in Persian, were only recently invented and, they felt, scarcely understood.

Nonetheless, when democratic rights were available, the popular classes frequently rushed to take advantage of them. After the reinstallment of the constitution in the Ottoman Empire in 1908, workers in numerous fields went on strike almost immediately, recognizing their improved legal position. During the constitutional period in early 20th-century Iran, peasants mobilized to protest mistreatment by local landowners, petitioning parliament and claiming rights as citizens. In the 1910s, Muslims in the four Senegalese cities that had been granted French citizenship began to exercise their voting rights in large numbers, and Indonesians exploited Dutch colonial regulations to found mass civic organizations such as Sarekat Islam.

Modernists' enthusiasm for democracy waned after World War I among Muslims as well as many other populations around the world, as leftist and fascist dictatorships took center stage. At this time, modernist political thought split into several streams. One of these streams was composed of secularist movements that adopted the modernists' goals but sought to limit the importance of Islamic faith in public life—examples include Atatürk in Turkey, Muhammad Reza Shah in Iran, and Amanullah Khan in Afghanistan. Another consisted of religious revivalist movements that adopted many of the modernists' tactics and goals but claimed to be pursuing a political path independent of Western models—examples include the two mass organizations founded in the late 1920s and early 1930s, Hasan al-Banna's Muslim Brotherhood in Egypt and Mawdudi's Jama'at-i Islami in India. Yet another was represented by liberal Islamic movements that continued to maintain the compatibility of Islamic faith and modernist ideals, including major proindependence parties such as Ahmad Dahlan's Muhammadiyah in Indonesia and Ahmadu Bello's Northern People's Congress in Nigeria.

Although the modernist movement fractured, much of its political thought remains widespread. Democracy is widely popular among Muslims, according to the World Values Survey and other polls. Parliaments meet in almost every Muslim-majority country and are considered crucial to the integration of state and society, even where parliament's members are not freely elected. Written legal codes are almost universal, and state-run judicial systems are now taken for granted, having wrested control from religious courts in almost every Muslim society over the past century. Large majorities of Muslims hold the state responsible for education, infrastructural investments, economic growth, and other duties that modernists first championed in the 19th century.

In other respects, however, the modernist movement failed. Muslim-majority countries on the whole are less democratic than other countries, according to cross-national statistical studies. The rule of law is incomplete in many Muslim societies. And modernism itself is often derided as overly Western-oriented and insufficiently authentic, even by some Muslim intellectuals who themselves espouse Western-derived global norms such as democracy and human rights.

See also constitutionalism; liberalism; modernity

Further Reading

Aziz Ahmad, *Islamic Modernism in India and Pakistan, 1857–1964*, 1967; Albert Hourani, *Arabic Thought in the Liberal Age, 1798–1939*, 1962; Adeeb Khalid, *The Politics of Muslim Cultural Reform: Jadidism in Central Asia*, 1998; Charles Kurzman, ed., *Modernist Islam, 1840–1940: A Sourcebook*, 2002; Şerif Mardin, *The Genesis of Young Ottoman Thought: A Study in the Modernization of Turkish Political Ideas*, 1962; Mansoor Moaddel, *Islamic Modernism, Nationalism, and Fundamentalism*, 2005; Itzchak Weismann, *Taste of Modernity: Sufism, Salafiyya, and Arabism in Late Ottoman Damascus*, 2001.

CHARLES KURZMAN

modernity

The idea of modernity combines a variety of vectors and paths of transformation: economic factors linked to the rise of capitalism, sociopolitical dynamics related to the formation of increasingly centralized and bureaucratized states, and cultural orientations putting a premium on individual autonomy and collective agency, on self-reflexivity, self-steering, and a capacity for creative innovation, and new, pervasive forms of solidarity. This complex yet well-profiled idea reflects in a first instance the historical experiences and achievements of European societies, or better, of some parts of northwestern Europe. It is also important to consider that the transformations that ushered in the advent of modernity concerned religion, both institutionally and conceptually. It was in modern transformations that religion became a clearly circumscribed—optimally, a privatized—sphere, one increasingly differentiated from the realm of politics.

The social science literature that, from the founders of sociology at large (Marx, Durkheim, and Weber) onward, has delineated the key traits of modernity (including its relations to religion) and has postulated that the historical breakthrough to modernity is a Western prerogative, focused on Western Europe and on some of its former settlement colonies overseas (mainly North America and Australia)—primarily because of some allegedly "Occidental" cultural and institutional conditions that did not exist or did not come to maturation in other civilizations. Such civilizations, including Islam, were by contrast considered lacking in one or more crucial features of modernity, in particular the fundamental capacity to spawn creative innovations and to liberate new transformative energies from the "shackles of tradition." According to this vision, non-Western civilizations could at best achieve limited degrees or dependent forms of modernity through their introduction from outside, via a modernization process induced from the West.

More recent theoretical work has revised both the assumption of the uniqueness of the West and the corresponding conception of modernity as singular. In order to reframe the issue of modernity from the perspective of Islamic political thought, a sound conceptualization of the relation between tradition and modernity cannot approach the former as a mere relic of premodern cultures that is destined to be either neutralized or erased in the course of modernization. Specifically, the relation between modernity and Islam cannot be reduced to an analysis of deficits to be measured by Islam's alleged insufficient capacity to supersede its rooting in tradition or in a set of combined traditions, by Islam's dependencies on Western hegemonic patterns of modernity, or by alleged Islamic idiosyncrasies reflected by distorted outcomes of a dependent modernization.

Questions such as "What went wrong?" with Islamic civilization vis-à-vis the modern world hegemonized by the West are the result of static and unilateral views of both tradition and modernity. The famous British Orientalist Bernard Lewis was not the first author to ask this type of question with regard to Islam, nor was 9/11 the first event that prompted such interrogations. The question has been repeatedly formulated from the perspective of a long-term Western hegemony extended over the entire modern world and therefore facing recurrent traumas (from the Indian revolt of 1857 through the oil embargo of 1973, to the terrorist attacks of 2001 and after) resulting in a continual challenge of this same hegemony, often occurring on a symbolical level more than on a material one. The formulation of the question therefore already presupposes that the Western path to modernity is unique, though exposed to challenges.

The heyday of modernization theory, which articulated ideas of modernity as monopolized by the West but exportable, under certain conditions, to the rest of the world, go back to the 1950s and 1960s. The approach suffered a lethal blow in the wake of various events unfolding on the global level during the 1970s and in particular the Iranian Revolution of 1978–79, which raised the banner of Islam against the Shah's authoritarian rule and Westernizing programs. Seeds for an alternative conception, according to which modernity is not a uniquely Western prerogative and cultural and religious traditions are not just detritus left behind by the waves of modernization, were sown in the decolonization struggles, which sparked reinterpretations and critiques of modern ideas and institutions. Their combined result was to challenge the West's monopoly over the definition of modernity.

With even greater intensity since after the demise of modernization theory, key voices within Western social sciences and in particular within social theory have concurred in observing that modernity was never singular, neither was it homogeneous, not even within Europe. A major contribution to make this simple insight productive in theoretical and comparative terms has been the development of a civilizational approach to modernity itself, according to which the civilizational heritage of a given country or macroregion has an impact on the type and outlook of the modernity to come. Yet even within this revisionist approach it is also admitted that modernity—as a global condition affecting cultural life and institutional forms as much as capitalist cycles and hegemonic contentions—equally impinges on a plurality of civilizational tracks differentiating the hegemonic West from the institutions and cultures developing in other macroregions like China, India, and the Islamic world. In spite of such significant theoretical revisions, the older patterns of Western appraisal of Islam vis-à-vis modernity that were cumulatively built over time have retained a considerable influence on a variety of levels, from scholarship to the media—not least, as mentioned earlier, due to the periodical reiteration of traumatic events.

The branches of scholarship that happened to deal with the issue of Islam's otherness from a Western viewpoint saw the light during the 19th century in coincidence with the European colonial encroachment upon the Muslim world. They underwent important changes during the 20th century, mainly as a consequence of the two world wars and of the ensuing processes of decolonization. Yet they were also influenced by earlier views of Islam

propagated by leading European thinkers who were not academic specialists within Islamic studies but who contributed to shaping the Enlightenment and post-Enlightenment self-understanding of the West—thinkers such as Hume, Voltaire, Hegel, and even Nietzsche. Both the discourse on Islam's insurmountable otherness on issues of modernity and the attempts to critique and revise it are therefore neither a merely scholarly enterprise nor the inexorable reflex of malign media campaigns. The debate has profound philosophical roots and widespread intellectual implications. Any attempt to develop a critical viewpoint should be aware of such deep ramifications in order to avoid falling into a facile counterhegemonic posture.

A host of historians and social theorists—from Ernest Renan through Max Weber to Rémi Brague—have provided the key link between intellectual manifestations of a Western modern self-understanding and scholarly programs for investigating specific cultural factors that were held responsible for the blockage or delay of the political and economic development within Muslim-majority societies. Within such a body of Western scholarship, it was argued that the doctrine of divine command proclaimed by Islam led Muslims and particularly the 'ulama' to deny a full legitimacy to government and therefore hindered a full-fledged, modern state formation. In a similar vein, the presuppositions to capitalist growth that enlivened the early modern sociopolitical formations of Western Europe have been considered too frail within Muslim lands. The cause for this deficit was often identified in cultural mechanisms of self-limitation of the entrepreneurial and innovative spirit. This self-limitation was in turn explained with the deeply religious commitments of both cultural elites and popular classes.

Such views have been elaborated upon within the specialized scholarship of Islamic studies. An influential antecedent to the discourse propagated by Bernard Lewis in the academic world of the post–World War II era is the work of another leading Orientalist of the 20th century, Gustave E. von Grunebaum. His approach capitalized on selected Weberian insights revolving around a keen understanding of Western cultural uniqueness and its universal normativity. Even more than Weber himself, von Grunebaum engaged in the study of Islam as a representative of the Western cultural elite deeply imbued with its civilizational values. While he was convinced that the Weberian approach held the key to understanding the West's rationalist spirit, he considered Islam to be at the mercy of the Western-led process of modernization. Not least, von Grunebaum followed Weber closely in explaining Islam's purportedly unsuccessful encounter with modernity by seeing in it a dilution of the inner impetus of Christian faith.

This idea aggravated Weber's derogatory view of the Islamic orientation toward immediate rewards in contrast to Christianity's focus on the "inner" realm of pure values. According to this interpretation, the inherent deficit of Islamic faith was magnified in the modern era by the fact that Islam did not undergo the process of self-renewal that the West had been going through since after the Protestant Reformation. This stress on reformation often became an obsessive theme in Western approaches to the issue of Islam and modernity. The Protestant Reformation was seen as anchored in a reform of the self that was facilitated by an increasing reflexivity and rationality. Von Grunebaum denied to Muslim cultural elites and political leaders such a capacity for intellectual renewal, which could enable them to successfully cope with the challenges and requirements of modernity.

Modernization theorists introduced some important distinctions into the picture. According to Manfred Halpern, the Muslim as a social actor is not completely paralyzed by the legacy represented by Islamic traditions. It was evident to him that many Muslim actors were not idle but on the move in postcolonial society. While the process and its predictable outcome amounted for him to a gradual collapse of Muslim culture, some key Islamic ideals may not only survive modernization but can even feed into it, if separated from the traditional system to which they originally belonged. Within this more dynamic picture, Islam appears ambivalently positioned toward modernity: while modernization theorists (wrongly) predicted the demise of Islamist forces, they did allow that selected elements of Islamic traditions could enliven the forces of change.

For all these Western scholars the ambivalence toward the West and Western modernity manifested by subsequent generations of Muslim leaders and thinkers, including the so-called modernists or reformists, was deeply problematic. What most Western observers neglected to see was a cumulative trend among Muslim reformers consisting in rejecting the view of either "Islam" or "modernity" conceived as comprehensive entities, as Western scholars were used to seeing them. The idea that Islam is internally plural and that modernity is a process not entrenched in a singular culture seemed alien to most Western observers, while it gradually became a main avenue of reasoning for key Muslim thinkers. A rare and early recognition of this insight came with the observation of Lothrop Stoddard (1883–1950), a non-Orientalist, who in spite of being a WASP supremacist wrote in the early 1920s that Muslim thinkers were not simply obsessed with the West but rather intent on developing "a new synthesis."

A more comprehensive appreciation of original Islamic approaches to modern thought as well as to modernity as a social process could only take form after the slow agony of modernization theory. A major change was prompted by the innovative work of younger Islamologists and historians. They saw that patterns of intellectual modernity, in their multiple ties to specific developments within capitalist production and markets, were seeing the light within the Muslim world prior to any overt confrontation with the encroaching Western modernity. They placed such developments in the context of comprehensive social processes and intellectual trends that linked Western Europe with the Muslim and in particular with the Ottoman world.

The two scholars who most coherently worked on the idea of largely endogenous seeds of an Islamic modernity were Peter Gran and Reinhard Schulze. In order to tackle the weakest point of the Orientalist argument about the decline of the Muslim world in the

modern era prior to the advance of the West on Muslim lands, they challenged head-on the "Napoleon's theorem"—namely, the assertion that the issue of modernity, with its spirit of enterprise and innovation, was first brought to the core of the Muslim world by Napoleon's occupation of Egypt and other parts of the Near East at the end of the 18th century. The main point of convergence between the work of Gran and Schulze is the intent to show the existence in 18th-century Ottoman society, including Egypt, of thriving bourgeois-like intellectual cultures, many of them significantly connected to some Sufi brotherhoods. According to the two scholars, such cultures reflected commercial and capitalist interests and revealed a new, genuinely modern emphasis on social autonomy and individual responsibility. Accordingly, the Islamic 18th century, far from being the stagnant counterpart to a flourishing European Enlightenment, might have manifested innovative dynamics both at the level of culture and politics.

In the debates that followed their scholarly challenge, Gran and Schulze also stressed that the analysis of texts is meaningful only if situated in the context of wider sociopolitical processes of transformation. Therefore, neglecting the sociopolitical context might lead students of Islamic civilization to lose touch with more general academic debates about the internal reform of tradition and the singularity versus the plurality of modernity. In other words, belittling the diversity of sociopolitical context encourages essentializing both Islamic traditions and Western modernity. The emergence of this new type of scholarship prefigured the possibility of interpreting the relation of Islam and modernity no longer as an oxymoron but as a theme in its own right, opening the way to thinking about the capacity of actors to creatively recombine endogenous resources with exogenous stimuli and challenges.

Secular Subjectivity and Social Solidarity

Against the deeper background of Western theorizing about the allegedly deficient capacity of Islamic civilization to fit into a modern world—not to mention its ability to initiate autonomous modern transformations—the new challenge strengthened the argument, supported by a general reflection on Islamic history (including a new attention to earlier works like *The Venture of Islam* of Marshall Hodgson), that a differentiation of state power and religious authority was integral to the development of Islamic civilization. Hodgson in particular anticipated interpretations that became familiar to a larger academic public only from the late 1970s onward, ranging from the critique of Orientalist worldviews to a plural and civilizational approach to modernity. Hodgson stated that at the dawn of the modern era, Islamic civilization reached the zenith not only of its political power but also of its cultural creativity. Key Muslim actors and institutions, he argued, worked to selectively blend the resources of power and culture that constitute a civilization within the three different but equally flourishing early modern Muslim empires: the Ottoman, the Safavid, and the Mughal or Timurid.

In the early 21st century, comparative civilizational analysts are revising the older bias of Western social theorists by valorizing selected Orientalist contributions like the work of Hodgson. As stated by Johann P. Arnason—a social theorist and leading practitioner of comparative civilizational analysis, who has thoroughly studied and commented on the work of Hodgson—the idea that any differentiation of religion and politics was alien to Islamic civilization has given way to the more nuanced view that this civilization displays specific trajectories of differentiation that cannot be measured on a homogeneous scale via a comparison with purported normal standards, usually taken from simplified Western models. Edward Said was right in suspecting that Orientalists were not alone with their essentialist bias concerning Islam. The mother of all essentialisms lies indeed in the way Western social scientists and social theorists have conceptualized religion and its role within modern societies. The work of revision within Western social theory concerning the issue of modernity is therefore no less crucial than the challenge launched by new historians and Islamologists.

In order to throw more light on the vexed question of the differentiation, or lack thereof, of religion and politics within Muslim societies, we need to extend our purview to the wider context that overloaded the study of religion in the West with heavy presuppositions closely tied to the Western self-understanding and its hegemonic discourse. In a variety of academic disciplines that attempted to locate the sources of human sociability, religion was identified as a key sphere of human endeavor, whose emergence basically coincided with the formation of organized community life. From comparative linguistics and comparative mythology through text criticism and history to anthropology and sociology, an army of Western scholars has worked since the 19th century to investigate the role of religion in the constitution of human society and the social bond. The issue of religion figured centrally in the genesis of sociology.

It was Karl Marx who defined religion as a crucial instrument of domination in human history and as a token of human alienation. Émile Durkheim and the school associated with his name reinterpreted religion as the pristine force of social cohesion through which the subject first alienates but then appropriates the power located in the collective world of social relations. According to this school, religion became the overarching category for investigating the nature of the collective forces providing cohesion to society via ever more abstract—and in this sense purportedly rational—models of solidarity. The idea itself of a modern society based on a rational division of labor became with Durkheim the key to postulate an evolutionist trajectory through which the integrative potential of traditional religion is transformed into a civic religion that is strictly functional to the maintenance of the social bond—a trajectory that sees its completion in Western, modern, and complex societies. In this perspective, secularization as a chief characteristic of modernization does not occur by suppressing religion but by transforming its cohesive potential in parallel with the deepening of the social division of labor. In the process, religion takes on increasingly abstract, and nonetheless civil, forms.

The purported role of a "civil religion" within modernity gained further prominence in the latter part of the 20th century, in

particular in the United States, where civil religion was interpreted as a cultural capital of society capable of reconciling tradition and modernity. This approach was also represented, though in original ways, in the work of the anthropologist Clifford Geertz, for whom the role of religion as a source of stability is found both in the most modern of Western societies—especially in those with a strong Protestant background, characterized by an increasing individualist ethos—and in the new postcolonial nations, including many Muslim-majority societies, where the cultural function of religion as a provider of collective identity comes to the fore. This interpretation overlapped with the idea, well represented within modernization theory, that elements of Islamic traditions were on their way to being reabsorbed as fragments of a new collective identity, in forms suitable to new development imperatives. Unlike the idea, dominant during the rise of European colonialism, that the Islamic doctrine of divine authority prevented a real legitimization of political power and justified the colonial supremacy of the West over Muslim lands, Geertz argued that in the postindependence polities of the Muslim world, cultural elites and political leaders might be able to culturally construct and politically legitimize new and sophisticated forms of social power and political organization—different from those of the West, but nonetheless modern or at least sufficiently compatible with the modern world.

The chief latent issue underlying the cohesion of modern, Muslim-majority societies, however, does not concern so much the role of "religion," on which Geertz focused his attention as the configuration of the domain of "politics." The specter of Western essentialism pushed out by the main door comes back through the window when it is assumed that a secular subjectivity aligned with the model nation-states of the modern West is surrogated within Muslim societies by hybrid formations favoring a basically authoritarian fabrication of a developmental ethos, whereby a conveniently reduced type of Islam remains a key component of collective identity. The relentless critique performed by Talal Asad, targeting a wide arch of Western scholarship stretching from Durkheim to Geertz, puts in evidence the vicious circle between the affirmation of secular subjectivity as the banner of Western culture and values and the reiteration of essentialist knowledge of the West's other, as incarnate in Islam. Western norms of modern governance remain both in the metropoles and in the former colonies connected to ideas of individual autonomy rooted in a secular subjectivity. Hereby the "secular" should not be equated with a rejection of "religion" but rather presupposes an essentialized, reformed religion as the necessary condition for the formation of self-governing agents.

Asad has stressed that practitioners of Islamic Studies often wrongly assumed that Islamic traditions had no notion of subjective inwardness, in spite of sufficient evidence of the importance of subjective intention and cultivation of the self, both in Islamic worship and in mysticism. Certainly, modern Western subjectivity is different in its emphasis on individual autonomy and dependence on state law, regulation, and administration, as well as on consumer choices mediated by the market. Asad warns, nonetheless, that based on a reiteration of such patterns across various stages of world politics (e.g., from the colonial to the postcolonial age), a full normalization of politics in Muslim-majority societies will always be deferred to some form of direct or indirect, benign or violent intervention by Western powers.

The historical reality is far more complex. Muslim intellectuals from the Maghrib to the Ottoman Empire viewed modern Europe not as culturally unique but as a frontier of new ideas and programs for the rational steering of society. The trauma of colonialism fractured this potentially positive perception of Europe, yet the continuous development of solidarity within modern European societies continued to impress subsequent generations of several Muslim reformers, for whom modern power could be attained within and through a variety of cultural settings. According to these Muslim reformers, there was nothing wrong with Islam per se, provided that its pristine forms of social cohesion and power were restored and reenergized. Yet most reformers remained caught in a polarizing dilemma, also evidenced by Asad's critique: Is the "organic solidarity" envisioned by Durkheim a legitimate goal for Muslim leaders intent on pushing for the reform of their societies? Does it necessarily require turning religion into mere civic morals? Or can it help instead retrieve the full power of Islamic normativity and even promote a transnational dimension of solidarity extended to the entire Islamic *umma* (community of believers)? Is the price to be paid the acceptance of the secular subjectivity of the citizen as reflected in the historic trajectory of Western nation-states: a type of subjectivity requiring a privatization of shari'a? While the latter option seems unattractive to the majority of Muslim intellectuals, all other responses risk becoming trapped in facile formulas of reconciliation of "tradition and modernity" that hide the node represented by the normative requirements of the secular subjectivity rooted in the Western historic models and experiences.

Premodern Forms of Collective Action and the Role of Sufism

Revising the postulates of the Western monopoly of modernity entails a questioning of its universally normative power. Western Europe accomplished a compromise between the state's control of the religious field and the sovereignty of the soul, between publicness and inwardness. This normative arrangement, however, does not match the historic dynamics through which the Islamic *dīn* (religion) was incorporated within sociopolitical structures. The *dīn* and the *dawla* (state) designated different, though at times overlapping, fields of social activity. Bernard Lewis's typical assertion that the state and the church are identical in Islam is fundamentally flawed, since neither "church" nor "state" are concepts that can be neatly translated into the institutional grammar of Islamic traditions. The conceptual pair *dīn* and *dawla* designates two poles of activity that permanently contribute to each other's definition while retaining their principled, though conditional, autonomy: they are not absolutely autonomous; rather, they are autonomous within the boundaries defined by Islam. Even at face value, the slogan *islām dīn*

wa-dawla (Islam is religion and state), which became particularly popular as a modern Islamic response to a state whose autonomy was compromised by colonial dependency, does not proclaim the identity of religion and state but the possibility of their concomitant and, optimally, mutual legitimation "in Islam." The problem in the formula is not an alleged identity of religion and state but rather a strong essentialization of Islam and of its univocal normative force—a presumption that was maintained with particular energy by Western Orientalists in the first place and by some Islamic actors concomitantly or subsequently.

Therefore, one cannot impute a deficit to Islamic civilization for having largely shunned the fully autonomous powers of Western models. Yet in the reiteration of historical processes under Western norms of autonomous agency—inscribed in constitutional formulas, sanctioned by human rights provisions, and prescribed in the form of good governance—this specific type of autonomy becomes an absolute value, in proximity of which any other tradition of self-governance is rarely recognized as fully legitimate from a Western viewpoint (be it "absolutist" or "relativist"). Modern associations invoking a specifically Islamic ethos and adopting organizational forms and funding patterns that refer directly or indirectly to Islamic tenets have had to prove their loyalty to the state in Egypt, while in France they have sometimes claimed a secular identity in order not to incur the suspicion of the authorities and of the public alike.

Invocations of an Islamic legitimacy of forms of organization cannot be reduced to a mere counteressentialist reflex prompted by the need to respond to the affirmation of the universality of Western standards. Once more we need the help of unbiased Orientalist scholarship to understand the relation of tradition and modernity in Islamic history. Hodgson stressed in particular the seminal role of Sufi movements, especially in the later phase of the Middle Periods, during the three centuries that preceded the modern era and the nearly simultaneous rise of what he termed the three dynamic and powerful "gunpowder empires" of the Muslim world: the Ottoman, the Safavid, and the Mughal or Timurid. According to Hodgson, Islamic civilization gained from the 13th to the 15th century the profile of a transstate ecumene, thanks to a steady expansion across the Afro-Eurasian landmass.

Orientalists before (but also after) Hodgson have mainly characterized this "medieval" period as an epoch of decadence and lack of creativity. It cannot be denied that in this phase, which followed the Mongol invasion of the mid-13th century, political domination was weak and fragmented. Yet at the same time, the cultural elaboration on the relationship between *siyāsa* (a term of Mongol origin that means sheer government) and shari'a (designating the comprehensive idea of Islamic normativity more than simply "law") reached a high point. During this period, Muslim society was a society of networks more than states, so that social governance and its legitimacy were effectively divorced from state power. In the Middle Periods, and especially in its latest phase, Sufi *ṭuruq* (brotherhoods) played a key role in Islam's expansion into the Eurasian depths—particularly into the Indian subcontinent and Southeast Asia—and across sub-Saharan Africa. Their flexible and semiformal model of organization and connectedness, of balancing competition, cooperation, and hierarchy, was well suited to the political characteristics of the epoch. As synthetically put by Hodgson at the end of this period, at the threshold of the modern era, thanks to the expansive capacity of this crystallizing model of soft governance, the dynamics of Islamic civilization exhibited a markedly hegemonic potential.

The most interesting question to ask from a contemporary perspective, which witnesses the erosion of the West-centered state system and the advent, in the wake of globalization, of new forms of governance and solidarity, concerns the aborted yet still latent potential of religious cosmopolitanism that Islamic civilization inherited from the Middle Periods and ambivalently invested into the structures of power of the modern Muslim empires. Viewed from the perspective of the seminal developments of the Middle Periods, these empires, in spite of displaying impressive political power, military organization, and promotion of high culture, and basing their power on specific patterns of differentiation of state and religion, could only partially inherit the creative impetus of the Middle Periods, when a cosmopolitan high culture thrived alongside a dense social autonomy balancing horizontal cooperation and solidarity with hierarchy and command—a pattern that facilitated the penetration of the Islamic message into the lifeworld of lower population strata across new territories.

Western scholars and Muslim reformers alike predicted that the Sufi networks would vanish as several colonial and postcolonial societies of the Muslim world adopted a greater separation between the religious sphere and a civic domain or "civil society." Yet in the colonial era some Sufi orders expanded their constituencies, and some actually participated in or even led movements of resistance against colonial occupation, most notably in North and West Africa and in Southeast Asia. Several scholars have noticed major shifts in some Sufi orders toward more formal and hierarchical modes of organization since the 18th century—a development that demonstrated their ability to push for social and even political change. While this thesis is well reflected in the previously examined work by Gran and Schulze, earlier scholars like Fazlur Rahman and John O. Voll already spoke of a distinctive "neo-Sufi" associational form characterized by a sociopolitical activism nurtured by a commitment to Islam's potential for mobilizing various social groups in order to implement Islamic ideals of justice. Some such Sufi groups cultivated the study of hadith in ways that are comparable to some puritan movements—like the Wahhabis—of a decidedly anti-Sufi inclination. The decentralized nature of studies of hadith and the latitude allowed within this branch of study to reinterpret norms of social interaction, including those affecting trade and business, appeared in some cases to further the interests of a rising commercial class. Some urban reformers of the 19th century seemed to be influenced by selective Sufi ideas even in the absence of solid organizational ties to any *ṭarīqa* or Sufi master. Those reformers who attacked Sufism stigmatized types of practices (like saint worshipping, shrine and grave visits, and above all the "abominable"

display of superstition and promiscuity at Sufi saints festivals) that most "neo-Sufi" leaders also shunned.

Sufi orders were overall in good health during the 19th and early 20th century and able to absorb the challenge of colonialism in order to partially renew their social goals and organizational forms; yet by the middle of the 20th century, during the formation of postindependence states, observers registered a state of stagnation if not an outward crisis of Sufism. Nonetheless, this moment of difficulty was overcome in the 1970s via the larger phenomenon commonly dubbed Islamic resurgence, which took a firmer root in a nonovertly political, "civic" field and therefore also favored a revival of Sufi types of affiliation. Nonetheless, especially in late-colonial and postindependence settings, Sufi orders in many countries underwent a process of bureaucratization through their subjection to a more centralized control under ultimate state supervision and patronage. In the new context, however, Sufi leaders often sought connection and influence with various, sometimes high echelons of the state bureaucracy. In this sense, while the formula of incorporation of *awqāf* (plural of waqf: "pious foundation") into the state administration was streamlined and could be roughly compared to secularization processes in European settings (whereby the first meaning of secularization was the confiscation of church properties by the state), the way Sufi orders renegotiated their space and autonomy in a postcolonial, nation-state setting was open to arrangements that did not necessarily erase the earlier autonomous dynamism of Sufism and in some cases even reinvigorated it. In republican Turkey, the Naqshbandis (almost reflecting a prototype of neo-Sufi ethos) reenergized themselves in the second half on the 20th century in spite of the thorough secularization measures of earlier republican governments. Most notable in Turkey is the capacity of Sufism to mutate into a new type of movement that is no longer formally a Sufi order but incorporates a rationalization of the Sufi ethos and its flexible organizational and disciplinary forms. This is the case of the Nur movement founded by Sa'id Nursi and its presently most successful spin-off initiated by Fethullah Gülen: increasingly pervasive in the media world and in the educational sector, aiming at the formation of new elites and audiences alike, imbued of a modern Islamic ethos, and active transnationally, not only in Turkey but also in several other countries of West and East.

Modern Politics and the Reform Program

In contrast to the pursuit of the social idea of human connectedness inspired to the "common good"—an idea that cuts across the divide between tradition and modernity—the prime theme of modernity lies in the issue of differentiation between societal spheres, a process governed by the new forms of power and regulation deployed by modern states. This process affected the original forms of organization and collective action historically promoted by Sufi orders in their pursuit of interconnectedness over distant spaces. The process of differentiation did not destroy or absorb the patterns of connectedness promoted by Sufism—but by affirming the centralization and monopolization of the state's power on the territory on which it exercised sovereignty, it inculcated in the state subjects the disciplines of the rational agent, increasingly identified with the social agent acting on the basis of narrowly defined personal interests (*homo economicus*). As an unexpected consequence of the process, these subjects started to reclaim more control of governance and tried to compensate the emerging dominance of economic rationales within social relations by mobilizing the ties of affection and solidarity entailed by ideals of civility—intended as a form of social intercourse, politeness, and interconnectedness that cuts across closed communities and confessional divides. The observation of the unfolding of such highly ambivalent processes in Muslim-majority societies first in the colonial era and then in the postindependence settings also drew the attention of observers to the programs of a host of self-proclaimed Muslim reformers. Many of them still saw in the Sufi ethic a resource, and not a hindrance, for encouraging a new ethos of participation.

Within Muslim societies, the path to modern transformations cannot be therefore reduced to an adaptationist twist of an older model of "Oriental despotism," which never existed except in the imagination of Western thinkers. Unless we want to identify the access to political modernity of Muslim-majority societies as a process entirely induced by colonial domination or indirect Western pressures (as in the case of the Ottoman Empire, whose kernel regions were never controlled by colonial powers), we should look at the transformations of the cohesive and mobilizing potential of discourses on the "common good" cutting across the conventional divide between traditional and modern social worlds. Islamic notions of the common good (*maṣlaḥa*) were appropriated by some early reformers in the 18th century (some of them linked to neo-Sufi groups) and were later reinvigorated both intellectually and politically by subsequent generations of thinkers and activists in the context of colonial and postcolonial politics, or, in the Ottoman Empire, in the framework of administrative reforms, known as Tanzimat, and which started in the 1830s.

It is noteworthy that the culture of those reformers who were also members of the high echelons of the state bureaucracy was particularly close to the *adab* tradition—distinct from the core Islamic traditions based on Qur'an and sunna—inherited from Persianate court culture. *Adab* denotes the catalogs of the ethical and practical norms of good life that were cultivated by a class of literati in the framework of life at court: a tradition that was central to Islamic civilization, even if detached from the core religious traditions. Far from being abandoned at the passage to the modern era, the cultivation of the *adab* tradition provided the background culture to the scribal class during the period, from the 18th century onward, when it increasingly acquired the ambitions of a modern bureaucracy. We might conceive of the transformations of *adab* as the cultural engine of a civilizing process in the sense highlighted by Norbert Elias: initiated in court milieus but with the potential to reach down the social ladder and encompass wider populations, and therefore as a substantial aid to "state-building." The upgrading of *adab* into the matrix for a self-sustaining civilizing process starting

in the era of the Tanzimat (during which printed administrative bulletins first saw the light) was followed by the rise of a full-fledged public sphere based on a largely free press and the emergence of new genres of public speech. This process suggests that conceptual syntheses of the essence of modernity in terms of either autonomy or self-mastery neglect the more complex social layering effected by a "civilizing process" also via the communicative sophistications allowed within a modern public sphere. Both phenomena are particularly well visible in a sociopolitical world, as in Ottoman and other Muslim, post-Ottoman and postcolonial societies, which are neither the modern incarnation of Oriental despotism nor the exact antithesis of liberal civil society.

By the time, in the late 19th century, when the reform discourse started to be formulated in the context of emerging public spheres by urban personalities who were in most cases both thinkers and activists and sometimes state servants, the Western diagnosis of the inherent deficits of Islamic cultural traditions was already gaining currency. Starting with Afghani (1838–97), reformers were faced with the task both to ground a shared cultural perspective and institute its communicative infrastructure in order to challenge their Western colonialist counterparts on their own terrain while relying on select elements of their own intellectual traditions and institutional legacies. With later reformers such as Muhammad ʿAbduh (1849–1905), the operational conditions were complicated by the fact that colonial (and later postcolonial) rule at the same time empowered the reform discourse and channeled it into a modern, positive view of the law as a key tool of reform controlled by the state.

The resulting visions could no longer be reconciled with the traditional approach to *maṣlaḥa*, in spite of the rising popularity of this concept among many Muslim reformers who were interested in its potential to provide the hub for a Muslim theory of social agency and autonomous judgment. The way the Islamic traditions ingrained into the newly emerging sphere that became the battleground of the civilizing process marks an interesting difference with regard to developments in northwestern Europe, where the moral subject was, initially, effectively integrated in the governance machine of the modern state before it claimed autonomy in the public sphere. In the Ottoman Empire and especially in Egypt, the public sphere, though still dependent from conditions dictated by the colonial regimes, developed from the beginning an autonomous potential distinct from the state by virtue of its reposing on a newly recombined discourse of shariʿa and *adab*—a discourse that, though focused on the building of a new moral subject, was not entirely functional to the sovereign domain of state law and was still to a large extent related to ideals of connectedness and self-governance. This is best illustrated by ʿAbdallah al-Nadim (1845–96), a committed Muslim reformer but also one major disseminator of *adab*, who defined virtue not just in terms of the canonical injunction *al-amr bi-l-maʿruf wa-l-nahī ʿan al-munkar* (commanding right and forbidding wrong) that is at the heart of the normative system of shariʿa, but as tied to economic development and "industriousness." *Adab* thus acquired a meaning close to "civility," understood as an ensemble of moral dispositions entailing good manners and mastery of the self as well as a sense of social circumstances. While initially reflecting a classic notion envisioning models of cultivation of the self, in the course of the reform process the concept of *adab* evolved into defining a quite homogeneous field of public morality that the state could not fully control by legislating measures.

Global Civil Society and Transnational Islam

The reform project has left a strong imprint on popular movements inspired by Islamic tenets until our era. Yet the rise of such movements since after the late 1920s can also be considered the symptom of a backlash in the attempt to autonomously articulate an Islamic modernity in the context of an ongoing colonial dependence and postcolonial weakness. Instead of increasing the power of the Islamic sphere through inculcating cultured behavior in the masses, as earlier reformers had tried to do, with the formation of Islamist sociopolitical movements like the Muslim Brothers, the reform program ended up justifying a more one-sided focus on the power of engineering a morality-based public culture. One major test of the development of the branch of Muslim reform that has morphed into modern Islamism has been whether it can renounce a prioritization of power as an instrument to enforce public morals and thus fit into modern visions of "civil society." Civil society is in the first instance the outcome of specific developments within northwestern Europe. The long erosion of ideological unity since medieval Christianity and the social fragmentation that resulted from the commercial and industrial revolutions led several modern authors, in particular those from the 18th-century Scottish Enlightenment, to view the social bond as resting on a combination of interest and affection and ultimately on mutual trust among individuals. This formulation replaced a more traditional notion of community as a partnership of faith in God among individuals. The emerging vision stressed new factors of cohesion in society, made "civil" by the simultaneously spontaneous and necessary bond of trust that linked individuals without any divine mediation. The "moral sense" theorized by the Scottish moralists was a form of pristine trust facilitating contractual exchange among private individuals and providing the necessary stability to social relationships spurned by the commercial and industrial revolutions.

Trust among individuals within civil society became the key tool to redefine a social bond increasingly exposed to the impersonality of factory work and of contract-based labor relationships within capitalist economies, as well as to the faceless bureaucracies that were replacing the arbitrary rule of absolutist autocrats. Civil society was considered distinct from the modern state, while it entered a rather symbiotic relationship with it. Optimally, civil society expresses legitimate interests and produces ties of solidarity, while the state guarantees the rules that protect those interests and provides a legal framework for warranting social order. Far from being an antistate, civil society contributes to both solidarity and governance from the bottom up. With the present processes of globalization, however, solidarity at the national level has been eroded, while governance gains ever more transnational contours.

In this sense, globalization as a whole denotes the long-term process of adaptation of practices, discourses, and institutions of a given society or civilization to standards dictated by the rationality of world capitalism and of the international political system of nation-states. The latter increasingly includes—especially since the 1990s—narrowly defined liberal norms, aligned with the governance standards of international organizations like the International Monetary Fund (IMF) and the World Bank. A response to the combined economic and political dynamics of globalization can be found at the level of sociopolitical movements that act on a global scale to challenge the hegemonic paradigms of globalization and propagate alternative global visions, typically subsumed under the slogan "Another world is possible" of the World Social Forum. To describe these developments, the term "global civil society" has been coined—an idea that happens to stress solidarity much more than ties of interest.

As a result, globalization does not weaken either solidarity or governance per se but deterritorializes and redeploys them across conventional borders. Solidarity in particular becomes less tied to locales and potentially more expansive, while governance can be either concentrated in transnational centers or delegated to local power centers less bound by conventional notions of citizenship. The obverse of this process is a looming sense of rootlessness that is caused by the weakening of the incorporation of individuals and groups into nation-state jurisdictions. Sociopolitical integration comes to increasingly depend on market rules and consumption preferences.

The contemporary unfolding of a globally Islamic, post-Westphalian sphere of connectedness, solidarity, and communication builds on the earlier illustrated historical experiences of global interconnectedness within Islamic civilization, while it also responds to Western norms raising the banner of civil society and global governance and to the deep ambivalence of the current processes of globalization, which create new dependences and constraints but also new occasions and spaces for collective action. Although the eyes of Western observers are mainly focused on so-called global jihadism and transnational networks of migration, Islamic globalism includes far more components and facets, which should be carefully taken into consideration. Underlying all forms of Islamic globalism is an abstract notion of a global *umma*, which superimposes social relations and political contests that are still mainly framed within nation-state frameworks and their narrow patterns of governance and solidarity.

In the extensive literature on Islam in Europe and in the West, several Muslim spokespersons and public intellectuals report a rising feeling of participation in a universal *umma*—a perception that is sharpened by critical events, from the Rushdie affair of 1989 to 9/11 and the ensuing "war on terror," which have nourished renewed patterns of Muslim global solidarity in the face of a threatening Western posture. This phenomenon is particularly intense in the Muslim diasporas of the West, and an increasing number of Muslim intellectuals who were born or reared in the West have led struggles for Muslim participation within global networks of solidarity. Such battles are often intended to transcend narrowly defined Muslim interests and to join broader efforts for global justice. While increasing attention has been paid to radical groups, particularly remarkable in this context is the flourishing of Sufism. Throughout Islamic history, one strength of Sufi networks was their capacity to support travelers across wide distances. Postcolonial labor migration has been, since the second half of the 20th century, similarly intertwined with the thriving of Sufi *ṭuruq* in the West. These orders are often linked with the regions of origins of the migrants, such as South Asia and West Africa, but sometimes initiate new networks that cut across traditional regional localizations and attract Western members, including practitioners and sympathizers who are not Muslims in the conventional sense.

To conclude, the significance of Islamic globalism at the present stage of entanglement of multiple modernities might support the decoupling of modernization from Westernization and a reconstruction of modernity along specific civilizational paths conforming to their foundational images, symbols, and discursive patterns. Mass cultural production can further this process but can also increase the chances of building new ties and coalitions across communal or national domains. The growing Islamic focus on transnational interconnectedness transcends a Eurocentric modernist approach to modernity confined within the rationales of nation-states or of new aggregations thereof, like the European Union.

See also civil society; globalizaton; international Islamic organizations; West, the

Further Reading

Said A. Arjomand, "Coffeehouses, Guilds and Oriental Despotism: Government and Civil Society in Late 17th to Early 18th Century Istanbul and Isfahan, and as seen from Paris and London," *European Journal of Sociology* 45, no. 1 (2004); Johann P. Arnason, "Marshall Hodgson's Civilizational Analysis of Islam: Theoretical and Comparative Perspectives," in *Islam in Process: Historical and Civilizational Perspectives*, vol. 7, *Yearbook of the Sociology of Islam*, edited by Johann P. Arnason, Armando Salvatore, and Georg Stauth, 2006; Talal Asad, *Formations of the Secular: Christianity, Islam, Modernity*, 2003; Karen Barkey, *Empire of Difference: The Ottomans in Comparative Perspective*, 2008; Dale F. Eickelman and James Piscatori, *Muslim Politics*, 1996; Shmuel N. Eisenstadt, "Fundamentalist Movements in the Framework of Multiple Modernities," in *Between Europe and Islam: Shaping Modernity in a Transcultural Space*, edited by Almut Höfert and Armando Salvatore, 2000; Clifford Geertz, *Islam Observed: Religious Development in Morocco and Indonesia*, 1971; Haim Gerber, "The Public Sphere and Civil Society in the Ottoman Empire," in *The Public Sphere in Muslim Societies*, edited by Miriam Hoexter, Shmuel N. Eisenstadt, and Nehemia Levtzion, 2002; Ralph D. Grillo, "Islam and Transnationalism," *Journal of Ethnic and Migration Studies* 30, no. 5 (2004); Robert W. Hefner, ed., *Remaking Muslim Politics: Pluralism, Contestation, Democratization*, 2005; Marshall G. S. Hodgson, *Rethinking World History: Essays on Europe, Islam and World History*, 1993; Bernard Lewis, *What Went Wrong? Western*

Impact and Middle Eastern Response, 2002; Saba Mahmood, "Secularism, Hermeneutics, and Empire: The Politics of Islamic Reformation," *Public Culture* 18 (2006); Şerif Mardin, *Religion, Society and Modernity in Turkey*, 2006; Muhammad Khalid Masud, Armando Salvatore, and Martin van Bruinessen, eds., *Islam and Modernity: Key Issues and Debates*, 2009; Brinkley Messick, *The Calligraphic State: Textual Domination and History in a Muslim Society*, 1993; Timothy Mitchell, *Colonizing Egypt*, 1988; Armando Salvatore, *Islam and the Political Discourse of Modernity*, 1997; Adam B. Seligman, *The Idea of Civil Society*, 1992; Georg Stauth, ed., *Islam, a Motor or Challenge of Modernity*, vol. 1, *Yearbook of the Sociology of Islam*, 1998; Martin van Bruinessen and Julia D. Howell, eds., *Sufism and the "Modern" in Islam*, 2007; John O. Voll, *Islam: Continuity and Change in the Modern World*, 1994; Björn Wittrock, "Social Theory and Global History: The Periods of Cultural Crystallization," *Thesis Eleven* 65 (2001); Muhammad Qasim Zaman, "The Scope and Limits of Islamic Cosmopolitanism and the Discursive Language of the 'Ulama'," in *Muslim Networks from Hajj to Hip Hop*, edited by Miriam Cooke and Bruce B. Lawrence, 2005; Sami Zubaida, *Law and Power in the Islamic World*, 2003.

ARMANDO SALVATORE

Mohammed, W. D. (1933–2008)

Wallace Delaney Mohammed, who later changed his name to Warith Deen (or W. D.), was the leader of the Nation of Islam, an American organization advocating black pride and independence. W. D. brought the Nation of Islam more in line with the mainstream of Sunni Islam, reversing or altering many of the more radical teachings of his father, Elijah Muhammad (1897–1975). Elijah, who took over leadership of the Nation of Islam when its founder, Muhammad Fard, mysteriously disappeared in 1934, introduced many unusual teachings. He taught, for example, that all white people are ruled by Satan but that Allah, who is black, permitted them dominion over Allah's people until the imminent apocalypse, in which all the "white devils" would be destroyed. He also taught that Fard was not a mere prophet but rather Allah embodied in human flesh.

Raised in the shadow of his father, W. D. quickly rose within the Nation of Islam's ranks, becoming the leader of its Philadelphia temple. In 1961, however, he received a three-year prison sentence for refusing the military draft. While in prison, W. D. assiduously studied the Qur'an and the sunna, which caused him to see glaring differences between his father's teachings and those of the rest of the Islamic world. Consequently, W. D. defected from the Nation of Islam upon his release from prison and formed a splinter group called the Afro-Descendant Upliftment Society. He rejoined the Nation of Islam after the assassination of Malcolm X in February 1963. Over the following years, W. D. was repeatedly expelled from the organization because of his dissenting teachings, but he succeeded his father as leader of the Nation of Islam after Elijah's death in 1975.

Upon taking control of the Nation of Islam, W. D. enacted several sweeping reforms. Rather than directly attacking his father's teachings, he altered them to fit mainstream Islamic belief. He claimed that Elijah's teachings were intended to bolster and elevate black Americans but that the teachings were purposefully rendered absurd so that followers would naturally seek a more enlightened path once they overcame their mental and physical oppression. He then opened up the Nation of Islam to all nonblack people, disbanded the militant wing of the Nation of Islam (the Fruit of Islam), and enacted educational reforms, including the study of the Qur'an and the five pillars of Islam. The Nation of Islam also went through several name changes, finally calling itself the American Society of Muslims. W. D.'s changes upset several of Elijah's closer followers, most notably Louis Farrakhan, who broke from W. D.'s organization in 1978 and later formed the "restored" Nation of Islam.

W. D. spent the later years of his life advocating a unified American Islamic community and interfaith efforts against poverty and injustice. He was honored with numerous awards and chairmanships from such notable leaders as U.S. president Bill Clinton, Egyptian president Anwar Sadat, and Pope John Paul II. He was also the first Muslim to offer morning prayers on the floor of the U.S. Senate.

See also Muhammad, Elijah (1897–1975); Nation of Islam

Further Reading

Herbert Berg, "Mythmaking in the African American Muslim Context: The Moorish Science Temple, the Nation of Islam, and the American Society of Muslims," *Journal of the American Academy of Religion* 73, no. 3 (2005); Zahid H. Bukhari, Sulayman S. Nyang, Mumtaz Ahmad, and John L. Esposito, eds., *Muslims' Place in the American Public Square: Hope, Fears, and Aspirations*, 2004; Edward E. Curtis IV, *Muslims in America: A Short History*, 2009; Richard Brent Turner, *Islam in the African-American Experience*, 1997.

ANDREW POLK

monarchy

Although independent local dynasties appeared on the periphery of the Abbasid caliphal body politic in Iran and Egypt in the latter part of the ninth century, the critical period for the recovery of the Persian idea of kingship and its development was the early tenth century, with the consolidation of a Persianate polity in Khurasan and Transoxiana (*mā warā'a l-nahr*) under the Samanids (819–1005). The Buyids (945–1062), who ruled independently in Iran later in that century, assumed the pre-Islamic Persian title of shah (king) and even the imperial *shāhānshāh* (king of kings).

The development of the Persianate concept of monarchy continued under the Ghaznavids (977–1086) in the 11th century. The father of Persian epic, Abu al-Qasim Firdawsi (d. 1020), summed up the emerging idea of monarchy in a famous verse, "Kingship and prophecy are two jewels on the same ring," alongside many other statecraft maxims such as "The king is the shadow of God on Earth." His *Shahnama* (*Epic of Kings*) made royal charisma (*farr-i izādī*), confirmed by the justice of the ruler, the basis of monarchy.

Meanwhile, Greek political science had been introduced to the Muslim world with the translations of works of Greek science and philosophy and was made central to the philosophical movement by one of its founding fathers, Abu Nasr al-Farabi (d. 950). Among the Iranian philosophers who sought to synthesize Greek political science and Persian statecraft in this period, Abu al-Hasan al-ʿAmiri (d. 991) is of particular interest. He modified Farabi's teachings to allow for a more harmonious reconciliation of Islam and philosophy by considering prophecy and kingship the two institutions vital for the preservation of the world. The Ghaznavid secretary and historian, Abu al-Fadl al-Bayhaqi (d. 1077), offers a concise statement on what he calls the two powers: "Know that God Most High has given one power to the prophets and another power to the kings; and He has made it incumbent on the people of the Earth to follow these two powers and thus to know God's straight path."

The Turkish Seljuqs, who replaced the Buyids in Baghdad in 1055 and defeated the Byzantine emperor, creating a vast empire from the Oxus to the Mediterranean, assumed the titles both of *shāhānshāh* and sultan, an abstract term meaning authority in the Qur'an, which was now assumed by the person of the ruler. Local rulers in Iran used the title shah, and those in the Arab countries used the equivalent title *malik* (king). The theory of prophecy and kingship as the two divinely ordained powers was reaffirmed in an important statement erroneously attributed to the great Sunni thinker Muhammad al-Ghazali in the 12th century: "Know and understand that God Most High chose two categories of mankind, placing them above others: the prophets and the kings. He sent the prophets to His creatures to lead them to Him. As for the kings, He chose them to protect men from one another and made the prosperity of human life dependent on them." The Turkic conception of kingship as a divine gift to the founder of the state also linked it to the establishment of the law (*törü*), but as the Seljuqs adopted the Persian conception of kingship and championed the Sunni restoration under the caliphate, the impact of the Turkic conception of the law had to wait for the Mongol invasion two centuries later. Meanwhile, a new idea emerged in the Seljuq period and subsequently gained greater currency: that of the "king of Islam," in such allocutions as *pādshāh-i islām*, *malik-i islām*, and *sulṭān-i islām*. This term was significant in dispensing altogether with the idea of the caliphate as the representative of Islam.

Monarchy thus developed under the Abbasid dynasty, but the relation between the two institutions was never free from tension. When the caliphate and the sultanate coexisted in Baghdad under the Buyids and the Seljuqs in the 11th and early 12th centuries, the Islamic jurists such as Mawardi and Ghazali developed a mode of subordination of monarchy to the caliphate as successor of prophecy and protector of the Islamic ethico-legal order anchored in the shariʿia. The juristic theory of the caliphate, however, did not find expression in the books of ethics and thus had limited currency, being confined to the circles of religious learning.

During the medieval and early modern period, Turkish slave generals established a Muslim monarchy in northern India early in the 13th century, with Delhi as its capital. The Delhi Sultanate lasted for some three centuries, until the conquest of India by the Timurid prince Zahir al-Din Babur (d. 1530) and the establishment of the Mughal Empire in 1526. After the overthrow of the Abbasids by the Mongols in 1258, the rulers of Muslim lands typically called themselves sultan and caliph, except in Mamluk Egypt (1250–1517), where a shadow Abbasid caliph was maintained until the Ottomans conquered Egypt. In addition to *shāhānshāh*, the Ottomans, the Safavids, and the Mughal rulers of India used *pādshāh* as an imperial title.

Monarchy (*salṭana*, *pādshāh*, *mulk*) was legitimated independently of the caliphate and its juristic theory and primarily on the basis of justice. The function of monarchy was to maintain order and rule with justice. As such, monarchy was compared to prophecy, the function of which was the salvation of humankind. Kings were thus necessary for cosmic order, just as were the prophets. A distinct literary genre on political ethic and statecraft grew and absorbed the philosophical strand, grounding the legitimacy of monarchy in its justice. A major synthesis of these ideas, *Akhlaq-i Nasiri* (The Nasirian ethics), was written in the 13th century by the Shiʿi philosopher and statesman Nasir al-Din al-Tusi. It had many imitators and became the standard work on political ethics and statecraft in the three early modern Muslim empires: the Ottoman, the Safavid, and the Mughal.

The idea of monarchy as sultanate spread eastward in the 15th century and survives in the 21st century in the federal states of Malaysia and in Brunei. With the spread of Islam into sub-Saharan Africa, some of the Muslim rulers assumed the title of sultan, and in 1841, the sultan of Oman transferred his court to Zanzibar across the Indian Ocean. The idea of constitutional monarchy was introduced into the Islamic world in the process of political modernization, with the Ottoman Constitution of 1876 and the Iranian constitution of 1906. The Ottoman sultanate was abolished in 1922 and the Iranian monarchy overthrown with the Islamic Revolution of 1979. A number of Muslim constitutional monarchies survive, however, notably in Morocco and Jordan.

See also caliph, caliphate; constitutionalism; patrimonial state; sultan

Further Reading

Saïd Amir Arjomand, "Evolution of the Persianate Monrachy and Its Transmission to India," *Journal of Persianate Studies* 2, no. 2 (2009): 115–36; Idem, "Legitimacy and Political Organization: Caliphs, Kings and Regimes," in *The New Cambridge History of Islam*, vol. 4, edited by R. Irwin and M. Cook, 2010; Linda T. Darling, "Islamic

Empires, the Ottoman Empire and the Circle of Justice," in *Constitutional Politics in the Middle East*, edited by S. A. Arjomand, 2008.

SAÏD AMIR ARJOMAND

Mongols

The Mongol conquests led by Chingiz Khan (ca. 1167–1227) produced the most extensive land empire in history, stretching from China in the east to Anatolia and Syria in the west. This vast but attenuated empire soon crystallized into two smaller states that adopted the cultures of the conquered populations, the Perso-Islamic Ilkhanid dynasty in Iran and the Sinicized Yüan dynasty in China, with the Golden Horde, a third offshoot, occupying southern Russia. By the time the Mongols, originally a forest people from Siberia, appeared on the world stage, they had become steppe nomads and intermarried with Turkic tribes; the Mongol conquests should thus properly be called the Turco-Mongol conquests and represent a second, far more devastating wave of westward expansion after the Turkic Seljuq invasion of Iran, Iraq, and Anatolia just over a century before. The conquerors' approach to administration was initially rudimentary and wholly centered on the distribution of booty; though they adopted existing bureaucracies wholesale for efficiency, their primary concern was to exploit the sedentary populations materially and financially, leading to the neglect of agriculture even as a source of revenue.

The driving force of these conquests was Temüjin, the son of a minor clan chieftain, who after a meteoric rise to power assumed the title Chingiz Khan, meaning oceanic or universal ruler, and was acclaimed as such at the tribal assembly (*quriltay*) of 1206. At this assembly he declared his mandate from Tengri (heaven) and his commitment to the sacred Yasa, or army and civilian code of law. By 1215 Chingiz had conquered northern China, and by 1223 Central Asia and Khurasan. The provocation of the Khwarazmshahid governor in Transoxiana, who rashly executed several Mongol ambassadors in 1218, had provided the excuse for a westward push in which most of the great cities of Transoxiana and Khurasan were razed and whole populations exterminated. Before his death in 1227, Chingiz divided his empire between his four sons according to the custom of Mongol chiefs, with the eldest receiving the territories farthest from the Mongolian heartlands and the youngest, designated as "guardian of the hearth," receiving the heartlands themselves. Thus Batu, the son of his eldest, Jochi, who had predeceased him, received western Siberia and the Qipchaq steppe, and from this base he founded the Blue Horde in southern Russia, while Batu's brother Orda founded the White Horde in western Siberia; the two would later unite to become the Golden Horde. The second eldest, Chaghatay, received Mogholistan and Transoxiana; in the 15th century, the Chaghatayids would come under Timurid sway. The third, Ögedey, became Chingiz's successor as Great Khan or emperor, though this office soon fell to the descendents of Toluy, the youngest son, whose own sons Möngke and Qubilay consolidated China under their rule first from Qara Qorum in Mongolia and then in Beijing.

Qubilay's brother Hulagu (r. 1256–65) meanwhile had been dispatched to assert Mongol control over the Islamic realms of western Asia. In Iran he broke the power of the Isma'ili Assassins at Alamut in 1256 and in 1258 sacked Baghdad and executed the last Abbasid caliph, Musta'sim (r. 1242–58), effectively putting an end to both the Abbasid line and the Sunni caliphate, largely symbolic by this time, as an exclusive institution. In the post-Mongol period, any upstanding ruler could lay claim to caliphal status. The Mongol advance was only halted by the Mamluks in Palestine in 1260 at the Battle of 'Ayn Jalut. Hulagu was appointed *īl khān*, or territorial or subordinate khan, over Iran, Iraq, Transcaucasia, and Anatolia by the Great Khan Möngke.

Despite an initial dilettantish interest in tantric Buddhism and Nestorian Christianity—indeed, at one point it was hoped in Europe that Persia would become part of a pan-Christian empire—the Ilkhanid line became both Islamicized and Persianized over the course of the next two generations and soon shed any practical connection to the Great Khans in the east. Their underlying shamanistic orientation persisted, however, and was frequently expressed in the form of devotion to charismatic Sufi shaykhs as authorities in matters of spirit and state. The high point of Mongol conversion to Islam is often associated with that of Ghazan Khan (r. 1295–1304), though his Islam, like that of the later Turco-Mongol elite, was a syncretist blend with Mongol custom and tradition.

Despite warfare and economic disturbance, the Ilkhanid period was materially prosperous and culturally and intellectually productive and saw the rise of Tabriz, Maragha, and Sultaniyya as centers of learning and science; vigorous trade led to a fresh influx of international influences, especially from China and Italy. Common hostility toward the Ilkhanids, however, led to an alliance between the Mamluks and the Golden Horde, which the Ilkhanids countered by attempting to create a coalition with European Christian powers, including the Crusaders in the Levantine littoral. The last great Ilkhanid ruler was Abu Sa'id (r. 1316–35), who made peace with the Mamluks, after which the dynasty devolved into a rivalry between petty khans; Iran and Iraq were soon divided among local dynasties such as the Jalayirids, Muzaffarids, Sarbidarids, and Karts. A generation later, Tamerlane (r. 1370–1405) reconquered these territories in his partially successful quest to reconstitute the Mongol Empire.

See also Abbasids (750–1258); China; Isma'ilis; Mamluks (1250–1517); Seljuqs (1055–1194); Sufism; Tamerlane (1336–1405); Timurids (1370–1506); al-Tusi, Nasir al-Din (1201–74)

Further Reading

Thomas Allsen, *Culture and Conquest in Mongol Eurasia*, 2001; Michal Biran, *Chinngis Khan*, 2007; David Morgan, *The Mongols*, 2007.

MATTHEW MELVIN-KOUSHKI

Morocco

Unlike many parts of the Middle East and North Africa, Morocco entered the modern era with a well-established tradition of Islamic monarchy represented by the ‘Alawi dynasty, which came to power in 1669. This indigenous monarchical tradition played a major role in the development of modern Moroccan political thought and behavior. Although French colonial analyses focused on the rupture between the dilapidated "medieval" political structures of the sultanate and the effective "modern" system they introduced during the protectorate (1912–56), it would be more correct to say that, while the Moroccan sultanate was in a state of collapse by the early 20th century, the 19th century witnessed a dynamic reinterpretation of many indigenous political concepts and the spontaneous formation of a resilient protonational community, which was reshaped in colonial and postcolonial times.

Central to this development was the contract that existed between the ‘Alawi sultans and their predominantly tribal subjects. The sultans demanded loyalty and revenues from their subjects in return for ensuring their welfare by means of the sultans' descent from the Prophet and their commitment to waging jihad. When the sultans failed to protect and provide, their subjects reserved the right to wage jihad against them, which, as armed tribesmen, they were well able to do. In the 19th century, recurrent popular jihads against the sultans for their inability to defend Morocco from European penetration played a powerful role in inculcating the principle of political reciprocity. The fact that the perceived threat to Morocco came from non-Muslims enhanced the religious dimension of these movements.

The imposition of the French and Spanish protectorates in 1912 further discredited the sultan and fostered the development of alternative political perspectives of European and Middle Eastern origin: secular nationalism, socialism, Salafism, Pan-Islamism, and Pan-Arabism. In the colonial context, Moroccans were naturally preoccupied with national liberation, but they sought it within a Pan-Islamic and Pan-Arab framework that combined recognition of Morocco's distinctive "national" history with participation in the fraternity of "Arab" states. Personal contacts existed between Moroccan nationalists and the famous Pan-Islamist Shakib Arslan in the 1930s. ‘Allal al-Fasi, Morocco's most famous national leader and a Salafi scholar, expressed in his memoirs the deep satisfaction he felt when the president of the League of Arab States declared that the Maghrib and Mashriq (i.e., North Africa and the Middle East) were the two indispensable wings of the same Arab bird.

While the Arabs of the Mashriq had to choose between religion and ethnicity, the conflation of Arab and Islamic identity posed no contradictions for Arabs in solidly Sunni Morocco. However, other ethnolinguistic groups—namely, the three main Berber communities—had to be subsumed within the new hegemonic Arabo-Islamic identity. The status of Morocco's culturally and economically important Jewish community was also ambiguous despite reassurances from nationalists, many of whom hoped for a secular republic. However, the sultan, Muhammad V, managed to activate his latent power and authority as a symbol of the Islamic Moroccan community and orchestrate a hybrid political system in which the Commander of the Faithful became a constitutional monarch who ruled rather than reigned.

In the half century since independence, Moroccan political thought internalized many global concepts of European origin. Some Moroccans have called for a more representative government, legal parity for men and women, and greater recognition of the Berber cultural contribution to shaping Moroccan identity. What is distinctive is the extent to which political discourse is shaped by Islam despite the existence of numerous secular political groups. In the early 21st century, monarchical legitimism still derived its power from the dynasty's status as descendents of the Prophet. The most successful rival political discourse was that of Islamism, which, as elsewhere, provided an authentic framework for articulating calls for social justice, a more equitable distribution of wealth, and a redress of the concerns of the frustrated urban middle and lower classes. Although Islamism has not attracted the same following in Morocco as in some other countries due to the monarchy's rival Islamic credentials, it is nonetheless a potent force.

See also colonialism; international Islamic organizations; modernity; North Africa

Further Reading

Amira Bennison, *Jihad and Its Interpretations in Pre-colonial Morocco*, 2002; Rahma Bourqia and Susan Gilson Miller, eds., *In the Shadow of the Sultan*, 1999; Henry Munson, *Religion and Power in Morocco*, 1993; John Waterbury, *The Commander of the Faithful: The Moroccan Political Elite—a Study in Segmented Politics*, 1970; Malika Zeghal, *Islamistes marocains: Le défi à la monarchie*, 2005.

AMIRA K. BENNISON

mosque

The mosque (*masjid*), which serves as the preferred site for prayer among Muslims, has a rich social and political history. From the time of the Prophet Muhammad, whose home in Medina, together with the adjoining courtyard, became the prototype for later designs, mosques have combined worship, instruction, administration, practical uses, and ritual activities with direct and indirect bearing upon the maintenance of order, popular mobilization, and the exercise of power. Although after Muhammad's death, the unity of religious and secular authority embodied by the Prophet could not be replicated, it is significant that this ideal combination of roles played a key part in the selection of Abu Bakr as the first caliph.

The Companions explicitly justified their choice by recognizing that Muhammad had designated him to lead the congregational prayer on numerous occasions when the Prophet himself was unable to do so. This symbolic link between the imam or prayer leader and the ruler underwent considerable variation over the following centuries, but the precedent it established remained a core principle in classical Islamic theories of political stability.

An early and enduring manifestation of the close conjuncture of secular and spiritual leadership is reflected in the architecture and design of the new capital cities founded or appropriated by the victorious forces in the course of establishing the new Islamic empire. A standard feature of this urban outline, which persisted through the Ottoman period, consisted of placing the governor's palace and the central mosque as a pair, marking the convergence of the administrative and ceremonial functions, at the heart of a city. In some cases, such as the Umayyad Mosque in Damascus and the Ayasofia Mosque in Istanbul, an existing Christian church was converted into a mosque, with remodeling and additions such as minarets and areas for ritual ablutions. In other instances, as happened in Basra, Kayrawan, and Cairo, conquering Arab leaders drew up plans for the first mosque at the center of a military camp. Historically, many Islamic dynasties have constructed immense monumental mosques to mark their authority, as seen, for example, in the Mughals' Jama Masjid in Delhi, the Abbasids' Great Mosque of Samarra, or, most recently, the Hassan II Mosque in Casablanca. The actual task of presiding over the prayer was, in time, delegated to others, but typically caliphs or their representatives continued to oversee the conduct of public religious ceremonies and thus legitimate their performance, whether by support, attendance, or through the invocation of a blessing upon the ruler by name spoken during the Friday prayer sermon.

The delivery of the sermon in the mosque as part of the obligatory Friday noon prayer, which the Prophet himself had originally performed, was also entrusted, upon his death, to the designated successor or caliph. Muslim rulers usually delegated this function to a scholar chosen for his eloquence and trustworthiness, but certain fixed conventions defining the classical forms of this oration continued to refer to the leader under whose auspices the preacher was speaking. For instance, the minbar, or mosque pulpit, retained importance as part of the formal procedure for recognizing the legitimacy of succession. Traditionally, the content of a Friday sermon reflected concern for the political order as well as the spiritual welfare of the community. Today, in most Muslim lands, a convergence of worldly and otherworldly concern continues to characterize sermon content, reflecting a wide range of variation from compliance and conformity to dissent and rebellion.

Another pattern that associates the administration of mosques with those governing a community derives from systems of patronage and oversight, including subsidies for the construction, the maintenance, and the staffing of a place of prayer. In general, Islamic legal conventions allow for a variety of particular edifices, large and small, to serve as mosques, but with a distinction made between the many ordinary mosques for everyday use and a limited number of generally much larger cathedral mosques. Traditionally, only these more spacious and often more celebrated mosques were authorized as sites for conducting the Friday noon prayer, a status designated by the term *jāmi'*. Typically, such privileged central mosques also had more resources, enabling them to provide enhanced worship services. Today, however, this distinction does not apply consistently. On the one hand, governments in most lands with Muslim majorities have instituted ministries or other bureaucratic agencies that seek to exercise some surveillance or control over the operation of mosques, often with special attention to any potentially incendiary content in sermons. These developments include a transfer, the pace of which varies considerably across the Islamic world, of the site of education from mosques to schools. On the other hand, a vast array of mosques funded, sometimes lavishly, by private donors or by benevolent societies rather than by the government have emerged over the last century, creating independent bases for preaching, instruction, and frequently for the provision of social services. The activities of the Society of Muslim Brothers and its later offshoots, ranging from medical clinics and vocational training facilities to transportation and financial cooperatives, provide perhaps the best known example of this trend.

A second important dimension of a mosque in the context of Islamic political culture is its reference to the model of the sanctuary in Mecca, the point of convergence for the hajj or pilgrimage. Symbolically, of course, every Muslim place of prayer is related to this original site, *al-Masjid al-Ḥarām*, by virtue of its directional orientation, which Muslims face when they pray. But Mecca also represents an emphasis on the enduring and transcendent unity of Muslims in a way that eludes any other earthly location, even Medina, the center of the early Islamic polity and first capital of the Islamic empire. Jerusalem, considered by Muslims to be the third most sacred site, is also venerated specifically by virtue of the Qur'anic allusion to the Prophet's mystical night journey, described as the visit to a mosque (17:1); this devotion later provided a concrete focus when the Umayyad caliphs constructed the Aqsa Mosque on the Temple Mount and the adjoining Dome of the Rock. The primary historical tendency has been to view both the mosques of Mecca and Jerusalem as focal points for spiritual promise rather than secular aspiration. However, in the context of the prolonged conflict between Israel and Palestine in the 20th and 21st centuries, a traditional religious site and symbol for all Muslims is frequently deployed as a popular nationalistic icon.

The Islamic revival that has surged dramatically and widely since the 1970s has also influenced the development and use of mosques. Mosque construction has increased exponentially in many Middle Eastern nations as well as the West and the former Soviet republics of Central Asia. Similarly, this movement has promoted the enhancement of mosques and the expansion beyond the traditional function of worship to the operation of schools, playgrounds, clinics, workshops, libraries, gyms, and performance venues. Many major European and American cities have recently acquired Islamic Centers that feature impressive architecture and décor and combine mosques with additional facilities for social and instructional

purposes. Not surprisingly, mosques have lately also advanced with measured enthusiasm into cyberspace, after having extended their reach through radio and television for decades.

See also Friday prayer; madrasa; preaching; pulpit

Further Reading

Martin Frishman and Hasan-Uddin Khan, eds., *The Mosque: History, Architectural Development and Regional Diversity*, 1994; Oleg Grabar, *The Formation of Islamic Art*, 1987; Muhammad Qasim Zaman, *The Ulama in Contemporary Islam: Custodians of Change*, 2002.

PATRICK D. GAFFNEY

Muʿawiya (602–80)

Muʿawiya b. Abi Sufyan b. Harb was a member of the powerful ʿAbd Shams clan of the Quraysh, a Companion of the Prophet, and the founder of the Sufyanid branch of the Umayyad dynasty, which ruled the Muslim Empire for almost a hundred years (661–750). Born in Mecca in 602 to Abu Sufyan b. Harb and Hind bt. ʿUtba bt. Rabiʿa, outspoken opponents of Muhammad and the early Muslim community before they converted to Islam in 630, Muʿawiya, it is believed, became a Muslim immediately before the conquest of Mecca by Muhammad in 629. After converting to Islam, Muʿawiya worked for a period as the Prophet's scribe, writing down some of the Qur'anic revelations that the Prophet received.

After the death of the Prophet and during the last year of Abu Bakr's reign (634), Muʿawiya was sent to Syria to support his half-brother Yazid, who had been dispatched there to lead the Arab troops against the Byzantines. ʿUmar b. al-Khattab (r. 634–44) appointed Muʿawiya commander of the forces besieging Caesarea on the Palestinian coast, which was eventually taken sometime between 637 and 640. Thereafter ʿUmar named Muʿawiya governor of Damascus in 640, and between 643 and 646, the territories of Jordan and Palestine were added to his governorship. In 647, ʿUmar's successor, ʿUthman b. ʿAffan (r. 644–56) charged him to invade Cyprus (647) in what was perhaps the largest use of maritime warfare and is seen by most historians as the inauguration of the Muslim navy.

Muʿawiya was thrust into the limelight with the assassination of ʿUthman in 656 by his refusal to step down as governor on the orders of ʿUthman's successor, ʿAli b. Abi Talib (r. 656–61). Muʿawiya's refusal was based on his demand that ʿAli punish ʿUthman's killers, a large number of whom were in ʿAli's camp. This confrontation escalated into a full-fledged war between Muʿawiya and ʿAli at the Battle of Siffin (657). This battle resulted in a stalemate, after which both parties agreed to an arbitration that also resulted in naught, although it did show Muʿawiya's skill in political maneuvering. After the assassination of ʿAli in 661 by the Khariji ʿAbd al-Rahman b. Muljam, Muʿawiya reigned for the next 20 years with very little or no opposition. According to the Islamic historical tradition, Muʿawiya reigned as caliph from the abdication of the caliphate by Hasan b. ʿAli (ca. 624–70) in 661 to his death in Damascus in 680. The Syrians had given him the oath of allegiance (*bayʿa*) even before Hasan's abdication, perhaps as early as 657.

As ruler, Muʿawiya instituted a number of centralizing reforms, such as the establishment of the chancellery and the bureau of the post. He allowed his governors to be semiautonomous, especially with regard to the moneys levied from these provinces. His ability to disarm former adversaries such as Hasan, or even turn them into loyal supporters, such as Ziyad b. Abih (623–73), was legendary. It is said that he took the *bayʿa* for his son Yazid a few years before his death in 680.

Muʿawiya is remembered for his *ḥilm* (forbearance), which is generally seen as an attribute that he inherited from his father, although it is conceivable that the Prophet was a greater influence on his forbearance, generosity, and political astuteness toward his enemies and followers alike.

See also ʿAli b. Abi Talib (ca. 599–661); civil war; Umayyads (661–750)

Further Reading

Stephen Humphreys, *Muʿawiya ibn Abi Sufyan: From Arabia to Empire*, 2006; Charles Pellat, "Le Culte de Muʿāwiya au IIIe siècle de l'hégire," *Studia Islamica* 6 (1956); Erling Ladewig Petersen, *ʿAlī and Muʿāwiya in early Arabic Tradition*, translated by P. Lampe Christensen, 1974; Abu Jaʿfar Muhammad b. Jarir al-Tabari, *The First Civil War* (*The History of al-Ṭabarī*, vol. 17), translated by G. R. Hawting, 1996; Idem, *Between Civil Wars: The Caliphate of Muʿāwiyah* (*The History of al-Ṭabarī*, vol. 18), translated by Michael G. Morony, 1987.

KHALED M. G. KESHK

mufti/grand mufti

A mufti is someone who issues fatwas, or religious opinions on points of Islamic law. The origins of the institution of *iftā'* (the act of giving a fatwa) lie in the rise of legal experts around the turn of the eighth century. In contrast to qadis, or government-appointed judges who decided legal cases on an ad hoc basis, muftis emerged as legal experts whose deliberations had legal value and who determined the acceptable range of opinion on concrete issues of Islamic law. According to this classical understanding, a mufti possessed legal authority on the basis of his recognized expertise in legal studies and was not necessarily affiliated with the government. "Mufti" can also refer, more specifically, to the office of the grand mufti—a bureaucratic position developed by the Ottoman government in the latter half of the 16th century. Also referred to as shaykh al-Islam,

the grand mufti was appointed by the sultan as the chief jurisconsult overseeing other scholars in a centralized hierarchy of madrasas (Muslim schools) and provincial courts. The office of grand mufti has lived on in the state governments that emerged from the former Ottoman Empire in the 20th century; for example, Shaykh ʻAli Gomaa is now the grand mufti of Egypt and Muhammad Rashid Qabbani is the grand mufti of Lebanon.

As early as 740, the authority to issue fatwas was commonly acknowledged as belonging solely to muftis. While some judges qualified as muftis, most did not. Therefore, the judge's role was relegated to deciding the facts of a pending case and applying the laws put forward by muftis. When faced with a case involving complex questions of Islamic law, the judge would request a mufti's opinion. While muftis provided an essential service within the legal system, their authority was epistemic, not based on holding a government office. This conception of legal authority began to change during the reign of Ottoman sultan Mehmed II (1451–81). Under Mehmed, the Ottoman government began to routinize Islamic law by organizing a hierarchical system of madrasas throughout the empire and by developing a bureaucratic apparatus that employed scholars as teachers, judges, and legal advisors to the central government. By the end of the 16th century, the government-appointed mufti of Istanbul was recognized as the grand mufti in charge of this apparatus.

The grand mufti's responsibilities changed in the course of the history of the Ottoman Empire but typically included serving as the sultan's personal religious advisor, appointing and dismissing provincial judges, teaching law, investigating charges of heresy, supervising religious endowments (waqf), and helping government administrators make state law (*qānūn*) compatible with Islamic law. With these responsibilities, the grand mufti acquired bureaucratic powers that increased his influence over other scholars. Yet the Ottoman system also made him, and the entire religious hierarchy beneath him, more beholden to the central government. The influence of the grand mufti was greatly curtailed during the Tanzimat (reforms) of the 19th century, as the Ottomans came to rely more on Western-trained civil bureaucrats to make and implement policy. The office of grand mufti survived the dissolution of the Ottoman Empire and is recognized in many nations of the Islamic world today, including Syria, Lebanon, Egypt, Tunisia, Saudi Arabia, Pakistan, India, Albania, and others. Indonesia has an interesting arrangement whereby the position of grand mufti is held by the Indonesian Ulama Council as a group. Al-Hajj Amin al-Husayni (d. 1974), the grand mufti of Palestine from 1921 to 1948, became well known for his opposition to Zionism, particularly during the Arab revolt from 1936 to 1939, and appears frequently in polemics regarding the Israel-Palestine conflict on account of his meeting Adolf Hitler in 1941 and having fled to Lebanon, Iraq, Italy, and then Germany to escape imprisonment by the British. Grand muftis still serve the important function of legitimating government policies, although contemporary Islamists often regard state muftis as government collaborators lacking proper religious authority.

See also judge; jurisprudence; shaykh al-Islam

Further Reading

Zvi Elpeleg and Shmuel Himelstein, *The Grand Mufti: Haj Amin el-Hussaini, Founder of the Palestinian National Movement*, 1993; R. C. Repp, *The Mufti of Istanbul: A Study in the Development of the Ottoman Learned Hierarchy*, 1986; Jakob Skovgaard-Petersen, *Defining Islam for the Egyptian State: Muftis and Fatwas of the Dār al-Iftā*, 1997.

JAMES BROUCEK

Mughals (1526–1857)

Founded by Zahiruddin Muhammad Babur (1483–1530), a Chaghatay Turkish ruler from what is now known as Central Asia, the Mughal Empire grew to control most of the Indian subcontinent over the next two centuries. Babur's victory at Panipat in 1526 over Ibrahim Lodi of the Delhi Sultanate is memorably recorded in his autobiography, the *Baburnama*. Babur bequeathed his empire to his son Humayun (d. 1556), who was unable to hold on to his father's domains. Humayun sought refuge with Shah Tahmasp I in Safavid Iran after losing northern India to the Afghan ruler Sher Shah Suri (d. 1545). With the help of the Safavid army, Humayun eventually established himself in India. The reigns of Humayun's successors, most notably Akbar (d. 1605), Jahangir (d. 1627), and Shah Jahan (d. 1666), saw the spread of Mughal political and cultural institutions into India's cities, shrines, and marketplaces. Successful assertions of local autonomy marked the reign of the Mughal emperor Aurangzeb (d. 1707), and the Mughal Empire also began to weaken because of the growing power of the English East India Company. Following an uprising against the British in 1857, India was placed under British rule, and the Mughal Empire was put to a formal end.

The multiethnic composition of Mughal courts demonstrates the heterodox nature of religious identity in the premodern Islamicate world. Babur brought with him a network of Central Asian nobles who were related to him by blood, by marriage, or through oaths of allegiance. Humayun brought with him members of the Persian elite, and Akbar began cultivating marital ties and military allegiances with the Hindu Rajputs (a warrior elite in India) as a means of securing a solid power base in India. Mughal patronage of local Sufi networks, most notably the Chishtis of Ajmer, and the Mughal elite's patronage of art, architecture, and literature are indicative of the many forms through which Mughal sovereignty was articulated. By appropriating local bases of spiritual authority such as the tombs of Sufis and building architectural monuments that wedded the spiritual authority of the king with a recognizable visual idiom, Mughal kings inscribed the landscape with articulations of their own power. In this, Mughal kings resembled their Ottoman and Safavid counterparts, as well as other Muslim and Hindu rulers of premodern India, all of whom saw themselves as

world rulers. Flourishing urban centers and port cities allowed for trade with Europe, Southeast Asia, and the Muslim world, and Mughal chronicles frequently mention the arrival of travelers and embassies from abroad, the splendor of Mughal cities, and the wealth of Mughal kings.

The syncretic and dynamic nature of the Mughal administrative apparatus has been seen as both contributing to the longevity of the empire and aiding in its devolution. Mughal methods of governance drew on existing Indian political norms, Islamicate legal and administrative codes, and a distribution of power among different ethnic and linguistic groups. The Mughal *mansabdārī* system, developed by Akbar, involved the assignment of positions to military leaders according to the number of troops they could provide in the event of war. Military officers were paid cash salaries or given an estate (*jāgīr*) to administer and from which to collect revenue. The historian Irfan Habib argues that the distribution of power to local elites, while useful for broadening the reach of the Mughal polity, led to the eventual fragmentation of the empire. Mughal campaigns into the Deccan, most notably under Aurangzeb, were met with a limited measure of success. The 18th century saw the weakening of Mughal power as the global economy came to be dominated by European powers and sea-based trade. By the time India was placed under the British Crown, the Mughal Empire had become a regional power, even though the Mughal king continued to command the symbolic loyalty that led to the uprising of 1857.

See also Akbar the Great (1556–1605); Aurangzeb (1618–1707); Babur, Zahir al-Din (1483–1530); Delhi Sultanate (1206–1526); India

Further Reading

Muzaffar Alam, *The Crisis of Empire in Mughal North India: Awadh and the Punjab, 1707–48*, 1986; M. Athar Ali, *Mughal India: Studies in Polity, Ideas, Society, and Culture*, 2006; Jos Gommans, *Mughal Warfare: Indian Frontiers and Highroads to Empire*, 2002; Irfan Habib, *The Agrarian System of Mughal India, 1556–1707*, 1999; J. F. Richards, *The Cambridge History of India: The Mughal Empire*, 1993.

TAYMIYA R. ZAMAN

Muhammad (570–632)

Muhammad's Career and Achievements

In Muslim belief, the religion of Islam is based on divine revelation and represents a divinely willed and established institution. In the perspective of history, the origins of Islam can be traced back to the prophetic career of Muhammad, its historical founder in the first third of the seventh century. Born around 570 in Mecca, a town in a rocky valley of the Hijaz—the northwestern quarter of the Arabian Peninsula—Muhammad began his prophetic proclamations circa 610. He appeared not as a mystic or visionary but as a prophet with the mission to convert the Quraysh, his fellow Arab tribesmen who had settled there.

The town of Mecca flourished on trade and commerce. It was built around a well, which provided a reliable yearlong water supply and held in its center the Ka'ba, the sanctuary of the Black Stone and seat of the tribal deity Hubal. Most importantly, it was a pilgrimage site where fairs and festivals were held every year. Muhammad's message to his fellow townsmen was based on the religious synthesis that had formed and fermented in him since his youth and that he understood to be the divine revelation that God had sent to him to proclaim. This message eventually became known as Islam, or "submission to God," and grew into a universal and missionary religion whose current followers represent about a fifth of the world's population. Muhammad experienced his revelations as inner promptings that inspired ad hoc utterances that he recited piecemeal to his listeners over about 20 years. These recitals were collected after his death in the Arabic Qur'an (literally, "recitation"), the holy book of Islam. They were couched in rhymed prose (*saj'*), a mode of expression that facilitated memorization and distinguished them from Muhammad's personal instructions.

Muhammad broke forth with his message, proclaiming faith in the one God (Allah), whose messenger he perceived himself to be. In God, the Prophet Muhammad recognized the divine creator of the universe and humanity as well as the final judge of all human beings on the Day of Judgment, which would bring this world to its end in an apocalyptic cataclysm. On that final day, all human beings would be raised in the general resurrection to account for their lives on Earth and enter into everlasting life in the world to come. The life offered in the hereafter would be either God's reward of eternal bliss in paradise for those who had surrendered to His will in this world, obeying His commandments and putting them into practice, or His punishment of never-ending suffering in hellfire for those who had acted against His will by violating the divine commands and interdictions.

For some ten-odd years, Muhammad tried to convert his fellow tribesmen at Mecca to his newly found faith of Islam. Rejected by the majority of the Quraysh, however, he took flight from Mecca with a small group of followers, becoming a tribal dissident who breached the bonds of common descent with his clan, and, in 622, immigrated to Medina, situated about 200 miles to the north. Medina was a cluster of fortresses and compounds scattered over a large area. It was known as Yathrib at the time, but it later came to be called "the city of the Prophet" (*madīnat al-nabī*) after Muhammad had settled there. Medina was an agricultural settlement inhabited by two major Arab tribes and three smaller Jewish tribes that had assimilated to the Arab way of life and its customs, adopting the Arabic language but not the beliefs of the pre-Islamic Arab tribal religion. Medina offered the emigrants (*muhājirūn*) the livelihood of its fields, palm groves, and orchards and extended to them the welcome of the helpers (*anṣār*), a group of Medinan Arabs who accepted Islam and became brothers in faith with the emigrants. Muhammad's emigration, known as the hijra and occurring in

September 622, became the moment in history in which the small Muslim community of Medina was launched on its meteoric rise; by the time of Muhammad's death, it had established its hold over the entire Arabian Peninsula. In the centuries after his death, both the religion and the empire of Islam spread over the Middle East, advancing westward along the North African shores of the Mediterranean into Spain and Sicily and pushing eastward across the Iranian plateau into Central Asia and the Indian subcontinent. The first day of the lunar year in which the hijra took place came to mark the beginning of the Muslim era, and the Muslim calendar reckons its own lunar calendar from this year.

Muhammad's time at Medina was characterized by a struggle for preeminence vis-à-vis the Meccan leadership of the Quraysh; his success in Medina represented a threat both to their authority and to their caravan trade that passed Medina on its route to Syria and Palestine. It also drew him into serious confrontations with the Jewish tribes of Medina, whose memory of their religious legacy was at variance with Muhammad's proclamation of events surrounding major biblical figures, such as Abraham and Moses. In addition, Muhammad faced the challenge of providing leadership for his Meccan emigrants and Medinan helpers while arbitrating issues between the two Arab tribes (the Aws and Khazraj and their clients) who had emerged exhausted after a long history of fraternal feuds and their ensuing blood revenge and adjudication of blood money. Especially in the first few years at Medina, Muhammad had to deal with the "waverers" (*munāfiqūn*): those Medinan Arabs on whose loyalty and zeal he could not rely and whom it took time to convert. Furthermore, he had to find a means of channeling the tribal raiding tradition of the Arab clansmen away from fraternal warfare and into the constructive building of a community.

At the end of his life in 632 in Medina, Muhammad was able to claim three major achievements: the foundation of the Muslim community (*umma*), the proclamation of the Arabic scripture (Qur'an), and the dynamism of the "struggle on the path of God" (jihad). For the first time in history, he had united all the Arabs living in the Arabian Peninsula into one *umma* based no longer on the tribal principle of blood kinship and descent from a common ancestor but rather on the religious basis of a common faith expressed in the Muslim profession of faith (*shahāda*) that "there is no god but Allah and Muhammad is his messenger." This achievement resembled a social revolution because it transformed Arab society from an unwieldy conglomeration of rivaling kinship groups into an ordered whole of individuals united by a common bond of faith. Rather than resting in the hands of freely elected tribal elders (shaykhs), community leadership rested thenceforth in the divinely chosen messenger (*rasūl*), to whom all owed obedience next to God. For the first time in history, Muhammad had given the Arabs a scripture in their own language that would remain the basis of their faith throughout the ages. It signified a religious revolution that uprooted the polytheistic beliefs and cultic practices of the pre-Islamic Arabs and substituted for them a strong monotheistic faith. The proclamations of this faith in the one God, understood as divine revelation, were written down and collected about two decades after the Prophet's death in the first Arabic book ever produced: the holy writ of the Qur'an. From now on, each Arab was charged to surrender to God alone and to justify his actions before God rather than seeking protection as a clan member and living in submission to the customs of his forefathers and tribal ancestors. For the first time in history, the tribal energy of the Arab clansmen, spent in the past on nomadic raids or tribal blood feuds, became directed toward the common goal of building a coordinated polity. This polity was to be driven by jihad, which marshaled all means, whether peaceful or militant, available to the members of the community. Jihad became the engine that, through conquest, empowered the Arabs to establish a global empire and, through proselytization, propelled Islam in its missionary thrust toward its goal of a universal religion.

Muhammad's Life from ca. 570 to 610

Western scholarship has studied the life of the Prophet assiduously and meticulously, beginning in earnest in the 19th century with F. Wüstenfeld and J. Wellhausen. The harvest of scholarship since then on the biography of the Prophet has been synthesized in two standard works: the one-volume masterpiece of F. Buhl, *Das Leben Muhammeds* (1934), and the two-volume set of W. M. Watt, *Muhammad at Mecca* (1953) and *Muhammad at Medina* (1956). Many studies, monographs, and articles have been added since World War II, but none has produced a radically new analysis that would change the basic assessment of Muhammad's achievements or alter the historical development of his career. Western scholarship is ultimately based on the principal work of the traditional Islamic biography of the Prophet, known as his "way of life" (*sīra*). This work of Ibn Ishaq (704–767), the famous *Sirat Rasul Allah* (Life of God's Messenger), is extant in the recension by Ibn Hisham (d. 833). Compiled more than a century after Muhammad's death, it portrayed the Prophet as a revered figure and the glorified founder of the religion. Other early Islamic works that include important information on the Prophet's life are those on his "campaigns" (*maghāzī*), such as the one by Waqidi (d. 823), as well as the history of Tabari (d. 923), which includes the valuable reports of ʻUrwa b. al-Zubayr (d. 712). The Qur'an itself offers limited historical data for the construction of Muhammad's biography. On the whole, the traditional biographical literature on Muhammad neglects the early phase of his life, focusing instead on his career as a prophet, which began with his call to proclaim the Qur'an in about 610. For the early period (ca. 570–610), only a small number of historical facts were recorded, such as those concerning his humble origins, his early career as a merchant, and his marriage to a widow in Mecca.

Muhammad was born into the family of the Banu Hashim, one of the clans of the Quraysh tribe. That his birth occurred in the "Year of the Elephant" (Q. 105:1–5), when Mecca was unsuccessfully threatened by a group of Abyssinian invaders, is not based on a reliable tradition. Because his name, Muhammad (worthy of praise), can be understood as an Arabic epithet, some scholars doubt whether this actually was his given name; yet it is the name by which he is mentioned four times in the Qur'an

(3:144; 33:40; 47:2; 48:29) without, however, being addressed by it directly. In general, Islamic literature addresses him by his Qur'anic titles—"the Prophet" (*al-nabī*) and "God's Messenger" (*rasūl Allāh*)—and frequently calls him "the Chosen One" (*al-muṣṭafā*) and honors him with the eulogies such as "peace be upon him" and "may God bless him and grant him salvation" after his name, while Muslim mystics tend to revere him as "the beloved of God" (*ḥabīb Allāh*). Muhammad grew up in poverty as an orphan, his father, ʻAbdallah, having died before his birth. Raised by his mother, Amina, and looked after by his grandfather, ʻAbd al-Muttalib, he may have spent a year with a wet nurse among the nomads. His mother died when he was six years old, and his grandfather died two years later. After passing into the custodianship of his uncle Abu Talib, the young boy showed an interest in the life of a trader and merchant, possibly making a trade journey to Syria while still a young man. Noticed for his business skills by Khadija, a well-to-do merchant's widow who was twice married before and possibly divorced, Muhammad became an agent in her employ. According to tradition, Khadija was 40 years old when she proposed marriage to him, and Muhammad was about 25 years of age. They had four daughters, who later were given in marriage to some of Muhammad's Companions, and several sons, all of whom died in infancy.

The legendary stories that Muhammad's breast was cleansed by angels shortly after his birth and that, in his youth, Muhammad placed the Black Stone in the wall of the Kaʻba during its reconstruction, thereby solving a squabble of the tribal elders of Mecca for the privilege of doing so, are later creations of tradition to signify immunity from sin and leadership qualities already manifested by Muhammad as a youth. Equally doubtful are encounters in his youth with a Christian monk, named either Bahira or Nastur, who is presented as prophesying Muhammad's later career. In his early life, Muhammad proved his mettle as a merchant, and he used a good portion of commercial vocabulary in his Qur'anic proclamations. He proved to be a responsible father, an energetic member of his clan, and a sound and capable person; this is in contrast to many discrediting assessments of his personality in European accounts from medieval times until today. Unfortunately, the traditional biographical literature tells us little about the provenance of the religious ideas Muhammad acquired during his early life. These ideas came from two principal sources: on the one hand from the religious environment into which he was born, the tribal Arab cult of pre-Islamic Arabia with its fatalistic notions and pagan practices that were observed in his hometown, and on the other hand from a medley of mainly Christian sectarian beliefs, certain Jewish practices, and some Manichean notions that he encountered during his youth in Mecca.

In Islamic historiography, the epoch of Arabia prior to the promulgation of Islam is generally called the age of "ignorance" (*jāhiliyya*), against which Islam is contrasted as the age of enlightenment and knowledge. The *jāhiliyya* was a time when the Arabs were known for their virtues of courage and bravery, their generosity and hospitality, their excesses in eating and drinking, their drinking songs and love poetry, their worship of idols and stone cults, and their beliefs in a variety of local and tribal deities, both male and female. Muhammad grew up in this environment of the *jāhiliyya*, as indicated by some scattered references in the Qur'an: he was found erring (93:3), did not know scripture and belief (42:52), offered animal sacrifices to deities (cf. 108:2), once brought a sheep as a sacrifice to the female deity al-ʻUzza, and believed in spirits (*jinn*) and demons (*shayāṭīn*). His uncle Abu Lahab, cursed in the Qur'an (111:1), was a violent defender of paganism, and his uncle and tribal protector Abu Talib never embraced Islam. Furthermore, Muhammad's early Qur'anic proclamations were expressed in cryptic rhymed prose that resembled the oracles of the pre-Islamic soothsayers (*kāhin*). To assert their truth, he would introduce them with oaths, swearing by natural phenomena, such as the heavens and the Earth, the sky and the constellations, the sun and the moon, the stars and the planets, the dawn and the forenoon, or the fig tree and the olive tree.

Muhammad speaks of the Jews and Christians with whom he came into contact cumulatively as "possessors of the scripture" (*ahl al-kitāb*) without specific reference to their religious differences. It is possible that the occasional reference to Sabaeans in the Qur'an (*Ṣābi'ūn*, 2:62; 5:69; 22:17) implies contact with Manicheans as well. The biblical lore of Jews and Christians made an overpowering impact on Muhammad; he firmly believed that his revelations agreed with the content of their original scriptures, and on occasion he asked them for clarification of his newly found ideas (Q. 10:94). In our present state of research, it is impossible to pinpoint the sources from the Jewish-Christian background that Muhammad may have had for his religious ideas. It is certain, however, that he received his knowledge by oral information and that he had not read the scriptures of Jews and Christians. In his time, the Bible had not yet been translated into Arabic, and Muhammad was unable to read either Hebrew or Greek. In fact, only one verse of the Bible (Psalms 37:29) is quoted verbatim in the Qur'an (21:105). As a merchant he may have had a rudimentary knowledge of Arabic writing and record keeping, though it is a general Muslim perception that he was illiterate (*ummī*—a term that in the Qur'an means not "illiterate" but rather denotes Muhammad as "the heathen prophet," *al-nabī al-ummī*; 7:157–58).

Most of the biblical lore included in the Qur'anic proclamations shows similarities with the Book of Genesis and signals midrashic or apocryphal origin. In the case of Christianity, it points to sectarian rather than normative and orthodox beliefs and possibly includes some traces of Manichean ideas. The significant number of Syriac and Ethiopic loan words in the Qur'an further document that Muhammad not only assimilated elements of biblical and extrabiblical lore but also absorbed some foreign ritual vocabulary. Furthermore, the Qur'an retains traces that reveal Muhammad's rather distinct knowledge of circumstances linked with Mount Sinai, its monastery, and the tradition of the burning bush (28:29–30; 44–6; 52:1–6; 95:2). It also shows some familiarity on his part with Christian prayer practices and some awareness of the lives of Christian hermits. There is not sufficient evidence, however, to

link Muhammad with particular Christian monks as his teachers. In general, all information about Christian themes and topics came to him by word of mouth, probably through contact with Christian traders or slaves in Mecca itself. Some scholars refer to accounts in Muslim tradition that signal Waraqa b. Nawfal, a cousin of his wife Khadija, as a possible channel of Christian ideas for Muhammad. Most of these accounts, however, treat him as one of the *ḥanīf*s, or seekers of a pure worship of God, who were dissatisfied with idol worship and inspired by an innate monotheistic belief. It should not be overlooked, however, that pre-Islamic Arabia was exposed on its borders to Christian beliefs. There were Christians living in Najran in Yemen in the south of the Arabian Peninsula, and Arab principalities had formed on the northern fringes of the Arabian desert: these included the Ghassanids, who adhered to a Monophysite creed, and the Lakhmids, who had adopted Nestorian beliefs.

Muhammad's Career in Mecca from ca. 610 to 622

In about 610 Muhammad began to proclaim his message at a decisive moment of his life when he suddenly broke through to the unshakeable conviction that he had to proclaim to the people of Mecca the inner promptings he received as the word of God. Muslim tradition places this event—"his call to prophecy"—in a cave on a mountain outside Mecca, when he was impelled to recite, "Recite in the name of your Lord who created . . ." (Q. 96:1–5). Tradition describes him as experiencing states of spiritual excitement and ecstatic seizures; at times he asked to be wrapped (Q. 73:1; 74:1) in a mantle, and his cryptic speech resembled the words of a magician (*sāḥir*) possessed by demonic forces (*majnūn*). According to tradition, he hesitated for an "interval" (*fatra*) of three years before he came forward publicly with his message, but then he continued fearlessly persevering in proclaiming it until his death. When explaining his revelations, Muhammad conceived of them as originating from an archetypal book (*umm al-kitāb*, Q. 43:3), a guarded tablet (*lawḥ maḥfūẓ*, Q. 85:22), kept in the presence of the angels, its noble scribes (Q. 80,15–16). Rather than reading this heavenly book, Muhammad received from it individual revelations of a few verses at a time, orally communicated to him by a spirit of revelation later identified as the angel Gabriel (Q. 2:97).

The content of his proclamations was focused on praise for God the Creator and the warnings of God the Judge, the one and only God, Allah. Muhammad saw himself as both a "warner" (*nadhīr*) of an apocalyptic end of the world followed by an eschatological punishment for unbelievers and a "bringer of good tidings" (*bashīr*) about God as the bountiful creator of the heavens and the Earth as well as the fashioner of each and every human being. His most prominent role was that of a prophet who proclaimed an uncompromising monotheism centered on God who had neither partners nor associates. He singled out the prophets of old as prototypical recipients of revelation in history and referred to them by their biblical names in Arabic, such as Nuh (Noah), Ibrahim (Abraham), and Musa (Moses), as well as certain heroes of pre-Islamic Arab lore. He made no reference, however, to any of the great prophets of the Bible, such as Isaiah, Jeremiah, or Ezekiel, yet he mentioned central figures of the gospels, such as Yahya (John the Baptist) and 'Isa b. Maryam (Jesus, son of Mary), the Messiah (*masīḥ*); he saw himself standing in line with these prophets of old as their final representative, the "seal of the prophets."

At first, Muhammad's proclamations were given little attention by most Meccans. They made an impact, however, on a small group who became his followers, honored in history as the first Muslim converts. Among them were his wife Khadija; his cousin 'Ali, a youth at the time; the well-to-do merchant Abu Bakr, who adhered to him with unswerving loyalty; as well as a handful of young men who would later play a significant role in the succession struggles to Muhammad's leadership of the community. One early convert to Islam, perhaps the first, was Zayd b. Haritha, a slave bought in Syria and given by Khadija to Muhammad, who freed and adopted him. Ten years younger than Muhammad, he hailed from the region of Dumat al-Jandal, an oasis halfway between Mecca and Damascus, where the idol Wadd was worshipped and a considerable Christian colony had found shelter. Until his death in 629 as standard bearer of the Muslim forces on an unsuccessful expedition at Mu'ta against Arabs on Byzantine soil in Transjordan, Zayd b. Haritha remained very close to the Prophet; his extreme solicitude for Muhammad may be seen in the fact that he divorced his wife Zaynab a few years after the hijra so that the Prophet might marry her.

The Meccans stiffened in their opposition to Muhammad's revelations when they realized that his message attacked their tribal religion and its polytheistic pantheon, threatening their authority and trade by challenging their tribal oligarchy and endangering their fairs. When their opposition turned into persecution, Muhammad sent a group of weaker followers away to seek the protection of the Christian ruler of Abyssinia in a migration (hijra), which occurred about 615 (most of these emigrants drifted back later to rejoin their Muslim brethren). In Mecca itself, Muhammad tried to gain the goodwill of the Meccans by accepting as special intercessors with God their three favorite female deities, whom they worshipped as "daughters of Allah." These three goddesses were al-Lat, a solar deity, who had her sanctuary in a valley near Tai'f, a neighboring town of Mecca; al-'Uzza, an astral deity, to whom animal sacrifices were made at her sanctuary in an acacia grove located in a valley on the road from Mecca to Tai'f; and Manat, the goddess of fate and death, whose sanctuary was a Black Stone on the road from Mecca to Medina. Realizing that the recognition of "daughters of Allah" harmed his radically monotheistic message, Muhammad withdrew this compromise and abrogated it by altering the relevant verses included in the Qur'an (53:19–23). The most trying hostile scheme of Muhammad's Meccan adversaries, however, occurred about 616, when the tribesmen of the Quraysh engaged in a full tribal boycott of the Banu Hashim, Muhammad's clan. Although most of the Banu Hashim, including his custodian Abu Talib, had not accepted Islam, the clan stood by Muhammad in loyalty to their tribal code of honor and protected him during this difficult period. Only his uncle Abu Lahab, together with

his wife, remained resolute in his hostility toward Muhammad (Q. 111:1). This boycott failed, however, because it proved to be more of a disruption to the communal life in Mecca than a successful step to silence Muhammad.

Most scholars place Muhammad's vision of a miraculous night journey (*isrā'*) in the later period of his life at Mecca. According to the legend, Muhammad was carried by a flying steed in the company of the angel Gabriel from the sacred area of the Ka'ba to the "farthest place of worship" (Q. 17:1), interpreted as either the temple precinct in Jerusalem or the place of prayer of the angels in heaven. Furthermore, Muslim tradition links the nocturnal journey with Muhammad's ascension to heaven (*mi'rāj*). This heavenly ascent, seen as initiation to his prophetic career, would need to be placed at the beginning of his Qur'anic proclamations. Though connected with a vision recorded in the Qur'an (53:1–18; 81:19–25) in which Muhammad is approached by a heavenly figure rather than being carried off, this would seem to refer to a separate experience. The interpretation of the Prophet's ascension to heaven as an ascent through the seven heavens into the very presence of God, with Muhammad passing beyond the spheres of other prophets (among them Adam, Jesus, Abraham, and Moses), is a further elaboration of Muslim tradition. According to the legend, Muhammad began his heavenly ascent from the rock in Jerusalem, which became associated with the Dome of the Rock, the symbol of Islam's triumph over Judaism and Christianity, erected in about 694 by the Umayyad caliph 'Abd al-Malik on the temple precinct of Jerusalem and opposite the hill crowned by the Church of the Holy Sepulcher.

Certain significant events occurred during the last third of Muhammad's prophetic activity in Mecca. In about 618, 'Umar b. al-Khattab, a young man of a certain social status, converted to Muhammad's cause and became one of his strongest supporters as well as the founder of the Arab Empire about a decade after Muhammad's death. 'Umar's joining of the Muslims in Mecca, however, was followed in the next year by the deaths of Khadija and Abu Talib, resulting in a loss of both deep personal and strong tribal support. Exhausted and discouraged by the obstinate opposition of the Meccans to his reforms and unsuccessful in his initiative to find a welcoming audience for his proclamations in Tai'f, Muhammad came to despair of converting his fellow townsmen, convinced that God had destined them to unbelief. At this point in time, he realized that he had to cut the blood bonds with his tribe and find a new theater for his message to be accepted. At this juncture, something happened that was beyond his control.

The settlement of Medina had reached an impasse in its communal life due to tribal warfare and bloodshed between the Aws and Khazraj, the two major Arab tribes living in the town together with three smaller Jewish tribes that were drawn into the altercations. Because of this predicament, the inhabitants of Medina were looking for a political leader who could arbitrate their tribal conflicts. Muhammad, for his part, was looking for a new environment that would be receptive to his teachings. Medina answered this need. It had been prepared for a monotheistic message and the vision of a history of prophets through the presence of the three Jewish tribes—the Banu Qaynuqa', Banu al-Nadir, and Banu Qurayza—who had settled in the town before the arrival of the Aws and Khazraj. At the same time, it offered Muhammad a platform to combine his role as a prophetical reformer with that of a political leader. It so happened that some peasants from Medina, who had come as pilgrims to Mecca, saw Muhammad as the person who could provide the solution to their communal strife. Muhammad found willing listeners for his message among them, and in 621, he met about a dozen of them on the hill 'Aqaba outside Mecca. A year later, a formal pledge was made at the same place between him and a group of 73 men and 2 women from Medina that they would receive him and his followers as brethren into their community and offer them their tribal protection by the force of arms if necessary. On the basis of this "pledge of war" (*bay'at al-ḥarb*), Muhammad had successive groups of his followers leave Mecca for Medina and then finally left the town himself with Abu Bakr and 'Ali, hiding in a cave, according to tradition, as the Meccans were in pursuit. The Meccans failed in their attempt to prevent Muhammad's group of fugitive dissidents from forming a new polity allied with other tribal groups in the neighboring town of Medina.

Muhammad's Career in Medina from 622 to 632

The emigration from Mecca to Medina in 622, known as the hijra, was to become a key historical event, marking as it did the decisive moment Muhammad became an exemplary political leader. Muhammad integrated the people of Medina into one cohesive community by subsuming the Arab tribal elements into his community and by eventually eliminating the Jewish tribes altogether from the town. With regard to the Arabs, Muhammad could rely on two groups: the *muhājirūn*, who were firmly identified with his message and had given up their livelihood and left their homes, and the *anṣār*, the group of tribesmen (mainly belonging to the Khazraj but some also to the Aws), who welcomed him and his followers into their midst and accepted Islam wholeheartedly. Henceforth the Muslim community of believers, established by and loyal to Muhammad, would be founded on these two groups who acquired rights of kinship with one another rooted not in common blood but rather in common faith. Many people of Medina, however, remained noncommittal toward Muhammad and as such were identified as "hypocrites" (*munāfiqūn*), turncoats on whose loyalty Muhammad could not rely, and "waverers," who irritated him because of their reluctant support and persistent doubt about his message. They were led by 'Abdallah b. Ubayy, a rather irresolute leader of the Khazraj who did not manage to organize them into an opposition to Muhammad; he did, however, incite the three smaller Jewish tribes to resist Muhammad but left them in the lurch when it came to blows.

It is not known whether the three Jewish tribes living in Medina, each of them about 500 to 800 men, were descendants from Hebrew stock or Arabs who had adopted Judaism. They spoke Arabic, lived according to Arab customs, and were organized as tribal units but

held to basic religious principles and practices of Judaism. Muhammad called the Jews (*yahūd*) "children of Israel," knew that they followed the laws of Moses, and was aware that they had their own scripture (called Tawrat in the Qur'an) and the psalms of David (called Zabur). Among the Jewish tribes that settled in Medina, the Banu Qaynuqa' lived in two strongholds in the southwest of the town, becoming clients of the Khazraj; as they did not possess any lands, they made their livelihood by trading. Muhammad perceived them as a challenge to his message, obstructing his way with their religious claims and mockeries of his person. He would eventually expel them from Medina after the Battle of Badr in 624, demanding that their arms and tools be left behind for the Muslims and taking a fifth of the spoils for himself. The Banu al-Nadir, believed to have come from Palestine at an unknown date, had connections with the Jews of the oasis of Khaybar and probably had an admixture of Arab blood in their veins. Though they bore Arabic names, they spoke their own peculiar dialect and lived in fortified compounds half a day's journey to the south of Medina. They were clients of the Aws and entered into alliance with Muhammad in the first year after the hijra. Muhammad, however, became suspicious of them and feared that they intended to kill him. Laying siege on them and cutting down their palm trees, he forced them to surrender and made them leave with their possessions to the oasis of Khaybar and Syria; he gave their lands to the emigrants and kept part of them for himself. The Banu Qurayza, related to the Banu al-Nadir, lived as agriculturalists of cereals and palms on lands outside the city to the southeast of Medina. They were known to have adhered firmly to Jewish traditions and had intermarried with Arabs, becoming allied with the Aws. After the Battle of the Trench (*khandaq*) in 627, they were made to surrender unconditionally; the men were put to the sword and their women and children sold as slaves. It remains a mystery why the Jewish tribes did not rally together to prevent their expulsion from Medina.

In Medina, facing the task of creating a united community—bringing together emigrants and helpers, overcoming the reluctance of the "waverers," and dealing with the Jewish tribes—Muhammad displayed considerable political acumen. After establishing a link of brotherhood between the emigrants and helpers, he realized that he needed a practical mechanism to form a true unity of highly different and incongruous elements of the Medinan society. He pursued this end soon after the hijra by promulgating a document, recorded in his biography, known as the "Constitution of Medina" (*ṣaḥīfat al-Madīna*); it may be considered authentic. This legal document drafted on Muhammad's initiative had two sections: the first defining the duties of the believers (*mu'minūn*), including both emigrants and helpers from various clans of the Aws and Khazraj, and the second guaranteeing the rights of the *yahūd* and their clients. It was a significant document of brotherly solidarity that formed the foundation for the communal life of the *umma*, now no longer based on the traditional tribal system of blood kinship groups. Indeed, it broke up the tribal system of Medina by severing links of some of its tribesmen, based on common blood, and bonded the helpers with the emigrants who belonged to the Quraysh, a separate blood kinship group. From now on, this new political order of society would make a radical distinction between those loyal to Muhammad and those who did not follow him. As a consequence, it fortified Muhammad's position as the highest authority, next to God, of the newly established community and demonstrated the eminent practical sense of purpose with which he established himself as the political leader of the new polity in Medina.

When Muhammad arrived in Medina, he came with the firm conviction of his status as the bearer of a revelation in Arabic that confirmed the revelations "the possessors of the scriptures" had received in their own languages. In this spirit he tried to win over the local Jews by adopting their fast on the day of atonement (*'āshūrā'*), introducing the midday prayer (*al-ṣalāt al-wusṭā*, Q. 2:238) in emulation of Jewish custom, easing the rules of ablutions before prayer, and maintaining the direction (*qibla*) of the ritual prayer (salat) toward Jerusalem. He soon realized, however, that he misjudged their openness to his message when they ridiculed his version of biblical stories due to discrepancies with their own traditional lore. In a religious sense, it was not possible for the Jewish tribes of Medina to welcome an Arab as their promised Messiah or accept Muhammad's claim to be "the seal of the prophets" (*khātam al-nabiyyīn*, Q. 33:40)—a title Mani (216–77), the founder of Manicheanism, had applied to himself—and whose coming Jesus is said to have predicted in the Qur'an under the name of Ahmad (Q. 61:6). Faced with overwhelming rejection from the Jews, Muhammad abruptly reoriented his religion, transforming it into an Arab religion focused on the sanctuary of the Black Stone in Mecca and dismissing the existing Jewish and Christian scriptures as a corruption of their original revealed form. He ordered that the direction of ritual prayer be changed toward the Ka'ba, making Mecca the hub of the true religion (Q. 2:144). He stressed Friday as the day of congregational prayer (Q. 62:9) yet not as a day of rest like the Sabbath because, in his view, God did not rest after his work of creation. Substituting for the fast on *'āshūrā'*, he instituted, following Manichean custom, the lunar month of Ramadan (Q. 2:183–5) as a month of fasting from daybreak until sunset requiring abstention from food, drink, and sexual intercourse during daylight hours. He introduced what was to become an essential element of the Muslim pilgrimage (hajj) by celebrating the day of sacrifice on the tenth day of the month of pilgrimage (Dhu al-Hijja) in Medina, and most of all, he identified Islam as a restoration of the primordial religion of Abraham (*millat Ibrāhīm*). Abraham, neither a Jew nor a Christian, thus became the prototype of the true Muslim and *ḥanīf*, the monotheist who had rejected all pagan polytheism. He now maintained that Abraham, assisted by his son Isma'il, had erected the Ka'ba (Q. 2:127) and celebrated the rites there that Muhammad sought to restore to their original purity.

Distancing himself somewhat from his identity as a prophet called to warn people of an oncoming apocalyptic judgment and to confirm the revelations other groups of people had received in their own languages before him, Muhammad now embraced his new role as legislator and leader of the burgeoning Muslim community. It

now became the duty of his followers to obey God and the Prophet. He pursued his newfound role not only in Medina but also in his relations with the Meccans, who constituted the major challenge he faced outside Medina. With Mecca as the focus of his religious thrust and with the responsibility of providing sustenance for his group of emigrants, Muhammad turned his attention to Mecca and focused the energies of the Arab tribesmen who were accustomed to raiding. His altercations with the Meccans, developing from skirmishes to full-fledged war, were driven by the idea of jihad, the all-out struggle on the path of God that demanded the total devotion of his Muslim followers such that they would go to war against the Quraysh of Mecca.

A new chapter began in the life of Muhammad and that of his community with a sequence of battles with the Meccans. A first instance of war was triggered by a raid made by some of Muhammad's followers on a caravan at the oasis of Nakhla. In it a Meccan was killed during the holy month of Rajab, in which raiding was forbidden by current pre-Islamic custom, and the spoils of his operations were taken to Medina. Emboldened by this success, Muhammad led a group of his Medinan followers in a new raid on a caravan of the Quraysh that was advancing from Syria to Mecca. In their attempt to ambush the caravan at Badr in 624, Muhammad's small contingent was forced to engage an army sent from Mecca to protect the caravan (Q. 3:123); surprisingly, however, they succeeded in routing the superior enemy, whose leader Abu Jahl was slain. Muhammad interpreted his glorious victory as divine confirmation of his religion and believed that angels fought at his side, enabling him to overpower the forces of the mighty commercial hub of Arabia. Islamic historiography upholds this day as a great watershed in the course of Muslim ascendancy as granted by divine assistance. To follow up on his victory, Muhammad not only expelled the Banu Qaynuqa' but, more importantly, sent letters to Bedouin tribes to contract alliances of mutual assistance with them, now recognized as a leader well beyond the confines of Medina. Trying to avenge their losses at Badr, the Meccans equipped an army of 3,000 men and sent them against Muhammad's forces in 625 under the leadership of Abu Sufyan, defeating them decisively at the hill of Uhud outside Medina (Q. 3:118, 121; 33:23). In this battle Muhammad was severely wounded and his uncle Hamza was killed. The Meccans, however, did not follow up on their victory and returned home thinking that they had put the upstart in Medina in his place; for his part, Muhammad expelled the Banu al-Nadir from the town and confiscated their possessions in order to replace the spoils his force had failed to secure in the battle.

Further harassed by Muhammad's raiders and realizing that their assessment of their victory at Uhud was premature, the Meccans assembled a force of Quraysh and tribesmen from the surrounding areas, specified as 10,000 men in the tradition, to advance against Medina in 627. Whether or not this was at the suggestion of a Persian by the name of Salman, Muhammad had a trench (*khandaq*) dug around the unprotected parts of Medina, which caused a long siege to drag on and gave Muhammad time to plot against the besieging force, who eventually lost heart and returned home without ever engaging in open battle. In the aftermath of the "Battle of the Trench," Muhammad felt free to deal harshly with the Banu Qurayza, executing their men and selling their women and children into slavery.

Still intent on bringing Mecca under his control, Muhammad called on a group of his followers in 628 to accompany him on a peaceful pilgrimage (*'umra*) to the Ka'ba in Mecca; in the process he tried to negotiate his way into the town. He encamped with his group at Hudaybiyya and sent 'Uthman b. 'Affan, who was related to the Meccan leadership, ahead to make arrangements for their peaceful passage. When 'Uthman did not return at first, Muhammad had his men swear an oath that they would fight for him to the last. This proved to be unnecessary when the Meccans offered the compromise proposal of a ten-year truce that would allow Muhammad to visit the town for a pilgrimage in the following year. Muhammad accepted this proposal, but his followers were disappointed by this apparent about-face, though history would later call it a stroke of brilliance on Muhammad's part to induce the Meccans to recognize a tribal dissident as an opponent of equal rank.

Muhammad made use of the lull in the struggle with the Meccans to capture the oasis of Khaybar in 628 and constrained its Jewish inhabitants to pay taxes every year. However, the tradition that holds that, in the same year, Muhammad began to send letters to the governor of Alexandria, the ruler of Abyssinia, the Byzantine emperor, and the Persian king, inviting them to adopt Islam, cannot be trusted. More certain is his dispatching of letters to chiefs of Bedouin tribes in different parts of Arabia, demanding that they join the fold of Islam, perform the ritual prayer, and pay the alms tax (zakat) incumbent on every Muslim. In the following year, 629, Muhammad performed the pilgrimage to the Ka'ba as agreed and welcomed Khalid b. al-Walid, later a great general of the Muslim conquests, into Islam. Khalid b. al-Walid proved his mettle soon thereafter in 630 when he subdued the inhabitants of Dumat al-Jandal and forced their leader to come to Medina to sign a treaty with Muhammad. Then in the Battle of 'Aqraba' in 632, Khalid b. al-Walid crushed the apostasy of the tribes after the Prophet's death and defeated Musaylima b. Thumama, the leader of the Banu Hanifa, who inhabited the oasis of Yamama in central Arabia. Musaylima rivaled Muhammad with his claim to be a prophet and to receive revelations from God the Merciful (*al-Raḥmān*). He aspired to be Muhammad's successor after his death, but when both of them met in Medina, the Prophet had him summarily dismissed, refusing to give him "even a splinter of a palm branch."

Using the pretext of a conflict that led to bloodshed between two tribal bands—one affiliated with him, the other with the Quraysh—Muhammad broke the ten-year truce of Hudaybiyya and set out to conquer Mecca at the head of an army of emigrants, helpers, and Bedouin tribesmen. They were met in the field by Abu Sufyan, the leader of the Quraysh, who accepted Muhammad's terms and received lavish gifts for himself and other chiefs of the Quraysh. The town of Mecca was opened to Muhammad's forces, and its

inhabitants nominally adopted Islam en masse; the idols were destroyed and some poets who had ridiculed Muhammad were executed. In 630, then, Muhammad achieved his ultimate victory, the conquest of Mecca, and was able to defeat a remaining hostile alliance of Bedouin tribes from central Arabia at Hunayn, after which the town of Ta'if was opened to him as well. Muhammad sent letters to various tribes, demanding that they adopt Islam and pay tribute, and he received their embassies in Medina. However, there were some signs of inner division among the Muslims, caused by a rival "mosque of dissension" (*masjid al-ḍirār*, Q. 9:108–9) where Muhammad, in his early years at Medina, used to perform a ritual prayer on the Sabbath. In fact, this mosque was the first established in Medina, founded by the exiled Abu ʻAmir, "the monk" (*al-rāhib*), of the clan ʻAmr b. ʻAwf, who lived in the compounds at Quba' in the southern part of the town. The unrest did not prevent Muhammad, however, from setting out in 630 on an expedition to Tabuk on the northern border of Arabia, where he received some petty Christian rulers and Jewish towns into Islam. New converts from tribes all over Arabia formally entered Islam—many out of fear, others more nominally than fervently—in hope of material and political advantages.

It is not fully clear to what extent Muhammad perceived his message to be a local or a universal one. At the beginning of his mission he directed his message primarily toward the people of Mecca (*qawm*), just as the prophets of old spoke to their own people, but he also addressed all of humanity (*al-nās*, *al-ʻālamūn*) without confining his audience to a specific group. The expeditions to Mu'ta and Tabuk across the northern borders of the Arabian Peninsula in the latter years of his career may indicate a shift in his consciousness toward a more universal applicability of his message. In addition, Muhammad sent letters from Medina to numerous Arab tribes in the desert demanding their conversion and received tribal delegations in Medina from all over Arabia in the last years of his life. They pledged their allegiance to his cause, a phase described by the Qur'an as being characterized by "men entering God's religion in throngs" (Q. 110:2). The actual spread of Islam beyond the confines of Arabia, however, did not occur during Muhammad's lifetime but would come about with astonishing rapidity during the age of the Muslim conquests that began shortly after his death. In 631, Muhammad sent Abu Bakr to Mecca to read a declaration of "exemption" (*barā'a*) from the hajj that excluded all pagans from performing it. Then, in 632, at the climax of his career, Muhammad performed his "Farewell Pilgrimage"—referred to in the Qur'an with the words "Today I have perfected your religion" (Q. 5:3)—that reformed some of the pagan rites and became the standard of the pilgrimage until today. On his way back to Medina from the pilgrimage, Muhammad had stopped at the watering place of Ghadir Khumm and, taking ʻAli b. Abi Talib by his hand, apparently signaled him to be his successor as leader of the Muslim community with the cryptic words, "For whomever I am the patron (*mawlā*), ʻAli is also his patron." A few months later, Muhammad died in Medina after a short fever in the lap of his beloved wife ʻA'isha on June 8, 632, a day that according to tradition saw an eclipse of the sun.

Throughout history all factions within Islam have maintained that prophecy, in the sense of the proclamation of a sacred scripture, had come to an end for all times with Muhammad's demise. In political terms, however, an intense struggle for succession began immediately during the preparations for his burial. Abu Bakr, ʻA'isha's father and an early Meccan convert, managed to secure the leadership, backed by the majority of the clans of the Quraysh, who acclaimed him as Muhammad's successor (*khalīfa*, or caliph) at the Portico of the Banu Saʻida. ʻAli, Muhammad's cousin, son-in-law, hero of many battles, and a man of great merits, was pushed aside despite his legitimate claim to being Muhammad's successor as champion of the family of the Prophet (*ahl al-bayt*) and leader of the Banu Hashim. A major bone of contention was that, during Muhammad's career at Medina, his family was assigned a certain religious privilege that entitled Muhammad and his kin to a fifth (*khums*) of the war booty as well as property (*fay'*) that came into possession of the community by means other than war. Upon his accession to leadership, Abu Bakr stripped the family of the Prophet of this entitlement and transferred it to the clans of the Quraysh, thereby solidifying their support for his caliphate (632–34). In this succession struggle lie the roots of the primary Islamic schism between the majority Sunnis and the minority Shiʻis, the party of ʻAli (Shiʻat ʻAli). In its origin, the ultimate issue driving the schism was political and material rather than religious and spiritual; in the history of the ideological development of orthodoxy and heterodoxy in Islam, however, it took on theological dimensions.

Muhammad as a Political Leader

That one man could achieve so much in such a short time is astounding. Muhammad can truly claim the status of one of humanity's greatest founders of religion who made a global impact over more than a millennium and whose cause continues to exert a worldwide attraction today. His message has stood the test of time for more than a thousand years, and his community has grown steadily over the centuries. Except in small corners of the Muslim world, Islam has never receded but rather has always expanded without losing any substantial region to any other religion. Throughout history, conversions from Islam to other religions have been rare and conversions to it plentiful.

Inasmuch as it can be gathered from the sources, Muhammad was a man of average height and sturdy build. He had a prominent forehead, a hooked nose, and black eyes. His hair was long and slightly curled and his beard was full and thick. His charming smile was endearing and his energetic stride difficult to keep pace with. He experienced periods of silence and withdrawal and was at times plunged into deep thought and meditation. He showed great self-control and spoke with clarity, frankness, and precision. He treated people with great friendliness, was fond of children, and was apt to break into tears during moments of grief and sadness. He lived in modest circumstances all his life and was known for his courage, impartiality, and resolve. Most of all, Muhammad was a deeply religious man whose strongest characteristic was, without doubt, his deep personal conviction that he was called by God.

This consciousness of a call from God gave him an unshakeable faith in his divine mission. On the strength of this conviction, he persisted in proclaiming his message of an uncompromising monotheism over more than 20 years in the face of all adversities and hostilities, whether in times of disappointment or in moments of success. He was a charismatic personality with enormous leadership qualities, stupendous political gifts, and persuasive diplomatic skills. He commanded intellectual superiority at critical moments of his career and was capable of savvy and executive decision making, even if this required an abrupt reversal of approach. He was a very practical man who found ways to compromise and adapt when presented with unforeseen circumstances. He showed an uncanny ability to maneuver through the labyrinth of tribal bonds, rivalries, and compacts. His strong personality gave him real power to influence others and win them over to his cause. After his death, his followers began to regard him as the model of the ideal Muslim and the perfect Prophet, placing him on the highest pedestal and attributing to him the qualities of impeccability and infallibility as well as the powers of intercession for his community at the Last Judgment.

Contrary to the oft-repeated claim that Muhammad functioned as a religious reformer and prophet in Mecca and became a political leader and statesman only in Medina, his qualities of political leadership were already evident during his Meccan days. From the beginning of his preaching in Mecca, Muhammad showed great political skills in building a network of followers woven together from family relations, young men belonging to influential clans of Meccan society, men nominally related to clans but without close ties to them, and a few older men of considerable social standing. It was essential for him to establish these bonds because, as an orphan, he lacked the natural protective power of the nucleus of his family and faced hostility from his uncles Abu Lahab, a determined opponent, and ‘Abbas, who joined his cause only reluctantly after the conquest of Mecca, while his uncle Abu Talib granted him loyal protection but never accepted Islam.

Muhammad's political acumen may also be seen in the way he strengthened his bonds with the core group of his followers through ties of marriage. Through his marriage with ‘A'isha, Abu Bakr's daughter, and Hafsa, ‘Umar's daughter, he established family bonds that tied him to the two caliphs who would succeed him at the head of his community. His marriages with widows of Companions who died in warfare or women who belonged to the group that early on had migrated to Abyssinia served to strengthen his bonds with his community early in the Medinan phase of his career. Other unions established links with a Jewish woman of the Banu al-Nadir in Medina and a Christian woman given to him by the ruler of Egypt. By giving his own daughters, Ruqayya and Umm Kulthum, to ‘Uthman in marriage, he forged a bond with a representative of an opposing clan who became his third successor. ‘Ali, the fourth caliph who became the leader of the Shi‘a, received Fatima, a third daughter from Muhammad's union with Khadija, as his spouse and also married the daughter of Muhammad's oldest daughter, Zaynab.

Two other political moves of great consequence include his decision to send a group of weaker members of his following in Mecca to Abyssinia and his decision to go with his group of emigrants as dissidents and fugitives on the hijra to Medina. The negotiations he held with the emissaries of the Medinans and the pledges he made with them shortly before the hijra paved the way for his subsequent political leadership in Medina. The draft of his first legal document soon after his arrival in Medina shows his sharp political insight into the new circumstances he and his followers faced in the new urban environment. It constituted the foundation of the social unity of the community established by Muhammad, integrated the Meccan immigrants with the Medinan helpers, and provided clauses of security for Jewish believers. With regard to military planning and strategy, Muhammad's political gifts may be seen in the way in which he calmly conducted the Battle of Badr, decided on an innovative form of defense at the "War of the Trench," and pragmatically reversed his position to arrive at a solution at the truce of Hudaybiyya. In the years after the conquest of Mecca, he exhibited shrewd political instincts in drafting the many treatises he concluded and in exacting tribute from the inhabitants of a number of oases, such as those with the people of Dumat al-Jandal in 630 and the Christians of Najran in northern Yemen in 631. In these later years of his activity he also forged alliances of mutual assistance and established ties of political dependence with many Arab tribesmen by sending a large number of delegations all over Arabia that served to tie them to his personal political authority. In all these political actions, Muhammad was led by a sense of flexible and adaptable pragmatism rather than by preset principles of political theory and may thus be considered a genius in the field of applied political practice.

See also Abu Bakr (ca. 573–634); ‘Ali b. Abi Talib (ca. 599–661); community; God; jihad; pilgrimage; prophecy; Qur'an; Quraysh; ‘Umar b. al-Khattab (ca. 580–644); ‘Uthman b. ‘Affan (ca. 579–656)

Further Reading

Tor Andrae, *Mohammed, the Man and His Faith*, 1936; Regis Blachère, *Le problème de Mahomet*, 1952; Frans Buhl, *Das Leben Mohammeds*, 1934; Alfred Guillaume, *The Life of Muhammad*, 1955; Harald Motzki, *The Biography of Muhammad: The Issue of the Sources*, 2000; Rudi Paret, *Muhammad und der Koran*, 1957; Maxime Rodinson, *Muhammad*, 1980; Uri Rubin, *The Eye of the Beholder*, 1995; William Montgomery Watt, *Muhammad at Mecca*, 1953; Idem, *Muhammad at Medina*, 1956.

GERHARD BOWERING

Muhammad, Elijah (1897–1975)

Before joining the great migration of African Americans to the northern United States in the 1920s, Elijah Poole witnessed the worst of the American South's racism, including poverty, Jim Crow

laws, and lynchings. Along with his fellow migrants, he discovered that racism was still a problem in the North, including his new home of Detroit, Michigan. His acute sensitivity to racism drew him to Wali Fard Muhammad's uniquely racial formulation of Islam. When Poole, renamed Elijah Muhammad, assumed the leadership of Fard Muhammad's Nation of Islam after the latter's disappearance in 1934, the racial problems of the United States completely infused the new leader's political thought and his understanding of Islam.

According to the teachings of Fard Muhammad that Elijah Muhammad developed over four decades, the original humanity was black. Some 6,600 years ago, one of their number, the diabolical genius named Mr. Yakub, set up a 600-year eugenics program to breed the evil white race. It was prophesied that this race would rule the world for 6,000 years. Although their evil ways were held in check for 1,000 years by the coming of the Prophet Muhammad, eventually they escaped the land of their banishment, Europe, and conquered and pillaged the rest of the nonwhite world. The greatest evil that the whites perpetrated was to capture Africans and enslave them in the Americas. In so doing, they robbed these blacks of their identities, including their natural language (Arabic) and their innate religion (Islam). They remained "lost" for 400 years under the white devil until Allah came in the person of Fard Muhammad to rescue this "Lost-Found Nation of Islam."

Given that his movement was conceived of as a nation, Elijah Muhammad had a fairly active political agenda. His political thought can be summarized by the slogan "Do for self." For him, this meant complete independence from whites: socially, religiously, economically, politically, and territorially. For example, blacks were not to befriend, much less intermarry with, their enemy. Christianity was a creation of whites to enslave blacks by teaching them to wait for justice in the hereafter and to worship a "white, blue-eyed" god. Instead, they should follow their innate religion, Islam. His economic program included Nation of Islam–owned farms, grocery stores, and restaurants. Elijah Muhammad taught his followers that the American government served only the interests of the whites, and it actively sought to control and destroy nonwhites. So he and his followers refused to vote or fight in its wars. Elijah Muhammad also demanded that the American government make reparations for slavery by giving African Americans a number of contiguous states within the continental United States. This was not just segregation but complete separation.

While Elijah Muhammad's "do for self" agenda was in some respects politically active, in other respects, he can be seen as advocating political quietism. His followers were told not to vote, because to participate in the political process was to be an "Uncle Tom." He saw the quest for civil rights and integration led by Martin Luther King Jr. (1929–68) as not only pointless but also dangerous. Despite his creation of the Fruit of Islam, a group of Nation of Islam's zealous young males trained in combat for self-defense, Elijah Muhammad repeatedly forbade the use of violence and the carrying of arms. Malcolm X (1925–65) became particularly frustrated by this lack of direct political action. Yet Elijah Muhammad maintained that the destruction of white society and its political structures would not come from him or through his followers' actions (violent or otherwise). The apocalyptic battle that would destroy white rule would be fought by Allah himself. Elijah Muhammad's duty was to prepare his followers to be independent and to separate them from whites lest they be destroyed by Allah along with whites.

Elijah Muhammad's movement was quickly reformed after his death in 1975. Under the leadership of his youngest legitimate son Warith Deen Mohammed (1933–2008), his vision of Islam and his racial political agenda were abandoned in favor of a more traditionally Sunni formulation. Nevertheless, Elijah Muhammad was enormously influential among African Americans. Long before slogans such as "black pride" and "black power" came into vogue, he not only advocated them but also effectively put them into practice.

See also Malcolm X (1925–65); Mohammed, W. D. (1933–2008); Nation of Islam; slavery

Further Reading

Herbert Berg, *Elijah Muhammad and Islam*, 2008; Claude Andrew Clegg III, *An Original Man: The Life and Times of Elijah Muhammad*, 1997; Elijah Muhammad, *Message to the Blackman in America*, 1965 (repr. 1992)

HERBERT BERG

Muhammad 'Ali (1769–1849)

Muhammad 'Ali, or more formally Muhammad 'Ali Pasha (Mehmed Ali), was an energetic and ambitious Ottoman governor of Egypt from 1805 to 1848. During his long career, he augmented Egypt's wealth, introduced long-lasting changes to its society, and embarked on an expansionist policy that gravely threatened the Ottoman Empire. Due to European opposition, however, the mini-empire he had founded had to be dismantled; in exchange, the Ottoman sultan granted him hereditary rule of Egypt.

Born in 1769 in the Macedonian town of Kavala, Muhammad 'Ali was dabbling in the tobacco trade when, in 1801, he joined an irregular military force that the Ottoman sultan dispatched to Egypt to evict the French army that had occupied the country three years earlier. Following the French evacuation in 1801, Muhammad 'Ali seized effective control of Cairo and forced the sultan in Istanbul to appoint him officially as governor of Egypt with the title of pasha in 1805.

Muhammad 'Ali moved fast to consolidate his control over Egypt by inviting many friends and relatives to settle in his new country

and appointing them in key positions within the provinces. Next, he moved to curtail the power of the merchants and the 'ulama' (religious scholars) by forcing some into exile and confiscating the property of others. He also put some of his opponents under house arrest. His decisive consolidation of power came in March 1811, when he invited rival warlords, Mamluks, to his citadel and had them massacred.

Gradually, Muhammad 'Ali imposed a monopoly over the sale of a large number of locally produced agricultural commodities. He then entered into negotiations with European merchants who had to deal with him and him alone if they wanted to trade with Egypt. Furthermore, throughout his second decade in power, he undertook a complete overhaul of the agricultural sector: he raised new taxes, conducted a thorough land survey, and ordered huge infrastructural projects the scale of which had not been seen in Egypt for centuries.

Aware of Istanbul's desire to dislodge him from power in Egypt, he attempted to raise troops from the Sudan in 1818. When these attempts proved unsuccessful, he started conscripting peasants from the Egyptian countryside in 1820 to 1821 and quickly appointed European officers to train the peasant soldiers. Conscription waves spread throughout the country, and within ten years the army reached the impressive figure of 130,000 troops. Numerous institutions were founded to supply this army with all its needs. Schools for infantry, cavalry, and artillery were opened to train army officers. These were followed by schools for metallurgy and agriculture. A number of "manufactories" were also founded to supply the army with uniforms, footwear, headgear, guns, and ammunition. A large educational hospital was opened that trained doctors and surgeons needed for the different regiments. A printing machine that had been founded in 1820 started printing military and medical books.

Using these well-trained troops, Muhammad 'Ali grudgingly lent a helping hand to the sultan in his fight against his Greek subjects who had broken out in a nationalist revolt in 1820. After initial successes that his army had achieved against the Greek rebels, a naval force of the British, French, and Russian navies sank the combined Egyptian-Ottoman fleet in Navarino Bay in October 1827.

Following the Greek debacle, the pasha resolved not to get embroiled in the sultan's struggles. In 1831, he even invaded Syria to establish a buffer area between his power base in Egypt and the sultan's in Anatolia. His troops faced ineffective resistance and soon crossed into Anatolia and gravely threatened Istanbul itself. Alarmed at his vassal's surprise advance, the Ottoman sultan sought help from Britain, and when this did not materialize, he turned to the Russians, who were only too eager to interfere in Ottoman affairs. In time, the British saw the pasha's bid for independence and expansionist policies as undermining the peace in Europe and seriously threatening their interests in Asia. In 1840, they convened a European conference in London that forced the pasha to withdraw from Syria, southern Anatolia, Crete, and Arabia. Finally, in 1841, the Ottoman sultan further limited Muhammad 'Ali's power by issuing a rescript ordering him to reduce the size of his army, but in return the sultan bestowed on him the hereditary rule of Egypt and the Sudan.

Said to be illiterate till the age of 40, Muhammad 'Ali was nonetheless a well-read man. He was in the habit of having his advisors read to him history books as well as European newspapers. He was a keen observer of the contemporary European scene, and despite not having ambassadors in any European capital, he was fairly well informed of the political situation in London, Paris, and St. Petersburg. Besides military training manuals and medical textbooks, the famous printing house he founded in Bulaq printed many Turkish and Arabic translations of European historical books and political biographies, most notably of Catherine the Great and Napoleon Bonaparte. He was also aware of Machiavelli's *The Prince*, although he was not keen on having it published, saying that it had nothing to teach him; he preferred, instead, to read Ibn Khaldun's *Muqaddima* (Prolegomena). Muhammad 'Ali was also curious to learn about Egypt's history and was particularly intrigued by the Pharaonic and the Ptolemaic periods, less so by the Mamluk and Ottoman ones. Above all, he was intimately familiar with Ottoman history and always looked at Istanbul to learn how to run his prized province. Specifically, he was keen to learn how the Ottomans attempted to use law (*qānūn*) in order to reinforce their rule by controlling members of the elite and by trading justice to the commoners in exchange for their production of the necessary surplus.

Dubbed as the "Founder of Modern Egypt," Muhammad 'Ali is often depicted as a strong man who stood up against Western imperialism. Having had imperial designs himself, however, it is probably more correct to see his legacy as changing Egypt's relationship with the Ottoman Empire, posing the gravest threat that the Ottoman Empire had faced in its history, instituting long-lasting socioeconomic changes in Egypt, and establishing a dynasty that ruled over Egypt for a hundred years.

See also colonialism; Egypt; Ottomans (1299–1924)

Further Reading

Henry Dodwell, *The Founder of Modern Egypt: A Study of Muhammed Ali*, 1931; Khaled Fahmy, *All the Pasha's Men: Mehmed Ali, His Army and the Making of Modern Egypt*, 1997; Idem, *Mehmed Ali: From Ottoman Governor to Ruler of Egypt*, 2009; Shafik Ghorbal, *The Beginnings of the Egyptian Question and the Rise of Mehemet Ali*, 1828; F. Robert Hunter, *Egypt under the Khedives, 1805–1978: From Household Government to Modern Bureaucracy*, 1984; Fred Lawson, *The Social Origins of Egyptian Expansionism During the Muhammad 'Ali Period*, 1992; Afaf Lutfi al-Sayyid Marsot, *Egypt in the Reign of Muhammed Ali*, 1984; Helen Rivlin, *The Agricultural Policy of Muhammad 'Ali in Egypt*, 1961; Judith Tucker, *Women in Nineteenth-Century Egypt*, 1985.

KHALED FAHMY

mujahidin. *See* jihad

Mulla Sadra (ca. 1572–1640)

Sadr al-Din al-Shirazi, commonly known as Mulla Sadra, is one of the most revered philosophers in Islam. Born Muhammad b. Ibrahim Qawami al-Shirazi to a wealthy family in Shiraz, southern Iran, on the return journey from his sixth pilgrimage to Mecca, he died in Basra, where his burial place was known until recent times.

Sadra's oeuvre does not include a treatise on political philosophy. A systematic examination of the principles of political philosophy is absent in his writings, and, contrary to classical political philosophy, he does not treat the concept "city" (*madīna*), or the "ideal city" (*al-madīna al-fāḍila*), as a subject of inquiry. There is no discussion of what constitutes a good or bad city, and there is neither a systematic examination of what justice is nor a theoretical concern with types of rule. Classical concepts such as "governance" (*siyāsa*), "political rule" (*ḥukūma*), and "management" (*tadbīr*) are never discussed in relation to the "virtuous city" (*al-madīna al-fāḍila*), while his discussion of the concept of "rule" relates to "divine management" (*tadbīr-i ilāhī*) generally and never to any specified political process, actual or theoretical. This means that Sadra's works can be described neither as political philosophy (*al-siyāsa al-madaniyya*) nor as practical philosophy (*al-falsafa al-'amaliyya*) in the classical sense. This does not mean that his new holistic philosophical system, "Metaphysical Philosophy" (*al-Ḥikma al-Muta'āliya*), is devoid of ideas and doctrines on political philosophy or theory; rather, it means that we have to glean his thoughts on the subject from different parts of his work.

Sadra's political thoughts focus on three themes: the authority and legitimacy of the learned (*'ālim*) philosopher-sage (*ḥakīm*), the source of inspirational knowledge that renews the foundations of science in every age, and governance by Shi'i imams who possess infallibility (*'iṣma*) and impart unrestricted knowledge to the most learned (*a'lam*). In all, the emphasis is on legitimizing the structure of Shi'i governance and establishing the "most learned" figure as the "source of imitation" (*marja' al-taqlīd*), an emerging Shi'i political institution later designated "ayatollah" (hierophant, lit. "Sign of God"). These themes are found in the classical theories of Farabi (d. 950) and Ibn Sina (d. 1037) and in the political doctrine of Shihab al-Din Yahya al-Suhrawardi (d. 1191).

The classical theory has a twofold core. First, it comprised an epistemology based on Aristotelian theories of intellectual knowledge according to which any person devoted to philosophical inquiry may gain access to objective knowledge and achieve union with the Active Intellect (*'aql fa''āl*), which acts as the giver of forms (*wāhib al-ṣuwar*) in Aristotelian epistemology, unrestricted by God's will. This theory of knowledge, later refined and reformulated by Ibn Sina into a unified theory of prophecy, is one of the most significant and enduring components of Islamic political philosophy. The second part of the theory is a practical philosophy that fuses the theories of intellectual knowledge in Aristotle's *De Anima* III and *Metaphysics* XII with the ideals of the perfect state in Plato's *Republic*, framed by the Islamic notion of just rule as the ultimate purpose of philosophy. Farabi had redefined Greek political philosophy in the context of Islamic monotheism and beliefs about prophecy and revelation, positing the ideal political order as one legislated by a prophet-lawgiver and reformed and upheld by the learned ('ulama'). This ensures just rule, a condition necessary for earthly and eternal happiness. Following Farabi's most popular work, *The Ideas of the Inhabitants of the Virtuous City*, Sadra mentions the doctrine of just rule and encourages philosophical discourse on prophecy and laws that affect the beliefs and practices of the Muslim community.

These form the classical components of Sadra's views and later help define the Shi'i political doctrine that invokes the "virtuous city" to describe just rule by the divinely inspired philosopher-ruler, who is progressively referred to as the "jurist-guardian" (*al-walī al-faqīh*).

The next components, perhaps the most essential of Sadra's political views, are founded on Suhrawardi's doctrine in which the political system is deemed meaningful if, and only if, a state, nation, or city embodies and in some *actual* manner manifests a divine dimension in its politics. According to Suhrawardi's illuminationist (*ishrāqī*) theory, legitimate rule is associated with a wholly other source, the "unseen realm" (*al-'ālam al-ghayb*), and is not shaped or initiated by the "sensed realm" (*al-'ālam al-maḥsūs*) or the "seen realm" (*al-'ālam al-shahāda*)—that is, the corporeal. Rulers in command of temporal rule, be they kings, sages, philosophers, or persons in a state of occultation, must possess and exhibit a sign of divine inspiration that displays a real relation with the "unseen" source of authority. Such rulers serve as a link between the world of sense perception and pure being and light from which all things emanate, political authority included. A ruler gains legitimacy by God's command (*al-ḥākim bi amr allāh*). This means that governance or *ḥukūma* can be justified if and only if it is through connection with the divine, or by the command (*amr*) of God.

The synthesis of earlier political philosophies with Illuminationist thought is revealed in Sadra's views, which combine the following elements: the theory of prophethood and the Islamic view of the miraculous powers of prophets (*anbiyā'*) and saints (*awliyā'*); the ancient Iranian concepts of royal "glory" (*kharra-yi kīyānī*), a sign of authority granted to legitimate rulers, and divine glory, which, as related by Suhrawardi, may be gained by *any* person who obtains wisdom (*ḥikma*) and in whom it will visibly radiate as a divine light (*farra-i izādī*); and an Islamic belief in saints and mystics who exercise awe-inspiring occult powers.

To conclude, Sadra's political doctrine may be summarized as follows: Any member of the 'ulama' who persists in the pursuit of

knowledge, preoccupies himself with the Divine Word, and immerses himself in remembering the attributes of the Shiʻi imams may gain unrestricted intellectual knowledge. Combining what is bestowed in the conjunction of the Active Intellect and acquired intellect (*ʻaql mustafād*) with intuitive inspirational knowledge, such a person acquires legitimate authority to rule. Authority will manifest itself upon the ruler as a radiating light that is visible to his subjects, who will consequently obey his commands as though issued by an infallible imam. The unrestricted knowledge associated with such a figure is also essential for the renewal and upholding of the principles of science, which in turn ensure enduring justice in the state.

See also al-Farabi, Abu Nasr (ca. 878–950); Ibn Sina, Abu ʻAli (ca. 980–1037); philosophy

Further Reading

Jalal al-Din Ashtiyani, *Sharh-i Hal wa-Araʼ-i Falsafi-yi Mulla Sadra*, 1981; Fazlur Rahman, *The Philosophy of Mullā Ṣadrā*, 1975; Hossein Ziai, "Source and Nature of Authority: A Study of Suhrawardī's Illuminationist Political Doctrine," in *The Political Aspects of Islamic Philosophy*, edited by Charles Butterworth, 1992.

HOSSEIN ZIAI

Mulla ʻUmar (b. 1959)

Mulla Muhammad ʻUmar is supreme leader of the Taliban, a disciplined and highly pious organization of madrasa (Muslim school) graduates emerging from the expansion of madrasa education in Pakistan during the 1960s that came to play a significant political role in Afghanistan since the 1990s. He has made few details of his life public, which serves to cultivate his spiritual stature as "Commander of the Faithful" (*amīr al-muʼminīn*), a title first held by ʻUmar b. al-Khattab (second caliphal successor to the Prophet Muhammad), and also to conceal his association with Pakistan's Inter-Services Intelligence (ISI). He was born, it is believed, in 1959 in Nodeh, a village in the province of Kandahar (another alleged birthplace is Singesar in the same province), and lived in Tarin Kowt in the province of Uruzgan for a period during the Soviet occupation of Afghanistan (1979–89). He is Pashtun, belonging to the Hotak clan of the Ghilzai tribe, and was raised in very simple circumstances. He apparently received enough of a madrasa education to be considered a religious authority, hence the title "mulla." Although he has no real depth as a religious scholar, his followers believe he is divinely sent, partly, it is claimed, because he receives guidance through dreams. He allegedly knows Arabic and was devoted to the teachings of ʻAbdallah ʻAzzam (d. 1989), a Palestinian figure who became the leader and ideological architect of the jihad against the Soviets and also the erstwhile mentor of Osama bin Laden. Mulla ʻUmar is highly reclusive and has not met with foreign journalists; even his physical features are not fully known, only that he is relatively tall and is missing one eye as a result of a wound suffered while fighting the Soviets in the 1980s.

After the fall of Soviet-installed President Najibullah Ahmadzai in 1992, Mulla ʻUmar founded a madrasa in Singesar. He was useful to the ISI in keeping the border roads clear, and he began to consolidate his power as a military leader. He recruited students from madrasas in Afghanistan and Pakistan, some of whom had been trained at ISI camps, for armed campaigns against the corruption and brutalities of warlords exploiting a post-Soviet society that had descended into chaos and civil disorder. Pursuing the goal of social order through a strict implementation of shariʻa, he was able to take control of the province of Kandahar in 1994 and then Herat in 1995. Kabul fell to his forces in 1996, at which point foreign radical groups that had conducted jihad against the Soviets began to return to Afghanistan, a development that would distort the national focus of the Taliban and drag it into the arena of global jihadism.

With power in the hands of the Taliban, Mulla ʻUmar became head of the Supreme Council, governing Afghanistan from September 1996 until November 2001. Taliban rule over the nation, known since October 1997 as the Islamic Emirate of Afghanistan, was recognized by Saudi Arabia, Pakistan, and the United Arab Emirates. Already in April 1996, Mulla ʻUmar had received the title of Commander of the Faithful, elected to the position by a large assembly of religious scholars from Pakistan, Iran, and Afghanistan, who symbolically robed him in a cloak alleged to have belonged to the Prophet Muhammad. Pious and ascetic, he did not personally head the government in Kabul but remained in Kandahar, apparently preferring the familiarity of his ancestral homelands to the urban life of the capital. He was, however, the ultimate authority of the political structure and issued decrees on a range of issues from local concerns to global jihad. Under his rule, the government pursued a strict and highly visible application of shariʻa: women were denied a public presence and were forbidden to pursue educational and professional opportunity; men were required to grow their beards to a specified length; adulterers were stoned to death; homosexuals were executed by being crushed under brick walls; murderers were executed by members of the victim's family; and the hands of thieves were amputated. He banned conversion from Islam upon pain of death and infamously ordered the destruction of the Buddha statues of Bamiyan in March 2001. In May 2001 he issued a decree requiring Hindus to wear a yellow patch, and in August 2001 he ordered the arrest of foreign nationals working for the nongovernmental organization Shelter Now International on charges of proselytism.

The religious prestige enjoyed by Mulla ʻUmar comes not from being recognized as a leading scholar of shariʻa but from a combination of spiritual aura and combat success. He was employed at one time as a madrasa teacher in Quetta, Pakistan, and then as a prayer leader in a mosque in Karachi, where he reportedly met Bin

Laden for the first time. The nature of the relationship between the two men, which developed during their time fighting the Soviets, is not clear. It is said that they cemented their alliance through marriage, but this is not confirmed. Mulla 'Umar did allow Bin Laden and his organization, al-Qaeda, to use Afghanistan as a base from which to promote its global jihadism, and he did defend Bin Laden against charges of orchestrating the 9/11 attacks, but their relationship was apparently marked by occasional tension. It is said that Mulla 'Umar denied Bin Laden authority that could be used to undermine him and also that some Taliban saw al-Qaeda as a distraction from their religious and political goals for Afghanistan. However, in general, the Taliban became more hostile to the West after the United States imposed sanctions on their regime in 1999, pushing them to align more closely with the jihadist ideology of al-Qaeda. Because of their association with al-Qaeda, the Taliban regime, upon which popular hopes for social order had been initially placed, quickly fell to U.S. attacks beginning in October 2001. However, while the Taliban was destroyed as a regime, its members quickly regrouped as a fighting force with Pakistani support, and Mulla 'Umar continued to act as a symbol of allegiance for a movement that effectively stymied international efforts to rebuild the nation and that even regained control of parts of the country. On the run since the fall of his government and wanted by the FBI for harboring al-Qaeda militants, Mulla 'Umar continued to issue statements on varied topics through different media. In April 2004, for example, he is said to have told a Pakistani journalist in a telephone interview that Bin Laden was alive and that the Taliban were in pursuit of U.S. soldiers. In June 2006 he saluted the martyrdom of Abu Mus'ab al-Zarqawi, the leader of al-Qaeda in Iraq, who had recently been assassinated by U.S. forces. In December 2006 he expressed confidence that foreign forces would be driven from Afghanistan. In April 2007 he called for more suicide attacks. Moreover, his prestige as leader of the Taliban seemed only to grow with the emergence of a Pakistani version of the Taliban. For example, Baitullah Mehsud (d. 2009), former leader of the Pakistani Taliban, swore allegiance to Mulla 'Umar.

As a result of the survival of the Taliban on both sides of the border, some have begun to consider Mulla 'Umar as part of the solution for restoring stability to Afghanistan. After a September 2007 suicide bombing in Kabul, for example, Hamid Karzai, the president of Afghanistan, offered to talk with the "esteemed" Mulla 'Umar. In January 2010 a retired ISI officer and graduate of Fort Bragg, Sultan Tarar, claimed that Mulla 'Umar, whom he once trained, was ready to turn against al-Qaeda, opening the door to national unity—that is, since Mulla 'Umar alone could end the legitimacy of al-Qaeda in the region, his role in the resolution of the national crisis would be vital. However, his willingness to work with the government came with conditions that were unlikely to be fulfilled—namely, the evacuation of foreign forces from the country and the refusal of a U.S. role in the process of restoring national unity.

See also Afghanistan; Pakistan; al-Qaeda; Taliban

Further Reading

Gilles Dorronsoro, *Revolution Unending: Afghanistan 1979 to the Present*, 2005; William Maley, *The Afghanistan Wars*, 2009.

PAUL L. HECK

Murji'is

The Murji'is were a religiopolitical group that emerged in Kufa in the second century of Islam and later spread to Khurasan. They formulated a unique position on the moral standing of the caliphs involved in the First Islamic Civil War, and in later times they were renowned for a theological position that measured faith by belief rather than acts. Heresiographers treat the latter as the most fundamental dogma of the Murji'is, giving less attention to their views on the caliphs.

The basic contention of the Murji'is was that human beings should not judge the caliphs who participated in the civil war, 'Uthman b. 'Affan and 'Ali b. Abi Talib; rather, that judgment should be deferred to God. In contrast, the two caliphs who ruled before the civil war, Abu Bakr and 'Umar b. al-Khattab, deserved praise and emulation, while anyone was free to take a stance on the (iniquitous) status of the Umayyad caliphs. The Murji'is argued for the suspension of judgment with respect to 'Uthman and 'Ali on the basis of the Qur'anic expression "and others are deferred to God's commandment" (9:106). By advocating this position, the Murji'is distanced themselves from Shi'is, who repudiated the caliphs preceding 'Ali (including 'Uthman); the 'Uthmanis, who repudiated 'Ali (the official Umayyad position); and the Kharijis, who denied the legitimacy of all the participants as well as the Umayyad caliphs. The Murji'is position was an attempt to avoid extreme partisanship on the issue of the caliphate and to advocate a return to unity among Muslims.

The Murji'is formulated the suspension of judgment doctrine on the basis of a unique epistemological principle: that something can be judged only on the basis of personal observation or unanimous testimony. Because the First Islamic Civil War was a disputed event that happened before their time, the Murji'is declined to pronounce on the rightness or wrongness of 'Uthman's and 'Ali's actions. The Murji'is accepted Abu Bakr and 'Umar as Rightly Guided Caliphs, however, because the members of the community were in agreement on this point.

The main opponents of the Murji'is were the Kharijis, who attempted to undermine the Murji'i position by showing that their epistemological position resulted in a rejection of tradition. The Kharijis argued that if the status of the Muslims who fought in the First Islamic Civil War was so uncertain, then the status of some of the Companions of Muhammad—the founders of tradition—was also uncertain. If the status of even the Companions was uncertain, then the Murji'is had lost their connection with God's messenger.

See also caliph, caliphate; civil war; Ibadis; Kharijis; Mu'tazilis; Shi'ism; theology

Further Reading

Michael Cook, *Early Muslim Dogma: A Source-Critical Study*, 1981; Patricia Crone and Fritz Zimmermann, *The Epistle of Salim Ibn Dhakwan*, 2001; Wilferd Madelung, "The Murji'a and Sunnite Traditionalism," in *Religious Trends in Early Islamic Iran*, 1988.

TARIQ JAFFER

Muslim Brotherhood

The Society of the Muslim Brothers (al-Ikhwan al-Muslimun) is a political movement whose ideology is based in Islamic principles. It was one of the most significant political opposition movements in the second part of the 20th century. Founded in Egypt in 1928 by Hasan al-Banna (1906–49), it produced offshoots elsewhere in the Middle East, such as in Palestine, Syria, Jordan, and Sudan, and influenced the ideologies of Islamist movements in Northern Africa.

In the 1940s, the Egyptian Muslim Brotherhood became the first mass grassroots political organization in the modern Middle East. Under the leadership of Banna, it sought recruits from the educated middle class and from the lower classes—who thereby gained a nonelitist access to politics—in contrast to the recruitment of politicians from higher socioeconomic backgrounds through patronage and clientele networks. This style of recruitment partially explains the extraordinary growth of the movement, in combination with Banna's focus on moral and religious education as well as on a practical vision of Islam reflected in active preaching and in the construction of schools and mosques. This vision brought to life many of the principles underlying reformist intellectual trends such as those inspired by Muhammad 'Abduh (1849–1905) and Rashid Rida (1865–1935). The Muslim Brotherhood has authoritarian forms of internal governance as well as administrative structures that resemble those of a political party. Banna was not in favor of parliamentary partisan life as it played out in Egypt between the two World Wars, however, and it was not until the end of the 20th century that the Egyptian Muslim Brotherhood and some of its offshoots located elsewhere attempted to become legal political parties.

The Muslim Brotherhood's history is marked by internal conflicts as well as by tempestuous relations with local regimes. A secret armed wing had existed since the end of the 1930s with the intention of fighting against British occupation, and its activities created tensions with the Egyptian government in the second half of the 1940s, leading to the assassination of Banna in 1949. The movement has often been repressed, which gave it its great martyrs, such as Banna himself. In particular, its harsh repression at the hands of Gamal Abdel Nasser's government in Egypt after a short alliance between the Muslim Brotherhood and the Free Officers' regime explains the radicalization of some of its members, as illustrated by the ideology of Sayyid Qutb (1906–66). Influenced by the Pakistani thinker Mawdudi (1903–79), Qutb insisted on political sovereignty (*ḥākimiyya*) as belonging exclusively to God and argued that it must not be usurped by the tyrant (*ṭāghūt*) presiding over the "societies of ignorance" (*jāhiliyya*). In Qutb's ideal polity, political power is not the result of human preferences: the political sovereign does not derive his power from God, but it is rather the law of God that is sovereign.

The more mainstream trend within the Muslim Brotherhood did not approve of the revolutionary appeal of such a doctrine. Although its members claim that the regimes governing their countries are not fully Islamic, they have preferred to compromise with them and have adopted a reformist stance. On the other hand, since the 1970s, some groups calling for immediate revolutionary action against "impious" regimes, such as al-Jihad, the group responsible for the assassination of the Egyptian president Anwar Sadat, were inspired by Qutb's doctrine, which they radicalized, and their strategy has been clearly denounced by the Muslim Brotherhood.

The mainstream Muslim Brotherhood does not have a homogeneous theology nor political ideology. Early on, the Muslim Brotherhood criticized the official religious institutions and their 'ulama' for neglecting their duty as guardians of Islam. However, leading members of the Muslim Brotherhood were also in contact with reformist 'ulama' from the mosque-university of Azhar, and, like them, sought a religious and political regeneration of their society. Anti-imperialism, the opposition to Christian missionary activism, and more generally the defense of Islam were at the heart of the early ideology of the Muslim Brotherhood, which articulated a strong critique of Western influence on Muslims. Banna blended Egyptian nationalism and Pan-Islamism, and the ambiguity produced by this combination remains important.

The Muslim Brotherhood was also radically opposed to Arabism and particularly to Ba'thism. Conflicts with Ba'thist regimes and political parties have run deep. In the 1950s, especially with Muslim Brotherhood members such as Egyptians Sayyid Qutb and Muhammad al-Ghazali and the Syrian Mustafa Siba'i, the theme of "Islamic socialism" and social justice became significant, reflecting a desire to reduce socioeconomic differences through redistribution of wealth while respecting private property. This reformist trend envisioned the role of the state as a central agency for welfare.

One of the most enduring elements of the Muslim Brotherhood's ideology has been the critique of secularism defined as the separation of religion and politics. Developing the idea that Islam must be a comprehensive way of life, their motto, "Islam is religion and world" (*al-Islām dīn wa-dunyā*), means that Islam must be applied to mundane problems. The political domain is particularly central since they believe that the political system organizing the life of the community must derive from Islam: Islam is "a religion and a

state" (*al-Islām dīn wa-dawla*). For Banna, political power was one of the "roots" of the sacred law, not one of its "branches," going back to the classical notion of *siyāsa shar'iyya* and applying it to the modern state. For the Muslim Brotherhood, the legitimate polity should be founded on Islamic legality. The political vision of Banna, which continues to influence the conception of politics of the Muslim Brotherhood, was the formation of a Muslim public opinion drawn by the principles of shari'a.

The Muslim Brotherhood primarily has focused on legal strategies of the Islamization of institutions and in particular of the state. While it originally showed some reluctance toward party politics, since the 1970s the mainstream Muslim Brotherhood has tried to form legalized parties in order to participate in electoral politics and in government. Whether legalized, as in Jordan and Morocco in the 1990s, or not, as in Egypt, the Muslim Brotherhood has shown a significant ability for electoral mobilization that derives from its denunciation of government corruption and authoritarianism, and more particularly its attention to social needs in domains where the state remains weak (health, education, charitable work). In Jordan and in Sudan, the Muslim Brotherhood governed the state or participated in governments after 1989, and in Morocco it governed at the local level since the end of the 1990s. Its inclusion in party competition and governance made the Muslim Brotherhood's ideologies more accepting of its governments, which it now wants to reform from within, with remarkable convergences between all the Muslim Brotherhood-inspired movements. The Brotherhood tended to see its respective political programs as animated by an "Islamic reference" (*marja'iyya Islāmiyya*) rather than by the desire to implement Islamic law, and it focused on the definition of an Islamic political ethics and citizenship. It also appealed to the expertise of the 'ulama' more than it used to and envisioned the 'ulama' as playing a significant role in policy decisions in its political programs. However, its normalization by the regimes of the Middle East remains a major point of contention among the Brotherhood, the larger public, and the state elite.

See also Azhar University; al-Banna, Hasan (1906–49); Ba'th Party; fundamentalism; Hamas; Mawdudi, Abu al-A'la (1903–79); Nasser, Gamal Abdel (1918–70); revival and reform; Sayyid Qutb (1906–66)

Further Reading

Marion Boulby, *The Muslim Brotherhood and the King of Jordan (1945–1993)*, 1999; Roxanne Euben, *Enemy in the Mirror: Islamic Fundamentalism and the Limits of Modern Rationalism: A Work of Comparative Political Theory*, 1999; Gilles Kepel, *Muslim Extremism in Egypt: Prophet and Pharaoh*, 1985; Brynjar Lia, *The Society of the Muslim Brothers in Egypt: The Rise of an Islamic Mass Movement (1928–1942)*, 1998; Olivier Carré et Gérard Michaud, *Les Frères Musulmans. Egypte et Syrie (1928–1982)*, 1983; Richard P. Mitchell, *The Society of the Muslim Brothers*, 1969; Malika Zeghal, *Islamism in Morocco: Religion, Authoritarianism, and Electoral Politics*, 2008.

MALIKA ZEGHAL

Muslim League

The Muslim League (ML) is the successor of the All-India Muslim League, which was founded in Dhaka on December 30, 1906, during the annual meeting of the Muhammadan Educational Conference under the leadership of Sir Sayyid Ahmad Khan (1817–98), its first honorary president. Following the partition in 1947, the All-India Muslim League was split into two organizations, the Pakistani Muslim League (ML) and the Indian Union Muslim League. The ML was instrumental in the creation of Pakistan as a Muslim state and has remained active in the political life of the subcontinent.

The objectives of the ML, as stated in its first resolution, were threefold: to foster Indian Muslims' loyalty to the British government, to protect and promote the rights of the Muslim minority in India while providing them with an adequate representation, and to prevent the rise of communal tensions between Muslims and Hindus. The ML was created as a reaction to the rising political influence of the Indian National Congress (INC), which was founded in 1885 to promote Indian participation and representation in government under British rule. The INC was perceived by many Muslims as an organization serving the interests of the Hindu majority to the detriment of Muslim Indians. Sayyid Ahmad Khan hoped to counterbalance this trend by providing Indian Muslims with their own representative body while asking them openly not to join the INC.

The ML has its origins in the Aligarh movement led by Sayyid Ahmad Khan since 1857. The movement had multiple stated objectives: to modernize Islam, to improve relations between Muslims and the British, to provide Western education to Indian Muslims, and to involve Indian Muslims more substantially in the administration of the country. The Muhammadan Anglo-Oriental College of Aligarh was established in 1877 to fulfill the educational purposes of the movement and to create politically active Muslim elites. The ML was born out of the first forum of the All-India Muslim Educational Conference held in 1906. Ahmad Khan initiated a movement of self-awakening and identity awareness for the Muslims of India. He formulated the "two-nation theory," known as the Ideology of Pakistan, arguing that Hindus and Muslims are two distinct peoples and nations that may not live in a single state. This theory later became the basis for the partition of India in 1947.

In its early years and under the leadership of Ahmad Khan, the ML adopted a policy of cooperation with the British in order to secure political rights for Muslim Indians. There were also efforts at a rapprochement with the INC. In 1916, Hindu-Muslim unity was symbolized through the signing of the Lucknow Pact, an agreement between the INC and the ML to combine their efforts to pressure the British for self-government. However, this unity was short-lived, and in 1929 Muhammad 'Ali Jinnah (1876–1948), a leader of the ML, proposed the "Fourteen Points" with the aim of protecting the political rights of Muslims. These points, adopted by the ML in 1929, included the creation of an independent Muslim province in

Sindh; the protection of the Muslim majority of Punjab, Bengal, and the North-West Frontier Province; and an adequate share for Muslims in government positions. These constitutional reforms were further promoted by Muhammad Iqbal (1877–1938), who, in his presidential address for the ML in Allahabad in 1930, suggested the idea of an independent state for Muslims in northwest India. Both the INC and the Deobandi 'ulama' (religious scholars) opposed the idea and defended a one-state solution.

In the mid-1930s, the former alliance between the ML and the INC came to a definitive end when the INC refused to admit ML representatives into its cabinets in the provinces. The growing power of the INC provoked suspicion among the ML that the INC would attempt to push for a Hindu agenda. On March 24, 1940, under Jinnah, the ML adopted the Lahore Resolution (commonly known as the Pakistan Resolution), which officially called for an independent Muslim homeland. The Muslim state of Pakistan was eventually established in 1947.

Following the creation of Pakistan, the newly named All-Pakistan Muslim League ruled Pakistan intermittently until the 1958 military coup and again in the 1960s, 1980s, and 1990s. After Jinnah's death in 1948, it suffered from internal splits, financial corruption, and a lack of a long-term political program. The ML has had a significant impact on modern Pakistani politics, however, and on most political parties formed in Pakistan after independence. Its importance is underlined by the fact that a number of political groups have used its name as a source of legitimacy.

See also India; Iqbal, Muhammad (1877–1938); Jinnah, Mohammad 'Ali (1876–1948); nationalism; Pakistan; Sayyid Ahmad Khan (1817–98)

Further Reading

Lal Bahadur, *The Muslim League*, 1954; Ayesha Jalal, *The Sole Spokesman: Jinnah, the Muslim League, and the Demand for Pakistan*, 1994; Sayyid A. S. Pirzada, ed., *Foundations of Pakistan: All-India Muslim League Documents, 1906–1947,* 1970; Matiur Rahman, *From Consultation to Confrontation: A Study of the Muslim League in British Indian Politics, 1906–1912*, 1970.

NASSIMA NEGGAZ

Mu'tazilis

The Mu'tazilis were the followers of a religious movement in early Islam called Mu'tazilism, founded in Basra by Wasil b. 'Ata' (d. 748–49) and his disciples in the late Umayyad period. Mu'tazilism evolved into a significant theological school, politically dominant during the ninth and tenth centuries, before experiencing a steady decline in the following centuries.

The origins of Mu'tazilism are highly controversial. According to some scholars, Mu'tazilism emerged out of a religiopolitical attitude during the First Islamic Civil War (*fitna*), specifically the Battle of the Camel (656) and the Battle of Siffin (657). A group of Muslims abstained from taking sides with 'Ali b. Abi Talib or his opponents and were called Mu'tazilis, from the Arabic *i'tazala*, meaning "to separate from" and "to dissociate oneself from." This historical attitude of "political neutrality" was later translated, on the doctrinal level, into a position of independence regarding the central question of Islamic theology at its beginnings: the status of the Muslim who committed a grave sin. Wasil allegedly was the first to place such a person between the status of the believer and the infidel, the so-called *manzila bayna al-manzilatayn*. A cloth merchant from Basra, he left the circle of his teacher, Hasan al-Basri (d. 728), after disagreeing with the teacher's views. With his disciples, he led a missionary organization spreading the views of the movement through travel and business activities. While other explanations have been suggested concerning the origins of the movement and the meaning of the term *mu'tazila*, this is the most commonly accepted one.

Mu'tazili doctrine is characterized by five principles, defined by Abu al-Hudhayl (d. 841): God's unity (*tawḥīd*), God's justice (*'adl*), divine retribution (*al-wa'd wa al-wa'īd*), the intermediate position concerning the Muslim sinner (*al-manzila bayna al-manzilatayn*), and commanding right and forbidding wrong (*al-amr bi-l-ma'rūf wa-l-nahy 'an al-munkar*). Each one of these principles carries significant doctrinal implications. Because of their understanding of *tawḥīd*, the Mu'tazilis considered God's inessential attributes, but also His speech (the Qur'an), to have been created. The second principle (*'adl*) entails the idea of human free will and responsibility. Because God is infinite justice, humans are the creators of their acts and are capable of distinguishing between good and evil. A fundamental aspect of Mu'tazili creed is the belief that human reason is able to demonstrate the existence of God rationally. Human reason and divine revelation are placed on an equal footing. Due to their rationalist approach and methods, the Mu'tazilis were opposed by the traditionalists who preached a literal reading of the Qur'an and traditions of the Prophet (hadith).

Scholars divide the development of Mu'tazilism into three main phases or periods: an incubation phase (eight century), a second period during which the movement was at its height both intellectually and politically at the Abbasid court (815–50), and finally a third period during which Mu'tazili thought was systematized (several centuries following). Under Wasil, the early Mu'tazilis were predominantly non-Arabs (*mawālī*), particularly Persians, who were not granted the same rights as Muslim Arabs despite their conversion. The movement and its early followers might have reacted to the difference of status between Arabs and *mawālī*. While it was rather politically neutral in its early years, the Mu'tazili movement took part in the 762 revolt led by the Shi'i Muhammad b. 'Abdallah al-Nafs al-Zakiyya against the Abbasid caliph. The failure of the revolt led to harsh persecution of the Mu'tazili movement and years of inactivity. However, Mu'tazilism was soon propelled to success due to the theological interest of the Abbasid

caliphs. While the viziers of Harun al-Rashid (r. 786–802), the Barmakid family, showed a predilection for theological disputes, Caliph Ma'mun (r. 813–33) imposed Mu'tazilism as a state doctrine and started an inquisition (*miḥna*) in 833. The Mu'tazilis, though not the instigators of the policy, provided the state doctrine with intellectual support, notably through the figure of Ahmad b. Abi Du'ad (d. 855).

Several explanations have been offered regarding the Abbasid support for the Mu'tazili doctrine. The Abbasid caliphs, argues Josef van Ess, saw in Mu'tazili rationality and dialectical methodology a potential way to transcend the fierce sectarianism that emerged from the early politico-theological disputes. Another explanation suggests that Mu'tazili political theory, grounded on the principle of the just ruler, justified the overthrow of the Umayyads by the Abbasids. The distinguished Mu'tazili jurist of the time, Abu 'Uthman 'Amr al-Basri (d. 869), known as "al-Jahiz," established that a tyrant imam is to be rebelled against and deposed. This position stands in contradiction to the traditionalists' emphasis on patience toward the imam and preference for stability against chaos. A third group of scholars argues that the Abbasid movement rested upon the early Mu'tazili theology of Wasil.

The *miḥna* continued under the caliphs Mu'tasim (r. 833–42) and Wathiq (r. 842–47) but was abandoned by Mutawakkil (847–61), who favored the traditionists, the scholars of hadith. Although Mu'tazilism was more influential in Iran, it declined in the early 13th century. Mu'tazili theology had a strong impact on Shi'ism, particularly on Zaydism and Twelver Shi'ism.

Mu'tazilism played a significant role in the development of Islamic theology and had a strong impact on the formation of traditionalist orthodoxy. While Mu'tazilism virtually disappeared after the Mongol invasion in the 13th century, it has experienced a comeback today through the work of modern scholars such as Fazlur Rahman or Harun Nasution, often labeled as "neo-Mu'tazilis."

See also Abbasids (750–1258); justice; Ma'mun (786–833); Qur'an; theology

Further Reading

Ann K. S. Lambton, *State and Government in Medieval Islam: An Introduction to the Study of Islamic Political Theory,* 1981; Richard C. Martin, Mark R. Woodward, and Dwi S. Atmaja, *Defenders of Reason in Islam: Mu'tazilism from Medieval School to Modern Symbol,* 1997; Albert Nasri Nader, *Le Systeme Philosophique des Mu'tazila,* 1956; J. A. Nawas, "A Reexamination of Three Current Explanations for al-Ma'mun's Introduction of the Mihna," *International Journal of Middle East Studies* 26, no. 4 (1994); J. A. Nawas, "The Mihna of 218 A.H./833 A.D. Revisited: An Empirical Study," *Journal of the American Oriental Society* 16, no. 4 (1996); Josef van Ess, *The Flowering of Muslim Theology,* 2006.

NASSIMA NEGGAZ

N

Nasser, Gamal Abdel (1918–70)

An Egyptian military commander and president of Egypt (1956–70), Nasser became a heroic figure whose charisma and nationalistic ideals moved the masses for decades and continue to endure in major parts of the Arab world. His political approach was characterized by nationalism, Pan-Arabism, and socialist ideas on how to lead the state and the economy. "Nasserism" is often cited as a political movement combining these ideologies that stands against Western imperialism and colonization and in favor of the emancipation of the Third World. Nasser was one of the founders and leaders of the Non-Aligned Movement, founded in Belgrade in 1961 as an international organization of states that chose not to align themselves with any powerful bloc during the cold war.

Nasser was born on January 15, 1918, into a modest family in Alexandria. His father, who worked as a post-office clerk, was from the village of Bani Murr in Upper Egypt, where Nasser spent part of his childhood. In 1933, he moved to Cairo to complete his secondary education and start a degree in law at Cairo University. The capital was fertile ground for Nasser to get involved in militant activities against both foreign domination and its support by local politicians. After the signing of the Anglo-Egyptian Treaty in 1936, Nasser interrupted his studies and joined the Royal Military Academy, which provided him with an outstanding social ladder. In the army he also met fellow dissident junior officers with whom he created the Free Officers movement in the aftermath of the 1948 Palestinian exodus. The Free Officers was a clandestine revolutionary movement committed to overthrow the monarchy and establish a new regime free of foreign influence.

Egypt's internal political life in the highly tense era of the 1940s and early 1950s provided the Free Officers with an excellent opportunity for political action. The well-known corruption of King Farouk's monarchy, the Arab defeat in Palestine, and the continuing British presence in Egypt all contributed to making change imminent. On July 23, 1952, following a series of anti-British riots during the events of Black Saturday on January 26 of that year, the Free Officers launched a coup d'état that overthrew King Farouk peacefully. The Republic of Egypt was proclaimed on June 18, 1953, with Muhammad Naguib (1901–84) as its first provisional president. After serving as chairman of the Revolutionary Command Council starting in 1954, Nasser was elected president of the young republic by a referendum on June 23, 1956.

Nasser and the Free Officers' political rule was characterized by a set of ideals rather than by a definite political program. Among their long-term goals were the liberation of Egypt from foreign presence and influence, the cleansing of the former autocratic political system and the creation of a modern and democratic one, and the dismantling of the former landowning elite and the establishment of a socialist economy. Internally, political and social reforms were launched to address these goals. The agrarian reform law of September 1952 established a limit of 200 *feddāns* of land per landowner (roughly 207 acres), severely limiting the reach of the powerful landowning families. Several reforms took on the modernization of religious institutions and put them under state control, curtailing significantly the authority and independence of the 'ulama' (religious scholars). Meanwhile, the newly established regime used a religious discourse to legitimize its rule, and the concept of "Islamic socialism" was created as a justification of the religious foundations of the socialist reforms of the state. Azhar University, the main religious-educational institution of Egypt, was thoroughly reformed and modernized; the mosque and the university became officially separated from one another by the reform law of 1961. Externally, Nasser signed an agreement with Britain in 1954 for the gradual withdrawal of the British forces from the Suez Canal. The compromising nature of the agreement led to strong criticism and opposition from the Muslim Brotherhood. Eventually, an assassination attempt on Nasser that same year triggered a severe repression of the Muslim Brotherhood by Nasser after an early alliance with it based on common anti-imperialist goals.

In February 1955, a devastating raid launched by Israel in Gaza made Nasser realize the importance of modernizing the military. After a failed arms agreement with the United States and Britain and the withdrawal of their pledge to finance the construction of a high dam project at Aswan, Nasser signed an arms agreement with Czechoslovakia, then acting as an intermediary for the Soviet Union. Following Egypt's deteriorating relations with the Western powers and its political alliance with the Soviet Union, Nasser announced the nationalization of the Suez Canal on July 26, 1956, a considerable achievement in the country's history. This decision quickly led to an Israeli invasion of Egypt in October 1956, followed by invasions by France and Britain a month later, in what was called the Tripartite Aggression. At that point, external affairs became a priority in Nasser's political agenda.

In *The Philosophy of the Revolution*, which he authored in 1954, Nasser highlighted the strong existing ties between the Arab world and the African continent and put forth the political and moral

responsibility of the Arab countries towards the "Dark Continent," which suffered from the dividing schemes of the "white man." After mentioning the first two circles of unity (Arab and African), Nasser envisioned a third level corresponding to a unified Islamic community, with Mecca as its religiopolitical center hosting an "Islamic-world-parliament."

In 1958, the Nasserist pan-Arab vision saw a concrete realization in the foundation of the United Arab Republic (UAR) encompassing Egypt and Syria. The dream of Arab unity was short-lived, however. In 1961 the UAR was dissolved, and in June 1967, the Arab states suffered a crushing defeat in the Six-Day War. Nasser died of a heart attack on September 28, 1970. The decline of Pan-Arabism saw the rise of Pan-Islamism throughout the Middle East.

See also Arab nationalism; Egypt; Muslim Brotherhood; Pan-Islamism; revolutions; socialism

Further Reading

Raymond William Baker, *Egypt's Uncertain Revolution under Nasser and Sadat*, 1978; Rami Ginat, *Egypt's Incomplete Revolution: Lutfi al-Khalil and Nasser's Socialism in the 1960s*, 1997; Joel Gordon, *Nasser's Blessed Movement: Egypt's Free Officers and the July Revolution*, 1997; Derek Hopwood, *Egypt, Politics and Society 1945–1990*, 1993; Gamal Abdel Nasser, *The Philosophy of the Revolution* [*Falsafat al-Thawra*], 1955; Robert Stephens, *Nasser: A Political Biography*, 1971.

NASSIMA NEGGAZ

nationalism

It is often assumed that an inherent contradiction exists between nationalism and Islam. On the one hand, nationalism is a product of secular Europe, which posits that human society should be organized along the dividing lines of language, kinship, and territoriality. On the other hand, Islam turns a community of believers into a political unit whose single religion should overpower any differences of culture, race, or geography. Nevertheless, the putative contradiction between Islam and nationalism did not prevent the inexorable global diffusion of the national state during the 19th and 20th centuries. Now, in the Islamic world no less than in the West, the national state provides the only viable unit of political organization.

The dramatic success of nationalism in the face of long-standing identities linked to Islam has puzzled scholars since Europe's decolonization of the Middle East, Africa, and Asia in the years following World War II. These debates have involved concerted efforts to identify not just the relationship between Islam and nationalism but also the meaning of nationalism itself. Earlier scholars conventionally understood nationalism as a political doctrine that stated the nation is the natural unit of human society, but this only begs the question of what the nation is and where the nation comes from. More recent work has focused less on nationalism as a set of ideas than on nationalism as a sociological phenomenon. This shift has been accompanied by a broader historiographical move away from a textualist, and often elitist, history-of-ideas approach to a perspective that focuses more squarely on subaltern practices and the popular imagination. Nationalism is no longer seen as a purely intellectual edifice: it is more often considered to be a constructed stage on which particular social performances are played out.

Nationalism as Idea

If nationalism is understood primarily as political ideology, one way to trace its spread from Europe to the Islamic world is to study how the language of "nation" penetrates local vernaculars and how it is absorbed by and eventually naturalized into political discourse. The Islamic world's exposure to modern nationalism effectively began with the French invasion of Egypt in 1798, when Napoleon Bonaparte (1769–1821) addressed the population as *al-umma al-miṣriyya*, a phrase that his learned Orientalist experts thought would adequately convey the intended meaning of the "Egyptian nation." But the word *umma* was more familiar in its Qur'anic context, where it referred to a whole community of believers rather than a delimited geographical body. Indeed, Muslims writing in the early and mid-19th century struggled to make sense of how the European Christians organized themselves politically. Terms such as *ṭā'ifa* (sect, segment), *milla* ([religious] denomination), and even *qabīla* (tribe) were all variously employed to describe the nations of Europe—sometimes in the space of a single text. As Ami Ayalon (1987) points out, the famous work *Takhlis al-Ibriz fi Talkhis Bariz* (*The Extraction of Gold in the Abridgement of Paris*, 1834) written by Egyptian chronicler Rifa'at al-Tahtawi (1801–73) interchangeably uses the words *milla*, *umma*, and *ṭā'ifa* to refer to the French people. Not until the growth of the Arabic printing press and the standardization of modern political terminology did *umma* become the generally accepted equivalent of a European "nation." Even then, the earlier religious connotations of *umma* remained intact, sustaining a certain ambiguity about the basis of European political identity.

Muslim writers in the second half of the 19th century often slipped between traditional religious and contemporary political understandings of nation. This ambiguity was instrumentally useful as Muslims sought to defend against the increasing encroachment of European powers into the Islamic world. Muslims in India and Central Asia called for aid and solidarity from their coreligionists, which inspired Sultan Abdülhamid II (d. 1918) to cast himself as the new caliph. The claim to unite a Muslim community faced with European advances in India, North Africa, and the Caucasus had evident rhetorical appeal. Yet political activists such as Afghani (1838–97) had no qualms about invoking the historical glories of particular peoples to galvanize them into action against the threat of foreign invasion. Elsewhere, Afghani couched his arguments in pan-Islamic terms, demonstrating what might be construed as a blatant disregard for the logical consistency of his overall position.

Nikkie Keddie (1969) offered an alternative position: that Afghani used religion for "protonationalist" purposes. By glorifying the Islamic past, opposing Islamic and Western cultures, and adopting a historicist perspective on civilizational progress, Afghani conceptualized "Islam" within a framework that was essentially nationalist.

In contrast, filtering out "Islamic" from "nationalist" elements was a challenge that equally confronted political nationalists in the mid-20th century. The ideologues of the Ba'th Party elaborated an understanding of the Arab nation that owed much to romantic German notions of nationalism as the organic expression of a vital linguistic and historical community. Yet if the Arabic language was to be the constitutive element of the Arab nation, it was impossible to ignore its sacred status as the language of Qur'anic revelation. As a consequence, even secular Ba'thism was obliged to incorporate the Islamic factor into its political formula. For the Christian Michel 'Aflaq (d. 1989), the genius of Islam was simultaneously the genius of the Arab people; 'Aflaq thought it would be dangerous to detach religion from nationality, as the Europeans had done. For secular Arab nationalists, differentiating between religious and nationalist culture was ill-advised, if not impossible. Both were equally part of the primordial Arab nation.

Nationalism as Political Practice

Once they ascend to the seat of power, political leaders have proved astute at avoiding a decisive choice between religious and nationalist principles. Such ostensible secularists as Syria's Hafiz al-Assad (in power 1970–2000) and Iraq's Saddam Hussein (in power 1973–2003) crushed religious opposition to their rule while donning the outer trappings of piety to appease any concerns about their ungodliness. Islamists have demonstrated a similar political dexterity at reconciling the apparently contradictory logics brought into play by attempting to construct a modern political project according to religious imperatives. This is most clearly demonstrated in the political theory and empirical practice of the Islamic Republic of Iran. Far from representing a return to the pristine principles of Shi'i jurisprudence, the Iranian doctrine of clerical rule enacts a radical departure from existing tradition. As Sami Zubaida (1989) has argued, Ayatollah Khomeini's (1902–89) argument for *wilāyat-i faqīh* (guardianship of the jurist) rests on a preeminently modern and implicitly *nationalist* conceptualization of "the people" as a distinct social entity and, more importantly, a political force. The rhetoric of the revolution owed more to political radicals such as Karl Marx (1818–83) and anticolonial activists such as Frantz Fanon (1925–61) than it did to Shi'i scholars. As the revolution became institutionalized, it increasingly conformed to the framework of the modern national state: the new constitution was modeled on that of the French Republic; the export of the revolution was reconsidered as it threatened to undermine the gains made by the regime; even the ideological basis of *wilāyat-i faqīh* proved flexible when faced with the thorny question of which scholar should succeed Khomeini after his death. While religion provided much of the symbolic content of Iranian politics after the revolution, the overall framework remained that of the modern national state.

A similar process of accommodation with existing national frameworks can be seen across a variety of Islamic movements in the 20th century. The Muslim Brotherhood is perhaps the most widespread of such movements in the Middle East. Founded in 1928, the Brotherhood's emphasis on social renewal and Islamizing the private sphere diverted its energies from working to unify the Islamic world after its dismemberment into separate national states at the hands of the colonial powers. While the Brotherhood did establish branches in a number of Arab states, each branch remained autonomous. There was little attempt to centralize control or to create an alternative to the existing system of national states. As a result, each individual branch developed in response to local, not transnational, conditions. The most notable example of this is the involvement of the Palestine Muslim Brotherhood in the formation of Hamas in 1987, completing the transition into a national(ist) movement. Lebanon's Hizbullah provides another example of how the reality of a particular state works to shape and delimit political programs within a recognizably nationalist political field. Although Hizbullah was initially inspired by the political radicalism of distant Iran in the mid-1980s, during the following decade it underwent a process of "Lebanonization" that witnessed its steady integration into the national political scene. This is not to say that Hizbullah gained unconditional support from all Lebanese as an uncontested representative of the nation, but that Hizbullah operated firmly within the organizational framework and social imaginary of the Lebanese national state.

Nationalism and Modernity

The commensurability between Islamist and nationalist political programs supports the notion that nationalism is more a constructed social phenomenon than it is the offspring of a particular intellectual genealogy. Since the 1980s, several theorists have articulated a "modernist" perspective that proposes that nationalism is the product of a variety of social processes such as urbanization, industrialization, modern educational practices, print capitalism, and innovative methods of social control (e.g., cadastral maps, surveys, and censuses). Ernest Gellner's *Nations and Nationalism* (1983) and Benedict Anderson's *Imagined Communities* (1991) have been influential in this regard. While Gellner, in particular, subscribed to the opinion that Islam was an island of resistance against the tide of nationalism sweeping the world, the necessary association between secularism and nationalism has been hotly disputed by other scholars studying the Middle East. As James Gelvin (1997) argues, "Popular nationalism and Islamism might be viewed as kindred oppositional movements that use a traditionalizing discourse to mobilize their constituents against those forms of cultural and political domination they view as alien." Seen from this angle, nationalism and Islam each act as avatars for anti-imperialism. Yet if contemporary Islamism is simply a particular expression of Third-World nationalism—a local variation on a larger theme of resistance—then the specific discursive configuration of nationalism and religion have little real significance. Accounts of nationalism as a sociological

phenomenon arguably neglect the *content* of nationalism as secondary to nationalism's structural function within the world-historical context.

In the early 21st century, the appearance of al-Qaeda seriously challenged the thesis that Islam and nationalism were on convergent paths. A transnational network apparently operating in the interstitial spaces of an increasingly globalized world, al-Qaeda rejected the modern system of national states and called for the unity of the *umma* to be restored under a new caliphate. But while al-Qaeda projected the image of being a free-floating structure detached from the institutional framework of the state, its achievements were always dependent on a real territorial base (first in Sudan, then in Afghanistan) and real state support (whether directly from Pakistan and Saudi Arabia, or indirectly from the United States). The image of its supposedly cosmopolitan, international membership masked the reality of its dependence on Saudi and Egyptian nationals to fill leadership positions. Far from heralding the end of the appeal of nationalism among Muslims, al-Qaeda illustrated the difficulty of constructing a modern political project along nonnational lines.

See also Arab nationalism; community; Pan-Islamism; al-Qaeda

Further Reading

Ami Ayalon, *Language and Change in the Arab Middle East*, 1987; James L. Gelvin, "Modernity and Its Discontents: On the Durability of Nationalism in the Arab Middle East," *Nations and Nationalism* 5, no. 1 (1999); Nikkie Keddie, "Pan-Islam as Proto-Nationalism," *Journal of Modern History* 41, no. 1 (1969); Anthony D. Smith, *Nationalism and Modernism: A Critical Survey of Recent Theories of Nations*, 1998; Sami Zubaida, *Islam, the People and the State*, 1989.

DANIEL NEEP

Nation of Islam

Whether the Nation of Islam is a political movement or a religious movement has been much debated by scholars. Within the movement, only Warith Deen Mohammed (the son of Elijah Muhammad) viewed the Nation of Islam (then under the leadership of Louis Farrakhan) as a social reform movement. All the other leaders of the Nation of Islam—Wali Fard Muhammad, its founder; Elijah Muhammad, its leader from 1934 to 1975; and Louis Farrakhan, who revived the movement after Warith Deen Mohammed reformed the Nation of Islam—saw no such distinction between the Nation's religion and its politics.

It is not always certain which teachings of the Nation of Islam go back to Fard Muhammad and which to his successor and sole transmitter, Elijah Muhammad. However, it does seem that Fard Muhammad first identified Islam with what he called the "original humanity," who were black. Thus the original and natural ruler of the world was the "blackman." This should not be understood to mean just Africans and their descendants. For Fard Muhammad all "original" people were Asiatics, with the distinction between Asia and Africa introduced by whites in order to divide and thereby conquer them.

Elijah Muhammad inherited and expanded on Fard Muhammad's racial understanding of religion, history, and politics but focused on the independence of African Americans. He encouraged them to set up their own economy and society and separate themselves entirely from white America. Even his strong emphasis on education and morality could be seen as a means of separating the races. Elijah Muhammad never used the term, but he advocated a kind of theocracy. He continually demanded obedience to himself—the "Apostle of Allah"—from his followers. And as he approached death, he believed the Nation of Islam needed no successor: the teachings of Allah as he had expounded them would suffice.

When Warith Deen Mohammed (then still named Wallace D. Muhammad) assumed the leadership of the Nation of Islam after his father's death in 1975, he radically transformed the movement, religiously and politically. He rapidly brought most of the beliefs and practices of the movement in conformity with more traditionally Sunni formulations of Islam. The anti-American statements and the demands for territorial separation between blacks and whites were also dropped. Although Warith Deen Mohammed frequently met with both American and Muslim political leaders and supported Muslim groups such as the Afghan mujahidin in the 1980s, the Palestinians, and the Kuwaiti refugees, he eschewed political activities. Instead he argued for interfaith dialogue and the unity of humanity. Unlike his father, he saw no problem with African American Muslims voting, running for office, or even joining the army. They were to be model citizens. His "solution" for the ills of the United States was Islam.

Louis Farrakhan strongly objected to the reforms of Warith Deen Mohammed. He returned to the beliefs of the Nation of Islam under Elijah Muhammad. However, Farrakhan was far more politically active. He supported Jesse Jackson's 1984 bid to be the Democratic presidential nominee and provided him with bodyguards. Farrakhan's most ambitious foray into politics came with his 1995 "Million Man March" on Washington, D.C. Although the purpose of the march was to advocate "unity, atonement, and brotherhood," it also included efforts to register African American men to vote and to convince them to engage in volunteerism and community activism. Several speakers also attacked the Republicans, who were depicted as hostile to welfare, Medicaid, and other programs that assisted poor African Americans.

The most recognizable and iconic political thinker to emerge from the Nation of Islam was also the one with the most ambivalent relationship with the movement: Malcolm X (1925–65). His

program of black nationalism and antiassimilation came directly from the Nation of Islam's political program. After his break with the movement, however, he was able to abandon its policy of political quietism. In fiery speeches such as the "Ballot or the Bullet" or demands for human rights for African Americans "by any means necessary," Malcolm X may have drawn on the political ideology of the Nation of Islam, but he also seemed poised to put it into action.

See also Malcolm X (1925–65); Mohammed, W. D. (1933–2008); Muhammad, Elijah (1897–1975)

Further Reading

Edward E. Curtis, IV, *Black Muslim Religion in the Nation of Islam, 1960–1975*, 2006; C. Eric Lincoln, *The Black Muslims in America*, 1994; Clifton E. Marsh, *From Black Muslims to Muslims: The Transition from Separation to Islam, 1930–1980*, 1984; Aminah Beverly McCloud, *African American Islam*, 1995.

HERBERT BERG

nation-state

The position of Islam toward nationalism and the nation-state has been subject to debate. According to some groups, the Qur'an overtly acknowledges and promotes nationalism and thus recognizes the nation-state. Such groups often cite Qur'an 49:13 ("O mankind! We divided you into nations [peoples] and tribes so that you may know each other better") to contend that nationalism is not destructive or divisive to religious unity but instead that the Qur'an acknowledges diversity and reinforces different languages and cultural practices to advance cohesive human relationships. For others, Islam opposes any type of schism, including those instigated by nationalist ideologies, which are often exclusionary, divisive, and thus incompatible with Islam. For this group, the Prophet's "farewell speech," which was delivered during his final pilgrimage in 632 and summarized the fundamental beliefs of Islam, not only denounced ethnic and racial domination but also declared Muslims as members of one unified community. Muhammad is reported to have said on this occasion, "An Arab has no superiority over a non-Arab; also a white has no superiority over a black—except through piousness. Every Muslim is a brother to every Muslim and Muslims constitute one brotherhood."

Discussion of these two principles continues to shape the policies endorsed by current Islamic movements. Some Islamic movements take a nationalist position by appropriating Islam as their main component, while others challenge national boundaries and seek to forge transnational ties based on the unity of and mutual responsibility for fellow Muslims under the *umma*—the global Islamic community. What form of the "state," if any, Islam endorses poses a more complicated question. The Qur'an offers detailed rules pertaining to social interactions and legal issues (e.g., divorce, collective decision making, inheritance, and the like) that are regulated by the modern state. The presence of these rules makes "the state" a more controversial term. While some perceive Islamic rules to be applicable and sustainable under any state, others subscribe to the establishment of an Islamic state that would solely uphold Qur'anic rules. Against this background of contesting interpretations, Islamic groups privilege different Islamic dictums while the national or international contexts give advantages to certain positions. For instance, early 20th-century anticolonial movements provided fertile ground for national Islamic movements and parties (e.g., the Pan-Malaysian Islamic Party in Malaysia), whereas the post-Iranian revolution context instigated the expansion of global *umma*-based movements (e.g., the Hizb-ut-Tahrir in Indonesia). Beyond their different forms, national-religious movements endorse the notion of the nation-state and share the view that nationalism serves as the first step toward resisting foreign influence and consolidating a broader range of Islamic identities. The views of *umma*-based political Islam on nationalism can be seen in the writings of Hasan al-Banna and Sayyid Qutb in the early 20th century. Qutb opposed nationalism in general and Arab nationalism specifically, stating that the "All-Wise God did not lead His Prophet . . . to free the Earth from Roman and Persian tyranny in order to replace it with Arab tyranny. All tyranny is wicked." In *Our Message*, Banna, the founder of the Egyptian Muslim Brotherhood, acknowledged the potential virtues of nationalism yet also declared, "Every region in which there is a Muslim . . . is our homeland."

In the face of contradictory trends of globalization, national and broader *umma*-based Islamic movements and parties coexist in many countries and vie for support. Jama'at-i Islami and the National Party in Bangladesh or Hizb-ut-Tahrir and the Islamic Action Front in Jordan exemplify movements that emphasize the universality of the *umma* and blend Islamic and nationalist ideologies. In many movements, one can see elements of contesting perspectives. For instance, the Muslim Brotherhood describes its goal as—in the words of one of its leaders—"achieving unification among Islamic countries," yet it also qualifies it by recognizing the critical importance of achieving this aim "mainly among Arab states, to liberate them from imperialism."

See also modernity; nationalism; Pan-Islamism

Further Reading

Said Amir Arjomand, ed., *From Nationalism to Revolutionary Islam*, 1984; Hasan al-Bannah, *What Is Our Message*, 2004; Asef Bayat, *Making Islam Democratic: Social Movements and the Post-Islamist Turn*, 2007; Robert W. Hefner and Patricia Horvatich, eds., *Islam in an Era of Nation-States: Politics and Religious Renewal in Muslim*, 1997; Sayyid Qutb, *Milestones*, 2003.

SULTAN TEPE

natural law

Natural law is a system of rights or justice held to be common to all humans and derived from nature rather than from the conventions of society. Its opposite is "positive law" in the sense of a law that has been "set" for a society either by itself, its rulers, or a higher, transcendent authority. Islamic revealed law (shari'a) is understood to be a positive law set by God. Muslim legal scholars, however, have always reflected on the relationship between shari'a and the legal systems of other communities and whether some moral and legal standards apply to all humans by virtue of being part of humanity. Here, the early Mu'tazila school argued that the rules of shari'a reflect an objective notion of justice that is accessible to all humans. Sunnis and many Shi'i thinkers oppose this view and argue that before the coming of Islam there was only limited moral guidance in this world and that valid moral judgments must be deduced from the Muslim revelation. Another question is whether considerations about God's creation (i.e., nature) can meaningfully contribute to shari'a's formulation.

In Islam, the subject of natural law is closely connected to discussions about Qur'an 7:172, in which God converses with Adam's offspring. God asks, "Am I not your Lord?" to which they collectively answer, "Yes, we bear witness." Some interpreters see here, together with Qur'an 36:60, the establishment of a covenant (*mīthāq*) between God and humanity that establishes certain basic legal obligations for all humans, such as acknowledging the existence of a single God and worshipping Him. These obligations were considered part of the "original human disposition" (*fiṭra*), which is mentioned in Qur'an 30:30 as well as in a famous hadith (prophetic tradition) about the reasons why not all people choose to become Muslims.

Al-Bukhari (d. 870) reports in his collection of hadith (*qadar* 3), "Every newborn is born according to the original disposition (*'alā al-fiṭra*) and his parents make him a Jew or a Christian." This hadith led to lively debates about whether Islam is part of the original disposition (i.e., the nature) of humans. A mainstream position was put forward by Ghazali (d. 1111), who argued that while some of Islam's doctrinal truths, such as monotheism or the existence of an afterlife, are part of that *fiṭra* and thus innate and instinctive to all humans, the normative obligations, such as the rites of Islam and its religious law, are not. God created humans in such a way that they could all reach the most basic doctrines of Islam without the assistance of a revelation. Like many rationalist Muslim theologians, Ghazali thought that humans could reach the basic doctrinal truths though rational arguments and that revelation points to this possibility. Such theologians also agree that the normative rules of Islam are not part of the original human disposition. If that were the case, even humans who had never heard of Muhammad's revelation could become Muslims and then revelation would be superfluous. The rites of Islam, such as the five daily prayers or fasting during Ramadan, are not instinctively plausible, nor can they be deduced from reason. The same applies to its law (shari'a). Yet this position still allows for reflections about the normative role of nature in divine legislation. In cases where the transmitted scriptural sources of shari'a are silent, the Islamic jurist may consider which ruling would maximize the common benefit of humans (*maṣlaḥa*) and in that decision reflections about what best befits human nature are quite common.

While agreeing on the instinctive element of the original human disposition, the Hanbali jurist Ibn Taymiyya (1263–1328) disagreed with Ghazali on the role of rational arguments and taught that they would not lead toward the truths found in the *fiṭra* but might, in fact, distract from it. Ibn Taymiyya developed an influential argument saying on the one hand that the *fiṭra* includes an intuitive faculty of knowing right from wrong where whatever is found to be right is the same as the basic moral teachings of Islam and its shari'a, while on the other hand arguing that the ritual obligations of Islam and the details of its revealed law are nonintuitive yet respond most perfectly to the requirements of the human *fiṭra*. Consequently, he stated that humans cannot become Muslims without the Qur'an. He believed that once Islam came into existence and once it is presented to humans without prejudice, however, they all will be compelled by its teachings and by the justice and suitability of its shari'a. Although this concept is different from the natural law tradition that evolved in the West, Ibn Taymiyya's concept of the relationship between the original human condition and Islam elevated shari'a to a system of law that is understood in very similar terms. Therefore, due to the way God created humans, shari'a is among all legal systems the one that most perfectly serves the condition of humans and of their societies.

Responding to Western debates about natural law, Muslim fundamentalist thinkers claim that Islam and its shari'a are in complete harmony with it. Mawdudi (1903–79), one of the first to express this idea, argued, however, that Islam and natural law are not identical, since shari'a is much more comprehensive and responds to more complex legal and moral problems than natural law. While natural law can satisfy the basic legislative needs of human societies, it cannot provide the basis for a truly fulfilling human life. Natural law, therefore, is only a part of shari'a. Here we find a modern expression of the classical position that shari'a cannot be developed by human reason but must be learned from Muhammad's revelation. Sayyid Qutb (1906–66), on the other hand, claims that shari'a is in complete agreement with natural law. Qutb follows Ibn Taymiyya in his understanding of the *fiṭra* as a disposition that allows humans to do both right and wrong. With the *fiṭra* comes an intuitive faculty to choose right actions over wrong ones. Shari'a responds to that disposition by recommending (or making obligatory) precisely those actions that the human would choose if he or she follows intuitive judgment (*ilhām*). This is why Qutb, like many Islamist thinkers, believed that all humans would adopt Islam and its shari'a if it were presented to them without prejudice. Following shari'a brings the human soul back to its original state and creates harmony among humans and between humans and their natural environment.

See also Ghazali (ca. 1058–1111); Ibn Taymiyya (1263–1328); Mawdudi, Abu al-A'la (1903–79); public interest; Sayyid Qutb (1906–66); shari'a

Further Reading

Anver M. Emon, *Islamic Natural Law Theories*, 2010; Geneviève Gobillot, *La fitra: La conception orignelle, ses interpretations et functions chez les penseurs musulmans*, 2000; Frank Griffel, "The Harmony of Natural Law and Shari'a in Islamist Theology," in *Shari'a: Islamic Law in the Contemporary Context*, edited by Abbas Amanat and Frank Griffel, 2007; Abul A'la Mawdudi, *The Islamic Law and Constitution*, 1960; Idem, *The Islamic Way of Life (Islām ka-niẓām-i ḥayāt)*, translated by K. Ahmad and K. Murad, 1986; Sayyid Qutb, *Milestones (Ma'ālim fī al-ṭarīq)*, 1990; A. Kevin Reinhart, *Before Revelation: The Boundaries of Muslim Moral Thought*, 1995.

FRANK GRIFFEL

Nazim Hikmet (1902–63)

Nazim Hikmet (whose rarely used surname was Ran), widely recognized as the best poet of the Turkish language in the 20th century, was born to a well-to-do family in then-Ottoman Salonica on January 15, 1902. After attending a French-language secondary school in Istanbul, he enrolled in the Naval Cadet School but was discharged at the age of 17 on account of ill health (or, according to another source, because he was a member of a group that opposed military training). Not long thereafter, he began writing poetry.

At that time, the Ottoman state had been defeated in World War I, its lands were partly occupied by Armenians in the East and Greeks in the West, and a struggle for liberation had been under way led by Mustafa Kemal Pasha (later to be called Atatürk [d. 1938]). Having strong nationalistic leanings, Nazim, together with a friend, traveled to Anatolia as a primary school teacher in early 1921 in order to join the liberation efforts. There he learned about the new Bolshevik revolution, which had spread to the Caucasus. He subsequently traveled to Baku, then to Moscow, where he attended the KUTV (the Communist University of the Toilers of the East) and became a Communist. Returning home in late 1924, he joined a Marxist circle in Istanbul and worked there semilegally until April 1925. The few articles he wrote for the journal *Aydınlik* (Clarté) consisted of stereotypical declarations of historical materialism.

As one of the leaders of the Turkish Communist Party (TKP), Nazim was sentenced in absentia to 15 years in prison, but he fled to Moscow in August 1925, where he gained fame as a poet and playwright. He participated in the Vienna Conference of May 1926, where he exhibited a stern secularist stand against a comrade who had a more lenient attitude toward people's traditions. He returned to Istanbul in late 1928. In the following year, the clandestine TKP suffered extensive arrests and was forced to reorganize. Nazim headed the opposition and was sentenced to four years in prison in March 1933. Pardoned in August 1934, he was purged from his party at the end of 1935 but continued his political activities; he also wrote more poems and plays and participated in filmmaking as a scenario writer. He was arrested in early 1938 and charged with inciting the cadets of the army to mutiny; another lawsuit was brought against him for disseminating communist propaganda in the navy. In total, he was sentenced to 28 years and 4 months in prison. He served the last of these sentences until mid-1950 and was readmitted to the party while he was still in prison. Fearing that he would be assassinated, he fled to the Soviet Union, where he spent the rest of his life. He became active in the World Council of Peace and also served as a member of the TKP External Bureau (Central Committee).

The pretext given for Nazim's dismissal from the TKP in the mid-1930s was his "Trotskite-police opposition," which is a usual cliché for refusal to obey party discipline. In fact, he was an ardent believer in equality and social justice and achieved, through his poetry and plays, much more than the center of the party did in disseminating these values to the public at large. His rebellious nature made him also oppose the personality cult dominant in the Soviet Union. It might be speculated that, had he lived in Russia rather than in Turkey in the 1930s, he would have ended up in the Gulag.

See also communism; Turkey

Further Reading

Erden Akbulut, *N.H. in Comintern Documents* (*Komintern Belgelerinde Nâzım Hikmet*), 2002; Memet Fuat, *Nazim Hikmet, Life, Psychological Frame, Lawsuits, Discussions, Doctrine, Poetical Development*, 2000.

METE TUNCAY

Nigeria

The Federal Republic of Nigeria, comprising 36 states and the federal capital territory of Abuja, as of 2008 had a population of 140,003,542. Nigeria is approximately 50 percent Muslim, 40 percent Christian, and 10 percent adherents of traditional religions. The country's north, composed of 19 states, is home to the Hausa, who make up the majority of the Muslim population in Nigeria.

Before the arrival of Islam, this northern region was ruled by the Hausa Bakwai—the Seven Hausa States. The earliest recorded Islamic influence came during the reign of Sarki (king) Yaji (r. 1349–85), when Mandigo traders traveled westward in search of Sudanese gold. The North African scholar 'Abd al-Karim al-Maghili arrived in Hausaland during the reign of Mohammad Rimfa (r. 1463–99), bringing with him the Maliki school of Islamic law, which now

dominates the region. Maghili's era—which is also associated with the spread of Sufism in the region—did not usher forth a stark transition from African traditions to literate Islamic ones; for the next three centuries the struggle between pagan and Islamic cultural and legal traditions would continue in Hausaland cities such as Katsina, Kano, Borno, and Zaria.

The Sokoto caliphate, founded in 1809 by the Fulani (Sheshu) Usman dan Fodio (also known by the Arabic name Ibn Fudi) marks the most important event in Nigerian Muslim modernity. A scholar and political leader, dan Fodio's loyalists defeated all major towns of the Hausa kingdom within six years, replacing them with Fulani emirates and establishing Sokoto as its capital. Dan Fodio combined a call for the renewal (*tajdīd*) of Islam—including a strict constructionist approach to Maliki law—with a political platform challenging the Hausa kingdom's rule. Dan Fodio cites excessive taxation, corruption, and suppression of Muslim practices as his casus belli in his work *Kitab al-Farq bayn Wilayat Ahl al-Islam wa-bayn Wilayat Ahl al-Kufr* (The difference between Muslim governance and governance by unbelievers).

British encroachment commenced with the foundation of the Inland Commercial Company in 1833 and culminated with colonial envoy F. D. Lugard's inauguration of the "Northern Region" at Lokoja on January 1, 1900. In March 1903, Sokoto was captured, marking the end of the caliphate. Having encountered a functioning Islamic legal system, the British pursued a policy of "indirect rule," allowing "native law and custom" to proceed undisturbed, save punishments deemed "repugnant to natural justice and humanity"—in practice a moratorium on the *ḥudūd*, or punishments found in the shari'a (Islamic law), including stoning and amputations.

Eight young civilians formed the Northern Elements Progressive Union (NEPA) in 1950 to challenge the amirs, who they argued had become instruments of the colonial administration. Despite NEPA's activities, however, the amirs' popular prestige was seriously eroded only with the achievement of independence in 1960 and especially when Nigeria transitioned into a republic united under a constitution in 1967. In 1999, Nigeria adopted a new constitution as it reinstated civilian rule under President Olusegun Obasanjo for the first time in 20 years. Section 38 calls for "freedom of thought, conscience and religion," which many northerners interpreted to sanction the reintroduction of shari'a—a view ardently protested by many of Nigeria's non-Muslims.

Claiming credit for this latest reintroduction of shari'a is a group known simply as Izala (full name Izalat al-Bid'a wa-Iqamat al-Sunna; "The removal of innovation and the uplifting of the sunna") founded in 1978 by Shaykh Ismaila Idris in Jos and one of Nigeria's largest Muslim organizations. Izala's ideological leader was Shaykh Abubakar Gumi (1922–92), the former grand-qadi (judge) of the north, whose anti-Sufi and anti-*bid'a* (innovation) views continue to exert great influence.

In 1999, Ahmed Sani Yerima, governor of Zamfara, reintroduced shari'a in his state amid massive popular support. But since then, the demand for shari'a has largely died down, though it still operates in many parts of the north in parallel or in combination with other legal systems. This can be attributed to politicization of the shari'a, which alienates many and only appeals to the most vulnerable. In addition, governors pay a political price if they attempt to mete out a scripturally sanctioned punishment, especially after two well-publicized stoning cases attracted international attention, embarrassing the state.

Nonetheless, the shari'a has played a role in sectarian violence, particularly in Kaduna, where in 2000 at least 400 were killed after shari'a was reimplemented, and most recently in Jos, where approximately 400 people were massacred in March 2010. Though some use the rhetoric of jihad to explain the violence, many view the underlying problem as the perennial failure of local and state governments to fairly distribute scarce resources within a federal system plagued by massive corruption.

See also Christian-Muslim relations; Dan Fodio, Usman (1754–1817); West Africa

Further Reading

Usman dan Fodio, *Ihya' al-Sunna wa-Ikhmad al-Bid'ah* [The revival of the sunna and the elimination of innovation], n.d.; Idem, *Kitab al-Farq bayn Wilayat Ahl al-Islam wa-bayn Wilayat Ahl al-Kufr* [The difference between Muslim governance and governance by unbelievers], n.d.; Philip Ostein, *Sharia Implementation in Northern Nigeria 1999–2006: A Sourcebook*, 2007; Abdullahi Smith, "The Early States of the Central Sudan," *History of West Africa*, vol. 1, edited by J. F. A. Ajayi and Michael Crowder, 1971; Ibraheem Sulaiman, *The Islamic State and the Challenge of History: Ideals, Policies and Operation of the Sokoto Caliphate*, 1987.

SARAH ELTANTAWI

Nizam al-Mulk (1018–92)

Abu 'Ali al-Hasan b. 'Ali b. Ishaq al-Tusi, generally known by his honorific title Nizam al-Mulk, was a scholar, statesman, and celebrated Persian vizier of two Seljuq dynasts, Alp Arslan (r. 1063–72) and his son, Malikshah (r. 1072–92). A manual of advice, the *Siyar al-Muluk* (The ways of kings), addressed to Malikshah, is generally attributed to him. There are early references to the work, for example in Ghazali's (d. 1111) *Nasihat al-Muluk* (Book of Counsel for Kings). The text was popular enough by the late 12th century for Nizami (d. ca. 1209) to signal his familiarity with the wording of the text by directly incorporating some phrases from it in his *Haft Paykar* (Seven Portraits).

Nizam al-Mulk was born in a village near Tus in Khurasan in the waning years of Ghaznavid rule (997–1186) and was assassinated near Isfahan in 1092, most probably on the orders of Malikshah. In spite of the perennial threat of Turkic invasions, as well

as Isma'ili-instigated occasional unrest in Baghdad and northern Iranian provinces, Nizam al-Mulk not only managed to hold onto the reins of power for three decades but also brought the Islamic empire, stretching from central Asia (Afghanistan) in the east almost to Egypt in the west, under uniform governance and put into place a vast network of able administrators and loyal acolytes in influential positions. Five of his sons, two of his grandsons, and one great-grandson held the office of vizier to one or another of the rulers after him, though none could reach his eminence. He is also credited with the establishment of privately endowed educational institutions, known as the Nizamiyya madrasas in several cities, including Nishapur, Baghdad, Isfahan, Mosul, Balkh, Herat, and Basra.

Although lionized in medieval sources for his justice, pragmatism, visionary rule, and political acuity, the details of his life and his policies remain sparse. A series of anecdotal reminiscences by foes or allies praise the vizier for his nonpartisanship, strong rule, and benevolence to religious luminaries. He was a follower of the Shafi'i school of law and Ash'ari theology, and his Nizamiyya were dedicated to the propagation of Shafi'i doctrine but without state policy being skewed in favor of the Shafi'i faction. According to a 12th-century Shi'i source, Nizam al-Mulk did not prohibit Shi'i notables from founding several madrasas for their own community in Rayy or Qazvin. And an early 13th-century Hanbali historian applauds Nizam al-Mulk's evenhandedness, recalling the vizier's severe rebuke of the head teacher of the Nizamiyya in Baghdad. In his classes, the instructor had lambasted the Hanbali creed, provoking riots in the city. Nizam al-Mulk reminded the scholar that the Nizamiyya had been established to disseminate learning and knowledge and not to foment sectarian discord. Should the schools fail in their primary function, he would have no choice but to close them down.

Nizam al-Mulk's book of advice, written according to the preface of the book around 1086 but referred to and cited only after his death, is among the later examples of the amalgam of pre-Islamic Iranian lore and literary and cultural tropes prevalent in the late antique world, including pseudo-Aristotelian lore and exempla and dicta culled from the Islamic tradition that dominated political thought in the medieval Islamic world. The introduction firmly sets the king in full command of his kingdom and the fate of his rule when it argues that, although divine selection places the king in office, the longevity and stability of his rule is contingent on his justice and openness to good counsel.

One of the most striking features of the *Siyar al-Muluk* is its long exposition of the dangers posed by heresiarchs. To that end, the vizier advises the king to keep abreast of intellectual currents in his realm and to familiarize himself with different traditions of thought so as to be cognizant of the political ramifications implicit in every religious dispute. Nizam al-Mulk chose, as an antidote to the rise of heresiarchs, the increasing sectarianism of the various Sunni schools and the spiritual appeal of the less legalistic and more philosophical tenets of the Isma'ili faith, to befriend Sufis throughout the empire and to publicize not only his association with spiritual leaders but also his preference for the Sufis among them. The medieval sources are replete with instances of the vizier's largesse toward the Sufi community.

It is both noteworthy and ironic that the virtues extolled in the *Siyar al-Muluk* were gathered not in the sultan but in the vizier himself. One of his contemporaries, the influential theologian Juwayni (d. 1085), hypothesized that the Abbasid caliphate and the Seljuq sultanate could both be abolished and the realm left solely to the care of the perfect vizier, Nizam al-Mulk.

See also Ghazali (ca. 1058–1111); Nizamiyya; Seljuqs (1055–1194)

Further Reading

'Izz al-Din ibn al-Athir, *The Annals of the Saljuq Turks: Selections from al-Kamil fi'l ta'rikh of 'Izz al-Din ibn al-Athir*, translated by D. S. Richards, 2002; Nizam al-Mulk, *The Book of Government or Rules for Kings*, translated by Hubert Darke, 1960; Neguin Yavari, "Polysemous Texts and Reductionist Readings: Women and Heresy in the *Siyar al-mulūk*," in *Views from the Edge: Essays in Honor of Richard W. Bulliet*, edited by Neguin Yavari, Lawrence Potter, and Jean-Marc Ran Oppenheim, 2004; Idem, "Mirrors for Princes or a Hall of Mirrors: Niẓām al-Mulk's *Siyar al-mulūk* Reconsidered," *Al-Masāq: Islam and the Medieval Mediterranean* 20, no. 1 (2008); Idem, "Niẓām al-Mulk," in *The Islamic World*, edited by Andrew Rippin, 2008; Idem, "Niẓām al-Mulk and the Restoration of Sunnism in Eleventh-Century Iran," in *Tahqiqat-i Islamī* 10, nos. 1–2 (1996).

NEGUIN YAVARI

Nizamiyya

The Nizamiyya (*Niẓāmiyya*) Madrasas (Muslim schools) were a network of colleges of Islamic law founded by the famous statesman Nizam al-Mulk (d. 1092) in the mid-to-late 11th century in the major cities of Iran, Iraq, and Syria, including Nishapur, Marv, Herat, Baghdad, Basra, Mosul, and Aleppo. The best known and most important of these was the Nizamiyya of Baghdad, which remained a premier institution of learning for several centuries and served as a model for numerous law colleges throughout the Islamic world. Nizam al-Mulk, vizier of the great Seljuq sultans Alp Arslan (r. 1063–72) and Malikshah I (r. 1072–92) and de facto ruler of the Seljuq Empire after the assassination of Alp Arslan and accession of Malikshah in 1072, planned, constructed, and endowed the various Nizamiyya colleges in an attempt to restore the traditional balance between the Hanafi and Shafi'i *madhhab*s (schools of law) that had existed in Iran for over a century but had been disturbed by the rise of the Seljuqs and their patronage of the Hanafi jurists, whom they favored at the expense of the Shafi'is. Tughril's vizier, Kunduri, had gone so far as to exile Shafi'i scholars from Khurasan; appoint Hanafi chief judges in Rayy; and appoint a Hanafi, 'Ali b. 'Ubaydallah al-Khatibi, as the chief judge

in Isfahan, which had traditionally been Shafi'i. Nizam al-Mulk's own position was that there were two acceptable legal *madhhabs*, the Hanafi and the Shafi'i, but he was determined to support scholars who belonged to the Shafi'i legal *madhhab* and were Ash'ari theologians, in counterweight to the Seljuqs' Hanafi protégés, in order to restore a proper balance to religious, intellectual, and political life of the community. He brought back to Khurasan exiled Shafi'i-Ash'ari scholars, including Ghazali's (d. 1111) famous teacher Juwayni, known as Imam al-Haramayn, whom he appointed to teach at the Nizamiyya in Nishapur, and Abu Bakr Muhammad b. 'Ali b. Hamid al-Shashi (d. 1093), whom he appointed to a teach at the Nizamiyya at Herat.

Construction of the Nizamiyya in Baghdad, the earliest of the Nizamiyya colleges west of Khurasan, began in 1065, and the college was completed and opened in 1067. While the endowment deed has not been preserved, some of its provisions are known from historical sources: the personnel of the college, including its professor of law, repetitor, preacher, librarian, stipendiary law students, and probably also its grammar teacher (*shaykh al-naḥw*), were required to adhere to the Shafi'i legal school in both *fiqh* (law) and *uṣūl al-fiqh* (legal theory or jurisprudence). The Nizamiyya of Baghdad became a significant model for other madrasas not only in Baghdad but also further west in Syria, Anatolia, and Egypt. It was rivaled by the Hanafi law college at the Shrine of Abu Hanifa, built by Alp Arslan's *mustawfī* (financial agent) Abu Sa'd also in 1057, and the Tajiyya law college, also Hanafi, completed in 1089 by Taj al-Mulk (d. 1093), the *mustawfī* of Malikshah. The Nizamiyya of Baghdad was probably a principal source of inspiration behind the construction of major Shafi'i madrasas under the Zengids and Ayyubids in Syria and Egypt. It remained the most impressive institution of learning in Baghdad throughout the 12th century and was admired by the traveler Ibn Jubayr (d. 1217), who visited Baghdad in 1185. It was superseded only by the sumptuous Mustansiriyya College, founded in 1234 by the Abbasid caliph Mustansir (r. 1226–42). The Mustansiriyya College was extremely well funded and based on a different model, including provisions for professors and students of all four Sunni legal *madhhabs*. The Nizamiyya declined after the founding of the Mustansiriyya and the Mongol conquest in 1258 and was probably defunct by the 15th century.

The Nizamiyya in its heyday attracted the most talented scholars available. The professor of law who taught there, the repetitor or assistant professor, the master of Arabic grammar, and the librarian were all outstanding scholars. Nizam al-Mulk first appointed Abu Ishaq al-Shirazi (d. 1083), the leading Shafi'i jurist of his day and author of *al-Tanbih* (The call to attention) and *al-Muhadhdhab* (The neatly arranged compendium), which continued to be used as textbooks of Shafi'i law for centuries after his death. The famous jurist and theologian Ghazali taught as professor of law at the Nizamiyya but gave up the position after four years as the result of a personal spiritual crisis, traveling to the Hijaz, Syria, and eventually returning to his native Khurasan. Other leading jurists who held the positions include Abu Nasr b. al-Sabbagh (d. 1084), author of the major textbook *al-Shamil* (The comprehensive work); Abu Bakr al-Shashi (d. 1114); 'Ali al-Tabari al-Kiya al-Harrasi (d. 1110); As'ad al-Mihani (d. 1129); Abu al-Mansur al-Razzaz (d. 1144–45); and Abu al-Najib al-Suhrawardi (d. 1168). Nizam al-Mulk retained the right to supervise the endowment and to make appointments and dismiss personnel as he saw fit, and this power passed to his descendants at his death but later became the right of the Abbasid caliph or the sultan. Frequent dismissals appear to have been contrary to common practice at the time, for appointments to professorships were often for life, and the large number of incumbents and their relatively short tenures is striking when compared with those of the Shrine College at Abu Hanifa. The law professors were usually Persians, and this condition may even have been stipulated in the endowment deed.

Similarly, the grammarians at the Nizamiyya were highly influential in the history of Arabic linguistic sciences and literary criticism. Abu Zakariyya al-Tibrizi (d. 1109), one of the first scholars to hold the position, is renowned for his commentaries on the classics of Arabic literature such as the *Hamasa* (Poems on bravery) of Abu Tammam, the poems of Mutanabbi, the *Mufaddaliyat* (Poems collected by al-Mufaddal), and also his recension of the ten *Mu'allaqat*, (The suspended odes). Al-Hasan al-Fasihi al-Astarabadi (d. 1110) held the position for a short time after Tabrizi's death but was dismissed when it was discovered that he was Shi'i and replaced with the outstanding linguist and lexicographer Abu Mansur al-Jawaliqi (d. 1144), who wrote, in addition to his famous dictionary *al-Mu'arrab* (Lexicon of Arabicized words), a commentary on Ibn Qutayba's *Adab al-Katib* (Instruction for the secretary). Another incumbent was Hibat Allah b. 'Ali b. al-Shajari (d. 1148), whose dictations, *al-Amali al-Shajariyya* (al-Shajari's dictations), remain widely read. Abu al-Barakat b. al-Anbari (d. 1181) was widely reputed to be the greatest grammarian of his day and wrote *Asrar al-'Arabiyya* (The secrets of Arabic), a book on grammar, as well as a biographical work devoted to literary figures, *Tabaqat al-Udaba'* (The classes of literary men). Another well-known incumbent, Abu Bakr Mubarak b. al-Dahhan al-Wasiti (d. 1219), is reported to have changed his affiliation from the Hanafi to the Shafi'i legal *madhhab* in order to take the position.

Nizam al-Mulk established the Nizamiyya, kept it under his personal control, and maintained it generously as an instrument of political policy. In his time and later, it successfully bolstered the position of Shafi'i law and Ash'ari theology in the societies of Iraq, Syria, and Egypt, and it played an important role in the Sunni revival, countering in some ways but corroborating in others the influence of the Hanafis and their patrons in the Turkish ruling class. It was an elite institution, and the sons of many prominent officials studied there and went on to distinguished careers in the chanceries and judiciaries of various dynasties. Among the prominent graduates of the institution were Ibn 'Asakir (d. 1175), the famous historian and hadith expert; 'Imad al-Din al-Katib al-Isfahani (d. 1201), who went on to a spectacular career as a secretary for Nur al-Din and then Salah al-Din in Syria and Egypt; and Muhyi al-Din al-Shahrazuri (d. 1190), who had been a classmate of 'Imad al-Din at the Nizamiyya under the professor Ibn al-Razzaz and who

led an equally spectacular career under the Zengids. He was appointed chief judge of Aleppo under Nur al-Din, but after Nur al-Din's death, he became the de facto ruler of northern Syria under the young Malik al-Salih Isma'il (1174–81).

See also Ghazali (ca. 1058–1111); jurisprudence; madrasa; Nizam al-Mulk (1018–92); al-Shafi'i, Muhammad b. Idris (767–820); shari'a

Further Reading

George Makdisi, "Muslim Institutions of Learning in Eleventh-Century Baghdad," *Bulletin of the School of Oriental and African Studies* 24, no. 1 (1961); Idem, *The Rise of Colleges*, 1981; As'ad Talas, *La Madrasa Nizamiyya et son histoire*, 1939.

DEVIN J. STEWART

Nizaris

One of two major communities of Isma'ili Shi'i Muslims, the Nizaris are dispersed as religious minorities in more than 30 countries of Asia, the Middle East, Africa, Europe, and North America. The Nizari Isma'ilis have recognized a line of imams or spiritual leaders, represented by the Aga Khan.

Upon the death of Mustansir (r. 1036–94), the eighth caliph of the Fatimid dynasty and the 18th Isma'ili imam, in 1094, his sons Nizar (1045–95) and Ahmad (1074–1101) disagreed over who should succeed their father, leading to a permanent schism in the Isma'ili movement and community. Nizar, Mustansir's original heir-designate, was set aside in favor of his younger brother (who ruled under the caliphal name of Musta'li) by the all-powerful Fatimid vizier Afdal b. Badr al-Jamali (d. 1121). Nizar's succession rights were championed in Iran by Hasan-i Sabbah (d. 1124), the chief Isma'ili *dā'ī*, or missionary, in the Seljuq dominions. Hasan had established himself at the fortress of Alamut in 1090, signaling the foundation of what was to become the Nizari Isma'ili state of Iran and Syria, and was then already pursuing an independent revolutionary policy against the Seljuq Turks in Iran. By upholding Nizar's rights, Hasan also founded the independent Nizari *da'wa*, or religiopolitical mission, on behalf of the Nizari imams, the descendants of Nizar.

The Nizari Isma'ilis failed in their general revolt against the Seljuqs, whose alien rule was detested by the Iranians. Despite their incessant offensives against the Nizaris, the Seljuqs failed to uproot the Nizari fortress communities as well.

From early on, the Nizaris affirmed as their central teaching the old Shi'i doctrine of *ta'līm*, or the necessity of authoritative teaching by the rightful imam of the time. This doctrine, with various modifications, provided the foundation for all subsequent Nizari teachings. Hasan-i Sabbah and his next two successors at Alamut ruled over the Nizari state and community as the *ḥujjas*, or chief representatives, of the Nizari imams who were then concealed and inaccessible to their followers. Starting with the fourth ruler of Alamut, Hasan II 'ala dhikrihi al-salam (r. 1162–62), Nizari imams emerged openly at Alamut to take charge of the affairs of their community. Hasan II proclaimed the *qiyāma*, or resurrection, which was interpreted symbolically and spiritually for the Nizaris. In *qiyāma* times, the Nizaris were expected to focus on the *bāṭin*, the inner meaning and spirituality of the religious commandments and prohibitions, rather than merely observing the *ẓāhir*, or the letter of the law.

The sixth lord of Alamut, Hasan III (r. 1210–21), attempted a daring rapprochement with the Abbasid-Sunni establishment, with obvious political advantages for the Nizaris who had been marginalized in their fortress communities as "heretics." He instructed the Nizaris to observe the shari'a in its Sunni form. The Nizaris evidently interpreted this command as the imposition of the Shi'i principle of *taqiyya*, or precautionary dissimulation, accepting any sort of accommodation to the outside world deemed necessary by the Nizari imam. Henceforth, the rights of Hasan III to Nizari territories were recognized by the Abbasid caliph, leading to peace and security for the Nizaris.

The political prominence of the Nizaris was finally ended by the Mongols. But the Nizaris survived the Mongol destruction of their state and fortress communities in 1256. Subsequently, the Nizaris of different regions, especially in Syria, Iran, Afghanistan, Central Asia, and South Asia, developed locally, concealing their religious identities rather strictly to safeguard themselves against persecution. They variously resorted to Sufi, Twelver Shi'i, Sunni, and Hindu disguises. At the same time, the Nizari imamate continued in the progeny of the last lord of Alamut, Rukn al-Din Khurshah (d. 1257).

By the 18th century, the Nizari imams, residing in Anjudan and other localities in Iran, had emerged from obscurity and acted as central leaders of their community. Some of these imams were also appointed as governors of the province of Kirman by the Qajar monarchs of Iran. By the 1840s, Hasan 'Ali Shah (1804–81), the first Nizari imam to bear the honorific title of Aga Khan, had permanently settled in British India. His successors, notably Sultan Muhammad Shah Aga Khan III (1885–1957) and Prince Karim Aga Khan IV, who succeeded his grandfather in 1957, achieved great success in modernizing their community. As a result, the Nizari Isma'ilis emerged in modern times as a progressive community of educated and prosperous Shi'i Muslims.

See also Fatimids (909–1171); imamate; Seljuqs (1055–1194); Shi'ism

Further Reading

Farhad Daftary, "Ḥasan-i Ṣabbāḥ and the Origins of the Nizārī Isma'ili Movement," in *Mediaeval Isma'ili History and Thought*, edited by F. Daftary, 1996; Idem, *The Ismā'īlīs: Their History and Doctrines*, 2nd ed., 2007; Marshall G. S. Hodgson, "The Ismā'īlī State," in *The Cambridge History of Iran*, vol. 5, *The Saljuq and Mongol Periods*, edited by John A. Boyle, 1968; Bernard Lewis, *The Assassins: A Radical Sect in Islam*, 1967; Azim Nanji, *The Nizārī Ismā'īlī Tradition in the Indo-Pakistan Subcontinent*, 1978.

FARHAD DAFTARY

nonviolence

The term "nonviolence" stands for two closely related concepts. *Strategic nonviolence* is a theory of political power as well as a set of techniques for winning conflicts through protests, noncooperation, defiance, and sanctions that fall short of physical or armed violence. *Principled nonviolence* is a theory of human nature as well as a set of values that aim at personal transformation so that all parties can meet their needs through peaceful means while establishing deeper connections. Since there are large areas of overlap between these two concepts, the difference between strategic nonviolence and principled nonviolence is sometimes seen as a matter of perspective.

The Islamic tradition of armed combat is well known. It can be seen in the extensive discussion of warfare in the Qur'an, the hadith, and jurisprudence (*fiqh*), as well as in the numerous instances of warfare throughout Muslim history that have been either inspired by or legitimized through religious beliefs and doctrines. As several scholars have demonstrated, however, there also is a parallel tradition of *nonviolence* in the Islamic heritage. Even though the term "nonviolence" has no equivalent in the classical Islamic vocabulary, studies by modern scholars provide evidence that many of the key elements that constitute the contemporary understanding of nonviolence have always been integral to Islam. By emphasizing these nonviolent elements of the Islamic tradition and by reinterpreting the meaning and relative significance of elements that promote violence, these scholars have offered fresh perspectives on issues of vital importance.

The use of nonviolent strategies played a central role in Muhammad's success as a religious and political leader. One of the key Qur'anic concepts in this regard is *ṣabr*, which denotes patience, perseverance, and persistence. The first 12 years of Muhammad's prophetic career were marked by an actively nonviolent response to opposition and persecution that helped in the formation and solidarity of the new *umma* (community of believers). Even during the period following Muhammad's emigration from Mecca to Medina (the hijra, in 622), which saw a number of battles and armed skirmishes, nonviolent methods of preaching, negotiating, and persuading were never abandoned. The treaty of Hudaybiyya, which secured a ten-year peace with the Quraysh and its allies, took place as a direct consequence of Muhammad's aggressively peaceful "march on Mecca" for the avowed purpose of performing the pilgrimage. Without bloodshed, this initiative forced the opposition into acknowledging Muhammad's status and allowed Muslims the opportunity to peacefully propagate the Islamic message. Even though the treaty of Hudaybiyya appeared to be a humble compromise at the time, the Qur'an declared it to be a "clear victory." The surrender of the Quraysh in 630 was made possible at least partly due to Muhammad's offer of amnesty for his former enemies; evidently, his aim was not to exterminate his opponents but to absorb them into the Muslim *umma*.

Both the Qur'an and the hadith offer significant resources for nonviolent resistance to oppression, particularly in the duty of "commanding right and forbidding wrong." A well-known hadith identifies the act of "speaking truth to power" as the noblest form of jihad. The notion of principled nonviolence is not foreign to the Islamic tradition, either, including the imperative of not harming another person, regardless of the cost to oneself. While the Qur'an allows just retaliation, it presents forgiveness as the supreme virtue. In the Qur'anic narrative of Cain and Abel, the latter dies while refusing to defend himself against his brother; a hadith report praises the nonresisting Abel as a role model for Muslims. A similar attitude of nonresistance was demonstrated by the third caliph, 'Uthman b. 'Affan, who refused to order his supporters to ward off the attacking rebels on the grounds they had not yet broken any laws. While these examples may appear as insignificant exceptions to the mainstream of juristic thought, they cannot be dismissed as ethically irrelevant.

An important hadith mandates disobedience to authorities where compliance would involve support for injustice or disobedience to God. The first caliph, Abu Bakr, is held by some to have established the Islamic social contract when he declared that the Muslim community was obligated to obey him only so long as he obeyed God, emphasizing the religious justification for what is now understood as the right to "civil disobedience." Such teachings contributed to a tradition of refusing allegiance and compliance to unjust rulers, of which Islamic history provides many illustrations. These typically are examples of conscientious *individuals* refusing to obey political authorities for the sake of holding on to truth rather than organized movements of civil disobedience.

The Tobacco Protests in Iran during the late 19th century was one of the earliest examples of successful nonviolent resistance carried out on a large scale. In the 20th century, perhaps the most spectacular instance of Muslim nonviolent resistance was seen in the collective struggle of the Iranian people that brought down the U.S.-backed regime of Reza Shah Pahlavi in 1979. In the course of the nationwide agitation, Ayatollah Khomeini explicitly prohibited the demonstrators from attacking anyone in uniform. The popular struggle in the ongoing "Green Revolution" in Iran, which began with mass protests in the wake of the 2009 presidential elections, is similar in tactics, for it too is based on nonviolent strategies. In the 1920s Khan Abdul Ghaffar Khan (1890–1988) and his nonviolent army of Khudai Khidmatgars challenged the British raj in what is now the Khyber Pakhtunkhwa Province in Pakistan. Khan's movement was based on his understanding of Muhammad's life and earned him the honorific title of "Frontier Gandhi."

In the Middle East, the Palestinian people have a long history of nonviolent resistance, initially against Jewish colonization and subsequently in response to Israeli occupation. The most dramatic instances of Palestinian mass resistance were seen during the First Intifada (1987–93), an uprising that was largely nonviolent. A number of contemporary Palestinian groups follow nonviolent strategies to resist Israeli occupation and to achieve freedom and statehood, often in collaboration with like-minded Jewish groups; these

include the international movement called Boycott, Divestment, and Sanctions (BDS) that emerged in response to the 2005 call by the Palestinian civil society for a campaign of economic pressure that will force Israel to comply with International Law and Palestinian rights. Other forms of nonviolent resistance, including the efforts to build civil society, have been waged in the midst of violent conflicts, such as those in Iraq and Afghanistan. The nonviolent prodemocracy uprisings in several Arab and Muslim countries that began in December 2010 have been collectively named "the Arab Spring." Mass civil insurrections nonviolently toppled the autocratic regimes in Tunisia and Egypt in January 2011 but led to civil war in Libya. Major nonviolent movements for democracy in Syria, Yemen, and Bahrain spread despite state repression. Significant protests took place in Algeria, Iraq, Jordan, Morocco, and Oman; there are signs of similar upheavals in Kuwait, Mauritania, and Saudi Arabia. As political awareness increases among Muslim communities, some observers expect to see an even more deliberate and organized application of both strategic and principled nonviolence at different levels of society and politics.

See also dissent, opposition, resistance; governance; jihad; quietism and activism; violence

Further Reading

Mohammed Abu-Nimer and Jamal A. Badawi, "Alternatives to War and Violence: An Islamic Perspective," in *Peace Movements Worldwide*, edited by Michael Nagler and Marc Pilisuk, 2011; Rabia Terri Harris, "Nonviolence in Islam: The Alternative Community Tradition," in *Subverting Hatred: The Challenge of Nonviolence in Religious Traditions*, edited by Daniel L. Smith-Christopher, 2007; Maxine Kaufman-Lacusta, *Refusing to Be Enemies: Palestinian and Israeli Nonviolent Resistance to the Israeli Occupation*, 2010; Mary Elizabeth King, *A Quiet Revolution: The First Palestinian Intifada and Nonviolent Resistance*, 2007; Maria J. Stephan, ed., *Civilian Jihad: Nonviolent Struggle, Democratization, and Governance in the Middle East*, 2010; Mazin B. Qumsiyeh, *Popular Resistance in Palestine: A History of Hope and Empowerment*, 2011; Stephen Zunes, "Peace Movements and the Middle East: The 1991 Gulf War and Aftermath," in *Peace Movements Worldwide*, edited by Michael Nagler and Marc Pilisuk, 2011.

AHMED AFZAAL

North Africa

In contrast to the Mashriq (the Middle East from Egypt eastward), the Maghrib (North Africa) was neither heavily Ottomanized nor urbanized on the eve of colonialism. With the exception of the Husaynid Beylik of Tunis (Tunisia), the region was predominantly tribal and greatly influenced by the religious brotherhoods that underwent a transformation in the late 18th to early 19th centuries. This transformation is associated with Ahmad b. Idris (d. 1837) and the idea of the *ṭarīqa muḥammadiyya*, the Sufi equivalent of Salafism, which advocated a return to the spiritual source, Muhammad, as a means to introduce a new centralized, activist, and orthodox type of Sufi organization ideally suited to the rural Maghribi milieu and similar areas such as the Sudan. In some regions, new brotherhoods such as the Sanusi in Cyrenaica fulfilled many of the functions of a state for their followers. In others, reformed brotherhoods such as the Qadiri, Darqawi, and Wazzani-Tayyibi challenged the authority of weakening indigenous regimes such as the 'Alawi sultans in Morocco or the Deys of Algiers and then went on to lead resistance movements conceptualized as jihads against the colonial intrusions of the French, Spanish, and Italians. Algeria's nationalist icon, 'Abd al-Qadir (d. 1883), emerged from this environment, as did 'Umar al-Mukhtar (d. 1931), the best-known leader of the Sanusi resistance to the Italian occupation of Cyrenaica. These movements established a particular strain of Islamic reformism that was later challenged but also adopted and manipulated by 20th-century Islamic thinkers.

Colonial rule was particularly harsh in French Algeria and, later and more briefly, in Italian Libya. Particularly in Algeria, which was under colonial rule longer than any other country in the region, traditional political institutions were swept away, creating a political vacuum that was extremely difficult to fill. In Morocco and Tunisia, established regimes managed to hold on under the "protection" of France (and Spain in northern Morocco). However, both the 'Alawi sultanate of Morocco and the Husayni Beylik of Tunis were greatly compromised by their subjection to an "infidel" power. In Tunisia this proved fatal and, as in Algeria, the old regime and the political discourse that accompanied it were swept away and new secular forms of political thought of a socialist but thoroughly nationalist persuasion triumphed. However, the Tunisian nationalist movement, headed by Habib Bourguiba (d. 2000), made headway only when Bourguiba started to use mosque networks, thereby implying, if not actually asserting, that Tunisian independence was an Islamic as well as a nationalist objective. In Morocco, the charismatic Muhammad V was able to use the conceptual framework developed by the 'Alawi sultans to set the country on a path to constitutional monarchy, despite the nationalist preference for a republic.

Despite the differences within each Maghribi state, there were also commonalities in the development of modern political thought across the region. As in the Middle East, the struggle for independence from European colonialism dominated the political agenda, and the adoption of ideologies such as socialism and communism depended on their national utility. Salafism, Pan-Islamism, and Pan-Arabism were more appealing because they implied mutual solidarity against the colonizer and were also more deeply rooted in the existing political culture of the Maghrib. In the Maghrib there was little conflict among the movements; the only significant religious minorities were the Jews and the Ibadis (of the Mzab region of Algeria). In both Morocco and Algeria, reformist 'ulama', inspired by the example of Muhammad 'Abduh in Egypt, were prominent in the nationalist movement. In Morocco, for instance, the nationalist

leader ‘Allal al-Fasi (d. 1974) was a traditionally educated Salafi scholar rather than a member of the French-educated elite, although he recognized the importance of learning French in the course of his political career.

Maghribi nationalists were thus, for the most part, Pan-Arabists and Pan-Islamists in that they perceived the Maghrib as an integral part of the Arabo-Islamic world. This approach was fostered by a new triangular relationship among the Maghrib, the Mashriq, and various European metropoles where intellectuals gathered. London, Paris, Vienna, and even Oslo provided forums where Maghribis met with Mashriqis, and indeed individuals from other colonized countries, to exchange ideas and express solidarity. The League of Arab States also played an important rhetorical role in this respect. Both ‘Allal al-Fasi and Bourguiba made extensive use of such networks and understood the political futures of their respective countries to be tied to the crystallization of Arab and Islamic blocs.

The Arabo-Islamic national identity in the Maghrib was a political development that, from a historical perspective, correlated with older concepts of *dār al-islām* (the abode of Islam) and the Maghrib's participation in its Arab-influenced high culture, but from a contemporary national perspective it downplayed the Berber ethnic component in Algeria and Morocco. Berber communities did not necessarily feel disadvantaged by the emphasis on the Maghrib as Arab during the struggle for independence, but hegemonic Arabization in Algeria and to a lesser extent in Morocco triggered the development of Berber cultural and political movements that sought a more pluralistic vision of national identity in the Maghrib.

This coincided with the rise of Islamism in the Maghrib in the 1980s, which appeared to privilege a hegemonic "Arab" interpretation of Islam over Berber forms of faith and culture. Islamism's main target, however, was the postindependence states of the Maghrib and their poor socioeconomic and political performance. As in other Muslim societies, Islamists presented Islam as the panacea for a range of social, political, and economic ills. In each Maghribi country, Islamism followed a slightly different trajectory, but in general Islamists sought to invest the nation-state with greater authenticity and moral accountability rather than to replace it. In Tunisia and Morocco, Islamism remained moderate. In Morocco's case, this reflected the religious prestige of the monarchy, although a more violent and radical minority emerged from the broader Islamist movement. In Algeria, opposition from the secular army forced a confrontation and civil war, but this was by no means an inevitable outcome based on the ideological premises of Algerian Islamism, which largely accepted modern political forms as in the rest of the Maghrib.

See also Algeria; colonialism; international Islamic organizations; Morocco; Ottomans (1299–1924)

Further Reading

Moshe Gershovich, *French Military Rule in Morocco: Colonialism and Its Consequences*, 2000; George Joffé, ed., *North Africa: Nation, State and Region*, 1993; Bruce Maddy-Weitzman and Daniel Zisenwine, eds., *The Maghreb in the New Century: Identity, Religion and Politics*, 2007; Rex O'Fahey, *Enigmatic Saint: Ahmad b. Idris and the Idrisi Tradition*, 1990; David Prochaska, *Making Algeria French: Colonialism in Bône, 1870–1920*, 1990; John Ruedy, ed., *Islamism and Secularism in North Africa*, 1996.

AMIRA K. BENNISON

North America

The exact number of Muslims in North America is unknown largely because the U.S. census does not inquire into religious affiliation. The Canadian census does, however, and in 2001 it identified nearly 600,000 Muslims in Canada. Estimates of Muslims in the United States are based either on telephone surveys or self-reporting, and they range widely from one million to seven million. Scholars estimate three million Muslims in the United States. There are also a few thousand Muslims in Mexico.

The first significant presence of Muslims in North America dates back to the colonial period, when some tens of thousands of Muslims from West and North Africa were brought as slaves to American shores. Although many enslaved Muslims practiced their religion in North America, they did not form enduring communities. Instead, they participated in the formation of slave religion and culture. A descendent of a Muslim slave, for example, recalled in the 1930s that her grandmother used to shout with other non-Muslim slaves at night and perform the Muslim ritual prayer by herself at sunrise.

At the turn of the 20th century, an estimated 60,000 to 75,000 Muslim immigrants from South Asia, Anatolia, Eastern Europe, and the Levant came to North America. They were mostly young men who planned to make money and return home. While many repatriated, others stayed and established roots. Between the two world wars, they founded mosques and Muslim funeral associations on both coasts and the Midwest. The first mosques in the United States were built in the Highland Park area of Michigan in 1921 (no longer in existence), in Ross, North Dakota, in 1929 (no longer a mosque), and in Cedar Rapids, Iowa, in 1934 (known as the "mother mosque").

The interwar period also witnessed the rise of indigenous movements that sought to establish a distinctive religious and national identity for black migrants to northern metropolises. The most prominent of these movements were the Moorish Science Temple and the Nation of Islam. These movements taught that the original religion of black Americans was Islam, of which they were robbed by whites during slavery. The movements called on black Americans to return to their "original religion" and to adhere to a black Muslim national identity through which they could help one another and improve their lot in North America. In short, they appropriated Islam

as a means of developing a national identity through which African Americans could shed the stigma of being black and participate in American modernity. In the 1950s and 1960s, while the civil rights movement focused on repealing segregation in the South, the Nation of Islam, mainly through its national spokesman, Malcolm X, vigorously criticized institutionalized racism in the North.

In the 1950s, American Muslims began to organize at a more national level through the formation of the Federation of Islamic Associations in the United States and Canada. As the United States came to play a more prominent role in Muslim-majority countries in the aftermath of World War II, they also sought an intermediary role between their countries of origin and the United States. In 1959, for example, the federation established formal relations with the United Arab Republic, and in 1961, they held their tenth annual conventions overseas in Lebanon and Egypt, where Egyptian and U.S. embassy representatives greeted them upon landing in Cairo.

The liberalization of U.S. immigration laws in the 1960s led to the large-scale immigration of Asian and African Muslims. Unlike earlier immigrants, many of these immigrants were educated or came to North America to attend universities. Some had become politicized by anticolonial and Islamist movements. In North America, they found the freedom and means to organize and to work toward the realization of a utopian Islamic community.

The most important American Muslim organization founded at this time was the Muslim Students Association of the United States and Canada (MSA, established in 1963). A number of prominent national Muslim organizations, such as the Islamic Circle of North America and the Islamic Society of North America, emerged out of the MSA. Some of the founding members of the MSA associated with such Islamist organizations as the Muslim Brotherhood and Jamaʻat-i Islami. MSA publications often presented Islam as an ideology that should shape every aspect of Muslims' individual and communal lives. North America, which had become home to Muslims from every corner of the world, proved an ideal testing ground for the realization of this utopian vision of Islamic society; it provided a context in which cultural differences that had shaped the practice of Islam for centuries could be sidestepped for the realization of a puritanical and idealized Muslim community. In practice, however, cultural differences endured.

Over the years, as activist Muslims who came to study in North America remained, found jobs, and started families, they became involved not only in the politics of their homelands but also in American politics. While there was much debate in the 1980s among Muslim activists about the degree to which participation in American politics was appropriate, given that it was likely to lead to cultural assimilation, events such as the Gulf War (1990–91), the World Trade Center bombing (1993), and the attacks of September 11, 2001, all of which increased hostility toward Muslims, led politically minded American Muslims to become more engaged in American political and civic life in order to protect their civil rights and to counter prejudice. Political and civic participation has thus helped the assimilation of Muslims in North America, and political and civic activists, both immigrant and African American, have been at the forefront of defining an American Islam.

See also Europe; Malcolm X (1925–65); Mohammed, W. D. (1933–2008); Nation of Islam

Further Reading

Edward Curtis IV, ed., *The Columbia Sourcebook of Muslims in the United States*, 2002; Kambiz GhaneaBassiri, *A History of Islam in America: From the New World to the New World Order*, 2010; Michael Gomez, *Black Crescent: The Experience and Legacy of African Muslims in the Americas*, 2005; Yvonne Haddad, "Muslims in U.S. Politics: Recognized and Integrated, or Seduced and Abandoned?," *SAIS Review* 21, no. 2 (2001); Larry Poston, *Islamic Daʻwah in the West: Muslim Missionary Activity and the Dynamics of Conversion to Islam*, 1992.

KAMBIZ GHANEABASSIRI

notables

The term *aʻyān*, or "notables," was used as early as the medieval period to denote the most distinguished inhabitants of a district or town. Under the Ottoman regime, the term indicated a class of people whose local influence throughout the imperial provinces bestowed them with an official status.

In *The Emergence of the Modern Middle East*, Albert Hourani, historian and specialist on the Middle East, has called urban notables the "natural" leaders of Muslim towns under the authority of the centralized Ottoman government in the late 19th century. In contrast to imperial rule in the capital, Istanbul, Ottoman power over provincial centers required local intermediaries familiar with the cultures and languages of Arab provinces. There were three types of notables: local politicians who exerted social power as religious authorities or 'ulama', leaders of local armed garrisons, or "secular notables" whose power derived from their families' reputations. In the Arab provinces especially, notables were members of a landowning bureaucratic class comprising urban families who resided in cities but who exercised power over rural hinterlands, a fact that contributed to the increasing dependence of rural populations on growing cities for administrative, social, and commercial services. A form of patrician politics developed, characterized both by the dependence of the countryside on urban families and by the political authority of those families. Leading families could act as independent agents or as semi-independent local authorities. They were subordinate to centralized monarchical powers for whom they served as representatives on behalf of local populations. The notables' influence was never totally uncontested, and resistance to them was exercised in journalistic and historical writing as well as through other forms of social organization that questioned the civic organization of cities.

Because urban notables did not compose institutional bodies, their exercise of power depended on their ability to balance their own authority and their cooperation with, and access to, monarchical power. As intermediaries between provincial populations and a ruler's court, notables were both advisors to the powers to which they were subordinate and leaders in their own right of the populations subordinate to them. This latter power depended on notables' maintenance of independence, from which they could derive their own social authority. Within such a dynamic, notables were both vulnerable and crucial: the balancing act they performed inevitably left them open to criticism from some groups, and their distinct power within their own societies made them necessary conduits of access for agents of imperial rule. For this reason, Hourani has characterized the actions of notables as ambiguous or potentially circumspect. Theirs was a position that could occasion, at different moments, their temporary ascendance to rule in the wake of revolution or their acquiescence to central rule when facing the risk of losing their own access to power. The three types of notables did not exercise power consistently or uniformly across the diverse Ottoman provinces. North African notables, for example, were able to rule under the auspices of the sultan but were able to appoint their own successors. In Syria, by contrast, a more delicate balance between notables and the governor's court was rooted in families with a long-standing tradition of military, social, and commercial power.

Scholarship on the historical roles notables played and on the social history of the cities of the Middle East has traditionally been a large part of Ottoman history. As historian Dina Rizk Khoury has argued in *The Urban Social History of the Middle East, 1750–1950*, scholars of regions where Ottoman power was weakest have tended to interpret that history through the influence of Arab states and have concluded that notables' political power was proof that Arab cities fell short of full integration into the empire. According to this line of argument, local factions transformed into "national" groups following the collapse of the Ottoman Empire. Rounding out this view, according to Khoury, is the broader one that takes into account other regions, such as western Anatolia and the Balkans. In part, this fuller picture is effected by access to a wider range of sources, Ottoman and Arab, and by a realignment of previous views that were either entirely local or entirely homogeneous with respect to Ottoman authority. The most recent scholarship strikes a middle course that emphasizes the fact that simple binaries do not account for the nuanced roles of notables throughout the Ottoman provinces.

See also masses

Further Reading

Albert Hourani, "Ottoman Reforms and the Politics of Notables," in *The Emergence of the Modern Middle East*, 1981; Dina Rizk Khoury, "Political Relations Between City and State in the Middle East, 1700–1850," in *The Urban Social History of the Middle East, 1750–1950*, edited by Peter Sluglett, 2008; Philip S. Khoury, *Urban Notables and Arab Nationalism: The Politics of Damascus 1860*, 2003; Elizabeth Thompson, *Colonial Citizens: Republican Rights and Paternal Privilege in French Syria and Lebanon*, 2000; Keith D. Watenpaugh, "Middle-Class Modernity and the Persistence of the Politics of Notables in Inter-war Syria," *International Journal of Middle East Studies* 35 (2003).

NANCY KHALEK

O

oath of allegiance

In classical thought, the oath of allegiance (*bay'a* or *mubāya'a*) derives from the oaths taken by the Prophet Muhammad from his followers. The six Qur'anic occurrences of the verb *bāya'a* (Q. 9:111; Q. 48:10 [in two places]; Q. 48.18; Q. 60:12 [in two places]) are understood to refer to these pledges. The general obligation to honor covenants also applies to oaths of allegiance (Q. 5:1; 16:91).

Bāya'a is the reciprocal form of *bā'a*, "to buy or sell," whence "to make a bargain" and "to give the oath of allegiance." Although alternative etymologies have been proposed, the *bay'a* probably was understood in these terms in early seventh-century West Arabia. Thus, the oath of allegiance is one of many religiopolitical relationships expressed in commercial language in the Qur'an, as they sometimes are in other Near Eastern religiopolitical traditions.

In the ancient and late antique Near East, oaths of allegiance entailed the recognition of a religious or political leader under the sanction of deities—or, as in this case, a deity—recognized by all parties to the agreement. The cultural form is an ancient one, of which Assyrian vassal oaths (late second millennium to first millennium BCE) are an early instance. The biblical *berīt* (Hebrew, "covenant"), which can denote both God's relationship with man and the related contract between a leader and his followers, is another important precedent.

After Muhammad's death, *bay'a* quickly became the name for the oath of allegiance to a new caliph and a synecdoche for the accession ritual. *Bay'a* also denoted the oath taken to the caliph's designated successor and oaths taken to other leaders. An early strand of Islamic thought emphasized the *bay'a*'s soteriological character: "Whoever dies without a *bay'a* upon his neck, dies a pagan death [*mītatan jāhiliyyatan*]" was attributed to the Prophet. For the Umayyad caliphs (661–750), the oath recognized their claim to represent God's covenant on Earth; the Abbasids (750–1258) adopted similar rhetoric. Prevalent ideas about the *bay'a*'s voluntary and reciprocal nature, however, are reflected in eighth-century traditions invalidating oaths sworn under duress and justifying rebellion against an impious ruler.

Sanctions for perjury of Umayyad oaths of allegiance varied but sometimes included loss of property and wives. From the early Abbasid period, these latter two penalties became common, together with a third sanction of expiatory pilgrimages. Such penalties perhaps reflect a traitor's loss of his rights as a Muslim (that the perjurer becomes an infidel is sometimes made explicit in Abbasid texts). Although classical legal theorists argued that religiously motivated Muslim rebels should not be executed, the caliphs often killed those who broke their oath and sometimes justified this with reference to the Qur'an (Q. 5:33). Capital punishment finds numerous precedents in ancient and late antique religiopolitical practice.

For the Imami Shi'is, who emphasized designation (*naṣṣ*) of legitimate authority, the oath of allegiance diminished in importance. In contrast, the Sunni theologian Abu Bakr Muhammad b. al-Tayyib al-Baqillani (d. 1013) held that the *bay'a* was constitutive of the caliphate, expressing the "choice" (*ikhtiyār*) of the "people of loosing and binding" (*ahl al-ḥall wa-l-'aqd*). Accepting the realities of a caliphate long dominated by military commanders, he asserted that the election of a qualified candidate by just one legitimate elector was a contract (*'aqd*) binding all Muslims, as was a "testamentary designation" (*'ahd*) by the previous incumbent. The contractual form of the oath, which resembled both commercial and marriage contracts, implied reciprocity, and the caliph had a minimum obligation to uphold Islam. Subsequent Sunni consensus on the oath of allegiance resembled Baqillani's formulation, although theorists debated the minimum number of electors.

The Prophetic *bay'a* continued, and continues, to be widely invoked in the election or recognition of caliphs and other leaders. In premodern times, practice varied according to circumstance. For example, in some cases written documents were required; other *bay'a*s were entirely oral. In the modern Islamic world the new term *yamīn al-walā'* (lit. "oath of allegiance") is often used of oaths taken by government representatives or the people to one or more of the nation, the constitution, and the head of state. Some states founded on more traditional principles, such as Kuwait and Morocco, retain some classical features of the *bay'a*, and the term itself. Some 20th-century theorists have argued that the elective dimension of the classical *bay'a* is equivalent to the democratic process. For political Islamists, the *bay'a* often determines membership in the organization.

See also authority; leadership; obedience

Further Reading

Patricia Crone, *Medieval Islamic Political Thought*, 2004; Ella Landau-Tasseron, "The Religious Foundations of the Bay'a in Premodern Islam," *Research Monographs on the Muslim World*, series no. 2, paper no. 4, May 2010; Andrew Marsham, *Rituals of Islamic Monarchy: Accession and Succession in the First Muslim Empire*, 2009; Roy Mottahedeh, *Loyalty and Leadership in an Early Islamic Society*, 2001.

ANDREW MARSHAM

obedience

Numerous Qur'anic verses directly command obedience to God and His messenger (Q. 3:32, etc.); several other verses spell out in detail that once the messenger has issued a command, it must be obeyed without reluctance (Q. 4:65; 33:36). In contrast, additional obedience to "those in authority among you (the Muslims)" is mentioned directly only in a single verse, where it is appended or subordinated to obedience to God and His messenger (Q. 4:59). The exegetical tradition plausibly explains this extension as referring to subordinate commanders on expeditions sent out from Medina by the Prophet; such lesser commanders also had to be obeyed in the Prophet's absence. Numerous hadith reports also reinforce the idea of obedience to those in authority, but some of these also place a serious limitation on such authority: obedience is required only provided that the command to be obeyed is not in conflict with the commands of God and the messenger, according to the following formula: "There is no obedience to any created being in disobedience to God." This formula occurs in the writing of 'Abd al-Razzaq b. Hammam al-San'ani (744–827), who cites it in a probably much older tradition regarding an incident in the Prophet's life, showing that it had become a formal doctrine already very early, thus representing a strong countercurrent of resistance against the pretensions of rulers among the nascent class of 'ulama' (religious scholars) and their followers.

Later, this doctrine became embodied in juristic doctrines about the sovereignty of the rulers and their right to obedience from their subjects: People must obey their ruler, especially if he is just. However, even if they do not like him or if he issues commands that are against their personal interests, they must still follow him. For most authorities, a ruler's personal corruption or deviance is an insufficient cause for disobedience as long as the ruler maintains Muslim public worship. In the case of military campaigns, when any insubordination could lead to defeat and death, the right to disobey is limited to those orders in which annihilation is likely; the commander thus cannot give his troops orders that would be suicidal for the army, nor can he order individuals to commit suicide.

The actual effects of these rules are similar to political arrangements in other times and places, for every political system requires organization, hierarchy, subordination, and obedience and uses ideological justifications to legitimate itself. In Islam, the absolute power of the ruler to command is limited by what is right according to God and the Prophet, primarily as interpreted by the 'ulama'. Commands contrary to Islamic law should not be obeyed. In practice, such restrictions had only a limited effect on rulers, government officials, and their retinues, as rulers held actual political power and often autocratically abused it. Nevertheless, the limits placed on obedience to unjust commands and rulers in Islamic law tended to weaken and compromise the legitimacy of the rulers and the state, undermining the ruler's and the state's effective power over the ruled and also giving some excuse for rebellion against an unjust ruler. Also, the ability of the rulers to command obedience from the people for self-aggrandizing projects such as state building was severely curtailed in Islamic law. Since the four legitimate taxes (zakat, *jizya*, *'ushr*, and *kharāj*) were completely insufficient for running a state, the rulers usually had to resort to illegitimate taxes or duties (*mukūs*) to keep the state going, which always put them in violation of the law. Such limitations impeded the growth of the institutions required by the intrusive modern bureaucratic state, an effect that continues to be felt in various Muslim polities.

See also authority; leadership; taxation; 'ulama'

Further Reading

Antony Black, *The History of Islamic Political Thought: From the Prophet to the Present*, 2001; L. Carl Brown, *Religion and State*, 2000; Michael Cook, *Commanding Right and Forbidding Wrong in Islamic Thought*, 2001; Abu al-Hasan al-Mawardi, *al-Ahkam al-Sultaniyyah: The Laws of Islamic Governance*, translated by Asadullah Yate, 1996.

KHALID YAHYA BLANKINSHIP

Ottomans (1299–1924)

The Ottomans, the dynasty that ruled the Balkans, Anatolia, and most of the Arab world for up to six centuries, inherited a political tradition from the Seljuqs and Ilkhanids that came from three sources: Islamic, based on the experience of the early Muslim community; Near Eastern, inherited from the pre-Islamic empires of the Middle East and Persia and developed under the Abbasids; and Turco-Mongol, based on the tribal chieftainships of Central Asia. This combined tradition reached them through Islamic political literature translated early in their rule and through their experiences on the steppes and under late Seljuq and Mongol or Ilkhanid government. From the Mongols they adopted world conquest as the purpose of rule, a purpose that dovetailed with Islamic monotheism's goal of world domination and conversion as well as Near Eastern methods of centralized bureaucratic administration. They also learned that rulers' law, reconciled with Islamic law and implemented in state courts, could create a political community extending beyond the Muslims to encompass all faiths. Their political literature suggests that they intended from the beginning to establish a just state fit for world dominion, belying the tendentious image of their pure tribal ethos in 15th-century chronicles and Turkish nationalist legends. By the 16th-century reign of Süleiman the Magnificent (r. 1520–66), it became possible to think with 'Ala' al-Din 'Ali Kinalizade (1510–72) that the Ottomans had succeeded in creating the just and virtuous government recommended by Plato.

Beyond these heterogeneous origins, Ottoman political thought was influenced by two sets of circumstances. One was the initial Ottoman conquests, which were made in Byzantine territory. At

first Muslims were in the minority, and it was imperative to harness the strength and skills of non-Muslims for the state. Ottoman rulers therefore allied with Christian powers, created non-Muslim military units, and brought non-Muslims into the palace and administration. Although many of the non-Muslims serving the state converted to Islam, some Muslims reacted against what they defined as the corruption brought by officials of non-Muslim origin into what they assumed to be more truly Islamic politics, and they made the assimilation of ideas and institutions from different sources an excuse for rejecting state policies. An opposition strain developed throughout Ottoman politics (as in earlier Muslim politics) that used Islamic piety and the tradition of "forbidding wrong" to critique the state and condemn rulers' pragmatic politics of incorporation as the source of the empire's political problems.

The other main influence on Ottoman political thought was the transition from the conquest state and expanding economy of the early centuries to the stable geography and challenged economy of the 16th and 17th centuries and then to the shrinking empire and modernization efforts of the 18th and 19th centuries. These changes, deemed a decline from the empire's original potential of world conquest, generated a literature of advice and reform that became the most prominent strand of Ottoman political literature, especially after the end of the 16th century when the major works were composed. By the 19th century, this literature had become preoccupied with the assimilation of Western political thought.

The earliest Ottoman political works were translations of classics from the Seljuq and Ilkhanid periods. The first original works were composed in the 15th century. A book of philosophical ethics by Ahmed b. Husam al-Din al-Amasi (early 15th century) dedicated to Mehmed I (r. 1413–20) contained a section on politics, as did a work in the tradition of Islamic ethics by Sinan Paşa (d. 1486), the grand vizier of Mehmed II (r. 1451–81). The genres of history and historical epic also became vehicles for political thought; the heroic poems of Taj al-Din Ibrahim b. Khizr Ahmedi (d. 1413) and Enveri (late 15th century), as well as histories written by men such as Oruj b. 'Adil (late 15th to early 16th century), Dervish Ahmed Aşikpaşazade (1400–ca. 1484), Tursun Beg b. Hamza Beg (d. after 1491), and Mehmed Neşri, conveyed their authors' attitudes toward the state, individual rulers, and specific policies. In the early 16th century, the Ottoman prince Abu al-Khayr Muhammad Korkud b. Bayazid (1470–1513) and the grand vizier Lutfi Paşa (1488–1562/3) wrote works of political advice in new styles. Several of these works, even some of the earliest, exhibited a theme that would become characteristic of Ottoman political thought: the greatness and virtue of government in the past (the Ottoman, Muslim, or Near Eastern past) and its sad decline in the present. Early in the empire's life, writers claimed that the "Byzantine" administrative complexity introduced by Bayazid I (r. 1389–1402) corrupted the purity of the nomad conquerors, causing them to lose divine favor. Measured against the ideal state of these writers' imaginings, all real political life demonstrated the validity of their theme of decline.

The discourse of decline gained sudden relevance in the disturbed conditions of the early 17th century and generated a flood of political writing. Administrators and statesmen such as Mustafa 'Ali b. Ahmed b. 'Abd al-Mawla (1541–1600), Göriceli Koca Mustafa Bey (Koçi Bey), and Mustafa b. Abdullah Hajji Khalifa Katib Çelebi (1609–57) blamed the government's inability to cope with climatic, economic, technological, and geopolitical changes on the decay of administrative rectitude and sought either to restore the administrative effectiveness of the past or to galvanize the sultan into seizing the reins of government and eliminating bureaucratic corruption by force. Meanwhile, critics in religious positions who followed the reformist preacher Kadızade pointed to sins and ethical deviations in the body politic, such as Sufi worship, the consumption of coffee and tobacco, and peace with Christian states, and sought to convert the ruler and his entourage to a more pious and traditional Islam. The debate over the causes of the observed problems continued unresolved; 18th-century governments attempted to address both sets of concerns through military-political reform and the preaching of Islam. Politics spread beyond the elites; a popular politics of artisans, urban migrants, and their Janissary protectors developed in the cities, and a politics of notables and tax farmers emerged in the provinces.

The assumptions about progress and development in 19th-century European political thought appeared to offer a way out of this endless spiral. It was therefore embraced enthusiastically, especially by officials responsible for the empire's survival. Others, especially those disadvantaged by economic change, saw it as another foreign intrusion. While reforming officials labored to implement bureaucratic modernization, an exiled liberal group called the Young Ottomans critiqued their efforts. In a civilization accustomed to autocratic rule, they generated a new political literature opposing top-down modernization and sultanic absolutism. Their ideas helped prepare the way for the republican government and popular politics of the 20th century. The Young Turk Revolution of 1908, reacting against the heavy-handed despotism of Abdülhamid II (r. 1876–1909), revived the nullified Constitution of 1876, and the last years of the empire were spent under constitutional rule.

See also bureaucracy; commanding right and forbidding wrong; justice; Tanzimat

Further Reading

Caroline Finkel, *Osman's Dream: The Story of the Ottoman Empire, 1300–1923*, 2005; Halil İnalcık, *The Ottoman Empire: The Classical Age, 1300–1600*, translated by Norman Itzkowitz and Colin Imber, 1973; Donald Quataert, *The Ottoman Empire, 1700–1922*, 2000; Stanford J. Shaw and Ezel Kural Shaw, *The History of the Ottoman Empire and Modern Turkey*, 1976.

LINDA T. DARLING

P

Pakistan

Pakistan was created on August 14, 1947, when the British partitioned the subcontinent and handed over power to the Dominions of India and Pakistan. The new state comprised the Muslim-majority areas of Sindh, Balochistan, West Punjab, the North-West Frontier Province (as it was known at that time), and East Bengal. A thousand miles of Indian territory divided its western and eastern wings. The refugee crisis that arose from the Partition and the war with India over the disputed territory of Kashmir in 1947–48 undermined the process of democratic consolidation, as did the death of the country's founding father, Mohammad 'Ali Jinnah, on September 11, 1948. The country from the outset also faced unresolved questions concerning the role of Islam in its public life. These were exacerbated by the presence of a sizeable Hindu minority in its eastern wing. The Bengali population also sought national recognition of their language on par with Urdu. The initial refusal to meet this demand was a source of tension between East and West Pakistan, which increasingly acquired economic and political dimensions.

The role of Islam in public life proved equally controversial. It was a factor in the delay in establishing a constitution until 1956. The role of the shari'a in governance continued to divide liberals and conservatives. Changes in the wider Muslim world since the early 1980s and the breakaway of East Pakistan in 1971 following civil war strengthened the forces of Islamization in Pakistan. Some commentators also link this with the role of the army, which cultivated the mullahs (teachers of law) to provide a base of legitimacy but also used militant jihadist groups for strategic purposes in its regional conflict with India.

The army controlled the administration of martial law for well over 20 years of Pakistan's existence, starting with the first military coup in 1958. At other periods, as in the 1990s and following the October 2002 elections, the military exerted a powerful influence behind the scenes. This entrenched position had negative effects on the country's economic development and its efforts to establish normal relations with India. The military's dominant presence reflected Pakistan's unstable geopolitical location. Each military intervention further entrenched the military presence not only in politics but also in the economic life of the country. Successive coup leaders justified their military intervention due to the political corruption and instability that existed at the time. The impact of martial law on civil society in part perpetuated the problem the army was claiming to solve. The fact that the army had a high concentration of officers and troops from the Punjab also undermined national cohesion, as it was seen as an occupying force in such regions as Balochistan and East Bengal.

Military leaders in Pakistan have differed considerably in their attitude toward Islam. Ayub Khan (r. 1958–69) and Pervez Musharraf (r. 1999–2008) were personally liberal and modernist in their approach. In contrast, Zia-ul-Haq (r. 1977–88) emphasized a Deobandi piety. Zia's attempt to legitimize his regime through Islamization intensified conflict with the large Shi'i minority. Zia also encouraged the proliferation of madrasas (schools); this, along with other effects of the Afghan conflict, such as the flood of weapons and Afghan refugees, profoundly affected Pakistan's subsequent development. It was also from Zia's time that the army, through its intelligence arm—Inter-Services Intelligence (ISI)—developed links with militant jihadist groups. This policy was reversed in the wake of the September 11, 2001, attacks on the United States but was a factor in the challenge to the state's authority in the tribal areas, in some of the ambiguities in the prosecution of the "war on terror," and in the rise of terrorist attacks within Pakistan. While Musharraf narrowly escaped assassination on a number of occasions, Benazir Bhutto was killed on December 27, 2007. She had returned from exile in a deal brokered by Musharraf in the face of considerable Western pressure.

Civilian leaders also displayed authoritarian tendencies that undermined democratic consolidation. Zulfiqar Ali Bhutto's populist regime (1971–77) became increasingly heavy-handed in its dealings with opponents. The use of the army to quell a tribal insurgency in Balochistan from 1973 onward enabled the army to recover from its public humiliation following defeat in the 1971 India-Pakistan War. Nawaz Sharif's second administration (r. 1997–99) was also marked by authoritarian tendencies that formed the backdrop to Musharraf's "reluctant" coup on October 12, 1999.

Despite hopes for democratic consolidation following the February 2008 elections and Musharraf's stepping down from power, President Asif Ali Zardari was initially reluctant to strip his office of the powers to dissolve the assembly. His government became mired in charges of corruption and incompetency. Pakistan thus more than 60 years after its creation continues to face problems of democratic consolidation, civil-military relations, and the establishment of a culture of religious and political tolerance that have beset it from birth.

See also Bangladesh; India; Iqbal, Muhammad (1877–1938); Jinnah, Mohammad 'Ali (1876–1948); Mawdudi, Abul al-A'la (1903–79)

Further Reading

Tariq Ali, *The Leopard and the Fox: A Pakistan Tragedy*, 2006; Stephen Philip Cohen, *The Idea of Pakistan*, 2006; Zahid Hussain, *Frontline Pakistan: The Path to Catastrophe and the Killing of Benazir Bhutto*, 2008; Owen Bennett Jones, *Pakistan: Eye of the Storm*, 2003; Shuja Nawaz, *Crossed Swords: Pakistan, Its Army and the Wars Within*, 2008; Ayesha Siddiqa, *Military Inc.: Inside Pakistan's Military Economy*, 2007; Ian Talbot, *Pakistan: A Modern History*, 2009.

IAN TALBOT

Palestine

In contemporary Arab nationalist and Islamist discourse, the term "Palestine" (*filasṭīn*) refers to an area delimited by the former British Mandate of Palestine (1923–48). This same territory more or less incorporates the modern state of Israel and the occupied West Bank and Gaza Strip. *Filasṭīn* first entered the Islamic politico-geographic lexicon following the Arab Muslim conquest of former Byzantine areas during the 630s. Adapting the Roman designation, Palestina Prima, the new rulers declared as *jund filasṭīn* (Military District of Palestine) an area situated between the Jordan River in the east and the Mediterranean coast to the west, Mount Carmel to the north, and Gaza to the south.

The significance of *filasṭīn* exceeded its administrative function. Muslims, generally, came to associate the region with Jerusalem, known in Arabic and Islamic texts as *madīnat bayt al-maqdis*, "City of the Holy Sanctuary." In contemporary Palestinian spoken Arabic, this designation reduces simply to al-Quds, "The Holy" (i.e., the Holy City). Asserting the Muslim attachment, Caliph ʿAbd al-Malik (r. 685–705) initiated the construction of the Aqsa Mosque and the Dome of the Rock on the platform that had once supported the Jewish temple. Jerusalem's importance declined after the Umayyad collapse in 750. Not until the Crusaders took Jerusalem in 1099 would *filasṭīn* again become central to Muslim political imagination. The massive expansion of *faḍā'il bayt al-maqdis* (the excellences of Jerusalem) literature—a type of propaganda meant to encourage Muslims to take up the jihad against the foreign invaders—played a significant role in this revival.

In the modern period, Palestine served as an important symbol and rallying point of the Arab nationalist and Islamist causes. During the 1930s and 1940s, Palestinian leaders such as al-Hajj Amin al-Husayni (1895–1974), mufti of Jerusalem and head of the Supreme Muslim Council and Arab Higher Committee, made Palestine a central issue in Muslim anticolonial consciousness globally by sending delegations to raise funds and solicit political support as far away as India. Husayni also actively courted the backing of the Egyptian Muslim Brotherhood, a group founded by Hasan al-Banna in 1928. Banna sent activists to organize chapters throughout Palestine. He also preached in Egypt on the threat of Zionism and the necessity of reviving the jihad to prevent the loss of Palestine to the Jews. Palestine, he declared, was an Islamic *waqf* (inalienable patrimony), and its defense was essential to the revitalization of the Islamic *umma* (community of all Muslims).

Whereas Banna's perspective was Islamic, secular Arab and Palestinian nationalists saw the defense of Palestine as a matter of preserving Arab rights, sovereignty, and honor in the face of European and American imperialism. Although the Islamic cultural heritage was a critical component of their historical consciousness, the secular nationalists, particularly the main factions comprising the Palestinian Liberation Organization, tended to construe Palestine not as primarily Islamic but as a "holy land" in which diverse religious groups—Muslims, Christians, Jews, Samaritans, and others—historically coexisted. Against the exclusive ethno-nationalist vision of Zionism, or the religiously exclusive idea of an Islamic state, the Palestinian secular-nationalists proposed a multi-sectarian democratic state.

By contrast, the Palestinian Islamist movements that emerged in the aftermath of the 1967 war—groups such as Shaykh Ahmad Yasin's (1937–2004) Islamic Collective (al-Mujammaʿ al-Islami, founded in 1973)—resisted the secular-nationalist dilution of Islam to a mere heritage shared by others, reasserting instead Banna's emphasis on the priority of the Islamic religious claim. In the 1980s, new groups like the Islamic Jihad and the Islamic Resistance Movement (Hamas) radicalized this perspective by asserting that the road to the *umma*'s revival lay in jihad to retake Jerusalem.

International jihadist groups also made Palestine a rallying cause. The leader of al-Qaeda, Osama bin Laden, declared in 2003, for example, that Palestine and Afghanistan constituted the most important arenas for jihad, since in both areas Muslims had the chance to weaken America and its staunchest ally, "the Jews." Significantly, Palestinian Islamist groups such as Hamas resisted cooperation with al-Qaeda. Although Hamas invoked transnational Islamic solidarity, its policies and practices focused almost exclusively on combating the Israeli occupation and liberating Palestinian territory rather than on a global struggle against the United States.

See also Arab nationalism; Arafat, Yasir (1929–2004); al-Banna, Hasan (1906–49); Bin Laden, Osama (1957–2011); Hamas; Jerusalem; jihad; Palestinian Liberation Organization (PLO); secularism

Further Reading

ʿAbd al-Fattah Muhammad El-Awaisi, *The Muslim Brothers and the Palestine Question: 1928–1947*, 1998; Osama bin Laden, *Messages to the World: The Statements of Osama bin Laden*, edited by Bruce Lawrence, 2005; Loren D. Lybarger, *Identity and Religion in Palestine: The Struggle between Islamism and Secularism in the Occupied Territories*, 2007; Beverley Milton-Edwards, *Islamic Politics in Palestine*, 1996; Shaul Mishal and Avraham Sela, *The Palestinian Hamas: Vision, Violence, and Coexistence*, 2000, reissued with updated introduction 2006.

LOREN D. LYBARGER

Palestinian Liberation Organization (PLO)

Decreed into existence by Arab leaders gathered at the First Arab Summit in Cairo, Egypt, in 1964, the Palestinian Liberation Organization (Munazzamat al-Tahrir al-Filastiniyya; PLO) functioned for nearly three decades as the primary framework of Palestinian political identity. Egyptian president Gamal Abdel Nasser (1918–70), preeminent tribune of pan-Arabism and convener of the First Arab Summit, originally intended the PLO to be an instrument for channeling Palestinian aspirations and buttressing Egypt's claim to leadership of the Arab cause. Israel's stunning victory in the Six-Day War of June 1967, however, weakened Nasser and diminished pan-Arabism as a viable option for addressing Palestinian grievances and goals.

The enfeebling of pan-Arabism after 1967 coincided with the emergence of Fatah—*fatḥ*, which means "conquest" or "opening," and is also an inverse acronym derived from the organization's Arabic name, Harakat al-Tahrir al-Watani al-Filastini (i.e., the Palestinian National Liberation Movement). Between 1968 and 1969, Fatah took control of the PLO, transforming the organization into a specifically Palestinian instrument of self-assertion. Formed in the late 1950s, Fatah was an indigenous Palestinian response to the perceived failures of leadership during the preceding decade, a period that had ended with the expulsion or displacement of approximately 750,000 Palestinians during the war of 1948. Fatah's founders—principal among them Yasir Arafat (1929–2004), Khalil al-Wazir (1935–88), Salah Khalaf (1933–91), and Khalid al-Hassan (1928–94)—represented a new generation of leaders who had personally experienced the expulsions. Sharing a common class background (petty bourgeois), as well, these individuals met one another while studying in the new state universities in Cairo and elsewhere.

In contrast with others of their generation who had aligned with Nasser-led pan-Arabism, Fatah's founders insisted that the Palestinians could not afford to wait for the Arab regimes to act. They had to seize the initiative themselves to liberate their homeland through independent armed struggle. Making good on the rhetoric, Fatah commandos launched their first raid against Israel on December 31, 1964. Although a failure in military terms, the event carried immense symbolic value. Dozens more actions followed. In the wake of the 1967 war, Palestinian refugee youths inspired by "the Palestinian Revolution" (*al-thawra al-filasṭīniyya*) flocked to PLO bases in Jordan to train as guerrilla fighters.

Eminently practical, the new leaders of the PLO accepted all volunteers regardless of their orientation as long as they demonstrated commitment to the baseline objective of national liberation. Underlying this pragmatic inclusiveness was a normative vision, reflected in official PLO documents like the amended covenant of 1968, that conceived of Palestinians as a multisectarian community (1) existing for generations within the territory once demarcated by the limits of the British Mandate of Palestine (1922–48); (2) sharing a common language (Arabic) and ties of affinity with other Arabic-speaking nations; (3) possessing attachments to the three major monotheisms—Islam, Christianity, and Judaism—and a tradition of religious coexistence within the Holy Land; (4) holding in common the customs of the now lost *fallāḥī* (peasant) past; and, most critically, (5) sharing the memory of violent dispossession during the 1948 war and a consequent commitment to reversing the expulsions and achieving the establishment of a single democratic state for all its citizens—Muslims, Christians, and indigenous Palestinian Jews—in the entirety of Palestine. These themes later underwent modifications in response to historical events that dictated political realism. In the wake of the 1973 war, for example, the Palestinian National Council meeting a year later deemphasized the restitution of all Palestine by instead calling for an independent national authority over any part of Palestinian territory that might be liberated.

Although faced with immense obstacles—Arab state interventions, violent Israeli reprisals, U.S. refusal to open a dialogue, a dispersed Palestinian population, and more—the PLO succeeded in asserting its claim to represent all Palestinians. By the end of the 1970s, the PLO had established an independent territorial base within Lebanon. Operating as a state within a state, the organization featured multiple social service agencies, military forces, and parliamentary and executive structures. It also had embassies in various countries and even attained observer status in the United Nations. The Israeli invasion of Lebanon in 1982 destroyed the PLO's base of operations, but the leadership managed to reestablish the organization in North Africa while also expanding its underground presence in the occupied Gaza Strip and West Bank.

The outbreak of the Intifada (uprising) in December 1987 greatly enhanced these efforts. A new generation of secular-nationalist leaders aligned with the PLO factions moved quickly to form the United National Command of the Intifada (al-Qiyada al-Wataniyya al-Muwahhada li-l-Intifada), while the PLO leadership outside capitalized diplomatically by opening a dialogue with the United States and declaring national independence in Gaza and the West Bank. At the same time, however, in a development that portended the demise of the dominance of PLO-style nationalism, revived Muslim Brotherhood forces responded to the Intifada and secularist attempts to control it by declaring the establishment of the Islamic Resistance Movement (Harakat al-Muqawama al-Islamiyya), better known as Hamas. (The Muslim Brotherhood received its start in Egypt during the 1920s. Advocating a return to piety, it pioneered mass politics as a path to Islamic sociopolitical revival in the Middle East. Beginning in the 1930s, it established branches across British Mandate Palestine, and its members fought alongside the Arab armies during the 1948 war. Yasir Arafat and Khalil al-Wazir, among others, were members of this movement before they established Fatah.) From the start, Hamas pursued an independent line in a bid to reframe Palestinian identity and resistance in Islamic terms. It succeeded in imposing its presence on the Palestinian political field, even during the Oslo Peace Process (1993–2000), an event that led to the formation of a Palestinian National Authority (PNA) in parts of the West Bank

and Gaza Strip. The PNA effectively displaced the PLO as the primary institutional framework of the secular-nationalist mainstream. The violent collapse of the Oslo process in 2000 alongside mounting popular frustrations with Fatah and the PNA, however, gave momentum to the Islamist opposition. In January 2006, Hamas won an outright majority in the Palestinian Legislative Council elections. Eighteen months later, faced with an internationally backed effort to arm and train Fatah forces, Hamas initiated a preemptive coup that routed Fatah and ended in a complete takeover of the Gaza Strip. While Fatah remained nominally in control of the West Bank territories that had been ceded to the PNA during the Oslo process, the ascendancy of Hamas in Gaza effectively ended the 40-year secular-nationalist monopoly over Palestinian politics.

See also Arab nationalism; Arafat, Yasir (1929–2004); Hamas; Palestine

Further Reading

Helena Cobban, *The Palestinian Liberation Organization: People, Power, and Politics*, 1984, reprinted 1992; Rashid Khalidi, *Under Siege: P.L.O. Decisionmaking during the 1982 War*, 1986; Loren D. Lybarger, *Identity and Religion in Palestine: The Struggle between Islamism and Secularism in the Occupied Territories*, 2007; Yezid Sayigh, *Armed Struggle and the Search for State: The Palestinian National Movement, 1949–1993*, 1997; Avraham Sela and Moshe Ma'oz, eds., *The P.L.O. and Israel: From Armed Conflict to Political Solution, 1964–1994*, 1997.

LOREN D. LYBARGER

Pan-Islamism

Pan-Islamism (1876) or Pan-Islam (1882) was an interpretative concept developed by Western observers to denote claims by Muslim public intellectuals and politicians to represent what they imagined to be a unified Muslim community (*umma*). Though some Western writers denied that this concept referred to anything real, and in spite of the fact that its use was extremely diverse, it deeply influenced the public opinion on Islam and Muslims, especially from 1880 to 1920. In scholarship, Pan-Islam or Pan-Islamism has been studied from 1900 onward. It was mostly Indian Muslim writers who, from the late 19th century, used the concept in a positive sense. Already in the 1870s, the Ottoman term *ittiḥād-i islām* (Union of Islam) was conceptually contextualized on the pattern of Western pan-ideologies, in particular pan-Slavism and pan-Germanism. The term itself had come into public use in the middle of the 1860s and soon spread to India and Iran. Originally there was no clear Arabic expression that reflected the Ottoman usage. Only at a later stage in the 19th century did Egyptian reformers coin terms like *waḥda islāmiyya* (Islamic Unity) or *jāmi'a islāmiyya* (Islamic Union). Nevertheless, already in the late 1870s Muslim reformers based in Egypt, notably Afghani (ca. 1838–97), identified Pan-Islamism as descriptive of a political and cultural agency whose claim was not to be restricted to specific national publics. Many Muslims and some Western writers were extremely critical of efforts to assemble the heterogeneity of Muslim public expressions under the single term Pan-Islam, as this only mirrored the Western construct of a "Muslim peril" (following clichés like the "yellow peril"). In fact, Pan-Islamism was often interpreted as an endeavor to unite Muslims under the despotic rule of the Ottoman sultan Abdülhamid II using Sufi orders and other religious groups or secret political associations, both creating a "widespread European anxiety about Muslim solidarity." In this sense, Pan-Islamism had been frequently used as a framework to contextualize Islam in the then-current realm of political imagination.

Although no longer used as an analytical tool to study Islamic political thought, Pan-Islamism can be discussed as a historical label for different and partly contradictory intellectual and political trends from the 1870s to the 1930s. Both Western observers and Muslims refer mainly to one of the following trends: (1) the claim of the Ottoman Empire to act as a representative of the Muslim world in its struggle with colonial powers; (2) the claim of specific social groups and communities, such as certain Sufi orders, to represent a network of internal solidarity and loyalty that transcend the nation-state boundaries; (3) the claim of Muslim public intellectuals that they represent Islam as a transnational cultural and even political order that should be reunified against the particularism and despotism of nation-states as well as against the dominion of Western colonial powers and, not least, against Christian missionary activities; and (4) a general cultural call for the "awakening of an Islamic conscience" and a striving for "free and complete expression of progress in Moslem societies."

All four trends have in common (1) a reference to the totality of the Muslim World and its "valorization" as a symbolic framework of political activity; (2) a definition of some sort of political, social, or cultural representation, either in the form of the Ottoman sultan or embodied by networks or institutions of Muslim intellectuals; and (3) a moral judgment on the Islamic past and on the contemporary state of Muslim societies. In fact, all three characteristics mirror the standards of secular ideological and religious cultural discourses that dominated the late 19th and early 20th centuries. This is why Western observers had no difficulty seeing these trends as equivalent to other pan-ideologies (e.g., pan-Slavism [1836], pan-Hellenism [1847], pan-Germanism [1850], pan-orthodoxy [Karl Marx; 1855], and pan-Europeanism [1856]).

Perceiving Islam as an immanent frame of political and cultural references was a common feature of public Islam and of Ottoman imperial ideology. Islamic currents subsumed under Pan-Islamism thus belonged to different social fields. As an imperial ideology, Pan-Islamism legitimated the power of the Ottoman sultan after the dramatic course of the Russo-Turkish War (1877–78), which resulted in the establishment of the Bulgarian state; the full independence of Romania, Serbia, and Montenegro; the Russian annexation of the Kars district; and the formation of a British protectorate over

Cyprus and of an Austrian-Hungarian protectorate over Bosnia and Herzegovina (established by the Treaty of Berlin in 1878). Its importance grew after the French occupation of Tunisia in 1881, the Greek annexation of Thessaly and South Epirus in 1881, and the British occupation of Egypt in 1882. The Ottoman ruling elites tried to compensate for these territorial losses with an appeal to a transnational Islamic identity, which would create general support for the Ottoman Empire in the emerging public opinion in Muslim societies. As an imperial ideology, Pan-Islamism did not have distinct normative content or irridentist claims but was conceived as a network of solidarity founded on the activities of individual agents. In some cases, this network incorporated Sufi orders (Madani, Rifa'i) whose elites were often called to Istanbul in order to directly work as an Ottoman agency.

The Ottoman propagation of Islamic unity did not, however, yield the response the empire might have expected. Ottoman Pan-Islamism faded out after 1910. In spite of massive propaganda, it had only limited success in mobilizing pro-Ottoman public opinion during the Italian-Turkish War (1911–12) and World War I. Consequently, Muslim public intellectuals came to stress the independence of Islam as an autonomous category of cultural and moral order based on ideas of Islamic unity. Apart from a few exceptions, such as the Khilafat movement in India (1919–24), the denationalized form of Pan-Islamism never served as an instrument for broader political mobilization but remained instead a framework for contextualizing particularistic political and cultural claims. In most cases, Islamic unity was construed as a symbolic field of solidarity that competed with other universalisms like Christianity, socialism, or, more generally, the West. Only rarely was this Islamic unity theoretically constructed, being taken instead as a self-evident form of religious solidarity and of a transnational Islamic public.

See also al-Afghani, Jamal al-Din (1838–97); Ottomans (1299–1924); revival and reform

Further Reading

Kemal H. Karpat, *The Politicization of Islam: Reconstructing Identity, Faith, and Community in the Late Ottoman State*, 2001; Nikki R. Keddie, "Pan-Islam as Proto-Nationalism," *Journal of Modern History* 41 (1969); Jacob M. Landau, *The Politics of Pan-Islam: Ideology and Organization*, 1990; Reinhard Schulze, "Citizens of Islam," in *Law and the Islamic World: Past and Present*, edited by C. Troll et al., 1995.

REINHARD SCHULZE

Pan-Malaysian Islamic Party (PAS)

The Pan-Malaysian Islamic Party (Parti Islam Se-Malaysia; PAS) emerged from a split between two factions, the 'ulama' and the political elite, within the Bureau of Religious Affairs of the conservative-nationalist Malay party (United Malays National Organisation; UMNO). On November 24, 1951, PAS was formed under the leadership of Haji Fuad Hassan, who was the head of the UMNO Bureau of Religious Affairs. In 1953 Fuad Hassan was replaced by Abbas Elias, a doctor by training who was also a member of the colonial medical services in British Malaya. By 1955 PAS was no longer linked to the UMNO party. Between 1956 and 1969, the combined leadership of Burhanuddin al-Helmy and Zulkiflee Muhammad helped turn PAS into a modern political organization. These leaders were largely responsible for turning the movement into a political party with a centralized organizational structure, a chain of command, and links with other Islamic parties and movements abroad. Under the leadership of Burhanuddin, PAS developed into an Islamist party that was both nationalist and anti-imperialist in its outlook. Burhanuddin's heroes and models were men of the day such as President Sukarno of Indonesia and Gamal Abdel Nasser of Egypt. He looked to the Bandung conference and the Pan-Arab alliance, rather than the Muslim community of Medina during the time of the Prophet, as models of collective political action. In 1969 Burhanuddin died after being put under detention without trial by the Malaysian government. PAS then came under the leadership of Mohamad Asri Muda, who was a staunch defender of Malay rights and privileges.

Between 1970 and 1982, Asri Muda turned PAS into an ethnocentric Malay-Muslim party concerned with the promotion of the status of Malay-Muslims in the country. But during that time Asri Muda's defense of Malay ethic rights also compromised PAS's Islamic credentials, and as a result other alternative Islamist movements such as the Malaysian Islamic Youth Movement (Angkatan Belia Islam Malaysia; ABIM) emerged. In 1982, PAS experienced an internal coup that led to the overthrow of Asri Muda and the rise of the "'ulama' faction" led by senior PAS 'ulama' like Tuan Guru Yusof Rawa and Tuan Guru Nik Aziz Nik Mat, as well as a number of ex-ABIM activists like Ustaz Fadzil Noor, Ustaz Hadi Awang, and Muhammad Sabu. The 1980s witnessed the first violent clash between PAS and the Malaysian government, as the Islamist party became more uncompromising in its demands. PAS's fortunes were mixed in the mid-1990s. At the 1995 general elections, it managed to retain control of the northern state of Kelantan but failed to make inroads anywhere else in the country. PAS made its biggest gains ever in the November 1999 elections, gaining control of two states. But in 2004 the party suffered another setback as a result of its support for the Taliban and its protest against the invasion of Afghanistan and Iraq, which reinforced the image of PAS being a radical Islamist party in the eyes of many ordinary Malaysian voters. At the elections of March 2008, PAS regained some of its losses as it joined the People's Alliance (Pakatan Rakyat) coalition and gained control of Kelantan as well as Perak and Kedah. In 2011 PAS was the second biggest Malay-Muslim party in Malaysia with an estimated one million members and supporters throughout the country. It remained committed to its goal of creating an Islamic state in Malaysia.

See also Malaysia; Southeast Asia

Further Reading

Zainah Anwar, *Islamic Revivalism in Malaysia: Dakwah among the Students*, 1987; Alias Mohamad, *Malaysia's Islamic Opposition: Past, Present and Future*, 1991; Idem, "The Pan-Malaysian Islamic Party: A Critical Observation," in *Southeast Asian Affairs*, 1978; Chandra Muzaffar, *Islamic Resurgence in Malaysia*, 1987; Farish A. Noor, *Islam Embedded: The Historical Development of the Pan-Malaysian Islamic Party PAS: 1951–2003*, 2 vols., 2004; Farish A. Noor, Martin van Bruinessen, and Yoginder Sikand, eds., *The Madrasa in Asia: Political Activism and Transnational Linkages*, 2008; Zainal Abidin Abdul Wahid, "Islamic Resurgence and Political Movements in Malaysia," paper presented at Ohio University, February 5, 1987.

FARISH AHMAD-NOOR

parliament

National parliaments, legislatures, assemblies, or councils exist in virtually all countries worldwide, including in all the approximately 50 Muslim-majority states and territories. Strictly speaking, parliament is a legislative body deriving from the political tradition of the United Kingdom and having a prime minister. However, national legislative or consultative bodies in different institutional settings (e.g., parliamentarianism, presidentialism, semipresidentialism) and political regimes (e.g., democratic and authoritarian) are often referred to as parliaments.

Democratic legislatures have as their primary function to propose, debate, and vote on bills. Authoritarian parliaments may play an advisory role as prescribed in their constitution (e.g., Oman) or may have more robust lawmaking prerogatives, which are limited, in practice, by the executive branch of government (e.g., Algeria).

Origins of Modern Parliaments

Democracy, or "rule by the many," first emerged in Athens, Greece, in the fifth century BCE. In a city-state, formal equality and self-government were attained through direct democracy—participation of free, adult males in a citizen's assembly. The impracticality of direct democracy in the large nation-states of 19th-century Europe necessitated the development of representative political institutions.

Parliaments in Authoritarian Countries

Parliamentary bodies vary according to the extent to which they embody the procedures of democracy or polyarchy, a term coined by Robert A. Dahl to mean a system in which the interests of every member of the polity are taken into equal consideration when making binding collective decisions. In *Democracy and Its Critics* (1989), Dahl describes polyarchy as having seven institutions: elected officials, free and fair elections, inclusive suffrage, the right to run for office, freedom of expression, alternative information, and associational autonomy. Democratic legislatures enjoy influence in policy making and institutional autonomy from the executive branch, are representative, and have the material and human capacity to undertake the complex tasks of lawmaking and oversight. Authoritarian parliaments are weak in comparison to the executive branch. Their members can usually provide particularistic benefits to their constituents but have little power to shape policy independent of the executive.

Emergence and Change in Parliaments in the Muslim World

Legislative bodies emerged in new states following the decolonization of Africa and Asia and have frequently been established by nationalist movements, suggesting that they confer legitimacy to nationalist and revolutionary claims and provide other organizational advantages. The Polisario Front, which contests Moroccan claims to the former Spanish Sahara, established the Sahrawi Arab Democratic Republic and the 101-seat Sahrawi National Council in 1976. The Palestinian National Authority also has a unicameral legislative body, the 132-seat, democratically elected Palestinian Legislative Council, successor to the Palestinian Liberation Organization's Palestinian National Council, established in 1964. The revolutionary Libyan Republic declared the Interim Transitional National Council on March 5, 2011, at the height of its conflict with Colonel Qaddafi's forces.

In *Legislative Politics in the Arab World* (1998), Abdo I. Baaklini, Guilain Denoeux, and Robert Springborg contend that Arab parliaments are not remnants of colonialism. Rather, the Ottoman Empire's first council emerged during the period of Sultan Selim III (r. 1789–1807), and instances exist in which colonial powers disbanded indigenous parliaments threatening colonial rule. Early republican experiments include the establishment of the first parliament in Egypt in 1866, Iran in 1906, and Iraq in 1922.

Legislative assemblies gained visibility as demands for political reform swept the globe beginning in the 1970s. The Federal National Council (Majlis al-Ittihad al-Watani) of the United Arab Emirates was established as an appointed body in 1971, but pressure from political opposition prompted limited reforms. In 2006, a group of voters consisting of less than 1 percent of the population elected half of the parliament's 40 members for the first time.

Variation in Parliaments in the Muslim World

Apart from the expression of Islamic principles in constitutional and legal instruments, which frequently refer to parliamentary life as an application of *shūrā* (consultation), parliaments in the Muslim world do not differ markedly in structure or function from those in other parts of the world. The number of chambers (i.e., bicameral or unicameral) and seats, term length, and electoral or appointment system vary little worldwide. The power of the parliament, however, varies as a function of the level of democracy. The preponderance of weak parliaments in the Muslim world corresponds to the high number of authoritarian regimes in the region.

Parliaments in the Muslim world vary widely in their power vis-à-vis the executive branch of government, as measured by the

Parliamentary Powers Index (PPI). On this scale, which ranges between 0 and 1, the weakest parliament in the Muslim world is the Somali Transitional Federal Parliament (PPI = 0), and the strongest is the Turkish Meclis (PPI = 0.78).

Among the world's weakest, the Saudi Consultative Council (Majlis al-Shura) functions in an advisory capacity to the king, who is both the head of the government and the head of state. Expanding the 12-member Consultative National Council established in 1924, the 60-member Majlis was created in 1993, and its membership gradually expanded to 150 appointed members. The Majlis cannot introduce bills, and promulgation of legislation is the sole prerogative of the king, who can disband the parliament at any time. Rather, it discusses proposed legislation before passing it to the parallel Council of Ministers. The Majlis has the power to summon ministers to debates pertaining to their jurisdiction (Article 22, Consultative Council Act).

Among the world's more powerful parliaments, Turkey's is part of a tradition of constitutionalism dating back to Ottoman rule. The unicameral Türkiye Büyük Millet Meclisi (Turkish Grand National Assembly) was established in the 1920s following the fall of the Ottoman Empire and the abolition of the caliphate. Turkey is a secular state, though the Islamist Justice and Development Party won an absolute majority of the seats for the first time in 2002; 18 women were elected to parliament in 1935. The Meclis (Parliament) enjoys the prerogatives and autonomy of a democratic parliament and can propose laws, elect the president, and remove the president and prime minister from office. Unlike many other countries in the region, Turkey does not have a gender quota, though 9.1 percent of the Meclis is made up of women (2007).

Parliaments and Islamic Political Thought

Debate about the role of parliaments in the modern Islamic state centers on the principle of *shūrā*, which existed as a practice in pre-Islamic Arabia and was used by the early Islamic community. *Shūrā* means collective decision making on matters of common interest. Two instances of *shūrā* are recorded in the Qur'an: the first an injunction to Muhammad to consult with his followers (3:159) and the second an exhortation for members of the community to engage in the praiseworthy act of consultation (42:38). Muslim scholars have debated the meaning and role of *shūrā* in modern Muslim political life. In *Tafsir Surat al-Shura* (Interpretation of sura 42, The Consultation [1973]), Sayyid Qutb (1906–66) argued that neither a parliament nor popular elections have a place; *shūrā* is optional and nonbinding consultation between a ruler and members of the elite. Although the caliph may consult with elites in order to achieve a wise and just ruling in keeping with God's law, he is neither elected by the council nor required to consult with them or take their advice as binding. The Qur'an and the sunna are sufficient sources of law, and no legislative function can be delegated to human beings.

In *The Principles of State and Government in Islam* (1961), Muhammad Asad (d. 1992) argued that the principles of *shūrā*, *ijtihād* (independent reasoning), and *ijmā'* (consensus), along with the Islamic values of justice, equality, and human dignity, are the basis for the application of representative democracy. Like him, Fathi Osman interprets *shūrā* as obligatory, citing it as an Islamic impetus for popular sovereignty exercised through the free election of a parliament and head of state. A legislature is required to make laws on matters not addressed by the Qur'an and sunna, including modern issues not encountered at the time of the Prophet and those on which jurists disagree, so long as they do not contradict any part of the shari'a.

See also democracy; elections

Further Reading

Muhammad Asad, *The Principles of State and Government in Islam*, 1961; Michaelle L. Browers, *Democracy and Civil Society in Arab Political Thought: Transcultural Possibilities*, 2006; John Bulloch, *The Shura Council in Saudi Arabia*, 1993; Khaled Abou El Fadl, ed., *Islam and the Challenge of Democracy*, 2004; M. Steven Fish and Matthew Kroenig, *The Handbook of National Legislatures: A Global Survey*, 2009; Fathi Osman, *Islam in a Modern State: Democracy and the Concept of Shura*, 2001.

LINDSAY J. BENSTEAD

patrimonial state

Patrimonialism is one of Max Weber's ideal types of political organization. It is a system of personal authority in which the ruler's servants are the holders of office and the administration of the kingdom is an extension of the management of the ruler's household. In medieval Muslim patrimonial states, Weber noted that the rulers' armies consisted of Turkish military slaves (mamluks). In Weber's view, this type of military force could be the source of chronic political instability, which made the Near East the classic location of nonlegitimate domination or what he called "sultanism." Although Weber's notion of sultanism as militarized, nonlegitimate domination can be misleading, his model of the patrimonial state fits the system of delegated authority as developed by the Abbasid caliphs and evolved with the emergence of independent Islamicate monarchies.

The Persianate polity, as it evolved under the Samanids in Khurasan and Central Asia (Transoxiana) in the ninth and tenth centuries, was divided into the *dargāh*, the household of the ruler or the court, and the *dīwān*, the bureaucracy, which consisted of several branches. The court was managed by the ruler's representative or deputy (*wakīl*) and an observer (*mushrif*), whose duty was to be aware of all that went on in the *dargāh* and report on it. The most important group among "the men of the *dargāh*" was the corps of military slaves, one of whom was appointed the chief chamberlain (*ḥājib-i buzurg*), who controlled access to the king. The corps of military mamluks was created by Isma'il b. Ahmad, the founder of the Samanid dynasty, and remained the most important element in

its military organization. The same corps of Mamluks supplied the security force under a police chief or captain of the watch (*ṣāḥib* or *amīr-i ḥaras*), either a slave general or a noble freeman, for maintaining law and order in the cities. Just as in Weber's ideal type, the policing of the cities was considered an extension of the duties of the guards who served at the court and protected the king. The Ghaznavid dynasty was founded by one of the Samanid Turkish mamluks. The Ghaznavids in the 11th and 12th centuries modeled it on that of the Samanids. The Ghaznavid patrimonial state was transplanted to India by the Ghurid military slave generals who founded the Delhi Sultanate in the early 13th century.

Meanwhile, another type of patrimonial regime developed with the formation of nomadic Turkic states in the 11th century—namely, the Qarakhanid kingdom in Central Asia and the Seljuq Empire in Iran, Iraq, Syria, and Anatolia. According to this conception, the kingdom was the patrimonial property of the whole family of the khan, the tribal chief, and was divided into appanages upon his death. The problem of succession, however, resulted in the disintegration of the nomadic Seljuq Empire, as it did with the Timurid Empire in the 15th century. Marshall Hodgson rejected Weber's ideal types of patrimonialism and, with better reasons, that of sultanism for these nomadic empires and offered two ideal types of his own in their place: the *a'yān-amīr* system in the Seljuq period and the military patronage state of the post-Mongol era. The first describes the regime that emerged with the development of the *iqṭā'* system of land tenure in which large land grants were made to the military elite. In this system, social power of the notables (*a'yān*) in towns and villages was subordinated to the domination of the military elite (*amīr*s) commanding the garrisons and using enormous landholdings for the maintenance of their tribal contingents. With the weakening of bureaucracy and decentralization of land assignments that resulted from the increase in the size of the *iqṭā'* and the amalgamation of fiscal revenue collection and prebendal grants for military and administrative service, the system developed in a military direction. Furthermore, the power of women in Turkic royal families, in interaction with the absence of primogeniture and indivisibility in nomadic kingdoms, laid the foundation for a novel political regime. The appanage of a young Seljuq prince was de facto governed by his tutor (*atabeg*), whom his widowed mother tended to marry. The *a'yān-amīr* system thus changed into an extremely decentralized system in the latter part of the 12th and early 13th centuries.

Hodgson's second ideal type for the post-Mongol period is the military-patronage state. It was modeled on the Mamluk sultanate in Egypt and Syria quite closely. The Mamluk amirs elected the sultan from their own ranks. As a consequence, the Mamluk kingdom was taken over as a whole by an elected sultan and never divided among the princes of the royal house as appanages. The Mamluk regime was strikingly similar to the Delhi Sultanate as an Islamicate polity under a complex system of collective rule by military slave-sultans. Given their relatively small number among the population, the Mamluk sultans of Egypt and Syria and their families developed an extensive network of patronage over civic and educational institutions through the civilian elite.

Despite his objection, however, Hodgson's "military-patronage state" can be considered a subtype of the Islamicate patrimonial state. In applying his model to the Ilkhanid and Timurid Turco-Mongolian empires in the 14th and 15th centuries, Hodgson noted the character of Yasa as the law of the military estate, of which the civilian population took no cognizance. The nomadic tribal confederations that established these empires transformed themselves into permanent ruling castes after conquest and remained rigidly separate from the civilian population to which they cultivated the ties of patronage by holding courts and founding endowments. Holding enormous undifferentiated land grants (*soyurghāl*) that did not distinguish between fiscal and prebendal elements, they became the landlords of the peasant masses. The pattern of social stratification under the Turco-Mongolian empires differed significantly from that of the Persianate polity of the Samanids and the Ghaznavids. For this reason, according to Hodgson, it should be considered a separate subtype of Islamicate patrimonial state—in fact, the latest. The bureaucratic class, secretaries of the chanceries who were the bearers of the culture of ethics and statecraft, dealt with the civic society and institutions of the kingdoms and provided a picture of the social hierarchy and stratification in terms of status by arranging different modes of address appropriate for different ranks within the civilian population. A rigid dichotomy of the military estate (*'askarī*) and the subjects (*ri'āya*) divided society into a dominant Turco-Mongolian estate on the one hand and the nonmilitary Persian or Tajik estate on the other, comprising both the urban strata and the peasantry.

See also endowment; household; monarchy

Further Reading

S. A. Arjomand, "Evolution of the Persianate Polity and its Transmission to India," *Journal of Persianate Studies* 2, no. 2 (2009); Idem, "The Law, Agency and Policy in Medieval Islamic Society: Development of the Institutions of Learning from the Tenth to the Fifteenth Century," *Comparative Studies in Society and History* 41, no. 2 (1999); M.G.S. Hodgson, *The Venture of Islam*, vol. 2, 1972; Max Weber, *Economy and Society*, edited by G. Roth and C. Wittich, vol. 2, 1978.

SAÏD AMIR ARJOMAND

patronage

"Patronage" can be defined either as kindness done to others, usually from a position of superiority, or the power to provide jobs for political and social advantage of those involved. This entry is divided into two sections: the first deals with patronage in the arts and the second with patronage in politics. The former is usually associated with the preindustrial period and the latter generally with the contemporary political situation, though neither is exclusively the case.

In the Islamic world, especially in the Middle Ages, when Islam was a world power, the arts—in the broadest sense of the word—were

patronized by the wealthy and particularly at the courts of various rulers of diverse Muslim societies. Poetry benefited the most from the patronage of the time: poets were paid handsome sums for exhibiting their literary works, which usually praised the benefactor or a feat connected with the benefactor in some fashion. The same also held for music and other art forms. Medieval sources are replete with stories of poets, musicians, or other artists being rewarded by the richer segments of society for their contributions. The manner in which patronage was practiced in the Islamic world differed from time to time and area to area, depending on the financial situation and the corresponding standard of living.

In the political arena, patronage belongs not only to the older but also to the contemporary Islamic world, the Middle East and North Africa in particular. Patronage is an important means used to buy loyalty to the state. As a result of the poor economic conditions in some of these countries, some even lagging behind sub-Saharan Africa, the state as an institution has gradually been retracting from the society it is meant to serve. Because the state cannot sustain all members of society, patronage is rampant. In concrete terms, contemporary leaders, especially in the Arab world, buy "loyalty" by extending financial favors and privileges to those who are affiliated with the state. In order to get anything done, a *wasṭa* is essential—literally a "connection" with someone who has by some means gained the favor of the ruler. In turn, this system of patronage binds the state's functionaries closely to the ruling elite. This balance of power provides stability, however fragile it might be. On the one hand, the numerous coups d'etat that took place in the 1950s and 1960s have ceased for the most part because of diminishing state control over the entire society; on the other hand, the maintenance of a patronage system closely concentrated on the ruler and the ruling elite has increased. Such a situation, which lacks civil society, transparency, and especially accountability, constitutes a serious obstacle for a process of democratization in the region.

See also loyalty; tribalism

Further Reading

Monique Bernards and John Nawas, eds., *Patronate and Patronage in Early and Classical Islam*, 2005; Ernst Gellner and John Waterbury, *Patrons and Clients in Mediterranean Societies*, 1977; Gavin R. G. Hambly, ed., *Women in the Medieval Islamic World: Power, Patronage, and Piety*, 1998; Allen Richards and John Waterbury, *A Political Economy of the Middle East*, 2007.

JOHN A. NAWAS

People of the Book

The Qur'anic phrase "People of the Book" (*ahl al-kitāb*) ordinarily connotes Jews and Christians but has also been used, particularly in later legal literature, to include a few other religious groups as well. The identifying quality is possession of a "book"—that is, recognition that the particular group has been the recipient of a previous divine revelation. The notion of "book" need not necessarily signify an actual physical entity or written product. Rather, its meaning can be more fluid, offering a sense of access to the knowledge that God gives to humans, whether recorded or not. Nevertheless, some Qur'anic uses of this phrase (Q. 4:153; 6:7; 17:93) clearly intend a scroll, codex, or similar material object. The related phrase, "source or mother of the book" (*umm al-kitāb*), which occurs three times in the Qur'an, carries a similar multivalence. Understandings of it also oscillate between the concept of a large celestial, primordial text and that of the totality of God's knowledge and will.

People of the Book is fundamentally a relational description. With this and similar phrases (e.g.,"those who were given the book," "those who recite the book before you"), the Qur'an self-consciously situates itself both chronologically and theologically within an extended sequence of divine revelations, all of which conveyed God's will and guidance. The Tawrat, Injil, and Zabur, to use the Qur'anic terms for the Hebrew Bible, the Christian New Testament, and the Psalms, respectively, convey earlier forms of this revelation, but it is an article of Muslim doctrine that the Qur'an constitutes the final and most comprehensive act of divine revelation. Discrepancies between the Qur'an and earlier scriptures are explained by the accusation of alteration (*taḥrīf*). Jews and Christians are charged with possession of corrupted versions of their original scriptures, although the long polemical debate on this issue expresses variant understandings of whether this corruption was deliberate or inadvertent and where, when, and by whose agency it happened. Complete disavowal of earlier scriptures was never the dominant position, however, because these texts were also valued for their predictive value. Medieval Muslim scholars compiled lists of biblical passages that were understood to announce Muhammad's advent and the subsequent military and political successes of his community. A similar ambivalence surrounds the People of the Book. Qur'an 10:94 urges consultation with them ("If you [Muhammad] are in doubt about what we have revealed to you, ask those who recite the book before you"), while other verses (e.g., Q. 3:64–65) accuse them of being in dispute or disagreement over the divine revelation.

As the revelation that abrogates all others, the Qur'an frequently criticizes the People of the Book and denounces numerous aspects of Jewish and Christian dogma. Both the hadith and subsequent theological and legal literature develop the Qur'anic discussion of aberrant doctrine, condemning beliefs such as those concerning the Incarnation and the Trinity that counter core concepts of Muhammad's message. Negative judgments about the religious attitudes and practices of the Jews and Christians may be found throughout the Qur'an, as well as prescriptive injunctions that mandate Muslim behavior toward the People of the Book.

Extra-Qur'anic literature expands on these scriptural mandates. The Constitution of Medina (*'ahd al-umma*) has been acknowledged as one of the earliest Islamic documents to address

interreligious relations, and it is followed by centuries of religio-legal literature that deals with the status and treatment of the People of the Book. A key theme of this literature is the control and even coercion of non-Muslim individuals and communities. Forms include a subordinate political and social position as "protected" peoples (*ahl al-dhimma*); financial encumbrance through a targeted taxation (*jizya*); legal restrictions in matters of marriage, inheritance, and other aspects of family and civil law; and physical avoidance to avert ritual impurity. The extent to which these forms of control and coercion have affected the lives of non-Muslims within Muslim societies has varied considerably and can be adequately assessed only when analyzed with chronological and geographical specificity. Nevertheless, the desirability or possibility of their contemporary reinstatement remains an active topic within Islamist political groups.

See also Christian-Muslim relations; minorities

Further Reading

Yohanan Friedmann, *Tolerance and Coercion in Islam: Interfaith Relations in the Muslim Tradition*, 2003; Jane Dammen McAuliffe, "The Qur'ānic Context of Muslim Biblical Scholarship," *Islam and Christian-Muslim Relations* 7, no. 2 (1996): 141–58; Uri Rubin, *Between Bible and Qur'ān: The Children of Israel and the Islamic Self-Image*, 1999; Jørgen B. Simonsen, *Studies in the Genesis and Early Development of the Caliphal Taxation System*, 1988.

JANE DAMMEN MCAULIFFE

philosopher-king

The Platonic concept of the philosopher-king, who combines philosophical knowledge with the capability to rule (Plato, *Republic,* V, 473c–e), reappears in Farabi's (d. 950) work on the "Perfect State." It became influential in later Islamic philosophical works, mostly through the mediation of Ibn Sina (d. 1037), who modified it and combined it with ideas taken from the originally Iranian-Sassanid Mirrors for Princes, which, since the translations of Ibn al-Muqaffa' (d. 757), developed practical rules regulating the behavior of rulers and ruled. Farabi concentrated on the intellectual qualities of the ruler, who, in his persuasion, should have the qualities of a prophet—a charismatic person whose intuition is inspired by the divine revelation, comparable to the revelations that the Prophet Muhammad received from God. Farabi, who apparently dreamed of a worldwide society with common faith and laws under the rule of a philosopher-prophet, did not mention in his *Perfect State* the Islamic prophet Muhammad and instead used the terms "prophet," "imam," and "first ruler" (*al-ra'īs al-awwal*), who must have particular ethical and intellectual qualities such as love of truth and justice, resoluteness and contempt of worldly things, the capacity to acquire knowledge, and the rhetorical ability to persuade others. He was convinced, in a much stricter manner than his Isma'ili forerunner Abu Hatim al-Razi (fl. early tenth century), of the universality of religion and belief in one God, the ultimate source of knowledge, which is promulgated by the ruler in the shape of laws, the guiding line of people in a hierarchically structured society. An alternative expression of these laws is "religion" (*milla*). Farabi expanded the Isma'ili combination of authority and prophecy, knowledge and divine inspiration, by introducing notions taken from Aristotelian epistemology and ethics. Actions of human beings are subject to the rules of laws imposed by the divinely inspired ruler-prophet. These actions, which are based on religious laws, are part of "religion" and mirror the divinely inspired knowledge of the ruler, a philosopher. Here, Farabi introduced his original idea of religion "imitating" philosophy and its universals. Religion becomes a picture of philosophy and, at the same time, religion is understood as an instrument used by philosophy. The practical prudence (*sophrosyne*) of Aristotle's *Nicomachean Ethics* appears to Farabi as religious laws, as religion that "imitates" the universals of philosophy. This imitation (*muḥākāt*) of philosophical knowledge is interpreted by Farabi as a kind of representation of the intelligible things through pictures that are the only way to develop a conception of theoretical insights. In consonance with Aristotle's persuasion that humans can only think through pictures based on the perceivable things, Farabi considers religion as the only way, as an "instrument" of theoretical philosophy, which is shaped and realized through the performance of the rules of religious laws. Farabi starts with Aristotle's concept of practical prudence, his assumption of an interrelation between human thought and perception, and his doctrine of an interdependence between theory and practice. Religion is not only "opinion," but also, according to Farabi, the only way to philosophical knowledge, which is moral insight in the shape of religious laws. The performance of religious laws leads the individual to supreme happiness (*al-sa'āda al-quṣwā*) and regulates the life of society, the city-state that requires the leader, an imam, and in which the people require their fellow-citizens. The Aristotelian notion of man as a political creature is integrated into a soteriological concept of a leader, a person with charismatic qualities, who with his intellectual and rhetorical qualities can lead the masses and persuade them from the prescriptions of religion. Here, religion appears as a picture, an imitation of universal knowledge, which is divinely inspired and becomes existent through the performance of the religious laws.

Farabi's notions reappear in modified form in the encyclopedia of the "Brethren of Purity" (tenth century) and in the later works of Ibn Sina, Ibn Bajja (d. 1138), Ibn Tufayl (d. 1185), Ibn Rushd (d. 1198), and Ibn Khaldun (d. 1406). Farabi's utopian state, which is guided by the ruler-prophet, a philosopher with prophetic qualities, became a model for human behavior in society and for the individual's path to welfare in the other world. As for Farabi, this ideal state is a generally valid model for humankind that becomes reality and receives its shape through the performance of its rules, or religious laws, and stresses both the cooperation of fellow-citizens—Ibn Khaldun's *'aṣabiyya*, or "solidarity"—and

the necessary qualities of the leader, who must be a philosopher and must have access to divinely inspired knowledge.

See also city (philosophical); Mirrors for Princes; philosophy

Further Reading

Aziz Al-Azmeh, *Muslim Kingship*, 1997; Patricia Crone, *God's Rule: Government and Islam*, 2004; Hans Daiber, "Political Philosophy," in *History of Islamic Philosophy*, vol. 2, edited by Seyyed Hossein Nasr and Oliver Leaman, 1996; Paul L. Heck, "Doubts about the Religious Community (*Milla*) in al-Fārābī and the Brethren of Purity," in *In the Age of al-Fārābī: Arabic Philosophy in the Fourth/Tenth Century*, edited by Peter Adamson, 2008.

HANS DAIBER

philosophy

In Islam, philosophy (*falsafa*) is reasoning about the physical and metaphysical worlds based on the Greek philosophical tradition, especially the works of Plato and Aristotle, received through the harmonizing interpretation of the Neoplatonists of late antiquity. The works most relevant to political thought were Plato's *Republic* and *Laws*, available in summary translations, and Aristotle's *Nicomachean Ethics*, translated in full. Aristotle's *Politics* was not translated, though parts of it seem to have been known, perhaps from anthologies or quotations in other works.

The Greek philosophical tradition was still alive in the Near East at the time of the Arab conquests, but little is known of the forms it took, except insofar as it had come to form part of Christian theology. Zoroastrian priests and other religious leaders may have found use for it, but its main exponents in late antiquity were doctors, astronomers or astrologers, alchemists, and secretaries. It was such educated laymen, not religious scholars, who were its main bearers in Islam as well.

The systematic translation of Greek works into Arabic began in the mid-eighth century, but it was not until around 900 that philosophy achieved prominence as a discipline in its own right. Since it was pursued by laymen and claimed to be an avenue to the highest truth and salvation based entirely on human reason rather than divine revelation, it was set for a head-on collision with Islam as understood by the religious scholars. Some early philosophers, notably the physician and alchemist Abu Bakr al-Razi (d. 925), rejected all revealed religion as false and dismissed the prophets as impostors, claiming that philosophy was the road to salvation for everyone. But most philosophers chose to avoid the clash by unifying philosophy and revealed religion. According to Farabi (d. 950), prophets were philosophers of such extraordinary worth that they had achieved contact with the Active Intellect: this was the source of their divine revelations. As prophets, they reformulated the absolute truths of philosophy in a language that everyone could understand, using myths, images, and metaphors and adapting their message to the particular conditions of their audience; as philosophers, they presented the eternal, universal, and unchanging truth as it was.

Some disagreement over the details notwithstanding, this solution was adopted by all later philosophers, including Ibn Sina (Avicenna, d. 1037) and Ibn Rushd (Averroes, d. 1198). Though it was a major intellectual achievement, it was rarely persuasive to the religious scholars for the obvious reason that it made the Prophet a self-made man rather than a person chosen by God and reduced his divine revelation to a popular version of the absolute truth. It implied that the philosophers were the true heirs of the Prophet and leaders of the Muslim community, and that the theologians, jurists, and other religious scholars were to take their cue from the philosophers as mere popularizers of their syllogisms. Indeed, the ruler himself should be a philosopher in Farabi's view. Failing that, a number of philosophers might rule together; this was Farabi's understanding of aristocracy (literally "the rule of the best"). In his view, it would be disastrous if philosophy had no representatives at the highest level of government. Instead of striving for happiness, the community would pursue unworthy aims such as wealth, military power, or mistaken impressions of the truth, all of which he illustrated in accounts of imperfect constitutions, in the loose sense of "ways of life," some adapted from Plato and Aristotle, others worked out by himself.

To modern readers, Farabi's political thought comes across as strangely unreal and decontextualized. He never gives historical or contemporary examples; he rarely mentions any names other than those of philosophers; and he has nothing to say about concrete forms of political organization, distribution of power, conflict resolution, or politics as a process. His interest lies entirely in the diverse views of the ultimate good to be pursued in this life, and government to him really meant spiritual direction. The battle he was fighting was for souls, not for the throne. Since the ultimate good in life followed from the ultimate nature of reality, all his "political" books devote more space to metaphysics than to the city that should reflect it. This was in keeping with the common understanding at the time. Whether known from reason or from revelation, the metaphysical world dictated how one should live on Earth, and concrete politics were far less important than identifying the road to eternal salvation.

Farabi's ideal community was necessarily authoritarian. A philosopher-king of the highest kind (i.e., a prophet) endowed with unique wisdom and understanding of what was best for everyone obviously had to be obeyed without question. The same was true of lesser philosophers in the absence of a supreme philosopher-ruler. Like Plato, Farabi would have liked everyone to follow the dictates of a small intellectual elite credited with superior insight and seen as indispensable for common welfare. Neither Greek nor Islamic philosophy ever extolled the virtues of democracy. The belief that the Greek philosophers were supporters of democracy is a modern lay misconception, and to Muslim philosophers, democracy was a constitution in which everyone was free to pursue

whatever aim in life he wanted, resulting in a highly diverse community. This struck them as self-evidently bad, since there was only one eternal truth and all those who ignored it would perish. Uniting people in the common pursuit of a single, overarching objective was the ideal to which philosophers and religious scholars alike subscribed. The shared objective took precedence in the vision of both.

The philosophers never achieved the primacy that Farabi hoped for. They never even succeeded in gaining regular representation in educational institutions, though logic did come to form part of the madrasa (institution of higher education) curriculum, especially in the eastern lands of Islam. In the absence of professorial chairs and schools, philosophers made a living as doctors, astronomers, and, to some extent, members of the bureaucracy. Despite all that, philosophy achieved great prominence in the 10th and 11th centuries, and it continued to exercise a major influence on Islamic thought thereafter, in part thanks to the fact that from the 11th century onward, Muslim theologians were often well read in it, whether they approved of it or not. Ghazali (d. 1111), often believed to be a mortal enemy of philosophy, explained that it was foolish to oppose it completely, since it included eminently useful sciences such as logic, mathematics, and the natural sciences. He presented philosophical writings on government and ethics in a somewhat unfavorable light, but it was only the metaphysics of the philosophers that he condemned, and only on a specific number of points. He was deeply influenced by Ibn Sina, probably beyond the limit he recommended in his pastoral works. By his time, it was above all in Spain, where Ibn Rushd was active, that there was interest in "political science," as the philosophers called their thoughts on communal life. Ibn Rushd, who wrote a commentary on Plato's *Republic*, which is extant only in Hebrew and which followed Farabi's own commentary, made an unprecedented attempt to relate philosophical constitutions to actual regimes. This played a role in the sociological theory of history developed by Ibn Khaldun (d. 1406), who was proudly aware of having developed a new science. However, his theory did not live on or receive further development, though it had its admirers in the Ottoman Empire. Farabi's political philosophy also left a deep imprint on Jewish thought, not least on that of Maimonides (d. 1204), who was born in Spain and who had a major impact on intellectual developments in Christian Europe.

Farabi's vision also had strong appeal to Shi'is, especially the Isma'ilis, because they shared his conviction that there was a man endowed with supreme wisdom not just in the past in the form of the Prophet but also in the present in the form of the imam. The Isma'ilis cast their imam (especially when he was absent) as the philosopher-king and saw themselves as sharing in his insights, identifying philosophy as esoteric knowledge inaccessible to the masses and themselves as the spiritual elite. Among those who saw themselves as such an elite were the anonymous authors of the tenth-century collection of epistles known as the *Rasa'il Ikhwan al-Safa'* (Epistles of the sincere or true brethren). The best-known Shi'i exposition of political philosophy is the *Nasirean Ethics* of the Imami (at some point Isma'ili) philosopher and scientist Nasir al-Din al-Tusi (d. 1274), who offered advice on the management of the self, the household, and the kingdom and who had many imitators.

From the 12th century onward, philosophy increasingly merged not only with theology but also with Sufism, but its later history is largely unknown, for lack of study rather than for lack of evidence. It is probably safe to say, however, that political philosophy never had much influence on politics on the ground. It is not likely to influence politics today, either. It still has its admirers, usually for its rationalism rather than its authoritarianism, but now as then, it is political visions based on divine revelation that have mass appeal. "Political science" in the modern sense of the term is a Western import.

See also al-Farabi, Abu Nasr (ca. 878–950); Ghazali (ca. 1058–1111); Ibn Rushd (1126–98); Ibn Sina, Abu 'Ali (980–1037); al-Tusi, Nasir al-Din (1201–74)

Further Reading

Patricia Crone, *Medieval Islamic Political Thought* [American title *God's Rule*], 2004; Al-Farabi, *Farabi on the Perfect State*, translated by Richard Walzer, 1985; Ibn Khaldun, *The Muqaddimah*, translated by F. Rosenthal, 1967; Ralph Lerner and Muhsin Mahdi, *Medieval Political Philosophy: A Sourcebook*, 1963; Seyyed H. Nasr and Oliver Leaman, *History of Islamic Philosophy*, 1996; Ibn Rushd, *Averroes' Commentary on Plato's 'Republic,'* translated by R. Lerner, 1974.

PATRICIA CRONE

piety and asceticism

Piety, the quality of a person's religious devotion, is a prominent feature in both legitimating and critiquing authority in Islam. Asceticism, the cultivation of austerity and rigorous self-discipline, is one of the most manifest forms of the expression of piety.

The distinctive form of piety in Islam is first given shape in the Qur'an, where religious exhortations are numerous. Furthermore, the anecdotal and narrative material of the scripture provides archetypal exemplars for pietistic imitation. Later elaborations of these Qur'anic depictions emphasized the spiritual particularities of certain figures, especially the prophets. For instance, in Sufi writings both John the Baptist and Jesus are paragons of asceticism. The most influential imitative model, however, was invariably the Prophet Muhammad himself, whose sunna was the preeminent source for emulation. The hadith literature attests to his rigorous religiosity as well as his consistent austerity in both body and wealth. This mimetic material has occupied a significant cultural space in Muslim societies and continues to do so.

Markers of Islamic piety include the meticulous maintenance of ritual observances, adherence to modest norms, and the possession

of spiritual charisma and wisdom. Asceticism, which is often connected to renunciation, can further entail demonstrating minimal concern for one's physical comfort or well-being, avoiding conventional means of earning a livelihood, abstaining from excesses, performing supererogatory prayers and fasts, adopting unconventional appearances, and physically or mentally withdrawing from society. These elements have figured prominently in the development of Islamic spiritual traditions, such as the Karrami and Sufi traditions. Stricter understandings of asceticism have also led to religious antinomianism and social deviance, as manifested by a group known as the Qalandars, who purposefully contravened normative conventions by adopting countercultural appearances and behavior. All of these modes of pietistic expression are pregnant with political potential and have been consciously and unconsciously displayed by public personas to curry favor with particular factions, demonstrate religious authenticity, or protest the perception of impiety.

Often, the memorialized lives of ascetics and mystics were cast as poignant social and political commentaries against the conditions of their respective eras. Such figures were frequently depicted as chastising rulers, avoiding political appointment, or withdrawing from the community altogether. Their acts of piety and asceticism are both correctives and critiques. Such characterizations, however, extend well beyond explicitly spiritual circles and are a hallmark of the 'ulama' (religious scholars) in general. Biographical records and chronicles are replete with references to a scholar's assiduous religiosity. Mentions of piety are often as important as mentions of position, accomplishment, and lineage in biographies. Pietistic descriptions serve to legitimate a person's social standing and scholastic projects, particularly important given the historically persistent sense of contestation and competition between various figures and schools of thought. In the modern era, a number of Islamist parties have wedded their political and social agendas to a pietistic, if not ascetic, way of life based on particular readings of the Qur'an and sunna.

The politicization of piety is also evident in the sphere of sovereignty. The legitimacy of a ruler was often buttressed with descriptions of his religious scrupulousness. Both the Rightly Guided Caliphs of the Sunni tradition and the Shi'i imams attest to this biographical convention. A sovereign could also consciously cultivate a persona of piety through public acts of worship. The ceremonial patronage of the hajj pilgrimage caravans and the attendance of congregational prayers were the two most prominent historical acts of this sort. A modern example is Egyptian president Anwar Sadat (d. 1981), who acquired a reputation of piety and was subsequently dubbed "the believing president" (*al-ra'īs al-mu'min*) by the Egyptian media in the early years of his presidency. In other cases, a pietistic portrait could accentuate a leader's exceptionalism, as in the case of the Umayyad caliph 'Umar b. 'Abd al-'Aziz (ca. 680–720). In that same historical vein, attributions of impiety have also been applied to mar the reputations of unfavorable past rulers, as seen in Abbasid portrayals of their caliphal predecessors, the Umayyads.

See also Muhammad (570–632); Sufism; sunna; 'ulama'; 'Umar b. 'Abd al-'Aziz (ca. 680–720)

Further Reading

Michael Cook, *Commanding Right and Forbidding Wrong in Islamic Thought*, 2000; Fred M. Donner, "Early Islamic Piety," in *Narratives of Islamic Origins*, 1998; Ahmet T. Karamustafa, *God's Unruly Friends*, 1994; Christopher Melchert, "The Transformation from Asceticism to Mysticism at the Middle of the Ninth Century C.E.," *Studia Islamica* 83, no. 1 (1996); John Renard, *Friends of God*, 2008.

MARTIN NGUYEN

pilgrimage

Pilgrimage in Islam takes three principal forms. The annual hajj and the year-round *'umra* involve travel to Mecca and its precincts, and *ziyāra* involves travel to the tombs of revered religious figures, notably Muhammad's grave in Medina. Jerusalem, as one of the three sacred precincts together with Mecca and Medina, also historically has been a pilgrimage destination.

Hajj and *'Umra*

The Qur'an enjoins all able believers to perform the hajj to Mecca, its sanctuary, and environs but does not detail the associated rituals. For these, Muslims rely on Muhammad's one hajj in 631 into which he incorporated many pre-Islamic practices, such as the circumambulation of the Ka'ba, the cubical stone structure that housed personal and tribal idols. The documents of treaties between tribes and succession documents such as that of the caliph Harun al-Rashid were also often stored in the Ka'ba. In 630, when Muhammad retook Mecca, his first act was to destroy the idols in the Ka'ba. Muslims hold that the Ka'ba (also called *bayt Allāh*, or "the House of God" or "Temple of God") was built by the first man and prophet, Adam, and then periodically rebuilt, most significantly by Abraham: this undergirds political rhetoric and interfaith discussion about Islam as an Abrahamic religion. Non-Muslims are, however, barred altogether from Mecca and Medina. Some Muslims, such as Osama bin Laden and al-Qaeda, have called for the removal of non-Muslims from the entire Arabian Peninsula, including foreign troops posted in Saudi Arabia and Yemen.

In the sixth century, Mecca prospered because of trade through the city and pilgrimage to its sanctuary, control of which was in the hands of Muhammad's tribe, the Quraysh. Such control conferred prestige, legitimacy, and jurisdiction; the Shi'i Fatimids, though based in Cairo, for instance, extended control over Mecca and Medina during their ascendancy. Modern Saudi monarchs, following Ottoman practice, have adopted the title "custodian of the two holy sanctuaries [Mecca and Medina]" (*khādim al-ḥaramayn*

al-sharīfayn). Guardianship came to include the obligation to appoint caravan leaders and guarantee safe passage for pilgrims. Other Muslim potentates have sought legitimacy through ceremonial acts such as sending ornamental keys for the Ka'ba door, official palanquins (*maḥmal*), or a brocaded drape for the Ka'ba (*kiswa*).

The hajj rituals—which include "halting" (*wuqūf*) at the plains of 'Arafat and Muzdalifa, the symbolic stoning of Satan and ritual animal sacrifice at Mina, and the circumambulation of the Ka'ba (*ṭawāf*) at Mecca, as well as a ritualized brisk walk (*sa'y*) between the mounts of Safa and Marwa—are performed by Muslims, male and female, from the world over, making it the only significant show of Muslim world unity. This is underscored by the fact that men of all ranks dress the same, in two pieces of unsewn cloth, and women dress in simple cotton garments called *iḥrām*. During the *'umra*, the pilgrim is in a sacralized state (also known as *iḥrām*), during which sexual intercourse, the cutting or shaving of hair, and the use of scented products are forbidden, but the *'umra* is short, lasting a few hours, whereas the hajj lasts from three to five days. *'Umra* rituals are confined to circumambulation, the brisk walk, and the cutting or shaving of hair to exit the sacralized state.

Sectarian and denominational differences are set aside during the hajj, and all pilgrims travel and worship together; in the past, many pilgrims stayed in Mecca and Medina for several months or years. The hajj consequently has long provided scholars of differing views the opportunity to meet and exchange ideas. Between the 10th and 12th centuries, for instance, North African pilgrims carried the Isma'ili ideas they encountered westward. In the 11th and 12th centuries, the Almoravid and Almohad movements are said to have been planned in Mecca. In the 17th century, returning pilgrims repatriated the books of the Southeast Asian Shaykh Yusuf al-Maqassari (d. 1699), who had been banished from Indonesia to Sri Lanka and then to the Cape by Dutch colonial authorities. In the 18th century, Indian pilgrims brought the ideas of Muhammad b. 'Abd al-Wahhab to the subcontinent, and in the 20th century, Malcolm X returned to the United States with a new understanding of egalitarian Islam and consequently broke away from Elijah Muhammad's separatist Nation of Islam.

Although never a political capital, Mecca has, nevertheless, at times been the site of political struggle. In Islam's first century, for instance, when 'Abdallah b. al-Zubayr disputed the caliphate, he sought sanctuary in Mecca and preached there against the ruling Umayyad caliph, 'Abd al-Malik; he also may have tried to control access to Mecca. According to one account, this prompted the caliph to build the Dome of the Rock in Jerusalem and to encourage pilgrimage to Jerusalem rather than to Mecca. Pilgrimage reverted to Mecca when Ibn al-Zubayr was killed in 692, but Jerusalem remains an important destination for the pious.

More recently, in 1979, 'Abdallah al-Qahtani proclaimed himself an awaited savior (*mahdī*) and with roughly 500 armed followers captured the Grand Mosque; hundreds, including hostages, died before the militants were subdued. In 1987, Iranian protesters (and bystanders) were killed by security forces after staging a demonstration.

Since ritual prayers are performed facing Mecca, every single Muslim, pilgrim or not, gains a sense of unity, community, and common purpose. Only 2 to 3 million out of some 1.5 billion Muslims perform the hajj each year, many of them repeat pilgrims. Thus most Muslims' actual experience of the hajj is only through national discourses. Sponsorship, regulation, and subsidy by governments politicizes those discourses and, in turn, the hajj itself. The fact that Saudi Arabia has been in charge of the hajj for the past century has meant that it, in particular, has wielded considerable political leverage. In the late 1960s, for instance, King Faisal successfully lobbied Muslim leaders about the need for a coalition of Muslim states (the Organization of the Islamic Conference [OIC]). It is through the OIC that international hajj quotas have been implemented. It was at the 2006 OIC meeting in Mecca that some Muslim leaders, outraged at cartoons of Muhammad published in a Danish newspaper, recalled their ambassadors to Denmark and called for a boycott of Danish products.

For some 20th-century intellectuals, the hajj is more a vehicle of resurgence and sociomoral reconstruction. For 'Ali Shari'ati, it is a prototype and metaphor for the individual, nonclerical production of religious knowledge. Muhammad Iqbal saw the hajj as a way to unite Muslims in order to destroy the indigenous idols of dogmatism and superstition and the Western idols of nationalism and consumerism.

Ziyāra

The veneration of deceased religious figures is widespread in the Islamic world, notably among Muslims who embrace Sufi practices. Pilgrims travel to seek blessings (*baraka*) from saintly figures' tombs and shrines, the custodians of which frequently wield power over pilgrims by controlling access.

Throughout Islamic history, however, many scholars have disputed the permissibility of such visits, holding that they are not part of prophetic practice (sunna) and thus constitute heresy and innovation (*bid'a*). Ibn Taymiyya, for instance, makes it clear that a visit to Muhammad's grave in Medina must be incidental to an *'umra* or hajj, and several important reform movements have made opposition to *ziyāra* a major platform.

In Shi'ism, *ziyāra* is made to the graves of the imams and their significant relatives and companions. The most important of these is at Karbala in Iraq, where Husayn, Muhammad's grandson through his daughter Fatima and his cousin 'Ali, was killed by the forces of Yazid I. With the removal of the Sunni Iraqi leadership in 2003, restrictions on visits to Karbala were lifted, and it received a million pilgrims in 2004.

See also Pillars of Islam

Further Reading

Azyumardi Azra, "Networks of 'Ulamā' in the Seventeenth-Century Ḥaramayn," in *The Origins of Islamic Reformism in Southeast Asia*, 2004; Robert R. Bianchi, *Guests of God: Pilgrimage and Politics in the Islamic World*, 2004; Amikam Elad, *Medieval Jerusalem and Islamic Worship: Holy Places, Ceremonies, Pilgrimage*, 1995; 'Ali al-Harawi, *A Lonely Wayfarer's Guide to Pilgrimage: 'Alī ibn Abī*

Bakr al-Ḥarawī's Kitāb al-Ishārāt ilā ma'rifat al-ziyārāt, translated and with an introduction by Josef W. Meri, 2004; Muhammad Iqbal, *Secrets of Collective Life*, translated by A. R. Tariq, 1977; F. E. Peters, *The Hajj: The Muslim Pilgrimage to Mecca and the Holy Places*, 1994; 'Ali Shari'ati, *Hajj*, 1977; Christopher S. Taylor, *In the Vicinity of the Righteous: Ziyāra and the Veneration of Muslim Saints in Late Medieval Egypt*, 1999.

SHAWKAT M. TOORAWA

Pillars of Islam

In a well-known tradition, Muhammad explains that Islam is "built on five [things]." Sunni Muslims have come to represent these five principles as "pillars" (*arkān*), evoking a physical structure. Preachers throughout the Muslim world frequently remind listeners that just as pillars alone do not make a building, so too must Muslims adopt other acts and practices to complete the edifice of their belief.

The Sunni Pillars

The five Sunni pillars (*arkān al-islām* or *arkān al-'ibāda*) are (1) testifying or witnessing that there is only God and that Muhammad is God's messenger (*shahāda*), (2) establishing the ritual prayer (*iqāmat al-ṣalāt*), (3) giving alms (*ītā' al-zakāt*), (4) fasting in the month of Ramadan (*ṣawm Ramaḍān*), and (5) making the pilgrimage to the Ka'ba in Mecca (*ḥajj al-bayt*) if one is able. For Maliki Sunnis, jihad, or struggle in the cause of Islam, is the fifth pillar, the *shahāda* being the foundation on which the other five pillars rest.

The *shahāda*—Islam's fundamental doctrinal statement—must be uttered at least once in one's lifetime. Those born Muslim do this from early childhood. For converts, this testimony marks an entrance into and membership in the Muslim community and polity, resulting in the immediate obligation to practice the remaining four pillars (in the case of recognized monotheists [the People of the Book], the almsgiving tax [zakat] replaces the poll tax [*jizya*] assessed by the state).

"Salat" refers to the five daily ritual prayers prescribed by God. These prayers (and times) are known as *fajr* (predawn), *ẓuhr* (postzenith), *'aṣr* (midafternoon), *maghrib* (postsunset), and *'ishā'* (nighttime). The specifics of the ritual prayer are derived entirely from prophetic practice. Most Shi'i denominations combine *ẓuhr* and *'aṣr* prayers and *maghrib* and *'ishā'* prayers, leading many Sunnis mistakenly to believe that Shi'is ignore a basic pillar. Though not one of the five prayers, the Friday congregational prayer replaces the zenith prayer and is also an obligation—one that brings Muslims together in congregational mosques. This ritual prayer is preceded by a sermon (*khuṭba*) and therefore has often been used by political authorities as a platform for the promulgation of state ideology or political doctrines. In the 21st century, many Muslim governments control or provide the text of Friday sermons.

Zakat, repeatedly enjoined in the Qur'an, where it is often paired with the performance of ritual prayer, is a form of charity that embodies the believer's commitment to the well-being of the larger community. It is assessed as a 2.5 percent almsgiving tax on accrued wealth, goods, and stock (excluding certain items, such as jewelry). As its literal meaning—purification—suggests, this (re) distribution of wealth is not only an important communal, fiscal, and sociopolitical act but also one that "purifies" wealth and the wealthy. If one does not have the means to pay zakat, then one is entitled to receive it. Organized collection of zakat began under Muhammad himself. When tribes that had pledged allegiance to Muhammad refused to contribute zakat to his successor Abu Bakr, the latter regarded them as apostates; Shi'is too deem that zakat should be turned over to the appropriate authorities. In time, jurists, who elaborated the provisions regarding zakat in great detail, would formalize the handing over of zakat to the state treasury (*bayt al-māl*). This practice has continued into modern times: in some Muslim countries, ministries or departments are in charge of collection and distribution; in others, nongovernment organizations do so. Recipients include not only the needy but also sometimes poorer countries.

Obligatory fasting (*ṣawm*) takes place the entire month of Ramadan, the ninth month in the Islamic lunar calendar. There are very few sectarian differences concerning the proper fast—which lasts from daybreak until sunset—but there is considerable disagreement about the method(s) to be used to determine the beginning and end of Ramadan (or any month). The issue centers on the new moon and whether it is to be sighted with the naked eye or through predictive astronomical data. Related are questions about the jurisdiction of a given pronouncement: does a sighting in Mecca bind someone in Medina, and if so, is this predicated on the fact that they are both part of the same political entity? Several countries and communities follow Saudi Arabia's start- and end-dates for Ramadan. Critics view this solidarity as politically or ideologically motivated and at odds with established jurisprudence. There have been numerous international conferences on the moon issue, which has been divisive internationally and, in some areas, such as India and the United States, nationally.

The hajj is the pilgrimage to Mecca and its precincts, required of all Muslims who are physically and financially able to make the trip only once in a lifetime. It takes place between the 8th and 12th days of the 12th Islamic month, Dhu al-Hijjah, or "pilgrimage month," which together with the months preceding and following were regarded as a time of "sacred truce," during which none were permitted to bear arms in the sacred precincts (*ḥaram*). Muslim pilgrims in fact perform the rituals in a sacralized state (*iḥrām*), which include the wearing of the *iḥrām*, the name given to the two pieces of unsewn cloth worn by men and the simple cotton garments worn by women.

The Shi'i Pillars

Twelver Shi'is have ten pillars (*furū' al-dīn*), which they call "branches" or "practices" (*furū'*). The six additional ones are a

20 percent tithe on profits, payable to the religious authorities (*khums*); struggle in the cause of Islam (jihad); commanding right (*al-amr bi-l-ma'rūf*); forbidding wrong (*al-nahy 'an al-munkar*); loving the *ahl al-bayt* (*tawallī*)—namely, the Prophet and his family (Fatima, 'Ali, Hasan, Husayn); and antipathy for the enemies of the Prophet and his family (*tabarru'*). As is clear from this additional list, all have direct social and political implications, and none but the last is especially Shi'i in character, as Sunnis too embrace the other practices as duties. To the five Sunni/Twelver Shi'i pillars (ritual prayer, almsgiving, fasting, pilgrimage, struggle), the Isma'ili Shi'is add two—*walāya*, or the devotion to God, the prophets, and the imams, and *ṭahāra*, or spiritual and physical purity—again not especially denominational, except for the inclusion of love of the imams in *walāya*.

See also Friday prayer; pilgrimage

Further Reading

Michael Cook, *Commanding Right and Forbidding Wrong in Islamic Thought*, 2001; Frederick M. Denny, *An Introduction to Islam*, 2010; Moojan Momen, *An Introduction to Shi'i Islam: The History and Doctrines of Twelver Shi'ism*, 1987; Andew Rippin, *Muslims: Their Religious Beliefs and Practices*, 2011; Abu al-Hasan Sadeq, *A Survey of the Institution of Zakah: Issues, Theories and Administration*, 1994.

SHAWKAT M. TOORAWA

pluralism and tolerance

Pluralism and tolerance are considered constitutive elements of good governance, especially liberal democracy as it developed in the late 19th and early 20th centuries. For this reason they are widely debated among modern Muslims, including Islamists of various persuasions. For the same reason, this entry will focus largely on modern debates. Pluralism and tolerance are clearly related and both cover a broad semantic field. They concern relations within the Muslim community, as well as between Muslims and non-Muslims, and are closely tied to understandings of freedom, liberty, and citizenship. However, there is a difference of emphasis between the two: Pluralism is discussed mostly with regard to the Muslim community, or *umma*, especially concerning the plurality of political views and interests and their institutionalization within civil society and a multiparty system. Discussions of tolerance, on the other hand, tend to focus on relations between Muslims and non-Muslims—more specifically Christians and Jews as the prime representatives of the People of the Book (*ahl al-kitāb*)—within a Muslim polity, or within an Islamic state.

On Method

The issue of (religious) authority has been of great relevance to Muslims from an early date, and it has always been controversial. As a result of mass education and new forms of mass communication spreading from the late 19th century onward, individuals, groups, and institutions who previously would not have been considered qualified to speak on Islam have asserted their right to do so. As a result, an unprecedented variety of speakers have made statements of uncertain status on Islam in general and pluralism and tolerance in particular. The 'ulama' (religious scholars) have by no means disappeared from the stage. But next to them, and often in competition with them, other voices employ different modes of expression, some of them decidedly modern. These include Islamic activists and intellectuals who share what has become known as the "Islamic discourse" (*al-khiṭāb al-islāmī*).

Islamists (*islāmiyyūn*, *uṣūliyyūn*) are defined here as a discursive community sharing a number of claims and assumptions: that Islam provides a comprehensive set of norms and values ordering human life in all its manifestations; that this set of norms and values derives solely from the Qur'an and the Prophetic traditions (sunna) and that it is enshrined in the shari'a; and that to follow other sources of normative guidance, such as modern political ideologies, amounts to *shirk*, or "associating" other powers with God. From this they conclude that for Islam to be fully realized within a given community or territory, the shari'a must be "applied" exclusively and in its entirety, and that the application of the shari'a makes Islam into a unique, self-contained, and all-embracing "order" or "system" (*niẓām*) competing with other ideological systems. Islamists pursue various strategies to realize their goals, nonviolent as well as violent, in contrast to the majority of Muslims, who reject violence except in cases of legitimate self-defense. Distinctions among Islamists, Muslim scholars advocating an "Islamic solution," and other Muslims speaking on Islam are less clear when it comes to the precise shape of the "Islamic order" in general and definitions of pluralism and tolerance in particular.

Many of the positions reviewed here are not strikingly original. However, they illustrate a specifically modern legal-cum-political reasoning that aims to be true to the Islamic heritage (*al-turāth*) and at the same time fully attuned to present realities. Global power relations clearly affect the style of writing and the thrust of the argument, giving it a defensive ring. Even authors expressing themselves strictly in Islamic terms, condemning the adoption of un-Islamic concepts, do so against the backdrop of a challenge posed by the West and modernity as defined by the West. This includes understandings of pluralism and tolerance as core elements of modernity and good governance. At the beginning of the 21st century, debate has become overshadowed by the threat of militant Islamism and the fear of terrorism, calling forth attempts to define "true Islam," which is not what its enemies claim it to be. Opposition to Islamist violence also informs reflections on the status of pluralism and tolerance among Muslims and between Muslims and non-Muslims.

Faced with Western demands on the one hand and Islamist militancy on the other, Muslim scholar-activists have attempted to define a "middle ground," *al-wasaṭiyya*, a concept that came to the fore in the 1990s and is widely identified with the Egyptian-born

scholar-activist Yusuf al-Qaradawi (b. 1926). The basis for this idea is Qur'an 2:143: "Thus, We have appointed you as a median nation (*wa-kadhālika ja'alnākum ummatan wasaṭan*), to be witnesses for mankind, and the Prophet to be a witness for you." Advocates of *al-wasaṭiyya* search for broader principles reflecting the essence of shari'a and at the same time responding to changing realities, enabling Muslims to find the "right place" between the extremes of Western demands for modernization in its own image and faith-based rejection of any kind of adjustment. Advocates of *al-wasaṭiyya* can build on solid support for the juste-milieu in classical Islamic scholarship and adapt key terms found in the *turāth* (the classical heritage), such as balance, moderation, and a pragmatic realism (*tawāzun*, *i'tidāl*, *iḥsān*). Men as different as Qaradawi and the Sudanese scholar-activist Hasan al-Turabi (b. 1932) propagate a "new *fiqh*," or jurisprudence, that takes into account conditions in the real world (*al-wāqi'iyya* and *al-maydāniyya*), focusing on the need to balance different interests and aspirations (*fiqh al-muwāzanāt*) and to establish a list of priorities (*fiqh al-awlawiyyāt*) that privileges the essence of Islam and the shari'a over what they see as trivialities. At the same time, like prominent authors of the Salafi reform movement of the late 19th and early 20th centuries, they emphasize the "ease of Islam" (*yusr al-islām*) that aims to make life easy for Muslims as well as non-Muslims and not to impose hardship on them (*yusr lā 'usr*)—a view neatly opposed to the rigor exercised by certain traditionalist scholars and radical Islamists.

In the debate on pluralism and tolerance, proponents of different positions, "radical" as well as "moderate," basically adopt the same reasoning: selective reference to the Qur'an and sunna, supplemented by even more selective use of Islamic history on the one hand and the Islamic scholarly tradition on the other and expressed in the language of Islamic jurisprudence. In contemporary Islamic discourse, the theological dimension is generally weak, whereas political considerations loom large. Shifts of register from theology to history or from theology to law are frequent and are often made with little regard for either text or context. They are especially marked in the debate on the legitimacy of a multiparty system and concepts of citizenship that reinterpret traditional notions of religious tolerance (or toleration) to extend equal civic and political rights to all residents of the "Islamic homeland," irrespective of religious affiliation. This requires considerable investment in reinterpreting the sources as well as the scholarly tradition.

Muslims confront the basic challenge to all believers in a personal God who has revealed himself in scripture: the fact that according to their own normative tradition, revelation is precisely located in time and place and yet universally valid for all times and places, unbounded by the confines of origin. For virtually all Muslim authors engaged in the debate on pluralism and tolerance, revelation (*waḥy*) is enshrined in the Qur'an and the Prophet's example, or *al-kitāb wa-l-sunna*. They pursue a textual approach to certain knowledge—but textual does not necessarily mean literal.

Most Muslim authors regard the sunna as part of revelation and look to the Prophet as well as members of the early Muslim community, the *salaf ṣāliḥ*, as role models for Muslims. In spite of much critical scholarship on the sunna, especially among Western authors, the life of the Prophet and the Prophetic traditions continue to be among the most popular sources of inspiration to Muslims. The sunna documents (or purports to document) the social norms and practices of Arab tribal society in seventh-century northwestern Arabia—practices that were informed by the Qur'anic message but that cannot easily be transferred across time and space to be implemented in highly diverse sociocultural settings. Tribal factions in seventh-century Arabia are not the same as modern political parties, the treatment of Jews in the oasis of Khaybar cannot be taken as a timeless model of tolerance, and the so-called Constitution of Medina is no blueprint for organizing the state of law in the modern period. Many Muslims are aware of these facts. Yet only a minority hold that the exemplary practice of the Prophet is not just embedded in a particular "space" but also tied to it and thus not timelessly valid and binding. The issue is relevant to all conceptualizations of the Islamic state or order, including understandings of pluralism and tolerance.

Even more sensitive is the status of the Qur'an as the primary source of normative guidance for Muslims of all times and places. With regard to Qur'anic exegesis (*tafsīr*), modern authors can build on the classical tradition, but openly or tacitly many also go beyond it. Classical exegetes did recognize that the Qur'anic text is occasionally ambiguous and too complex to be ever fully exhausted by human minds; the Qur'an itself says so in more than one place. Certain features of the Qur'anic narrative and the hermeneutical strategies of Qur'anic exegesis, such as the use of metaphor, figurative speech, self-referentiality, and allegorical interpretation, are relevant to present discussions. However, these discussions are largely limited to academic circles. In a broader context, which tends to be more openly political, other methods of Qur'anic exegesis stand out more prominently, one based on contextualization and the other on abstraction. Both seek to define a hierarchy of commands and rules, one by placing them on a chronological scale, the other by assessing their validity within the overall context of revelation.

Contextualization includes, first, the exegetical subdiscipline of the "circumstances of revelation" (*asbāb al-nuzūl*), which aims to establish the context, or "seat in life," of all textual references, and second, abrogation (*naskh*, *al-nāsikh wa-l-mansūkh*), which seeks to ascertain their chronological sequence, with later revelations superseding earlier ones. Contextualization is a recognized element of both Qur'anic exegesis, *tafsīr*, and legal reasoning, *fiqh*, and indeed is indispensable to these disciplines. In contrast to most classical scholars, however, modern authors like the Egyptian lawyer Muhammad Sa'id al-'Ashmawi (b. 1932), an outspoken critic of the "application" of the shari'a, use contextualization as a tool not only to correctly locate specific rulings but also to restrict their binding force to this context. In doing so, they attempt to expand the scope of rational inquiry without abandoning the textual framework of the Qur'an (and sunna). There are obvious problems with this approach. One concerns history or rather historiography: the Qur'an

does not represent a linear narrative and therefore does not establish an undisputed chronological sequence of divine commands and rulings. At best, this may be done with the aid of other materials, including the sunna and the Life of the Prophet (*sīra*), both of which, however, were not written down at the same time as the Qur'an. Very few Muslim scholars have ventured to deconstruct the historiography concerning the age of the Prophet and the early community. Seen from the perspective of modern historical source criticism, contextualization rests on shaky ground. Seen from the perspective of tradition-bound scholars, it threatens to undermine the foundations of Muslim belief.

Abstraction offers ample opportunities to rethink the Qur'anic message, especially when combined with contextualization, and it is widely employed in present debates on pluralism and tolerance. Here, too, modern authors can build on the Islamic scholarly tradition. A majority hold that the shari'a is divine law in the sense that it was laid down by God (or his messenger, Muhammad, which is generally less clearly stated), with respect to its fundamentals and certain specific rulings. The challenge is to identify these fundamentals, or universal principles, in order to do justice to the "spirit" of Islam and the shari'a rather than merely following its letter. These fundamentals or universal principles have been largely identified with the "objectives" of the shari'a (*maqāṣid al-sharī'a*), or its "finality." They have also been linked to the concepts of the common good or public interest (in modern terminology, *maṣlaḥa 'āmma*) and of certain underlying goods or benefits (*maṣāliḥ*) to be protected by the shari'a: religion (i.e., Islam), life, offspring, property, and intellect; often honor has been included in the list as well. In ways that are not always clear, the distinction between fundamentals and nonfundamentals has also been related to the distinction between general and specific rules (*'āmm* and *khāṣṣ*). While the fundamentals or universal principles constitute the unchanging essence of Islam and the shari'a, their realization is contingent on time, place, and circumstance. As a result, the shari'a is considered fixed and unchangeable in its essence but flexible in its detailed rules and regulations.

The distinction between the fixed and the flexible (*al-thābit wa-l-mutaghayyir*), between the basics and secondary matters, and between universals and specifics is crucial to modern conceptions of an Islamic order and more particularly to discussions of tolerance, equality, and citizenship. According to some, universal principles carry greater weight than specific injunctions of the Qur'an and sunna, and in case of conflict, can even supersede or suspend explicit textual injunctions (*naṣṣ*) if this serves the common good. Reference to *siyāsa shar'iyya*, or governance in accordance with the shari'a, and to respected theoreticians of *maṣlaḥa*, from Ghazali (d. 1111) to Abu Ishaq al-Shatibi (d. 1388), cannot obscure the fact that modern interpretations are set in a context quite different from the one inhabited by Ghazali or Shatibi. The rationalist, if not openly utilitarian, logic employed by writers such as 'Ashmawi to root modern understandings of liberty, pluralism, and tolerance in the normative tradition renders them vulnerable to critique from Islamists and Islamic scholars alike, who defend what they see as unchanging "divine law" against human whims and interests, especially because those whims and interests seem to be inspired by foreign models.

The Unity of the Community

The crucial importance of unity (*waḥda*) to Islamic thought past and present is undisputed. There are numerous references to unity in the Qur'an, and they are liberally quoted by modern authors. At the core is Qur'an 3:103–5:

> O believers, fear God as He should be truly feared, and die not except as Muslims. And hold fast, all of you, to the rope of God and do not fall into dissension (*lā tafarraqū*). Remember God's bounties upon you, when you were enemies to one another, and how He brought harmony to your hearts so that, by His blessing, you became brothers . . . Let there be among you a group who call to virtue, who command the good and forbid vice. These shall indeed prosper. Do not be like those who scattered (*tafarraqū*) and fell into dissension (*ikhtalafū*) after manifest signs had come to them. These shall meet with terrible torment.

Qur'an 23:52 states simply, "This, your nation, is a single nation and I am your Lord. So fear Me." Qur'an 30:31–32 warns people not to be "among those who associate other gods with Him, those who have sundered their religion and turned into sects, each sect happy with what they have." Some modern authors refer to the doctrine of *tawḥīd*, denoting the unity of God, in order to explain the overriding need for the unity of the community, or *al-jamā'a*. Critics have spoken of "political *tawḥīd*." In legal theory (*uṣūl al-fiqh*) the emphasis on unity corresponds to the principle of *ijmā'*, the consensus of the Muslim community as expressed by its religious scholars or the first generations of Muslims. (For Twelver Shi'is, or Imamis, consensus has to be endorsed by the imams.) Many modern authors leap from religious doctrine and legal principle to historical practice: virtually all believe that at the beginning there was unity—a community firmly united around the Prophet as its sole spiritual and political leader—and that only later did unity yield to differentiation, giving rise to theological, legal, and political schools (*madhāhib*), sects (*milal*), or parties (*aḥzāb*).

The unitary vision can entail the rejection of all divergence of opinion, critique, or opposition to the dominant doctrines and practices as a menace to and sin against not just the given sociopolitical system but the divinely ordained order at large. Many writers do indeed view differentiation as fragmentation, entailing a weakening of the community of Muslims, as exemplified by the first and second civil wars, or *fitna*s, of the first century after the hijra (the migration of the Prophet and his Companions from Mecca to Medina). If broad moral-cum-religious categories such as true and false (*ḥaqq* and *bāṭil*), right and wrong (*ma'rūf* and *munkar*), or permissible and forbidden (*ḥalāl* and *ḥarām*) are employed to evaluate political opinions and decisions; if there is only one truth

and only one correct "position of Islam" on any given issue; and if this truth can be clearly identified by the community of Muslims or a given group of Muslims, then critique and diversity cannot be admitted as legitimate, nor can it be institutionalized. Legitimate plurality remains confined to what the powers-that-be define as consistent with the public order. Many would not rule out plurality and diversity altogether but still perceive them as destructive and divisive. There is a widely shared feeling that Muslims should overcome internal divisions and restore the pristine unity of the age of the Prophet. Attempts to bring about a rapprochement between Sunni and Shi'i Muslims (*taqrīb*) and to create a unified *fiqh* beyond the established schools of law and theology testify to this quest for unity.

The Logic of the Nation-State

Idealization of the early *umma* as an undivided community has been reinforced by the colonial experience and the opposition to Zionism, Israel, and the West as the perceived enemies of Islam. It has been further enhanced by the imprint of the modern nation-state. Modern authors are heirs to a legacy of conceptionalizing the community, homeland, and nation that was created by Salafi authors and activists, from Afghani (1838–97) to Hasan al-Banna (1906–49), largely in opposition to colonial domination. Even in the present era of globalization and mass migration, or perhaps precisely because of these phenomena, many (and not only Muslims) continue to think of Islam and the Muslim community in territorial terms, evoking the boundary between the "territory of Islam" (*dār al-islām*), in which the shari'a is enforced by the prince or state, and the "territory of war" (*dār al-ḥarb*), in which this is not the case, either because the rulers are not Muslim or because they, though nominally Muslim, fail to apply the shari'a. Even those who, in recognition of present realities, acknowledge a third category, the "territory of truce" (*dār al-ṣulḥ*) or the "territory of treaty" (*dār al-'ahd*), in which the state of war between Islamic and non-Islamic territories has been suspended, adhere to a territorial logic.

Building on the binary notions of *dār al-islām* versus *dār al-ḥarb*, Salafi authors have proposed a territorial concept of Islam as the homeland (*waṭan*) of all Muslims as well as of the non-Muslims living in their midst. Thus in 1934, Banna, the founder of the Egyptian Muslim Brotherhood, wrote in a newspaper editorial that "every piece of land where the banner of Islam has been hoisted is the fatherland of the Muslims" (Krämer, 2010, p. 105). From earlier authors, he borrowed the neologism *al-jinsiyya al-islāmiyya* ("Islamic nationality") to describe the bond uniting all residents of the Islamic homeland. By the same token, earlier Salafi reformers had declared patriotism to be "part of faith" (*ḥubb al-waṭan min al-īmān*). Because of the close link between the Arabs and Islam in the formative period, relations between Arabism and Islam retained a special character throughout the 20th century. As a result, the vocabulary employed—especially in the context of tolerance and citizenship, with its characteristic combination of terms taken from the Islamic tradition (*umma, jamā'a*) on the one hand and modern political vocabulary (*waṭan, jinsiyya*) on the other—suggests a certain level of conceptual confusion.

From Plurality to Pluralism

In spite of the high value attached to unity (of both the Muslim *umma* and the modern nation-state), most contemporary Muslim thinkers acknowledge plurality and diversity as facts of life willed by God and sanctioned by the Qur'an. The recognition of plurality and diversity, however, does not necessarily entail a recognition of pluralism, which makes diversity into a founding principle of social and political organization and allows for its institutionalization through voluntary associations ("civil society"), political parties, and bodies of parliamentary representation. The important distinction between plurality and pluralism is not always made, though the key terms—difference or divergence of opinion (*ikhtilāf*), plurality (*tanawwu'*), and pluralism (*ta'addudiyya*)—permit such a differentiation. On the theoretical as well as the practical level, there exist a range of positions, even among Islamists, that can be roughly divided into two opposing camps: one deeply suspicious of, or indeed opposed to, plurality and pluralism as menacing to Muslim integrity, power, and unity, and the other supporting plurality and pluralism as contributing to Muslim strength and creativity, rendering Islam, as the well-known formula has it, valid for all times and places. Even among the latter, finer distinctions emerge as soon as the legitimacy of a plurality of *interests* rather than mere *opinions* is addressed.

Opposition to plurality and pluralism is characteristic of militant Islamic groups and their spokespersons, while support of plurality and pluralism is common among Muslim thinkers and activists advocating a moderate, pragmatic course. The most widely shared view would seem to be that plurality and diversity are legitimate as long as they involve nonantagonistic groups operating "within the framework of Islam." Put simply, Muslim society and the Islamic state are conceived of as plural but not pluralistic. Differing opinions and interests should be balanced and harmonized to reflect the ideals of the equilibrium and the *juste milieu*. This limits both plurality and pluralism, though the actual imposition of restrictions may be subject to pragmatic considerations, including political reason weighing the options in light of the public interest, or what is identified as such.

Advocates of pluralism point to the elements of diversity in the religious, legal, and historical heritage of the Muslim community as one of the very sources of its strength and resilience. They quote the Qur'an and sunna, and, like their opponents, they do not hesitate to translate ethicoreligious concepts into sociopolitical ones. The most popular reference is Qur'an 49:13: "O mankind, We created you male and female, and made you into nations and tribes that you may come to know one another. The noblest among you in God's sight are the most pious." Potentially more powerful, though less often cited, is Qur'an 5:48:

> For every community We decreed a law and a way of life. Had God willed, He could have made you a single

> community—but in order to test you in what He revealed to you. So vie with one another in virtue. To God is your homecoming, all of you, and He will then acquaint you with that over which you differed.

In addition, there is a famous Prophetic saying (hadith) according to which the "diversity of opinion among [the learned of] my community is a blessing (*ikhtilāf* [*'ulamā'*] *ummatī raḥma*)." Though the hadith is considered weak, which restricts its legal force, it is often quoted in the literature on Islamic political thought, and pluralism and tolerance more specifically. The tradition of scholarly controversy, together with its specific body of literature (*kutub al-ikhtilāf*), is still known in erudite circles and serves to legitimize a plurality of views, even if antagonistic—provided they do not transgress the bounds of religion and morality.

As in other contexts, the shift from theology to law to politics is readily made. Thus the existence of the different Sunni and Shi'i schools of law (*madhhab*, pl. *madhāhib*) and of local legal practices (*'urf*, *'āda*) are often assimilated to political parties. The same is not true of the theological schools, which, at least among modern authors, are widely seen as divisive. Thus Qaradawi insists on the need to transcend the boundaries of the established schools of theology and law in order to create an inclusive vision of Islam that is meaningful to all Muslims. In various contexts, he asserts that what he practices is *ijtihād*, or independent reasoning on the basis of the Qur'an and sunna, freed from the ties to any particular *madhhab* with its specific rules and assumptions. Qaradawi acknowledges the historical embeddedness of *fiqh* and the controversies of its practitioners. In contrast to many others, he welcomes the existing plurality of legal opinions found in the legal tradition, but he also considers them a matter of the past that is no longer a concern for present-day Muslims, who should harness their energies to make Islam relevant to their own lives and those of others.

In the domain of politics, even conservative authors who take care not to be seen as borrowing from outside the Islamic tradition advocate consultation, or *shūrā*, as a key principle of political organization, enjoined by the Qur'an and incumbent on Muslim rulers past and present. *Shūrā* is premised on a plurality of opinions, at least within the community and within what is generally referred to as the "framework of Islam." *Shūrā* is a flexible device that allows for a variety of interpretations, all relevant to the issues of pluralism and tolerance. Some see it as mere advice to the ruler, similar to "good counsel," or *naṣīḥa*; others view it as the foundation of multiparty parliamentary democracy. Definitions of *shūrā* can be purely pragmatic, but they can also be based on philosophical reflection, for even though there may be only one truth, there is no guarantee that humans will be able to attain it with certainty. The Tunisian Islamist thinker and activist Rachid al-Gannouchi (b. 1941) is a prominent champion of this line of thinking. It has also been put forth in the context of Islamist self-critique. The Qur'anic text permits more than one reading. Accordingly, no individual or group of Muslims can have a monopoly on truth, or exert a tutelage (*wiṣāya*) over their fellow Muslims. This argument, which for lack of a better term might be called egalitarian, is directed against all kinds of religious authorities, from the Sunni 'ulama' of Azhar University in Cairo to the Shi'i leaders of the Islamic Republic of Iran. It is also directed against Islamist movements, first and foremost the Egyptian Muslim Brotherhood, whose claim to leadership over the "Islamic awakening" (*ṣaḥwa*) has been squarely repudiated by Islamist leaders such as Gannouchi and Turabi. Both insisted that Islamist activists, like all Muslims, have to interact with local realities if they wish to make their vision of Islam relevant to their own societies. Interaction with local conditions necessarily results in a plurality of interpretations.

Debate is therefore legitimate and indeed necessary. Under the conditions of modern mass society, debate may have to be institutionalized in voluntary associations and political parties to become effective. However, there is little agreement even among Islamists concerning institutionalization. Views range from a grudging recognition of political associations and parties as the lesser evil (compared to clandestine activities of undesirable political forces) to full acceptance of political pluralism as healthy and legitimate. Some recognize voluntary associations or even trade unions but not political parties. Others express more liberal views. The names adopted by Islamist organizations reflect this diversity of opinions. Many call themselves *jamā'a*, *jam'iyya*, or *tajammu'*, all derivatives of a verbal root stressing unison, to highlight their faith in unity; the Muslim Brotherhood (Jam'iyyat al-Ikhwan al-Muslimin) is a prime example. Some call themselves "front" (*jabha*), using a more openly modern label to transport a similar message; examples include the Algerian Front Islamique du Salut and the Sudanese National Islamic Front or the Islamic Action Front in Jordan. Yet others call themselves parties, such as the Islamic Liberation Party (Hizb al-Tahrir al-Islami), founded in the early 1950s by the Jordanian Taqi al-Din al-Nabhani; the Malaysian Parti Islam Se-Malaysia (PAS), also established in the early 1950s; or the Tunisian Nahda Party (Hizb al-Nahda), founded in 1989 by Gannouchi.

However, the choice of the term "party" does not in itself signal an acceptance of political pluralism, as shown by the Hizb al-Tahrir or the Lebanese Hizbullah; at least in its early years, the latter was firmly opposed to a multiparty system. According to the binary vision adopted by both organizations, there are only two "parties" (or rather groups or communities): the party of God (*ḥizb allāh*) and the party of the devil (*ḥizb al-shayṭān*), or, with a significant change of register, the party of the downtrodden (*al-mustaḍ'afūn*) and the party of the arrogant (*al-mustakbirūn*). The former refers to Qur'an 5:56 ("Whoso takes God and His Messenger and the believers for allies, the party of God shall be victorious") and Qur'an 58:19, 22 ("They are the party of Satan and the party of Satan are assuredly the losers. . . . They are the party of God, and the party of God shall surely win through"). The latter uses categories popularized by the leaders of the Islamic Revolution in Iran. Here as elsewhere the argument rests on a transfer of ethicomoral notions to the sociopolitical field. Thus the Qur'anic condemnation of whims and desires (*hawā*, pl. *ahwā'*) is used to denounce political parties and

associations premised on a particular interest (*maṣlaḥa*) at the expense of the common good or public weal, resulting in a collective weakening of the Muslim community or the nation. Gannouchi is one of the few distinguished Islamist authors to defend interests as a legitimate component of political action and organization.

At one end of the spectrum, the prominent Egyptian lawyer and Islamist intellectual Muhammad Salim al-ʻAwwa (b. 1942) openly declared himself in favor of pluralism. In an article on "political pluralism" published in 1993, he wrote that pluralism means the recognition of diversity and that this diversity is an "expression of the marvelous divine achievement." With regard to political organization he argued that if one "recognises the pluralistic nature of humans, and recognises their rights to disagree and differ, one must inevitably, and without much effort, recognise pluralism in the political sphere." To reject political pluralism and to adopt monism, or a unitary vision, he continued, usually leads to an unjust despotic rule or tyrannical government. The reference to the Qur'anic verses sanctioning plurality cited earlier comes out clearly, as does the seemingly effortless change of register from theology to politics.

In spite of some verbal stridency, pragmatism features prominently in modern Islamic discourse. The Egyptian Muslim Brotherhood, for example, under changing conditions gradually moved from a principled rejection of multipartyism to an acceptance of a multiparty system—provided that it stays within the framework of Islam. In the face of British colonialism, the Muslim Brotherhood propagated national unity combined with the denunciation of party politics or factionalism (*ḥizbiyya*). Faith, Banna declared, is unity; fragmentation and disunity equal unbelief (*kufr*). Considering that in Egypt the interwar period has often been called the age of party politics, this was not a minor point. Yet the Muslim Brotherhood was not alone in criticizing "partyism" and partisanship. Saʻd Zaghlul, the leader of the Wafd Party founded in 1918, did the same, claiming for the Wafd the role of representative of the nation at large; by the 1930s, the critique had become commonplace. For Banna, politics (but not party politics) was an integral part of Islam. In 1938, he sent an open letter to the king and leading politicians, which was later published under the title *Nahwa al-Nur* (To the light), urging them to dissolve all parties and to create a united front. Still, there is no compelling link between this dualistic vision pitting right against wrong and the endorsement of a one-party system as it was espoused especially during the 1950s and 1960s by Islamists in particular communities and countries. Changed sociopolitical circumstances resulted in modified political thinking. By the mid-1990s, the Egyptian Muslim Brotherhood had largely revised its earlier positions on multipartyism, exchanging earlier rejection for cautious endorsement.

At the same time, most authors would rule out the possibility that political parties explicitly representing non-Muslims (such as Christian parties) be recognized in the framework of an Islamic order. Lebanon, with its system of institutionalized confessionalism, or sectarianism (*ṭā'ifiyya*), is a special case; set quotas for non-Muslims and other minorities in countries such as Iran or Jordan do not allow for political parties to form on a confessional basis. The same applies to political parties based on what are labeled un-Islamic principles, such as Marxism, communism, or fascism. But this does not exclude the possibility of cooperation under certain circumstances, notably under conditions of duress, in which the established legal principle of necessity, or *ḍarūra*, can be invoked. Here the crucial distinction between the fundamentals of religion (*aṣl*) and its derivatives (*furūʻ*) comes into play. It allows for recognizing the existing plurality and diversity of opinion and interest without abandoning the ideal of unity. In a similar context, the noted Islamic scholar H.A.R. Gibb has spoken of "tolerance for the sake of unity" (Gibb, 1962, p. 15).

From Toleration to Tolerance

Tolerance covers a broad spectrum of positions, from toleration of the Other to respect for his or her beliefs and practices to the full recognition of these beliefs and practices as equally viable and legitimate. The Arabic *tasāmuḥ* does not distinguish between toleration on the one hand and tolerance on the other. Toleration can be based on pragmatic considerations and made contingent on certain conditions; it is thus revocable. It can be granted by autocratic rulers and authoritarian states irrespective of their own beliefs and ideologies. Toleration can also reflect philosophical insight into the impossibility of ascertaining truth, similar to the argument made by Gannouchi and others in the context of pluralism. Both pragmatic toleration and philosophical reflection can come together but need not do so. In modern debates, it is often conditional toleration that authors, especially Islamist authors, have in mind when they invoke tolerance as the distinguishing feature of Islam and any polity based on it. Respect for the Other as a different expression of toleration and tolerance presupposes a certain degree of familiarity among the different parties, especially concerning their religious beliefs and practices. However, respect need not translate into specific legal and political arrangements granting equal religious, civic, and political rights to the latter.

By contrast, tolerance in the sense of full recognition of the Other is inconceivable without such legal and political arrangements translating religious recognition into rights of citizenship. In the modern period, tolerance thus defined has been associated with human rights, freedom, and liberty. Tolerance entails recognition of individual self-determination in diverse fields of life, including the free choice of lifestyle and religion, the right to practice this lifestyle or religion, and the right to either change or relinquish them altogether. Tolerance thus bears on individual and collective rights and liberties in both the private and the public spheres and is premised on a differentiation between religion, morals, law, and the constitution. The distinction many authors make between the public and the private domain, with the private sphere protected against outside intrusion and intervention, is remarkable in light of contemporary debates on whether the distinction between public and private in Western contexts is relevant to Muslim contexts. Discussions of sexual freedom and apostasy suggest that it is indeed highly relevant to the latter.

Tolerance among Muslims

Even for innovative authors such as 'Awwa, there are limits to tolerance and diversity. These limits, defined by God's law and revelation, inform (or ought to inform) Muslim understandings of freedom, liberty, and tolerance. Freedom in its various dimensions—freedom of conscience, religion, thought, and expression; freedom of association; academic and artistic freedom—is widely discussed among contemporary Muslims. Personal freedom, entailing free individual choice, bears on concepts of tolerance and pluralism. With regard to personal freedom, 'Awwa, who supports political pluralism and tolerance toward non-Muslims that treats them as citizens, not as protected subjects, shows himself as much more conservative. In a monograph on Islamic penal law he argued that

> the Islamic concept of personal freedom is entirely opposed to that of the post-war generation in the West. Personal freedom, according to the Islamic concept, is permissible only in respect to matters not regulated by the injunctions and prohibitions laid down in the Qur'an and the Sunna, which are expressions of the Divine Will. (El Awa, 1982, p. 18)

This does not address the question of how the community or the state should deal with transgression and whether under certain circumstances it might be tolerated, but it does underscore the necessity to distinguish among different fields to which individual groups and authors may apply different standards of rigor or leniency or toleration and tolerance.

The distinction between public and private is equally relevant to another key issue affecting tolerance among Muslims: the change of religion, which continues to be labeled as apostasy (*ridda*), suggesting the illegitimate nature of the act. Many would argue that within the Muslim community, public debate must fall short of any radical critique of religion or its dominant interpretations, which is readily denounced as blasphemy, heresy, or apostasy, raising the issue of *takfīr*, or the exclusion from the community of Muslims. Modern Muslim authors are concerned not so much with the theological dimension (the definition of apostasy and how it can be distinguished from sin, unbelief, heresy, or blasphemy) but with its impact on the body politic. Discussions of apostasy provide a striking illustration of territorial logic and the modern nation-state's impact on much of contemporary Islamic discourse. Thus in a tract devoted to the issue of apostasy, Qaradawi claimed that the Muslim who openly declares his apostasy transfers his allegiance from his own community and homeland to another and thereby threatens the foundation of collective identity.

According to him, the apostate does not simply abandon the community; he joins the enemy, an act not to be tolerated. Lacking compelling evidence from the Qur'an and sunna to support the identification of religious conversion and high treason, Qaradawi follows standard practice by invoking memories of the historical *ridda*, the secession of Arab tribes after Muhammad's death, which he describes as treason on both religious and political grounds. Like many others, Qaradawi looks at apostasy from the perspective of the community, not the individual making a personal choice, and he identifies Islam with individual and collective identity. This has obvious consequences for conceptions of religious tolerance and the status of non-Muslims in a Muslim polity or Islamic state.

The Status of Non-Muslims

The Qur'an describes other religions in its own terms, and these terms have been adapted by Muslim scholars of the formative and classical periods; modern Muslims still use basically the same vocabulary. Monotheism and a book of revelation are the crucial criteria by which the Qur'an distinguishes between several categories of believers (*mu'minūn* and *muslimūn*) and unbelievers (*kuffār*): the People of the Book, which include the Christians, the Jews, the Zoroastrians, and the mysterious Sabeans; the polytheists or pagans (*mushrikūn*); and the hypocrites (*munāfiqūn*), who pretend to be Muslims while actually conspiring against the Muslim community. Qur'anic rulings on the theological and legal status of non-Muslims as well as on how Muslims should interact with non-Muslims are not entirely consistent. Interpretation rests on the methods of contextualization and abstraction outlined earlier. Some Qur'anic verses describe the commonalities of all believers; others draw a clear line between Muslims, the People of the Book, and pagans. Thus Qur'an 109:6 states, "O unbelievers! I do not worship what you worship, nor do you worship what I worship; nor will I ever worship what you worship, nor will you ever worship what I worship. You have your religion, and I have mine." Qur'an 5:48 makes a similar statement. Both could be taken as the basis of respect and religious tolerance, although they are by no means unequivocal. As for the modes of interaction among the adherents of different faiths, Qur'an 2:256 famously decrees that "there is no compulsion in religion," whereas Qur'an 9:29 calls on Muslims to "fight those who do not believe in God or the Last Day, who do not hold illicit what God and His Messenger hold illicit, and who do not follow the religion of truth from among those given the Book, until they offer up the tribute, by hand, in humble mien." Several verses warn Muslims not to take non-Muslims as their friends and allies, while others instruct them to act justly toward them and to respect their treaties with them.

In view of such diversity, modern authors rely on classical theological and legal scholarship to put forth the position of Islam on the status and treatment of non-Muslims in Islamic or Muslim society. Modern authors still discuss *dhimma*, the protection granted to non-Muslims living permanently under Muslim rule; *jizya*, the poll tax to be paid by all able-bodied adult non-Muslim males in exchange for protection; the rules of interaction, including intermarriage, the possibility of sharing a table and of consuming foodstuffs produced or meat slaughtered by the non-Muslim Other, and the risks of ritual pollution; the freedom of religious practice, including the construction and restoration of sites of worship; and (partial) autonomy within the Islamic polity, best known from the late Ottoman Empire as the millet system. Most of these issues are dealt with in the so-called Treaty of 'Umar,

attributed to the second caliph, 'Umar b. al-Khattab (r. 634–44), and possibly composed in the eighth century. Modern writings are often apologetic in nature; religious polemic informed by theological issues has become rare. According to prevalent perceptions, tolerance was practiced from the time of the Prophet and the pious ancestors (*al-salaf al-ṣāliḥ*) up to at least Ottoman times. While early Muslim history is frequently invoked, the actual experience of coexistence, if not conviviality—not only in Andalus or in Fatimid Egypt but in various other times and places, too—is rarely explored. The conceptual framework is shaped by the territorial state, and the non-Muslims concerned are by and large local Christians. Muslim minority groups within Muslim-majority societies, such as Alevis in Turkey, Shi'is in Saudi Arabia or Morocco, or Sunnis in Iran, are hardly ever covered under the heading of tolerance. The status of Hindus and Buddhists is rarely discussed outside of South Asia and Southeast Asia, and contributions of South Asian or Southeast Asian Muslim intellectuals tend to be ignored by their Middle Eastern homologues. Reception is slightly better among Muslim intellectuals and activists residing in the West. New religious communities such as the Mormons or Jehovah's Witnesses are largely excluded from discussion and denied recognition and legal protection.

Discussions of tolerance accorded to non-Muslims under Islam, therefore, tend to be limited to the People of the Book in general and to Christians and Jews in particular. Within this narrow field, however, the range of positions is wide: At one end of the spectrum are those scholar-activists who are prepared to tolerate Christians and Jews as *dhimmīs*, subjects of the Muslim state or ruler protected on the condition that they acknowledge the superiority of Islam and the Muslim community and, as a token of this recognition, pay the *jiyza* "with humble mien" (Q. 9:29). They exclude non-Muslims from political participation and representation as well as all positions involving power and authority over Muslims (*wilāya*), including the judiciary, the military, and high state offices, which are classified as religious because in one way or another, they are charged with applying the shari'a. The distinction between "religious" and "nonreligious" spheres and offices at work here is intriguing given the Islamist conviction that Islam does *not* separate religion from politics—the bedrock of antisecular argument. It appears that within the framework of Islamic rule, as exemplified by the application of the shari'a, distinct fields or domains operate according to a different logic, provided that this logic does not contradict the "fundamentals" of Islam and the shari'a. Still, this is a minority view, mostly to be found among militant Islamist groups and theoreticians. At the other end of the spectrum are those scholars, intellectuals, and political activists who recognize Christians and Jews as citizens of the (Muslim or Islamic) nation-state with equal rights and duties, grant them autonomy in personal-status matters, and bar them only from the office of president, to which only male Muslims can be appointed. This position is much more common than the former, though also more diversified. Statements on the status of Jews must be seen in light of political conflict with Zionism and Israel rather than the principle of religious tolerance only. The same applies to anti-Semitism, which in certain milieus has arisen mainly as an element of the critique of Zionism and Israel or Israeli state policies.

In certain contexts, non-Muslims residing in Islamic territory are described as *dhimmīs* of the Muslim community, enjoying protection (*dhimma*) against the payment of dues and taxes including the *jizya*; in other contexts, they are described as *muwāṭinūn*, variously to be translated as compatriots or citizens. According to classical *fiqh*, relations between Muslims and non-Muslims are based on a contract involving reciprocal rights and duties, which were unequal, reflecting the religious and political superiority of Muslims. Except for certain militant Islamist activists, modern authors commonly assert that non-Muslims enjoy essentially the same civic and political rights and duties as Muslims, referring to the formula "same rights, same duties" (*lahum mā lanā wa-'alayhim mā 'alaynā*), which is also known in classical *fiqh*, especially the Hanafi tradition. Accordingly, Islam guarantees non-Muslims protection of their lives, bodies, property, and honor as well as respect for their religious freedom, covering the fundamental goods or benefits (*maṣāliḥ*) protected under the shari'a. In the framework of the modern nation-state, it also offers them social benefits such as old-age pensions. It is only in the religious field that they cannot be considered equal.

With regard to politics, some authors argue that the protection accorded non-Muslims under Islam is the same as what is today described as nationality or citizenship (*jinsiyya*). They interpret the *jizya* as an equivalent of zakat or a substitute for military service. Accordingly, non-Muslims could not be expected to fight for Islam and the Muslim community, a fight identified as jihad, in the premodern era; however, the nature of jihad was transformed in the process of anticolonial struggle and modern nation building. Non-Muslims who joined their Muslim fellow countrymen in the fight against colonialism and for the nation earned the rights of citizenship, making special payment of *jizya* obsolete. Not all authors claim that the *muwāṭinūn min ghayr al-muslimīn* (non-Muslim countrymen and women) enjoy full equality with their Muslim compatriots in all spheres of life. Instead, they elaborate on justice, equity, and religious freedom properly understood, which does not force non-Muslims to convert but allows them to retain their cultural authenticity just as it protects the cultural authenticity of Muslims. In return, non-Muslims have to respect the religious sensibilities of the Muslims. Proselytizing missions among Muslims cannot be tolerated, highlighting once again the shifting meanings of toleration and tolerance.

See also minorities; modernity; revival and reform

Further Reading

S. Ghalib Khan al-Abbasi and A. de Zayas Abbasi, *The Structure of Islamic Polity. Part I: The One-Party System in Islam*, 1952; Mohammed Salim al-Awa, "Political Pluralism from an Islamic Perspective," in *Power-Sharing Islam?*, edited by Azzam Tamimi, 1993; Mark Cohen, *Under Crescent and Cross*, 1994; Hamid Dabashi, *Theology of Discontent: The Ideological Foundation of the Islamic*

Revolution in Iran, 1993; Mohamed S. El-Awa, *Punishment in Islamic Law: A Comparative Study*, 1982; Rainer Forst, *Toleranz im Konflikt: Geschichte, Gehalt und Gegenwart eines umstrittenen Begriffs*, 2003; Yohanan Friedmann, *Tolerance and Coercion in Islam: Interfaith Relations in the Muslim Tradition*, 2003; H.A.R. Gibb, *Studies on the Civilization of Islam*, edited by Stanford Shaw and William R. Polk, 1962; Bettina Gräf and Jakob Skovgaard-Petersen, eds., *The Global Mufti: The Phenomenon of Yusuf al-Qaradawi*, 2009; Gudrun Krämer, *Gottes Staat als Republik. Reflexionen zeitgenössischer Muslime zu Islam, Menschenrechten und Demokratie*, 1999; Idem, *Hasan al-Banna*, 2010; Birgit Krawietz, *Hierarchie der Rechtsquellen im tradierten sunnitischen Recht*, 2002; Johanna Pink, *Neue Religionsgemeinschaften in Ägypten. Minderheiten im Spannungsfeld von Glaubensfreiheit, öffentlicher Ordnung und Islam*, 2003; Josef van Ess, *Theologie und Gesellschaft im 2. und 3 Jahrhundert Hidschra*, vol. 1, 1991; Muhammad Qasim Zaman, *The Ulama in Contemporary Islam: Custodians of Change*, 2002.

GUDRUN KRÄMER

police

In the premodern Islamic world, responsibility for carrying out police functions for maintaining public safety and enforcing the law was distributed among several institutions and jurisdictions. The primary ones included the *shurṭa* (police, military, and prosecutorial arms of the ruling authorities); *maẓālim* (jurisdiction within institutions designed to offer recourse for injustices of public officials, redress contraventions of justice in the courts, and impose criminal sanctions); and *ḥisba* (jurisdiction whose officials had the mandate to inspect market practices, offenses against public morality, and the like). Though none of these institutions are mentioned in the Qur'an, the legal and theoretical basis for them is firmly entrenched in the Islamic tradition by a combination of practical necessity and scriptural interpretation. The Qur'an outlines a series of moral precepts for the Muslim community, commands Muslims to "obey God and his Messenger and those in authority over you" (4:59), and insists on a duty to command right and forbid wrong (*amr bi-l-ma'rūf wa-nahy 'an al-munkar*; 3:104). Through a doctrine called *siyāsa*, roughly the "governance of the public sphere," medieval Muslim jurists-*cum*-political theorists drew on such Qur'anic verses to accord Muslim rulers broad discretion over issues of governance in the public interest (*maṣlaḥa*), including matters of public safety and law enforcement. The idea was that the government had a basic obligation to uphold Islamic law as an expression of divine will for a moral and just society and that the ruler was best equipped to preside over this task.

The most common term used to discuss the police was *shurṭa*. The *shurṭa* carried out police functions from the earliest period of Islamic history. Early on, the *shurṭa* was evidently an elite military force, or special troops chosen specifically to serve the caliph or governor of a particular region. The second caliph, 'Umar b. al-Khattab (r. 634–44), reportedly employed a night patrol (called *'asas* or *ṭawāf*), which performed a function later taken on by the *shurṭa*: policing and domestic military duties both day and night. The fourth caliph and first Shi'i imam, 'Ali b. Abi Talib (r. 656–61), is said to have employed a *shurṭa* as a military guard following the Battle of Siffin, where he fought Mu'awiya (r. 661–80), the first caliph of the Umayyad dynasty, in 657 during the First Civil War (*fitna*). Some historical sources report that the third caliph, 'Uthman b. 'Affan (r. 644–56), had a *shurṭa* as a personal guard, though if he did, the guard was wholly ineffective in preventing his assassination.

By the time of Mu'awiya's reign, the *shurṭa* was an established institution that carried out recognizable police functions in Iraq's major regions. Historical sources report that in Kufa in 663, the *shurṭa* surrounded the house of a Khariji rebel leader, arresting him and his coconspirators; in Basra in 665, the governor Ziyad b. Sufyan established a *shurṭa* of 4,000 men responsible for enforcing law and order; and in Karbala in 680, the *shurṭa* played a leading role in the assassination of Husayn b. 'Ali, the grandson of Muhammad and the third Shi'i imam. The *shurṭa* in these later instances was distinguished from the ruler's personal bodyguard (*ḥaras*), which guarded the caliph or governor, and from the army (*jaysh*), which protected the community from external threats.

Under the Abbasids (r. 750–1258) and the Spanish Umayyads (r. 756–1031), the role of the *shurṭa* expanded. Its head, the *ṣāḥib al-shurṭa* (also *walī al-jarā'im* in Spain), was charged not only with maintaining law and order but also with helping to adjudicate it. He investigated crime, made arrests, and conducted pretrial interrogation procedures—alongside the *muḥtasib* (the agent responsible for market inspection)—for both the qadi and *maẓālim* courts; adjudicated misdemeanors over which the ruler had wide discretion (*ta'zīr*); supervised the imposition of retaliation for bodily injuries and homicides (*qiṣāṣ*); and sometimes imposed criminal sanctions (*ḥudūd*). In some instances, the *shurṭa* was subordinate to the local judge (qadi). For example, in 11th-century Córdoba, he attended the sessions (*majlis*) of the local judge, consulted him on major matters, and had deputies (*a'wān*) whom the local magistrate (*ḥākim*) helped select for judicial duties. Likewise, in Fatimid Cairo (r. 969–1171), the *shurṭa* was called *ma'ūna* (a helping body) for its role in aiding the magistrates in performing judicial tasks. In other instances, however, the *shurṭa* dispensed justice without recourse to the qadis. By the 10th and 11th centuries in both eastern and western Islamic lands, the *shurṭa* was divided into at least two different branches of jurisdiction—major (*kubrā* or *'ulyā*) and minor (*ṣughrā*). Andalusian sources also identify a third area, the "intermediate" jurisdiction (*wusṭā*), beginning in the 11th century. The higher branches seem to have had expansive authority over all crimes among both notables and commoners, while the lower were confined to handling petty crimes among the masses; the middle jurisdiction was a bit obscure but perhaps handled issues and social strata in between the other two.

In addition to policing and judicial duties, the head of the *shurṭa* had other responsibilities. These included strategy consultations with the local ruler, diplomatic missions (e.g., accompanying Christian delegations wanting to meet with the caliph or an area governor), military activities, and executive duties (i.e., serving as acting governor in the ruler's absence). Thus the *ṣāḥib al-shurṭa* was also called *ṣāḥib al-madīna* in Spain, where he assumed governorship and diplomatic duties; in Mamluk Cairo and elsewhere, he was called *wālī al-madīna* (city chief), *wālī al-qāhira*, or *walī al-shurṭa*, where his role was more militaristic. During the time of the Crusades in 1169 in Damascus and Egypt, the police were called the *shiḥna*, and the chief helped combat Crusaders. During Ottoman times, the so-called police-chief (*walī al-shurṭa*) took on a more administrative role. In the modern Arab world, *shurṭa* is the common term for police.

See also governance

Further Reading

Fred M. Donner, "The *Shurṭa* in Early Umayyad Syria," in *The Fourth International Conference on the History of Bilād al-Shām*, edited by M. Adnan Bakhit and Robert Schick, 1989; Boğaç Ergene, ed., *Judicial Practice: Institutions and Agents in the Islamic World*, 2009; Hugh Kennedy, *The Armies of the Caliphs: Military and Society in the Early Islamic State*, 2001; Émile Tyan, *Histoire de l'organisation judiciaire en pays d'Islam*, 2nd ed., 1960.

INTISAR A. RABB

political ritual

The ceremonies and performances conducted by Muslim political leaders to demonstrate their authority and religious legitimacy became common under the Abbasid and Fatimid dynasties, especially rulers' titles, dress, and court and prayer ceremonies. These particulars are generally discussed under the rubric of *adab* (etiquette) and appear as distinct sections in larger works on Islamic government, Mirrors for Princes, and so on. Likewise, the terms *rusūm* or *marāsim*, defined either as "protocol" or as "ceremonies," are used in the main medieval works that document these practices.

Lineage was already important in pre-Islamic Arabia, and titles formed an integral part of a prominent figure's reputation. In the political context, lineage might also offer legitimacy. The descendants of the Prophet emphasized their pedigree by appending to their name the title of *al-sayyid* (the master) or *al-sharīf* (the noble). In the 11th century, the Buyids introduced the controversial titles *malik* (king) and *malik al-mulūk* (king of kings). The latter had particularly problematic connotations, since a famous hadith attributes to the Prophet the statement, "The most abhorrent of names before God is that of 'king of kings.'" Scholars have interpreted this gesture by the Buyids as an attempt either to revert to pre-Islamic Persian titulature or to distance the ruler from religious responsibility.

In the medieval period, several regular occasions provided opportunities for rulers to demonstrate their legitimacy. Perhaps the two most important such occasions were the Friday and holiday prayers, since it was customary to mention the ruler's name in the accompanying sermon (*khuṭba*). During the Friday sermon, the preacher would cite the current ruler's name and recite blessings for him. This invocation of the ruler's name parallels his mention in inscriptions on the coins (*sikka*) minted during his reign as well as his mention on textiles made in the ruler's atelier (*ṭirāz*). In the ninth century, it became customary for the ruler to lead prayers at the central mosque of his capital, thus displaying his religious and political clout, and for his name to be pronounced in the *khuṭba* of a secondary mosque.

Similarly, holidays proved fitting contexts for rulers to display their authority. For the Fatimids and Buyids, celebration of the festival of Ghadir Khumm was regarded as the most direct evidence of their legitimacy. On that day in the year 632, the Prophet was said to have pronounced his cousin and son-in-law, 'Ali b. Abi Talib, as his heir. Shi'i governments would mark the occasion by decorating the city and proclaiming 'Ali's special status as the Prophet's legitimate successor. Similarly, the Fatimid procession at the New Year's celebration was a powerful display of authority, particularly in the context of the contestation for power among the caliph, the army, and the vizier. The vizier would ride on horseback with his sons and brothers before him and would be followed by the caliph and his party. The caliph would be carried on a sedan chair and would exchange slight bows with the vizier toward the end of the procession. Their places in the lineup were said to have reflected their ranks. Medieval historian Paula Sanders notes that while the vizier's power stemmed from the caliph, his actual powers in terms of government emerged from the trust of his troops. Therefore, national and religious holidays served not only to legitimate the sources of power but also to restore and define the internal dynamics of the government.

Different religious rulers also demonstrated their legitimacy by wearing or displaying the Prophet's insignia when appearing in public. According to Dominique Sourdel, this tradition first became apparent during the Abbasid caliphate, when the caliph would wear the Prophet's cloak (*burda*), hold the Prophet's scepter (*qaḍīb*), and carry a copy of the Qur'an (*muṣḥaf*).

In the political context, pledges (*bay'a*) played an important role in articulating trust in a ruler. The *bay'a* was an important practice that dates from the death of the Prophet, when Abu Bakr assumed the caliphate, and the ceremony became a prominent feature in the assumption of Sunni caliphal rule. Under Shi'i governments, it served merely as a gesture of loyalty rather than an official marker of power. During the Buyid reign, pledges were the most prominent way for a ruler to informally obligate and instruct government functionaries regarding their tasks.

In the modern period, rituals are commonly performed by governments to articulate their connection to Islam. Iran confers the highest political and religious authority on the supreme leader (*rahbar*)—a position that has thus far been filled by descendants of the Prophet. They too adopt the title *sayyid* and wear a black turban as a sign of this pedigree. Strict enforcement of the dress code serves as an expression of the country's religious nature. Women are required to wear a chador, a concealing black cloak, and hijab, a headscarf, as an outward sign of the obligation to preserve modesty and piety.

In contemporary Morocco, the sultan also adopts certain traditional practices to display his legitimacy. In 1962 Sultan Muhammad V introduced the pledge, which subsequent leaders make upon assuming power. Moreover, since 1962, kingship is conferred upon descendants of the Prophet, and only sons may succeed the reigning king. The king's public ritual sacrifice of two sheep (one for himself and one for the Moroccan people) every year on the festival of sacrifice ('Id al-Adha) associated with the annual pilgrimage to Mecca is a powerful symbol of his sovereignty under the aegis of Islam.

Parallel to rituals of legitimacy, in the modern period certain novel rituals are introduced to maintain the religious spirit of the country. In Iran, the Basij, the official paramilitary group, plans religious events and suppresses opposition. In Saudi Arabia, the *muṭawwi'īn* are officially charged with ensuring prayer attendance—sometimes by harsh means—thus monitoring the nation's religious culture.

See also 'Ashura'; bureaucracy

Further Reading

M. E. Combs-Schilling, *Sacred Performances: Islam, Sexuality, and Sacrifice*, 1989; Jacob Lassner, *The Shaping of 'Abbāsid Rule*, 1980; Andrew Marsham, *Rituals of Islamic Monarchy: Accession and Succession in the First Muslim Empire*, 2009; Roy Mottahedeh, *Loyalty and Leadership in an Early Islamic Society*, 2001; Paula Sanders, *Ritual, Politics and the City in Fatimid Cairo*, 1994; Muhammad Qasim Zaman, *Religion and Politics Under the Early 'Abbāsids: The Emergence of the Proto-Sunnī Elite*, 1997.

JACOB OLIDORT

preaching

Announcing the message of Islam, which the Qur'an refers to as a call or an invitation (*da'wa*), represents preaching as an activity that all Muslims are expected to practice (Q. 16:125). In this broad sense, engaging in religious discourse in order to instruct, edify, admonish, exhort, counsel, inspire, or proselytize is understood to be identified closely with the general mission of the entire *umma*, or the community of the faithful. In some contexts, including both classical and contemporary works, this emphasis on the public presentation of Islam as a universal vocation is accompanied by the recognition that, formally speaking, Islam does not have a clergy, which therefore confers the duty of preaching, in a general sense, upon all believers.

Nevertheless, the emergence of preaching, in the narrower and more specialized application of the term, dates from the earliest period of Muhammad's response to God's revelation, since, to a large degree, much of what is contained in the Qur'an and the sunna might be characterized as constituting preachment. This diffuse work of addressing people in God's name, however, soon came to be framed in a particular ritual setting that fixed the standard occasion for delivering a sermon in the mosque, originally meaning the courtyard of Muhammad's house in Medina, at the Friday noon prayer, which free male Muslims were obligated to attend. This precedent has since been codified in the Islamic legal tradition that regards the Friday prayer service, including the valid performance of the sermon, as a defining feature of a properly constituted Islamic community.

Traditionally, the right to deliver this Friday sermon was specified as the prerogative of the Prophet's successor, who would either preach himself or delegate others to do so in his name. Accordingly, the content of the sermon was meant to embrace both sacred and secular issues. Likewise, over time, formal oratorical elements and a certain language style came to be incorporated into the practice that required considerable knowledge and skill, leading to the rise of scholarly professionals who tended to occupy the posts of preachers. Among the elements prescribed as necessary for the sermon was a formula of blessing that explicitly mentioned the name of the ruler, under whose auspices the preacher was presiding. This requirement came to take on exceptional importance at many points, especially in times of political instability, when a preacher was obliged either to confirm his old loyalty or to signal a shift of allegiance to a rival.

In nations with Muslim majorities, mosque preaching continues to have an inherent potential for addressing political as well as religious themes. Accordingly, various mechanisms are employed to regulate the conduct of preachers who, for the most part, comply with policies of the state whose institutions train, subsidize, and supervise them. Preachers expressing dissent, however, typically may still find relative freedom of expression in mosque preaching, which provides ample opportunity to convey critical views through such devices as selective omissions and leading rhetorical allusions.

See also commanding right and forbidding wrong; Friday prayer; mosque; propaganda; pulpit

Further Reading

Jonathan Berkey, *Popular Preaching and Religious Authority in the Medieval Islamic Near East*, 2001; Jacques Waardenburg, "Islam as a Vehicle of Protest," in *Islamic Dilemmas: Reformers, Nationalists and Industrialization*, edited by Ernest Gellner, 1985.

PATRICK D. GAFFNEY

privacy

The conceptual dichotomy of private and public life is anchored in the Western social sciences; no exact translation of this pair of opposites exists in any of the Islamic languages. As a minimal definition, privacy in the Islamic context refers to the right to remain concealed (*ḥaqq al-sitr*) and protected from unwanted intrusion. The inviolability of territory is only one of several dimensions in this definition. In addition, the concept of privacy in Islamic societies relates to the highly developed notions of the inviolability (*ḥurma*) of the human body, regardless of location, and of the inviolability of a person's or group's honor (*sharaf*) that is derived from moral and religious integrity (*'adāla*). Such rights protect a person's privacy even when he or she enters into the public sphere of government control. The line that separated private from public in traditional Islamic societies was defined by the social and historical context, and traditions of political thought about privacy in Islam likewise differed in important respects according to the various perspectives adopted in jurisprudence (*fiqh*); in the ethico-theological tradition; and by those writing under the patronage of political power, the authors of chancery documents, Mirrors for Princes, chronicles, panegyric poetry, and the like.

Political Elites as Private Bodies

Privacy as defined earlier could be claimed not only by the subjects of political rule but also by those in power. Medieval Islamic governments, especially after the militarization of society in large parts of the Islamic world beginning in the tenth century, were largely disconnected from their subjects. Political elites conceived of themselves as an autonomous and extrajudicial "private" body. The men of the regime (*khawāṣṣ*)—namely, all those who were distinguished (*khāṣṣ*) by their share in the task of governing—together inhabited a self-regulatory realm of reward and punishment that was strictly separate from the public arena of the commoners (*'awāmm*). The sphere of the *khawāṣṣ* was internally stratified according to closeness to the ruler who presided over it. Different degrees of proximity to the ruler included participation in court ceremonies and audiences, membership in the group of the ruler's boon companions and intimate advisors, and access to the ruler's harem (usually restricted to close relatives).

Political writers of the premodern period gave rulers the power to discipline the *khawāṣṣ* at their discretion; the ruler must educate (*rawwaḍa*) and lead (*sāsa*) them but at all times protect their privacy. The court secretary Ibn Hamdun (d. 1166) judged that an offense committed by a member in the private realm of the court (*dhanb al-sirr*) required a punishment meted out in private (*'uqūbat al-sirr*). Only on the extreme occasion when the *khawāṣṣ* fell from grace—for example, when they had revolted against their patron—could they lose the privilege of being disciplined within the confines of the court; medieval chronicles occasionally mention the ritual ejection and public display in the city of disgraced amirs after their execution at court.

Levels of Inviolability of the Ruled

Jurists and ethical writers of Islam defended the right to concealment of the subjects, which was always precarious under the conditions of military government in medieval Islam. The Qur'an (24:27) states, "Do not enter houses other than your own unless you have asked permission and greeted the inhabitants!" There is also a general injunction not to pry and spy on people (49:12). As Eli Alshech argues in his article on the evolution of the notion of the domestic sphere, around the tenth century, Islamic legal doctrine underwent a change from a mechanical, occupancy-based notion of privacy to the interpretation of privacy as a value in itself, regardless of legal claims to rightful tenancy. Transgressions against privacy, such as acts of voyeurism, were increasingly threatened with punishment. Jurists aimed such restrictions not only at ordinary citizens but also, and perhaps primarily, at the agents of the repressive state apparatus. Medieval legal manuals detailing the duties and prerogatives of the government-appointed market inspector and censor of morals (*muḥtasib*) specifically stipulate that the *muḥtasib* is entitled to prosecute only openly visible and apparent wrongdoings (*munkarāt ẓāhira*). He is not allowed to spy on people in their homes or violate their property rights (*ḥuqūq al-irtifāq*).

Islamic law also emphasizes the right and the duty to protect the inviolability (*ḥurma*) of the human body. A free man's "zone of shame" (*'awra*) is defined as the area between the navel and the knees; a free woman's is the whole body except the face and hands (and, according to others, the feet and forearms). These body parts are to be covered, but rules tend to be less strict in relation to family members. In general, among members of Muslim society, relational standing rather than the sanctity of specific places seems the key to understanding privacy in Islamic law. The jurists' concern for the inviolability of the human body can also be seen in their broad condemnation of punitive mutilation (*tamthīl*; with the shari'a punishments for theft and brigandage—namely, the amputation of hands and feet—as an exception) and in their refusal (with some post-Mongol exceptions) to allow judicial torture.

The ethos of protecting private behavior from the intrusive gaze of others, or even of keeping sins hidden and not divulging them to the public, is anchored in both the Qur'an and hadith; it is a hallmark of all later Islamic legal and ethical writings. On the other hand, discretionary state punishment based on the interest of the state (*siyāsa*), particularly the practice of ignominious parading (*tashhīr*), the medieval Muslim equivalent of the Western pillory, was often aimed directly at destroying the convicted person's honor and reputation. Jurists of the classical period usually opposed such transgressions against people's right of privacy, although they tended to distinguish between different levels of honorability: the less honor was at stake, the more public state punishments could be. According to the Hanafi jurist Abu Bakr b. Mas'ud al-Kashani (d. 1189), descendants of the Prophet and

the jurists must only be made to suffer a private reprimand from the judge. Noblemen (*ashrāf*) are to receive a reprimand from the judge in the public setting of the court. The middle classes (*awsāṭ*) are punished with reprimand in the judge's court and with imprisonment. Finally, the nether classes (*sifla*) suffer public reprimand, imprisonment, and beating.

See also city (philosophical); commanding right and forbidding wrong; government; holy places; honor; household; human rights; individualism; Mirrors for Princes; patrimonial state; public interest; public opinion; quietism and activism; veil

Further Reading

Eli Alshech, "'Do Not Enter Houses Other Than Your Own': The Evolution of the Notion of a Private Domestic Sphere in Early Sunnī Islamic Thought," *Islamic Law and Society* 11, no. 3 (2004); Michael Cook, *Commanding Right and Forbidding Wrong*, 2000; Jans-Peter Hartung, *Court Cultures in the Muslim World: Seventh to Nineteenth Centuries*, 2010; Mohamed Kerrou, ed., *Public et privé en Islam*, 2002; Yaron Klein, "Between Public and Private: An Examination of *Ḥisba* Literature," *Harvard Middle Eastern and Islamic Review* 7 (2006); Christian Lange, "Legal and Cultural Aspects of Ignominious Parading (*Tashhīr*) in Islam," *Islamic Law and Society* 14, no. 1 (2007); Christian Lange and Maribel Fierro, "Spatial, Ritual and Representational Aspects of Public Violence in Islamic Societies (1st–19th Centuries CE)," in *Public Violence in Islamic Societies*, 2009.

CHRISTIAN LANGE

propaganda

Propaganda, defined as the systematic spreading of information, ideas, and rumors in the effort to help or harm a particular group or cause, plays an integral role in the activism of modern Muslim groups for social, religious, and political purposes. Their understanding and use of it is rooted in the classical concept of *da'wa*, which means "call or invitation" in the Qur'an and hadith (prophetic tradition) as well as in everyday parlance. The term *da'wa* is most commonly used to describe religious missionary activity, and a missionary or proselytizer is termed a *dā'ī*, or "one who calls or invites." In the modern period, state-sponsored *da'wa* has allowed certain interpretations of Islam, such as the Saudi version of the Salafi trend within Sunni Islam, to gain a global following. Muslim political groups, both religious nationalist and transnational, have adopted classical principles of *da'wa* and applied them to modern politics.

In the medieval period there are several examples of the use of *da'wa* to further political goals. In the mid-eighth century, Abu Muslim (d. 755) was sent to the region of Khurasan to propagate and plan a revolt on behalf of the Abbasids, a family claiming descent from the Prophet Muhammad, against the ruling Umayyad dynasty. Another notable example is the movement of the early Shi'i rebel Mukhtar (d. 687), who led a revolt against the Umayyads from 685 to 687 in the name of Muhammad b. al-Hanafiyya, though the latter did not support it. In the second half of the ninth century, the Fatimids, a family claiming descent from the Prophet's family through his daughter Fatima, dispatched missionaries across the Muslim world to win converts for their cause—namely, the right to assume the roles of spiritual and temporal ruler, combining them into one position, that of "imam-caliph." By 875, Fatimid missionaries had established footholds in North Africa, Syria, Yemen, Iran, Bahrain, and Central and South Asia. The *dā'ī* Abu 'Abd Allah al-Shi'i converted the Kutama Berbers of North Africa to Fatimid Isma'ili Shi'ism, allowing the Fatimids to move from Salamiyya, Syria, where they were threatened by the Abbasid dynasty, to greater safety in Tunisia, where they built their empire.

Propaganda of many types allowed premodern rulers in Islamic societies to bolster legitimacy, mobilize the populace, and suppress dissent. Political propaganda often touted the outstanding qualities and accomplishments of the ruler, especially his generosity, charity, justice, clemency, piety, devotion, abstention from sinful behavior, dedication to the faith, bravery, and exertion in defending the Muslim community and in championing the believers. Authors often announced these qualities explicitly in panegyric poetry, court chronicles, campaign narratives, biographies, diplomatic correspondence, and the introductions and dedications of treatises on diverse topics. Rulers also implicitly propagated similar messages by the construction of mosques, colleges of Islamic law, Sufi centers, hospitals, and so on; lavish support of the annual pilgrimage caravan; and refurbishment of places of worship in the main cities of their realm and at prominent shrines such as in Mecca, Medina, Jerusalem, or Karbala. Public ceremonies on holy days or during the month of Ramadan, including donations or free banquets, served a similar role. Rulers also enhanced their images as pious by public acts of personal repentance, such as Shah Tahmasp's *Edict of Sincere Repentance* in 1556, when he swore off drinking wine, listening to music, and so on, or visible acts of devotion, such as Shah 'Abbas I's barefoot pilgrimage from Isfahan to Mashhad in 1601 or the contemporary Moroccan king's televised sacrifice of two sheep on 'Id al-Adha (the festival of the annual pilgrimage to Mecca), one for himself and one symbolically for the Moroccan people. Rulers also boosted their images as defenders of the faith by sponsoring campaigns against public immorality and heretical views, closing down brothels and wine taverns, executing or punishing heretics, or burning the books of the Shi'is and the Mu'tazilis, as occurred upon Mahmud of Ghazna's conquest of Rayy in 1029, and philosophy books, as occurred in the Andalus under the Almohads.

Propaganda denouncing enemies of the realm or the faith has often served for the establishment of political legitimacy, political mobilization, and social control. The Abbasids and the Seljuqs made use of propaganda in the form of sponsored polemics about their Isma'ili rivals, both Fatimid and Nizari. In formally signed public documents, they proclaimed that the Fatimids' genealogy

was forged. They also propagated what are collectively known as the "black legends," which accused the Isma'ilis of involvement in black magic, sexual deviance, and heresy. Many Muslim rulers such as the Hamdanid Sayf al-Dawlah bolstered their legitimacy by touting their victories in warfare against the Christian Byzantines. When the Fatimids conquered Egypt and most of Syria in the mid-tenth century, they continually announced that the main purpose behind the occupation was their dedication to conducting jihad against the Byzantines, in contrast to the failure of the current rulers in the region to pursue it vigorously. Propaganda played an enormous role in mobilizing Muslim forces to combat the Crusades, and it resulted in the authorship of many works on the virtues of jihad and the merits of Jerusalem and other holy sites in the Levant. The Zengids, and particularly Nur al-Din, developed what has been termed the unified jihad, a vigorous propaganda campaign against not only the Crusaders but also the Shi'is, on the logic that the latter weaken the Muslim community from within and are potential allies with the enemy from without. A particularly striking act of Nur al-Din was his commission of a lavish minbar, the pulpit from which the Friday sermons were read, intended to be installed at the mosque at the Dome of the Rock upon the eventual reconquest of Jerusalem from the Franks. In the 16th century, the Twelver Shi'i Safavid dynasty, aided by religious scholars from Jabal 'Amil in Syria, used *da'wa* to convert much of Iran's Sunni majority to Shi'i Islam. They enhanced their legitimacy by denouncing their Sunni neighbors, the Ottomans and the Uzbeks, as heretical foes. The Ottomans and the Uzbeks reciprocated, having fatwas issued declaring the Safavid Shi'is heretics and denouncing them in many polemical works.

Contemporary propaganda, in the form of multimedia and written releases, is an integral political tool for Muslim political ("Islamist") groups. Religious-nationalist groups such as the Egyptian Muslim Brotherhood (al-Ikhwan al-Muslimun) and the Lebanese Shi'i party Hizbullah have long used propaganda to build support for their social, religious, and political platforms. Transnational Islamist militants, popularly and self-referentially called *jihādīs*, have adopted media and propaganda tactics started by religious-nationalist groups and greatly expanded them to fit their own needs. From its founding in 1928, the Egyptian Muslim Brotherhood has published newsletters, newspapers, and magazines to propagate the movement's views. The movement continues to publish such materials but has since also wholeheartedly adopted the use of new technologies such as the Internet, running Arabic- and English-language websites. As part of its Internet strategy, the Ikhwan employs a team of its younger members as bloggers.

Hizbullah, which began as a national resistance movement against Israel's occupation of a large swath of southern Lebanon in the 1980s and 1990s, has evolved into a sophisticated political movement with national and regional influence. The party's growth has been aided significantly by its media outlets, key among them its satellite television station Al-Manar (The beacon), which began broadcasting in 1991. Hizbullah also publishes the newspaper *Al-Intiqad* (Criticism) and runs a radio station, Al-Nur, as well as several websites in Arabic, Hebrew, English, Persian, Spanish, and French.

The earliest transnational *jihādī* literature was published in the 1980s by various groups participating in the war against the Soviet Union's occupation of Afghanistan (1979–89). Thousands of foreigners, many of them Arab Muslims, traveled to Afghanistan in order to aid the various factions of Afghan mujahidin, or warriors of the faith. One of the most influential of these was 'Abd Allah 'Azzam, a Palestinian Sunni religious scholar who had completed a doctorate in Islamic law at Egypt's famed Azhar University, who was a key fundraiser for the anti-Soviet cause. He founded the Markaz al-Khidmah li-l-Mujahidin al-'Arab (Service Bureau for Arab Mujahidin) in Peshawar, Pakistan, which aided Arab fighters going to Afghanistan, many of whom entered via Pakistan. 'Azzam and his supporters also published propaganda materials, including the magazine *Al-Jihad* (The struggle), in which the exploits of the mujahidin were recounted.

Al-Qaeda and many other transnational jihad groups have their own media outlets through which they produce and distribute propaganda materials. Since 2003–4, the majority of this material is distributed online through a handful of web forums and affiliated websites, including the Ansar al-Mujahidin (Partisans of the warriors of faith) forum. Releases are made available for download via file-sharing websites, where copies are uploaded dozens of times and the URLs published in the forums. Major releases are advertised with animated banners, and forum users then upload the files to non-jihad websites such as Internet Archive and YouTube.

Al-Qaeda Central's (AQC) al-Sahab (The clouds) Foundation for Media Production is the premier jihad media outlet and regularly produces sophisticated videos through which its leaders broadcast their ideology and address their supporters, potential supporters, and enemies. Among its most sophisticated productions is the video series *Rih al-Jannah* (Wind of paradise), which highlights the group's martyrs in Afghanistan and Pakistan. As of this writing, it consists of five installments. Jihad videos mesh image and spoken word, including martial music in the form of *anāshīd* (religious and political anthems).

Despite al-Sahab's preeminence, other major jihad media outlets connected to other groups, many of them al-Qaeda allies and affiliates, exist, including al-Qaeda in the Islamic Maghreb's (AQIM) al-Andalus Media, al-Qaeda in the Arabian Peninsula's (AQAP) Al-Malahim Media, and the Islamic State of Iraq's al-Furqan Media. Many of these groups publish monthly or bimonthly Internet magazines, including *al-Samud* (Afghan Taliban) and *Sada al-Malahim* (AQAP). Several major "independent" jihad media outlets and distribution networks also exist, chief among them the Global Islamic Media Front (GIMF) and the al-Fajr Media Center, which distributes releases from AQC, AQAP, and AQIM. The GIMF produces translations of Arabic and Urdu-language releases from various transnational jihad groups, including AQC, and publishes essays and monographs from a host of jihad scholars and ideologues. Jihad propaganda is regularly produced in Urdu,

Pashtu, Uzbek, Turkish, Dari, German, Uighur, Russian, Chechen, and French, in addition to Arabic and English, by various groups, each of which favors the native language(s) of its key support bases.

See also fundamentalism; jihad; media; Pan-Islamism; preaching

Further Reading

Jarret Brachman, *Global Jihadism: Theory and Practice*, 2008; David Commins, *The Wahhabi Mission and Saudi Arabia*, 2006; Farhad Daftary, *The Assassin Legends: Myths of the Isma'ilis*, 1995; Sumaiya Hamdani, *Between Revolution and State: The Path to Fatimid Statehood*, 2007; Brynjar Lia, *Architect of Global Jihad: The Life of Al Qaeda Strategist Abu Mus'ab al-Suri*, 2008; Hanna Rogan, *Al-Qaeda's Online Media Strategies: From Abu Reuter to Irhabi07*, 2007; Devin R. Springer, James L. Regens, and David N. Edger, *Islamic Radicalism and Global Jihad*, 2009.

CHRISTOPHER ANZALONE

prophecy

Prophecy is one of the key facets of the Islamic creed. In a famous hadith report, belief in the prophets or messengers of God is assigned the fourth rank among the six main articles of faith: belief in God, angels, scriptures, prophets, Judgment Day, and destiny. According to the Qur'an, a prophet will be sent to each nation (10:47; 16:36). The function of the prophet (*nabī*) or messenger (*rasūl*), the definition of prophecy (*nubuwwa*), and the definition of a prophetic message (*risāla*) are among the central questions of Islamic theology, philosophy, and mysticism. Disagreements among scholars on these issues have had consequential bearings on their conception of key notions such as sin, free will, and human nature. Many theologians have argued that since the Qur'an stresses that God will not punish any nation until a prophet is sent to them (17:15), the nations in which no prophet has been sent are exempt from blame for sin on the grounds that they have not yet been informed of God's laws.

Defining the role of the prophet and the significance of prophecy was central to the development of Islamic political thought. Muhammad, the Prophet of Islam, was not only the spiritual and religious leader of the first Muslim community but also its political leader. Since emulating the customary acts of the Prophet (sunna) is one of the main principles of Islamic faith and practice, this twofold role led Muslim thinkers to inquire about the relationship of spiritual wisdom to politics and to develop an Islamic view of the ideal leader and the ideal political system. This interest made medieval Muslim scholars—especially philosophers—amenable to Plato's theory of the philosopher-king and his preference for a knowledge-based aristocracy as the ideal form of the perfect state. It also triggered many scholarly attempts, in both classical and modern eras, to interpret the dual role that the Prophet played in the course of his mission in order to show that the close relationship between politics and religion in Islam does not lead to theocratic despotism.

Interpretation of the spiritual and political leadership of Prophet Muhammad also played a decisive role in the formation of the doctrine of the imamate in Shi'i Islam versus the notion of the caliph in the Sunni tradition. For Shi'is, the Prophet's role as mediator and interpreter of the word of God is one of the key justifications of the doctrine. This conception radically contrasts with the Sunni notion of the caliphate, at least according to classical Sunni theology. According to most Sunni theorists, the caliphs did not lay claim to ultimate or divine authority. This allowed later Muslim thinkers to conceive of a historical bifurcation of his spiritual and political leadership and contributed, for instance, to the emergence of the notion of the shaykh or master in Sufism, the mystical tradition of Islam.

Muslim theologians treated the topic of prophecy under five main rubrics: the definition and function of prophecy, miracles and justifications of prophecy, the definition and function of divine messages, proof of Muhammad's prophecy, and the human nature of prophets. Prophecy is described in the Qur'an as an expression of God's mercy and compassion toward humankind. Because God cares for humans, the beings he chose to be his vicegerents on Earth, he sends messages to guide them to the absolute truth of all beings: himself. The prophet is the one who receives this message; thus anyone who receives the messages of God achieves a dimension of prophecy. The Qur'an mentions three main ways in which the message of God may be conveyed to humankind. The first is true vision (*al-ru'yā al-ṣāliḥa*), the second is God's direct speech to the messenger, and the third and most common way is through Gabriel, the angel of revelation.

Most Muslim scholars distinguish between the function of a messenger (*rasūl*) and that of a prophet (*nabī*). The messenger is sent with a specific scripture and preaches a specific religion, such as Moses and the Torah, Jesus and the Gospel, and Muhammad and the Qur'an. The prophet, in contrast, preaches only the general message of the unity of God and is sometimes sent to remind humanity of the messages conveyed to them earlier, through previous messengers. The famous Mu'tazili theologian 'Abd al-Jabbar (d. 1025) challenged this notion, arguing that the messenger and the prophet are essentially identical. However, the distinction between messenger and prophet afforded Muslim thinkers, and especially mystics, some freedom in dealing with the notion of prophecy (*nubuwwa*). Many mystics, for example, bolstered their claims regarding the authority of Sufi shaykhs because of their participation in prophecy through visions.

Like Jewish and Christian theologians, Muslim theologians considered miracles the absolutely crucial proofs of prophecy. 'Abd al-Jabbar defines four main characteristics of miracles in his theological manual *Sharh al-Usul al-Khamsa* (Commentary on the five fundamental principles). Miracles must point to the divine power underlying them, temporally follow the claim to prophecy, support

the nature of the message, and violate the laws deemed natural and immutable. Miracles are generally divided into material and rational categories, and the miracle of Islam is of the second type. In Islam the miracle proving the veracity of the Prophet Muhammad's mission is the scripture itself, the Qur'an.

Muslim theologians addressed the proof of the prophecy of Muhammad in various ways. In *Ma'arij al-Quds fi Madarij Ma'rifat al-Nafs* (The ladder to God in the plains of knowing one's soul), Ghazali (d. 1111) holds that while it is impossible to define a prophetic message exactly, the truth of a message can be proven both rationally and effectively. In Ghazali's view, God grants prophets the honor of receiving divine messages as a form of grace. A contrasting approach was primarily concerned with proving that Muhammad was necessarily and indisputably a messenger through a systematic rational analysis, taken up by 'Abd al-Jabbar in his lengthy work *Tathbit Dala'il al-Nubuwwa* (Confirming the evidence of prophecy).

Some of the most interesting contributions to the Islamic theory of prophecy are found in theological, philosophical, and mystical discussions of the human nature of the Prophet. The Qur'an's description of Muhammad as an ordinary man and its assertion that prophets are essentially a select set of people led Muslim thinkers to analyze prophets ontologically and psychologically as perfect humans. Muslim philosophers appropriated Platonic and Aristotelian psychology, ethics, and politics and sought to harmonize them with Islamic religious concepts, especially the concept of prophecy. According to Farabi (d. 950), the prophet, like the philosopher, seeks to actualize his humanity by acquiring both practical and theoretical wisdom. Since he, like the philosopher-king, is concerned mainly with the most exalted human activities, or in Aristotle's language, thinking the forms or universal ideas that are in fact divine thoughts, the prophet is capable of leading his community to perfection. In order to assume this role as guide, however, the prophet must have a unique imaginative faculty that allows him to represent universal rational ideas in an immediate, practical way so that his people might understand, even if they are incapable of the rational inquiry practiced by expert philosophers. Strong imagination is thus an essential dimension of prophecy.

This naturalistic view of prophecy and prophetic psychology led to a similar perspective on religion and its role in society. In *Kitab al-Milla* (The book of religion), Farabi uses the term *ri'āsa* (leadership or rule) to refer to religion. Similarly, he refers to the Prophet as the first leader or ruler of the community. Practical and theoretical wisdom, the main components of philosophy, are both required for the preservation of the virtuous religion that was revealed to the first ruler, the Prophet. However, philosophy remains superior to religion, for what the Prophet merely received as revelation and represented to his people through his imagination can be demonstrated rationally through philosophy. For Farabi, the true heirs of the Prophet are philosophers, and the best extrapolation of prophecy is rational inquiry, on both theoretical and practical levels.

Adopting the same Aristotelian framework, Ghazali analyzes the psychology of the prophet in *Ma'arij al-Quds fi Madarij Ma'rifat al-Nafs*. He argues that what sets the prophet apart from other humans is not only his possession of theoretical and practical wisdom but also his possession of a strong imagination that enables him to represent rational, universal ideas to his people in tangible, sensible terms. The prophet is thus a perfect human who can use all his faculties, especially the rational and imaginative faculties, in the best way possible to attain happiness and lead his community to its attainment as well.

In his seminal work *Fusus al-Hikam* (The bezels of wisdom), the mystic and philosopher Ibn al-'Arabi (d. 1240) addresses the concept of the prophet from a radically existential perspective as the perfect human (*al-insān al-kāmil*). The first chapter of his work presents the human-divine relationship as the most fundamental ontological reality, for the divine cannot be divine unless his divinity is recognized as such by a being with free will. The fulfillment of humanity consists in letting the absoluteness of the divine manifest itself in all its possible forms—as absolute justice, absolute beauty, and so on. There are as many possible divine manifestations as there are divine names. Through spiritual, philosophical, and contemplative exercise, the perfect human manages to let the divine names manifest themselves in each and every experience of his or her life. Ibn al-'Arabi's distinctive use of the term *walī* (saint) to refer to the prophets stems from the essential equation of the two categories in his thought. The only difference between prophets and other saints is that they have special or exclusive prophecy (*nubuwwat ikhtiṣās*), whereas saints have general prophecy (*nubuwwa 'āmma*). Special prophecy is the grace God bestows upon the prophets to convey His special messages and laws to mankind. In Ibn al-'Arabi's ontology, prophecy is the highest, most perfect level of being human, and he interprets the entire history of prophecy as a series of attempts to perfect the fundamental human–divine relationship that constitutes the essence of human existence. Ibn al-'Arabi associates each prophet with a specific wisdom that reflects the way in which that prophet managed to let the divine manifest Himself through his life. Muhammad is the seal of the prophets because he is the prophet whose life best manifested the divine attributes. In other words, Muhammad achieved the highest level of human perfection.

See also al-Farabi, Abu Nasr (ca. 878–950); free will; Ghazali (ca. 1058–1111); human nature; philosophy; theology

Further Reading

Abu al-'Ila 'Afifi, *The Mystical Philosophy of Ibn al-'Arabī*, 1938; Muhyi al-Din b. al-'Arabi, *Bezels of Wisdom*, translated by R.W.J. Austin, 1980; Charles E. Butterworth, *Al-Farabi: The Political Writings*, 2004; William Chittick, *Ibn al-'Arabi: Heir to the Prophets*, 2005; Abu Nasr Muhammad al-Farabi, *On the Perfect State: Ārā' Ahl al-Madīna al-Fāḍila*, translated by Richard Walzer, 1986; Abu Hamid al-Ghazali, *On the Soul: Ma'ārij al-Quds fī Madārij Ma'rifat al-Nafs*, translated by Yahya Abu Risha, 2001; Al-Qadi 'Abd al-Jabbar, *Tathbīt Dalā'il al-Nubuwwa*, translated by Gabriel Reynolds, 2010; Muhsin Mahdi, *Al-Farabi and the Foundation of Islamic Political Philosophy*, 2001.

AHMED ABDEL MEGUID

public interest

Throughout Islamic history one finds tensions between political and religious leaders over the right to determine and enact the public interest—a question situated at the intersection of politics, law, and religion. Islamic political authorities have always been concerned with policies that serve the interest of society as a whole. The second caliph ʿUmar b. al-Khattab (r. 634–44), for instance, justified keeping the conquered land of southern Iraq under state control and with a land tax (*kharāj*) because that would serve the public good (*khayr*, *ʿumūm al-nafʿ*). During the first few centuries of Islam, political authorities controlled the discussion of the public interest—the Arabic word frequently used was *maṣlaḥa*, literally "well-being" or "welfare"; but with the weakening of the caliphate after the tenth century, Islamic legal scholars challenged the dominance of secular authorities by defining public interest in religious terms. Ghazali (ca. 1058–1111) was the first jurisprudent to articulate that the objective of the divinely revealed law is to protect humankind's *maṣlaḥa* by preserving their religion, life, intellect, progeny, and offspring; whatever benefits these five basic necessities of human existence constitutes a *maṣlaḥa*, and whatever does not runs counter to the interest of Muslim society. Grounding the determination of public interest in the religious law (i.e., the shariʿa) meant not only that decisions by political authorities received legitimacy by being in agreement with the divine purpose of the law but also that religious scholars (ʿulamaʾ) had greater say in the public policies of the state. Various jurists after Ghazali refined and enlarged his concept of public interest to the point that it became the overriding principle to determine all rulings not explicitly addressed in the revealed sources of Islamic law (cf. Shatibi [d. 1388]).

After about the 14th century, Muslim writings on public interest were dominated by the concept of *siyāsa sharʿiyya*—articulated in detail by the Hanbali scholars Ibn Taymiyya (1263–1328) and Ibn Qayyim al-Jawziyya (d. 1350). This concept emphasizes that all political policies have to be governed by the religious law and that the political ruler and his functionaries have to implement policies and conduct state affairs in consonance with it. In contrast to the concept of *maṣlaḥa*, *siyāsa sharʿiyya* envisions the whole of the political sphere to be guided by religious consideration and to follow the procedures of Islamic law (*fiqh*). This view leaves little room for the ruler to use purely political expediency in determining state policies in areas in which he hitherto was granted exclusive and discretionary authority—even if only by his de facto power—namely, extra-qadi jurisdiction, penal law (especially *taʿzīr*), and the administration of the state. While the regime of *siyāsa sharʿiyya* provides religious scholars with greater power in political affairs and the ability to curtail governmental excesses, close cooperation between political and religious authorities also implicates the latter in state policies and allows for vesting laws promulgated out of political considerations with the mantle of religious legitimacy.

In the modern period, the tug of war between religious and political leaders over the sphere of law has been won mostly by the political authorities. Islamic law and its traditional practice have been marginalized in its application mainly to personal status law. In order to reinsert Islamic law into the public sphere, Muslim intellectuals have turned toward the concepts of *maṣlaḥa* and *siyāsa sharʿiyya* to accommodate the desire of the state for all-inclusive authority while retaining an Islamic identity. The state receives its authority to legislate, administer justice, and implement its policies by doing so in the public interest (*maṣlaḥa*) within the limits of the shariʿa. Depending on interpretation and political circumstances, *maṣlaḥa* may be optimistically seen as a check on unlimited state power or pessimistically viewed as a mere rubber stamp for its abuses. For instance, reinstating the Ottoman Constitution in 1908 was hailed as a way to uphold the people's *maṣlaḥa*; the abolition of polygamy in Tunisia in 1956 was justified in the name of public interest, serving the country on its way to modernization; and the Syrian jurist Muhammad Saʿid Ramadan al-Buti (b. 1929) supported the state's right to restrict freedom of speech with the argument that the *maṣlaḥa* of the people's intellect is thereby preserved from deviation and error.

See also Ghazali (ca. 1058–1111); governance; Ibn Taymiyya (1263–1328); shariʿa; ʿulamaʾ

Further Reading

Ibn Qayyim al-Jawziyya, Muhammad b. Abi Bakr, *The Legal Methods in Islamic Administration*, translated by Alaeddin Kharofa, 2000; Ibn Taymiyya, Ahmad b. ʿAbd al-Halim, *Ibn Taymiyya on Public and Private Law in Islam: or Public Policy in Islamic Jurisprudence*, translated by Omar A. Farrukh, 1966; Abdullahi Ahmed An-Naʿim, *Islam and the Secular State: Negotiating the Future of Shariʿa*, 2008; Felicitas Opwis, "Islamic Law and Legal Change: The Concept of *Maṣlaḥa* in Classical and Contemporary Islamic Legal Theory," in *Shariʿa: Islamic Law in the Contemporary Context*, edited by Abbas Amanat and Frank Griffel, 2007.

FELICITAS OPWIS

public opinion

In theory, Muslims have always been free to speak their minds. Islam grants individual believers the freedom to interpret God's commandments on their own, without the intermediation of a clerical class. Nevertheless, from the early days of Islam, Muslims have been pressured to weigh what they say and to refrain from expressing views liable to anger powerful groups. Consequently, in no Muslim-governed state has public opinion, which aggregates publicly expressed individual views, ever conveyed the distribution of actual thoughts and true preferences. It also has reflected the prevailing structure of political power. Incentives

to avoid expressions unfavorable to the political status quo have been particularly strong and public opinion most heavily distorted under centrally controlled regimes.

On matters pertaining to religion, organized repression of Muslim masses has never assumed the extreme form epitomized by the Spanish Inquisition. Nevertheless, Muslim-governed states of the past discouraged, and also punished, nonconformist interpretations of Islam. Under the threat of persecution, even some of the greatest Muslim philosophers, including Ibn Rushd (Averroes), Ghazali, and Farabi, disguised their most controversial views, including those bearing on politics.

States of the Muslim world tend to be repressive by contemporary political standards. One indication is their poor standings in global indexes of political freedom prepared annually by Freedom House, an international nongovernmental organization that conducts research and advocacy on democracy, political freedom, and human rights. On a 0 (best) to 7 (worst) scale, the population-weighted average of the 2009 civil liberties index was 4.46 for the Organization of Islamic States (OIS) and 1.53 for the Organisation for Economic Cooperation and Development (OECD), the club of advanced industrialized countries. As for the press freedom index, which runs from 0 (best) to 100 (worst), it was 63.42 for the OIS and 25.35 for the OECD. Another indication of strong repression is that many Muslim states tightly restrict polls aimed at identifying public opinion scientifically through anonymous surveys. Still another indication is that individual citizens exercise great caution in speaking to reporters and researchers on politically controversial issues.

In countries with regimes exceptionally intolerant of dissent, such as Libya, Tunisia, and Syria, reliable opinion surveys are practically impossible. In less repressive Arab regimes, Arab Barometer, an organization led by American-based scholars, has started to conduct scientific polling. Beyond Arab countries, public opinion surveys have been conducted regularly in a few countries, including Turkey and Indonesia. On social, political, economic, and religious matters, surveys in both Arab and non-Arab countries point to substantial differences between the actual preferences of the masses and those of incumbent regimes.

Where pollsters have been able to inquire about political preferences, public opinion tends to be highly favorable to democracy. It has been suggested that this pattern, documented through the World Values Survey, an academic project that conducts periodic investigations to assess cultural trends around the world, reflects a yearning for religious freedom rather than for expressive liberties generally. Another hypothesis is that the surveys reveal not deep-rooted attitudes but marginal preferences, which are high precisely because of limited political freedoms.

In the Muslim world, freedom of speech tends to be especially constrained and public opinion particularly difficult to measure on matters related to Islam. Islamist violence against those considered hostile to Islam induces self-censorship even in secular states such as Turkey and Syria. In some countries, including Egypt, Saudi Arabia, and Iran, states have a tacit bargain with religious bodies whereby the latter uphold religious taboos and persecute religious nonconformists with impunity in return for granting the political status quo Islamic legitimacy. Secular regimes of the modern Muslim world limit freedom of speech on religion in their own ways by punishing public challenges from Islamists to the secularist-preferred interpretations of Islam.

See also censorship; civil society; democracy; freedom

Further Reading

Timur Kuran, *Private Truths, Public Lies: The Social Consequences of Preference Falsification*, 1995; Kanan Makiya, *Republic of Fear: The Politics of Modern Iraq*, 1998; Mansoor Moaddel, ed., *Values and Perceptions of the Islamic and Middle Eastern Publics*, 2007; Trevor Mostyn, *Censorship in Islamic Societies*, 2002; Charles K. Rowley and Nathanael Smith, "Islam's Democracy Paradox: Muslims Claim to Like Democracy, So Why Do They Have So Little?" *Public Choice* 139, no. 3 (2009); Mark Tessler and Amaney Jamal, "Political Attitude Research in the Arab World: Emerging Opportunities," *PS: Political Science and Politics* 39, no. 3 (2006).

TIMUR KURAN

public sphere

The idea of the public sphere is Greco-Roman in origin, although its institutionalization in Western history is more specifically Roman, since it reflects the experience of the Roman republic. The Latin adjective *publicus* (public) and the simultaneously normative and material spaces it demarcates are framed in a polar relationship with *privatus* (private). Both refer, quite concretely, to a good or thing—that is, *res*. The Roman republic is the *res publica* (public good) or also, in one word, *respublica*. The Roman characterization of the "public" and its articulation in a social sphere delimit a new type of collective bond detached from the primordial forms of authority that singled out domains of exclusive possession and embodied the patriarchal origin of the private sphere.

The notion of the public was first Christianized in the European Middle Ages (*respublica christiana*) and then became a key idea within modern transformations, first through movements of reform within Christianity, then in the emergence of a bourgeois world spearheaded by the intellectual vanguards of the Enlightenment. In such narratives, the rise of a Western modern public sphere is tied to the formation of a *civil society*.

The best-known contemporary theorist of the public sphere, Jürgen Habermas, provides evidence that bourgeois gathered mostly for mundane and self-interested reasons rooted in private concerns—to discuss stock exchange trends or prices of colonial commodities, for example—in such places as English coffeehouses. But in debating

such problems, they started to deliberate on ways to protect their private interests from potential abuses of the ruler. In the process, a modern public sphere emerged beyond the legalistic presuppositions of a classic *res publica* by carving out autonomous and potentially critical spaces of debate. Such dynamics emphasize rationality and openness in deliberation. The resulting crystallization of a "public opinion" facilitated by the diffusion of newspapers reflected the often conflicted yet broadly cohesive processes of forming a rational consensus about the common good within an increasingly differentiated modern society, with the bourgeoisie at its center.

The inclusiveness implied by such a narrative has been subject to criticism. The formation of public spheres also reflects patterns of exclusion—of workers, women, and other nonelite groups. Alongside a bourgeois, liberal-democratic public sphere, there have always been a plethora of "alternative" public spheres that challenged the former's hegemonic pretensions. This development also affected the colonial and postcolonial Muslim-majority world. The view of the modern state as representing the general interest of society is also the result of the process of emergence of public spheres. At this level, the Western prototypes and the Muslim colonial and postcolonial versions of the public sphere show a high degree of convergence. Voices in the public sphere might be critical of state policies, yet they are ingrained into its governance mechanisms through their contribution to the education of the responsible citizen, while they also try to make state policies more just, democratic, and egalitarian.

The notion of the public sphere rests, then, on the idea of arguing, acting, and deliberating in common through a rational pursuit of collective interest. Activity within such a sphere requires a fair degree of transparency of communication among the actors involved in the process. This is why the public sphere is a wider and, at the same time, more specific concept than that of civil society. While a civil society always produces a public sphere, the opposite is not necessarily true, because a public sphere can exist without a civil society—particularly because in some historical instances and contemporary cases the self-interested, liberal, and bourgeois type of agency that aids the formation of civil society is not a necessary condition for a public sphere to emerge and thrive. The public sphere is not just a site of fruitful communication and orderly representation of interests mediated by open communication; it is also an arena where inherited notions of social justice and social order are elaborated on and contested. Habermas underplayed the role of religious traditions, and in particular of radical protest movements, in the conflicted formation of modern public spheres. He neglected the mechanisms through which the social and communicative activity within public spheres reshapes traditional norms and concepts of justice and order.

The idea of the public sphere is therefore at the same time culturally embedded and comparable across various civilizations. Yet the way a sense of the public contributes to social life varies considerably, depending on several factors: modalities of transaction over the definition of the common good; the search for equitable solutions to collective problems; shifting boundaries of inclusion and exclusion; background notions of personality, responsibility, and justice; but also the degree of legitimacy of existing states and their capacity to control, manipulate, or repress autonomous public sphere dynamics.

An enlarged focus on the genesis of public spheres opens the door to a comparative look at various trajectories of their emergence within civilizations situated outside of the Western core of modernity. The ubiquity of public spheres and their autonomous dynamics outside of the West works against the idea of Oriental despotism, according to which the moral cohesion of a community is engineered by the despot. A sense of viable public spheres can be supported by Muslim identities in a variety of Muslim-majority societies. Islamic reformers have worked particularly well with the communicative instruments and normative tools of the public spheres since the end of the 19th century. The semiformal articulation of the public sphere through the press was particularly suitable to the reform discourse and to its ambivalent relationship toward the institutional structure of the colonial and postcolonial states. Islamist voices inherit this type of vocation and extend it to a wider circle of participants and activists.

A particular articulation of the public sphere in an Islamic context has been called "public Islam," whereby Islamic tenets are used to justify the cohesion of Muslim-majority societies irrespective of the whims of autocrats, whether traditional or modern. Many of the characteristics of traditional Muslim public spheres—their moral cohesiveness, the multiplicity of informal ties therein, or the possibilities of eruption of crowdlike confrontation—have persisted and evolved: given the basic premises of the modern state as well as of modern communication, they have undergone dramatic changes. New social actors such as professionals, intellectuals, and media experts have emerged, often in close relation with modern forms of collective action—whether social movements or political parties. Concomitantly several new religious groups or movements—from Sufi orders to modern Islamist networks—have carved out distinct public spaces by becoming largely disembedded from traditional Islamic institutions.

While the emergence of new cultural and political actors in a variety of public spheres attests to a potential of democratization, it can also exacerbate their confrontation with modern political regimes. As a result, the autonomy of the public spheres can be severely undermined. In this ambivalent process, Islam has often become the hub of a unique public sphere, based on a complex tradition, aware of the modern conditions of communication and connectedness, and nesting in spaces tensely coexisting with an official sphere dominated by the state and state-controlled media.

In sum, the public sphere cannot be understood as the exclusive prerogative of modern, Western societies or of mature democracies based on formalized templates of individual rights and political participation. Semiformal articulations of Muslim identities can also facilitate the emergence of public spheres, while the coercive and institutional power of the modern state may both further and limit this potential.

See also civil society; modernity

Further Reading

Michael Gasper, *The Power of Representation: Publics, Peasants and Islam in Egypt*, 2009; Charles Hirschkind, *The Ethical Soundscape: Cassette Sermons and Islamic Counterpublics*, 2006; Armando Salvatore and Dale F. Eickelman, eds., *Public Islam and Common Good*, 2004; Armando Salvatore, *The Public Sphere: Liberal Modernity, Catholicism, Islam*, 2007.

ARMANDO SALVATORE

pulpit

The traditional elevated platform specifically used by preachers in the Islamic tradition (minbar) has its origins in the example of the Prophet Muhammad, who customarily delivered his sermons while standing on a wooden dais located at the front of the mosque adjoining his house in Medina. This pulpit, which also contained a seat, is believed to have been associated with the raised ceremonial chair of a judge or the throne of a ruler. Thus, while it offered some practical benefit insofar as it enabled the speaker's voice to be better heard, it also expressed a symbolic statement of authority. This first pulpit was also apparently portable, as history records that later successors of the Prophet moved it so they could use it in other mosques.

The perceived importance of the pulpit increased with the continuing development of a fixed ritual order for the Friday noon prayer service, which included the delivery of a sermon from this special podium. Hence, the mere presence of the pulpit in a mosque announced its privileged status since, traditionally, the Friday noon prayer service was restricted to one location, or in a large city, perhaps including a few carefully distinguished central mosques. Likewise, the prestige and thus the influence of such a mosque was often enhanced by the size, shape, and artistic quality expressed in its pulpit. While the general contours of this mosque furnishing were defined by traditional precedent, the architectural ingenuity and skilled craftsmanship displayed in the execution of particular classical versions, in wood, stone, or ceramic tiles, have made an appreciation of their particular features a notable subcategory in the history of Islamic art.

Typically, in its classic form, a mosque pulpit is aligned against the wall that marks the direction toward which the congregation faces in lining up for prayer, usually to the left of the empty niche (*miḥrāb*) marking the orientation toward Mecca. The speaker mounts the pulpit by steps that lead to a flat base, behind which is a bench or seat that the preacher occupies briefly according to set rubrics. It is reserved for use at the Friday noon prayer and only by the designated preacher. Hence, access to the authoritative pulpit is often a matter of considerable political sensitivity, and its regulation is normally entrusted to a religious ministry in states with predominantly Muslim populations.

While Muslims still widely maintain a profound respect for the mosque pulpit and what it represents, the premise that the Friday noon prayer service, together with the sermon, may be conducted only in designated mosques has largely faded. In its place, a less formal view of the pulpit has emerged. Among many Muslims, a strong reformist impulse has arisen that favors a return to simplicity, which has led to a markedly diminished style of ceremonial furnishings. In this spirit, many new or recently remodeled mosques have installed merely token pulpits, or the preacher stands on the floor, although often equipped with a microphone.

See also Friday prayer; mosque; preaching

Further Reading

Richard T. Antoun, *Muslim Preacher in the Modern World: A Jordanian Case Study in Contemporary Perspective*, 1989; Asghar Fathi, "The Islamic Pulpit as a Medium of Political Communication," *Journal for the Scientific Study of Religion* 20, no. 1 (1981).

PATRICK D. GAFFNEY

punishment

Punishment in an Islamic context is a crucial element within the larger notion of God's justice (*'adl*). For justice to prevail, evil must be punished just as good must be rewarded, both in this world and in the afterlife. God judges humankind on the Day of the Resurrection, while judges and rulers dispense punishments on Earth. Muslim conceptions of political leadership stress the leader's responsibility to maintain justice and uphold the law, which entails actively punishing wrongdoing. God's punishment of a disobedient life is internment in hell.

Even in the Qur'an, hell has many names, and later it was frequently described as having seven levels, reminiscent of the *Inferno* of Dante, who indeed cribbed his vision of hell from Islamic sources. Muslims who died with unrepented mortal sins (*kabā'ir*) spent a terminal period in hell before ascending to paradise; others became eternal denizens. Punishment in hell was imagined first as environmental. Hell was a vast, volcanic landscape full of fetid winds, acid rain, and burning brimstone. The hellbound were subjected to these conditions and harassed by serpents and scorpions. Hell was also a prison and torture chamber. Hell's wardens were gruesome angels (*zabāniya*) who busied themselves meting out punishments particular to the various sins of the damned.

In Islamic law, punishments can be divided into three separate categories: crimes with fixed penalties (*ḥudūd*), retaliation (*qiṣāṣ*), and discretionary punishment (*ta'zīr*). Crimes with fixed penalties are murder (*qatl*), theft (*sariqa*), brigandage or highway robbery (*ḥirāba* or *qaṭ' al-ṭarīq*), adultery and fornication (*zinā*), false accusation of adultery (*qadhf*), drinking wine (*shurb al-khamr*), and

apostasy (*irtidād* or *ridda*). The punishments for these crimes are stipulated in the Qur'an or the sunna, and they are thus nonnegotiable and fixed, even though there are various positions on precisely what the punishments should be. Reciprocal retaliation (*qiṣāṣ*) for murder or injury is allowed, at least in principle, by Islamic law. However, the case of bodily injury even up to death is often treated as a tort, where the victim or the victim's family receives a settlement (*diya*) from the perpetrator. Discretionary punishment covers all other kinds of crimes and torts. A judge adjudicates between the claimants and renders a judgment at his discretion; these punishments may include admonition, fines, public humiliation, incarceration, flogging, or even the death penalty.

Muslim legal theorists did not advance a distinct theory of penology, the study of crime and punishment, explicitly. The desirability of restitution and retribution certainly was prominent, given that achieving justice was the goal of punishment. However, deterrence can also be found mentioned alongside as a positive result of punishment, thought of as a contribution to social order. Rehabilitation of a criminal through punishment, while occasionally mentioned, was not a prominent dimension of Muslim legal thinkers' views on punishment.

See also apostasy; blasphemy; justice; rights

Further Reading

Mohamed S. El-Awa, *Punishment in Islamic Law*, 2000; Christian Lange, *Justice, Punishment, and the Medieval Muslim Imagination*, 2008; Rudolph Peters, *Crime and Punishment in Islamic Law: Theory and Practice from the Sixteenth to the Twenty-First Century*, 2005.

NICHOLAS G. HARRIS

Q

Qadaris

The verb *qadara* in Qur'anic usage means God's power to determine all events; the noun *qadar* denotes the eternal decree of God. Oddly enough, the term Qadaris (*qadariyya*) was given in early sources to a group of theologians in the late seventh and early eighth centuries, mainly from Basra and Syria, who believed the opposite: that evil cannot be created by God but is determined by the human being, and accordingly, if humans have free will then God's foreknowledge is at variance with this freedom.

The debate on this subject has its roots in Qur'anic discourse, where it is ambivalent whether divine guidance entails enforcement: "God thereby leads many astray, and guides many. But the dissolute alone He leads astray" (Q. 2:25–26; 2:7; 4:109; 99:8). Moreover, it carries on the pre-Islamic fatalistic view—namely, that everything is predestined by the forces of time (*dahr*). But it also shows hints of the acculturation process of Muslims within the multicultural Hellenistic, Byzantine, and Iranian milieu. The Qadari movement could be seen both as a political reaction against the Umayyad dynasty, who maintained that their rule was decreed by God, and as a group of pious individuals reflecting on the design of God's salvation plan. Their doctrine spread in various centers of the empire and underwent a process of elaboration, ultimately leading to more intricate theological systems during the later part of the eighth century.

Hadith compendia attest to the existence of this group and the controversy over predestination or "free will" as early as the last quarter of the seventh century in Syria during the reign of 'Umar b. 'Abd al-'Aziz (r. 717–19). *Ṭabaqāt* books and history works from the early ninth century give the impression that these issues were ardently debated in Syria and in Basra before a consensus was reached concerning belief in divine decree and determination during the late eighth and early ninth centuries, mainly among Sunni scholars. Nevertheless, most of the material and reports are of doubtful authenticity and represent later views of historians and heresiographers.

The earliest advocates of the tenet of "asserting the value of human activity" (that evil cannot be created by God and thus the human being is responsible for his or her actions) include Ma'bad al-Juhani al-Basri (executed in 704), Hasan al-Basri (d. 728), Ghaylan al-Dimashqi and Salih b. Suwayd (both executed ca. 732), and Makhul al-Dimashqi (d. 731). Two of these thinkers are from Basra; the others are Syrians. The origins of this tenet are obscure. The Syrian religious scholar Awza'i (d. 773) claims that Ma'bad and Ghaylan were the first to speak of *qadar* and that this precept was formulated under Christian influence. Modern scholarship also argues to that effect, finding similarities with John of Damascus on the issue that human beings had been created with their own power by God.

All these names are related in one way or another to Hasan al-Basri and his circle. Yet Hasan al-Basri was a quietist, whereas Ma'bad joined the revolt of Ibn al-Ash'ath in 702, and Ghaylan and Salih b. Suwayd were politically active against Umayyad rule in Syria. The Qadaris did not form a homogeneous group but should rather be seen as a loose collection of political activists as well as early rational theologians.

The *qadar* controversy in Syria was seen primarily as a political movement calling for egalitarianism and for social and political justice, thus threatening the social order with its opposition to the Umayyad ideology. Later, the Umayyad caliph Yazid III (d. 743), who came to power as a result of an insurrection backed by the Syrian Qadaris, formulated a radical program that threatened the foundation of Umayyad legitimacy. However, Murad argues against an exaggerated association of Qadarism with political activism. In Basra, on the other hand, Qadari ideas spread mainly among pious ascetics; later, during the eighth century, it became to a large extent the "ideology of the middle class," as the prominent scholar of Islam Josef van Ess maintains.

Modern scholars agree that Hasan al-Basri held Qadari views, although later Sunni scholars made great efforts to rehabilitate his image by claiming that he held some Qadari ideas early in his life but that he turned away from them soon after. Later Mu'tazilis see him as their major forerunner. The alleged exchange of letters between Hasan al-Basri and some of his contemporaries concerning the issue of *qadar* are most probably a later forgery. The authorship of the two anti-Qadari epistles attributed to 'Umar b. 'Abd al-'Aziz and Hasan b. Muhammad b. al-Hanafiyya is also contested.

See also Mu'tazilis; theology

Further Reading

Michael Cook, *Early Muslim Dogma: A Source-Critical Study*, 1981; György Fodor, "Some Aspects of the Qadar-Controversy in Early Islam," *The Arabist: Budapest Studies in Arabic* 1, no. 57–65 (1988); Richard M. Frank, "The Structure of Created Causality According to al-Aš'arī," *Studia Islamica*, 25, 13–75 (1966); Suleiman Ali Mourad, *Early Islam between Myth and History: Al-Ḥasan al-Baṣrī (d. 110H/728CE) and the Formation of His Legacy in Classical Islamic Scholarship*, 2006; Hassan Qasim Murad, "Jabr

and Qadar in Early Islam: A Reappraisal of Their Political and Religious Implications," in *Islamic Studies Presented to Charles J. Adams*, 1991; Daud Rahbar, *God of Justice: A Study in the Ethical Doctrine of the Qur'ān*, 1960; H. Ringgren, *Studies in Arabian Fatalism*, 1955; Josef van Ess, *Theologie und Gesellschaft im 2. und 3. Jahrhundert Hidschra: Eine Geschichte des religiösen Denkens im frühen Islam*, vols. 1–4, 1991–96; William Montgomery Watt, *The Formative Period of Islamic Thought*, 1973; Idem, *Free Will and Predestination in Early Islam*, 1948; A. J. Wensinck, *The Muslim Creed: Its Genesis and Historical Development*, 1932.

MAHER JARRAR

Qaddafi, Muʿammar (1942–2011)

Born in the Libyan desert, Muʿammar al-Qaddafi was the only surviving son of a poor Bedouin family. With formal schooling available only in larger population centers, his early education was limited to traditional religious subjects taught by local tribal teachers.

Qaddafi finished his secondary schooling in the coastal town of Misurata, where he recruited like-minded students to a political philosophy based on Islam, social equality, and Arab unity. Realizing that the army was the only organization in the country capable of overthrowing the monarchy, Qaddafi enrolled in the Royal Military Academy in Benghazi, graduating in 1965.

Having become an admirer of Egyptian president Gamal Abdel Nasser in the 1960s, Qaddafi formed the Libyan Free Unionist Officers, a group of some 70 army officers that overthrew the Libyan monarchy on September 1, 1969. Once they had seized power, Qaddafi became commander in chief of the armed forces and de facto head of state. The early policies of the revolutionary government reflected Qaddafi's deep Islamist roots, together with his strong support for Arab nationalism. The consumption of alcohol was banned, nightclubs were closed, churches were converted into mosques, Islamic punishment was adopted in principle if not always in fact, and Arabic was decreed the only language acceptable for official communications.

In late 1972, Qaddafi began to give his strain of Arab nationalism a theoretical underpinning in his Third Universal Theory, which advocated a third way between capitalism and communism, concluding that socialism was the optimal system for Libya.

In the first volume (1975) of *The Green Book*, Qaddafi's three-part political manifesto and ideological guide, he emphasized the role of religion in society without making any specific mention of the role of Islam. In the second volume (1978), he explored the economic dimensions of the Third Universal Theory, and in the third (1979), he developed its social concepts.

The reformist elements of Qaddafi's approach to Islam, including the revival of Islamic law, a rejection of the hadith, and the purely human role of the Prophet, were a deliberate attempt to reduce the role of the 'ulama' (religious scholars) in Libya. As the regime moved to make Islam a domestic and international instrument of the revolution, Qaddafi used the process of legal reform to centralize control over all aspects of religious life in Libya and to take control of the waqf property (religious endowments), destroying the cultural and political autonomy of the 'ulama' and reducing the influence of the Sanusi Sufi order that had been allied with the Libyan monarchy.

Qaddafi was largely successful in neutralizing the traditional religious leadership and the Islamist opposition to the regime fragmented under constant pressure from government security forces. Various Islamist opposition groups, including Excommunication and Withdrawal (al-Takfir wa-l-Hijra), Islamic Jihad, Islamic Liberation Party, Islamic Martyrs' Movement, Libyan Islamic Group, and the Muslim Brotherhood, continued to be active in Libya; however, none of them posed a serious threat to the Qaddafi regime.

On December 21, 1988, Pan Am Flight 103 from London to New York was destroyed by a bomb over Lockerbie, Scotland, killing 243 passengers, 16 crew members, and 11 people on the ground. Qaddafi's security forces were suspected of having planned the bombing and, on January 31, 2001, Abdel Basset 'Ali al-Megrahi, a Libyan agent, was given a life sentence for his involvement in the bombing. He was released, however, on August 20, 2009, by the Scottish government on humanitarian grounds. In 2007, Ayman al-Zawahiri, al-Qaeda's second-in-command, condemned Qaddafi as an enemy of Islam and announced that the Libyan Islamic Group had joined al-Qaeda.

See also North Africa

Further Reading

Mahmoud Mustafa Ayoub, *Islam and the Third Universal Theory: The Religious Thought of Mu'ammar al-Qadhadhafi*, 1987; George Joffé, "Qadhafi's Islam in Historical Perspective," in *Qadhafi's Libya, 1969–1994*, edited by Dirk Vandewalle, 1995; Ann Elizabeth Mayer, "Islamic Resurgence or New Prophethood: The Role of Islam in Qadhadafi's Ideology," in *Islamic Resurgence in the Arab World*, edited by Ali E. Hillal Dessouki, 1982; Amal Obeidi, *Political Culture in Libya*, 2001; Mu'ammar al-Qaddafi, *The Green Book*, 1975; Ronald Bruce St John, *Libya: From Colony to Independence*, 2008; Idem, *Libya: Continuity and Change*, 2011; Dirk Vandewalle, *A History of Modern Libya*, 2006.

RONALD BRUCE ST JOHN

al-Qaeda

Al-Qaeda (*al-Qā'ida*) is a militant Islamist network founded by Osama bin Laden (1957–2011) in Pakistan around 1988 or 1989. Its initial purpose was to provide moral and financial assistance to Afghani war veterans who fought against the communist Red Army

and to pursue jihad after the retreat of the Soviets from Afghanistan. Its name comes from the Arabic word *qā'ida* ("the foundation" or "the base") and refers to a military base that would act as a vanguard to reach an ideal society where an Islamic state prevails. Al-Qaeda came to worldwide public attention after the deadly attacks of September 11, 2001, on the World Trade Center in New York and the Pentagon in Washington, D.C.

The Birth of al-Qaeda: The Afghan Volunteer Warriors

Al-Qaeda was born in the midst of the Afghan resistance to the Soviet invasion in the late 1980s. Its ideological founder was 'Abdallah 'Azzam (1941–89), a Palestinian political activist and member of the Muslim Brotherhood. 'Azzam grew up in the Palestinian territories and received a PhD in Islamic law from Azhar University in Cairo in 1973. He later taught at King 'Abd al-'Aziz University in Saudi Arabia and in Pakistan. When the Soviet Union invaded Afghanistan in December 1979, 'Azzam issued a fatwa (legal opinion) declaring that jihad against an occupying power was a *farḍ 'ayn* (i.e., an individual obligation upon every Muslim) rather than a *farḍ kifāya* (an obligation falling upon the community as a whole). In Pakistan, he met with Bin Laden, a young and wealthy Saudi businessman who had relocated to the region to help organize the Arab Afghan volunteers for jihad. In 1984, both men founded the Maktab Khadamat al-Mujahidin al-'Arab (MAK, translated as "Afghan Services Bureau") to raise funds and recruit foreign volunteers for the war against the Soviets. The MAK, which was a forerunner of al-Qaeda, received considerable financial support not only from Bin Laden but also from other sources, such as the United States, the United Kingdom, Saudi Arabia, Egypt, Pakistan, and other Muslim states. The U.S. Central Intelligence Agency (CIA) in particular provided the group with covert funds to help defeat the Soviet Union in the context of the cold war. After the volunteer army eventually forced the Soviet Union to withdraw its troops in 1989, the MAK's agenda expanded globally, its name was changed to al-Qa'ida al-'Askariya (the military base), and its mission was redefined: to oppose the military and economic intervention of non-Muslim states in predominantly Muslim lands.

The Ideological Roots of al-Qaeda: Doctrine and Main Figures

Ideologically, al-Qaeda drew on a core of Islamic sources and scholars. The Egyptian scholar Sayyid Qutb (1906–66) had a significant impact on the founders of al-Qaeda. Bin Laden had read Qutb's works at a young age and had attended lectures by his brother, Muhammad Qutb, who at the time was a popular professor of Islamic studies in Saudi Arabia. By declaring that a Muslim leader who did not rule according to God's principles was an apostate, Sayyid Qutb framed an ideology of *takfīr* (excommunication) that became a cornerstone in al-Qaeda's doctrinal system; he is often considered to have established the theoretical foundations for radical Islamist organizations. Others who helped shape the ideology of the group include the aforementioned 'Abdallah 'Azzam and Ayman al-Zawahiri, an Egyptian surgeon and leader of Egyptian Islamic Jihad. The organization's ideology can be seen as a merger between Bin Laden's interest in expelling foreigners from Muslim lands (the far enemy) and Zawahiri's obsession with fighting off the Egyptian state (the near enemy). In 1988, Sayyid Imam al-Sharif (b. 1950), known as Dr. Fadl, provided the jihadist movement with a practical guide to prepare for jihad: *Al-'Umda fi I'dad al-'Udda [li-l-Jihad]* (*The Essentials of Making Ready [for Jihad]*). The book became one of the most important texts in the training of prospective jihadists.

Al-Qaeda has drawn on selective sources in the Islamic tradition, such as the early hadith scholar Ahmad b. Hanbal (780–855) and the medieval jurist Ibn Taymiyya (1263–1328). The group also endorsed certain doctrines of Salafism and Wahhabism. Because of its adoption of the concept of *takfīr*, al-Qaeda has often been compared to the early Kharijis.

Al-Qaeda also found theoretical and practical inspiration in several modern militant organizations that acted as its forerunners, such as the Ikhwan that rose against King 'Abd al-'Aziz b. 'Abd al-Rahman b. Sa'ud (1876–1953) in Saudi Arabia in the 1920s and the Egyptian al-Takfir wa-l-Hijra (Excommunication and Withdrawal), created in 1969 by Shukri Mustafa (1942–87).

Al-Qaeda's Organizational Development and Structure: A Cluster Network

Following the end of the Soviet-Afghan War (1978–89), Bin Laden returned to Saudi Arabia. When Iraq invaded Kuwait in 1990, he offered his services to the Saudi government to organize volunteers to fight the Iraqi troops in Kuwait. Saudi Arabia turned down his offer and instead allowed U.S. armed forces to deploy into its territory. This decision, backed by the Saudi clerical establishment, radicalized al-Qaeda and shifted its focus: the Saudi government was declared apostate and became the first enemy. Bin Laden went into exile in Sudan, where he expanded the movement with new training facilities and infrastructure. In 1996, he was expelled from Sudan and returned to Afghanistan, then under the control of the Taliban. A declaration of war against the United States and its allies was issued in 1998 through a fatwa calling for their deaths in order to free Muslim lands. That same year Bin Laden created the World Islamic Front for Global Jihad against Christian Crusaders and Zionist Jews, an umbrella organization to bring together scattered jihadist groups. As a result of the attacks of September 11, 2001, the U.S. led a bombing campaign in Afghanistan in October 2001, which dispersed the movement's leadership and changed its tactics. Al-Qaeda continued to function as a decentralized cluster of various groups operating independently in different geographical locations.

Though the current structure of al-Qaeda remains a mystery, it is certainly a loose network, with a horizontal organizational structure composed of various cells that also operate vertically. Al-Qaeda has managed to make use of modern technologies for its recruitment and propaganda. It has created its own media outlet, As-Sahab Foundation for Islamic Media Publication, which distributes and promotes the group's messages. It has also achieved a wide Internet presence, reaching a global audience for its views and controlling its public image.

Al-Qaeda Today

Al-Qaeda is believed to have carried out several major terrorist attacks worldwide: on tourist resorts in Aden, Yemen (1992); on the World Trade Center in New York (1993); on two U.S. embassies in Tanzania and Kenya (1998); on the *U.S.S. Cole* in Yemen (2000); and on the World Trade Center in New York and the Pentagon in Washington, D.C. (2001). Al-Qaeda has achieved its goal of attracting world attention to its cause and spreading fear among its enemies. It has established bases in various parts of the world, such as North Africa and Asia. The Anglo-American invasion of Iraq in 2003 even created a fertile ground for recruitment for the network, which has not been dismantled since the beginning of the U.S.-led war on terror in 2001.

The network, however, demonstrates significant weaknesses. It remains a relatively small movement with no mass appeal. Its tactics, particularly the killing of innocents, have been condemned by Muslims worldwide. Al-Qaeda also suffers from steady internal dissensions. Sayyid Imam al-Sharif, a former member of the group, severely condemned its violent tactics in *Guiding Jihad Action in Egypt and in the World Today*, published in 2007. On May 1, 2011, U.S. president Barack Obama announced that Osama bin Laden had been killed in Abbottabad, in Pakistan, in an operation led by U.S. Navy Seals and CIA operatives.

See also Bin Laden, Osama (1957–2011); fundamentalism; Ibn ʻAbd al-Wahhab, Muhammad (1703–92); jihad; Kharijis; Mulla ʻUmar (b. 1959); Muslim Brotherhood; Sayyid Qutb (1906–66); al-Zawahiri, Ayman (b. 1951)

Further Reading

Fawaz A. Gerges, *The Far Enemy: Why Jihad Went Global*, 2009; Bruce Lawrence, ed., *Messages to the World: The Statements of Osama bin Laden*, translated by James Howarth, 2005; Brynjar Lia, *Architect of Global Jihad: The Life of Al-Qaeda Strategist Abu Mus'ab al-Suri*, 2008; Laura Mansfield, *His Own Words: A Translation of the Writings of Dr. Ayman al-Zawahiri*, 2006; Lawrence Wright, *The Looming Tower: Al-Qaeda and the Road to 9/11*, 2006.

NASSIMA NEGGAZ

Qajars (1789–1925)

Under the Qajars, Iran was gradually transformed from a decentralized tribal monarchy into a modern secular constitutional state with a strategic and economic role in international politics.

The Turkmen Qajar tribe, thought to have settled in the Caspian coastlands during the Mongol period, first rose to prominence as part of the Turkmen tribal army known as the Qizilbash, or Redheads, that brought Isma'il I (r. 1501–24) to power as founder of the Safavid dynasty (1501–1722); Qajar khans subsequently occupied important positions in the Safavid state. After the disintegration of the Safavid empire in the early 18th century, the Qajar Qavanlu clan, led by Agha Muhammad (r. 1789–97), first expanded across northern Iran, proceeding to displace the Zands to the south and the Afsharids to the east. Qajar rule marked the first time since the Safavids and the brief rule of Nadir Shah (r. 1736–47) that Iran was united under one shah. Agha Muhammad moved his capital to Tehran in 1786.

The reign of his successor, Fath ʻAli Shah (r. 1797–1834), was characterized by courtly opulence and openness to European cultural, military, and economic influence. Fath ʻAli Shah entered into regular diplomatic relations with Britain and Napoleonic France, both of which had strategic interest in Iran, given its position as gateway to the east. His requests for aid against the advance of imperial Russia along Iran's northern borders were disregarded, however, and in the Treaty of Turkmanchay of 1828 Iran was forced to relinquish its claim to territories in eastern Armenia and the Caucasus and to facilitate Russian commercial interests in Iran. Efforts to reextend Iran's borders eastward into Afghanistan likewise failed due to the unwillingness of the British to compromise their buffer against Russian or French incursion into India. Throughout the Qajar period, Iran was politically and economically subject to shifting Russian and British interests; the nation's vulnerability was further compounded by royal extravagance, haphazard attempts at modernization, and financial and administrative mismanagement, which led to deep foreign indebtedness and economic strangling.

Recognizing this vulnerability, Nasir al-Din Shah (r. 1848–96) encouraged foreign powers to invest in Iran but failed to undertake the necessary financial and administrative reform to make such a policy successful. Various concessions (e.g., the Reuter concession, 1872–73; lottery concession, 1889; tobacco concession, 1890–92) granted to the British provoked popular protest and Russian intervention, leading to the cancellation of the Reuter and tobacco monopolies. Such protests, reflecting widespread resentment both of the corruption of the ruling elite and of foreign control, came to a head during the reign of Muzaffar al-Din Shah (r. 1896–1907) with the Iranian Constitutional Revolution of 1905–11, which resulted in a constitution limiting the powers of the monarch and a parliamentary system of governance. Its royal power thus circumscribed, the Qajar house became entirely dependent on Russian support in its efforts to counteract the new constitution.

During World War I, Russian and British troops occupied northern and southern Iran, respectively, further exacerbating the already debilitating political disarray in the country. This balance of power shifted with the Bolshevik revolution of 1917, which led to a temporary Russian withdrawal from northern Iran. British troops accordingly moved in from the south, and the Anglo-Persian Agreement of 1919 proposed Iran as a British protectorate; however, the treaty was highly unpopular in Iran and contested by the other Allied countries as granting the British an imperial monopoly, and it was never ratified. In 1921, during the rule of Ahmad Shah (r. 1909–25), the British backed a coup d'état by the Persian Cossack Brigade that successfully toppled the cabinet and formed a new government. Reza Khan, the commander of the Persian Cossacks,

rose quickly in government as a virtual military dictator, becoming first minister of war and then prime minister; in the latter office he persuaded the National Assembly to depose the Qajars, with the intention of forming a republic on the model of Atatürk (r. 1923–38). The clerics, however, fearing the erosion of their influence as had happened to their counterparts in Turkey, prevailed upon Reza Khan to retain the monarchy, and he was accordingly elected the first shah (Reza Shah, r. 1925–41) of the Pahlavi line.

See also Mongols; Safavids (1501–1722)

Further Reading

Abbas Amanat, *The Pivot of the Universe: Nasir al-Din Shah Qajar and the Iranian Monarchy, 1831–1896*, 1997; Peter Avery, Gavin Hambly, and Charles Melville, eds., *The Cambridge History of Iran*, vol. 7, *From Nadir Shah to the Islamic Republic*, 1991; Lord George N. Curzon, *Persia and the Persian Question*, 1892; Ann K. S. Lambton, *Qājār Persia: Eleven Studies*, 1987.

MATTHEW MELVIN-KOUSHKI

al-Qaradawi, Yusuf (b. 1926)

Yusuf al-Qaradawi, one of the most recognized and revered jurists of modern Sunni Islam, was born in a small village in Western Egypt on September 9, 1926. He moved to Cairo as a child and studied at Azhar's primary, middle, and secondary schools, and then at the faculty of religion at Azhar University. He excelled in his studies, which culminated in 1973 with a PhD. His dissertation was on the concept of zakat (charity) and is considered one of the best scholarly treatises on the subject. He visited Qatar in 1961 and eventually settled there, obtaining Qatari citizenship (he also retained his Egyptian citizenship).

Qaradawi is the author of more than a hundred works, many of which have had worldwide influence on Islamic political thought. His most popular book, *al-Halal wa-l-Haram fi al-Islam* (The lawful and prohibited in Islam), demonstrates some of the primary reasons for his appeal—namely, discarding antiquated rulings; concentrating on contemporary issues; and rewriting classical Islamic legal manuals in a modern, accessible style that is easily understood by readers. Another popular work, *Islamic Awakening between Rejection and Extremism*, outlines some of his critiques of the modern Islamist movements. One of his most recent works (some would argue his magnum opus) is the two-volume *Fiqh al-Jihad* (The legal rulings of jihad), in which he argues against a militant interpretation of jihad and presents a moderate view of the rules of warfare in Islam.

Along with his academic career, Qaradawi has excelled as a preacher and a leading public intellectual in all forms of media, including a popular television show called *al-Shari'a wa-l-Hayat* (Shari'a and life) on the Qatar-based Aljazeera channel and a website that documents his writings, appearances, fatwas (religious opinions), and other activities.

Qaradawi has participated in numerous Islamic academic committees throughout the world, appeared regularly at international conferences, and traveled to most Muslim (and many non-Muslim) countries. He has won many prestigious awards, including the King Faisal Award for Islamic Studies in 1994. He became the head of the European Council for Fatwa and Research and established a reputation as a leading jurist on modern Islamic economics.

Qaradawi's informal relationship with the Muslim Brotherhood led to his imprisonment by the Egyptian authorities on three occasions. He did not take an official role within the hierarchy of the movement, however, despite multiple offers to do so.

Qaradawi was banned from visiting a number of Western countries (including the United States and the United Kingdom) because of specific fatwas he issued—in particular, one that justified suicide bombings in Israel under certain circumstances. The Muslim world, however, widely views him as a moderate scholar who opposes religious extremism and senseless violence and a champion of positive reform.

See also jihad; media; revival and reform

Further Reading

Bettina Gräf, "Shaykh Yūsuf al-Qaradāwī in Cyberspace," *Die Welt des Islams* 47, nos. 3–4 (2007); Ana Belen Soage, "Sheikh Yūsuf al-Qaradawi: A Moderate Voice from the Muslim World?" *Religion Compass* 4, no. 9 (2010).

YASIR QADHI

al-Qarafi, Shihab al-Din (1228–85)

A major 13th-century Maliki scholar, Shihab al-Din al-Qarafi (Abu al-'Abbas Ahmad b. Idris) wrote on the relationship between law and political domination in early Mamluk Egypt. Though an Ash'ari in theology, he devoted little scholarly attention to rationalism and focused his major writings on law and legal theory: *al-Dhakhira* (The treasure), a massive compendium of Maliki *fiqh* (Islamic law); *Sharh Tanqih al-Fusul* (Examining Razi's chapters on legal theory) and *Nafa'is al-Usul fi Sharh al-Mahsul* (The precious principles in Razi's compendium on legal theory), both commentaries on Fakhr al-Din al-Razi's work on legal theory, *al-Mahsul*; and *Kitab al-Furuq* (The book of legal case studies), which focused on legal precepts. Beyond these, Qarafi's most significant (and unique) contribution to Islamic political thought was his *Kitab al-Ihkam fi Tamyiz al-Fatawa 'an al-Ahkam wa-Tasarrufat al-Qadi wa-l-Imam* (Distinguishing legal opinions from binding decrees and discretionary actions of judges and caliphs).

The premodern Islamic state had no law of its own and thus depended on shari'a to legitimate its use of power. Shari'a, however, was not a monolith but a composite of multiple, equally orthodox interpretations. This raised the question of the relationship between Islamic law, its authoritative interpreters, and the Muslim state, particularly where the latter favored one school of law over the others. For under such circumstances, the state's monopoly on executive authority threatened to denude the remaining schools of practical import. Qarafi's solution to this was essentially to cast each school of law as a corporate entity whose views were "constitutionally" protected as constituents of the larger composite of orthodox Islamic law. On this understanding, the state could not violate the views of any school without violating shari'a as a whole.

Qarafi recognized the state's prerogative to favor whatever school it saw fit. But it could not refuse to implement the rulings of those it appointed (e.g., a judge or alms collector from another school); nor could it impose the view of its favored school outside cases adjudicated by its judges in court; nor could it, generally speaking, standardize the religious law in areas where there were standing disagreements among the schools. None of this was to negate the rather broadly defined discretionary authority of the state; in fact, Qarafi not only recognizes but actually expands this authority. This, however, was for the purpose of denying the state's every proclamation the full force of law. On the one hand, he compares some state pronouncements to the nonbinding legal opinions (fatwas) issued by muftis, while he contrasts others with the binding decrees (*ḥukm*) of judges and other state officials. In this way, Qarafi asserts that one can challenge and ignore any number of state pronouncements, including declarations of jihad, on the grounds that such pronouncements do not constitute a *ḥukm* but are only nonbinding opinions or provisionally binding but legally challengeable dicta (*taṣarruf*).

This counterintuitive move of granting the state the right to issue fatwas raised problems of its own. If state proclamations, having adopted a school of law, came to enjoy a presumption of authority and protected status, routine state operations could extend legal authority into virtually every aspect of life, producing in effect a "tyranny of law." In other words, while open to challenge, social, economic, cultural, political, and even practical views could be subjected to legal contemplation and presumed to admit of "correct" answers at shari'a. In the face of this, Qarafi set out to define the limits of law and the boundary separating law from nonlaw, so as to restrict the legal authority and jurisdiction of the state and the schools of law to that which could be genetically traced to the actual sources of the religious law. Based on this clarification, there could be no concrete, unassailably correct shari'a rule dictating, for example, economic policy, medical licensing, or speed limits.

A meaningful assessment of Qarafi's relevance to modern Islamic political thought might begin by considering the following. First, he seeks to protect the rights of individuals not as individuals but as members or followers of "corporate" schools of law. Second, he assumes legal pluralism (i.e., recognizing the application of different legal regimes to different segments of society) to be a normative arrangement that does not threaten the sovereignty of states. Third, his theory defines the ideal political order primarily in negative terms, in other words, what authority states (or jurists) are *not* authorized to claim. Finally, the "secular," or worldly, space opened up by his perspective on shari'a is clearly meant to serve and complement rather than challenge or impugn religion.

See also jurisprudence; al-Razi, Fakhr al-Din (1149–1209); shari'a

Further Reading

Sherman A. Jackson, "From Prophetic Actions to Constitutional Theory: A Novel Chapter in Medieval Muslim Jurisprudence," *International Journal of Middle East Studies* 25 (1993); Idem, *Islamic Law and the State: The Constitutional Jurisprudence of Shihāb al-Dīn al-Qarāfī*, 1996; Idem, "Legal Pluralism and the Nation-State: Between Medieval Romanticism and Modern Pragmatism," *Fordham International Law Journal* 24 (2007); Idem, "Sharī'ah, Democracy and the Modern Nation-State: Some Reflections on Islam, Popular Rule and Pluralism," *Fordham International Law Journal* 27, no. 1 (2004).

SHERMAN A. JACKSON

Qarmatians

A dissident faction of the early Isma'ilis, the Qarmatians (Arabic, *Qarāmiṭa*) were named after Hamdan Qarmat, the first chief Isma'ili *dā'ī* (missionary) in Iraq.

The early Isma'ili movement appeared in Iraq and many other regions of the Islamic world from the 870s. The primary revolutionary objective of the Isma'ilis, as millenarian Shi'i Muslims, was to uproot the Abbasids and bring about fundamental world change at the hands of the Mahdi, who would close the era of exoteric Islam, bring out the inner meaning of the law, conquer the world, and rule with justice. The Mahdi was Muhammad b. Isma'il b. Ja'far al-Sadiq, the seventh in a line of imams starting with 'Ali b. Abi Talib. The bulk of the early Isma'ilis denied his death and awaited his imminent return from hiding. The early Isma'ili *da'wa* (mission) was centrally directed by 'Alid leaders who later claimed to have hidden their correct identity. They acted as the chief representatives (*ḥujjas*) of the hidden Muhammad b. Isma'il. Qarmat, the chief *dā'ī* in southern Iraq and all other *dā'īs* propagated the *da'wa* on this basis. The Isma'ilis of Iraq and adjacent regions were called Qarmatians after their first local leader.

In 899, soon after his accession to the central leadership of the Isma'ili movement, 'Abdallah, the future founder of the Fatimid caliphate, claimed the imamate openly for himself and his predecessors. He later explained that to hide their identity, all the true imams in the progeny of Ja'far al-Sadiq adopted the name Muhammad b. Isma'il as a collective code name in addition to other pseudonyms while assuming the rank of *ḥujja* of the hidden Mahdi. The doctrinal

reform of ‘Abdallah split the Isma‘ili movement into two rival factions. Some accepted the reform and acknowledged the imamate of ‘Abdallah and his predecessors as well as his successors in the Fatimid dynasty. Others, including the communities in Iraq, Iran, Bahrain, and some of the Isma‘ilis in Yemen, retained their original doctrine and prepared for the imminent return of the hidden Muhammad b. Isma‘il. Henceforth, the term "Qarmatian" came to be more specifically applied to those dissident Isma‘ilis who did not acknowledge ‘Abdallah and the later Fatimid caliphs as imams.

The Qarmatians found their main stronghold in eastern Arabia, then called Bahrain. There, in the same eventful year of 899, the *dā‘ī* Abu Sa‘id al-Jannabi (d. 913) established a Qarmati state. He was succeeded by a number of his sons, including Abu Tahir al-Jannabi (d. 944). The Qarmatians of Bahrain engaged in pillaging raids into Iraq, as well as drawn-out hostilities with the Abbasids and the Fatimids. Abu Tahir's raids culminated in his attack on Mecca in 930 during the pilgrimage season. The Qarmatians massacred the pilgrims and carried off the Black Stone of the Ka‘ba to al-Ahsa', their capital in Bahrain, to symbolize the end of the era of Islam. In 931, Abu Tahir recognized a young Persian as the expected Mahdi, to whom he turned over the reins of power. The early disastrous end of this episode weakened the doctrinal basis of the Qarmatians of Bahrain, also diminishing their influence over other Qarmatian communities.

The Qarmatians eventually returned the Black Stone in 950 in exchange for a large sum of money paid by the Abbasids and not, as held by some anti-Fatimid authorities, in response to the Fatimid caliph-imam al-Mansur bi-llah's request. The Qarmatians of Bahrain and elsewhere did not acknowledge ‘Abdallah (‘Ubaydallah) al-Mahdi (d. 934) as the expected Mahdi, nor did they regard any of his successors in the Fatimid dynasty as their imams. The Isma‘ilis of the Jibal region in Persia continued to be a branch of the Qarmatians. There, the fifth *dā‘ī* of Rayy, Abu Hatim al-Razi (d. 934), corresponded with Abu Tahir and like him expected the reappearance of Muhammad b. Isma‘il as the Mahdi. In Khurasan and Transoxiana, too, the dissident Qarmatian view persisted after the advent of the Fatimids. The *dā‘ī* Muhammad b. Ahmad al-Nasafi (d. 943) reaffirmed the Mahdiship of Muhammad b. Isma‘il in his *Kitab al-Mahsul* (Book of the yield), which also introduced a type of Neoplatonic philosophy into Isma‘ili (Qarmati) thought.

By the time the Qarmatian state of Bahrain was finally uprooted in 1077 by local tribesmen, the Qarmatian communities elsewhere, which had continued to expect the return of the hidden Mahdi, had disintegrated or were won over to the side of the loyal Isma‘ili *da‘wa* propagated on behalf of the Fatimid caliph-imams. Condemned by the Muslim majority as unspeakable heretics or worse, the Qarmatians of Bahrain have also been praised in modern times for the communal and egalitarian principles that were important elements in the social and political organization of their state.

See also Isma‘ilis; Shi‘ism

Further Reading

Farhad Daftary, *The Ismā‘īlīs: Their History and Doctrines*, 2007; Heinz Halm, *The Empire of the Mahdi: The Rise of the Fatimids*, translated by M. Bonner, 1996; Wilferd Madelung, "The Fatimids and the Qarmaṭīs of Baḥrayn," in *Mediaeval Isma‘ili History and Thought*, edited by F. Daftary, 1996.

FARHAD DAFTARY

quietism and activism

In premodern history, both Sunni and Twelver Shi‘i attitudes toward illegitimate authorities were predominantly quietist. "Quietism" can be generally defined as passivism in politics, while its antonym, "activism," entails active involvement in the political affairs, thus affecting political power and its policy. In the Twelver tradition, the central symbol of political thought is the martyrdom of Imam Husayn, the grandson of Prophet Muhammad, who was killed along with his Companions and many of the Prophet's family members at the Battle of Karbala in 680 on order of the Umayyad caliph Yazid I (r. 680–83). This tragedy elicited profound emotions of grief and a deep conviction of historical injustice. As a result, many Shi‘is believed that a ruler could not be powerful and moral at the same time, so they chose morality and renounced all political action. Convinced that political power is beyond reform, they practiced dissimulation (*taqiyya*), concealing their faith for self-protection from their non-Shi‘i opponents. Government was to be accommodated, not overthrown. This attitude became consolidated in the Twelver tradition with the doctrine of the Occultation of the Twelfth Imam (*ghayba*). In 874 it was held that the Twelfth Imam, out of fear for his safety, had gone into occultation and could be contacted only by a representative; this came to be known as the Lesser Occultation (*al-ghayba al-ṣughrā*). In 941, after a series of four representatives, in what would be termed the Greater Occultation (*al-ghayba al-kubrā*), it was held that ordinary contact with the Twelfth Imam was no longer possible. Because the Twelfth Imam could no longer serve as a rallying point for rebellion, and because his explicit permission was held to be necessary for any uprising, the struggle to depose the illegitimate usurper of the imamate and install the rightful imam fell into abeyance.

In contrast, as the majority, Sunnis had no need to practice dissimulation. However, they also practiced a policy of quietism toward corrupt leadership. Sunnis thought that the proper response to an oppressive government was to endure it. A famous hadith of the Prophet instructed the Muslims to obey the leader, even if he were an Ethiopian slave. Another widespread maxim held that 60 years of tyranny was better than one hour of civil strife (*fitna*): God is the ultimate ruler of the community, and as long as guidance can be freely dispersed and practiced among the believers, which was the task of the ‘ulama', it was more important to avoid conflict with power and keep the community together. They considered rulers to serve merely as shields for the *umma* (community of believers), protecting it against external enemies. An oppressive or

sinful ruler was to be admonished or cajoled and ultimately could be deposed if he failed to uphold Islamic law, became physically disqualified, or lost his probity. However, there was no systematic means for deposing a ruler other than rebellion and strife. In that case, it was deemed preferable to endure the ruler's tyranny rather than inciting civil strife in the *umma*. If he failed to reform, however, it was deemed preferable to endure his tyranny or iniquity rather than rebel.

In contrast, the Kharijis and Zaydi Shi'is adopted an activist stance. Like the Twelvers, they denounced the current rulers as illegitimate, but they held that it was a fundamental obligation to remove usurpers and tyrants and to install a legitimate imam. The Kharijis were the most adamant in this regard, holding that the member of the community with superior merit should be elected to the caliphate. If someone else were in power, or even if the legitimate imam himself lost his superior status through sinful behavior, the current ruler should be removed, by open rebellion if necessary. The Zaydi view was somewhat similar, except that the legitimate imam had to be a descendant of the Prophet and learned in the religious sciences; rebellion and the establishment of a legitimate state was an absolute requirement for legitimate rule. The need to keep the community together was no reason to submit to oppressive rule. These positions had dire consequences for those who espoused them, and it is no accident that Khariji and Zaydi communities survived in remote regions, including Oman, Yemen, and the Mzab region in Algeria.

The 20th century witnessed a dramatic shift in the Shi'i position from quietism to revolutionary activism. The historical tragedy of Imam Husayn was reinterpreted as a revolutionary symbol for the struggle against oppression. The martyrdom of Imam Husayn set an eternal role model for the suppressed Shi'is and inspired an activist ideology that equated morality with political action, condemned the quietist tradition within Shi'i Islam, and culminated in the Iranian Revolution (1978–79). In 1971 and afterward, Ayatollah Khomeini (d. 1989) set forth the political doctrine of the guardianship of the jurist (*wilāyat al-faqīh*), which grants the Shi'i 'ulama', specifically the leading jurist (*faqīh*), the prerogative of the religious and political leadership roles that, according earlier Twelver doctrine, had been to a large extent restricted to the Hidden Imam. Khomeini's activist legacy may be seen outside Iran in the Lebanese Hizbullah, which started as a resistance movement against the Israeli occupation and then became a political party and joined the Lebanese national government in 2005.

The modern period has also witnessed Islamic activism among Sunnis, but it has most commonly targeted reform rather than the overthrow of current political orders. Sunni activist movements have developed in the context of decolonization as a reaction to oppressive regimes that tend to criminalize involvement in politics and use strategies of control, co-option, and repression to curb any resistance movement. Islamic activists react by submerged or hidden networking that aims mainly to bring about a change in the social and intellectual environment of the youth. Adherents to such movements frame activism as a moral obligation and embrace an ideology that mandates participation as a moral duty. Groups such as Jama'at-i Islami in India and the Muslim Brotherhood in Egypt emphasize fairness and social justice and offer an image of a moral community living in accordance with God's rules. The Muslim Brotherhood has not openly fought the Egyptian regime and has not overturned existing relations of economic and political domination in Egypt. Rather, they accept the status quo with the hope of incremental, gradual change and focus mainly on social activities, because the latter represent a less risky alternative than directly confronting the state's oppressive power.

The year 2011 witnessed a tremendous change in the understanding of the concept of statehood and citizenship. For the first time, we witness citizens determined to actively topple oppressive regimes and have a direct say on the affairs and destiny of their state. Millions of people from different socioeconomic and religious backgrounds protested against dictatorships through organizing campaigns of civil resistance featuring peaceful demonstrations and labor strikes. The January 25 Egyptian revolution, which endured 18 days of clashes between state oppressive forces and civilians resulting in loss of life and great casualties on the latter's side, managed to overthrow President Husni Mubarak's regime. The success of the Tunisian revolution in December 2010 sparked the Egyptian uprisings whose success in return sparked a series of civil protests across the Arab world against oppressive regimes in Yemen, Libya, and Bahrain. While analysts are trying to uncover the reasons behind the revolutions, the fact that they were largely driven by a majority of Arab youth who saw themselves as "agents of change" reflects the success of Islamic activists in introducing the desired change in their societies from a passive quietist culture into an active self-determined one.

See also dissent, opposition, resistance; dissimulation; nonviolence; rebellion; violence

Further Reading

Rainer Brunner, "Shiism in the Modern Context: From Religious Quietism to Political Activism," *Religious Compass* 3, no. 1 (2009); Patricia Crone, *God's Rule: Government and Islam—Six Centuries of Medieval Islamic Political Thought*, 2004; Mazen Hashem, "Contemporary Islamic Activism: The Shades of Praxis," *Sociology of Religion* 67, no. 1 (2006); Quintan Wiktorowicz, *Islamic Activism: A Social Movement Theory Approach*, 2004.

KATRIN JOMAA

Qur'an

The Qur'an, the holy book of Islam, is the most recent of the major sacred scriptures to have appeared in human history. It includes the prophetic proclamations of Muhammad (570–632) in

Arabic, collected after his death in definitive written form and meticulously transmitted through the centuries. More than a billion Muslims around the globe consider the Qur'an to be the eternal word of God, who "sent down" the scripture as his final divine revelation and commissioned Muhammad to be the last prophet to proclaim his divine will for all of humanity to follow.

Muslims believe that as the most perfect and ultimate form of divine revelation, the Qur'an represents the final stage in a process through which divine speech is translated as scripture. In essence there is only one timeless revelation reiterated by the prophets, God's messengers throughout the ages, without any contribution of their own. From Adam, through Abraham, Moses, David, and Jesus, to Muhammad, the messengers are considered human beings as well as divinely chosen mouthpieces of revelation. God is the speaker of the Qur'an and Muhammad its recipient; the Qur'an itself is considered the verbatim word of God, revealed in clear Arabic to Muhammad.

Clearly understood, faithfully proclaimed, and accurately recited by Muhammad in historical time, the Qur'an, according to the normative Muslim view, was memorized with exact precision and also collected in book form by Muhammad's followers after his death. Then it was recited and copied with painstaking care in continuous transmission from generation to generation. Today, as in the past, the Qur'an is copied and recited in Arabic; it is pronounced only in Arabic in Muslim ritual worship by Arabs and non-Arabs alike. It cannot be rendered adequately into any other tongue, and, in the Muslim view, all translations are crutches, at best helpful explanations of its original intention and at worst doubtful makeshifts, obscuring its true meaning. Inasmuch as Muslims believe that the Qur'an has been preserved unchanged over time in its pristine Arabic, they also believe that it is superior to all other scriptures solely because of the faulty form in which other scriptures have been transmitted and preserved by their respective communities.

The Qur'an exhibits a significant relationship to the biblical tradition and echoes themes found in the epigraphical writings of Judaism and Christianity. No single collection of normative, midrashic, or apocryphal biblical writings, however, has been identified as the major source on which the Qur'an might directly depend. There is no evidence that this tradition had been translated into Arabic by the time of Muhammad, either as a whole corpus or in the form of single books. It is the widely shared view among historians of religion that Muhammad's knowledge of the biblical tradition came principally, if not exclusively, from oral sources. This oral lore, enriched by extrabiblical additions and commentary, was communicated to Muhammad in his mother tongue. However, it ultimately originated in traditions recorded mainly in Syriac, Ethiopian, and Hebrew, as evidenced by the vocabulary of foreign origin to be found in the Arabic Qur'an. Mainly, this foreign vocabulary had already been assimilated into the Arabic religious discourse of Muhammad's native environment.

The Qur'an is the first book-length production of Arabic literature and as such stands at the crossroads of the pre-Islamic oral, highly narrative, and poetical traditions of the Arabic language and the written, increasingly scholarly prose tradition of the subsequently evolving civilization of Islam. The beginnings of this transition in the Arabic language from the oral to the written tradition can be tied to the time and person of Muhammad and are clearly reflected in the rhymed prose style of the Qur'an. This rhymed prose (*saj'*), the mode of speech of the oracles uttered by the pre-Islamic soothsayer (*kāhin*), is a characteristic of the Qur'an, the first Arabic document of any length to exhibit this form of speech in written form. The roots of the Qur'an as the first Arabic book may also be detected in its content. In its verses, the Qur'an captures many topics that had formed an important part of the worship and cult of the nonscriptural tribal religion practiced in pre-Islamic Arabia. There is no doubt that the religious practice of Mecca exerted the most influence on the vision of Arab tribal religion that Muhammad acquired in his early life.

The Qur'an exerts a powerful spell on its listeners. It has a presence in everyday Muslim life, with its verses visible on the walls of mosques or inscribed in the hearts of men and women. For centuries, it has been copied in precious manuscripts and printed in definitive editions published all over the Islamic world. The Qur'an accompanies the Muslim believer from birth to death, and a copy of the book is kept in a special place in Muslim households. Words of the Qur'an are whispered into the ears of newborn children, daily prayers are taken from its verses, and particular words of its praise of God are exclaimed at set points in the daily routine of Muslims. All Muslims learn to recite essential passages of the Qur'an by heart from an early age and turn to them throughout their adult life. Some scholars commit its entire text to memory, and blind men often make it their profession to recite the Qur'an by heart at funerals and other special occasions.

Historical Origin and Development of the Qur'an

The most common translation of the Arabic word *qur'ān* is "recital," connoting that Muhammad heard the words from God and recited them without specific reference to a written text. If understood as rooted in a Syriac loanword, *qur'ān* would mean "a reading," such as a reading aloud of scripture in a liturgical context. In the actual text of the Qur'an, the word *qur'ān* refers to separate revelations made piecemeal to Muhammad or, more generally, to the revelation (*tanzīl*) that was sent down by God (specifically in the month of Ramadan). When it is understood to mean a book, the word *kitāb* (scripture) is used synonymously with "the Arabic Qur'an" that was revealed or, generally, as the manifest scripture that includes the wondrous "signs" (*āya*) sent down to manifest and expound God's power. The Qur'an calls itself a *dhikr* (admonition) and *ḥikma* (wisdom) as well as a *furqān* (salvation, discrimination) and even *sūra* ("section," i.e., a piece of revelation). Originally referring to component parts of the revelation, the terms *sūra* and *āya* eventually were chosen to denote "chapter" and "verse" of the Qur'an, respectively.

According to Qur'anic evidence, Muhammad understood his revelations as coming from a heavenly archetype, called "the mother of the scripture" (*umm al-kitāb*), that is described in the Qur'an as

a well-guarded tablet, to be touched only by the pure angels—lofty leaves in the hands of noble scribes, unrolled sheets of parchment inscribed by the reed pen, a holy writ comprising all happenings in the universe. This heavenly scripture contains not only what is revealed through the Qur'an but also what previously has been revealed through the law (Tawrat) of Moses and gospel (Injil) of Jesus. Jews and Christians—"the people of the Scripture"—altered their own holy books, effecting serious discrepancies between their scriptures and the authentic Qur'an. Muhammad did not read this heavenly book but rather received words of revelation from it that no one may alter. They were brought down by the "spirit of holiness" (identified with the angel Gabriel) and induced trancelike moments of meditation or ecstatic states in which the shaken Muhammad had to be wrapped in a mantle. The words that he received were predominantly auditions rather than visions, some traces of visions in a few suras notwithstanding. The promptings came piecemeal and were couched in verses of rhymed prose. Some of these verses were clear and obvious, others obscure and ambiguous, but all of them were clearly distinct from Muhammad's ordinary words.

It is widely assumed that Muhammad proclaimed the Qur'an in the dialect of the people of Mecca and that the language of the Qur'an and its style originated from one particular person, Muhammad, rather than from a group of disparate individuals. Because Muhammad would add new revelations to the earlier ones throughout his career, when he died, there was not yet a collection of revelations in final form. Muslim tradition records the names of Ubayy b. Ka'b (d. between 640 and 656) and Zayd b. Thabit (d. between 662 and 675) as two followers who served Muhammad as scribes in Medina. In addition, Muhammad's wives Hafsa and Umm Kulthum could write, while his wives Umm Salama and 'A'isha could read but not write. Tradition also mentions that 'Abdallah b. Abi Sarh, foster brother of the third caliph 'Uthman b. 'Affan, claimed to have served Muhammad as a scribe and induced him on occasion to change the wording.

The actual collection of the Qur'an in book form was principally the work of Zayd b. Thabit, who knew Syriac and arithmetic. He was an expert on the division of inheritances during the time of Muhammad. He collected ransoms and calculated taxes during the caliphate of Abu Bakr, prepared written orders for the distribution of supplies during the caliphate of 'Umar b. al-Khattab, and oversaw the treasury during 'Uthman's caliphate. He was given the task of collecting the material that existed on various primitive writing materials and in the memoirs of men and wrote it down on "sheets" of uniform size (*ṣuḥuf*). Though there is some conflict in the traditions on this point, this collection seems to have been a process that may have begun during the caliphate of Abu Bakr and was furthered by the caliph 'Umar, whose daughter Hafsa (d. 665), a widow of Muhammad, is portrayed as the guardian of the *ṣuḥuf*. This process of collection came to a head during the caliphate of 'Uthman, who entrusted a commission, headed by Zayd b. Thabit, with the standard collection of the Qur'an in its rudimentary book form, considered the original copy of the Qur'an. It is known as the 'Uthmanic codex (*muṣḥaf*) and was established about 15 to 20 years after the Prophet's death.

Next to this standard codex established in Medina, tradition also attributes particular collections of the Qur'an to Companions of Muhammad that showed a somewhat different order of suras. Ubayy b. Ka'b's collection had two additional suras and 'Abdallah b. Mas'ud's (d. 652) lacked the last two suras of the 'Uthmanic codex. For a short time, these private collections enjoyed a measure of authority in Syrian towns of Damascus and Homs and in the Iraqi towns of Kufa and Basra. They disappeared, however, after the 'Uthmanic codex had imposed uniformity as the authoritative standard, a standard in which Zayd's commission seems to have made the final order of the suras, many of which existed in a set order since the time of the Prophet while others show marks of having been put together in the final redaction. The order of the suras, 114 in number, was based on the principle of roughly decreasing length, which had the longest chapters in the beginning of the book and the shortest at its end. The short first sura, al-Fatiha ("the Opening"), numbering seven verses, was placed at the head of this authoritative standard, on which all Qur'ans are based.

Each of the individual chapters of the Qur'an is introduced by the formula, "In the name of God, the Merciful, the Compassionate" (except for the ninth sura, which might originally have formed a unit with the preceding chapter). The formula is also found once in the body of the Qur'an, at the head of Solomon's letter to the queen of Sheba. Immediately following this formula at the head of 29 suras, there are mysterious letters that are disconnected and convey no obvious meaning. Some of them occur only once and others are put together in patterns of two to five letters. Scholars have suggested a great variety of explanations about the meaning of these letters, but none of them has been accepted as probable, although they belong to the earliest stage of the Qur'anic redaction and cannot be explained as additions by later hands. The Qur'an does not refer to its suras by numbers; rather, each chapter has a particular name (or in some cases is known under a few different names). These names are clearly later additions to the Qur'an and were derived from catchwords that figure in the first few verses of a sura or are derived from a characteristic or odd word in the body of a sura. The division of the chapters into numbered verses, mainly based on rhyme, is likewise a later phenomenon that was not yet in use in the early centuries of the transmission of the Qur'an. The numbered verses, just like the numbers of the suras, have become standard, however, in the Qur'an copies in print today, although Muslims prefer to quote the suras by their names rather than their numbers.

The Analysis of the Qur'an in Scholarship

The 'Uthmanic codex established by the commission headed by Zayd b. Thabit was written in a rudimentary form, a "*scriptio defectiva*" constituting merely a consonantal skeleton lacking diacritical marks that distinguish certain Arabic consonants from one another. Oral recitation was needed to ascertain the intended pronunciation of the text by the addition of short vowels for its vocalization. As the Qur'anic orthography developed incrementally over more than two centuries and as the linkage between the consonantal skeleton and the oral recitation became increasingly robust, the deficiencies

of the Arabic script were gradually overcome. The variants of recitation, the vast majority being of a minor nature, were either reconciled or accommodated, and the written text became increasingly independent of its linkage to oral pronunciation. This process culminated with the *scriptio plena*, the fully vocalized and pointed text of the Qur'an. This text may be considered a *textus recepetus, ne varietur* with the proviso that no single clearly identifiable textual specimen of the Qur'an was ever established or accepted with absolute unanimity.

The final, fully vocalized and pointed text of the Qur'an, accepted as normative and canonical, may best be understood as a construct underlying the work of Abu Bakr b. Mujahid (d. 936), who restricted the recitation of the Qur'an to seven correct readings, termed *aḥruf* (literally, "letters") on the basis of a popular tradition. Ibn Mujahid accepted the reading *(qirā'a)* of seven prominent Qur'an scholars of the eighth century and declared them all to be based on divine authority. In 934 the Abbasid establishment promulgated the doctrine that these seven versions were the only acceptable forms of the text and all others forbidden. Nevertheless, "three after the seven" and "four after the ten" ways of reading were added somewhat later to form, respectively, 10 or 14 variant readings. Finally, each of the ten ways of reading was eventually accepted in two slightly varying versions (*riwāya*), all of which, at least theoretically, belong within the spectrum of the *textus receptus, ne varietur*. For all practical purposes, only two versions are in general use today—that of Hafs (d. 805) from 'Asim (d. 744), that is, Hafs's version based on 'Asims's way of reading, which received official sanction when it was adopted by the Egyptian standard edition of the Qur'an printed in 1924, and that of Warsh (d. 822) from Nafi' (d. 785), that is, Warsh's version based on Nafi''s way of reading, which is followed in North Africa with the exception of Egypt.

From the mid-19th century, Western scholars began to engage in serious literary research on the Qur'an, linking the scholarly findings of traditional Muslim scholarship with the philological and text-critical methods that biblical scholarship was developing in Europe. An intensive scholarly attempt was made to arrive at a chronological order of Qur'anic chapters and passages that could be correlated with the development and varying circumstances of Muhammad's career. This Western chronological approach to the Qur'an achieved its climax in the highly acclaimed *Geschichte des Qorans* (History of the Qur'an) by Theodor Nöldeke (1860), which was later revised and expanded by F. Schwally (1909 and 1919) and again by G. Bergsträsser (1938). The chronological sequencing of the suras elaborated by Western Qur'anic scholarship largely adopted the distinction of traditional Muslim scholarship between Meccan and Medinan suras already worked out in the *Itqan fi 'Ulum al-Qur'an* (Securing Qur'anic exegesis) by Jalal al-Din al-Suyuti (d. 1505), the major Muslim reference work on the Qur'anic sciences. However, it further subdivided the Meccan phase of Muhammad's proclamation of the Qur'an into three distinct periods. R. Bell, in his *The Qur'ān* and, posthumously, *A Commentary on the Qur'an*, took a radically different approach. He abandoned the chronological division into Meccan and Medinan periods and designed a disjointed dating system for individual verses in the Qur'an taken as a whole.

The overriding goal of the chronological framework of the Qur'an as elaborated in Western scholarship was to divide the Qur'anic proclamation into four distinct periods—Mecca I, Mecca II, Mecca III, and Medina. It linked these periods with a vision of the gradual inner development of Muhammad's prophetic consciousness and political career that Western scholarship had determined through biographical research on the life of Muhammad in conjunction with its research on the Qur'an. In general, the fourfold division of periods of the Qur'anic proclamation proceeded on the basis of two major principles. It related Qur'anic passages source-critically to historical events known from extra-Qur'anic literature, and it systematically analyzed the philological and stylistic nature of the Arabic text of the Qur'an passage by passage. It also placed clear markers between the Meccan periods at the time of the emigration to Abyssinia (about 615) and Muhammad's disillusioned return from Ta'if (about 620), and it retained the emigration in 622 as the divide between Meccan and Medinan suras.

The group of 48 short suras classified as belonging to the first or early Meccan period were identified by a similarity of style that gives expression to Muhammad's initial enthusiasm in a language that is rich in images, impassioned in tone, uttered in short and rhythmic verses, marked by a strong poetic coloring, and containing about 30 oaths or adjurations that introduce individual suras or passages. They are driven by a heightened awareness of the apocalyptic end of this world and God's final judgment of humanity. They include Muhammad's vehement attacks against his Meccan opponents for adhering to the old Arab tribal religion and his vigorous rebuttals to their damaging accusations against his claim of divine inspiration when they dismissively characterized him as a soothsayer (*kāhin*), sorcerer (*sāḥir*), poet (*shā'ir*), and a man possessed (*majnūn*).

The suras of the second or middle Meccan period, 21 in number, have longer units of revelation, which are more prosaic and do not exhibit a clearly distinct common character. They mark the transition from the excitement of the first phase to a Muhammad of greater calm who aims to influence his audience by parenetic proofs selected from descriptions of natural phenomena, illustrations from human life, and vivid depictions of paradise and hellfire. The stories of earlier prophets and elements from the story of Moses in particular are cited as admonitions for his enemies and as encouragement for the small group of his followers. The place of the oath is taken by introductory titles such "This is the revelation of God!" and by the frequently recurring "Say!" (*qul*), the divine command for Muhammad to proclaim a certain Qur'anic passage. The name *al-Raḥmān* (the Merciful), a name for God in use prior to Islam in southern and central Arabia, although rejected by the pre-Islamic Meccans, is frequently employed yet dies out in the third period.

The suras of the third or late Meccan period, also 21 in number, cannot be seen as standing in any kind of inner chronological

order. They exhibit a broad prosaic style with rhyme patterns that become more and more stereotyped, frequently ending in *-ūn* and *-īn*. In addressing his followers as a group, Muhammad frequently employs the formula, "O you people" (*yā ayyuhā al-nās*). Muhammad's imagination seems to be subdued; the revelations take on the form of sermons or speeches and the prophetic stories repeat earlier ideas. Overall, this group of suras could be understood to reflect Muhammad's exasperation at the stubborn resistance to his message on the part of his fellow Meccan tribesmen.

The suras of the Medinan period, 24 in number, follow one another in a relatively certain chronological order and reflect Muhammad's growing political power and his shaping of the social framework of the Muslim community. As the acknowledged leader in spiritual and social affairs of the Medinan community that had been torn by internal strife prior to his arrival, Muhammad's Qur'anic proclamation becomes preoccupied with criminal legislation; civil matters such as laws of marriage, divorce, and inheritance; and with the summons to warfare against opponents. Various groups of people are addressed separately by different epithets. The believers, the Meccan emigrants (*muhājirūn*) and their Medinan helpers (*anṣār*), are addressed as "you who believe," while the Medinans who distrusted Muhammad and hesitated in converting to Islam are called "hypocrites" (*munāfiqūn*). The members of the Jewish tribes of the Qurayza, Nadir, and Qaynuqa' are collectively called Jews (*yahūd*), and the Christians are referred to by the group name of Nazarenes (*naṣārā*). More than 30 times—and only in Medinan verses—the peoples who have been given a scripture in previous eras are identified collectively by the set phrase "the People of the Book" (*ahl al-kitāb*). They are distinguished from the *ummiyyūn* (gentiles) who have not been given a book previously but from among whom God selected Muhammad, called *al-nabī al-ummī* (the "gentile" prophet) in a late Meccan passage, as his messenger. A significant group of Qur'anic passages from Medinan suras refers to Muhammad's break with the Jewish tribes and his subsequent interpretation of the figure of Abraham, supported by Ishmael, as the founder of the Meccan sanctuary. Abraham is henceforth depicted as the prototypical Muslim (*ḥanīf*) who represents the original pure religion designated "the religion of Abraham" (*millat Ibrāhīm*), now reinstated by Muhammad.

The most radical chronological rearrangement of the suras and verses of the Qur'an, undertaken by R. Bell, concluded its elaborate hypothesis with many provisos. Bell suggested that the composition of the Qur'an followed three main phases: a "sign" phase, a "Qur'an" phase, and a "book" phase. The earliest phase of sign passages (*āyāt*) represents the major portion of Muhammad's preaching at Mecca, of which only an incomplete and partially fragmentary amount survives. The Qur'an phase included the later stages of Muhammad's Meccan career and about the first two years of his activity at Medina, a phase during which Muhammad was faced with the task of producing a collection of liturgical recitals (*qur'ān*). The book phase belonged to his activity at Medina and began at the end of the second year after the emigration, from which time Muhammad set out to produce a written scripture (*kitāb*). In the present Qur'an each of these three phases, however, cannot be separated precisely, because sign passages came to be incorporated into the liturgical collection and earlier oral recitals were later revised to form part of the written book. Regarding the redaction of the Qur'an during Muhammad's lifetime, the starting point for the Qur'an as sacred scripture, in Bell's view, had to be related to the time of the Battle of Badr in 624. For Bell, this was the watershed event, while the emigration did not constitute a great divide for the periodization of the suras.

None of the systems of chronological sequencing of Qur'anic chapters and verses has been accepted universally by contemporary scholarship. Nöldeke's sequencing and its refinements have established a rule of thumb for the approximate order of the suras in their chronological sequence. Bell's hypothesis has established that the final redaction of the Qur'an was a complex process of successive revisions of earlier material, whether oral or already available in rudimentary written form. In many ways, Western Qur'anic scholarship reconfirmed the two pillars on which the traditional Muslim views of Qur'anic chronology were based. First, the Qur'an was revealed piecemeal, and, second, it was collected into book form on the basis of both written documents prepared by scribes on Muhammad's dictation and Qur'anic passages preserved in the collective memory of his circle of Companions. All methods of chronological analysis, whether traditional Muslim or modern Western, agree that the order of the suras in Muhammad's proclamation was different from the order found in the written text we have today, where, in general, the suras are arranged according to decreasing length.

Political Elements in the Qur'an

As can be seen from his prophetical career, Muhammad's political actions were directed by an instinct for pragmatism. The Prophet did not act on the basis of preset principles of political theory but rather demonstrated a flexible and adaptable political practice. Examples of Muhammad's political documents are the Constitution of Medina, the treaty of Hudaybiyya, and the documents of alliances with Arab tribes. The Qur'an, however, is foremost a religious message rather than a document of political theory. The Qur'an is an expression of Islamic beliefs, doctrines, rituals, laws, and practices; it is not a textbook of political theory, nor does it provide a system for political thought. Rather, it offers certain themes that constitute scattered building blocks for the eventual historical development of political thought in Islam. These elements do not represent a complete foundation or an articulated framework for the emergence of a systematic political vision in Islam, although some of them became cornerstones in the eventual political theories developed by Muslim thinkers over the centuries. The number of such elements is small, and, compared to the weight they carry in contemporary Islamic political thought, they appear to be at best stepping stones for political theories.

The core of the Islamic creed, the twofold Muslim profession of faith (*shahāda*)—"There is no god but God, and Muhammad

is God's messenger" (*lā ilāha illā Allāh wa-Muḥammad rasūl Allāh*)—is intensified by the Qur'anic command, "Obey God and obey the messenger" (Q. 4:59) that is also embedded in the most articulate passage of the Qur'an on obedience and authority (Q. 24:47–56). The Shi'is augment this profession of faith by adding "and 'Ali is God's guardian" (*walīy Allāh*) and interpret the Qur'anic phrase "and those in authority among you" (Q. 4:59) as validating the authority of their imams as rulers of the community after the Prophet. The categorical command of obedience implies two basic dimensions for Islamic political thought. It defines the vertical axis of authority that intrinsically links obedience to God with obedience to the Prophet, intertwines the power of divine rule with human governance, and requires unquestioning submission to God combined with absolute allegiance to the Prophet. Furthermore, it marks the horizontal axis of an inextricable interrelation of religion and politics in Islam, the immutable religion (*al-dīn al-qayyim*, Q. 12:40) that the Prophet perfected (Q. 5:3) and proclaimed as the religion of submission to God, Islam.

The crux of the creed is Muhammad's self-perception as a prophet that developed from his early preaching in Mecca, where he presented himself as the reformer of the pre-Islamic tribal religion. He believed himself a "messenger" (*rasūl*) called by God for an Arab monotheistic and revealed religion that confirmed the revelations other peoples had received in their languages. In proclaiming his message, he drew inspiration from the example of earlier messengers (*rusul*), prophets (*nabīyyūn*), and biblical patriarchs, as well as leaders known from old Arab lore. Established in Medina after the hijra (emigration), he applied the term "prophet" (*nabī*) consciously to himself. Henceforth he had himself addressed as "O Prophet!" (*yā ayyuhā al-nabī*, Q. 33:45), and he understood himself as *al-nabī al-ummī* (Q. 7:157–58), the final prophet, and "the seal of the prophets" (*khātam al-nabiyyīn*, Q. 33:40). The authority of the earlier biblical prophets, who founded a community, was rooted in the covenant (*mīthāq*, *'ahd*) God had made with them. Yet only one passage, based on the small phrase "and with you" (*wa-minka*, Q. 33:7), refers to a covenant relationship with God on the part of Muhammad. Post-Qur'anic traditions recognized the tenuousness of this basis and tried to bolster it through legends such as the angelic cleansing of Muhammad's chest and his miraculous ascension to heaven (*mi'rāj*), symbols of a divine covenant with Muhammad.

The biblical background of the covenant is evident in Qur'anic references to God's covenant with pivotal prophetical figures of the Qur'an. On the day of the primordial covenant (Q. 7:172), humanity professed monotheism as its pledge in response to God's self-disclosure as their Lord at the dawn of creation. Since the dawn of creation, according to the Qur'an, God has made a covenant with humanity that is reinstituted from prophet to prophet throughout religious history. Although they are recipients of a covenant for their people, in the Qur'an the prophets are not immune to sin. Adam, "the father of the human race," carries in his loins the symbol of God's covenant, his progeny, the human race, as "the children of Adam," until the Day of Resurrection (Q. 7:172). Yet Adam broke the covenant together with Eve by eating from the tree of paradise (Q. 20:115)—an act, however, for which he repented. The symbol of Noah's covenant is the ark in which he is rescued together with his people (Q. 33:7). Abraham, the prototype of the true Muslim (*ḥanīf*, Q. 3:65–70), abandons the worship of astral deities (Q. 6:76–79), breaks the idols (Q. 21:58–67), builds the Ka'ba, and institutes the pilgrimage as the symbol of his covenant but violates the covenant through three lies: feigning illness (Q. 37:89), denying culpability (Q. 21:63), and passing his wife off as his sister (according to tradition). Joseph, whose mark of the covenant is his inspired ability to interpret dreams, showed his readiness to commit sin with the wife of the Egyptian (Q. 12:24) but was divinely protected from acting on it. Moses, in his encounter with God on Mount Sinai, receives the tablets as the symbol of his covenant (4:142–45), and in his desire to see God, he falls to the ground as if struck by lightning as the mountain is crumbled to dust (4:142–45). But he breaks the covenant by slaying another human being without any right to blood revenge, while his followers, "the Children of Israel," break the covenant made at Sinai through their idolatry of the calf (Q. 2:63).

David, who represents the covenant in his receiving the psalms (Zabur), slaying of Goliath, and appointment as God's viceroy (*khalīfa*) to dispense justice, asks for God's forgiveness (Q. 38:24). Solomon, heir to David's throne, receives as a symbol of his covenant immense knowledge and wisdom, giving him power over humans and demons (*jinn*) and the capacity to understand the speech of birds and command the wind. Solomon had to repent for idolatry (Q. 38:34). Jesus, the son of Mary, the Messiah and the recipient of the Gospel (Injil), is spirit from God (*rūḥun minhu*) and his word (*kalimatuhu*, Q. 4:171) as well as God's servant (*'abd Allāh*). He has his symbol in the power to give life by raising the dead and breathing life into figures of clay (Q. 3:47; 5:110). The Qur'an rejects the crucifixion of Jesus but accepts the ascension in an earthly body: "They did not kill him nor crucify him, but it was made to seem so to them" (*shubbiha lahum*, Q. 4:157). His death on the cross as a sign of defeat is therefore denied in the Qur'an, but his being raised to life directly from the cross is granted (Q. 4:158). It is God Himself who says in the Qur'an, "O Jesus, I am going to take you and raise you to Me" (*mutawaffīka wa-rāfi'uka*, Q. 3:55). This position resembles the Gnostic Christian belief that only a counterfeit (simulacrum) of Jesus was crucified.

In the Qur'an, Muhammad stands in the line of the prophets, who are human beings with all their foibles and flaws and their sins and acts of disobedience before God. In the Qur'an Muhammad expressly states, "I am only a mortal like you" (Q. 18:110), who receives forgiveness for all the sins of his life, "may God forgive you your past sin and your sin that is to come" (Q. 48:2). Tradition explains that Muhammad was "erring" (Q. 93:7) when he toyed with a compromise of his monotheism by accepting three Meccan female deities as divine intercessors next to God, sacrificed to a heathen goddess before his call, and married Zayd's wife. The Qur'an portrays Muhammad as a human being as well as the carrier of a revelation and leader of his community. In post-Qur'anic

literature, he was put on a pedestal; ranked above all other prophets before him; and attributed the power of intercession on the Last Day, sitting next to God on the divine throne. In his ascension to heaven, he passes beyond the other prophets who each rule one of the seven spheres. His colloquy with God, associated with his ascension to heaven and linked with his encounter of God's presence at the Lote Tree of the boundary (Q. 53:13–18), becomes the symbol of his covenant through the divine institution of the five daily prayers. Through association with the famous light verse (Q. 24:35), Muhammad is perceived created as "light from light" and taking the place of Adam—the last prophet taking the place of the first—as he swears his oath of fealty to God on behalf of all of humanity. His message, reconfirming the religion of Abraham, surpasses it by reflecting most perfectly the light of the innate primal religion (*fiṭra*, Q. 30:30), enshrined in all human beings since the dawn of creation.

There is hardly any emphasis in the Qur'an on Muhammad as a political leader or lawgiver. The Qur'an, however, juxtaposes the background of the history of the prophets and their covenants with the oath of allegiance, a ceremony rooted in a pre-Islamic tribal institution. Obedience to God is linked with obedience to the Prophet, and obedience to the Prophet is made manifest through entrance into the community by an oath of allegiance. The formal gesture of the oath of allegiance (*bay'a*) was the ceremonial handclasp. Exchanged with the Prophet, it implied a pledge of fealty to God (Q. 48:10). The *bay'a* guaranteed the gift of God's protection and reward, mediated by the Prophet, in exchange for the loyalty of the person who joined Muhammad's community and surrendered to God. It possessed the character of a contractual agreement rooted in the ceremonial of pre-Islamic commercial transactions. In this sense, submission to God became symbolized by "grasping the firmest handle" (*al-'urwa al-wuthqā*, 2:256), an act that meant abandoning idolatry and doing good works. "Whoever surrenders his face to God and does good, has grasped the firmest handle" (Q. 31:22).

New converts to Islam enter into the community by swearing allegiance to the Prophet, who represents the covenant humanity made with God at the dawn of creation and the fashioning of Adam as father of the human race. Sworn by an individual entering the fold of Islam, this oath manifests two aims. It recognizes the authority of the person to whom it is given and expresses the adherence to the message of the person who represents and proclaims it. On the power of this oath, the Qur'an prescribes fighting to Muhammad's followers in Medina and demands that military commands be obeyed (Q. 22:39–40). When decisive action had to be taken during crucial moments of his cause, formal oaths of allegiance were made to Muhammad (Q. 48:10). Such vows of obedience became the norm when Muhammad's polity in Medina grew in numbers (Q. 9:11–12), although the Qur'an indicates that Muhammad did not always find it easy to enforce compliance (Q. 9:38–57; 9:81–106). A particular case is the oath of allegiance to the Prophet sworn by women, traditionally linked with the treaty of Hudaybiyya that includes as its conditions the core commands of the Decalogue (Q. 60:12). The treaty made between Muslims and pagans at the sacred mosque of Mecca, however, is a pact (*'ahd*) and hence does not imply an oath of allegiance (Q. 9:7).

Three particular terms in the Qur'an, *umma*, *khalīfa*, and jihad, have become highly valued fulcrums of Islamic political thought in Islamic history, although they do not appear in a prominent position in the Qur'an itself. The term *umma* (community), appearing about 60 times in the Qur'an, is a loanword from Hebrew and Aramaic that refers to groups of people who are included in the divine plan of salvation. In the view of the Qur'an, humanity consists of a plurality of communities, each to whom God sends messengers to guide and test them (Q. 6:42), but the messengers are usually attacked and accused of lying. When each *umma* is brought to judgment on the Last Day, God will call upon their respective messengers to give witness against those who did not follow their message (Q. 4:41). The Qur'an explains the plurality of the communities from the divine will. Originally, God created one *umma* (Q. 10:19), but humanity became disunited because of their malice and rancor. In the Meccan suras, the Qur'an envisages the Arabs of Mecca as forming an *umma*; in the Medinan suras a new "community surrendering to God" (*umma muslima*, Q 2:213) is founded on a religious basis that bids to honor and forbids dishonor (Q. 3:104, 110). The famous statement of the Prophet, "My community (*umma*) will never agree upon an error," is a post-Qur'anic tradition. Only twice does the Qur'an mention the related term, "the party of God" (*ḥizb Allāh*, 5:56; 48:22), and the term *jamā'a*, later so prominent and used to denote the whole body of the believers as a unified "community," does not appear in the Qur'an at all. The Qur'anic term, *milla* (religious community), an Aramaic or Hebrew loanword, appears 15 times in the Qur'an and 8 times as "Abraham's religion," in which sense it is applied to Muhammad's community. As such, however, it means "religion" and does not imply the aspect of solidarity and unity that is so predominant in Islamic political thought.

Another Qur'anic term that has only tenuous Qur'anic moorings with regard to political authority is the notion of *khalīfa*, which appears only twice in the singular in the Qur'an and seven times in the plural. With reference to Adam, the Qur'an says, "I am setting a viceroy in the Earth" (Q. 2:30), and with reference to David, the Qur'an says, "We have appointed you a viceroy in the Earth" (Q. 38:26). The Qur'anic reference to Adam represents a divine address to the angels who are being told by God that Adam, and with him the human race, will be their "successor" (*khalīfa*) inhabiting the Earth. The passage about David as "successor" has a political and juridical meaning in that David is commissioned by God to judge justly between people. The notion itself does not imply the idea of the caliph, conceived as representative of God's messenger or even as shadow of God on Earth, although in later political theories the term took on a politically charged meaning and, in Sunni interpretation, became the key term for the caliph as head of the Muslim polity, called somewhat ineptly the "vicar of God's messenger" (*khalīfat rasūl Allāh*). For their idea of supreme leadership, the Shi'is have erected impressive theological

theories around the term "imam" (leader), which appears in the Qur'an seven times in the singular and five times in the plural. It refers to Abraham as "a leader for the people" (Q. 2:124); to the Book of Moses as "a model" (Q. 11:17; 46:12); to the prophets raised from the progeny of Adam, who will give witness about the conduct of their communities on the Day of Judgment (Q. 17:71); to pious Muslims as leaders in faith; and to both righteous and unjust leaders. Both Sunnism and Shi'ism employed the term *imāma* (leadership, imamate) for their theological discourse on leadership and authority.

Similarly, in the Qur'an, jihad, a highly prominent slogan of Islamic political thought, means "struggle" or "striving," which, coupled with the notion of fighting "in the path of God" (*fī sabīl Allāh*, Q 2:190; cf. 9:24; 60:1), gained its predominantly political meaning of "warfare" through post-Qur'anic interpretation. As used in the Qur'an (the verbal noun, *jihād*, occurs but four times in the Qur'an: 9:24; 22:78; 25:52; 60:1), only a small portion of the term's semantic range can be linked with warfare. On the contrary, the majority of the relevant passages point to an origin in the pre-Islamic tribal perception that one must demonstrate oneself deserving of the deity's reward through hardship, pilgrimage, poverty, and perseverance in trials and tribulations. Rather, the Qur'an expresses warfare mainly by employing a semantic field that expresses the order to fight and slay the infidels (*qitāl*), as exemplified in Qur'an 9:1–14. There is no doubt that the Prophet encouraged his followers to fight and proclaimed fighting as a divine command, and Qur'an 22:40 may be the first Medinan verse that deals with fighting the unbelievers. Many other verses exhort the believers to fight "with their possessions and their selves." Those who "are slain or die in the path of God" (Q. 3:157–58) are promised eternal reward—they will be "living with their Lord" and rejoicing "in the bounty that God has given them" (Q. 3:169–70), while those who are not willing to fight are threatened with hellfire (Q. 9:81). Exhortations to fight and participate in warfare can be found many times in the Qur'an (e.g., Q. 4:84; 8:65), but it was not the term "jihad" that was their standard Qur'anic expression.

There is no one coherent doctrine of warfare in the Qur'an, and exegetes found it difficult to reconcile ambiguous and contradictory verses given both the inconsistent Qur'anic terminology on warfare and Muhammad's increasingly hostile relations with the Meccans that developed into open warfare after his emigration to Medina. Muslim exegesis tried to resolve these ambiguities and contradictions through the use of certain methodological techniques, particularly theories of abrogation and specification that regarded Qur'an 9:5 and 9:29 as ultimately superseding earlier verses. The basis for these theories may be found in the Qur'an itself in a passage (Q. 4:76–77) that implies an inner-Qur'anic evolution with regard to warfare. When relevant Qur'anic verses are read chronologically, one may construct four stages in the evolution of Qur'anic exhortations to warfare. Before his emigration to Medina, Muhammad was instructed by God to pardon the unbelievers and to desist from engagement in warfare. After the hijra, however, his followers were given permission to retaliate for injustices they had suffered from the Meccans (Q. 22:39–40). As the altercations with the Meccans increased, they were exhorted to fight against unbelievers as long as they observed certain conditions. Then they were given the divine command to rescind all treatises with the unbelievers and fight them unconditionally (Q. 9:1–4). Finally, God's ultimate and unconditional command to engage in warfare was given expression in the "sword verse" (Q. 9:5) with regard to the unbelievers and the "poll tax verse" (Q. 9:29) with regard to "the People of the Book." A group of Qur'anic verses (Q. 2:216; 4:71; 9:38–41; 9:120–22) provide the basis for the legal definition of jihad as a collective duty (*farḍ kifāya*) and not an individual obligation (*farḍ 'ayn*) that became the normative principle elaborated by the scholars of Islamic law.

The Qur'an not only exhorts to warfare but also stipulates a series of specific conditions that served as the basis for later Islamic thought on the purpose of warfare and the definition of a just war. A good number of Qur'anic verses counsel patience and forbearance with respect to the unbelievers, warn Muslims to avoid fighting, recommend forgiveness and generosity, and advise arguing with opponents in a peaceful manner, while other verses warn unbelievers of God's vengeance (Q. 3:19). Warfare against idolaters who are to be converted to Islam is differentiated from fighting against the People of the Book—whether they are Jews, Sabians (i.e., Manicheans or Mandeans), or Christians (Q. 2:62; 5:69,82)—who are identified as enjoying a measure of tolerance. The famous and oft-quoted verse, "There is no compulsion in religion" (*lā ikrāha fī al-dīn*, Q. 2:256), however, does not proclaim the principle of tolerance as the Qur'anic ideal—it simply states that compelling acceptance of religion must prove a futile exercise in the face of obstinacy. As purposes for warfare other than subjection and nominal conversion, the Qur'an mentions revenge for violation of treaties and retaliation for attacks of adversaries as well as self-defense and the defense of weak members of the community. Exemption from warfare is granted to the physically handicapped (Q. 4:17). Other verses deal with the treatment of prisoners and safe conduct. Qur'an 8:67 exhorts the Prophet not to take prisoners—a norm judged to be abrogated by Qur'an 47:4, which accepts ransom for prisoners or offers outright pardon. Other very specific stipulations would be added in Islamic tradition, such as the interdiction against killing enemy noncombatants (women, children, and the elderly); mutilating bodies; harming infrastructure such as buildings and fruit trees; and embezzling spoils. The idea of "holy war," however, is not present in the Qur'an at all, although warfare may be considered sacred to a certain extent because it is commanded and rewarded by God under certain conditions.

The Legacy of the Qur'an

Throughout its entire text, the Qur'an intertwines two basic traditions, the pre-Islamic tribal and the Judeo-Christian, through loanwords drawn from Aramaic, Syriac, or Hebrew and assimilated by the Arabic of the Qur'an. This power of association has been noted earlier in the typological history of messengers and prophets that include central biblical figures next to leaders and

heroes of pre-Islamic Arabian lore. Similarly, the celestial messengers among the angels show an association with the spirits and demons (*jinn*) of tribal Arabia, as can be seen in the figure of the devil that merges Shaytan with Iblis (i.e., *diabolos*), the fallen angel. The intertwining of these traditions can also be seen in some of the central rituals of the Qur'an, the "pillars of religion," as for instance the daily ritual prayer, the obligation of almsgiving, the month of fasting, and the yearly pilgrimage. Ritual prayer (salat) combines recitation of scripture and liturgical worship at precise times of the day with gestures of submission offered in the direction of the sanctuary of the Ka'ba. The twin institution of almsgiving (zakat) links the practice of benevolence and charitable righteousness toward the poor and needy with taxes levied on property, crops, and merchandise, and it is collected for the necessities of warfare and from the dues paid by tribes adopting Islam. The ritual obligation of fasting (*ṣawm*) assimilates aspects of monastic asceticism and abstinence with the Arab month of Ramadan, established in the tradition of sacred months during which bloodshed was prohibited in pre-Islamic tribal Arabia. The Muslim pilgrimage (hajj) merges tribal festival traditions at the Meccan sanctuary and on the hill of 'Arafat with the story of Abraham and his sacrifice.

At the death of Muhammad, Abu Bakr (d. 634), the first caliph and Muhammad's direct successor, is said to have coined the slogan "Whosoever has worshiped Muhammad—Muhammad is dead. Whosoever has worshiped God—God lives and will not die." His message was that although Muhammad had died, God's word would endure. No new prophet was required to come and renew his message.

What counted throughout history was the membership in the community based on the Qur'an and the memory of the Prophet's sayings and actions, as demonstrated by two early monuments of Islam. The construction of the Dome of the Rock in Jerusalem in 692 was established as a sign of triumph over the power of the Byzantine Empire, facing the ruins of the Christian landmark, the Church of the Sepulchre, on the opposite hill of the city. Inscribed on the Dome's walls were words taken from sura 112, the Qur'anic manifesto aiming at Christianity: "Say, He is God, One. God, the Impenetrable, who has not begotten, and has not been begotten, and equal to Him is not any one." The Umayyad Mosque of Damascus, standing in the place of the destroyed church of John the Baptist, would bear the inscription of the year 706, "Our Lord is God alone, our religion is Islam and our Prophet is Muhammad," where the person of the Prophet seems to overshadow his message, the Qur'an. Although the Prophet proclaimed the Qur'an, Islam became supremely a religion of the book. The word of the Qur'an has a much greater weight in Islam than the New Testament does in Christianity, for in Islam the dogma of *incarnatio*, the Word become flesh, is transformed into the belief of *inlibratino*, the Word become book. Jesus did not manifest the urge to compose a book; Mani (216–76), the founder of Manicheanism, had done so, and Muhammad would proclaim the final holy book. The Qur'an was not "good news" proclaimed by a group of narrators but instead God's own speech, warning and reminding humanity of God's presence in his word.

The Qur'an came into being at a time of a paradigm shift in human history when myth was overtaken by history, and when, in Arabia, a book of parchment overpowered graffiti on the rocks. Breaking into the bright light of history from the dark ages of the Arab past, the Arabic language of the Qur'an became the idiom of a newly arrived "third world," pushing a wedge between the Greco-Roman and Indo-Persian culture zones. When the Qur'an entered the scene of world history, Judaism and Christianity read their respective Bibles in translations, rather than in the original idioms of Moses or Jesus. The Arabic Qur'an, however, has remained steady and fixed until the present in the idiom of its messenger and the language of the listeners to whom it had been addressed. Although the Qur'an was not a wholly coherent book, with its evidence of abrogation, and had weaknesses of repetition, it became understood as eternal by virtue of being the divine speech. It came to be regarded as the normative scripture of Islam, possessing inimitability (*i'jāz*) and rhetorical superiority even if linguistic elegance was granted to Arabic poetry.

As scripture the Qur'an was identical with the word of God recorded since eternity and, in the view of some, known in its entirety by Muhammad even before he was called to come forth as a prophet. By reproducing the word of God in this world, prophecy separated it from God as his revelation. As text it recorded the trace (*rasm*) that divine speech left in this world through its letters and consonants, distinguished by diacritical marks and carrying vowel signs. As divine speech it was considered the actual inner speech of God, eternal in nature and revealed from on high as sounds that were God's own voice (*ṣawt*) and his own pronunciation (*lafẓ*). God's speech, which had been heard in different historical epochs by other prophets, now was spoken forth by Muhammad, either directly as God's mouthpiece in the ecstatic utterances of the early Meccan period or mediated by Gabriel, the angel of revelation who "brought it down upon your heart" (Q. 2:97), in the extended passages of the Medinan period of its proclamation. The stage was thus set for the "Trial" (*miḥna*, 833–48), the great theopolitical struggle about the nature of the Qur'an defined by the antagonists as centering on the issue of the "created" versus "uncreated" nature of the word of God, a divisive contention Muhammad himself had neither anticipated nor offered guidance in either direction.

See also exegesis; Muhammad (570–632)

Further Reading

R. Bell, *The Qur'ān*, 2 vols., 1937–39; Idem, *A Commentary on the Qur'an*, 1991; J. Burton, *The Collection of the Qur'ān*, 1977; M. Cook, *The Koran: A Very Short Introduction*, 2000; J. Jeffery, *The Qur'an as Scripture*, 1952; J. D. McAuliffe, *The Cambridge Companion to the Qur'ān*, 2006; A. Neuwirth, *Der Koran als Text der Spätantike: Ein europäischer Zugang*, 2010; R. Paret, *Der Koran: Kommentar und Konkordanz*, 1977; F. Rahman, *Major Themes of the Qur'an*, 1980; N. Robinson, *Discovering the Qur'an*, 1996;

J. Wansbrough, *Quranic Studies*, 1977; W. M. Watt, *Introduction to the Qur'an*, 1970; S. Wild, *The Qur'an as Text*, 1996.

GERHARD BOWERING

Quraysh

Quraysh is the name of the tribe in Mecca to which the Prophet Muhammad belonged. (The adjectival form is "Qurashi," though modern authors often use "Qurayshi.") Quraysh were genealogically related to the Kinana, whose pedigree went back to the Mudar, a branch of the north Arabian tribes. One of their pre-Islamic ancestors, Qusayy b. Kilab, is said to have united them five generations before Muhammad and to have established their supremacy in Mecca, securing the guardianship of its shrine, the Ka'ba, for them. Quraysh and some other tribes were grouped together under the term *hums*, said to refer to their observance of certain religious taboos; tribes not observing these taboos were termed *hilla*. After Qusayy's death, conflict reportedly broke out between his sons over the sacred offices of the Ka'ba, resulting in the formation of two opposed alliances: the Ahlaf around 'Abd al-Dar and the Mutayyabun around 'Abd Manaf. The tradition wavers between exalting Quraysh as the ancestors of Muhammad and denigrating them as infidels who fought against him, with the result that they are presented both as proto-Muslims who kept monotheism alive when the rest of Arabia was sunk in polytheism and as rank pagans who put the deity Hubal and a plethora of other idols in and around the Ka'ba. The name "Quraysh" occurs only once in the Qur'an, in the short sura 106, which mentions their "winter and summer journeys" (traditionally interpreted as trading journeys) and alludes to a hunger and a fear from which God has freed them. The name also appears in the so-called Constitution of Medina, which was drawn up in Medina a few months after Muhammad's hijra (emigration). Here it stands not only for those who still resisted him as unbelievers but also for the Muhajirun.

The tradition presents Quraysh as making a living as traders in pre-Islamic times. The trade was founded by Hashim, Muhammad's great-grandfather, who secured permission to trade in Syria from the Byzantine emperor (more probably a local governor) and negotiated agreements with the tribes on the way. They supplied many of the goods, described as leather, hides, and other pastoralist products, as well as perfume. In addition to Syria, Qurashi traders are said to have been active in Yemen, Iraq, Ethiopia, and Egypt. They played a leading role in the rise of Islam, both as supporters and as enemies of Muhammad, and after his death they took over the leadership of the community he had founded. All the caliphs down to the Mongol conquest of Baghdad in 1258 were drawn from Quraysh, in conformity with an expectation that appears to have been established early and that was soon formulated as a legal requirement. The requirement was disputed by the Kharijis and some groups of south Arabian (Yemeni) descent. Supporters of the doctrine affirmed the special status of Quraysh in traditions from the Prophet and his Companions, which extolled their virtues and asserted that "the imams are of Quraysh." In other traditions Quraysh appear as true heirs of Abraham and Ishmael and as divinely chosen from among the rest of the Arabs. The traditions also reflect conflicts within Quraysh over the issue of Muhammad's successor and the right to the caliphate. Sunni traditions extol the virtues of Abu Bakr and 'Umar b. al-Khattab, while Shi'i hadith disparage them in favor of 'Ali b. Abi Talib. The rise of the Abbasids is reflected in traditions that denigrate the ancestor of the Umayyads, Umayya b. 'Abd Shams b. 'Abd Manaf, stressing his inferiority to Hashim.

Though the rule that the caliph must be of Quraysh was upheld even after the Abbasids had been reduced to puppet rulers in Egypt, many jurists from the 11th century onward were willing to consider the possibility of a non-Qurashi caliph, and the Zaydi Maqbili (d. 1696) explicitly ruled that choosing a Qurashi was merely a custom, not a legal requirement. In practice the caliphal title had by then been adopted by rulers who were not even Arabs, let alone Qurashis (notably the Seljuqs and the Ottomans). Later, Javanese, Indian, and African rulers were also to style themselves caliphs. Today, "Qureshi" is a common surname, especially in Pakistan, and numerous families all over the Muslim world, including the Hashimites to whom the king of Jordan belongs, claim descent from 'Ali and the Prophet's daughter Fatima, but as a tribe Quraysh have disappeared. That the caliph need not be a Qurashi was endorsed by the Egyptian legal scholar Abu Zahra in 1976.

See also caliph, caliphate; genealogy; tribalism

Further Reading

P. Crone, *Medieval Islamic Political Thought*, 2004; Eadem, "Quraysh and the Roman Army: Making Sense of the Meccan Leather Trade," *Bulletin of the School of Oriental and African Studies* 70 (2007); M. J. Kister, "Mecca and Tamīm," *Journal of the Economic and Social History of the Orient* 8 (1965); Michael Lecker,*The "Constitution of Medina": Muḥammad's First Legal Document*, 2004; Wilferd Madelung, *The Succession to Muḥammad: A Study of the Early Caliphate*, 1997; Uri Rubin, *Between Bible and Qur'ān: The Children of Israel and the Islamic Self-Image*, 1999.

PATRICIA CRONE

R

racism

Racism, or the belief that race is a primary determinant of human abilities and that racial differences produce an inherent superiority of a particular race over others, is foreign to Islam as a proselytizing religion that spread to all corners of the world with an essentially egalitarian and meritocratic spirit: "We have created you all out of a male and a female, and have made you into nations and tribes, so that you might come to know one another. Verily, the noblest of you in the sight of God is the one who is most deeply conscious of Him" (Q. 49:13).

Historically, however, there is ample evidence of prejudices directed by Muslims against particular groups of people, such as in the environmental explanations of human traits in the work of Sa'id al-Andalusi, who asserted in 1068 with regard to sub-Saharan Africans that "because the sun remains close to their heads for long periods, their air and their climate have become hot: they are of hot temperament and fiery behavior. Their color turned black, and their hair turned kinky. As a result, they lost the value of patience and firmness of perception. They were overcome by foolishness and ignorance. These are the people of Sudan who inhabited the far reaches of Ethiopia, Nubia, the Zanj, and others."

Another way of justifying prejudices directed against Africans was by reference to the "curse of Ham." In the Book of Genesis (9:20–27), Noah gets drunk one day after the flood and falls asleep naked in his tent. Ham, the son of Noah and father of Canaan, sees his father naked and tells his two brothers outside. Shem and Japheth take a cloak, lay it on their shoulders, walk backward, making sure that they would not see Noah naked, and cover his body. When Noah wakes up and learns what Ham has done to him, he says, "Cursed be Canaan, a slave of slaves shall he be to his brothers." This curse, which is apparently a product of the Hebrews' conquest of the "land of Canaan" around 1200 BCE and the subsequent enslavement of the Canaanites, evolved into new forms as Middle Eastern societies started to use African slaves. By the sixth century, both Christian and Jewish traditions in the Middle East had added blackness to Noah's curse. In the Muslim adaptation of the story, the curse fell on Ham, Canaan's father, who was regarded as the ancestor of all Africans in Muslim sources. Blackness was added to servitude in some Islamic versions of the story as well.

A vocal response to these environmental and Biblico-exegetical attempts to justify racial prejudices came from, among others, an African-Ottoman jurist Mullah 'Ali (d. 1622–23). According to 'Ali, the diversity of human skin colors is not a matter of accident; thus it is neither environmental nor punishment for a deed but stems rather from the beginning of the creation: "Among [other] signs of [God] is the creation of the heavens and the Earth, and the variety of your languages and of your colors" (Q. 30:22). Blackness was inherent in the essence of Adam, not unlike the blackness that is inherent in white sugar, as suggested by the Persian Sufi Najm al-Din Razi (d. 1256): "From the first state of raw sugar to that of treacle, lucency and whiteness gradually decrease until only darkness and blackness remain. He who is unaware of the art of the sugar merchant will not know that he obtains these several and different products from the same sugar; he will deny the fact and say that black treacle could never have emerged from the white, translucent sugar. He will not know that blackness and darkness were inherent in the particle of the sugar."

While these discussions suggest the existence of racial prejudices and an intellectual discourse both in support of and in opposition to them, it is much harder to decide whether it was race and racism—as contemporary readers understand them—that were at stake. Although there are studies that attempt to make a case for an ancient origin for racism (such as Benjamin Isaac's *The Invention of Racism in Classical Antiquity*), there is a major qualitative difference between ethnocentrism and xenophobia, which have existed in many societies since ancient times, on the one hand, and modern racism, which crystallized in the "scientific racism" of physical anthropology in the late 19th century, on the other.

Broadly speaking, while there is overwhelming evidence for the existence of racial prejudices in the medieval and early modern Islamic world, the continuing access of Africans to major leadership roles in what one would today call "majority white" Muslim societies (as in the case of the aforementioned Mullah 'Ali, who became chief justice of the European provinces of the Ottoman Empire in 1621–22) suggests that race was not understood as a rigid biological category that would disqualify one from equal membership in society.

See also East Africa; genealogy; North Africa; Ottomans (1299–1924); slavery; South Africa

Further Reading

Sa'id al-Andalusi, *Science in the Medieval World: Book of the Categories of Nations*, edited and translated by Sema'an I. Salem and Alok Kumar, 1991; Bernard Lewis, *Race and Slavery in the Middle East: An Historical Enquiry*, 1990; 'Abd Allah ibn Muhammad Najm al-Din Razi, *Path of God's Bondsmen from Origin to Return*,

translated by Hamid Algar, 1982; Baki Tezcan, "Dispelling the Darkness: The Politics of 'Race' in the Early Seventeenth Century Ottoman Empire in the Light of the Life and Work of Mullah Ali," in *Identity and Identity Formation in the Ottoman World: A Volume of Essays in Honor of Norman Itzkowitz*, edited by Baki Tezcan and Karl K. Barbir, 2007.

BAKI TEZCAN

Rahman, Fazlur (1919–88)

Fazlur Rahman was one of the 20th century's foremost Muslim intellectuals and scholars whose ideas on modern Islamic thought reached a global audience of elites through his prolific and courageous writings. He was born on September 21, 1919, to the Malik family in the Hazara district of British India, now part of Pakistan. On his death on July 26, 1988, in Chicago, Fazlur Rahman was described by Wilfred Cantwell Smith, the doyen of western Islamicists with strong ties to South Asia, as "a person of integrity; a religious man with a brilliant mind using it as part of his religion. He was a moral person; a serious Muslim motivated by deep concern for his culture and his people."

Fazlur Rahman's father, Mawlana Shihab al-Din, had orthodox leanings and was associated with the anticolonial scholar-activist Mawlana Mahmud al-Hasan (d. 1920), better known as "Shaykh al-Hind." Mawlana Mahmudul Hasan was affiliated with the Deoband madrasa now located in India. The young Fazlur Rahman studied the traditional Muslim scholastic texts that were featured in the traditional Nizami curriculum with his father, including law (*fiqh*), dialectical theology (*kalām*), prophetic traditions (hadith), Qur'an exegesis (*tafsīr*), logic (*manṭiq*), and philosophy (*falsafa*). He then attended Punjab University in Lahore, where he received a BA and an MA in Arabic. In 1946, he went to Oxford to work with Professor Simon van den Bergh. His dissertation was a translation, critical edition, and commentary on a section of Ibn Sina's work on psychology, *Kitab al-Najat* (Book of salvation). In 1950 Fazlur Rahman began teaching Persian and Islamic philosophy at Durham University, and in 1958 he left England to teach at the Institute of Islamic Studies at McGill University in Montreal.

Three years later, Fazlur Rahman embarked on an ambitious project. Pakistan under General Ayyub Khan had renewed its efforts at state formation with plans to revive the national spirit with political and legal reforms. Fazlur Rahman was asked to lead the project. At the newly formed Central Institute of Islamic Research, he first became a visiting professor and later director over a seven-year period, from 1961 to 1968. The policy side of the job meant that Fazlur Rahman's views were often open to public scrutiny, and his intellectual labor in the service of social reform was thus drawn into the messy political fray of Pakistan in the 1960s. Political parties and religious groups opposed to Ayyub Khan targeted Fazlur Rahman's scholarly views in order to scuttle the proposed social and cultural reforms. Some of the critical legal and religious issues he attempted to redress involved the status of interest on deposits in banks, zakat (the compulsory alms tax), the mechanical slaughter of animals, family law, and family planning. But his views on the authority of prophetic reports (hadith) and prophetic practice (sunna) and his reflections on the nature of revelation drew the greatest ire. After a turbulent period that adversely affected his health and his leadership role at the Central Institute for Islamic Research and the Advisory Council for Islamic Ideology, Fazlur Rahman resigned. After a short spell as visiting professor at the University of California, Los Angeles, he was appointed in 1969 as professor of Islamic thought at the University of Chicago, where he stayed until his death, having been named as of 1986 the Harold H. Swift Distinguished Service Professor.

Fazlur Rahman's intellectual legacy is captured in his prolific writings ranging from philosophy to contemporary questions in Islamic thought such as human rights, women's rights, education, religion and politics, law and ethics, medicine, and the role of history and hermeneutics, all of which culminated in his efforts to make the Qur'an the centerpiece of a Muslim interpretative framework. Continuing the modernist tradition of Muhammad 'Abduh (d. 1905) of Egypt and the poet-philosopher of prepartition India, Muhammad Iqbal (d. 1938) was in his view a worthwhile cause. In the Western academy, especially in North America, Turkey, Indonesia, and of late in parts of the Arabic-speaking world, his views and interpretations have become the subject of scholarly debate and are used for the purposes of social reform.

See also modernism; Pakistan; revival and reform

Further Reading

Frederick Mathewson Denny, "Fazlur Rahman: Muslim Intellectual," *Muslim World* 79, no. 2 (1989); Ebrahim Moosa, "Introduction," in *Revival and Reform in Islam: A Study of Islamic Fundamentalism*, edited by Ebrahim Moosa, 2000.

EBRAHIM MOOSA

al-Razi, Fakhr al-Din (1149–1209)

A leading proponent of the late Ash'ari theological school that developed in Iran and Central Asia in the 12th through 16th centuries, Muhammad b. 'Umar Fakhr al-Din al-Razi is known primarily for his contributions to Sunni theology and Qur'anic exegesis, on which he wrote prolifically, in addition to writing on jurisprudence, philosophy, medicine, and astrology. He was born in Rayy, Iran, and after studying in Maragha he spent the remainder of his life debating with intellectuals of various types throughout Central Asia. He received patronage from both the Khwarazmshahs and the Ghurids, dynasties that were hostile to one another.

Although Razi did not compose a work on rulership or governance, he did address various political issues in his works on theology, philosophy, and Qur'an commentary. In so doing, he made significant contributions to the development of Islamic political thought. His views in this area were influenced by those of the Mu'tazilis as well as of the philosopher Ibn Sina.

The central concept of Razi's political thought is prophecy. Following the basic principles of Muslim theology, he held that prophets are human beings through whom God communicates with humankind. Among these prophets are messengers who bring new versions of God's laws, and thus new religions. Razi wrote that the prophets who communicate God's laws should be invested with political authority. He also argued that prophets are infallible, although he admitted that they could commit major sins before, and unintentional sins after, their prophetic missions.

Razi's political theory, which he discussed under the rubric of "practical science," was shaped by the philosophical tradition in Islam. In accordance with Ibn Sina's teaching on prophecy, he held that prophets are a sociopolitical necessity, since only prophets are capable of introducing laws that organize human life. Also following Ibn Sina, he defined prophecy as a perfection of the human soul. According to this teaching, a prophetic soul is one that has developed its imaginative and intellective faculties such that it may receive intelligible forms from the higher heavenly souls. It is the prophet's intellectual perfection that places him in a position to legislate and direct the Muslim community.

On the issue of the leadership of the Muslim community and the political concept of the imamate, topics that he addressed in his *Compendium* and *Book of Forty Questions*, Razi polemicized against the postulates of Twelver Shi'i theologians. These theologians have argued that the imamate is a logical consequence of God's benevolence or grace, and it is incumbent upon God by virtue of his benevolence to invest mankind with an imam, just as it is incumbent upon God to send prophets to humankind. Following his Ash'ari colleagues as well as many Mu'tazili scholars, Razi held that the imamate is necessary only as a matter of tradition and scripture. Also in opposition to Twelver Shi'i ideas, Razi held that it is incumbent upon the intellectuals of the Muslim community, not upon God, to designate an imam, by way of election.

Razi addressed the issue of the moral status of jihad against non-Muslims in his commentary on the Qur'an. In his milieu, many saw a tension between supporting jihad against non-Muslims and maintaining the Qur'anic precept that "there is no compulsion in religion" (2:256). The great majority of scholars interpreted this verse to mean that, while compulsion in religion was valid at the political level, it was inappropriate and futile to attempt to compel inner conviction. Under the influence of the Mu'tazilis, Razi interpreted the verse to mean that God intends that individuals have choice in religious belief. He argued that this world is an abode of trial or testing and that compulsion in religion at the level of conviction would nullify this idea. The use of compulsion in conversion, he argued, is incompatible with the moral responsibility that has been granted by God to human beings in this world.

See also Ash'aris; caliph, caliphate; Central Asia; exegesis; Ghurids (1009–1215); Ibn Sina, Abu 'Ali (980–1037); imamate; jihad; jurisprudence; Mu'tazilis; philosophy; Shi'ism; theology

Further Reading

Patricia Crone, *God's Rule: Government and Islam*, 2004; Fathalla Kholeif, *A Study on Fakhr al-Din al-Razi and His Controversies in Transoxiana*, 1966; Ann Lambton, *State and Government in Medieval Islam*, 1981.

TARIQ JAFFER

rebellion

Rebellion is action undertaken by a group aiming to replace the government in a state or to secede from the state to form a new one. Direct references to rebellion are not found in the Qur'an, but there are numerous references to hypocrites (*munāfiqūn*) in Medina who publicly accepted Islam while continuing to oppose Muhammad, more through subversion than in open revolt. The Qur'an (9:107) alludes to a "mosque of dissension" (*masjid al-ḍirār*) erected on the outskirts of Medina "by way of mischief and infidelity—to disunite the believers." This building was demolished on Muhammad's orders before the plotters' schemes could materialize. Rebellions marked the caliphates of Abu Bakr, 'Uthman b. 'Affan, and 'Ali b. Abi Talib. The Umayyad dynasty lasted barely 90 years before it was overthrown by an Abbasid revolt, and the Abbasids themselves had faced numerous rebellions already by the late ninth century.

Rebellion was, therefore, a timely and troubling issue for classical political and legal theorists. With the goal of preventing civil strife (*fitna*) and disorder or corruption (*fasād*), the theorists banned nearly all challenges to the established ruler. Qur'an 4:59, which reads, "Obey God and obey the Messenger and those in authority among you," along with numerous hadith reports, was marshaled by scholars to prohibit revolt against the caliph or the sultan, regardless of how he had come to power. Disobedience to a ruler's commands was permitted only when the ruler contravened Islamic law in accordance with the hadith that states, "No obedience to the created in opposition to the Creator." An errant ruler should be admonished, counseled, and suffered patiently by his subjects rather than challenged by force. Only in extreme circumstances, such as when a ruler abandoned Islamic law altogether or committed apostasy, should the Muslim subjects overthrow him. Ibn Taymiyya (d. 1328), for example, declared jihad obligatory against the Mongol conquerors of the Abbasid Empire, who, despite their conversion to Islam, ruled by the Yasa, the Mongol tribal law, rather than the shari'a. He castigated rebellion, however, against Muslim rulers over mainly political grievances.

Classical sources generally treat rebellion (*baghy*) as a type of criminal activity along with apostasy (*ridda*) and brigandage

(*ḥirāba*), yet they devote considerable attention to differentiating the way rebels are to be treated compared to apostates, highway robbers, or pirates. People were deemed rebels if they formally withdrew from the Muslim community (*khurūj*) by disavowing allegiance to the ruler, provided a reasonable religious pretext for their disobedience (*ta'wīl*), and constituted a group with demonstrated power to challenge the state (*shawka*). If they met these criteria, they were subject to treatment under the laws governing the suppression of rebels (*aḥkām al-bughāh*). Because these laws were based largely on precedents set by 'Ali in dealing with his enemies, especially the Kharijis, there was general agreement between Sunni and Shi'i legal schools on these matters. As Mawardi writes in *al-Ahkam al-Sultaniyya* (The ordinances of government), fighting rebels differs from fighting infidels, apostates, and brigands in eight ways: the intent is to deter rather than kill rebels; they should not be pursued when they are retreating; their injured may not be killed; captured rebels may not be killed; their property may not be seized and their women and children may not be enslaved; the aid of *dhimmīs* (protected communities) cannot be sought in fighting rebels; the Muslim commander may not give them assurances of an indefinite truce or conclude a peace treaty in return for monetary payment; and their homes and farms may not be despoiled. Clearly, the goal of these strictures was to rehabilitate rebels back into the body politic as quickly and completely as possible.

The political quietism proposed in the classical theory was always in tension with more popular themes of renewal (*tajdīd*) and reform (*iṣlāḥ*), which led periodically to violent movements aimed not only at overthrowing corrupt rulers but also at purifying society. One such insurrection was the Wahhabi revolt in 19th-century Arabia that in many ways laid the intellectual basis for the Muslim revivalist movements of the 20th century. To the Wahhabi creed of purging Islam of internal, heretical innovations (*bid'a*), 20th-century activists added the goal of thwarting Western political and cultural domination of Muslim countries. Thus modern writers espouse not so much rebellion but revolution, in the sense of a thoroughgoing sociopolitical change in norms and institutions.

Sayyid Qutb, in his influential essay *Ma'alim fi al-Tariq* (Milestones), never openly declares jihad against the Egyptian or any other Muslim government, but his argument that Muslim societies are in a state of *jāhiliyya* (ignorance) akin to that against which the Prophet fought has obvious revolutionary implications. 'Abd al-Salam Faraj, the author of *al-Farida al-Gha'iba* (The absent duty), the manifesto of Anwar Sadat's assassins, took Qutb's views to their logical conclusion. Citing Ibn Taymiyya, Faraj declared the Egyptian government to be an apostate regime; thus rebellion against it was a religious obligation. In responding to this document, the 'ulama' (religious scholars) of Azhar University denounced Faraj's justification of tyrannicide by resorting to classical arguments that so long as a ruler was a Muslim and did not interfere with the performance of Islamic obligations in the country, rising up against him was prohibited.

A number of Shi'i theorists also figure prominently in contemporary debates on the legitimacy of rebellion. For centuries, Shi'i 'ulama' generally espoused dissimulation (*taqiyya*) and compliance with political authorities, tracing this policy back to the views of the sixth imam, Ja'far al-Sadiq. The views of Ayatollah Khomeini fundamentally challenged this legacy. Beginning in the 1940s with criticism of the two Pahlavi shahs, Khomeini moved to open defiance and by the late 1960s called for the regime to be overthrown. In *Hukumat-i Islami* (Islamic government), published in 1970, Khomeini outlines his theory of *wilāyat al-faqīh* (guardianship of the jurist). At the end of the treatise, he calls for tyrannical rulers (*ṭāghūt*) to be overthrown through civil disobedience and for the creation of parallel Islamic institutions. Similarly, the most prominent lay intellectual of the revolution, 'Ali Shari'ati, focused on mobilizing a grassroots movement led by the youths. Shari'ati criticized what he labeled "Safavi Shi'ism," after the Safavid dynasty, characterizing it as an ideology of quietism and political repression. True Shi'ism, Shari'ati argued, was "'Alavi Shi'ism," after 'Ali b. Abi Talib: a dynamic, politically active faith that required action to implement a just Islamic order.

See also coup d'état; dissent, opposition, resistance; quietism and activism

Further Reading

Khaled M. Abou El Fadl, *Rebellion and Violence in Islamic Law*, 2001; J.J.G. Jansen, *The Neglected Duty: The Creed of Sadat's Assassins*, 1986; Ruhallah Khomeini, *Islam and Revolution: Writings and Declarations of Imam Khomeini*, translated by Hamid Algar, 1981; J. L. Kraemer, "Apostates, Rebels and Brigands," *Israel Oriental Studies* 10 (1980); Fazlur Rahman, "The Law of Rebellion in Islam," in *Islam in the Modern World*, edited by Jill Raitt, 1983.

SOHAIL H. HASHMI

representation

As a concept in political analysis, "representation" can refer to a variety of forms of decisions, judgments, and actions made on behalf of a larger group of persons by a smaller group (including a group of one). For the term "representation" to be appropriate, there must be some sense not only that the decisions of the smaller group are binding on the larger group (a relationship better expressed by the idea of "authority") but also that the smaller group is making decisions for the larger group by appointment or designation, or in the best interests of the larger group. Nonetheless, representation and authority are clearly companion concepts as long as the decisions of representatives are enforced on the larger population as legitimate, binding rules.

In classical Sunni political thought, perhaps the predominant emphasis was on communal unity (*ahl al-sunna wa-l-jamā'a*) and

the avoidance of the twin evils of sectarianism and civil strife. This pragmatic conception of political life is consistent with a willingness to accommodate a great many departures from the ideal, as long as social life is preserved and no heterodox doctrine is imposed on the populace. Here, the only conception of legitimacy or representation in operation is that of a man with the capacity to redeem the populace from uncertainty and disorder. However, this bare-bones Sunni quietism is not, perhaps, most characteristic of the Sunni political *vision*. That vision is itself a realistic one in that it is nonutopian and noncharismatic, but its primary features are a concern for legitimacy in the wielding of power by some humans over other humans. This is Sunnism as a *justificatory project*, according to which the highest social goal to which humans can strive in this life is to govern their affairs with as much certainty as possible that this is the way required by God.

The caliph, or imam, is the primary representative institution in this vision. The concern with its legitimacy is shown by the efforts made by classical and medieval jurists to prove its necessity by both reason and revelation. Tellingly, Mawardi (974–1058) refers to the imamate as a "collective duty" (*farḍ kifāya*), like going to war or pursuing religious knowledge, "according to which the mass of people are exempted once it is undertaken by someone with the proper qualifications." This reveals that the caliphate was regarded as a representative institution and also something about the concept of representation in classical Sunnism: acting "on behalf" of someone is seen not only as a principal-agent relationship according to which the principal is owed something but also as a way of discharging something that the principal himself owes.

Of course, the representative nature of the imamate was linked not only to what the imam was doing and how (e.g., Mawardi's list of "ten public duties" that the imam must discharge, including the general duty of "enforcing [not creating] the law") but also to how he came into office. The Sunni scholars came to describe the imamate as "elective." Of course, in reality, this was a pious fiction designed to distinguish Umayyad and Abbasid dynastic rule from Shi'i claims. However, the origins of that fiction were in the institution of the *ahl al-ḥall wa-l-'aqd*, the "people who loosen and bind." These were the notables who acted as representatives of the community of the Muslims, who act on their behalf in appointing (and deposing) a caliph or another ruler. Their necessary qualifications were to be Muslim, male, mature, free, "just" (sufficiently pious and trustworthy), and capable of judging who is best qualified to hold the office. Sometimes this body of men was referred to as a *shūrā* (council), according to the pre-Islamic Arabian tradition. A *shūrā* can refer more broadly, however, to any council of advisors around a decision maker, such as a ruler, judge, or military commander. A permanent assembly of such representative advisors is often called a *majlis al-shūrā*, especially in modern times.

But if Sunnism is to be understood as defining political legitimacy and authority mostly in terms of fidelity to law, then the representative class par excellence is that of the 'ulama' (religious scholars). They are regarded as the guardians, transmitters, and interpreters of religious knowledge, of Islamic doctrine and law; the term also embraces those who fulfill religious functions in the community that require a certain level of expertise in religious and judicial issues, such as judges and preachers.

The 'ulama' can be regarded as a representative class in a number of important ways. First, as with the caliphate, the pursuit of knowledge—specifically knowledge of the divine law—is a collective obligation. In devoting themselves toward the search for God's law, the scholars are discharging this obligation on behalf of the entire Muslim community. Second, in defining the content of law independently from the executive authority, the scholars are, in fact, representing the masses in the articulation of the limits of executive political authority. Third, to the extent that Sunnism sees religious knowledge as dispersed throughout the community (rather than concentrated in an imam), the scholars are the articulation and realization of this claim. Fourth, in practical terms, the scholars were often seen as the de facto voice of the people against the corruption (political and moral) of the elites. Fifth, in constituting themselves as a class, the scholars established themselves through public institutions extended through time, such as the legal schools and the madrasas (religious seminaries).

In the modern Islamic world, of course, it is harder to distinguish Islamic political thought from actual political practice. Representative bodies of various kinds have been established in all postcolonial contexts, usually with reference to *shūrā* when the aim is to suggest continuity with Islamic traditions (and to limit democratic expectations), or "delegates" (*nuwwāb*) when the aim is to suggest democratic constitutionalism. Among revivalist or Islamic thinkers, it is common to find calls for some kinds of representative institutions alongside calls for the full restoration of the shari'a and "God's sovereignty." Thus, in the works of such thinkers as Mawdudi (d. 1979), Yusuf al-Qaradawi (b. 1926), Hasan al-Turabi (b. 1932), and Rachid al-Ghannouchi (b. 1941), one finds the endorsement of elections for those entrusted with implementing the shari'a and even for representatives to "legislative" bodies to form policies on matters not settled by revelation.

See also elections; government; parliament

Further Reading

Raja Bahlul, "People vs. God: The Logic of 'Divine Sovereignty' in Islamic Democratic Discourse," *Islam and Muslim-Christian Relations*, 11 (2000); Patricia Crone, *God's Rule: Government and Islam: Six Centuries of Medieval Islamic Political Thought*, 2005; Wael Hallaq, *Origins and Evolution of Islamic Law*, 2005; Abu al-Hasan al-Mawardi, *The Ordinances of Government: A Translation of al-Aḥkām al-Sulṭāniyya w'al-Wilāyāt al-Dīniyya*, translated by Wafaa H. Wahba, 1996; Bernard Weiss, *The Spirit of Islamic Law*, 1998; Muhammad Qasim Zaman, *The Ulama in Contemporary Islam: Custodians of Change*, 2007.

ANDREW F. MARCH

republicanism

Republicanism is a relatively new term in Islamic philosophical discourse. The idea of a representative government resembling what today is called a republic (*jumhūrīyya*) first appeared in 19th- and 20th-century Islamic thought. The term "republic" was first used to refer to a Muslim-majority country with the establishment of the Republic of Turkey in 1922–23.

Muslim thinkers who argue in favor of republicanism as a preferred political system justify this relatively new idea with reference to classical Islamic sources and doctrines. The most important of these doctrines is the Qur'anic principle of *shūrā* (consultation). Sura 42 of the Qur'an, called al-Shura, encourages mutual consultation. Elsewhere in the Qur'an (3:159), Muhammad is urged to consult with the members of his community (in spite of their faults) when making important decisions. This principle of consultation has become a primary justification for the arguments of prorepublican Muslims.

Early proponents of republican government in Muslim-majority countries included the Young Ottomans, who operated in Turkey in the late 19th century. One of their most common strategies was to demonstrate support for more democratic forms of government in Islamic teaching by identifying parallels between Qur'anic teachings and the terms familiar to liberal political discourse. Namık Kemal (1840–88) was a member of the Young Ottomans who argued that the principle of *shūrā* could be used to justify representative forms of government. Another early supporter of republican principles was Muhammad 'Abduh (1849–1905), who argued that consultation is crucial for a just government, as it provides individual rulers with access to the greater intelligence that comes from the collective community. Muhammad Rashid Rida (1865–1935) was more explicitly republican in his adoption of the principle of *shūrā*. Rida proposed a group of representatives of the general population to choose, consult with, and have the power to remove the ruler. Rida argued that this model was fully compatible with the traditional Islamic caliphate, as the caliph could benefit from consultation with community representatives and Muslim jurists, so long as their advice did not contradict Qur'anic teachings.

The rise of republican discourse among Muslim thinkers was also connected to Arab nationalist and Pan-Islamic movements. Afghani (1838–97), a major figure in the history of Pan-Islamism and of modern Islamic thought more generally, argued that Muslims could seek truth in both revelation and reason. Afghani argued that a revival of Islam, uniting all Muslims in one community, would include a revival of reason as a source of guidance and also of more representative forms of government. Rida also argued strongly in favor of a united Islamic community; the collective intelligence of the Muslim community as a whole would far outweigh any national grouping.

Many contemporary Islamic countries are called republics, including Turkey, Lebanon, Syria, and Indonesia, among others. In 1956, Pakistan was the first country to adopt the title of "Islamic Republic," which subsequently was used by many other nations including the Shi'i-dominated Islamic Republic of Iran, established in 1979, and the post-Taliban Islamic Republic of Afghanistan. The legal structures of these countries are characterized by a high degree of variety, demonstrating the wide array of possibilities that can be captured by republicanism in the Islamic context.

See also 'Abduh, Muhammad (1849–1905); al-Afghani, Jamal al-Din (1838–97); democracy; elections; Rida, Muhammad Rashid (1865–1935)

Further Reading

Antony Black, *The History of Islamic Political Thought: From the Prophet to the Present*, 2001; Hamid Enayat, *Modern Islamic Political Thought*, 1982; Sylvia G. Haim, ed., *Arab Nationalism: An Anthology*, 1962; Malcolm H. Kerr, *Islamic Reform: The Political and Legal Theories of Muhammad 'Abduh and Rashid Rida*, 1966.

ROSEMARY B. KELLISON

revival and reform

Revival and reform, *tajdīd* and *iṣlāḥ*, are terms widely disseminated across a range of genres in Muslim literature. They are found in commentaries of prophetic traditions, political discourses, debates about shari'a, and the integrity of learning and scholarship. Often these key words are rhetorically invoked in exhortations of moral awakening in order to advance a Muslim social and political gospel. Over time, these terms have been used together to represent a concept that links newness and creativity (renewal/revival) to wholeness and integrity (*iṣlaḥ*, reform). Whether the "renewal and reform" is aimed at the collective or the individual or both, the discourse of revival and reform addresses stability and change, the mutable and immutable in Muslim thought. In this larger semantic framework, two things loom large: political theology and the integrity of the learned tradition. Renewal and revival (*tajdīd*) stem from the root *j-d-d*, to make new, to innovate, to refresh and resuscitate. One may think of reform as a discourse of improvement, recovery, and healing. Indeed, *iṣlāḥ* (repair) is derived from the Arabic root *ṣ-l-ḥ*, which means to mend, restore, and improve.

Plain readings of the proof texts suggest that renewal will not only resuscitate the body politic of both community and society but also heal and restore the brokenness of the moral order. This restorative aspect made this conceptual category attractive and appealing to all kinds of public actors who advanced a political, spiritual, and intellectual agenda for the betterment of both individuals and society.

The key report attributed to the Prophet Muhammad on the question of renewal states, "Indeed, at the beginning of every century God dispatches to this confessional community (*umma*) a person who will renew its *dīn*—salvation practices (religion)." Another

report on the topic says, "God shows benevolence to the people who are part of His order of *dīn* at the beginning of every century by dispatching a man from my family who will clarify to them matters related to their salvation practices (*dīn*)."

Paradox, however, lies at the heart of the renewal-reform concept. A countervailing concept, called illicit innovation (*bid'a*), appears to ascribe dire consequences to expressions of newness and creativity. Generally, the prophetic statement "all innovation leads to misguidance" is understood to suggest that innovation in matters of *dīn* were forbidden. Thus alterations to normative standards of behavior (sunna) as well as those concepts associated with these normative practices were viewed as an egregious disruption of the paradigm of salvation. Even supplementing or altering the practices of *dīn*, without reference to the broader purposes of the Islamic ethics (shari'a), was frowned upon. Over time new paradigmatic shifts occurred that tolerated alteration to the practices of *dīn*, provided that they cohered with the overall goals of the shari'a. The tension generated by the enthusiasm to promote renewal-reform, on the one hand, and the proscription of illicit innovation in matters of *dīn*, on the other, required some explanation. The two conceptual categories were not polarities but rather mutually constitutive. Renewal and reform was a providential promise for the continued betterment of God's approved faith community. This forward-looking momentum was sustained by traditions attributed to the Prophet, which said, "The parable of my community is like that of rain. It is not known whether the best part is when it begins to rain or when it ends." Twelver Shi'i Islam has a strong messianic dimension in the expectation of the return of the political-spiritual leadership of the imam who went into occultation, but it has no tradition of centennial renewal. Sunni Islam, however, rooted its notion of perpetual low-key messianism in the idea of centennial renewal. Coupled with the sentiment of a melancholic exilic framework (namely, "true" Islam's estrangement in the world), this cluster of concepts constituted Sunni Islam's political theology.

Political theology, in the words of contemporary theorist Jan Assmann, is the "ever-changing relationships between political community and religious order, in short, between power [or authority: Herrschaft] and salvation [Heil]." Muslim thinkers such as Mawardi articulated a similar idea somewhat differently through the prism of leadership and governance: "Leadership (*imāma*) was designed in order to succeed the role of prophecy by protecting the order of salvation (*dīn*) and managing the affairs of the world." There was a conjunction of the religious order and the political order for these Muslim thinkers, too. But what made Muslim political theology so different from its counterpart in Christianity was that the political-theological in Islam was intimately related to the idea of prophecy. With the death of the Prophet Muhammad, the responsibility of his mission passed on to those who were designated as the guardians of the knowledge produced by prophecy, namely revelation. Since salvation was a core idea of Islam, the knowledge of practices was integral to the order of revelation. The semi-sacrosanct character of the discursive tradition, in turn, elevated the status and power of the scholars ('ulama'), the mediators of the learned tradition. The learned in Islam were seen as the true heirs of prophetic charisma. Statements attributed to the Prophet suggested that the learned "were analogous to the prophets among the Israelites." Given the equivalence between the learned and the prophets of yore, the power and authority of tradition was inseparable from Muslim political theology. And given this rather elevated status of the learned, the tradition that they managed and interpreted also acquired a certain semi-sacrosanct status.

Another way of putting this was that the Prophet in Islam had two bodies that paralleled his two primary earthly roles. The first was the Prophet's political body in his capacity as God's messenger, who established a political order that favored the transcendent good. The second was his moral body in his role as teacher of wisdom and the transcendent good (*yu'allimuhum al-kitāb wa-l-ḥikma*), whose embodied life (sunna) became the reference point of imitation. After Muhammad's death, the political body was continuously articulated through the concept of stewardship (*khilāfa* in Sunnism or imamate in Shi'ism), and the body of knowledge provided by the Prophet lived on in the Islamic knowledge tradition.

Reform and the Meaning of Tradition

The concept of reform was put to different uses by a range of Muslim actors and social movements. One can thus pose several questions: What do Muslims mean by revival and reform across time? What are the goals of revival and reform? Did revival and reform resonate differently over time and serve different functions at distinct periods of Muslim history?

Any conception of Muslim reform was intimately connected to tradition. To reform a tradition was to recover it, in order to rehabilitate it to its original form. If one understood tradition as a continuing moral argument that authoritatively connected a community's memory of the past to its present and future, then reform was the process of restoring that tradition, of sustaining the promise of its continued repetition and also inventing it simultaneously. Reform in Islam, therefore, did not have a singular meaning or trajectory. Modernist presumptions about reform imagined it to be progressive and incremental. To the contrary, apart from some recent modernist discourses, reform in Islam was usually mobilized to "re-form" what was already in place, to restore the original form of a practice or an idea to shield it from the specter of change and newness. Any attempt to restore an original form, however, was always vulnerable to the possibility of creating something new instead of restoring the original. Therefore reform, even when it ostensibly sought to resist change, could not escape the inherent dynamism of creativity and change.

In order for a project of reform to authorize itself, it had to identify an object of reform, a fractured object that was available and in need of healing, mending, and improvement. In that sense, reform was integral to the story of Islam from its very beginnings. Reform was in many ways at the heart of Prophet Muhammad's career.

Moreover, the divine revelation transmitted through the Prophet told a particular story of moral fracture, disintegration, and chaos about the place and time in which it was revealed. The seventh-century Arabic context, so the story went, was enveloped by the corruptions of unbelief, polytheism, and idolatry. People valorized ancestral authority over divine command, tribal customs over divinely sanctioned law. The revelation of the Qur'an, as embodied in the figure of the Prophet, intervened to mend, resolve, and reform that disorder.

The philosopher/historian Quentin Skinner wrote that certain modes of inquiry rest on what he called "a question and answer space." Skinner maintained that a proposition was only properly understood if the question that elicited an answer was properly identified and articulated. The meaning of a proposition, in other words, was relative to the question it answered and could not, as a consequence, be discovered by lifting it out of the discursive process or milieu of which it was a constitutive part. In order to conceptualize the narrative plot of Muslim reformist discourses, one must examine the nature of the questions the reformists imagined alongside the answers they provided. More precisely, the moral argument for submitting to the absolute sovereignty of the divine represented an answer to a society crippled by polytheism and idolatry. This original story of contestation between those who affirmed and detracted from divine sovereignty served as the paradigmatic narrative plot that haunted almost all subsequent moments of Muslim reform, in both the premodern and modern periods.

Indeed, the authority of any project of reform depended on its ability to establish the relevance of its own question and answer space within the context of the Prophet's time. Reform then emerged as the trope of reenacting the narrative drama of prophetic time in a new context or present. Such instances of narrative "translation" populate the intellectual history of premodern Islam.

Ibn Khaldun: History and Change

In his magnum opus, the *Muqaddima* (Prolegomena), the historian and polymath Ibn Khaldun (1332–1406) demonstrated that apocalyptic narratives in the prophetic traditions were by and large not reliable. Often the predictions made about the end times in the prophetic traditions were of a political character. Reports predicted the political fate of pious and impious rulers and the rise and fall of dynasties with great specificity and detail. Ibn Khaldun treated many of these reports as spurious. He used his skills as a historiographer of the hadith literature to show that some of the material recorded in the books of prognostications (*malāḥim*) were either weak reports or tied to the sectarian conflicts endemic to early Islam.

Acutely aware that many of these discourses were constructed, Ibn Khaldun then examined some of the narratives that explained the messianic coming of the guide or Mahdi before the apocalypse. Often these narratives, he stated, were deeply coded with political agendas that gave power to those who wielded them: "The time, the person, place, everything is indicated in these many spurious and arbitrary proofs. Then the time passes without a trace of the predictions coming true. Then they fabricate another narrative replete with linguistic equivocations, along with imaginary and astrological claims!" The idea of the imminent advent of a person who would renew both the moral values of the faith community (*aḥkām al-milla*) and the principles of truth (*marāsim al-ḥaqq*) was prevalent among his Sufi contemporaries, Ibn Khaldun wrote. He claimed to have been in touch with relatives of some saintly figures who expected the arrival of such a renewer at the beginning of the eighth Islamic century, corresponding to the 14th century on the Gregorian calendar. Ibn Khaldun did not cite any authority, such as a prophetic report about the centennial renewer from the collection of Abu Dawud, a collection with which he was familiar. Rather, Ibn Khaldun implied that such activities of renewal were part of the practice of the Sufis. He reminded his readers that charismatic authority on its own was insufficient to gain power. One needed something more fundamental in order to institutionalize change: hegemonic power. He explicitly stated, "No religious or political propaganda can be successful, unless hegemonic power (*shawka 'aṣabiyya*) prevail in order to support such religious and political aspirations and to defend them against adversaries until God's will materializes in these matters." Central to Ibn Khaldun's theory for any religious or political transformation to successfully occur was the need to be in a position to wield what he called group solidarity (*'aṣabiyya*): in other words, the acquisition of hegemonic power was necessary in order to make things happen. Any religious call or political mission had to be backed up by a form of social solidarity that became the basis and vehicle for the transmission of ideas.

Religion, in Ibn Khaldun's view, played a central role in leavening the hegemonic political power he regarded as fundamental to social organization. Political authority, what he called royal authority, needed some kind of compelling appeal that was provided by religion, which held people together. In fact, one might say that Ibn Khaldun used the notion of religion in the sense of an ideology. Arabs in their state of nature were uncontrollable, he said, and their traits were tailor-made for anarchy and the ruin of civilization. Then something transformative happened that rendered them capable of governance. That elixir, in his view, was *dīn*, a set of practices and behaviors central to salvation, which transformed the community that adopted it. He described the way *dīn* shaped both the individual subject and the community attached to it. Inspired by a Qur'anic expression of *sibghat Allāh* (the color of God), Ibn Khaldun freely used the expression *sibgha dīniyya* (religious coloration) to describe the deep transforming experience a people derived from prophecy or from their engagement with religion. "Arabs are by nature remote from political leadership," he said. "They attain power only once their nature has undergone a complete transformation under the influence of some religious coloring that wipes out all such [negative qualities] and causes the Arabs to have a restraining influence on themselves."

Even though Ibn Khaldun did not give much weight to prophetic materials, he was aware of the potential and limits of social reform based on religion. He was aware of reform initiatives taken

by figures in North Africa whose theopolitical platform was to propagate the truth and reestablish the prophetic traditions. Ideally, such changes required the moral correction of humanity (*iṣlāḥ al-khalq*), but often such efforts, he claimed, resulted in superficial changes. The rhetorical keystroke of the reform initiatives was to connect people to the sunna of the Prophet Muhammad and to instruct them to desist from living a life of sin, he said. The rate of successful change in some of the folk he had observed, he admitted, was limited. Some merely desisted from a life of highway robbery and brigandage without really changing their conduct when they adopted a religious ethic. While such cessation of sin was by all accounts noteworthy, Ibn Khaldun's larger point was that internalizing a religious ethic required additional education. Merely raising the standard of the sunna and rooting out the wrongs were not sufficient.

Premodern Imaginaries of Reform

The sunna played a key role in the earliest discourses on renewal and the healing of the faith community. A report in the book of Abu Dawud stated, "Indeed, God deputes to this faith community (*umma*) at the beginning of every century one who will renew its salvific practices (*dīn*)." This pithy statement captured the redemptive utopia of Islam and also structured its sense of history. Not only did providence play an important role in the self-understanding of the faith community, human agency was explicitly affirmed in the renewal process. Furthermore, temporality and human agency were inseparable, while Islam as a faith was equipped with a reformist gospel. In other words, Islam as a discursive project was a human-God partnership or covenant. In order to keep the faith community vibrant and to render it temporally relevant, it would require a regular process of renewal—but the nature of this process and the spheres in which it would take place were points of contention among Muslims.

Given that the idea of revival and reform animated the Muslim moral and political imagination from a very early period, it also produced an illustrious genealogy of actors and players who had occupied the role of "renewer(s) of the age." The career of the jurist and eponymous founder of the Shafi'i school of Sunni law, Muhammad b. Idris al-Shafi'i (d. 820), was one such example. Shafi'i's project of reform was animated by his desire to fashion the model of the Prophet into a coherent, universal, and consistent object of knowledge. Shafi'i's offer of a system and a method to retrieve the epistemological body of the Prophet—namely, the sunna—catapulted him into prominence as a centennial renewer (*mujaddid*). His principal intervention was to introduce a hermeneutical understanding to the prophetic reports (hadith) and to end the reign of crass literalism perpetrated by the partisans of hadith. Moreover, he sought to counter the unbridled rational opinion advanced by the advocates of rationality—namely, the Hanafi scholars of Iraq. Shafi'i's dissatisfaction was directed at what he perceived to be the potential ethical chaos that might result from a plurality of models or bodies of the Prophet. The central dilemma that Shafi'i sought to address was this: how must a community affirm and embody the memory of the Prophet's model in a world that was becoming more and more distant from that prophetic past? Fashioning an answer to this question was central to multiple projects of reform, revival, and ethics in Islam. Moreover, with the movement of time, this question became increasingly pressing, and it engaged several Muslim scholars in the generation following the foundational architects of Islamic law and moral reasoning such as Shafi'i. Among the Shafi'is, Ibn al-Surayj (d. 918), Juwayni (d. 1085), and Ghazali (d. 1111) all became known as centennial renewers for their labors in recasting the body of knowledge in the Muslim tradition.

An excellent illustration of this trend can be found in the reformist project of Ibrahim al-Shatibi (d. 1388), the 14th-century Andalusian jurist aligned with the Maliki School of law. If Shafi'i's signature achievement was to systematize the knowledge of prophetic norms, then for Shatibi it was the elucidation of the underlying objectives that sustained the philosophical and doctrinal dimensions of Islamic law. Shatibi's most meticulous treatment of this project was found in his well-known magnum opus *al-Muwafaqat* (Concordances), although almost all his works were inspired by this central theme in some way.

Shatibi's conception of reform was driven by his attempt to align the practical implementation of law to its moral foundations. He argued that divine law could not be divorced from a larger program of ethics. For Shatibi, divine revelation was not a composite of haphazard discourses that lacked any cause or intentionality. On the contrary, revelation and the order that it generated were grounded in certain indispensable deeper objectives (*maqāṣid*), such as the safeguarding of life, property, salvational potentiality, intellect, and lineage. When law became separated from these objectives, Shatibi argued, it ceased to serve the welfare of the people for whom it was intended. In that situation, law no longer performed its primary purpose, to serve human interests in both this life and the next. Shatibi elaborated on this principle in his work that is now known as the discourse on the "objective-driven understanding of law and jurisprudence" (*al-fiqh al-maqāṣidī*). At the heart of Shatibi's legal reform, as exemplified in the category "objectives of the law," was his desire to establish a correlation between the values attached to particular practices and the higher ethical objectives that those values were supposed to foster and fulfill. Shatibi perhaps most emphatically articulated the foundational premise that informed his understanding of reform in Islam when he wrote, "[Divinely revealed] laws have all been established to preserve human beings' interests both in this life and the life to come." He further elaborated this principle when he said, "Normative rulings are intended to realize the welfare [of a community] and to repel harm and corruption. These, then [i.e., the realization of welfare and the repelling of harm], are the desired effects of normativity." To be engaged in reform signified, for Shatibi, the labor of preserving the synchronicity between the normative limits of the law and the ethical objectives that those limits were intended to secure. In other words, Shatibi sought to protect the marriage between law and ethics in Islam from separation or divorce.

But what kind of narrative about the past's relationship to the present (and the future) enabled the urgency of such agendas of moral reform? Shatibi provided some clues in his highly poignant introduction to his most extensive work on the concept of heretical innovation (*bid'a*), *al-I'tisam* (The adhering). Here Shatibi told a particular story about the tension produced by the polarities of normativity versus heresy in Islam through a narrative about becoming estranged from the world. Shatibi's prophetic report has a melancholic mood. "Islam began as a stranger and will return as a stranger like it began, so blessed were the strangers." Shatibi narrated his own struggles against the heretical innovations prevalent in his time, such as offering a benediction (*du'a*) after formal prayers, and his resultant marginalization from the mainstream of his society. His suffering was unmistakably similar to the Prophet Muhammad's estrangement from society in the early years of his mission as God's messenger. In confronting heresy and adhering to the sanctioned path, according to Shatibi, one also became estranged from the sinful society.

In his political and theological writings in the 14th century, Ibn Taymiyya (1263–1328) used the hadith about the coming of a centennial renewer as a sign of the promised awakening and renewal of the *dīn* in two slightly different contexts. In a letter to the Crusader leader of Cyprus, he explained the virtues of Islam and commented on a number of practices and recent experiences of the Muslims. The Mamluk sultans, he explained, routed the Mongols, who had declared their loyalty to Islam but then reneged in their conduct and obstinate pagan beliefs. In terms of the providential promise, Ibn Taymiyya stated, God sent the "armies of God" in the shape of the Mamluks in order to protect the community of Muslims from sure destruction. In this instance he invoked the hadith about awakening and renewal after the Muslim political entity was saved from destruction at the hands of enemies. In another citation of the same hadith, Ibn Taymiyya talked about messianic times, when Islam would become estranged from the world for some time until it was announced again to the world. Under such conditions, according to the authority of another hadith report, the true people of faith would stand up for the truth, fearless of the consequences and suffering they might endure at the hands of their adversaries. Ibn Taymiyya then cited the hadith that promised the revival of Islam in every century, creating an association between the estrangement of Islam and the parallel awakening and renewal. In other words, the symbolism of the rise and fall or the decline and renewal of Islam as a faith community was not absent from the historical narrative of Muslim thinkers themselves.

The tradition of renewal was connected to one of the central functions of prophecy: to share divine wisdom with humanity. Often the prophetic report about renewal of religion was connected to the traditions of learning and the discursive practices of Islam. Hence the learned of Islamdom were on par, in terms of function and service rendered, with the prophets of the children of Israel.

All commentaries on the centennial renewal report insisted that the primary function of the act of renewal was to ensure that the sunna displaced the heretical innovations (*bid'a*) that had superseded it in social practices and customs. Semantically, the concept of sunna was a continuation of the pre-Islamic sensibility or custom. After the advent of Islam, all customs pointed toward monotheism. Yet the sunna was a serious element of continuity in the Muslim community, for whatever was true and just was embodied in the sunna. As Ignaz Goldziher described the sunna in relation to the Arabs, "The sunna was their law and their sacra." Sunna could be understood as tradition, provided the latter also signified a strong sense of obligation. So when the sunna was tied to the person and identity of the Prophet Muhammad as the lawgiver and moral exemplar for Muslims, it also signified the completion of an ideal. As an ideal, the sunna represented how Muslims felt about the Prophet Muhammad. Imitating Muhammad was thus an essential part of proper Islamic living to simulate the representative feelings for the charismatic authority. Since the sunna became the accepted model of proper living, displacing the sunna was a sure sign of delinquency and signaled an intent to disavow the life practices ushered in by Islam.

Yet Muslim jurist-theologians quickly realized that idealizing the sunna as a cultural phenomenon was not practical. The sunna had to be sifted from the amalgam of reports gathered over time, then understood, rationalized, and turned into an interpretive logic as well as a charismatic reference point. One outcome was *fiqh*, literally the task of understanding the statements of the sunna and the Qur'an to constitute the core teachings of Muslim practice. Simultaneously, Islam's scriptural statements had to be understood in the light of changing times. This became one of the most challenging tasks for Muslims over the centuries and became especially acute in the rapidly changing historical period of modernity.

Reform in Modernity

It is now well accepted among scholars of Islam that tradition and modernity are not inherently opposed. Instead of approaching tradition as a field of discourses, types of knowledge, and norms that became irrelevant or outdated in the wake of modernity, it is more accurate to approach tradition as a continuing moral argument that has undergone particular shifts and transformations in new political and institutional conditions. Indeed, it might be most accurate to think of modernity also as a particular kind of tradition with its own expectations, sensibilities, and dreams of a good life. Some characteristics of modernity include the valorization of a "rational" subject unencumbered by the burden of myth and superstition, a renewed emphasis on the capacity of the individual to attain knowledge, and the articulation of a political theology that resists hierarchies and that champions the promise of a radically egalitarian ethos. Western colonialism transformed the discursive terrain in which Muslim actors and discourses could advance their projects of reform. Indeed, the career of the Muslim reform tradition also transformed in dramatic ways while it confronted the new conceptual and discursive terrain of Western colonial modernity. Most significantly, the modern episode in the tradition of Muslim reform took place in a postimperial context, when Muslim political

power in various parts of the world, from the late 18th century onward, either had collapsed or was steadily dwindling. But ironically, this loss of political power served as a major catalyst for the intensification of intellectual activity among reform-minded Muslim scholars. Contrary to a rise-and-fall model of history that equated political loss to intellectual decline, the reformist tradition in Islam showcased a remarkable degree of intellectual fermentation during periods of political decline. Various reformist movements in such regions as Central Asia, the Middle East, and South Asia attest to this trend.

A hallmark of the Muslim reform tradition in the modern era was a renewed emphasis on protecting the absoluteness of divine sovereignty not only as an incontrovertible theological dogma but also as a moral imperative in everyday life. Several devotional practices, such as seeking the intercession of the Prophet and saints, visiting shrines of deceased saints in order to seek redemptive intercession, and attending birth and death ceremonies of charismatic pious figures, all emerged as objects of intense polemics and contestations. The legitimacy of these practices had been debated before the modern period: even in the premodern era, the problem of how a community should guard divine sovereignty from all potential human competitors produced much debate and differences among Muslim scholars. The political and institutional conditions in which these battles were fought in modern times, however, had almost entirely changed. There were two main traditions or thought styles that most decisively shaped the contours of Muslim reformist thought in the modern era. Broadly conceived, these traditions can be called Muslim modernism and Muslim maximalism, or what is generally known as the Salafi tradition. Although the sources of knowledge that informed these two traditions were different, the recipe for religious and social reform offered by the custodians of these traditions shared certain key ingredients.

Perhaps most significantly, each placed a renewed emphasis on the Qur'an and the sunna as the only authentic sources of religious practice. They offered a scathing critique of devotional and popular practices that threatened divine sovereignty. There were perhaps two defining features of Muslim reformist thought in modernity. Remarkably, on these two foundational points, Muslim modernist and Salafi thinkers seem to be in total agreement. The famous 20th-century Indian poet-philosopher Muhammad Iqbal (d. 1939) was unambiguous in his chastisement of a worldview that placed antinomian mysticism above a commitment to treating the social and moral ills of this world. Iqbal reminded his readers in his classic *The Reconstruction of Religious Thought in Islam* that, after having received ultimate proximity with the divine during his famous ascension, the Prophet chose to return to this world. What the modern Muslim needed, Iqbal pleaded, was precisely this spirit of return to the world in order to address its challenges. Such a spirit was only possible, Iqbal argued, with an attitude that was inspired by the revolutionary ethos of the Qur'an. The reinvigoration of the self, the elevation of the self, required a renewed emphasis on the primacy of the Qur'an as the foundational source of Islamic practice. If such a project of reform required that certain nonessential rituals and customary conventions be jettisoned in order to serve moral and social change, then Iqbal was prepared to sacrifice them. "This one prostration which you consider to be a burden, relieves a person of a thousand other prostrations," Iqbal famously wrote. Iqbal's view, shared by several other Muslim modernists of his generation, emphasized transcendence articulated in a rationally grounded idiom. The way to confront the crisis of meaning caused by Western modernity, colonialism, and the larger processes of industrial capitalism was to recover that spirit of submission to a transcendent authority that had enabled Islam to emerge as a revolutionary ideological force at its beginnings.

Similarly, the famous 19th-century Egyptian reformer Muhammad 'Abduh's (d. 1905) conception of reform focused on retrieving an egalitarian ethos of a transcendent authority that for him had become corrupted by an overweening degree of dependence on hierarchies of human authority. As he stated most clearly in his well-known work *Risalat al-Tawhid* (The epistle on unity), his primary objective was "freeing the minds of Muslims from the chains of belief in authority because God has not created humankind in order to be led by a halter." 'Abduh's primary target was the principle of conforming to canonical authority (*taqlīd*), which, in his view, had vitiated the capacity of the ordinary believer to apply his reason and intellect in interpreting the foundational sources of religion. Unlike Iqbal, 'Abduh was trained in the traditional canonical sources of law at the prestigious Azhar University in Cairo. Despite, or perhaps because of, his traditional training, however, 'Abduh was convinced that in order to challenge the looming threat of Westernization (*taghrīb*) and colonialism with any integrity, it was imperative to reject any practice that did not value rational inquiry over dogmatic following, egalitarianism over submission to authority.

The Algerian thinker Malek Bennabi (d. 1973), building on the intellectual threads spun by Afghani, 'Abduh, and Iqbal, offered a critique of both Salafist and modernist reform projects. Bennabi lamented that the drive of Salafist reformism adopted a retrograde character, directing its intellectual energies to the past and providing imprints and templates that were "incompatible with the exigencies of the present and the future." The modernist reformers, he complained, uncritically adopted European ideas; they were obsessed with how they could be acquired but lacked the curiosity to know "how they were created." What Bennabi found lacking in all Muslim reformist thought was the absence of a doctrine of culture. Without developing a sense of culture, he believed that all "Iṣlāḥism [reformism] propagates a complacent symbolism that dreams of transforming the condition of life by communicating, above all, the taste for 'Muslim things' and Arab 'belles-lettres.'" The reformist movement did not know how to "transform the Muslim soul or to translate into reality the 'social function' of the religion." However, reformists were successful, he wrote, in making Muslims realize their position in the world, what he called the "secular drama." He argued that only by posing the problem of culture generally could the Islamic renaissance emerge from its embryonic state.

Apart from South Asia and the Middle East, a similar trajectory of Muslim modernist reform is found in Soviet Central Asia. In the 19th century, a small number of intellectual elites in such urban centers as Bukhara, Tashkent, and Samarqand established what came to be known as the Jadid (new) movement. At the heart of this movement was an attempt to establish the compatibility of scientific rationality and the foundational sources of Islam, mainly the Qur'an and sunna. Moreover, in ways similar to their modernist counterparts in South Asia and the Middle East, the Jadids sought to eradicate the influence of local customs, conventions, and rituals that in their view lacked a precedent in the Qur'an and sunna. Again, reform for them involved the separation of "local culture" from "authentic religion." The most crucial variable in enabling such a process of reform, for the Jadids, was education of both the religious and secular varieties. Therefore, prominent 19th- and 20th-century Jadid thinkers such as Munawwar Qari (d. 1933) and Mahmud Behbudi (d. 1919) were defiant in their call to adopt "new methods" of education in both secondary schools and institutions of higher learning. Their vision for Central Asian Muslims was unabashedly modern; the cultivation of a new civil society required discarding old myths, rituals, and superstitions and the need to embrace a rationally sound subjectivity. The enlightenment project of relegating older traditions to irrelevance seemed very real and possible to Jadid scholars like Qari and Behbudi. Their project of reform not only took place in the shadow of Soviet hegemony but also was heavily inspired by the Marxist-Communist narrative of progress and modernization in society. But they differed from the Soviet model in their belief that Islam was inherently compatible with scientific rationality. Hence they resisted the Soviet drive to completely eradicate religion from the public sphere.

Apart from these modernist discourses that emerged either as a response to or in the shadow of Western colonialism, another major trend of Muslim reform in the modern period was the maximalist or puritanical tradition, usually called Salafism. Literally, the term "Salafism" referred to the argument that only the body of norms that originated during the patristic community of the Prophet could be regarded as authoritative in Islam. In a move not all that different from Muslim modernist thinkers, puritanical reformers such as the well-known Muhammad b. 'Abd al-Wahhab (d. 1787) in Arabia and the lesser-known Shah Isma'il (d. 1831) in India also argued for a return to the Qur'an and the sunna as the exclusive reservoirs for an authentic religious normativity. What distinguished these puritanical reformers from their modernist counterparts was the degree to which they conceived of reform as equivalent to guarding the absoluteness of divine sovereignty. A mindset of constant rivalry between human and divine norms was central to their social imaginaries (norms regulating social existence), much more pronounced than in modernist thinkers like Iqbal or 'Abduh. A significant part of the reform project advanced by thinkers like Ibn 'Abd al-Wahhab and Shah Isma'il centered on such issues as the limits of prophetic intercession, the legitimacy of visiting shrines of dead saints, and the capacity of the Prophet to know the unknown, among other doctrines.

On each of these issues, their position was informed by a political theology that amplified divine sovereignty, even if that meant casting the humanity of the Prophet as a fallible subject. Theirs was a larger program to perpetuate social egalitarianism. They downplayed the Prophet's miraculous qualities and emphasized that his prophetic authority was enabled by the perfection of his humanity. Similarly, the authority of saints and other pious figures to perform such acts as interceding on behalf of sinners also had to be restrained in order to preserve a radical difference between divine and human authority. The zeal of such thinkers to guard the absoluteness of divine sovereignty not only inspired a number of important movements within Muslim reformist thought but also generated a great deal of controversy, polemics, and a fair number of rebuttals.

One of the more interesting developments was the emergence of traditionalist reform-minded scholars who inhabited seemingly antithetical genealogies of Islamic thought. On the face of it, it appeared as certain reform-minded scholars were bringing together new hybrid traditions and incommensurable discourses. Among them is Ibrahim b. al-Hasan al-Kurani, but one can also include Shah Waliullah of Delhi and also later Indian traditional scholars such as Anwar Shah Kashmiri, among others, who were strong admirers of Ibn Taymiyya and also liberally drew on, and defended, the teachings and insights of Ibn al-'Arabi. Ibn Taymiyya's salafist-nominalism combined with Ibn al-'Arabi's dizzying immanentist metaphysics would appear to be strange bedfellows. But some reform-minded scholars including the Ghumari brothers ('Abdullah and Ahmad Ghumari) of North Africa combined their reverence for the family of the Prophet (*ahl al-bayt*) with their Sunni traditionalism. All this suggests that multiple logics (heterologies) were at play in certain reformist strains of thought that might be antithetical to more systematic thinkers of reform. But it might well be that these contradictions are the product of a larger modernist template in which things that appear to be antithetical can have perfect synchrony in practice.

Contemporary Debates on Reform

In late 20th-century India, the rector of the Darul Uloom of Deoband, Qari Muhammad Tayyab (d. 1988), offered a narrative of revival and reform that represented a traditional perspective of the 'ulama'. Tayyab argued that there were two means by which the path of *dīn* was providentially protected. The first was through powerful personalities who represented the preservation of *dīn*. The second was through the inner spirit of *dīn*, which naturally shielded it from any subversive threat.

Tayyab argued that human mentality changed over the duration of a century and that significant intergenerational changes had occurred. As a result, he wrote, new modes of thinking and new experiences unfolded in a progressive manner. In every generation, therefore, was a risk and a legitimate fear that the next generation of the Muslim community might jettison the imprint of the previous generation. The primary concern, Tayyab explained, was to prevent the original and traditional imprint from becoming anachronistic for

the new generation. For this reason the teachings of the faith had to be continuously explained and interpreted in the light of the new and altered mentality, and for this reason individuals were providentially deputed to the world to serve as centennial renewers.

Anwar al-Jundi (d. 2002), a prominent Egyptian advocate of revival and reform in the tradition of major reformers such as Ibn Hazm, Ghazali, Ibn Taymiyya, and Ibn Khaldun, described each of these figures as "correctors of concepts and renewers of Islamic thought." Each one had made a specific methodological intervention to the intellectual tradition that gave integrity to the teachings of Islam in terms of the challenges of their respective times. Ibn Hazm, said Jundi, combated the distortion produced by the overuse of analogy and paved the way back to the straightforward and plain meaning of the Qur'an. The prevalent predisposition toward blind imitation of authority (*taqlīd*) was another distortion that Ibn Hazm opposed. Ghazali chose to work in the area of education and culture, Jundi explained, and brought the spiritual and legal into a meaningful integration. At the same time, Ghazali also combated the excessive claims of philosophy and the Muslim philosophers. Ibn Taymiyya, in turn, evaluated all Islamic thought on the touchstone of the truth of the Qur'an. Whatever could not sustain the scrutiny of the Qur'an and the sunna could be discarded, according to Jundi's reading of Ibn Taymiyya. Ibn Khaldun turned against the empty verbal polemics of his day that contributed to the lack of originality in Islamic thought. Ibn Khaldun's intervention was to give empirical observation a respectable place in the epistemological framework of religious thought, Jundi argued.

For Jundi and many advocates of reform in the modern period, the rebuttal of the idea of following ancient discursive authority of the law schools (*taqlīd*) was one of the most important rhetorical markers of the reform movement. Instead of following authority, they advocate *ijtihād*, or independent thinking. However, often *ijtihād* meant following a variety of legal opinions instead of one law school. And instead of following the canonical authority of a law school and its interpretations, in the sphere of moral teachings and ethics, the reformists sometimes resorted to plain readings derived from the Qur'an and sunna but more often fell back on the opinions of ancient schools.

The U.S./European wars in Afghanistan and Iraq against a range of Muslim groups from terrorists and militants to religious revivalists and pietists has had a major impact on the discourse of revival and reform. If certain Muslims in the 19th and 20th centuries were suspicious of the agenda of revivalism and reform as a vehicle for Westernization advanced by European colonizers, then in the early 21st century, discourses of revival and reform have become deeply politicized and polarizing within Muslim societies where some see revival and reform as a bridgehead for new crusades against Islam. For instance, after the U.S. invasion of Iraq in 2003, the Egyptian public intellectual Muhammad 'Imara wrote a pamphlet titled *Religious Discourse: Between Islamic Reform and American Subversion* (*al-Khitab al-Dini bayna al-Tajdid al-Islami wa-l-Tabdid al-Amrikani*), in which he identified himself as a protagonist of an Islamic reformist agenda. Renewal was not only a rational necessity, said 'Imara, but also a part of the "tradition (*sunna*), necessity (*ḍarūra*) and universal rule (*qānūn*)." He argued that without renewal, the chasm between "thought (*fikr*), ethics (*fiqh*), Islamic discourse (*al-khiṭāb al-Islāmī*)," which represent the shari'a on the one hand and the demands of societal change on the other, would only widen. 'Imara also argued that a unifying agenda of reform was impossible, and hence diversity would be a hallmark of any such project. However, he was highly skeptical of what he called the American-financed reform projects that supported Muslim secularists, Marxists, and mercenaries, whose purpose he viewed as the replacement of Muslim religious discourse with secularism. 'Imara's rhetoric, however exaggerated, has gained traction in contexts where conflict with the West has reached new levels of antagonism.

'Imara's focus was on the disagreement within Muslim circles over the rights to and limits of reform. But 'Imara chose a demonic rhetoric to describe his Muslim intellectual adversaries, similar to the way anthropologist Saba Mahmood charged certain Iranian and Arab Muslim thinkers of tailoring their reforms to American imperial designs. Among the targets of these critics were figures such as Nasr Hamid Abu Zayd (d. 2010), Hasan Hanafi, Khalil 'Abd al-Karim (d. 2002), and the pivotal Iranian reformist thinker Abdolkarim Soroush, who were engaged in fairly far-reaching criticisms of traditional Muslim discursive and interpretative paradigms. 'Imara invoked the authority of Afghani and 'Abduh in order to distinguish genuine reform from what he suspected was the bacillus of subversive reforms. This overheated debate has echoes of early and mid-20th-century debates in Egypt, where such thinkers as Taha Husayn (d. 1973), 'Ali 'Abd al-Raziq (d. 1966), Qasim Amin (d. 1908), and Muhammad Ahmad Khalafallah (d. 1977) were demonized as hostile and subversive elements who attempted to undermine the authentic inherited narrative of Islamic thought. One of the perpetual challenges for Muslim reformers was to know where to draw the line in the realm of ideas.

Revival and reform also became the pretext for a largely sterile but earnest debate among academics in the Western academy during the 1980s over the larger political implications of revival and reform. Fazlur Rahman, the Pakistani scholar and émigré to the United States, observed a neo-Sufi revivalist tradition that in his view combined spirituality with activism, a move away from the passive, world-denouncing, ascetic Sufism of old. While some scholars, such as John Voll, agreed with him, others, including Rex O'Fahey, Bernard Radtke, Reinhard Schulze, and Ahmad Dallal, voiced alternative viewpoints. Their fundamental disagreement with the Fazlur Rahman and Voll thesis was that it tried to explain a range of revivalist Sufi practices under a singular rubric—neo-Sufism—whereas the actual story was much more complex. Rahman and Voll's detractors argued that Muslim intellectuals and social reform movements in the 18th century were generating revivals independent of European influences in creative and innovative ways that defied the charges of decline.

Conclusion

Revival and reform have been integral to Islam from its very beginnings. The idea of reform relates to mending a fractured present in order to generate something entirely new or to rehabilitate an original form. Whether reform seeks to renew or rehabilitate, it is always a creative and dynamic process that produces change and newness. The various projects of reform in the intellectual and social history of Islam both converged and diverged on important points. Almost all moments of reform engaged with certain authoritative discourses and bodies of knowledge such as the Qur'an, sunna, and traditions of canonical law. However, every moment of reform articulated varied points of emphasis on what reform entailed. For example, the conception of reform for premodern luminaries Ibn Khaldun and Shatibi was very different compared to later figures. Ibn Khaldun was captivated by the necessity of cultivating social solidarity, while Shatibi's concern was to synchronize the law with its fundamental objectives. Both of these thinkers engaged in what might be called reform, but the specific trajectories of reform differed significantly. Reform in Islam remains variegated, diverse, and unpredictable.

Fundamental to thinking about the question of reform in Islam is the role of memory and how that memory relates to the founder, the Prophet Muhammad, and the revelation, the Qur'an. The "body" of the Prophet, whether discursive, political, or mystical, remains a central reference point. In order for reform to be credible, however, reformers often strive to connect the memory of the past with the fractured and the always incomplete present. But a set of contentious and hotly debated questions remains. How much of the past should inform a project of reform and recovery? Can reimagining, reforming, and reviving political theology be constrained by boundaries and limits? How does the knowledge of the tradition relate and converse with modernity? Answers to these fundamental questions have varied significantly, depending on the individual agents of reform, as well as specific political, cultural, and material conditions. Therefore, in the modern period, developments such as colonialism and the eventual rise of the nation-state, the emergence of print, and the consolidation of such institutions of state building as the census all transformed the Muslim reform tradition in profound ways. These shifts in the political and institutional terrain enabled new trajectories of reform and brought into central view particular questions of authoritative debates (such as the humanity of the Prophet) with an unprecedented intensity and vigor. Like any other aspect of Islam, the Muslim reform tradition is neither monolithic nor predictable. Rather, reform in Islam is continually invested with and divested of particular meanings, knowledge, and aspirations at specific junctures in history.

See also fundamentalism; messianism; modernity

Further Reading

Charles Adams, *Islam and Modernism in Egypt: A Study of the Modern Reform Movement Inaugurated by Muhammad 'Abduh*, 1968; M. Bennabi, *Islam in History and Society*, translated by A. Rashid, 1991; David Commins, *Islamic Reform: Politics and Social Change in Late Ottoman Syria*, 1990; A. Dallal, "The Origins and Objectives of Islamic Revivalist Thought, 1750–1850," *Journal of the American Oriental Society* 113 (1993): 341–59; Samira Haj, *Reconfiguring Islamic Tradition: Reform, Rationality, and Modernity*, 2009; B. Haykal, *Revival and Reform in Islam: The Legacy of Muhammad al-Shawkani*, 2003; N. Levtzion and J. O. Voll, ed., *Eighteenth-Century Renewal and Reform in Islam*, 1987; B. D. Metcalf, *Islamic Revival in India: Deoband, 1860–1900*, 1982; R. Peters, "Idjtihad and Taqlid in 18th and 19th Century Islam," in *Die Welt des Islams* (2000); Fazlur Rahman, *Revival and Reform in Islam: A Study in Islamic Fundamentalism*, edited by Ebrahim Moosa, 2000; J. O. Voll, "Foundations for Renewal and Reform," in *The Oxford History of Islam*, edited by J. Esposito, 1999.

EBRAHIM MOOSA AND SHERALI TAREEN

revolutions

Revolution is a transformation of the social, political, economic, or religious structures in a society, carried out, most frequently, by revolts of the less powerful or disenfranchised against ruling authorities. This transformation can occur in a single locale over a period of days or extend across a wide geographical region over a period of decades. Revolutions signal or embody a crisis of the status quo. Revolutions may involve a political crisis for existing regimes of power and authority that cannot respond effectively to challenges from external or internal actors or coalitions of actors. Sometimes revolutions are led by intellectuals, elites, military cadres, or members of the middle class, but quite often, revolutions begin at the grassroots level through the discontent of the masses or dispossessed.

Revolutions and revolutionary thinking have had a place within Islamic thought since the Prophet Muhammad first overturned the prevailing cultural, political, and religious status quo of the Arabian Peninsula by establishing new institutions of governance, law, and society in Medina in 622. The boundaries of revolution in Islam are defined, first and foremost, by Qur'anic injunctions, regardless of the ideological commitments of the various Muslim revolutionary thinkers. There is a revolutionary quality to the Qur'an itself: beyond being the direct word of God, the Qur'an offers itself as a witness to itself, as revelation and instruction unlike any other, and as reliable guidance for the purpose of establishing a righteous social and political order under the specific theological, ethical, and human framework of belief in the one God. Muslim revolutionaries throughout history have cited various verses of Islam's sacred text in order to justify and validate revolution as authentically Islamic and have rejected the admonitions attributed to the Prophet Muhammad regarding the *fitna* (trial) of rebellion against unjust rulers. According to many of these thinkers, the mission of Qur'anic revelation is to provide a revolutionary ideology, sufficient unto itself, that can transform people and free them from the shackles of unjust cultural and social practices. Modern-day Islamic revolutions

or revolutions of Muslims in their various locales have therefore been influenced significantly by the early establishment of the Islamic social order under Muhammad and his successors; the ideology of revelation as revolutionary; Marxist thought; and to a lesser extent, the revolutionary ethos ushered into the modern world by the peasantry overthrowing of the old aristocratic order during the French Revolution. Early theorists of revolution in Islam include Ibn Khaldun, who proposed the Mahdist theory, which argues that at the end of time, after a period of social and moral disorder and crisis, a redeemer or guide called the "Mahdi" will arrive who will lead a revolution of justice and reinstitute the Islamic Golden Age. This theory is shared by Shi'i and Sunni Islam, and there have been numerous Mahdist movements throughout history, which have been led by charismatic leaders proclaiming themselves as the Mahdi. Other theorists of revolution include Afghani, who endorsed an early form of Islamic liberation theology. Some of the most influential 20th-century revolutionary thinkers include 'Ali Shari'ati, Sayyid Qutb, Ayatollah Khomeini, Muhammad 'Abduh, Sultan Galiyev, and Mawdudi.

Within Islamic political thought are two general streams of revolutionary writings and activities: one that relies on the principle of Islam as a comprehensive system, often as a reaction to Western colonialism (realized, for example, in the writings of Qutb or the activities of the Muslim Brotherhood), and one that employs Islamic thought while appropriating Western notions of revolution and political-economic transformation (along the lines of Marxist or socialist thought). The latter stream may be found, for example, in the writings of Shari'ati, who provided some of the ideological basis for the Iranian Revolution of 1979, which witnessed the collaboration of Marxist and Islamic activists in overthrowing the Western-backed, secular regime of Shah Muhammad Reza Pahlavi.

Inspiration for the revolutionary trend that seeks to establish an Islamic state or caliphate derives from several ideas: (1) the eternal and absolute sovereignty of God, who liberates Muslims from human bondage, guarantees the victory of believers and affirms their brotherhood, and gives Muslim authorities the power to administer the laws of God; (2) the divine origin of the Qur'an, which ensures the truth and eternal status of Qur'anic revelation and the guidance of Muslims; (3) the unique status of the Islamic *umma* (community of believers), which will lead society to righteousness and justice because it has a mandate from God; (4) righteousness as a precondition of vicegerency and success in administration (the word *khilāfa*, "caliphate," referring to morally upright practice and trusteeship of society); (5) Islamic consciousness, which entails recognition of the superiority of Islam compared to all other ways of life and necessitates refusal of, or even rebellion against, defeatism, colonial appropriation of land and people, subservience, irrelevance, injustice, and evil; (6) the necessity of establishing a political and religious order on Earth that ensures the worship of God alone; and (7) the comprehensiveness, uniqueness, and sufficiency of the Islamic system for all humanity. When Muslim societies fall into decadence, foreign rule, economic servitude, or faithless disorder, for example, change in the form of revolution is necessary to restore God's will on Earth and the ideal of a just social order. The rule of righteousness and justice is achieved through political appropriation of power to oversee and implement the social, cultural, and economic transformation of society. An influential verse of the Qur'an that commands people to accept responsibility and accountability for every action has served as the basis for much Islamic revolutionary thinking on the logic that God will not change the condition of a people until they strive to change their own conditions (Q. 13:11; see also 8:53). The oppressed are, therefore, responsible for their condition and are accountable for their weakness in the face of their oppressor, whom they have enabled. The revolutionary process is made possible through commitment, collective work or collaboration, education, conviction, purity of thought and action, and jihad (struggle; activity and devotion to transformation). Struggle is necessary and violence potentially unavoidable for the achievement of justice.

Revolutions in Islamic history have included the Abbasid revolution that overthrew the Umayyad caliphate in the eighth century; the Sufi revolution of Shaykh Abu Hafs 'Umar al-Suhrawardi, who aided the spread of Sufism and brought political legitimacy to Sufism in the 13th century; the Islamic revolution of the Songhay Empire beginning in the 11th century; the Algerian War from 1954 to 1962; and the Iranian Revolution of 1979. The puritan elements in the Iranian Revolution—a noteworthy revolution for the current generation—sought to replace the morally lax and disordered political system with a new moral order and parochially rejected cosmopolitanism and Western culture. Some modern-day Islamist groups, such as Hizbullah in Lebanon and Hamas in Palestine, view their struggle against occupation and political corruption as revolutionary work that employs a type of Islamic liberation theology toward the ends of social, political, and economic freedom from Western-backed interventions in the Islamic world.

See also coup d'état; fundamentalism; jihad; military; quietism and activism; rebellion

Further Reading

Said Amir Arjomand, "Iran's Islamic Revolution in Comparative Perspective," *World Politics* 38, no. 3 (1986); Idem, "Revolution in Early Islam: The Rise of Islam as Constitutive Revolution," in *Islam in Progress: Historical and Civilizational Perspectives*, edited by Johann P. Arnason, Armando Salvatore, and Georg Stauth, 2006; John Foran, "Theories of Revolution Revisited: Toward a Fourth Generation?" *Sociological Theory* 11, no. 1 (1993); Yvonne Yazbeck Haddad, "Qur'anic Justification for an Islamic Revolution: The View of Sayyid Qutb," *Middle East Journal* 37, no. 1 (1983); Thomas Hodgkin, "The Revolutionary Tradition in Islam," *Race and Class* 21, no. 3 (1980); Jacob Lassner, "The 'Abbasid Dawla: An Essay on the Concept of Revolution in Early Islam," *Shi'ism*, edited by Etan Kohlberg, 2003; Roberto Marin-Guzman, "Arab Tribes, the Umayyad Dynasty and the 'Abbasid Revolution," *American Journal of Islamic Social Sciences* 21, no. 4 (2004).

MELISSA FINN

Rida, Muhammad Rashid (1865–1935)

A Syro-Egyptian publicist, publisher, and anticolonial activist of the Arab Renaissance (*al-nahḍa*), Rida founded the influential Cairo-based Pan-Islamist journal *al-Manar* (The lighthouse; 1898–1935) as well as a host of educational societies and political organizations, both public and secret. Known as an Islamic reformer, he was the self-proclaimed heir and biographer of Muhammad ʻAbduh (whose partial exegesis of the Qur'an he edited and serialized as *Tafsir al-Manar*) and the frustrated disciple of Afghani (who died before Rida could join him). While his sociopolitical commitments were enactments of the reforms called for in his journal, his trademark advocacy of a critical return to the Qur'an and prophetic traditions (the so-called Method of the Pious Predecessors, *manhaj al-salaf al-ṣāliḥ*, which earned him his Salafi designation) evolved no scholarship. Rather, it laid the discursive foundations of the emerging public sphere of his time.

Born to a Sunni family of Sayyids in the coastal town of Qalamun near Tripoli in the then-Syrian province of the Ottoman Empire, Rida learned to read and write and memorized the Qur'an at the local school before briefly moving to Tripoli's Turkish-language government school. He then spent eight years at the private school of the Azhari shaykh Husayn al-Jisr, which offered a blend of the Islamic and positive sciences, graduating in 1892. Prior to his emigration to Cairo (1897), he contributed to several Tripolitan and Beiruti newspapers while furthering his education both at the hands of scholars and in the columns of scientific popularization journals such as *al-Muqtataf* (The selected).

It was the reading of Afghani's and ʻAbduh's subversive and short-lived Parisian newspaper *al-ʻUrwa al-Wuthqa* (The firmest bond) that ultimately gave him a sense of purpose, inspiring him to publish a reformist journal that would guide the world's Muslims on the path of unity, progress, and civilization. From Ghazali's *Ihya' ʻUlum al-Din* (The revivification of the religious sciences), the second most influential reading of his youth, Rida retained a commitment to reorganize Islamic sciences but disowned Sufism, which he squarely equated with devious popular religiosity in the wake of a traumatic experience with the Naqshbandis.

Rida grew up witnessing the gradual encroachments of the Western powers on the territories of Islam. While missionarism and colonialism were the biggest external foes, the servility toward the past of the ʻulama' and the uncritical emulation of the West by the Europeanized (*mutafarnijūn*) constituted the biggest internal ills and were subsumed by the double-edged concept of imitation (*taqlīd*). When it came to combating missionarism, however, Rida had no qualms with imitation. He thus pioneered an Islamic missionary institute (Dar al-Daʻwa wa-l-Irshad, 1912), which included in its curricula the sociology of the papacy and the patriarchate, and he oversaw the establishment of a Muslim replica of the Young Men's Christian Association (Jamʻiyyat al-Shubban al-Muslimin, 1927). A fervent Ottoman constitutionalist, Rida saw in the caliphate the only defense against the increasing powers of the nation-state with its reliance on foreign legal codes. Up until ʻAbduh's death (1905), he therefore relentlessly exhorted the ʻulama' to codify the shariʻa and advocated a synthesis in legal rulings among the four Sunni schools of law (*talfīq*). After ʻAbduh's death, Rida's pledge not to engage in politics (ʻAbduh's condition for supporting *al-Manar*) became obsolete, and he openly thrust himself into the fray. At the heart of Western civilization and progress, Rida had recognized the power of organizations.

In 1905, he organized the Ottoman Society for Consultation (Jamʻiyyat al-Shura al-ʻUthmaniyya). In 1908, he spared no speeches or articles in favor of the reinstated Ottoman Constitution. In 1911, however, despairing of the anti-Arab policy of the Committee of Union and Progress, he founded the Society for Arab Union (Jamʻiyyat al-Jamiʻa al-ʻArabiyya), a Pan-Arab secret society that defended the interests of the Arab provinces of the Ottoman Empire. In 1912, he cofounded the Party for Ottoman Decentralization (Hizb al-la Markaziyya al-Uthmaniyya). Although he was on the margins of Egyptian politics, he played an active role in Syrian politics, from the Young Turk Revolution (1908) until his death (1935). As president of the Syrian Congress (1920), he negotiated Syrian independence with the British and the French. He was a member of the Syrian-Palestinian Delegation in Geneva in 1921, sat on the political committee in Cairo during the Great Syrian Revolt of 1925–26, and participated in the Islamic Conferences of Mecca (1926) and Jerusalem (1931).

Perceived as a crucial opinion maker by contemporary political players, he was contacted by the British during World War I to spread the idea of independence among the Arabs. He also communicated the Arab opposition to the creation of an independent Jewish state to the representatives of the Egyptian and Levantine Jewish communities and corresponded with Chaim Weizmann, the first president-to-be of Israel. He even managed to remain on good terms with both Sharif Husayn of Mecca and ʻAbd al-ʻAziz b. Saʻud, envisioning the latter as the most capable leader of a revived caliphate (and a much-needed patron for a permanently indebted *al-Manar*).

Rida's later shift from Ottomanism to Wahhabi Arabism was more pragmatic than doctrinal—his publication of Hanbali authors such as Ibn Taymiyya (d. 1328) notwithstanding. More broadly, his championing of premodern scholars, whose ideas he selectively paraphrased or flagrantly distorted, was consistently elusive. An example of selective paraphrase is his treatment of Najm al-Din al-Tufi (d. 1316) and Abu Ishaq al-Shatibi (d. 1388), the most radical exponents of the legal theory concept of public interest (*maṣlaḥa*), while distortion is evinced in his portrayal of the 18th-century Yemeni reformer Muhammad al-Shawkani as a supporter of legal analogy (*qiyās*). A new professional in search of legitimacy, Rida affiliated himself with authorities who afforded him the concepts needed to mold public opinion and to push for political institutions that would resist wholesale Westernization: *maṣlaḥa* allowed him to speak in the name of the public good and *qiyās* to justify all-out legislation on an Islamic basis. By "journalizing" not only Islamic legal

concepts but also genres such as the fatwa, Rida ultimately severed a formidable jurisprudential corpus from its procedural basis, reducing it to a limited and ready-to-use lexicon. A pragmatic move aimed at confronting external and internal challenges to Muslim society in a colonial setting, Rida's "Salafi turn" in effect empowered the future postcolonial literate masses to Islamicize indefinitely.

See also 'Abduh, Muhammad (1849–1905); Ghazali (ca. 1058–1111); Ibn Taymiyya (1263–1328); Syria

Further Reading

Ahmad Dallal, "Appropriating the Past: Twentieth-Century Reconstruction of Pre-Modern Islamic Thought," *Islamic Law and Society* 7, no. 1 (2000); Mahmoud Osman Haddad, "Arab Religious Nationalism in the Colonial Era: Reading Rashîd Ridâ's Ideas on the Caliphate," *Journal of the American Oriental Society* 117, no. 2 (1997): 253–77; Dyala Hamzah, "Muhammad Rashid Rida or: The Importance of Being (a) Journalist," in *Religion and Its Other: Secular and Sacral Concepts and Practices in Interaction*, edited by Heike Bock, Jörg Feuchter, and Michi Knecht, 2008; Albert H. Hourani, *Arabic Thought in the Liberal Age, 1798–1939*, 1983 [1962]; Malcolm H. Kerr, *Islamic Reform: The Political and Legal Theories of Muhammad 'Abduh and Rashid Rida*, 1966; Umar Ryad, *Islamic Reformism and Christianity: A Critical Reading of the Works of Muḥammad Rashīd Riḍā and His Associates (1898–1935)*, 2009; Simon Wood, *Christian Criticisms, Islamic Proofs: Rashid Rida's Modernist Defense of Islam*, 2008.

DYALA HAMZAH

Rightly Guided Caliphate (632–61)

The first four rulers after Muhammad's death in 632 came to be regarded in later (Sunni) historiography as the "Rightly Guided Caliphs" (*al-khulafā' al-rāshidūn*). They comprised Abu Bakr (r. 632–34, allegedly the first male Muslim after Muhammad); 'Umar b. al-Khattab (r. 634–44, who introduced the Islamic calendar starting with the Prophet's emigration from Mecca to Medina, i.e., the hijra); 'Uthman b. 'Affan (r. 644–56, to whom Sunni tradition ascribes the compilation of the text of the Qur'an); and 'Ali b. Abi Talib (r. 656–61, who became the progenitor of Shi'ism). They not only belonged to the same tribe as the Prophet (the Quraysh) but were also closely related to him by marriage: Abu Bakr and 'Umar were his fathers-in-law, and 'Uthman was the Prophet's son-in-law, as was 'Ali, who also was his cousin. The era of the Rightly Guided Caliphs is marked by two main characteristics that had a decisive influence on Islamic history: a rapid expansion of Islamic rule on the one hand and a severe crisis of legitimacy on the other, which finally led to the split of the Muslim community into religiopolitical factions that only later became tangible as Sunnis and Shi'is.

Within a few years after Muhammad's death, the Islamic realm underwent a geographical expansion beyond the Arabian Peninsula that is largely unparalleled in history. By the year 661, Muslims ruled over Mesopotamia (conquered in 633), Palestine and Syria (634–40), Iraq (636–41), Egypt (639–42), Persia (640–42), parts of North Africa (647), Armenia (652), and Cyprus (654) and had laid the foundation for the later Muslim empire stretching from Andalus to Central and South Asia. The military activities, however, did not take place under a central supreme command. None of the early caliphs distinguished himself as an army leader, and the title *amīr al-mu'minīn* (Commander of the Faithful), which was first assumed by 'Umar, always remained more of a claim than a reality. Instead, the conquests were carried out by local leaders such as Khalid b. al-Walid, and the tribal entities acted largely on their own authority. Being rulers without sufficient troops of their own, the caliphs could never be sure of the loyalty of these armies; not even the provincial governors were reliable in this regard. It is not by chance that 'Uthman was defenseless in the face of opposing tribal groups and was finally murdered in 656.

The early conquests entailed two other developments with longstanding consequences. One was the establishment of a central administrative system begun under 'Umar, who formed an institution for the distribution of the incoming booty, the so-called *dīwān*. The other was the shift of the center of gravity away from the Arabian Peninsula: 'Ali moved the capital from Medina to Kufa in southern Iraq, and later, under the Umayyads and Abbasids, it was transferred to Damascus and Baghdad. Henceforth, the Arabian coastal area of the Hijaz as the cradle of Islam fell into political oblivion and remained present in Muslim memory only as the spiritual center and the site of the annual pilgrimage.

Following Muhammad's death in 632, not only did prophetic guidance of the nascent Islamic community come to an abrupt halt, but the political leadership also had to be reformulated, as the Prophet had apparently not left any explicit instructions on how to organize his succession. The so-called wars of apostasy (*ridda*) immediately after his death, when several tribes broke away from Medina and counterprophets appeared on the stage, were easily halted by Abu Bakr, but the ensuing crisis of legitimacy left far more enduring marks on the Muslim community. Throughout the early period, there was no unanimity on how the leader should be elected or what the basis of his legitimacy should be. (Abu Bakr was appointed by acclamation, 'Umar by designation, and 'Uthman by consultation.) In general, the genealogical tribal principle was predominant, while outstanding service to Islam played only a secondary role.

The crisis came to a head when 'Uthman was killed by his opponents, who had not acknowledged the legitimacy of his rule and accused him of favoritism and other transgressions. His murder provoked what came to be known as the First Civil War (*fitna*, lit. "affliction, trial"), the single most crucial event in Islamic history in that it was the starting point of the deep split within the Muslim community. It was only later that the emerging two main parties could be identified as Sunnis and Shi'is; in the context of the

early period it is more appropriate to define them as adherents of ‘Uthman and adherents of ‘Ali, respectively. The two groups represented contrasting approaches to the question of the legitimacy of succession. The adherents of ‘Uthman recognized the third caliph's rule as legitimate, denying that he had forfeited his position by his transgressions and stressing that he was elected by a council (*shūrā*) after ‘Umar's death. The followers of ‘Ali, who seem initially to have stressed ‘Uthman's transgressions, soon came to narrow the circle of claimants to the caliphate to the direct descendants of the family of the Prophet (*ahl al-bayt*), which eventually came to mean descendants of ‘Ali and Fatima, daughter of the Prophet. The power struggle was finally decided in favor of the adherents of ‘Uthman. ‘Ali's brief rule, which bore the marks of a countercaliphate, was challenged by a number of oppositional currents and was finally replaced by the Umayyad dynasty, which restored the claim to ‘Uthmani leadership. By then the adherents of ‘Ali had split by the defection of the so-called Kharijis, who rejected ‘Ali as no better than ‘Uthman and who were willing to accept as leader of the community only the most meritorious Muslim, disregarding ancestral affiliations. Around 700 another party emerged in the Murji'is, who suspended judgment with regard to the relative status of ‘Ali and ‘Uthman without accepting the Umayyads.

The concept of the Rightly Guided Caliphate is a later construction of Islamic theology based on the retrospective need for a unified community. It was only in the formation of the hadith in the ninth century that the thesis of four primary caliphs was finally acknowledged and ‘Uthman and ‘Ali were equally regarded as legitimate rulers; this process coincided with the general canonization of the Companions of the Prophet (*ṣaḥāba*) and even entailed occasional attempts to add a fifth ruler to the Rightly Guided Caliphs (either Hasan b. ‘Ali or ‘Umar b. ‘Abd al-‘Aziz). Nevertheless, it was too late by then to reverse the basic split of the community: the ‘Alids that evolved into Shi‘ism rejected the legitimacy of the first three caliphs (as well as the testimony of most *ṣaḥāba*) by claiming that the Prophet himself had designated ‘Ali as his successor and that caliphal rule had therefore been usurped. Finally, the era of the Rightly Guided Caliphs was completely transfigured in modern Islam (especially after the formal abolition of the caliphate in 1924) when Islamist currents in particular started defining it as the golden age of Islam, which they planned on restoring. An epoch that had been highly controversial (three of the four caliphs died at the hands of a murderer) now acquired a normative character.

See also Abu Bakr (ca. 573–634); ‘Ali b. Abi Talib (ca. 599–661); succession; ‘Uthman b. ‘Affan (ca. 579–656); ‘Umar b. al-Khattab (ca. 580–644)

Further Reading

Asma Afsaruddin, *The First Muslims: History and Memory*, 2008; Patricia Crone, *Medieval Islamic Political Thought*, 2004; Fred McGraw Donner, *The Early Islamic Conquests*, 1981; Safa Khulusi and Sabiha al-Dabbagh, *Al-Khulafa' ar-Rashidun: The Rightly-Guided Khalifs*, 1990; Wilferd Madelung, *The Succession to Muḥammad: A Study in the Early Caliphate*, 1997; Albrecht Noth, *The Early Arabic Historical Tradition: A Source-Critical Study*, 1994; Abu Ja‘far Muhammad b. Jarir al-Tabari, *The History of al-Ṭabarī (Ta'rīkh al-rusul wa'l mulūk)*, vols. 10–17, 1985–98.

RAINER BRUNNER

rights

Rights exist de facto as social norms in any society with a minimum of social differentiation or hierarchy, whether such societies have developed concepts of rights or not. Premodern Islamic legal thought developed a concept of rights in a technical legal sense. Premodern Islamic political thought also recognized certain rights, though these are distinct from legal rights in the sense of specific, enforceable obligations. The extent to which premodern Islamic religious discourses contributed to modern rights discourses among Muslims is debatable, but the two trends reveal a complex and sometimes productive fusion of Islamic and Western notions of rights.

Legal Rights

Islamic law, like any sophisticated legal system, confers many different kinds of rights, such as those regarding property, the sanctity of the person, marriage, and access to courts. Such rights, like rights found in other legal systems, comprise privileges, claims, powers, and immunities, each of which has a correlative (no claim, duty, liability, and disability, respectively) and an opposite (duty, no claim, disability, and liability, respectively). For example, under Islamic sales law (*buyū‘*), a buyer's right to rescind a sale upon visual inspection of the sales goods (*khiyār al-ru'ya*) includes the privilege not to purchase the goods—that is, the buyer has no duty to purchase the goods and the seller has no claim against the buyer for not doing so. It also includes the claim against the buyer to sell the goods if they meet the buyer's approval upon such inspection, which entails the seller's correlative duty to sell them to the buyer. The Islamic legal system also recognizes procedural rights of litigants in civil matters and of defendants in criminal matters, and these can have important substantive consequences. Such rights include the impartiality of the judge and of witnesses and in criminal matters the requirement that the court fully observe strict evidentiary rules and exculpatory doctrines.

Islamic law classifies certain kinds of claim rights, which imply a duty or liability on the part of someone other than the holder, under the term *ḥaqq* (pl. *ḥuqūq*; compare Hebrew *ḥuqqīm*, "laws," as in Exodus 18:16, "God's laws"). The word *ḥaqq* appears very frequently in the Qur'an in the sense of "truth" or "what is correct." Sometimes it is also used in ways that are relevant to a concept of rights: it can refer to certain claims against believers for the performance of duties (Q. 2:180, 241, concerning bequests and divorce,

respectively) and against their property (Q. 17:26; 51:19; 70:24, concerning claims of the poor to charity). In two closely related passages, it refers obliquely, in a prohibition against homicide, to the right to impose capital punishment (Q. 6:151; 17:33). It can also refer generally to the authority to engage in certain acts, though in such passages it is always used in a negative construction to indicate that the behavior in question was engaged in unlawfully or without right. For example, several persons or groups are said to have behaved arrogantly—in other words, contrary to God's injunctions—without right or justification (Q. 7:146; 10:23; 28:39; 42:42; 46:20). Others are accused of having killed the prophets without right or justification (Q. 2:61; 3:21; 3:112; 3:181; and 4:155; see also 5:116; 7:33; and 11:79, which contain similar negative constructions in other contexts).

In post-Qur'anic Islamic law, *ḥuqūq* in the sense of claim rights fall into three distinct groups. Some of these rights are private (i.e., held by individuals); some are owed to God, being claims against humans to avoid matters that are divinely prohibited and to perform acts that are divinely commanded; and some straddle both categories. In regard to all three categories of rights or claims, judges have jurisdiction, on behalf of the state, to award recovery or punishment, as appropriate, depending on the right involved. As Ibn Rushd (Averroes, d. 1198) puts it, "It is widely agreed that the judge can rule in regard to any kind of right, whether it be a right of God or a right of individuals, and that he is the representative of the supreme political leader in that regard." Private rights, or the rights of individuals (*ḥuqūq al-ādamiyyīn* or *ḥuqūq al-'ibād*), generally arise where there has been a civil wrong, such as a breach of contract. They entitle the holder to seek recovery or redress through litigation. Such rights constitute claims against other private individuals. The rights of God (*ḥuqūq Allāh*) may be divided into two kinds: those that arise from violations of Islamic criminal law and those that reflect God's claim against humans that they perform certain religious obligations. In the former case, God's rights extend specifically to the small number of crimes described in Islamic law, especially those mentioned together with a specific punishment in the Qur'an, referred to collectively as *ḥudūd* (limits): theft (Q. 5:38); unlawful sexual intercourse (Q. 4:15–16; 4:25; 24:2); false or unsupported accusation of unlawful sexual intercourse (Q. 24:4); and "brigandage" (*ḥirāba*), a residual category that covers other transgressions against persons and property, especially outside of urban areas (Q. 5:33). Others that are implied by the Qur'an, mandated in prophetic tradition, or historically viewed as theologically serious violations of public order, such as wine drinking, apostasy, refusal to pray, and insulting the Prophet or his Companions, may be included here as well. The right in such cases is God's claim against the defendant for corporal or capital punishment. Such punishment, even capital punishment, is thought by some to expiate the crime, which is considered to be a sin. The fact that the state has the right to enforce these criminal laws and so to inflict punishment on God's behalf has suggested to some that these are public rights exercised by the state on behalf of the community. These divine public rights also resemble private rights to the extent that they arise from the commission of an offense.

The state also retains a right—strictly, a power—to inflict a lesser discretionary corporal punishment called *ta'zīr*, which may not exceed the lowest of the prescribed *ḥudūd*-based corporal punishments. Such discretionary punishment may be meted out in cases where conviction for a *ḥadd* offense is impossible because of exculpatory doctrines or strict evidentiary requirements or for general transgressions of public order not addressed by the law. It is unclear whether this residual right to punish, in either case, inheres in the state or is exercised by the state on God's behalf. Whether *ta'zīr* is God's right or simply the state's exercise of a de facto power (entailing the perpetrator's correlative liability for punishment), it owes its existence in part to the difficulty of obtaining criminal convictions under Islamic law. This difficulty could be characterized as a right of defendants that involves an immunity and a correlative disability on the part of the state.

In contrast to the claims of God that arise from behavior that God has prohibited, other claims of God pertain to the performance of religious obligations, behavior that God has mandated. In such cases God enjoys the right to expect positive compliance with the mandated conduct and thus has a claim right against believers, all other things being equal, for the successful performance of such acts. Although such divine claims may pertain to private worship, such as prayer, they are also connected with the public sphere, and the creation of appropriate conditions for their successful performance are thus viewed as the responsibility of the state, as in the case of the collection of canonical taxes (zakat), making provision for holding the Friday congregational prayer (*ṣalāt al-jum'a*), infrastructural initiatives that ease or assist with the pilgrimage (hajj), or the prosecution of holy war (jihad). An individual's failure to perform such obligations is not usually something over which courts have jurisdiction unless accompanied by public disavowal of the obligations themselves, which could subject the person in question to liability for *ta'zīr*.

Whether a given obligation is classified as a duty pursuant to a right of God or of humans can have consequences. For example, in the case of zakat, whose proceeds are distributed to the needy, there is a disagreement over whether paying the tax is a religious obligation (and thus one of God's rights) or a claim held by the poor against those with sufficient wealth (and thus a right belonging to humans). In the former case, as a religious obligation, the right could only be "enforced" against those otherwise endowed with the legal capacity to perform religious obligations in general: sane adults, but not, for example, minors. If the right is one that belongs to humans, then the restrictions related to the capacity to perform religious obligations would not apply, and a larger class of persons would be subject to the tax (e.g., minors).

The Islamic law of torts—*jināyāt* (offenses) or often simply *diyyāt* (blood money payments)—gives rise to rights that encompass both a private and a public or divine dimension. Private right holders in such cases (certain injured persons or heirs of victims of wrongful killing) enjoy a right to retaliation in serious cases and to

compensation in less serious cases. The right of retaliation includes the power to waive infliction of equivalent physical harm or to accept compensation in lieu thereof. Such retaliation is generally carried out by the state in order to satisfy the private claim and also to satisfy the public claim against the defendant on God's behalf, as well as to discourage resort to self-help and vigilantism.

Is there a coherent, even if latent, conception or philosophy of rights under Islamic law, whether such rights are designated as *ḥaqq* or merely de facto recognized under law? Since the *ḥuqūq* are viewed primarily as claims that, if proved, lead to the restoration of something, they do not fit easily within the "will theory of rights," according to which an individual's rights carve out a sphere of choices and freedom of action. It may be that they accord better with an interest or benefit theory, in which rights further the interests of, or benefit, their holders—for example, by restoring a claimant, after a wrong, to the previous status quo, but even this is difficult to decide with certainty. On the other hand, God—who is omnipotent, transcendent, and utterly self-sufficient—has neither interests nor a need for rights to enjoy absolute sovereignty, at least according to premodern Islamic theology. Nor does it seem reasonable to speak of God as a beneficiary of legal remedies. It has been noted that religious legal systems pose problems for the analysis of rights in terms of interests or will.

If the latent underpinning of rights in Islamic law is closest to an interest theory of rights, does that mean that there are "natural rights" in Islamic law? The question has become controversial in the field of Islamic studies. Islamic legal theory (*uṣūl al-fiqh*), both Sunni and Shi'i, is highly positivist in the sense that answers to legal questions are grounded in specific passages in revealed texts (Qur'an, prophetic traditions). For Sunnis, rights and obligations are created by God and spelled out, in varying degrees of clarity, in texts sent down by God. The criterion for the validity of such rights is, for most Sunni jurists, simply their existence in or link with those texts. Shi'is, however, inherited much of their theology from the early rationalist movement of the Mu'tazilis, who held, as Shi'i legal theorists do, that reason may be used to discover the law—a view that is at least compatible with a notion of natural rights. It has been argued that Islam in general, or Sunni Islam in particular, has neither a theory of natural law nor a theory of natural rights. Recent scholarship has begun to reexamine this claim. A. Kevin Reinhart argues, based on an examination of legal theory texts, that the existence of a range of views makes the question at least nuanced. Anver Emon, who reexamines Sunni legal theorists and expressly equates *ḥuqūq al-ādamiyyīn* with "interests," argues that despite Sunni denials of the force of natural law arguments, juristic discretion rested on assumptions compatible with or even informed by ideas of natural law and natural rights.

Rights of Those Disadvantaged by the Law

Islamic law expressly recognizes that persons and other beings who lack full legal capacity or may be otherwise legally or socially disadvantaged—for example, the disabled, women, minor orphans, slaves, non-Muslims, and even animals—nonetheless enjoy rights. Such rights are not, however, necessarily defined as *ḥuqūq* or separately conceptualized as rights. Although the physically disabled are only rarely expressly disadvantaged by Islamic law, Muslim jurists did recognize that they were entitled to accommodations in many though not all instances in regard, for example, to religious obligations that otherwise presuppose full physical capability. However, according to Mawardi (d. 1058) in his treatise on government, physical disabilities do prevent otherwise qualified candidates from becoming or remaining caliph. Those with mental disabilities are precluded under Islamic law from engaging in financial transactions for their own protection, but the mentally retarded (*ma'tūh*, as opposed to the insane, *majnūn*) are allowed to marry according to some modern fatwas. Perhaps these accommodations can be regarded as rights in view of modern legislation specifically conferring rights on the disabled such as the U.S. Americans with Disabilities Act or the UN Declaration on the Rights of Disabled Persons. Although women suffer from certain legal disabilities under Islamic law—a diminished capacity to testify, asymmetrical divorce rights, certain rules of ritual purity, diminished inheritance rights, and others—they also enjoy certain express protections under Islamic law. For example, even though rules of marriage and divorce disadvantage women in important respects, women enjoy specific rights as spouses, including the right to material support (*nafaqa*, which extends to food, lodging, and clothing). It has been argued that informal but consistent judicial cognizance of women's disabilities under Islamic family law contributed to an increased willingness to enforce strictly those marital rights that women did have. Orphaned children, though lacking full legal capacity as minors, are protected against predations on their property by ethical injunctions in the Qur'an requiring fair dealing by their guardians (e.g., Q. 6:152). Slaves also enjoy certain rights even within the context of servitude, including the de facto ability to own property, the right to resist forced conversion to Islam, and the right not to be married to someone against their will. Non-Muslim subjects of Muslim-ruled states are generally considered protected persons (*dhimmīs*) and are, within certain limits, entitled to practice their religion without undue interference and free from forced conversion, in exchange for the payment of a special tax. Enforcement of such protections varied with political circumstances; conversely, *dhimmīs* could forfeit their protections by failing to observe the restrictions to which they were subject. Non-Muslims suffered other specific legal disabilities as well, such as being precluded from inheriting from their Muslim relatives according to Islamic inheritance law (though, according to some jurists, they could receive otherwise lawful bequests) or, in the case of men, from marrying Muslim women (though non-Muslim women could, under Sunni law, marry Muslim men). In light of emerging contemporary concerns about animals' welfare, it is worth mentioning that the law also allowed for legal intervention in cases of animal mistreatment. This responsibility belonged to the *muḥtasib*, an inspector in charge of public health, safety, and morals whose jurisdiction extended to market practices and public works. Certain pietistic currents in religious thought and the

depiction of apparently sentient animals in the Qur'an (e.g., sura 27, "The Ants") also engendered reflection on whether human dominion over animals, though widely assumed to be divinely imposed, was justified.

Political Rights

Political rights as conceived by premodern Muslim thinkers involved limitations on state power and as such perhaps imply a will theory of rights, in contrast to the legal rights previously discussed. For the most part, such political rights did not involve participation in political decision making but instead rested on the idea that free subjects of Muslim-ruled states were entitled to two things: the application of Islamic law and otherwise to be left alone by the state. Government by rule of law, independent of an individual ruler's whim, would contribute to the realization of a just social, legal, and political order. Conceptions of the rule of law were thus related to the full recognition, application, and enforcement of divine public and private *ḥuqūq*.

The "right" to live under a government that applied and enforced Islamic law was expressed early on as a result of disputes, including civil wars, over legitimacy of rule and attendant doubts about rulers' claims to religious authority. Such doubts contributed in part to the emergence of private specialists in piety who gradually evolved into the separate class of religious scholars ('ulama'), who focused, among other tasks, on the development of criteria for evaluating behavior in religious terms, for example, by systematically formulating theological criteria for salvation and the rules of Islamic law. The resulting bifurcation of temporal and religious authority led to a lowering of expectations in regard to rulers and a strengthening of the idea that the scholars' discourse was the primary site of relevant concepts of ethics. It undoubtedly also contributed to the formulations of some ideas about limits on state (or the ruler's) power. Several modern scholars (e.g., Noah Feldman, Wael B. Hallaq) have suggested that the distinctive relationship between the state and the clerical institution in premodern Islamic societies evolved, after early disappointments, into a system of checks on government, grounded in the scholars' moral authority, that could perhaps be construed as further implying some individual political rights and even a kind of constitutional order.

As early as the mid-eighth century, the Iranian political advisor and litterateur 'Abdallah b. al-Muqaffa' (d. ca. 756) noted the currency of the phrase "No obedience to any creature who is disobedient to the Creator" (*lā ṭā'ata li-makhlūq fī ma'ṣiyat al-khāliq*). The phrase was understood to mean that no obedience was required toward impious rulers, at least in regard to their impious acts, and thus expressed the idea that a ruler could be disobeyed, and perhaps deposed, on religious grounds. Although countertendencies urged obedience even to impious Muslim rulers under the theory that political stability could be more important than the adherence to principle, the phrase discussed by Ibn al-Muqaffa' implies increasing recognition of the zone between private conduct and state authority and of refinements in religious and ethical criteria for assessing the rectitude of state action.

There were generally four hallmarks of right rule, which entailed obedience to political authority: enforcement of criminal law (*iqāmat al-ḥudūd*), prosecution of jihad, preservation of sexual morality (*furūj*), and protection of private property (*ḥurmat al-amwāl*). These may be restated as rights: free Muslim citizens have the right to expect that government will enforce God's law. This expectation may be related to concerns about personal or communal salvation, but one can imagine more specific concerns as well. For example, the protection of private property expresses the specific concern that the government will not unlawfully confiscate the private property of Muslims except according to law—this is the right to be free from unlawful misappropriation (*ghaṣb*) by political authorities. After all, the persons and property of free Muslims are inviolate (*ḥarām*) under Islamic law. Such inviolability (*ḥurma*) may be expressed as a right (either a privilege or an immunity for individuals) and its correlatives (either no claim or a disability on the part of the state). Such ideas accord well with a will theory of rights.

Against this background, it is possible to isolate some additional discrete ideas in Islamic legal and political thought that perhaps deserve the term "right." Elites, especially scholars, claimed for themselves the right (and sometimes the duty) to provide ethical advice (*naṣīḥa*) to rulers. Indeed, according to one maxim, "Religion consists of the provision of sound advice" (*al-dīn al-naṣīḥa*). In addition, all subjects were, at least in theory, entitled to appeal directly to the ruler or his representative for the redress of wrongs (*maẓālim*). In regard to the enforcement of the law, limits were placed on the state's ability to invade private property to make arrests for crimes of morality, in other words, those involving intoxicants, frivolous entertainment (e.g., music or dancing, in the view of the socially conservative), and sexual immorality. Jurists also sought to impose limits on the state's power in regard to certain armed rebellions that had a plausible claim of theological support (*ta'wīl*). Such rules allowed the state to fight the rebels but required that property and even weapons be returned to rebels once order had been restored. This could be characterized as the rebels' immunity from, and the state's correlative disability in regard to, gross mistreatment exceeding the minimum force required to restore civil order.

Some Contemporary Notions of Rights

Modern conceptions of rights, which rest on the idea that individuals have inherent rights of various kinds, especially political rights consisting mostly of privileges and immunities against the state, are indebted to the American and French revolutions. In Muslim-ruled states of the early modern period, ideas of liberty and equality factored into a number of programs of constitutional reform, occasionally justified under principles of Islamic law. Throughout the 19th century, the greatest of the Muslim absolutist empires, the Ottomans, extended state power into the lives of individuals, bypassing those intermediary groups through which the Ottoman state had traditionally ruled and fostering ideas of social and legal equality, at least for males, and perhaps of individual duties and protections. The Tunisian statesman and reformer Khayr al-Din al-Tunisi (d. 1890) argued

for constitutional liberties, portrayed as shari'a-compliant, as part of a program of political and religiocultural renewal. The Iranian Constitution of 1906, which took aim against local autocratic government and external imperialist threats, established procedures for electing a representative assembly, including a right to vote for men of certain social classes. Although modeled on the Belgian Constitution of 1831, it was supported by Muslim clerics and required that legislation adopted by the assembly conform to Shi'i interpretations of Islamic law. Such trends—in combination with experiences of colonialism, incipient nationalisms, projects of Islamic reform, modernization, modernity, and the emergence of the post–World War II world order that included international agreements enshrining individual rights under international law—all contributed to modern rights discourses in the Islamic world. It should be emphasized that not all such rights discourses are "Islamic," though some are self-consciously so.

In the modern period, the term *ḥaqq* has come increasingly to translate the word "right" (and the French *droit*) in all the latter's various connotations, so that the term's semantic field has changed to some degree in Arabic. That change has affected usage within both secular and Islamic discourses on rights more generally. The semantic proximity of the Arabic word *ḥaqq* to the English word "right" is nonetheless suggested by the ease with which the Modern Standard Arabic phrase *ḥuqūq al-insān* (lit. "rights of the person") translates to the English phrase "human rights." The term figures prominently in the names of two of the oldest human rights organizations in the Arab world: the Palestinian human rights organization Al-Haq (al-Haqq) and the Egyptian Organization for Human Rights (al-Munazzama al-Misriyya li-Huquq al-Insan), both of which seek to ensure adherence to international standards of human rights and humanitarian law.

The internationalization and universalization of the concepts of rights—civil, human, and political—have also affected Islamic rights discourses. For example, in the 1990s a Saudi organization that protested against government policies called itself in English the Committee for the Defense of Legitimate Rights and in Arabic al-Lajna li-l-Difa' 'an al-Huquq al-Shar'iyya. In Arabic, the adjective *shar'ī* is ambiguous and can mean "legitimate," either in the sense of "according to law" or in the sense of "according to the shari'a." This ambiguity was useful in the group's attempt to portray itself to a religious, Saudi constituency as urging the impartial application of Islamic law and to Western observers as a Saudi human rights organization. The term "rights" (*ḥuqūq*) apparently made sense to both audiences. In recent decades, too, movements to reform family law as it affects women have appealed simultaneously to international law and shari'a as binding transnational standards mandating equality of treatment in domestic legal systems. Islamicizing constitutions have offered a particularly interesting arena for official rights discourses that deploy a language of both liberal and Islamic legitimacy. The preamble to the Iranian Constitution (*Qanun-i Asasi*) of 1979 (as amended in 1989), for example, speaks of women's rights as human rights (*ḥuqūq-i insānī-yi khud*) and proclaims in Article 3.14 that a goal of the state is to secure the rights of all men and women (*ta'mīn-i ḥuqūq-i hamah-yi jānibah-yi afrād az zan wa-mard*).

The governments of some Muslim-majority states, aided in some cases by religious scholars, have also attempted to generate international human rights instruments that adhere to what are claimed as Islamic standards. These have been promulgated in response to international human rights discourses that expressly or implicitly call into question certain rules of Islamic law, such as those that expressly disadvantage women in areas of family law. These efforts have resulted in documents such as the 1981 Universal Islamic Declaration of Human Rights and the 1993 Cairo Declaration on Human Rights in Islam. The documents in question have not been adopted by any Muslim-majority country but seem instead designed to provide a rhetorically useful, politically advantageous, and theologically satisfying response to perceived competition from secularizing international human rights discourses. In such documents, as in Islamicizing constitutions, unqualified affirmations of rights are usually qualified by reference to unspecified Islamic principles so that the scope of the rights in question remains unclear. As Mohammed Arkoun has noted, such documents underscore a "very confused ideological situation" in which "the colonial fact poses problems for both the West and Muslim countries," making it "difficult to speak to a Muslim audience today about the Western origin of human rights without provoking indignant protests." Still, as Arkoun points out, the fact that such efforts are undertaken is itself potentially significant and could yet form part of a "critical reexamination and reworking of the concept of *Truth-Right* (*al-ḥaqq*) and of its foundations" in order to "go beyond the mimetic competition, essentially ideological, between traditional religion and civil religion."

See also hadith; punishment; shari'a; 'ulama'

Further Reading

Khaled Abou El Fadl, *Rebellion and Violence in Islamic Law*, 2001; Al-Haq, accessed March 30, 2010, http://www.alhaq.org; Mohamed Arkoun, *Rethinking Islam: Common Questions, Uncommon Answers*, 1994; Antony Black, *The History of Islamic Political Thought*, 2001; Michael Cook, *Commanding Right and Forbidding Wrong in Islamic Thought*, 2000; Patricia Crone, *God's Rule: Government and Islam*, 2004; Egyptian Organization for Human Rights, accessed March 30, 2010, http://en.eohr.org; Anver Emon, *Islamic Natural Law Theories*, 2010; Noah Feldman, *The Fall and Rise of the Islamic State*, 2008; Wael B. Hallaq, *Sharī'a: Theory, Practice, Transformations*, 2009; Internetprojekte, "Iran—Constitution," accessed March 30, 2010, http://www.servat.unibe.ch/icl/ir00000.html; Abu al-Hasan 'Ali al-Mawardi, *The Ordinances of Government*, translated by W. Wahba, 1996; Ann Mayer, *Islam and Human Rights: Politics and Tradition*, 2006; Ministry of Foreign Affairs, Islamic Republic of Iran, "Constitution," http://www.mfa.gov.ir/cms/cms/Tehran/fa/Tourism/Constitution.htm; A. Kevin Reinhart, *Before Revelation: The Boundaries of Muslim Moral Thought*, 1995; Judith Tucker, *In the House of the Law: Gender and Islamic Law in Ottoman Syria and Palestine*, 1998.

JOSEPH E. LOWRY

royal court

The royal court in Islamic societies encompasses bureaucracy, literary production, public display of sovereignty, and the patronage of arts, sciences, and religious institutions. One of the earliest models for the organization of an Islamic "royal court" comes from the Abbasid caliphate. Under the caliph Abu Ja'far al-Mansur (r. 754–75), an elaborate bureaucratic system of government offices (*dawāwīn*) was established that would allow for the successful government and financial administration of his burgeoning empire. By the time of the caliph Harun al-Rashid (r. 786–809), this system had expanded to include a flowering court culture with the caliph at its center. Texts such as the 11th-century *Rusum Dar al-Khilafah* (*The Rules and Regulations of the Abbasid Court*) outline in great detail the extent of these bureaucratic responsibilities, as well as the colorful experience of everyday life at court. The royal court was governed by strict rules of behavior dictating highly controlled access to the caliph or ruler. Surrounding him were a number of figures (often formally employed as bureaucrats) such as the *nadīm*, or drinking companion, who joined the ruler in entertainments such as chess games and hunting. The *adīb*, an erudite man well read in science, culture, history, and languages, is perhaps best exemplified by the famous al-Jahiz (d. 868). Some of these men could be called *ẓarīf* to note their elegance and refinement. Over time, as Islamic societies began to expand into areas increasingly distant from the Hijaz, foreign court customs, notably Persian, were absorbed into the Islamic paradigm.

The royal household included numerous pages, servants, entertainers, cooks, and craftsmen. The palace of the Islamic world thus became an increasingly complex space, evolving from the early Umayyad *dār al-imāra* (palace of government) model into the more elaborate and formal *dār al-khilāfah* (caliphal palace) model. Architecture played an important role in court life as a means to regulate access to the ruler, as a public display of sovereignty, and as a locus for royal ceremonies. The Ottoman Topkapi Saray, constructed on the order of Mehmed II to be built on top of the Byzantine acropolis, provides an excellent example of these functions, with its multiple gates and courtyards and increasingly restrictive access to royal spaces culminating in the royal harem at the heart of the complex.

Artistic patronage was another important aspect of the outward expression of the royal court. Courtly patronage of the arts and sciences could include undertaking monumental building projects such as the Süleymaniye Mosque in Ottoman Istanbul or the Taj Mahal in Mughal Delhi. But while pious projects such as Qur'an manuscript production or the construction of a new mosque were important undertakings, all manner of luxury items were commissioned under the auspices of the royal court. Costumes, ceremonial weapons, poetic anthologies, culinary utensils, and jewelry were presented as gifts at court and produced in royal workshops closely associated with the palace. Luxury manuscripts of Abu al-Qasim Firdawsi's *Shahnama* (Book of kings) demonstrate the central role that Persianate models of kingship and courtly life played in the development of the Islamic royal court. Examples such as the Safavid *Tahmasp Shahnama* or the Ilkhanid *Demotte Shahnama* lavishly depict the contemporary courtly milieu as the setting for historical episodes, thus creating a connection with the imagined royal past while underscoring the magnificence of the ruler's court.

See also bureaucracy; Mirrors for Princes; political ritual

Further Reading

Abu al-Qasim Firdawsi, *Shāhnāmah*, edited by Jalal Khaliqi Mutlaq, 8 vols., 1987–2002; Hilal al-Sabi', *Rusūm dār al-Khilāfah: The Rules and Regulations of the 'Abbāsid Court*, translated by Elie A. Salem, 1977; Ahmad b. al-Rashid b. al-Zubayr, *Book of Gifts and Rarities*, translated by Ghada al Hijjawi al-Qaddumi, 1996.

ROSE E. MURAVCHICK

S

al-Sadr, Muhammad Baqir (1935–80)

Born in 1935 to a leading Shi'i clerical family in Iraq, Sadr studied with the leading *mujtahids* (jurists) in the holy city of Najaf, notably Abu al-Qasim Kho'i and Muhammad Reza al-Muzaffar, and began to teach in Najaf in 1963. Sadr had to be careful about politics under Saddam's repressive regime, and his relations with Ayatollah Khomeini, who was then in exile in Najaf, were cordial but not close. After the Islamic Revolution, however, Iran's Arabic radio broadcasts referred to him as the "Khomeini of Iraq." Saddam Hussein ordered the execution of Sadr and his sister Amina, known as Bint al-Huda, on April 8, 1980.

In 1959, at the high point of the Iraqi Communist Party's influence, Sadr, a seminarian at the time, entered the public sphere with the publication of his *Falsafatuna* (Our philosophy). He emerged as a leader of the Shi'i reform movement with the publication of another widely circulating book, *Iqtisaduna* (Our economics), in 1968. These two books were written in response to the Marxist challenge, and probably also that of Sunni ideologues, notably Mawlana Abu al-A'la Mawdudi, and demonstrated Sadr's fascination with ideology and Marxist-inspired system-building. In *Iqtisaduna*, Sadr seeks to identify the principles of the Islamic economic system in point-by-point contrast to capitalism and socialism. Sadr justified private property as the fruit of labor and offered a sharp distinction between worked land and dead land. Public property occupied the predominant position in his economic system, and the state was assigned the function of exploiting natural resources and implementing large-scale economic projects for the benefit of the entire society. Similarly, in his writings on Islamic interest-free banking, Sadr advocated state control of the banking sector, where the forbidden category of *ribā* (interest) is replaced with modified forms of the permissible principle of *muḍāraba* (joint ventures between capital and enterprise).

The Marxist influence is also discernible in Sadr's political thought. He characterized the traditional Shi'i *marja'iyya* (being an authoritative source of imitation) as "ideological leadership" and the jurist holding this position as "the supreme representative of Islamic ideology." In *Iqtisaduna*, Sadr conceived of a discretionary area subject to the (legislative) authority of the ruler, since Islam allowed the *walī al-amr* (the person invested with authority) to exercise *ijtihād* according to the needs and interests of society. Sadr divided the rules of the shari'a into four categories in 1976. Sadr identified the last of these categories as the rules pertaining to public conduct; the rules covered the conduct of the *walī al-amr* according to the principles of *wilāya al-'āmma* (general mandate). Sadr deftly avoided the thorny discussion of the referent of the term *walī al-amr*; we are left to guess whether the *walī al-amr* is the ruler (sultan) of the medieval jurists, or the (Hidden) Imam. At that stage, he did not accept Khomeini's theory of *wilāyat al-faqīh*, though later the term could be equated with Khomeini's theocratic *faqīh*, as is the case in the Islamic Republic of Iran. In a note proposing a constitution for an Islamic republic in Iran, written a week before the final collapse of the monarchy, Sadr put the general deputyship (*al-niyāba al-'āmma*, of the Hidden Imam) that pertains to the supreme jurist (*al-mujtahid al-muṭlaq*) in place of *wilāya al-'āmma* as the mandate to rule, and the supreme jurist as *marja'* in place of the ruler (*walī al-amr*) of his earlier writings. He thus offered a clear legal formulation of the *wilāyat al-faqīh* as the mandate of the jurist to rule, one that is more precise than the vague statement put forward by Khomeini a decade earlier. As an Islamic legislature for Iran, Sadr proposed a *majlis ahl al-ḥall wa-l-'aqd*, to function in conjunction with the principle of constitutional supervision of the *walī al-amr*, who was the "deputy of the [Hidden] Imam."

See also Iraq; revival and reform; Shi'ism

Further Reading

Chibli Mallat, *The Renewal of Islamic Law: Muhammad Baqer as-Sadr, Najaf and the Shi'i International*, 1993; Muhammad Baqir as-Sadr, *Lessons in Islamic Jurisprudence*, translated by R. P. Motahhedeh, 2003.

SAÏD AMIR ARJOMAND

Safavids (1501–1722)

The Safavids originated as the leaders of a Sufi order named after its founder, the mystic Shaykh Safi al-Din (1252–1334) and centered in Ardabil in Azerbaijan. Originally apolitical Sunnis, they became involved in politics and turned Shi'i in the 15th century, when they began to recruit followers among the Turkoman tribes of what are now the borderlands of Turkey, Syria, and Iran. These followers, known collectively as "Redheads" (Qizilbash), were extreme Shi'is, and it was with them that Isma'il, the founder of the political dynasty, conquered Tabriz in 1501. They constituted the main military force of the Safavids throughout the 16th century and remained powerful (though decreasingly so) throughout the lifetime of the dynasty.

Isma'il succeeded in establishing an empire that stretched from the Euphrates to the Oxus (or Amu Darya), but his defeat by the Ottoman sultan Selim I at the Battle of Chaldiran in 1514 brought an end to expansion. A long series of Ottoman-Safavid wars ensued until 1639, when the Treaty of Zuhab confirmed the surrender to the Ottomans of the original Qizilbash heartland in Anatolia and also of Baghdad and Iraq. The Safavids were generally outmatched by the Ottoman armies and on more than one occasion lost large swaths of territory, including Tabriz, their capital. The Ottomans' extended lines of communication from their capital in Istanbul constrained their capacity to conduct campaigns so far to the East. This allowed the Safavids repeatedly to survive, regroup, and reconquer lost lands. Tahmasp I (r. 1524–76) transferred the capital from Tabriz to Qazvin, which was farther from the Ottoman threat, and in 1598 'Abbas I (r. 1587–1629) moved it again to Isfahan in central Iran, farther still from the Ottoman frontier.

In the east the Safavids were engaged in frequent warfare with the Shaybanids for control of Khurasan and, in the first half of the 17th century, with the Mughals, with whom they contested Afghanistan and especially Qandahar. Territorially, the Safavid Empire was the first polity whose shape broadly resembles that of modern Iran. Like most medieval Iranian dynasties, the Safavids governed through a combination of Turkish military strength and Persian (or Tajik) administrative know-how.

The most significant long-term outcome of Safavid rule was their forcible imposition of Imami or Twelver Shi'ism. Initiated by Isma'il, this policy remains a puzzle. Other than Isma'il's boyhood exile in Gilan, the Safavids had no previous connection with Imami Shi'ism, whose beliefs and practices differed from both the extreme Shi'ism of the Qizilbash (and the young Isma'il himself) and the Sunnism of the vast majority of Iranian Muslims. No previous Muslim ruler, whether Sunni or Shi'i, had ever imposed his own religion on the general populace. The Qizilbash maintained their extreme Shi'i beliefs and practices, but the Iranian population they had conquered was coerced into adopting Imamism, a lengthy process that resulted in the emigration from Iran (mostly to India) of a considerable number of clerical and intellectual elites and the suppression of most Sufi orders. Successive Safavid shahs patronized a new Shi'i religious establishment, endowing shrines, mosques, and madrasas, especially the shrines of the eighth imam Reza in Mashhad and of his sister Fatimah in Qum. The religious differences between the Shi'i Safavids and the Sunni Ottomans, Shaybanids, and Mughals figured prominently in propaganda, while religious affinity played a role in the Safavids' alliance with the Shi'i Deccan Sultanates.

Many Twelver Shi'i 'ulama' remained ambivalent toward Safavid claims to legitimacy, for in principle, a legitimate government could be exercised only by the imam, and the Safavids could not claim to be imams, since the 12th and last of them had gone into hiding long ago and would remain there until the Day of Judgment. The Imami 'ulama' fully acknowledged the need for government, but however meritorious its dispenser, he could never be more than a *sulṭān jā'ir*, a wrongful or illegitimate ruler. Basing their ideas partly on the supposed descent of the Safavids from 'Ali b. Abi Talib and partly on their support of Shi'ism, a sufficient part of the clerical establishment supported Safavid claims to the right to rule. The technical illegitimacy of the Safavids nonetheless had important implications. In the absence of the imam, his functions were widely held to be suspended. The shah could not take over these functions, and the Imami 'ulama' had not previously claimed them either. Endowed with political support, however, they began to envisage themselves as representing the imam in some respects. This line of thinking eventually culminated in Ayatollah Khomeini's theory of *wilāyat al-faqīh*, or the government (or guardianship) of the jurist.

For much of the 16th century, the Safavid state was threatened by a series of internal conflicts among the Qizilbash tribes and by succession disputes; these allowed the Ottomans and Uzbeks to invade virtually unopposed. The 42-year reign of 'Abbas I marked both a turning point and the apogee of the Safavid era. He succeeded in restoring internal order, defeating external enemies, and making Isfahan one of the most magnificent capital cities of the age. He curbed the power of the Qizilbash by relying increasingly on Georgian and Armenian *ghulāms* (royal slaves) in both the army and administration; concentrated royal control over revenues by converting lands from state (*mamālik*) to royal (*khāṣṣah*) status; and promoted trade by establishing security on the roads, investing in infrastructure, and co-opting the services of Armenian merchants (forcibly transported to Isfahan) and the West European merchants and companies that visited Iran in significant numbers during his reign.

Artistic and cultural life, especially painting and architecture, flourished in the Safavid state down to the reigns of Sulayman (r. 1666–94) and Sultan Husayn (r. 1694–1722), when problems mounted. In 1722 a rebellion by the Sunni Ghilzai Afghans in Qandahar brought down the dynasty, but it did not restore Sunnism in Iran. During two centuries of Safavid rule, Imami Shi'ism apparently had taken firm root.

See also 'Abbas I (1571–1629); guardianship of the jurist; Shi'ism

Further Reading

Norman Calder, *Interpretation and Jurisprudence in Medieval Islam*, 2006; Peter Jackson and Laurence Lockhart, eds., *The Cambridge History of Iran*, vol. 6, *The Timurid and Safavid Periods*, 1986; Rudolph Matthee, *The Politics of Trade in Safavid Iran: Silk for Silver, 1600–1730*, 1999; David Morgan, *Medieval Persia, 1040–1797*, 1988; Andrew Newman, *Safavid Iran: Rebirth of a Persian Empire*, 2006.

EDMUND HERZIG

Sa'id Nursi (1877–1960)

Born in eastern Anatolia and of Kurdish descent, the Qur'anic exegete and theologian Bediüzzaman Sa'id Nursi lived through the final decades of the Ottoman Empire, its collapse and dissolution after World War I, and the first 37 years of the secular Turkish

Republic. It was an era during which the Muslim world faced major intellectual and political challenges, including secularization, colonization, and failure of traditional structures. Nursi's scholarly writings and public engagements throughout his life reflected a deep concern for Islamic revival.

Referring to an inner transformation he went through around age 45, Nursi divided his life into "Old Sa'id" and "New Sa'id" phases. In the "Old Sa'id" phase (1890–1922), Nursi was a public intellectual and an erudite scholar who taught and wrote about Qur'an interpretation (*tafsīr*) and theology (*kalām*). While critical of nationalism, Nursi supported the constitutional government that sought to limit the sultan's power. He argued that the era of one caliph acting on behalf of the entire community is over and that a representative government is needed. Nursi also supported the abolishing of the special status of religious minorities, a change that made all citizens equal before the Ottoman state. Though committed to a religious revival of the caliphate, he distinguished between its religious foundations and day-to-day transactions of governance and argued that, according to the shari'a, minorities may become governors and have equal say in the parliament.

Old Sa'id was also enthusiastic about progress in the sciences and what he considered as the end of dogmatism in Europe. He proposed educational reforms to the Ottoman sultans Abdülhamid (d. 1918) and Mehmet Reshad (d. 1918), aiming at putting the traditional madrasa (seminary) training, Sufism (*tasawwuf*), and the modern sciences in dialogue with each other. But the eruption of World War I interrupted his endeavors: the Russians invaded his town, and he lived for two years as a prisoner of war in Russia.

In 1922 when many were celebrating Turkish nationalist victory over European colonial powers, Nursi wrote about a serious danger infiltrating the community: the positivistic attitude, which pretended to explain the world in materialistic terms, would soon undermine the faith of many. His understanding of Islamic revival radically shifted with this birth of the "New Sa'id." He now argued that revival was not about sociopolitical reform or establishing a caliphate capable of uniting Muslims across the globe. Rather, the urgent task was reviving the hearts and minds of Muslims in the light of the Qur'an. He argued that belief based on imitation will not survive in the modern age, and to ensure the happiness of the people in this world and the next, belief based on investigation had to be expounded and put forth.

New Sa'id forbade himself any political engagement. He found it harmful to have any political agenda while trying to serve the Qur'an. While he admitted that political power could be useful for restraining evil people from corrupting society, Nursi contended that such people were a minority; the majority of people who strayed from the "truth" were actually willing to find a way out of their confusions but did not know how. The "light" of the Qur'an had to be made available to them without any connection to politics, lest they think that the call to the Qur'an was a means for gaining power. According to Nursi, even if the majority chooses to apply the social aspects of shari'a as a collective, the service to belief should continue relentlessly, as it is the most important and yet the most neglected aspect of the religion.

New Sa'id lived much of his life in prison and in exile (1925–56), persecuted by the secularist state for having invested in religious revival. During this difficult period, Nursi composed the *Risale-yi Nur* (literally, "Epistle of light"), a 6,000-page collection seeking to expound the Qur'an and nurture a life infused with belief and love of God. He also sought to revive *kalām* and offer a Qur'anic theology that speaks to the modern age. His writings, banned by the state, were secretly disseminated and hand-copied by thousands of people, many of whom were also persecuted.

After decades of political disengagement, in 1950 Nursi voted for the Democratic Party in the first multiparty elections in Turkey, signaling his support for the relaxation of state despotism, which led to the lifting of the ban on his writings in 1956. This was also a period when most Muslim countries were gaining independence from colonial rule. Nursi encouraged solidarity across Muslim communities in the world. He also called for an interfaith solidarity to uphold faith in God and resist moral collapse, which he felt was demonstrated by the horrors of the two World Wars.

The grassroots movement founded around *Risale-yi Nur*, the Nur movement, continued to grow after Nursi's death in 1960, and the *Risale* found an international audience in translation.

See also revival and reform; Turkey

Further Reading

M. Said Ramadan Al-Buti, "Bediuzzaman Said Nursi's Experience of Serving Islam by Means of Politics," in *Proceedings of Third International Symposium on Said Nursi: The Reconstruction of Islamic Thought in the Twentieth Century and Bediuzzaman Said Nursi*, 1997, 105–14; Ahmet Davudoglu, "Bediuzzaman and the Politics of 20th Century Muslim World," *Proceedings of Third International Symposium on Said Nursi: The Reconstruction of Islamic Thought in the Twentieth Century and Bediuzzaman Said Nursi*, 1997, 286–311; Zeynep Akbulut Kuru and Ahmet T. Kuru, "Apolitical Interpretation of Islam: Said Nursi's Faith-Based Activism in Comparison with Political Islamism and Sufism," *Islam and Christian-Muslim Relations* 19, no. 1 (2008): 99–111; Nursi Studies, http://www.nursistudies.com; Ibrahim Abu Rabi', *Islam at the Crossroads: On the Life and Thought of Bediuzzaman Said Nursi*, 2003; Risale-i Nur: A Contemporary Interpretation of the Qur'an, http://www.saidnur.com; Colin Turner and Hasan Horkuc, *Makers of Islamic Civilization: Said Nursi*, 2009.

ISRA YAZICIOGLU

Saladin (1138–93)

Abu al-Muzaffar Yusuf b. Ayyub, known in Europe as Saladin from his honorific title *Ṣalāḥ al-Dīn* (Reformer of the Religion), was the founder of the Ayyubid dynasty, which ruled over Egypt,

upper Iraq, most of Syria, and Yemen during the 12th and 13th centuries. He acted as the vizier of Egypt between 1169 and 1171, and sultan between 1174 and 1193. He is known, particularly in the West, for being the most prominent opponent of the crusaders and for the capture of Jerusalem from the Kingdom of Jerusalem in 1187.

A Kurd from Dvin, in Armenia, he was born in Tikrit, near Baghdad, where his father, Najm al-Din Ayyub, was governor and his uncle, Asad al-Din Shirkuh, a state functionary for the Seljuqs. Following an incident involving Shirkuh's killing of a Christian, the two brothers left Tikrit for Mosul in 1138 and started working for the Zangids. After serving at the court of Zangi, the amir of Mosul, the brothers worked for Nur al-Din Mahmud, Zangi's son and ruler of Damascus.

Saladin spent his formative years in Damascus and participated in several Syrian military expeditions in Egypt to defend the Fatimid caliphate against the forces of the Kingdom of Jerusalem. After the death of his uncle Shirkuh in 1169, he was appointed commander of the Syrian forces and vizier of Egypt. Saladin gradually secured his position in Egypt, both against the external threats of the crusaders' armies and the internal threats of the partisans of the Fatimid dynasty. In 1171, after consolidating his power base, he officially abolished the Shi'i Fatimid caliphate of Egypt and proclaimed the return to Sunni Islam. Upon the death of Nur al-Din in 1174, Saladin extended his rule to Damascus, Homs, and Hama. He further consolidated his power over the remainder of Syria following the death of Isma'il al-Malik al-Salih, Nur al-Din's heir, in 1181. By 1186, he had unified the Muslim territories of Egypt, Syria, and Mesopotamia under his rule and was ready to face the crusaders' threat.

The motives behind Saladin's expansionist policy have received numerous and often contradictory interpretations in both contemporary and later accounts. While some saw in that policy an attempt to unify Muslim territory against the existing threats of the crusaders in preparation for jihad, as Qadi al-Fadil (d. 1199) believed, others denounced it as an act of betrayal on the part of a self-promoting Kurd who turned against his own masters, as one sees it described in Zangid sources.

In 1187, Saladin gathered all his Muslim allies and declared a jihad against the Christian crusaders who had invaded parts of the Middle East, including the Holy Land. As commander of the Muslim forces, he soundly defeated the crusader states at the Battle of Hattin in July 1187 and regained large parts of the territory invaded, except for the city of Tyre. On October 2, 1187, Saladin entered the besieged city of Jerusalem with no significant resistance and restored Muslim rule. The civility of his army has been contrasted with the crusaders' brutality eight decades earlier. The capture of Jerusalem would trigger the Third Crusade and a series of new attacks launched by the Christian armies in the Middle East. In 1192, after long negotiations, Saladin signed a peace agreement with the king of England, Richard the Lionheart, recognizing the Frankish coastal gains between Acre and Jaffa. He died a few months later in Damascus, in March 1193, after a serious illness.

Saladin's legacy is marked both by his military achievements against the crusaders externally and by his socioreligious policies internally. In the Muslim territories under his rule, Saladin created a considerable number of institutions of learning, such as religious schools (madrasas), legal colleges, hospitals, and Sufi retreats. He founded several pious endowments to encourage religious learning and to promote Sunni orthodoxy, particularly in post-Fatimid Egypt. In Jerusalem, he restored the Dome of the Rock and the Aqsa Mosque to Muslim use.

Saladin has become the object of myths in both the West and the Muslim world. The abundant literature encompasses exalted descriptions on the part of his admirers and more hostile views on the part of his opponents. A number of features are, however, widely recognized and mentioned in the literature: his chivalry, his generosity, and his fair treatment of religious minorities, notably the Christian population of Jerusalem. Saladin's legacy is still alive in the contemporary Arab and Muslim world. Twentieth-century Arab nationalism and modern Islamic movements have used him as a symbol and a source of inspiration for his successful unification of the Muslim territories.

See also Ayyubids (1169–1250); Crusades; Fatimids (909–1171); jihad; madrasa

Further Reading

Abdul Rahman Azzam, *Saladin,* 2009; Hamilton Gibb, *The Life of Saladin: From the Works of 'Imad al-Din and Baha' al-Din*, 1973; Margaret Jubb, *The Legend of Saladin in Western Literature and Historiography*, 2000; Malcolm Cameron Lyons and D.E.P. Jackson, *Saladin, the Politics of the Holy War* 1982; Hannes Mohring, *Saladin: The Sultan and His Times, 1138–1193,* translated by David S. Bachrach, 2008; D. S. Richards, *The Rare and Excellent History of Saladin*, translated by Baha' al-Din Ibn Shaddad, 1964.

NASSIMA NEGGAZ

Salafis

The Salafi designation is contested in the scholarly literature as well as among some Muslims, and because of this there is considerable confusion about to whom it applies and the nature of its doctrines. A historically grounded definition maintains that Salafis adhere to a literalist theology that rejects allegorical interpretation and reason-based arguments and claim to be faithful to the teachings of the theological Hanbalis or the *ahl al-ḥadīth*. Salafis insist that their beliefs are identical to those of the first three generations of Muslims, *al-salaf al-ṣāliḥ* (pious ancestors), from whom they take their name. Their attention is directed at convincing other Muslims of the superiority of Salafi teachings and of the need to abandon reprehensible innovations (*bida'*) allegedly not rooted in Islam, such as superstitious beliefs and the intercessionary practices associated with the

cult of dead saints. Sufis and Shi'is in particular are the target of Salafi polemical attacks for partaking in forms of unbelief (*kufr*) by not being faithful to a strict conception of God's oneness (*tawḥīd*). Salafism's most prominent premodern authorities are Ibn Taymiyya (d. 1328), his student Ibn Qayyim al-Jawziyya (d. 1350), and a number of reformist scholars who followed in their footsteps, such as Muhammad b. 'Abd al-Wahhab (d. 1792) and Muhammad al-Shawkani (d. 1834), among others. Because Salafis are concerned with theological purity, they engage in exclusionary practices that can attain the level of excommunication (*takfīr*) of fellow Muslims, and embedded in this is the potential for direct action against individuals or institutions.

In legal matters, Salafis are divided between those who, in the name of independent legal judgment (*ijtihād*), reject strict adherence (*taqlīd*) to the four Sunni schools of law (*madhāhib*) and others who remain faithful to these. All Salafis, however, claim that an *ijtihād* based on a probative proof text (*dalīl*) that contradicts an established school's opinion is to be accepted as superior. Moreover, they insist that the canonical hadith corpus, which provides the vast majority of proof texts, is to be considered unconditionally authoritative. In the realm of politics, Salafis do not adhere to any particular ideology—some are quietists whereas others are activists. A commitment to a distinctive creed is Salafism's most characteristic and unifying marker of identity in addition to its followers' effort to reform the beliefs and practices of other Muslims.

In the late 19th and early 20th centuries, the label Salafism was applied to a group of modernizing and rationalist scholars, such as Afghani (1838–97) and Muhammad 'Abduh (d. 1905). These scholars, however, did not share the literalist theology of the premodern Salafis and were engaged in a project of uplifting Muslim society from a state of decay by finding the philosophical resources that would accomplish this. Legal reform through *ijtihād* formed part of this effort, but not the puritanical theology that lies at the core of Salafi teachings. Furthermore, while the relationship with the West that Afghani and 'Abduh expressed was rivalrous, it also involved adopting and learning from the West's intellectual and scientific achievements.

Salafis are closely identified with the Wahhabis of Saudi Arabia because of a shared theological orientation and because the Wahhabis have claimed to be Salafis from the early 20th century, if not before. The Kingdom of Saudi Arabia adheres to a Salafi interpretation of Islam, and its promotion and defense have been a source of legitimacy for its ruling family since the mid-18th century. From the 1920s Saudi monarchs regularly patronized Salafis in Egypt, Syria, Iraq, South Asia, and elsewhere and subsidized the publication of this movement's books. Independent of the Saudi connection, Salafis have also had an autonomous history and presence in several countries where they formed associations to promote their respective projects, which tended to focus on religious reform rather than an activist political agenda. In India, for example, the Salafis established the Jam'iyyat Ahl-i Hadith (1906), whereas in Egypt they established the Jama'at Ansar al-Sunna al-Muhammadiyya (1926). Similar Salafi organizations exist in a number of other countries, including in the West.

The development of a distinctive Salafi political ideology has been in progress since the mid-20th century and has yet to coalesce into a dominant current. This began with the government of Saudi Arabia's promotion of Pan-Islamism against the ideologies of communism and Arab nationalism that threatened its legitimacy while also funding institutions and programs that spread globally a Salafi interpretation of Islam. New self-declared Salafi groups emerged in the 1970s, some of which combined Salafi theology with tenets of the Muslim Brotherhood to form new hybrid ideologies and programs for political action. The more radical of these groups argued on the basis of their interpretation of Ibn Taymiyya that it is permissible to engage in *takfīr* against individuals and groups and, if necessary, to rebel against a state that is not ruling in accordance with the shari'a. From the Muslim Brotherhood, especially the works of Sayyid Qutb (d. 1966), they obtained a conceptual framework and organizational strategies with which to launch attacks on governments that do not base their rule and laws on Islamic foundations. In Egypt, one such group was the Islamic Jihad (Jama'at al-Jihad al-Islami), which was established in 1979 by Muhammad 'Abd al-Salam Faraj (d. 1982, author of *The Neglected Duty* [*al-Farida al-Gha'iba*]). In Saudi Arabia, Juhayman al-'Utaybi's group, al-Jama'a al-Salafiyya al-Muhtasiba, was formed in 1975 and led a millenarian revolt that included the brief seizure of the great mosque in Mecca in 1979. Since then a plethora of Salafi political groups has been formed, including al-Qaeda and its various affiliates.

Not all Salafi groups preach violent action. Most, in fact, reject the forms of violence advocated by al-Qaeda, and Salafism can best be described as politically fragmented. Three streams can be distinguished in terms of political engagement: (1) the Salafi jihadists, who advocate direct action against the dominant order, including specific states, and wish to re-create the historic caliphate (al-Qaeda exemplifies this tendency); (2) the activists (Harakis), who engage in nonviolent political activism in order to advance specific goals (the Ahl-i Hadith in India and the "Awakening Islamists" in Saudi Arabia [Sahwis] are typical of this stream); and (3) the traditionalists (Taqlidis), who, as quietists, shun all forms of overt political action and argue for obedience to Muslim rulers in order to avoid civil strife (*fitna*). Most Salafis tend to belong to the last group, seeking to transform society through the purification and education of individuals and not through the toppling of the established political order.

See also 'Abduh, Muhammad (1849–1905); Ibn 'Abd al-Wahhab, Muhammad (1703–92); Pan-Islamism; Saudi Arabia

Further Reading

David Commins, *The Wahhabi Mission and Saudi Arabia*, 2006; Johannes J. G. Jansen, *The Neglected Duty*, 1986; Malcolm Kerr, *Islamic Reform*, 1966; Roel Meijer, ed., *Global Salafism*, 2009; Madawi al-Rasheed, *Contesting the Saudi State: Islamic Voices from a New Generation*, 2006.

BERNARD HAYKEL

Samanids (819–1005)

The Samanid dynasty was the most important political power of the eastern Islamic world between the years 900 and 999. The Samanid family originated with their eponymous eighth-century founder, Saman-khuda, who was apparently one of the local landowning gentry of the Balkh region in northeastern Khurasan. The family first rose to political prominence in the early ninth century, when the four grandsons of Saman, having won the caliph Ma'mun's favor, were appointed to senior governorships, three of which were located in the neighboring Central Asian border province of Transoxania.

It was in Transoxania during the following generation that the founder of the dynasty emerged as a major power: Isma'il b. Ahmad (r. 892–907), great-grandson of Saman and a noted *ghāzī* (border warrior against the infidels), unified the entire province under his rule. In the year 900 Isma'il conquered the Saffarids, which until that time had been the major power of the eastern Islamic world, and subsequently incorporated virtually all the Islamic lands of that time from Khurasan eastward into his realm. The dynasty continued to dominate the eastern Islamic world until the dismembering of its realm in 999 at the hands of the ethnically Turkic Qarakhanids and Ghaznavids.

The Samanid dynasty occupies a critical place in Islamic history and political thought. First, the Samanids presided over the revival of the Persian language, culture, and political tradition and their incorporation into Islamic political discourse. Thus the Samanids were responsible not only for the literary and administrative revival of the Persian language but also for having made it into one of the classical Islamic languages, alongside Arabic, and the primary language of government in the Islamic world from Iran eastward. The Samanids also revived pre-Islamic Persian political ideals and concepts, adapting them to the new Islamic norms and culture. Thus, for example, it was the Samanids who imparted Islamic respectability to ancient Iranian regal titles such as *shāhānshāh* (king of kings), the title of the ancient pre-Islamic Iranian monarchs.

Second, the Samanids established the model of Islamic governance and political legitimization for every succeeding premodern Muslim polity that arose in the wake of Abbasid political dissolution, particularly the precedent of establishing one's legitimacy as ruler through assuming and executing the dual core duties of a ruler in Islamic political thought: namely, "commanding right and forbidding wrong" within the borders of the Islamic world and waging jihad against the non-Muslims, both inside and outside of those borders. In the Samanid case, this jihad was directed primarily against the Turkic peoples to their north and east. As a result, the Samanid model of government became paradigmatic in Islamic political thought. Isma'il b. Ahmad is portrayed as the ideal Muslim ruler in many classic medieval Islamic literary works, including Nizam al-Mulk's famous Mirror for Princes.

Third, the dynasty is, correctly, viewed as a bulwark of political Sunnism—in fact, virtually the only significant Sunni dynasty in the entire Middle East at this time—in an age of Shi'i political ascendancy. Throughout much of the tenth century, the other major Muslim political powers were the Shi'i Buyid and Fatimid dynasties. Moreover, the Samanid realm was the bastion not only of Sunnism but also of autochthonous Iranian political rule; its downfall inaugurated a millennium of Turkic domination of the eastern Islamic world.

Finally, the Samanid dynasty played a leading role in the Islamization of Central Asia—an effort that was crowned with success in the mid-tenth century when a mass conversion of the Turkic peoples bordering the Samanid lands occurred. This enduring Samanid legacy secured the dominance of Islam in the Central Asian steppes and ensured that the first invading waves of Turco-Mongol nomads, beginning with the Qarakhanids and then the Seljuqs, entered the Islamic world as Muslims.

See also Abbasids (750–1258); commanding right and forbidding wrong; *ghāzī*; Seljuqs (1055–1194); *shāhānshāh*

Further Reading

Vasilii Vladimirovitch Barthold, *Turkestan Down to the Mongol Invasion*, 1968; Richard N. Frye, *Bukhara: The Medieval Achievement*, 1965; Idem, "The Sāmānids," in *The Cambridge History of Iran*, vol. 4, edited by R. N. Frye, 1975; Numan N. Negmatov, "The Samanid State," in *History of Civilizations of Central Asia IV, Part One: The Historical, Social, and Economic Setting*, edited by M. S. Asimov and C. E. Bosworth, 1999; Jürgen Paul, "The State and the Military: The Samanid Case," *Papers on Inner Asia* 26 (1994); Deborah G. Tor, "The Islamization of Central Asia in the Sāmānid Era and the Reshaping of the Muslim World," *Bulletin of the School of Oriental and African Studies* 72, no. 3 (2009); Eadem, "The Mamlūks in the Military of the Pre-Seljūq Persianate Dynasties," *IRAN: Journal of the British Institute of Persian Studies* 46 (2008); W. Luke Treadwell, "*Shāhānshāh* and *al-Malik al-Mu'ayyad*: The Legitimation of Power in Sāmānid and Būyid Iran," in *Culture and Memory in Medieval Islam: Essays in Honour of Wilferd Madelung*, edited by Farhad Daftary and Josef W. Meri, 2003.

D. G. TOR

Saudi Arabia

Saudi Arabia has been an important locus and sponsor of Islamic reformist thought and activism since the 1920s, even before the kingdom was officially established in 1932. Its founder, King 'Abd al-'Aziz b. 'Abd al-Rahman Al Sa'ud (Ibn Sa'ud, d. 1953), saw himself as heir to the Wahhabi movement that had emerged in central Arabia in the 18th century and dominated much of the

Arabian Peninsula until the state it helped create was destroyed by the Ottomans in 1818. Wahhabism, which Ibn Sa'ud labeled Salafism from as early as the 1910s if not before, is the religious ideology in whose name he united the disparate regions and tribes of Arabia. Its sponsorship by the state and the claim to implement Islamic law represent the bases for the legitimacy of the Al Saud dynasty into the early 21st century. Wahhabis seek to reform "errant" Muslims, leading them away from the reprehensible innovations (*bid'a*) and superstitious practices that they are accused of having adopted. In Arabia, these involve beliefs and practices that Wahhabis deem to be polytheistic (*shirk*) and to contain elements of unbelief (*kufr*). They include such practices as worship at certain trees and the graves of holy men, as well as seeking the intercession or aid of dead or living persons and abandoning the ritual obligations of the faith (e.g., prayer, fasting, alms, pilgrimage). Wahhabi scholars argue for a return to the original teachings of the Qur'an and the sunna of the Prophet Muhammad, which they claim are embodied in the Wahhabis' strict monotheistic creed centered on God's unicity (*tawḥīd*). Wahhabis have not hesitated to use excommunication (*takfīr*) of persons accused of deviating from *tawḥīd* or to engage in armed struggle against them (jihad). In addition, Sufis and Shi'is, and to a lesser extent Ash'aris, have been singled out by Wahhabis as theological deviants and are regularly attacked in polemical writings, sermons, and various other media. It is the Wahhabi practice of *takfīr* and the potential violence it entails that have engendered the ire of other Muslims and their condemnation of the Saudi Arabian government.

While sponsoring Wahhabi scholars and teachings, the Saudi royal family has continuously had to balance the religious zeal of its foundational and legitimating doctrine with the pragmatic constraints of ruling a territorial nation-state. The first test of this came when the Bedouin-origin paramilitary force called the Ikhwan (Brotherhood) rebelled against Ibn Sa'ud's rule in the late 1920s, accusing him of not being faithful to the tenets of Wahhabism. He crushed this movement militarily because its repeated acts of violence on the frontiers of Iraq, Kuwait, and Jordan threatened retaliation from imperial Great Britain. But he also dispensed with the Ikhwan because their value as shock troops of an expanding Saudi state had diminished by the late 1920s and because their leaders were challenging his authority. Through the late 1960s, Saudi Arabia's religious scene was dominated by traditional Wahhabi scholars, led by the mufti (legal specialist) Muhammad b. Ibrahim Al al-Shaykh (d. 1969), who deferred to the dictates of the royal family.

In the 1950s a new threat emerged for Saudi Arabia in the form of Arab nationalism and republican socialism, as promulgated by President Gamal Abdel Nasser (1918–70) of Egypt. The Egyptian government's persecution of members of the Muslim Brotherhood led many of them to seek refuge in Saudi Arabia in the 1950s and 1960s, and here they found employment in the then-nascent administrative bureaucracy and in teaching and religious institutions. Accused by Nasser of representing backward and reactionary forces, Saudi Arabia, under the rule of King Faisal b. 'Abd al-'Aziz Al Sa'ud (d. 1975), developed and sponsored Pan-Islamic ideologies and institutions to ward off the threats from Nasserism and socialism. This effort, which became known as the Islamic Solidarity Movement (Harakat al-Tadamun al-Islami), led to the establishment of the Islamic University in Medina (1961) and the Muslim World League (1962), among other Islamic missionary, educational, and religious institutions. Saudi Arabia, especially after accruing massive wealth from the oil booms of the 1970s, devoted considerable resources to these institutions with the aim of promoting a Salafi brand of Islam and emphasizing the Islamic legitimacy of its ruling family and political regime.

In 1979 three critical events took place that intensified Saudi Arabia's effort to bolster its Islamic legitimacy. Two of these, the Iranian Revolution under the leadership of Ayatollah Khomeini (1902–89) and the seizure of the great mosque in Mecca by a group of millenarian Sunni zealots, directly threatened the religious legitimacy of Saudi Arabia. The third, the Soviet invasion of Afghanistan, provided an opportunity for Saudi Arabia to burnish its Islamic credentials by financially and politically supporting the Afghan resistance.

In the 1980s the Saudi government adopted more austere social and religious domestic policies, and this period corresponded with the rise of a more politicized generation of Saudi Islamist activists and thinkers. These Islamists were strongly influenced by the teachings of the Muslim Brotherhood and subscribed to a new hybrid ideology—one that combined the activism of the Muslim Brotherhood with the theological zeal of Wahhabism. Labeled Sahwis (Awakeners), they began a campaign of criticism of the Saudi regime's pro-Western political orientation, especially after Iraq's invasion of Kuwait in 1990 and the arrival of hundreds of thousands of U.S. troops to defend Saudi Arabia. The official Saudi religious establishment, which was led by Grand Mufti 'Abd al-'Aziz b. Baz (d. 1999), had issued a fatwa (religious opinion) legitimizing the foreign military presence, and this led to a steady decline in its prestige and authority in the eyes of many in Saudi Arabia as well as among Salafi and Islamist networks abroad. Concurrently, certain circles of Sahwis and Salafis became increasingly radicalized, and a number of these rallied to the call of al-Qaeda and joined its ranks in Afghanistan. The latter declared the Saudi royal family to be "apostate" rulers who should be toppled through violent means, and its religious leaders were described as corrupt and unprincipled lackeys and labeled pejoratively "scholars of the sultan."

The events of 9/11 represented a watershed in Saudi Arabia's religious politics, especially after al-Qaeda took aim at Saudi Arabia in a series of suicide bombing attacks in 2003. Since that time a change in rhetoric, religious appointments, funding, and policies has occurred. The effort aimed at tempering the intolerance and zeal of Wahhabism and its representatives while attacking al-Qaeda and its affiliates as an "errant group" that has many of the attributes of the heretical Kharijis.

See also Ibn 'Abd al-Wahhab, Muhammad (1703–92); Mecca and Medina

Further Reading

David Commins, *The Wahhabi Mission and Saudi Arabia*, 2006; Thomas Hegghammer, *Jihad in Saudi Arabia*, 2010; Stephane Lacroix, *Awakening Islam*, 2011; Madawi al-Rasheed, *Contesting the Saudi State*, 2006; Joshua Teitelbaum, *Holier than Thou: Saudi Arabia's Islamic Opposition*, 2000.

BERNARD HAYKEL

Sayyid Ahmad Khan (1817–98)

There are three main categories under which Sayyid Ahmad Khan, or "Sir Sayyid," as he is known in South Asia, can be classified: as an architect of the Two-Nation Theory, which led to the partition of India and the creation of Pakistan; as a great "modernist" thinker who interpreted Islam in a rational, scientific manner and established a college to foster Western sciences among Muslims; and as a "deviant" or "heretic," since he emphasized, inter alia, direct recourse to the Qur'an, bypassing the weighty institution of hadith (prophetic tradition), and held that heaven and angels were mere metaphors. Broadly, these categories also characterize his roles respectively as a political activist, educator, and theologian. However, it is his image as an architect of the Two-Nation Theory and of "Muslim separatism" that has probably been the most controversial over the decades. All such classifications of Khan, however, reflect more about analysts' understandings and ideologies than about the figure himself.

Born in Delhi, Khan had a prestigious lineage, as members of his paternal and maternal families enjoyed high positions under the Mughal Empire. Khan's mother's family admired Shah 'Abdulaziz (d. 1824), a key reformist figure and the son of Shah Waliullah (d. 1762), who Shaikh Muhammad Ikram, author of *Muslim Civilization in India*, called "the greatest Islamic scholar India ever produced." Khan thus grew up in an environment of deep piety, free from superstition and local customs then prevalent among what his associate and biographer Altaf Husain Hali called "ignorant Muslims." Early on, he read books by Shah Isma'il (d. 1831) that liberated him from, according to Hali, the "fetters of *taqlīd* (imitation)." At the age of 20, and against his elders' wishes, Khan joined the service of the British and became a subjudge in 1841. In 1844 he wrote *Archeological History of the Ruins of Delhi*, which won him a fellowship from the Royal Asiatic Society. While Khan was posted at Bijnaur, the 1857 anti-British revolt erupted and crucially shaped his thoughts.

In 1858 Khan wrote *The Causes of the Indian Revolt*, in which he criticized the nonrepresentation of Indians in the Legislative Council of India, the British government's support of the Christian missionaries in India, and the law necessitating the resumption of revenue-free land. This pamphlet may be described as a call for democracy, for Khan wrote in it, "This voice . . . can never be heard, and this security never acquired, unless the people are allowed a share in the consultations of the Government." Two years later, Khan published *The Loyal Mohammedans of India*, and it was clear that, in the aftermath of the revolt, his concerns about Muslims only sharpened. Given the havoc inflicted on Muslims by the British after the revolt, and the British portrayal of Muslims as disloyal and fanatic (by such people as W. W. Hunter in his *The Indian Musalmans: Are They Bound in Conscience to Rebel against the Queen?*), Khan aimed at fashioning a nonantagonistic atmosphere between the British and Muslims. In order to allow India's Muslims to improve their lot, he established in 1875 a "Muslim Cambridge," the Muhammadan Anglo-Oriental (MAO) College. He also took on the charges of violence and barbarism leveled against Islam by the missionaries, who, according to Hali, believed that it was "their natural right to spread Christianity in British India." These missionaries considered Muhammad's biography, as authored by Sir William Muir, the basis for disgracing the Muslims' faith and for converting Muslims to Christianity. As a rebuttal to Muir, Khan published his *Life of Mohammad* in 1870, demonstrating in it his immersion in both Western scholarship and comparative theology, as well as classical Islam. In this tract, as in others, his main addressee was not the community of Muslims per se but "human society in general." He also wrote commentaries on the Bible and the Qur'an.

Khan considered the traditional Muslim educational system as almost redundant. His intellectual project—exemplified in MAO—was to craft an Islamic theology in consonance with European rationalism. Islam, he averred, is in line with modern science and "nature" and its laws. While he advocated the cause of modern education, he was also aware of its foul sides, particularly with regard to its impact on religion. And it was the modern educated stratum of society that he viewed as his main audience. In this regard, Hali narrates that a traditional theologian came to him once desiring to see his commentary on the Qur'an. Khan told him that if he believed in monotheism, the prophecy of Muhammad, and life in the hereafter, he did not need to see his commentary, since it was meant for the modern educated Muslims who had developed doubts about the fundamentals of Islam.

The ethos he and his colleagues helped fashion—through activism, speeches, print circulations, and a variety of other institutional mechanisms—is known as the Aligarh Movement. This novel ethos, or the perception thereof, left a deep impact in multiple arenas: historiography, Urdu language and literature, Western education, the conduct of public debates, and so on. The sine qua non of this ethos was a distinct way of dealing with the mythological to foreground that which is human. For instance, Khan urged Urdu poets to go past "love and imagination" and address "real events" and "visible objects." He favored "natural poetry," which "contained criticism of life and was purposeful." It is this aspect of Khan's momentous and multifaceted life that is probably far more significant than the twin labels of an "architect of the Two-Nation Theory" and "a British loyalist"—after all, the so-called nationalists, from Surendranath Banerjee and Tarakrishna Haldar to Mohandas Gandhi, have all been British loyalists.

Given his rational interpretation of Islam, Khan is often described as a Muslim Martin Luther. One can begin to appreciate the irony of such a description from the fact that Gilbert Genebrard accused Luther and other German reformers of introducing Islam into Christianity, and Martinus Alphonous Vivaldus likened Lutheranism to Muhammadenism because, like Muhammad, Lutherans rejected saint worship and allowed divorce. As for Khan's modernism, Hali held that his ideas were barely new: Khan only spread that which was common in the history and traditions of Islam among the most learned few scholars.

See also Aligarh; modernism; revival and reform

Further Reading

G.F.I. Graham, *The Life and Work of Sir Syed Ahmed Khan*, 1974; Altaf Husain Hali, "Sayyid Ahmad Khān aur Mazhab," *Aligaṛh Magazine* (1971); Shaikh Muhammad Ikram, *Muslim Civilization in India*, 1964; Sir Sayyid Ahmad Khan, *Intekhaab Mazaameen: Aligarh Institute Gazette*, edited by Asghar Abbas, 1982; Idem, *Life of Mohammad*, 2002; David Lelyveld, *Aligarh's First Generation: Muslim Solidarity in British India*, 1978; Idem, "Disenchantment at Aligarh: Islam and the Realm of the Secular in Late Nineteenth Century India," *Die Welt des Islams* 22, no. 4 (1984); Hafeez Malik, "Sayyid Ahmad Khan's Contribution to the Development of Muslim Nationalism in India," *Modern Asian Studies* 4, no. 2 (1970).

IRFAN AHMAD

Sayyid Qutb (1906–66)

Sayyid Qutb was one of the most influential Islamists of the 20th century. He was born in 1906 in a village in Asyut Province in Upper Egypt and attended the recently established government school there. In 1921, he went to Cairo to attend secondary school and later enrolled at Dar al-'Ulum, a teacher training institute, graduating in 1933. He then joined the Ministry of Education, working as a teacher and then as an official until 1952. In 1936, he was transferred from the provinces to Helwan, near Cairo, where he established a home and brought his mother, brother, and two sisters to live with him. He was thus responsible for a family although he never married. His brother, Muhammad Qutb (b. 1912), was to become a well-known Islamist in his own right.

In Cairo, Sayyid Qutb became active on the literary scene and was for some time a disciple of the prominent writer 'Abbas Mahmud al-'Aqqad (1889–1964). Between 1924 and 1954, he published about 125 poems and almost 500 articles on literature, social and political issues, and education in various newspapers and literary journals. Among these articles was a series in the 1930s defending 'Aqqad from his conservative critics and a long article in 1939 critiquing Taha Hussein's book, *The Future of Culture in Egypt*, a well-known defense of Westernization. In his critique, he stressed the need to retain and renew Egyptian and Arab culture. During this period, he showed concern for social problems but was not revolutionary or particularly anti-Western.

After the end of World War II, Qutb, like many others, began to write passionately against European and American imperialism and the political corruption and economic inequality that afflicted Egypt. In the late 1940s, he also published a number of books, including a book on literary criticism and an account of his childhood (translated as *A Child from the Village*). In 1945 and 1948, he published two books dealing with the literary style of the Qur'an but not passing judgment on religious issues.

Through 1947, Qutb's writings were consistently secular and nationalist with a strong concern for social justice. Religion appears as a necessary and potentially positive force but not as a comprehensive guide for society. This changed abruptly in 1948, when he began to write clearly Islamist articles and also wrote a book, *Social Justice in Islam*. Little is known of the immediate reasons for this change.

From late 1948 to mid-1950, Qutb was in the United States on a government-sponsored study tour. He was impressed by American technology but horrified by the people's moral and cultural level.

Returning to Egypt, he began to cooperate with the Muslim Brotherhood but apparently became a member only in 1953. He wrote for Islamist and secular journals, revised *Social Justice*, and wrote two other Islamist books. In 1952, he began writing his commentary on the Qur'an, *In the Shade of the Qur'an*. When he joined the Muslim Brotherhood, he became one of its leading spokespersons and edited its journal for a time. Qutb now expressed his concerns for social justice and independence from imperialism mostly in Islamic terms but was willing to cooperate with secularists for common goals. While he criticized the political leaders, he considered Egyptian society as a whole to be Islamic. He also looked for an "Islamic bloc" of nations that would counterbalance capitalism and communism.

When, in July 1952, the Free Officers under Gamal Abdel Nasser (1918–70) took power, both Qutb and the Muslim Brotherhood at first supported them but soon withdrew this support. In October 1954, after an attempt to assassinate Nasser, the Muslim Brotherhood was banned, some of its leaders were executed, and many were imprisoned, including Qutb. He spent almost all of his prison time in the prison hospital because of poor health and was allowed to continue his writing and to have contact with fellow Muslim Brothers in prison.

His Islamism now became much more radical, and it is generally assumed that the harsh treatment that he and others suffered was a major reason for this. He completed *In the Shade of the Qur'an* in 1959 and then began to rewrite it in a more radical form, completing it through al-Hijr (sura 15) before his death. He also wrote other books during this period, including *Islam and the Problems of Civilization* (1962) and *Characteristics of the Islamic Worldview* (1962).

In May 1964, he was released from prison, and in November he published his best-known book, *Milestones*, which was considered a call for Islamic revolution and was soon banned. A new and more radical edition of *Social Justice* was also published the same year. He became the guide of a secret group of young Muslim Brothers not only to direct them in a program of intellectual and moral preparation but also to help them procure weapons claimed to be for self-defense. In August 1965, he was arrested and convicted of plotting against the government. The main evidence against him appears to have been *Milestones*. He was executed on August 29, 1966, thus becoming a martyr in the eyes of many.

Qutb's later Islamist writings are more radical than his earlier ones in several ways. They are more uncompromisingly theocentric. Only God's will counts, and only God has sovereignty (*ḥākimiyya*). Society is either ruled according to God's shari'a or it is *jāhiliyya*, actively opposed to God. There is no middle ground, no room for cooperation with secularists, and no room for compromise on social institutions. They must be based purely on God's laws and not on human ideas. In fact, Qutb considers all the societies of the time to be *jāhiliyya*. Islam must therefore be started over again, as it was in the time of the Prophet Muhammad, by small groups that will devote years to absorbing the basic truths of Islam, and then will confront *jāhiliyya*. *Jāhiliyya* will almost certainly respond with violence and God will determine the outcome.

Qutb has influenced later generations, both through his example as a martyr and through his writings, which have been widely translated and disseminated.

His later ideas divided the Muslim Brotherhood in the 1960s, with the majority rejecting them but smaller and more violent offshoots, such as the so-called Takfir wa-l-Hijra, Jihad, and al-Gama'a al-Islamiyya in Egypt continuing his legacy in varying ways. He has influenced al-Qaeda, especially through Ayman al-Zawahiri (b. 1951), its deputy leader. Whether he would have approved of their more violent tactics is hard to say but seems doubtful. Radical groups in other countries have also reflected his influence, and more moderate Muslims also read and appreciate his writings, especially his Qur'an commentary.

See also al-Banna, Hasan (1906–49); Egypt; Faraj, Muhammad 'Abd al-Salam (1954–82); fundamentalism; al-Gama'a al-Islamiyya; *jāhiliyya*; Muslim Brotherhood; al-Qaeda; al-Zawahiri, Ayman (b. 1951)

Further Reading

Adnan Musallam, *From Secularism to Jihad: Sayyid Qutb and the Foundations of Radical Islamism*, 2005; Sayyid Qutb, *A Child from the Village*, translated by John Calvert and William Shepard, 2004; Idem, *Social Justice in Islam*, translated by John Hardie, translation revised by Hamid Algar, 2000; Idem, *In the Shade of the Qur'an*, 18 vols, translated by M. A. Salahi et al., 1999–2009.; vol. 30, 1979; Idem, *Milestones*, translated by M. M. Siddiqui, 1990.

WILLIAM E. SHEPARD

secularism

Controversies surrounding secularism in Islamic political thought are often exacerbated by the ambiguity and different understandings of the concept.

Secularism is usually understood to mean the institutional separation between religion and state or, according to a common expression in the West, between church and state. The latter formula might suggest that secularism is irrelevant to Islam because Islam, in principle, has no equivalent to a church. But in theory as well as in practice, the separation between religion and state can take on various forms that do not hinge on the typical historical background of Christian societies. It can mean, for instance, that the state has to remain neutral toward religion and should refrain from favoring one particular faith. In that sense, whether Muslim societies have ecclesiastical institutions that resemble a church is beside the point—even when the answer is far from self-evident—because the goal of secularism is simply to create or preserve autonomous political spaces that are free from religious regulation, influence, or interference. The key here is the profane or worldly character of these spaces. Indeed, the dominant translation of "secularism" in Arabic is *'almāniyya*, which is believed to derive from the word "world" (*'ālam*). But to define secularism in terms of neutral spaces and institutional separation leaves much room for debate. How much state neutrality or autonomy is necessary to warrant the use of the term "secular"? The institutional definition of secularism is thus, in some measure, a matter of opinion and perspective.

Secularism has also been defined as the process whose aim is to expose the growing irrelevance of religious traditions in the face of rationality and the scientific method. While this understanding of secularism entails the reduction of religion's role and importance within society, it often assumes that religious beliefs and practices will recede as well. For this reason, it has been a source of great concern among a wide range of Muslim activists and has sometimes been dubbed "irreligiousness" (*al-lā dīniyya*). Here positivism and the competition between religion and science are key: the second translation of secularism in Arabic is *'ilmāniyya*, which derives from the word "science" (*'ilm*). But despite their differences, the scientistic and institutional conceptions of secularism are not mutually exclusive. They can easily intersect, and both have been used to justify anticlerical and antireligious measures, as was the case in Turkey under Atatürk (1881–1938). Hence, it is easy to understand why many Muslim opponents of secularism have mixed up *'almāniyya*, *'ilmāniyya*, and irreligiousness, out of either genuine confusion or rhetorical strategy.

Some scholars speak of secularism to refer to the modern sociological phenomenon whereby traditional religious beliefs, practices, and identities are reconstructed and individualized. This can lead to the idea that religious belief has become an option rather

than a given. Although some have argued that this aspect of secularism does not exist in Muslim societies, certain thinkers, such as the Egyptian judge and writer Qasim Amin (1863–1908), have in fact recognized the right not to believe in God. Yet such ideas never gained wide acceptance socially and politically. Even the liberal Egyptian constitution of 1923 fell short of enshrining this type of secularism.

In view of these difficulties, an obvious question arises: is there—or can there be—an Islamic notion of secularism? Those who answer in the negative often argue that Islam covers all facets of life, including state and politics, and that anyone who challenges this axiom should not be considered Muslim. In their view, secularism is a modern concept that first emerged in Europe and did not become an object of debate until after Western political ideas started to gain ground in Muslim societies in the 19th century. Secularism, they argue, is the product of Westernization and intellectual colonialism; it is foreign to Islamic authenticity.

Muslim proponents of secularism argue that Islamic history is replete with examples of de facto secularism. In the Middle Ages and early modern period, the state often failed to abide by all religious norms, it was unable to control all religious scholars and their sources of revenue, wars were regularly fought for nonreligious reasons, and extracanonical laws and taxes were commonplace. Traditionally, however, Muslim scholars either turned a blind eye to the gaps between the ideal and the actual or called for the reconciliation of state policies with Islam. The Egyptian scholar ʻAbd al-Raziq (1888–1966) caused a shock when he broke with this tradition in 1925. In his *Islam and the Principles of Governance,* ʻAbd al-Raziq argued that the Islamic political ideal was not the fusion but rather the separation between religion and state. The formative texts of Islam, he maintained, did not dictate a particular form of governance or polity. As for the Prophet, his political actions and decisions were responses to specific circumstances that should not be confused with his religious mission.

In the 21st century, a number of Muslim thinkers continue to defend the validity and even the necessity of institutional secularism. The Iranian thinker Abdolkarim Soroush argues that political norms and institutions should be open to rational evaluation and removed from the realm of the sacred to prevent rulers from turning their understanding of politics into religious dogma. A similar desire to free Islam from the grip of political arbitrariness can be found in the work of the Sudanese-born scholar Abdullahi An-Naʻim, who maintains that the coercive enforcement of religion contradicts the nature of Islam. Therefore, he believes that the establishment of a neutral secular state, combined with the use of civic reason and the promotion of autonomous religious spaces, constitutes the best means to guarantee an Islamic way of life.

See also civil society; public sphere

Further Reading

Abudullahi An-Naʻim, *Islam and the Secular State: Negotiating the Future of Shariʻa*, 2008; Olivier Roy, *Secularism Confronts Islam*, 2007; Abdolkarim Soroush, *Reason, Freedom, and Democracy in Islam: Essential Writings of Abdolkarim Soroush*, 2000; Charles Taylor, *A Secular Age*, 2007; Nazik Saba Yared, *Secularism and the Arab World (1850–1939)*, 2002.

HENRI LAUZIÈRE

Seljuqs (1055–1194)

The Seljuqs were the ruling family of a band of Turkish tribal nomads that seized power in the Islamic heartlands after defeating the Ghaznavid ruler and his forces in battle (1040). During its zenith in the 11th century, Seljuq rule was acknowledged in most of the Islamic world, from the Mediterranean Sea to the Indian borderlands, and from Anatolia to the Persian Gulf.

The Seljuq dynasty reached its height during the reigns of Sultan Alp Arslan (r. 1063–72) and his son Malikshah (r. 1072–92), largely due to the skill and extraordinary abilities of their vizier, Nizam al-Mulk (d. 1092). During Alp Arslan's reign, the Seljuqs inflicted a crushing defeat on the Byzantine Empire at the Battle of Manzikert (1071). As a result of this victory, Anatolia was flooded with waves of Turkish nomads, beginning the process of the Turkification of Anatolia, which eventually led to the downfall of the Byzantine Empire and its replacement by the Muslim Ottomans. Among the most important of the Muslim polities established in Anatolia as a result of Manzikert was the Seljuq sultanate of Rum (1081–1307), which formed a separate polity from that of the eastern or Great Seljuq sultanate and was ruled by a rival branch of the Seljuq family.

After the death of Malikshah in 1092, the Seljuq empire began unraveling due to infighting among the various Seljuq princes, although in the early 12th century the empire experienced a revival in the East under the strong rule of Sultan Sanjar b. Malikshah (r. 1097–1157), who emerged as supreme sultan in 1118; he was widely recognized as the most powerful Muslim ruler of his time. Sanjar met his downfall in 1153, when he was defeated and subsequently taken prisoner by the unruly Turkish nomads who had originally elevated the Seljuqs. After this event the Great Seljuq realms disintegrated, breaking into a number of petty states ruled by *atabegs*, Seljuq military commanders who had been given charge of a young Seljuq prince, until the final extinction of the Seljuq sultanate in 1194.

The Seljuq period wrought profound political changes and, in consequence, significant developments in Islamic political thought. As the rulers of the first massive Turkish tribal migration, the Seljuqs faced the difficult task of balancing the role of tribal chieftain with that of a settled ruler in the Perso-Islamic tradition, a problem they never satisfactorily resolved and one that was to confront all subsequent Turkic rulers up to and including the Ottomans.

The Seljuqs were long portrayed as champions of Sunni Islam for several reasons. They constituted a bulwark against the rival

Isma'ili Shi'i Fatimid caliphate, the predominant power in the Muslim lands from Syria westward. Further, they put an end to over a century of Shi'i Buyid control of the Abbasid caliphate. Finally, they subsidized Sunni madrasas (religious seminaries) while also engaging in brutal military campaigns to combat both covert Isma'ili proselytizing and the open revolt of the Isma'ili Assassins, which threatened to destabilize the Seljuq lands.

At the same time, the experience of conquest by nomads was a bitter one for all Muslims, and, instead of restoring political power to the Abbasid caliphate, the Seljuqs continued to hold the reins of power. This caused great tension between the Abbasid caliphs and the Seljuq sultans throughout the 11th and 12th centuries, resulting in political murder on several occasions. Power in the hands of the Seljuqs also posed an unprecedented difficulty for political theorists, among religious jurisprudents and Seljuq administrators alike, who were forced to elaborate new theories regarding the theoretical bases of the sultan's authority and to redefine the proper relations between caliph and sultan. Thus, the Seljuq era produced some of the classic manuals of medieval Islamic political thought, in both the Mirrors for Princes (statecraft advice manuals) and religious genres, written by figures such as Ghazali (ca. 1058–1111), Juwayni (d. 1085), and Nizam al-Mulk.

Perhaps the most important development in both political theory and practice that occurred under the Seljuqs was the sea change in relations between the government and the Sunni religious scholars. Whereas the original Sunni ideal was the complete independence, even aloofness, of the 'ulama', or religious clerics, from the government, the Sunni 'ulama' of Seljuq times, panicked by the Isma'ili threat, were glad to accept Seljuq patronage. This growing dependence of the 'ulama' on the government led to the gradual subservience of the 'ulama' and their subsumption under state control. Over the centuries, this state of affairs was sometimes seen as discrediting the 'ulama' and played a role in modern times in the birth of the Salafi movement, which, among other tenets, disavows any religious scholar who maintains ties with the government.

See also Abbasids (750–1258); Fatimids (909–1171); Isma'ilis; madrasa; Sunnism

Further Reading

C. E. Bosworth, "The Political and Dynastic History of the Iranian World (A.D. 1000–1217)," in *The Cambridge History of Iran, Volume 5: The Seljūq and Mongol Periods*, edited by J. A. Boyle, 1968; Claude Cahen, *The Formation of Turkey: The Seljukid Sultanate of Rūm: Eleventh to Fourteenth Century*, translated by P. M. Holt, 2001; Carole Hillenbrand, "The Power Struggle Between the Seljūqs and the Isma'ilis of Alamūt, 487–518/1094–1124: The Seljūq Perspective," in *Medieval Isma'ili History and Thought*, edited by Farhad Daftary, 1996; George Makdisi, "The Sunni Revival," in *Islamic Civilisation 950–1150*, edited by D. S. Richards, 1973.

D. G. TOR

al-Shafi'i, Muhammad b. Idris (767–820)

Muhammad b. Idris al-Shafi'i is important for the large corpus of early legal texts preserved in his name, for central contributions to early Islamic legal theory, and as the namesake of the Shafi'i school of legal thought (*madhhab*). He is not known as a political theorist, but his placement of hadiths (traditions from the Prophet, the main source of Islamic law together with the Qur'an) at the center of the law's structure contributed to the process by which scholarly authority supplanted that of the caliphs. Scholarly control over the study, transmission, and elaboration of the sources of Islamic law—especially the hadith—allowed scholars to become the exclusive discoverers and formulators of that law and to attribute its authority to God and the Prophet.

Indirect glimpses of Shafi'i's political views occasionally surface in his writings. In his *Risala* (a work on legal theory) he justifies juristic reliance on the *khabar al-wāḥid* (a hadith report transmitted by only one person in Muhammad's generation) by analogizing from the fact that the earliest Muslims delegated political authority to individuals, and he names, presumably with approval, the caliphs Abu Bakr, 'Umar b. al-Khattab, and 'Uthman b. 'Affan. Some of his views on positive law place constitutional limits on caliphal authority (e.g., in dealing with rebels), but they are well within the mainstream of proto-Sunni legal thought.

The tradition preserves hints of an inclination toward Shi'ism. In the chapter on Muslim rebels (*ahl al-baghy*) of his *Kitab al-Umm* (his main work on positive law), Shafi'i cites a tradition favoring lenient treatment, the *isnād* (chain of transmitters), which consists of three Shi'i imams: Ja'far al-Sadiq, Muhammad al-Baqir, and 'Ali Zayn al-'Abidin. The tradition itself has Marwan b. al-Hakam (Umayyad caliph, r. 684–85) praise another Shi'i imam, Husayn b. 'Ali. Mild sympathy for Shi'i political aspirations would be consistent with the views of other early heroes of Sunnism, such as the Medinan jurist Malik b. Anas (d. 795), Shafi'i's most important teacher (in terms of both fame and frequency of citation in Shafi'i's works) and namesake of another of the four Sunni *madhhabs*.

Like most other aspects of his life, details of Shafi'i's contacts with the holders of power remain murky. According to some traditions, he traveled to Yemen, possibly assisting a local judge, but other traditions portray him as traveling there for study or even for pro-Shi'i agitation. A state connection is possible, since he seems to have discussed the taxation of non-Muslim communities while there. One cluster of narratives portrays him in Baghdad displaying his wit before the caliph Harun al-Rashid (r. 786–809), but this may be a literary topos. He does seem to have traveled to Egypt in the company of the Abbasid governor's son in 814, but evidently this contact did not avail him, and he was compelled to rely on the generosity of a colleague when he settled in Egypt shortly thereafter. While in Egypt, Shafi'i seems to have been active in local politics in regard to the appointment of local officials. The student

who became the primary transmitter of Shafi'is writings, Rabi' b. Sulayman al-Muradi (d. 884), was employed by the state as a prayer caller (muezzin). After Shafi'i's death, during the continuing prosecution of the Mu'tazili-inspired inquisition (*miḥna*) under the caliph Wathiq (r. 842–47), it is reported that his students were barred from the congregational mosque in Old Cairo (Fustat). However, in a typical portrait of a proto-Sunni religious figure, Shafi'i's earliest biographer, the hadith scholar Ibn Abi Hatim al-Razi (d. 938), emphasizes neither political views nor political (or any other of his worldly) entanglements, concentrating instead on piety and commitment to Prophetic tradition as a source of law.

See also caliph, caliphate; hadith; imamate; jurisprudence; Malik b. Anas (712–95); shari'a; Shi'ism; sunna; Sunnism; 'ulama'

Further Reading

Kecia Ali, *Imam Shafi'i: Scholar and Saint*, 2011; Eric Chaumont, "*al-Shāfi'ī*," in *Encyclopaedia of Islam*, 2004; Patricia Crone and Martin Hinds, *God's Caliph*, 1986; Majid Khadduri, *Islamic Jurisprudence*, 1961; Joseph E. Lowry, *Early Islamic Legal Theory*, 2007; Christopher Melchert, *The Formation of the Sunni Schools of Law*, 1997; Ibn Abi Hatim al-Razi, *Adab al-Shafi'i wa-Manaqibuhu*, 1953; Joseph Schacht, "On Shāfi'ī's Life and Personality," in *Studia Orientalia Ioanni Pedersen . . . Dicata*, 1953; Idem, *The Origins of Muhammadan Jurisprudence*, 1967; Muhammad b. Idris al-Shafi'i, *al-Risala*, in *Kitab al-Umm*, edited by 'Abd al-Muttalib, 2008; Idem, *Kitab al-Umm*, 1990.

JOSEPH E. LOWRY

shāhānshāh

Used by the Achaemenid, Parthian, and Sasanian kings, *shāhānshāh*, an ancient Iranian title meaning "king of kings," fell into a centuries-long abeyance with the Muslim conquest of Iran in the seventh century. In the ninth century, however, the collapse of the Islamic form of government, the universal caliphate, forced the new rulers and dynasties that arose to look for alternative political models outside the Islamic tradition; thus, throughout virtually the entire Islamic world, including the non-Iranian lands, the Sasanian model was embraced as the paradigm of rulership.

This phenomenon included among its manifestations the revival, in the early tenth century, of the ancient title of *shāhānshāh*, which at that time was still considered impious by many clerics, since it recognized someone other than God as the "king of kings." The first to adopt it were heterodox Daylamite dynasties, the Shi'i Buyids among them. The greatest ruler of this dynasty, 'Adud al-Dawla, dubbed himself "King of Islam *shāhānshāh*." But Sunni dynasts, too, embraced the title, even in an official context as in the case of the Samanids, and the Ghaznavid rulers were addressed as *shāhānshāh* by their court poets.

In the 11th century, under the Seljuqs, the title became an integral part of the ruler's nomenclature; on their coins the Seljuqs arrogated to themselves both the formerly caliphal title of "sultan" and the Sasanian imperial title *shāhānshāh*, frequently modified by the Buyid-era addition "King of Islam." As a result, general use of the title *shāhānshāh* became widespread throughout the Persianate world, including India, from the later Middle Ages through the modern period, and was adopted at various times by the rulers of such major dynasties as the Mughals, Safavids, Qajars, and Pahlavis.

Some scholars have viewed the recrudescence of this and other aspects of the ancient Iranian political heritage as an alien and essentially inassimilable element in Islamic political thought. Others maintain that the incorporation of the ancient Persian ideal of rulership into Islamic political thought after the ideological failure of the caliphate was a successful adaptation and that these neo-Sasanian political ideals were assimilated harmoniously into Islamic culture and political life.

See also Buyids (945–1062); Mughals (1526–1857); Safavids (1501–1722); Seljuqs (1055–1194); sultan

Further Reading

C. E. Bosworth, "The Heritage of Rulership in Early Islamic Iran and the Search for Dynastic Connections with the Past," *Iran* 11 (1973); D. G. Tor, "The Long Shadow of Pre-Islamic Iranian Rulership: Antagonism or Assimilation?" in *Late Antiquity: Eastern Perspectives*, edited by Teresa Bernheimer and Adam Silverstein, 2011.

D. G. TOR

Shahnama

Abu al-Qasim Firdawsi's *Shahnama* (Book of kings) is a Persian poem of about 50,000 lines completed in 1010 and dedicated to Sultan Mahmud of Ghazna. Though the story, written by a Shi'i Muslim, culminates in the death of the last Sasanian king and the conquest of Iran by Muslim Arab armies, the *Shahnama* is not an overtly Islamic text. It concerns the "matter" of Iran, its pre-Islamic myths, legends, and history, as translated from Middle Persian texts into Arabic and New Persian prose. Firdawsi began the work of versifying this material circa 977.

In the tenth century, Persophone courts at the edges of Abbasid territory established Persian as a vernacular literary language. In heroic and archaizing style, Firdawsi memorialized the mythical and epic history of imperial Iran, celebrating Achaemenid-Parthian-Sasanian traditions of kingship and statecraft, martial and aristocratic values, and the continuity of an Iranian polity. Firdawsi claimed to bring Persia to life through his *Shahnama*. The work came to function as an icon of legitimate political authority with dynasties ruling in Persia proper (the Ilkhanids, Timurids,

and Safavids) and well beyond (the Seljuqs, Ottomans, and Mughals), who commissioned lavishly illustrated copies of the text. In constructing a 20th-century nation-state, the Pahlavi dynasty also mined the *Shahnama* for symbols of Iranian nationalism and imperial continuity.

The *Shahnama* begins with the primordial Pishdadian dynasty, whose nine kings rule for over two millennia, engaging in cosmic combat to defeat the minions of Ahriman (in the reign of Kiumars), discover fire (reign of Hushang), tame the demons (reign of Tahmures), and build a cultured Edenic civilization (reign of Jamshid) before hubris leads to the usurpation of the Iranian throne by an Arab (reign of Zahhak). Zahhak succumbs to satanic temptation and becomes an oppressive tyrant, until freedom and justice are restored by Feridun. Feridun's sons fall into conflict over the succession, embroiling Iran and Turan in an unending feud. Rustam, a princely warrior of Zabolestan, stalwartly defends the Iranian throne during the wars with Turan and helps establish the legendary Kayanid dynasty, which merges, after the advent of Zoroaster (or Zarathustra, the founder of the dualistic Iranian religious tradition, Zoroastrianism) and the demise of Rustam, into the quasihistorical Achaemenid kings, Darius II (Darab) and Darius III (Dara). Alexander the Great is revealed to be the son of Darab; thus his victory over Persia does not constitute foreign conquest but continuity. He was followed by the last 30 kings of the *Shahnama*, which briefly mentions the Parthians before turning its focus to the Sasanians.

The prelapsarian king, Jamshid, is presented as establishing a static and hierarchical social structure (actually Indo-Iranian in origin), consisting of four classes: priests, warriors, farmers, and artisans. Cosmic retribution is exacted from those who would attempt to overturn this "natural" order (e.g., Mazdak), or to kill kings (e.g., Mahuy) or crown princes (e.g., Rustam). Even the evil king Zahhak, once overthrown, is protected from execution by an intervening angel, who orders the Iranians to chain Zahhak in a mountain cave. Authority to rule derives from royal descent, defined primarily through the father (many of the queen mothers are non-Iranian). But the ruler must also possess the royal *farr*, a supernatural charisma that manifests itself as a halo, light, or totemic animal and may disappear if the king succumbs to sin or hubris (as did Jamshid). Dynasties may change when the *farr* alights upon royals not born in the reigning bloodline who are nominated to the throne by the nobility (e.g., Kay Qobad) or who usurp it (e.g., Sasan). The *Shahnama* states that rule by women will not go well, but in fact the queens (Homay, Puran, Azarm) do prove able and just monarchs.

The ideal royal virtues include wisdom, honor, equanimity, bravery, and martial prowess, but Firdawsi often depicts something rotten in the state of Persia. He does not glorify the kings but shows their character flaws, which frequently lead to tragedy for those around them. The best princes (Siawash, Isfandiar) die before taking the throne, and the ideal king (Kay Khusraw) abdicates for fear of succumbing to hubris and abusing his power. The *Shahnama* worldview is thus deeply pessimistic, even tragic: though the creator God gives humankind the gift of mind/wisdom, it is rather fate and the relentless maw of time that govern human history.

See also Ghaznavids (977–1086); Samanids (819–1005)

Further Reading

Olga Davidson, *Poet and Hero in the Persian Book of Kings*, 1994; Dick Davis, *Epic and Sedition: The Case of Ferdowsi's Shāhnāmeh*, 1992; John Miles Foley, ed., *A Companion to Ancient Epic*, 2005; Theodore Noeldeke, *The Iranian National Epic, or the Shahnamah*, 1930; A. Shahpur Shahbazi, *Ferdowsi: A Critical Biography*, 1991.

FRANKLIN LEWIS

Shah Waliullah (1703–62)

One of the most important religious scholars of Muslim South Asia, Shah Waliullah was a prolific writer in both Arabic and Persian. His political theory is largely found in two comprehensive works—*Hujjat Allah al-Baligha* (The conclusive argument from God) and *al-Budur al-Bazigha* (Full moon appearing on the horizon)—and in a third book about the caliphate, *Izalat al-Khafa' 'an Khilafat al-Khulafa'* (Removing rancor in issues concerning the caliphate), written near the end of his career. Waliullah was a synthetic thinker, and his political ideas reflect the Islamic tradition of idealistic works, such as Farabi's *Virtuous City*, and are based on Platonic ideas of the ideal state as well as classical Islamicate works on government, such as Mawardi's rules for the caliph. On occasion, he offers practical observations and critiques of existing policy and governance in response to circumstances of later Mughal rule in India.

A notable and original feature is Waliullah's formulation of human civilization as developing through four stages of sociopolitical order, for which he coined the term *irtifāqāt*. These progressive stages are described as (1) humans following natural and instinctive patterns in primitive groups, (2) the emergence of orderly family life and rules for social exchange in communities, (3) the rise of the division of labor and local political systems of kingship, and (4) the highest political order based on a single caliph dominating regional rulers. In *Hujjat Allah*, the qualifications for the caliph are initially discussed in pragmatic terms (vol. 1) and later in symbolic and religious terms (vol. 2). In *Izalat al-Khafa'*, Waliullah takes up the discussion of the caliphate of the first four Islamic rulers in greater detail, in part to refute Shi'i claims, perhaps as a response to an ascendancy of Shi'i power in his contemporary North India.

In this work Waliullah defines three categories of the caliphate in terms of language drawn from a hadith report:

The *khilāfa khāṣṣa*, the "elite" or special caliphate, is ultimately restricted to the period of the first four successors of the Prophet. Their rule was marked by (1) the actual presence of the caliph as

the authority and (2) the achievement of complete control over the *umma* (community of believers). Because ʻAli b. Abi Talib's rule was marked by dissent, his stature is somewhat ambiguous here; in another section, a distinction is made between the first three caliphs who ruled at a time of "mercy" (*raḥma*), as opposed to the crisis and dissent (*fitna*) that emerged during ʻAli's rule.

The *khilāfa ʻāmma*, or "general" type of caliphate, either lacks the consensus of the entire Muslim community, fails to achieve its internal quality of embodiment of (*tashabbuh*) of the Prophet's model in responding to people's needs and implementing the divine mandate, or has a ruler that is deficient in his knowledge of the shariʻa. Still, external elements of establishing the religion may effectively be fulfilled by the "general" caliph, although this ruler is not at the same level in *tashabbuh* of the prophetic legacy that marked the initial phase. This general level of the caliphate is required for two beneficial aims (*maṣāliḥ*): one political, in other words, for the sake of defense and justice, and the other to enforce compliance with the shariʻa. There is also the suggestion that consensus (*ijmāʻ*) on matters of policy and religion emerges institutionally from the ruler's decree, with or without scholarly consultation. During this period following the tenure of the Rightly Guided Caliphs, the ruler is not envisioned as coming from the ʻulamaʼ (religious scholars) class, although according to certain passages in Waliullah's works, *al-Tafhimat al-Ilahiyya* (Divine instructions) and *Fuyud al-Haramayn* (Visions received in the two holy cities), the religious scholars are the bearers of an "inner" caliphate (*al-khilāfa al-bāṭina*), continuing the Prophet's teaching role in the sense of transmitting religious learning as well as moral and spiritual exhortations and authority. Meanwhile, the "external" caliphate (*al-khilāfa al-ẓāhira*) is fulfilled by the political ruler who exercises the aforementioned functions of defense, control, and enforcement.

The final type of caliphate, the *khilāfa jābira*, or "oppressive" caliphate, is undesirable, although quietism on the part of the populace is generally enjoined unless the ruler goes so far in injustice or apostasy that he must be resisted and overthrown.

Waliullah's more practical discussions of the necessary infrastructure, policies of remuneration, fair taxation, and so on occur both in some of his political letters and in specific passages in his longer works. In his discussion of rules for kings, he draws on Islamicate advice or wisdom literature to treat topics such as the superior qualities possessed by an ideal ruler and the ruler's need to recognize and reward competence and to weed out treachery.

Waliullah's criticism of economic and social injustices have been seized on by thinkers such as the Pakistani scholar ʻUbaydallah Sindhi (d. 1944), who casts Waliullah as an economic reformer promoting social justice or even a socialist agenda. Waliullah has also been construed as an incipient Islamic political activist and a progenitor of the 20th-century freedom movement in India. This latter image has been contested across Indian and Pakistani scholarship. He certainly lived in turbulent times: after the death of Aurangzeb, the last strong Mughal emperor, in 1707, a sequence of ten kings occupied the throne during the remainder of Waliullah's life. In 1739, Delhi was sacked by the Persian Nadir Shah. When Delhi and the rest of northern India were subsequently threatened by the rise of Hindu clans known as Jats and Marathas and by the Sikhs, Waliullah tried in his letters to encourage Muslim notables to take a stand. Most successful among these were Ahmad Shah Abdali, an Afghan king, and Najib al-Dawla, the leader of a Pathan clan, the Rohillas, who joined forces to decisively defeat the Marathas at the Battle of Panipat in 1761.

Khaliq Ahmed Nizami (d. 1998) published *Shah Wali Allah ki Siyasi Maktubat* (Political letters of Shah Wali Allah), in which he collected the messages written by Waliullah to various Muslim rulers of his age, requesting them to come to the aid of Indian Muslims against non-Muslim forces in India. Waliullah did not address the threat from the British East India Company, although the British were to rule Delhi within a few decades of his death. Later, his son and successor, Shah ʻAbd al-ʻAziz (d. 1823), issued two notable fatwas (religious opinions) that were accommodating to British rule. The first declared India to be *dār al-ḥarb* (the abode of war), since it facilitated Indian Muslims' adapting to new rules of interest-based finance and land tenure. The second fatwa permitted Indian Muslims to work for the British.

Waliullah was a noted scholar and teacher with a wide circle of pupils, some of whom are linked directly with the establishment of the Deoband madrasa. His grandson, Shah Ismaʻil Shahid (d. 1831), is known primarily for his involvement in the Mujahidin movement against the Sikhs led by Sayyid Ahmed Barelvi (d. 1831). This has led some scholars to conclude that a "Waliullahi" movement for political and religious reform inspired later Muslim nationalist and reformist trends in the subcontinent.

See also India; revival and reform

Further Reading

Aziz Ahmed, "An Eighteenth Century Theory of the Caliphate," *Studia Islamica* 28 (1968); J. M. S. Baljon, *Religion and Thought of Shah Wali Allah Dihlavi*, 1986; Ahmad Dallal, "The Origins and Objectives of Islamic Revivalist Thought, 1750–1850," *Journal of the American Oriental Society* 113, no. 3 (1993); Muhammad al-Ghazali, *The Socio-Political Thought of Shah Wali Allah*, 2001; Marcia K. Hermansen, trans., *The Conclusive Argument from God: Shāh Walī Allāh of Delhi's Ḥujjat Allāh al-Bāligha*, 1996.

MARCIA HERMANSEN

Shamil (1797–1871)

Shamil was the third and most successful imam (r. 1834–59), or leader of the Muslim resistance to the Russian conquest of Chechnya and Daghestan and ruler of the imamate (Islamic state) it established.

Born in the *aʼul* (village) of Gimry, Shamil displayed from early childhood interest in religious studies. He, together with his

older friend and distant relative Ghazi Muhammad (the future first imam), studied with various ʻulama' in Daghestan, the most famous of whom was Saʻid al-Harakani (d. 1834), and then joined the Khalidi branch of the Naqshbandi-Mujaddidi Sufi brotherhood. Both he and Ghazi Muhammad were disciples (*murīds*) of Jamal al-Din al-Ghazi-Ghumuqi (1788–1869) but were given licenses (*ijāza*) to propagate the brotherhood (*ṭarīqa*) by his master, Muhammad al-Yaraghi (1770–1838). Shamil remained loyal and obedient to Jamal al-Din until his last day in the Caucasus. He married his mentor's daughter and gave two of his daughters to Jamal al-Din's sons. Jamal al-Din, on his part, supported Shamil in his bid for leadership and during the entire period of his rule.

During his first three years as imam, Shamil was busy establishing his authority over rival claimants to leadership and the population at large. Here, his master's support was of crucial importance. So was the imam's low profile in his negotiations with the Russians. In 1837 the Russians tried to destroy him but were forced to sign a truce. Two years later Shamil escaped a crushing defeat with his family and a few followers, but he rose to new heights of power and success in the following years.

At the peak of his power, Shamil controlled most of Daghestan and Chechnya and sent *nā'ib*s (lieutenants) to the Circassians in the Western Caucasus, the most successful of whom was Muhammad Amin (active 1848–59). In 1845, Shamil dealt a painful blow to a huge Russian expeditionary force under Count Vorontsov, and in the following year he tried to join forces with the Circassians. He repeated such attempts up to, and during, the Crimean War (1853–56).

Understanding the odds he was up against, Shamil, like his predecessors, tried to secure Ottoman assistance, but the Sublime Porte denied it. During the early 1840s, however, assistance came from Muhammad ʻAli, the pasha of Egypt. In the period leading to the Crimean War it seemed as if both Shamil and the Ottomans were moving toward cooperation. Shamil's serious attempts to join forces with the Ottoman army at the beginning of that war, however, were met with a feeble Ottoman response. The Ottomans abandoned such attempts completely following their defeats on the Anatolian front and pressure from the British ambassador.

With the lessons of the Crimean War in mind, the Russians concentrated on conquering Chechnya and Daghestan. The Chechens and Daghetsanis were in the meantime greatly demoralized after the Ottomans failed to join them during the war and thereafter abandoned them in the Paris peace treaty of March 1856, which concluded the Crimean War. Beginning in 1857, successive Russian offensives from three sides gradually reduced Shamil's imamate, which collapsed in 1859, forcing Shamil's surrender.

In captivity, Shamil was treated with respect and allocated a house in Kaluga and later in Kiev. In 1869, he was allowed to leave for hajj, the pilgrimage to Mecca. He settled in Medina and died in 1871 on his way to another visit to Mecca. His eldest surviving son, Ghazi Muhammad, became a general in the Ottoman army and led a Caucasian division in the Russo-Ottoman War (1877–78). His other son, Shafiʻ Muhammad, was a general in the Russian army. His grandson Sait (Saʻid) Shamil joined the 1920 rebellion against the Bolsheviks in Daghestan and was one of the only two survivors who returned to Turkey.

During his long reign, Shamil completed the structure of the imamate, the foundations of which had been laid by his predecessors, Ghazi Muhammad (1829–32) and Hamza Bek (1832–34). The imam stood at the head of both the lay and the religious hierarchies and claimed full sovereignty, assuming the title *amīr al-mu'minīn* (Commander of the Faithful). He was assisted in running the state by a *dīwān* (privy council), which included Jamal al-Din. The lay hierarchy below the imam included in descending order *mudirs* and *nā'ibs*, who were simultaneously governors, military commanders, and tax collectors for *bayt al-māl* (the treasury). The religious hierarchy included muftis (jurists) and qadis (judges), who were independent of the *nā'ibs* and accountable only to the imam. The backbone of the army were the *murtaziqa* (supported, provided for)—a standing army of one soldier per ten households who provided for all his family's needs—but in the late 1840s an artillery corps and an Ottoman-style regular infantry, the *niẓām*, were also set up.

Contrary to the established view, the main aim of Shamil's movement was not jihad (holy war) but *tanfīdh* (implementation) of the shariʻa. Jihad was merely a tool for *tanfīdh*, in addition to a means for self-defense against occupation by unbelievers. Correspondingly, the imamate was based on Islamic law—according to his (and his followers') interpretation. Shamil thus made a major effort that the taxes and the expenses of *bayt al-māl* approximate as far as possible the stipulations of the shariʻa, and an important part of the stipulations of the *niẓām*—Shamil's "secular" legislation (by-laws, not to be confused with the infantry unit of a similar name)—dealt with (re)interpretations of the provisos of the shariʻa. As both an *ʻālim* (scholar) and a Naqshbandi disciple, Shamil personally made an effort to live according to the shariʻa and to demonstrate that all his actions as leader matched the dictates of the sacred law.

From an early stage in the struggle, the Russians used Daghestani and Middle Volga Region ʻulama' in their service in order to discredit Shamil and his movement on Islamic grounds. The most important of these ʻulama' were Harakani, Mirza ʻAli al-Akhdi (d. 1858), and Yusuf al-Yakhsawi (d. 1871). But Shamil and his followers easily dismissed them as traitors to Islam. Of more consequence was Sulayman Efendi, a *nā'ib* in Shamil's imamate who defected to the Russians and produced in 1846 a list of Shamil's transgressions and deviations from the shariʻa. This prompted Shamil to put on record both his history and the legal justifications for his actions. Both of these projects were carried out by well-known ʻulama'.

Muhammad Tahir al-Qarakhi, who served for a while as Shamil's secretary, wrote the chronicle titled *Bariqat al-Suyuf al-Daghistaniyya fi baʻd al-Ghazawat al-Shamiliyya* (The glitter of Daghestani swords in some of Shamil's raids), which recorded Shamil's version of the events. Murtada ʻAli al-Uradi (d. 1865), who also served for a short time as Shamil's secretary, wrote *al-Murghim* (The compulsory) and *Risala fi al-Hijra* (Treatise on emigration), which summarized the legal point of view of the imam and his supporters.

According to this point of view, an imam is a *farḍ kifāya* (collective duty), which means that the Muslims must always have at least one leader. Territories too far removed from one another or from the center to effectively assist each other should have their own imam. All Muslims in the imam's domain have to accept his authority. Those who disobey him are *bughāt* (rebels), and those who reject the rule of the shari'a are *murtaddūn* (apostates). Hijra—that is, emigration from *dār al-ḥarb* (abode of war) to *dār al-islām* (abode of Islam)—is compulsory if called upon by the imam. Those who remain in *dār al-ḥarb* are *bughāt*, while collaborators with the infidels are *murtaddūn*. The killing of *ahl al-ridda* (apostates) takes priority over the killing of *ahl al-ḥarb* (infidels not recognizing the sovereignty of the Islamic state). If those *ahl al-ridda* are beyond the reach of the imam, their property may be seized or destroyed, and their marriages, commercial contracts, and inheritance rights are null and void. It is permitted to raid the houses of the *bughāt*, to pillage and destroy them, and to evict their inhabitants by force into *dār al-islām*. If dictated by *maṣlaḥa* (the benefit of the Muslim community), *bughāt* may be killed too.

The principle of *maṣlaḥa* grants unrestricted authority to the imam. He has the right of *ijtihād* (independent reasoning on the basis of the Qur'an and sunna) with regard to legislation and to *ta'zīr* (punishments for criminal offenses), including inflicting the death penalty and punishing upon suspicion, without the sufficient proof required by Islamic law. Indeed, Shamil used this authority in both his "secular" legislation—the *niẓām*—and in substituting the *ḥudūd* (punishments fixed by the shari'a) with other punishments.

The physical and spiritual backbone of the movement and the imamate were the Khalidis. It is, therefore, natural that the real challenge to the imamate came from another *ṭarīqa* that started to spread in Chechnya and Daghestan in the late 1850s: the Qadiris. Shaykh Kunta Hajji al-Michiki al-Iliskhani (ca. 1830–67), who introduced it to the Caucasus, offered people exhausted by 30 years of war and deprivation a third alternative to the two presented by Shamil—either to be true believers and resist or to surrender and become apostates. Kunta Hajji said that being a good Muslim depended on one's personal behavior, not on resistance. Furthermore, he stated that resistance to the Russians was a sin and predicted the fall of the imamate and the captivity of Shamil. Unable to counter these arguments, the imam sent Kunta Hajji on another hajj, but the message had fallen on fertile ground and contributed to the downfall of the imamate.

Almost completely forgotten in the wider Muslim world and in the West, Shamil became a hero to many in the former Soviet Union, and his figure generated controversy in Soviet historiography. His heritage is claimed by various, often opposing, political, ethnic, and ideological groups and movements in the Caucasus.

See also brotherhoods; Central Asia; Ottomans (1299–1924); Sufism

Further Reading

Moshe Gammer, *Muslim Resistance to the Tsar: Shamil and the Conquest of Chechnia and Daghestan*, 1994; Idem, "Shamil in Soviet Historiography," *Middle Eastern Studies* 28, no. 4 (1992); Michael Kemper, "Khalidiyya Networks in Daghestan and the Question of Jihad," *Die Welt des Islams* 42, no. 1 (2002); Idem, "The North Caucasian Khalidiyya and 'Muridism': Historiographical Problems," *Journal of the History of Sufism* 5 (2006); Alexander Knysh, "Sufism as an Explanatory Paradigm: The Issue of the Motivations of Sufi Movements in Russian and Western Historiography," *Die Welt des Islams* 42, no. 2 (2002); Anna Zelkina, *In Quest of God and Freedom: The Sufi Response to the Russian Advances in the North Caucasus*, 2000.

MOSHE GAMMER

shari'a

The shari'a (*sharī'a*) is the revealed, sacred law of Islam, though the primary term for law in the Qur'an is arguably *dīn*, ordinarily translated as "religion." Law is an essential feature of revealed religion in both the Qur'an and Islamic thought in general, and the term shari'a is used with reference not only to Islam but also to Judaism and Christianity, because all three are conceived as having a divinely given law. According to later jurists, 500 verses of the Qur'an, termed *āyāt al-aḥkām* (verses of rulings), treat legal subjects, including matters relating to prayer, fasting, alms, pilgrimage, permitted food, marriage, divorce, inheritance, slavery, and trade. This represents roughly one-thirteenth of the sacred text.

Fiqh (literally, "understanding") is the term for the human effort to work out God's law on particular issues. Like shari'a, with which it is often contrasted, it is translatable as law, but whereas shari'a refers primarily to God's regulation of human behavior, and thus the ideal, *fiqh* always stands for the human approximation of this ideal, the law as actually found in the books. Because it etymologically means "comprehension," *fiqh* is often translated as "jurisprudence" in English, but usually it corresponds to law, referring to the actual rules in the books. Jurisprudence, the science or methods of interpretation through which one determines the law, corresponds more closely to *uṣūl al-fiqh* (literally, "the roots of the law"), the science devoted to the hermeneutics of Islamic law.

For the vast majority of Muslims, law has determined—and still determines today—what Islam is. This distinguishes Islam from Christianity, which does not actually have a revealed law and in which theology is the queen of religious sciences; Judaism likewise stresses the importance and centrality of the law. The "clergy" of Islam, like the rabbis of Judaism, are jurists rather than theologians, and it is their study of the law and competence in addressing legal questions that gives them authority. Many other claimants to authority have coexisted with them in the course of history, but, for more than a millennium, jurists have been among the groups most successful in gaining acceptance for their claims.

The Law in the Books

Islamic law is not embodied in a single authoritative code but rather held to reside in the vast array of legal texts, based ultimately on legal responsa issued by recognized jurists over the course of history. A responsum (fatwa) is an opinion solicited from a legal authority on a specific legal question. In the early sources, opinions are often solicited by one jurist of another ("I asked so-and-so about the case of . . .") or by a student or a layperson; in later times, fatwas were typically issued in response to questions by laypersons. Not all opinions were considered equal: the most authoritative opinions were those issued by *mujtahids*, jurists endowed with the ability acquired through intense legal study to derive independent legal rulings directly from the sources (*ijtihād*). Of the books recording these opinions, some were (and are) considered more important than others, but no one book gained the overriding authority of a work such as the *Shulchan Aruch* (The set table) of Joseph ben Ephraim Karo (d. 1575), which has served as the nearly exclusive basis for the elaboration of Jewish law over the past four centuries.

The law books divide their subject matter into set topical chapters that, already in the ninth century, followed a standard order, with some variations, that facilitated the location of particular legal topics in relatively large works without fixed pagination and often without indexes or tables of contents. The chapters fall into three large categories: *'ibādāt* (acts of worship); *mu'āmalāt* (transactions or contracts); and *qaḍāyā* (court cases). The *'ibādāt* sections start with ritual purity (*ṭahārah*), a prerequisite for ritual prayer and other acts of devotion, and proceed to discuss prayer itself, the first act of devotion since it is performed daily; this is followed by fasting, performed during at least one month of the year, the alms tax (zakat), which must be given once a year, and the pilgrimage, which must be performed once in a lifetime by those who are able to undertake it. The chapter order in the *mu'āmalāt* section is not as rigidly fixed, but it always appears after the *'ibādāt* section. Major topics include sales, marriage, divorce, inheritance, renting, pawning, sharecropping, partnerships, agents, slavery, deposits, found property, foundlings, endowments, and so on. The third section includes chapters on crimes, judicial procedure, and court cases. The crimes known as *ḥudūd* are those for which fixed punishments are sanctioned by the Qur'an, and they are generally held to be seven in number: apostasy, adultery, false accusation of adultery, burglary, highway robbery, sedition, and drinking alcohol.

The law books regulate many matters of ritual that one could scarcely hope to enforce. Muslims are not tried in court for failing to perform ablutions properly, even though the discussion of ritual purity is usually one of the longest sections in any given law book. Most actual court cases have to do with matters governed by contracts and agreements between individuals, such as business transactions of all types. In addition, the law does not simply regulate what is forbidden, obligatory, or permissible but rather seeks to rank all human acts in moral terms on a five-tiered scale: *ḥarām* (forbidden), *makrūh* (reprehensible, discouraged), *mubāḥ* (allowed), *mustaḥabb* (recommended), and *wājib* (obligatory).

The Sources of the Law

On what did the scholars base their responsa? The substance of their rules was often indebted to existing systems, both Arabian and Near Eastern (a conglomeration of systems of diverse origin, including Jewish, Byzantine, and Sassanian law), but this does not tell us on what basis the rules were counted as Islamic. Some will have been formulated by the caliphs, whose decisions seem initially to have been accepted as authoritative. In later times this was true only of those caliphs who were also Companions of the Prophet, notably 'Umar b. al-Khattab (r. 634–44), who is held to have made important contributions to the law. The laws relating to *dhimmīs* (non-Muslim communities under Muslim rule) must also have derived from caliphal decrees, even though the documents attributed to them are not always genuine. By most accounts, however, Islamic law was elaborated by thinkers who stood outside the government and were opposed to or at least stood aloof from it and who did not accept the decrees of the caliphs as a source of law. In the earliest material, their rules often rest on nothing but their considered opinion (*ra'y*); their decision is recorded, but their reasoning is not explained. Stringent principles for the derivation of law soon made their appearance, however.

The science of the *uṣūl al-fiqh* proposed that the law must be derived from an ordered series of sources, of which most Sunni jurists eventually accepted four: (1) the Qur'an; (2) the sunna (the customary way of the Prophet Muhammad), which was understood to be preserved in the hadith (recorded reports about the Prophet's words and deeds); (3) consensus (*ijmā'*); and (4) legal analogy (*qiyās*) or the exhaustive independent consideration of a legal question (*ijtihād*). The idea of an ordered list of sources originated in the eighth century and is seen in checklists presented in instructions for judges. The first extant work of *uṣūl al-fiqh*, the *Risala* of Shafi'i (d. 820), presents a sophisticated system of legal hermeneutics, but his system is based on the idea that there is only one source of the law: revelation. Revelation includes both the Qur'an and the corpus of prophetic hadith, but to Shafi'i they combined to form a coherent whole. This is quite a bit different from the later four-source theory. Jurists writing after Shafi'i interpreted his work anachronistically, in some cases even rearranging the text in order to bring it in line with the later conventions of the *uṣūl al-fiqh* genre. As the four-source theory gained ground, "considered opinion" as a basis of the law was eclipsed and suppressed in favor of a stricter reliance on texts; "opinion" came to be associated with whim or wild speculation. It survived in a disciplined form as *qiyās*, analogical reasoning from a known, determined case to a similar, undetermined case, but some jurists continued to oppose that too.

Consensus is usually negative and retroactive: the lack of dissenting opinions over the past generation is a sign that consensus exists. The body of acceptable opinion is thus made up of two parts, consensus and disputed points (*khilāf*), both within a particular legal school and between them, for variant opinions are allowed on those points of law for which a consensus does not exist. Lists of the requirements of a master jurist often stress that he must be aware of areas of consensus in the law—this is similar

to a call for the necessity of examining relevant precedent before deciding a case.

Madhhabs and Madrasas

Two institutions that contributed to making the law central to Islamic societies and creating continuity over space and time are the *madhhab*, or the legal school (in the sense of a tradition of legal study based on a stable body of doctrine), and the madrasa, or college of law. The circles behind the legal schools organized and regularized the transmission of legal knowledge and interpretive authority, which have survived until the present day, and their activities represent a significant step in the professionalization of the jurists as a class. They solidified in the course of the ninth and tenth centuries, and four Sunni schools survive to this day: the Hanafi, named after Abu Hanifa (d. 767); the Maliki, named after Malik b. Anas (d. 795); the Shafi'i, named after Shafi'i (d. 820); and the Hanbali, named after Ahmad b. Hanbal (d. 855). But there were others as well, including the Dawudi *madhhab*, named after its founder Dawud b. 'Ali b. Khalaf al-Isfahani (d. 884), which was also called the Zahiri *madhhab* on account of the principle of reliance on the prima facie reading (*ẓāhir*) of revealed proof texts, and the Jariri, named after Muhammad b. Jarir al-Tabari (d. 923). In addition to these six, several non-Sunni legal schools arose. These included the Twelver Shi'i school, called the Imami *madhhab*, after their adherence to the teachings of their 12 imams, or Ja'fari, in reference to the sixth imam, Ja'far al-Sadiq (d. 765); the Zaydi Shi'i *madhhab*, named after the martyred rebel imam Zayd (d. 740); and the Ibadi Khariji school, named after 'Abdallah b. Ibad (d. 708), all of which were established by the 11th century, making nine in total. The Zahiri and Jariri schools had died out by the 12th century and were absorbed into the Shafi'i school, leaving the Imami, Zaydi, Ibadi, and the four well-known Sunni schools: Hanafi, Maliki, Shafi'i, and Hanbali. Isma'ili Shi'is developed their own legal tradition under the Fatimid caliphate (909–1171), chiefly in the work of the outstanding jurist Qadi al-Nu'man (d. 974), but their legal *madhhab* differs from the others in institutional terms because of continued access to and dependence on the teachings of an inspired imam. While the Shi'i and Khariji legal traditions preserved early doctrines that differed from those of the Sunni schools, such as the Twelver Shi'is' acceptance of *mut'a* or temporary marriage, the professionalization of the jurists as a class and the institution of the *madhhab* had the effect of making their systems of legal education and interpretation resemble those of the Sunnis more and more over time.

The main centers of formation of the schools were Fustat in Egypt and Baghdad in Iraq. The Hanafi school was supported by the Abbasid caliphs and associated with their rule until the late 12th century (when several caliphs adopted the Shafi'i school); later, it became the preferred school of all major Turkish dynasties, spreading in Central Asia, Anatolia, and India and in Syria and Egypt under the Ottomans. The Shafi'i school was strong in Iraq, Syria, Egypt, Arabia, and, later, Indonesia; that of the Malikis was strong in Egypt and dominant in North Africa, sub-Saharan Africa, and Andalus, where the Umayyad rulers supported it. The Hanbali school, more limited in scope, boasted adherents in some towns of Palestine, Syria, and Iraq. In modern times, it was chosen by adherents of the Wahhabi movement that grew in tandem with the Saudi state and through them became influential throughout the Islamic world. Iran was split between Hanafis and Shafi'is until the Safavids succeeded in converting most of the populace to Shi'i Islam. The remaining Sunnis—for the most part Kurds—are Shafi'is. The Twelver, Zaydi, and Khariji *madhhabs* developed primarily in Iraq and Baghdad in particular, gained ground during the Buyid period (945–1055), and spread to Iran and other areas from there. *Madhhab* allegiance has remained to this day a matter of region and has been influenced in many cases by political rule, illustrating the dictum that "people adopt the religion of their rulers."

The madrasa represents another milestone in the professionalization of the jurists. The madrasa originated in Khurasan—eastern Iran—in the tenth century and traveled west into Iraq, Syria, Egypt, North Africa and east into Central Asia, India, and beyond. It was an organization embodied in a physical building dedicated to legal education through the establishment of an endowment. Agricultural land or rental properties that produced an annual income were placed in a charitable endowment in perpetuity, and the funds were used to pay for the maintenance and upkeep of the building, for the salary of a law professor (*mudarris*), and for monthly stipends for law students. Like the European universities, such as that of Bologna, it grew out of the needs of out-of-town law students. Previously, many prominent jurists had taught their lessons in a mosque, and an adjacent inn provided convenient lodging for students who were not local. This often continued to be the case, but the madrasa combined these two functions: a typical madrasa was a two-story building with an open courtyard. Lessons would be held on the ground floor in alcoves designed for teaching purposes, and the upper floor served as a dormitory for the stipendiary students and sometimes the *mudarris*. By the late 11th century, a number of madrasas had been founded in Baghdad; the most impressive of them was the Nizamiyya, one of a series of such institutions founded by the famous Seljuq vizier Nizam al-Mulk. The Zengids and Ayyubids made the madrasa a prominent feature of the major cities of Syria and Egypt, where they spread its influence in the 12th century. It continued moving west, and the Marinids established numerous madrasas in Morocco in the 14th century. At the same time, madrasas also spread into Anatolia, Central Asia, India, and beyond.

The spread of the madrasa did not initially change the nature of legal study, for the curriculum, stages of study, and methods of teaching apparently remained the same. They did, however, serve visibly to increase the power and prestige of jurists by raising the status of the *mudarris*, and they increased societal support for legal education as a whole, especially on account of the stipends accorded to law students. In addition, they bolstered the institution of the legal school, since each madrasa was devoted to the teaching of the law according to a single school, with one law professor

teaching stipendiary students belonging to the same school. Over time, the madrasa came to dominate legal education, and access to the judiciary came to be controlled primarily by the law professors, who would recommend their students to the chief judge of the district for patents of probity—essentially, a document from the local judge attesting that a student was of good character and had a clean moral record and was thus not barred from holding positions of legal responsibility—and then, probably, for the certificate of permission to teach law and grant legal opinions.

Legal Education and Careers

The study of the law in the 10th to 14th centuries was divided into three stages: preparatory studies, including Arabic grammar, rhetoric, and logic; the legal doctrine of the particular school to which one belonged, studied in epitomes; and the disputed points of the law, legal hermeneutics, and dialectic—the rules of legal debate. Advanced students often became the disciples of a master jurist, studying with him for many years and eventually composing a commentary called a *ta‘līqa*, based on the lectures of the professor. In recognition that a student had completed his legal education, the master jurist conferred on him a diploma termed *ijāzat al-tadrīs wa-l-iftā’* (certificate to teach law and grant legal opinions). This diploma established the student's qualifications as a jurist or *faqīh* able to analyze legal questions, as a mufti or jurisconsult entitled to answer legal questions from the lay public, and as a scholar of law able to teach law students of his own.

One of the functions of the system of legal education was to provide legal experts to serve in the judiciary. At a low level, a scholar who had a good basic knowledge of the law and a patent of probity could obtain work as a private notary who drew up documents such as marriage, divorce, sales, and other contracts or as an official witness, notary, or clerk attached to a judge's court. A more experienced jurist could serve as a deputy judge and eventually as a judge in his own right. After the 11th century, more and more salaried positions as law professors (*mudarris*) or repetitors (*mu‘īd*, essentially an assistant professor) became available. Jurists who had a good knowledge of mathematics could also make a living as inheritance law experts (*faraḍī*), who, like notaries for marriage and divorce contracts, were often in high demand.

The relative ranking of the jurists within a given legal school in a city was generally known, though it was not official. A pecking order was established not only by debate, authorship, teaching, and serving as judges but also by the public activity of granting fatwas and endorsing, revising, correcting, or denouncing the fatwas of other jurists. The top living jurist within a given *madhhab* was termed *ra’īs* (chief) or foremost jurist. The hierarchy was theoretically independent of specific offices such as that of chief judge, but rank and office often tended to go together. The endowment deeds of a number of madrasas specified that the law professor at the madrasa should be the top Shafi‘i legal scholar of the time. Related to this juristic hierarchy was the controversy over *ijtihād*. Theorists such as Yahya b. Sharaf Nawawi (d. 1277) wrote that the jurists were to be ranked according to various levels of *ijtihād*, often with one or more of the top ranks empty. While the texts of jurisprudence present this as a theoretical exercise about past jurists, it also reflects an understanding that contemporary jurists form a hierarchy of authority.

Rival Authorities

The legal schools served not only to establish regular methods of textual transmission and legal education but also to exclude other groups from participation in the elaboration of law. In the ninth and tenth centuries, the main contenders for religious authority among the scholars were the theologians (*mutakallim*s). The jurists took the view that every believer should know a basic catechism: there is one God, the Prophet Muhammad is the messenger of God, the Qur'an is God's word, and so on. Beyond that, theology was necessary only to defend Islam from heretics, and an advanced knowledge of theology was not required for the populace at large or important for their daily lives and worship. The theologians, by contrast, held that the law merely treated details whereas theology dealt with the large, important questions. Mu‘tazili theologians explicitly stated that the study of hadith and law were subordinate to the study of theology.

The conflict between the two groups, jurists and theologians, is nowhere more evident than in the *miḥna* (literally, trial, tribulation, often called "inquisition") of the mid-ninth century, in which the theologians in cooperation with the caliph Ma'mun and his successors sought to impose the doctrine that the Qur'an was created by God at a particular point in historical time (rather than being eternal) on the officials and prominent scholars of the empire. The theologians lost this battle, but they regained ground through the patronage of later rulers. By the tenth century, however, the legal schools had grown so powerful that the theologians had to declare allegiance to one of them in order to legitimate their scholarship. In general, the Mu‘tazilis chose the Hanafi school, while the Ash‘aris chose that of Shafi‘i. A tenth-century Mu‘tazili is said to have encouraged his students to join different schools in order to populate them all with proponents of Mu‘tazilism. The Mu‘tazili school of theology waned in the 11th and 12th centuries, and with it, the authority of theologians in general. It lived on in part in the Twelver and Zaydi Shi‘i traditions, whose leading scholars were profoundly influenced by Mu‘tazili theology between the 9th and 11th centuries, but in those traditions as well, religious authority came to be based on the study of law rather than theology. While theology continued to be an important Islamic science, it was relegated to a subordinate and ancillary position.

There was also some conflict between jurists and hadith experts. The *ahl al-ḥadīth* were scholars of reports concerning the words and deeds of the Prophet Muhammad, which they examined in order to determine his exemplary or normative behavior, or sunna. They believed that these rules determined the law for contemporary Muslims. They rejected the use of rational inquiry independent of such texts for the elaboration of the law, and they were able to maintain a distinct authority in the ninth and tenth centuries, compiling many legal works termed *Sunan*, which arranged hadith reports by

legal chapter. Jurists who were more inclined to rational inquiry decried the *ahl al-ḥadīth* as uncritical, simple-minded collectors who were incapable of understanding the implications of the texts they transmitted. By the end of the 11th century, the hadith scholars had lost much of their former authority and came to be subsumed under the legal scholars. Signs of this development include statements that the fully qualified jurist need not have memorized hadith reports but should know where to look them up in standard reference works.

Other rivals of the jurists were the philosophers and Sufi masters (who were rivals themselves). Both groups tended to see themselves as elites, holding that their understanding of the world was only accessible to a few; those who were not adept at rational analysis (according to the philosophers) or not sensitive to the spiritual world of the unseen (according to the Sufis) could make do with following the dictates of the jurists and simply performing their religious obligations in the ordinary fashion. This identified the jurists as low-level leaders, somewhat like school teachers in relation to professors. The jurists responded by often denouncing the philosophers as unbelievers, but the Sufis were a more prevalent and persistent threat. Their claim to access to divine knowledge through paths other than study of the law threatened to undermine the jurists' authority, leading one 16th-century scholar to remark to a Sufi friend that the jurists and the Sufis were mentioned right next to each other in the Qur'an, in the verse that reads, "Are the two equal: those who know and those who do not know?" (Q. 39:9); he obviously took "those who know" to mean the legal scholars. The jurists did come to terms with Sufis who adhered to the law, and they often joined them, too, but they vigorously condemned those who claimed that the ordinary rules concerning religious obligations did not apply to them because they were in direct communion with the divine, often charging them with antinomianism—categorical disregard for the law—and belief in reincarnation and divine immanence. They also accused Sufis of vices such as laziness, excessive dependence on others, dancing and singing, and pederasty and tended to react adversely to their apparently blasphemous ecstatic statements. Fierce debates raged over the mystical poetry of Ibn al-Farid (d. 1235), which many jurists declared heretical. Defenders of the poetry, who also included jurists, insisted that one could not interpret the ecstatic and inspired statements of the Sufis literally, for the true meaning was incomprehensible to the uninitiated. Sufism has continued to be extremely influential in many areas in the Muslim world, and Sufi groups continue to risk conflicts with representatives of juristic authority, such as in Pakistan, where their shrines have been bombed by Salafi zealots, or in Iran, where the Islamic Republican government has disbanded several Sufi orders in the last decade.

Caliphs

The jurists' most important rivals in the first centuries were the caliphs, who claimed religious authority in legal and theological matters alike. The rivalry between them came to a head in the "inquisition" of the mid-ninth century, a battle that the caliphs lost along with the theologians. Nonetheless, they never lost their religious authority completely. They retained some room for maneuver through their control of the judiciary, the main institution that applied the law; the chief judges (*qāḍī al-quḍāt*) they appointed were prominent ideologues with authority throughout the empire and had tremendous influence on legal doctrine and practice. In the late 10th and early 11th centuries, the caliph Qadir (991–1031) made a number of attempts to enhance his religious authority and was particularly active in denouncing the public presence of Mu'tazili theology and Twelver and Isma'ili Shi'ism. In league with Hanbali and other conservative Sunni theologians, he repeatedly and publicly promulgated, in 1018 and subsequent years, the Qadiri Creed, a document that declared Mu'tazili and Shi'i theology heretical and prohibited debate with their scholars. His policy was continued by Qa'im, his son and successor. Even until the late Abbasid period, dynasts throughout the central Islamic lands regularly sought the caliph's recognition of their position and even his sanction for their military campaigns against the Byzantines and others. The idiosyncratic caliph Nasir (r. 1180–1225), who endeavored to revive the glory of the early Abbasid caliphate by placing himself at the pinnacle of all societal structures of authority, wrote four *ijāzah*s or certificates authorizing the activities of the four Sunni schools, granting one to the leading jurist of each one of them. Much later, in the Treaty of Kuchuk-Kainardja, signed in July 1774 between the Ottoman sultan Abdülhamid I (1774–89) and the Russian empress Catherine the Great (1762–96), the Ottomans recognized the independence of Crimea but insisted that the sultan remained the spiritual leader of the Tartars on the grounds that he was the caliph of the Muslims. This may be seen as a move to counter Russian and French claims to represent the cause of Christian minorities within the Ottoman Empire, similarly claiming jurisdiction over Muslims outside the official boundaries of Islamdom. Whatever the reasoning behind it, the condition nevertheless indicates a strong claim to religious authority on the part of the caliph many centuries after the heyday of the Abbasids.

As far as the caliph's relations with the jurists are concerned, it could be said that a compromise was reached whereby the jurists claimed direct jurisdiction over private law while recognizing the caliphs' (and eventually other rulers') control over public law; the jurists publicly supported the legitimacy of the government, while the rulers supported the jurists as a class. This was possible because the shari'a leaves large parts of the law relatively undeveloped, particularly public law (except for taxation, a constant bone of contention). Rulers thus had some freedom to act, and they imposed a wide variety of systems of civil, criminal, and even tax law throughout Islamic history. The most famous is the *Qanun* of the Ottoman sultans. Collected by Mehmed the Conqueror in the mid-15th century, this code was revised in 1501 and again in the mid-16th century by Sultan Süleiman; it dealt primarily with the organization of government and the military, taxation, and treatment of the peasantry.

Jurists periodically attempted to assert broader control, arguing that the ruler, even when acting on his own, was required to adhere closely to the dictates of the shari'a. They made such arguments in works under the generic rubric of *siyāsa shar'īyya* (public policy

that conforms to the shari'a), including such works as *al-Siyasa al-Shar'iyya* (The book of governance according to the shari'a) by Ibn Taymiyya and *al-Turuq al-Hukmiyya* (Methods of rule) by Ibn Qayyim al-Jawziyya. Such works stressed the authority of the jurists as a professional class and the obligation of the caliph or ruler to heed their advice and carry out their dictates. They occasionally admitted that the caliph could decide legal questions on his own, but only if he were himself a qualified jurist.

Similarly, many premodern reform movements emphasized the importance of adherence to the law on the part of the ruler and/or the populace in general, or the necessity of ridding society of beliefs and practices that were inauthentic accretions contradicting the law in its pure form. Such movements included the Almohad movement that held sway in North Africa in the 12th and 13th centuries, the Wahhabi movement founded in central Arabia by Muhammad b. 'Abd al-Wahhab (d. 1792), the Sanusi movement in 19th-century Libya, the thought of Indian Muslim reformers such as Shaykh Ahmad Sirhindi (d. 1624) and Shah Waliullah (d. 1762), and so on. The same logic led to public expressions of repentance and atonement on the part of rulers who promised to turn over a new leaf, giving up wine drinking, dancing girls, illegal taxes, and other un-Islamic practices. One dramatic example of this was the Edict of Sincere Repentance promulgated by the Safavid monarch Shah Tahmasp in 1556, in which he forswore not only alcohol and other vices but also the patronage of painting and other secular arts.

Judges and Muftis

Judges (qadis) theoretically arrived at their verdicts independently of outside interference, but they were appointed directly by the ruler, and thus in a sense they were his representatives and beholden to him. The position of judge was considered morally dangerous by many, not least of whom were the jurists themselves. A judge was often under considerable pressure to violate the law in order to enforce the ruler's will or justify his actions or those actions of influential and powerful viziers or army commanders, and stories abound of prominent scholars refusing the office in order to avoid such a predicament. Many jurists were also reluctant to accept a salary that could have been acquired through illegal taxes or through seizure or extortion. In addition, the office presented many opportunities for increasing one's income in less than honest ways. The judge and other court officials often lined their pockets by charging various fees for hearing cases and processing documents, not to mention by accepting gifts and bribes to influence the outcome of cases. A judge was often in charge of the property of orphans and other individuals who were wards of the court, lost property, unclaimed estates, and so forth and could divert funds for his own benefit or that of his accomplices. He often became the trustee of endowments, a position that usually paid 10 percent of the annual endowment income, or he could appoint relatives or friends as trustees or sell these positions for bribes or kickbacks. The same was true of various salaried positions funded by endowment income, such as professorships at madrasas and positions as Qur'an readers and imams at mosques. Many judges accumulated a large number of such endowed positions in the course of their career and had deputies carry out the duties associated with them. Perhaps the largest income, though, came from selling deputy judgeships for the various subdistricts within his territory. Aspiring judges were often ready to pay large sums for such deputyships because they knew they would be able to recoup their investment in a short time. In short, if they could stay in office for a considerable period, chief judges could accumulate vast fortunes, and it is likely that many appointees paid a huge fee or bribe to the ruler for the office. Indeed, the sums involved were so significant that the later Fatimid caliphs' urgent need for funds was provided, to a large extent by the payments involved in a rapid succession of appointments to the position of chief judge. A judge who remained unsullied by venality was deserving of comment.

Judges adjudicated cases that appeared before them but did not investigate and bring cases to trial unless a private citizen filed a suit. Another legal arm of the government was the *muḥtasib* or "market inspector," who was in charge of inspecting weights and measures, preventing fraud in economic transactions, setting prices, and preventing hoarding and price gouging for basic commodities. He was also in charge of public morality and was responsible for closing down wine taverns and houses of ill repute. Also important were the *shurṭa* or police, who actively sought to prevent crime, investigate incidents of crime, and bring criminals to justice. Grievance courts were a standard feature of Islamic governments and were intended to be an avenue for the redress of wrongs committed by government officials and the like. This court was ideally presided over by the ruler himself, but a specific judge was often appointed to represent him. While the official appointed as judge of the grievance court was often a qualified jurist, he was not required to apply Islamic legal rules in a strict fashion and often had wide discretion to resolve disputes as he saw fit.

Jurisconsults (muftis) remained relatively freer of government control than judges, but eventually they too became government-appointed officials. Muftis were (and are) supposed to grant fatwas to lay Muslims on legal questions having to do with personal devotion, ritual practice, marital issues, commercial disputes, or other issues. Since such consultation should ideally be free of charge and accessible to all, Mirrors for Princes regularly suggest that the ruler should pay stipends to muftis so that they could carry out their service without asking for payment; from the 12th century onward, the Zengid, Ayyubid, and Mamluk rulers of Syria and Egypt provided state-appointed muftis to answer the legal questions of the public at large.

In tenth-century Khurasan, prominent jurists began to be recognized as the leading muftis of their cities, each one of them under the title of shaykh al-Islam (master of Islam). At first an informal position, it became an official government appointment in later centuries and spread throughout Iran, Central Asia, India, Anatolia, and then to Syria and Egypt. The shaykh al-Islam of the capital city came to wield enormous power and was viewed as the highest legal authority in the realm under such dynasties as the Ottomans, Safavids, Uzbeks, and Mughals. He not only answered thousands

of petitions from the laity but also oversaw all the shaykhs al-Islam in the cities of the empire and sanctioned the policies and actions of the ruler. In the 16th century, the position of the Ottoman shaykh al-Islam was integrated fully into the government bureaucracy, and along with him the entire network of shaykhs al-Islam in provincial cities. Many Muslim states such as Egypt and Pakistan continue to appoint grand muftis who are responsible for answering questions of public import.

In the Twelver Shi'i system, the jurists successfully maintained more independence from the government, in part because they were less dependent on the income of endowments, which could more easily by confiscated or controlled by the government. Instead, the Shi'i scholarly establishment was supported by the payment of the *khums* (literally, "fifth"), an income tax paid by lay believers directly to the leading Shi'i scholars, which often crossed borders and remained inaccessible to rulers. Even though religious authority is understood to reside in the imam, the authority of Twelver jurists has grown steadily since the tenth century, when the Twelfth Imam was said to have gone into occultation. In 874 the 11th imam died in Samarra, Iraq. A series of four representatives maintained contact with his son, the Twelfth Imam, who remained in hiding, during a period known as the Lesser Occultation. In 941 the last of the four representatives died without designating a successor, and it was held that the Twelfth Imam was now in Greater Occultation: ordinary communication with the Twelfth Imam was cut off, as he circulated incognito among the believers. Since then, Twelver jurists gradually arrogated to themselves many of the prerogatives of the Twelfth Imam, making ever-stronger claims concerning their own religious authority. In the 13th century, they accepted the concept of *ijtihād*, claiming the exclusive right to determine the correct rulings on legal questions through legal study and investigation. In the 16th century, the theory developed that the leading jurists' authority derived from the fact that they had been designated the general representatives of the Hidden Imam. A hierarchy was established among the jurists in which the top rank is occupied by a *marja' al-taqlid* (reference for adoption of opinions), who serves as an authority for lay believers and is now termed *āyat allāh 'uẓmā* (a greater sign of God). This process culminates in Ayatollah Khomeini's theory of the comprehensive authority of the jurist (*wilāyat al-faqīh*), according to which the leading jurist is actually responsible for political rule, which goes against the theories of many earlier Shi'i legal thinkers, who argue that certain prerogatives of the Hidden Imam, such as direct political rule, the conduct of jihad, taxation, and the establishment of Friday prayer, are in abeyance until he reveals himself.

The Law and the Family

Unsurprisingly, the shari'a assumes a patriarchal system in which the head of the family is male. Paternity determines what family one belongs to, and in Sunni law a person's male agnatic relatives form part of the extended family. The law of inheritance grants them the remnant of the estate when it is not exhausted by the fixed shares (a rule rejected in Shi'i law), and they are also responsible for paying blood money for injury or death (except in Hanafi law). Laws regarding child custody are based on the premise that the natural allegiance of a child is to the father's side of his or her family, and custody always reverts to the father even though very young children may remain with their mothers temporarily.

Men are generally dominant over women. While men and women are held to believe in the same way and to have roughly equal religious obligations, one may argue that in a blunt, practical sense, a woman's value is half that of a man of similar status. According to the traditional system of blood money payments, which likely goes back to pre-Islamic customs in pagan Arabia, a free Muslim woman is worth 50 camels, exactly one-half the price of a free Muslim man and equal in value to a Jewish or Christian male or a male slave. Similarly, a daughter's share of inheritance from her parents is half that of a son, and the testimony of a woman in court is worth one-half of the testimony of a man. Nevertheless, women have many rights under Islamic law, including the right to own and dispose of property without the interference of their husbands, something that women in Western societies did not have until quite recently. Husbands are required to pay for the food, shelter, clothing, and upkeep of their wives and children, while wives are not required to use any of their own property or income, even if it is vast, to support the family.

Slavery is accepted as a legitimate institution, though there are rules for the humane treatment of slaves, and slaves are not merely property but also individual agents. They can be Muslims and have the same religious obligations as other Muslims, such as fasting and regular prayer. They may marry and they may own property, though, technically, until they gain their freedom, their property belongs to their master. Many apologists claim that Islam set out to abolish slavery gradually, basing this idea on the Qur'anic verses that urge emancipation of slaves as a means to atone for infractions of religious obligations.

All free men are generally awarded the same rights and duties, but there are a few exceptions. The law of marriage equality (*kafā'a*, literally, "suitability") stated that a man had to be of appropriate status to marry a woman of high status and could be used to annul the marriage of an heiress who ran off with a servant or the local butcher. Some held that a non-Arab was not a suitable partner for an Arab woman, nor an ordinary man for a woman descended from the Prophet. The descendants of the Prophet (termed *sayyid*s or sharifs) are also distinguished from other Muslims in some other respects, but the vast respect they enjoyed in medieval Muslim society had little to do with the law.

Modernity

During the 19th and 20th centuries, most of the Islamic world came under the direct rule of colonial powers, especially France and Britain but also Holland, Italy, Portugal, and Russia (later the Soviet Union). Colonial rule and the modern nation-states that followed in the mid-20th century had far-reaching effects on the law enforced in those areas. From 1850 onward the traditional

legal system was increasingly replaced by codes based on European models, and traditional Islamic law was largely restricted to ritual, family, and inheritance law. With the new codes came a system of law depending on constitutions, codes, and statutes, together with a new system of secular legal education and a new class of legal professionals; Saudi Arabia was the only country to have a shari'a court system in 2011. The jurists in the traditional system lost their monopoly on organized education and saw their social power and status plummet. In nearly every nation in the Muslim world, the endowment properties that had funded most of the institutions of Islamic legal education were confiscated by the colonial powers and then the modern nation-state. Most members of the class of jurists, including the top religious authorities, became government employees.

In colonial India, the British sought to apply the law of the various religious communities to their members and thereby prevent the unfair imposition of Hindu law on Muslims, so that they created "Anglo-Muhammadan law" for the Muslims. In so doing, they inadvertently turned Islamic law into code law, for they chose the Hanafi work *al-Hidaya* by Burhan al-Din al-Marghinani (d. 1197) for the administration of Hanafi Muslims in India, translated it into English, and used it as the nearly exclusive reference for Islamic law. Similar developments occurred in Dutch Indonesia and elsewhere.

The modern period witnessed many attempts to change Islamic law and debates about how it could be done. Muslim reformers such as Muhammad 'Abduh (d. 1905) and Rashid Rida (d. 1935) argued for modern jurists' freedom to adapt rules from other legal schools to those of their own, a process called *talfīq* (piecing together). A prominent example of *talfīq* put into practice was the use of principles borrowed from Maliki law to reform the Hanafi law of divorce in the Anglo-Muhammadan legal system. Another method was *takhayyur*, granting jurists the freedom to choose from all the opinions found in the traditional corpus, including those of other schools and minority views within one's own. This generated the new field of *fiqh muqāran* (comparative law), the study of similar issues across the different schools.

Others argued for a rethinking of the hermeneutics of Islamic law, generally presented as a form of *ijtihād*, which takes on here a new sense allowing traditional rules to be set aside and permitting those with secular education to participate. Muhammad 'Abduh argued that laws should change with the times and the conditions of the societies to which they apply; since reason and revelation are intended to be in harmony, independent rational inquiry should be used to revise and reform the law as needed. Many liberal proposals have involved the rejection or limitation of one or more of the "sources" on which law was based. 'Ali 'Abd al-Raziq (d. 1966) and others argued for the rejection or limitation of consensus; some, such as the Shi'i thinker Murtada Mutahhari (d. 1979), denounced *qiyās*; Ahmed Mansour, leader of the contemporary Ahl al-Qur'an movement in Egypt, has argued for the rejection of hadith, seeking the law in the Qur'an alone; and some would even limit the sources to the suras, or chapters of the Qur'an, revealed at Mecca (which would yield almost complete freedom, since they contain practically no legislation). Radical proposals of this sort have met with limited success and have often been vehemently rejected.

Strategies for reform that do not throw out any of the traditional bases of the law but rather urge an emphasis on lesser-known aspects of medieval Islamic legal hermeneutics have met with better acceptance from traditional legal authorities. Proponents of these strategies have championed a more expansive and aggressive use of the concepts of public interest (*maṣlaḥa*) or "the objectives of the law" (*maqāṣid al-sharī'a*). Frequent recourse is also had to the traditional principle of *al-barā'a al-aṣlīyya* (original permissibility), according to which something is considered permissible unless a text states that it is not.

Political Islam

The late 20th century has called for the application rather than change of the shari'a that multiplied throughout the Muslim world, becoming the basis for myriad political campaigns, resistance movements, and even revolutions. This is usually seen as a response to the failure of secular nation-states to keep up with the economic aspirations of Muslim populations, and it was also seen as an attempt to return to culturally authentic forms of government, social organization, and regulation of public behavior in the face of a perceived cultural invasion from the West. Drawing on leftist anticolonialist thinkers from Europe, the new leaders couched their push for the application of the shari'a in terms of a resistance struggle, believing that the shari'a would guarantee social and economic justice by replacing despotic, self-interested rulers with pious officials reined in by the revealed law. Khomeini and many other activists stressed the corruption and predatory nature of the secular rulers in the Islamic world, who were enriching themselves at the expense of the Muslim populace and not using oil wealth and other resources to improve the lot of the common people, something they claimed a return to Islamic law would change. Modern reformers and activists claim that Islamic law provides an answer to all possible questions, an idea captured in the common slogan *al-Islām huwa al-ḥall* (Islam is the solution).

In a number of ways, these calls for the implementation of shari'a are quite different from the periodic insistence of premodern reform movements that the ruler should adhere strictly to the sacred law; they cannot be interpreted as pure traditionalism, for the Muslim world has irrevocably changed. The modern, bureaucratic nation-state exerts a level of invasive control over the populace that its premodern precursors never had; modern education and administration have depersonalized the context in which the law used to be studied and applied. Just as the veils required for women in Iran do not resemble those worn by their precolonial counterparts, so the Islamic regime imposed on them differs starkly from a traditional Islamic state. Similarly, when Zia-ul-Haq (d. 1988) undertook a series of Islamizing reforms to appease Islamists in Pakistan, including a new law that required banks to deduct zakat automatically, this was something unprecedented in Islamic history. In addition,

Western concept categories and modes of thought have indelibly affected those of Muslims, who are reacting to this "colonization of their minds" by seeking their identity in Islam. Jihad, traditionally a duty to expand and defend the borders of the Islamic world, is now understood as part of a broader defense of Muslims against cultural imperialism.

The urge to find culturally authentic forms is prominent in the continuing attempts to apply Islamic law to modern economic institutions, including corporations, bank accounts, mortgages, stock exchanges, and insurance of all kinds, throughout the Islamic world. These present a challenge for several reasons. The corporation, an economic entity that can act as a fictional person, does not exist in Islamic law, which assumes that all economic actors are individuals, partnerships, or agents for individuals or partners. Islamic law traditionally forbids both the taking and payment of interest, termed *ribā*. It forbids the unequal assumption of risk, such as the buying or selling of something the value of which is unknown because of contingency for a fixed price, as this is akin to gambling. It is understood in medieval legal texts that one lends money as a favor or act of piety in order to help a fellow believer and should expect no profit in return. This created, and continues to create, an economic problem, as the use of loans is a necessary part of any economic system. One avenue of reinterpretation of the traditional laws is to argue that *ribā* in the Qur'an and hadith did not refer to all interest but rather to exorbitant interest or usury, so that reasonable interest is excluded from the prohibition. For bank accounts, theorists have often resorted to the concept of *muḍāraba*, a type of sleeping or limited partnership, whereby the account holder essentially shares in the profit of the bank's investments. Of course, this arrangement is often understood to require, though, that the interest rate not be fixed and that the account holder lose money if the bank's investments are not profitable. Similar shari'a-compliant banking and financial instruments have become a major area of investigation and legal innovation and interpretation, and economic globalization is having an enormous effect on traditional business structures, from halal pizza chains to banking conglomerates and multinational corporations.

The calls for the application of shari'a have had major political effects starting in the 1970s, when the Egyptian and Syrian Constitutions were amended to name Islamic law as their basis. The Iranian Revolution of 1979 and the subsequent establishment of the Islamic Republic was a watershed, for they proved that it was possible to topple a secular regime and replace it with a theocratic Islamic one. It was also in 1979 that Zia-ul-Haq began his Islamicizing reforms, establishing benches charged with delivering verdicts in accordance with Islamic law, reviving the amputation of the hand for theft; the stoning of married adulterers; the flogging of unmarried fornicators; and a fine of 5,000 rupees or imprisonment, or both, for Muslims who sold or drank alcohol. He also instituted a blasphemy law prohibiting disparagement of the Prophet, his family, his Companions, and other prominent symbols of Islam; forbade the Ahmadis to call themselves Muslims or use Islamic rituals; and prosecuted Shi'is and Pakistani Christians under the blasphemy law. These laws remain on the books.

Forms of the shari'a have likewise been instituted in Saudi Arabia, Iran, Sudan, Northern Nigeria, and Afghanistan, where Mulla Muhammad 'Umar, the leader of the Taliban movement, became de facto head of state during Taliban rule (1996–2001), styling himself Commander of the Faithful. All these cases of Islamization of the law are primarily symbolic, focusing on visible issues associated with Muslim identity and morality such as women's clothing in public and the enforcement of *ḥudūd* punishments. Entire new codes of law have not been introduced. Even in Iran, where an ideologically based theocratic regime is in place and new legislation is checked for violation of the shari'a by the Council of Experts, the laws already on the books remain unchanged until they are challenged for some other reason.

Calls to implement the shari'a meet with resistance from various quarters, including women's organizations and advocates of human rights and religious freedom. Muslim minorities such as Shi'is in Afghanistan and Pakistan or Baluchi and Kurdish Sunnis in Iran have in fact been subject to regular abuse by regimes intent on applying shari'a law, and Coptic Christians look upon the application of shari'a in Egypt with some trepidation, since it threatens to strip them of gains they made under colonial regimes and later nation-states in favor of the restrictions associated with *dhimmī* status. Indeed, their perception is that their Muslim compatriots are already treating them according to many of the medieval rules associated with *dhimmī* status, even though this contradicts the Egyptian Constitution and other laws.

Discussions of the merits or flaws of Islamic law often suffer from a failure to distinguish between several levels of what may be held to represent "Islam" or Islamic legal rules, conflating (1) what is stated in the Qur'an, (2) what is stated in the legal works of one or more legal schools, (3) the idealized or exemplary behavior of Muslims, (4) the actual or nonexemplary behavior of Muslims, and (5) local customs in a particular area inhabited by Muslims, which often diverge from Islamic law. In some cases, the problems do not arise from the law itself but rather from the way it functions. For example, Islamic law provides a wife with a right to her entire dower (*mahr*), including any deferred amount, in case of a divorce initiated by the husband. Requiring a large deferred dower in the contract is a way for a bride's family to provide a sort of divorce insurance for her or to provide for her significant wealth to support herself in case divorce actually occurs. In practice, though, a husband who decides to divorce his wife but does not wish to pay an enormous deferred *mahr* to her may simply mistreat her until she promises to relinquish her claim to the *mahr* in exchange for being released from the marriage. Ensuring that the law function as it should is a problem whatever the legal system may be.

Throughout Islamic history, the shari'a has played a crucial role in defining Islam, determining the boundaries of Islamic orthodoxy and shaping societal institutions, including political rule. Its hegemony has not been total, however, and it has had to contend with and adapt to other systems of thought and social and political

organization. The impact of colonialism and the rise of the secular nation-state in the Islamic world did much to limit the purview of the shari'a, and some observers in the 20th century imagined that its influence, along with that of religion in general, would steadily decline. However, the failure of secular nationalisms to support steady material progress and to keep up with the expectations of the populace led to a turn toward religion, and adherence to the shari'a became a key component of identity politics in the modern Muslim world. It is bound to remain an important feature of political movements in Muslim nations that stress cultural authenticity and independence in the face of Western political, economic, and cultural dominance. The shari'a, though, is not a monolithic and static category: governments are defining and applying it in diverse ways, and modern thinkers are revising and formulating its concrete rules and its hermeneutic methods, drawing both on the rich historical legacy of Islamic legal thought and on Western theories and legal models.

See also authority; caliph, caliphate; family; judge; jurisprudence; madrasa; punishment

Further Reading

Khaled Abou El Fadl, *Speaking in God's Name: Islamic Law, Authority and Women*, 2001; Norman Calder, "Al-Nawawī's Typology of Muftīs and Its Significance for a General Theory of Islamic Law," *Islamic Law and Society* 3, no. 2 (1996): 137–64; Wael B. Hallaq, *A History of Islamic Legal Theories: An Introduction to Sunni Uṣūl al-Fiqh*, 1997; Idem, *An Introduction to Islamic Law*, 2009; Idem, *The Origins and Evolution of Islamic Law*, 2005; Idem, *Sharī'a: Theory, Practice, Transformations*, 2009; Colin Imber, *Ebu's-Su'ud: The Islamic Legal Tradition*, 1997; George Makdisi, *The Rise of Colleges*, 1981; Muhammad Khalid Masud, Brinkley Messick, and David S. Powers, eds., *Islamic Legal Interpretation: Muftis and their Fatwas*, 2005; Christopher Melchert, *The Formation of the Sunni Schools of Law, 9th–10th Centuries*, 1999; Joseph Schacht, *An Introduction to Islamic Law*, 1964; Idem, *Origins of Muhammadan Jurisprudence*, 1950; Devin J. Stewart, *Islamic Legal Orthodoxy: Twelver Shiite Responses to the Sunni Legal System*, 1998; Knut S. Vikør, *Between God and Sultan: A History of Islamic Law*, 2005; Bernard Weiss, *The Spirit of Islamic Law*, 1998; Roland Knyvet Wilson, *A Digest of Anglo-Muhammadan Law*, 1895.

DEVIN J. STEWART

Shari'ati, 'Ali (1933–77)

Known as one of the major ideologues of the Islamic Revolution in Iran, 'Ali Shari'ati was influential in channeling much of the revolutionary fervor of a large segment of the Iranian youth at the intersection of Islam and mostly leftist Western ideologies.

Shari'ati was born in the northeastern town of Mazinan, close to Mashhad (Iran) on November 24, 1933. His father, Muhammad-Taqi Mazinani Shari'ati, was strongly influenced by the intellectual and political currents of his time and attempted to merge his traditional understanding of Islam with new ideas such as those espoused by the secular critic of religion, Ahmad Kasravi, or the concepts of social justice and equality promoted by the Tudeh party. The result was a highly unorthodox vision of Islam that drove Shari'ati's father toward secular teaching instead of membership in the clergy. He was instrumental in founding the Center for the Propagation of Islamic Truths (*Qanun-i Nashr-i Haqa'iq-i Islami*), where he held his first lectures while still a high school student in Mashhad.

Shari'ati's formative years coincided with a period of political unrest in Iran. While he was strongly influenced by the nationalist movement of Prime Minister Mohammad Mossadeq, he remained rooted in the religious culture of his youth. This ambivalence was to remain with Shari'ati and become one of his trademarks. During those years, Shari'ati also came into contact with the Movement of God-Worshipping Socialists (Nahdat-i Khoda Parastan-i Socialist), an organization founded in 1945 among university students. According to this movement, socialism, strong religious sentiments, and nationalism need not be mutually exclusive. Islam is seen by this movement as an internationalist idea that provides the philosophical underpinnings of socialism as an economic system and a frame of reference for social action, picturing an authentic, progressive, and liberating Shi'ism. Shari'ati's later writings are strongly influenced by this revolutionary sociopolitical program that was deeply anchored in Islamic culture, while simultaneously discarding Islamic ritual and quietism associated with the traditional religious establishment.

Shari'ati enrolled at the Teacher's Training College of Mashhad in 1950 and subsequently worked as a teacher for several years. In 1955, he began to study literature at Mashhad University. Even before entering the university, Shari'ati had joined a student cell of Mahmud Taleqani's National Resistance Movement (Nahdat-i Muqawamat-i Milli), which had evolved by 1954 into the Iranian People's Party (Hizb-i Mardim-i Iran). At the university, he became involved in clandestine propaganda activities and was known as a political agitator. But he also expanded his writing activities and published a translation of Abu Dharr al-Ghifari's (d. 652) philosophies by a contemporary Egyptian writer, 'Abdul-Hamid Jawdat al-Sahhar, which laid the cornerstone of Shari'ati's own line of thinking. By his own admission, he was so intrigued by Abu Dharr, who was an early convert to Islam remembered for his strict piety, that he interspersed the translation with his own comments and reflections and finally published the text in 1955 under the title *Abu Dharr al-Ghifari, the God-worshipping Socialist*, a clear reference to the movement he had joined some years back. He molded the historical person Abu Dharr to suit his own time, making him the first "Islamic socialist" who aided the downtrodden, stood up for the authentic meaning of Islam, and became the first martyr to his convictions. Shari'ati's take on Abu Dharr is symptomatic of his subsequent method of work: ahistorical, nonmethodological, and

using conceptual transformations to suit his own needs. In addition to translations of Arabic and Western books—among them a Farsi rendition of Frantz Fanon's *The Wretched of the Earth*—Shariʿati started his prolific publishing of political treatises as well as mystical, autobiographical writings. Among the political treatises he wrote and published was a series called The Median School of Islam (*Maktab-i Wasita-i Islam*), in which he praised Islam as a third option between communism and capitalism.

From 1959 to 1964, Shariʿati pursued his studies at the Sorbonne on a state scholarship, attaining a doctorate in 1964 in Persian literature (not in sociology, as is often mistakenly assumed). His stay in France was intellectually formative in that he became acquainted with the Western political, sociological, and philosophical currents of the day. In addition, he joined the Union of Iranian Students in France and the Confederation of Iranian Students in Europe and the United States and thus became involved in the budding Iranian exile politics against the Pahlavi regime.

Upon his return to Iran, Shariʿati was detained for a short period of time. After he was released, he worked as a teacher and finally lectured at the Department of History at Mashhad University in the spring of 1966, thanks to the intervention of some influential academic personalities. Soon he established a reputation as a charismatic orator and innovative teacher, and his students were intrigued by his blend of scientific Western methods and Islamic principles. He presented ideal Islam as an egalitarian, democratic, and revolutionary ideology. Transcripts of his course notes were distributed and eventually collected in 1969 under the title *Islamshinasi*. This collection found its way to intellectual circles in Tehran, where it was hotly debated. His popularity aroused the suspicion of the regime, and in 1968 he was dismissed from the university. He started to lecture both openly and clandestinely until he found his forum at the newly built religious institute Husseiniye-ye Ershad in Tehran, where he drew increasing numbers of listeners from the educated, urban middle class. In November 1972, Husseiniye-ye Ershad was closed on the grounds of subversive activities against the interests of the state, and Shariʿati went into hiding. Following periods of detainment and house arrest, he finally managed to leave Iran and died under suspicious circumstances in Southampton, England, shortly afterward on June 18, 1977.

Most of Shariʿati's immense written output was originally delivered in the form of speeches and often lacks coherence and defies classification. Yet these writings provide an easily understandable blueprint for action clothed in known Shiʿi terminology and affirm cultural self-assertion. Those concepts that were instrumental in mobilizing large and diverse segments for revolutionary change refer to the role of martyrdom (*jihād wa-shahādat*); the revolutionary participation of women (*Fatima Fatima ast*); the distinction between a quietist, ritualistic Shiʿism and one that is the vehicle for revolution (*tashayyuʿ-i safawī wa-tashayyu'-i ʿalavī*); and the all-important issue of personal choice and individual responsibility that accords more importance to the intellectual and makes the intervention of the clergy obsolete. Thus, while Shariʿati eased the way for the advent of the Islamic Revolution, his ideas differ markedly from Ruhollah Khomeini's concept of the "guardianship of the jurist" (*wilāyat al-faqīh*) in which the clergy play the dominant role in fulfilling the vision of a theocratic Islamic Republic. Shariʿati remains a controversial personality. His critics on the Left dismiss his ideology for its lack of scientific reasoning and reliance on "metaphysics"—a synonym for religious thinking in leftist circles. The religious establishment, on the other hand, voices its objections to Shariʿati's unorthodox Islamic interpretations and the negative role he assigned to the clergy.

See also Iran; revival and reform; revolutions; Shiʿism; socialism

Further Reading

S. Akhavi, *Religion and Politics in Contemporary Iran: Clergy-State Relations in the Pahlavi Period*, 1980; H. E. Chehabi, *Iranian Politics and Religious Modernism: The Liberation Movement of Iran under the Shah and Khomeini*, 1990; H. Dabashi, *Theology of Discontent: The Ideological Foundations of the Islamic Revolution in Iran*, 2006; A. Rahnema, *An Islamic Utopian*, 2000; A. Shariʿati, *Collected Works in 35 Volumes*, 1984–90.

SCHIRIN H. FATHI

al-Shawkani, Muhammad b. ʿAli (1760–1834)

A scholar, judge, and reformer who played a central role in the Sunnification of the Zaydi imamate and the religious landscape in Yemen, Shawkani is also important for his influence on modern Salafis, who praise him for abandoning Zaydi Shiʿism, for rejecting the authority of the established schools of law (*madhhab*), and for his originalist interpretation of the Qur'an and the hadith, the sources of revelation. Shawkani is the last great figure in the Sunni- and hadith-oriented lineage of scholars that emerged in Yemen with Muhammad b. Ibrahim al-Wazir (d. 1436) and is a prominent authority for the Salafi version of Islam that is promoted by the modern state in Yemen. His oeuvre, which includes over two hundred titles in numerous Islamic fields, relies heavily on the teachings of Sunni traditionists (*ahl al-hadīth*), including Ibn Taymiyya and Ibn al-Qayyim but also Ibn Hajar al-ʿAsqalani. He advocated a revamping of Islamic law; in particular he condemned *taqlīd*, or the strict adherence to the established opinions of the schools of law. Shawkani strongly believed that Muslims should systematically practice independent judgment (*ijtihād*) for obtaining rulings and opinions, and his methodology stresses the explicit meaning of the texts of revelation (i.e., Qur'an and sunna). He saw in *ijtihād* a panacea for the ills that afflicted the Muslim community, which he argued were due to having distanced itself from the principal sources of law. In his interpretive method, Shawkani can be considered a radical in that he rejected the principle of juristic consensus (*ijmāʿ*) and most forms of

analogical reasoning (*qiyās*) while claiming that his methodology obtained greater certainty of God's will and therefore had greater authoritativeness. He dismissed speculative theology (*kalām*) and reason-based arguments as idle talk and was a staunch Salafi in matters of creed.

Shawkani's most widely referenced book is his hadith-based legal manual titled *Nayl al-Awtar fi Sharh Muntaqa al-Akhbar* (Attaining the aims in commenting on the choicest traditions). Modern Salafis favor it because it provides proof texts from the hadith corpus for its legal opinions. He also wrote an influential work on legal theory titled *Irshad al-Fuhul* (Guidance to the luminaries), a biographical dictionary titled *al-Badr al-Tali* (The rising moon), and a commentary on the Qur'an titled *al-Fath al-Qadir* (Victory of the Almighty), as well as numerous shorter treatises on a panoply of topics. In Yemen his most controversial work is a detailed legal critique of Zaydi law titled *al-Sayl al-Jarrar* (The raging torrent), in which Shawkani undermines the canonical legal manual of the school, *Kitab al-Azhar* (The book of flowers). His books, especially those on the Qur'an and on hadith-based law, continue to be taught widely throughout the Muslim world.

For modern Muslim reformers, Shawkani is a towering figure not only because of his powerful criticism of the failings of the scholastic tradition and synthetic style but also because of his successful reformist project in Yemen. The dominant tradition in 18th-century highland Yemen was Zaydism, one of the branches of Shi'ism. Shawkani made the case that many Zaydi theological and legal teachings had no basis in revelation but rather consisted of the unsubstantiated opinions of the imams and therefore had to be rejected. By the mid-18th century, Yemen was ruled by a dynasty of imams called the Qasimis, who supported scholars like Shawkani because he legitimized their dynastic form of rule while at the same time he managed the state's judicial apparatus as chief judge. In contrast with the Zaydi insistence that the state be ruled by a qualified imam and that unjust rulers be removed forcibly if necessary, Shawkani favored a quietist political posture that favored obedience even to one who lacked the qualifications enumerated in Zaydi law. As chief judge from 1795 until 1834, Shawkani instituted his reformist project and placed many of his students in positions of influence, who then carried on his intellectual legacy into the early 21st century. With the state favoring scholars with this Sunni orientation, the Zaydis were unable to stop the influence of Shawkani and his hadith-centered students and followers. The Zaydis continue to insist that their imams, as members of the Prophet's family, are more authoritative sources for religious teachings than the Sunni canonical hadith collections on which Shawkani's interpretive methodology is so heavily focused.

Zaydis saw Shawkani as seeking to destroy Zaydism in order to create a legal school and sect in the tradition of the Salafis or the *ahl al-ḥadīth*. The modern Yemeni state has indeed pursued an anti-Zaydi policy and justifies this under the broad label of Islamic reform and by invoking Shawkani's teachings. Shawkani also had a profound influence on the *ahl al-ḥadīth* on the Indian subcontinent in the 19th century, especially on scholars such as Siddiq Hasan Khan of Bhopal, and Shawkani's views and works remain influential in Saudi Arabia and wherever else Salafis are to be found.

See also revival and reform; Salafis; Yemen

Further Reading

Husayn 'Abdullah Al-'Amri, *The Yemen in the 18th & 19th Centuries*, 1985; Ahmad Dallal, "Appropriating the Past: Twentieth Century Reconstruction of Pre-Modern Islamic Thought," *Islamic Law and Society* 7, no. 3 (2000); Bernard Haykel, *Revival and Reform in Islam: The Legacy of Muhammad al-Shawkani*, 2003.

BERNARD HAYKEL

al-Shaybani, Muhammad b. al-Hasan (749–805)

Muhammad b. al-Hasan al-Shaybani was an early Muslim jurist who was the most important progenitor of the Hanafi school of law. His father is said to have been a non-Arab *mawlā* or client of the Arab tribe of Shayban from Upper Mesopotamia who moved to Damascus, enlisted there in the Umayyad army, and was stationed at Wasit in Iraq, where Shaybani was born. Shaybani himself chose a different career as a student of Muslim religious knowledge. At an early age, he immigrated to the Muslim metropolis of Kufa and later to its great successor and the capital of the Abbasid caliphate, Baghdad. As one of the main early jurists of the Iraqi school of law, Shaybani is said to have been the student of its eponymous founder, Abu Hanifa (699–767), but this is barely possible, as Abu Hanifa was unavailable—in prison—from 763, when Shaybani was only about 14 years old. Rather, Shaybani was the student of Abu Yusuf (732–98), Sufyan al-Thawri (716–78), and Awza'i (706–74). Shaybani also studied for three years with Malik b. Anas (712–95), the great exponent of the Madinan school of law, taking from him his legal compendium *al-Muwatta'* (The trodden path), of which Shaybani produced his own version. Shaybani also produced a highly polemical work, *Kitab al-Hujja 'ala ahl al-Madina*, in which he defined his own Iraqi school's legal positions against those of the Medinan school.

Politically, Shaybani is almost always portrayed together with the caliph Harun al-Rashid (r. 786–809). In 792, Rashid asked him for a religious approval that would permit the caliph to execute an 'Alid rebel who had been given a promise of safety in exchange for surrendering, but Shaybani refused, and his opinion was hence ignored by the caliph. Nonetheless, when the caliph left for the Syrian town of Raqqa in 796, he summoned Shaybani to accompany him and to serve as judge, which Shaybani did until Rashid dismissed him in 803. It is probably this service with the caliph that led to Shaybani being described as chief judge (*qāḍī al-quḍāt*), a position that had not yet been clearly defined. Shaybani then returned to Baghdad, but in 805 he was again summoned by the caliph to accompany him to Khurasan. Shaybani, however, died on the way, in the city of Rayy, which is modern Tehran. It is clear that Rashid

respected Shaybani and that Shaybani found serving the caliph acceptable. However, that did not stop Shaybani from sometimes opposing the caliph.

The writings attributed to Shaybani are extensive and indeed probably more voluminous than all other Muslim writings produced until his time combined. One of his most important works is his *Kitab al-Siyar* (The great book on the rules of war), the earliest Muslim treatise on foreign relations, including laws of war and peace. Despite his obvious interest in the state, Shaybani's works are still surprising for assigning a limited role to the state and especially the ruler, who nevertheless makes the decisions about war and peace. Still, it is clear that the idea of the independence of the religious scholar from the ruler was cultivated by Shaybani, despite his close ties to Rashid.

Shaybani also played a significant role as teacher and informant to Muhammad b. Idris al-Shafi'i, the founder of the Shafi'i school of law. In particular, his writings emphasize that traditions traceable to the Prophet Muhammad are the strongest legal proofs after the Qur'an, a feature incorporated by Shafi'i into his famous legal principles (*uṣūl*).

See also Abbasids (750–1258); Abu Hanifa (699–767); Abu Yusuf (ca. 731–98); jurisprudence; al-Shafi'i, Muhammad b. Idris (767–820)

Further Reading

Muhammad b. al-Hasan Shaybani, *The Islamic Law of Nations: Shaybānī's Siyar*, translated by Majid Khadduri, 1966; Idem, *The Kitāb al-Āthār of Imam Abū Ḥanīfah*, translated by Abdassamad Clarke, 2006; Idem, *The Muwaṭṭa' of Imam Muḥammad*, translated by Mohammed Abdurrahman and Abdus Samad Clarke, 2004; Idem, *The Shorter Book on Muslim International Law*, translated by Mahmood Ahmad Ghazi, 1998.

KHALID YAHYA BLANKINSHIP

shaykh, *pīr*

The Arabic term "shaykh" and the Persian term *pīr* both have the principal meaning of a person of advanced age, generally older than 50 years. This primary meaning has been extended to a secondary meaning of "master," and especially "spiritual master," by virtue of the fact that one may become a master only after a lifetime of work. It is also an honorific title given to one's teacher or mentor. The most common social context of both shaykh and *pīr* is in the hierarchy of Sufism. In this case, the shaykh/*pīr* is one who has traveled the mystical path (*ṭarīqa*) and mastered its various states (*aḥwāl*) and stations (*maqāmāt*). Once an individual has mastered the path and is qualified to teach the doctrines of Sufism to novices and train them, he or she takes on the title shaykh/*pīr* (*shaykha* in the case of women).

The training of novices may take many forms. The shaykh/*pīr* might assign the novice spiritual exercises, litanies, prayers, or chants to be performed under the shaykh's guidance. In other instances, the shaykh/*pīr* may assign the novice seemingly degrading tasks in order to inculcate humility in the novice and conquer the ego-self. In all cases the novice is meant to follow the directives of his or her shaykh/*pīr* without question and bind himself or herself to the master. This is exemplified in the well-known Sufi aphorism, "The novice should be in the hands of the *shaykh* as a corpse in the hands of the mortician." This master–disciple relationship became one of the more distinctive elements of Sufism, the importance of which can be gleaned from another aphorism, "One who does not have a *shaykh* takes Satan for his *shaykh*." As Sufi practices became increasingly institutionalized after the 11th century, Sufis began to differentiate between *shaykh al-ta'līm* and *shaykh al-tarbiya*. The former refers to "the teaching *shaykh*," or a master who conveys general knowledge of the Sufi path to many individuals, while the latter refers to "the training *shaykh*," a master who takes on disciples and personally trains them in the Sufi way.

The institutionalization and organization of Sufism after the 11th century would have significant consequences for the Sufi shaykh/*pīr*. With the emergence of formal, organized brotherhoods, the shaykh/*pīr* became the spiritual leader of large groups of people, which attracted the attention of political rulers. While most shaykhs and *pīrs* were not directly involved in politics, a number of examples highlight the political potential of the shaykh/*pīr*.

By the 11th century, Seljuq authorities were patronizing and supporting influential Sufi shaykhs by building and endowing hospices (*khawāniq*, sing. *khānaqāh*) for them and their students. The Ayyubid and Mamluk sultans after them continued this practice in Egypt and greater Syria, creating the office of *shaykh al-shuyūkh*, or the "master of masters." The *shaykh al-shuyūkh* was appointed, usually for life, to oversee all the Sufi activities under the ruling authorities' jurisdiction. This patronage has continued up to the present day, and a number of governments have full-time positions for Sufi shaykhs, including Egypt, Syria, and Sudan, among others.

Sufi shaykhs and *pīrs* may also serve important roles as advisors to political figures. It is often related that the Seljuq vizier Nizam al-Mulk (d. 1092) sought counsel with a number of Sufi shaykhs, including Abu Sa'id b. Abi al-Khayr (d. 1049). While the Chishtis in South Asia were generally politically quietist, Suhrawardi shaykhs were prominent political advisors at the court of the Delhi Sultanate. Likewise, the Ottoman Janissaries were often affiliated with the Bektashi order, and their shaykhs were prominent members of the Ottoman court in Istanbul.

In addition to their roles as political counselors, a number of shaykhs/*pīrs* have been influential in bringing Islam to new regions. The *wali songo*, or nine Sufi saints, were supposed to have brought Islam to Indonesia from South Asia and converted the population of Java in the 15th century, although much of this is legend. In the 19th century, Sanusi shaykhs in Cyrenaica and Sahili shaykhs in Somalia were instrumental in bringing Islam to those regions. Various subbranches of the Qadiris in sub-Saharan Africa during the

19th century were the vehicles for a number of charismatic shaykhs to proselytize and propagate Islam in Nigeria, Mali, and Senegal. In South Asia *pīrs* of the Chishti, Suhrawardi, and Naqshbandi orders trained their disciples to act as missionaries to the local non-Muslim population and are widely credited with bringing Islam to much of the Indian subcontinent. In Central Asia and the Caucasus, Sufi shaykhs, particularly of the Qadiris and Naqshbandis, traveled into mountainous and isolated regions to spread Islam and teach Sufism.

In some cases the shaykh/*pīr* becomes a political leader in his own right. As the hereditary *pīrs* of a Sufi order, the Safavid shahs, such as Isma'il I (1501–24), were simultaneously rulers and spiritual masters. This was a potent combination, as the Safavid troops, a federation of Turkic tribes termed collectively the Qizilbash (Redheads) because of the distinctive red headgear they wore, were bound to obey their shah/*pīr*, to whom they had sworn multiple allegiances. This was a significant factor in the success of the Safavid armies in conquering much of present-day Iran. Between 1824 and 1859, Imam 'Ali Shamil (d. 1871), a Daghestani Naqshbandi, commanded an Islamic state in the area that was the center of the anti-Russian struggle. While Shamil was not the primary Naqshbandi shaykh, his followers saw him as their temporal guide and would chant the *dhikr* (invocation of God's name) in their marches into battle. The Sammani order played an important role in the founding of the Mahdist state in Sudan, led by the shaykh Muhammad Ahmad b. 'Abdallah (d. 1885). 'Abdallah was granted authority to initiate others into the Sammani brotherhood in 1861. In 1881 once he had gathered a sufficiently large number of disciples, he declared himself the Mahdi (savior) and, with an army of loyal disciples, launched a successful offensive against the Egyptian-British occupation of Sudan.

See also brotherhoods; Sufism

Further Reading

Arthur Buehler, "Overlapping Currents in Early Islam: The *Sufi Shaykh* and the Shī'ī Imam," *Journal of the History of Sufism* 3 (2001–2): 279–97, 355; S. Digby, "The Sufi Shaykh and the Sultan: A Conflict of Claims to Authority in Medieval India," *Iran* 28 (1990): 71–81; Marshall Hodgson, *The Venture of Islam: Conscience and History in a World Civilization*, vol. 2, 1974; Ahmet Karamustafa, *Sufism: The Formative Period*, 2007; Margaret Malamud, "Gender and Spiritual Self-Fashioning: The Master-Disciple Relationship in Classical Sufism," *Journal of the American Academy of Religion* 64 (1996): 89–117.

NATHAN HOFER

shaykh al-Islam

The term "shaykh al-Islam," literally "master of Islam," originated as an honorific title for outstanding scholars of the Islamic sciences but also has been used to designate the chief jurisconsult of a city or realm. The term suggests that the official thus designated was so learned in the religious sciences, especially Islamic law, that he was in effect the teacher of the entire Muslim community and that the authority of his opinions was unassailable or unmatched among his contemporaries. The term has been applied in this sense to such historic figures as Malik b. Anas, Ahmad b. Hanbal, Ibn Taymiyya, and Hajar al-'Asqalani, among others. The Egyptian historian and hadith expert Muhammad b. 'Abd al-Rahman al-Sakhawi complained in the 15th century that it had been overused and applied to many who did not actually deserve it.

The history and the exact nature of the office are somewhat obscure before the 16th century, but it apparently originated in Khurasan in the tenth century, where the major cities each had a scholar, called a shaykh al-Islam, who was not a government appointee but was recognized by his peers as an authority. One of the early holders of this title was Abu Sa'd al-Khargushi (d. 1016), a wealthy Ash'ari preacher and Shafi'i jurist of Nishapur, known for his piety and asceticism. After the 11th century, the position became a regular government appointment throughout the Persianate sphere, including the central lands of the Islamic world. The office was developed in an effort to create for the mufti (jurisconsult) an office that paralleled and supplemented that of the qadi (judge), a policy somewhat at variance with classical Islamic legal theory, which envisaged the independence of the mufti from government control. The shaykh al-Islam of the capital city, like the chief judge (*qāḍī al-quḍāt*), was responsible for those appointed to the same position in the other cities of the realm. Historical sources mention a shaykh al-Islam under the sultan of Delhi Iltumish (1211–36). The Abbasid caliph Nasir (1180–1225) designated Abu Hafs 'Umar al-Suhrawardi (d. 1234), his confidant and a renowned Sufi master, shaykh al-Islam in 1200. Similarly, the Ilkhanid sultan Ahmad Teguder appointed 'Abd al-Rahman, his spiritual advisor, shaykh al-Islam. Timur (r. 1370–1405) appointed the title shaykh al-Islam of Samarqand to the Hanafi jurist 'Abd al-Malik al-Marghinani, a descendant of Burhan al-Din al-Marghinani, author of *al-Hidayah* (The book of guidance), the famous text of Hanafi law.

The title appears not to have been used in this fashion by the Zengids, Ayyubids, or the Mamluks, who founded a new institution called the House of Justice (Dar al-'Adl) in an attempt to bolster the prestige of the grievance court and at the same time sponsor the public granting of fatwas, legal responsa or answers to legal questions of the lay populace, the first in Damascus circa 1163 and the last in Cairo in 1315. Terminology differed in North Africa as well, where the chief mufti of a realm was simply termed the mufti of the capital city, such as the mufti of Fez or of Marrakesh.

The institutionalization of the office reached a peak under the Ottomans, but it was also a prominent office under the Safavids, Uzbeks, and Mughals. In the 15th century the shaykh al-Islam was a highly respected jurist whose position remained outside the learned hierarchy, untainted by the secular associations of judgeships and similar positions, who served in some sense as a check on the authority of the sultan. In the course of the 16th century, the office was consolidated and incorporated into the learned hierarchy, especially under the shaykh al-Islam Abu al-Su'ud (d. 1574), who spent

29 years in office under sultans Süleiman I (r. 1520–66) and Selim II (r. 1566–74). The shaykh al-Islam generally acceded to this office after a long *cursus honorum* of teaching and judicial appointments in the empire's major cities. Standing at the pinnacle of the learned hierarchy, he was charged with broad oversight not only of the muftis but also of the professors and judges of the realm, a responsibility held in earlier times by the *qāḍī-'askars*, originally judges over the governing military class. Ironically, the incorporation of the office into the state apparatus seems to have diminished the power of the incumbents and their ability to critique the government. Incumbents after Abu al-Su'ud had short tenures.

One of the main duties of the Ottoman shaykh al-Islam was to answer a monumental number of legal questions submitted by the public, and a bureaucracy termed the *fetvahane* was established to accomplish this quickly. Before being viewed by the shaykh al-Islam himself, questions were drafted, after the 16th century, by a permanent staff of clerks headed by the superintendent of fatwas (*fetva amini*), who removed extraneous information, replaced actual names with pseudonyms, and brought the point of law at issue into relief. The shaykh al-Islam was able to answer a very large number of fatwas in this manner, sometimes as many as 1,400 in one day. The shaykh al-Islam's office received all manner of questions: requests for clarification on matters of correct religious observance; commercial and property disputes; issues of general social concern such as the legality of coffee or tobacco; and important matters of state, such as queries from the sultan seeking justification for war. Holders of the office played an important role in anti-Safavid propaganda, justifying Ottoman wars against the Safavids in the 16th and 17th centuries on the grounds that the Qizilbash, the Turkmen tribal warriors who formed the core of the Safavid armies, were actually unbelievers on account of their heterodox beliefs and therefore legitimate targets of jihad. They also sanctioned the introduction of new technologies such as the printing press, the telegraph, railroads, and Western arms of various types. The last Ottoman shaykh al-Islam, Mustafa Sabri Efendi, held the office until 1922, when he was exiled to Egypt.

In the Safavid Empire, the shaykh al-Islam of the capital city—Tabriz, then Qazvin, then Isfahan—fulfilled a role similar to that of the Ottoman shaykh al-Islam, though the cadre of religious scholars had a less hierarchical structure and often held the office for life. One of the main roles fulfilled by the Safavid incumbents of the office was responding to ideological attacks from their Ottoman counterparts and other Sunni polemicists. Their fatwas were likewise important in justifying war against the Ottomans in the West and the Uzbeks of Transoxania in the East. In the late 17th century, the Safavid government made a structural change similar to the change in the Ottoman office more than a century earlier: the shaykh al-Islam of Isfahan was recognized as the titular head of the entire cadre of religious scholars in the realm, thus acquiring some of the prerogatives of the *ṣadr*, an official who corresponded roughly to the Ottoman *qāḍī-'askar*. In recognition of the change, he acquired the new title *mullā-bāshī*, "chief of religious scholars," an office established in 1712–13 by Shah Sultan Husayn (r. 1694–1722) for the jurist Muhammad Baqir Khatunabadi. The *mullā-bāshī*'s office continued to exist under Nadir Shah (r. 1736–47) and the Qajar dynasty (1794–1925), but in the late Qajar period it became a more ceremonial sinecure in which the incumbent served as a tutor for royal princes.

In the modern period, various governments of Islamic nations have appointed grand muftis who fulfill the functions of the shaykh al-Islam. Institutions also have been founded to regulate fatwas and to ensure that only trained scholars with government-approved qualifications have the authority to issue them. Among these institutions are the Dar al-Ifta' al-Misriyya (The Egyptian Organization for Granting Legal Opinions), founded by the Egyptian government in 1895 and headed by the grand mufti of Egypt, and the Jedda-based Islamic Fiqh Academy (Majma' al-Fiqh al-Islami al-Dawli), founded in 1988 by the 57-nation Organization of the Islamic Conference in reaction to what was seen as a proliferation of irresponsible and incompetent fatwas.

See also mufti/grand mufti; shari'a

Further Reading

Richard Bulliet, "The Shaikh al-Islam and the Evolution of Islamic Society," *Studia Islamica* 35, no. 1 (1972); Colin Imber, *Ebu's-su'ud: The Islamic Legal Tradition*, 1997; R. C. Repp, *The Müfti of Istanbul: A Study in the Development of the Ottoman Learned Hierarchy*, 1986; Devin J. Stewart, "The First *Shaykh al-Islām* of the Safavid Capital Qazvin," *Journal of the American Oriental Society* 116, no. 3 (1996).

DEVIN J. STEWART

Shi'ism

"Shi'ism" is the English term given to the sectarian movement referred to in early Arabic sources as Shi'at 'Ali (the party of 'Ali), or simply the "Shi'a." The Shi'a identified themselves as supporters of the leadership claims of 'Ali b. Abi Talib, the son-in-law and cousin of the Prophet Muhammad, whom they saw as the rightful successor to Muhammad as leader of the Muslim community. Whether 'Ali viewed himself in the same terms is difficult to assess, since he did not embark on an open rebellion against the first caliphs of the Muslim empire following Muhammad's death in 632. The claim that 'Ali was the rightful leader (or imam) after Muhammad was based on reports in which the Prophet expresses his high regard and (arguably) his preference for 'Ali over his other Companions. The reliability and interpretation of these reports has become a topic of extensive sectarian dispute between the Shi'a and their opponents (primarily the later Sunnis). 'Ali did eventually become caliph in 656, though he had to face extensive opposition during his reign, and he was

eventually murdered in 661. In the century and a half following 'Ali's death, there were a series of rebellions in the name of 'Ali and his descendants. All of these movements, in one way or another, were appealing to the central Shi'i political idea that the members of the family of the Prophet had somehow been blessed with particular leadership skills—for some groups, these qualities were sufficiently unique to make the imams a breed apart from the ordinary folk. Members of the Prophet's family have, by some process of divine designation, acquired particular qualities and rights, among which is the right to govern. This, at least, indicates the basics of Shi'i political theory developed in this early period, and it contrasts with the emerging Sunni (and Khariji) notions of good leadership and political legitimacy. Some subsequent Shi'i groups proclaimed the imams to be a manifestation of God or to have a divine nature in an incarnational sense. These beliefs were unacceptable to other Shi'a and also viewed as dangerously heretical by the mainstream Sunnis. In the heresiographical literature, the groups associated with these incarnational beliefs were labeled *ghulāt* (extremists).

Central to all the Shi'i political ideas at this time was the notion of an imam as a political leader designated by God (through an inheritance of the Prophet's designation to 'Ali) but lacking political power. It seems that for all the Shi'a the imam must be a relative of the Prophet Muhammad. How far this description might extend was disputed. Was the son of 'Ali by a slave girl a candidate for legitimate leadership (as was claimed in Mukhtar's rebellion in support of Muhammad b. al-Hanafiyya in 686)? Was a descendent of 'Abbas, the Prophet's uncle, acceptable (as was claimed by the Abbasid movement, which came to power in 750)? The rebellion against the Abbasids by a grandson of Hasan (the eldest son of Imam 'Ali), Muhammad b. 'Abdallah al-Nafs al-Zakiyya (d. 762), and the continued opposition to the Abbasids by other Shi'i groups show that most did not consider this extension of the "Prophet's descendants" (*ahl al-bayt*) acceptable. Other debates among the Shi'a at the time included whether an imam (or his representative) must rebel against the usurping caliphate of the Umayyads (and later the Abbasids). The Shi'a had examples of imams who had been quietist (such as Hasan) and examples of those who had taken up arms (the most famous being Husayn, 'Ali's second son and the third imam, at Karbala in 680). Additional accretions to these fundamental Shi'i ideas in the early period included the idea of an imam who had disappeared and would return at some time to establish legitimate government and abolish the corrupt system of the Umayyads (and later Abbasids). For example, Muhammad b. al-Hanafiyya is said to have disappeared (and not died), and the appeals of other Shi'i leaders in this early period were tinged with messianic expectation.

As well as all the rebellious movements challenging the Umayyads and the Abbasids, there was a more quietist Shi'i position associated with a group given the title "Imamis" in the heresiographical literature. According to these writers, the Imamis traced a line of imams beginning with imams 'Ali, Hasan, and Husayn and then followed by generational descendents of Husayn. The line continues with Husayn's son 'Ali Zayn al-Abidin, 'Ali's son Muhammad al-Baqir, and Muhammad's son Ja'far al-Sadiq. For the Imamis, while the current political power was illegitimate, the imams did not wish to endanger themselves or the true community of followers by openly rebelling. Proper government would be established at some future point, and rebellious activity was fruitless (and for some even forbidden). After the death of Imam Sadiq, the Imamis followed Musa al-Kazim, Sadiq's son by a slave woman. The decision was controversial, and some of the Shi'a considered a separate line of descendents (through Ja'far's deceased son Isma'il) acceptable, giving birth to the Isma'ili Shi'a. The Imamis recognized five more imams after Musa in a father-son sequence. The last of these, the Twelfth Imam after the Prophet, was Muhammad b. al-Hasan al-Mahdi, who, according to Imami accounts, disappeared in 874. The Imamis then became known as the Twelvers (*ithnā 'ashariyya*), since their 12th and last imam disappeared and, according to Imami theology, will reappear at some point in the future. The Twelvers went on to become the most numerous Shi'i sect with a distinctive political theory. Twelver legal literature (*fiqh*) explored the operation of proper Islamic rule through an elucidation of rules supposedly derived from sources (in particular the Qur'an and the sources describing the sunna, or example of the Prophet). In effect, the limitation of these sources left much to the individual jurist's creativity. In the Imami tradition, the ideal government was one led by the imam himself. However, this rarely happened when the imams were present (only 'Ali actually held political power, and even then his authority was hardly absolute). When there were no longer imams because they were in hiding (*ghayba*), the operation of particular elements of the law became problematic in the jurists' views. For example, a legitimate collection or distribution entity was required for valid taxation: not only for religious taxes such as zakat (the alms tax) and *khums* (the special Shi'i "one fifth" tax) but also for other valid taxes such as *kharāj* (the land tax). In the absence of the imam, no such entity exists. The first jurists, such as Muhammad b. al-Hasan al-Tusi (d. 1067), offered various solutions, including burying the wealth in a secret place to await the return of the imam or distributing the wealth oneself to the deserving recipients. Over time, one solution became dominant in *fiqh* literature: the individual believer could (and for some jurists, must) give his religious taxes to a suitably qualified jurist (i.e., a *mujtahid*) to distribute. Imami jurists proposed a theory of *niyāba*, or delegation, whereby certain sayings of the imams were reinterpreted to demonstrate that the imams themselves had delegated to the jurists the right to collect and distribute taxes, convene Friday prayer, and perform other duties for which a legitimate imam was required. During the Safavid period in Iran, a number of jurists gave the state a sort of limited legitimacy by sanctioning its activities as "legal" (*shar'ī*), though they still argued that the ideal state is one led by the imam himself. This was a controversial move, and many Imami Shi'i jurists continued to argue that the state was de jure illegitimate and that a truly pious believer would avoid all contact with it. The debate continues

into the early 21st century, but it has been given an added twist by the introduction of the revolutionary theory of *wilāyat al-faqīh* (the guardianship of the jurist). Imami jurists had always avoided making an outright claim to political power, even if some of them at times came close to sanctioning actual political rule by a temporal power. In the mid-20th century, Ayatallah Khomeini began to develop a theory whereby the role of the jurists within Shi'i society might be expanded to include direct political rule. He put forward this theory in the context of the rule of Muhammad Reza Shah Pahlavi in Iran, who had embarked on a series of policies that were undermining the traditional authority of the scholarly class in the name of modernization. Khomeini took an established jurisprudential concept, such as the notion that the jurist (*faqīh*) has control of the assets of an orphaned minor, and expanded it to legitimize the seizure of power by the scholarly class. In the same way that the jurist has legitimate power over the orphan's property (in order to protect it from being seized by the unscrupulous and unworthy), the *faqīh* also has rights to take political control in order to prevent the assets of the nation from being wasted by the corrupt. This idea of direct clerical rule was quite novel within Imami Shi'i law and underpinned much of the political structures of postrevolutionary Iran, where *wilāyat al-faqīh* is the theoretical basis for the political system. The debate over the legitimacy of Khomeini's theory has dominated modern Shi'i political thought, with a sizable body of juristic opinion (particularly from those based outside of Iran) arguing that the statement is invalid and unscriptural.

The two other major Shi'i groups that survived from the early period, the Zaydis and the Isma'ilis, also devised distinctive political theories, and both of these groups experienced internal fissures. The Zaydis were named after a grandson of Imam Husayn, Zayd b. Ali, who led an ill-fated revolt against the Umayyads in 740. His rebellion may have failed, but his movement gave rise to a number of subsequent groups of scholars and activists. The Zaydis generally did not recognize the Imami doctrine of the designation (*naṣṣ*) of one imam by the previous one. For some Zaydis, there had never even been a designation of 'Ali by the Prophet; rather, 'Ali and his descendents had the right to rule because they were intrinsically the most meritorious (*al-afḍal*). For others, only 'Ali and his two sons had been designated. After Husayn, all the descendents of 'Ali and his wife, Fatima, were eligible for the imamate, and this explains why there was no need for a designation of Zayd himself. The imam was the person who combined the qualities of lineage (from 'Ali and Fatima), learning, and worthiness, and, most crucially, who had rebelled against the unjust government of the day. Zaydi statelets appeared in northern Iran and in Yemen. In Yemen, the Zaydis established dynastic rule in north Yemen that survived until 1962, when an Arab nationalist revolution overthrew the last Zaydi imam. The militant activism of the Zaydi tradition continued in the 21st century through the movement associated with the Yemeni rebel Husayn Badr al-Din al-Huthi (d. 2004), though it is not clear whether his political ideas included the reestablishment of the Zaydi imamate.

The Isma'ilis emerged only a century or so after Muhammad b. Isma'il's death (or disappearance in the early ninth century), and in its early phase it seems to have been primarily a spiritual rather than political movement. There were inevitable political manifestations, however. First, there was the emergence of the revolutionary Qarmatians, and then later the Fatimids and their successors. The Qarmatians established a rebel state in eastern Arabia, which broke free of the Abbasid Empire and (most infamously) raided Mecca and removed the Black Stone of the Ka'ba in 930. Their origins certainly lay in a form of Isma'ilism that had broken away and developed its own messianic and millenarian tendencies. The Fatimids, on the other hand, appeared in North Africa in the early tenth century as a military force under the leadership of 'Abdallah al-Mahdi, who claimed 'Alid descent. For the Fatimids, the caliph of their empire (which spread out across North Africa with its capital in Cairo) was the imam—theoretically a sinless, divinely designated leader descended from the Prophet through Fatima. Even before the Ayyubid capture of Egypt in 1169, the Fatimid Isma'ilis had experienced offshoots that established separate communities claiming the lineage of different descendents of the Fatimids. While some of these communities were subsequently politically active (most famously the Nizari Isma'ilis in Iran, renowned for assassinating leading political figures), the post-Fatimid Isma'ili intellectual tradition was less concerned with politics, returning instead to spiritual and philosophical questions. The different Isma'ili groups have survived into the modern period, the largest being the Nizaris under the spiritual direction after 1957 of their 49th imam, Karim Husayni, who has the honorific title of Agha Khan.

The Shi'i movement did not have a detailed political theory worked out from its inception. Much of its theory developed out of Shi'i historical experiences, and the need to justify history, rather than any abstract contemplation by theorists. Its basic premises, however, such as the legitimacy of 'Ali's claim to be the Prophet's successor and the importance of Muslim leadership being drawn from the Prophet's family and their descendents, provided subsequent thinkers with an ideological base from which to develop a variety of conflicting and competing political theories. Furthermore, the various Shi'i groups defined their political stance in relation not only to each other but also to the wider Muslim (particularly Sunni) intellectual landscape. This variety has survived into the modern period and demonstrates the continued potency and popularity of the basic tenets of Shi'ism.

See also Isma'ilis; Qarmatians; Sunnism; Zaydis

Further Reading

Juan Cole, *Sacred Space and Holy War: The Politics, History and Culture of Shi'ite Islam*, 2005; Patricia Crone, *Medieval Islamic Political Thought*, 2004; Robert Gleave, "Recent Research into the Early History of Shi'ism," *History Compass* 7, no. 6 (2009); Wilferd Madelung, *Religious Trends in Early Islamic Iran*, 1988.

ROBERT GLEAVE

Shu'ubis

The term *Shu'ūbiyya* is most often used to refer to a movement, social and cultural in tenor, that originated in the eighth century and that stood for the equality of Arabs and non-Arabs in Muslim society, or even the non-Arabs' superiority. The movement had its roots among the non-Arab court secretaries that served the Abbasid caliphs. Its proponents, known as Shu'ubis, were skilled orators and talented poets, overwhelmingly of Iranian origins, and centered in Baghdad. At times they employed incendiary rhetoric. Although not widespread, the Shu'ubis and the opposition they generated reflected broader tensions in Muslim society between Arabs and non-Arabs. The Shu'ubis aimed neither to overthrow the Abbasid government nor to advance a political program.

A central tactic of Shu'ubis was apparently to assert the irrelevance of Arab descent as a criterion for precedence in Muslim society. An anonymous statement suggests the style of rhetoric employed by Shu'ubis. It quotes Qur'an 23:12 to argue that all people are the offspring of one man (Adam), as well as Qur'an 49:13, which states, "The most noble among you before God is the most pious." It is from the latter verse, which mentions *shu'ūb* (peoples), that the Shu'ubis' name derived. This statement also mentions that the Prophet, during his Farewell Pilgrimage to Mecca, reiterated the common descent of humanity and the equality of Arabs and non-Arabs. At the same time, the statement undermines traditional bases for Arab pride. For example, it alleges the corruption of Arab genealogies by citing the Arabs' own pre-Islamic poetry as evidence for raids in which women passed back and forth between tribes.

The movement is commonly mentioned in scholarship on early Islam. The most important early study was completed by Ignaz Goldziher, who placed the Shu'ubis in the context of the growth of "foreign elements in Islam" and the growing displacement of Arabs from powerful positions. With the emergence of independent dynasties within the caliphate beginning in the ninth century, these foreign elements ultimately achieved foreign rule, breaking not only the caliphate's power but "also that of the nation from which this institution stemmed." For H.A.R. Gibb, the Shu'ubis represented a movement among court secretaries with loyalties to pre-Islamic values. These secretaries sought to "remold" the political and social institutions of the Islamic empire and the "inner spirit of Islamic culture." If successful, the secretaries would have achieved the subordination of Arabic and Islamic elements to "the old Perso-Aramaean culture." The Shu'ubis' concern with social status has also been much remarked on by scholars (including Roy Mottahedeh, Susanne Enderwitz, and Louise Marlow). Most recently, Patricia Crone characterized Shu'ubism as a form of "post-colonialism," with the argument that the Shu'ubi movement "was a literary attack on the Arabs and their heritage by assimilated natives who were heard with increasing frequency" after the Abbasid revolution in 750. What was at stake was "self-respect and, above all, the character of the culture that converts were now sharing with the conquerors." The Shu'ubi movement has also received significant attention from scholars working in Arabic and Persian. A Shu'ubi phenomenon also apparently emerged in Andalus, and the term has had a currency in certain modern contexts as a pejorative label applied, for example, to opponents of Pan-Arab nationalism.

Few sources contemporary with the Shu'ubis survive. In analyzing the Shu'ubis, scholars, by necessity, have relied heavily on works written by the Shu'ubis' opponents. These works include a book-length refutation by Ibn Qutayba (d. ca. 889). Although of Iranian ancestry, as were many of their opponents, Ibn Qutayba was bothered by the way that Shu'ubis ridiculed Arabs as less civilized than Persians and explained why, for example, Arabs have eaten camel fur and lizards. He praised Arabs for their cultural traits and practices and cited several statements by the Prophet himself to support the superior status of Arabs in Muslim society. For Ibn Qutayba, humans are all the same before God, but in the present world, differences exist, and so, too, there are superior and inferior individuals and peoples (*umam*).

Classical Arabic authors generally are unsympathetic to the Shu'ubis. When biographers identify individuals as Shu'ubis, for example, they allege bias against Arabs and give no indication that Shu'ubis held egalitarian views, as the Shu'ubi statement cited earlier might suggest. As one biographer of Sahl b. Harun (d. ca. 830), an Abbasid courtier who was likely a Shu'ubi, stated, Sahl "felt great bias for the *'Ajam* [Persians] against the Arabs; he was extreme in that."

Some scholars have raised doubts about the importance of the Shu'ubi movement as a historical phenomenon, instead viewing it as a term to describe anti-Arab bias and particular ways of expressing it.

See also kinship

Further Reading

Patricia Crone, "Post-Colonialism in Tenth-Century Islam," *Der Islam* 83, no. 1 (2006); H.A.R. Gibb, "The Social Significance of the Shuubiya," in *Studies on the Civilization of Islam*, edited by Stanford J. Shaw and William R. Polk, 1962; Ignaz Goldziher, *Muslim Studies*, vol. 1, edited by S. M. Stern, translated by C. R. Barber and S. M. Stern, 1967; Sami A. Hanna and George H. Gardner, "'Al-Shu'ūbiyyah' Up-Dated: A Study of the 20th Century Revival of an Eighth Century Concept," *Middle East Journal* 20, no. 3 (Summer 1966); Göran Larsson, *Ibn García's Shu'ūbiyya Letter: Ethnic and Theological Tensions in Medieval al-Andalus*, 2003; James T. Monroe, *The Shu'ūbiyya in al-Andalus: The Risāla of Ibn García and Five Refutations*, 1970; Roy P. Mottahedeh, "The Shu'ūbīyah Controversy and the Social History of Early Islamic Iran," *International Journal of Middle Eastern Studies* 7, no. 2 (April 1976).

SARAH BOWEN SAVANT

al-siyāsa al-sharʿiyya. *See* governance

slavery

Chattel slavery was a well-established reality of political, legal, and social life in the pre-Islamic world. The advent of Islam did not change this; the revelations of the Qur'an and the Prophet Muhammad's sunna accepted slavery as an ordinary aspect of human existence. Yet the Qur'an and the Prophet explicitly recognized the humanity of the enslaved, seeking to ameliorate suffering and injustice and encouraging emancipation. Many modern jurists have therefore argued that one of the purposes of the Qur'anic revelation was to bring about the gradual disappearance of slavery and the advent of a society free of slavery. While a fair reading of the texts might support this view, the actual history of slavery and slave trading in the Muslim world belies this perspective. The slave trade and the suzerainty of slave-holding regimes in the Islamic heartlands flourished for more than 1,300 years after the death of the Prophet; in many places slavery and slave trading were robust, a source of great wealth, a sinew and building block for the construction of empire, and a central feature of Muslim political, legal, military, economic, and social life. Significantly, vestiges of slavery and slave trading, taking the form of human trafficking practices using transportation routes established in the 18th and 19th centuries, as well as forced labor regimes and extremely brutal forms of domestic servitude, still remain in some parts of the contemporary Muslim world, particularly in the Persian Gulf and the Arabian Peninsula, and on the Indian subcontinent.

Slavery and slave trading flourished in the early modern and modern eras because of a curious paradox created by the Islamic law. The classical law, developed by Muslim jurists over a 300-year period following the death of the Prophet, considerably reformed pre-Islamic slave systems. Under these pre-Islamic systems, one could enter the state of enslavement in a number of ways, including capture in war, birth, self-sale and sale by parent or guardian, as punishment for crime, as satisfaction for debt, as expiation for sin, and as a foundling or other disenfranchised person without means of support. The classical shariʿa reduced the means by which one could be lawfully enslaved to just two: birth from two lawfully enslaved parents or capture as a prisoner in a lawful jihad. All other forms of enslavement were abolished. Furthermore, no Muslim could be lawfully enslaved (although conversion to Islam after enslavement did not automatically result in emancipation). The Qur'an expressly permitted marriage between enslaved and free, observing that marriage to a Muslim slave is preferable to marriage to an unbelieving free person. The Qur'an also declared the emancipation of slaves to be an act of great piety, entitling the believer to reward in the afterlife. Interpreting these provisions and others like them, the jurists concluded that there should be a presumption of human freedom in all social and political affairs (*al-aṣl huwa al-ḥurriyya*), and any reasonable doubt with respect to one's servile status should be resolved in favor of emancipation. The jurists also declared that the children of unions between slave and free were also free and that the mother of such children (*umm al-walad*) was entitled to freedom at the death of her owner. This was an important rule in elite households, where a man might own large numbers of concubines. Heads of state in the Muslim world often traced their heritage to a slave mother. It is said that 34 of the 37 Abbasid caliphs were born of such relationships.

Islam's ameliorative approach to slavery thus resulted in frequent emancipation and great fluidity in social movement of persons who had once been enslaved, paradoxically creating a constant demand for more slaves. This demand was satisfied by entrepreneurs, slave traders, and unscrupulous marauders and plunderers who illegally captured and transported fresh slaves to the Muslim cosmopolitan centers from many distant places, including West and East Africa, the Balkans, the Caucasus, the Asian Steppes, India, and the islands of Southeast Asia. The classical law was essentially ignored, and many individuals, particularly women and children, were violently uprooted and relocated to the central lands of the Muslim world. Africans were particularly vulnerable to slave raiding, but by no means were they the only victims. The great majority of slaves in the Muslim world performed domestic household duties, but many worked as soldiers and sailors, concubines, agricultural and mining laborers, or as servants of governments.

The presence of significant numbers of enslaved persons in the Islamic heartlands, particularly military slaves, had a profound effect on Islamic political thought. In 1250, military slaves (mamluks) of the Ayyubid dynasty based in Cairo overthrew the sultan and established their own dynasty, which lasted for almost 300 years (1250–1517), deriving its success from the continuation of the codes of behavior established under the traditions of slave soldiery. Another dynasty of slaves and former slaves was established in Delhi, lasting for almost 100 years (1206–90). Similar events occurred in other places, and it is fair to say that military slaves were influential in a number of Islamic centers of power for nearly a millennium, from the rise of the Abbasid caliphate beginning in the eighth century until the decline of the Ottoman Empire at the end of the 19th century.

Military slavery and concubinage were not the only aspects of the Muslim slave systems that influenced political thought. Medieval and premodern jurists developed elaborate rules governing the commercial buying and selling of slaves, the resolution of disputes over slaves arising out of insolvency, the liability of slaves for crimes, the disposition of prisoners of war, and myriad other circumstances, making slavery an important aspect of the Islamic

legal and political culture. This feature of the culture remained part of the political milieu in the major centers of Islamic thought until well into the 20th century. In fact, the conventional historical wisdom tells us that there was never any significant indigenous impetus for the abolition of slavery in the Muslim world and that slavery and slave trading came to an end in the Muslim world only because of the abolitionist edicts of colonialist Western governments and the persistent efforts of antislavery activists, particularly the British. While there is considerable truth in this assertion, it cannot be said that Muslim thinkers played no role in abolition. It was difficult to eradicate the old thinking among religious conservatives, but a number of 19th- and early 20th-century liberal Muslim scholars and political leaders, notably Ahmed Bey (1784–1850) in Tunisia, Sayyid Ahmad Khan (1817–98) and Sayyid Ameer 'Ali (1849–1928) in India, and Muhammad 'Abduh (1849–1905) and Rashid Rida (1865–1935) in Egypt, were critical of slaving and slave trading by Muslims and sometimes vigorously sought to influence public opinion to end it. This struggle to make Muslims aware of the history of slavery and abolition in the Islamic world and to eliminate the vestiges of slavery and slave trading, referred to earlier, continues to this day.

See also Delhi Sultanate (1206–1526); equality; jihad; Mamluks (1250–1517); military; Ottomans (1299–1924); racism; rights; women

Further Reading

David Ayalon, *Islam and the Abode of War: Military Slaves and Islamic Adversaries*, 1994; William Gervase Clarence-Smith, *Islam and the Abolition of Slavery*, 2006; Patricia Crone, *Slaves on Horses: The Evolution of the Islamic Polity*, 1980; Bernard Freamon, "Slavery, Freedom and the Doctrine of Consensus in Islamic Jurisprudence," *Harvard Human Rights Journal* 111 (1998); Murray Gordon, *Slavery in the Arab World*, 1989; Bernard Lewis, *Race and Slavery in the Middle East: An Historical Enquiry*, 1990; Ronald Segal, *Islam's Black Slaves: The Other Black Diaspora*, 2001; Ehud R. Toledano, *Slavery and Abolition in the Ottoman Middle East*, 1998.

BERNARD K. FREAMON

socialism

The modern concept of socialism (*ishtirākiyya*), which involves state regulation, if not ownership, of the means of production and distribution, was introduced to the Muslim world in the 19th century, probably in the Ottoman Empire during the reform period known as the Tanzimat (1839–77). The word *ishtirākiyya* comes from the root *sh-r-k*, which denotes sharing. The Young Ottomans, as the reform-minded intellectuals were known, diffused the concept and doctrines of socialism among themselves, and through the media their ideas spread into Egypt and the Fertile Crescent. Socialist political groups emerged in Turkey after the collapse of the Ottoman Empire after World War I, but the regime of Mustafa Kemal Atatürk, Turkey's president, exerted constant pressure on these entities in the early to mid-1920s. Socialism and communism were understood to be bedfellows, so the repression of the Turkish Communist Party tended to reverberate and extend to the socialists as well. It was only after the Turkish military coup in 1960 that Turkish socialists acquired a new lease on life.

Meanwhile, in the Arab lands of the Middle East, Egyptian, Syrian, and Lebanese writers such as Salama Musa (d. 1958) and Shibli Shumayyil (d. 1917) published their interpretations of European socialist thought and practice in newspaper essays and articles. By the late 1940s and the 1950s, socialism came to be examined in the context of Arab society and politics, and some of its principal exponents were the Syrian Michel 'Aflaq (d. 1989) and the Jordanian Munif al-Razzaz (d. 1984), Arab nationalist writers of the Ba'th Party. Meanwhile, professional men of religion or pious laypersons such as the Syrian Mustafa al-Siba'i (d. 1964), the leader of the Syrian branch of the Muslim Brotherhood, and the Egyptian Sayyid Qutb (d. 1966), the main ideologue of the Egyptian branch of the Muslim Brotherhood, began writing about socialism in the context of the principles of Islam. In Iran, the cleric Mahmud Taliqani argued that the best attributes of socialism were already to be found in Islam, a line of argument similar to that of Siba'i and legions of others writing on this topic, both Sunni and Shi'i. In contrast, Qutb and the Pakistani thinker Abul al-A'la Mawdudi (d. 1979) argued that all secular ideas were inherently inimical to Islamic thought and practice. Even so, in their view, "Islam" introduced these same principles centuries ago, and the rest of the world was merely belatedly catching up.

Many Muslims have attested that the Islamic scriptures are redolent with themes of egalitarianism, a bedrock concept in socialism. They also alleged that "social justice" (*al-'adāla al-ijtimā'iyya*) is endemic to Islamic belief and used the expression "joint mutual responsibility" (*al-takāful al-ijtimā'ī*) to capture the spirit of this principle. But the phrase *al-'adāla al-ijtimā'iyya* is a neologism generated by pious Muslims in the face of writings in non-Islamic social theory, and it was absent from Islamic discourse—whether juristic or theological—until the late modern period. As David Miller, author of *Principles of Social Justice*, has shown, the concept of social justice emerged in Western political discourse itself only in the late 19th century, even though its genesis might be found in 18th-century writings.

Those responsible for crafting a theory of social justice assumed first of all that every individual is entitled to a claim of fairness. Second, they held that a clearly articulated society with identifiable members must exist in order to assess whether individual members were obtaining their fair share of goods, services, and opportunities. Third, they agreed that sophisticated measures were necessary to make that determination accurately. Fourth, they maintained that an

institution (typically, the state) must be able to operate in a manner that would ensure as close an approximation to social justice as possible. Finally, they believed that rational, nonreligious justifications should be provided for each individual's claim to entitlements, presumably on the argument that religiously based justifications risked omitting entitlements for those who did not profess the mainstream religion of the group.

In the juristic theories of the classical Muslim legists, these conditions and considerations were absent. Indeed, the main concern of these jurists was to identify the caliphate as divinely ordained and its task to ensure the ability of the believer to worship God according to the strictures of the holy law, as opposed to an organizational framework for enforcing the right of individuals to pursue their interests.

Nonetheless, socialism was the preferred model for Muslim writers in the contemporary period. During the Soviet era, Muslim political theorists maintained that "Islam," which they tended to reify, avoided the excesses of communism and capitalism. They cited scripture, such as Qur'an 11:143: "We have made you a middle-most nation so that you may act as witness over man." These Muslim writers saw a community of the middle way, as it were, as God's deliberate creation, which alone could ensure justice, equity, balance, and moderation. In other words, in their view "Islam" avoided extremism. The extremism of communism was its putative brutality against individuals, and the extremism of capitalism was its alleged valorization of greed.

Such interpretations have routinely been made by political leaders and professional men of religion. Among the former are Libyan ruler Mu'ammar Qaddafi (d. 2011), whose famous *Green Book* referred to Islam as "the third international theory," and Iranian leader Ayatollah Khomeini (d. 1989), who demonized communism and capitalism as the work of Satan. Popular Muslim preachers, such as Yusuf al-Qaradawi (b. 1926), Muhammad al-Ghazali (d. 1996), and Shaykh Muhammad Mutawalli Sha'rawi (d. 1998)—all Egyptians—have echoed such ideas.

Although socialism in the writings of authors in the Muslim world was undercut to some degree by the collapse of the communist systems in Europe and the Soviet Union in the late 1980s and early 1990s, its appeal did not vanish. Indeed, to the degree that capitalism was perceived as a threat, a number of Muslim writers upheld the advantages they saw in socialism. But socialism held little appeal for many other Muslims, given its association with secular thought and the suppression of organized Islamic activities by some political leaders in the Muslim world who professed Arab socialism, such as President Gamal Abdel Nasser (d. 1970) in Egypt or the Ba'thist leaders in Syria and Iraq from the 1960s into the 21st century.

See also Ba'th Party; capitalism; communism; economic theory; individualism

Further Reading

Shahrough Akhavi, "The Dialectics of Contemporary Egyptian Social Thought: The Traditionalist and Modernist Discourses of Sayyid Qutb and Hasan Hanafi," *The International Journal of Middle East Studies* 29, no. 3 (1997); Albert Hourani, *Arabic Thought in the Liberal Age, 1798–1939*, 1962; David Miller, *Principles of Social Justice*, 1999.

SHAHROUGH AKHAVI

solidarity

The Qur'an explicitly mentions *ta'āwun*, which means solidarity or cooperation: "And be in solidarity with each other in righteous works and Godwariness, and do not support one another in sin and transgression" (Q. 5:2). The text is also replete with references to related notions of unity and community. In Qur'an 3:110, for instance, God calls the believers the best community brought forth for the benefit of humankind. Indeed, the rise of Islam in seventh-century Arabia ushered in a radical paradigm shift in existing notions of solidarity: from one based on strict adherence to centuries-old tribal loyalties to one based on faith wedded to righteous conduct. Throughout the history of Islam, solidarity has been expressed in varied, interwoven ways: politically, socially, economically, and religiously.

Pan-Islamic identity is one of the most enduring manifestations of Muslim solidarity in the contemporary world. The Islamic reformist and anti-imperialist activist Afghani (d. 1897) played a pioneering role in fostering Pan-Islamic sentiment. Drawing on the Qur'anic notion of the *umma*—that the faithful constitute a community, irrespective of language or race—Afghani urged Muslims to stand united against European rule. The Ottoman sultan Abdülhamid II (d. 1918) also picked up the banner of Pan-Islam, calling on Muslims from India to North Africa to rebel against their occupiers. Muslims in the 20th century kept the call of Pan-Islamic resistance alive, such as the Lebanese activist Shakib Arslan (d. 1946), who became a fiery voice of anti-imperial Muslim unity in the 1920s and 1930s. Though most Muslim countries achieved political independence by the mid-20th century, the global balance of power shifted from Europe to the United States. The ensuing dominance of America in the Middle East in general, and U.S. support for Israel in particular, has played a vital role in sustaining a keen sense of solidarity among Muslims.

While most forms of Islamic solidarity have been based on the appeal to Muslims to support other Muslims, the concept of solidarity increasingly has been invoked for such causes as gender justice, gay rights, religious pluralism, the struggle against apartheid, and the destigmatization of people living with HIV and AIDS. Sisters in Islam (SIS) is a case in point. Formed in 1988 in Malaysia, the organization undertook gendered readings of the Qur'an to argue for the full inclusion of women in social, economic, religious, and political life. Under the leadership of Zainah Anwar, SIS became a formidable force within Malaysian society and for Muslim women

in other parts of the world. Positive Muslims (PM) is another example. Established in South Africa in 2000, the faith-based organization increased awareness about HIV and AIDS within the Muslim community, emphasizing compassion and love for those afflicted. In addition to combating the stigma associated with the disease, particularly within Muslim circles, PM provided counseling and safe spaces for people living with HIV and AIDS. Solidarity has also been approached through the framework of religious pluralism, most notably by the South African liberation theologian Farid Esack (b. 1956). Reflecting upon his own experiences in the antiapartheid struggle, which had a markedly interreligious character, Esack put to paper a Qur'anic theology of liberation that embraced the religious Other, calling for interfaith solidarity against oppression.

See also Abdülhamid II (1842–1918); apartheid; colonialism; equality; justice; Pan-Islamism; tyranny

Further Reading

Selim Deringil, *The Well-Protected Domains: Ideology and the Legitimation of Power in the Ottoman Empire, 1876–1909*, 1998; Farid Esack, *Qur'an, Liberation and Pluralism: An Islamic Perspective of Interreligious Solidarity against Oppression*, 1997; Toshihiko Izutsu, *Ethico-Religious Concepts in the Qur'an*, 2002; Nikki R. Keddie, *An Islamic Response to Imperialism: Political and Religious Writings of Sayyid Jamal al-Din al-Afghani*, 1983.

SHADAAB RAHEMTULLA

source of emulation

For more than a century, the term *marja' al-taqlīd*, or "source of emulation," has been used to designate the highest position of clerical authority in Twelver Shi'i Islam, indicating that the jurist-scholar (*faqīh*) acts as the primary source (*marja'*) of religious instruction and imitation (*taqlīd*) for lay followers (*muqallids*). In addition to providing instruction in following the dictates of Islamic law, the *marja'* is also responsible for the collection of religious taxes (zakat and *khums*) and their redistribution to the networks of charitable institutions, seminaries, and students over which he presides. Despite this clear hierarchical structure, the *marja'* achieves his position not through a formal institution but instead through what sociologist Said Arjomand calls a "hierarchy of deference" wherein the community of *mujtahids*, jurists capable of issuing religious opinions (fatwas), acknowledges the superior learning (*a'lamiyya*) of a particular jurist and chooses him as their own religious reference. (Although given his own capability, a *mujtahid* does not need to follow a *marja'* but does so out of respect.) This process can lead to the presence of single or multiple sources of emulation in any given period. Of course, in addition to excelling in all areas of Islamic scholarship and especially in jurisprudence, a *marja'* must be *ṣāliḥ* (pious) and *'ādil* (of just character).

The institutionalization of the *marja' al-taqlīd*, like other major developments in contemporary Shi'ism, coincided with the rapid decentralization of Iranian social and political structures under the Qajar dynasty (1789–1925). It was also the outgrowth of the fracturing of the Twelver Shi'i community as seen in the rise of Shaykhism and Babism, the religious movements originating with Shaykh Ahmad al-Ahsa'i and Sayyid 'Ali Muhammad Shirazi, respectively, that ultimately led to the development of the Baha'i religion. However, the doctrinal underpinnings of the institution and the clerical authority that supports it are rooted in the classic jurisprudential struggle to define a legitimate hermeneutical method of discerning Islamic legal ordinances during the Occultation of the Twelfth Imam. Identifying the basis of the authority of Twelver Shi'i jurists—who act as the curators of the divine law—as the general representatives (*al-nā'ib al-'āmm*) of the Imam therefore becomes a necessary attendant question. These classic jurisprudential debates were reinvigorated during and after the Safavid period (1501–1722) in what has come to be known as the Akhbari-Usuli conflict.

Deriving its name from the term for texts or reports (*akhbār*) of the imams' words or deeds, the Akhbari school restricted the basis of the law to scriptural proof texts, quotes from sacred literature, arguing that legal injunctions and ordinances could not surpass or limit what was explicitly recorded in the Qur'an or in the reports of the Prophet and his legitimate successors, the Twelver imams. The Akhbari school thus rejected *ijtihād,* even when performed by a highly qualified jurist, as a source of law. In contrast, the Usuli school, a label that derives from *uṣūl al-fiqh* or "the roots of the law," argued that a process of legal interpretation that included rational operations was the best method to understand God's law in shifting contexts and thus ensure the application and survival of the Divine Law throughout time. This logic also underlies the mandate that only a living *marja'* can offer a religious opinion and that it is forbidden for the lay Shi'i to follow the opinions of a past authority. Building upon the efforts of Agha Muhammad Baqir al-Bihbihani (d. 1793), who managed to cast Akhbaris as heretics, the Usuli jurist Shaykh Muhammad Hasan al-Najafi (d. 1849) is credited with heralding the demise of the most recent Akhbari intellectual movement. After his time, Akhbarism survived only in marginal settings in the Shi'i world, particularly in Bahrain.

These theological debates were concomitant with structural changes in the world of 19th-century Shi'i jurists. For example, in addition to providing intellectual grounds for the defeat of Akhbaris, Najafi was also the first *mujtahid* to delegate his clerical authority to lower-ranking scholars in other urban centers. Having a network of representatives, he thus created a centralized system of *khums* collection and legal administration that provided a source of income and political power that surpassed formal political boundaries and ensured clerical independence from state authorities. He also was the first to appoint a successor, Ayatollah Murtada al-Ansari (d. 1864)—generally recognized as the first to bear the title *marja' al-taqlīd*—as the chief *mujtahid* of the Twelver community. Between Najafi and Ansari's jurisprudential

and administrative contributions lie the clearest precedents for the contemporary Shi'i hierocracy. It is no surprise, then, that Ansari's student and successor, Ayatollah Hasan al-Shirazi (d. 1895), used the power vested in him by such a system in his famous fatwa against the tobacco concession granted to the British by the shah of Iran in 1891.

With the consolidation of the clerical establishment, doctrinal justification of religious authority naturally became a topic of Usuli jurisprudence. Among the first to provide coherence to the otherwise ambiguous arrangement of general clerical authority (*al-wilāya al-'āmma*) was Mulla Ahmad al-Naraqi (d. 1829) in a wide-ranging treatise on Shi'i jurisprudence titled *'Awa'id al-Ayyam* (Expectations of the millennium). True to his Usuli schooling, Naraqi justified the authority of Twelver Shi'i jurists on more rational grounds (*dalīl 'aqlī*) than on explicit textual authority. He wrote, for example, "It is obvious and understood by every common or learned man, that when the messenger of God was on a trip, someone behind him is assigned as his substitute, successor, trustee, [or] proof. . . . This person would be accorded all the powers that the Prophet enjoyed over his community." Naraqi's vision was foundational to Ayatollah Khomeini's infamous treatment of the issue in his exposition of the doctrine of "the guardianship of the jurist" (*wilāyat al-faqīh*), according to which the constitution of a legitimate state depends on its being headed by a just jurist. Like Naraqi and other Usuli scholars, Khomeini justified his position on the issue through a combination of rational arguments and scriptural proof texts. His elaborations on Naraqi's points should not be seen, then, as a spontaneous innovation. Rather, in the 150 years between Naraqi and Khomeini, the question of *wilāyat al-faqīh* had become an important question in Usuli jurisprudence that leading scholars addressed in different ways.

Khomeini's joint occupation of the positions of both the singular temporal leader (*rahbar*) and *marja' al-taqlīd* was a unique development in Twelver Shi'i Islam. Both before and after Khomeini's occupation of the position of head of state, other sources of emulation in and outside of Iran were divided in their support of *wilāyat al-faqīh*, and the doctrine never received the unanimous sanction that its supporters sought. The requirement that the *rahbar* be the leading *marja'* was dropped from the Iranian Constitution shortly before Khomeini's death in 1989, and though 'Ali Khamene'i, Khomeini's successor as head of state, eventually became recognized by his devotees as a *marja'*, his status as such remains a heated point of contention among many clergy and lay followers. Ironically, the fusion of state and religious institutions in the Iranian experiment has had the counterintuitive effect of further decentralizing the Shi'i religious establishment. Whereas the *marja' al-taqlīd* in much of the 19th and 20th centuries was an office held exclusively by one figure, in the early 21st century there were multiple sources of emulation throughout the Shi'i world, divided once again on the question of the relationship between political and religious authority.

See also authority; guardianship of the jurist; imamate; Khomeini, Ayatollah (1902–89); Shi'ism

Further Reading

Said Amir Arjomand, ed., *Authority and Political Culture in Shi'ism*, 1988; Mehdi Khaliji, *The Last Marja: Sistani and the End of the Traditional Religious Authority in Shiism*, 2006; Ruhollah Khomeini, *Islam and Revolution: The Writings and Declarations of Imam Khomeini*, trans. Hamid Algar, 1981; Ahmad Kazemi Moussavi, "The Establishment of the Position of Marja'iyyat-i Taqlid in the Twelver-Shi'i Community," *Iranian Studies* 18, no. 1 (1985); Linda Walbridge, *The Most Learned of the Shi'a: The Institution of the Marja' Taqlid*, 2001.

ABBAS BARZEGAR

South Africa

The first group of Muslims came to the Cape in successive waves from 1658 to the end of the 18th century. Most of them came from the Malay Archipelago and the coastal regions of India as servants, slaves, and political exiles. The most prominent religious figures among them were Shaykh Yusuf (d. 1699), a Sufi thinker who died several years after his exile to the Cape, and Imam 'Abdallah b. Qadi 'Abd al-Salam, better known as "Tuan Guru" (d. 1807), an Islamic philosopher, Sunni theologian, and mystic who was banished to Robben Island in 1780. Upon his release in 1791, he established the first mosque (Awwal Mosque) and school (madrasa) in the Bo-kaap. The early Muslims generally were not militant, but they were not slow to confront the colonial state if they felt that their Islamic faith and practices were threatened.

With the emergence of the secular Turkish Republic in 1924, the classical concept of the caliphate and sultanate came to an end. With the Salafi scholars, however, especially Muhammad 'Abduh and Rashid Rida, Islam as an ideology was revived in response to the needs of a modern Muslim nation-state. Hasan al-Banna, Sayyid Qutb, and Mawdudi were representatives of this Islamic revival. These scholars, among others, had a profound impact on Muslim political thought in South Africa.

Political Thought during Apartheid

The first notable South African leader to be inspired by the teachings of Banna and Qutb was Imam 'Abdallah Haron (d. 1969), whose sermons at the Stegman Road mosque emphasized the social message of Islam. The imam was critical mainly of the racial inequality and social injustice of the apartheid regime. Consequently, he was arrested and killed by the state security police on September 27, 1969. Attendance at his funeral was overwhelming, and soon he became a symbol of the revolutionary message of Islam, especially for the Muslim Youth Movement (MYM), established in 1970; the Muslim Students Association (MSA), established in 1974; and the Qibla movement, founded in 1980. After the Iranian Revolution

of 1979, these movements developed a culture of commemoration of the imam's martyrdom, which became a catalyst for social programs that sought to bring about transformation from complacency to activism against apartheid.

After the Iranian Revolution of 1979, the MYM was interested not only in the writings of Mawdudi and Qutb but also in those of ʿAli Shariʿati (d. 1977) and Ayatollah Khomeini (d. 1989). It did not see the Iranian model of establishing an Islamic state as something to be emulated in South Africa, however, and preferred to focus on Islamic education and training. By 1982 the MYM's members expressed reservations about the Shiʿi vilification of the first three caliphs in Islam. Thus the MYM accommodated the teachings of Shariʿati but not Shiʿi theology. A graduate of the Sorbonne, Shariʿati was inspired by existentialism and Marxism. He denounced not only Western capitalism and imperialism but also the Shiʿi teaching of the Hidden Imam who will return to the world to rectify the injustices. In his view, the clerics used that idea to justify a passive Islam rather than the evolutionary Islam exemplified by the martyrdom of Imam Husayn. He believed instead that Islam's mission was the liberation of the "oppressed" (*mustaḍʿafīn*), who included the poor and the exploited in Iran and elsewhere in the Third World.

Other Islamic resurgent organizations emerged in the South African Muslim community that challenged the MYM ideology. Achmat Cassiem, a leading antiapartheid activist who also had been imprisoned on Robben Island, was inspired by the Iranian Revolution and the ideological thought of Shariʿati. He launched the Qibla Mass Movement, which married the revolutionary message of the Iranian Revolution with local, antiapartheid politics. Qibla worked closely with the Pan-Africanist Congress (PAC), a group that had broken away from the African National Congress (ANC) in 1959 to espouse an Africanist program as opposed to a nonracial one based on the Freedom Charter of 1955.

Another example of a resurgent organization that resisted the political direction of the MYM was the Call of Islam, founded by Mawlana Farid Esack. This organization, committed to the struggle against the injustice of apartheid, aligned itself with the United Democratic Front (UDF) in 1983. The UDF represented a cross section of the South African cultural and religious organizations opposed to the apartheid state. Like Qibla, it espoused a clear, unequivocal political program and addressed the broader liberation struggle. While Qibla worked with the PAC, the Call of Islam remained aligned with UDF and, by extension, the ANC. By contrast, the MYM merely identified itself as the local manifestation of the global Islamic movement but did not make antiapartheid activity central to its program.

Furthermore, the Call of Islam drew its inspiration from the South African experience and not from international Islamic movements. It was committed to the creation of a nonracial, nonsexist, democratic, and just South Africa. It searched for a South African Islam, not one inspired by "outside" models as in the case of Qibla and the MYM. The Call of Islam presented Islam as social conscience linked to mass democratic movements. Imam Hasan Solomons, a member of the Muslim Judicial Council (MJC, established in 1945), also became attracted to the contextual approach to Islam and therefore joined the Call of Islam. Subsequently, the MYM sought to express Islam in the local context of the struggle for social justice against apartheid.

Political Thought during Democracy

The turning point in the history of Islamic political thought and practice in South Africa came in 1994, which marked the end of apartheid and the inception of democracy. The new democracy protected human rights, including gay and abortion rights. Although the legalization of abortion and the granting of equal rights to gay people were perceived as contrary to Islamic morality, Islamic political parties that campaigned against these measures in 1994 did not gain much support from Muslims. Taking into account that Muslims constituted only 1.46 percent of the total population, their support for these Islamic political parties was still well below the national average. Like the MYM and Qibla, who projected the utopian vision of an Islamic state, the Islamic political parties projected the vision of a utopia with an emphasis on Islamic morality; however, they showed little sign of attempting to respond to the real ethical challenges of a democracy that wants to protect the rights of all citizens.

Ebrahim Rasool, a former MYM and UDF member, was elected as the premier of the Western Cape in August 2004. Rasool was committed to religious pluralism, not to the "fundamentalist" Islamic discourse that avoided the real challenges of society. For him, just as the religious leaders developed a theology of liberation during the struggle against apartheid, so developing a theology of complementing religion with politics was now crucial for guiding religiously diverse communities. Thus he saw no contradiction between being a politician and having a religious identity. A politician with a religious identity could be more sensitive to the concerns not only of his own religious community but also of others.

The MJC supported the 2009 elections on the grounds that, for a Muslim minority, an Islamic state in a non-Muslim country was unrealistic. Thus they argued that Muslims should support the political party that served Muslim objectives, which included the establishment of a just and moral order for all South Africans. Furthermore, they argued that Muslims should become an integral part of the political structures of the country and participate in shared values but without sacrificing their Islamic principles.

From the preceding information, we can conclude that the Islamic political thought of persons and organizations in South Africa changed in accordance with the changes in the sociopolitical conditions of the country. During the apartheid era, Muslims made a significant contribution to the struggle for justice in South Africa for all South Africans. After the establishment of a democratic state, Muslims came to terms with the new challenges of a secular constitution that protected the rights of all its citizens. Muslim religious

leaders encouraged the support of political parties that could also serve Muslim objectives but cautioned against sacrificing Islamic principles and values as a result of that support.

See also apartheid; al-Banna, Hasan (1906–49); Khomeini, Ayatollah (1902–89); Mawdudi, Abul al-A'la (1903–79); Sayyid Qutb (1906–66); Shari'ati, 'Ali (1933–77)

Further Reading

Farid Esack, "Three Islamic Strands in the South African Struggle for Justice," *Third World Quarterly* 10, no. 2 (1988); Muhammad Haron, *The Dynamics of Christian-Muslim Relations in South Africa (ca 1960–2000): From Exclusivism to Pluralism*, 2006; Lubna Nadvi, "South African Muslims and Political Engagement in a Globalising Context," *South African Historical Journal* 60, no. 4 (2008); Abdulkader Tayob, "Islamic Politics in South Africa between Identity and Utopia," *South African Historical Journal* 60, no. 4 (2008).

YASIEN MOHAMED

Southeast Asia

Islam is represented in almost all of the modern nation-states that make up Southeast Asia, whether as the hegemonic faith in Indonesia, Malaysia, or Brunei, or as that of a noticeable, often marginalized minority in such entities as Burma, Thailand, Cambodia, and the Philippines.

Though Islam perhaps was known to some of the peoples traversing the waters between China and India in the first centuries after the death of Muhammad, there is no firm evidence of it being taken up as the religion of state in Southeast Asia until the 13th century, when North Sumatran ports such as Perlak and Pasai, in the present-day Indonesian province of Aceh, adopted Islam, followed by numerous polities along both sides of the Strait of Malacca. Of these, Malacca, a Ming vassal that seems to have formally adopted Islam at the opening of the 15th century and emerged as the primary entrepôt in the straits, played a pronounced role in the further dissemination of Islam in the western reaches of the archipelago. The north coast ports of Java, Islamized around the same time, ensured that Islam penetrated the still-Indianized hinterland of that island and the spice-rich eastern part of the Indonesian archipelago.

Wherever Islam spread, the Arabic script was adopted, and Malay (often known as Jawi) emerged as the primary vehicle of regional scholarship. Scholars would travel as far afield as Mecca, supported by rulers eager to connect their lineages to that of the Prophet. By the beginning of the 17th century, these same rulers sought official titles from the Sharifs of Mecca, and in keeping with international trends, they also invested in connections with specific Sufi orders. Thus the Shattari order, often associated in Southeast Asia with the teachings of the Gujarati Muhammad b. Fadl Allah al-Burhanpuri (d. 1620), attained official favor in many parts of Sumatra and Java, particularly after the return to Aceh from Arabia of the Acehnese 'Abd al-Ra'uf al-Sinkili (1615–93) in the latter part of the 17th century.

Esoteric Sufi teachings were not necessarily encouraged for the broader population, however. Legal codes such as the *Undang-undang Melaka* (The laws of Malacca) often urged commoners to abstain from deliberate emulation of their rulers' dress and rituals and sometimes royally endorsed campaigns attempted to limit Sufi practices, especially those deemed to stray from Islamic norms. Allegedly antinomian preachers were repeatedly condemned for revealing the secrets of Sufism to the masses, as was the case with a campaign led by Nur al-Din al-Raniri (d. 1658) in Aceh in the 1630s.

As such campaigns were supported by an increasing number of local rulers, such as those of Gowa, South Sulawesi (Islamized ca. 1605), ever more Southeast Asians took to the study of *fiqh* (almost uniformly that of the Shafi'i *madhhab* [school of law]), which encouraged the ongoing dialogue with visiting scholars from the holy cities, Gujarat, the Hadhramaut, and Ottoman Cairo. Southeast Asia is remarkable for following a single *madhhab* and, until the Iranian Revolution, for having practically no Shi'i communities. This uniformity notwithstanding, the increasing penetration of the Europeans in the region from the early 16th century was not met by unified political action. After their conquest of the Muslim port of Manila in 1570, the Spanish effectively pushed back the frontiers of politically autonomous Islam to the southern reaches of the Philippines, while their Portuguese and later also Dutch competitors engaged in a long series of conquests and conversion, leaving the Southern Moluccas a patchwork of Muslim and Christian settlements.

Meanwhile, in the Malay lands and Java, sultans such as Iskandar Muda of Aceh (r. 1607–36) and his contemporary Agung of Mataram, Java (r. 1613–45), expanded their territories at the expense of Muslim rivals rather than the Western interlopers. In subsequent centuries their own domains and authority would be eaten away by the Dutch East India Company in the 18th century or Great Britain and the Netherlands in the 19th century. By the 1770s, however, the independent entrepôt of Palembang in South Sumatra had become a center of the Sammani Sufi order, said to have been at the heart of the resistance to both English and Dutch attacks in the distant wake of the Napoleonic Wars.

The rise of the Sammanis at Palembang had been inspired in part by one of that port's most famous sons, 'Abd al-Samad al-Falimbani (1719–89), who was composing Malay glosses of Ghazali's works in Mecca in the 1770s and also sending letters to Javanese rulers urging active jihad against the Dutch. While the latter intercepted these letters and grew more wary of Islam's political force, they were nonetheless taken aback by the religious rhetoric and effective resistance launched during the Java War of 1825–30 and by the Padri War that ravaged West Sumatra in the early 1800s before turning into an anticolonial conflict in the 1830s. In the case of Java in particular, it was apparent that the forces of

the leading rebel Prince Dipanagara (1785–1855) included many people connected to the large, and relatively recent, network of Islamic schools (*pesantren*).

Such schools were furthermore spreading throughout the region at large. Although they were divided somewhat between those of Malay lands and those of Java and satellite isles such as Madura, they all sent ever more aspiring scholars and pilgrims on the hajj and into the arms of Sufi teachers, particularly the Naqshbandis, who were reasserting their place in Ottoman society after the Wahhabi occupation of the holy cities in the first quarter of the century. Travels, whether between schools or to Mecca, also engendered networks of kinship that could foster connections between politically aware subjects of British, Dutch, Spanish, and even Thai regimes in the region at large. (The Thais were conquering territories down the Malay Peninsula at the time.) With the opening of the Suez Canal in 1869 and the increasing propagation of printed materials via Singapore, Mecca was rendered an ever more accessible refuge and fount of religious authority for Southeast Asian subjects. During the drawn-out Dutch attempt to annex the remains of Aceh in 1873, the local fighters, many bearing Sufi amulets, were the talk of the day in the holy city.

With the almost wholesale annexation of Southeast Asian territories and strong-armed incorporation of the last independent rulers of the Archipelago as clients, some Muslim activists linked themselves to Cairo and the rhetoric of religious reformism to seek political redress. Then, with the belated birth of Islamic periodicals at the opening of the 20th century, well-connected Muslims in the Dutch sphere began to establish welfare societies, schools, and associations. On Java this culminated in the establishment of the trade-oriented Sarekat Islam and the Cairo-oriented reformist movement Muhammadiyah in 1912, but there were like-minded activists elsewhere, too. They were countered by more conservative associations, such as the Nahdatul Ulama, founded in 1926 around a core of East Javanese 'ulama' with little liking for either the modernist pretensions to religious leadership or the disdain for Sufi orders that was gaining support in once-more Wahhabi Mecca.

Matters were somewhat different, however, in the British sphere, where local rulers were effectively made the final arbiters of Islamic law for their subjects after the Pangkor Treaty of 1874. Some encouraged the links to Cairo and the ongoing codification of Islamic law in their names, thereby winning a respect they retained under the Japanese occupation and the independence that followed in the decades after World War II.

By contrast, the Japanese occupation of 1942–45, which had radically reorganized Indonesian society and elevated such nationalists as Sukarno (1901–70) before the attempted return of the Dutch, left little formal political space for Islam. The assembly hurriedly convened in 1945 to debate the future of the state and ultimately decided not to declare it Islamic (causing this to be taken up as the aim of the Darul Islam insurgencies that broke out in West Java, Aceh, and Sulawesi in the 1950s). The Islamic parties, forcibly merged under the Japanese in the all-encompassing body known as Masyumi (an acronym for the Majelis Syuro Muslimin Indonesia, or "Consultative Council of Indonesian Muslims"), were divided on questions of strategy, with the Nahdatul Ulama withdrawing to contest the elections of 1955.

The final crushing of the Darul Islam by the early 1960s and the silencing of Masyumi's leaders by President Sukarno seemingly heralded the last gasps of Islamist activism in Indonesia. Even with the active collaboration of Muslim youth organizations in the countercoup that toppled Sukarno in 1965–66, political Islam received little encouragement during the long reign of President Suharto (1921–2008), though he did encourage the de facto Islamization of the regime in the 1990s. Islamic political parties only reemerged in the wake of his downfall in 1998. Once again the spectrum of Islamic political offerings was widespread, ranging from accommodating parties allied to the older Muhammadiyah and Nahdatul Ulama to the more strident, globally oriented Hizb ut Tahrir and the Partai Keadilan Sejahtera (PKS), formed under the Suharto administration in emulation of the Muslim Brotherhood in Egypt. The latter group in particular seemed poised to make major gains after a series of corruption scandals in 2000 brought down Abdurrahman Wahid (1940–2009), formerly the head of Nahdatul Ulama and all too briefly the first Muslim intellectual president of the republic.

In the meantime, growing interreligious conflict in the Moluccas saw other nonstate Islamic actors enter the fray to act in the name of Indonesian Islam, from the Salafi-inspired Laskar Jihad (disbanded in the wake of the Bali bombing of 2004) to the more opaque Jemaah Islamiyah, led by old hands from the Darul Islam and recruited from among their descendants. The actions of the latter grouping, which courted funding and support from international Islamists while prosecuting a series of deadly bombings (most spectacularly in Bali in 2004 and Jakarta in 2003 and 2009), seemed calculated to engage a constituency that went far beyond any national boundaries, linking members in Malaysia, Indonesia, and the Southern Philippines.

With the effective neutralization of the main actors of the Jemaah Islamiyah network by the police and of a significant number of minority seats taken in parliament by such parties as PKS in recent years, it would be tempting to say that the problem of Muslim politics seems to have been resolved (for the moment) in Indonesia, with its open public sphere. In Malaysia, where an ascendant Malay majority is increasingly flexing its muscles either in support of the current paternalistic state ruled by the United Malays National Organization or as its most vocal opposition in the Pan-Malaysian Islamic Party (PAS, Parti Islam Se-Malaysia), Islam and politics also remain inextricably but peacefully linked. By contrast the situation remains fraught for the populations of Southern Thailand and, to a lesser degree, the Southern Philippines, which have both witnessed insurgencies and repressions over the last decades. Indeed, the long-running violence in Southern Thailand in particular shows little sign of abating, though it may be seen less as a manifestation of global jihad than as a function of older Malay claims to sovereignty founded on Islam.

See also Indonesia; Malaysia

Further Reading

Azyumardi Azra, *The Origins of Islamic Reformism in Southeast Asia Networks of Malay-Indonesian and Middle Eastern 'Ulama' in the Seventeenth and Eighteenth Centuries*, 2004; R. Michael Feener, *Muslim Legal Thought in Modern Indonesia*, 2007; Michael Laffan, *The Makings of Indonesian Islam: Orientalism and the Narration of a Sufi Past*, 2011; Duncan McCargo, *Tearing Apart the Land: Islam and Legitimacy in Southern Thailand*, 2008; Farish A. Noor, *Islam Embedded: The Historical Development of the Pan-Malaysian Islamic Party PAS: 1951–2003*, 2 vols., 2004; M. C. Ricklefs, *A History of Modern Indonesia since c. 1200*, 4th ed., 2008; William R. Roff, *The Origins of Malay Nationalism*, 2nd ed., 1995; Martin van Bruinessen, "Genealogies of Islamic Radicalism in Post-Suharto Indonesia," *South East Asia Research* 10, no. 2 (2002).

MICHAEL LAFFAN

sovereignty

The theme of sovereignty (*ḥākimiyya*) featured prominently in modern Islamic political thought during the mid-to-late 20th century in the context of emerging debates on the moral basis of legitimate political authority in the postcolonial era. Theoreticians of political Islam, seeking to construct an authentic Muslim identity in the face of growing Westernization and secularization policies, seized upon the theme of sovereignty to anchor their concept of an "Islamic state" and to contrast it philosophically with Western capitalist and Eastern socialist political systems. In the view of these Muslim thinkers, the critical difference with other political systems was that sovereignty in a Muslim polity belonged exclusively to God and not to the people. The objective of political life was not to fulfill the whims of human beings, they argued, but to discover God's will as guided by the Qur'an, the traditions (sunna) of the Prophet Muhammad, and the provisions of Islamic law.

The internal logic of this God-as-sovereign approach to politics was rooted in a traditional understanding of Islam. According to the Qur'an, "Governance belongs to God" (Q. 12:40), and those "who do not rule in accordance with what God has revealed are unbelievers" (Q. 5:47). The Qur'an uses the following adjectives to describe God: "the arbitrator" (*al-ḥakam*), "the eternal possessor of sovereignty" (*mālik al-mulk*), and "the bringer of judgment" (*al-ḥasīb*). Moreover, as a monotheistic religion, Islam holds the doctrine of the oneness of God (*tawḥīd*) as foremost in the profession of faith, integrating all domains of human existence, including the religious and the political. This approach to politics has posed a huge challenge for modernist Muslims seeking to reconcile Islam and democracy where popular sovereignty, according to international norms, is supreme.

The first major debate of the 20th century on sovereignty occurred during the Iranian Constitutional Revolution of 1905–11. The idea of a constitutional monarchy raised two pressing questions: (1) do democracy and a secular constitution have any legitimacy in a Muslim society, and (2) where does political sovereignty lie? A major public debate ensued wherein some senior clerics supported the revolution, arguing that a democratic constitution was compatible with Islamic norms because of the limits it placed on political tyranny. Others argued the opposite view, focusing on the supremacy of shari'a over constitutional law.

Ayatullah Khomeini's theory of the rule of Islamic jurist (*wilāyat al-faqīh*) draws upon this idea of the supremacy of the sovereignty of God. The constitution of the Islamic Republic of Iran that emerged after the 1979 Iranian Revolution tried to reconcile clerical sovereignty with popular sovereignty, but it clearly gave supremacy and veto power to the former in case of a clash between the two.

While Sunni Islamists reject a special role for the clergy in their vision of an Islamic state, they fully agree with the elevation of the sovereignty of God over popular sovereignty. The two most influential Sunni theoreticians of this concept are Sayyid Qutb (1906–66) and Mawdudi (1903–79). In his influential treatise *Milestones*, Qutb maintained that only a group of enlightened and committed thinkers and activists could lead the Muslim world out of the state of pagan materialism (*jāhiliyya*) toward a just society under the sovereignty of God.

Mawdudi developed a more detailed political theory than Qutb. He sought to reconcile the supremacy of divine sovereignty with the modern reality of popular sovereignty. He observed that Islam is the very antithesis of secular Western democracy and coined the term "theo-democracy," which he described as "divine democratic government, because under it the Muslims have been given a limited popular sovereignty under the suzerainty of God." In this theoretical model, which became widely popular among Sunni Islamists during the late 20th century, the entire Muslim population is involved in politics, but within the framework of the Qur'an and the sunna, while the executive is constituted by the general will of the Muslims, who have the right to depose it within the framework of Islamic law.

As the foregoing suggests, both mainstream Sunni and Shi'i Islamists share a particular skepticism toward full popular sovereignty. In the various political models proposed by both groups, there has been a call for the creation of a council of religious experts to ensure that the legislation that emerges from democratically elected parliaments does not violate Islamic norms. The most explicit and robust manifestation of this is in the Iranian Council of Guardians (Shura-i Nigahban), an appointed oversight body dominated by clerics that has veto power over parliamentary deliberations. Similarly, the 2007 draft platform of the Egyptian Muslim Brotherhood, while less intrusive, called for an elected body of senior religious scholars to advise the president and parliament. This provision led to considerable controversy within Egypt, and it was dropped in the 2011 updated version of this document.

The development of Islamic political thought in the late 20th and early 21st centuries on the question of democracy has led to greater

theorizing on the tension between popular and divine sovereignty. In the context of reformist Shi'i Islam, Iranian philosopher Abdolkarim Soroush sought to reconcile the two by affirming that, in essence, "the voice of the people is the voice of God."

Developing this theme further, Abdelwahab El-Affendi criticized the Islamist obsession with the sovereignty of God, noting that it has created a false obsession among Muslims while ignoring that which is central in political life: the question of human agency, the horizontal relationships between people, and the question of who should exercise authority here and now. Responding to the Islamist fear that full popular sovereignty could lead to the erosion of Islamic values, and hence the need for a religious oversight council, El-Affendi noted that in a Muslim society, most people will want to rule themselves according to values that reflect their indigenous traditions. It is up to the community to determine what these values should be and not merely one segment of the community.

See also authority; democracy

Further Reading

Khaled Abou El Fadl, *Islam and the Challenge of Democracy*, edited by Joshua Cohen and Deborah Chasman, 2004; Abdelwahab El-Affendi, "Democracy and Its (Muslim) Critics: An Islamic Alternative to Democracy?" in *Islamic Democratic Discourse: Theory, Debates, and Philosophical Perspectives*, edited by M. A. Muqtedar Khan, 2006; Sharough Akhavi, *The Middle East: The Politics of the Sacred and the Secular*, 2009; Hamid Enayat, *Modern Islamic Political Thought*, 1982; Roxanne Euben and Muhammad Qasim Zaman, eds., *Princeton Readings in Islamist Thought: Texts and Contexts from al-Banna to Bin Laden*, 2009; Nader Hashemi, "Religious Disputation and Democratic Constitutionalism: The Enduring Legacy of the Constitutional Revolution on the Struggle for Democracy in Iran," *Constellations* 17, no. 1 (2010).

NADER HASHEMI

Spain and Portugal (Andalus)

Andalus (Spain and Portugal) was initially a province of the Umayyad caliphate, based in Syria. The arrival of the Umayyad 'Abd al-Rahman I in Córdoba in 756, after escaping from the Abbasids, led to independent rule—a trend toward autonomy that had already begun under the previous Arab governors. It took more than 150 years for one of the descendants of the first Córdoban Umayyad amir to proclaim himself caliph. 'Abd al-Rahman III did so in 929, mainly as a reaction against the proclamation of the Fatimid caliphate in Ifriqiya in 909, which obliged him to develop a rival political and religious ideology. The rise to effective power of the Yemeni Arab Ibn Abi 'Amir—acting as chamberlain and helped by the fact that the third caliph, Hisham II, was a minor—and his descendants posed the problem of their legitimization, achieved mostly through jihad. Military reforms aiming at weakening the old conquest elites involved increased importation of Berber troops from North Africa. Dissatisfaction with these developments eventually led to civil wars—which sources tend to present as the result of enmity between Berbers and Andalusis—and to the "abolition" (*ibṭāl*) of the caliphate in Córdoba in the year 1031. Political fragmentation gave rise to a varying number of party kingdoms, whose rulers had different backgrounds and found different ways of legitimizing their power without ever claiming the caliphate. Only the Maghribi Hammudids—who claimed 'Alid (Idrisid) descent—obtained recognition as caliphs in a reduced area and for a short period. Coins struck at the time mention "the imam *'abd Allāh* [servant of God], Commander of the Faithful," a useful formula that did not refer to any specific caliph but merely implied acknowledgment of the Sunni doctrine regarding the need for an imam as supreme leader of the community of believers. When after 1087 the Berber Almoravids started incorporating Andalus into their empire, they kept the same formula, while their leader limited himself to adopting the title Commander of the Muslims. The recognition of Almoravid rule by the Abbasid caliphs led eventually to the new formula "the imam *'abd Allāh* [servant of God] the Abbasid," attested in a coin minted in 1140. The Almoravids were by then fighting a new Berber movement, that of the Almohads, founded by a messianic figure (Ibn Tumart), whose successor 'Abd al-Mu'min officially proclaimed himself caliph in 1147. 'Abd al-Mu'min developed a revolutionary policy that involved the creation of new political and religious elites and the assimilation of Almohad rule to God's command (*amr Allāh*). His successors reigned in Andalus until the Christian advance greatly reduced the territory under Muslim rule, with Córdoba and Valencia conquered in 1236 and Sevilla in 1248. The resulting power vacuum was filled by various local notables, such as Abu 'Abdallah Muhammad b. Yusuf b. Hud, known as Ibn Hud, who followed the Almoravid model by proclaiming himself Commander of the Muslims in Murcia in 1228, and Muhammad b. Nasr (Muhammad I, also known as Ibn al-Ahmar), who entered Granada in 1238 and made it his capital from which he extended his rule to Almería and Malaga, thus establishing the Nasrid kingdom. Almost three centuries later, in 1492, it was conquered by the Catholic kings, thus ending Muslim rule in the Iberian Peninsula. The existence of a Muslim population living under non-Muslim rule (the so-called Mudejares) gave rise to different legal opinions about whether this was in accordance with Islamic law. The Mudejar population was eventually forced to convert and finally was expelled from the Iberian Peninsula between 1609 and 1616.

Andalusi scholars sometimes produced works reacting to the political developments of their time. The Zahiri scholar Ibn Hazm (d. 1064)—from positions usually understood as pro-Umayyad—devoted a lengthy section of his book on religions and sects to the issue of who is entitled to the imamate (leadership) of the community, while in other works he argued for the illegitimacy and illegality of Taifa politics. Coinciding with Almoravid rule, two Andalusi scholars—Muradi (d. 1095) and Turtushi (d. 1126)—wrote Mirrors

for Princes, Ibn ʻAbdun reflected in his *ḥisba* (commanding right and forbidding wrong) work the tendency of qadis (judges) to assume power in their towns in moments of a power vacuum, and Abu Bakr b. al-ʻArabi (d. 1148) elaborated his political thought within Ashʻarism. Almohad rule favored philosophical political thought, as shown by both Ibn Tufayl (d. 1185) and Ibn Rushd (d. 1198), within a tradition going back to Ibn Bajja (Avempace; d. 1138). Sufi involvement in politics—with Ibn Qasi (d. 1151) becoming a political leader thanks to his army of *murīdūn* during the disintegration of Almoravid rule—or just the fear of such possibility led to the persecution of Ibn Barrajan (d. 1141) and Ibn al-ʻArif (d. 1141), and to the emigration under the Almohads of many Andalusi Sufis such as Abu Madyan (d. 1197), Ibn al-ʻArabi (d. 1240), and Ibn Sabʻin (d. 1270). Under the Nasrids, Ibn al-Khatib (d. 1375) reflected in his political writings his own experience as a member of the ruling circles, and Ibn al-Azraq (d. 1491) heavily relied on Ibn Khaldun's *Muqaddima* in his *Bada'iʻ al-Silk*. Andalusi political thought still awaits a monographic study, analyzing both works such as those mentioned and the reception and assimilation of non-Andalusi thinkers and writers.

See also Berbers; caliph, caliphate; imamate; North Africa; Sufism; theology

Further Reading

Michael Cook, *Commanding Right and Forbidding Wrong in Islamic Thought*, 2000; Maribel Fierro, *Abd al-Rahman III, The First Cordoban Caliph*, 2005; Eadem, "The *Qadi* as Ruler," in *Saber religioso y poder político actas del Simposio Internacional (Granada, 15–18 octubre 1991)*, 1994; Mercedes García-Arenal, *Messianism and Puritanical Reform: Mahdis of the Muslim West*, 2006; M. Cruz Hernández, *Historia del pensamiento de al-Andalus*, 2 vols., 1985; P. S. van Koningsveld and G. A. Wiegers, "The Islamic Statute of the Mudejars in the Light of a New Source," *Al-Qantara* 37 (1996); Miguel Asín Palacios, *Abenházam de Córdoba y su historia crítica de las ideas religiosas*, 5 vols., 1927–32; Janina Safran, *The Second Umayyad Caliphate: The Articulation of Caliphal Legitimacy in al-Andalus*, 2000; Peter C. Scales, *The Fall of the Caliphate of Córdoba: Berbers and Andalusis in Conflict*, 1994; D. Urvoy, *Pensers d'al-Andalus. La vie intellectuelle à Cordoue et Sevilla au temps des Empires Berberes (fin XIe siècle–début XIIIe siècle)*, 1990; D. Wasserstein, *The Caliphate in the West: An Islamic Political Institution in the Iberian Peninsula*, 1993.

MARIBEL FIERRO

succession

The fact that the Prophet Muhammad died in 632 without a surviving male heir ensured that succession in the nascent Islamic state, that of the Rightly Guided Caliphs, would not be based on simple heredity. A survey of later Islamic dynasties shows a number of distinct modes of succession, varying with region, period, and other factors; by and large, succession by primogeniture, which became the dynastic norm in premodern Europe, was followed relatively infrequently.

The legitimate leadership of the Islamic polity—the caliphate or imamate—after the Prophet Muhammad died became the subject of violent dispute in the early decades of the Islamic state and defined the major Muslim sectarian divisions, which produced two distinct narratives regarding the rightful rulers over the early Islamic polity. Sunni orthodoxy upheld the principle of acclamation, whereas Shiʻi orthodoxy favored designation or appointment. While succession to the universal caliphate is no longer a central issue in Islamic politics, views of the early disputes over succession became matters of theological doctrine and remain the subject of polemics.

Historical reports supporting the Sunni construction of Islamic salvation history agree that Muhammad did not designate a successor, leave an heir, or transfer political authority by covenant; at the same time, he did not repudiate political leadership. Nonselection of a successor apparently allowed for a flexible form of government, distinguishing the Islamic political system from contemporary forms of hereditary rule. Almost immediately following the Prophet's death, a political successor and leader of the Muslim community (*umma*) was installed without the use of force. While the Prophet's body was being prepared for burial, factions from the dominant Arab tribes of Medina, the *anṣār*, and their Meccan immigrant counterparts, the *muhājirūn*, gathered at a garden called Saqifat Bani Saʻidah in Medina to deliberate on the leadership issue. By most accounts, this brief public meeting was heated, tense, and nearly raucous. Without an explicit prophetic political directive or legal proof text to guide the assembly, the *anṣār* and *muhājirūn* each argued that the successor should come from their respective ranks because of their prominent services to Islam. A general agreement prevailed on Arab heritage, Islam, male gender, and nonslave status, but the particular choice of leader was contested. The *anṣār* proposed a two-ruler solution—"a leader (*amīr*) from us and a leader from you"—but it was rejected outright by the *muhājirūn* in favor of one ruler from the *muhājirūn*. Meanwhile, outside the Saqifa, Muhammad's uncle, ʻAbbas b. ʻAbd al-Muttalib, reportedly attempted to give the oath of allegiance (*bayʻa*) to ʻAli b. Abi Talib, thereby recognizing the Prophet's household (*ahl al-bayt*) as rightful successors, but garnered no support. Finally, Abu Bakr was elected as "the successor (*khalīfa*) of the Messenger of God," allegedly on the grounds of two widely acknowledged moral and social characteristics: his standing as Muhammad's closest and most trusted Companion and a shared Quraysh Arab heritage.

Toward the end of Abu Bakr's brief tenure (632–34), he reportedly chose ʻUmar b. al-Khattab as his successor after consulting prominent members of the community. ʻUmar's longer reign (634–44) ended with his assassination, but before he died, he had appointed a council comprised of six *muhājirūn* elders to elect his

successor. This ad hoc electoral body chose ‘Uthman b. ‘Affan (644–56). After a 12-year tenure as caliph, ‘Uthman was also assassinated and died before making any provisions for his successor. ‘Ali b. Abi Talib was acclaimed as caliph, but conflict soon broke out because of ‘Ali’s failure to bring ‘Uthman’s assassins to justice, implicating him in the plot in the view of some of his opponents. ‘Ali’s rule witnessed a civil war and the first political schism in Islam, creating three distinct groups: the Shi‘is, who were his supporters; the Kharijis, ‘Ali’s supporters who later turned against him because he negotiated with the enemy; and the ‘Uthmanids or Umayyads, who denounced ‘Ali’s caliphate. The reign of the first four caliphs altogether did not exceed 30 years and ended with ‘Ali’s assassination, after which Mu‘awiya founded the Umayyad dynasty (661–750) with its capital at Damascus. Sunni Islam arose as a compromise between the views of Shi‘is and the Umayyads on the issue of succession in particular. Later Sunni views stressed that the succession was based on acclamation and the moral excellence of the caliphs, but also to some extent on tribal affiliation—the caliph had to be from the Quraysh tribe. It became a standard Sunni creed that these first four caliphs were all “Rightly Guided” and that the chronological sequence of their accession to the office matched their moral superiority among the Companions of the Prophet: Abu Bakr was first in terms of moral merit, then ‘Umar, then ‘Uthman, then ‘Ali. It is often overlooked that the first four caliphs were all related to the Prophet by marriage.

According to the heresiographer Abu al-Fath Al-Shahrastani (d. 1153), Shi‘is are “those who follow ‘Ali in particular and assert his imamate and caliphate by appointment (*waṣiyya*) and delegation (*naṣṣ*) made either openly or secretly, and who believe that the imamate does not depart from his descendants.” Shi‘is agree that the caliphate rightly belonged to the Prophet’s descendants through ‘Ali and Fatima, “the People of the House” (*ahl al-bayt*), but are divided, as a result of succession disputes, into numerous splinter groups or sects. The most historically important of these Shi‘i groups are the Zaydis, Isma‘ilis, and Imamis. All of them adhere to ‘Ali, but they differ on the number of legitimate imams and the manner and line of succession. The Zaydis maintain that any descendant of the Prophet can assume the imamate, provided that his claim is public and backed by force. In other words, the imam must rise up and establish a state. Their appellation derives from the name of Zayd (grandson of ‘Ali b. al-Husayn who was the grandson of ‘Ali), who led an unsuccessful revolt against the Umayyad regime and was killed in 740. The Imamis, or Twelvers, hold that the rightful leader of the Muslim community had to be a descendant of ‘Ali’s son Husayn and, as their doctrine developed, had to be designated explicitly by the previous imam. In accordance with this doctrine, they stress that the Prophet had explicitly designated ‘Ali his successor at Ghadir Khumm while returning to Medina from the Farewell Pilgrimage (i.e., his last and only pilgrimage to Mecca), shortly before he died. A crisis occurred around 874 when their 11th imam, Hasan al-‘Askari, died, apparently without issue. The doctrine came to be that his son, the Twelfth Imam, had gone into hiding and could be contacted only through a representative; this was termed the Lesser Occultation. After the fourth representative died in 941 without designating a successor, it was held that the Greater Occultation had begun: the believers could no longer contact the imam, even through a representative. Circulating incognito in the Muslim world because of the danger to himself and his adherents posed by the Sunni majority, and with his life miraculously prolonged by God, he would reveal himself as the *mahdī* (“Guided One”) toward the end of time, filling the Earth with justice. The Isma‘ili Shi‘is emerged in the late ninth century, posing a revolutionary threat to Muslim leaders. Their view of succession resembled that of the Twelvers but they held that the sixth imam, Ja‘far al-Sadiq (d. 765), had been succeeded by his son Muhammad b. Isma‘il, who remained in occultation. Their doctrine stresses the possibility that the identity of the current imam could be hidden, even for several generations, before being revealed. The dominant Khariji view came to be that any Muslim who did not commit major sins could accede to the caliphate and revolt against any leader of the community who sinned.

The issue of political succession became an issue of theological difference not only among the various Shi‘i groups but also among the Sunnis, Shi‘is, and Kharijis. The Twelver and Isma‘ili Shi‘is regard the first three caliphs—Abu Bakr, ‘Umar, and ‘Uthman—as usurpers. The Zaydis, at least in the early period, accepted the legitimacy of Abu Bakr and ‘Umar but rejected ‘Uthman. The Kharijis accepted the legitimacy of Abu Bakr and ‘Umar but rejected both ‘Uthman and ‘Ali. Sunni theologians have denounced as heretics anyone who denies the legitimacy of any of the Rightly Guided Caliphs and even one who denies that their order of superiority follows the chronological order of their succession.

Hereditary rule was introduced to the Islamic polity with the establishment of the Umayyad dynasty. Mu‘awiya, the former governor of Damascus, who became universal caliph by default when ‘Ali was assassinated in Kufa, Iraq, had his followers swear a *bay‘a* to his son Yazid, thereby recognizing him as heir apparent. (Although it should be noted there that, upon the death of his father ‘Ali, Hasan became caliph by acclamation, but after a few months, he abdicated to Mu‘awiya in order to avoid civil war in the year known as the “Gathering” [*‘ām al-jamā‘a*] circa 661, since it unified Muslim rule.) This move worked, and Yazid indeed succeeded his father. When Yazid’s son Mu‘awiya abdicated, the rule passed to an uncle, Marwan b. al-Hakam. Rule remained among the descendants of Marwan for the remainder of the dynasty, but the nature of succession changed somewhat. The caliphs appointed two heirs apparent, ostensibly in order to keep rule within the family in case one died or proved unacceptable, but they would try to depose one or more of the heirs apparent in order to favor their own sons as they sensed that they were reaching the end of their reign.

The Abbasid caliphs (750–1258) continued the practice of naming an heir apparent, usually preferring their sons though not necessarily the eldest, but succession disputes were frequent among the sons, brothers, and cousins of the previous caliph. The most

famous succession dispute is undoubtedly that which caused a four-year civil war (809–13) between Amin (r. 809–13) and Ma'mun (r. 813–33), sons of Harun al-Rashid (r. 786–809). Ma'mun was the elder son, but Harun probably appointed Amin because his mother belonged to the Abbasid family, while Ma'mun's mother was a Persian woman. The war divided the entire empire in two, with Amin in control of the west, including Iraq and Syria, and Ma'mun in control of the east, including Iran. Ma'mun's forces eventually succeeded in capturing Baghdad and beheaded Amin. In a surprising move, Ma'mun named as his heir apparent 'Ali al-Rida, the eighth imam of the Imamis, while also recognizing Rida's son Muhammad as the next in line for the caliphate. 'Ali al-Rida died in 818, before this succession came to pass, but for a time it appeared that Ma'mun (r. 813–33) intended to restore caliphal rule from the Abbasid line—descendants of the Prophet's uncle 'Abbas—to the line of 'Ali.

The rise of the Seljuq dynasty (11th to 14th century) in the central Islamic lands introduced another type of political apparatus and mode of succession. The nomadic Turks created an appanage state, rule by family federation in which the paramount member of the family assigned male relatives parts of the conquered domain as semiautonomous realms. Thus the great Seljuq, Malikshah I (1072–92), divided up most of Iran, Iraq, Syria, and Anatolia among his relatives and also among his leading generals, creating several Seljuq states as well as the dynasties of the Saltuqids (1071–1202), Danishmendids (1086–1178), and others in Anatolia. This mode of succession usually required continual expansion by conquest to have any longevity; the empire was prone to fall apart into several warring kingdoms upon the death of the paramount ruler. After the death of Malikshah in 1092, for example, the Seljuq realm split between his brother and four sons, who immediately began internecine warfare.

The Mamluk dynasty in Egypt and Syria (1250–1517) provides another distinct, and unusual, mode of succession. Rule was restricted to Turkish warriors who had been bought as slaves and trained in the barracks of a military commander, also a slave. The offspring of these slave warriors were excluded from the office of sultan and other posts of high command, so hereditary succession was ruled out. Instead, the heir to the throne tended to be one of the protégés of the former sultan, who formed a tight and loyal group, unless a rival faction succeeded in ousting the incumbents.

Succession in the long-lived Ottoman dynasty (1299–1924) varied over time, but its modes of successions were formative. Beginning with the reign of Mehmed II (r. 1444–46, 1451–81) in the 15th century, a fratricidal system of succession that may be described as survival of the fittest son—and not necessarily the eldest—became the norm. The Ottoman sultans' practice was to assign governorships to the princes in order to prepare them for rule. When the sultan died, the princes would race with their supporters to Istanbul, the capital, in order to vie for the succession. The victorious prince would then have all of his brothers and half brothers immediately killed to prevent future coups d'état by rival claimants to the throne. Beginning in the 17th century, the fratricidal system was modified to one of permanent house arrest. Surviving brothers were confined for life to apartments in the harem of the Topkapi palace that came to be known as the *Kafes*, or "cage." Kept under constant surveillance by palace personnel, they were prevented from producing an heir by having access only to barren concubines. At the same time, there was a shift from succession by sons to one of agnatic seniority in the Ottoman family, so that a brother often succeeded instead of a son. This system remained in place until the end of the empire in 1924, despite attempts in the 19th century to establish primogeniture as the principle of succession.

Beginning in the 19th century a number of royal dynasties in the Muslim world, influenced by Western models, adopted primogeniture as their official modes of succession. They included the Muhammad 'Ali dynasty of Egypt, the Alaoui dynasty of Morocco, the Hashemi dynasty of Jordan, the Pahlavi shahs of Iran, and others. Other monarchies, such as those of Saudi Arabia and the Gulf countries, maintained a looser mode of succession related to traditional tribal systems of leadership, whereby primogeniture was not strictly required. An heir was chosen by a flexible system of agnatic seniority from among the deceased ruler's brothers, sons, or even nephews, who were viewed as highly competent and capable of bolstering the legitimacy of the dynasty and galvanizing support among the various factions within the ruling family.

See also authority; Rightly Guided Caliphate (632–61); Shi'ism; Sunnism

Further Reading

Patricia Crone, *Medieval Islamic Political Thought*, 2004; Joseph A. Kechichian, *Succession in Saudi Arabia*, 2001; Ann K. S. Lambton, *State and Government in Medieval Islam*, 1981; Wilferd Madelung, *Succession to Muhammad: A Study of the Early Caliphate*, 1998; Al-Shahrastani, *Al-milal wa-n nihal*, 2 vols., 1988; W. Montgomery Watt, *Islamic Political Thought*, 1968.

FIAZUDDIN SHU'AYB

Sudan

The history of the interaction between Islam and politics in Sudan traditionally begins with the anticolonial revolution led by the "Mahdi" Muhammad Ahmad (a former Sufi turned messianic leader claiming to be the "rightly guided one," a figure from Muslim eschatology) in 1881. According to those who celebrate the current political order, it pauses for about 100 years, and then resumes with the Revolution of National Salvation (*thawrat al-inqādh al-waṭanī*) in 1989, which brought to power General 'Umar Hasan Ahmad al-Bashir with the backing of the National Islamic Front (NIF) and its erstwhile leader Hasan

al-Turabi. President Ja'far Numayri's imposition of the shari'a in September 1983 is another convenient starting point for what is understood to be the current wave of Islamization. A more careful appraisal of Sudanese history, however, suggests that the relationship between Islam and politics in Sudan has been a consistent and complex feature of the development of the political order since at least the 16th century. Starting with the mutually beneficial relationship of Sudanese Sufi shaykhs with the leaders of the Funj kingdom of Sinnar and continuing during Turkish-Egyptian rule in the 19th century, Islamic politics wove through even British colonial efforts. Governor General Francis Reginald Wingate (r. 1899–1916) indeed deserves a seat among the great reformers of Sudanese Islam. It was under his initiative that the British created a new scholarly religious class ('ulama') in Sudan, which they hoped to appropriate, while suppressing the remnants of ecstatic Mahdism and other "local" varieties of Islam from which they feared a reemergence of Islamic political fervor. In the immediate postindependence years, political rule vacillated between a party affiliated with the Sufi Khatmi order (which went by several names) and a party affiliated with the sons (and religious organization) of the aforementioned "Mahdi" (Hizb al-Umma). "The Revolution of National Salvation" brought to power an offshoot of the Muslim Brotherhood for the first time, the NIF, which experimented with projects to create an Islamic economy, education system, legal apparatus, and social order, funneling significant resources to such projects. Since the coming of the Revolution of National Salvation, Islamic politics has by no means been stagnant, as the Islamic political project of the early revolution has been reworked to meet the demands of an ever-changing political context.

It is in this fertile ground that Sudanese Islamic political thought has flourished. The luminaries of the modern period—individuals such as Hasan al-Turabi (b. 1932), the liberal Muslim reformer and "post-Sufi" Mahmoud Mohamed Taha (d. 1985), and the leader of the Umma Party Sadiq al-Mahdi (b. 1936)—are well covered in the modern literature. Less attention has been paid to the unique situation of a large class of Sudanese intellectuals who were perhaps the first in the Sunni world to put the ideas of resurgent 20th-century Muslim Brotherhood–style Islamism into practice with the foundation of the Islamic state in 1989. The period from 1989 until the present has provided a laboratory in which the utopian ideas of the Islamic Movement (*al-ḥaraka al-islāmiyya*) were reformulated in order to respond to realities on the ground. Forced to confront the religious and cultural diversity of Sudan (made up of more than 100 languages, a sizable Christian population, and followers of tribal-based religious systems), and an international and regional political landscape that responded negatively to Sudanese reforms, these Islamist thinkers had to factor in variables unimagined by their earlier brethren who had never tasted power. Despite the notoriety of thinkers like Turabi, the Revolution of National Salvation and its project of social reform (called by the intellectuals who led the movement the Civilization Project, *al-mashrū' al-ḥaḍārī*) has received little scholarly attention, and its leaders' agenda of Islamic renewal remains hidden in the pages of government reports of ministries such as Social Planning (Wizarat al-Takhtit al-Ijtima'i), in local periodicals, or in the multitude of cultural products produced by the government or its allies such as poetry and song.

Moreover, Sudanese Islamic intellectuals outside of the NIF and its offshoots, such as the leaders of Salafi groups, like Ansar al-Sunna and the shaykhs of myriad Sufi orders, put barely a word to the page, and thus their politically relevant thought is little known outside of Sudanese circles. Indeed, the true range of Sudanese Islamic political thought outside of the ruling Islamist elite has mostly gone unnoticed in scholarly literature, with the notable exception of the trend begun by Taha, the Republican Brotherhood movement.

Since the signing of the Comprehensive Peace Agreement (CPA) in 2005 with the majority non-Muslim and southern Sudan People's Liberation Movement (SPLM) and the reorganization of the state it occasioned, some scholars have heralded the end of the Islamic experiment or the beginning of "post-Islamism," as if a failure of the ideas of an intellectual such as Turabi amounted to the failure of Muslim politics more broadly. A closer look at this period reveals that the problems faced by the ruling elite when it had to harmonize its vision of the Islamic state with political realities on the eve of the short-lived experiment with national unity, did not lead to a dead end for Islamic politics but rather to a new flourishing thereof. Muslim organizations from Sufis to Salafis took the opportunity that this opening of the political window afforded to offer new interventions into models of Islamic statehood, public order, and the proper relationship between religion and politics. With the separation of the south on July 9, 2011, some members of the ruling party in the north have promised to cancel the multicultural provisions of the Sudanese Constitution now that the non-Muslim southerners are "gone" and indeed are celebrating separation as a new birth for the project of Islamic statehood more broadly. In the new Republic of South Sudan, the southern Muslim minority is putting forth its vision for the role of Islam in this avowedly secular state, and its positions span from an embrace of a religion-blind secularism as the best way to achieve equal rights for all south Sudanese, to armed rebellion demanding 30 percent representation for Muslims in the new government. It is undeniable that Islamic political thought will play an important role in Sudan's immediate future in both the north and the south.

See also Mahdi of the Sudan (1844–85); Taha, Mahmoud Mohamed (1909–85); al-Turabi, Hasan (b. 1932)

Further Reading

Abdelwahab el-Affendi, *Turabi's Revolution: Islam and Power in Sudan*, 1990; Einas Ahmed, "Political Islam in Sudan: Islamists and the Challenge of State Power (1989–2004)," in *Islam and Muslim Politics in Africa*, edited by Benjamin Soares and Rene Otayek, 2007; Alex De Waal and A. H. Abdel Salam, "Islamism, State Power and *Jihad* in Sudan," in *Islamism and its Enemies in the Horn of*

Africa, edited by Alex de Waal, 2004; Daisuke Maruyama, "Sufism and Tariqas Facing the State: Their Influence on Politics in the Sudan," *Orient: Reports of the Society for Near Eastern Studies in Japan* 46, 2011; Neil McHugh, *Holy Men of the Blue Nile: The Making of an Arab-Islamic Community in the Nilotic Sudan, 1500–1850*, 1994; Noah Salomon, "The Salafi Critique of Islamism: Doctrine, Difference and the Problem of Islamic Political Action in Contemporary Sudan," in *Global Salafism: Islam's New Religious Movement*, edited by Roel Meijer, 2009; Ruediger Seesemann, "Between Sufism and Islamism: The Tijaniyya and Islamist Rule in Sudan," in *Sufism and Politics: The Power of Spirituality*, edited by Paul Heck, 2007; T. Abdou Maliqalim Simone, *In Whose Image? Political Islam and Urban Practices in Sudan*, 1994; Gabriel Warburg, *Islam, Sectarianism and Politics in Sudan since the Mahdiyya*, 2003.

NOAH SALOMON

Sufism

Sufism (*taṣawwuf*) is the mystical current of thought in Islam, the individual mystic being known as a Sufi. Among the Companions of the Prophet Muhammad were persons who wanted to strive for more than the outward observance of the religious law and the customs founded by the Prophet. While fulfilling their religious duties, they also paid attention to what was happening to their souls and tried to harmonize these internal experiences with the external observances through asceticism and renunciation of the world. As a result of the great conquests, secularization of life and luxury, contrary to the ideals of the original Islamic community, became widespread, and the ascetics believed that the truly God-fearing person could save himself from such temptations only by withdrawing from the world.

The representatives of the ascetic movement wore rough woolen cloth (*ṣūf*) as a visible reaction against people who wore more luxurious clothing and possibly also as an imitation of the Christian monks.

In the eighth century, a fringe group of the movement called *ṣūfiyya* emerged. They developed views about the love of God, citing the Qur'an (5:54): "He loves them, and they love Him." They intensified this relation by playing music and reciting and listening to love poems (*samāʿ*). For the *ṣūfiyya*, God was the beloved celebrated in these poems, and the love relation described in them was their relation to God. Listening to these poems often put them in a state of ecstasy (*wajd*), brought about in particular by the exercise of *dhikr allāh* (recollection of God).

A Sufi was poor (*faqīr*), renounced this world, and devoted himself to the ardent service of God. In his eyes, an even greater enemy was his base self (*nafs*), experienced as the seat of all evil lusts, which impeded real renunciation of the world and exclusive surrender to God. It was therefore his task to exercise self-training in order to do away with the self and all impulses of its will. The final obliteration of personal activity was experienced as an absorption, a cessation of being, in God (*fanāʾ*). A road (*ṭarīq* or *ṭarīqa*, the later word for "dervish order") along which the mystic traveled (*sulūk*) led to this goal. In the internal experience, it led across a number of way stations (*manāzil*), locations (*maqām*), and situations (*ḥāl*). Already in early times, many interpreted this road as a journey toward God through the macrocosmos.

A center of intellectual mysticism developed in the Abbasid capital of Baghdad under the leadership of Junayd (d. 910), to whose authority almost all later Sufism refers. Other prominent early mystics include Sahl al-Tustari (d. 896) in Basra and the famous Hallaj, whose exaggerated and challenging sayings provoked the state authorities, leading to his execution in Baghdad in 922.

The 10th and 11th centuries were a period of consolidation in which great collections and textbooks appeared that gave Sufism its final orthodox tone. The writings of Sarraj (d. 988), Sulami (d. 1021), and Qushayri (d. 1074) collected information about Sufism and Sufis. Classical Sufism found a certain culmination in the activities of Ghazali (d. 1111). Originally a theologian, he converted to mysticism after a crisis in his life. In his main work, the *Ihya' ʿUlum al-Din* (Revival of the religious sciences), he accomplished a synthesis of theological science and mysticism. Increasingly, the Persian language was also used in Sufi literature, which until far into the tenth century had been written only in Arabic. Sufism was to be of particular importance for the Persian poetry of ʿAttar (d. 1220), Rumi (d. 1273), and Jami (d. 1492) and later in Turkish, Urdu, and other languages.

Since early times, Sufism was enriched by admitting non-Islamic ways of thinking, above all Neoplatonism. A broad influence set in only much later, however, through the works of Shihab al-Din Yahya al-Suhrawardi (d. 1191), who was from Persia, and Ibn al-ʿArabi (d. 1240), who was from Spain but died in Damascus. Suhrawardi joined mystical experiences with older Iranian traditions. Ibn al-ʿArabi drew up a Neoplatonic-Gnostic system dominated by the idea of the unity of all beings (*waḥdat al-wujūd*). Later, opposition arose against aspects of Sufism, which Ibn Taymiyya (d. 1328) considered as abuses.

Mystic life was increasingly cultivated in the orders (*ṭuruq*), which have been its characteristic home. The orders originated in the 12th and 13th centuries, during which Sufi groups were formed with fixed rules and a hierarchal leadership.

The most important orders, each with suborders and secondary branches, are the Qadiris (found throughout the entire Islamic world, with the exception of Shiʿi Iran); Kubrawis (who were spread throughout Central Asia); Naqshbandis (who arose in Central Asia and spread to India, the Caucasus, Kurdistan, and South Arabia); Khalwatis (who were spread throughout the Ottoman Empire and grew in Egypt and the rest of the Arab world from the 17th to 18th centuries, with branches, such as the Sammanis and Tijanis, that are important to more recent history in Africa); Shadhilis (who arose chiefly in North Africa); Mevlevis, known as "the whirling dervishes" (who traced their origin to Rumi but were founded in the 14th century and were influential within the Ottoman Empire); and Bektashis (who are said to have been founded by an Anatolian saint, Hajji Bektash [d. ca. 1270], and developed in the Ottoman Empire).

The orders generally have fixed, written rules, which usually include the following points:

The order's affiliation. They state the order's affiliation (*silsila*), which is traced back from the present leader to the Prophet Muhammad and may comprise 30 to 40 degrees. These affiliations are frequently not very historical; in the various orders, they often coincide from the Prophet onward to the foundation of the specific order in the 13th to the 15th century, but after that date, differentiation appears.

The conditions and rituals for admission into the order. Some orders take men and women, some only men. The novice owes the shaykh unconditional obedience in the affairs of everyday life.

Instructions for the use of the formulas for the dhikr *(remembrance of God)*. These deal with the regulation of breathing, the rhythms in which these formulas must be recited, and the speed at which they must be performed.

*Instructions regarding seclusion (*khalwa*)*. The Sufi often withdraws for a length of time, which may span weeks, in a special, screened-off, small room in order to devote himself to *dhikr* exercises. Precise instructions are given for the site and the arrangement of space, the length of the seclusion, the sequence of the formulas and litanies, the prescriptions for posture, and practical points such as maintenance and cleanliness.

Advice. Often advice is also given concerning the relations between the members of the order.

The most important practice of the Sufis and of the Sufi communities is the *dhikr*, and with some orders music and dance play a large role. These were rejected by the theologians, as well as by Ibn Taymiyya and his school; others, like Ghazali, accepted music (*samā'*) but rejected dance.

In early times, even during the Prophet's lifetime, *dhikr* could involve picturing God in one's mind and thinking of Him, for which purpose meetings were held. The early *ṣūfiyya* recited certain formulas in common. Later, *dhikr* means to have God's name (*allāh*) always present and to pronounce it while paying attention to certain breathing techniques. This recital of God's name could lead to a state of ecstasy accompanied by visions. At times, the schools or orders developed specific methods for remembering God. Upon admission into the order, these methods were "implanted" into the novice by the teacher (*talqīn al-dhikr*).

Many prominent teachers and personalities of Sufism attained sainthood soon after their deaths, some even during their lifetimes. They were said to have supernatural knowledge and the power to work miracles, and their tombs often became places of pilgrimage. Garlands of stories and legends developed about their lives and works, forming the basis of hagiographies.

The model for miracle-working saints was the Prophet Muhammad himself, to whom supernatural features were ascribed by the Sufis. The Prophet's life (*sīra*) and his sayings and actions (sunna) were an example to follow. The Sufis not only imitate the Prophet with body and soul (*imitatio Muhammadi*) but also exert theselves to keep Muhammad ever-present in their thoughts and feelings, and this practice could be so intense that the Sufis thought they saw Muhammad in person and heard his words and advice. They were convinced that Muhammad lives on after his death in a transformed existence, and in later times the term "Muhammad's path" (*ṭarīqa muḥammadiyya*) was used in this context.

The mystical path is in principle open to every Muslim. According to the Sufis, therefore, anyone can arrive at higher forms of religious knowledge. On the other hand, Shi'is, for whom religious authority and knowledge are associated with degrees of consanguinity with the Prophet Muhammad through the imams, were hostile to the "democratic" idea of knowledge upheld by the Sufis.

Groups founded on the basis of strong "ideological" ties were capable of developing strong sociopolitical powers. For example, a shaykh with a charismatic personality could receive from worldly rulers rich gifts that he might use to further the worldly influence of his order. He might win the loyalty of entire tribes if, as often happened, he succeeded in the role of peacemaker in tribal society. He might establish a community around his rule that swore allegiance to him. The state of Sanusi in Libya, for instance, emerged on the basis of its peacemaking function. If the power of the order was directed outwardly in military undertakings, such as was the case with the Safavids at the end of the 15th century in Iran, it was even possible for an empire to form.

European observers in the 19th century, especially colonial officials whose job it was to watch over Islamic opposition movements, noticed this strong group solidarity. They noted that Sufi shaykhs and groups often supported resistance to European colonialization. One example is the famous Shamil in Daghestan, who organized resistance to the Russian conquest. In North Africa, there were the Sanusis and the amir 'Abd al-Qadir, who was a member of the Qadiris. The so-called *littérature de surveillance* produced by the colonial officials created the image of a dark conspiracy across an immense international network led by secretive Sufi shaykhs against European civilization. This literature, often based on the most unreliable sources, exerted a considerable influence on European scholarship.

In contemporary times, many Western-oriented Muslim reformers see dervish orders as a cause of weakness and decadence in the Muslim world. In Turkey, orders have been prohibited since 1925. For the so-called fundamentalists, such as the Wahhabis, who are dominant in Saudi Arabia, Sufism is an aberration of what they see as the true form of Islam. The Wahhabis view the veneration of shaykhs, an essential feature of the orders, as a form of idolatry, the suppression of which they consider to be pleasing to God. Consequently, Sufi orders are also forbidden in Saudi Arabia, and the Saudi regime spends sizable sums of money throughout the Islamic world to combat the influence of Sufi orders. Several orders have moved their center from post-revolutionary Iran to Western countries, especially England and America. The internal Sufi discussion concerning this double challenge by Western rationalism and Islamic fundamentalism has scarcely begun.

See also brotherhoods; shaykh, *pīr*

Further Reading

Julian Baldick, *Mystical Islam*, 1989; Richard Gramlich, *Die Wunder der Freunde Gottes*, 1987; Louis Massignon, *Essai sur les origines du lexique technique de la mystique musulmane*, 1955; Alexandre Popovic and Gilles Veinstein, *Les Voies d'Allah*, 1996; J. Spencer Trimingham, *The Sufi Orders in Islam*, 1971.

BERNDE RADTKE

al-Suhrawardi, Abu Hafs ʿUmar (ca. 1145–1234)

Shihab al-Din Abu Hafs 'Umar al-Suhrawardi was a celebrated 13th-century Sufi master of Baghdad who, in addition to directing a number of the city's endowed residential lodges for Sufis, was a popular preacher, jurist, prolific author, and court diplomat of the ambitious 34th Abbasid caliph Nasir (r. 1180–1225). Hailing from a Persian-speaking family of Shafi'i scholars and Sufis who had made a name for themselves in Baghdad, he eventually drew the attention of the caliph, who in 1183—probably acting on the influence of his mother, Zumurrud Khatun (d. 1202 or 1203)—installed him as director of a newly endowed Sufi lodge known as the Ribat al-Ma'muniyya. As he routinely did with a number of Baghdad's more prominent Sufis and 'ulama', the caliph would call upon Suhrawardi over the next 30 years to conduct no less than four diplomatic missions in support of his *al-da'wa al-hādiya* (guiding call), a wide-ranging and sophisticated religiopolitical campaign aimed at reasserting and revivifying the long since de jure authority of the Abbasid caliphs.

In 1192 Suhrawardi was sent to the strategically important Armenian town of Akhlat in order to secure the loyalty of its military governor, a strategy that the caliph had already employed to great effect upon his accession in 1180. Similarly, in 1207–8, he sent Suhrawardi to the Ayyubid courts of Syria and Egypt, where he not only delivered caliphal diplomas and robes of honor but also conveyed the ceremonial trousers (*sirwāl*) marking initiation into the caliph's newly centralized *futuwwa* (chivalric) order. A later mission to the camp of the rebellious Khwarazm Shah 'Ala' al-Din Muhammad (r. 1200–20) in 1217–18 proved less successful, but in 1221 Suhrawardi found a much friendlier reception at the court of the Seljuqs of Rum in Konya, where he ceremoniously presented the illustrious 'Ala' al-Din Kayqubad (r. 1219–37) with the caliphal tokens of investiture. Owing to the caliph's support, Suhrawardi succeeded toward the end of his life in managing at least five separate endowed Sufi lodges in Baghdad as well as drawing around himself a sizable group of often well-positioned associates, students, and disciples.

Replicating the practice of the Great Seljuqs, and in an effort to legitimate their rule, both the caliph and his competitors systematically drew upon the popular religious and moral authority held by urban Sufi masters and 'ulama' such as Suhrawardi, often to measurable effect. As but one figure in a much larger group of Sufis and 'ulama' whom the caliph drew upon in support of his grand political aims, Suhrawardi is significant not for any particular contribution to the caliph's program but rather as a particularly well-documented example of someone important to the public and political life of the age. Although recent research has shown that previous scholarship overstated Suhrawardi's personal role in the far-reaching political agenda of the caliph (as he was neither the caliph's court theologian nor did he systematically propagate a new theory of the caliphate based on its unification with Sufism and the *futuwwa*), the Sufi master was nonetheless vigorous in support of his patron. He publicly affirmed allegiance to the Abbasid caliphate as an article of faith and was keen to buttress the caliph's carefully crafted image as a member of the 'ulama' by programmatically quoting hadith transmitted on his authority. As evinced in a polemical text against students of Greek philosophy he wrote near the end of his life, the *Idalat al-'Iyan 'ala al-Burhan* (Directing the sight toward decisive proof), Suhrawardi extended this support to the caliph's successor, Mustansir (r. 1226–42), characterizing the new caliph as a fully actualized Sufi and the institution of the caliphate itself as a mystical link between God and the Muslim community at large.

See also Abbasids (750–1258); caliph, caliphate; chivalry; Sufism; 'ulama'

Further Reading

A. Hartmann, *an-Nasir li-Din Allah (1180–1225): Politik, Religion, Kultur in der späten Abbasidenzeit*, 1975; Erik S. Ohlander, *Sufism in an Age of Transition: 'Umar al-Suhrawardī and the Rise of the Islamic Mystical Brotherhoods*, 2008.

ERIK S. OHLANDER

suicide

Suicide (*qatl nafs*, *intiḥār*) is strictly prohibited in the Islamic tradition. The Qur'an is ambiguous on the matter: in 4:29, "do not kill your selves" may refer to infighting between believers, not suicide, and in 2:195, "make not your hands contribute to your destruction" does not necessarily refer to self-killing. Tradition (hadith), however, clearly condemns suicide as a grave sin. Suicide has always occurred in the Muslim world but has remained relatively rare. Contemporary Muslim populations have very low official suicide rates, and quantitative studies suggest that belief in Islam reduces suicide rates more than belief in any other major religion.

While suicide is universally condemned by Islamic legal authorities, self-sacrifice for the good of Islam may be praised as martyrdom. This ambiguity has generated debates throughout Islamic history over self-sacrificial behavior in combat. In classical times debates centered on *inghimās*, the storming of an enemy

target by an individual or small group at very high risk of death. Most medieval jurists condoned *inghimās* provided that certain conditions were met: the context must be one of legitimate jihad, the attacker's intentions must remain pure, and the attack must carry real military benefits. Irregular operations such as the assassinations by Azraqi Kharijis and Nizari Isma'ilis (known as the Assassins)—operations that usually involved the death of the attacker—were widely condemned.

Modern suicide bombings have revived this debate. Suicide bombing as a tactic was first introduced in the early 1980s by Shi'i militants in Lebanon. During the 1980s, Shi'i militants launched some 40 suicide bombings in Lebanon and Kuwait. The tactic was introduced to Sunnism in April 1993 by the Palestinian Islamist group Hamas, who, along with Palestinian Islamic Jihad, would launch close to 30 suicide bombings against Israel in the mid-1990s. Beginning in 2000, the number of attacks, perpetrating groups, and target countries all increased exponentially. Between 2000 and 2008, Islamist groups perpetrated around 1,500 suicide bombings, primarily in Palestine, Iraq, Afghanistan, and Pakistan.

The introduction of suicide tactics in the early 1980s was linked to the rise, in the previous decade, of Shi'i Islamism as articulated by clerics such as Ayatollah Khomeini, Muhammad Baqir al-Sadr, and Muhammad Husayn Fadlallah. Departing from traditional Shi'i quietism, these ideologues reinterpreted the martyrdom of the Prophet's grandson Husayn at Karbala as an ideal of self-sacrifice to be emulated in the modern world for the promotion of Islam. Revolutionary Iran promoted "martyrdom-seeking" (*istishhād*) as a virtue during the Iran-Iraq War, and the first modern "martyrdom-seeking operation" is said to have been a November 1980 attack on an Iraqi tank by a 13-year-old Iranian. Hamas's adoption of suicide bombings was directly inspired by the Lebanese group Hizbullah but also reflected the development of a Sunni Islamist discourse on martyrdom during the 1980s jihad in Afghanistan. Revolutionary Islamists in 1970s Egypt and Syria did not develop a suicide-martyrdom ideology; in fact, until the late 2000s, groups fighting Muslim regimes rarely undertook suicide operations. The causes of the growth in the 2000s remain a subject of debate; some scholars stress the role of non-Muslim military interventions in the Muslim world, others the spread of a cult of martyrdom, and yet others intergroup tactical learning.

Suicide bombing was initially more controversial in the Sunni world than in Shi'ism, where *istishhād* was sanctioned from the top of the clerical hierarchy. The Sunni debate, particularly intense in 1996 and 2002 following bombing waves in Israel, tended to pit Muslim Brotherhood ideologues (such as Yusuf al-Qaradawi) against official clergy in Egypt and Saudi Arabia. The second Palestinian intifada caused a clear shift in clerical as well as popular attitudes in favor of suicide bombings against Israel. Suicide bombings outside Israel are more controversial, especially since al-Qaeda attacks have resulted in substantial Muslim deaths and injuries.

In addition to the pragmatic argument that military asymmetry forces the weaker side to use irregular tactics, proponents of such attacks typically rely on three theological arguments. First, they say that the conditions for martyrdom are present, since the attacker's intention is pure and the tactic causes major damage, including instilling fear in the enemy's ranks. Second, they argue that Qur'an 4:29 is qualified by 4:30 ("whoever does this aggressively and unjustly, We will soon cast him into fire"), and that the classical story of the "People of the Ditch" (Q. 85:4–10), in which a believer instructed disbelievers how to kill him, in order to convince the latter of God's power, invalidates the distinction between direct and indirect self-killing. Third, they compare suicide bombings to *inghimās*. This involves a controversial interpretation of the Qur'an passage (Q. 9:111) where the phrase "they fight in Allah's way, so they slay and are slain" has been used by opponents to argue that the killing of the enemy must precede the death of the attacker, whereas in a suicide bombing the perpetrator dies before his victims.

See also jihad; martyrdom; terrorism

Further Reading

David Cook, *Martyrdom in Islam*, 2007; Bernard Kenneth Freamon, "Martyrdom, Suicide, and the Islamic Law of War: A Short Legal History," *Fordham International Law Journal* 27 (2003); Farhad Khosrokhavar, *Suicide Bombers, Allah's New Martyrs*, 2005; *Maghreb-Machrek*, no. 186 (2005); Assaf Moghadam, *The Globalization of Martyrdom: Al Qaeda, Salafi Jihad, and the Diffusion of Suicide Attacks*, 2008; Robert Pape, *Dying to Win: The Strategic Logic of Suicide Terrorism*, 2005; Franz Rosenthal, "On Suicide in Islam," *Journal of the American Oriental Society*, no. 66 (1946); David Jan Slavicek, "Deconstructing the Shariatic Justification of Suicide Bombings," *Studies in Conflict and Terrorism* 31, no. 6 (2008).

THOMAS HEGGHAMMER

Süleiman the Magnificent (1494–1566)

Süleiman the Magnificent was one of the most influential Ottoman sultans. His long reign (r. 1520–66), in terms of political imagination, falls into two distinct periods. The first, extending to roughly 1550, is dominated by a millenarian and messianic discourse as justification for universal monarchy. The second is characterized by the articulation and elaboration—institutional, cultural, and administrative—of a distinctively dynastic and Sunni Muslim imperial identity both within and without Ottoman borders.

The scene for the threats and crises that Süleiman faced in the first years following his accession was set by the brief but eventful reign of his father Selim (r. 1512–20). Selim established his reputation for martial ferocity by leading an army from Istanbul to Çaldıran in eastern Anatolia to confront and defeat the Safavid Shah Isma'il (r. 1501–24) in 1514. Isma'il's successful messianic claims,

in an Anatolia that the Ottomans did not yet control, rivaled Selim's own equally grandiose and messianic ambitions. In the following years (1515–17) Selim pursued his quest for recognition as the astrologically foretold and widely expected *ṣāḥib-qirān* (the Master of the Auspicious Conjunction and millennial world conqueror) by swiftly overrunning southeastern Anatolia, Syria, and Egypt. He advanced as far as Cairo, where the last Mamluk sultan was captured and executed.

Süleiman inherited the tremendous challenges represented by the simultaneous enormity and instability of his charismatic father's ideological legacy. He had first to establish both his personal prestige and a measure of actual authority over nominal dominions now twice the size of those Selim had inherited in 1512. After proving his political and martial credentials with the capture of Belgrade (1521) and Rhodes (1522), Süleiman elevated his own slave and confidant Ibrahim to the grand vizierate in 1523. For the next ten years Süleiman and the adherents to his cause pursued a program of self-consciously imperial expansion, based on the cultivation of a messianic image. A central theme of the prophetic literature current throughout the Mediterranean at this time was the capture of Rome and the recognition of Süleiman as the Last World (or Roman) Emperor of Christian and, latterly, Muslim apocalyptic tradition. The military high points of this program included the conquest of much of the Hungarian kingdom (1526); the siege of Vienna (1529); the German Campaign (Sefer-i Alaman, 1532), which sent Ottoman raiders into the Friuli and Carinthia; and the Campaign of the Two Iraqs (Sefer-i Irakeyn, 1533–36), which established direct Ottoman control from the northern Euphrates to the Persian Gulf.

Following Ibrahim Pasha's death (at Süleyman's command) in 1536, Süleiman's image as the uncontested *ṣāḥib-qirān* was ever more richly articulated. He was identified simultaneously as the renewer (*mujaddid*) of the tenth Islamic century, the 30th *quṭb al-aqṭāb* (Axis Mundi), the one awaited for at the end of history who would realize a single society over which perfect justice reigned. This aura of prophetic kingship, reuniting universal temporal and spiritual authority, secured Ottoman dynastic legitimacy and expressed claims to supremacy over non-Muslim rivals and to priority in the Islamic world.

After the mid-1540s this new imperial persona and program was increasingly defined with reference to Islamic and Hanafi identity. It was embodied further in the form of a more bureaucratic administrative and judicial apparatus supervising the application of both *kanun* (sultanic prerogative and decree) and shari'a. The Ottoman pairing of *kanun* and shari'a was informed at once by the dynastic experience and the particular realities of the Ottoman Empire. Within a single reign, a military conquest venture based in the Balkans, where a small and heterogeneous Muslim military elite controlled substantially non-Muslim populations, was transformed into an empire. Within imperial Ottoman society Muslims of various sectarian and legal affiliations constituted a majority, and increasingly well-defined, protected non-Muslim communities formed a plurality.

See also Ottomans (1299–1924)

Further Reading

Virginia H. Aksan and Daniel Goffman, eds., *The Early Modern Ottomans: Remapping the Empire*, 2007; Esin Atıl, *The Age of Sultan Süleyman the Magnificent*, 1987; Cornell Fleischer, *Bureaucrat and Intellectual in the Ottoman Empire: The Historian Mustafa Âli (1541–1600)*, 1986; Halil İnalcık and Cemal Kafadar, eds., *Süleymân the Second and His Time*, 1993; Metin Kunt and Christine Woodhead, eds., *Süleyman the Magnificent and His Age: The Ottoman Empire in the Early Modern World*, 1995; J. M. Rogers and R. M. Ward, *Süleyman the Magnificent*, 1988.

CORNELL FLEISCHER AND KAYA ŞAHİN

sultan

The word "sultan" in Arabic means, literally, "authority." The term appears in the Qur'an 37 times, both in the straightforward sense of authority or power over others (e.g., Q. 14:22; 17:33; 69:29) as well as in the sense of authentication, permission, or proof that a claim is true (e.g., Q. 27:21; 30:35; 37:157; 55:33), and in both cases is usually seen as granted by God. On seven occasions, "sultan" is something possessed by Moses (e.g., Q. 11:96: "We had indeed sent Moses with Our signs and a manifest authority"; similarly, Q. 23:45; 4:153; 28:35; 40:23; 44:19; 51:38). The term is never used in explicit personal attribution to any other apostolic figure in the Qur'an.

The Concretization of "Sultan" in the Early Islamic Period

With the collapse of the Abbasid caliphate, a process beginning in the mid-ninth century and completed in the first part of the tenth century, governing authority devolved upon a series of autonomous rulers, and, as caliphal authority devolved, so (more slowly) did the epithets associated with the caliphal position. By the late tenth century, the term "sultan" had begun to be applied as an appellation, not an official title, to various noncaliphal rulers; it was never used as a title on the coinage or on official inscriptions before the Seljuqs.

"Sultan" as a Title

The autonomous Sunni Muslim potentates who arose and arrogated power to themselves in the central caliphal lands from the mid-ninth century through the early 11th century were faced with a dilemma regarding the title they should adopt for themselves: mainstream Islamic law and theology at this time left no theoretical room for any sovereign ruler other than the caliph, and the Arabic term for king, *malik*, is a negative one in Islamic political parlance.

Thus most of the autonomous Sunni rulers of the ninth and much of the tenth century were known officially as amirs or commanders in order to maintain the pious fiction that their power and authority were delegated by the universal caliph, although the Buyids, for

instance, adopted the slightly more descriptive title *amīr al-umarā'* ("commander of the commanders," a parallel construction to the caliphal "commander of the faithful"). Terms based on the ancient Iranian titles of *shāh* or *pādishāh* (king) and *shāhānshāh* (king of kings) were also employed, both by the Buyids and other dynasties, but these Persian titles obviously lacked a Qur'anic resonance and aura of Islamic legitimation.

Many of the literary sources attribute to Mahmud of Ghazna (r. 998–1030) the first adoption of the title "sultan." It is probably more correct, however, to state that he is the first ruler named to whom this term is applied as a title, although he himself never employed it in self-reference. That is, before the mid-11th century this use of the term "sultan" as a title meaning "ruler" was limited to speech, literary works, and documents addressed to the ruler. Independent rulers did not at the time use "sultan" as a title when referring to themselves in the official titulature of coins and inscriptions, nor in official documents they issued. The Fatimid caliphs are also addressed by this epithet in a late tenth century-literary dedication.

The Adoption of the Title by the Seljuqs

A major change in the use of the term "sultan" came about in the mid-11th century with the coming of the Seljuq Turkmen dynasty, who conquered the Islamic heartlands and became the first Sunni dynasty to rule directly over the Abbasid caliphs. The Seljuqs soon made the epithet "sultan" into the official title of the ruler and the preferred one on their official coinage and inscriptions—an example that was followed shortly thereafter by their rivals the Ghaznavids, whose rule was now confined largely to India.

The Seljuqs apparently used this caliphal epithet as an official title in a deliberate fashion, in order to stake their claim to universal political authority as a counterpart to the caliph's universal but symbolic religious headship as imam of the Muslim ecumene. The Seljuq reordering of the Islamic world, signaled by their adoption of the title "sultan," heralded a new political reality: it was no longer possible to maintain that some powerful Sunni would one day restore rule to the caliph. Although they were unquestionably a Sunni dynasty, the Seljuqs made no pretense that they were simply one among the caliph's many commanders, holding delegated authority over a limited area at the caliph's behest and positing that the caliph would, at least theoretically, one day be freed from outside control.

Rather, the Seljuqs actually did "free" the caliphs from heterodox control—and, far from restoring rule to the caliph's hands, they promptly placed him under their own sway while arrogating to themselves all political power. Moreover, the Seljuq sultans openly aimed at a universal, independent, and dual caliphal-sultanic authority, in which the caliph was deprived of all temporal power and the sultans actually ruled. The title "sultan" in Seljuq hands, therefore, constituted a usurpation not only of the title but also of the substance of caliphal political authority; it signaled a claim to be the temporal counterpart to a caliphal role that was meant to be limited thenceforth purely to the spiritual sphere.

This constituted a decisive break with Islamic political theory up until that time and a de facto separation of the temporal and spiritual roles of government. This disturbing new political reality elicited in response the writing of a flurry of innovative works of political philosophy—most notably those of Juwayni (d. 1085), Ghazzali (d. 1111), and Fakhr al-Din al-Razi (d. 1209)—during the Seljuq era and shortly thereafter, all of which attempted to supply a theological rationale for the new division of power and authority in the Islamic lands. Historically, this division of authority and rule between the caliphate and sultanate resulted in perpetual tension and even outright hostility between the representatives of the two institutions and to the unremitting efforts of the Abbasid caliphs to reassert their political sway.

Given this new definition of the role of a sultan, it is unsurprising that the Seljuqs themselves used the term "sultan" only for princes of the blood. Since their empire was ruled as a family confederation, however, there were always numerous sultans at any given time. They distinguished therefore between "sultan" (in the sense of ruler or the embodiment of authority) or subordinate regional prince on the one hand and the great sultan or *Sulṭān al-mu'aẓẓam* (the sovereign ruler or the most powerful embodiment of authority) on the other.

The appropriation of erstwhile caliphal epithets by and for the Seljuqs was not limited to the term "sultan" but also extended to such titles as *ẓill Allāh fī al-arḍ* (the shadow of God on Earth) and *khalīfat Allāh* (God's deputy) to the sultans. This trend only accelerated after the extinction of the caliphate in the mid-13th century, reaching its logical culmination in the late 15th and early 16th centuries, when the title most closely associated with the caliphal office, *amīr al-mu'minīn* (Commander of the Faithful), was officially employed by Ottoman sultans such as Bayazid II and Süleiman I in formal inscriptions on public edifices, including, for instance, the Grand Mosque of Medina and the Jerusalem Citadel.

The Later Middle Ages and Modern Times

With the disintegration of Seljuq rule in the 12th century, the title "sultan" became universal, and by the 13th century, from Anatolia and Egypt to India, Central Asia, and Sumatra, it was used to denote any independent Muslim ruler. With the exception of the Mongol polities, which invariably preferred Turkic and Persian titles, most of the major late medieval Muslim principalities—including the Mamluk Sultanate of Egypt, the Delhi Sultanate, and the Ottoman Sultanate—employed this title for their governing figure. By the 16th century, it came to be used even in Shi'i Iran, where the Safavid and Qajar rulers, while preferring to be known by the Persian title of "shah," are occasionally called "sultan" on their coins. At the Western end of the Islamic world, the title was adopted for the first time, in the 18th century, by the rulers of Morocco.

In the 20th century, however, as a result of European influence and the desire to accrue prestige on the broader world stage, many Muslim rulers exchanged traditional Muslim titles such as amir, sultan, and sharif, for the previously eschewed "king." These include the current and former ruling dynasties of, for instance,

Egypt, Jordan, and Morocco, although one still finds a small handful of Muslim rulers, such as the sultans of Brunei and Oman, who continue to employ the more traditional Islamic term.

It is important to note that all the earlier meanings of the term, particularly both the abstract concept of "authority" and the impersonal reified use of "sultan" for "the authorities," at all times continued and still continue to coexist with the later personalized and titular significations.

See also Abbasids (750–1258); Delhi Sultanate (1206–1526); Ghazali (ca. 1058–1111); *ghāzī*; Ghaznavids (977–1086); Mamluks (1250–1517); Ottomans (1299–1924); Seljuqs (1055–1194); *shāhānshāh*

Further Reading

W. Barthold, "Caliph and Sultan," translated by N. S. Doniach, *The Islamic Quarterly* 7 (1963); Idem, *Turkestan Down to the Mongol Invasion*, translated by T. Minorsky and edited by C. E. Bosworth, 1968; C. E. Bosworth, "The Titulature of The Early Ghaznavids," *Oriens* 15 (1962); Patricia Crone, *Medieval Islamic Political Thought*, 2004; H.A.R. Gibb, "Some Considerations on the Sunni Theory of the Caliphate," in *Studies on the Civilization of Islam*, 1962; S. D. Goitein, "Attitudes towards Government in Islam and Judaism," in *Studies in Islamic History and Institutions*, 1966; Ann K. S. Lambton, *State and Government in Medieval Islam: An Introduction to the Study of Islamic Political Theory: The Jurists*, 1981; Bernard Lewis, *The Political Language of Islam*, 1988; Émile Tyan, *Institutions du droit public Musulman: II. Sultanat et califat*, 1956.

D. G. TOR

sunna

"Sunna" is a term of pre-Islamic origin for established custom, the approved practice handed down from the past. In Islam, sunna came to mean the practice of the Prophet, whose example all Muslims should follow: in effect, Islamic law. Initially, the Prophet's sunna was not sharply distinguished from that of his Companions and other righteous figures of the past, who were assumed to have acted as he did or in his spirit when they had innovated. The righteous figures in question seem to have included the caliphs, regarded as sources of sunna by virtue of their office, but their role had been rejected by 750, when the Umayyads were replaced by the Abbasids. Initially, the sunna was inferred from Qur'anic rulings (on the assumption that the Prophet and other moral exemplars had followed them); from the behavior of upright people; and from short reports, known as hadiths, recording their words or acts on a particular occasion. Such reports began to proliferate in the course of the first Islamic (*hijrī*) century, with reports from the Companions predominating. Their validity as sources for Islamic law was disputed. Muhammad b. Idris al-Shafi'i (d. 820) is usually held to have been the first major proponent of the belief that "sunna" meant the sunna of the Prophet as documented in the hadith alone, with reports about the Companions as a subsidiary source. This eventually came to be generally accepted. In the course of the century after Shafi'i's death, the reports from which the Prophet's sunna was known, by then circulating in very large numbers, were sifted and tested for authenticity on the basis of the chain of transmitters attached to them, and several collections of those deemed authentic were made from the mid-ninth century onward. Six of these became canonical. In principle, Islamic law is based on both the Qur'an and hadith, but in practice the hadith was by far the more important source. Though the word "sunna" came invariably to conjure up that of the Prophet, it also continued to be used in its old sense of established practice without reference to any particular authority, as when a particular practice was deemed to have "become sunna."

The concept of sunna as the practice of the Prophet documented in the hadith is fundamental to Sunnism. It concentrated all religious authority in one man in the past and effectively ruled out that supreme religious authority could ever be acquired by anyone in the present. Muhammad did have such authority, but only because his knowledge was of divine origin, and as the seal of the Prophet he was the last recipient of revelation. After his death, his message was preserved in the Qur'an and hadith, which were, and are, accessible to everyone. Religious authority rested on mastery of these two sources and associated disciplines, achieved in varying degrees by the scholars, who were in principle just learned laymen and who often disagreed. In practice, the scholars did come to be institutionally separate from the laity in the course of time, and something in the nature of a religious hierarchy also emerged. But though some scholars were more authoritative than others, no one person or body was empowered to sit in final judgment of what was or was not Islamic law and doctrine. Determining and interpreting the will of God was a cumulative endeavor fraught with uncertainty, and the only final arbiter was consensus (*ijmā'*), an entirely informal and retrospective mechanism consisting in the observation that the community had in practice acted in accordance with a particular rule for so long that the rule in question must count as vindicated. The Prophet is on record as having said that "my community will not agree on an error," and the ultimate arbiter of what did or did not count as Islamic was in fact the community. There could be no equivalent of papal authority in Sunni Islam and also no "Caesaropapism." This is still the case. Accordingly, Sunni Islam cannot quickly be made to turn around or change direction, nor does it have the vulnerability of communities dependent on a leadership defined by special descent, status, or office.

It is above all in its concept of religious authority that Sunni Islam differs from Shi'ism. Like all Muslims, Shi'is accept the sunna of the Prophet as authoritative, but they see their imams as continuing it as authorities in their own right, not just as mere transmitters of the hadith documenting the sunna. To Shi'is, the divine guidance mediated through a human being (prophet or

imam) could never be cut off. The Imamis eventually ruled that the Twelfth Imam had gone into occultation in 874, so that to them as to the Sunnis, religious authority came to rest on fallible scholarly learning, but by then they had developed a different corpus of the hadith and a different law. Both the Zaydis and the Isma'ilis continued to concentrate religious authority in imams in the here and now, with the proviso that there might be periods without such imams (or without such imams in the open) in between.

Even within Sunnism the classical concept of sunna was never unchallenged. Sufis claimed religious authority as saints endowed with supernatural powers rather than book learning, the value of which they sometimes rejected altogether. Scholars, too, might claim to be saints or, more drastically, to be the messiah (Mahdi), thereby endowing themselves with supreme authority that was not normally available. In modern times the very concept of the Prophet's sunna has become an object of debate, with much discussion of the authenticity of the hadith and even outright rejection of it in favor of exclusive reliance on the Qur'an. Some of the most influential thinkers in modern times have been laymen without scholarly training. But the classical distribution of religious authority still prevails.

See also hadith; al-Shafi'i, Muhammad b. Idris (767–820); Sunnism; 'ulama'

Further Reading

Daniel W. Brown, *Rethinking Tradition in Modern Islamic Thought*, 1996; Jonathan A. C. Brown, *The Canonization of al-Bukhārī and Muslim: The Formation and Function of the Sunnī Ḥadīth Canon*, 2007; Idem, *Hadith: Muhammad's Legacy in the Medieval and Modern World*, 2009; Patricia Crone, *Medieval Islamic Political Thought*, 2004; G.H.A. Juynboll, *The Authenticity of the Tradition Literature: Discussions in Modern Egypt*, 1969; Bernard G. Weiss, *The Spirit of Islamic Law*, 1998.

PATRICIA CRONE

Sunnism

Sunnism is the form of Islam to which the majority of contemporary Muslims (close to 90 percent) adhere. In formal terms Sunnism is defined by acceptance of the authoritative nature of the Prophet's sunna (paradigmatic behavior and beliefs) as transmitted through his Companions and by recognition of the first four caliphs (Abu Bakr, 'Umar b. al-Khattab, 'Uthman b. 'Affan, and 'Ali b. Abi Talib), drawn from the Companions, as legitimate caliphs and moral exemplars. By contrast, the Kharijis do not recognize the third and the fourth caliphs, and most forms of Shi'ism do not recognize the first three. The Khariji and Shi'i positions rendered all later caliphs illegitimate, a view once seen as tantamount to the entire community living in sin: a legitimate caliph was required for the performance of public religious duties such as the Friday prayer, the conduct of jihad, and the execution of certain punishments known as *ḥudūd*. The Sunnis preferred to differentiate between practical requirements and moral perfection and so adopted less utopian standards for legitimizing a claimant to the office of the caliph, but even these standards were difficult to enforce. The Sunnis thus chose to recognize anyone who seized power as the caliph as long as he was a Qurashi (a member of the tribe of the Prophet), partly to minimize bloodshed and partly to ensure that they would retain some moral hold on the state. Sunnis do not consider caliphs after the first four as moral exemplars, nor were their actions, executive proclamations, or decisions on points of law regarded as having any value as precedents, so their often reprobable behavior did not endanger Islamic norms.

The Sunnis tended to hold that all de facto holders of public power (initially caliphs, thereafter sultans and amirs) were to be obeyed, whether formally legitimate or not and regardless of their mode of government, however unjust, unless they violated God's commands. Resistance, according to the Sunni view, should be passive rather than armed; the martyrdom of individuals was preferable to the large-scale bloodshed and general instability that accompanied revolt. All Muslims eventually came to live under rulers who were technically illegitimate in terms of the stipulations laid down for the caliphate (or, as it is usually called in this context, the imamate). But the Sunnis went further than others in accommodating these rulers, and in so doing they made most of Islamic history their own.

Like other Muslims, however, they lived under unstable regimes, many of them established by the pastoralist tribes that formed a warlike base outside the cities or beyond the borders of the Muslim world. These tribesmen often seized power by invasion (e.g., the Almohads or Almoravids in Andalus, and the Seljuqs, Mongols, and Safavids in the east), or they supplied the bulk of soldiers for existing armies, as free men or slaves, usually monopolizing political and military offices as well, leaving only the bureaucracy and religious affairs in the control of the existing urban elites. Determined though the Sunnis were to domesticate all regimes (as long as they were Muslim) and make them serve the cause of Islam as best they could, their relationship with these regimes was balanced by both cultural and political alienation from them.

Historically the bearers of Sunnism are religious scholars who are in principle learned laymen rather than religious specialists marked off from the laity by special gifts or institutional affiliation, making for a dispersed pattern of religious authority. But keeping the community together is a fundamental Sunni value, and internal disagreement never reached the point of producing enduring schisms.

Religious scholars ('ulama') are authoritative only to the extent that they master the Qur'an and hadith (the mass of short reports recording aspects of the sunna), as studied and interpreted through the sciences devoted to them, most prominent among these being the study of the shari'a. It is their learning, and that alone, which sets the scholars apart from everyone else. In terms of legal doctrine, this means that the ultimate legal authority is vested in the Qur'an

and the hadith (both treated as revelation) rather than in an office or a person endowed with special sanctity, whether by descent or special grace, such as the Shi'i imam or holy men.

It was around 800 that the Qur'an and authenticated hadith reports came to be seen as the sole legitimate source of Islamic legal norms reflective of God's will. The theory is best exemplified in the thought of Shafi'i (d. 820). Although he was motivated primarily by the desire to overcome regionalism, his jurisprudential system denied the political ruler the ability to create Islamic law. Sunni scholars held that the ruler could issue administrative rules and other regulations, but he could not create legal institutions or norms that reflected the divine will. Authorized by his own ability to engage in competent interpretation (*ijtihād*), the ruler could, however, decide which legal rule the courts were to apply when juristic interpretation yielded several legitimate interpretations, as they usually did. In the past, many dynasties used this ability to favor a particular legal school (often the Hanafi).

The *Siyāsa Shar'iyya* Tradition

While Sunni religious scholars were more accommodating of de facto rulers than their Shi'i counterparts, the public law they taught was often impracticable and highly idealized. They made up for this by granting rulers wide authority to make discretionary rules for the sake of public order. The administrative and criminal law generated in this way was deemed to be merely instrumental, devoid of the moral authority of Islamic law. The 14th-century jurists Ibn Taymiyya and his student Ibn al-Qayyim, however, sought to place this law, and public policy in general, on a firmer moral footing and bring it into the purview of the shari'a by modifying some of the inflexible and impractical rules. The outcome was labeled *siyāsa shar'iyya*, or shari'a-oriented governance. Ibn Taymiyya and Ibn al-Qayyim hoped to engender greater cooperation between lay Muslims, religious scholars, and rulers by orienting all of them toward establishing a just society in conformity with a broader vision of the shari'a. *Siyāsa shar'iyya* thus does not represent a reluctant move to accommodate alien rulers but rather an attempt at further integration of society and political elites.

The Rise of the Activists

In the early 20th century, Sunnism saw an unprecedented form of politics: the mass political movement. This is perhaps best exemplified by the rise of the Muslim Brotherhood in Egypt, founded in the late 1920s, to national prominence during the events preceding and following the Egyptian Revolution of 1952. Abandoning the quietist attitude that had prevailed in much of the scholarly establishment even in the colonial period, and taking advantage of Sunnism's relative lack of formal authority, the Muslim Brotherhood refused to trade legitimacy for patronage by normalizing or accommodating the foreign, non-Muslim occupation of Egypt. Backed by laymen and led by one, Hasan al-Banna, they demanded an immediate end to British presence on Egyptian soil and at the very least a more public display of Islamic symbols and application of Islamic norms, if not the application of the shari'a as the law of the land.

In the aftermath of the end of formal colonial occupation in the late 1940s and 1950s, two Sunni thinkers emerged who were to exert an enormous influence on Islamic political thought: Mawdudi of Pakistan and Sayyid Qutb of Egypt. Both thinkers gave a more concrete form to the amorphous demands of movements such as the Muslim Brotherhood. Neither was a religious scholar by profession. Mawdudi, though trained in the Islamic sciences at an early age, was a journalist, while Qutb, who worked as a literary critic in his early life, had no formal religious training at all. Unlike medieval Sunni scholars, who tended to have a realistic conception of political possibilities, both thinkers had a utopian streak. Both sought to mobilize all Muslims for the transformation of Muslim society from its present state of Western-inspired decadence and corruption to a state of perfect individual and collective obedience to God's will. In their view, Muslim rulers must actively seek to uphold and implement the shari'a to count as legitimate: mere confessional membership in the Muslim community did not suffice. Mawdudi provided a more detailed account of a government that could count as Islamic than Qutb, who was content to assert that it was only through subservience to God and obedience to Him that human beings could break their servitude to one another. Both, however, stressed that sovereignty belonged to God alone and inferred that rulers whose government failed to accord with His will had to be actively resisted. Qutb advocated open rebellion; Mawdudi did not. Mawdudi further proposed that only God could legislate and that Islam required all Muslims to work actively for the establishment of an Islamic state. Such a state would have a representative institution charged with the function not of legislating but rather of discovering God's law and offering advice to the executive on the best way to implement it. The political programs of many Islamist movements of the 1960s through the 1990s were rooted in Mawdudi's and Qutb's ideas, but the most radical movements of the early 21st century have gone well beyond them by extending the legitimacy of revolt to attacks on the foreign powers that sustain the corrupt regimes of the postcolonial Muslim world. On the other hand, the vast majority of Sunni Islamist thinkers and political movements have categorically rejected Qutb's call for rebellion against illegitimate regimes. These movements tend either to adopt participation in the electoral process to acquire political power or else to channel their energies into the provision of social services for the poor. Recent Sunni Islamist thinkers have also moved away from the idea that belief in God's exclusive sovereignty excludes the possibility of democratic government. The popular religious scholar Yusuf al-Qaradawi, in fact, insisted that voting is a perfectly acceptable method for the Muslim community to decide issues relevant to their common good, specifically where there are historical differences of opinion in Islamic law.

See also consensus; hadith; *ijtihād* and *taqlīd*; jurisprudence; shari'a; sunna

Further Reading

Mohammed Ayoob, *The Many Faces of Political Islam: Religion and Politics in the Muslim World*, 2007; Antony Black, *The History of*

Islamic Political Thought: From the Prophet to the Present, 2001; L. Carl Brown, *Religion and State*, 2000; Patricia Crone, *Medieval Islamic Political Thought*, 2004; Hamid Enayat, *Modern Islamic Political Thought*, 2001; Roxanne Leslie Euben and Muhammad Qasim Zaman, eds., *Princeton Readings in Islamist Thought: Texts and Contexts from al-Banna to Bin Laden*, 2009; Roy Jackson, *Mawlana Mawdudi and Political Islam: Authority and the Islamic State*, 2011.

MAIRAJ SYED

Syria

Syria (*Shām*, "the left-handed region," when one faces the rising sun in the Arab heartlands) falls naturally into an eastern mountain range along the Mediterranean with its major cities of Damascus and Aleppo and into a western section with a plain of steppes and deserts. Prior to the Muslim conquest, Syria had been a wealthy Roman province (64–300), with Antioch as its capital, and had continued to flourish in its golden age during the Byzantine period (300–634). Conquered by Muslim Arab forces in 635–36, Syria became the center of the Arab Empire under the Umayyad dynasty, with Damascus as its seat of government (658–750). During the first phase of the Abbasid Empire (750–945), with Baghdad as the seat of the caliph, Syria lost its central position to Iraq, became the principal Muslim province bordering on the Byzantine Empire to its north, was drawn into tribal conflicts between southern and northern Arabs, faced attempts by Muslim rulers of Egypt to extend their hegemony over its territory, and became the theater of competing Sunni-Shi'i influence. During the second phase of Abbasid rule (945–1258), Syria initially experienced a period of renaissance under local dynasties, foremost among them the Shi'i dynasty of the Hamdanids ruling from Aleppo, at the same time coming under the increasing influence of the Isma'ili Fatimid dynasty, which sought to extend itself from its base in Cairo, the capital of its counter-caliphate. With the Sunni revival patronized by the Turkic Seljuq sultans after their takeover of Baghdad in 1055, Syria soon came under the control of Seljuq *atabegs* (tutors), among them the Turkic Zengids of Aleppo and the Kurdish Ayyubids of Damascus. The Ayyubid Saladin brought Fatimid rule to an end in 1171 and defeated the Crusaders at Hattin in 1187, thereby restoring Jerusalem to Muslim control and firmly establishing Sunni rule over Syria.

At the time of the Mongol invasions of the Iranian lands that brought the Abbasid caliphate in Baghdad to its end in 1258, the Mamluks succeeded to the rich heritage of the Ayyubids in both Egypt and Syria after having definitively arrested the Mongol advance westward in 1260 at the Battle of 'Ayn Jalut. For its part, Syria flourished under Mamluk rule as a land of prosperity and a center of learning but was dealt a harsh blow by Tamerlane's invasion in 1401, which devastated Aleppo and Damascus. Thereafter Syria's culture declined, and the country was conquered in 1516 by the Ottoman Turks, who had established themselves in Anatolia and the Balkans and had conquered Constantinople in 1453, renaming it Istanbul and taking it as the capital of their expanding empire. Under the Ottomans, Syria continued for three centuries as a province ruled by Turkish pashas, administrators appointed by the Ottoman sultans, while much of local urban politics was dominated by the powerful influence of prominent Arab families, such as the 'Azms.

Over the centuries, Greater Syria (including the regions of today's Palestine, Lebanon, and Jordan) made significant contributions to Islamic culture and civilization out of proportion to its geography and population within the spectrum of the Muslim world. Umayyad caliphs built the first great monuments of Islamic architecture: the Dome of the Rock in Jerusalem and the Umayyad Mosque in Damascus. Syrian Nestorian Christians, foremost among them Hunayn b. Ishaq al-'Ibadi (d. 873), were the principal translators of Greek works of philosophy and science into Arabic. During Abbasid times the great Arab poets Mutanabbi (d. 965) and Ma'arri (d. 1058), the philosopher Farabi (d. 950), and the anthologist of Arabic poetry Abu al-Faraj al-Isfahani (d. 967) flourished in Aleppo. Ibn 'Asakir's (d. 1175) magisterial history of Damascus and Ibn al-'Arabi's (d. 1240) definitive synthesis of Sufi mysticism were both completed in Damascus. In Mamluk times Damascus produced a plethora of scholars, among them the ideologue Ibn Taymiyya (d. 1328), the historian Dhahabi (d. 1348), the biographer Safadi (d. 1363), and the exegete Ibn Kathir (d. 1373). In modern times the Academy of Damascus, founded in 1919, and the Arab Academy began an active literary production under the aegis of Arab nationalism.

During World War I the British wrested Syria from Ottoman control with the help of an Arab army, and the five provinces of Syria became a French mandate after the war; the French influence was more pervasive in the region of Mount Lebanon, and France accordingly declared it a separate Lebanese republic in 1926. A year prior, the People's Party was formed to work for Syrian independence and national unity. The outbreak of World War II prevented total independence from being realized, but with the departure of the last French soldiers in 1946, Syria gained full sovereignty and adopted a new civil code in 1949, replacing the Ottoman code of the *Mecelle*. After World War II and articulated in opposition to foreign rule, Arab nationalism emerged as the leading ideology and allowed Syrians of all confessions—Sunni, Shi'i, 'Alawi, Druze, and Christian—to unite against European powers whose colonial presence all over the globe was steadily eroding. This secular and nationalist trend, however, encountered the opposition of grassroots organizations, cultural institutions, and benevolent associations that had developed between the two world wars in several cities in Syria, characterized overall by a strong Islamist trend that sought to combat immoral foreign influence and propagate Salafi religious education. Two movements took the lead in Syrian society: the secularist and nationalist Ba'th Party and the traditionalist and Islamist Muslim Brotherhood. On the political front, military coups followed in rapid succession, one of which established a

brief union with Egypt in 1954 as the United Arab Republic. This was overturned in 1961, followed by a military coup in 1963 that firmly established Ba'thist military autocracy. Islamist uprisings in 1964 and 1973 were put down by force. The Syrian Arab Republic took part in the Six Day War in 1967, during which it lost the Golan Heights to Israel.

In 1970 Hafiz al-Assad, a military man and a Ba'thist belonging to the 'Alawi sect, seized power and was sworn in as president. Under his rule a progressive front of political parties was granted a semblance of political freedom, but power remained in the hands of the military and secret police. In 1973 Syria joined Egypt in a surprise attack on Israel in the so-called October War; in 1975 Syrian troops were dispatched to restore order during the Lebanese Civil War. In 1982 an Islamist uprising in Hama was ruthlessly quelled and Syrian troops clashed with the Israeli army in its invasion of Lebanon. The Ta'if Accords of 1989, drafted under Saudi and American patronage, legitimized the Syrian military presence in Lebanon, but Syria did not enter into a peace agreement with Israel, despite American support to this end. Assad died in 2001 and was succeeded as president of Syria by his son Bashar. The governments of France and the United States pushed for the withdrawal of Syrian troops from Lebanon by isolating Syria diplomatically. When the Lebanese prime minister Rafiq al-Hariri was assassinated in Beirut in 2005, suspicion turned to Syria as the instigator together with Hizbullah, the most influential Shi'i party of Lebanon. After a massive popular demonstration in Beirut on March 14, 2005, Syria withdrew its troops from Lebanon, and a UN resolution established an international tribunal to prosecute those responsible for Hariri's death. As of early 2011, Syria had begun to experience the first signs of popular protest for greater freedoms that had begun to shake the Arab Middle East since January of that year, in Tunisia and Egypt in particular.

The wave of unrest in the Arab Middle East that began in Tunisia and Egypt as the "Arab Spring" erupted in March 2011 in Dara'a in southern Syria and soon found its center in Homs, the third most populated city of the country. The regime of Bashar al-Assad decided to crack down on the uprising with brutal military force, while making empty promises of political reform. By December 2011, the regime, led by the minority 'Alawi constituency and supported by its military and elite security forces, faced a growing opposition of Sunnis, representing the majority of the people, who attempted to establish a Syrian National Council in exile and began to form a Free Civil Army, led by defectors from the Syrian military. The United States, the Arab League, and neighboring Turkey favored the opposition but were unwilling to be involved militarily, while Russia and China tried to keep the regime in place through diplomatic maneuvering. The insurgency also burst out in northwestern Syria, focused on the town of Idlib, but it did not engulf Aleppo or most of Damascus. By early 2012, the conflict had resulted in more than 9,000 dead and thousands displaced, many of them finding refuge in Turkey and Lebanon. Neighborhoods in Homs were violently destroyed, and many inhabitants of smaller towns and villages were driven out. The country appeared on the verge of a civil war but became locked in a stalemate between the overwhelming firepower of the regime and the determination of the unprepared and ill-equipped opposition. Efforts by the United Nations through a special envoy and its tentative six-point peace plan led to a precarious cease-fire that diminished the fighting but did not shift the regime. In April 2012, after much diplomatic haggling, a group of United Nations observers entered the country to monitor the cease-fire. Nevertheless, the threat of a severe humanitarian crisis remained as demonstrations and government shelling continued and violence flared up all over the country.

See also Abbasids (750–1258); Baghdad; Egypt; al-Farabi, Abu Nasr (ca. 878–950); Ibn Taymiyya (1263–1328); Jordan; Lebanon; Ottomans (1299–1924); Saladin (1138–93); Seljuqs (1055–1194); Tamerlane (1336–1405)

Further Reading

Umar F. Abd-Allah, *The Islamic Struggle in Syria*, 1983; J. F. Devlin, *Syria, Modern State in an Ancient Land*, 1983; Raymond A. Hinnebusch, *Authoritarian Power and State Formation in Ba'thist Syria*, 1990; Philip K. Hitti, *History of Syria*, 1951; Philip S. Khoury, *Syria and the French Mandate: The Politics of Arab Nationalism*, 1987; P. Seale, *The Struggle for Syria*, 1987; A. L. Tibawi, *A Modern History of Syria*, 1969.

GERHARD BOWERING

T

Tablighi Jama'at

Arguably the largest Islamic faith movement in the contemporary world, the Tablighi Jama'at (Jama'at al-Da'wa wa-l-Tabligh, "The Party of Preaching and Proselytizing") operates in many countries and has directly influenced the religious practice of millions of Sunni Muslims. According to the movement's teachings, all Muslims are encouraged to devote a minimum of one-tenth of their lives (2.5 hours per day, 3 days per month, and 40 days per year) to nurturing within themselves and calling other Muslims toward six qualities: certainty of belief in the Muslim profession of faith, timely prayer (salat) with concentration and devotion, a basic knowledge of the obligations of Islam combined with the remembrance of God, service to other Muslims, purification of intention, and "going out in the path of God" for the sake of *da'wa* (preaching, in this case to fellow Muslims). These six qualities are said to be derived from the lives of the Companions of the Prophet, and it is through their implementation that, according to believers, the Muslim community is expected to one day return to a proper Islamic order, which in turn would inspire much of the non-Muslim world to convert to Islam as well. In pursuit of these goals, ad hoc bands of itinerant Muslim preachers devote their own time and resources to the Tablighi cause, often traveling to distant and foreign lands "in the path of God" to revive their own faith and that of other wayward Muslims. The Jama'at's loosely defined global membership base is drawn from a broad array of ethnic and socioeconomic backgrounds and is largely filled by nonscholars, as *da'wa* to Muslims is seen as a form of "commanding right and forbidding wrong" and is thus an individual obligation and not simply the duty of a scholarly elite. Women may also participate in Tablighi activities, albeit under stricter guidelines and in the company of their husbands, fathers, or sons.

Both in the path of God and in a member's home, books on the virtues of devotional works (*faḍā'il*) form the primary manuals for daily piety. Arabic-speaking *jama'at*s are instructed to read from Imam Nawawi's (d. 1278) *Riyad al-Salihin* (Gardens of the righteous), while all other language groups rely on Muhammad Zakariyya al-Kandhalawi's (d. 1982) *Faza'il-i A'mal* (Merits of righteous deeds, originally *Tablighi Nisab* or "curriculum") in its original Urdu or in translation. Muhammad Yusuf al-Kandhalawi's (d. 1965) *Hayat al-Sahaba* (The lives of the Companions) also plays an instrumental role in inspiring the activities of Tablighi participants. The Tablighi leaders who guide the functioning of the movement, however, pass on much of their teachings through nonliterary means. All participants are encouraged to undertake, at least once in a lifetime, a four-month initiatory pilgrimage to the Indian subcontinent in order to learn Tablighi norms from their source.

The Tablighi Jama'at originated as an indirect response to the Hindu *shuddhi* movement of North India in the 1920s. Muhammad Ilyas (d. 1944), a scholar of the Deobandi reformist tradition, received a vision during his pilgrimage to Mecca in 1925–26 and returned to Delhi to redirect his late father's proselytizing activities among the semi-Islamized Meos of the Mewat region to the southwest of Delhi. In the few years before his death, Ilyas would develop a proselytizing methodology that has come to form the crux of the Tablighi *da'wa* principles. Working out of a mosque complex near the Nizamuddin shrine in Delhi that has remained the global Tablighi headquarters to this day, he attracted a devoted core of preachers numbering in the thousands. The Tablighi movement was next led by Muhammad Yusuf al-Kandhalawi, who shaped it into an international movement. Subsequently, under the leadership of In'am al-Hasan (d. 1995), control of the Jama'at shifted toward wealthy Gujarati merchants who were able to provide the capital for further global penetration. Since Hasan's death, Tablighi leadership around the world has generally moved toward a more decentralized consultative (*shūrā*) structure. Two secondary global headquarters exist today in Raiwind, Pakistan (near Lahore), and Dhaka, Bangladesh.

The Tablighi Jama'at remains nominally apolitical, though it has played some role in the Islamization of many Muslim societies and minority communities across the globe, sometimes with distinctly political repercussions.

See also Deobandis; preaching; quietism and activism; revival and reform; 'ulama'

Further Reading

Muhammad Khalid Masud, ed., *Travellers in Faith: Studies of the Tablighi Jama'at as a Transnational Islamic Movement for Faith Renewal*, 2000; Barbara D. Metcalf, "'Traditionalist' Islamic Activism: Deoband, Tablighis, and Talibs," *ISIM Papers*, no. 4 (2002); Sayyed Abul Hasan Ali Nadwi, *The Life and Mission of Maulana Muhammad Ilyas*, 1983; Yoginder Sikand, *The Origins and Development of the Tablighi Jama'at (1920–2000)*, 2002.

MATTHEW B. INGALLS

Taha, Mahmoud Mohamed (1909–85)

While Mahmoud Mohamed Taha founded and led a political party that worked toward the independence of Sudan, he devoted his life to leading his followers to a new understanding of Islam that had emerged from his own Sufi training. Taha essentially eschewed politics as he focused on his movement to redirect Muslims to the teachings of the Prophet Muhammad, but in a Sudan that had never experienced completely secular governance, Taha and his movement were frequently confronted with the political consequences of their beliefs.

Taha was born in 1909 in the Blue Nile village of Hijaleej, about 100 miles south of Khartoum. He was raised surrounded by the intense Sufi teaching atmosphere of Sudan's Gezira region, but he never affiliated himself with a particular sect. He received the best Western education a man in colonial Sudan could obtain, studying engineering at Gordon Memorial College, the precursor of the University of Khartoum. He found work in Sudan's growing railroad sector and also in the many agricultural schemes started by the British. He also joined the Graduates Congress, the Khartoum University alumni group that stimulated and organized much of Sudan's independence activity.

Sudan's struggle for independence from Anglo-Egyptian control was largely dominated by the Umma Party, followers of the 19th-century Mahdi, and the Democratic Unionist Party of the Khatami Sufi sect. The former sought to rule Sudan through the descendants of Muhammad Ahmad al-Mahdi, and the latter had close ties to Egypt. Taha wanted Sudan to be free and independent of these influences, and to that end he founded in the early 1940s the Republican Party, whose objective was to found a Republic of Sudan. Taha was elected president of the Republican Party at its first meeting, and the group quickly published its manifesto, "Say, This Is My Path!," which advocated party principles that spoke to Islamic ideals. Taha and several other party members were arrested by the colonial police for distributing pamphlets, becoming Sudan's first political prisoners. The group was released quickly, but Taha himself soon again ran afoul of colonial proscriptions. A woman was arrested near Taha's hometown for performing on her young daughter female circumcision, an ancient and non-Islamic practice that was still common throughout the Horn of Africa and Egypt but that had been banned by the British colonial authorities. Taha led a demonstration at the Hassaheisa jail where the woman was held; he was arrested and sentenced to a two-year term, under the impression that Taha was in support of female circumcision. Taha's point, however, which would become a cornerstone of his later movement's work, was that the British could not legislate Sudanese morality and that female circumcision would continue in Sudan until girls and women were given equal access to education.

Sudan achieved its independence on January 1, 1956, but Taha spent the 1950s formulating his New Islamic Mission, the religious movement that grew out of his political party. The movement was popularly known as the Republican Brotherhood, in recognition of its party roots, and most of Taha's early followers were members of his party.

Taha's postprison time in retreat generated the themes of his New Islamic Mission. He studied the Qur'an and came out with an understanding of the qualitative difference between the Meccan and Medinan verses of the Qur'an. The Medinan verses, he said, were meant for the unsettled society of the Medinan era and included much of the Qur'an's revelations about war, the obedience required of women to men, and strict social controls, while the Meccan verses, which contained the Prophet's own sunna, or personal conduct, were meant to be practiced by all humankind all the time, which Taha called Islam's "second message."

Taha spelled out this Islamic social philosophy in his best known book, *The Second Message of Islam* (1967, trans. 1987). Through the 1960s and 1970s he continued to lecture around the country and to attract a small group of men and women, known as the Republican Brothers and Sisters, to his teachings. He was taken to court or tried on charges related to "apostasy" over these two decades, and Taha emerged invigorated in each case. His small movement grew a little; his followers took on his writings and speeches, particularly after he was banned from speaking in public or publishing his work, and distributed about two million copies of Republican tracts all over Sudan, largely through individual sales.

When Sudan's president Ja'far al-Numayri declared his version of the shari'a as state policy in 1983, the Republican Brotherhood launched a public attack on these laws, considering them dangerous in a multireligious secular society. About 70 members of the group, including Taha and four women from the Republican Brothers and Sisters, were arrested in 1983 and were released about 18 months later. They immediately took to the streets again with a new pamphlet, and Taha and four of his followers were arrested on "apostasy" charges. The four followers were forced to denounce their leader on national television in early January 1985. Taha, who would not recant, was tried and convicted of apostasy. He was executed by hanging at the age of 76 on January 18, 1985, before a crowd of 10,000 onlookers. The Arab Human Rights Organization declared that day "Arab Human Rights Day."

See also excommunication; Sudan

Further Reading

Abdullahi An-Na'im, *Toward an Islamic Reformation*, 1990; Steve Howard, "Mahmoud Mohamed Taha: A Remarkable Teacher in Sudan," *Northeast African Studies* 10, no. 1 (1988); Idem, "Mahmoud Mohammed Taha and the Republican Brotherhood: Transforming Islamic Society," *Journal for Islamic Studies* 21 (2001); Mahmoud Mohamed Taha, *The Second Message of Islam*, translated by Abdullahi An-Na'im, 1987.

STEVE HOWARD

Taliban

The term *ṭālibān* is the Persian plural form of the Arabic word *ṭālib* (seeker or student). As a general term, *ṭālibān*, or its Arabic equivalents *ṭullāb* or *ṭalaba*, refers to madrasa students. Since 1994, Da Afghanistan da Talibano Islami Tahrik (Islamic Movement of Taliban of Afghanistan), or "Taliban," has become known internationally as the name chosen by a hitherto unknown group formed mainly from the ranks of the Afghan mujahidin—resistance groups fighting the Soviet forces and their proxy governments in Kabul from 1978 to 1992. As a political-military organization, the Taliban came to the scene of Afghan politics in Kandahar in 1994 with direct military and diplomatic support from Pakistan and was initially backed with financial and political support from Saudi Arabia. The original leaders and members of the Taliban claimed to be madrasa students from schools run mainly by Pakistan's Jamiat-Ulama-i Islam (Assembly of Islamic Clergy).

Consolidation of Power: 1994–96

The Taliban gained international notice in early November 1994 when the group freed a convoy of Pakistani trucks commandeered by a local Afghan mujahidin group; in the same month, they captured Kandahar. The Taliban became the de facto government of Afghanistan in September 1996 when it seized control of the Afghan capital, Kabul, ousting the nominal government headed by President Burhan al-Din Rabbani. Mulla Muhammad ʿUmar Mujahid, who had in April 1996 proclaimed himself *amīr al-mu'minīn* (Commander of the Faithful), became the ruler of Afghanistan. With the capture of Mazar-i Sharif, the last significant Afghan city not under its control, in May 1997, the Taliban was recognized by Pakistan, Saudi Arabia, and the United Arab Emirates as the legitimate ruler of Afghanistan. This transformed the internal structure of the Taliban movement from loose pockets of fighters led by a consultative council in which Mulla ʿUmar was first among equals, into a theocratic regime with power consolidated under one figure. The change of the Taliban's method of governance to a centralized, autocratic system is also attributed to the increasing ties between Mulla ʿUmar and al-Qaeda leadership. Al-Qaeda wanted to establish a presence in Afghanistan through access to and control over an identifiable group of leaders. Osama bin Laden had arrived in Jalalabad, Afghanistan, in 1996 before the Taliban had control of that city.

In August 1998, the bombings of two U.S. embassies in Africa by affiliates of Bin Laden, and the Taliban's refusal to surrender him, prompted the United States to launch cruise missile attacks on suspected terrorist camps in Afghanistan and to spearhead an international effort to isolate the Taliban through unilateral and UN sanctions. The fate of the leadership of the Taliban and al-Qaeda became interconnected while their strategies remained divided: the former were more concerned with internal affairs of Afghanistan while the latter concentrated on expanding its international reach.

Demise and Resurgence: 2001–10

The September 11, 2001, terrorist attacks in the United States were immediately attributed to al-Qaeda. The U.S.-led war of retaliation resulted in the removal of the Taliban government from power and the routing of al-Qaeda forces from Afghanistan. However, the majority of both organizations' leadership reached safe havens in neighboring Pakistan.

Beginning in 2002, insurgents opposed to the Western-backed government in Afghanistan began armed operations and propaganda campaigns. These insurgents, who formally referred to themselves as mujahidin, were popularly referred to as the Taliban. This neo-Taliban became increasingly active in the eastern and southern parts of Afghanistan and fed on the lack of coordination of foreign objectives and efforts in Afghanistan; profits from the uncontrolled narcotics trade; foreign financial support; and weakness, corruption, and, not infrequently, the absence of the Afghan government. Over the following years, it managed to become more than a menace, morphing into a full insurgency, with increasing reliance on suicide attacks and terror tactics.

The neo-Taliban is not a monolithic group, nor do all of its elements share a common vision for the future of Afghanistan. The insurgency consists of a loose unofficial alliance of the following: former Taliban leaders (known as the Quetta Shura Taliban); elements of pre-Taliban mujahidin leaders and commanders (mainly elements of Hizb-i Islami led by Gulbuddin Hekmatyar and loyalists of Jalal al-Din Haqqani, a former commander affiliated to Hizb-i Islami of Muhammad Yunus Khalis); al-Qaeda and other nonindigenous organizations; Pakistan-based Taliban offshoots such as Tahrik-i Taliban Pakistan; Pashtun political leaders sensing loss of power and legitimacy; narcocriminals; and opportunist warlords benefiting from lack of governance in their areas of operation. By 2010, from among these groups, the Quetta Shura of Taliban (in the south), Haqqani's network (in the southeast), and Hekmatyar's Hizb-i Islami (in the northeast) were the most militarily active elements and as a collective had become what is generally referred to as the Taliban.

The main demands of the neo-Taliban focus on the withdrawal of foreign forces from Afghanistan and the restoration of a stricter interpretation of Islam in that country. However, there is no coordinated position or vision for the future of the Afghan state or the fate of the political structure established after the 2001 defeat of the original Taliban regime, either within the Quetta-based Taliban itself or among the various active insurgents.

The strength of the insurgency in Afghanistan and the inability of the Afghan government to gain widespread national legitimacy forced elements of Kabul's power structure to look for peace with elements of the neo-Taliban movement as early as 2002. Afghanistan's international partners reluctantly joined the reintegration process leading to official meetings between elements of

the neo-Taliban and the Afghan government and including formal discussions between the Afghan government and members of Hekmatyar's Hizb-i Islami. These meetings increasingly resembled the talks from the 1990s to bring about a peaceful, shared system of governance for Afghanistan in which each Afghan party and its foreign patron jockeyed for more power. In 2010, NATO's International Security Assistance Force and its troop-contributing states sought an honorable exit strategy that would leave behind an Afghan government with at least minimal exercise of sovereignty over major urban centers of the country and some capability to prevent it from becoming an incubator for international terrorist organizations such as al-Qaeda. The neo-Taliban, for its part, seemed inclined to wait out the military phase of the international commitment in Afghanistan with aspirations to reemerge as a major political player a decade after its total defeat.

See also Afghanistan; Deobandis; madrasa; Mulla ʻUmar (b. 1959); Pakistan; al-Qaeda

Further Reading

Robert D. Crews and Amin Tarzi, eds., *The Taliban and the Crisis of Afghanistan*, 2008; Antonio Giustozzi, ed., *Decoding the New Taliban: Insights from the Afghan Field*, 2009; Ahmed Rashid, *Taliban: Militant Islam, Oil and Fundamentalism in Central Asia*, 2000; Abdul Salam Zaeef, *My Life with the Taliban*, edited by Alex Strick van Linschoten and Felix Kuehn, 2010.

AMIN TARZI

Tamerlane (1336–1405)

The last great nomadic conqueror to come out of the Central Asian steppe after Chingiz Khan (r. 1206–27), Tamerlane aimed to reestablish the vast Mongol Empire on a dual Chingizid and Sunni base of authority. He is remembered to this day as a figure of romance and horror, a supremely charismatic, erudite, and ferocious razer of cities who often built pyramids of the skulls of his victims. His name is properly Temür, a Turkic name meaning "iron"; such European forms as Tamerlane or Tamburlaine come from the Persian *Tīmūr-i Lang*, Timur the Lame, referring to battle wounds to his right arm and right leg sustained during a raid in his youth. Though his territorial conquests rivaled those of the Mongols, Temür styled himself only as amir, or commander, and *güregen*, or royal son-in-law, through his marriage to a princess of the Chingizid line, and ruled through a puppet khan of the Chaghatay; this political front was not continued under his descendants, who ruled as Timurid sultans in their own right.

Despite his illiteracy, Temür was an avid patron of learning and poetry, and Ibn Khaldun, who famously met Temür in Damascus, describes him as intelligent and fond of scholarly debates. In the course of his conquests he transported many scholars and artists to Samarkand and created a brilliant court there, with special attention to religious scholarship, monumental architecture, and historical writing; with this precedent, the long Timurid century in Iran (1370–1507) witnessed a cultural efflorescence under the patronage of Timurid rulers and princes. In creed Temür was a Sunni of the Seljuq brand, though with pronounced ʻAlid sympathies, and like the Mongol Ilkhanids he showed special deference to Sufi masters and included them in his retinue.

After rising to power within the nomadic confederation of the Ulus Chaghatay in Transoxiana, Temür embarked on a series of wide-ranging campaigns between 1382 and 1405. From his base in Transoxiana, with Samarkand as his capital, he succeeded in subjugating Iran, Iraq, Syria, and Anatolia to the west (including a major defeat of the Ottomans in 1402); the steppe of the Golden Horde and Russia to the north; and India to the south. He died on campaign against China. Yet he was an inefficient conqueror; most of his campaigns were undertaken for the sake of booty and to demonstrate his supremacy within the Islamic world, and he often had to resubjugate rebellious territories.

The government established by Temür continued the Seljuq and Ilkhanid pattern, with separate administrative spheres or *dīwān*s for the seminomadic Turkic amirs as military elite on the one hand and settled Persian bureaucrats on the other; the latter, termed the *dīwān-i aʻlā*, administered financial affairs, tax collection, and aspects of local government, among other responsibilities. True to its nomadic roots, the dominant Turkic component of Temür's government was constituted by his family and personal following whose loyalty attached to him directly and who in return received leading administrative offices in the new empire. Temür curbed the apparent arbitrariness of tribal politics and its tendency toward warfare with the administrative structures and imperial ideology he inherited from the Mongol Empire; his highly personal government was thus not without system but had the advantages of political fluidity and institutional confusion, with the ultimate basis of rule being consent. However, Temür bent this nomadic-imperial template to his own ends by subverting and realigning all political structure to sole dependency on his own person and destroying the existing tribal aristocracy. His death accordingly led to a long and debilitating succession struggle between his sons and their factions in which much of the vast territory he conquered was lost to Timurid control. Equally debilitating was the ideological crisis that emerged following Temür's death, which shook the uneasy marriage of Chingizid and Sunni principles of government appealing simultaneously to Mongol dynastic law (Yasa) and Islamic shariʻa. Nevertheless, during the 15th century this Perso-Islamic Turco-Mongol culture became entrenched in the Near East and at the beginning of the 16th century would give rise to the three great empires of the early modern era, Ottoman, Safavid, and Mughal.

See also Central Asia; China; Ibn Khaldun (1332–1406); India; Mughals (1526–1857); Ottomans (1299–1924); Safavids

(1501–1722); Seljuqs (1055–1194); shari'a; succession; sultan; Sunnism; Timurids (1370–1506)

Further Reading

Beatrice F. Manz, *The Rise and Rule of Tamerlane*, 1989; Justin Marozzi, *Tamerlane: Sword of Islam, Conqueror of the World*, 2004.

MATTHEW MELVIN-KOUSHKI

Tanzimat

The plural of the Arabic verbal noun *tanẓīm*, which means "arranging," "regulating," or "reforming," the term "Tanzimat" historically refers either to the Ottoman Gülhane Hatt-ı Hümayunu (Noble Edict of the Rose Chamber) of November 3, 1839, or to the era beginning with the announcement of this imperial decree and ending in 1871 or 1876. The edict, prepared by Grand Vizier Mustafa Reşid Pasha and issued by Sultan Abdülmecid (r. 1839–61), promised new laws that would guarantee the right to life and property, prohibit bribery, and regulate the levying of taxes and the conscription and service time of soldiers. The edict further pledged to enact legislation that would outlaw execution without trial, confiscation of property, and violations of personal chastity and honor. It also undertook to abolish tax farming and to establish an equitable draft system. The text of the decree draws inspiration from the 6th, 7th, 13th, and 17th articles of the French *Déclaration des Droits de l'Homme et du Citoyen*. There are also conspicuous similarities to the Virginia Bill of Rights of 1776. Accordingly, the proclamation may be viewed as the belated Ottoman response to the New Order that emerged in Europe in the wake of the American Independence and the French Revolution. It represents the culmination of the reform process begun under Sultan Mahmud II (d. 1839) and the launching point for a bold new program of change.

Codification of law, restructuring of institutions, centralization of government, and formation of a new state ideology were major components of the Tanzimat era. The regulation of life in the empire entailed the adoption of modified versions of Western (especially French) legal texts, such as the Ottoman penal code of 1858, which was adapted from the French penal code of 1810. One major exception was the *Majalla*—a comprehensive compendium of Hanafi *fiqh* (canonical jusriprudence)—which, along with other codifications, produced a dualism in the Ottoman legal system. New civil courts (*Niẓāmiye*) were established alongside the old shari'a courts, which continued to function. The *Majalla* coexisted with the new legal system inspired by the West within the new court system.

The Tanzimat era gave momentum to the radical reform of the bureaucracy begun by Sultan Mahmud II. By the 1870s, the Ottoman administrative structure closely resembled its European counterparts. In the process of implementing an ambitious program of top-down transformation, the Sublime Porte acquired unprecedented power at the expense of the court and the religious establishment, becoming the dominant force in Ottoman politics. Inspired by the Austrian prince Metternich, Ottoman statesmen such as 'Ali and Fu'ad Pashas established a bureaucratic dictatorship through which they administered the empire until 1871, when Sultan Abdülaziz (d. 1876) began to reclaim the powers of the court.

In an effort to reverse the fragmentation of the empire, the Tanzimat statesmen placed great emphasis on centralizing Ottoman administration. They crushed surviving local dynasts in Anatolia and Rumelia, reconquered remote and loosely held regions such as Yemen and 'Asir, obliged local Arab leaders in the Arabian peninsula to pledge allegiance to the sultan, and reestablished central government in areas under the control of local chieftains and notables in Albania and Kurdistan.

To increase the cohesiveness of their multinational empire in the age of nationalism, the reformers strove to create a new identity that superseded religious and ethnic divisions. Accordingly, they replaced the official ideology of the state, Islam, with a secular ideology, Ottomanism. As embodied in the Ottoman Law of Nationality of 1869, the new legal term "Ottoman" replaced the old distinction between Muslims and non-Muslims (*dhimmīs*). At the same time, the Tanzimat statesmen did not aspire to eliminate the traditional Ottoman *millets* (religious communities) entirely and instead attempted to reform them from within. First the Greek Orthodox (1862), then the Armenians of the Apostolic Church (1863), and finally the Jews (1865) received new organic regulations, which granted representation within religious communities. Finally in 1870, the state recognized the Bulgarians as an independent *millet* under the administration of an exarch.

The Tanzimat era produced drastic changes in the economic realm as well, which resulted in a policy of laissez-faire first embodied in the Anglo-Ottoman Commercial Treaty of 1838. The Tanzimat era abolished forced labor, afforded legal recognition to ownership of private land, monetarized the economy, dissolved the *timar* (fief) system definitively, and standardized tax collection. The official abrogation of tax farming following the issuance of the Noble Edict of the Rose Chamber proved less enduring, however, and the sharp decline in revenues compelled a swift return to this traditional practice in 1841–42.

Although some historians date the end of the Reforms era to the death of the great reformer Mehmed Emin Ali Pasha in 1871, the commonly accepted date is 1876, when Sultan Abdülhamid II promulgated the first Ottoman Constitution.

See also modernism; Ottomans (1299–1924)

Further Reading

Roderic Davison, *Reform in the Ottoman Empire, 1856–1876*, 1963; M. Şükrü Hanioğlu, *A Brief History of the Late Ottoman Empire*, 2008.

M. ŞÜKRÜ HANIOĞLU

al-Tawhidi, Abu Hayyan (ca. 950–1023)

Abu Hayyan al-Tawhidi, ʻAli b. Muhammad b. al-ʻAbbas, is one of the most accomplished and creative writers of Arabic classical prose in the medieval period. Born to a poor family, probably in Baghdad, in the early tenth century, he associated in his early life with Sufis and then became a professional manuscript copyist. His profession gave him close association with books and encouraged him to pursue higher education in the Arabic linguistic and religious sciences. This education, together with a burgeoning literary talent, made him aspire to improve his social position, and he thus traveled to Rayy (near modern Tehran) three separate times in 12 years (968–80), seeking the patronage of three of its successive, powerful viziers: Abu al-Fadl b. al-ʻAmid (d. 970), his son Abu al-Fath (d. 976), and al-Sahib b. ʻAbbad (d. 995). All his journeys were resounding failures that filled him with frustration and resentment and led him to write a book, *Akhlaq/Mathalib al-Wazirayn* (The slanders of the two viziers; published in Damascus, 1965), in which he exposed the vices of the three viziers he had encountered. Back in Baghdad, he finished a ten-volume literary anthology, *al-Basa'ir wa-l-Dhakha'ir* (Insights and treasures; Beirut, 1988), and, more importantly, added to his education a Greek dimension by attaching himself to a circle of Aristotelian philosophers, about whose discussions he wrote in yet another book, *al-Muqabasat* (Acquisitions; Baghdad, 1970). During this period, he finally attained literary and scholarly recognition from the vizier Ibn Saʻdan (d. 985), who made Abu Hayyan his private interlocutor, educator, and informant; Abu Hayyan's three-volume book *al-Imtaʻ wa-l-Mu'anasa* (Pleasure and enjoyment; Cairo, 1939–44) is a record of his conversations with the vizier. After the vizier's death, and still poor, Abu Hayyan possibly sought patronage in Shiraz, but no success is recorded there. In his 80s, he wrote a book on friendship, his *al-Sadaqa wa-l-Sadiq* (On friensdhip and friends; Damascus, 1964), in which he complained bitterly about his lack of friends and persistent destitution, and another book, *al-Isharat al-Ilahiyya* (Divine intimations; Beirut, 1973), in which he addressed God with meditative pieces in a pronounced Sufi vein. In 1010, he burned his books and wrote a poignant letter describing the forbidding existential circumstances that had led him to undertake that heinous act. He died in Shiraz 14 years later in 1023, leaving behind the 6 books mentioned above, along with 6 additional books and 10 letters and treatises, some of which have not survived and are known to us by title or citation.

Abu Hayyan's contribution to Islamic political thought is to be culled not only from a letter of advice he wrote to Ibn Saʻdan (included in his *Imtaʻ*) but also from almost all his works, where his political opinions are scattered, and from his experience as a political observer as well as a client to several patrons and politicians. It is because of the latter aspect of his experience that this contribution centers on analyzing, uniquely from the point of view of intellectuals, the dilemma faced by intellectuals: whether to attach themselves to the politically powerful, knowing that they are more accomplished than the powerful. Theoretically, forging such attachments by intellectuals is wrong, according to Abu Hayyan, given the religious, moral, and practical perils they pose to intellectuals. In the real world, however, intellectuals cannot but forge such attachments, because intellectuals are subject to the weaknesses of human nature, and they desire to put their knowledge into practice, spread their values among wide audiences, and earn sufficient prominence in society to protect themselves from the negative consequences of poverty and cynicism. These attachments must, however, be based on mutual respect between politicians and intellectuals, and politicians must give intellectuals complete freedom of expression and direct, unfiltered access to them and also allow them to participate in drawing state policy. In return, intellectuals must grant politicians access to their vast knowledge, help them bring to politics the precepts of religion, and act as intermediaries between them and the people. In the final analysis, a good politician is someone who knows how to recruit the right persons for his administration, who makes firmness and generosity the foundations of his rule, and who is kind to the common people, since it is he who holds the keys to the people's prosperity or decline.

See also Mirrors for Princes

Further Reading

Ihsan ʻAbbas, *Abu Hayyan al-Tawhidi*, 1956; Marc Bergé, *Pour un humanisme vécu: Abū Ḥayyān al-Tawḥīdī*, 1979; Wadad Kadi, "ʻAlāqat al-mufakkir bi-l-sultān al-siyāsī fī fikr Abī Ḥayyān al-Tawḥīdī," in *Studia Arabica et Islamica*, edited by Wadad Kadi, 1981; Eadem, "Abū Ḥayyān al-Tawḥīdī: A Sunni Voice in the Shīʻī Century," in *Culture and Memory in Medieval Islam, Essays in Honour of Wilferd Madelung*, edited by Farhad Daftary and Josef W. Meri, 2003.

WADAD KADI

taxation

The Islamic system of taxation represents an attempt to reconcile the actual practices of taxation with Islamic principles and to harmonize the potential dissonance between administrative and religious concerns.

During the time of Muhammad, there was no established system of taxation. The community's income was based on ad hoc support for specific purposes, on donations, and on part of the booty from raids. In addition, an alms tax (zakat or *ṣadaqa*) was levied on Muslims, while subdued tribes or communities had to pay a tribute called *jizya*. With the early Islamic conquests, the situation changed. The Muslims concluded treaties of submission with conquered cities, which varied widely with respect to the taxes or tributes to be

paid. They also inherited the elaborate tax systems of the Byzantine and the Sasanian empires and at first relied on the same personnel and the same administrative procedures in collecting the taxes. The diversity and heterogeneity of these systems accounts for many discrepancies in the legal rulings and in the use of technical terms in the literature on taxation.

From the eighth century onward, jurists made various attempts to develop an Islamic concept of taxation based on the Qur'an and the examples set by the Prophet Muhammad and the first caliphs. Although the jurists disagreed in many details, the theoretical framework of the classical taxation system is rather uniform, relying on a more or less fixed corpus of scriptural sources. This theoretical framework did not change fundamentally in the centuries to come, although it did not comply with the fragmented practice of actual taxation.

The development of an Islamic tax system can also be interpreted as the emancipation of legal thinking from the constraints of practical politics. While in early Islamic times rulers did not face serious religious opposition when they fixed taxes, scholars now reduced the religiously sanctioned options of raising taxes or imposing new ones. Although numerous taxes and customs duties were levied, they were mostly disapproved of by the jurists. It was only in Ottoman times that the rulers succeeded in controlling the legal community more effectively and therefore received religious sanction for their fiscal measures.

The Islamic laws of taxation are based on the legal status of the taxable land, on the one hand, and on the communal or religious identity of the taxpayer, on the other hand. All Muslims were liable to an alms tax on a specified part of their property. Non-Muslims under Islamic dominion (*dhimmīs*) had to pay a poll tax (called *jizya* like the tribute of earlier time) of a fixed amount. The land tax (*kharāj*), which accounted for the largest part of the state revenue, was at first imposed only on non-Muslims but was soon considered to be incumbent on the land and therefore due on Muslims as well.

The various taxes were different in character and served different purposes. Zakat is a religious duty—in fact, one of the Five Pillars of Islam—and served the purification of the giver. It was meant to contribute to the reduction of social and economic disparities, and it was to be paid even if there was no legitimate government to collect it. *Jizya*, on the other hand, was intended, among other things, to demonstrate the inferior status of the *dhimmī*. Other taxes, like the land tax, did not have specific religious connotations.

At least in theory, the revenues from the different taxes were to be kept in separate accounts, since there were religious sanctions as to their respective distribution. During classical times, the military and the palace administration accounted for most of the expenditures of the state. As the revenues depended heavily on the amount of land to be taxed, both territorial losses and the practice of assigning land to military leaders decreased revenues and made tax assessment a difficult task.

In modern times, some Muslim states attempted to reintroduce an Islamic system of taxation; mostly this involved the levying of zakat in addition to other, not specifically Islamic taxes, such as income tax. The revenue from zakat usually amounted only to a small percentage of the total tax revenue. In contemporary Islamist discourses, writers call for the reintroduction of zakat for Muslims and the imposition of *jizya* for non-Muslims.

See also economic theory; *jizya*

Further Reading

Abu 'Ubayd al-Qasim b. Sallam, *The Book of Revenue* (*Kitāb al-Amwāl*), translated by Imran Ahsan Khan Nyazee, 2002; Nicolas Aghnides, *Mohammedan Theories of Finance*, 1916; A. Ben Shemesh, *Taxation in Islam*, 3 vols., 1958–69; Daniel C. Dennet, *Conversion and the Poll Tax in Early Islam*, 1950; Baber Johansen, *The Islamic Law on Land Tax and Rent: The Peasants' Loss of Property Rights as Interpreted in the Hanafite Legal Literature of the Mamluk and Ottoman Periods*, 1988; Frede Lokkegaard, *Islamic Taxation in the Classical Period*, 1950; Abu al-Hasan al-Mawardi, *The Ordinances of Government* (*al-Aḥkām al-Sulṭāniyya w'al-Wilāyāt al-Dīniyya*), translated by Wafaa H. Wahba, 1996.

ANDREAS GÖRKE

terrorism

Terrorism is a politically charged concept with no commonly accepted definition. First used to describe state repression during the French revolution, the term later became associated with indiscriminate political violence by rebel groups and other nonstate actors. The label "terrorist" has pejorative connotations and is used by political actors, usually states, to delegitimize their militant opponents. Western legal definitions of terrorism were first formulated in the late 20th century and differ among countries. Social scientific definitions also vary but share three core criteria: that terrorism has *political* aims, targets *noncombatants*, and has a *communicative* dimension. Its symbiotic relationship with mass media distinguishes terrorism from other forms of political violence and makes it a fundamentally modern phenomenon.

Terrorism as such is not treated in the Islamic legal tradition. The root of the modern Arabic word for terrorism (*irhāb*) features in the Qur'an (8:60) in the general sense of "striking fear in the enemy," but *irhāb* never emerged as a distinct conception of warfare or as a legal category (although many contemporary Muslim states have Western-inspired antiterrorist legislation). However, the rich Islamic legal tradition on warfare considered certain forms of violent activism and certain military tactics as illegitimate.

Classical Muslim jurists distinguished, from a *jus ad bellum* (right to wage war) perspective, among three forms of violent activism: jihad (war against non-Muslims), *baghy* (rebellion against Muslim rulers; Q. 49:9), and *ḥirāba* (brigandry; Q. 5:33). Jihad was legitimate but subject to caliphal authorization or specific casus belli such as outside invasion.

Both *baghy* and *ḥirāba* were considered illegitimate, but only *ḥirāba* carried severe sanctions. Rebels (*bughāt*) of a certain number (*shawka*) with a reasonable cause (*ta'wīl*) should be stopped but not punished. *Ḥirāba* connoted senseless violence by small groups spreading fear in the general population (*al-mufsidūn fī al-arḍ*) and thus represents the Islamic legal notion closest to terrorism. Jurists often disagreed on the classification of specific militants, notably the late seventh-century Kharijis, as rebels or brigands. The name "Khariji" itself thus eventually became a general term for illegitimate militants with a meaning close to "terrorist."

Jurists also developed detailed guidelines for conduct in jihad (*jus in bello*). These rules reflected a concern for proportionality and discrimination and were analogous, though not identical, to those of the Western just war tradition. Fighters should not cause more bloodshed or material destruction than necessary for the achievement of their objective. They should use clean tactics and avoid killing noncombatants, as suggested by the prophetic tradition: "do not cheat or commit treachery, nor should you mutilate or kill children, women, or old men." Treaties should be respected and prisoners of war well treated until their fate was decided. Irregular tactics such as abductions, poisoning of water wells, arson, torture, and rape were condemned and associated with *ḥirāba*.

Not all these prohibitions were absolute, however. For certain situations, many medieval jurists approved of tactics that violated these principles. This included the use of indiscriminate weapons such as catapults against besieged cities or the launch of night raids in which low visibility put noncombatants at risk. Attacks on enemy armies that used Muslims as human shields were generally permitted. Deception (*khidā'*) was sanctioned if practiced upon non-Muslims who had broken truces. Most jurists (except Hanafis) allowed for the execution of male prisoners of war if the commander deemed it beneficial. The sanctioning of such tactics by at least some jurists, combined with their occasional use in the Prophet Muhammad's own campaigns, was later exploited by modern militants in their attempts to justify terrorist tactics.

Islamists were latecomers to the modern history of terrorism. Although the "secret apparatus" of the Egyptian Muslim Brotherhood had carried out bombings in the 1940s, terrorist activity by Islamists took substantial proportions only in the late 1970s, by which time secular militants such as the Palestinian Liberation Organization and the German Rote Armé Fraktion had established the principal methods associated with modern terrorism, such as bombings, hostage-takings, hijackings, and assassinations. However, Islamist terrorist activity steadily increased in frequency and brutality, and by the 2000s the majority of high-casualty attacks worldwide were undertaken by Islamists.

The modern history of Islamist terrorism began in Syria and Egypt in the 1970s, where militants conducted numerous attacks on government targets, including the successful assassination of Egyptian president Anwar Sadat in 1981. In the 1980s, Shi'i Hizbullah undertook spectacular suicide bombings and hostage takings against Westerners in Lebanon and elsewhere. The 1990s saw extensive use of terrorist tactics, notably by the Groupe Islamique Armé in Algeria, al-Gama'a al-Islamiyya in Egypt, Hamas in Israel, Abu Sayyaf in the Philippines, Lashkar-e-Taiba in Kashmir, and Lashkar-e Janghvi in Pakistan. In the 1990s, Sunni militancy globalized, first with Armed Islamic Group of Algeria (GIA) attacks against France, then with al-Qaeda's operations against America, which culminated with the attacks on September 11, 2001. In the 2000s, al-Qaeda and related groups launched mass-casualty suicide bombings across the globe, notably in Bali, Istanbul, Riyadh, Madrid, London, Amman, Sharm el-Sheikh, and Islamabad, but nowhere more than in post-2003 Iraq. The abduction and murder of the American journalist Daniel Pearl in Pakistan sparked a wave of hostage takings from 2002 onward, especially in Iraq. Chechen militants took mass hostages in a Moscow theater in 2002 and at a Beslan school in North Ossetia in 2004. Although Islamists have executed hostages, they rarely tortured, raped, or mutilated them. Islamists have not successfully used chemical, biological, nuclear, or radiological weapons, but al-Qaeda has declared its intention to use, and attempted to develop, such weapons. In 2003 the radical Saudi cleric Nasir al-Fahd issued a fatwa sanctioning their use against Western civilians.

Islamist militants usually reject the label "terrorist." Instead they view themselves as mujahidin engaged in a legitimate defensive jihad against unbelievers. They circumvent *jus ad bellum* restrictions by arguing that the urgency of the infidel threat and the absence of a caliphate abrogate the need for caliphal authorization and individualize the duty for jihad. In the cases where the enemy is Muslim, militants resort to excommunication (*takfīr*) and declare these Muslims infidel. *Jus in bello* principles are sidestepped in different ways. Civilians are denied noncombatant status because they vote, pay taxes, work for the government, or may be called to serve in the military. Radical rulings on human shields or on night raids are exploited to justify noncombatant collateral damage. Visas are not considered pledges of security because they are issued by illegitimate authorities. Suicide bombings are framed as martyrdom-seeking operations, not self-killing. Mass casualty attacks are justified as a proportional response to infidel killing and oppression of Muslims.

Some activists have nevertheless embraced the terrorist label. The Palestinian ideologue 'Abdallah 'Azzam (d. 1989) wrote, "If preparations for *jihād* are terrorism, then we are terrorists." With reference to the Qur'an (8:60), the Saudi cleric Hamud al-Shu'aybi (d. 2002) ruled terrorism a duty in jihad. The Syrian ideologue Abu Mus'ab al-Suri considered "the *jihād* of individual terrorism" a crucial strategic option for today's mujahidin. "*Irhābī*" and "terrorist" are common nicknames on radical Islamist discussion forums on the Internet.

The late 2000s saw a Muslim public backlash against terrorism, partly in reaction to high Muslim civilian casualties. Mainstream Islamic scholars began to articulate a legal discourse banning terrorism, and several radical ideologues called for more discriminate tactics. Polls showed that most Muslims denounced al-Qaeda's tactics as terrorism. Fewer Muslims, however, condemned mass-casualty attacks against Israeli civilians in the context of the Palestinian Israeli conflict.

See also Bin Laden, Osama (1957–2011); jihad; martyrdom; nonviolence; al-Qaeda; rebellion; violence

Further Reading

Khaled Abou El Fadl, *Rebellion and Violence in Islamic Law*, 2001; David Cook, *Understanding Jihad*, 2005; Bruce Hoffman, *Inside Terrorism*, 2006; Johannes Jansen, *The Neglected Duty: The Creed of Sadat's Assassins and Islamic Resurgence in the Middle East*, 1986; Gilles Kepel, *Jihad: The Trail of Political Islam*, 2003; Majid Khadduri, *War and Peace in the Law of Islam*, 1966; Barry Rubin and Judith C. Rubin, *Anti-American Terrorism and the Middle East: A Documentary Reader*, 2004; David Aaron Schwartz, "International Terrorism and Islamic Law," *Columbia Journal of Transnational Law* 29, no. 3 (1991).

THOMAS HEGGHAMMER

theocracy

Theocracy (divine rule, from Greek θεός/*theós* [God] and κρατεi/*kratia* [rule]) is a system of government in which religious and political authority are merged and which is ruled according to religious laws. The fact that the corresponding Arabic term *ḥukūma dīniyya* denotes "religious government" rather than "divine rule" reveals the limited applicability of notions of theocracy in various traditions of Islamic thought.

A defining opposition with reference to theocracy is that between imamate and kingship, between rule according to the limits laid down by God and one indifferent to any such limits. The following saying, addressed to the second caliph, 'Umar b. al-Khattab (d. 644), reveals this opposition: "A caliph only takes what is due and spends it where it is meant to be spent, whereas a king oppresses people by arbitrarily taking from some and giving to others." It is with reference to this understanding of just rule, based on sacred law, that invocations of the right of disobedience in early Islam may be understood. Religious law was seen as a check on political power. For instance, certain strands of Mu'tazili thought allowed for the right to disobey the ruler and to depose him when he broke the law. The Kharijis, like some Mu'tazilis, even preferred a non-Arab caliph on the grounds that, lacking strong tribal ties, he would be easier to depose than an Arab.

Religion as State Law in Islamic Political Thought

As a system of rule, theocracy requires some basic rules of government. Constitutional law, however, emanates neither historically nor conceptually from the schools of law (*madhhab*, pl. *madhāhib*) that emerged in the ninth century. Muslim scholars therefore have developed a variety of methodologies that derive from traditional Islamic roots for a basic law of the state. The Charter of Medina (ca. 624) is often portrayed as the first Islamic constitution. Shi'is also regard the rulings of the first Shi'i imam, 'Ali b. Abi Talib (d. 661), as important principles of rule. However, neither the Charter of Medina nor the principles of rule that 'Ali stipulated in his writings present blueprints for a theocracy.

In what is regarded as the classic Sunni treatment of the subject, the Shafi'i jurist Mawardi (d. 1058) in his treatise *al-Ahkam al-Sultaniyya* (The ordinances of government) postulates sovereignty on the basis of the Qur'an and the sunna. In this model of government, which Mawardi developed to justify and support Abbasid rule in the context of contending claims to rule by warlords in Egypt and Iraq, the caliph is installed by investiture (*bay'a*). He thereby relies on collective and formal acknowledgment on the part of the 'ulama' as well as the *ahl al-ḥall wa-l-'aqd* (those who loosen and bind). Here, too, the caliph must govern in the framework of, and with guidance from, religious law.

Whither Theocracy: The Empirical Relationship between State and Religion

Commonly held views about the unity of state and religion in Islam (*al-islām dīn wa-dawla*) are contested by scholars and must be qualified historically as the exception rather than the rule. Some date the separation of religion and state to the emergence of the class of 'ulama' from the ninth century onward. Possessing semi-autonomous sources of financial and social support frequently allowed the 'ulama' to maintain a degree of independence from the caliph. Others date the separation of state and religion to the time of the Buyid intervention in Baghdad in 945 that terminated the Abbasid caliph's dual role as the temporal and spiritual leader of the *umma* (community of believers).

The bifurcation of the legal system into shari'a and *maẓālim* courts (*dīwān al-maẓālim*, board of grievances) in early Abbasid times can be seen as solidifying separate realms of religion and state, as it created a separation of "religious" and nonreligious courts, implicitly acknowledged a source of law outside of the Qur'an and the sunna, and stipulated a limited application of religious law. The very concept of *siyāsa* (politics, government) indicates a realm of administration and generation of rules in areas where no jurisprudence could be derived from the Qur'an and the sunna.

Characteristically, in the Ottoman Empire, sultans made ordinances that were complements to shari'a regulations but were not equal and not superior to shari'a. As a political ethics, shari'a functioned here too as a limit on executive rule rather than as a constituent to theocratic government.

Theocracy and the Modern State

Departing from the tradition of shari'a as a political ethics limiting executive rule, the 20th century saw the rise of juristic theories of theocracy as a state based on Islamic law. Due to the absence of Islamic constitutional thought, such juristic theories of theocracy, proposed by Islamist thinkers from Sayyid Qutb to Hasan al-Banna and from Mawdudi to Ayatollah Khomeini, have all reverted to civil law types of legal systems in order to envision their Islamic states.

Even though ten Muslim-majority countries designated themselves "Islamic states" in 2010 (Afghanistan, Bahrain, Brunei, Iran, Maldives, Mauritania, Pakistan, Qatar, Saudi Arabia, and Yemen—comprising about 28 percent of the populations living in Muslim-majority states), strictly speaking none can be characterized as a theocracy, in that religious and political authority is not congruent (e.g., Saudi Arabia) or constitutional and republican elements limit religiopolitical authority (e.g., Iran). Indeed, the public law of the ten Islamic states incorporates numerous elements not specifically drawn from Islamic legal traditions. Dutch scholar Johannes Jansen consequently argues that it is not the reinterpretation of the Qur'an and the sunna that lies at the basis of theocratic formulations but the assumption that the Qur'an and the sunna have little to offer by way of constitutional law. Malcolm Kerr speaks here of the "empty spaces" in the sources, Konrad Dilger of the "silence of the legislator."

The public law of today's so-called Islamic states takes various forms. Saudi Arabia, which declares the Qur'an to be the country's constitution, has since 1992 adopted a Basic Regulation, placing quasiconstitutional limits on political authority. Political authority is primarily exercised by the king and the royal family, although the 'ulama' exercise legal authority by issuing fatwas on social and political matters and, following a strict Hanbali/Wahhabi tradition, by controlling shari'a courts.

The 1956 Constitution of Pakistan stipulated that no law shall be enacted that is repugnant to the injunctions of Islam as laid down in the Qur'an and the sunna. When a law was in conformity with the Qur'an and the sunna, the constitution allocated the decision-making power not to a council of religious scholars but to the National Assembly. The legal system was further Islamized when in 1980 military ruler Zia-ul-Haq decreed an Islamic legal code to be applied through shari'a courts. In 1991, the competitively elected National Assembly continued the Islamization process when passing a shari'a bill introduced by Nawaz Sharif's government.

A further case of a self-proclaimed Islamic state with yet another public law framework emerged in the late years of Ja'far Nimeiri's regime (1969–85) in Sudan, in alliance with the Sudanese Muslim Brothers led by Hasan al-Turabi. Passed as part of the emergency law of 1984, an Islamization project of the legal system was embarked upon that kept the existing public law framework largely intact and concentrated on Islamizing the criminal justice system by forming Islamic courts and applying *ḥudūd* punishments.

The 1979 Iranian Constitution provided perhaps the most ambitious project by creating a novel public law framework for an Islamic state by combining Shi'i concepts of government with republican traditions. Based on the Constitution of the French Fifth Republic (1958), the 1979 Iranian Constitution provides for a number of directly elected republican institutions, such as the presidency and the parliament, as well as the possibility of referenda as direct expressions of public will. Simultaneously, it also recognizes that the supreme leader (*rahbar*) has oversight over the three branches of power, requires of legislation to be "consistent with Islamic law" probed by a council of clerical and civil jurists (the "Guardian Council"), and recognizes divine sovereignty. As Asghar Schirazi, among others, has shown, the notion of the guardianship of the jurist (*wilāyat al-faqīh*) applied in the 1979 constitution constituted a radical reinterpretation of the conventional meaning of *wilāya* and thus a jurisprudential revolution in itself. Whereas in Ja'fari jurisprudence, *wilāya* had referred to the legal authority by the 'ulama' to act for orphans, the insane, and minor women who had no legal guardian, in the 1979 constitution this notion was expanded from the private to the public realm and narrowed from the collectivity of the 'ulama' to an individual: a high-ranking *faqīh*. This high-ranking *faqīh* would guard over and conciliate between the branches of power, command the army, and appoint the chief of the judiciary, among other matters. While the original constitution did not foresee a mechanism for constitutional reform, the amended constitution of 1989 invested the supreme leader with the initiating and certifying power of every constitutional amendment process and every referendum.

Beside the ten states designating themselves Islamic states, an additional 12 have chosen to declare Islam the official state religion, encompassing 30 percent of the population living in Muslim-majority states. Among these, the consequences for the status of religious law in the legal system vary from case to case. In some, it is limited to private law, and in particular family law, such as in Jordan and Malaysia. In other cases, the jurisdiction on the basis of religious law is broader, as in Yemen, where article 46 of the constitution provides judges with discretionary powers to interpret shari'a and apply punishments that may not necessarily be proscribed by positive law. Further, which institution is mandated to interpret the meaning and scope of religious law differs. In Egypt the role of interpreting the meaning of "shari'a" has fallen to the Supreme Constitutional Court, a body made up of judges typically not trained in Islamic law. In Pakistan the constitution specifically assigns this role to the Federal Shariat Court.

The juristic theory of shari'a poses fundamental challenges to legal reform and the accommodation of changing norms in jurisprudence. In Sunni-majority countries as well as in the Islamic Republic of Iran after 1988, the reform of codified Islamic law therefore often has been justified with reference to "public interest" (*maṣlaḥa 'āmma*). As a principle or method of law, *maṣlaḥa* derives its validity from the idea that the fundamental purpose of legislation is to secure the common good. In the classical view, *maṣlaḥa* applies only when the shari'a is silent on a given issue or when it can be proven that exigency requires the temporary suspension of certain legal practices prescribed by shari'a. For the doctrine of *maṣlaḥa* to be valid, the necessity should be reasonably certain; it should benefit the public at large, not only a certain segment of the population; it should not conflict with explicit or implicit Islamic ordinances; it should be rational and acceptable to people of sound intellect; and it should relieve or prevent hardship for the people. Expounding a different view, Khomeini, as the supreme leader of the Islamic Republic of Iran, decided in 1988 that the doctrine of *maṣlaḥa* permitted the temporary suspension

of the primary rulings of Islam in emergencies or conditions of overriding necessity. He thereby empowered his own office to unilaterally revoke Islamic law where it was perceived to be contrary to public interest. To determine public interest, Khomeini created the Expediency Discernment Council in 1988, which was written into the 1989 amendments to the constitution. This novel adoption of *maṣlaḥa*, hitherto rejected in Shi'i thought, as a legal principle justifying both the reform of the fundamental laws of the state and the suspension of legal practices prescribed by shari'a can be interpreted as the attempted prioritization in legislation of pragmatism over dogma, while still remaining, at least formally, in the juridical framework of an Islamic state.

See also democracy; government; secularism; shari'a

Further Reading

Patricia Crone, *God's Rule: Government and Islam, Six Centuries of Medieval Islamic Political Thought*, 2004; Konrad Dilger, "Das Schweigen des Gesetzgebers als Mittel der Rechtsfortbildung im Bereich des islamischen Rechts," in *Festschrift für H. R. Roemer. Die Islamische Welt zwischen Mittelalter und Neuzeit*, edited by Ulrich Haarmann and Peter Bachmann, 1979; Hans-Georg Ebert, "Tendenzen der Rechtsentwicklung," in *Der Islam in der Gegenwart*, edited by Werner Ende and Udo Steinbach, 1996; Muhammad Hashim Kamali, *Principles of Islamic Jurisprudence*, 1995; Malcolm Kerr, *Islamic Reform: The Political and Legal Theories of Muhammad 'Abduh and Rashid Rida*, 1966; Asghar Schirazi, *The Constitution of Iran: Politics and the State in the Islamic Republic*, 1998.

MIRJAM KÜNKLER

theology

Theology in Islam is defined equally by its reason-based dialectical method (*kalām*), from which its name derives (*'ilm al-kalām*), and by its topic of inquiry. It developed in response to the realities Muslims faced after the death of their prophet, when they came face to face with the intellectual and religious milieus of the newly conquered populations while at the same time grappling with problems of their own. The dialectical method they adopted had long been current in the Near East, where it was used above all in public disputations. The Muslims continued to debate many of the same questions, notably monotheism versus dualism, free will, cosmology, and the nature and limits of knowledge. One question, however, was quite new, engendered by the crisis of succession after Muhammad's death: who was entitled to the leadership of the community (*imāma*)? This question, which was highly divisive in both theological and political terms, in turn generated new questions regarding human-divine interaction, and some of these also had a political dimension. Thus the murder of 'Uthman b. 'Affan in 656 and 'Ali b. Abi Talib's acceptance of arbitration with Mu'awiya raised the question whether a grave sinner was still a member of the Muslim community or an unbeliever and what constituted faith. The solutions ranged from banishing a grave sinner from the community of believers (thus the Kharijis)—a position that would remain marginal in Muslim political thought—to accepting him or her as a full member on the grounds that faith did not include acts (thus the Murji'is, who prefigure Sunnism). The issue of free will and predestination acquired political relevance, too. The proponents of free will did not prevail in Sunnism, but the methods and questions they posed to those in power (the Umayyads) would have a lasting impact on the development of the doctrine of human action in that their positions posed the questions that the predestinarians had to answer before they could finalize their doctrine. Investigation into the nature of free will was part of the larger systematic inquiry into the nature of God and His attributes—in this particular case, His justice (rejected by all dualists, to whom a just God could not be a creator of evil)—that would later dominate theological inquiry. But God's attributes acquired political relevance again under the Abbasids in connection with the question of whether the Qur'an (God's speech) was preeternal or created in time. Even theodicy, epistemology, physics, and cosmology sometimes acquired political importance. Most theological problems were debated partly by reason-based *kalām* and partly by authority-based hadith (prophetic tradition), and the question of which of the two carried the greater weight was also a major issue. In the Islamicist literature, "theology" usually translates as *kalām*, however.

Theology and Orthodoxies

Although theology in the sense of *kalām* played a crucial role in the fashioning of Islamic doctrines, it largely disappeared as an independent science in Sunnism and survived, under substantial doctrinal restrictions, only in Twelver and Zaydi Shi'ism. The Sunnis opted instead for hadith-based traditionalism as a reliable source of their doctrines. In Shi'ism, the imam's authority allowed for a contained acceptance of theology, though not without the resistance of many Shi'i traditionalists.

The marginalization of *kalām* was a drawn-out process spanning the entire period from the early centuries to the dawn of the modern age. Hostility to theology had begun already in the eighth century, when the proto-Sunni traditionalists (*ahl al-ḥadīth*) opposed the doctrine of free will as represented by the Qadaris and later the Mu'tazilis, the latter being the most significant representatives of theology in Islamic history. In the ninth century, the traditionalists omitted hadith advocating free will from the canonical collections, which provided next to scripture the reservoir for their doctrinal positions. Their influence grew after the failure of Ma'mun's so-called inquisition (*miḥna*), which sought to impose not only the Jahmi and Mu'tazili doctrine that the Qur'an was created but also the method of reason-based theological argumentation for interpreting scripture. Traditionalism came to the fore in the 10th to 12th centuries, when it was supported by the Abbasid

caliph Qadir (d. 991, famed for issuing the Qadiri Creed) and thereafter by the Seljuqs, who used madrasas as an instrument for linking up with, and ensuring the support of, the Sunnis. Despite the wish of the traditionalists to dissociate themselves from theology as practiced by Mu'tazilis, however, there arose in the second part of the ninth century groups best exemplified by Abu al-Hasan al-Ash'ari (d. ca. 934), who created a Sunni traditionalist theology. Ash'ari theology (and also that of the Maturidis) generated a long fight within traditionalism (including Hanbalism), which frequently overlapped with important political moments, exemplified by the trials and careers of the traditionalists Ibn 'Aqil (d. 1119) and Ibn Taymiyya (d. 1328). The traditionalist theology affected a wide range of disciplines from Sufism (especially via the doctrine of the divine attributes) to Islamic philosophy and science, and its legacy continues to be felt.

Major elements of theology, specifically Mu'tazili theology, survived fully in Shi'ism, most importantly the doctrine of divine justice, but others were strongly circumscribed by the doctrine of the *imāma*, notably the doctrine of promise and threat (relating to the rewards and punishments of the afterlife) and the status of the grave sinner. It is to the Zaydi preservation of Mu'tazili manuscripts that we owe much of our knowledge about Mu'tazilis today.

See also Ahmad b. Hanbal (780–855); free will; inquisition; Kharijis; Murji'is; philosophy; Shi'ism; Sufism; Sunnism

Further Reading

Josef van Ess, *Theologie und Gesellschaft im 2. und 3. Jahrhundert Hidschra: Eine Geschichte des religiösen Denkens im frühen Islam*, 1997; Sabine Schmidtke, "Neuere Forschungen zur Mu'tazila unter Besonderer Berücksichtigung der Späteren Mu'tazila ab dem 4./10. Jahrhundert," *Arabica* 45, no. 4 (1998); Idem, *The Theology of al-'Allāma al-Ḥillī (d. 726/1325)*, 1991.

RACHA EL OMARI

Thousand and One Nights

The *Thousand and One Nights*, also known as the *Arabian Nights*, is a story collection, containing Indian, Persian, Greek, Arabic, and other elements and popularized in Europe through 18th- and 19th-century English and French translations. It is a perennial source of musical, dramatic, and cinematic adaptations. The earliest known Arabic manuscript of *Nights* dates to the ninth century, although Arabic authors identify the tales as Persian. The Persian tales, in turn, are evidently based on Sanskrit originals. Like other Arabic works in the Indo-Iranian tradition, notably the animal fables *Kalila and Dimna*, attributed to the sage Baydaba or Bidpai, *Nights* presents itself as a work of advice to kings. Its stories unfold in a world ruled by despots. The most important of these is King Shahriyar, who, betrayed by his wife, marries and executes one virgin after another. His murderous compulsion provides the pretext for the tales told by Shahrzad, the learned daughter of the king's vizier. After volunteering to marry the king, she saves her own life by telling stories and leaving them incomplete, thereby forcing him to spare her for another day. Her stories—or at least those that form the core of the collection—provide the king with object lessons in the use and abuse of power. Many stories in *Nights* feature brutal despots, among them the imaginary king Yunan, who wrongly executes the sage Duban and—in a denouement of great symbolic importance—is himself killed by the poison-soaked pages of a volume bequeathed to him by the sage. Kings are thus advised to heed their advisors and to submit to the lessons found in books. Not all the exemplary stories are negative: some feature (relatively) benevolent despots who—perhaps significantly—tend to be historical figures rather than mythical kings from far-off lands. The best known of these historical figures is the Abbasid caliph Harun al-Rashid (r. 786–809), who in the stories takes to the streets of Baghdad in disguise in order to examine the condition of his subjects. Typically, he is rescued from the ensuing predicaments by his resourceful vizier Ja'far al-Barmaki (also a historical figure, d. 803). After revealing himself as caliph, Rashid rewards the just and punishes the wicked. The motif of caliph as folk hero is present in tenth-century historical sources but in *Nights* apparently represents a later idealization of the early Abbasid period. This idealization was embraced by European readers, who pronounced themselves enamored of what the English poet Alfred, Lord Tennyson (d. 1892) called the "golden prime / of good Haroun Alraschid." To the extent that it tells tales of bad kings and offers good kings advice on how to do their job, *Nights*—or at least the core stories around which the collection grew—may be read as a criticism of the institution of monarchy. Yet the collection, which brings together stories from many times and places, should not be understood as providing an accurate account of political and social life in any particular premodern society. In modern times, the characters and situations of *Nights* have served the purpose of political allegory in several works of Arabic literature (e.g., Naguib Mahfouz's *Arabian Nights and Days*).

See also Abbasids (720–1258)

Further Reading

Husain Haddawy, *The Arabian Nights*, 1992; Robert Irwin, *The Arabian Nights: A Companion*, 2004; Muhsin Mahdi, *The Thousand and One Nights (Alf layla wa-layla) from the Earliest Known Sources*, vol. 1–3, 1984–95; Naguib Mahfouz, *Arabian Nights and Days*, translated by Denys Johnson-Davies, 1995; Alfred Tennyson, "Recollections of the Arabian Nights," in *Poems, Chiefly Lyrical*, 1830.

MICHAEL COOPERSON

Timurids (1370–1506)

Timurid political thought was shaped by an ideal combining Aristotelian ethics with the pre-Islamic "circle of justice." According to this the ruler depends on the army, which requires revenue; revenue is provided by the subjects, who depend on justice; justice is ensured by the ruler. The Timurids also honored the imperial ideologies of the Islamic caliphate and the Mongol Empire. Order in society was provided by an absolute ruler, sanctioned by God, governing through an administration divided into separate spheres—the men of the sword, largely Turco-Mongolian, and the men of the pen, mostly Persian bureaucrats. In practice the division between military and civilian, Persian and Turco-Mongolian, was less clear.

In his treatise *Akhlaq-i Muhsin* (The ethics of Muhsin; 1501–2) the Timurid scholar Husayn al-Wa'iz al-Kashifi, building on Nasir al-Din al-Tusi, presented the function of the ruler as the maintenance of justice—here meaning social order—keeping men in their proper places and curbing natural aggression. In practice, for city populations, a ruler's justice meant the promotion of economic welfare and security in return for taxation. Suffering under an oppressive or unsuccessful ruler, city notables might switch allegiance, and historians describe such action as reasonable.

When the Timurid founder Timur (Tamerlane, r. 1370–1405) rose to power, Chingizid rule had ended in Transoxiana and Iran, but in most regions power remained with Turco-Mongolian commanders loyal to both Islamic and Mongol traditions. Since Timur was not descended from Chingiz Khan, Mongol tradition did not permit him to assume the sovereign title "khan." He used the title amir (commander), ruled through a puppet khan, and increased his status by marrying into the Chingizid house. At the same time he gathered prominent 'ulama' at his court, honored Sufi shaykhs, and justified many campaigns as protection of the shari'a.

The end of the Abbasid caliphate and then of Chingizid rule encouraged experimentation with new ideologies and the rise of messianic movements like the Hurufis and the Nurbakhshis, which challenged existing rulers. Perhaps partly in response, the Timurids developed charismatic and religious claims. Timur emphasized his personal charisma, adopting the title *ṣāḥib-qirān* (Lord of the Auspicious Conjunction) and encouraging stories about his spiritual power. By the end of Timur's reign, the force of Chingizid legal tradition was declining and Timur did not replace his second puppet khan when he died circa 1402–3. His successor Shahrukh (1409–47) ruled without a khan and announced in some quarters that he was abrogating the Mongol dynastic code. Some of Shahrukh's historians referred to him as *mujaddid*, or centennial renewer of religion.

During the same period the Timurids elaborated their Chingizid genealogical ties, developing a new myth that increased the dynasty's separate prestige. Timur's ancestor Qarachar Barlas, a relative of Chingiz Khan, had been chief commander to Chingiz's son Chaghatay; he was now reported to have been Chaghatay's chief advisor and to have passed his position to his descendants. This myth reached its full development under Shahrukh. He and later Timurid rulers could now assume Islamic and Mongol sovereign titles previously reserved for the puppet khan, most notably that of sultan (sovereign ruler). Shahrukh was also referred to as *khaghan* (great khan) in contemporary histories, and used the term *khilāfat* (caliphate) on some coins. The Timurid synthesis of Islamic and Mongol traditions was appealing to later dynasties such as the Mughals, Safavids, and Uzbeks, and a number adopted elements of Timurid legitimation.

See also Mongols; Tamerlane (1336–1405); al-Tusi, Nasir al-Din (1201–74)

Further Reading

Shahzad Bashir, *Messianic Hopes and Mystical Visions: The Nūrbakhshīya between Medieval and Modern Islam*, 2003; Anne Broadbridge, *Kingship and Ideology in the Islamic and Mongol Worlds*, 2008; Beatrice Forbes Manz, *Power, Politics and Religion in Timurid Iran*, 2007; Maria Subtelny, "A Late Medieval Persian *Summa* on Ethics: Kashifi's *Akhlāq-i Muḥsinī*," *Iranian Studies* 36 no. 4 (2003); John E. Woods, "Tīmūr's Genealogy," in *Intellectual Studies on Islam: Essays Written in Honor of Martin B. Dickson, Professor of Persian Studies, Princeton University,* edited by Michel M. Mazzaoui and Vera B. Moreen, 1990.

BEATRICE FORBES MANZ

torture

Torture, the infliction of physical or psychological pain or suffering on a person in custody of the law for the purpose of extracting a confession, or for punishment, is traditionally seen as part of Islamic political and legal thought. It may be considered as the outcome of a political conception of justice and a judicial tradition centered on physical punishment as rehabilitation.

Classical Islamic penal law distinguishes between two categories of offenses: crimes against "the rights of God" punishable by the *ḥudūd*, or "limits," sentences specified in scriptural sources for fornication, calumny, banditry, burglary, and drinking alcohol and other crimes that arise out of transactions between individuals. The law sets high standards of proof for sentences against fornication or repeated theft and banditry. Nevertheless, stoning (lapidation) for adulterers, men or women, is a "fixed sentence," the application of which is unavoidable. Similarly, crucifixion can be meted out to bandits, although jurists disagree over whether it should occur before or after the death of the accused. Where offenses differ from

those covered by *ḥudūd*, they are punished according to *ta'zīr* (or chastisement) laws, which are left to the discretion of the ruler or the judge, usually the head of the police (*ṣāḥib al-shurṭa*), and thus open to arbitrariness. *Ta'zīr* sentences range from flogging and imprisonment to banishment but can also include the death penalty. Their extension to all criminal acts deemed inimical to public order, frequently for political reasons, has resulted in judicial torture, a preferred method of *siyāsa shar'iyya* (governance). Intentional wounding or murder is punished by *qiṣāṣ* law, comparable to private justice, which enables the victim or his kin to opt for retaliation instead of compensation.

Classical Muslim jurists evinced skepticism about the validity of torture as a method of proof. They argued that a judge can ascertain only the truthfulness of verbal testimony and not of facts, emphasized unconstrained and free testimony as guarantee of credibility, and insisted on the observance of formal procedure as a safeguard against arbitrariness. Nevertheless, recourse to judicial torture became routine from the end of the tenth century on as a result of changes in judicial practice, including a relaxation of rules of evidence, the vagaries of political power, and the blurring of functions between the judge (qadi), the head of the police, and the magistrate in charge of military justice (*qāḍī al-'askar*). Torture was also carried out extrajudicially by tax collectors, who frequently ordered individuals suspected of tax evasion to be exposed to the sun (with oil poured on their heads or jars suspended from their necks) or held in stress positions until payment was secured. The practice of *muṣādara*, or confiscation, institutionalized under the Abbasids, compelled public officials as well as rulers' political rivals, frequently with the use of torture, to divulge their (often) illegally obtained wealth for confiscation by the government. The *tannūr*, a machine comprised of a heated cylinder internally spiked with nails, invented by ninth-century vizier Ibn al-Zayyat (769–848), was one of the devices used against such officials. In spite of attempts at codifying penal law made by the Ottomans, recourse to torture did not diminish.

In the modern era, shari'a penal law has long been enforced in Saudi Arabia in accordance with a strict legal doctrine, as well as in Qatar. Under the influence of colonial rule, a number of countries, such as Algeria, Tunisia, Egypt, Jordan, and Syria, adopted Western-inspired penal codes and constitutions that prohibit torture. Nevertheless, torture frequently is used as a method of investigation by police and security services against political prisoners and persons of both sexes suspected of acts of terror and dissidence. Techniques of torture vary in degrees of sophistication but follow a pattern featuring sexual humiliation (including rape), physical and mental degradation, sensory deprivation, and disruption of psychological processes.

The emergence of faith-based political movements throughout the Muslim world beginning in the 1970s brought demands for a reinstitution of Islamic penal law as an assertion of political identity. Yemen, the United Arab Emirates, Iran, Libya, Sudan, Pakistan, and Northern Nigerian states adopted codified forms of the shari'a. Codification of Islamic penal law varies from country to country and frequently exacerbates inconsistencies inherent in the classical legal tradition. It has resulted in expansive definitions of offenses, selective fixing of *ta'zīr* sentences, lax rules of evidence, minors' criminal liability, and increased discretionary powers afforded to judges. Codified law enforces physical punishment and pain with various degrees of severity, as exemplified by public flogging, judicial cross amputation of the right hand and left foot (occasionally ordered under anesthesia or a physician's supervision), crucifixion, lapidation, and retaliation in cases of intentional homicide or wounding.

The use of torture, whether under shari'a law or modern penal code, violates the 1984 Geneva Convention against Torture and Other Cruel, Inhuman or Degrading Treatment or Punishment, to which these states (except the Islamic Republic of Iran) are signatories. It further contradicts conceptions of human rights and declarations formulated by the United Nations, as well as Islamic organizations.

Human rights organizations reported acts of collective torture in Jordan's Swaqa prison in August 2007 and abuse of capital punishment in the Islamic Republic of Iran (which also executes minors), Saudi Arabia, Iraq, Yemen, and Pakistan. Several countries, including Egypt, Jordan, Syria, and Morocco, also participated in a U.S.–sponsored program that transfers individuals suspected of acts of terror to friendly countries willing to use torture as a method of interrogation against them. Initiated in 1995 during the presidency of Bill Clinton, the program was expanded by President George W. Bush (2000–8) and retained by the Obama administration.

See also human rights; punishment; terrorism

Further Reading

Baber Johansen, "Vérité et Torture. Ius commune et droit musulman entre le Xe et XIIIe siècle," in *De la Violence*, edited by Françoise Héritier, 1996; Idem,"La découverte des choses qui parlent. La légalisation de la torture judiciaire en droit musulman (XIIIe–XIV siècles)," *Enquête* 7 (1998); Ann Elizabeth Mayer, *Islam and Human Rights: Tradition and Politics*, 4th ed., 2007; Rudolph Peters, *Crime and Punishment in Islamic Law: Theory and Practice from the Sixteenth to the Twentieth Century*, 2005.

MARNIA LAZREG

trade and commerce

Politics and trade have been closely intertwined in the Islamic world since the dawn of Islam. Perhaps the best known example of this connection is spelled out in the work of Montgomery Watt, who claimed that Mecca was the center of a vast trade hub across the Arabian Peninsula at the time of Muhammad. In this view, it was the social and moral disorder created by commercial wealth that facilitated the initial spread of Islam. Patricia Crone forcefully

argues against this thesis, suggesting that Meccan trade centered on humble goods, such as leather, clothing, and animals—not the types of goods that foster immense wealth or attract merchants from far away. It is clear, however, that the expansion of trade in the first few Islamic centuries was intimately tied to the growing power and stability provided by Islamic empires.

The Arab conquests of the seventh and eighth centuries, extending as far west as the Iberian Peninsula and North Africa and as far east as India, provided security and a unifying language and religion under which trade blossomed. This period is considered the Golden Age of Islam, and the success of trade was dependent on the rise of new Islamic polities. An agricultural revolution followed from the Arab conquests as a new set of crops and agricultural techniques were introduced, especially from India. The agricultural surplus and local agricultural trade that followed permitted the rapid growth of cities throughout the Islamic world. Likewise, the relative security provided by the Umayyads (661–750), Abbasids (750–1258), and Fatimids (909–1171) allowed for the unprecedented movement of people, ideas, and goods over huge areas. The flow of goods was extremely important to the development of cities and wealth in the early Islamic period. The importance of trade is perhaps best seen in the design of the Abbasid capital of Baghdad. It was located on the Tigris River and connected to the Euphrates River by canal, allowing shipments from the Mediterranean to be transported downstream toward the Persian Gulf and imports from India shipped upstream. Baghdad was constructed in a circular manner, with four gates leading outward to the major trading routes: Iran and Transoxiana in the northeast, Syria in the northwest, lower Mesopotamia in the southeast, and Egypt in the southwest. In part because of its role as a center of trade, Baghdad became one of the largest and most important cities in the world, with 500,000 to one million inhabitants. Many of the important Muslim cities in Persia and Central Asia, such as Nishapur, Samarkand, Tashkent, Kandahar, and Kabul, were depots on trade routes connecting Baghdad to China. Many of these cities existed before the Islamic conquest, while others such as Fustat, Qayrawan, Fez, and Tunis were the creation of the conquest or of later dynasties.

The caravans that traversed these trade routes were often extraordinarily large, employing numerous camels to carry goods over land. In the early Islamic period, the primary goods traded were spices, textiles, and glass from China; gold from Ethiopia; and slaves from Sudan and Ethiopia. In conjunction with these caravans, a bevy of financial instruments and arrangements arose to facilitate trade. Among the most important of these was the bill of exchange (*suftaja*), which allowed merchants to travel from one land to another without having to carry specie. The *suftaja* predated its important European counterpart by centuries. Other financial instruments created in the early Islamic period include transfers of debt (*ḥawāla*) and orders of payment (*ruq'a* or *sakk*). Trade was often financed through partnerships, structured according to Islamic law generally as sleeping partnerships (*muḍāraba*, or "mutual loan") or *'inān*, in which both partners invested some capital. Although direct lending at interest (*ribā*) was illegal, it was easy to circumvent antiusury laws through legal fictions or partnerships. Documented evidence suggests that direct lending at interest did prevail at certain times and places in the Ottoman Empire.

Beginning in the 13th and 14th centuries, the center of trade slowly moved from the Islamic world to Europe—and with it, political and economic power. Some of this relative decline in trade can be directly attributed to political authorities. For example, the Egyptian Mamluks were notorious for squeezing revenues out of the spice trade, hence encouraging merchants to find alternate routes. A huge problem for the Mamluks was finding ways to divert trade from the Far East to Europe through the Red Sea instead of overland through Central Asia or (eventually) around the southern tip of Africa. The broader shift was one from the Middle East to the Italian city-states, placing the Islamic world more in the role of the "periphery" than in centuries past. Differing reactions to this sea change between the Mamluks and the Ottomans were among the key factors determining Islamic political power in the late medieval and early modern periods. The Mamluks, who controlled the most powerful Islamic state between the fall of the Abbasids and the rise of the Ottomans in the 15th century, did not integrate themselves (at least, relative to the Ottomans) in the new patterns of world trade, instead turning inward. The Ottomans, on the other hand, readily accepted many of the new goods coming from Europe—including firearms and artillery—and were able to defeat the Safavids and Mamluks, taking control of much of the Middle East, North Africa, and the Balkan Peninsula for centuries.

As in earlier Islamic empires, the security and rule of law offered by the rapid rise of the Ottoman Empire was a boon to trade and among the primary reasons for the early expansion of wealth of the empire. Ottoman policy was specifically designed to nurture the merchant class. Unlike farmers, whose actions were highly regulated by the state, merchants were free to accumulate and invest as much capital (*māl*) as desired. Indeed, merchants were largely viewed favorably by political authorities and as such were accorded a privileged position. As the primary holders of ready money, merchants were used to make loans to the state, ensure revenues through customs charges, and act as agents and ambassadors. On the other hand, merchants and moneylenders often faced hostility from the broader population. This was especially true in the smaller cities, where guilds dominated production, which was primarily in local markets. Within the guilds, excessive profit was frowned upon, and merchants were frequently demonized as speculators who drove up the price of raw materials or hoarders who caused coinage shortages.

Trade played an important role in Ottoman relations with the West. Although the Ottomans were able to threaten Europe numerous times in the 15th and 16th centuries—getting as far west as the gates of Vienna—their power in relation to the European powers began to wane by the end of the 16th century as trade imbalances grew. Perhaps most famously, the weakened Ottomans allied themselves with the French and English (against their mutual enemy the Habsburgs of Austria and Spain) through trade agreements known as "capitulations," whereby the French and English were granted

the right to trade with reduced customs duties. The capitulations persisted for centuries and were symbolic of diminishing Ottoman power relative to Europe. By the end of the 18th century, it was clear that Europe was far in front politically and economically. Areas vital to Eurasian trade that had once been firmly in Islamic hands—such as intermediating Chinese-Indian and European spice and silk trades—were controlled by Europeans. The loss of the revenues associated with taxation of such trade greatly weakened the Ottoman Empire.

Enormous changes have occurred since the fall of the Ottoman Empire in the early 20th century. European nations attempted with varying levels of success to colonize much of the Islamic world, in many cases redrawing geopolitical boundaries. Yet trade still plays an extremely important role in the politics of the Islamic world. In the Middle East in particular, trade in oil has provided excessive wealth and has been used by some polities, such as Iran, to provide a level of stability in the face of an otherwise unpopular regime. A primary challenge of the 21st century for the oil-based economies of the Islamic world will be how they handle—both politically and economically—the worldwide transition away from oil as the essential fossil fuel and the immense political ramifications of this change.

See also economic theory; globalization

Further Reading

Patricia Crone, *Meccan Trade and the Rise of Islam*, 1987; Ronald Findlay and Kevin H. O'Rourke, *Power and Plenty: Trade, War, and the World Economy in the Second Millennium*, 2007; Albert Hourani, *A History of the Arab Peoples*, 1991; Halil İnalcık, "Capital Formation in the Ottoman Empire," *Journal of Economic History* 29, no. 1 (1969); Andrew W. Watson, *Agricultural Revolution in the Early Islamic World: The Diffusion of Crops and Farming Techniques 700–1100*, 1983; W. Montgomery Watt, *Muhammad at Mecca*, 1953.

JARED RUBIN

traditional political thought

In terms of political thought, as in so many other respects, Muslims today could be said to be bilingual. On the one hand, they speak the global political language of Western derivation marked by key concepts such as democracy, freedom, human rights, and gender equality; on the other hand, they still have their traditional political idiom, formed over 1,400 years of Islamic history and marked by concepts such as prophecy, imamate, and commanding right and forbidding wrong. The Islamic tradition is alien to most Western readers. What follows is an attempt to familiarize them with it to make it easier for them to follow the other entries in this volume.

The single most important difference between contemporary Western political thinking and the Islamic tradition is that contemporary thought focuses on freedom and rights whereas the Islamic tradition focuses on authority and duties. This separates contemporary political thought from that of all premodern societies, not just that of the Islamic world. Premodern political thought centered on authority and duties because government, law and order, and the agreeable forms of life that they make possible were precious goods that could not be taken for granted. How to maintain political unity, social stability, and collective welfare were more urgent problems than protecting the interests of minorities and individuals.

Islamic political thought is based on the assumption that humans are fundamentally antisocial animals constrained by their own needs to live in societies. By nature, it was said, human beings are given to the ruthless pursuit of their own interests at the cost of everyone else; without government the strong would eat the weak, and the social bonds required for reproduction and coexistence would unravel. In the European tradition this view is represented by Thomas Hobbes (d. 1679), who, writing at the time of the English Civil War, famously said that life in a state of nature would be "solitary, poor, nasty, brutish and short." Yet man was also a social (or political) animal, the Muslims said, using Aristotle's no less famous phrase. What they meant was that humans had to come together and collaborate so that they could engage in division of labor and satisfy their many diverse needs. Even to produce a loaf of bread required cooperation; nobody could satisfy all his or her needs on his or her own, and without communal life, nobody would be free to pursue higher aims. How then was it possible for political society to be established? According to Hobbes, the creation of political society required an agreement whereby people surrendered their sovereignty to a single individual, the king. This was also the Muslim view. But whereas Hobbes envisaged people as signing away their freedom to a human king, the Muslims held them to sign it away to God, the king of the universe. In other words, God solved the problem by sending a prophet bearing a divine law; those who accepted this law would form a community together, ruled by God as represented by the Prophet and his successors. God, an infinitely superior and impartial party, defined the rules of communal life. Vis-à-vis God humans had no freedom at all, but by following God's law, they were freed from the tyranny of other human beings.

Prophets

To the Muslims, the answer to the question of how authority was to be created thus lay in divine revelation. Religion was the key to the creation of political society, not in the sense that it should legitimate an existing power structure but rather in the sense that it could supply such a structure. This reflected their own historical experience, for the Muslim community had in fact been created by a prophet, Muhammad, who had preached to the Arabs and freed them from tribal anarchy by uniting them in allegiance to God and His law. It

also reflected an ancient tradition in the Near East, well known to Westerners from the case of Moses, who led his people out of Egypt at the command of God and founded the polity that was eventually to become the Davidic monarchy that lies at the heart of the Jewish political tradition.

More than anything else, it is probably this fusion of the religious and the political that makes Islamic political thought a closed book to modern Westerners, accustomed as they are to thinking of religion and politics as belonging in separate compartments. Their thinking also has long historical roots. Christianity grew up inside the Roman Empire as a religion that transcended ethnic, social, and political divisions. The Christians abandoned the Jewish political tradition, remembering Jesus as having said that His kingdom was not of this world; and as subjects of the Roman Empire they left government to Caesar. Later they converted Caesar to Christianity, took over the empire, and Christianized it: this was the closest they could get to fusing religion and politics. But the empire was still a structure originating outside Christianity, with a history stretching back into pagan times, and however entangled their jurisdictions became, state and church always remained distinct. This is what allowed for their gradual separation in modern times, and it is thanks to this separation that modern Westerners find it difficult to envisage politics as intrinsically religious: they always react by trying to separate the two, wondering whether this or that is *really* religious or *really* political or seeing the religious element as mere wrapping for secular aims. But Islam shares with secular belief systems such as nationalism or communism the feature that it can *define* political aims, not just legitimate them (though of course it can do that, too).

Religion serves to create authority because people defer to the divine. They throw themselves to the ground in fear and awe in encounters with God or angels; they go down on their knees and kiss the hands or feet of religious leaders such as the Pope or ayatollahs. A man of God can gather people around him without any need for armies and police; people come to him of their own accord, attracted by his sanctity, and directed by him, they can take political action. The reader who still finds it hard to envisage a prophet as a political leader could do worse than read Naguib Mahfouz's *Children of Gebelawi*, an allegorical novel about human history from the expulsion of paradise to the modern age set in the slums of Cairo. It brilliantly captures the prophets as political activists in the portraits of Moses and Muhammad, both very vivid, whereas that of Jesus is flat and lifeless: he was only a spiritual leader. Needless to say, the Muslims saw the prophets as spiritual figures, too; Muhammad, the object of immense devotion, was eventually to be elevated to a quasi-divine position in Sufism. But this was not meant as a denial of his political role. In the period after the Mongol invasions, holy men and leaders of Sufi orders also came to found states in the Middle East and North Africa; it is thanks to the leader of a Sufi order that Iran is a Shi'i country today. Holy men led the resistance to Western colonialism in several parts of the Muslim world as well.

Like everyone else, medieval Muslims took their own historical experience to be paradigmatic and so assumed that polities were normally founded by prophets bringing revealed law. (There had also been prophets of other kinds, but we can ignore them here.) When Plato and Aristotle were translated into Arabic, their Muslim readers understood their accounts of Greek lawgivers as descriptions of prophets. They thereby inaugurated a philosophical tradition of political thought that became highly influential in the Middle East among Muslims, Christians, and Jews alike and also came to play a role in medieval Europe via Jewish intermediaries. Muslim philosophers subscribed to the idea that all polities rested on religious law brought by a prophet. In the 14th century, two thinkers (Ibn Taymiyya and Ibn Khaldun) noted that they were wrong: it was perfectly possible to base a polity on man-made rather than revealed law, and many people had in fact done so, they observed. Eventually, this was to become all too well known, for the peoples in question included the Europeans, and it was when they rose to world dominance that the idea of a purely man-made law and political order had to be taken seriously. From a traditional Muslim point of view, it looked like a recipe for anarchy and oppression.

Caliphs and Imams

Having created authority by recourse to the concept of prophets, the Muslims faced the problem of how to maintain it when Muhammad died in Medina in 632. They reacted by establishing the caliphate or imamate. A caliph was a "deputy of God" (*khalīfat Allāh*), another direct representative of God on Earth; just as God and his subordinates, the angels, rule the created world, so the deputy and his subordinates, his governors, rule the part of humanity that has submitted to God. An imam is somebody whose example is to be followed in religious and moral matters; a prayer leader is an imam, for instance. Applied to the head of state, the term stressed his presumed moral perfection, the quality that caused others to follow him and entitled him to high office; in principle he was the most meritorious Muslim of his time (*al-afḍal*). Most Muslims held that the first caliphs in Medina had been such paragons of virtue. Having embarked on conquests, however, the caliphs came to preside over a huge empire that rapidly gave them political interests and personal tastes at variance with those of their subjects, and they were soon deemed undeserving of their office. The problems posed by morally flawed and increasingly tyrannical occupants of the caliphal office generated three civil wars between 656 and 750 and led to the emergence of the three main groups into which the Muslims are still divided: the Kharijis (now an insignificant minority represented only by the Ibadis); the Shi'is (Zaydis, Imamis, Isma'ilis and others, perhaps 10 percent of Muslims today); and the Sunnis (around 90 percent of Muslims today), a residual category formed around the scholars who called themselves *ahl al-sunna wa-l-jamā'a* and whom Western scholars usually call Traditionalists.

The First Civil War (656–61) was won by the Umayyads, who moved the capital from Medina to Syria. Both the Kharijis and the

Shi'is regarded the Umayyads as usurpers, but they fully accepted that the legitimate head of the community would be a caliph in the sense of deputy of God and imam, a moral exemplar endowed with overriding religious authority. They differed radically about everything else about him. According to the Kharijis, moral perfection was assessed by the community. Any free Muslim man might be deemed to possess it and so qualify for the highest office, but he had to be deposed if he lost his superior merit. It obviously would not be possible to run an empire on this basis. The Shi'is, on the other hand, took the view that moral perfection was to be found only in the Prophet's family, and the Imami Shi'is limited the pool of candidates to one particular line in which the imamate passed from father to son so that the identity of the true leader of the community was always known. This man was the true caliph in the here and now, endowed with overriding, indeed infallible, authority in matters of law and doctrine. He was never put to the test of actually having to govern, however, and in 874 the 12th of the line was deemed to have gone into hiding, from which he would not emerge until the end of times. To the Imami Shi'is, the imams had become more important as religious than as political figures. The imams kept their political role in Zaydi Shi'ism, but here as in Kharijism, they did so in a form incompatible with stable government. It was only on the tribal fringes that the Kharijis and the Zaydis enjoyed a measure of political success.

In effect, then, both the Kharijis and the Shi'is retained the ideal of morally perfect government by divorcing it from political reality. By contrast, the Traditionalists, eventually followed by the vast majority of Muslim thinkers, accepted that the head of state could not be morally perfect and that one had to look elsewhere for imams in the sense of paragons of virtue. Their solution was to redefine the nature of the caliphal office so as to detach religious guidance from it. God was still the ultimate source of all authority, but He had no direct representatives on Earth any more, they said; Muhammad was the last, and all authority now came from him, not directly from above. In their opinion the caliphal title stood for "successor of the messenger of God" (*khalīfat rasūl Allāh*), and this, they said, was the form in which the first caliph had adopted it. (In practice, the only caliphs to have used this version seem to be the early Abbasids, who adopted it along with the title of imams, not instead of it.) When Muhammad died, his political position had passed to the caliphs and his religious leadership to his Companions, the Traditionalists said; the latter had passed on their knowledge of what Muhammad had said and done to the religious scholars ('ulama').

A religious scholar was a person who had acquired knowledge (*'ilm*) of the Qur'an and the hadith, in other words, the reports of what Muhammad said or did on particular occasions. These were the primary sources of Islamic law and doctrine. The law (shari'a) on which the Muslim community was based was divine, not only in the sense of being in accordance with God's will but also in the sense of being actually given by Him. God had revealed His will in the Qur'an, His own words. But the Qur'an needed both interpretation and supplementation, and the question was who was authorized to provide it. The early caliphs apparently thought that they were, but they were overruled by the scholars, who held the key supplement to the Qur'an to be the hadith as expounded by themselves. With the victory of the scholars, Islamic law came to be a law elaborated by private scholars rather than the government, like Jewish law. The shari'a seeks to establish what is obligatory, allowed, and forbidden in the eyes of God and also what is morally preferable or disapproved within the category of the allowed. This is an endeavor full of uncertainty and disagreement, for although God's will is eternal and unchanging, every scholar is just a fallible human being, and scholarly interpretations differ. Some scholars are more learned and authoritative than others, but nobody can settle controversial questions on behalf of all. Every juristic decision is uncertain and provisional until it has been accepted by so many for so long that it counts as validated by consensus. Consensus is the ultimate authority, for although every scholar is individually fallible, collectively they cannot go wrong: "My community will never agree on an error," as the Prophet is believed to have said.

Where the Imami Shi'is concentrated religious authority in the imam, the Sunnis thus dispersed it in the community. When the Twelfth Imam went into hiding, much the same pattern came to prevail in Imami Shi'ism. The caliph was only the executor of the law; his legitimacy no longer rested on moral superiority but rather on his ability to cooperate with the scholars. Though he was to be replaced by rulers of other types and new religious leaders were to appear in the form of Sufis, this was essentially the division of labor that prevailed in the Sunni world until modern times.

Islamic history is punctuated by the periodic appearance of religious leaders who tried to concentrate religious authority in their persons again in order to introduce radical religiopolitical change. Most commonly, they would claim to be the Mahdi, the savior expected to appear at the end of times, but they might also cast themselves as the "renewer" (*mujaddid*) expected to appear in every century or claim a special relationship with God as Sufis; some even claimed prophetic status or divinity, though this put them beyond the pale. There were also attempts by political rulers to organize the religious scholars within their realm on a hierarchical basis, notably in the Ottoman Empire. Something in the nature of a hierarchy also developed in Shi'i Iran. But the dispersed pattern was the default mode, and in the Sunni world it still prevails.

Amirs, Kings, and Sultans

In 750 the Umayyad caliphs were replaced by the Abbasids, who were members of the Prophet's family (though not 'Alids) and who moved the capital from Syria to Iraq, where their dynasty survived until 1258. In practice, their power began to disintegrate already in the ninth century, when autonomous rulers took over the provinces and they themselves were reduced to mere puppets at the center. The new rulers used secular titles such as king, amir (governor), or sultan (power, authority), and since there were no

provisions in the religious law for wielders of power other than the caliph and his delegates, most of the new rulers tried to legitimate their position by seeking a letter of appointment from the caliph, acknowledging that all legitimate power came from him. In 1258, however, the Mongols conquered Baghdad and put the caliph to death without setting up another in his place. The succession of men who were both relatives of the Prophet and rulers of the community (*umma*) that the Prophet had founded thus came to an end. The Muslim world had long ceased to be a single political unit by then, but now it did not even have a single figurehead any more. For all that, the Muslims continued to feel that they lived in a single Muslim society.

In fact, a caliphate of sorts did survive, for the sultans of Mamluk Egypt (1250–1517) enthroned an Abbasid as caliph in Cairo, but this caliphate was both politically impotent and devoid of general recognition. Its significance lies mainly in the fact that when the Ottomans conquered Egypt in 1517, they claimed the caliphal title for themselves. By then the title was devalued currency, for many others had claimed it, too, often without fulfilling the legal requirement that the caliph must be a member of Muhammad's tribe (Quraysh). But though the Ottomans did not fulfill this requirement either, they came close to reuniting the Muslim world, and this, as well as their control of the holy cities of Mecca and Medina, made their claim to caliphal status meaningful. It came as a shock to many when Atatürk abolished the Ottoman caliphate in 1924. All rulers of the Islamic world today are either kings, amirs, sultans, or presidents, with the partial exception of Iran; there the head of state, ranking above the president, is simply called leader (*rahbar*), popularly "supreme leader," a new title coined in the Iranian Revolution of 1979. There are, however, still Muslims who dream of reestablishing the caliphate, associated as it is with the heyday of Islamic power.

Political Freedom

The early Muslims had a strong sense that Islam had arrived to free mankind not only from tribal anarchy but also from kings, meaning those who ruled in accordance with their own whims rather than God's dictates. ("King" was a term of abuse when contrasted with caliph or imam, though not otherwise.) When the conquests endowed the caliphs with imperial power, the Muslims accused them of "turning the caliphate into kingship" and vigorously resisted what they perceived as despotic rule. But three civil wars over less than a hundred years deprived most of them of their taste for activism. All rulers turned into kings, as some observed; fighting to replace one with another was too costly in terms of lives, general security, and Muslim solidarity to be worth it. What then were the alternatives? A rebel in eastern Iran in the 730s experimented with ideas of setting up an institution to control the local governor, a few thinkers around 800 held that it might be possible to do without a ruler altogether, and the Mu'tazili theologian Nazzam (d. ca. 845) thought that it might be best to replace the caliph with a federation of locally elected rulers. But nothing came of these ideas.

The Traditionalists around whom the Sunnis were formed held that it was best simply to tolerate tyranny while at the same time withdrawing as much of communal life as possible from the caliph's control. In their view even a morally flawed and oppressive ruler had to be obeyed as long it did not entail a violation of God's command. The ruler's moral status did not affect the law, they said (in disagreement with the Shi'is). Even a sinful ruler could lead the prayer or conduct holy war, and participation carried the same divine rewards as when they were led by a righteous imam. One was not to rebel, since the rightly guided nature of the community did not depend on the head of state, and keeping the community together was all important. The only remedies against oppressive rulers were hellfire sermons and books of advice designed to inculcate virtue. A great many of such were produced, but needless to say their effectiveness was limited.

The jurists writing in the 11th and 12th centuries did hold that a wrongful caliph could be deposed. There were even some who held that it was a religious duty to do so. But they did not specify who should determine when or on what grounds a caliph merited deposition or how his removal was to be effected. Those who had chosen him should remove him, they said, but this simply delegated the task to whoever wielded power and influence at the center at any given time. It was never suggested that the courts should play a role in the proceedings, and there were no other formal institutions, such as a privy council or parliament, to which the task could be assigned. When the caliph lost his power to upstart rulers, even the principle that the head of state could be deposed was abandoned. God raised them up, it was said, and God would raise up others in their stead if they sinned. There is nonetheless an interesting example of a local ruler by the name of Ahmad Khan being taken to court, deposed, and executed in Samarqand (now Uzbekistan) in 1095. The charge was a heresy so grave that it amounted to apostasy. Of this he was probably innocent, but he had been a terrible oppressor, and a conviction of apostasy was an effective way of securing his removal. Why the military leaders who formed part of the coalition against him did not simply assassinate him, the normal solution, is not clear, but it did not set a precedent.

Tyranny was bearable because large parts of life were not affected by the state at all. The main way in which the government made its presence felt was through taxation, here as elsewhere a heavy burden on the peasantry. It was also a constant bone of contention between rulers and scholars, for the scholars had elaborated the fiscal law of the shari'a in such a way that did not allow enough resources for the state in such a way that rulers were forced to impose additional taxes, which the scholars denounced as uncanonical (*maks*). The taxes went to finance the state apparatus, war, building projects, and cultural life, especially at the court. But schooling, educational training, funding, loans, health care, and the running of local affairs—all these and many other things now taken over or supervised by the state—were then in the hands of family, neighbors, friends, religious scholars, and local notables, with only intermittent attention by the government at best and often none at all. The closer

one came to the center of power, the more dangerous life became (while at the same time becoming vastly much more rewarding in material terms); a great many of those who rose to powerful positions came to a violent end. But though others certainly suffered from time to time, the main problem posed by government was not usually that it was oppressive but rather that it was arbitrary and inefficient. General insecurity and local oppressors were probably more of a problem to most than the tyranny of kings, though these factors are not easily separated.

The modern state brought higher levels of security, but it also assumed a far greater role in people's lives than was formerly the case, and in combination with modern means of communication and surveillance, this transformed the old-style tyrants into dictators of a new and more totalitarian kind.

Religious Freedom

In a society based on religious law, there evidently cannot be religious freedom in the modern sense that anybody is free to choose whatever religion (if any) that he or she prefers. What Muhammad had founded was a community of believers, not a territorial state, and a community of believers it remained, even though it was eventually divided into many states. There was no room in it for unbelievers.

It is nonetheless possible to speak of religious freedom in the Islamic world. The Muslims themselves never used the expression "religious freedom" until they learned it from the West; indeed, it has an offensive ring to it from a traditional point of view, suggesting as it does that people have no obligations to their creator. But there were in fact mechanisms whereby adherents of divergent beliefs, whether infidel or just heretical, could be accommodated. As regards the former, unbelievers could be accepted as protected peoples (*dhimmīs*), at least if they were Jews, Christians, or Zoroastrians; even pagans qualified according to some legal schools. *Dhimmīs* were entitled to practice their ancestral religion and manage their own internal affairs under Muslim sovereignty, though they were subject to certain conditions, including payment of a special tax that was meant as a mark of humiliation. This was a right granted to communities, not to individuals, and individuals retained it only as long as they retained their ancestral faith. If they wished to convert, they could in principle do so only to Islam. Entrance into the Muslim community was open to all, but the exit was closed, so that once people had become Muslims, they were not allowed to convert to another religion at all. Apostasy was a betrayal of the community and punishable by death. A Muslim who converted to another religion would be safe only if he left the Islamic world for a country professing the religion for which he had betrayed his own.

Regarding fellow Muslims, the schisms between Kharijis, Shi'is, and the majority Muslims were deeply regretted by all involved, but the majority rarely tried to impose their own views on the minorities, except in the sense that the latter risked harassment when they ventured out of their own quarters (adherents of different beliefs tended to segregate physically). Local fighting between Sunni and Shi'i quarters was common at times, but the government took military action against dissident communities only when the latter took to arms themselves. Virulent though their polemics were, the three branches of Islam in effect accepted one another as legitimate in the sense that nobody had the right to eradicate the others by force. The habit of toleration inculcated by the recognition of non-Muslim communities may have made it easier to accept the presence of sectarian communities as well. It was only when religious leaders set out to seize political power and reform the world that the pattern of toleration was broken, usually because all normal political and social relations were thrown into turmoil, not because the leaders saw themselves as called upon to eliminate other religious groups. The only major exception is the Safavids (1501–1732), who imposed Shi'ism on Iran and engaged in the forcible conversion of Christians and Jews as well.

The fundamental schisms apart, Muslims tolerated divergent beliefs by distinguishing between external observance and inner conviction and insisting on the former alone for purposes of membership. All Muslims were expected to observe the rules relating to food, marriage, divorce, inheritance, purity, and ritual, meaning the five daily prayers (which can be performed anywhere), the weekly Friday prayer (a public ritual that men must perform in a *jāmi'* or "cathedral mosque"; whether women can or must is disputed), the annual fast (observed by all healthy adults), the pilgrimage to Mecca once in a lifetime for those who had the means to undertake it, and the annual payment of alms. These rituals served visibly to mark out the community from others. Their neglect might be tolerated as long as it was intermittent rather than systematic, but principled denial of their validity amounted to apostasy.

Most Muslims, however, soon came to supplement this "external" religion, as some called it, with religion of a more personal kind, such as philosophy, mysticism, or esotericism, which established a direct relationship between the individual and God. (Philosophy was not a secular pursuit directed against religion but rather a rival form of it.) Only the Traditionalists did their best to live by the Qur'an and hadith, and even they were gradually sucked into Sufism, all dominant in the post-Mongol world. Since the new forms of religion were pursued by individuals in search of their own private salvation, they often brought their adherents into conflict with the law. All downplayed the importance of the law one way or the other by holding salvation to lie in spirituality or human reason or in the mixture of the two known as theosophy. The law was deemed to be no more than a first step on the ladder to the truth, or just a metaphorical version of the absolute truth for those unable to understand higher things. In some cases, the law was not even deemed a metaphorical version of the truth but simply a utilitarian institution required for social life or even chains and fetters that had to be cast off by those in search of salvation. There were also those who accepted the law as a genuine but temporary form of religion that would be swept away when the Mahdi came to transfigure the world, so that all would be able to experience the truth directly and worship God of their own accord

without the need for all the paraphernalia of institutionalized religion. Such views were widely perceived as attacks on the very foundations of Muslim society, but most of them could be tolerated as long as the "external" religion was respected and the private convictions were handled with discretion.

Freethinkers could discuss their views with like-minded individuals in private salons, in learned gatherings at the court, and to some extent in books and even more so in poetry, where things could be put ambivalently. One could also debate radical propositions as if for the sake of argument alone or voice them as part of *mujūn*. *Mujūn* was playful behavior or writing that violated the normal rules of propriety, an accepted part of the high culture which allowed people to say things that bordered on the blasphemous, the scurrilous, or the pornographic as long as they did so with literary elegance and wit and had a good sense of where to stop. There was no institutionalized confession of sins, no inquisition, and no prying into people's hearts. The authorities were responsible for the maintenance of the society in which Muslim law was practiced and without which there could be no salvation, but they were not responsible for the salvation of individuals, and what people concealed in their innermost consciences was between them and God.

In short, freedom lay essentially in privacy. The public sphere was where public norms had to be maintained, where there might be censors or private persons fulfilling the duty of "commanding right and forbidding wrong" who would break musical instruments, pour out wine, and separate couples who were neither married nor closely related. But their right to intrude into private homes was strictly limited. Here the veils came off. What went on privately was not meant to become public knowledge, and those who knew one's private life should not reveal it. Casting a veil over other people's faults was as virtuous as covering one's own; one certainly should not wash dirty linen in public. A sin that was kept secret only harmed the person who had committed it, as it was said, whereas once it was revealed, it had to be denounced lest everyone be harmed by it (in that it would weaken public norms). For the same reason, it was wrong to give clear accounts of heretical views. All these attitudes were deeply ingrained in the Near East and by no means limited to Muslims.

Again, the modern state ruined the traditional pattern. It imposes its law directly on all inhabitants of a particular territory regardless of faith and awards citizenship on the basis of criteria of secular origin, in principle awarding all citizens the same rights and duties, so that Muslims, non-Muslims, Sunnis, and Shi'is were brought out of their separate communities as members of the same national state. The national and the religious principle now coexist uneasily in the Muslim world. At the same time nationalism highlighted ethnic cleavages hitherto masked by religious fellowship. Tensions formerly defused by segregation and hierarchical ordering (with the Muslims on top) thus became difficult to contain. In addition, the home ceased to be a castle shielding the family from external intrusion. The faces and voices of the outside world, including the government, came to be seen and heard on radio, television, cassettes, and so on, and the old respect for boundaries was eroded. After the Iranian Revolution, the religious police would routinely raid private homes. Thanks to the modern economy, even the family itself is changing, as women are entering the work force and rebelling against their traditional subordination, while a growing number of the young are escaping parental supervision in cyberspace, which offers instant access to both peers and the rest of the world. All this is inevitably affecting political thought.

Outsiders

Like many other peoples, the premodern Muslims conceived of the world in which their own norms prevailed as a haven of peace and safety surrounded by threatening outsiders lacking in civilized standards; they called the former "the abode of Islam" and the latter "the abode of war." Again like many, they saw themselves as called upon to expand their haven of peace and moral rectitude so that others, too, could enjoy its benefits. Unlike the Greeks, Romans, Chinese, French, British, and others who have entertained comparable ideas but like the Spanish, the Muslims saw themselves as bringing not only benefits in this world but also salvation in the next, obedience to God being the key to both. Expanding the sovereignty of God was the aim of jihad, the Muslim form of holy war. Once brought under Muslim law, non-Muslim populations could retain their religion as *dhimmīs*, but it was hoped that they would convert, and many invariably did with the passing of time. The jurists identified jihad primarily as missionary warfare.

To the Christians, jihad has always been a stumbling block. Jesus did not use force to establish, or even to defend, himself but rather died as the victim of coercive power; the early Christians also preferred martyrdom to the use of arms. By contrast, Muhammad waged war to establish his message and died as the leader of a polity, whereupon his followers set out to conquer the world. This contrast has figured in Christian polemics against Islam for over a thousand years, often in a manner suggesting that holy war is the opposite of no war, whereas in fact it is merely the opposite of secular war (i.e., war lying outside the religious domain). The Muslims elevated one type of war to religious status, whereas their Christian counterparts assigned all war along with politics to a compartment separate from that of religion. But this does not mean that the Christians stopped fighting wars of expansion or even that they refrained from doing so in the name of religion.

The Muslim jurists identified jihad as a duty imposed on the community rather than the individual, except when it was conducted for the defense of Islam rather than its expansion, and it was typically discharged by the ruler and his troops. Volunteering was highly meritorious, however, and jihad was lawful even without official direction or authorization. Self-help was also authorized against other Muslims when they were deemed to be apostates. If a religious scholar declared a certain person to be an infidel, any Muslim could kill him with impunity. (A person found guilty of unbelief by

a court would normally be executed by the authorities.) Muslims frequently declared one another to be infidels, often, it would seem, without anything happening, presumably because the declarations were confined to books. If they were widely publicized, however, the alleged infidel might be no better off than the outlaw in medieval European society. Self-help was likewise authorized in the maintenance of public morality. Any Muslim could, indeed should, command right and forbid wrong by counseling people if he saw them acting contrary to what he knew to be the law or even by using force, though this was a contentious issue.

The early jurists who divided the world into an abode of Islam and an abode of war took it for granted that a Muslim could not live permanently outside the Islamic abode. To be a Muslim was to live under the sovereignty of God as represented by a Muslim ruler upholding Islamic law. In practice, however, Muslims soon came to live as (usually commercial) minorities in other countries, while conversely parts of the Muslim world eventually came to be ruled by non-Muslims in the form of Crusaders, Mongols, and Europeans, so the abode of Islam came to be understood as anywhere that Islam could be openly practiced; political sovereignty was not required. Today a full third of all Muslims live as minorities under non-Muslim sovereignty.

These developments have put an end to jihad of the traditional type. In the later 19th century, the Muslims of British India began to reinterpret the duty as purely defensive, and this has become the prevalent view today; many Muslims even deny that it has ever meant expansionist war, dismissing the traditional concept of jihad as an Orientalist invention. Instead, a new type of global jihad has appeared. That, too, is cast as defensive and thus defined as as an individual duty, not simply a communal one that can be discharged by some on behalf of all. Conducted by way of self-help without government direction, it is distinguished by systematic disregard of traditional boundaries. The same is true of self-help against apostates. When the Shi'i Ayatollah Khomeini declared the novelist Salman Rushdie to be as an apostate, many tried to kill him, even though Rushdie lived in England rather than a Muslim state (and had never been Shi'i). Similarly, offensive Westerners such as the Dutch filmmaker Theo van Gogh or the Danish cartoonists who drew mocking images of Muhammad were treated as if they were *dhimmīs* under Muslim rule. All these cases are exceptional, but they illustrate the flux into which traditional concepts have been thrown by modern changes.

Overview

Religion in the broad sense of appeals to the supernatural has played a major role in all political thought wherever it is found, but there is no denying that it is particularly prominent in Islam. In line with this, Muslim thinkers display strong awareness of the degree to which reality is shaped by constructions put on it and of the power to be derived from working people's minds. In that sense they could be said to be the true heirs of the Christians, who succeeded in taking over the Roman Empire armed with nothing but the power of their convictions. Islamic political thought is also unusual in the degree to which it endorses self-help, as opposed to reliance on political or ecclesiastical authorities, and not just in matters involving the use of force. The standard example is the lunar calendar. Even illiterates can handle it because the beginning and end of each month is established on the basis of a sighting of the new moon rather than astronomical calculation (though scientists liked to engage in that, too). The religion is institutionally lightweight; indeed, there is a vision in some juristic writings of every Muslim as personally responsible for the maintenance of Muslim norms for himself and his neighbors—a view often in a state of tension with authoritarian respect for social and political hierarchies.

The historical roots of this vision lie partly in the tribal heritage of Arab conquerors who founded Muslim society in the Middle East and partly in the colonial past of the provinces in which they established their first capitals. As tribesmen from a stateless society, the Arabs were used to managing their own affairs without recourse to political and ecclesiastic hierarchies, and having been ruled by Greeks and Persians for close to a thousand years, the inhabitants of Syria and Iraq, as well as Egypt, had a long tradition of living communal lives separate from those of their imperial masters without renouncing obedience to them. When the Muslims discovered that their own caliphs kept turning into kings, most of them in effect opted for the same solution: what mattered was communal life, not the state, which they saw as a mere protective envelope; certainly, this envelope had to be maintained, but in terms of the morally significant domains of life, the believers took charge of themselves. This gave Islamic political thought a very different character from that of Western Christendom, where an immense amount of attention was devoted to a hierarchical institution, the church.

See also authority; caliph, caliphate; government; minorities

Further Reading

Patricia Crone, *Medieval Islamic Political Thought*, 2005.

PATRICIA CRONE

Transoxiana

"Transoxiana" (*mā warā' al-nahr*) designates the territory between the rivers Oxus (Amu Darya) and the Jaxartes (Sir Darya), roughly equivalent of most of modern Uzbekistan and Tajikistan (but not including Khwarazm on the north and Farghana on the south). More generally, it sometimes refers to everything beyond the Oxus, all the way to China—that is, a general name for Central Asia.

Before the Muslim conquest, the region between the Oxus and the Jaxartes was not under direct imperial rule (although Turks

and Chinese competed for nominal sovereignty) but was divided among city-states, most important of which were Bukhara and Samarqand, and nomads living in the deserts around these cities. The main income of the city-states came from long-distance trade along the Silk Roads, conducted mainly by Sogdian traders. The region was highly diverse religiously, ethnically, and linguistically, though most of the population spoke Iranian languages.

Muslim invasions into Transoxiana began in the seventh century, but the region was conquered by the Umayyad governor of Khurasan Qutayba b. Muslim (705–15). It has retained close connections with Khurasan, Khwarazm, and Farghana, also conquered by Qutayba, ever since. Conversion to Islam had begun already in Umayyad times (660–750), but the integration of Transoxiana into the Muslim empire began in earnest under the Abbasids (750–1258). In early Abbasid times several rebellions that united sectarian Islamic and non-Islamic religious dissent from politicosocial resentment at Arab domination took place in Transoxiana, the most renowned of which was the rebellion of Hashim b. Hakim (known as al-Muqanna', the Veiled One) in 777–79. Yet Transoxiana's importance for Islamic political thought was mainly in two later periods: the Samanid (819–1005) and the Timurid (1370–1501).

The Samanid period, in most of which Transoxiana and Khurasan were ruled from Bukhara, was a time of economic and intellectual efflorescence. It saw the rise of New Persian to the status of literary language and the recording of Iranian literature and traditions that culminated in Abu al-Qasim Firdawsi's *Shahnama* (Book of kings, completed under the dynasty after the Samanids, the Ghaznavids), an epic and Mirror for Princes that has remained significant for Iranian and Turkic Muslim rulers ever since. The Samanids also actively promoted the Islamization of the Turks, and the Turkic dynasties that replaced them (and that began the region's Turkicization), mainly the Qarakhanids (ca. 950–1213) and Seljuqs (ca. 1055–1194), used Samanid models for their administration.

The Mongol period was the watershed in the history of Muslim Transoxiana, introducing into the region the Chingizid political tradition, which remained valid there until the 18th century. As one of the first regions to be conquered by the Mongols, in the 1220s, Transoxiana's resources—human and material—were channeled to the needs of the ever-growing empire, thereby eliminating a considerable segment of the region's elites, artisans, and soldiers. Marginalized under the rule of the Chaghatayid khanate (ca. 1260–1347, descendants of Chingiz Khan's son, Chaghatay), Transoxiana came to full bloom under Tamerlane (r. 1370–1405), who replaced the decaying Chaghatayids, made Samarqand his capital, and strove to revive the Mongol Empire. Tamerlane created a new form of legitimation, which combined Chingizid, Muslim, and personal elements, and used monumental building and historiography to strengthen it. This legitimation became a model for future rulers in the region and beyond (the Timurids, the Mughals in India, Nadir Shah in Iran and Transoxiana, the Kokand Khanate in Farghana). With the political and economic decline of the region from the 18th century onward, Tamerlane also became Transoxiana's popular hero and political symbol, a precedent to his prominent position in contemporary Uzbekistan. Another political tradition, developed mainly under the Timurids, was the leading role of Sufi shaykhs, especially of the Naqshbandi order, in the region's economic and political life: in 15th-century Transoxiana the Naqshbandi Khwaja Ahrar became the factual ruler of the region, more powerful than the Timurid princes, whose capital had by then moved to Khurasan.

Under the Chingizid Uzbeks, who deposed the Timurids in 1501, Chingizid political concepts were revived. Thus only descendants of Chingiz Khan could become legitimate khans, and the Yasa, the collection of laws ascribed to Chingiz Khan, remained valid, especially in the fields of political and criminal matters and court etiquette, coexisting with the shari'a. The decline of the Chingizid concepts throughout the 18th century led to the rise of non-Chingizid rulers; thus the Manghit emirate of Bukhara replaced the declining Chingizids in 1753. Yet only the Russian conquest of 1865 brought modern political concepts into the region.

See also Central Asia; Mongols; Mughals (1526–1857); Samanids (819–1005); *Shahnama*; Tamerlane (1336–1405); Timurids (1370–1506); Umayyads (661–750)

Further Reading

Yuri Bregel, "The New Uzbek States: Bukhara, Khiwa and Kokand: c. 1750–1886," in *The Cambridge History of Inner Asia, vol. 2, The Chinggisid Age*, edited by Nicola Di Cosmo, Peter B. Golden, and Allan Frank, 2009; Étienne de la Vaissière, *Sogdian Traders: A History*, 2005; Richard N. Frye, *Bukhara: The Medieval Achievement*, 1996; Beatrice F. Manz, *Power, Politics and Religion in Timurid Iran*, 2007; Robert D. McChesney, *Central Asia: Foundations of Change*, 1996; Svat Soucek, *A History of Inner Asia*, 2000.

MICHAL BIRAN

treason

In common parlance, "treason" refers to the act of betraying one's country to the benefit of another, usually an enemy or a rival. Historically, in English common law, this understanding was denoted by "high" treason, as opposed to "petty" treason, which could entail a servant killing his master, a wife killing her husband, or adultery between a servant and his master's wife. Throughout its usage, however, "treason" has been largely synonymous with "sedition"; the difference between the two words—namely, that treason carries the additional connotation of allegiance to a foreign power—is a

modern convention. Practically speaking, treason would typically include such acts as political assassination, sabotage, and military desertion.

Examples of treason in Islamic history are many and varied. Perhaps the first prosecution of treason in Islamic history belongs to the first caliph, Abu Bakr (r. 632–34). Following the Prophet Muhammad's death, a group of Muslim tribes in the Najd refused to pay the alms tax (*ṣadaqa*) to the caliph in Medina. Abu Bakr considered this a kind of treason—more precisely, apostasy (*ridda*)—and sought to bring the rebels back into the taxpaying fold by force.

This episode adds an important dimension to the definition of treason in an Islamic context. Was treason against a ruler also considered a religious transgression? Certainly, one can imagine that any ruler would favor such a conflation, but the question could be, and was, easily turned around. Was "treason" against a tyrannical ruler a religious duty? There is no clear answer to this question, and opinions among Muslims have been varied. Nor was there a standard response to treason from medieval rulers. Some groups rebelling against caliphs were punished with extreme prejudice, while others were granted clemency.

The period known as the First Civil War (*fitna*; 656–61) was also thick with examples of treason. The caliph ʻUthman b. ʻAffan was murdered by treasonous mutineers dissatisfied with his leadership of the community. ʻAli b. Abi Talib was acknowledged as caliph by many, but ʻUthman's relative Muʻawiya dismissed ʻAli's leadership, claiming that ʻAli was complicit in ʻUthman's assassination. ʻAli's camp regarded Muʻawiya as a traitor, while Muʻawiya's camp regarded ʻAli as guilty of treason against ʻUthman. In the midst of the battle between the two forces, Muʻawiya's troops sued for arbitration, to which ʻAli agreed. Some of ʻAli's stalwart supporters felt that his capitulation to a traitor (Muʻawiya) was itself betrayal, and they deserted him, thus forming the Kharijis. The arbitration did not go well for ʻAli's claim, prompting accusations of treason against the arbitrators. However, shortly thereafter a Khariji assassinated ʻAli, and Muʻawiya became caliph.

This early episode proved extremely divisive. For subsequent generations, it was also a painful and disquieting memory, given that some Companions of the Prophet had fought and killed others. While intrigue and the threat of treason always lurked in the courts and corridors of power, these two very different early examples of treason in Islamic history certainly further complicated Muslim attitudes toward political legitimacy, the possibility of rebellion, and loyalty.

See also apostasy; rebellion

Further Reading

Khaled Abou El Fadl, *Rebellion and Violence in Islamic Law*, 2001; Patricia Crone, *God's Rule*, 2004; Wilferd Madelung, *The Succession to Muḥammad*, 1996.

NICHOLAS G. HARRIS

Treaty of ʻUmar

The Treaty of ʻUmar is the title given to the canonical document that sets forth the rules and restrictions pertaining to non-Muslims living under Muslim rule. Various other documents were intended to serve the same purpose but have not been accorded the same authority. Although it was not always systematically or strictly enforced between the 9th and the 11th centuries, the Treaty of ʻUmar seems progressively to have become the accepted norm in later centuries.

A treaty allegedly signed between the Muslim conquerors and the Christians of one city following the Islamic conquest, the document lists a series of obligations made by the conquered in return for the assurance of protection (*amān*) given to them by the Muslims. It includes clauses regarding the obligation to host the Muslims and to be loyal to them; a prohibition on building new prayer houses; a list of restrictive measures regarding religious customs such as refraining from beating a clapper (*nāqūs*) loudly as a call to prayer, praying loudly, forming processions on holidays and for funerals, displaying crosses and lights on the roads, and selling pigs and wine; clauses regarding behavior in the presence of Muslims, such as the obligation to respect the Muslims and to give them priority on the road as well as in seating and the prohibition of burial next to them, peeking into their houses, and the possession of Muslim slaves; and a series of clauses requiring the adoption of differentiating signs (*ghiyār*), including an obligation to wear the girdle (*zunnār*) and distinct clothing and the prohibitions of resembling Muslims in appearance, using saddles, adopting seals in the Arabic language, bearing arms, and teaching Christian children Arabic.

Traditionally attributed to ʻUmar b. al-Khattab (r. 634–44), the document in its final form is a later product portraying a state of established coexistence between Muslims and non-Muslims and was formed, according to most scholars, sometime around the end of the eighth or beginning of the ninth century. Opinions are divided over the process of its formation. While Arthur Stanley Tritton and Antoine Fattal regard the document as a product of jurists of the ninth century, other scholars such as Salo Baron, Norman Stillman, and Habib Zayyat claim that the ʻUmar referred to is the Umayyad caliph ʻUmar b. ʻAbd al-ʻAziz (r. 717–20), in whose days the initial document was forged. Bernard Lewis, Albrecht Noth, and Mark Cohen believe that many of the clauses in the document reflect the conditions of the immediate postconquest period, although all agree that it underwent a process of elaboration and editing at the hands of later jurists.

Noth, who proposed an early date for the Treaty of ʻUmar, suggested that it initially aimed at protecting the Muslim minority from the non-Muslim majority. However, in its final form the treaty reflects the transformation undergone by Muslim society, from insecure and at times rejected conquerors to secure and confident lords and masters. Thus while the initial conquest

agreements represented a tolerant, minimally invasive approach, demanding in general only the payment of the *jizya* (poll tax) in return for *amān* and the inhabitants' right to observe their ancient customs, the Treaty of 'Umar replaced these with an intolerant and restrictive approach. The document reflected the new social order, according to which the Muslims were the superior, ruling class, while the non-Muslims were the inferior and humiliated class. This new order was entrenched in the ethos of class-stratified Sasanian society, which was now turned to the advantage of the Muslim rulers. Like Sasanian society, Muslim society distinguished between the ruling class and the subject class through distinguishing marks such as clothes and paraphernalia, riding habits, and privileges in the public sphere.

See also minorities; 'Umar b. 'Abd al-'Aziz (ca. 680–720); 'Umar b. al-Khattab (ca. 580–644)

Further Reading

Mark Cohen, "What Was the Pact of 'Umar? A Literary-Historical Study," *JSAI* 23 (1999); Milka Levy-Rubin, *Non-Muslims in the Early Islamic Empire: From Surrender to Coexistence*, 2011; Idem, "*Shurut 'Umar* and Its Alternatives: The Legal Debate on the Status of the *Dhimmīs*," *Jerusalem Studies in Arabic and Islam* 30 (2005); Albrecht Noth, "Problems of Differentiation between Muslims and Non-Muslims: Re-Reading the 'Ordinances of 'Umar'," in *Muslims and Others in Early Islamic Society*, edited by Robert Hoyland, translated by Mark Muelhaeusler, 2004; Arthur Stanley Tritton, *The Caliphs and Their Non-Muslim Subjects*, 1930.

MILKA LEVY-RUBIN

tribalism

Islam was born in a tribal environment, and tribes have played a large role in Islamic history. Except, however, in the work of the great historian and sociologist Ibn Khaldun (d. 1406), tribalism—the values and attitudes that are characteristic of tribes—has not been an important topic in Islamic political theory. Nor is it likely to become so, for even in places where the tribes were once dominant, they are mostly no longer important actors. Yet tribalism, at least in some regions, continues to influence the way that people think about politics and indeed about other topics.

Although the word "tribe" has never been defined in a satisfactory fashion, scholars who write about the Middle East and North Africa agree, broadly speaking, as to which groups should be called tribal. In this usage, which will be followed here, virtually all nomads are tribal, but not all tribes are nomadic.

This entry focuses on the Middle East and North Africa, with particular attention to the Arabic- and Berber-speaking parts of the region.

Tribalism and Islam

Islam is hostile to tribalism, and this hostility goes back to the time of Muhammad. He wanted to convert not only his fellow townspeople but also the Bedouin tribes of Arabia. The new religion offered a view of the world that centered on the supernatural—God, the afterlife, and the Day of Judgment—and that demanded revolutionary changes in people's behavior and beliefs. The Bedouin, however, were down-to-earth people, with little interest in things they could not perceive and a deep attachment to their ancestral way of life. The Prophet did not have an easy time with them.

Eventually all the Bedouin converted to Islam, although those who remained nomads retained many of their traditional values and practices. Some medieval Arab historians, writing centuries after the nominal conversion, used the term *muslimūn* (Muslims) to refer to the settled population as opposed to the *'arab* (Bedouin). Islamic religious literature generally shows them in a poor light, and Islamic law either prohibits many of their customs (e.g., blood revenge carried out on someone other than the perpetrator) or else makes no allowance for them. For example, virtually every Bedouin tribe has its own particular territory, but Islamic law does not recognize tribes as corporate entities and therefore cannot entertain any territorial claim that a tribe might make.

Until well into the 20th century there were still Bedouin whose way of life was un-Islamic, even though they mostly felt a deep loyalty to their faith. Many pious Muslims have been of the opinion that nomads cannot not be good Muslims. When the Saudis, for instance, reestablished their kingdom at the beginning of the 20th century and encouraged the spread of Wahhabi doctrines among the tribes of Arabia, they attempted at the same time to settle the nomads. But old customs are tenacious, and the authorities in Saudi Arabia, a state that more than any other in the Arab world attempts to follow Islamic law, still find it necessary to recognize tribal territories. Discrimination between individuals according to their tribal (or other) origin, something that has generally been condemned by Islam, remains a significant feature of Saudi life.

The only region where there were nomads who followed the prescriptions of Islamic law as strictly as possible was the Western Sahara, where the Zawaya tribes maintained high standards of piety, and indeed religious scholarship, for centuries. The Western Sahara was also inhabited by other Arabic-speaking nomads, notably those referred to as the warrior tribes. The Zawaya looked on them as little better than infidels.

The History of Tribes in the Islamic Middle East and North Africa

Until the 20th century there had, throughout the Islamic period, been a flow of tribespeople from the Arabian Peninsula into the Fertile Crescent. This flow began well before the appearance of the Prophet Muhammad, but up to the time of his death it was on a modest scale. The conquests that followed the demise of the Prophet were accompanied by a massive outpouring as the Muslims destroyed the Sasanian Empire (Iran and the eastern part of

the Fertile Crescent) and took over much of the territory of the Byzantine Empire (the western part of the Fertile Crescent, Egypt, and some coastal regions of North Africa).

The population of the new Muslim empire was made up predominantly of townspeople and peasants (i.e., nontribal agriculturalists). The Arab tribes, which soon fell to fighting among themselves, remained a significant force for many decades after the conquest, but the cities and villages of the new Muslim empire did not generally suffer lasting damage. Arabic became the dominant language in the Fertile Crescent and Egypt but not further east. Apart from the Arabs, the main tribal elements in the previously Sasanian and Byzantine domains of Asia were the speakers of various Iranian languages, notably the Kurds, the Lurs, and the Baluch. They do not seem to have been particularly numerous or influential in the early Islamic period, but during the era of extreme political fragmentation in the late 10th and early 11th centuries a number of short-lived Kurdish principalities appeared in eastern Anatolia and western Iran.

A second tribal flood burst out of Arabia in the 10th century, when the Bedouin again flowed north, especially into Iraq. Certain Isma'ili groups (the Qarmatians) made their influence felt on the Bedouin during these years, but the degree to which this influence can be linked to the migration is uncertain. At the same time the Arab tribes of northern Syria grew stronger, and some of them may have moved east across the Euphrates. In the late 10th and early 11th centuries these Bedouin groups founded a number of small states in the Fertile Crescent. This was accompanied by considerable destruction and population decline, as is shown, among other things, by the archeological evidence. At least in the western part of the Fertile Crescent there was a revival of urban life some 200 years later, though it has been suggested that there was further substantial Bedouin immigration from Arabia around the year 1200.

The third, and last, great Bedouin emigration began in the late 17th century and continued until early in the 19th century. It occurred at a time when the Ottoman Empire was weak, and in its later stages it was linked to the Wahhabi movement. This wave, which brought the Shammar and 'Anize tribes into the Syrian steppes, determined the tribal composition of the region as it remains to this day. All indications are that it was accompanied both by a decline in the overall population and by an increase in the proportion of nomads in that population.

Bedouin tribes reached Egypt at the time of the Islamic conquests and were reinforced in the centuries that followed. Some of the tribespeople lost their tribal identity, but others, especially those in Upper Egypt, did not. At least from the 14th century onward, the tribes were powerful, and sometimes dominant, in Upper Egypt, and they remained so until early in the 19th century.

It was from Egypt that the Muslims conquered the Maghrib. Here, in contrast to the East, they found a rural population that was itself largely tribal. These rural people—nomads and sedentaries—mostly spoke, and continued to speak, Berber languages. Only in the middle of the 11th century did Arab tribespeople begin to appear in large numbers in the Maghrib. The first wave consisted of tribes that had long been resident in Egypt, and their advance, which was accompanied by considerable destruction, is known to history as the invasion of the Banu Hilal. The Bedouin gradually moved westward, reaching Morocco at the end of the 12th century and entering the Western Sahara in the 15th century. There they eventually extended about as far east as Timbuktu. Before the arrival of the tribes, the Arabic language in North Africa had been confined largely to the cities; now Arabic spread to the countryside, and there came into being the pattern that exists to this day, in which, very broadly speaking, Arabic is spoken in the plains and Berber in the mountains.

Arab tribes also flowed into the northern parts of the present-day states of Sudan and Chad, a region referred to here as eastern Sudan. They began to enter this part of Africa in large numbers in the 14th century, mostly traveling up the Nile from Egypt. Once south of the Sahara they spread westward, eventually reaching as far as Lake Chad.

Wherever they went, the Arabs mixed sooner or later with the local population, which in Africa was either Berber or black. The term "Arab tribe" is used here simply to refer to a tribe whose native language is Arabic; in many cases it is clear that the ancestors of what is now an Arab tribe were mostly non-Arabs. These Arab tribes often show cultural traits that are characteristic of the local people rather than of the inhabitants of the Arabian Peninsula. In the case of Africa one might mention, for instance, the prevalence of monogamy in the Western Sahara and the use of drums as tribal symbols in eastern Sudan.

The second great reservoir of tribes, after Arabia, was Central Asia. Turkic nomads began moving westward across Iran into Azerbaijan and Anatolia from about the year 1000, and in the last decades of the century they entered Anatolia in large numbers. Anatolia had suffered greatly during the preceding centuries, but though the population was thin, it apparently did not include, at the time of the Turkic invasions, a high proportion of tribal people. After the first wave of Turkic tribes in the 11th century, there was a second one in the 13th century, the result of Mongol pressure from the East. In contrast to what happened in North Africa, the arrival of the nomads in Anatolia was not accompanied by lasting demographic or economic decline. Some of them, indeed, turned back to the East: between the 14th and 16th centuries there were three waves of Turkic nomads, associated respectively with the Qara Quyunlu, the Aq Quyunlu, and the Safavids, that moved from Anatolia to Iran. Of the tribespeople who remained in Anatolia, many became sedentary. Those who continued as nomads generally spent the winter on the Mediterranean coast or on the northern fringes of the Fertile Crescent and then moved into the mountains and spent the summer with their flocks on the interior plateau. The Ottoman authorities made some use of the nomads as soldiers but also invested considerable effort in attempts to settle them, beginning in the 17th century.

Incomparably the most destructive of the tribal invaders were the Mongols, who swept over Iran and the eastern half of the Fertile Crescent in the 13th century. The Mongols, unlike the Turks and the

Arabs, left no lasting linguistic heritage in the region. At least from this time on, both Iraq and Iran were thinly settled countries with large tribal populations; the population levels of the early Islamic centuries were not to return before modern times.

The Tribal Population in 1800

The preceding section gives only a schematic view of events; at the local level there were innumerable ups and downs over these many centuries. It is likely, however, that in relation to earlier periods of Islamic history, the populations of the Arab world and Iran reached a new low, and the proportion of tribespeople a new high, some time in the decades around 1800. These are significant years, for they mark the time when Western influence on the Middle East begins to have revolutionary effects.

The population of all the Arab lands, from Morocco to Iraq, and including the Berbers, may have been about 15 million in 1800; a more miserly estimate gives a similar figure for all the Arab lands plus Anatolia, and even the most generous would not set the Arab and Berber population above 20 million. The area covered by present-day Turkey contained at most about 10 million people, while the population of Iran was perhaps five or six million. To put these figures in proportion, it is worth noting that the population of India was at this time perhaps 200 million (with a wide margin for error), while the population of China, for which the evidence is much better, is generally agreed to have been not less than 300 million.

The people of the territory covered by present-day Iran, Turkey, Israel, and the Arab states were divided, in the first place, between town and country. Here we are confronted not only by factual problems but also by conceptual ones, since there is no wholly satisfactory way of drawing the line between urban and rural settlements. But by almost any measure, at least 80 percent of the population was rural in 1800.

Next, there is the delicate question as to what proportion of the rural population was tribal. Many nomadic Turkomans still inhabited Anatolia in the 18th century, and eastern Anatolia also contained many Kurdish tribespeople. Quantitative estimates, however, are few, and the rural population of early 19th century Anatolia, though it appeared sparse to European observers, was evidently denser than that of any area of similar size in the Arab lands or Iran. It is only in parts of central and eastern Anatolia that the nomads were dominant.

For Iran, an estimate from the beginning of the 19th century that about half the population was nomadic seems to be generally viewed as plausible, as does another that about a quarter of the population remained nomadic at the beginning of the 20th century. Even without allowing for the possibility of sedentary people who were tribally organized, this implies that more than half the rural population of Iran was tribal in 1800.

In the Arab world there were extensive regions where almost the whole rural population was tribal in 1800. It goes practically without saying that this was true of the Western Sahara, eastern Sudan, and Libya. In Morocco and Algeria there was a large, and in some places quite dense, Berber population in the mountains, most of it sedentary, some of it more or less nomadic, and all of it tribal. The plains of Morocco, Algeria, and Tunisia were largely occupied by Arab tribes, and even those whose main occupation was agriculture were not fully sedentary. Each agricultural tribe had a territory, only part of which was cultivated in a given year; the people lived in lightly built huts that they would move from time to time. One of the main reasons for moving was to allow one area of the territory to lie fallow while another was cultivated. The most urbanized area of the Maghrib was Tunisia, the only part of the region where there was a significant number of Arab villages in the plains that probably had roots in the pre-Hilalian population. Yet even in Tunisia it is believed that in the 19th century nomads constituted a majority of the population.

Turning now to the east, it is clear that the great majority of the population of the Arabian Peninsula was tribal in 1800. Perhaps half of that population lived in the Yemen, mostly in stable, long-established mountain villages, but here too tribal organization was predominant. The situation in Iraq was, broadly speaking, similar to that in Algeria and Morocco, with the Kurds taking the place of the Berbers. In the territories controlled by the present-day states of Syria, Jordan, Lebanon, and Israel (Greater Syria), the tribes were somewhat less prominent, at least in those regions that lie not more than a hundred miles or so from the Mediterranean. The cities were particularly strong in this region, and here, as in most places in the Middle East, there were peasants in the immediate vicinity of each city. Beyond the immediate environs of the cities, however, the flatlands were everywhere dominated, or at least menaced, by the Bedouin. What distinguishes Greater Syria is that peasants were also to be found in at least some of the mountain regions, the Maronites of Mount Lebanon being the best known group of this kind.

'Ali al-Wardi (1913–95), an eminent Iraqi sociologist who proposed ideas similar to those expressed here, viewed Egypt, and especially Lower Egypt, as the only Arab country in which sedentary influences clearly outweighed nomadic ones. There is much to be said for this view. Upper Egypt is to this day a region with marked tribal traits, but Lower Egypt, even in 1800, retained a large peasant population.

Tribal Influences

During the long centuries when they dominated much of the countryside, the Bedouin had a marked influence on the nontribal population. Peasants adopted many elements of Bedouin culture. So, for instance, the traditional kinship structures and laws of the Palestinian villagers are merely variants of the corresponding institutions among the nomads, and there can be little doubt about who influenced whom. The age-old hostility between the desert and the sown land was no barrier. Mark Sykes, an English traveler, wrote of the Syrian peasants, "Their manners and customs are borrowed from the Bedawin, whom they dread as their hereditary foes, and against whom until lately they have had to defend themselves" (*Dar ul-Islam*, 1904). Like so many other Islamic peoples, these peasants

were often proud to proclaim themselves descendants of the old Arab tribes.

Even towns and cities were not always immune to tribal influence. One of the most striking examples comes from Iraq: the Muslims of Baghdad ceased at some point to speak their ancient urban Arabic and instead adopted a Bedouin dialect. A similar process took place in a number of cities in North Africa, where almost all the rural dialects of Arabic are of Bedouin origin. Bedouin forms of social organization sometimes penetrated the towns. Agreements relating to the payment of blood money that are clearly based on Bedouin models are recorded for Nazareth in the 19th century and for Najaf early in the 20th century.

In some places, certain institutions of tribal society still retain their vigor in the early 21st century, above all where governments are weak. This is amply illustrated by recent events in the Sudan, Yemen, Iraq, and Palestine, where tribes or clans have often appeared as political forces. Even in a firmly governed country like Egypt, a large amount of dispute settlement, especially in the south, takes place according to the *ḥaqq al-'arab*, the villagers' version of Bedouin law.

It is not, however, institutions that constitute the most important part of the tribal heritage of the Arab (and Berber) world but rather values and attitudes. This is an idea that has often been adumbrated, though it has been developed at length only in the work of Wardi. It would be desirable to specify these values and attitudes with precision, to offer good evidence that they are widely held in the relevant population, and then to prove that they originated among the tribes. In practice, unfortunately, none of these things can be done, but many of the suggestions that have been raised in this context are nevertheless worthy of attention.

One common observation is that those who cultivate the soil in the Arab lands, unlike their fellows in other parts of the world, show little interest in, or little respect for, agriculture as an activity. There are clear exceptions to this, notably in the mountainous areas and in parts (at least) of Egypt, but there is no doubt that the attitude is widespread. It can plausibly be ascribed to nomadic influence.

Two other frequently made observations are that "extreme individualism" is prevalent among the Iranians and Arabs and that these same people "develop intense loyalty to certain small units, such as the family, the clan, the tribe, or the religious sect," but not to large ones, notably the state (Charles Issawi, "Economic and Social Foundations of Democracy in the Middle East," *International Affairs* 32, 1956). Issawi does not discuss the question of just how these qualities can coexist, but perhaps what those who have made these observations have in mind can best be captured by substituting the word "assertiveness" for "individualism" and by remembering that it is not uncommon for someone who is assertive in one relationship to be just the opposite in another. Assertiveness is not a trait that one would expect among peasants, but it is characteristic of many Middle Eastern tribes, which stress respect for the autonomy of the individual man. This respect is perhaps linked to the facts that where the tribes flourish, there is no effective central authority, and that a nomad and his family form a mobile and fairly independent economic unit. The absence of an authority that maintains the peace also helps explain the loyalty to a small group, which often consists of agnates: a man depends on such a group to defend his vital interests, not least his physical integrity and that of his dependents.

Wardi viewed the central feature of Bedouin culture as *taghālub*, by which he meant something like competitive striving for domination, and he argued, mainly with respect to Iraq, that this had been inherited or adopted by the sedentary population, though often in a debased form. The Bedouin, writes Wardi, whether as an individual or as a member of his tribe, "wants to be the despoiler and not the despoiled, the transgressor and not the victim of transgression, the giver and not the receiver, the one whom others seek out and not the one who seeks out others, the one who makes demands and not the one of whom demands are made, the one who helps others and not the one who seeks help, the protector and not the one who seeks protection" (*Dirasa fi Tabi'at al-Mujtama' al-'Iraqi* [A treatise on the nature of Iraqi society]).

The tribal environment was one in which it was necessary always to broadcast the message *nemo me impune lacessit* (no one attacks me with impunity). Every man was armed, and the absence of security meant that a man always had to be ready to use his arms. Disgrace would follow a failure to resort to violence when—in the local view—it was demanded. The emphasis on individual rights and the continual fear of their being infringed meant that disputes were frequent and protracted and the spirit of cooperation limited in scope. These features have also often been observed in the peasant societies of the Middle East. Thomas Russell, a British police officer with decades of experience, wrote of the Egyptian peasant that "brought up from childhood to stories of violence . . . he almost welcomes an affront so as to demonstrate to the world his manliness in avenging it" (*Egyptian Service*, 1949). Cathie Witty, an American anthropologist who studied disputes in a village in the Biqa Valley of Lebanon, wrote of the women that "they are quick to anger, as are men, and they engage in conflict with a vitality and tenacity that usually astounds Westerners" (*Mediation and Society*, 1980).

Much of South and East Asia entered the modern era with a relatively dense population that consisted largely of peasants. The Arab world and Iran started with a thin population that consisted largely of tribespeople. In the Arab world, moreover, even many of the peasants were suffused with tribal values. These are not the values characteristic of peasants in, say, India or China, and it may be that some of the difficulties that the Arabs and Iranians have faced in adapting themselves to the changes of the last two hundred years are a result of having started with a society in which the broad masses of the population were heirs to values and attitudes that have their roots in a tribal, rather than a peasant or urban, society.

See also ethnicity; genealogy; household; kinship; solidarity

Further Reading

Najwa Adra, *Qabyala—The Tribal Concept in the Central Highlands of the Yemen Arab Republic* (PhD diss., Temple University, 1982); Werner Caskel, *Die Bedeutung der Beduinen in der Geschichte der Araber*, 1953; Kurt Franz, *Vom Beutezug zur Territorialherrschaft: Das lange Jahrhundert des Aufstiegs von Nomaden zur Vormacht in Syrien und Mesopotamien, 286–420/899–1029*, 2007; Ignaz Goldziher, *Muslim Studies*, vol. 1, 1967; Stefan Heidemann, "Arab Nomads and Seljuq Military," in *Shifts and Drifts in Nomad-Sedentary Relations*, edited by Stefan Leder and Bernhard Streck, 2005; Anne K. S. Lambton, "The Tribal Resurgence and the Decline of the Bureaucracy in Eighteenth Century Persia," in *Studies in Eighteenth Century Islamic History*, edited by Thomas Naff and Roger Owen, 1977; William Marçais, "Comment l'Afrique du Nord a été arabisée," in William Marçais, *Articles et conférences*, 1961; X. de Planhol, *Kulturgeographische Grundlagen der islamischen Geschichte*, 1975; Yossef Rapoport, "Invisible Peasants, Marauding Nomads: Taxation, Tribalism, and Rebellion in Mamluk Egypt," *Mamluk Studies Review* 8 (2004); 'Ali al-Wardi, *Dirasa fi Tabi'at al-Mujtama' al-'Iraqi*, 1965.

FRANK H. STEWART

Tunisia

In March 1956, both Morocco and Tunisia were granted independence as France focused its colonial efforts in North Africa on keeping a firm grip over Algeria. The first 30 years of independent Tunisia were marked by the leadership of Habib Bourguiba (1903–2000), a French-educated lawyer referred to as *al-mujāhid al-akbar* (the Supreme Combatant), who became the dominant figure in the Tunisian nationalist movement and the architect of modern Tunisia. His philosophy of state building rested on a reformist platform. Although Tunisia was often viewed in the Western media as a secular state, Bourguiba insisted that he was a proponent of a reformist, progressive, and rational Islam, and Article 1 of the 1959 Tunisian constitution stated the Islamic identity of Tunisia.

Bourguiba's views on religion were first reflected in the country's adoption of a code in August 1956 that outlawed polygamy and gave women rights not accorded in traditional Islamic law. Tunisian women had the right to vote and to be candidates in municipal and general elections. The one major exception to this feminist trend was the adherence (with minor amendments) to Islamic law in matters of inheritance because of clear Qur'anic texts relevant to the issue. Bourguiba focused on the establishment of a modernist educational system and the extension of health care to the rural areas. Religious endowments (known as *ḥubūs*) were dissolved and the traditional religious schooling system was abandoned. Centers of family planning were created in the early 1960s. Until his removal in 1987, Bourguiba was the undisputed ruler of Tunisia and his party, the Neo-Destour (renamed in 1964 the Socialist Destourian Party), the overwhelming political force with no distinction between the authority of the state and the party. On July 25, 1957, Tunisia was declared a republic, thus ending the rule of the Husayni dynasty (1705–1957). The Tunisian constitution reflects a powerful presidential system tailored to Bourguiba's stature. He was the head of state, the leader of the ruling party, the social reformer, and the modern-day reformist theologian. The position of mufti of the Republic, theoretically the highest religious position in Tunisia, was kept but was hollowed of any authority. This became evident in the early 1960s when the mufti was dismissed because he did not adhere to Bourguiba's view that Tunisia was in the midst of a national jihad to overcome underdevelopment. During the same period, orders were issued for businesses and institutions to operate during the month of Ramadan according to the same schedule as the rest of the year. In the 1980s and following the success of the Iranian Revolution (1978–79), the Bourguiba regime took repressive measures to curb the influence of religiously oriented movements. This perceived threat, together with Bourguiba's advanced age and poor health, led to an atmosphere of court intrigue and competition over who would succeed Bourguiba. On November 7, 1987, Zine El-Abidine Ben Ali, then prime minister, staged a bloodless coup by declaring Bourguiba medically unfit to continue as head of state. Article 57 of the Tunisian constitution made the prime minister the automatic successor to the presidency in case of vacancy. Bourguiba ended his days under virtual house arrest in his native town of Monastir, where he died on April 6, 2000.

Zine El-Abidine Ben Ali's professional background was rooted in the military and civilian security services. During his 23 years in power, Ben Ali continued Bourguiba's social policy, granting further legal rights to women: creation of family judgeships, premarital agreements allowing joint property, and other benefits for women with children in cases of divorce. His rule, dubbed as the period of *Taghyīr* (Change), made an effort to erase Bourguiba from Tunisian collective memory, starting with, in 1988, changing the name of the Socialist Destourian Party into the Constitutional Democratic Rally. Any manifestation of political Islam was harshly repressed, and the movement leaders faced either exile or long jail sentences. This trend reached its height after the September 11, 2001, terrorist attack in the United States and the subsequent passage of Tunisia's antiterrorist laws. Ben Ali's regime was increasingly viewed as having reduced the country to a repressive police state, and some dubbed it a kleptocracy for its rampant corruption. High unemployment rates, especially among university graduates, added to the general discontent. Ben Ali and his family fled to Saudi Arabia on January 14, 2011, as a result of a revolution sparked by the self-immolation of a street vendor in the town of Sidi Bouzid on December 17, 2010.

See also Egypt; nation-state; North Africa

Further Reading

Nicolas Beau and Catherine Graciet, *La régente de Carthage: Main basse sur la Tunisie*, 2009; Nicolas Beau and Jean-Pierre Tuquoi,

Notre ami Ben Ali: L'envers du "miracle tunisien," 1999; Mounira M. Charrad, *States and Women's Rights: The Making of Postcolonial Tunisia, Algeria and Morocco*, 2001; Derek Hopwood, *Habib Bourguiba of Tunisia: The Tragedy of Longevity*, 1992; Kenneth J. Perkins, *A History of Modern Tunisia*, 2004; Norma Salem, *Habib Bourguiba, Islam, and the Creation of Tunisia*, 1984.

ADEL ALLOUCHE

al-Turabi, Hasan (b. 1932)

Born in 1932 to a well-known family of religious notables in the town of Kassala in eastern Sudan, Hasan al-Turabi is one of the most intriguing figures among the Islamic thinkers and political activists of the 20th century. In his childhood and youth, he received a basic training in the traditional Islamic disciplines at the hands of his father, a judge (qadi), whose occupation kept the family constantly on the move. On the completion of his secondary school education in 1950, Turabi enrolled at the University of Khartoum, where he came in close contact with the Muslim Brotherhood, which had just started to set up local branches in the Sudan. In 1957, shortly after Sudan's national independence, Turabi left the country to continue his studies abroad, earning a master's degree from the University of London and a PhD in law from the Sorbonne, thus acquiring in-depth knowledge of Western legal systems and thought.

After his return to the Sudan in 1964, Turabi, now the dean of the Faculty of Law at the University of Khartoum, became immersed in Sudan's politics and continued to be politically active throughout his life. The political wing of the Sudanese Muslim Brotherhood at the time was the Islamic Charter Front (ICF), and Turabi emerged as one of its foremost activists, campaigning against the "Communist threat" and seeking support for the adoption of an Islamic constitution. Despite serious setbacks, such as the failure of the parliament to endorse the constitution proposed by the ICF in 1968 and the socialist and secular orientation of the military regime under Ja'far al-Numayri (1969–85), Turabi never gave up on his agenda of establishing an Islamic state in the Sudan.

After Numayri took power, Turabi was arrested on charges of treason and spent several years in prison. In the 1970s he emerged as the pioneer of what he and his fellow activists called the "Islamic movement." He authored more than ten books and numerous articles, outlining his ideas about "Islamic renewal" (*tajdīd*), the key concept in Turabi's thought, and dealing with diverse topics such as the Islamic political system, Islam and art, Islam and women, humanism, and Islam and the West. What sets Turabi apart from many of his contemporaries within political Islam is his attempt to synthesize Islamic doctrine and some aspects of Western political thought, such as devolution of power, federalism, and democracy (though not a multiparty system). He aimed at creating a new model that reconciled religious principles with the changing realities of modern life. Turabi left considerable room for the reinterpretation of Islam, arguing that, with few exceptions reflecting the eternal components of the divine message, everything could be subject to revision. This position earned him the reputation of a liberal thinker within contemporary Islamism, as well as the enmity of the more conservative-minded leaders within the Islamist spectrum.

Although Turabi consistently emphasized that the path to the Islamic state was only through education and raising an Islamic awareness among all citizens, his political strategies revealed that he also had an acute concern for power. Many observers noted a pattern of mismatch between his proclamations, which emphasized that the Islamization of the individual has to precede the Islamization of the state, and his actions, which suggest that he sought to assume political power first and then impose an Islamic political system that would ultimately lead to the full Islamization of Sudanese society. This contradiction runs as a central thread throughout Turabi's political career. As many observers have noted, Turabi always gave the impression of being moderate and soft-spoken in his public announcements, but his name is intimately connected to the so-called September Laws that introduced a shari'a-based penal code under President Ja'far al-Numayri in September 1983, a move that rekindled the fire of the civil war between the Northern regime and the Sudanese Peoples' Liberation Army (SPLA).

During the democratic interlude from 1985 and 1989, Turabi became the leader of the National Islamic Front (NIF), a political party that propagated the establishment of an Islamic state in the Sudan. The party was moderately successful in the 1986 elections but was unable to prevent the rapprochement between the government and the SPLA through democratic means. Turabi was widely perceived as the driving force behind the military coup of 1989 led by General 'Umar al-Bashir, who was still in power as of 2011. Turabi appeared as the chief ideologue of the new Islamist order, although he served another term in prison immediately after the coup. During the 1990s he was the founder and secretary general of the Popular Arabic and Islamic Congress (PAIC), an international forum for well-known Muslim radicals with its headquarters in Khartoum. As the éminence grise behind the regime he was instrumental in declaring the civil war against the SPLA a jihad, a move accompanied by compulsory conscription for the so-called Peoples' Defense Forces. The enactment of new shari'a laws and the promulgation of a new, "Islamic" constitution completed the picture of "God's rule in the Sudan." Turabi was finally stripped of his political influence, imprisoned, and kept under house arrest after losing a power struggle against President 'Umar al-Bashir in 1999, whose regime subsequently displayed a more moderate orientation.

Turabi's legacy is ambiguous. Hailed as a liberal and innovative Islamist thinker by some, seen as a cynical power broker and pillar of the "NIF dictatorship" by others, accused of directing an

international terrorist network by the United States during Bill Clinton's presidency, admired for his intellectual rigor and skillful pragmatism by his supporters, and disparaged as a secularist in Islamic garb by more conservative Islamists, he invariably caused a stir with his controversial pronouncements. In a series of public lectures after 2003, Turabi declared that the Muslims who died in the war against the SPLA could not be considered martyrs, thus denying that the war fulfilled the Islamic legal requirements for a jihad; he maintained that the consumption of alcohol should not be punishable under Islamic law; and he supported the idea that a woman could lead men in ritual prayer or become president in an Islamic state. Many Sudanese saw him as an enfant terrible whose "Islamic Project" has run its course. A definite assessment of his legacy, however, will depend on his reception by future generations of Islamic intellectuals.

See also revival and reform; Sudan

Further Reading

Abdelwahab El-Affendi, *Turabi's Revolution: Islam and Power in Sudan*, 1991; Millard J. Burr and Robert O. Collins, *Revolutionary Sudan: Hasan al-Turabi and the Islamist State, 1989–2000*, 2003; Abdullahi Ali Ibrahim, "A Theology of Modernity: Hasan al-Turabi and Islamic Renewal in Sudan," *Africa Today* 46 (3–4); Judith Miller, "Global Islamic Awakening or Sudanese Nightmare? The Curious Case of Hasan Turabi," in *Spokesmen for the Despised: Fundamentalist Leaders of the Middle East*, edited by R. Scott Appleby, 1997; John O. Voll, "Hasan al-Turabi: The Mahdi-Lawyer," in *Makers of Contemporary Islam*, edited by John L. Esposito and John O. Voll, 2001.

RÜDIGER SEESEMANN

Turkey

Turkey is a transcontinental state located mostly (291,773 sq. mi.) in Southwest Asia and partly (9,174 sq. mi.) in Europe. Bordered by three seas—the Black Sea to the north, the Aegean Sea to the west, and the Mediterranean to the south—Turkey serves as a geographic and cultural bridge between Asia and Europe. Its estimated population in 2007 was 73 million, of which 99.8 percent were Muslim. Although the Ottoman Empire ruled from Istanbul after 1453, Ankara became the capital of the Republic of Turkey in 1923.

The Ottoman state had been a multifaith, polyethnic empire up until World War I, but the mass deportation of Armenians in 1915 and the forcible population exchange between Greece and Turkey in 1923–26 produced a nation-state overwhelmingly inhabited by Muslims, most of whom consider themselves ethnically Turkish. Sunnis constitute a strong majority of the population, but there is also a sizable 'Alawi minority as well as pockets of Shi'is and Nusayris. Small Greek Orthodox, Armenian (Lusavorchakan and Catholic), and Jewish communities remain mainly in the big cities, while significant Kurdish populations inhabit the eastern and southeastern parts of Anatolia. Due to intensified internal migration after 1950, large numbers of Kurds now live in the major cities of western Turkey as well. The partition of the Ottoman Empire also turned small concentrations of Arabs and Turks into minorities on either side of Turkey's borders with Iraq and Syria.

Although Turkey is but one of the many successor states of the Ottoman Empire, it is commonly considered to be the heir of that historic polity. With one brief exception in the 1920s and 1930s, the Turkish establishment embraced this perception and viewed the republic as the legitimate successor to the empire and its former glory. In the aftermath of the Balkan wars of 1912–13, the empire that once straddled three continents and included such far-flung regions as Hungary, Yemen, Egypt, and Eritrea lost substantial territory to a number of breakaway nation-states and shrank to become a principally Asiatic country. The Ottoman defeat along with the Central Powers in 1918 brought about the final partition of the empire. The threat of further partition, embedded in the Sèvres Treaty of 1920, forced Turkish nationalists to fight for their independence in Anatolia between 1919 and 1922. The war, fought mainly against Greece, ended in a Turkish victory that yielded recognition of the boundaries of the new nation-state in the Lausanne Treaty of 1923. This treaty left the decision on the fate of the former Ottoman province of Mosul to the League of Nations, which awarded Mosul to Iraq in 1925. Since then, the single major change in Turkey's borders took place in 1939 when Turkey annexed the former Sanjak of Alexandretta (Hatay), which had been ceded to Syria under the French Mandate.

For centuries, the Ottoman Empire was the main Sunni power of the Muslim world. Following the conquest of the Arab provinces in the early 16th century, the Ottoman sultans formalized this position by assuming the title of caliph, which they used increasingly from the 19th century onward. Although Turkey inherited the caliphate, the republican leadership abolished the institution in March 1924, thereby bringing to an end a 1,300-year-old Muslim tradition. The abolition of the caliphate constituted a landmark event in the history of the Turkish Westernization movement. In contrast to the more cautious Ottoman tradition of reform, in which the ruling elite sought to Westernize the empire while keeping Islamic institutions intact, the republican leadership, led by Mustafa Kemal Atatürk, adopted a radical program aimed at sidelining Islam completely in the new Turkish society, which was to be governed by lay institutions guided by an intensely secular ideology. As part of their project, the republican elite strove to fashion a new Turkish identity based on ethnicity in place of religion. Turkey became the first officially secular Muslim country in 1937, although it had already been so in practice since at least 1928.

A central part of the republican agenda was the creation of new political institutions. In 1921, the Turkish Grand National Assembly adopted a new constitution. In November 1922, it abolished

the sultanate. On October 29, 1923, the leaders of the nationalist movement proclaimed the Turkish Republic. In 1922, Mustafa Kemal had established the People's Party (later called the Republican People's Party, or RPP), which dominated the political scene until the end of World War II. No genuinely free elections were held until 1950. Since then, however, regularly contested elections precipitated the fall of the RPP from its erstwhile position of dominance, and Turkey enjoyed a pluralistic multiparty regime. The advent of electoral politics notwithstanding, the army and the civilian bureaucracy maintained a form of tutelage over the state. The military, which viewed itself as the guardian of Kemalist ideology, launched two major coups in 1960 and 1980, intervened directly in politics in 1971, and intervened less directly (the so-called postmodern coup) in 1997. More recently, the Turkish military threatened to intervene in the presidential elections in 2007. Although secular centrist parties traditionally have dominated Turkish politics, the elections of 2002 produced the first pro-Islamist government in modern Turkish history. The Justice and Development Party, a moderate Islamist party, won a second and more decisive election victory in 2007 and gained a majority in the Turkish Grand National Assembly, the legislative body, and full control over the executive branch of government.

Turkey is the 17th largest economy in the world, with a gross domestic product (GDP) of $361.1 billion (at official exchange rates), GDP per capita of $8,900, and a real growth rate in GDP of 6.1 percent for 2006. Despite measures toward economic liberalization following the switch to a multiparty system, the Turkish economy of the 1960s and 1970s remained protectionist, etatist, and still heavily dependent on agriculture. Extensive reforms carried out in the 1980s, however, brought about major structural change. In the early 21st century, the agricultural sector produced less than 10 percent of Turkish GDP, and Turkey had one of the world's freest market economies.

To date, Turkey is the only Muslim country to have joined major Western institutions and alliances. Turkey joined the European Council in 1949, the Organisation for Economic Cooperation and Development in 1961, the Organization for Security and Cooperation in Europe in 1973, and the North Atlantic Treaty Organization (NATO) in 1952. It became an associate member of the European Economic Community in 1963 and received full membership candidate status from the European Union in 1999. Negotiations on accession to the European Union began in 2005.

See also Central Asia; Ottomans (1299–1924)

Further Reading

Sibel Bozdogan and Resat Kasaba, eds., *Rethinking Modernity and National Identity in Turkey*, 1997; Andrew Mango, *The Turks Today*, 2004; Ziya Onis, *State and Market: The Political Economy of Turkey in Comparative Perspective*, 1993; Erik J. Zurcher, *Turkey: A Modern History*, 2004.

M. ŞÜKRÜ HANIOĞLU

al-Tusi, Nasir al-Din (1201–74)

A philosopher, scientist, and major Shi'i theologian contributing to both the Isma'ili and Twelver traditions, Nasir al-Din al-Tusi wrote one of the most influential Persian medieval works on politics, ethics, and statecraft—namely, the *Akhlaq-i Nasiri* (*Nasirean Ethics*).

Abu Ja'far Muhammad al-Tusi was born into a scholarly Twelver Shi'i family in Tus in 1201. He began his studies in Arabic, the Qur'an, the hadith, and jurisprudence with his father and continued his education in Nishapur, Baghdad, and Mosul, studying with leading jurists and philosophers. In 1233, in pursuit of patronage, he accepted a commission to write a work on ethics and politics framed within Isma'ili theology for the governor of Kuhistan, Muhtasham Nasir al-Din. This work was the *Akhlaq-i Muhtashami* (Ethics for Muhtasham). Two years later, he wrote the *Akhlaq-i Nasiri* for Nasir al-Din. It drew on Abu 'Ali Ahmad b. Muhammad b. Miskawayh's (d. 1030) *Tahdhib al-Akhlaq* (The refinement of ethics), an Arabic naturalization of Aristotle's *Nicomachean Ethics*, and on the works of Ibn Sina (d. 1037) and Farabi (d. 950) on politics as well as Persian works of homiletics and statecraft. He spent more than 20 years with the Isma'ilis, acting as a missionary and benefiting from the excellent library in Alamut. This was his most productive period, in which he wrote major works in philosophy and mystical ethics such as the commentary on Ibn Sina's *al-Isharat wa-l-Tanbihat* (Pointers and reminders) and *Aghaz-u Anjum* (The origins and the final destinations).

After the fall of Alamut in 1256 and the siege of Baghdad two years later, both of which his detractors claimed he had connived, he joined the Mongol entourage of Hulagu, who provided him with a new observatory and academic complex in Maragha, Azerbaijan, making it a major center for philosophical and scientific learning. Toward the end of his life he returned to Baghdad and wrote some further works in Twelver Shi'i theology. He died in Baghdad in 1274 and was buried in the shrine complex of the seventh and ninth Shi'i imams in the Kazimiyya section of the city.

Tusi's contribution to politics and political thought lies not only in his Persian works and in his primary interest in both theoretical philosophy (metaphysics) and practical philosophy (ethics and politics) but also in his practice as a vizier to the Mongols. His works on politics fall within the Aristotelian tradition of virtue ethics being located in a polity that facilitates the production of flourishing happiness (*sa'āda*). The *Akhlaq-i Nasiri* is divided into three discourses. The first is divided into two parts: one on moral psychology and the nature of the soul as the seat of moral will and agency and the other on virtue ethics that focuses upon the notion of the Aristotelian mean and justice as a primary virtue. This has clear implications for politics, as he makes clear later in the text. This first part is, broadly speaking, a Persian paraphrase of Miskawayh's *Tahdhib al-Akhlaq*. The second discourse concerns the regulation of household affairs (*tadbīr-i manzil*) and includes important

discussions on mutual rights within the family and household as the basic units of societies and polities. The third discourse addresses Platonic conceptions of politics with philosophers as political leaders and the need for hierarchy and a clear role for different strata in society in advising the ruler. This examination of statecraft is all the more remarkable not only for its insistence on justice as a central political virtue but also for its emphasis on Aristotelian notions of friendship and Neoplatonic ideas of love and sympathy as fundamental elements in the fostering of harmony within society. This *akhlāq* tradition of placing interpersonal virtue ethics within the context of political thought had an important impact, and imitations were written for various subsequent rulers such as the *Akhlaq-i Jalali* (The Jalalian ethics), written by Jalal al-Din Dawani (d. 1502) for the Turkoman Aq Quyunlu ruler Uzun Hasan, and the *Akhlaq-i Muhsini* (Ethics for Muhsin), written by Husayn al-Wa'iz al-Kashifi (d. 1504) for the son of the Timurid ruler of Herat, Sultan Husayn Bayqara. Later works were written for Mughal and Safavid rulers, and even the *Jami' al-Sa'adat* (Compendium of happiness), written by Mulla Mahdi Naraqi (d. 1794), shows the influence of Tusi's work.

See also al-Farabi, Abu Nasr (ca. 878–950); Ibn Sina, Abu 'Ali (980–1037); philosophy

Further Reading

Ghulamhusayn Ibrahimi Dinani, *Nasir al-Din Tusi: Faylasuf-i Guftagu*, 2007; Nasrollah Pourjavady and Zhiva Vesel, eds., *Dānishmand-i Ṭūs/Naṣīr al-Dīn Ṭūsī: Philosophe et savant du XIIe siècle*, 1997; Nasir al-Din al-Tusi, *The Nasirean Ethics*, translated by G. M. Wickens, 1964; Idem, *Paradise of Submission: A Medieval Treatise on Ismaili Thought*, edited and translated by Sayyid Jalal Badakhchani, 2005.

SAJJAD H. RIZVI

tyranny

Tyranny is to act in a deeply unjust and cruel manner. Oppression (*ẓulm*), usually by someone in a position of state power, is the defining feature of tyranny. The Qur'an uses several words for tyranny, including *'uluww* (Q. 17:4), as well as *ẓulm*, and refers to the tyrant or the tyrannical as *ẓallām* (Q. 3:182; 8:51; 22:10; 41:46; 50:29) and *jabbār* (Q. 11:59; 14:15; 50:45). A crucial aspect of the Qur'anic understanding of tyranny is that it is created wholly by humans: God does not commit injustice (Q. 4:40; 28:5–6, 45:22), but people perpetrate the oppression of others. Indeed, one of the 99 divine epithets is *al-'adl* (the Just). Moreover, because every soul is accountable before God on the Day of the Resurrection (Q. 7:8–9 3:30; 45:28–31), the oppressor not only commits injustice against others but also ultimately wrongs himself or herself. Despite the Qur'an's condemnation of tyranny, numerous Muslim rulers have appealed to Islamic principles, motifs, and propaganda to justify various forms of oppression, to prolong their rule, and to perpetuate the status quo. Sunni Islamic law and theology generally require obedience even to an oppressive and sinful ruler as long as he outwardly upholds the shari'a as the law of the land and Islam as his own religion. A major motivation behind this stance is the view that the lack of a strong central authority will lead to *fitna*, widespread public conflict or a general state of disorder and lawlessness in society, a principle encapsulated in the maxim, "Sixty years of tyranny are better than an hour of civil strife." In addition, in classical Islamic law and theology, the legitimacy of institutions of public welfare such as the treasury of the Muslim community, the judiciary, and the defense forces are dependent on the legitimacy of the ruler; there was thus a strong incentive for theorists of the Sunni majority such as Ghazali (d. 1111) to uphold the legitimacy of a tyrant, because the alternative would entail an admission that all institutions dependent on appointment by the ruler were null and void, and society would cease to function properly. The Umayyads and Abbasids even fabricated hadith reports that promoted obedience to the ruling monarch and branded any opposition as Islamically deviant. At the same time, though, Islamic political theory and the practical discourse on kingship stressed a social contract by the dictates of which rulers were obligated to uphold justice and eradicate injustices in the territory under their control. Medieval Islamic governments set up special courts to deal with "injustices" (*maẓālim*) that were not addressed by the courts of ordinary judges, including abuses of power by government officials.

Early Islamic discourse strongly associates tyranny with kingship, which is seen as entailing the subordination of public interest and of the Muslim community's material and religious welfare to the interests or whims of the ruler. In the early centuries, the title of "king" was opposed to the caliph or imam, defined as the legitimate leader of the Muslim community, who takes his duties toward the believers seriously and puts their interests before his own. Thus when the Abbasids and later Muslims described the Umayyads as kings, this was equivalent to denouncing them as illegitimate tyrants, even though the title "king" later became popular among Muslim rulers such as the Ayyubids (1171–1250). Similarly, the well-known hadith report in which the Prophet allegedly predicts that the caliphate will last 30 years, after which there will be kings, is to be understood as a condemnation of all the caliphs after the first four as tyrants.

Non-Sunni theologies and countless historical rebellions against the existing status quo, particularly on the part of Shi'i and Khariji groups, have been predicated on the idea that the current ruler is an illegitimate caliph or imam, a usurper whose rule is by definition tyrannical and who should be replaced with the legitimate imam. Sunni legal and theological doctrine stresses the obligation to criticize the oppressive ruler for unjust deeds or violations of Islamic law and to attempt to convince him to change his ways, though obedience to a tyrant is required when such critiques are impossible, dangerous, or ineffective. Most Sunni authorities held that rebels

who have a plausible cause for rebellion, including those who are rebelling against a tyrannical ruler, should be treated with leniency or granted amnesty if possible.

Critiques of oppression and tyranny constitute a core theme of contemporary Islamic political thought. In the 20th century, tyranny for most Muslims manifested itself on two levels: foreign domination of the historic heartlands of Islam, first by European powers such as Britain and France and later by the United States, and domestic dictatorships, such as the governments of Egypt, Morocco, and Saudi Arabia. These twin tyrants—the external and the internal—have shaped contemporary Islamic discourse on injustice. The speeches of Osama bin Laden (d. 2011) effectively encapsulate this trend. Though his violent tactics do not represent the vast majority of Muslims, his grievances and sense of victimhood are widely shared by others. Bin Laden's concerns were essentially twofold: American policies in the Middle East, most notably support for the Israeli occupation of Palestine and sanctions imposed on the Iraqi people, and "un-Islamic" and deeply authoritarian Muslim regimes.

Contemporary readings of the Islamic heritage have become a powerful weapon of resistance against tyranny. Drawing on the Qur'an and early Islamic history for guidance, Muslim thinkers have sought to apply an understanding of episodes in Islam's salvation history to their own struggles in the present. Writing against the Nasserist regime in Egypt, the Islamic activist Sayyid Qutb (d. 1966), building on the ideas of his South Asian contemporary Mawdudi (d. 1979), used the term *jāhiliyya* to refer to the state. Conventionally defined as "the age of ignorance," the Qur'anic term *jāhiliyya* refers to the paganism of pre-Islamic Arabia, characterized by false worship, sin, bloody warfare, and gross inequity. By equating the contemporary Egyptian government with the *jāhiliyya*, Qutb thus sought to delegitimate the regime as un-Islamic and to call for its overthrow. The assassination of the Egyptian president Anwar Sadat (d. 1981) by the militant group Jihad is another telling example. After shooting Sadat, one of the assassins cried out triumphantly, "I am Khaled al-Islambuli. I have killed Pharaoh, and I do not fear death." By connecting the rule of Sadat with that of Pharaoh—who embodied tyranny and corruption in the Qur'an (Q. 10:83; 28:4), as in the Hebrew Bible (Exodus 1:8–22)—Islambuli underscored the oppressive policies of the regime.

See also colonialism; equality; ethics; human rights; imperialism; justice; masses; rebellion; revolutions; solidarity; torture

Further Reading

Farid Esack, *Qur'an, Liberation and Pluralism: An Islamic Perspective of Interreligious Solidarity against Oppression*, 1997; Toshihiko Izutsu, *Ethico-Religious Concepts in the Qur'an*, 2002; Gilles Kepel, *Muslim Extremism in Egypt: Prophet and Pharaoh*, 1985; Nizam al-Mulk, *The Book of Government or Rules for Kings: The Siyar al-Muluk or Siyasat-Nama of Nizam al Mulk*, translated by Hubert Darke, 2001.

SHADAAB RAHEMTULLA

U

Uighurs

With a population of over nine million, the Uighurs (also spelled Uygurs or Uyghurs) are the second largest ethnic Muslim group in the People's Republic of China after the Hui. They are mainly concentrated in a northwest province of China (officially known as the Xinjiang Autonomous Region but called Eastern Turkistan by Uighur nationalists). Originating from Tiele-Turkic nomads in the steppes of the northwestern Mongolia Plateau around 300 BC, the Uighurs migrated to northwestern China around the mid-ninth century after the Uighur empire (774–840) was overthrown by the Kyrghiz tribe as a result of a famine and civil war; they settled mainly in contemporary Gansu, Xingjiang, and west of Tieshan Mountain. The Uighurs' Islamic identity began with the Qarakhanid Khanate (around 960–1209, also spelled Karakhanid), the West Turkic dynasty established by a group of those migrated Uighurs based in Transoxiana and Tarim Basin of Central Asia. From their conversion to Islam in 934 under the rule of Sultan Satuq Bughra Khan (920–56) until the later years of Mughal rule in Chinese Turkistan (late 15th century), Islam gradually replaced Shamanism, Buddhism, Manicheanism, and Nestorian Christianity and became the sole religion of the Uighurs living in Xinjiang.

The political thoughts of Uighur Muslims can be viewed in three historical stages: (1) Islamic statecraft and virtue politics during the Qarakhanid dynasty; (2) religious activism and quasi theocracy during the rule of the Eastern Chaghatay and Yarkand khanates (also known as Mughulistan) from the late 14th century to the late 17th century; and (3) modern ideologies of Pan-Islamism, pan-Turkism, and Uighur nationalism from the late 19th century into the early part of the 21st century. The first stage of the Islamization of Xinjiang under the Turkic and Mongol khans resulted in a blossoming of indigenous Uighur literature and culture by absorbing influences from Indo-Persian, Islamic, Chinese, and even ancient Greek traditions. Yusuf Khass Hajib's *Wisdom of Royal Glory* (*Kutadgu Bilig*), completed in 1069 in Kashgar and often acclaimed as a Mirror for Princes, is a long prose work on political virtues, statesmanship, religion, and the art of war and was first presented to the prince of Kashgar in the hope that it would guide his rulership. This masterpiece was originally written in the Uighur language (mid-Turkish) and contains the authentic folk cultures of the different Turkic peoples, with the ambition to reconcile the diverse traditions of the region, including Islamic, Indo-Persian influence. By featuring four major characters who represent four virtues or principles—the king Rising Sun (justice), the vizier Full Moon (fortune), the sage Highly Praised (wisdom), and the ascetic Wide Awake (piety)—in a poetic story of the king's search for the best way of life as he asks others how to rule, *Kutadgu Bilig* recommends Islam as the protector of law and grounds the institution of justice on virtues, fortune, and religious piety. The work emphasizes that piety and wisdom are keys to a good kingship and echoes the perennial debate between Islam and politics by asking whether it is better to withdraw into solitude for religious contemplation or actively engage in worldly affairs. Ultimately, the author advocates for a symbolic but not actual withdrawal from politics, or "solitude in the multitude," in order to live a fulfilling life and attain success in the hereafter.

The second stage is related to Sufi orders and the reform-minded Khojas (religious-political leaders) during the Eastern Chaghatay (13th to 16th century) and Yarkand (1514–1680) khanates. Xinjiang was fully Islamicized by the 15th century, and most of the population ruled by the Chaghatayid (the Turkic Mughals related to Chaghatay Khan, the second son of Chingiz Khan) converted to Islam as a result of their ruler Tughluq Temur's (1347–63) embrace of Islam and the mass *da'wa* (Islamic missionary activity) by the Sufi shaykhs and missionaries. During the Yarkand Khanate (established by Sultan Said Khan, a relative of the Chaghatay nobles), branches of the Naqshbandis, a Sufi order originating from Central and South Asia, were able to seize control of political affairs with their religious activism and revivalism. One important leader, Baha' al-Din, taught that Sufis need not seclude themselves from the political community in order to maintain a strong relationship with God. The Naqshbandis rejected religious quietism and accelerated their missionary efforts in search of political support to advance their religious influence among the Mongol nomads and Uighur oasis dwellers. Their teachings had a pronounced Sunni bent that combined political activism, adherence to the law, and propagation of the religion, and soon became a divisive banner in the political struggles between two powerful Naqshbandi groups, Aq Tagh and Kara Tagh, whose leaders, called Khojas in the Turkic language, wielded both spiritual and political power and pushed the Chaghatay and Yarkand khans to adopt their brands of Islam. One prominent doctrine of Naqshbandis among the Uighurs (developed by Khoja Taj ad-Din), especially in the Altishahari and Mawarannahr branches, is the emphasis on "miracles" (*karāmāt*) and the veneration of saints and their tombs. Those tendencies were banished and labeled heretic in the 18th century when neo-orthodox fundamentalists became one of the major ideological sources for Uighur resistance

against the Zungaria Mongols' domination (1680–1756) and the Manchurian occupation from China (1756–1864).

The third stage witnesses the rise of modern Uighur nationalism in the context of pan-Islamism and pan-Turkism under the rule of a series of Chinese authorities: the late Manchurian Qing dynasty (1880–1911), Chinese warlords during the Republic era (1911–49), and Communists (1949–). In 1864, the Uighurs revolted against the rule of Manchurian officials, who mainly used begs (Turkic landlords) and Khojas to exercise indirect control, and they established a Kashgaria kingdom under Yaqub Beg (1820–77), who declared a holy war to expel Chinese-speaking Muslims and Han merchants from the region. Starting in the late 19th century, after the death of Yaqub Beg and the subsequent reconquering of the area by the Chinese, Uighur merchants and overseas students gradually introduced the ideas of pan-Turkism and Pan-Islamism, which nurtured widespread separatist sentiment. When Chinese warlords ruled Xinjiang (1911–49), progressive Uighur intellectuals adopted Islamic and Turkic modernism to promote enlightenment of Turkic peoples and national awareness through education, teaching Islam along with modern natural science. On November 12, 1933, a short-lived Eastern Turkestan Islamic Republic was established under the leadership of Khoja Niyaz, which became the important symbol of modern Uighur nationalism. Its constitution reflects its Islamic character with a modernizing and nationalizing ideology: its first clause announces governance in accordance with shari'a, whereas the second clause stresses democracy. The Second Eastern Turkestan Republic (founded in 1944 and led by Ahmatjan Qasimi), which also embodied both Islamic and secular political principles in its constitution, eventually collapsed after Chinese communists took control of Xinjiang in 1949. During communist rule, and especially during the Cultural Revolution, both Muslim and Uighur identities were suppressed, and class struggles became the dividing line among the Uighurs. Following the independence of the Central Asian countries in the early 1990s, Uighur nationalism, an umbrella identity to unite claims of an Islamic state, pan-Turkism, or simply Uighur independence, has revived and gained international concern. For example, according to documents released by the Chinese government and the U.S. Department of State, the East Turkistan Islamic Movement is a mujahidin organization of Uighur separatists whose ideology is to free Xinjiang from China and convert all Chinese to Islam. Although Islamic "extremism and fundamentalism" was sometimes blamed for the riots and bombings that have taken place in Xinjiang since the 1990s, it is those more secular and nationalistic claims that are gaining wider audience, thanks to Uighurs in exile, such as the successful businesswoman Rabiya Qadir, who has emerged as the main advocate of separatism in democratic terms.

See also China; Mongols

Further Reading

Joseph Fletcher, *Studies on Chinese and Islamic Inner Asia*, 1995; Yusuf Khass Hajib, *Wisdom of Royal Glory (Kutadgu Bilig): A Turko-Islamic Mirror for Princes*, translated by Robert Dankoff, 1982; Ho-dong Kim, *Holy War in China: The Muslim Rebellion and State in Chinese Central Asia, 1864–1877*, 2004; James A. Millward, *Euroasian Crossroads: A History of Xinjiang*, 2007; Justin Jon Rudelson, *Oasis Identities: Uyghur Nationalism along China's Silk Road*, 1997; Li Sheng, *History and Current Situation of Chinese Xinjiang (Zhongguo xinjiang lishi yu xiangzhuang)*, 2006.

SHAOJIN CHAI

'ulama'

The Arabic term *'ulamā'* (sing., *'ālim*) refers to Muslim scholars specializing in the Islamic religious sciences. A number of other terms are often used to characterize the particular focus of a scholar's work, among them *muḥaddith* (concerned with the study of the hadith reports attributed to the Prophet Muhammad), *mufassir* (an exegete of the Qur'an), and *faqīh* and mufti (a scholar of Islamic law and a jurisconsult, respectively). The term "'ulama'" usually is understood to encompass these somewhat narrower categories. The boundaries between "religious" and "secular" learning were less clearly delineated in premodern Islam than they have been in the modern world, and those recognized as 'ulama' sometimes made significant contributions to fields of knowledge lying well beyond the aforementioned areas. Further, the same person might well be a scholar of Islamic law, a theologian, a philosopher, and a Sufi. In modern times some "new religious intellectuals"—that is, people who are educated not at institutions of traditional Islamic learning but rather at Western or Westernized colleges and universities and who are active contributors to religious discourse—have sometimes claimed that they, too, should be considered as 'ulama'. As the Sudanese Islamist Hasan al-Turabi (b. 1932), who received a doctorate in law from the Sorbonne, put it, "Because all knowledge is divine and religious, a chemist, an engineer, an economist, or a jurist are all ulama." Despite occasionally blurred boundaries, The term "'ulama'" is usually understood as those who claim religious authority on the basis of their grounding in the Islamic religious sciences. This entry focuses on such traditionally educated religious scholars.

The 'Ulama' in Medieval History

The origins of the 'ulama' are to be traced to those figures of the first generations of Islam who had come to be seen by their contemporaries and successors as especially knowledgeable in matters relating to the Qur'an, as sources of information on the life and teachings of the Prophet Muhammad, and as jurists. By the early eighth century, scholarly circles had begun to emerge in several major Islamic towns in Arabia, Syria, Iraq, and elsewhere. Statements attributed to the Prophet and to his Companions also began to be collected with much vigor during the second century of Islam (roughly the eighth century), though it would take many generations of scholarly

contestation before the authority of hadith reports attributed to the Prophet Muhammad (as distinguished from statements ascribed to his Companions and other early Muslims or the evolving juridical discourses of particular scholarly circles) would be recognized as a source of legal norms second to the Qur'an.

Many prominent scholars of early Islam worked under the patronage of the rulers. One notable example is Muhammad b. Shihab al-Zuhri (d. 742), who served several Umayyad caliphs and was instructed by the caliph 'Umar b. 'Abd al-'Aziz (r. 717–20) to collect normative traditions (*sunan*, best understood here, as Wael Hallaq has observed, as reports relating to the teachings and practices not just of the Prophet but also of other early figures). Another example is Muhammad b. Ishaq (d. 767), the author of an early biography of the Prophet, which he composed at the behest of the second Abbasid caliph Mansur (r. 754–75) as part of a larger history of the world. Abu Yusuf (d. 798), a founding figure in the history of the Hanafi *madhhab*, or school of law (named after his teacher, Abu Hanifa [d. 767]), served as an influential judge in Baghdad and wrote a treatise on taxation for the Abbasid caliph Harun al-Rashid (r. 786–809). Medieval biographical dictionaries are replete with instances of scholars visiting caliphs and other notables, receiving their gifts, and benefiting in sundry other ways from royal patronage.

Yet the emergence of religious scholars also represented a multifaceted challenge to the ruling elite. For one thing, many scholars were willing to lend their support to trends and movements hostile to the political establishment. This was the case especially with those who came to be allied with various Shi'i groups in the late Umayyad and early Abbasid period. But even those not so allied were sometimes opposed to particular policies adopted by the caliphs and their officials, from unjust taxation to the failure to conform to the ideals and norms as they were being articulated in these scholarly circles. Quite apart from specific instances of scholarly disaffection, the fact that the scholars had come to represent an increasingly independent locus of authority in Muslim society was a cause of much apprehension on the part of the ruling elite. It was independent in the sense that, unlike the judges appointed by the state, the scholars did not need authorization from the caliph to do their work, for example, responding to people's queries on matters of law, interpreting the Qur'an, collecting hadith reports, and engaging in theological debates. From the mid-eighth century onward, the scholars also began defining the position of the caliph in such a way that it lacked any privileged authority in religious as opposed to political matters.

The most serious challenge to the increasing influence of the 'ulama', as represented by the scholars of hadith, came from the Abbasid caliph Ma'mun (r. 813–33). Toward the end of his reign he instituted an "inquisition" (the *miḥna*) requiring the scholars to affirm the "createdness" of the Qur'an. Though ostensibly intended to guard the cardinal Islamic doctrine of the oneness of God against any coeternal competitors, hence the caliph's insistence that the Qur'an be regarded as the created rather than uncreated (and, by implication, eternal) word of God, this ingenious test is better seen as an effort to put the increasingly assertive scholars in their place by affirming the caliph's prerogative to articulate correct beliefs. The *miḥna* eventually was terminated during the reign of caliph Mutawakkil (r. 847–61), its end signaling caliphal recognition of the 'ulama' collectively as the authoritative guardians of the evolving religious tradition. The caliph was scarcely divested of "religious" functions with the end of the *miḥna*, however. One of the primary functions, and justifications, of government was, after all, the upholding of the shari'a; several influential jurists writing on government stipulated that the caliph should be knowledgeable in matters of the law to the rank of a scholar capable of arriving at independent legal opinions (*ijtihād*). Irrespective of whether these jurists seriously expected the caliphs to have such legal expertise, stipulations of this sort suggest the degree to which the scholars had come to define what constituted legitimate political authority as well as the centrality of their own vocation to all Islamic matters.

The 'ulama' also wrote themselves into medieval constitutional theory by stipulating that they were the people responsible, either exclusively or together with other notables, for choosing the ruler. In practice, of course, the 'ulama' had little say in who ruled the polity and, in keeping with their generally quietist politics, the jurists studiously avoided discussing the mechanisms through which a corrupt, incompetent, or irreligious ruler should be removed from office. Yet this quietism did not quite extend to the degree where the ruler could necessarily take the 'ulama' for granted. The ruling elite needed political legitimacy, which came not from popular will or good governance but rather, in considerable measure, from the allegiance of the religious scholars. Moreover, as observed by Jonathan Berkey, given the fact that the medieval political and military ruling classes often had shallow roots in the societies over which they ruled, the 'ulama', with much deeper local roots, could serve as a constraint of sorts on the arbitrary exercise of power even as they helped mediate between the ruling elite and their subjects. Nor, by the same token, did the scholars' concern with political stability mean that they were necessarily wedded to a particular ruler: a successful challenger to an existing regime could very well receive the same endorsement from the scholars as had his predecessor. As Khaled Abou El Fadl has shown, many medieval jurists also argued that while it was wrong to rebel against constituted political authority, Muslim rebels did nonetheless have political rights. They were not to be treated by the rulers in the manner of mere brigands but rather as people with an "interpretation," albeit an incorrect one, that had led them to adopt a particular course of action. Such reasoning was not merely an effort to distinguish wrongheaded Muslim rebels from either the brigands or the non-Muslim foes; it was also an implicit warning to the rulers that the jurists' quietist worldview could nonetheless countenance an alternative to the existing political dispensation.

Inasmuch as they sought to exercise some degree of restraint on the political elite, the jurists, and the 'ulama' in general, remained vulnerable to political pressure and influence. This made

for an often tense relationship between the religious and the political elite. The social institutions and the scholarly culture of the 'ulama' do nonetheless seem to have served them well in trying to safeguard the space they had been carving out for themselves since the ninth century. For instance, the institution of the waqf, or the charitable endowment, was understood as existing in perpetuity, so that, even when established by members of the ruling elite, it was expected to be rather more resistant to political interference than might have been the case otherwise. It was such waqf endowments that helped sustain Islamic institutions of learning, the madrasas, which had begun to appear in Muslim societies in the late 11th century.

Religious scholarship also made for a remarkable cosmopolitanism in the world of the 'ulama': for all their local roots, many among the 'ulama' traveled widely and, despite the limitations of a manuscript culture, their work could enjoy broad recognition. Among other things, this cosmopolitanism served again to limit the degree to which the ruling elite could regulate, even when so inclined, the activities and discourses of the 'ulama'. The very nature of the scholarly tradition of the 'ulama' was, furthermore, resistant to political encroachment. With the veritable canonization of particular collections of hadith reports and with the crystallization of their schools of law, complete with their agreed-upon methods and their authoritative norms, the scholars were keen not to leave the door ajar for political manipulation of their tradition. Contrary to how Muslim modernists as well as an earlier generation of Western observers viewed the medieval Islamic scholarly tradition, mechanisms for rethinking legal norms and adapting them to changing needs did continue to exist. For their part, the rulers were seldom at a loss in finding pliant scholars who would endorse this or that measure. Nonetheless, in constructing an elaborate scholarly tradition and anchoring their identity and authority in it, the 'ulama' sought to guard it from political and other vicissitudes. To the extent that the 'ulama' can be seen as a key component of a public sphere in medieval Islamic societies, their scholarly tradition and attendant socioreligious roles were crucial to it.

A significant exception to the pattern of 'ulama'-state relations discussed here is represented by their position in the Ottoman Empire. The Ottoman 'ulama' comprised a veritable religious establishment that was headed by the shaykh al-Islam (the grand mufti) who belonged, as did the sultans, to the Hanafi school of law. The close identification of the 'ulama' with the state carried important dividends: their leading madrasas were richly endowed, the Hanafis comprised the dominant school even in regions whose Muslim inhabitants belonged to other schools of law, and the shaykh al-Islam was one of the most powerful officials in the empire. The close relationship with the political elite also had very considerable costs, however: in the 17th and early 18th centuries, as Madeline Zilfi has noted, no fewer than three shaykhs al-Islam were executed, and others came close to that fate. And the demise of the Ottoman Empire in the early 20th century meant that the fate of the Ottoman religious establishment, too, was sealed.

The 'Ulama' in the Modern World

The 'ulama' have faced major challenges in all Muslim societies since the 19th century. Among the most significant was the onset of European colonial rule, which, in many cases, spelled the end of Muslim political authority. While many among the 'ulama' had maintained their distance from the governing elite, they depended on the government for the upholding of Islamic law. The sultan did not need to be virtuous for the 'ulama' to serve as judges in his administration or to attend to various aspects of intellectual and religious life in society. The advent of colonial rule jeopardized the practice of Islamic law as never before, however. With the establishment of British colonial rule in India, for instance, the scope of Islamic law was gradually reduced to matters of personal status (e.g., marriage, divorce, and inheritance), which is what the "shari'a" came to mean in British India. But even this limited body of Islamic law was administered by judges who were usually non-Muslim. The judges based their decisions on a small set of "authoritative" Islamic legal texts, but they did so while being guided by norms of English common law. The 'ulama' tended to see the resulting jurisprudence—the "Anglo-Muhammadan law"—as nothing but a travesty of the shari'a. Many among them considered it illegitimate for people to have recourse to colonial courts even for such routine matters as the dissolution of a marriage, which meant further restrictions on the practice of Islamic law even in areas that the colonial administration had officially recognized.

Colonialism brought new institutions not just in the judicial realm but also, among others, in that of education. Even as many madrasas and related institutions declined with the drying up of earlier forms of financial patronage, not the least the disintegration of what had once been substantial waqf endowments, a new generation of Muslims began to be educated in modern institutions of Western learning. Such institutions had only limited space for Islamic learning. In part, this was because their raison d'être was to provide Muslims with the sort of education that would help them succeed in the colonial economy, and in part, it had to do with the highly critical stance the founders of such institutions adopted toward the traditionalist 'ulama', holding them responsible for the cultural and intellectual decline of Islam. But it also had to do with the 'ulama''s own suspicion of such modern institutions, which they saw not merely as trespassing on their territory—in this instance, education—but as yet another instrument of a colonial enterprise bent on the very destruction of Islam.

Despite the lack of any sustained formal training in the Islamic sciences, those educated in such modern institutions have had a keen interest in Islamic matters. But their engagement with Islam—as Muslim modernists, Islamists, and other new religious intellectuals—has been of a decidedly different sort than the manner in which the 'ulama' have tended to understand and interpret their religious tradition. By the same token, the products of these modern institutions of learning have often taken a dim view of the intellectual tradition of the 'ulama' and of their relevance, thus representing a serious challenge to the authority and social influence of the 'ulama'.

A related challenge has come from the fact that print and information technologies, in tandem with the impact of mass education, have made the sources of religious knowledge far more accessible to larger groups of people than had ever been the case before the early 20th century. The 'ulama' have never been a cohesive social or religious group and, despite considerable overlaps between "religious" and other forms of learning in medieval Islam, their claims to authority were sometimes vigorously contested by the philosophers, the Sufis, members of the urban cultural elite, and popular preachers, just as scholars of hadith and law might contest the claims of, say, the theologians. The degree to which modern Islam has seen what Dale Eickelman and James Piscatori have characterized as the "fragmentation" of religious authority is nonetheless unparalleled. Also unprecedented is the power and reach of the modern state, which has been far less willing to allow the 'ulama' to have the sort of social and religious autonomy that they had so jealously guarded in many premodern Muslim societies.

It was common for observers of Muslim societies in the mid- and late 20th century to assume that the 'ulama' had fared altogether badly in the face of such challenges. Adherents of modernization and secularization theories had little doubt that the 'ulama' and their institutions were mere relics of the past waiting to be swept aside by the forces of Westernization. They were not entirely wrong in this view. In Turkey under Atatürk, the institution of the shaykh al-Islam had been abolished, as noted earlier, and the madrasas and Sufi orders were closed down. In Morocco and Tunisia, long-established madrasas such as the Qarawiyyin in Fez and the Zaytuna in Tunis underwent radical transformations at the behest of the ruling elite. So did Azhar University in Egypt: the reforms of 1961, representing a culmination of decades of governmental effort at regulation, sought simultaneously to transform this venerable seat of Sunni learning into a modern university (with faculties of Arabic and Islamic studies now part of a much broader educational mandate) *and* to make it more fully subservient to the government. Even in Iran, where the 'ulama' and their madrasas were considerably freer of state regulation than they were in many Sunni countries because of structures of religious authority peculiar to Shi'ism, the 'ulama''s institutions saw sharp decline under the Pahlavi dynasty.

The Iranian Revolution (1978–79) was a major corrective to conventional wisdom. A seemingly strong and Westernized regime was overthrown by a massive movement that was not merely suffused with a religious idiom but also led by traditionally educated religious scholars, who then proceeded to occupy a prominent place in the Islamic Republic. Together with developments in Pakistan, Saudi Arabia, Afghanistan, Egypt, and elsewhere in the Muslim world, the Iranian Revolution helped draw the attention of scholars, policy analysts, and other observers to Islamism. Yet given that Sunni Islamists have tended to be drawn not from the ranks of the 'ulama' but rather from those of the college- and university-educated, a recognition of the limits of modernization theories did not immediately translate into attention to the 'ulama' and their institutions in Sunni societies. It has come to be increasingly recognized, however, that Sunni 'ulama'—and the 'ulama' in general—continue to be an important facet of Muslim politics and the public sphere and that it is difficult to understand contemporary Islam in all its complexity without serious attention to them.

Some of the very forces that posed severe challenges to the 'ulama' and, in many cases, marginalized them have, paradoxically, served to bring them back into prominence. The onset of colonial rule in India goaded the establishment not only of the Westernizing Muhammadan Anglo-Oriental College (later Aligarh Muslim University) in 1875 but also, a few years earlier, of a new madrasa in the North Indian town of Deoband. While the founders of the Aligarh college wanted Muslims to effectively compete with their Hindu compatriots by learning the language and the ways of the new rulers, those of the Deoband madrasa sought to defend Muslim identity through a renewed focus on Islamic learning. Unlike earlier institutions of Islamic learning in India and elsewhere, the Deoband madrasa was sustained not by the support of rich and powerful patrons but rather by the donations of ordinary people. Though admitting of different permutations, this pattern was followed by other institutions throughout South Asia and beyond. "Deobandi" madrasas—so called because they adhere to a shared approach to Islam anchored in the study of hadith and Hanafi law—now number in the tens of thousands, though significant numbers of madrasas belonging to other doctrinal orientations also dot the religious landscape in South Asia.

While mass education and print and information technologies have made it possible for people to access normative religious texts on their own, unaided by the 'ulama', and to compete with the 'ulama' in the production of religious discourse, the very same developments have also enabled the 'ulama' to disseminate their writings in new ways and to reach new audiences. Though many among the 'ulama' have resisted governmental efforts to open up their madrasas and related institutions to modern, secular learning, they have come to benefit from such learning as well. At Azhar University in Cairo, as Malika Zeghal has shown, the opening of new faculties devoted to the modern sciences has contributed to the ability of at least some 'ulama' to interact with greater facility with college- and university-educated Islamists than would otherwise have been the case. Some of the most influential of the contemporary 'ulama'—for example, Muhammad Taqi 'Uthmani (b. 1943) of Pakistan and the Egyptian religious scholar Yusuf al-Qaradawi (b. 1926), who moved to the oil-rich Persian Gulf emirate of Qatar in the early 1960s—have come to base their authority not only on a demonstrated mastery of the Islamic tradition but also on their putative ability to make it relevant to contemporary circumstances, which, in turn, is recognized as depending on their understanding of the modern world. The prominence Qaradawi enjoyed in the early years of the 21st century had to do, in considerable measure, with his dexterous use of the Internet and satellite television, together with the opportunities made available long ago by print, to reach multiple audiences well beyond the Arab Middle East.

Notwithstanding the challenges posed by the modern state to the autonomy of the 'ulama', the ability of individual governments to regulate their institutions has also varied significantly. There is a marked contrast, for instance, between successful governmental efforts toward integrating Islamic institutions of learning into the educational mainstream in Indonesia and the halting and far from effective attempts of successive Pakistani governments to do the same. In Egypt, for its part, the ability of an authoritarian regime to make Azhar University amenable to its will has come at the cost of having to cede oversight of the religious public sphere to it, sometimes at considerable international embarrassment to a regime keen to project a "liberal" image.

Fragmentation and Rearticulations of Authority

The discourses and practices of the 'ulama' have been subject to significant countervailing pressures in modern Islam, revealing—as might be expected for a still-active scholarly community with deep roots in history—elements of both continuity and change. In many cases, the most distinctive of their institutions, the *madhhab*, has tended to decline in terms of the authority it carries over the lives of the people, even as new institutions and practices have continued to emerge in efforts to standardize belief and practice in new ways. For a millennium since their beginnings in the ninth century, the *madhhab*s have provided the normative legal framework in which the Sunnis (and Shi'is) have led their lives. Since the late 19th century, the 'ulama' tied to particular schools of law have been fiercely challenged by those who seek to base all belief and practice squarely on the foundational texts—the Qur'an and the normative example of the Prophet—as well as the practices of Islam's first generations (the *salaf*), rather than on the agreed-upon doctrines of the medieval schools. The Salafis, as these putative adherents of the forebears style themselves, have differed much among themselves. They include those who have sought to rethink particular norms in the conviction that "true" Islam, as enshrined in the Qur'an and the practices of the first Muslims, can be shown to be in much greater accord with modern liberal sensibilities than it is with traditional religious practices. But the Salafis also include those who reject a good deal of the ideas, practices, and institutions characteristic of the modern world on grounds of their perceived incompatibility with the foundational texts. Either way, the Salafi view that Muslims should follow the unalloyed teachings of the foundational texts and the example of the pious forebears rather than the doctrines and hermeneutical approaches of the medieval schools of law has had considerable resonance in many Muslim circles, and it has done much to undermine the authority of the *madhhab*. So have the legislative initiatives of the modern state, given that modern Islamic legislation and codifications of the law have tended to draw on the resources of the schools of law as a whole rather than those limited to any particular *madhhab*.

It would nonetheless be an exaggeration to conclude that the schools of law have ceased to matter much in contemporary Islam. In some regions, notably South Asia, most Muslims still identify themselves as Hanafis—that is, as adherents of the Hanafi school of law; it is as Hanafi scholars that Deobandis, and many other Sunni scholars, articulate their claims to authority in this region. Even in contemporary Saudi Arabia, a Salafi orientation toward the foundational texts tends to be combined with a continuing reliance on the norms of the Hanbali school of law. Yet the schools of law carry less overarching authority than they did a century ago, even in regions whose inhabitants continue to adhere to them, with the result that the 'ulama', whose authority was long tied to the *madhhab*, have had to look for alternative loci of authority.

These alternatives have assumed many forms, but common to them is the tendency toward a new institutionalization of authority. Building on previous juridical hierarchies, the Dar al-Ifta' al-Misriyya (The Egyptian Organization for Granting Legal Opinions) was established in Egypt in 1895 as a way of both standardizing the issuing of juridical opinions and giving them an official imprimatur. In India, the Deoband madrasa had established its own Dar al-Ifta' two years prior to the Egyptian namesake. In more recent decades, a number of "*fiqh* academies" have been established to provide forums for collective deliberation on matters of Islamic law (*fiqh*). Some, notably the International Islamic Fiqh Academy in Jeddah, Saudi Arabia (established in 1983 under the auspices of the Organization of the Islamic Conference), brings together scholars from the Muslim world at large. Others, such as India's Islamic Fiqh Academy (founded in 1989), are limited to one country, though it, too, seeks to foster ties with scholars elsewhere. More recent institutional ventures include the European Council for Fatwa and Research, founded in 1997 under the leadership of Qaradawi with a view to providing legal guidance to increasingly substantial numbers of Muslims living in Europe, as well as the International Union of Muslim Scholars, founded in 2004 with Qaradawi again as its founding president.

Though such institutions do not necessarily seek to supplant the *madhhab*—the Dar al-Ifta' of Deoband is the juridical arm of the Hanafi madrasa, and even members of transnational *fiqh* academies are not required to relinquish their legal affiliations—they do occupy some of the space that the school of law would have inhabited, and often still does, for its adherents. They are equally a facet of the increasing standardization of religious norms and practices that have been witnessed not just in Islam but also, as C. A. Bayly has observed, in many other religious traditions in the modern world. In medieval Islam the *madhhab*—and the expectation that all but the most distinguished jurists would adhere strictly to its established norms and methods (a practice known as *taqlīd*)—had itself represented efforts toward standardization of doctrine. While standardization and institutionalization are not new to the culture of the 'ulama', they have come to assume distinctive forms in the modern world.

Another expression of this standardization is an increasing interest in the idea of collective fatwas and, indeed, of "collective *ijtihād*." While *ijtihād* has long been viewed as the exercise of an individual jurist's mental faculties and legal acumen to arrive at new rulings on matters not hitherto regulated by the foundational texts, the 20th century has seen increasing initiatives toward making this a collective venture. In part, this is an effort to answer

rhetorical objections of those among the 'ulama' who have long opposed *ijtihād* on the grounds both that their abilities did not match those of their incomparably more learned predecessors and that encouraging possibilities of *ijtihād* would open the door to willful manipulation of the sacred law in an age of rampant intellectual and moral decline. Against such objections, still not without resonance in particular circles, collective *ijtihād* offers the possibility of pooling together the resources of scholars who would supposedly be inadequate on their own but are more credible as a collective. By the same token, it is also a very visible effort to bring together traditionally educated religious scholars and "experts" in modern, secular domains, underscoring the oft-repeated claim that Islam can provide guidance on all matters, including those that go well beyond the traditional religious expertise of the 'ulama'. In recent years, particular regimes have also sought to encourage collective, quasi-official venues of fatwas as a means of reining in the diverse voices in the public sphere and, increasingly, in cyberspace.

Yet modern initiatives toward standardization and institutionalization—sometimes as a way of facilitating state regulation of Islam and sometimes as a way of resisting it—often exist side by side with an increasing fragmentation of authority, with the 'ulama''s assertions and interpretations being questioned by ever-increasing numbers of educated men and women in light of their own access to the foundational texts and their diverse bodies of knowledge. The 'ulama' themselves are to be found on both sides, sometimes simultaneously. Thus even as many jurists among them are part of institutional forums of collective *ijtihād* and of collective fatwas, some of the very same scholars continue to issue fatwas on their own individual authority as well. Standardization and institutionalization, on the one hand, and individualization and fragmentation, on the other, have continued to shape the discourses, practices, and institutions of the 'ulama' as well as their claims to authority. As much as they would have liked it to be the case, the 'ulama' of medieval Muslim societies were scarcely unchallenged in their claims to authority. Such challenges have only grown in range and intensity in modern and contemporary Islam. Yet they have not necessarily marginalized the 'ulama', and, in local, regional, and global contexts, many among them have continued to lay claim to, and not unsuccessfully compete with others for, authority and influence within and outside the religious sphere.

See also authority; fundamentalism; jurisprudence; knowledge; shari'a; shaykh al-Islam

Further Reading

Khaled Abou El Fadl, *Rebellion and Violence in Islamic Law*, 2001; Aziz Ahmad, "The Role of Ulema in Indo-Muslim History," *Studia Islamica* 31 (1970); C. A. Bayly, *The Birth of the Modern World, 1780–1914*, 2004; Peri Bearman et al., eds., *The Islamic School of Law*, 2005; Jonathan Berkey, *The Formation of Islam*, 2003; Michael Cook, *Commanding Right and Forbidding Wrong in Islamic Thought*, 2000; Patricia Crone, *God's Rule: Government and Islam*, 2004; Patricia Crone and Martin Hinds, *God's Caliph: Religious Authority in the First Centuries of Islam*, 1986; Dale F. Eickelman and James Piscatori, *Muslim Politics*, 1996; Wael B. Hallaq, *The Origins and Evolution of Islamic Law*, 2005; Sherman Jackson, *Islamic Law and the State: The Constitutional Jurisprudence of Shihab al-din al-Qarafi*, 1996; George Makdisi, *The Rise of Colleges*, 1981; Barbara D. Metcalf, *Islamic Revival in British India: Deoband, 1860–1900*, 1982; Stefan Reichmuth, *The World of Murtada al-Zabidi (1732–91): Life, Networks and Writings*, 2009; Jakob Skovgaard-Petersen, *Defining Islam for the Egyptian State: Muftis and Fatwas of the Dār al-Iftā*, 1997; Muhammad Qasim Zaman, "The Ulama and Contestations on Religious Authority," in *Islam and Modernity: Key Issues and Debates*, edited by M. K. Masud et al., 2009; Idem, *The Ulama in Contemporary Islam: Custodians of Change*, 2002; Malika Zeghal, *Gardiens de l'Islam: Les ulama d'al-Azhar dans l'Egypte contemporaine*, 1995; Madeline C. Zilfi, *The Politics of Piety: The Ottoman Ulema in the Post-Classical Age (1600–1800)*, 1988.

MUHAMMAD QASIM ZAMAN

'Umar b. 'Abd al-'Aziz (ca. 680–720)

Despite a very short caliphate (717–20), 'Umar b. 'Abd al-'Aziz ('Umar II) occupies a specific place in the Islamic tradition. Although the Umayyads were generally portrayed negatively in Abbasid historiography, 'Umar II is remembered as a moral exemplar and a truly pious caliph.

Prior to his caliphate, 'Umar served as governor of Medina for more than five years (706–12) during the caliphate of al-Walid b. 'Abd al-Malik (r. 705–15). Although he was eventually dismissed from office under the pressure of the powerful governor of Iraq, Hajjaj b. Yusuf (d. 714), 'Umar notably supervised the expansion of the Prophet's Mosque in Medina at the caliph's request and governed the city in close collaboration with the Medinan religious scholars and jurists (*fuqahā'*), with whom he developed strong links. He became the eighth Umayyad caliph under rather murky circumstances, as he was designated a successor by Sulayman b. 'Abd al-Malik (r. 715–17), perhaps under the influence of his éminence grise, Raja' b. Haywa (d. 730). Sulayman's decision generated profound discontent among the sons of 'Abd al-Malik, especially Hisham, who wanted to keep the caliphate in their father's lineage, thus revealing the intense competition between the various branches of the Umayyad family.

'Umar II's first decision as caliph was to recall from the field Maslama b. 'Abd al-Malik, who had embarked, at Sulayman's orders, on a disastrous siege of Constantinople. He also seems to have considered recalling other Muslim armies, as in the case of recently conquered Spain, for instance, before abandoning this project. This has often been interpreted in modern scholarship as an attempt by 'Umar II to end Muslim expansion. The picture, however, is more complicated. For although his caliphate witnessed an imperial

contraction, 'Umar II sent troops against the Turks and the Khariji rebels in Iraq and continued the practice of annual summer campaigns against Byzantium.

'Umar II's fiscal policies are symptomatic of the main challenges faced by the Umayyad caliphate at the time—namely, finding new sources of income to compensate for the slowing down of the conquests and taking into account the expectations of new Muslim converts, who were eager to be placed on an equal footing with long-established Muslims. Particularly noteworthy from this perspective is a famous but obscure document attributed to 'Umar II, his so-called fiscal rescript, in the form it is preserved in Ibn 'Abd al-Hakam's (d. 815) later biography of the caliph. This text has generated varying interpretations, but its authenticity has not been questioned. It makes clear that 'Umar II tried to increase the state's resources, notably by reassessing the status of lands and the taxes due on them and by giving a moral dimension to the government. At the same time, the caliph was intent on improving the situation of new converts. He therefore decided to grant them the same fiscal status as that of their fellow Muslims, even though this could increase the incentive to conversion and lead to a reduction in state revenue. And, in fact, the *dhimmīs* who converted to Islam during 'Umar II's caliphate were no longer required to pay the head tax (*jizya*). This placed significant pressure on non-Muslim communities, and Christian sources usually complain about 'Umar II's anti-Christian policies, even if his piety is duly acknowledged. Such fiscal policies were short-lived, however, as they were largely abandoned by his successors. On his way to Aleppo, 'Umar II died in 720 in Dayr Sim'an, where he was buried. The ruins of his tomb, of uncertain date, are still visible today, and occasionally attract some pilgrims and visitors.

As 'Umar II's policies departed significantly from previous Umayyad practice, he has been portrayed by some modern scholars, such as M. A. Shaban, as a "radical reformer." His image in Muslim and non-Muslim sources overall is quite fascinating. In the Muslim sources, he is depicted as the fifth Rightly Guided Caliph, a new 'Umar b. al-Khattab, and the model caliph in terms of piety, generosity, asceticism, and sense of justice—one who ardently tried to follow the example of the Prophet and his Companions. Indeed, 'Umar II played a significant role in the promotion of the Prophet's sunna and the sunna of his successors. This attitude generated strong opposition from the Qadaris, with whom 'Umar II had serious theological disagreements. 'Umar II is furthermore credited with playing a role in the recording of the Prophet's traditions (hadith), and a *musnad* is even attributed to him, although it is considered unreliable by hadith critics. 'Umar II is also famous for the pseudo-correspondence that he supposedly had with the Byzantine emperor Leo III (r. 717–41). Moreover, a large body of letters attributed to the caliph is also preserved in Muslim and Christian sources, and some of these have serious claims to authenticity.

'Umar II is portrayed in some Muslim sources as the Mahdi (eschatological savior) or the *mujaddid* (renewer) of the Muslim community, and some evidence suggests that he indeed viewed himself as such. This messianic status is closely connected with the fact that he was the caliph during the year 100 of the hijra, a year of intense apocalyptic expectations in the Islamic tradition. The same was apparently true of his predecessor Sulayman, who was expected to be the caliph in 100 AH but died before that year. 'Umar II's eschatological dimension is echoed in his nickname, *al-ashajj*, "the scarred one": he had been scarred as a consequence of an accident in his childhood, but that was subsequently viewed as a herald to his function as a renewer who fills the Earth with justice.

It would appear that 'Umar II's image was largely elaborated in the context of emerging Malikism relatively early, as of the eighth century. This is clearly seen in the elevated place he occupies in Malik b. Anas' (d. 795) *Muwatta'*, as well as in the *Sirat 'Umar ibn 'Abd al-'Aziz*, compiled by Ibn 'Abd al-Hakam, one of the architects of Malikism in Egypt. His image as an almost "holy" caliph is also very early: he is remembered as a very special person in both Muslim (Sunni and Shi'i alike, as he is praised by the latter for having stopped the practice of cursing 'Ali b. Abi Talib in the Friday sermons) and non-Muslim sources. Such a highly positive image may explain why, in the troubled aftermath of the Abbasid revolution, his grave was spared by the Abbasids, in contrast to the tombs of his fellow Umayyads.

See also 'Ali b. Abi Talib (ca. 599–661); apocalypse; Mahdi; Malik b. Anas (712–95); Muhammad (570–632); Qadaris; Rightly Guided Caliphate (632–61); Shi'ism; sunna; Sunnism; 'Umar b. al-Khattab (ca. 580–644); Umayyads (661–750)

Further Reading

W. W. Barthold, "Caliph 'Umar II and the conflicting reports on his personality," *Islamic Quarterly* 15 (1971); Antoine Borrut, "Entre tradition et histoire: genèse et diffusion de l'image de 'Umar II," *Mélanges de l'Université Saint-Joseph* 58 (2005); Hamilton A. R. Gibb, "The Fiscal Rescript of 'Umar II," *Arabica* 2 (1955); Gerald R. Hawting, *The First Dynasty of Islam: The Umayyad Caliphate*, 2002; Robert G. Hoyland, "The Correspondence of Leo III (717–741) and 'Umar II (717–720)," *Aram* 6 (1994); M. A. Shaban, *Islamic History: A New Interpretation, Vol. I: A.D. 600–750 (A.H. 132)*, 1971.

ANTOINE BORRUT

'Umar b. al-Khattab (ca. 580–644)

A towering personality of nearly unrivaled stature in Sunni Islam, 'Umar b. al-Khattab influenced the institutions and creation of the early Islamic polity—both as a caliph and a prominent Companion of the Prophet. He is popularly known as *al-Fārūq*, a title traditionally interpreted to mean "he who distinguishes right from wrong." Arguably, due to his oversight of the earliest phases of the Islamic

conquests outside peninsular Arabia, ‘Umar’s practical influence on the early Islamic polity can be seen to surpass even that of Muhammad himself. For posterity, ‘Umar’s formative role secured him the status of the incarnation of the ideal caliph, causing the many political leaders who succeeded him to associate their own practices with those of ‘Umar.

Virtually no major political institution of the early Islamic polity lacks the mark of ‘Umar’s acute political strategy. This applies equally to the minutiae of Islamic civil and criminal law and the larger features of the Islamic polity, such as the institution of Islamic judiciary and the marking of time by the *hijrī* calendar, beginning with Muhammad’s emigration (hijra) from Mecca and Medina in 622. Even the idea of the caliphate itself—especially as a linchpin institution uniting the entirety of the Muslim community (*umma*) and occupied exclusively by a member of the Prophet’s tribe, the Quraysh—emerges out of the united efforts of Abu Bakr (d. 634), Abu ‘Ubayda b. al-Jarrah (d. 639), and ‘Umar to maintain the political unity of Muhammad’s community in the wake of his death. As caliph, a position to which Abu Bakr appointed him before his own death in 634, ‘Umar imparted to the burgeoning Islamic polity its essential features and oversaw the transformation of the Medinan polity from one mainly preoccupied with the challenges of incorporating the inhabitants of the Arabian Peninsula into a single polity to a state that conquered Byzantine Egypt and Syria in the West and considerable Sasanian territories in the East.

‘Umar organized this enterprise of conquest principally on a meritocratic basis, leaning heavily on the prominent and capable emigrants (*muhājirūn*) who undertook the hijra from Mecca to Medina in 622. Preferring that the early Muslims not intermingle with the conquered populations, ‘Umar stipulated to the early Qurashi commanders that they establish their own garrison cities (*amṣār*) so as to avoid diluting the nascent, and thus still vulnerable, ethos of the Islamic conquest polity. From the *amṣār*, the early Arabian conquerors lived as the collective recipients, rather than the managers, of a massive tax base consisting of land taxes (*kharāj*) and poll taxes (*jizya*) culled from the local, conquered populations. ‘Umar, ostensibly basing his policy on earlier Sasanian models, distributed the wealth of these conquered lands through a system of regularized salaried pay (*‘aṭā’*) distributed according to a registry of warriors known as the *dīwān*. Within ‘Umar’s polity, the greatest political virtue and merit was that of precedence (*sābiqa*) in converting to Islam, and accordingly, one’s pay rate ideally corresponded with how early one converted to Islam and participated in the conquests. From these newly settled garrison cities—Kufa and Basra in Iraq in particular, but also Fustat in Egypt, as well as other settlements postdating ‘Umar’s caliphate—there swiftly emerged among the conquerors a new Islamic elite that rivaled in political and religious influence the historically more entrenched tribal elites. It was a dynamic system that propelled the conquests, but it was also one with acute contradictions that would eventually contribute to the undoing of the caliphate of ‘Umar’s successor, ‘Uthman b. ‘Affan (d. 656).

‘Umar’s leadership throughout the entirety of this process emanated from distant Medina, which he allegedly never left, except for one trip to Syria circa 636–38 in order to oversee the conquest of Jerusalem. Although traditions concerning this event are complex and often contradictory, focus often falls on the origins of an important political document known variously as “the Treaty of ‘Umar” (*‘ahd ‘Umar*) or “the Stipulations of ‘Umar” (*al-shurūṭ al-‘umariyya*), of which there exist many versions, resulting from ‘Umar’s negotiations with the local Christian inhabitants. This document has often been seen by Muslim legists as distilling the stipulations and restrictions to be placed on Jews, Christians, and other religious communities coexisting with Muslims in an Islamic state.

All of these accomplishments were no mean feat for a figure, even if known for his sternness, incorruptibility, and overpowering will, who began in Mecca as a person of little real political power. Although not among the first converts in Mecca, ‘Umar did join the ranks of the believers in Muhammad’s message at an early date, despite his initially strident and even violent opposition to the early movement. Tradition relates that his conversion transpired thanks in large part to his sister Fatima’s prior conversion and to Muhammad’s own prayers that God should strengthen Islam with ‘Umar’s support. Little evidence exists, however, for ‘Umar’s prominence in the Meccan period prior to the hijra, perhaps due to his lineage from a minor clan of the Quraysh, the ‘Adi b. Ka‘b. Upon his arrival in Medina, ‘Umar was swift to place himself in a good position politically with the city’s inhabitants through marriage alliances with locally prominent families. Sunni tradition highlights instances in which ‘Umar’s opinion on a matter presaged or prompted the revelation of Qur’anic verses—even when his opinions ran contrary to those of the Prophet himself. (Q. 2:125; 33:5; and 66:6 are the most famous, but tradition lists more than 30 other instances known as *muwāfaqāt ‘Umar*.)

‘Umar was a consummate political tactician without whom much of the success of the early Islamic conquests would probably not have taken place. The process, though not entirely under his control, was marked by his bold direction and his appointment and dismissal of its leaders. This is perhaps most observable in his unilateral discharge of Khalid b. al-Walid from command, indisputably the most effective and successful of all the military commanders of the Islamic polity. However, this can also be seen as his effort to marginalize the role and leadership of the Prophet’s clan, the Banu Hashim, and particularly his son-in-law ‘Ali b. Abi Talib, one of the many reasons for which Shi‘is have historically reviled him and sought to diminish the prominence of his persona.

Glorious as it was, the caliphate of ‘Umar ended bloodily and abruptly at the end of an assassin’s blade. Tradition alleges that ‘Umar foresaw the troubles to arise from the increased visibility and strength of non-Arab clients (*mawālī*; sing. *mawlā*) among the ranks of the early Islamic elite, particularly in the caliphal capital, Medina; indeed, his assassin was one such *mawlā*. He did not appoint his successor as Abu Bakr had done but instead bequeathed to his community one further institution: he transformed the

pre-Islamic, Arabian consultative assembly, or *shūrā*, into a method for choosing the next caliph by appointing a quorum of prominent Qurashi Companions of the Prophet to choose the next caliph from among their own ranks.

See also caliph, caliphate; Companions of the Prophet; Rightly Guided Caliphate (632–61); succession

Further Reading

Sean Anthony, "Dionysius of Tell Maḥrē's Syriac Account of the Assassination of 'Umar ibn al-Khaṭṭāb," *Journal of Near Eastern Studies* 69, no. 2 (2010); Heribert Busse, "'Omar's Image as the Conqueror of Jerusalem," *Jerusalem Studies in Arabic and Islam* 8 (1986); Mark R. Cohen, "What Was the *Pact of 'Umar*? A Literary-Historical Study," *Jerusalem Studies in Arabic and Islam* 23 (1999); Avraham Hakim, "'Umar b. al-Khaṭṭāb and the Title *Khalīfat Allāh*," *Jerusalem Studies in Arabic and Islam* 30 (2005); Tayeb El-Hibri, *Parable and Politics in Early Islamic History: The Rashidun Caliphs*, 2010; M. J. Kister, "Notes on an Account of the Shūrā Appointed by 'Umar b. al-Khaṭṭāb," *Journal of Semitic Studies* 9, no. 2 (1964); Wilferd Madelung, *The Succession to Muḥammad*, 1997.

SEAN W. ANTHONY

Umayyads (661–750)

The Umayyads were a dynasty of caliphs who ruled the Muslim empire between 661 and 750. They descended from a clan of the Quraysh that had led the opposition to Muhammad in Mecca under the leadership of Abu Sufyan.

The Umayyads ruled from Damascus in Syria, as it was difficult to manage the conquered lands from Medina, the original capital in Arabia. They had to cope with enormous changes wrought by the conquests, notably the massive influx of new non-Arab members into the Muslim community, the divergent aspirations of Arab populations settled in different regions, significant regional priorities, a variety of religious communities that had been established before the conquests, and the political and economic consequences of these phenomena and processes. They tried to cope by centralizing their power, refining their governmental system, and establishing a professional army. Their measures brought some short-term solutions, but in the process they enhanced the erosion of the positions of Arab tribal chiefs, the rivalries among tribal groups, and the emergence of religious leadership, all of which eventually contributed to their demise.

The beginning and the end of Umayyad rule were effected through civil wars. After the Prophet Muhammad had died in 632, four of his Companions succeeded one another as caliphs, assuming office through various mechanisms, including appointment and election (632–61). Three of these four caliphs, known as the Rightly Guided Caliphs, were assassinated, and a civil war (656–61) effectively brought Mu'awiya, the first Umayyad caliph, to power in 660. Hoping to prevent additional civil wars and eager to perpetuate Umayyad power, Mu'awiya introduced hereditary succession (from father to son, brother to brother, or between more distant relatives) that was put into practice by two branches of the Umayyad dynasty: first the Sufyanids (661–84) and then the Marwanids (684–750). This measure, as well as other policies carried out by Mu'awiya, raised opposition that challenged Umayyad authority. Upon the death of Mu'awiya (680), civil war broke out, first on a small scale on the accession of his son and then more generally in 684. The Marwanids assumed power, putting an end to the civil war in 692 yet not to the continued rivalry of Arab tribal groups (the Qays and Kalb in particular). In 750, the Abbasid revolution put an end to Umayyad rule and made hereditary succession the norm for their rule of the Muslim empire.

In spite of the enormous internal challenges, the Umayyads succeeded in expanding the Arab-Muslim empire they founded, westward and eastward, across North Africa into Spain and across the Iranian plateau into Central Asia and India. They established effective ways of administration for the vast empire by appointing enterprising governors in the heart of the newly conquered regions and managed to integrate whole blocks of newly attracted ethnic groups into its polity. The height of Umayyad power became symbolized by the magnificent and triumphal Dome of the Rock they had erected on the temple precinct of Jerusalem in 691.

The Abbasids portrayed their predecessors as oppressors of Muslims and transgressors against Islam. This propaganda influenced much of Muslim scholarship and subsequently many modern scholars, which characterizes the Umayyads as purely political, and even secular-minded, Arab rulers who turned *khilāfa* or *imāma*, the rule of the Rightly Guided Caliphs, into *mulk*, Arab kingship. However, whatever their personal piety or impiety, the Umayyads' position was not purely political but on the contrary conceived religiously as the deputyship of God. Speeches and letters by these caliphs, as well as panegyrics by their poets and officials, especially from the reigns of 'Abd al-Malik (r. 684–705) onward, show that the Umayyads saw history as revolving around obedience to God's authority based on the Qur'an and the leadership of the Prophet Muhammad. Drawing on the Qur'an, they envisaged God as having been known to humankind from the beginning of history through prophets and messengers He had sent to communicate His will. The first of these prophets was Adam, the very first man created by God, but humanity erred time and again. God repeatedly sent prophets to deliver His message and establish communities of believers, but these always erred in their turn. This cycle of error and amendment ended with Islam. Muhammad came to be seen as the seal of the prophets and his successors, the caliphs, as God's deputies, entrusted with interpreting, implementing, and protecting the religion as well as managing the affairs of God's community so that it would not err. Each caliph was seen as directly chosen by God to serve as His agent, though in practice he had received his office from his predecessor or through civil war.

At the same time the caliphs presented themselves as heirs to the Prophet Muhammad, upholding his legacy and following his tradition. The Umayyads thus saw themselves as both political and religious leaders, and although they carried no prophetic message, they conceived of themselves as the interpreters of the sacred law, laying down rules to meet new problems and situations. Obeying the Umayyads and their laws was tantamount to obeying God and became the only way to ensure the right implementation of God's religion on Earth. To explain why God should choose His deputies from among the Umayyads, the caliphs stressed their kinship with the Rightly Guided Caliph 'Uthman b. 'Affan (r. 644–56), claiming that he had been a legitimate caliph and unjustly slain. Since the Rightly Guided Caliphs had derived their authority from their Companionship with the Prophet, the first Umayyads also stressed that they had been close to him, although their clan had in fact opposed him until the end of his life. The main sources of Umayyad legitimacy thus were their deputyship of God, their closeness to the Prophet, and their kinship with 'Uthman.

See also civil war; Mu'awiya (602–80); succession

Further Reading

Patricia Crone, *Medieval Islamic Political Thought* [American title *God's Rule*], 2004; Patricia Crone and Martin Hinds, *God's Caliph*, 1986; Gerald Hawting, *The First Dynasty of Islam: The Umayyad Caliphate AD 661–750*, 1986; Wadad Kadi, "The Religious Foundation of Late Umayyad Ideology," in *Saber Religioso y Poder Politico*, edited by Manuela Marin and Mercedes Garcia-Arenal, 1994; Uri Rubin, "Caliphs and Prophets," in *Method and Theory in the Study of Islamic Origin*, edited by Herbert Berg, 2003; Moshe Sharon, "The Umayyads as *ahl al-bayt*," *Jerusalem Studies in Arabic and Islam* 14 (1991).

ELLA LANDAU-TASSERON

usurper

"Usurper" is a Western term rendering a variety of Arabic expressions for an illegitimate ruler. In the first two centuries (ca. 650–850), the Arabic term was normally "king" (*malik*) as opposed to "imam," the latter being a ruler who conformed to the requirements of the law by being a member of Muhammad's tribe (or closer family, according to the Shi'is, or anyone, according to the Kharijis and others), distinguished by certain characteristics including greater virtue than anyone else, and who was the ruler of the entire Muslim world endowed with the titles of caliph and commander of the faithful. The usurper was a person or, more commonly, an entire dynasty that had wrongfully assumed the caliphal position or taken control of some part of the Muslim world without the caliph's consent. Thus the Umayyad caliphs (661–750), especially Mu'awiya (r. 661–80), the first Umayyad ruler, are said to have turned the imamate into mere kingship by having assumed a position to which they had never been entitled or by unjust and tyrannical behavior. "Kingship" conjured up arbitrary government in accordance with private interests (*ahwā'*), as opposed to faithful adhesion to God's law, representing the interests of the community at large, and it was considered to have been characteristic of the Byzantines and Persians before the rise of Islam whom the Muslims had come to replace.

In the Abbasid period (750–1258), the problem was more commonly rulers who had taken control of some part of the Muslim world by military might (*ghalaba*, *qahr*, *istīlā'*), such as the Buyids (945–1055) or Seljuqs, and who called themselves kings (in a flattering sense), amirs, or sultans. There was a fair amount of juristic agonizing over their constitutional position among the Sunnis, though it was clear that they had to be accepted as legitimate in the simple sense of falling within the purview of the shari'a so that they could be seen as bound by it. The rulers themselves often regularized their status by seeking, and usually receiving, recognition by the caliph.

The Imami Shi'is differed in that their doctrine of the imamate made it impossible for them, until recent times, to bestow technical legitimacy on any rulers other than their own imams, of whom only one ('Ali b. Abi Talib) had been caliph in actual fact and the last of whom was deemed to have gone into hiding in 874. But the significance (or even the truth) of this point is often disputed. The Imamis certainly did not have any doubt that actual rulers were required, however illegitimate they might be in strictly legal terms. How far rulers were considered legitimate, in the broader sense of their ability to uphold the ideals of the community, seems to have depended largely on their behavior, in the eyes of Sunnis and Imamis alike.

Rebels taking over by force from noncaliphal rulers were not normally seen as usurpers but simply as men raised up (and eventually deposed) by God as he wished. They might still be denounced as oppressors, but when, in a highly unusual case in 1095, an oppressive king of Samarqand was taken to court and executed, the charge was not of tyranny but rather of apostasy. The extreme solution to illegitimate government known in the Western political tradition as tyrannicide (i.e., killing a ruler whose behavior violated the common conception of the law) was endorsed only by the Kharijis, who identified their own ancestors as those Muslims who had killed the unrighteous (*ẓālim*) caliph 'Uthman b. 'Affan (r. 644–56), and by some Mu'tazilis. A great many rulers met a violent end but not usually at the hands of subjects taking the law into their own hands.

See also authority; Shi'ism; succession; Sunnism

Further Reading

Norman Calder, "Legitimacy and Accommodation in Safavid Iran: The Juristic Theory of Muḥammad Bāqir al-Sabzavārī (d. 1090/1679)," *Iran* 25 1987; Patricia Crone, *Medieval Islamic Political Thought* [American title *God's Rule*], 2004; Tilman Nagel, *Staat und Glaubengesellschaft im Islam*, 1981.

PATRICIA CRONE

'Uthman b. 'Affan (ca. 579–656)

The third of the four Rightly Guided Caliphs, 'Uthman b. 'Affan's caliphate began after his election by a *shūrā* (consultative) council of six Qurashi Companions, whom his predecessor, 'Umar b. al-Khattab (ca. 580–644), appointed as he lay dying. 'Uthman was an early Companion of the Prophet, and his personal wealth, meticulous dress, and graceful manner garnered him a reputation as a man of finesse rather than a man of hard-boiled military grit and religious austerity like his peers and rivals. 'Uthman's caliphate lasted 12 years (644–56) but ended traumatically when he was assassinated in Medina. His death marks both the first regicide of a Muslim leader at Muslim hands and the inauguration of the First Islamic Civil War (*fitna*). The civil war ensuing after his death was largely between the faction that considered 'Uthman a martyr killed unjustly (*maẓlūm*) and the faction that reviled 'Uthman as a lax ruler who had forfeited his right to the leadership of the community by his many misdeeds (*aḥdāth*) or as the usurper of 'Ali b. Abi Talib's (d. 661) right and, therefore, was justly killed as a wrongdoer (*ẓālim*). These two warring factions, the pro-'Uthmanis (represented by Mu'awiya [d. 680] in Syria and Talha b. 'Ubayd, Zubayr b. 'Awwam, and 'A'isha bt. Abi Bakr in the Hijaz) and the pro-'Alids/Hashimids, or Shi'at 'Ali (represented by 'Ali and his supporters in Iraq and Egypt), are the earliest ancestors of three major sectarian divisions of Islam: Sunnism, Shi'ism, and Kharijism/Ibadism. Mu'awiya's victory over the Hashimid party in 661 marked the dynastic ascendance of 'Uthman's clan, the Umayyads, who dominated the caliphate until 750.

Historians have often interpreted 'Uthman's election by the *shūrā* as rooted not so much in his proven capacity for leadership in relation to the other candidates—for in this quality he was lacking—but rather his status as the Prophet's son-in-law. 'Uthman had married two of the Prophet's daughters, Ruqayya and Umm Kulthum (hence his nickname *Dhū al-Nūrayn*, "the possessor of the two lights"). 'Uthman's marriages thus rendered him the most capable counterweight to 'Ali b. Abi Talib, the figurehead of Muhammad's clan, the Banu Hashim, whose influence the other participants in the *shūrā* sought to mitigate. His victory over 'Ali accorded him unparalleled status as the first caliph chosen by a consensus of his peers—Abu Bakr's so-called election was regarded as just but, nonetheless, an ad hoc maneuver (*falta*) hardly worth repeating—and this status seems to have instilled within him a profound sense of *divine* election as well. This notion comes to the fore in the subsequent attribution to him, almost certainly after his death, of the title of God's caliph (*khalīfat Allāh*) and his belief that the caliphate was a garment (*qamīṣ*) with which God had clothed him.

Commensurate with 'Uthman's high conception of his caliphal office were his numerous efforts to effectuate a modicum of centralized authority as the Medinan polity adapted to the postconquest phase of consolidating its holdings in the provinces in Iraq, Syria, and Egypt. The contradictions this entailed, balancing centralized authority and the Arab tribemen's desire for local autonomy in the provinces, embroiled his caliphate in conflict. Most emblematic of this was 'Uthman's codification of the Qur'anic text, from which all present-day Qur'ans ostensibly derive, whereby he established a Medinan codex (*muṣḥaf*) and ordered for rival codices, particularly those in Iraq, to be burned and eliminated. Although he did so at the cost of alienating the Qur'an readers (*qurrā'*)—the new piety-minded Islamic elite who would later lead the call for his abdication—this achievement, if it is indeed to be accorded the historical weight given to it by the Muslim sources, certainly proved to be his most important contribution, inasmuch as it has provided the perennial basis for Muslim identity and faith across sectarian divides until this day.

Traditionally divided into two six-year divisions, one good and the other bad, 'Uthman's caliphate initially enjoyed prosperity and success in the first Muslim naval defeat of the Byzantines at the Battle of the Masts, the conquest of the final Sasanian province, and the execution of their last shah, Yazdegerd III (d. 651). However, the era of sweeping conquests came to an end, and the second half of 'Uthman's caliphate, rife with internal dissent, entered a downward spiral. Although tradition attributes this decline to certain legendary incidents (e.g., 'Uthman's loss of the Prophet's signet ring in the well of Aris and the feigned conversion of the Jew 'Abdallah b. Saba' who plotted his downfall), the actual causes of political dissent during 'Uthman's caliphate emerged from policies and actions that alienated nearly every sector of the early *umma* to some degree.

Although the list of 'Uthman's misdeeds is long, the most controversial among them is the allegation of nepotism. The provincials' main grievances were directed against what seems to be 'Uthman's reversal of 'Umar's Islamic meritocracy, which had fostered leadership on the basis of Islamic precedence (*sābiqa*). In contrast, 'Uthman used the strength of tribal notables and appointed unscrupulous Umayyad kinsmen to positions of power across the empire. Exacerbating this reversal of policy, 'Uthman instituted a land exchange in which prominent Qurashi landholders granted their ancestral Hijazi properties to 'Uthman for the conquered crown lands of Iraq. The provincials opposed these measures insofar as these crown lands had, under 'Umar, served as the basis of their salary—'Uthman's land policy effectively converted their communal property into the private estates of tribal sharifs to whose largesse and good graces the provincials would subsequently be beholden. The Medinans, already separated by rival groups among the Companions of the Prophet, aligned themselves with various factions of the disaffected, and their opposition to the caliph deepened as a result of what they perceived to be 'Uthman's squandering of monies of the treasury on his personal interests and kinsmen, his laxity in religious observances, his severe beating and exile of outspoken critics, and his appointment of an uncle exiled by the Prophet as overseer of the markets in Medina. When the provincials from Iraq and Egypt marched on Medina to call for 'Uthman's abdication, these factors combined to form the perfect storm. The Egyptian faction, led by the first caliph's son

Muhammad b. Abi Bakr (631–58), besieged the caliph's house on June 17, 656, and murdered him virtually unimpeded.

See also caliph, caliphate; Companions of the Prophet; Rightly Guided Caliphate (632–61); succession

Further Reading

Patricia Crone, "*Shūrā* as an Elective Institution," *Quaderni di Studi Arabi* 19 (2001); G. R. Hawting, "The Significance of the Slogan '*lā ḥukma illā lillāh*' and the Reference to the 'Ḥudūd' in the Traditions about the Fitna and the Murder of 'Uthmān," *Bulletin of the School of Oriental and African Studies* 41, no. 3 (1978); Martin Hinds, "Kūfan Political Alignments and Their Background in the Mid-Seventh Century A.D.," *International Journal of Middle East Studies* 2, no. 4 (1971); Idem, "The Murder of the Caliph 'Uthmān," *International Journal of Middle East Studies* 3, no. 4 (1972); R. Stephen Humphreys, trans., *The Crisis of the Early Caliphate* (*The History of al-Ṭabarī*, vol. 15), 1990; Idem, "Qur'anic Myth and Structure in Early Islamic Historiography," in *Tradition and Innovation in Late Antiquity*, edited by R. M. Clover and R. S. Humphreys, 1989; Wilferd Madelung, *The Succession to Muḥammad*, 1997; Harald Motzki, "The Collection of the Qur'an: A Reconsideration of the Western Views in Light of Recent Methodological Developments," *Der Islam* 78 (2001).

SEAN W. ANTHONY

utopia

A Latinate construct coined by Sir Thomas More (d. 1535) to signal an impossible, ideal community, utopia is a category of analysis external to Islamic discourses. Depending on the social theories on which the scholar draws in describing Islamic political thought as "utopian," this term might carry a positive or negative valence, linked either to the history of European totalitarianism or the possibility of progressive change. A number of social phenomena and intellectual projects in Islamic history may be profitably understood as utopian.

Like Sir Thomas More, the Muslim philosopher Farabi (ca. 878–950) drew on Plato's *Republic* to depict a program for an ideal community in *al-Madina al-Fadila* (The virtuous city) and other political works, including *al-Siyasa al-Madaniyya* (Perfect political rule). Farabi's ideal city is defined by human cooperation with the aim of becoming virtuous and attaining happiness through the perfection of reason. While all citizens have some commonality in their idea of the good life, only a few can fully perfect the virtuous self. Farabi's recovery of Platonic and Aristotelian philosophical approaches was not merely an Islamic replication of earlier Greek works but instead an attempt to harmonize Greek philosophy with Islamic theories of divine law. Farabi's writings therefore formed an influential source for much of later Islamic political thought, including middle-period works such as the *Akhlaq-i Nasiri* (*The Nasirean Ethics*) of Nasir al-Din al-Tusi (d. 1274) and, less directly, Ayatollah Khomeini's idea of the "rule of the jurist" (*wilāyāt al-faqīh*) in the 20th century.

While the majority of Muslims have drawn on the example of Muhammad and those following him as ethical exemplars, the Salafi reformists view the Sunni golden age as particularly exemplary. Drawing on the works of the Hanbali scholar Ibn Taymiyya (d. 1328), the Salafi movement of the 19th and 20th centuries called for a return to tradition, largely as represented by the first three generations of Muslims. In *Islams and Modernities*, Aziz al-Azmeh distinguishes between the historical utopia of the golden age as an exemplary model and the negation of history in utopian attempts to re-create that golden age. In Azmeh's reading, the utopianisms of radical Islamists or fundamentalists such as the Egyptian Sayyid Qutb (d. 1966) and the Pakistani Mawdudi (d. 1979) negate the passage of history entirely and impute the condition of *jāhiliyya* (the age of ignorance, preceding Muhammad's prophetic mission) to the present historical moment.

The final type of Islamic utopianism situates itself around the coming of the Islamic messiah or Mahdi. Though not solely attributable to Shi'i communities, scholars have focused on messianic utopianism in Shi'i Islam rather than in Sunni Islam. According to Twelver Shi'i doctrine, the Twelfth Imam disappeared in 874, and his occultation (*ghayba*) will last until the end of time, when he returns as the Mahdi. Throughout Shi'i history, both preceding the disappearance of the Twelfth Imam and following it, the death or disappearance of an imam has often been read as a sign of a coming apocalypse. As Said Amir Arjomand has argued, the assumption of authority by Shi'i jurists following the disappearance of the Twelfth Imam represents a rationalization of this cycle, though it was later disrupted with the rise of the Safavid dynasty. Shi'i Iranian movements of the 20th and 21st centuries have demonstrated messianic expectations as well, most notably in the identification of Ayatollah Khomeini as an imam but additionally in the Hujjatiyyeh movement and in Iranian president Mahmoud Ahmadinejad's (2005–) chiliastic readings of his own presidency.

Messianic ideas appeared early in Islamic history in Sunni circles as well. While the term "Mahdi" does not appear in the Qur'an itself and signified a religiopolitical leader rather than messianic deliverer in the earliest period of Islam, movements during the Umayyad and Abbasid periods set the template for later discussions of the Mahdi. 'Abdallah b. al-Zubayr's (d. 692) revolt against the Umayyads defined the typology of messianic figures for later Islam and became linked to the term "Mahdi" through pre-Abbasid Shi'i claims to rule, in particular those of Ibn al-Hanafiya (d. 700–701). Outside of specifically Shi'i theories of the imam's return, by the ninth century most Sunni Muslims had accepted the theory of a Mahdi as well. Although the figure never occupied a central place in Sunni scholastic discussions, numerous Sunni messianic movements appeared over the course of Islamic history. These Sunni movements generally emphasized the renewal of Islamic law—a notable contrast to claims for a new

religious dispensation seen in Shi'i messianism. In the modern period, one Sunni messianic movement of particular importance was the 18th-century Sudanese Mahdis, led by Muhammad Ahmad al-Mahdi (d. 1885). The Sufi-inspired Mahdis fought off Turco-Eygptian rule and established a short-lived Islamic state from 1885 until the Anglo-Egyptian reconquest of 1898. Other significant Sunni movements of the late middle and modern periods include the Mahdi of Jawnpur (d. 1505) in India and Shehu Usman dan Fodio (d. 1817), along with numerous others, in West Africa.

See also Mahdi; messianism; revival and reform

Further Reading

Abbas Amanat, *Apocalyptic Islam and Iranian Shi'ism*, 2009; Said Amir Arjomand, *The Shadow of God and the Hidden Imam: Religion, Political Order, and Societal Change in Shi'ite Iran, from the Beginning to 1890*, 1984; Aziz al-Azmeh, *Islams and Modernities*, 2009; Muhsin Mahdi, *Alfarabi and the Foundation of Islamic Political Philosophy*, 2001; Vanessa Martin, *Creating an Islamic State: Khomeini and the Making of a New Iran*, 2003.

KATHLEEN FOODY

V

veil

The veil, also referred to as "hijab" or "purdah"—words that literally mean "curtain"—has various meanings in the Islamic context. In Sufism, for instance, it can refer to a barrier that interferes with a person's search for God. The terms are popularly used, however, to refer to women's seclusion in the private sphere or to a form of dress. This dress can take the form of a head scarf, but it can also cover other body parts through loose, enveloping garments worn on top of a woman's clothing. This entry focuses primarily on veiling as a form of dress.

Veiling and the seclusion of women have a pre-Islamic origin and a long history in the regions surrounding Arabia. These practices were institutionalized in Mesopotamia in order to make a distinction between "good women" and "bad women" in pre-Christian times and became a characteristic of the upper class in various cultures—such as the Hellenic, Christian, Persian, Byzantine—in the Mediterranean Middle East and beyond by the time of Islam's advent in Arabia. It also existed as a marker of social status in the urban areas of Arabia at this time.

Veiling initially was prescribed only for the Prophet Muhammad's wives, and later as a marker of all "believing women" in order to distinguish them from nonbelieving women so that they would not be harassed (Q. 33:59). The practice was largely limited to the Prophet's wives during his lifetime but became more widespread over time. Commonly suggested sociological reasons for veiling include the desire to emulate the Prophet's wives; the increased wealth of Arab families, who took pride in knowing that the women in their families no longer had to work outside the home; and Islam's spread into neighboring lands, where veiling already existed as a marker of social status.

For Muslims who see the veil as a religious symbol and a sign of piety, such sociological reasons are reductive and take attention away from the role religious faith plays in the adoption of this practice. A survey of ethnographic studies published between 1990 and 2010 strongly suggests, however, that to simply label the veil as a religious symbol simplifies a complex reality no less than arguments that draw solely upon sociological reasons. Paying attention to the sociopolitical context in which veiling occurs—both in a particular moment and across time—is essential to bring out the multiple meanings of veiling.

The veil and varying degrees of seclusion in the private sphere continue to be seen as a marker of economic status in many societies. Yet women of varying economic status also have been known to take it up as they enter the public sphere to pursue their education, go to work, or engage in other activities. The veil becomes a means of appeasing family concerns as the women venture out in public, for it marks them as respectable and moral individuals. The belief is that this sign of morality, which also hides their body, will protect them from sexual harassment in public and serve as a signal to men to not bother them. Veiling in this context becomes a ticket to increased participation in the public sphere and, as such, has the potential to lead to social, economic, or political empowerment. Some women also seem to take up the veil so as not to stand out among other veiled women, because it is a tradition to do so in their community, or as a way of holding on to "traditional" values when migrating to urban areas or whenever those values are felt to be under attack. Some women believe that it prevents them from being treated as sex objects. Others say that men have a low threshold of control when they see unveiled women, and it is women's responsibility to veil themselves in order to prevent "chaos" in society.

These reasons do not detract from the fact that veiling is sometimes *also* a manifestation of religious faith—a practice justified by the belief, among many Muslims in general and among religious revivalist movements around the world in particular, that veiling is an Islamic tenet. While some Muslim women do not feel the need to justify their wearing of the veil, others are vocal in highlighting religious reasons for it without, however, excluding social benefits of the sort mentioned earlier. Regardless of whether women veil primarily for religious reasons or not, a close association between the veil, Islam, and Muslim women has developed over time.

Non-Muslim observers have played a significant role in highlighting the connections between the veil, Islam, and Muslim women, but in particular ways. The Orientalist discourse, particularly during the Romantic Era, marked the veil as exotic, while the colonial discourse depicted it as a marker of women's oppression. For some women it *is* forced oppression. However, the veil's link with oppression in the colonial narrative, as well as non-Muslim attacks on the veil and what it symbolizes—a group's boundaries and tradition, both commonly mapped on the female body—have led some Muslims to use the veil as a symbol of resistance to imperialism, whether colonial or postcolonial. In the Algerian liberation struggle, for example, Algerians resisted the French colonists' desire to control the country by affirming the veil as a symbol of their culture and identity. The veil has also been used as a symbol of resistance to authoritarian regimes. In the course of the Iranian Islamic Revolution from 1978 to 1979, many women decided to don the veil as a way to challenge an autocratic establishment that had

banned the veil many decades earlier. The banning of the head scarf in French public schools and the reaction of some Muslim women who deliberately began wearing it as a marker of their religious identity in response to this ban or in response to their belief that Islam and Muslims were being attacked in a post-September 11, 2001, world further illustrates the fraught relationship between the veil, Muslim identity, and politics.

See also women

Further Reading

Sadaf Ahmad, *Transforming Faith: The Story of Al-Huda and Islamic Revivalism Among Urban Pakistani Women*, 2009; Leila Ahmed, *Women and Gender in Islam*, 1992; John Bowen, *Why the French Don't Like Headscarves*, 2007; Fadwa El Guindi, "Veiling Resistance," in *Feminist Postcolonial Theory: A Reader*, edited by Reina Lewis and Sara Mills, 2003; Homa Hoodfar, "The Veil in Their Minds and on Our Heads: Veiling Practices and Muslim Women," in *Women, Gender, Religion: A Reader*, edited by Elizabeth Castelli, 1997; Saba Mahmood, *Politics of Piety: The Islamic Revival and the Feminist Subject*, 2005; Fatima Mernissi, "The Meaning of Spatial Boundaries," in *Feminist Postcolonial Theory: A Reader*, edited by Reina Lewis and Sara Mills, 2003.

SADAF AHMAD

violence

The question of violence (and, by implication, nonviolence) was one of the first major political issues confronted by the early Muslim *umma*, or community. Indeed, the consequences of the Muslim community's earliest and most traumatic ruptures—those occasioned by ʿAli b. Abi Talib and Muʿawiya's great *fitna* or civil war (the First Islamic Civil War, 656–61)—brought the problem of violent conflict and its alternatives to the attention of early Muslim theorists of communal integrity and provoked a series of intriguing responses. Meanwhile, the larger political universe into which Islam was born, and in which its earliest intellectuals recalled a primordial Islamic past upon which to base normative political ideals, had been one characterized by political violence in its many forms long before the birth of the Prophet Muhammad. The political landscape of Mesopotamia, the Middle East, and the Mediterranean had for more than a millennium constituted a single vast stage upon which successive empires and their subjects had pondered violence as both a destructive and productive force within the lives of human communities. Not surprisingly, the violence inherent in the politics of an empire left a profound impression upon the intellectual traditions of local Christianities and rabbinic Judaisms. As Islam evolved in dialogue with these communities, it would join an ongoing discussion concerning the role of violence—whether committed or forsaken, given or received—as a central component of religious, communal, and, inevitably, political legitimacy.

Among the first historical memories of the early Muslim community was the early seventh-century clash of superpowers that brought the Roman and Sasanian Persian empires to the battlefields of the Middle East one final time. Early works of Qur'anic exegesis, for example, recalled that Muhammad's besieged community of Abrahamic monotheists in the Arabian city of Mecca had cheered their "brothers the Romans" in this conflict, even as the polytheists of Mecca rooted for the Persians, whom, we are told, they looked upon as their own champions in the faraway war. What is significant about this and similar passages of very early Muslim texts is what they suggest about the ways in which the early Muslim *umma*—perhaps not the actual early seventh-century members of Muhammad's community, but their successors of a century or so later—imagined the intersection of empire, belief, and violence; the role of a polity based in religious truth was, in part, to wage war against unbelief and its champions. This was a model of an empire current in seventh-century Roman imperial ideology, as the court poetry and material culture of the time of the emperor Heraclius show, and it remained a compelling model of imperial piety among Christian communities scattered throughout Egypt and the Middle East long after the Muslim conquests.

But even if this had not been the case, the Qur'an itself—revealed, Muslim dogma insists, during Muhammad's time of trials and struggle against the unbelievers of Arabia—is (like the Torah) unflinching in its characterization of God's polity as one obliged to accept war as a means of defending God's truth in the face of God's enemies. In the Qur'an, however, the most frequently recurring analog for the English term "violence" is *ẓulm* and variants of the root *ẓ-l-m*. The terms derived from this root signal the idea of "oppression" and "transgression." Perhaps inevitably, then, the idea of violence in Islamic legal theory features prominently a tension between violence as a means of resisting oppression and the necessity of mitigating the oppressive consequences of violence waged in the service of Islam and the Muslim *umma*.

Whatever the relation of the revelations recorded in the Qur'an to the spread of Muhammad's followers beyond the confines of Arabia—scholarly opinion is divided on this matter—the political realities confronted by Muslims living through the first Islamic centuries were shaped by the explosive Arab conquests that began in the years immediately following Muhammad's passing (632) and resulted in a vast territorial empire by the middle of the first century of the Islamic era. What in fact prompted the conquests is hotly debated and beyond the scope of this entry, but the fact of the conquests left the very early Muslim community with the task of narrating a history of its origins and with the task of so narrating the conquests' events as to understand them as evidence of God's divine plan. Accordingly, the realities of conquest—killing, destruction, enslavement, dispossession, and horror—were necessarily accommodated to a metanarrative of piety and godly virtue rewarded, and the evils of abusive and violent empires punished. This presented the early Muslim community with a host of moral,

ethical, and theoretical difficulties as it looked upon its own evolving imperial power in the eighth and ninth centuries of the Common Era and sought to contain the violence inherent in projects of imperial expansion and domination.

Further complicating the question of violence and nonviolence in early Islamic political thought was the fact that political, religious, and social legitimacy within the Muslim *umma* and the Islamic imperial hierarchy often rested upon the perception that an individual or group of individuals had retained, as much as possible, the character of those men who were recalled as founders and champions of the early Muslim *umma*. These were men who were recollected by later Muslims to have been "like mounted raiders by day and monks by night." They were scrupulously pious, honest, and loving with their fellow Muslims, and with their enemies intransigent, uncompromising in matters of religious scruple, and violent in defense of God's one community. They were, after all, men who through their "strivings" had upended both the power hierarchies of Arabia and the ancient imperial systems of the Middle East and Iran and who had claimed by means of the sword and prayer the sprawling new domain bequeathed to their descendents. Living in the wake of revelation and godly conquest, Muslims in the centuries immediately after Muhammad's death now struggled to build a stable polity upon the example left by the Prophet and his Companions, who were understood as the primordial heroes of the new Muslim empire.

By the second century after the hijra (the period in which the earliest Muslim texts were compiled), a major theme regarding violence and nonviolence within the Muslim polity had begun to emerge. That theme was one of restraint and the moral importance of mitigating the violence that had permeated imperial politics for millennia before the birth of Muhammad. Works on the law of war, for example, emphasized the relative mercy to be shown to women, children, noncombatants, and captives. Families of captives, for example, were not to be split apart. The killing of children and women was absolutely forbidden. There was to be no compulsion of religion for those taken in war or those who had become protected subjects of the Muslims through surrender.

Elsewhere, in works of legal advice, this theme of restraint as the best part of justice emerges in practical advice given by scholars and jurists regarding the meting out of punishment or chastisement. In the *Kitab al-Muharaba* (The book of warfare) of the Maliki scholar 'Abdallah b. Wahb (743–812), for example, one encounters a series of questions concerning the ways in which one should handle captured Khariji rebels. The answers to these questions stress that the Kharijis are only to be killed if they have killed and that it is best to try to reason with them, or to find someone to whom they will listen. Elsewhere, in Ahmad b. Hanbal's responses to legal queries, not only is a nonviolent approach to wrongdoers emphasized repeatedly, but also Muslims are encouraged to handle transgressions of Islam's normative strictures themselves, through nonviolent "commanding and forbidding," rather than risk exposing fellow Muslims, no matter how sinful, to the potential violence of the government.

In the Middle Ages, the violence undertaken by representatives of government power was beheld with a great deal of ambivalence; religious and legal scholars foresaw the damnation of policemen, government torturers, and even those sovereigns who ordered unjust violence against their subjects. As in earlier periods, however, perceptions of violence ran in close tandem with perceptions of the relative justice or injustice with which any given act was undertaken. Central to many Muslim's reservations about the role of rulers in the use of violence as a means of preserving civic order or redressing crime was the incertitude that these rulers, and, more specifically, their representatives, could be assumed to act in accordance with justice.

Similarly, in the first centuries after the advent of the Muslim community, consensus over the place of rulers as leaders of just or "holy" campaigns of warfare—jihad—was also frequently elusive. This did not hamper caliphal or dynastic leaders' ability to wage wars of succession or political rivalry, of course. Indeed, Muslim rulers from the seventh century on, just like their counterparts in Byzantium or Western Europe, waged war frequently and in some periods almost constantly. The violence inherent in these wars was not, however, considered "Islamic" by legal scholars and traditionalists unless they met certain relatively narrow criteria. Throughout the Middle Ages, in fact, the formulations of such early theorists of religiously appropriate violence as 'Abdallah b. al-Mubarak remained deeply influential. It was to such formulations, which took into account what were understood as specifically Islamic theories of violence and its alternatives, that Muslims turned at the outbreak of the Crusades as a means of mobilizing a mass response to the European invaders.

Muslim communities have struggled with questions of violence and nonviolence in the often radically changed political circumstances of modern times. One key example comes from the life and legacy of the Egyptian political theorist Sayyid Qutb (d. 1966). Thinking and writing during decades of postcolonial upheaval in Egypt, Qutb drew upon the Qur'anic concept of *jāhiliyya*, or the pre-Islamic time of idolatry and ignorance, to describe what he understood as contemporary Muslim society's decadence. Qutb prescribed a rigorous cleansing of modern Muslim society on the model of the Prophet's cleansing of pre-Islamic Arab society. Within this schema, however, some self-confessed Muslims were to be understood as having reverted to unbelief. A troubling question emerged: What role would violence play in the cleansing, Islamic reform of Egyptian society Qutb envisioned? After Qutb's execution by the regime of President Gamal Abdel Nasser in 1966, his followers struggled to answer precisely this question. For some, individuals who diverged from their own rigorist understanding of "proper Islam" (a group that constituted most of Egyptian society) were to be rejected as Muslims and punished with violence as unbelievers. For others, it was only the repressive Nasser regime itself against which violence was necessary. For still others, Qutb's call was understood to have been for a spiritual—and nonviolent—war against the temptations of contemporary society. In time, divergent interpretations of Qutb's belief resulted in multiple, diverse, and in

some cases sharply opposed theories concerning violence and nonviolence in the politics of the present world. In all cases, such theories and their real-world consequences derived from the confluence of very early Islamic thought concerning violence and nonviolence necessarily interpreted in light of contemporary circumstances, events, and intellectual trends.

See also jihad; nonviolence; quietism and activism; rebellion; Sayyid Qutb (1906–66)

Further Reading

Khaled Abou El Fadl, *Rebellion and Violence in Islamic Law*, 2001; Michael Bonner, *Aristocratic Violence and Holy War: Studies on the Jihad and the Arab-Byzantine Frontier*, 1996; Michael Cook, *Commanding Right and Forbidding Wrong in Islamic Thought*, 2001; Giles Kepel, *Jihad: The Trial of Political Islam*, 2002; Christian Lange, *Justice, Punishment and the Medieval Muslim Imagination*, 2008; Thomas Sizgorich, *Violence and Belief in Late Antiquity: Militant Devotion in Christianity and Islam*, 2009.

THOMAS SIZGORICH

vizier

Having first entered the English lexicon in the 16th century, "vizier" derives from the Arabic *wazīr* (pl. *wuzarā'*), the conventional meaning of which translates roughly to "helper" or "aide." Such would appear to be the meaning intended in Qur'an 20:29 and 25:35, in which God makes Aaron a *wazīr* to Moses; a usage closer to the later, technical meaning of the word appears in a hadith of the Prophet that is found in the collections of Abu Dawud and Ahmad b. Hanbal. As a political term, the vizierate (*wizāra*) emerged during the Abbasid period as the highest political office beneath the caliph. In its technical sense, then, *wazīr* can be translated conveniently as "minister," capturing both its earliest institutional understanding and its contemporary usage by various governments throughout the Muslim world.

As has been demonstrated persuasively by S. D. Goitein in *Studies in Islamic History and Institutions*, the vizierate did not originate from an earlier Persian model, neither institutionally nor etymologically. Rather, the office traces its origins to an Arabian custom in which the emancipated slave of an Arab chieftain would serve as primary educator to his ex-master's child, remaining a critical advisor, protector, and confidant to the latter upon the chieftain's death. The personal nature of this relationship between freedman and the household of his lord helps to account for the institutional fluidity that the vizierate retained, particularly in its early history, as the relative power of the vizier shifted markedly from one caliphal reign to the next.

While use of the Arabic *wazīr* to denote "helper" can be found in pre-Islamic poetry, it was the Abbasid propagandist Abu Salama al-Khallal's (d. 750) assumption of the title "helper (*wazīr*) of the house of Muhammad" in the immediate aftermath of the Abbasid revolution that would set the stage for the official use of the term only a few decades later. The second Abbasid caliph Mansur (r. 754–75) had appointed Abu 'Ubaydallah al-Ash'ari (d. 786–87) as the personal scribe and steward to his young son and successor Mahdi (r. 775–85). When Mahdi ascended to the caliphate, Ash'ari served as de facto vizier under him, while it was this latter figure's successor Ya'qub b. Dawud (d. 803) who stands as the first person to receive the formal title of *wazīr* in the caliph's letters and official correspondences. From that point forward, the Abbasid vizier continued—albeit at times precariously—to serve in the highest civilian position beneath the caliph until the emergence of the office of *amīr al-umarā'* (supreme military commander) in the early tenth century.

In subsequent centuries, the vizierate reached a new apogee of institutional influence under Turkish and Mongol conquerors, as a new class of expatriate sultans depended on savvy viziers to assist in ruling lands that were otherwise unknowable to them. However, even the greatest Seljuq vizier Nizam al-Mulk (d. 1092) acknowledged that a sultan's ruling entirely by proxy was unethical, and the image of the vizier serving as de facto ruler while the true sultan idled his days away is not a wholly accurate historical picture, as Goitein rightly concludes.

The *Qawanin al-Wizara* (Laws of the vizierate) and the celebrated *Ahkam al-Sultaniyya* (Ordinances of government) of Mawardi (d. 1058), in addition to the slightly earlier *Tuhfat al-Wuzara'* (Gift of the vizierate) of Abu Mansur al-Tha'alibi (d. 1039), present arguably the best theoretical treatment of the vizierate in premodern Islamic constitutional law. Following Mawardi's more refined categories, the vizierate in fact comprises two distinct offices—namely, the "vizierate of unrestricted delegation" (*wizārat al-tafwīḍ*) and the "vizierate of implementation" (*wizārat al-tanfīdh*). The vizier of unrestricted delegation, for his part, functions as the imam's (i.e., the principal ruler's) proxy in all but three capacities: he cannot appoint a successor to the imamate (i.e., the caliphate or sultanate, depending on the historical circumstances); he cannot request the imam's resignation; and he cannot relieve another of the imam's appointees of his post. Beyond these three restrictions, the vizier of unrestricted delegation enjoys comprehensive oversight of the Muslim commonwealth and may serve in any other capacity to which the imam himself has a right. Accordingly, multiple viziers of unrestricted delegation may not exist simultaneously, for pragmatic reasons, while the imam must stay informed of his vizier's decisions and must review them as necessary. Moreover, the imam must select such a vizier from among those subjects who are most knowledgeable of military and administrative affairs and who possess a general familiarity with the dictates of Islamic law (shari'a). Such breadth of knowledge is not a necessary qualification for the imamate itself.

The vizier of implementation, in contrast, serves merely as an aid in executing the decisions of the imam, and Mawardi acknowledges that only in those instances where this figure's opinion is sought by the imam does his service truly merit the title of vizier.

Therefore, the qualifications for the vizierate of implementation remain far less stringent than those for the vizierate of unrestricted delegation. Those qualifications that are expressly stipulated by the jurists function primarily to ensure a transparent line of communication from the imam to the vizier to the populace and vice versa. Because the vizer of implementation lacks administrative autonomy, there may be several such viziers at any given time, as this multiplicity does not undermine the functioning of government but rather enhances it.

While many Muslim-majority nations have appropriated the Arabic *wazīr* as a title for their various ministers, this "constitutional vizierate" shares little to no institutional continuity with its premodern counterpart for historical reasons that are beyond the scope of this article. Among Islamist thinkers, discussions of the vizierate as a cornerstone of the Islamic state have been largely abandoned in favor of an idealized scholar-caliph who seeks advice from a consultative assembly of experts (*shūrā*). That the Salafi intellectual backdrop to Islamism might find little to stake in an institution that traces its entire existence to the second Islamic century may help to explain Islamist reticence with regard to the vizierate. But perhaps a more obvious explanation is that in the absence of a single, unifying caliphate, discussions of the vizierate are effectively moot.

See also bureaucracy; caliph, caliphate; government; leadership; Mawardi (974–1058); Nizam al-Mulk (1018–92)

Further Reading

S. D. Goitein, "Appendix: On the Origin of the Term Vizier," in *Studies in Islamic History and Institutions*, 1968; Idem, "The Origin of the Vizierate and Its True Character," in *Studies in Islamic History and Institutions*, 1968; Ibn Khaldun, *The Muqaddimah*, translated by Franz Rosenthal, 1958; Abu 'l-Hasan al-Mawardi, *The Ordinances of Government*, translated by Wafaa H. Wahba, 2000; Dominique Sourdel, *Le vizirat ʻabbāside de 479 à 936 (132 à 324 de l'hégire)*, 1959–60.

MATTHEW B. INGALLS

W

welfare state. *See* public interest

West, the

Although Muslims have resided in parts of Europe for centuries, and many slaves taken from Africa to North America were Muslims, the question of Islam in the West rose in importance after World War II. European countries encouraged workers from North and West Africa, South Asia, and Turkey to add their labor power to the postwar recovery, and most of those workers were Muslims. By the late 1960s, many of those workers had settled in Europe with their families. Immigration to the United States increased at about the same time, and Muslims, particularly from South Asia, were among those who settled there. Among the new arrivals were many Muslim scholars who offered opinions about how ordinary Muslims were to live religious lives in lands where they were minorities and where not all Islamic religious institutions were available. At the same time, many African American Muslims were turning from the specific teachings of the Nation of Islam toward a more broadly distributed Sunni Islam. Contemporary scholars of diverse origins increasingly provide opinions through broader networks that stretch across the Atlantic and include scholars from non-Western centers of learning.

Muslims have posed questions about (1) the legitimacy of participating in Western political institutions and (2) how best to adapt their individual, everyday behavior to their new, non-Islamic environments. One major response has been the call to develop "legal theory for Muslim minorities" (*fiqh al-aqalliyyāt*) or a distinct jurisprudence for Muslims living as minorities in non-Muslim societies. In Europe the idea has been most closely associated with Yusuf al-Qaradawi, a scholar born in 1926 in Egypt who was educated and taught at Azhar University before moving to Qatar, where he created a faculty of shari'a and became well-known through his books, his website, and his broadcasts on Aljazeera television. He played a major role on the popular website Islam Online and in the European Council for Fatwa and Research, an association of scholars mainly living in (although not originating from) European countries. Qaradawi also wrote of the "*fiqh* of balances" (*fiqh al-muwāzanāt*) to point to the need to balance minor evils against greater or longer-term benefits to Muslims. He drew on this imperative to argue (in 1999, through the European Council) that Muslims unable to find interest-free loans could borrow at interest for a first home. He drew on the arguments advanced by Ghazali (d. 1111) and Abu Ishaq al-Shatibi (d. 1388) that Muslims should above all advance the objectives (*maqāṣid*) of revelation. Qaradawi employed Shatibi's three-level hierarchy of necessities, needs, and improvements: "when interests (*maṣāliḥ*) conflict, a low-level interest is sacrificed for the sake of a higher-level interest." In the bank interest matter, it was the prohibition of *ribā* (interest) that was sacrificed for the sake of stable Muslim families and thus religious lives.

In North America, the idea of a "*fiqh* for minorities" has been promoted through the Islamic Society of North America (ISNA), and in particular by the Iraqi scholar Taha Jabir al-Alwani, although in later writings Alwani recommended that scholars should rebuild *fiqh* from values and rights in the Qur'an rather than through the idea of Muslim minorities, perpetuating the older distinction between the *dār al-islām* (abode of Islam) and the *dār al-ḥarb* (abode of war). Many contemporary Muslims express discomfort with this way of viewing the world; some refer to the protection given to religious minorities by international law and propose *dār al-'ahd* (abode of covenant), *dār al-da'wa* (abode of predication), or *dār al-shahāda* (abode of witness), emphasizing the possibilities open to Muslims in these lands.

Much of the debate among scholars living in the West concerns *how* to determine general principles or objectives, not *whether* such activity should take place. Whereas Qaradawi couched his fatwa (legal opinion) within the several schools of *fiqh* and ended by exempting some Muslims in the West from the rules of *fiqh*, other scholars argue that *fiqh* is and should be universal but that its universal dimensions are at the level of general principles. The Swiss scholar Tariq Ramadan, for example, together with many scholars active in England, France, and Belgium, argued that one could consider a civil marriage to already contain most or all of the elements of an Islamic marriage (consent, witnesses, a contract), and therefore it could constitute a marriage in Islamic terms. Tareq Oubrou, based in Bordeaux, emphasized the distinction between obligatory ritual (*'ibādāt*) and social norms (*mu'āmalāt*) and contended that the former does not change but the latter may be realized either as law or as ethics, depending on the political context within which one lives. In Western countries, Muslims must "ethicize" these norms.

Though touted as providing support for progressive views, this approach can lead to more prohibitive view of the law (e.g., a traditional view that all abortions are forbidden because of the need to

protect life, one of the five necessities, as opposed to a juristic view that abortion is permissible until a certain point in gestation). But by seeking equivalents between Western and Islamic institutions, it can legitimate full political and social participation in Western countries.

This line of reasoning starts from general principle and seeks support in schools of *fiqh* only in a secondary fashion, and so it has been criticized by some *fiqh* scholars such as the Syrian Sa'id Ramadan al-Buti, for whom the call for a *fiqh* for minorities is part of the "plot aiming at dividing Islam." But he also distinguishes between what he sees as the false idea of special dispensations for those Muslims who live in Europe or North America and the idea that "whenever there is a hardship exceeding the moral limit, the legal permission which warrants canceling it persists." In other words, the easing of rules due to hardship has nothing to do with where a Muslim lives but rather depends on his or her specific circumstances. As this debate shows, Muslims in the West look for learned political and social opinions from a global array of scholars and institutions.

See also Europe; globalization; jurisprudence; North America; shari'a

Further Reading

Khaled Abou El Fadl, *Islam and the Challenge of Democracy*, 2004; Taha Jabir al-Alwani, *Towards a Fiqh for Minorities: Some Basic Reflections*, 2003; Andrew March, *Islam and Liberal Citizenship: The Search for an Overlapping Consensus*, 2009; Muhammad Khalid Masud, *Islamic Legal Philosophy: A Study of Abu Ishaq al-Shatibi's Life and Thought*, 1977; Tariq Ramadan, *Radical Reform: Islamic Ethics and Liberation*, 2009.

JOHN BOWEN

West Africa

The development of Islamic political thought in the *bilād al-sūdān* ("the lands of the blacks") of sub-Saharan West Africa was linked with the development of Islam as a legitimating factor in state development in this region. There were three major theological positions regarding the relationship with non-Muslims (or "bad Muslims"): accommodation and peaceful coexistence, withdrawal from political power, and jihad. They correspond roughly with three distinct historical periods.

In the age of "empires," from the 11th to the 18th centuries, Muslims constituted a minority of the population. Even when rulers acknowledged Islam as a religion of the court, they had to balance Islam and local religions. Muslim scholars were mostly confined to courts and a few centers of long-distance trade. The major issue was "how Islamic" the state was, which in turn depended on how Muslim rulers negotiated the role of Islam at their courts. A tradition of peaceful coexistence of Muslims and non-Muslims was represented by the Jakhanke, a group of scholars originally from Ja (Dia) or Jakha (Diakha) in Mali. The Jakhanke stressed the importance of Islamic learning—in particular, the memorization of the Qur'an and the teaching of *tafsīr* (long commentaries), based on the *tafsīr al-jalālayn* of Mahalli and Suyuti. An important feature of Jakhanke teachings was the rejection of proselytization and jihad. Muslims living among non-Muslims had an obligation to cultivate the pure teachings of Islam as individuals. A different and rather militant tradition of Islam was represented in the same period by North African Muslim scholar Muhammad b. 'Abd al-Karim al-Maghili (d. 1503), who visited the cities of Kano in 1492 and Katsina and Gao in 1498. In two texts, later titled *Taj al-Din fi ma Yajib 'ala l-Muluk* (The crown of religion: On the duties of kings) and *As'ilat Asqiyya wa-Ajwibat al-Maghili* (The questions of the Askia and Maghili's responses), which were to become important texts for Muslim reformers in the centuries to come, Maghili expounded on the principles of Islamic government. He also came to advise the emperor of Songhay, Askia Muhammad Turé (r. 1493–1528), on the principles of Islamic rule. Turé had invited Maghili to his court in order to get support for his claim that the deposition of the preceding Sunni dynasty had been legitimate on the grounds that the last Sunni emperor, Sonni 'Ali, had tolerated un-Islamic practices. Maghili supported Turé's position by arguing that Sonni 'Ali had to be regarded as an unbeliever due to his unorthodox religious practices. Maghili also argued that a ruler who oppressed his people and raised un-Islamic taxes could be fought by means of a jihad.

In a second epoch, from the late 17th century to the onset of colonial rule, Muslim scholars started to criticize the allegedly un-Islamic policies of the rulers of the Sudanic kingdoms, especially the enslavement of Muslims. Since most of these rulers were Muslims, opposition to their rule was often based on theological argumentation leading to their *takfīr* (excommunication). In a series of movements of jihad, religious scholars gained political power for the first time in the history of the *bilād al-sūdān*, and Islam became the only source of political legitimacy in the new "Islamic" states. While only a few texts on Islamic theology had been written by Sudanic scholars before the 18th century, the need to justify *takfīr* and jihad led to an explosion in the production of such texts. Also, a mass movement of conversion to Islam transformed Muslim minorities into majorities in major parts of the *bilād al-sūdān* in the 19th century. A paradigmatic religious scholar-cum-leader of a jihad in this period was Usman dan Fodio (1754–1817), who was born in Maratta in the kingdom of Gobir, the paramount Hausa state of the region. Around 1794 he became the leader of a small but growing *jamā'a* (religious community) in Degel/Gobir. Inspired by Maghili's writings, he identified a number of local religious practices as "un-Islamic innovations" (*bida'*, sing. *bid'a*) in a series of texts such as *Ihya' al-Sunna wa-Ikhmad al-Bid'a* (The revival of the sunna and the elimination of innovation), *Kitab al-Farq* (The book of difference), and his major work, *Bayan Wujub al-Hijra 'ala al-'Ibad wa-Bayan Wujub Nasb al-Imam wa-Iqamat al-Jihad* (Clarifying the obligation for the believers to emigrate, to nominate the imam, and to lead the jihad; 1806). He came to the conclusion, however, that most local religious practices, though

reprehensible (*bid'a*), did not constitute a basis for *takfīr*: Muslims guilty of them could still be regarded as mere "sinners" rather than infidels. *Takfīr* would be legitimate only if a Muslim intentionally violated the prescriptions of the faith and defended these practices in public. On the basis of his inclusive definition of faith and unbelief (*īmān* and *kufr*), dan Fodio was able to identify most Muslims in Hausaland as true Muslims. Only those rulers who tolerated the reprehensible practices of their populations had to be classified as unbelievers, against whom jihad was not only lawful but also a religious obligation.

In a third historical era, from the coming of colonial rule to postcolonial times, Muslims formed the majority of the population in many sub-Saharan states but had to find ways to accommodate secular colonial and postcolonial governments. In the colonial period, Islam was seen by many as a theology of resistance against the Christian colonizers. At the same time, reformist Muslim scholars began to blame the Sufi brotherhoods for the backwardness of Muslims and to advocate reform (*iṣlāḥ*), inspired by movements of reform in North Africa and Egypt. Thereafter Muslim societies in sub-Saharan West Africa saw the emergence of a spectrum of Muslim reformist orientations. The most prominent movements were those that combated Sufi concepts of the faith while advocating modernization of Muslim societies in an "Islamic" guise (e.g., the Jama'at Izalat al-Bid'a wa-Iqamat al-Sunna in Nigeria and Niger, the Jama'at Ibad al-Rahman in Senegal, and a number of Ansar al-Sunna movements in Ivory Coast and Mali). Far less important were activist movements that were less concerned with Islamic religious practices than with the advocacy of an "Islamic" revolution (e.g., the Islamic movement and the Muslim Students' Society in Nigeria) or quietist movements such as the Jama'at al-Tabligh in various West African countries. Criticisms of Sufi religious practices, such as those offered by Abubakar Gumi (d. 1992) or Cheikh Touré (d. 2005), remained a prominent feature of reformist discourse in the 20th century. Gumi's *al-'Aqida al-Sahiha bi-Muwafaqat al-Sharī'a* (The right faith according to the prescriptions of the shari'a) was paradigmatic of these religious reform efforts. While attacking Sufi tenets of the faith, contemporary Muslim reformers have at the same time mostly accepted both colonial and postcolonial regimes, although demands for the reintroduction of aspects of the shari'a, such as "Islamic penal law," suspended during most of the colonial and postcolonial periods, have surfaced in Senegal and Nigeria.

See also Dan Fodio, Usman (1754–1817); jihad; shari'a; Sudan

ROMAN LOIMEIER

Westernization

Since the mid-19th century, Muslim political philosophers and social reformers have understood and debated Westernization in the context of colonial encounters. In various ways, they have pondered how to distinguish the experience of colonialism from modernity and Westernization. Many associated modernity, either in promoting or rejecting it, with Westernization, while others have emphasized the conceptual and practical distinctions between the two.

One of the early proponents of modernity as Westernization was the Indian Muslim educator and social reformer Sir Sayyid Ahmad Khan (1817–98). In 1875, he founded the Muhammedan Anglo-Oriental College with a mission to promote modern education brought to India by the British. He believed that Muslim Indians would eventually benefit from British Imperial rule and that, in the final instance, Westernization would bring modernity and prosperity to his fellow Muslims.

Mustafa Kemal Atatürk (1881–1938) left the most enduring legacy among those who regarded Westernization as an inevitable consequence of modernity. He advanced the most comprehensive project, known as Kemalism, for the modernization of Turkish society. He believed that nation building in Turkey required Westernization both in governance (i.e., secular republicanism) and in its foundational worldview, in science and the Enlightenment rationalism.

Those who remain skeptical of Westernization today have their intellectual roots in the Salafi movement of the mid-19th century. Despite their shared nostalgia for the departed earthly glory of pristine Islam, Salafists diverge radically on how to realize the revitalization of Islam under the condition of modernity. Those who espoused a literal reading of the Qur'an and the hadith, increasingly gravitated toward a Wahhabi puritanism and a total rejection of modernity as a Western conspiracy against Islam. Others who followed the teachings of Afghani (1838–97) believed that the Islamic Renaissance of the Middle Ages afforded the West the essential principles of the Enlightenment. By emphasizing the Islamic roots of modernity, Afghani put forward a critique of the traditionalist 'ulama', who regarded Westernization as the inevitable consequence of modernity and thereby condemned any attempt to rearticulate Islamic scriptures within the contemporary context. Concurrently, he chastised those who promoted modernity without emphasizing its Islamic distinctions. He particularly ridiculed Sir Ahmed Khan, whom the British championed as the intellectual force behind the modernization of India. Afghani thus argued that modernity was a Western project neither in its origin nor in its global implications. He believed that benefiting from Western science and technology must bring Muslims closer to, rather than alienate them from, their cultural identity. This assertion became a recurring theme in the Islamic movements of the 20th and 21st centuries.

While rejecting Westernization, Afghani's disciple Muhammad 'Abduh (1849–1905) and Hasan al-Banna (1906–49), the Egyptian founder of the Muslim Brotherhood, followed Afghani's anticolonial assertion of the congruity of Islam with modernity. Through a return to the wellsprings of Islam, Banna considered the mission of the Brotherhood to be enabling Muslims to restore their religion's power and stand firm against what he called "intrusive tendencies" such as secular liberalism and Marxism. However, after World War II,

with the rise of postcolonial nationalisms and the establishment of the state of Israel, the Brotherhood and other Islamic movements gradually adopted a culturally protectionist ideology based on puritan renditions of Islam.

The South Asian Muslim scholar and political leader Mawdudi (1903–79) and the Egyptian teacher and political activist Sayyid Qutb (1906–66) for the first time theorized Westernization as a comprehensive ideology of *jāhiliyya* (pagan ignorance). Rather than a reference to the pre-Islamic Arabian Peninsula, they interpreted *jāhiliyya* as an omnihistorical state of being, now manifested in the West, that threatens Muslims' way of life. By characterizing Westernization as the expression of *jāhiliyya*, Mawdudi and Qutb situated Islam in a mutually exclusive relationship with the West. In contrast to Mawdudi, Qutb developed the critique of *jāhiliyya* into a revolutionary program against the ideological and political dominance of the West. He chastised the advocates of Westernization for their indiscriminate recognition of its unbounded rationalism, which he held responsible for depleting modern life of any ethical norms and spiritual values.

Whereas the concept of *jāhiliyya* gave rise to an Islamic critique of Westernization, the notion of *gharbzādagī* (Weststruckness, or plagued by the West), coined originally by an Iranian philosopher, Ahmad Fardid (1909–94), made this critique more readily available to a wider community, both Muslim and secular. Fardid traced the ontological roots of *gharbzādagī* to ancient Greece. He defined, in an ahistorical fashion, all of world history as the struggle between idolatrous impurity (*tāghut*) and the sanctity of the divine. From the moment human beings strove to place themselves in the position of God, they became alienated from themselves. The desire to act like God, Fardid opined, belongs solely to Western civilization. Godlike Westerners have spread their idolatrous ideas around the world, either in the form of ancient Greece's polytheism or modern humanism. Either way, Fardid insisted, the result was the same: the incessant Weststruckness of the world by blood and iron or words and ideas. It was another Iranian social critic and writer, Jalal Al-i Ahmad (1923–69), who transformed Weststruckness into a postcolonial critique. In order to address the particular predicament of colonialism and dependency, Al-i Ahmad historicized *gharbzādagī* rather than underscoring the essential differences between the East and the West. He considered Weststruckness to be a disease that infected the soul and the body of colonized people. Echoing a sentiment that was shared by many postcolonial revolutionaries such as Frantz Fanon and Aimé Césaire, Al-i Ahmad believed that Weststruckness had turned the colonized into strangers in their own land.

Ali Shari'ati (1933–77) and other key ideologues of the Iranian revolution further appropriated this revolutionary reinterpretation. Accordingly, Shari'ati considered the West to be neither an indivisible totality nor a degenerate essence beyond redemption. Rather, he developed a universal conception of Weststruckness as a plague that has infected all humanity, regardless of geographic locations or religious affiliations. For Shari'ati and Al-i Ahmad, *gharbzādagī* induced alienation both through the instrumental rationality of capitalism and by the violence of colonialism. They negated the *imposition* of Western modernity while they promoted a *critical* reengagement with, rather than an apologetic view of, Islam and Muslim traditions. They called Westernization the appropriation of Western social norms and institutions divorced from the historical consciousness and cultural particularities of Muslim societies.

See also al-Afghani, Jamal al-Din (1838–97); Atatürk, Mustafa Kemal (1881–1938); Mawdudi, Abul al-A'la (1903–79); Muslim Brotherhood; Sayyid Qutb (1906–66); West, the

Further Reading

Jalal Al-i Ahmad, *Occidentosis: A Plague from the West*, translated by Hamid Algar, 1984; Mehrzad Boroujerdi, *Iranian Intellectuals and the West: The Tormented Triumph of Nativism*, 1996; Roxanne L. Euben, *Enemy in the Mirror*, 1999; Behrooz Ghamari-Tabrizi, *Islam and Dissent in Postrevolutionary Iran: Abdolkarim Soroush, Religious Politics and Democratic Reform*, 2008; Nikki Keddie, *An Islamic Response to Imperialism: Political and Religious Writings of Sayyid Jamal ad-Din al-Afghani*, 1983; Charles Kurzman, ed., *Modernist Islam, 1840–1940: A Sourcebook*, 2002.

BEHROOZ GHAMARI-TABRIZI

women

A look at Muslim historical sources illustrates that the role of gender in Islamic political thought has been varied and complicated. The complex relationship between gender and Islamic political thought will be considered here through a few snapshots: the Qur'an, female contemporaries of Muhammad, medieval Islamic scholarship, and modern Muslim women.

Women in the Qur'an

Several women are mentioned in the Qur'an, some of whom demonstrate a strong independent spirit. They are held responsible for their own salvation, apart from their husbands or male relatives. The stories of these women trump the patriarchal gender norms of a seventh-century Arabian context in which the Qur'an was purportedly revealed. Such women include Eve (Q. 20:117–23); the wives of Noah, Lot, and Pharaoh (Q. 66:10–12); Sarah, the wife of Abraham (Q. 11:71–73; 51:29–30); Moses' mother (Q. 28:7, 13) and sister (28:10–11); Potiphar's wife (Q. 12:23–32); and Mary, the mother of Jesus (Q. 19). All references to these women are made through their relations to the central male figures in their lives, be they husbands, fathers, sons, or brothers. Mary is the only woman who is mentioned by name in the Qur'an and has a chapter named after her.

The story of the Queen of Sheba is especially noteworthy, since she represents the only positive, nonmonotheistic model of political leadership in the Qur'an (27:15–44). Although the Queen of Sheba is never mentioned by name in the Qur'an, she is identified by her

political role as a ruler whose power rivaled that of the prophet and king Solomon. She was the queen of a people called "Saba" (Sheba), a prosperous nation of sun worshipers. All descriptions of the Queen in the Qur'an are salutary; her wisdom and power are highlighted in the story through her pragmatic, diplomatic, and consultative leadership. In the Qur'anic story, the queen's encounter with Solomon occurs in the context of an aggressive unilateral threat delivered by Solomon's avian emissary, named Hudhud. In the missive, Solomon announced the oneness of God and called the queen to submit through Solomon to this God ("Do not exalt yourselves against me and come to me in submission," Q. 27:31). Contrary to her chieftains' counsel favoring military confrontation, the queen opted to pursue diplomatic negotiations with Solomon by offering him gifts. When Solomon rejected these gifts, seeing them as an insult, and then threatened war, the queen visited Solomon personally. After a series of interactions, in which she passed a test devised by Solomon, she successfully avoided war by submitting, not *to* Solomon as he had suggested, but *with* him, to the "Lord of the worlds" (Q. 27:44). While the story of the Queen of Sheba is powerful and meaningful for modern Muslim political thought, its meaning and significance was contested in medieval Qur'anic exegesis.

Although the Qur'an can be seen as challenging patriarchal gender norms through the example of the earlier-mentioned women, it also can be seen as confirming these norms through other stories (e.g., Q. 60) and through its legal dictates. Qur'anic legal verses dealing with marital discord (Q. 4:34), polygamy (Q. 4:3), the higher rank of men over women (Q. 2:228), and women's testimony (Q. 2:282) establish an asymmetrical relationship between men and women in both private and public spheres. Premodern Muslim scholars regularly cited such verses to limit women's participation in the public sphere and the political process. At the same time, the Qur'an speaks of the spiritual equality of believing men and women (Q. 33:35), promising them similar rewards in the hereafter. While some verses suggest that women become polluted during menstruation (Q. 2:222), other verses warn against devaluing the birth of a daughter over that of a son (Q. 16:58–59) and condemn female infanticide (Q. 81:8–9).

Another complex set of verses, which have become highly politicized in contemporary Muslim thought, revolve around the seclusion of women and the appropriate attire when they are in public spaces. One verse in the Qur'an commands Muhammad's wives to "stay in [their] homes" and not to make a "dazzling display" of themselves, a practice that the verse associates with the pre-Islamic "time of ignorance" (*jāhiliyya*; Q. 33:33). The believers are further instructed to speak to Muhammad's wives from behind a screen (*ḥijāb*; Q. 33:53). Muhammad's wives, daughters, and "believing women" are also instructed to "draw their outer garments [sing. *jilbāb*] over their person" when in public in order to be both "recognized" and to avoid being molested (Q. 33:59). The Qur'anic text also exhorts both men and women to observe modesty but further specifies that believing women should "draw their veils [sing. *khimār*] over their bosoms" and "not display their beauty except that which is apparent" (Q. 24:30–31). Although these verses do not provide specific instructions about what Muslim women should wear, or which parts of their body they should cover, medieval Muslim exegetes and jurists concluded that it was obligatory for a Muslim woman to cover her entire body, including, in most cases, her face. In practice, however, the dress code of Muslim women has varied significantly in different social, cultural, and historic moments, where social and economic factors have played a significant role in the determination of women's public attire.

Muhammad's Contemporaries: Wives and Companions

The independent personalities of women who appear in the Qur'an are reflected in the stories of early Muslim women as recorded in Islamic history. Muhammad's wives played key political roles during the lifetime of Muhammad and the early generations of Islam. His first wife, Khadija, was the first convert to Islam and helped launch his prophetic career through tangible social, economic, and political support. Muhammad was monogamous during his marriage to Khadija, though he was continuously polygamous after her death. Muhammad regularly consulted his wives about political affairs, most famously taking the advice of Umm Salama (d. ca. 680) about how to lead his community after concluding the treaty of Hudaybiyya (628). Muhammad's youngest wife, 'A'isha (d. 678), became intellectually and politically active after his death. She is responsible for the transmission of the second largest number of prophetic traditions in Sunni hadith literature. She publicly condemned the policies and person of the third caliph, 'Uthman b. 'Affan (ca. 579–656), and fought against his successor, 'Ali b. Abi Talib (d. 661). 'A'isha personally led an army of 3,000 against 'Ali but lost to him in the Battle of the Camel (656). She had a contentious relationship with Muhammad's daughter Fatima (d. 633), who was married to 'Ali. Fatima, the mother of Muhammad's grandsons Hasan (d. 669) and Husayn (d. 680), is highly venerated by both Sunnis and Shi'is, although Shi'is have a special reverence for her.

'A'isha's leadership of a military campaign was unique, though women were regularly present on the battlefield. Several female Companions of Muhammad fought alongside men, including Nusayba bt. Ka'b, who is credited with saving Muhammad's life several times during the Battle of Uhud (625). Women also played key roles in the transmission of the Qur'an. Hafsa (d. 665), Muhammad's widow and the daughter of the second caliph, 'Umar b. al-Khattab (ca. 580–644), was instrumental in the transmission of the text of the Qur'an. The Qur'anic text itself formalized the inclusion of women into the religious-political community of early Muslims by citing the specific words that women spoke when taking an oath of allegiance (*bay'a*) to Muhammad (Q. 60:12). Even though the words of the oath highlight the gendered responsibilities of women, focusing on the control of sexuality ("You will not commit adultery or kill your children"), it is nevertheless significant that women were required to state their independent fealty to Muhammad and the community of believers.

The role of women in the mosque was contested in the early Muslim community and reflected the tension surrounding women's

political leadership. The mosque in the early Muslim community was more than a religious center. It was also a center of communal life, political administration, and adjudication. The fact that Muhammad appointed Abu Bakr to lead the prayer in the mosque as Muhammad lay on his deathbed was used by Abu Bakr's supporters to legitimate his political succession to Muhammad and reign as the first caliph. By the same token, it is significant that Muhammad appointed a person to chant the call for prayer (*mu'adhdhin*) for the household of Umm Waraqa, who, for her part, led her household in prayer. In the contemporary period, much has been made of whether this represents Muhammad's approval of women-led prayer. At the heart of the debate is whether Umm Waraqa was given a special dispensation to lead her specific mixed-gender household or if her example points to a general permission for women to lead men in prayer.

The debate in the early community about women's political participation was reflected in the imposition and removal of a physical gender barrier in the mosque. 'Umar instituted a gender-segregating barrier in the mosque in Medina and reportedly discouraged women from regularly attending the mosque for prayers. 'Uthman removed the barrier upon assuming power. Despite 'Umar's general attitude of discouraging women from participating in the mosque, women still played a public and political role during his reign. For instance, while delivering a Friday sermon, 'Umar proposed limiting the acceptable dower (*mahr*) that could be offered to wives in marriage, and a woman stood up to interrupt him. She challenged his proposition by citing a verse in the Qur'an that makes it acceptable to offer wives a "heap of gold" (Q. 4:20) as *mahr*. 'Umar responded to this by saying, "The woman is right and 'Umar is wrong." Despite 'Umar's strong desire for gender segregation, during his rule a woman was able to challenge and prevail against the caliph's proposition.

In modern conversations about women's political leadership, a particular tradition attributed to Muhammad has become especially controversial. Muhammad is reported to have said, "Never shall a folk prosper who delegate their affairs to a woman." Although this report seems to contradict the Qur'anic story of the Queen of Sheba, whose people were prosperous, it has been used in multiple ways to argue against women's political and religious leadership. It has also been used to caution against the use of overtly misogynistic prophetic reports when determining the role of women in contemporary Muslim society. The feminist scholar Fatima Mernissi used this prophetic report to advocate for increased text criticism of prophetic reports, while Mohammad Fadel, a professor at the University of Toronto, used this same report to promote "hermeneutical historicism" as the primary approach to deal with traditional texts that appear ethically problematic at first glance.

Women in Medieval Islam

Women's political and religious authority was restricted in the medieval period, especially as compared to their role in early Islam. Leila Ahmed, a pioneer in the field of gender studies in Islamic studies, has shown that scholars in the medieval period were almost entirely male and were products of their sociohistorical context. They produced Qur'anic exegesis and Islamic legal works that reinstituted existing patriarchal norms and, in many cases, expanded the patriarchy of the Qur'anic text to map onto their own patriarchal contexts. Consequently, discussions of female political authority assumed that women should not hold political positions due to what were seen as their physical and intellectual deficiencies. The discussion of essential gender differences often echoed and borrowed from the thought of Hellenistic philosophers and sometimes reflected Aristotelian understandings of gender as differentiated by temperatures of "hot" and "cold."

Women's position in the medieval public sphere was challenged in several ways. Their access to political leadership was disputed through the hadith, which warned against delegating the affairs of the community to a woman. The potential for women to serve as caliph was uniformly denied in Islamic law, though their role as judges was more contested. Karen Bauer's work on the debate regarding female judges illustrates the predominant thought on women's leadership in the medieval period. Most Sunni jurists prohibited women from being judges, although some Hanafi and Maliki jurists allowed women to adjudicate in civil cases. The opposition against female judges was based on four broad arguments. Two of the arguments were based on Qur'anic texts, one on a prophetic tradition, and one on a social argument. The Qur'anic text arguments used 4:34's assertion that "men are in authority (*qawwāmūn*) over women because God has preferred (*faḍḍala*) some over others" to argue that women could not be in a position of authority over men because God preferred men to women and gave them authority over women. The second Qur'anic text used in these discussions was 2:282, which states that the testimony of one male is equivalent to that of two women, particularly in financial transactions. The text was interpreted to mean that because the testimony of two women was equivalent to the testimony of one man, women could not adequately judge the testimony of men. The prophetic report used to limit women's authority was the one warning against a woman leading a community. Finally, the social argument against female judges was that being a judge would allow women to interact with men, which could only result in social and sexual chaos.

These scholarly debates aside, there are some examples of female judges in the medieval period. One of them was the mother of the Abbasid caliph Muqtadir (d. 932), who held a weekly court in the tenth century. There are also some examples of female rulers of Muslim empires, such as Razia Sultana (d. 1240), ruler of the sultanate of Delhi in India, and the Mamluk queen Shajarat al-Durr (d. 1259) in Egypt. Additionally, despite the arguments regarding women's intellectual weaknesses, several Muslim women gained prominence as religious teachers and scholars in Muslim history. Some of them reached the highest level of spiritual authority, such as Rabi'a al-Basri and Ibn al-'Arabi's (d. 1240) female teacher Fatima bt. al-Muthanna. In the traditional sciences, Umm Hani (d. 1466) is an example of an acclaimed teacher who taught men

multiple subjects including grammar, history, and hadith studies. Recent studies have detailed the lives of such female figures who appear in the written works of male scholars. One fecund genre for such study is biographical literature, where female figures appear as noteworthy scholarly figures. Research conducted by Ruth Roded, Marilyn Booth, and Devin J. Stewart shows that even though the number of these women is small, especially in comparison to the male scholars cited in the biographical literature, it is nevertheless important that female scholars were able to attain scholarly prominence in patriarchal contexts, where the education of women was not the norm.

Modern Muslim Women

The relationship between women and political authority in the modern period is embedded in the discourse of colonialism. Since the encounter of much of the Muslim world with modernity coincided with the economic and political project of Western colonialism, the two have become intertwined in popular Muslim imagination. To compound the issue, a major moral argument in support of colonialism was the emancipation of Muslim women from the oppression of Muslim men. Colonists such as Lord Cromer (d. 1917) in Egypt championed the cause of Muslim women by encouraging unveiling, while at the same time restricting their participation in the public sphere to roles he considered especially suited for women, such as midwifery as opposed to medicine. Such disingenuous rhetoric for female emancipation on the part of the colonists (Cromer having also headed the antisuffragist movement in Britain) tended to tie the feminist movement to the colonial enterprise such that advocating for feminist causes became tantamount to supporting colonialism. As a result, women's public and political participation in the modern world is fraught with postcolonial trauma.

Still, the 20th and 21st centuries have witnessed several feminist movements in the Muslim world. In Egypt women have been increasingly active members of society and politics; they played key roles in anticolonialist movements and participated in the public discourse regarding the creation of a postcolonial nationalist identity. Women began working in and contributing to newspapers in the late 19th century, and by the early 20th century, women's journals, such as *Al-'Afaf* (Honor) and *Fatat al-Sharq* (Women of the east), began to appear alongside feminist organizations such as the Society for the Advancement of Women, the Intellectual Association of Egyptian Women, and the Egyptian Feminist Union. Women collaborated with male politicians, and they participated in demonstrations and riots alongside men, though Egyptian women were not given the vote until 1957 when Rawya 'Atiya (d. 1997), the first female member of parliament in the Arab world, was elected. Egyptian political and feminist movements were sometimes spearheaded by secular feminists such as Huda Sha'rawi (d. 1947) and Saiza Nabarawi (d. 1985), who were comfortable using both Egyptian and Western ideas to fight for Egyptian women's rights. Other, more conservative feminists also emerged, such as Malak Hifni Nassef (d. 1918) and Zainab al-Ghazali (d. 2005), who were more interested in developing an Egyptian Islamic feminism that was independent of Western influence. 'A'isha 'Abd al-Rahman (d. 1996), who wrote under the pen name Bint Shati', became the first female to write a commentary on the Qur'an.

In the modern period, "Muslim women" as an abstract, essentialized entity has become a measuring stick for "progress" as well as an embodiment of "authentic" Islamic values. Western political rhetoric often cites the treatment of Muslim women to argue for the "progress" or "backwardness" of Muslim-majority countries. The view that Afghan women were oppressed and in need of saving played an important role in the moral rationale for the American invasion of Afghanistan in 2001. Muslim political movements and governments likewise use the concept of the "ideal" Muslim woman to evaluate the influence of either "Westernization" or "authentic" Islamic values. In Afghanistan, the Taliban used their treatment of Afghan women as the physical embodiment of their version of "authentic" Islam. In this way, Afghan women were used by both the Taliban and the U.S. government to project varied images of themselves; the Taliban used women's bodies to demonstrate their commitment to a pure, unadulterated Islam, while the U.S. government used the image of these same women to establish their commitment to human rights.

Simplified constructions of "the veil" offer a useful example of the politicization of Muslim women. Many governments have used the veil to demonstrate their own commitment to either Islamic piety or secular values. In Saudi Arabia, for instance, Islamic law is interpreted as requiring women in public to cover their entire bodies with a loose robe (*'abāya*), and women are usually expected to cover their faces by wearing a face veil (*niqāb*). In Iran, women must similarly cover their entire bodies, but the *niqāb* is not required. Whereas women are required to dress in a concealing manner in Saudi Arabia and Iran as a sign of the country's fidelity to Islamic law, France prohibits women from dressing in this manner, making the face veil a punishable offense, as a sign of that country's commitment to secular values. A similar debate took place in Canada's province of Quebec, where Bill 94 proposed to deny women who chose to wear the *niqāb* access to public services. In both cases, a key argument was that the *niqāb*, even when worn by choice, subjugated Muslim women, who needed to demonstrate their belief in gender equity, assimilation, and liberal democracy by renouncing certain types of dress. In Turkey the head scarf is officially banned in public settings, though the ban is not strictly enforced, and the head scarf is seen as a litmus test for one's religiosity and commitment to secularism. The method of gauging women's freedom and independence as directly proportional to how much they are covered was called into question by the mass demonstrations in 2011 in Egypt, Libya, Bahrain, and Yemen, wherein veiled and nonveiled women have played and continue to play key public roles.

Stereotypical images of women and gender in Muslim societies do little to capture their complexity or shed light on the meaning of women's increasing visibility in the public spheres for evolving understandings of Islam. Some Muslim women have become highly

visible in the politics of postcolonial nation-states. The Muslim-majority countries of Indonesia, Pakistan, Bangladesh, and Turkey have democratically elected female presidents and prime ministers in the past three decades. Muslim women are also active in other political and public offices in many Muslim-majority countries. Some Muslim countries have designated a specific number of seats for women in their houses of parliament. Such countries include Afghanistan, Bangladesh, Egypt, Iraq, Jordan, Morocco, Pakistan, and Syria.

Yet important as they are, such examples do not necessarily reflect an egalitarian shift in modern Islamic discourse. Just as patriarchal norms did not necessarily translate into the obliteration of the possibility of female leadership, observed female political and religious authority does not translate into egalitarian religious norms. However, the contrast between normative texts and social values in the modern period has led to a contestation of religious authority. In the case of gender, egalitarian social and political Muslim values are fundamentally at odds with inherited patriarchal norms. This discord gives rise to what can be called the egalitarian-authoritarian paradox. The paradox is that religious authority is gained by connecting oneself to the inherited tradition. This means that those who support a gender-egalitarian vision of Islam compromise their religious legitimacy if they break from the patriarchal tradition. However, if they root themselves in the inherited patriarchal tradition, they must compromise their commitment to gender egalitarianism and opt for the gender complementarity model at the expense of gender equality.

Muslim women are beginning to reclaim religious authority amid this dilemma by both breaking from the patriarchal tradition and simultaneously insisting on their religious legitimacy. An example of this was the 2005 mixed-gender Friday prayer led by Amina Wadud in New York City. Recognizing that leading men and women in prayer represents religious, political, and social authority, Wadud attempted to reclaim women's authority in Islam by leading men and women in ritual prayer. Although females had led the Friday prayer before, most notably in South Africa, the New York City prayer elicited responses from scholars and leaders across the globe. Most condemned the prayer, while others, such as Khaled Abou El Fadl and Abdennur Prado of the Catalonian Islamic Board, issued opinions of wholehearted support. Shaykh 'Ali Goma'a of Azhar University in Cairo issued a fatwa that appeared to support the prayer, but he later clarified that he was only recounting the positions of some historical scholars who approved of female-led prayer and that none sanctioned a woman leading the Friday prayer. Whatever the particular reactions to the prayer, the event changed the discourse of gender in Islam by forcing a conversation in liberal and conservative circles alike about female religious and political authority. Issues of women's leadership are at the heart of modern Muslim discourse in the contemporary period and will help determine the future direction of Muslim communities.

See also colonialism; fundamentalism; modernity; veil

Further Reading

N. Abbott, *Two Queens of Baghdad: Mother and Wife of Harun al-Rashid*, 1946; L. Ahmed, *Women and Gender in Islam*, 1992; K. Ali, *Sexual Ethics and Islam*, 2006; K. Bauer, "Debates on Women's Status as Judges and Witnesses in Post-formative Islamic Law," *Journal of the American Oriental Society* 130, no. 1 (2010): 1–21; J. P. Berkey, *The Transmission of Knowledge in Medieval Cairo: A Social History of Islamic Education*, 1992; M. Booth, *May Her Likes Be Multiplied: Biography and Gender Politics in Egypt*, 2001; A. Chaudhry, "The Ethics of Marital Discipline in Pre-Modern Qur'anic Exegesis," *Journal of the Society of Christian Ethics* 30, no. 2 (2010): 123–30; M. Fadel, "Is Historicism a Valid Strategy for Islamic Law Reform? The Case of 'Never Shall a Folk Prosper Who Have Appointed a Woman to Rule Them,'" *Islamic Law and Society* 18 (2011): 131–76; F. Malti-Douglas, *Woman's Body, Woman's Word*, 1991; F. Mernissi, *Beyond the Veil: Male-Female Dynamics in Modern Muslim Society*, 1987; Idem, *The Forgotten Queens of Islam*, 1993; R. Roded, *Women and Islam in the Middle East*, 2008; D. Stewart, "Women's Biographies in Islamic Societies: Mirza Abd Allah al-Isfahani's Riyad al-Ulama'," in *Biography in the Middle East*, edited by Louise Marlowe, forthcoming; A. Wadud, *Inside the Gender Jihad: Women's Reform in Islam*, 2006.

AYESHA S. CHAUDHRY

Y

Yemen

Until the republican revolution in 1962, the political history of Yemen was dominated by the Zaydi imamate. The imamate's doctrine posits a revolutionary vision of rule by any Fatimid descendant of the Prophet Muhammad who has the qualifications to become an imam and is able to rise militarily against an unjust ruler. The last Zaydi imams to rule Yemen were of the Hamid al-Din family, who adopted a monarchical form of government in the 1920s and established the Mutawakkili Kingdom of Yemen, a political order that stood in tension with traditional Zaydism that had, in theory if not always in practice, rejected dynastic kingship. Yemen's relative political isolation was broken in the first half of the 20th century when Yemenis were sent to study in Egypt and Iraq and thus were exposed to the political ideologies of Islamism and Arab nationalism, which they imported back home. In the 1940s an Algerian member of the Muslim Brotherhood, al-Fudayl al-Wartalani (d. 1959), arrived in Yemen at Hasan al-Banna's behest with the aim of spreading this movement's views. This appears to have had an effect on some Yemenis who in turn led the so-called Constitutional Revolution of 1948. Although Imam Yahya b. Muhammad Hamid al-Din was assassinated, this attempt at toppling the Hamid al-Din imams was quickly thwarted with the resumption of power by Imam Ahmad b. Yahya Hamid al-Din (d. 1962).

Nonetheless, the Muslim Brotherhood's influence and presence continued in Yemen, represented formally since 1990 by important elements within a political party called the Yemeni Congregation for Reform (al-Tajammu' al-Yamani li-l-Islah) and by ideologues such as Shaykh 'Abd al-Majid al-Zindani. The Yemeni Congregation for Reform has been in and out of power in the guise of a coalition partner in government or in opposition in parliament, and the influence of the Muslim Brotherhood on Yemen's politics has been nominal and symbolic, though it has been more significant with respect to the content of the school and university curricula.

The 1962 revolution in Yemen led to a civil war that ended in 1970 with the coming to power of a leadership (e.g., President 'Abd al-Rahman al-Iryani) that adhered to the teachings of an indigenous Salafi movement, similar in many respects, but not identical, to the teachings of the Wahhabi movement in central Arabia. Historically, the two most prominent scholars of this movement were Muhammad b. al-Amir al-San'ani (d. 1769) and Muhammad al-Shawkani (d. 1834), both of whose teachings are constitutive of the republican form of Salafism that was imposed in Yemen since the early 1970s. In terms of doctrine, this Sunni reformist movement advocated a literal interpretation and exclusive reliance on the Qur'an and sunna, shunning the *taqlīd* (emulation) of the four established schools of law in favor of an absolute form of *ijtihād* (independent legal reasoning). As to theology, it rejected the Mu'tazili doctrines that the Zaydis uphold as well as their doctrine of the imamate.

By adhering to this version of Salafism, the republican leadership effectively ended their conflict with the Saudi Arabian authorities, who had supported the Hamid al-Din–led Zaydis throughout the civil war. Furthermore, this Salafism constituted an ideology that the Republicans claimed would unite Yemenis around indigenous reformist teachings that allegedly transcended sectarian identities as well as jurisprudential and legal differences. The result of this, however, was that traditional Zaydis ended up being marginalized and at times persecuted by this government-sanctioned form of Islam. The Saudi Arabian authorities welcomed this turn of events and, since the early 1970s, subsidized a parallel system of Islamic education in Yemen, the so-called Institutes of Knowledge (*al-ma'āhid al-'ilmiyya*), as well as sponsoring a Salafi revival in the country that had a transformative effect on the nature of religiosity and practice, in former South Yemen as well. A number of Salafi shaykhs emerged in the process, among whom Muqbil al-Wadi'i (d. 2001) was considered the most important.

The spread of Salafism, whether through Saudi Arabia's sponsorship or that of the central government in Sanaa, led to forms of resistance from some Zaydis as well as from certain Sufis from the Hadhramaut and other regions of South Yemen. While not claiming to revive the legacy and teachings of the imamate, some Zaydis engaged in political efforts to protect their heritage and identity by creating a political party called Hizb al-Haqq. Others, known as the Huthis, engaged in an armed rebellion against the central government. The Sufis, mainly of the Ba 'Alawi order, established educational institutions to preserve and spread their teachings. Among these was Habib 'Ali al-Jifri, who established an institution called the Tabah Foundation in Abu Dhabi and through which he hoped to propagate a version of Islam more ecumenical and "modern" than Salafism.

See also al-Shawkani, Muhammad b. 'Ali (1760–1834); Zaydis

Further Reading

Laurent Bonnefoy, "Salafism in Yemen: A 'Saudisation'?" in *Kingdom Without Borders*, edited by Madawi al-Rasheed, 2009; Paul Dresch, *A History of Yemen*, 2000; Bernard Haykel, *Revival and Reform in Islam*, 2003; Barak Salmoni, Bryce Loidolt, and Madeleine Wells,

Regime and Periphery in Northern Yemen, 2010; Jillian Schwedler, *Faith in Moderation*, 2006.

BERNARD HAYKEL

Young Turks

The phrase "young Turks" was first used by Charles MacFarlane in 1828 to refer to the generation of young Ottomans being brought up under a Western educational system at the time. Over the ensuing 80 years, "young Turks" took on various meanings and was applied to quite diverse groups of people. In 1855, Abdolinimo Ubicini coined the phrases "jeune Turquie de Mahmoud" (young Turks of Mahmoud) and "jeune Turquie d'Abdul Medjid" (young Turks of Abdülmecid) in an attempt to describe the reforming Ottoman statesmen under Sultans Mahmud II (d. 1839) and Abdülmecid (d. 1861). Hippolyte Castile made the first use of the capitalized expression "Young Turks" in 1857, a concept that refers to a group of 19th-century Ottoman intellectuals and statesmen akin to the Giovani Italia of Mazzini. Various Ottoman sources register that several reform-minded young bureaucrats were called "jeunes" in 1861. When, in 1867, a number of leading Ottoman intellectuals fled the Ottoman capital to organize an opposition movement in Paris, the European press labeled them Young Turks.

The exiles themselves adopted this title as the name of their movement. The Egyptian prince Mustafa Fazıl, who financed the movement, used the phrase *grand parti de la Jeune Turquie* in his letter to the sultan inviting him to carry out extensive reforms. In their official program, these dissidents called themselves *Jeune Turquie*, as contrasted with the *Vieux Turcs*, a term they applied to the conservative statesmen of the time. In Turkish historiography, this first Ottoman opposition movement abroad is referred to as the "Young Ottoman movement."

In the 1870s, the terms "Young Turk" and "Young Turkey Party" were employed once again, especially in British and French diplomatic correspondence. This time, they referred to those statesmen and bureaucrats who promoted the constitutional regime. Following the end of the short-lived constitutional regime in 1878, the opponents of Sultan Abdülhamid II's regime came to be called Young Turks (*Jön Türk* in Turkish). The Ottoman Freemasons named their political branch "Committee of Young Turkey at Constantinople" in 1893. By 1895, the French publication of the main opposition organization, the Ottoman Committee of Union and Progress, was published as *organe de la Jeune Turquie*. From this point on, the phrase "Young Turk" was used to denote Ottoman opposition organizations dominated by Muslim dissidents. Despite some confusion in the European press at the time, the term did not encompass the opposition groups formed by Armenians, Macedonians, and other non-Muslim minorities. The sultan issued an imperial decree in July 1901 banning use of the phrase "Young Turks" in official correspondence and in the press, on the grounds that it aggrandized individual opponents by according them the status of a social group. Henceforth, officials and journalists adopted the term "agitator" in place of Young Turk.

After 1908, the term fell out of use within the empire, with the exception of the names of several newspapers. However, European and American journalists and scholars continued to use the phrase to refer to the governments formed following the revolution of 1908, which reinstated the constitutional regime; this has created some confusion, since both adherents and opponents of the ruling Committee of Union and Progress had belonged to the Young Turk movement that came to an end in 1908.

The Young Turk Movement and Its Major Political Ideas

Although opposition to Abdülhamid II's (r. 1876–1909) regime started on the morrow of the dismissal of the Ottoman parliament in February 1878, for more than a decade the Young Turk movement did not go further than the publication of a few journals in Europe. In 1889, the main Young Turk organization, originally named the Ottoman Union Committee, was established in the Royal Medical Academy. The name was changed to the Ottoman Committee of Union and Progress in 1895 after protracted negotiations between the original founders and Ahmed Rıza (1858–1930), a staunch positivist who proposed Auguste Comte's (1798–1857) famous dictum "Order and Progress."

Until 1902, the Ottoman Committee of Union and Progress operated as an umbrella organization with various "activist" branches promoting revolutionary tactics and a branch in Cairo initially dominated by the 'ulama'. At the Congress of Ottoman Liberals, held in February 1902 in Paris, a major schism developed between the member organizations over the question of foreign intervention in the service of revolutionary change in the empire. The argument resulted in the dissolution of the Committee of Union and Progress as an alliance. The majority faction, led by the sultan's brother-in-law Mahmud Celaleddin Pasha (1843–1903), and his two sons, Sabahaddin (1879–1948) and Lutfullah Beys (1880–1973), allied itself with the Armenian and Albanian committees, and promoted the idea of a coup d'état to be carried out with British assistance. The minority splinter group, composed of the "activists" led by Ahmed Rıza, adopted a Turkist policy. They allocated a central role to ethnic Turks, as the dominant ethnic group, in the future of the empire, and categorically opposed any foreign intervention in Ottoman politics. The majority faction underwent reorganization in 1905 under the leadership of Sabahaddin Bey, who, influenced by the *Science sociale* movement and especially renowned French pedagogue and founder of L'École des Roches Edmond Demolins (1852–1907), advocated decentralization and private initiative. He founded the League of Private Initiative and Decentralization in that year and worked toward creating a mutual understanding with the non-Muslim organizations, especially the Armenian Revolutionary Federation (the Dashnaktsutiun).

The Turkist faction also underwent reorganization in 1905 under the leadership of Bahaeddin Şakir (1874–1922), who gave it the

new name Ottoman Committee of Progress and Union (CPU). The CPU now adopted an even stronger activist agenda. In 1907, it merged with the Ottoman Freedom Society, established by army officers and bureaucrats in Salonica in 1906. This merger proved crucial for the effort to expand the influence of the movement within the Ottoman armies of European Turkey. In 1908, with the help of these armies, the Ottoman CPU carried out the constitutional revolution, which marked both the end of Abdülhamid II's regime and the terminus of the Young Turk movement.

Since members and sympathizers of organizations dominated by Muslim opponents of the sultan were all called Young Turks, the designation should not necessarily be taken to imply a shared pool of ideas. For instance, both Muslim clerics and ardent positivists worked side by side in various "Young Turk" organizations. However, many Young Turks, including the original founders of the Ottoman Committee of Union and Progress, were adherents of mid-19th-century German materialism who admired the famous German popular materialist Ludwig Büchner (1824–1899). Darwinism and social Darwinism also deeply influenced many Young Turks. Several Young Turk leaders promoted positivism. Almost all members of the movement were influenced by French popular sociologist Gustave Le Bon (1841–1931) and his theories about the phenomenon of the crowd, which shaped the elitist outlook of the Young Turks.

Following the reorientation of the Ottoman Committee of Union and Progress toward political activism in 1905, many of these ideas were shelved. Instead, the leaders of the movement promoted more popular ideas, such as a variant of the ideology of Ottomanism, which allocated a dominant role to the Turks in Ottoman politics and opposed European economic penetration and political intervention.

The Young Turk movement is mistakenly equated with the activities of the Committee of Union and Progress that carried out the Young Turk Revolution of 1908. European and American scholarship goes further, referring to the Ottoman Second Constitutional Period (1908–18) as the "Young Turk" era. According to the accepted view in Turkish scholarship, however, the Young Turk movement came to an end with the revolution of 1908.

See also Ottomans (1299–1924); Turkey

Further Reading

M. Şükrü Hanioğlu, *Preparation for a Revolution: The Young Turks, 1902–1908*, 2001; Idem, *The Young Turks in Opposition*, 1995; Şerif Mardin, *The Genesis of Young Ottoman Thought: A Study in the Modernization of Turkish Political Ideas*, 1962.

M. ŞÜKRÜ HANIOĞLU

Z

Zahiris

The Zahiris (*Ẓāhiriyya*) were a literalist school of law established by Dawud b. ʿAli b. Khalaf al-Isfahani (d. 884) in Iraq. It claimed adherents among not only common believers but also a number of prominent theologians, jurists, hadith anthologists, and mystics such as Ibn al-ʿArabi (d. 1240). Its teachings spread into Central Asia, Iran, Sindh, Oman, and Andalusia, where an Almohad-championed movement against the Malikis brought the Zahiri school to its peak of influence during the 12th and 13th centuries. However, the school's influence in Andalus and elsewhere declined with the fall of the Almohads, and by the 16th century it had practically died out.

The prominent Andalusian scholar Ibn Hazm (d. 1064) codified Zahiri doctrines, and his surviving works represent our primary source of information for the school. Ibn Hazm categorically rejected the use of individual judgment (*ra'y*) and analogical reasoning (*qiyās*) in the juridical process and went so far as to favor a weak hadith over *qiyās* in his legal method. He considered the literal (*ẓāhir*) sense of the text to be legitimate only in determining whether an act fell under one of the five legal categories—namely, (1) obligatory, (2) recommendable, (3) permissible, (4) reprehensible, and (5) forbidden. In practice, Zahiri jurists did yield to practical pressure by applying *qiyās*, though overall their literalism gave rise to a relatively simpler jurisprudence.

Ibn Hazm's reasoning with regard to commodities that are subject to usury is emblematic of the Zahiri spirit. The analogical Maliki and Hanafi schools, for instance, understand the commodities subject to the practice of usury in hadith literature—gold, silver, wheat, barley, dates, and raisins—to represent larger classes of goods to which usury applies. Bearing in mind the legal cause (*ʿilla*) behind the prohibition of usury, and making use of *qiyās*, these schools extend the religious proscription of usury to include commodities that the Prophet did not originally stipulate. Ibn Hazm, acknowledging only the literal import of sacred texts, forbids the practice of usury only with regard to the six commodities mentioned by the Prophet and contends that the extrapolations of the other schools amount to speculative arbitrariness. Underlying this position is the understanding that juridical rulings are uniquely determined by God's unrestricted and unfathomable will and not some motive that we can grasp. Had it been divinely willed that usury should be forbidden with regard to other articles, the Qur'an or hadith would have made it explicit.

Zahiri hostility toward the prevailing schools of law, especially the Hanafi and Maliki ones, is evident in Ibn Hazm's uncompromising scripturalism. Moreover, in advocating the Zahiri cause, Ibn Hazm denounced uninformed imitation of a school or religious authority (*taqlīd*). He understood the legal principle of scholarly consensus (*ijmāʿ*) to mean the consensus of the Prophet's Companions (*ṣaḥāba*) only, and not that of later learned jurists in general. He argued that after the Companions' death, the jurists became so widespread and numerous that determining their consensus was impossible. Finally, it should be noted that Ibn Hazm applied Zahiri principles to Qur'anic sciences and theology as well, though he was unable to establish those domains as essential to the school.

See also Almohads (1130–1269); Ibn Hazm (994–1064); jurisprudence; shariʿa

Further Reading

Camilla Adang, *Beginnings of the Zahiri Madhhab in al-Andalus,* in P. Bearman, R. Peters, and F. Vogel, *The Islamic Schools of Law*, 2005; Ignaz Goldziher, *The Ẓāhirīs: Their Doctrine and Their History, A Contribution to the History of Islamic Theology*, translated by Wolfgang Behn, 1971; Abdel-Magid Turki, "al-Ẓāhiriyya," in *Encyclopaedia of Islam,* 2nd ed., edited by P. Bearman, T. Bianquis, C. E. Bosworth, E. van Donzel, and W. P. Heinrichs, 2010; Idem, *Polémiques entre Ibn Ḥazm et Bāǧī sur les principes de le loi musulmane*, 1976.

YOUSEF CASEWIT

al-Zawahiri, Ayman (b. 1951)

The radical Egyptian Islamist Ayman al-Zawahiri was born in Cairo on June 19, 1951, to Dr. Muhammad Rabie al-Zawahiri and Umayma ʿAzzam. The Zawahiri and ʿAzzam families enjoyed an aristocratic rank in Egyptian society that included physicians, university professors, and high-ranking religious and political notables. Zawahiri was raised in Maʿadi, an upper-class suburb south of Cairo, where he was exposed at an early age to a broad range of different political currents and ideologies. Throughout his life, he was an active member and chief ideologue of a number of different violent political organizations, including Egyptian Islamic Jihad and al-Qaeda.

Zawahiri was introduced to the ideas of Sayyid Qutb, the infamous ideologue of the Muslim Brotherhood whose work

Milestones has been regarded as a blueprint for transnational Islamic militancy, through his maternal uncle Mahfouz ʻAzzam, who himself served as Qutb's personal lawyer and trusted confidant. Qutb's assassination in 1966, which had a deep effect on Zawahiri, contributed in part to Zawahiri's active involvement, at the early age of 15, in a clandestine militant cell that sought to overthrow the Egyptian government and pursue a model of Islamic governance. The cell matured in 1974, as Zawahiri was finishing his medical education, when it converged with other similar militant networks that together later formed the Egyptian Islamic Jihad. Then named simply al-Jihad, the group was under the direct leadership of ʻAbd al-Salam al-Faraj, who, along with Khaled Islambouli, was directly responsible for the assassination of Egyptian president Anwar al-Sadat in 1981.

Zawahiri was one of over three hundred defendants tried for conspiracy in the assassination. The trial lasted three years and resulted in Zawahiri's release, after he was charged and convicted of illegal weapons possession. He emerged from his prison experience as an articulate voice for the militants and eventually assumed leadership of the Egyptian Islamic Jihad. Zawahiri left Egypt for Saudi Arabia in 1985, where he practiced medicine in Jeddah. Shortly after, he arrived in Afghanistan in order to contribute to the jihad against the Soviet invasion taking place there. In fact, Zawahiri had already been exposed to the Afghan jihad effort through two trips to Pakistan in 1980 and 1981, where he had offered medical services to Afghan refugees under the auspices of the Red Crescent. The return to Afghanistan in 1986 provided the opportunity for Zawahiri to cultivate a relationship with Osama bin Laden.

As the Afghan-Soviet struggle subsided, Zawahiri, along with Bin Laden, sought refuge in Sudan under the patronage of Hasan al-Turabi and established operational bases between Khartoum and Yemen. However, in 1996 Zawahiri, members of Islamic Jihad, and Bin Laden's group were expelled from Sudan after the failed assassination attempt on the Egyptian president Husni Mubarak a year earlier. Zawahiri and Bin Laden both found refuge in Afghanistan, then under the control of the Taliban. The alliance between the two leaders strengthened, and they issued a joint fatwa (religious opinion) in 1998 under the auspices of the "World Islamic Front against Jews and Crusaders," which served as a virtual declaration of war against the United States and its allies. By this point Zawahiri's organization, Egyptian Islamic Jihad, had formally merged with Bin Laden's al-Qaeda. Zawahiri was tried in 1999 in absentia and sentenced to death by an Egyptian court in what has come to be known as the Returnees from Albania case.

Until Bin Laden's death in 2011, Zawahiri was seen as the strategic and operational commander of al-Qaeda by most global intelligence services. On June 16, 2011, Zawahiri was announced as the new head of al-Qaeda by the organization's consultative assembly. At the time of writing he was under worldwide sanctions by the United Nations, and there was a $25 million bounty for him from the United States. His whereabouts are unknown, but he is largely believed to be in hiding in Pakistan's Federally Administered Tribal Areas in the northwest of the country.

Zawahiri assumed the role of unofficial spokesman of radical political Islam since his imprisonment in the 1980s. His writings and proclamations are voluminous and extensive. One of the most important ideological statements he authored is a polemical history of the Muslim Brotherhood in Egypt titled *The Bitter Harvest: The Brotherhood in Sixty Years* (1991). Part history, part intra-Islamist critique, the text scorns the official policies and leadership of the Brotherhood since its founding up to the present. He condemns the Brotherhood's alleged collusion with Egypt's successive secular governments in the 20th century as well as its recognition of, and participation in, secular governing institutions such as representative parliament and elections. He praises Sayyid Qutb and other members of the Brotherhood who did not follow the official line of the Brotherhood as the true representatives of Islamic political action. In *The Bitter Harvest*, Zawahiri increasingly deploys, even if implicitly, the rhetoric of *takfīr* (excommunication), which in his theological apparatus legitimates violent action.

In addition to hundreds of speeches, pamphlets, and short treatises, he wrote a memoir titled *Knights under the Prophet's Banner* (2001), which provides detail on the formation and development of Islamic Jihad in Egypt and its later convergence with al-Qaeda. At the same time it condemns other Islamist activists for not pursuing the path of violent action he advocates. One of his targets of criticism, Muntasir al-Zayyat, a prominent Islamist lawyer and former cell mate of Zawahiri's, wrote a critical biography of Zawahiri in 2002, *Ayman al-Zawahiri as I Knew Him*. Together, the two texts provide some of the most important primary material on the evolution of Egyptian Islamic radicalism.

In order to gain an appreciation of Zawahiri's rhetorical and theological appeal, it is important to read Zawahiri's writings in light of the classic Islamic exegetical and legal traditions. A cursory look at one example is revealing; consider the treatise "Loyalty and Enmity: An Inherited Doctrine and Lost Reality" (*Al-Wala' wa-l-Bara': ʻAqida Manqula wa-Waqiʻ Mafqud*), written in 2002.

In the first section of the text Zawahiri provides the theological and legal justification for the doctrine of loyalty and enmity, which mandates Muslims to commit socially and politically to the worldwide Muslim community (*umma*) over and against any association with non-Muslims. He begins with the Qur'anic verse, "Let not the believers take for friends or helpers unbelievers rather than believers: whoever does this shall have no relationship left with Allah—unless you but guard yourselves against them, taking precautions. But Allah cautions you to fear Himself. For the final goal is to Allah" (Q. 3:28). He invokes this verse in order to describe a permanent mode of tension between Muslims and non-Muslims, which may be marked by outright warfare (jihad), cordial demeanor, or dissimulation (*taqiyya*), depending on context. Zawahiri grounds the treatise in the Qur'an, hadith, and quotes from prominent scholars (ʻulama') from the classical tradition, which together rhetorically function to promote a sense of undisputed orthodoxy. For example, he begins with the tenth-century Muslim polymath Muhammad b. Jarir al-Tabari (d. 923), who is recognized by many Muslims as Sunni Muslim par excellence. He then draws upon Ibn Taymiyya's

(d. 1328) ideas, which have been used by modern radicals to justify their violent positions against secular Muslim rulers. However, throughout the text he weaves together statements and opinions of classical scholars across centuries of Islamic intellectual history. The cumulative rhetorical effect is to create the semblance of an undeniable historical consensus, to which only Zawahiri and his allies remain loyal.

In the second section of the text, Zawahiri discusses the relevance of the doctrine of loyalty and enmity to the contemporary political context and identifies those who have "deviated" from the mandate. His first target of criticism is the entire "clique" of Muslim rulers who "have placed their armies into the service of the new Crusading campaign against the Islamic umma" (Zawahiri, 2002, 101). He then identifies state-sponsored 'ulama' (scholars) and lay intellectuals as the "rulers' henchmen." He calls them the "Sultan's ulema" who "sign fatwas delivered from the palace, to legitimize this seizure, this pillaging, this Crusader overlordship" (106). He holds this class responsible for "distracting" the youth from their true religious duty of jihad.

The repeated reference to medieval images such as the Crusades or the invading Mongols paints a picture that the majority of contemporary Muslims are out of step with their "heritage." Zawahiri uses this trope effectively. At one point he asks rhetorically, "So, what would al-Tabari, Ibn Hazam, and Ibn Taymiyya say if they were made witness to American planes, troops, and their allies launching off from the [Arabian] Gulf to strike Muslims in Iraq?" (Zawahiri, 2002, 92). Zawahari's recourse to the imagery and symbolism of a mythical Islamic imperial past is one of the cornerstones of his rhetorical allure. Deeper analysis of Zawahiri's writings in the context of classical Islamic theological and legal traditions will likely reveal more about the ideological and aesthetic appeal of his message.

See also Egypt; fundamentalism; jihad; al-Qaeda

Further Reading

Nimrod Raphaeli, "Ayman Muhammad Rabi' al-Zawahiri: The Making of an Arch Terrorist," *Terrorism and Political Violence* 14, no. 4 (2002); Ibrahim Raymond, *The Al-Qaeda Reader*, 2007; Lawrence Wright, *The Looming Tower: Al-Qaeda and the Road to 9/11*, 2006; Ayman Zawahiri, "Loyalty and Emnity," in *The Al-Qaeda Reader*, translated by Raymond Ibrahim, 2002; Montasser al-Zayyat, *The Road to al-Qaeda: The Story of Bin Laden's Right-Hand Man*, 2004.

ABBAS BARZEGAR

Zaydis

The Zaydis, Twelvers, and Isma'ilis form the major contemporary Shi'i communities. In 2010 there were approximately 13 million Zaydis worldwide, with the greatest number in northern Yemen, which served as the bastion for a Zaydi state from 897 until the republican revolution of 1962. Shorter-lived Zaydi states also existed in Iran and North Africa. Zaydism goes back to the failed uprising in 740 of Zayd b. 'Ali, the great-great-grandson of the Prophet Muhammad. Zayd's revolt against the Umayyad regime set the pattern for further Zaydi insurgencies against the Umayyads and Abbasids, and Zayd became the symbol of the revolutionary movement within Shi'ism.

The Zaydis are commonly said to stand closest to Sunnism of all the Shi'i groups, and in some sense this is true, particularly with respect to the question, critical to Shi'ism, of the imamate, the succession to Muhammad. The qualifications of legal learning, masculine gender, physical integrity, moral character, and courage required of Zaydi imams mirror those set down by Sunni jurists for the caliph, with the important difference that the Zaydis require descent on the father's side from one of Muhammad's grandsons, Hasan and Husayn. Once in office, the Zaydi imams, like the Sunni caliphs, are regarded primarily as administrators rather than inspired religious teachers. (According to Zaydis, only 'Ali and his two sons, Hasan and Husayn, whom they regard as infallible, were directly appointed imams by Muhammad.) The path to office is another matter. While Sunni caliphs are elected by representatives of the *umma* (community of believers), the Zaydi imam elects himself, in the sense that a candidate for the imamate decides whether he is under a religious obligation to assert his claim, and political success or failure does not settle the matter. Rule does not make an unqualified candidate imam, and the rightful imam retains his office even when the people fail to support him as they are obligated to do. Some of the most highly respected Zaydi imams in fact have devoted far more time to scholarship than to governance.

Zaydi theorists generally regard the question of which rival claimant, if any, is the rightful imam as admitting of an unambiguous answer, known to God, but not necessarily to the rival claimants themselves, their contemporaries, or later Zaydis. It is thus not possible to draw up an uncontroversial list of Zaydi imams. In theory Zaydi imams, apart from their lineage, are self-made men, although de facto dynastic succession was not entirely foreign to Zaydi history, and in 1926 the Zaydi imamate in Yemen officially became a monarchy.

The Zaydi imam is invested with enormous authority. Unlike other legal scholars, he can at his discretion give his determinations the binding force of law, a principle that extends even to determining the framework of the imamate itself. Zaydi imams act as constitutional framers, legislators, judges of last resort, and commanders in chief. Among the prerogatives of the imam are the imposition of the *ḥudūd* punishments, the collection of Islamic taxes, and the use of coercive measures to insure compliance with affirmative religious duties such as prayer.

Although Zaydi doctrine holds that there will always be a qualified candidate for the imamate, circumstances may make a claim to office untimely. In such cases the community may find itself headed by a so-called *muḥtasib*, who need not meet all the requirements of an imam such as prophetic descent. Like the imam, the *muḥtasib* is

charged with "commanding right and forbidding wrong" but outside of warfare is restricted in his use of force to averting wrongs, not to the enforcing of positive duties.

For some centuries Zaydism suffered significant erosion, as a number of influential thinkers abandoned Zaydism for Sunnism. The best known of these are Muhammad b. Isma'il al-San'ani (d. 1769), Muhammad b. 'Ali al-Shawkani (d. 1834), and more recently Muqbil al-Wadi'i (d. 2001). In addition to a scathing critique from within, Zaydism has suffered inroads from Wahhabism. After the 1962 Yemeni revolution, traditional Zaydis found themselves marginalized by the state, when not in armed opposition to it, as in the case of the so-called Huthi rebellion that began in 2004. Since the mid-1990s, there has been a noteworthy political and intellectual resurgence of Zaydism, including a lively debate on the future of the imamate.

See also imamate; al-Shawkani, Muhammad b. 'Ali (1760–1834); Shi'ism; Yemen

Further Reading

Michael Cook, *Commanding Right and Forbidding Wrong in Islamic Thought*, 2000; Patricia Crone, *God's Rule: Government and Islam*, 2004; Bernard Haykel, *Revival and Reform in Islam: The Legacy of Muhammad al-Shawkani*, 2003; Wilferd Madelung, *Der Imam al-Qāsim ibn Ibrāhīm und die Glaubenslehre der Zaiditen*, 1965.

ARON ZYSOW

Zia-ul-Haq (1924–88)

General Zia-ul-Haq (1924–88) was president of Pakistan from 1978 until his death under mysterious circumstances in a plane crash on August 17, 1988.

Born in 1924, Zia-ul-Haq fought in the Indian army during World War II and subsequently rose through the ranks of the Pakistani military, eventually being appointed Joint Services Chief of Staff under Prime Minister Zulfikar 'Ali Bhutto in 1976. On July 5, 1977, Zia-ul-Haq overthrew Bhutto in a coup code-named Operation Fair Play, exploiting widespread public sentiment that Bhutto's Pakistan People's Party (PPP) had rigged the March 1977 elections.

Zia wasted no time in promoting himself as an Islamically guided leader. He met publicly with Mawdudi and worked to garner the support of Mawdudi's party, the Jama'at-i Islami. Zia would later benefit politically from the Soviet invasion of Afghanistan in December 1979. After that invasion Mawdudi preached a legitimate jihad against the Soviet state, and Zia threw his support behind the Afghani mujahidin (the loose array of fighters who went out for jihad against the Soviet armies).

The legal "Islamization" of Pakistan was already well under way before Zia took office. Islam was declared to be the "state religion" of Pakistan in the Constitution of 1973 and required, among other things, certain officials to take an oath affirming the finality of Muhammad's prophethood. The following year, Bhutto amended the constitution to declare the Ahmadis non-Muslims. In 1977 Bhutto also banned alcohol, gambling, and nightclubs, partly to appease the Jama'at-i Islami, who were critical of his administration.

While Bhutto likely sought to conciliate his critics, it is generally believed that Zia's efforts to integrate shari'a-based regulations into every aspect of Pakistani law and society were genuine rather than merely political calculations. Zia declared in 1978 that Pakistan's laws would be thereafter based on *Niẓām-i Muṣṭafā*, the "system of the Prophet." He set up a Federal Shari'at Court in 1978 and a special bench of the Supreme Court that could challenge the shari'a compliance of previous legislation. In 1979 he imposed Islamic laws for the punishment of crimes including drinking alcohol, theft, prostitution, adultery, and bearing false witness. In 1980 Zia began the Islamization of Pakistan's economy, introducing the government collection of zakat (alms tax) and *'ushr* (the land tax).

On April 26, 1984, Zia amended the Pakistan Penal Code to forbid Ahmadis from calling themselves Muslims. Strong opposition to the Ahmadis had been a staple policy of Mawdudi's Jama'at-i Islami since its inception. However, tensions between Zia and the Jama'at arose in 1985, when Zia organized elections for national and provincial assemblies and sought the support of the Muslim League. The Jama'at then accused him of pressing Islam into the service of political ends. Elections proceeded smoothly, and 1988 saw Zia at the height of his power, when his support for the Afghan mujahidin paid off with the Soviet defeat in April. Then, in May 1988, Zia abruptly dissolved the National Assembly and his cabinet, accusing them of impeding the Islamization process; and on June 15, 1988, he promulgated the Enforcement of Shariat Ordinance to counteract what he perceived as impediments to implementing shari'a. This was one of the last acts in Zia's Islamization agenda before his death the following August.

See also Jama'at-i Islami; Pakistan

Further Reading

Khalid Mahmud 'Arif, *Working with Zia: Pakistan's Power Politics, 1977–88*, 1995; Shahid Javed Burki and Craig Baxter, eds., *Pakistan under the Military: Eleven Years of Zia ul-Haq*, 1991; Seyyed Vali Reza Nasr, *The Vanguard of the Islamic Revolution: The Jama'at Islami of Pakistan*, 1994; Lawrence Ziring, "Public Policy Dilemmas and Pakistan's Nationality Problem: The Legacy of Zia ul-Haq," *Asian Survey* 28, no. 8 (1988).

BRANNON INGRAM

Index

Main articles are indicated by **bold** page numbers.

Index

Index